SAINT THOMAS AQUINAS

SUMMA THEOLOGIAE
PRIMA SECUNDAE, 71-114

Translated by Fr. Laurence Shapcote, O.P.
Edited by John Mortensen and Enrique Alarcón

SUMMA THEOLOGIAE

Volume 16
Latin/English Edition of the Works of St. Thomas Aquinas

The Aquinas Institute for the Study of Sacred Doctrine
Lander, Wyoming
2012

This printing was funded in part by donations made in memory of:
Marcus Berquist, Rose Johanna Trumbull, John and Mary Deignan,
Thomas and Eleanor Sullivan, and Fr. John T. Feeney and his sister Mary.

This printing was also made possible by a donation from Patricia Lynch,
and by a donation made in honor of Fr. Brian McMaster,
and in gratitude to the Very Rev. Romanus Cessario, OP, STM

Published with the ecclesiastical approval of
The Most Reverend Paul D. Etienne, DD, STL
Bishop of Cheyenne
Given on November 10, 2012

Publisher's Cataloging-in-Publication data

Thomas Aquinas, St., 1225?-1274
  Summa Theologiae Prima Secundae, 71-114 / Saint Thomas Aquinas; edited by John Mortensen, Enrique Alarcón;
  translated by Fr. Laurence Shapcote, O.P.
  p. 536 cm.
  ISBN 978-1-62340-009-5

1. Thomas, Aquinas, Saint, 1225?-1274 -- Summa theologiae -- Prima Secundae -- 71-114.   2. Catholic Church --
Doctrines -- Early works to 1800. 3. Theology, Doctrinal - -Early works to 1800.   I. Title. II. Series

BX1749.T512 2012
230´.2--dc23   2012953833

Notes on the Text

Latin Text of St. Thomas

The Latin text used in this volume is based on the Corpus Thomisticum text of the Fundación Tomás de Aquino <www.corpusthomisticum.org>. This text is based on the Leonine Edition, transcribed by Fr. Roberto Busa SJ, and revised by Dr. Enrique Alarcón and other editors and collaborators of this bilingual edition. © 2012 Fundación Tomás de Aquino, Pamplona. Used with permission.

English Translation of St. Thomas

The English translation of the *Summa Theologiae* was prepared by Fr. Laurence Shapcote, O.P. (1864-1947), of the English Dominican Province. It has been edited and revised by The Aquinas Institute and its collaborators.

DEDICATED WITH LOVE TO
OUR LADY OF MT. CARMEL

Contents

Summa Theologiae
Prima Secundae, 71-114

QUESTION 71

OF VICE AND SIN CONSIDERED IN THEMSELVES

Consequenter considerandum est de vitiis et peccatis. Circa quae sex consideranda occurrunt, primo quidem, de ipsis vitiis et peccatis secundum se; secundo, de distinctione eorum; tertio, de comparatione eorum ad invicem; quarto, de subiecto peccati; quinto, de causa eius; sexto, de effectu ipsius.

Circa primum quaeruntur sex.

Primo, utrum vitium contrarietur virtuti.

Secundo, utrum vitium sit contra naturam.

Tertio, quid sit peius, utrum vitium vel actus vitiosus.

Quarto, utrum actus vitiosus possit esse simul cum virtute.

Quinto, utrum in omni peccato sit aliquis actus.

Sexto, de definitione peccati quam Augustinus ponit, XXII contra Faustum, *peccatum est dictum vel factum vel concupitum contra legem aeternam.*

We have in the next place to consider vice and sin: about which six points have to be considered: (1) Vice and sin considered in themselves; (2) their distinction; (3) their comparison with one another; (4) the subject of sin; (5) the cause of sin; (6) the effect of sin.

Under the first head there are six points of inquiry:

(1) Whether vice is contrary to virtue?

(2) Whether vice is contrary to nature?

(3) Which is worse, a vice or a vicious act?

(4) Whether a vicious act is compatible with virtue?

(5) Whether every sin includes action?

(6) Of the definition of sin proposed by Augustine (*Contra Faust.* xxii): *Sin is a word, deed, or desire against the eternal law.*

Article 1

Whether Vice Is Contrary to Virtue?

AD PRIMUM SIC PROCEDITUR. Videtur quod vitium non contrarietur virtuti. Uni enim unum est contrarium, ut probatur in X Metaphys. Sed virtuti contrariantur peccatum et malitia. Non ergo contrariatur ei vitium, quia vitium dicitur etiam si sit indebita dispositio membrorum corporalium, vel quarumcumque rerum.

PRAETEREA, virtus nominat quandam perfectionem potentiae. Sed vitium nihil nominat ad potentiam pertinens. Ergo vitium non contrariatur virtuti.

PRAETEREA, Tullius dicit, in IV de Tusculanis quaest., quod *virtus est quaedam sanitas animae*. Sanitati autem opponitur aegritudo vel morbus, magis quam vitium. Ergo virtuti non contrariatur vitium.

SED CONTRA est quod dicit Augustinus, in libro de perfectione iustitiae, quod *vitium est qualitas secundum quam malus est animus.* Virtus autem est qualitas quae facit bonum habentem, ut ex supradictis patet. Ergo vitium contrariatur virtuti.

RESPONDEO dicendum quod circa virtutem duo possumus considerare, scilicet ipsam essentiam virtutis; et id ad quod est virtus. In essentia quidem virtutis aliquid considerari potest directe; et aliquid ex consequenti. Directe quidem virtus importat dispositionem quandam alicuius convenienter se habentis secundum

OBJECTION 1: It would seem that vice is not contrary to virtue. For one thing has one contrary, as proved in *Metaph.* x, text. 17. Now sin and malice are contrary to virtue. Therefore vice is not contrary to it: since vice applies also to undue disposition of bodily members or of any things whatever.

OBJ. 2: Further, virtue denotes a certain perfection of power. But vice does not denote anything relative to power. Therefore vice is not contrary to virtue.

OBJ. 3: Further, Cicero (*De Quaest. Tusc.* iv) says that *virtue is the soul's health.* Now sickness or disease, rather than vice, is opposed to health. Therefore vice is not contrary to virtue.

ON THE CONTRARY, Augustine says (*De Perfect. Justit.* ii) that *vice is a quality in respect of which the soul is evil.* But *virtue is a quality which makes its subject good,* as was shown above (Q55, AA3,4). Therefore vice is contrary to virtue.

I ANSWER THAT, Two things may be considered in virtue—the essence of virtue, and that to which virtue is ordained. In the essence of virtue we may consider something directly, and we may consider something consequently. Virtue implies *directly* a disposition whereby the subject is well disposed according to the mode of its nature:

modum suae naturae, unde philosophus dicit, in VII Physic. quod *virtus est dispositio perfecti ad optimum; dico autem perfecti, quod est dispositum secundum naturam.* Ex consequenti autem sequitur quod virtus sit bonitas quaedam, in hoc enim consistit uniuscuiusque rei bonitas, quod convenienter se habeat secundum modum suae naturae. Id autem ad quod virtus ordinatur, est actus bonus, ut ex supradictis patet.

Secundum hoc igitur tria inveniuntur opponi virtuti. Quorum unum est peccatum, quod opponitur sibi ex parte eius ad quod virtus ordinatur, nam peccatum proprie nominat actum inordinatum, sicut actus virtutis est actus ordinatus et debitus. Secundum autem quod ad rationem virtutis consequitur quod sit bonitas quaedam, opponitur virtuti malitia. Sed secundum id quod directe est de ratione virtutis, opponitur virtuti vitium, vitium enim uniuscuiusque rei esse videtur quod non sit disposita secundum quod convenit suae naturae. Unde Augustinus dicit, in III de Lib. Arb., *quod perfectioni naturae deesse perspexeris, id voca vitium.*

Ad primum ergo dicendum quod illa tria non contrariantur virtuti secundum idem, sed peccatum quidem contrariatur secundum quod virtus est operativa boni; malitia autem secundum quod est bonitas quaedam; vitium autem proprie secundum quod est virtus.

Ad secundum dicendum quod virtus non solum importat perfectionem potentiae quae est principium agendi, sed etiam importat debitam dispositionem eius cuius est virtus, et hoc ideo quia unumquodque operatur secundum quod actu est. Requiritur ergo quod aliquid sit in se bene dispositum, quod debet esse boni operativum. Et secundum hoc virtuti vitium opponitur.

Ad tertium dicendum quod, sicut Tullius dicit, in IV de Tusculanis quaest., *morbi et aegrotationes partes sunt vitiositatis,* in corporibus enim morbum appellant totius corporis corruptionem, puta febrem vel aliquid huiusmodi; aegrotationem vero, morbum cum imbecillitate; vitium autem, cum partes corporis inter se dissident. Et quamvis in corpore quandoque sit morbus sine aegrotatione, puta cum aliquis est interius male dispositus, non tamen exterius praepeditur a solitis operationibus; in animo tamen, ut ipse dicit, haec duo non possunt nisi cogitatione secerni. Necesse est enim quod quandocumque aliquis interius est male dispositus, habens inordinatum affectum, quod ex hoc imbecillis reddatur ad debitas operationes exercendas, quia unaquaeque arbor ex suo fructu cognoscitur, idest homo ex opere, ut dicitur Matth. XII. *Sed vitium animi,* ut Tullius ibidem dicit, *est habitus aut affectio animi in tota vita inconstans, et a seipsa dissentiens.* Quod quidem invenitur etiam absque morbo vel aegrotatione, ut puta cum aliquis ex infirmitate vel ex passione peccat. Unde in plus se habet vitium quam aegrotatio vel morbus, sicut etiam virtus in plus se habet quam sanitas, nam sanitas etiam quaedam virtus

wherefore the Philosopher says (*Phys.* vii, text. 17) that *virtue is a disposition of a perfect thing to that which is best; and by perfect I mean that which is disposed according to its nature.* That which virtue implies *consequently* is that it is a kind of goodness: because the goodness of a thing consists in its being well disposed according to the mode of its nature. That to which virtue is directed is a good act, as was shown above (Q56, A3).

Accordingly three things are found to be contrary to virtue. One of these is *sin,* which is opposed to virtue in respect of that to which virtue is ordained: since, properly speaking, sin denotes an inordinate act; even as an act of virtue is an ordinate and due act: in respect of that which virtue implies consequently, viz., that it is a kind of goodness, the contrary of virtue is *malice*: while in respect of that which belongs to the essence of virtue directly, its contrary is *vice*: because the vice of a thing seems to consist in its not being disposed in a way befitting its nature: hence Augustine says (*De Lib. Arb.* iii): *Whatever is lacking for a thing's natural perfection may be called a vice.*

Reply Obj. 1: These three things are contrary to virtue, but not in the same respect: for sin is opposed to virtue, according as the latter is productive of a good work; malice, according as virtue is a kind of goodness; while vice is opposed to virtue properly as such.

Reply Obj. 2: Virtue implies not only perfection of power, the principle of action; but also the due disposition of its subject. The reason for this is because a thing operates according as it is in act: so that a thing needs to be well disposed if it has to produce a good work. It is in this respect that vice is contrary to virtue.

Reply Obj. 3: As Cicero says (*De Quaest. Tusc.* iv), *disease and sickness are vicious qualities,* for in speaking of the body *he calls it* disease *when the whole body is infected,* for instance, with fever or the like; he calls it sickness *when the disease is attended with weakness*; and vice *when the parts of the body are not well compacted together.* And although at times there may be disease in the body without sickness, for instance, when a man has a hidden complaint without being hindered outwardly from his wonted occupations; *yet, in the soul,* as he says, *these two things are indistinguishable, except in thought.* For whenever a man is ill-disposed inwardly, through some inordinate affection, he is rendered thereby unfit for fulfilling his duties: since *a tree is known by its fruit,* i.e., man by his works, according to Mt. 12:33. But *vice of the soul,* as Cicero says (*De Quaest. Tusc.* iv), *is a habit or affection of the soul discordant and inconsistent with itself through life*: and this is to be found even without disease and sickness, e.g., when a man sins from weakness or passion. Consequently vice is of wider extent than sickness or disease; even as virtue extends to more things than health; for health itself is reckoned a kind of virtue (*Phys.*

ponitur in VII Physic. Et ideo virtuti convenientius opponitur vitium quam aegrotatio vel morbus.

vii, text. 17). Consequently vice is reckoned as contrary to virtue, more fittingly than sickness or disease.

Article 2

Whether Vice Is Contrary to Nature?

AD SECUNDUM SIC PROCEDITUR. Videtur quod vitium non sit contra naturam. Vitium enim contrariatur virtuti, ut dictum est. Sed virtutes non sunt in nobis a natura, sed causantur in nobis per infusionem aut ab assuetudine, ut dictum est. Ergo vitia non sunt contra naturam.

PRAETEREA, ea quae sunt contra naturam, non possunt assuefieri, *sicut lapis nunquam assuescit ferri sursum*, ut dicitur in II Ethic. Sed aliqui assuefiunt ad vitia. Ergo vitia non sunt contra naturam.

PRAETEREA, nihil quod est contra naturam, invenitur in habentibus illam naturam ut in pluribus. Sed vitia inveniuntur in hominibus ut in pluribus, quia, sicut dicitur Matth. VII, *lata est via quae ducit ad perditionem, et multi vadunt per eam.* Ergo vitium non est contra naturam.

PRAETEREA, peccatum comparatur ad vitium sicut actus ad habitum, ut ex supradictis patet. Sed peccatum definitur esse *dictum vel factum vel concupitum contra legem Dei*; ut patet per Augustinum, XXII contra Faustum. Lex autem Dei est supra naturam. Magis ergo dicendum est quod vitium sit contra legem, quam sit contra naturam.

SED CONTRA est quod Augustinus dicit, in III de Lib. Arb., *omne vitium, eo ipso quod vitium est, contra naturam est.*

RESPONDEO dicendum quod, sicut dictum est, vitium virtuti contrariatur. Virtus autem uniuscuiusque rei consistit in hoc quod sit bene disposita secundum convenientiam suae naturae, ut supra dictum est. Unde oportet quod in qualibet re vitium dicatur ex hoc quod est disposita contra id quod convenit naturae. Unde et de hoc unaquaeque res vituperatur, *a vitio autem nomen vituperationis tractum creditur*, ut Augustinus dicit, in III de Lib. Arb.

Sed considerandum est quod natura uniuscuiusque rei potissime est forma secundum quam res speciem sortitur. Homo autem in specie constituitur per animam rationalem. Et ideo id quod est contra ordinem rationis, proprie est contra naturam hominis inquantum est homo; quod autem est secundum rationem, est secundum naturam hominis inquantum est homo. *Bonum autem hominis est secundum rationem esse, et malum hominis est praeter rationem esse,* ut Dionysius dicit, IV

OBJECTION 1: It would seem that vice is not contrary to nature. Because vice is contrary to virtue, as stated above (A1). Now virtue is in us, not by nature but by infusion or habituation, as stated above (Q63, AA1,2,3). Therefore vice is not contrary to nature.

OBJ. 2: Further, it is impossible to become habituated to that which is contrary to nature: thus *a stone never becomes habituated to upward movement* (*Ethic.* ii, 1). But some men become habituated to vice. Therefore vice is not contrary to nature.

OBJ. 3: Further, anything contrary to a nature, is not found in the greater number of individuals possessed of that nature. Now vice is found in the greater number of men; for it is written (Matt 7:13): *Broad is the way that leadeth to destruction, and many there are who go in thereat.* Therefore vice is not contrary to nature.

OBJ. 4: Further, sin is compared to vice, as act to habit, as stated above (A1). Now sin is defined as *a word, deed, or desire, contrary to the Law of God*, as Augustine shows (*Contra Faust.* xxii, 27). But the Law of God is above nature. Therefore we should say that vice is contrary to the Law, rather than to nature.

ON THE CONTRARY, Augustine says (*De Lib. Arb.* iii, 13): *Every vice, simply because it is a vice, is contrary to nature.*

I ANSWER THAT, As stated above (A1), vice is contrary to virtue. Now the virtue of a thing consists in its being well disposed in a manner befitting its nature, as stated above (A1). Hence the vice of any thing consists in its being disposed in a manner not befitting its nature, and for this reason is that thing *vituperated*, which word is derived from *vice* according to Augustine (*De Lib. Arb.* iii, 14).

But it must be observed that the nature of a thing is chiefly the form from which that thing derives its species. Now man derives his species from his rational soul: and consequently whatever is contrary to the order of reason is, properly speaking, contrary to the nature of man, as man; while whatever is in accord with reason, is in accord with the nature of man, as man. Now *man's good is to be in accord with reason, and his evil is to be against reason*, as Dionysius states (*Div. Nom.* iv). Therefore human virtue, which makes

cap. de Div. Nom. Unde virtus humana, quae hominem facit bonum, et opus ipsius bonum reddit, intantum est secundum naturam hominis, inquantum convenit rationi, vitium autem intantum est contra naturam hominis, inquantum est contra ordinem rationis.

AD PRIMUM ergo dicendum quod virtutes, etsi non causentur a natura secundum suum esse perfectum, tamen inclinant ad id quod est secundum naturam, idest secundum ordinem rationis, dicit enim Tullius, in sua rhetorica, quod *virtus est habitus in modum naturae rationi consentaneus*. Et hoc modo virtus dicitur esse secundum naturam, et per contrarium intelligitur quod vitium sit contra naturam.

AD SECUNDUM dicendum quod philosophus ibi loquitur de his quae sunt contra naturam, secundum quod esse contra naturam opponitur ei quod est esse a natura, non autem secundum quod esse contra naturam opponitur ei quod est esse secundum naturam, eo modo quo virtutes dicuntur esse secundum naturam, inquantum inclinant ad id quod naturae convenit.

AD TERTIUM dicendum quod in homine est duplex natura, scilicet rationalis et sensitiva. Et quia per operationem sensus homo pervenit ad actus rationis, ideo plures sequuntur inclinationes naturae sensitivae quam ordinem rationis, plures enim sunt qui assequuntur principium rei, quam qui ad consummationem perveniunt. Ex hoc autem vitia et peccata in hominibus proveniunt, quod sequuntur inclinationem naturae sensitivae contra ordinem rationis.

AD QUARTUM dicendum quod quidquid est contra rationem artificiati, est etiam contra naturam artis, qua artificiatum producitur. Lex autem aeterna comparatur ad ordinem rationis humanae sicut ars ad artificiatum. Unde eiusdem rationis est quod vitium et peccatum sit contra ordinem rationis humanae, et quod sit contra legem aeternam. Unde Augustinus dicit, in III de Lib. Arb., quod *a Deo habent omnes naturae quod naturae sunt, et intantum sunt vitiosae, inquantum ab eius, qua factae sunt, arte discedunt.*

a man good, and his work good, is in accord with man's nature, for as much as it accords with his reason: while vice is contrary to man's nature, insofar as it is contrary to the order of reason.

REPLY OBJ. 1: Although the virtues are not caused by nature as regards their perfection of being, yet they incline us to that which accords with reason, i.e., with the order of reason. For Cicero says (*De Inv. Rhet.* ii) that *virtue is a habit in accord with reason, like a second nature*: and it is in this sense that virtue is said to be in accord with nature, and on the other hand that vice is contrary to nature.

REPLY OBJ. 2: The Philosopher is speaking there of a thing being against nature, insofar as *being against nature* is contrary to *being from nature*: and not insofar as *being against nature* is contrary to *being in accord with nature*, in which latter sense virtues are said to be in accord with nature, in as much as they incline us to that which is suitable to nature.

REPLY OBJ. 3: There is a twofold nature in man, rational nature, and the sensitive nature. And since it is through the operation of his senses that man accomplishes acts of reason, hence there are more who follow the inclinations of the sensitive nature, than who follow the order of reason: because more reach the beginning of a business than achieve its completion. Now the presence of vices and sins in man is owing to the fact that he follows the inclination of his sensitive nature against the order of his reason.

REPLY OBJ. 4: Whatever is irregular in a work of art, is unnatural to the art which produced that work. Now the eternal law is compared to the order of human reason, as art to a work of art. Therefore it amounts to the same that vice and sin are against the order of human reason, and that they are contrary to the eternal law. Hence Augustine says (*De Lib. Arb.* iii, 6) that *every nature, as such, is from God; and is a vicious nature, insofar as it fails from the Divine art whereby it was made.*

Article 3

Whether Vice Is Worse Than a Vicious Act?

AD TERTIUM SIC PROCEDITUR. Videtur quod vitium, idest habitus malus sit peius quam peccatum, idest actus malus. Sicut enim bonum quod est diuturnius, est melius; ita malum quod est diuturnius, est peius. Sed habitus vitiosus est diuturnior quam actus vitiosi, qui statim transeunt. Ergo habitus vitiosus est peior quam actus vitiosus.

OBJECTION 1: It would seem that vice, i.e., a bad habit, is worse than a sin, i.e., a bad act. For, as the more lasting a good is, the better it is, so the longer an evil lasts, the worse it is. Now a vicious habit is more lasting than vicious acts, that pass forthwith. Therefore a vicious habit is worse than a vicious act.

PRAETEREA, plura mala sunt magis fugienda quam unum malum. Sed habitus malus virtualiter est causa multorum malorum actuum. Ergo habitus vitiosus est peior quam actus vitiosus.

PRAETEREA, causa est potior quam effectus. Sed habitus perficit actum tam in bonitate quam in malitia. Ergo habitus est potior actu et in bonitate et in malitia.

SED CONTRA, pro actu vitioso aliquis iuste punitur, non autem pro habitu vitioso, si non procedat ad actum. Ergo actus vitiosus est peior quam habitus vitiosus.

RESPONDEO dicendum quod habitus medio modo se habet inter potentiam et actum. Manifestum est autem quod actus in bono et in malo praeeminet potentiae, ut dicitur in IX Metaphys., melius est enim bene agere quam posse bene agere; et similiter vituperabilius est male agere quam posse male agere. Unde etiam sequitur quod habitus in bonitate et in malitia medium gradum obtineat inter potentiam et actum, ut scilicet, sicut habitus bonus vel malus praeeminet in bonitate vel malitia potentiae, ita etiam subdatur actui. Quod etiam ex hoc apparet, quod habitus non dicitur bonus vel malus nisi ex hoc quod inclinat ad actum bonum vel malum. Unde propter bonitatem vel malitiam actus, dicitur habitus bonus vel malus. Et sic potior est actus in bonitate vel malitia quam habitus, quia propter quod unumquodque tale, et illud magis est.

AD PRIMUM ergo dicendum quod nihil prohibet aliquid esse simpliciter altero potius, quod tamen secundum quid ab eo deficit. Simpliciter enim potius iudicatur quod praeeminet quantum ad id quod per se consideratur in utroque, secundum quid autem quod praeeminet secundum id quod per accidens se habet ad utrumque. Ostensum est autem ex ipsa ratione actus et habitus, quod actus est potior in bonitate et malitia quam habitus. Quod autem habitus sit diuturnior quam actus, accidit ex eo quod utrumque invenitur in tali natura quae non potest semper agere, et cuius actio est in motu transeunte. Unde simpliciter actus est potior tam in bonitate quam in malitia, sed habitus est potior secundum quid.

AD SECUNDUM dicendum quod habitus non est simpliciter plures actus, sed secundum quid, idest virtute. Unde ex hoc non potest concludi quod habitus sit simpliciter potior in bonitate vel malitia quam actus.

AD TERTIUM dicendum quod habitus est causa actus in genere causae efficientis, sed actus est causa habitus in genere causae finalis, secundum quam consideratur ratio boni et mali. Et ideo in bonitate et malitia actus praeeminet habitui.

OBJ. 2: Further, several evils are more to be shunned than one. But a bad habit is virtually the cause of many bad acts. Therefore a vicious habit is worse than a vicious act.

OBJ. 3: Further, a cause is more potent than its effect. But a habit produces its actions both as to their goodness and as to their badness. Therefore a habit is more potent than its act, both in goodness and in badness.

ON THE CONTRARY, A man is justly punished for a vicious act; but not for a vicious habit, so long as no act ensues. Therefore a vicious action is worse than a vicious habit.

I ANSWER THAT, A habit stands midway between power and act. Now it is evident that both in good and in evil, act precedes power, as stated in *Metaph*. ix, 19. For it is better to do well than to be able to do well, and in like manner, it is more blameworthy to do evil, than to be able to do evil: whence it also follows that both in goodness and in badness, habit stands midway between power and act, so that, to wit, even as a good or evil habit stands above the corresponding power in goodness or in badness, so does it stand below the corresponding act. This is also made clear from the fact that a habit is not called good or bad, save insofar as it induces to a good or bad act: wherefore a habit is called good or bad by reason of the goodness or badness of its act: so that an act surpasses its habit in goodness or badness, since *the cause of a thing being such, is yet more so*.

REPLY OBJ. 1: Nothing hinders one thing from standing above another simply, and below it in some respect. Now a thing is deemed above another simply if it surpasses it in a point which is proper to both; while it is deemed above it in a certain respect, if it surpasses it in something which is accidental to both. Now it has been shown from the very nature of act and habit, that act surpasses habit both in goodness and in badness. Whereas the fact that habit is more lasting than act, is accidental to them, and is due to the fact that they are both found in a nature such that it cannot always be in action, and whose action consists in a transient movement. Consequently act simply excels in goodness and badness, but habit excels in a certain respect.

REPLY OBJ. 2: A habit is several acts, not simply, but in a certain respect, i.e., virtually. Wherefore this does not prove that habit precedes act simply, both in goodness and in badness.

REPLY OBJ. 3: Habit causes act by way of efficient causality: but act causes habit, by way of final causality, in respect of which we consider the nature of good and evil. Consequently act surpasses habit both in goodness and in badness.

Article 4

Whether Sin Is Compatible with Virtue?

Ad quartum sic proceditur. Videtur quod actus vitiosus, sive peccatum, non possit simul esse cum virtute. Contraria enim non possunt esse simul in eodem. Sed peccatum quodammodo contrariatur virtuti, ut dictum est. Ergo peccatum non potest simul esse cum virtute.

Praeterea, peccatum est peius quam vitium, idest actus malus quam habitus malus. Sed vitium non potest simul esse in eodem cum virtute. Ergo neque peccatum.

Praeterea, sicut peccatum accidit in rebus voluntariis, ita et in rebus naturalibus, ut dicitur in II Physic. Sed nunquam in rebus naturalibus accidit peccatum nisi per aliquam corruptionem virtutis naturalis, sicut monstra accidunt corrupto aliquo principio in semine, ut dicitur in II Physic. Ergo etiam in rebus voluntariis non accidit peccatum nisi corrupta aliqua virtute animae. Et sic peccatum et virtus non possunt esse in eodem.

Sed contra est quod philosophus dicit, in II Ethic., quod *per contraria virtus generatur et corrumpitur*. Sed unus actus virtuosus non causat virtutem, ut supra habitum est. Ergo neque unus actus peccati tollit virtutem. Possunt ergo simul in eodem esse.

Respondeo dicendum quod peccatum comparatur ad virtutem sicut actus malus ad habitum bonum. Aliter autem se habet habitus in anima, et forma in re naturali. Forma enim naturalis ex necessitate producit operationem sibi convenientem, unde non potest esse simul cum forma naturali actus formae contrariae; sicut non potest esse cum calore actus infrigidationis, neque simul cum levitate motus descensionis, nisi forte ex violentia exterioris moventis. Sed habitus in anima non ex necessitate producit suam operationem, sed homo utitur eo cum voluerit. Unde simul habitu in homine existente, potest non uti habitu, aut agere contrarium actum. Et sic potest habens virtutem procedere ad actum peccati. Actus autem peccati, si comparetur ad ipsam virtutem prout est habitus quidam, non potest ipsam corrumpere, si sit unus tantum, sicut enim non generatur habitus per unum actum, ita nec per unum actum corrumpitur, ut supra dictum est. Sed si comparetur actus peccati ad causam virtutum, sic possibile est quod per unum actum peccati aliquae virtutes corrumpantur. Quodlibet enim peccatum mortale contrariatur caritati, quae est radix omnium virtutum infusarum, inquantum sunt virtutes, et ideo per unum actum peccati mortalis, exclusa caritate, excluduntur per consequens omnes virtutes infusae, quantum ad hoc quod sunt virtutes. Et hoc dico propter fidem et spem, quarum habitus remanent informes post peccatum mortale, et sic non sunt virtutes. Sed peccatum veniale, quod non contrariatur caritati nec excludit

Objection 1: It would seem that a vicious act, i.e., sin, is incompatible with virtue. For contraries cannot be together in the same subject. Now sin is, in some way, contrary to virtue, as stated above (A1). Therefore sin is incompatible with virtue.

Obj. 2: Further, sin is worse than vice, i.e., evil act than evil habit. But vice cannot be in the same subject with virtue: neither, therefore, can sin.

Obj. 3: Further, sin occurs in natural things, even as in voluntary matters (*Phys.* ii, text. 82). Now sin never happens in natural things, except through some corruption of the natural power; thus monsters are due to corruption of some elemental force in the seed, as stated in *Phys.* ii. Therefore no sin occurs in voluntary matters, except through the corruption of some virtue in the soul: so that sin and virtue cannot be together in the same subject.

On the contrary, The Philosopher says (*Ethic.* ii, 2,3) that *virtue is engendered and corrupted by contrary causes*. Now one virtuous act does not cause a virtue, as stated above (Q51, A3): and, consequently, one sinful act does not corrupt virtue. Therefore they can be together in the same subject.

I answer that, Sin is compared to virtue, as evil act to good habit. Now the position of a habit in the soul is not the same as that of a form in a natural thing. For the form of a natural thing produces, of necessity, an operation befitting itself; wherefore a natural form is incompatible with the act of a contrary form: thus heat is incompatible with the act of cooling, and lightness with downward movement (except perhaps violence be used by some extrinsic mover): whereas the habit that resides in the soul, does not, of necessity, produce its operation, but is used by man when he wills. Consequently man, while possessing a habit, may either fail to use the habit, or produce a contrary act; and so a man having a virtue may produce an act of sin. And this sinful act, so long as there is but one, cannot corrupt virtue, if we compare the act to the virtue itself as a habit: since, just as habit is not engendered by one act, so neither is it destroyed by one act as stated above (Q63, A2, ad 2). But if we compare the sinful act to the cause of the virtues, then it is possible for some virtues to be destroyed by one sinful act. For every mortal sin is contrary to charity, which is the root of all the infused virtues, as virtues; and consequently, charity being banished by one act of mortal sin, it follows that all the infused virtues are expelled *as virtues*. And I say on account of faith and hope, whose habits remain unquickened after mortal sin, so that they are no longer virtues. On the other hand, since venial sin is neither contrary to charity, nor banishes it, as a consequence, neither does it

ipsam, per consequens etiam non excludit alias virtutes. Virtutes vero acquisitae non tolluntur per unum actum cuiuscumque peccati.

Sic igitur peccatum mortale non potest simul esse cum virtutibus infusis, potest tamen simul esse cum virtutibus acquisitis. Peccatum vero veniale potest simul esse et cum virtutibus infusis, et cum acquisitis.

Ad primum ergo dicendum quod peccatum non contrariatur virtuti secundum se, sed secundum suum actum. Et ideo peccatum non potest simul esse cum actu virtutis, potest tamen simul esse cum habitu.

Ad secundum dicendum quod vitium directe contrariatur virtuti, sicut et peccatum actui virtuoso. Et ideo vitium excludit virtutem, sicut peccatum excludit actum virtutis.

Ad tertium dicendum quod virtutes naturales agunt ex necessitate, et ideo, integra existente virtute, nunquam peccatum potest in actu inveniri. Sed virtutes animae non producunt actus ex necessitate, unde non est similis ratio.

expel the other virtues. As to the acquired virtues, they are not destroyed by one act of any kind of sin.

Accordingly, mortal sin is incompatible with the infused virtues, but is consistent with acquired virtue: while venial sin is compatible with virtues, whether infused or acquired.

Reply Obj. 1: Sin is contrary to virtue, not by reason of itself, but by reason of its act. Hence sin is incompatible with the act, but not with the habit, of virtue.

Reply Obj. 2: Vice is directly contrary to virtue, even as sin to virtuous act: and so vice excludes virtue, just as sin excludes acts of virtue.

Reply Obj. 3: The natural powers act of necessity, and hence so long as the power is unimpaired, no sin can be found in the act. On the other hand, the virtues of the soul do not produce their acts of necessity; hence the comparison fails.

Article 5

Whether Every Sin Includes an Action?

Ad quintum sic proceditur. Videtur quod in quolibet peccato sit aliquis actus. Sicut enim meritum comparatur ad virtutem, ita peccatum ad vitium comparatur. Sed meritum non potest esse absque aliquo actu. Ergo nec peccatum potest esse absque aliquo actu.

Praeterea, Augustinus dicit, in libro de Lib. Arb., quod *omne peccatum adeo est voluntarium, quod si non sit voluntarium, non est peccatum.* Sed non potest esse aliquid voluntarium nisi per actum voluntatis. Ergo omne peccatum habet aliquem actum.

Praeterea, si peccatum esset absque aliquo actu, sequeretur quod ex hoc ipso quod aliquis cessat ab actu debito, peccaret. Sed continue aliquis cessat ab actu debito, ille scilicet qui nunquam actum debitum operatur. Ergo sequeretur quod continue peccaret, quod est falsum. Non ergo est aliquod peccatum absque actu.

Sed contra est quod dicitur Iac. IV, *scienti bonum facere et non facienti, peccatum est illi.* Sed non facere non importat aliquem actum. Ergo peccatum potest esse absque actu.

Respondeo dicendum quod quaestio ista principaliter movetur propter peccatum omissionis, de quo aliqui diversimode opinantur. Quidam enim dicunt quod in omni peccato omissionis est aliquis actus vel interior vel exterior. Interior quidem, sicut cum aliquis vult non ire ad Ecclesiam quando ire tenetur. Exterior autem, sicut cum aliquis illa hora qua ad Ecclesiam ire tenetur, vel

Objection 1: It would seem that every sin includes an action. For as merit is compared with virtue, even so is sin compared with vice. Now there can be no merit without an action. Neither, therefore, can there be sin without action.

Obj. 2: Further, Augustine says (*De Lib. Arb.* iii, 18): So true is it that every sin is voluntary, that, unless it be voluntary, it is no sin at all. Now nothing can be voluntary, save through an act of the will. Therefore every sin implies an act.

Obj. 3: Further, if sin could be without act, it would follow that a man sins as soon as he ceases doing what he ought. Now he who never does something that he ought to do, ceases continually doing what he ought. Therefore it would follow that he sins continually; and this is untrue. Therefore there is no sin without an act.

On the contrary, It is written (Jas 4:17): *To him . . . who knoweth to do good, and doth it not, to him it is a sin.* Now *not to do* does not imply an act. Therefore sin can be without act.

I answer that, The reason for urging this question has reference to the sin of omission, about which there have been various opinions. For some say that in every sin of omission there is some act, either interior or exterior—interior, as when a man wills *not to go to church*, when he is bound to go—exterior, as when a man, at the very hour that he is bound to go to church (or even before), occupies

etiam ante, occupat se talibus quibus ab eundo ad Ecclesiam impeditur. Et hoc quodammodo videtur in primum redire, qui enim vult aliquid cum quo aliud simul esse non potest, ex consequenti vult illo carere; nisi forte non perpendat quod per hoc quod vult facere, impeditur ab eo quod facere tenetur; in quo casu posset per negligentiam culpabilis iudicari. Alii vero dicunt quod in peccato omissionis non requiritur aliquis actus, ipsum enim non facere quod quis facere tenetur, peccatum est.

Utraque autem opinio secundum aliquid veritatem habet. Si enim intelligatur in peccato omissionis illud solum quod per se pertinet ad rationem peccati, sic quandoque omissionis peccatum est cum actu interiori, ut cum aliquis vult non ire ad Ecclesiam, quandoque vero absque omni actu vel interiori vel exteriori, sicut cum aliquis hora qua tenetur ire ad Ecclesiam, nihil cogitat de eundo vel non eundo ad Ecclesiam.

Si vero in peccato omissionis intelligantur etiam causae vel occasiones omittendi, sic necesse est in peccato omissionis aliquem actum esse. Non enim est peccatum omissionis nisi cum aliquis praetermittit quod potest facere et non facere. Quod autem aliquis declinet ad non faciendum illud quod potest facere et non facere, non est nisi ex aliqua causa vel occasione coniuncta vel praecedente. Et si quidem causa illa non sit in potestate hominis, omissio non habet rationem peccati, sicut cum aliquis propter infirmitatem praetermittit ad Ecclesiam ire. Si vero causa vel occasio omittendi subiaceat voluntati, omissio habet rationem peccati, et tunc semper oportet quod ista causa, inquantum est voluntaria, habeat aliquem actum, ad minus interiorem voluntatis. Qui quidem actus quandoque directe fertur in ipsam omissionem, puta cum aliquis vult non ire ad Ecclesiam, vitans laborem. Et tunc talis actus per se pertinet ad omissionem, voluntas enim cuiuscumque peccati per se pertinet ad peccatum illud, eo quod voluntarium est de ratione peccati. Quandoque autem actus voluntatis directe fertur in aliud, per quod homo impeditur ab actu debito, sive illud in quod fertur voluntas, sit coniunctum omissioni, puta cum aliquis vult ludere quando ad Ecclesiam debet ire; sive etiam sit praecedens, puta cum aliquis vult diu vigilare de sero, ex quo sequitur quod non vadat hora matutinali ad Ecclesiam. Et tunc actus iste interior vel exterior per accidens se habet ad omissionem, quia omissio sequitur praeter intentionem; hoc autem dicimus per accidens esse, quod est praeter intentionem, ut patet in II Physic. Unde manifestum est quod tunc peccatum omissionis habet quidem aliquem actum coniunctum vel praecedentem, qui tamen per accidens se habet ad peccatum omissionis.

Iudicium autem de rebus dandum est secundum illud quod est per se, et non secundum illud quod est per accidens. Unde verius dici potest quod aliquod peccatum

himself in such a way that he is hindered from going. This seems, in a way, to amount to the same as the first, for whoever wills one thing that is incompatible with this other, wills, consequently, to go without this other: unless, perchance, it does not occur to him, that what he wishes to do, will hinder him from that which he is bound to do, in which case he might be deemed guilty of negligence. On the other hand, others say, that a sin of omission does not necessarily suppose an act: for the mere fact of not doing what one is bound to do is a sin.

Now each of these opinions has some truth in it. For if in the sin of omission we look merely at that in which the essence of the sin consists, the sin of omission will be sometimes with an interior act, as when a man wills *not to go to church*: while sometimes it will be without any act at all, whether interior or exterior, as when a man, at the time that he is bound to go to church, does not think of going or not going to church.

If, however, in the sin of omission, we consider also the causes, or occasions of the omission, then the sin of omission must of necessity include some act. For there is no sin of omission, unless we omit what we can do or not do: and that we turn aside so as not to do what we can do or not do, must needs be due to some cause or occasion, either united with the omission or preceding it. Now if this cause be not in man's power, the omission will not be sinful, as when anyone omits going to church on account of sickness: but if the cause or occasion be subject to the will, the omission is sinful; and such cause, insofar as it is voluntary, must needs always include some act, at least the interior act of the will: which act sometimes bears directly on the omission, as when a man wills *not to go to church*, because it is too much trouble; and in this case this act, of its very nature, belongs to the omission, because the volition of any sin whatever, pertains, of itself, to that sin, since voluntariness is essential to sin. Sometimes, however, the act of the will bears directly on something else which hinders man from doing what he ought, whether this something else be united with the omission, as when a man wills to play at the time he ought to go to church—or, precede the omission, as when a man wills to sit up late at night, the result being that he does not go to church in the morning. In this case the act, interior or exterior, is accidental to the omission, since the omission follows outside the intention, and that which is outside the intention is said to be accidental (*Phys.* ii, text. 49,50). Wherefore it is evident that then the sin of omission has indeed an act united with, or preceding the omission, but that this act is accidental to the sin of omission.

Now in judging about things, we must be guided by that which is proper to them, and not by that which is accidental: and consequently it is truer to say that a sin can be

possit esse absque omni actu. Alioquin etiam ad essentiam aliorum peccatorum actualium pertinerent actus et occasiones circumstantes.

AD PRIMUM ergo dicendum quod plura requiruntur ad bonum quam ad malum, eo quod *bonum contingit ex tota integra causa, malum autem ex singularibus defectibus*, ut Dionysius dicit, IV cap. de Div. Nom. Et ideo peccatum potest contingere sive aliquis faciat quod non debet, sive non faciendo quod debet, sed meritum non potest esse nisi aliquis faciat voluntarie quod debet. Et ideo meritum non potest esse sine actu, sed peccatum potest esse sine actu.

AD SECUNDUM dicendum quod aliquid dicitur voluntarium non solum quia cadit super ipsum actus voluntatis, sed quia in potestate nostra est ut fiat vel non fiat, ut dicitur in III Ethic. Unde etiam ipsum non velle potest dici voluntarium, inquantum in potestate hominis est velle et non velle.

AD TERTIUM dicendum quod peccatum omissionis contrariatur praecepto affirmativo, quod obligat semper, sed non ad semper. Et ideo solum pro tempore illo aliquis cessando ab actu peccat, pro quo praeceptum affirmativum obligat.

without any act; else the circumstantial acts and occasions would be essential to other actual sins.

REPLY OBJ. 1: More things are required for good than for evil, since *good results from a whole and entire cause, whereas evil results from each single defect*, as Dionysius states (*Div. Nom.* iv): so that sin may arise from a man doing what he ought not, or by his not doing what he ought; while there can be no merit, unless a man do willingly what he ought to do: wherefore there can be no merit without act, whereas there can be sin without act.

REPLY OBJ. 2: The term *voluntary* is applied not only to that on which the act of the will is brought to bear, but also to that which we have the power to do or not to do, as stated in *Ethic.* iii, 5. Hence even not to will may be called voluntary, insofar as man has it in his power to will, and not to will.

REPLY OBJ. 3: The sin of omission is contrary to an affirmative precept which binds always, but not for always. Hence, by omitting to act, a man sins only for the time at which the affirmative precept binds him to act.

Article 6

Whether Sin Is Fittingly Defined As a Word, Deed, or Desire Contrary to the Eternal Law?

AD SEXTUM SIC PROCEDITUR. Videtur quod inconvenienter definiatur peccatum, cum dicitur, *peccatum est dictum vel factum vel concupitum contra legem aeternam*. Dictum enim, vel factum, vel concupitum, importat aliquem actum. Sed non omne peccatum importat aliquem actum, ut dictum est. Ergo haec definitio non includit omne peccatum.

PRAETEREA, Augustinus dicit, in libro de duabus animabus, *peccatum est voluntas retinendi vel consequendi quod iustitia vetat*. Sed voluntas sub concupiscentia comprehenditur, secundum quod concupiscentia largo modo sumitur, pro omni appetitu. Ergo suffecisset dicere, peccatum est concupitum contra legem aeternam; nec oportuit addere, dictum vel factum.

PRAETEREA, peccatum proprie consistere videtur in aversione a fine, nam bonum et malum principaliter considerantur secundum finem, ut ex supradictis patet. Unde et Augustinus, in I de Lib. Arb., per comparationem ad finem definit peccatum, dicens quod *peccare nihil est aliud quam, neglectis rebus aeternis, temporalia sectari*, et in libro octoginta trium quaest., dicit quod *omnis humana perversitas est uti fruendis et frui utendis*.

OBJECTION 1: It would seem that sin is unfittingly defined by saying: *Sin is a word, deed, or desire, contrary to the eternal law*. Because *Word*, *deed*, and *desire* imply an act; whereas not every sin implies an act, as stated above (A5). Therefore this definition does not include every sin.

OBJ. 2: Further, Augustine says (*De Duab. Anim.* xii): *Sin is the will to retain or obtain what justice forbids*. Now will is comprised under desire, insofar as desire denotes any act of the appetite. Therefore it was enough to say: *Sin is a desire contrary to the eternal law*, nor was there need to add *word* or *deed*.

OBJ. 3: Further, sin apparently consists properly in aversion from the end: because good and evil are measured chiefly with regard to the end as explained above (Q1, A3; Q18, AA4,6; Q20, AA2,3): wherefore Augustine (*De Lib. Arb.* i) defines sin in reference to the end, by saying that *sin is nothing else than to neglect eternal things, and seek after temporal things*: and again he says (Qq. lxxxii, qu. 30) that *all human wickedness consists in using what we should*

Sed in praemissa definitione nulla fit mentio de aversione a debito fine. Ergo insufficienter definitur peccatum.

PRAETEREA, ex hoc dicitur aliquid esse prohibitum, quia legi contrariatur. Sed non omnia peccata sunt mala quia prohibita, sed quaedam sunt prohibita quia mala. Non ergo in communi definitione peccati debuit poni quod sit contra legem Dei.

PRAETEREA, peccatum significat malum hominis actum, ut ex dictis patet. Sed malum hominis est contra rationem esse, ut Dionysius dicit, IV cap. de Div. Nom. Ergo potius debuit dici quod peccatum sit contra rationem, quam quod peccatum sit contra legem aeternam.

IN CONTRARIUM sufficit auctoritas Augustini.

RESPONDEO dicendum quod, sicut ex dictis patet, peccatum nihil aliud est quam actus humanus malus. Quod autem aliquis actus sit humanus, habet ex hoc quod est voluntarius, sicut ex supradictis patet, sive sit voluntarius quasi a voluntate elicitus, ut ipsum velle et eligere; sive quasi a voluntate imperatus, ut exteriores actus vel locutionis vel operationis. Habet autem actus humanus quod sit malus, ex eo quod caret debita commensuratione. Omnis autem commensuratio cuiuscumque rei attenditur per comparationem ad aliquam regulam, a qua si divertat, incommensurata erit. Regula autem voluntatis humanae est duplex, una propinqua et homogenea, scilicet ipsa humana ratio; alia vero est prima regula, scilicet lex aeterna, quae est quasi ratio Dei. Et ideo Augustinus in definitione peccati posuit duo, unum quod pertinet ad substantiam actus humani, quod est quasi materiale in peccato, cum dixit, dictum vel factum vel concupitum; aliud autem quod pertinet ad rationem mali, quod est quasi formale in peccato, cum dixit, contra legem aeternam.

AD PRIMUM ergo dicendum quod affirmatio et negatio reducuntur ad idem genus, sicut in divinis genitum et ingenitum ad relationem, ut Augustinus dicit, in V de Trin. Et ideo pro eodem est accipiendum dictum et non dictum, factum et non factum.

AD SECUNDUM dicendum quod prima causa peccati est in voluntate, quae imperat omnes actus voluntarios, in quibus solum invenitur peccatum, et ideo Augustinus quandoque per solam voluntatem definit peccatum. Sed quia etiam ipsi exteriores actus pertinent ad substantiam peccati, cum sint secundum se mali, ut dictum est, necesse fuit quod in definitione peccati poneretur etiam aliquid pertinens ad exteriores actus.

AD TERTIUM dicendum quod lex aeterna primo et principaliter ordinat hominem ad finem, consequenter autem facit hominem bene se habere circa ea quae sunt ad finem. Et ideo in hoc quod dicit contra legem

enjoy, and in enjoying what we should use. Now the definition is question contains no mention of aversion from our due end: therefore it is an insufficient definition of sin.

OBJ. 4: Further, a thing is said to be forbidden, because it is contrary to the law. Now not all sins are evil through being forbidden, but some are forbidden because they are evil. Therefore sin in general should not be defined as being against the law of God.

OBJ. 5: Further, a sin denotes a bad human act, as was explained above (A1). Now man's evil is to be against reason, as Dionysius states (*Div. Nom.* iv). Therefore it would have been better to say that sin is against reason than to say that it is contrary to the eternal law.

ON THE CONTRARY, the authority of Augustine suffices (*Contra Faust.* xxii, 27).

I ANSWER THAT, As was shown above (A1), sin is nothing else than a bad human act. Now that an act is a human act is due to its being voluntary, as stated above (Q1, A1), whether it be voluntary, as being elicited by the will, e.g., to will or to choose, or as being commanded by the will, e.g., the exterior actions of speech or operation. Again, a human act is evil through lacking conformity with its due measure: and conformity of measure in a thing depends on a rule, from which if that thing depart, it is incommensurate. Now there are two rules of the human will: one is proximate and homogeneous, viz., the human reason; the other is the first rule, viz., the eternal law, which is God's reason, so to speak. Accordingly Augustine (*Contra Faust.* xxii, 27) includes two things in the definition of sin; one, pertaining to the substance of a human act, and which is the matter, so to speak, of sin, when he says *word, deed,* or *desire;* the other, pertaining to the nature of evil, and which is the form, as it were, of sin, when he says, *contrary to the eternal law.*

REPLY OBJ. 1: Affirmation and negation are reduced to one same genus: e.g., in Divine things, begotten and unbegotten are reduced to the genus *relation,* as Augustine states (*De Trin.* v, 6,7): and so *word* and *deed* denote equally what is said and what is not said, what is done and what is not done.

REPLY OBJ. 2: The first cause of sin is in the will, which commands all voluntary acts, in which alone is sin to be found: and hence it is that Augustine sometimes defines sin in reference to the will alone. But since external acts also pertain to the substance of sin, through being evil of themselves, as stated, it was necessary in defining sin to include something referring to external action.

REPLY OBJ. 3: The eternal law first and foremost directs man to his end, and in consequence, makes man to be well disposed in regard to things which are directed to the end: hence when he says, *contrary to the eternal law,* he includes

aeternam, tangit aversionem a fine, et omnes alias inordinationes.

AD QUARTUM dicendum quod, cum dicitur quod non omne peccatum ideo est malum quia est prohibitum, intelligitur de prohibitione facta per ius positivum. Si autem referatur ad ius naturale, quod continetur primo quidem in lege aeterna, secundario vero in naturali iudicatorio rationis humanae, tunc omne peccatum est malum quia prohibitum, ex hoc enim ipso quod est inordinatum, iuri naturali repugnat.

AD QUINTUM dicendum quod a theologis consideratur peccatum praecipue secundum quod est offensa contra Deum, a philosopho autem morali, secundum quod contrariatur rationi. Et ideo Augustinus convenientius definit peccatum ex hoc quod est contra legem aeternam, quam ex hoc quod est contra rationem, praecipue cum per legem aeternam regulemur in multis quae excedunt rationem humanam, sicut in his quae sunt fidei.

aversion from the end and all other forms of inordinateness.

REPLY OBJ. 4: When it is said that not every sin is evil through being forbidden, this must be understood of prohibition by positive law. If, however, the prohibition be referred to the natural law, which is contained primarily in the eternal law, but secondarily in the natural code of the human reason, then every sin is evil through being prohibited: since it is contrary to natural law, precisely because it is inordinate.

REPLY OBJ. 5: The theologian considers sin chiefly as an offense against God; and the moral philosopher, as something contrary to reason. Hence Augustine defines sin with reference to its being *contrary to the eternal law*, more fittingly than with reference to its being contrary to reason; the more so, as the eternal law directs us in many things that surpass human reason, e.g., in matters of faith.

QUESTION 72

OF THE DISTINCTION OF SINS

Deinde considerandum est de distinctione peccatorum vel vitiorum. Et circa hoc quaeruntur novem.

Primo, utrum peccata distinguantur specie secundum obiecta.

Secundo, de distinctione peccatorum spiritualium et carnalium.

Tertio, utrum secundum causas.

Quarto, utrum secundum eos in quos peccatur.

Quinto, utrum secundum diversitatem reatus.

Sexto, utrum secundum omissionem et commissionem.

Septimo, utrum secundum diversum processum peccati.

Octavo, utrum secundum abundantiam et defectum.

Nono, utrum secundum diversas circumstantias.

We must now consider the distinction of sins or vices: under which head there are nine points of inquiry:

(1) Whether sins are distinguished specifically by their objects?

(2) Of the distinction between spiritual and carnal sins;

(3) Whether sins differ in reference to their causes?

(4) Whether they differ with respect to those who are sinned against?

(5) Whether sins differ in relation to the debt of punishment?

(6) Whether they differ in regard to omission and commission?

(7) Whether they differ according to their various stages?

(8) Whether they differ in respect of excess and deficiency?

(9) Whether they differ according to their various circumstances?

Article 1

Whether Sins Differ in Species According to Their Objects?

AD PRIMUM SIC PROCEDITUR. Videtur quod peccata non differant specie secundum obiecta. Actus enim humani praecipue dicuntur boni vel mali per comparationem ad finem, ut supra ostensum est. Cum igitur peccatum nihil aliud sit quam actus hominis malus, sicut dictum est, videtur quod secundum fines peccata debeant distingui specie, magis quam secundum obiecta.

PRAETEREA, malum, cum sit privatio, distinguitur specie secundum diversas species oppositorum. Sed peccatum est quoddam malum in genere humanorum actuum. Ergo peccata magis distinguuntur specie secundum opposita, quam secundum obiecta.

PRAETEREA, si peccata specie differrent secundum obiecta, impossibile esset idem peccatum specie circa diversa obiecta inveniri. Sed inveniuntur aliqua huiusmodi peccata, nam superbia est et in rebus spiritualibus et in corporalibus, ut Gregorius dicit, in libro XXXIV Moral.; avaritia etiam est circa diversa genera rerum. Ergo peccata non distinguuntur specie secundum obiecta.

SED CONTRA est quod peccatum est dictum vel factum vel concupitum contra legem Dei. Sed dicta vel facta vel concupita distinguuntur specie secundum diversa

OBJECTION 1: It would seem that sins do not differ in species, according to their objects. For acts are said to be good or evil, in relation, chiefly, to their end, as shown above (Q1, A3; Q18, AA4,6). Since then sin is nothing else than a bad human act, as stated above (Q71, A1), it seems that sins should differ specifically according to their ends rather than according to their objects.

OBJ. 2: Further, evil, being a privation, differs specifically according to the different species of opposites. Now sin is an evil in the genus of human acts. Therefore sins differ specifically according to their opposites rather than according to their objects.

OBJ. 3: Further, if sins differed specifically according to their objects, it would be impossible to find the same specific sin with diverse objects: and yet such sins are to be found. For pride is about things spiritual and material as Gregory says (*Moral.* xxxiv, 18); and avarice is about different kinds of things. Therefore sins do not differ in species according to their objects.

ON THE CONTRARY, *Sin is a word, deed, or desire against God's law.* Now words, deeds, and desires differ in species according to their various objects: since acts differ

13

obiecta, quia actus per obiecta distinguuntur, ut supra dictum est. Ergo etiam peccata secundum obiecta specie distinguuntur.

RESPONDEO dicendum quod, sicut dictum est, ad rationem peccati duo concurrunt, scilicet actus voluntarius; et inordinatio eius, quae est per recessum a lege Dei. Horum autem duorum unum per se comparatur ad peccantem, qui intendit talem actum voluntarium exercere in tali materia, aliud autem, scilicet inordinatio actus, per accidens se habet ad intentionem peccantis; *nullus enim intendens ad malum operatur,* ut Dionysius dicit, IV cap. de Div. Nom. Manifestum est autem quod unumquodque, consequitur speciem secundum illud quod est per se, non autem secundum id quod est per accidens, quia ea quae sunt per accidens, sunt extra rationem speciei. Et ideo peccata specie distinguuntur ex parte actuum voluntariorum, magis quam ex parte inordinationis in peccato existentis. Actus autem voluntarii distinguuntur specie secundum obiecta, ut in superioribus ostensum est. Unde sequitur quod peccata proprie distinguantur specie secundum obiecta.

AD PRIMUM ergo dicendum quod finis principaliter habet rationem boni, et ideo comparatur ad actum voluntatis, qui est primordialis in omni peccato, sicut obiectum. Unde in idem redit quod peccata differant secundum obiecta, vel secundum fines.

AD SECUNDUM dicendum quod peccatum non est pura privatio, sed est actus debito ordine privatus. Et ideo peccata magis distinguuntur specie secundum obiecta actuum, quam secundum opposita. Quamvis etiam si distinguantur secundum oppositas virtutes, in idem rediret, virtutes enim distinguuntur specie secundum obiecta, ut supra habitum est.

AD TERTIUM dicendum quod nihil prohibet in diversis rebus specie vel genere differentibus, invenire unam formalem rationem obiecti, a qua peccatum speciem recipit. Et hoc modo superbia circa diversas res excellentiam quaerit, avaritia vero abundantiam eorum quae usui humano accommodantur.

by their objects, as stated above (Q18, A2). Therefore sins, also differ in species according to their objects.

I ANSWER THAT, As stated above (Q71, A6), two things concur in the nature of sin, viz., the voluntary act, and its inordinateness, which consists in departing from God's law. Of these two, one is referred essentially to the sinner, who intends such and such an act in such and such matter; while the other, viz., the inordinateness of the act, is referred accidentally to the intention of the sinner, for *no one acts intending evil,* as Dionysius declares (*Div. Nom.* iv). Now it is evident that a thing derives its species from that which is essential and not from that which is accidental: because what is accidental is outside the specific nature. Consequently sins differ specifically on the part of the voluntary acts rather than of the inordinateness inherent to sin. Now voluntary acts differ in species according to their objects, as was proved above (Q18, A2). Therefore it follows that sins are properly distinguished in species by their objects.

REPLY OBJ. 1: The aspect of good is found chiefly in the end: and therefore the end stands in the relation of object to the act of the will which is at the root of every sin. Consequently it amounts to the same whether sins differ by their objects or by their ends.

REPLY OBJ. 2: Sin is not a pure privation but an act deprived of its due order: hence sins differ specifically according to their objects of their acts rather than according to their opposites, although, even if they were distinguished in reference to their opposite virtues, it would come to the same: since virtues differ specifically according to their objects, as stated above (Q60, A5).

REPLY OBJ. 3: In various things, differing in species or genus, nothing hinders our finding one formal aspect of the object, from which aspect sin receives its species. It is thus that pride seeks excellence in reference to various things; and avarice seeks abundance of things adapted to human use.

Article 2

Whether Spiritual Sins Are Fittingly Distinguished from Carnal Sins?

AD SECUNDUM SIC PROCEDITUR. Videtur quod inconvenienter distinguantur peccata spiritualia a carnalibus. Dicit enim apostolus, ad Galat. V, *manifesta sunt opera carnis, quae sunt fornicatio, immunditia, impudicitia, luxuria, idolorum servitus, veneficia,* etc., ex quo videtur quod omnia peccatorum genera sunt opera carnis. Sed peccata carnalia dicuntur opera carnis. Ergo non sunt distinguenda peccata carnalia a spiritualibus.

OBJECTION 1: It would seem that spiritual sins are unfittingly distinguished from carnal sins. For the Apostle says (Gal 5:19): *The works of the flesh are manifest, which are fornication, uncleanness, immodesty, luxury, idolatry, witchcrafts,* etc. from which it seems that all kinds of sins are works of the flesh. Now carnal sins are called works of the flesh. Therefore carnal sins should not be distinguished from spiritual sins.

PRAETEREA, quicumque peccat, secundum carnem ambulat, secundum illud Rom. VIII, *si secundum carnem vixeritis, moriemini; si autem spiritu facta carnis mortificaveritis, vivetis*. Sed vivere vel ambulare secundum carnem, videtur pertinere ad rationem peccati carnalis. Ergo omnia peccata sunt carnalia. Non ergo sunt distinguenda peccata carnalia a spiritualibus.

PRAETEREA, superior pars animae, quae est mens vel ratio, spiritus nominatur, secundum illud Ephes. IV, *renovamini spiritu mentis vestrae*, ubi spiritus pro ratione ponitur, ut ibi Glossa dicit. Sed omne peccatum quod secundum carnem committitur, a ratione derivatur per consensum, quia superioris rationis est consentire in actum peccati, ut infra dicetur. Ergo eadem peccata sunt carnalia et spiritualia. Non ergo sunt distinguenda ad invicem.

PRAETEREA, si aliqua peccata specialiter sunt carnalia, hoc potissime intelligendum videtur de illis peccatis quibus aliquis in corpus suum peccat. Sed sicut apostolus dicit, I ad Cor. VI, *omne peccatum quodcumque fecerit homo, extra corpus est, qui autem fornicatur, in corpus suum peccat*. Ergo sola fornicatio esset peccatum carnale, cum tamen apostolus, ad Ephes. V, etiam avaritiam carnalibus peccatis annumeret.

SED CONTRA est quod Gregorius, XXXI Moral., dicit quod *septem capitalium vitiorum quinque sunt spiritualia, et duo carnalia*.

RESPONDEO dicendum quod, sicut dictum est, peccata recipiunt speciem ex obiectis. Omne autem peccatum consistit in appetitu alicuius commutabilis boni quod inordinate appetitur, et per consequens in eo iam habito inordinate aliquis delectatur. Ut autem ex superioribus patet, duplex est delectatio. Una quidem animalis, quae consummatur in sola apprehensione alicuius rei ad votum habitae, et haec etiam potest dici delectatio spiritualis, sicut cum aliquis delectatur in laude humana, vel in aliquo huiusmodi. Alia vero delectatio est corporalis, sive naturalis, quae in ipso tactu corporali perficitur, quae potest etiam dici delectatio carnalis.

Sic igitur illa peccata quae perficiuntur in delectatione spirituali, vocantur peccata spiritualia, illa vero quae perficiuntur in delectatione carnali, vocantur peccata carnalia; sicut gula, quae perficitur in delectatione ciborum, et luxuria, quae perficitur in delectatione venereorum. Unde et apostolus dicit II ad Cor. VII. *Emundemus nos ab omni inquinamento, carnis et spiritus*.

AD PRIMUM ergo dicendum quod, sicut Glossa ibidem dicit, illa vitia dicuntur opera carnis, *non quia in voluptate carnis perficiantur, sed caro sumitur ibi pro homine, qui dum secundum se vivit, secundum carnem vivere dicitur*; ut etiam Augustinus dicit, XIV de Civ. Dei.

OBJ. 2: Further, whosoever sins, walks according to the flesh, as stated in Rm. 8:13: *If you live according to the flesh, you shall die. But if by the spirit you mortify the deeds of the flesh, you shall live*. Now to live or walk according to the flesh seems to pertain to the nature of carnal sin. Therefore carnal sins should not be distinguished from spiritual sins.

OBJ. 3: Further, the higher part of the soul, which is the mind or reason, is called the spirit, according to Eph. 4:23: *Be renewed in the spirit of your mind*, where spirit stands for reason, according to a gloss. Now every sin, which is committed in accordance with the flesh, flows from the reason by its consent; since consent in a sinful act belongs to the higher reason, as we shall state further on (Q74, A7). Therefore the same sins are both carnal and spiritual, and consequently they should not be distinguished from one another.

OBJ. 4: Further, if some sins are carnal specifically, this, seemingly, should apply chiefly to those sins whereby man sins against his own body. But, according to the Apostle (1 Cor 6:18), *every sin that a man doth, is without the body: but he that committeth fornication, sinneth against his own body*. Therefore fornication would be the only carnal sin, whereas the Apostle (Eph 5:3) reckons covetousness with the carnal sins.

ON THE CONTRARY, Gregory (*Moral.* xxxi, 17) says that *of the seven capital sins five are spiritual, and two carnal*.

I ANSWER THAT, As stated above (A1), sins take their species from their objects. Now every sin consists in the desire for some mutable good, for which man has an inordinate desire, and the possession of which gives him inordinate pleasure. Now, as explained above (Q31, A3), pleasure is twofold. One belongs to the soul, and is consummated in the mere apprehension of a thing possessed in accordance with desire; this can also be called spiritual pleasure, e.g., when one takes pleasure in human praise or the like. The other pleasure is bodily or natural, and is realized in bodily touch, and this can also be called carnal pleasure.

Accordingly, those sins which consist in spiritual pleasure, are called spiritual sins; while those which consist in carnal pleasure, are called carnal sins, e.g., gluttony, which consists in the pleasures of the table; and lust, which consists in sexual pleasures. Hence the Apostle says (2 Cor 7:1): *Let us cleanse ourselves from all defilement of the flesh and of the spirit*.

REPLY OBJ. 1: As a gloss says on the same passage, these vices are called works of the flesh, not as though they consisted in carnal pleasure; but flesh here denotes man, who is said to live according to the flesh, when he lives according to himself, as Augustine says (*De Civ. Dei* xiv, 2,3).

Et huius ratio est ex hoc, quod omnis rationis humanae defectus ex sensu carnali aliquo modo initium habet.

ET PER HOC etiam patet responsio ad secundum.

AD TERTIUM dicendum quod in peccatis etiam carnalibus est aliquis actus spiritualis, scilicet actus rationis, sed finis horum peccatorum, a quo denominantur, est delectatio carnis.

AD QUARTUM dicendum quod, sicut Glossa ibidem dicit, *specialiter in fornicationis peccato servit anima corpori, intantum ut nihil aliud in ipso momento cogitare homini liceat.* Delectatio autem gulae, etsi sit carnalis, non ita absorbet rationem. Vel potest dici quod in hoc peccato etiam quaedam iniuria fit corpori, dum inordinate maculatur. Et ideo per hoc solum peccatum dicitur specialiter homo in corpus peccare. Avaritia vero quae in carnalibus peccatis connumeratur, pro adulterio ponitur, quod est iniusta usurpatio uxoris alienae. Vel potest dici quod res in qua delectatur avarus, corporale quoddam est, et quantum ad hoc, connumeratur peccatis carnalibus. Sed ipsa delectatio non pertinet ad carnem, sed ad spiritum, et ideo secundum Gregorium, est spirituale peccatum.

The reason of this is because every failing in the human reason is due in some way to the carnal sense.

THIS SUFFICES for the Reply to the Second Objection.

REPLY OBJ. 3: Even in the carnal sins there is a spiritual act, viz., the act of reason: but the end of these sins, from which they are named, is carnal pleasure.

REPLY OBJ. 4: As the gloss says, *in the sin of fornication the soul is the body's slave in a special sense, because at the moment of sinning it can think of nothing else*: whereas the pleasure of gluttony, although carnal, does not so utterly absorb the reason. It may also be said that in this sin, an injury is done to the body also, for it is defiled inordinately: wherefore by this sin alone is man said specifically to sin against his body. While covetousness, which is reckoned among the carnal sins, stands here for adultery, which is the unjust appropriation of another's wife. Again, it may be said that the thing in which the covetous man takes pleasure is something bodily, and in this respect covetousness is numbered with the carnal sins: but the pleasure itself does not belong to the body, but to the spirit, wherefore Gregory says (*Moral.* xxxi, 17) that it is a spiritual sin.

Article 3

Whether Sins Differ Specifically in Reference to Their Causes?

AD TERTIUM SIC PROCEDITUR. Videtur quod peccata distinguantur specie secundum causas. Ab eodem enim habet res speciem, a quo habet esse. Sed peccata habent esse ex suis causis. Ergo ab eis etiam speciem sortiuntur. Differunt ergo specie secundum diversitatem causarum.

PRAETEREA, inter alias causas minus videtur pertinere ad speciem causa materialis. Sed obiectum in peccato est sicut causa materialis. Cum ergo secundum obiecta peccata specie distinguantur, videtur quod peccata multo magis secundum alias causas distinguantur specie.

PRAETEREA, Augustinus, super illud Psalmi, incensa igni et suffossa, dicit quod *omne peccatum est ex timore male humiliante, vel ex amore male inflammante.* Dicitur etiam I Ioan. II, quod *omne quod est in mundo, aut est concupiscentia carnis, aut concupiscentia oculorum, aut superbia vitae,* dicitur autem aliquid esse in mundo, propter peccatum, secundum quod mundi nomine amatores mundi significantur, ut Augustinus dicit, super Ioan. Gregorius etiam, XXXI Moral., distinguit omnia peccata secundum septem vitia capitalia. Omnes autem huiusmodi divisiones respiciunt causas peccatorum. Ergo videtur quod peccata differant specie secundum diversitatem causarum.

OBJECTION 1: It would seem that sins differ specifically in reference to their causes. For a thing takes its species from that whence it derives its being. Now sins derive their being from their causes. Therefore they take their species from them also. Therefore they differ specifically In reference to their causes.

OBJ. 2: Further, of all the causes the material cause seems to have least reference to the species. Now the object in a sin is like its material cause. Since, therefore, sins differ specifically according to their objects, it seems that much more do they differ in reference to their other causes.

OBJ. 3: Further, Augustine, commenting on Ps. 79:17, *Things set on fire and dug down*, says that *every sin is due either to fear inducing false humility, or to love enkindling us to undue ardor.* For it is written (1 John 2:16) that *all that is in the world, is the concupiscence of the flesh, or the concupiscence of the eyes, or the pride of life.* Now a thing is said to be in the world on account of sin, in as much as the world denotes lovers of the world, as Augustine observes (*Tract. ii in Joan.*). Gregory, too (*Moral.* xxxi, 17), distinguishes all sins according to the seven capital vices. Now all these divisions refer to the causes of sins. Therefore, seemingly, sins differ specifically according to the diversity of their causes.

SED CONTRA est quia secundum hoc omnia peccata essent unius speciei, cum ex una causa causentur, dicitur enim Eccli. X, quod *initium omnis peccati est superbia*; et I ad Tim. ult., quod *radix omnium malorum est cupiditas*. Manifestum est autem esse diversas species peccatorum. Non ergo peccata distinguuntur specie secundum diversitates causarum.

RESPONDEO dicendum quod, cum quatuor sint causarum genera, diversimode diversis attribuuntur. Causa enim formalis et materialis respiciunt proprie substantiam rei, et ideo substantiae secundum formam et materiam specie et genere distinguuntur. Agens autem et finis respiciunt directe motum et operationem, et ideo motus et operationes secundum huiusmodi causas specie distinguuntur; diversimode tamen. Nam principia activa naturalia sunt determinata semper ad eosdem actus, et ideo diversae species in actibus naturalibus attenduntur non solum secundum obiecta, quae sunt fines vel termini, sed etiam secundum principia activa; sicut calefacere et infrigidare distinguuntur specie secundum calidum et frigidum. Sed principia activa in actibus voluntariis, cuiusmodi sunt actus peccatorum, non se habent ex necessitate ad unum, et ideo ex uno principio activo vel motivo possunt diversae species peccatorum procedere; sicut ex timore male humiliante potest procedere quod homo furetur, et quod occidat, et quod deserat gregem sibi commissum; et haec eadem possunt procedere ex amore. Unde manifestum est quod peccata non differant specie secundum diversas causas activas vel motivas; sed solum secundum diversitatem causae finalis. Finis autem est obiectum voluntatis, ostensum est enim supra quod actus humani habent speciem ex fine.

AD PRIMUM ergo dicendum quod principia activa in actibus voluntariis, cum non sint determinata ad unum, non sufficiunt ad producendum humanos actus, nisi determinetur voluntas ad unum per intentionem finis; ut patet per philosophum, in IX Metaphys. Et ideo a fine perficitur et esse et species peccati.

AD SECUNDUM dicendum quod obiecta, secundum quod comparantur ad actus exteriores, habent rationem materiae circa quam, sed secundum quod comparantur ad actum interiorem voluntatis, habent rationem finium; et ex hoc habent quod dent speciem actui. Quamvis etiam secundum quod sunt materia circa quam, habeant rationem terminorum; a quibus motus specificantur, ut dicitur in V Physic. et in X Ethic. Sed tamen etiam termini motus dant speciem motibus, inquantum habent rationem finis.

AD TERTIUM dicendum quod illae divisiones peccatorum non dantur ad distinguendas species peccatorum; sed ad manifestandas diversas causas eorum.

ON THE CONTRARY, If this were the case all sins would belong to one species, since they are due to one cause. For it is written (Sir 10:15) that *pride is the beginning of all sin*, and (1 Tim 6:10) that *the desire of money is the root of all evils*. Now it is evident that there are various species of sins. Therefore sins do not differ specifically according to their different causes.

I ANSWER THAT, Since there are four kinds of causes, they are attributed to various things in various ways. Because the *formal* and the *material* cause regard properly the substance of a thing; and consequently substances differ in respect of their matter and form, both in species and in genus. The *agent* and the *end* regard directly movement and operation: wherefore movements and operations differ specifically in respect of these causes; in different ways, however, because the natural active principles are always determined to the same acts; so that the different species of natural acts are taken not only from the objects, which are the ends or terms of those acts, but also from their active principles: thus heating and cooling are specifically distinct with reference to hot and cold. On the other hand, the active principles in voluntary acts, such as the acts of sins, are not determined, of necessity, to one act, and consequently from one active or motive principle, diverse species of sins can proceed: thus from fear engendering false humility man may proceed to theft, or murder, or to neglect the flock committed to his care; and these same things may proceed from love enkindling to undue ardor. Hence it is evident that sins do not differ specifically according to their various active or motive causes, but only in respect of diversity in the final cause, which is the end and object of the will. For it has been shown above (Q1, A3; Q18, AA4,6) that human acts take their species from the end.

REPLY OBJ. 1: The active principles in voluntary acts, not being determined to one act, do not suffice for the production of human acts, unless the will be determined to one by the intention of the end, as the Philosopher proves (*Metaph.* ix, text. 15,16), and consequently sin derives both its being and its species from the end.

REPLY OBJ. 2: Objects, in relation to external acts, have the character of matter *about which*; but, in relation to the interior act of the will, they have the character of end; and it is owing to this that they give the act its species. Nevertheless, even considered as the matter *about which*, they have the character of term, from which movement takes its species (*Phys.* v, text. 4; *Ethic.* x, 4); yet even terms of movement specify movements, insofar as term has the character of end.

REPLY OBJ. 3: These distinctions of sins are given, not as distinct species of sins, but to show their various causes.

Article 4

Whether Sin Is Fittingly Divided into Sin Against God, Against Oneself, and Against One's Neighbor?

AD QUARTUM SIC PROCEDITUR. Videtur quod inconvenienter peccatum distinguatur per peccatum quod est in Deum, in proximum, et in seipsum. Illud enim quod est commune omni peccato, non debet poni quasi pars in divisione peccati. Sed commune est omni peccato quod sit contra Deum, ponitur enim in definitione peccati quod sit contra legem Dei, ut supra dictum est. Non ergo peccatum in Deum debet poni quasi pars in divisione peccatorum.

PRAETEREA, omnis divisio debet fieri per opposita. Sed ista tria genera peccatorum non sunt opposita, quicumque enim peccat in proximum, peccat etiam in seipsum et in Deum. Non ergo peccatum convenienter dividitur secundum haec tria.

PRAETEREA, ea quae sunt extrinsecus, non conferunt speciem. Sed Deus et proximus sunt extra nos. Ergo per haec non distinguuntur peccata secundum speciem. Inconvenienter igitur secundum haec tria peccatum dividitur.

SED CONTRA est quod Isidorus, in libro de summo bono, distinguens peccata, dicit quod *homo dicitur peccare in se, in Deum, et in proximum.*

RESPONDEO dicendum quod, sicut supra dictum est, peccatum est actus inordinatus. Triplex autem ordo in homine debet esse. Unus quidem secundum comparationem ad regulam rationis, prout scilicet omnes actiones et passiones nostrae debent secundum regulam rationis commensurari. Alius autem ordo est per comparationem ad regulam divinae legis, per quam homo in omnibus dirigi debet. Et si quidem homo naturaliter esset animal solitarium, hic duplex ordo sufficeret, sed quia homo est naturaliter animal politicum et sociale, ut probatur in I Polit., ideo necesse est quod sit tertius ordo, quo homo ordinetur ad alios homines, quibus convivere debet. Horum autem ordinum secundus continet primum, et excedit ipsum. Quaecumque enim continentur sub ordine rationis, continentur sub ordine ipsius Dei, sed quaedam continentur sub ordine ipsius Dei, quae excedunt rationem humanam, sicut ea quae sunt fidei, et quae debentur soli Deo. Unde qui in talibus peccat, dicitur in Deum peccare, sicut haereticus et sacrilegus et blasphemus. Similiter etiam secundus ordo includit tertium, et excedit ipsum. Quia in omnibus in quibus ordinamur ad proximum, oportet nos dirigi secundum regulam rationis, sed in quibusdam dirigimur secundum rationem quantum ad nos tantum, non autem quantum ad proximum. Et quando in his peccatur, dicitur homo peccare in seipsum, sicut patet de guloso, luxurioso et prodigo. Quando vero peccat homo in his quibus ad proximum ordinatur, dicitur peccare in

OBJECTION 1: It would seem that sin is unfittingly divided into sin against God, against one's neighbor, and against oneself. For that which is common to all sins should not be reckoned as a part in the division of sin. But it is common to all sins to be against God: for it is stated in the definition of sin that it is *against God's law*, as stated above (Q66, A6). Therefore sin against God should not be reckoned a part of the division of sin.

OBJ. 2: Further, every division should consist of things in opposition to one another. But these three kinds of sin are not opposed to one another: for whoever sins against his neighbor, sins against himself and against God. Therefore sin is not fittingly divided into these three.

OBJ. 3: Further, specification is not taken from things external. But God and our neighbor are external to us. Therefore sins are not distinguished specifically with regard to them: and consequently sin is unfittingly divided according to these three.

ON THE CONTRARY, Isidore (*De Summo Bono*), in giving the division of sins, says that *man is said to sin against himself, against God, and against his neighbor.*

I ANSWER THAT, As stated above (Q71, AA1,6), sin is an inordinate act. Now there should be a threefold order in man: one in relation to the rule of reason, insofar as all our actions and passions should be commensurate with the rule of reason: another order is in relation to the rule of the Divine Law, whereby man should be directed in all things: and if man were by nature a solitary animal, this twofold order would suffice. But since man is naturally a civic and social animal, as is proved in *Polit.* i, 2, hence a third order is necessary, whereby man is directed in relation to other men among whom he has to dwell. Of these orders the second contains the first and surpasses it. For whatever things are comprised under the order of reason, are comprised under the order of God Himself. Yet some things are comprised under the order of God, which surpass the human reason, such as matters of faith, and things due to God alone. Hence he that sins in such matters, for instance, by heresy, sacrilege, or blasphemy, is said to sin against God. In like manner, the first order includes the third and surpasses it, because in all things wherein we are directed in reference to our neighbor, we need to be directed according to the order of reason. Yet in some things we are directed according to reason, in relation to ourselves only, and not in reference to our neighbor; and when man sins in these matters, he is said to sin against himself, as is seen in the glutton, the lustful, and the prodigal. But when man sins in matters concerning his neighbor, he is said to sin against his neighbor, as appears in the thief and murderer. Now the

proximum, sicut patet de fure et homicida. Sunt autem diversa quibus homo ordinatur ad Deum, et ad proximum, et ad seipsum. Unde haec distinctio peccatorum est secundum obiecta, secundum quae diversificantur species peccatorum. Unde haec distinctio peccatorum proprie est secundum diversas peccatorum species. Nam et virtutes, quibus peccata opponuntur, secundum hanc differentiam specie distinguuntur, manifestum est enim ex dictis quod virtutibus theologicis homo ordinatur ad Deum, temperantia vero et fortitudine ad seipsum, iustitia autem ad proximum.

AD PRIMUM ergo dicendum quod peccare in Deum, secundum quod ordo qui est ad Deum, includit omnem humanum ordinem, commune est omni peccato. Sed quantum ad id quod ordo Dei excedit alios duos ordines, sic peccatum in Deum est speciale genus peccati.

AD SECUNDUM dicendum quod quando aliqua quorum unum includit alterum, ab invicem distinguuntur, intelligitur fieri distinctio non secundum illud quod unum continetur in altero, sed secundum illud quod unum excedit alterum. Sicut patet in divisione numerorum et figurarum, non enim triangulus dividitur contra quadratum secundum quod continetur in eo, sed secundum quod exceditur ab eo; et similiter est de ternario et quaternario.

AD TERTIUM dicendum quod Deus et proximus, quamvis sint exteriora respectu ipsius peccantis, non tamen sunt extranea respectu actus peccati; sed comparantur ad ipsum sicut propria obiecta ipsius.

things whereby man is directed to God, his neighbor, and himself are diverse. Wherefore this distinction of sins is in respect of their objects, according to which the species of sins are diversified: and consequently this distinction of sins is properly one of different species of sins: because the virtues also, to which sins are opposed, differ specifically in respect of these three. For it is evident from what has been said (Q62, AA1,2,3) that by the theological virtues man is directed to God; by temperance and fortitude, to himself; and by justice to his neighbor.

REPLY OBJ. 1: To sin against God is common to all sins, insofar as the order to God includes every human order; but insofar as order to God surpasses the other two orders, sin against God is a special kind of sin.

REPLY OBJ. 2: When several things, of which one includes another, are distinct from one another, this distinction is understood to refer, not to the part contained in another, but to that in which one goes beyond another. This may be seen in the division of numbers and figures: for a triangle is distinguished from a four-sided figure not in respect of its being contained thereby, but in respect of that in which it is surpassed thereby: and the same applies to the numbers three and four.

REPLY OBJ. 3: Although God and our neighbor are external to the sinner himself, they are not external to the act of sin, but are related to it as to its object.

Article 5

Whether the Division of Sins According to Their Debt of Punishment Diversifies Their Species?

AD QUINTUM SIC PROCEDITUR. Videtur quod divisio peccatorum quae est secundum reatum, diversificet speciem, puta cum dividitur secundum veniale et mortale. Ea enim quae in infinitum differunt, non possunt esse unius speciei, nec etiam unius generis. Sed veniale et mortale peccatum differunt in infinitum, veniali enim debetur poena temporalis, mortali poena aeterna; mensura autem poenae respondet quantitati culpae, secundum illud Deut. XXV, *pro mensura delicti erit et plagarum modus*. Ergo veniale et mortale non sunt unius generis, nedum quod sint unius speciei.

PRAETEREA, quaedam peccata sunt mortalia ex genere, sicut homicidium et adulterium, quaedam vero ex suo genere sunt peccata venialia, sicut verbum otiosum et risus superfluus. Ergo peccatum veniale et mortale specie differunt.

OBJECTION 1: It would seem that the division of sins according to their debt of punishment diversifies their species; for instance, when sin is divided into *mortal* and *venial*. For things which are infinitely apart, cannot belong to the same species, nor even to the same genus. But venial and mortal sin are infinitely apart, since temporal punishment is due to venial sin, and eternal punishment to mortal sin; and the measure of the punishment corresponds to the gravity of the fault, according to Dt. 25:2: *According to the measure of the sin shall the measure be also of the stripes be.* Therefore venial and mortal sins are not of the same genus, nor can they be said to belong to the same species.

OBJ. 2: Further, some sins are mortal in virtue of their species, as murder and adultery; and some are venial in virtue of their species, as in an idle word, and excessive laughter. Therefore venial and mortal sins differ specifically.

PRAETEREA, sicut se habet actus virtuosus ad praemium, ita se habet peccatum ad poenam. Sed praemium est finis virtuosi actus. Ergo et poena est finis peccati. Sed peccata distinguuntur specie secundum fines, ut dictum est. Ergo etiam distinguuntur specie secundum reatum poenae.

SED CONTRA, ea quae constituunt speciem, sunt priora, sicut differentiae specificae. Sed poena sequitur culpam, sicut effectus eius. Ergo peccata non differunt specie secundum reatum poenae.

RESPONDEO dicendum quod eorum quae specie differunt, duplex differentia invenitur. Una quidem quae constituit diversitatem specierum, et talis differentia nunquam invenitur nisi in speciebus diversis; sicut rationale et irrationale, animatum et inanimatum. Alia autem differentia est consequens diversitatem speciei, et talis differentia, etsi in aliquibus consequatur diversitatem speciei, in aliis tamen potest inveniri in eadem specie; sicut album et nigrum consequuntur diversitatem speciei corvi et cygni, tamen invenitur huiusmodi differentia in eadem hominis specie.

Dicendum est ergo quod differentia venialis et mortalis peccati, vel quaecumque alia differentia sumitur penes reatum, non potest esse differentia constituens diversitatem speciei. Nunquam enim id quod est per accidens, constituit speciem. Id autem quod est praeter intentionem agentis, est per accidens, ut patet in II Physic. Manifestum est autem quod poena est praeter intentionem peccantis. Unde per accidens se habet ad peccatum, ex parte ipsius peccantis. Ordinatur tamen ad peccatum ab exteriori, scilicet ex iustitia iudicantis, qui secundum diversas conditiones peccatorum diversas poenas infligit. Unde differentia quae est ex reatu poenae, potest consequi diversam speciem peccatorum; non autem constituit diversitatem speciei.

Differentia autem peccati venialis et mortalis consequitur diversitatem inordinationis, quae complet rationem peccati. Duplex enim est inordinatio, una per subtractionem principii ordinis; alia qua, salvato principio ordinis, fit inordinatio circa ea quae sunt post principium. Sicut in corpore animalis quandoque quidem inordinatio complexionis procedit usque ad destructionem principii vitalis, et haec est mors, quandoque vero, salvo principio vitae, fit inordinatio quaedam in humoribus, et tunc est aegritudo. Principium autem totius ordinis in moralibus est finis ultimus, qui ita se habet in operativis, sicut principium indemonstrabile in speculativis, ut dicitur in VII Ethic. Unde quando anima deordinatur per peccatum usque ad aversionem ab ultimo fine, scilicet Deo, cui unimur per caritatem, tunc est peccatum mortale, quando vero fit deordinatio citra aversionem a Deo, tunc est peccatum veniale. Sicut

OBJ. 3: Further, just as a virtuous act stands in relation to its reward, so does sin stand in relation to punishment. But the reward is the end of the virtuous act. Therefore punishment is the end of sin. Now sins differ specifically in relation to their ends, as stated above (A1, ad 1). Therefore they are also specifically distinct according to the debt of punishment.

ON THE CONTRARY, Those things that constitute a species are prior to the species, e.g., specific differences. But punishment follows sin as the effect thereof. Therefore sins do not differ specifically according to the debt of punishment.

I ANSWER THAT, In things that differ specifically we find a twofold difference: the first causes the diversity of species, and is not to be found save in different species, e.g., *rational* and *irrational, animate*, and *inanimate*: the other difference is consequent to specific diversity; and though, in some cases, it may be consequent to specific diversity, yet, in others, it may be found within the same species; thus *white* and *black* are consequent to the specific diversity of crow and swan, and yet this difference is found within the one species of man.

We must therefore say that the difference between venial and mortal sin, or any other difference is respect of the debt of punishment, cannot be a difference constituting specific diversity. For what is accidental never constitutes a species; and what is outside the agent's intention is accidental (*Phys.* ii, text. 50). Now it is evident that punishment is outside the intention of the sinner, wherefore it is accidentally referred to sin on the part of the sinner. Nevertheless it is referred to sin by an extrinsic principle, viz., the justice of the judge, who imposes various punishments according to the various manners of sin. Therefore the difference derived from the debt of punishment, may be consequent to the specific diversity of sins, but cannot constitute it.

Now the difference between venial and mortal sin is consequent to the diversity of that inordinateness which constitutes the notion of sin. For inordinateness is twofold, one that destroys the principle of order, and another which, without destroying the principle of order, implies inordinateness in the things which follow the principle: thus, in an animal's body, the frame may be so out of order that the vital principle is destroyed; this is the inordinateness of death; while, on the other hand, saving the vital principle, there may be disorder in the bodily humors; and then there is sickness. Now the principle of the entire moral order is the last end, which stands in the same relation to matters of action, as the indemonstrable principle does to matters of speculation (*Ethic.* vii, 8). Therefore when the soul is so disordered by sin as to turn away from its last end, viz., God, to Whom it is united by charity, there is mortal sin; but when it is disordered without turning away from God, there is

enim in corporalibus deordinatio mortis, quae est per remotionem principii vitae, est irreparabilis secundum naturam; inordinatio autem aegritudinis reparari potest, propter id quod salvatur principium vitae; similiter est in his quae pertinent ad animam. Nam in speculativis qui errat circa principia, impersuasibilis est, qui autem errat salvatis principiis, per ipsa principia revocari potest. Et similiter in operativis qui peccando avertitur ab ultimo fine, quantum est ex natura peccati, habet lapsum irreparabilem, et ideo dicitur peccare mortaliter, aeternaliter puniendus. Qui vero peccat citra aversionem a Deo, ex ipsa ratione peccati reparabiliter deordinatur, quia salvatur principium, et ideo dicitur peccare venialiter, quia scilicet non ita peccat ut mereatur interminabilem poenam.

AD PRIMUM ergo dicendum quod peccatum mortale et veniale differunt in infinitum ex parte aversionis, non autem ex parte conversionis, per quam respicit obiectum, unde peccatum speciem habet. Unde nihil prohibet in eadem specie inveniri aliquod peccatum mortale et veniale, sicut primus motus in genere adulterii est peccatum veniale; et verbum otiosum, quod plerumque est veniale, potest etiam esse mortale.

AD SECUNDUM dicendum quod ex hoc quod invenitur aliquod peccatum mortale ex genere, et aliquod peccatum veniale ex genere, sequitur quod talis differentia consequatur diversitatem peccatorum secundum speciem, non autem quod causet eam. Talis autem differentia potest inveniri etiam in his quae sunt eiusdem speciei, ut dictum est.

AD TERTIUM dicendum quod praemium est de intentione merentis vel virtuose agentis, sed poena non est de intentione peccantis, sed magis est contra voluntatem ipsius. Unde non est similis ratio.

venial sin. For even as in the body, the disorder of death which results from the destruction of the principle of life, is irreparable according to nature, while the disorder of sickness can be repaired by reason of the vital principle being preserved, so it is in matters concerning the soul. Because, in speculative matters, it is impossible to convince one who errs in the principles, whereas one who errs, but retains the principles, can be brought back to the truth by means of the principles. Likewise in practical matters, he who, by sinning, turns away from his last end, if we consider the nature of his sin, falls irreparably, and therefore is said to sin mortally and to deserve eternal punishment: whereas when a man sins without turning away from God, by the very nature of his sin, his disorder can be repaired, because the principle of the order is not destroyed; wherefore he is said to sin venially, because, to wit, he does not sin so as to deserve to be punished eternally.

REPLY OBJ. 1: Mortal and venial sins are infinitely apart as regards what they *turn away from*, not as regards what they *turn to*, viz., the object which specifies them. Hence nothing hinders the same species from including mortal and venial sins; for instance, in the species *adultery* the first movement is a venial sin; while an idle word, which is, generally speaking, venial, may even be a mortal sin.

REPLY OBJ. 2: From the fact that one sin is mortal by reason of its species, and another venial by reason of its species, it follows that this difference is consequent to the specific difference of sins, not that it is the cause thereof. And this difference may be found even in things of the same species, as stated above.

REPLY OBJ. 3: The reward is intended by him that merits or acts virtually; whereas the punishment is not intended by the sinner, but, on the contrary, is against his will. Hence the comparison fails.

Article 6

Whether Sins of Commission and Omission Differ Specifically?

AD SEXTUM SIC PROCEDITUR. Videtur quod peccatum commissionis et omissionis specie differant. Delictum enim contra peccatum dividitur, Ephes. II, ubi dicitur, *cum essetis mortui delictis et peccatis vestris*. Et exponit ibi Glossa, *delictis, idest dimittendo quae iubentur; et peccatis, scilicet agendo prohibita*, ex quo patet quod per delictum intelligitur peccatum omissionis, per peccatum, peccatum commissionis. Differunt igitur specie, cum ex opposito dividantur, tanquam diversae species.

OBJECTION 1: It would seem that sins of commission and omission differ specifically. For *offense* and *sin* are condivided with one another (Eph 2:1), where it is written: *When you were dead in your offenses and sins*, which words a gloss explains, saying: '*Offenses*,' by omitting to do what was commanded, and '*sins*,' by doing what was forbidden. Whence it is evident that *offenses* here denotes sins of omission; while *sin* denotes sins of commission. Therefore they differ specifically, since they are contrasted with one another as different species.

PRAETEREA, peccato per se convenit quod sit contra legem Dei, ponitur enim in eius definitione, ut ex supradictis patet. Sed in lege Dei alia sunt praecepta affirmativa, contra quae est peccatum omissionis; et alia praecepta negativa, contra quae est peccatum commissionis. Ergo peccatum omissionis et peccatum commissionis differunt specie.

PRAETEREA, omissio et commissio differunt sicut affirmatio et negatio. Sed affirmatio et negatio non possunt esse unius speciei, quia negatio non habet speciem; *non entis enim non sunt neque species neque differentiae,* ut philosophus dicit. Ergo omissio et commissio non possunt esse unius speciei.

SED CONTRA, in eadem specie peccati invenitur omissio et commissio, avarus enim et aliena rapit, quod est peccatum commissionis; et sua non dat quibus dare debet, quod est peccatum omissionis. Ergo omissio et commissio non differunt specie.

RESPONDEO dicendum quod in peccatis invenitur duplex differentia, una materialis, et alia formalis. Materialis quidem attenditur secundum naturalem speciem actuum peccati, formalis autem secundum ordinem ad unum finem proprium, quod est obiectum proprium. Unde inveniuntur aliqui actus materialiter specie differentes, qui tamen formaliter sunt in eadem specie peccati, quia ad idem ordinantur, sicut ad eandem speciem homicidii pertinet iugulatio, lapidatio et perforatio, quamvis actus sint specie differentes secundum speciem naturae. Sic ergo si loquamur de specie peccati omissionis et commissionis materialiter, differunt specie, large tamen loquendo de specie, secundum quod negatio vel privatio speciem habere potest. Si autem loquamur de specie peccati omissionis et commissionis formaliter, sic non differunt specie, quia ad idem ordinantur, et ex eodem motivo procedunt. Avarus enim ad congregandum pecuniam et rapit, et non dat ea quae dare debet; et similiter gulosus ad satisfaciendum gulae, et superflua comedit, et ieiunia debita praetermittit; et idem est videre in ceteris. Semper enim in rebus negatio fundatur super aliqua affirmatione, quae est quodammodo causa eius, unde etiam in rebus naturalibus eiusdem rationis est quod ignis calefaciat, et quod non infrigidet.

AD PRIMUM ergo dicendum quod illa divisio quae est per commissionem et omissionem, non est secundum diversas species formales, sed materiales tantum, ut dictum est.

AD SECUNDUM dicendum quod necesse fuit in lege Dei proponi diversa praecepta affirmativa et negativa, ut gradatim homines introducerentur ad virtutem, prius quidem abstinendo a malo, ad quod inducimur per praecepta negativa; et postmodum faciendo bonum, ad quod inducimur per praecepta affirmativa. Et sic

OBJ. 2: Further, it is essential to sin to be against God's law, for this is part of its definition, as is clear from what has been said (Q71, A6). Now in God's law, the affirmative precepts, against which is the sin of omission, are different from the negative precepts, against which is the sin of omission. Therefore sins of omission and commission differ specifically.

OBJ. 3: Further, omission and commission differ as affirmation and negation. Now affirmation and negation cannot be in the same species, since negation has no species; for *there is neither species nor difference of non-being*, as the Philosopher states (*Phys.* iv, text. 67). Therefore omission and commission cannot belong to the same species.

ON THE CONTRARY, Omission and commission are found in the same species of sin. For the covetous man both takes what belongs to others, which is a sin of commission; and gives not of his own to whom he should give, which is a sin of omission. Therefore omission and commission do not differ specifically.

I ANSWER THAT, There is a twofold difference in sins; a material difference and a formal difference: the material difference is to be observed in the natural species of the sinful act; while the formal difference is gathered from their relation to one proper end, which is also their proper object. Hence we find certain acts differing from one another in the material specific difference, which are nevertheless formally in the same species of sin, because they are directed to the one same end: thus strangling, stoning, and stabbing come under the one species of murder, although the actions themselves differ specifically according to the natural species. Accordingly, if we refer to the material species in sins of omission and commission, they differ specifically, using species in a broad sense, insofar as negation and privation may have a species. But if we refer to the formal species of sins of omission and commission, they do not differ specifically, because they are directed to the same end, and proceed from the same motive. For the covetous man, in order to hoard money, both robs, and omits to give what he ought, and in like manner, the glutton, to satiate his appetite, both eats too much and omits the prescribed fasts. The same applies to other sins: for in things, negation is always founded on affirmation, which, in a manner, is its cause. Hence in the physical order it comes under the same head, that fire gives forth heat, and that it does not give forth cold.

REPLY OBJ. 1: This division in respect of commission and omission, is not according to different formal species, but only according to material species, as stated.

REPLY OBJ. 2: In God's law, the necessity for various affirmative and negative precepts, was that men might be gradually led to virtue, first by abstaining from evil, being induced to this by the negative precepts, and afterwards by doing good, to which we are induced by the affirmative precepts. Wherefore the affirmative and negative precepts do

praecepta affirmativa et negativa non pertinent ad diversas virtutes, sed ad diversos gradus virtutis. Et per consequens non oportet quod contrarientur diversis peccatis secundum speciem. Peccatum etiam non habet speciem ex parte aversionis, quia secundum hoc est negatio vel privatio, sed ex parte conversionis, secundum quod est actus quidam. Unde secundum diversa praecepta legis non diversificantur peccata secundum speciem.

AD TERTIUM dicendum quod obiectio illa procedit de materiali diversitate speciei. Sciendum est tamen quod negatio, etsi proprie non sit in specie, constituitur tamen in specie per reductionem ad aliquam affirmationem quam sequitur.

not belong to different virtues, but to different degrees of virtue; and consequently they are not of necessity, opposed to sins of different species. Moreover sin is not specified by that from which it turns away, because in this respect it is a negation or privation, but by that to which it turns, insofar as sin is an act. Consequently sins do not differ specifically according to the various precepts of the Law.

REPLY OBJ. 3: This objection considers the material diversity of sins. It must be observed, however, that although, properly speaking, negation is not in a species, yet it is allotted to a species by reduction to the affirmation on which it is based.

Article 7

Whether Sins Are Fittingly Divided into Sins of Thought, Word, and Deed?

AD SEPTIMUM SIC PROCEDITUR. Videtur quod inconvenienter dividatur peccatum in peccatum cordis, oris, et operis. Augustinus enim, in XII de Trin., ponit tres gradus peccati, quorum primus est, cum carnalis sensus illecebram quandam ingerit, quod est peccatum cogitationis, secundus gradus est, quando sola cogitationis delectatione aliquis contentus est; tertius gradus est, quando faciendum decernitur per consensum. Sed tria haec pertinent ad peccatum cordis. Ergo inconvenienter peccatum cordis ponitur quasi unum genus peccati.

PRAETEREA, Gregorius, in IV Moral., ponit quatuor gradus peccati, quorum primus est culpa latens in corde; secundus, cum exterius publicatur; tertius est, cum consuetudine roboratur; quartus est, cum usque ad praesumptionem divinae misericordiae, vel ad desperationem, homo procedit. Ubi non distinguitur peccatum operis a peccato oris; et adduntur duo alii peccatorum gradus. Ergo inconveniens fuit prima divisio.

PRAETEREA, non potest esse peccatum in ore vel in opere, nisi fiat prius in corde. Ergo ista peccata specie non differunt. Non ergo debent contra se invicem dividi.

SED CONTRA est quod Hieronymus dicit, super Ezech., *tria sunt generalia delicta quibus humanum subiacet genus, aut enim cogitatione, aut sermone, aut opere peccamus.*

RESPONDEO dicendum quod aliqua inveniuntur differre specie dupliciter. Uno modo, ex eo quod utrumque habet speciem completam, sicut equus et bos differunt specie. Alio modo, secundum diversos gradus in aliqua generatione vel motu accipiuntur diversae species, sicut aedificatio est completa generatio domus, collocatio autem fundamenti et erectio parietis sunt species incompletae, ut patet per philosophum, in X Ethic.; et idem

OBJECTION 1: It would seem that sins are unfittingly divided into sins of thought, word, and deed. For Augustine (*De Trin.* xii, 12) describes three stages of sin, of which the first is *when the carnal sense offers a bait*, which is the sin of thought; the second stage is reached *when one is satisfied with the mere pleasure of thought*; and the third stage, *when consent is given to the deed*. Now these three belong to the sin of thought. Therefore it is unfitting to reckon sin of thought as one kind of sin.

OBJ. 2: Further, Gregory (*Moral.* iv, 25) reckons four degrees of sin; the first of which is *a fault hidden in the heart*; the second, *when it is done openly*; the third, *when it is formed into a habit*; and the fourth, *when man goes so far as to presume on God's mercy or to give himself up to despair*: where no distinction is made between sins of deed and sins of word, and two other degrees of sin are added. Therefore the first division was unfitting.

OBJ. 3: Further, there can be no sin of word or deed unless there precede sin of thought. Therefore these sins do not differ specifically. Therefore they should not be condivided with one another.

ON THE CONTRARY, Jerome in commenting on Ezech. 43:23: *The human race is subject to three kinds of sin, for when we sin, it is either by thought, or word, or deed.*

I ANSWER THAT, Things differ specifically in two ways: first, when each has the complete species; thus a horse and an ox differ specifically: second, when the diversity of species is derived from diversity of degree in generation or movement: thus the building is the complete generation of a house, while the laying of the foundations, and the setting up of the walls are incomplete species, as the Philosopher declares (*Ethic.* x, 4); and the same can apply to the

etiam potest dici in generationibus animalium. Sic igitur peccatum dividitur per haec tria, scilicet peccatum oris, cordis et operis, non sicut per diversas species completas, nam consummatio peccati est in opere, unde peccatum operis habet speciem completam. Sed prima inchoatio eius est quasi fundatio in corde; secundus autem gradus eius est in ore, secundum quod homo prorumpit facile ad manifestandum conceptum cordis; tertius autem gradus iam est in consummatione operis. Et sic haec tria differunt secundum diversos gradus peccati. Patet tamen quod haec tria pertinent ad unam perfectam peccati speciem, cum ab eodem motivo procedant, iracundus enim, ex hoc quod appetit vindictam, primo quidem perturbatur in corde; secundo, in verba contumeliosa prorumpit; tertio vero, procedit usque ad facta iniuriosa. Et idem patet in luxuria, et in quolibet alio peccato.

AD PRIMUM ergo dicendum quod omne peccatum cordis convenit in ratione occulti, et secundum hoc ponitur unus gradus. Qui tamen per tres gradus distinguitur, scilicet cogitationis, delectationis et consensus.

AD SECUNDUM dicendum quod peccatum oris et operis conveniunt in manifestatione, et propter hoc a Gregorio sub uno computantur. Hieronymus autem distinguit ea, quia in peccato oris est manifestatio tantum, et principaliter intenta, in peccato vero operis est principaliter expletio interioris conceptus cordis, sed manifestatio est ex consequenti. Consuetudo vero et desperatio sunt gradus consequentes post speciem perfectam peccati, sicut adolescentia et iuventus post perfectam hominis generationem.

AD TERTIUM dicendum quod peccatum cordis et oris non distinguuntur a peccato operis, quando simul cum eo coniunguntur, sed prout quodlibet horum per se invenitur. Sicut etiam pars motus non distinguitur a toto motu, quando motus est continuus, sed solum quando motus sistit in medio.

generation of animals. Accordingly sins are divided into these three, viz., sins of thought, word, and deed, not as into various complete species: for the consummation of sin is in the deed, wherefore sins of deed have the complete species; but the first beginning of sin is its foundation, as it were, in the sin of thought; the second degree is the sin of word, insofar as man is ready to break out into a declaration of his thought; while the third degree consists in the consummation of the deed. Consequently these three differ in respect of the various degrees of sin. Nevertheless it is evident that these three belong to the one complete species of sin, since they proceed from the same motive. For the angry man, through desire of vengeance, is at first disturbed in thought, then he breaks out into words of abuse, and lastly he goes on to wrongful deeds; and the same applies to lust and to any other sin.

REPLY OBJ. 1: All sins of thought have the common note of secrecy, in respect of which they form one degree, which is, however, divided into three stages, viz., of cogitation, pleasure, and consent.

REPLY OBJ. 2: Sins of words and deed are both done openly, and for this reason Gregory (*Moral.* iv, 25) reckons them under one head: whereas Jerome (in commenting on Ezech. 43:23) distinguishes between them, because in sins of word there is nothing but manifestation which is intended principally; while in sins of deed, it is the consummation of the inward thought which is principally intended, and the outward manifestation is by way of sequel. Habit and despair are stages following the complete species of sin, even as boyhood and youth follow the complete generation of a man.

REPLY OBJ. 3: Sin of thought and sin of word are not distinct from the sin of deed when they are united together with it, but when each is found by itself: even as one part of a movement is not distinct from the whole movement, when the movement is continuous, but only when there is a break in the movement.

Article 8

Whether Excess and Deficiency Diversify the Species of Sins?

AD OCTAVUM SIC PROCEDITUR. Videtur quod superabundantia et defectus non diversificent species peccatorum. Superabundantia enim et defectus differunt secundum magis et minus. Sed magis et minus non diversificant speciem. Ergo superabundantia et defectus non diversificant speciem peccatorum.

PRAETEREA, sicut peccatum in agibilibus est ex hoc quod receditur a rectitudine rationis, ita falsitas in speculativis est ex hoc quod receditur a veritate rei. Sed non diversificatur species falsitatis ex hoc quod aliquis dicit

OBJECTION 1: It would seem that excess and deficiency do not diversify the species of sins. For excess and deficiency differ in respect of more and less. Now *more* and *less* do not diversify a species. Therefore excess and deficiency do not diversify the species of sins.

OBJ. 2: Further, just as sin, in matters of action, is due to straying from the rectitude of reason, so falsehood, in speculative matters, is due to straying from the truth of the reality. Now the species of falsehood is not diversified by

plus vel minus esse quam sit in re. Ergo etiam non diversificatur species peccati ex hoc quod recedit a rectitudine rationis in plus vel in minus.

PRAETEREA, *ex duabus speciebus non constituitur una species*, ut Porphyrius dicit. Sed superabundantia et defectus uniuntur in uno peccato, sunt enim simul quidam illiberales et prodigi, quorum duorum illiberalitas est peccatum secundum defectum, prodigalitas autem secundum superabundantiam. Ergo superabundantia et defectus non diversificant speciem peccatorum.

SED CONTRA, contraria differunt secundum speciem, nam contrarietas est differentia secundum formam, ut dicitur in X Metaphys. Sed vitia quae differunt secundum superabundantiam et defectum, sunt contraria, sicut illiberalitas prodigalitati. Ergo differunt secundum speciem.

RESPONDEO dicendum quod, cum in peccato sint duo, scilicet ipse actus, et inordinatio eius, prout receditur ab ordine rationis et legis divinae; species peccati attenditur non ex parte inordinationis, quae est praeter intentionem peccantis, ut supra dictum est; sed magis ex parte ipsius actus, secundum quod terminatur ad obiectum, in quod fertur intentio peccantis. Et ideo ubicumque occurrit diversum motivum inclinans intentionem ad peccandum, ibi est diversa species peccati. Manifestum est autem quod non est idem motivum ad peccandum in peccatis quae sunt secundum superabundantiam, et in peccatis quae sunt secundum defectum; quinimmo sunt contraria motiva; sicut motivum in peccato intemperantiae est amor delectationum corporalium, motivum autem in peccato insensibilitatis est odium earum. Unde huiusmodi peccata non solum differunt specie, sed etiam sunt sibi invicem contraria.

AD PRIMUM ergo dicendum quod magis et minus, etsi non sint causa diversitatis speciei, consequuntur tamen quandoque species differentes, prout proveniunt ex diversis formis, sicut si dicatur quod ignis est levior aere. Unde philosophus dicit, in VIII Ethic., quod *qui posuerunt non esse diversas species amicitiarum propter hoc quod dicuntur secundum magis et minus, non sufficienti crediderunt signo.* Et hoc modo superexcedere rationem, vel deficere ab ea, pertinet ad diversa peccata secundum speciem, inquantum consequuntur diversa motiva.

AD SECUNDUM dicendum quod intentio peccantis non est ut recedat a ratione, et ideo non efficitur eiusdem rationis peccatum superabundantiae et defectus propter recessum ab eadem rationis rectitudine. Sed quandoque ille qui dicit falsum, intendit veritatem occultare, unde quantum ad hoc, non refert utrum dicat vel plus vel minus. Si tamen recedere a veritate sit praeter intentionem, tunc manifestum est quod ex diversis causis aliquis movetur ad dicendum plus vel minus, et secundum hoc diversa est ratio falsitatis. Sicut patet de iactatore, qui superexcedit dicendo falsum, quaerens gloriam; et

saying more or less than the reality. Therefore neither is the species of sin diversified by straying more or less from the rectitude of reason.

OBJ. 3: Further, *one species cannot be made out of two,* as Porphyry declares. Now excess and deficiency are united in one sin; for some are at once illiberal and wasteful—illiberality being a sin of deficiency, and prodigality, by excess. Therefore excess and deficiency do not diversify the species of sins.

ON THE CONTRARY, Contraries differ specifically, for *contrariety is a difference of form*, as stated in *Metaph.* x, text. 13,14. Now vices that differ according to excess and deficiency are contrary to one another, as illiberality to wastefulness. Therefore they differ specifically.

I ANSWER THAT, While there are two things in sin, viz., the act itself and its inordinateness, insofar as sin is a departure from the order of reason and the Divine law, the species of sin is gathered, not from its inordinateness, which is outside the sinner's intention, as stated above (A1), but one the contrary, from the act itself as terminating in the object to which the sinner's intention is directed. Consequently wherever we find a different motive inclining the intention to sin, there will be a different species of sin. Now it is evident that the motive for sinning, in sins by excess, is not the same as the motive for sinning, in sins of deficiency; in fact, they are contrary to one another, just as the motive in the sin of intemperance is love for bodily pleasures, while the motive in the sin of insensibility is hatred of the same. Therefore these sins not only differ specifically, but are contrary to one another.

REPLY OBJ. 1: Although *more* and *less* do not cause diversity of species, yet they are sometimes consequent to specific difference, insofar as they are the result of diversity of form; thus we may say that fire is lighter than air. Hence the Philosopher says (*Ethic.* viii, 1) that *those who held that there are no different species of friendship, by reason of its admitting of degree, were led by insufficient proof.* In this way to exceed reason or to fall short thereof belongs to sins specifically different, insofar as they result from different motives.

REPLY OBJ. 2: It is not the sinner's intention to depart from reason; and so sins of excess and deficiency do not become of one kind through departing from the one rectitude of reason. On the other hand, sometimes he who utters a falsehood, intends to hide the truth, wherefore in this respect, it matters not whether he tells more or less. If, however, departure from the truth be not outside the intention, it is evident that then one is moved by different causes to tell more or less; and in this respect there are different kinds of falsehood, as is evident of the *boaster*, who exceeds in telling untruths for the sake of fame, and the *cheat*, who

de deceptore, qui diminuit, evadens debiti solutionem. Unde et quaedam falsae opiniones sunt sibi invicem contrariae.

AD TERTIUM dicendum quod prodigus et illiberalis potest esse aliquis secundum diversa, ut scilicet sit aliquis illiberalis in accipiendo quae non debet, et prodigus in dando quae non debet. Nihil autem prohibet contraria inesse eidem secundum diversa.

tells less than the truth, in order to escape from paying his debts. This also explains how some false opinions are contrary to one another.

REPLY OBJ. 3: One may be prodigal and illiberal with regard to different objects: for instance one may be illiberal in taking what one ought not: and nothing hinders contraries from being in the same subject, in different respects.

Article 9

Whether Sins Differ Specifically in Respect of Different Circumstances?

AD NONUM SIC PROCEDITUR. Videtur quod vitia et peccata diversificentur specie secundum diversas circumstantias. Quia, ut dicit Dionysius, IV cap. de Div. Nom., *malum contingit ex singularibus defectibus*. Singulares autem defectus sunt corruptiones singularum circumstantiarum. Ergo ex singulis circumstantiis corruptis singulae species peccatorum consequuntur.

PRAETEREA, peccata sunt quidam actus humani. Sed actus humani interdum accipiunt speciem a circumstantiis, ut supra habitum est. Ergo peccata differunt specie secundum quod diversae circumstantiae corrumpuntur.

PRAETEREA, diversae species gulae assignantur secundum particulas quae in hoc versiculo continentur, *praepropere, laute, nimis, ardenter, studiose*. Haec autem pertinent ad diversas circumstantias, nam praepropere est antequam oportet, nimis plus quam oportet, et idem patet in aliis. Ergo species peccati diversificantur secundum diversas circumstantias.

SED CONTRA est quod philosophus dicit, in III et IV Ethic., quod *singula vitia peccant agendo et plus quam oportet, et quando non oportet*, et similiter secundum omnes alias circumstantias. Non ergo secundum hoc diversificantur peccatorum species.

RESPONDEO dicendum quod, sicut dictum est, ubi occurrit aliud motivum ad peccandum, ibi est alia peccati species, quia motivum ad peccandum est finis et obiectum. Contingit autem quandoque quod in corruptionibus diversarum circumstantiarum est idem motivum, sicut illiberalis ab eodem movetur quod accipiat quando non oportet, et ubi non oportet, et plus quam oportet, et similiter de aliis circumstantiis; hoc enim facit propter inordinatum appetitum pecuniae congregandae. Et in talibus diversarum circumstantiarum corruptiones non diversificant species peccatorum, sed pertinent ad unam et eandem peccati speciem.

Quandoque vero contingit quod corruptiones diversarum circumstantiarum proveniunt a diversis motivis. Puta quod aliquis praepropere comedat, potest provenire ex hoc quod homo non potest ferre dilationem cibi,

OBJECTION 1: It would seem that vices and sins differ in respect of different circumstances. For, as Dionysius says (*Div. Nom.* iv), *evil results from each single defect*. Now individual defects are corruptions of individual circumstances. Therefore from the corruption of each circumstance there results a corresponding species of sin.

OBJ. 2: Further, sins are human acts. But human acts sometimes take their species from circumstances, as stated above (Q18, A10). Therefore sins differ specifically according as different circumstances are corrupted.

OBJ. 3: Further, diverse species are assigned to gluttony, according to the words contained in the following verse: *Hastily, sumptuously, too much, greedily, daintily*. Now these pertain to various circumstances, for *hastily* means sooner than is right; *too much*, more than is right, and so on with the others. Therefore the species of sin is diversified according to the various circumstances.

ON THE CONTRARY, The Philosopher says (*Ethic.* iii, 7; iv, 1) that *every vice sins by doing more than one ought, and when one ought not*; and in like manner as to the other circumstances. Therefore the species of sins are not diversified in this respect.

I ANSWER THAT, As stated above (A8), wherever there is a special motive for sinning, there is a different species of sin, because the motive for sinning is the end and object of sin. Now it happens sometimes that although different circumstances are corrupted, there is but one motive: thus the illiberal man, for the same motive, takes when he ought not, where he ought not, and more than he ought, and so on with the circumstances, since he does this through an inordinate desire of hoarding money: and in such cases the corruption of different circumstances does not diversify the species of sins, but belongs to one and the same species.

Sometimes, however, the corruption of different circumstances arises from different motives: for instance that a man eat hastily, may be due to the fact that he cannot brook the delay in taking food, on account of a rapid

propter facilem consumptionem humiditatis; quod vero appetat immoderatum cibum, potest contingere propter virtutem naturae potentem ad convertendum multum cibum; quod autem aliquis appetat cibos deliciosos, contingit propter appetitum delectationis quae est in cibo. Unde in talibus diversarum circumstantiarum corruptiones inducunt diversas peccati species.

Ad primum ergo dicendum quod malum, inquantum huiusmodi, privatio est, et ideo diversificatur specie secundum ea quae privantur, sicut et ceterae privationes. Sed peccatum non sortitur speciem ex parte privationis vel aversionis, ut supra dictum est; sed ex conversione ad obiectum actus.

Ad secundum dicendum quod circumstantia nunquam transfert actum in aliam speciem, nisi quando est aliud motivum.

Ad tertium dicendum quod in diversis speciebus gulae diversa sunt motiva, sicut dictum est.

exhaustion of the digestive humors; and that he desire too much food, may be due to a naturally strong digestion; that he desire choice meats, is due to his desire for pleasure in taking food. Hence in such matters, the corruption of different circumstances entails different species of sins.

Reply Obj. 1: Evil, as such, is a privation, and so it has different species in respect of the thing which the subject is deprived, even as other privations. But sin does not take its species from the privation or aversion, as stated above (A1), but from turning to the object of the act.

Reply Obj. 2: A circumstance never transfers an act from one species to another, save when there is another motive.

Reply Obj. 3: In the various species of gluttony there are various motives, as stated.

QUESTION 73

OF THE COMPARISON OF ONE SIN WITH ANOTHER

Deinde considerandum est de comparatione peccatorum ad invicem. Et circa hoc quaeruntur decem.

Primo, utrum omnia peccata et vitia sint connexa.

Secundo, utrum omnia sint paria.

Tertio, utrum gravitas peccatorum attendatur secundum obiecta.

Quarto, utrum secundum dignitatem virtutum quibus peccata opponuntur.

Quinto, utrum peccata carnalia sint graviora quam spiritualia.

Sexto, utrum secundum causas peccatorum attendatur gravitas peccatorum.

Septimo, utrum secundum circumstantias.

Octavo, utrum secundum quantitatem nocumenti.

Nono, utrum secundum conditionem personae in quam peccatur.

Decimo, utrum propter magnitudinem personae peccantis aggravetur peccatum.

We must now consider the comparison of one sin with another: under which head there are ten points of inquiry:

(1) Whether all sins and vices are connected with one another?

(2) Whether all are equal?

(3) Whether the gravity of sin depends on its object?

(4) Whether it depends on the excellence of the virtue to which it is opposed?

(5) Whether carnal sins are more grievous than spiritual sins?

(6) Whether the gravity of sins depends on their causes?

(7) Whether it depends on their circumstances?

(8) Whether it depends on how much harm ensues?

(9) Whether on the position of the person sinned against?

(10) Whether sin is aggravated by reason of the excellence of the person sinning?

Article 1

Whether All Sins Are Connected with One Another?

AD PRIMUM SIC PROCEDITUR. Videtur quod omnia peccata sint connexa. Dicitur enim Iac. II, *quicumque totam legem servaverit, offendat autem in uno, factus est omnium reus*. Sed idem est esse reum omnium mandatorum legis, quod habere omnia peccata, quia, sicut Ambrosius dicit, *peccatum est transgressio legis divinae, et caelestium inobedientia mandatorum*. Ergo quicumque peccat uno peccato, subiicitur omnibus peccatis.

PRAETEREA, quodlibet peccatum excludit virtutem sibi oppositam. Sed qui caret una virtute, caret omnibus, ut patet ex supradictis. Ergo qui peccat uno peccato, privatur omnibus virtutibus. Sed qui caret virtute, habet vitium sibi oppositum. Ergo qui habet unum peccatum, habet omnia peccata.

PRAETEREA, virtutes omnes sunt connexae quae conveniunt in uno principio, ut supra habitum est. Sed sicut virtutes conveniunt in uno principio, ita et peccata, quia sicut amor Dei, qui facit civitatem Dei, est principium et radix omnium virtutum, ita amor sui, qui facit civitatem Babylonis, est radix omnium peccatorum; ut patet per Augustinum, XIV de Civ. Dei. Ergo etiam

OBJECTION 1: It would seem that all sins are connected. For it is written (Jas 2:10): *Whosoever shall keep the whole Law, but offend in one point, is become guilty of all.* Now to be guilty of transgressing all the precepts of Law, is the same as to commit all sins, because, as Ambrose says (*De Parad.* viii), *sin is a transgression of the Divine law, and disobedience of the heavenly commandments.* Therefore whoever commits one sin is guilty of all.

OBJ. 2: Further, each sin banishes its opposite virtue. Now whoever lacks one virtue lacks them all, as was shown above (Q65, A1). Therefore whoever commits one sin, is deprived of all the virtues. Therefore whoever commits one sin, is guilty of all sins.

OBJ. 3: Further, all virtues are connected, because they have a principle in common, as stated above (Q65, AA1,2). Now as the virtues have a common principle, so have sins, because, as the love of God, which builds the city of God, is the beginning and root of all the virtues, so self-love, which builds the city of Babylon, is the root of all sins, as Augustine declares (*De Civ. Dei* xiv, 28). Therefore all vices and

omnia vitia et peccata sunt connexa, ita ut qui unum habet, habeat omnia.

SED CONTRA, quaedam vitia sunt sibi invicem contraria, ut patet per philosophum, in II Ethic. Sed impossibile est contraria simul inesse eidem. Ergo impossibile est omnia peccata et vitia esse sibi invicem connexa.

RESPONDEO dicendum quod aliter se habet intentio agentis secundum virtutem ad sequendum rationem, et aliter intentio peccantis ad divertendum a ratione. Cuiuslibet enim agentis secundum virtutem intentio est ut rationis regulam sequatur, et ideo omnium virtutum intentio in idem tendit. Et propter hoc omnes virtutes habent connexionem ad invicem in ratione recta agibilium, quae est prudentia, sicut supra dictum est. Sed intentio peccantis non est ad hoc quod recedat ab eo quod est secundum rationem, sed potius ut tendat in aliquod bonum appetibile, a quo speciem sortitur. Huiusmodi autem bona in quae tendit intentio peccantis a ratione recedens, sunt diversa, nullam connexionem habentia ad invicem, immo etiam interdum sunt contraria. Cum igitur vitia et peccata speciem habeant secundum illud ad quod convertuntur, manifestum est quod, secundum illud quod perficit speciem peccatorum, nullam connexionem habent peccata ad invicem. Non enim peccatum committitur in accedendo a multitudine ad unitatem, sicut accidit in virtutibus quae sunt connexae, sed potius in recedendo ab unitate ad multitudinem.

AD PRIMUM ergo dicendum quod Iacobus loquitur de peccato non ex parte conversionis, secundum quod peccata distinguuntur, sicut dictum est, sed loquitur de eis ex parte aversionis, inquantum scilicet homo peccando recedit a legis mandato. Omnia autem legis mandata sunt ab uno et eodem, ut ipse ibidem dicit, et ideo idem Deus contemnitur in omni peccato. Et ex hac parte dicit quod qui offendit in uno, factus est omnium reus, quia scilicet uno peccato peccando, incurrit poenae reatum ex hoc quod contemnit Deum, ex cuius contemptu provenit omnium peccatorum reatus.

AD SECUNDUM dicendum quod, sicut supra dictum est, non per quemlibet actum peccati tollitur virtus opposita, nam peccatum veniale virtutem non tollit; peccatum autem mortale tollit virtutem infusam, inquantum avertit a Deo; sed unus actus peccati etiam mortalis, non tollit habitum virtutis acquisitae. Sed si multiplicentur actus intantum quod generetur contrarius habitus, excluditur habitus virtutis acquisitae. Qua exclusa, excluditur prudentia, quia cum homo agit contra quamcumque virtutem, agit contra prudentiam. Sine prudentia autem nulla virtus moralis esse potest, ut supra habitum est. Et ideo per consequens excluduntur omnes virtutes morales, quantum ad perfectum et formale esse virtutis, quod habent secundum quod participant prudentiam, remanent tamen inclinationes ad actus virtutum, non

sins are also connected so that whoever has one, has them all.

ON THE CONTRARY, Some vices are contrary to one another, as the Philosopher states (*Ethic.* ii, 8). But contraries cannot be together in the same subject. Therefore it is impossible for all sins and vices to be connected with one another.

I ANSWER THAT, The intention of the man who acts according to virtue in pursuance of his reason, is different from the intention of the sinner in straying from the path of reason. For the intention of every man acting according to virtue is to follow the rule of reason, wherefore the intention of all the virtues is directed to the same end, so that all the virtues are connected together in the right reason of things to be done, viz., prudence, as stated above (Q65, A1). But the intention of the sinner is not directed to the point of straying from the path of reason; rather is it directed to tend to some appetible good whence it derives its species. Now these goods, to which the sinner's intention is directed when departing from reason, are of various kinds, having no mutual connection; in fact they are sometimes contrary to one another. Since, therefore, vices and sins take their species from that to which they turn, it is evident that, in respect of that which completes a sin's species, sins are not connected with one another. For sin does not consist in passing from the many to the one, as is the case with virtues, which are connected, but rather in forsaking the one for the many.

REPLY OBJ. 1: James is speaking of sin, not as regards the thing to which it turns and which causes the distinction of sins, as stated above (Q72, A1), but as regards that from which sin turns away, in as much as man, by sinning, departs from a commandment of the law. Now all the commandments of the law are from one and the same, as he also says in the same passage, so that the same God is despised in every sin; and in this sense he says that whoever *offends in one point, is become guilty of all*, for as much as, by committing one sin, he incurs the debt of punishment through his contempt of God, which is the origin of all sins.

REPLY OBJ. 2: As stated above (Q71, A4), the opposite virtue is not banished by every act of sin; because venial sin does not destroy virtue; while mortal sin destroys infused virtue, by turning man away from God. Yet one act, even of mortal sin, does not destroy the habit of acquired virtue; though if such acts be repeated so as to engender a contrary habit, the habit of acquired virtue is destroyed, the destruction of which entails the loss of prudence, since when man acts against any virtue whatever, he acts against prudence, without which no moral virtue is possible, as stated above (Q58, A4; Q65, A1). Consequently all the moral virtues are destroyed as to the perfect and formal being of virtue, which they have insofar as they partake of prudence, yet there remain the inclinations to virtuous acts, which inclinations, however, are not virtues. Nevertheless it does

habentes rationem virtutis. Sed non sequitur quod propter hoc homo incurrat omnia vitia vel peccata. Primo quidem, quia uni virtuti plura vitia opponuntur, ita quod virtus potest privari per unum eorum, etsi alterum non adsit. Secundo, quia peccatum directe opponitur virtuti quantum ad inclinationem virtutis ad actum, ut supra dictum est, unde, remanentibus aliquibus inclinationibus virtuosis, non potest dici quod homo habeat vitia vel peccata opposita.

Ad tertium dicendum quod amor Dei est congregativus, inquantum affectum hominis a multis ducit in unum, et ideo virtutes, quae ex amore Dei causantur, connexionem habent. Sed amor sui disgregat affectum hominis in diversa, prout scilicet homo se amat appetendo sibi bona temporalia, quae sunt varia et diversa, et ideo vitia et peccata, quae causantur ex amore sui, non sunt connexa.

not follow that for this reason man contracts all vices of sins—first, because several vices are opposed to one virtue, so that a virtue can be destroyed by one of them, without the others being present; second, because sin is directly opposed to virtue, as regards the virtue's inclination to act, as stated above (Q71, A1). Wherefore, as long as any virtuous inclinations remain, it cannot be said that man has the opposite vices or sins.

Reply Obj. 3: The love of God is unitive, in as much as it draws man's affections from the many to the one; so that the virtues, which flow from the love of God, are connected together. But self-love disunites man's affections among different things, insofar as man loves himself, by desiring for himself temporal goods, which are various and of many kinds: hence vices and sins, which arise from self-love, are not connected together.

Article 2

Whether All Sins Are Equal?

Ad secundum sic proceditur. Videtur quod omnia peccata sint paria. Hoc enim est peccare, facere quod non licet. Sed facere quod non licet, uno et eodem modo in omnibus reprehenditur. Ergo peccare uno et eodem modo reprehenditur. Non ergo unum peccatum est alio gravius.

Praeterea, omne peccatum consistit in hoc quod homo transgreditur regulam rationis, quae ita se habet ad actus humanos, sicut regula linearis in corporalibus rebus. Ergo peccare simile est ei quod est lineas transilire. Sed lineas transilire est aequaliter et uno modo, etiam si aliquis longius recedat vel propinquius stet, quia privationes non recipiunt magis et minus. Ergo omnia peccata sunt aequalia.

Praeterea, peccata virtutibus opponuntur. Sed omnes virtutes aequales sunt, ut Tullius dicit, in paradoxis. Ergo omnia peccata sunt paria.

Sed contra est quod dominus dicit ad Pilatum, Ioan. XIX, *qui tradidit me tibi, maius peccatum habet.* Et tamen constat quod Pilatus aliquod peccatum habuit. Ergo unum peccatum est maius alio.

Respondeo dicendum quod opinio Stoicorum fuit, quam Tullius prosequitur in paradoxis, quod omnia peccata sunt paria. Et ex hoc etiam derivatus est quorundam haereticorum error, qui, ponentes omnia peccata esse paria, dicunt etiam omnes poenas Inferni esse pares. Et quantum ex verbis Tullii perspici potest, Stoici movebantur ex hoc quod considerabant peccatum ex parte privationis tantum, prout scilicet est recessus a ratione, unde simpliciter aestimantes quod nulla privatio susciperet

Objection 1: It would seem that all sins are equal. Because sin is to do what is unlawful. Now to do what is unlawful is reproved in one and the same way in all things. Therefore sin is reproved in one and the same way. Therefore one sin is not graver than another.

Obj. 2: Further, every sin is a transgression of the rule of reason, which is to human acts what a linear rule is in corporeal things. Therefore to sin is the same as to pass over a line. But passing over a line occurs equally and in the same way, even if one go a long way from it or stay near it, since privations do not admit of more or less. Therefore all sins are equal.

Obj. 3: Further, sins are opposed to virtues. But all virtues are equal, as Cicero states (*Paradox.* iii). Therefore all sins are equal.

On the contrary, Our Lord said to Pilate (John 19:11): *He that hath delivered me to thee, hath the greater sin*, and yet it is evident that Pilate was guilty of some sin. Therefore one sin is greater than another.

I answer that, The opinion of the Stoics, which Cicero adopts in the book on Paradoxes (*Paradox.* iii), was that all sins are equal: from which opinion arose the error of certain heretics, who not only hold all sins to be equal, but also maintain that all the pains of hell are equal. So far as can be gathered from the words of Cicero the Stoics arrived at their conclusion through looking at sin on the side of the privation only, in so far, to wit, as it is a departure from reason; wherefore considering simply that no privation admits

magis et minus, posuerunt omnia peccata esse paria. Sed si quis diligenter consideret, inveniet duplex privationum genus. Est enim quaedam simplex et pura privatio, quae consistit quasi in corruptum esse, sicut mors est privatio vitae, et tenebra est privatio luminis. Et tales privationes non recipiunt magis et minus, quia nihil residuum est de habitu opposito. Unde non minus est mortuus aliquis primo die mortis, et tertio vel quarto, quam post annum, quando iam cadaver fuerit resolutum. Et similiter non est magis tenebrosa domus, si lucerna sit operta pluribus velaminibus, quam si sit operta uno solo velamine totum lumen intercludente. Est autem alia privatio non simplex, sed aliquid retinens de habitu opposito; quae quidem privatio magis consistit in corrumpi, quam in corruptum esse, sicut aegritudo, quae privat debitam commensurationem humorum, ita tamen quod aliquid eius remanet, alioquin non remaneret animal vivum; et simile est de turpitudine, et aliis huiusmodi. Huiusmodi autem privationes recipiunt magis et minus ex parte eius quod remanet de habitu contrario, multum enim refert ad aegritudinem vel turpitudinem, utrum plus vel minus a debita commensuratione humorum vel membrorum recedatur. Et similiter dicendum est de vitiis et peccatis, sic enim in eis privatur debita commensuratio rationis, ut non totaliter ordo rationis tollatur; alioquin malum, si sit integrum, destruit seipsum, ut dicitur in IV Ethic.; non enim posset remanere substantia actus, vel affectio agentis, nisi aliquid remaneret de ordine rationis. Et ideo multum interest ad gravitatem peccati, utrum plus vel minus recedatur a rectitudine rationis. Et secundum hoc dicendum est quod non omnia peccata sunt paria.

AD PRIMUM ergo dicendum quod peccata committere non licet, propter aliquam deordinationem quam habent. Unde illa quae maiorem deordinationem continent, sunt magis illicita; et per consequens graviora peccata.

AD SECUNDUM dicendum quod ratio illa procedit de peccato, ac si esset privatio pura.

AD TERTIUM dicendum quod virtutes sunt aequales proportionaliter in uno et eodem, tamen una virtus praecedit aliam dignitate secundum suam speciem; et unus etiam homo est alio virtuosior in eadem specie virtutis, ut supra habitum est. Et tamen si virtutes essent pares, non sequeretur vitia esse paria, quia virtutes habent connexionem, non autem vitia seu peccata.

of more or less, they held that all sins are equal. Yet, if we consider the matter carefully, we shall see that there are two kinds of privation. For there is a simple and pure privation, which consists, so to speak, in *being* corrupted; thus death is privation of life, and darkness is privation of light. Such like privations do not admit of more or less, because nothing remains of the opposite habit; hence a man is not less dead on the first day after his death, or on the third or fourth days, than after a year, when his corpse is already dissolved; and, in like manner, a house is no darker if the light be covered with several shades, than if it were covered by a single shade shutting out all the light. There is, however, another privation which is not simple, but retains something of the opposite habit; it consists in *becoming* corrupted rather than in *being* corrupted, like sickness which is a privation of the due commensuration of the humors, yet so that something remains of that commensuration, else the animal would cease to live: and the same applies to deformity and the like. Such privations admit of more or less on the part of what remains or the contrary habit. For it matters much in sickness or deformity, whether one departs more or less from the due commensuration of humors or members. The same applies to vices and sins: because in them the privation of the due commensuration of reason is such as not to destroy the order of reason altogether; else evil, if total, destroys itself, as stated in *Ethic.* iv, 5. For the substance of the act, or the affection of the agent could not remain, unless something remained of the order of reason. Therefore it matters much to the gravity of a sin whether one departs more or less from the rectitude of reason: and accordingly we must say that sins are not all equal.

REPLY OBJ. 1: To commit sin is lawful on account of some inordinateness therein: wherefore those which contain a greater inordinateness are more unlawful, and consequently graver sins.

REPLY OBJ. 2: This argument looks upon sin as though it were a pure privation.

REPLY OBJ. 3: Virtues are proportionately equal in one and the same subject: yet one virtue surpasses another in excellence according to its species; and again, one man is more virtuous than another, in the same species of virtue, as stated above (Q66, AA1,2). Moreover, even if virtues were equal, it would not follow that vices are equal, since virtues are connected, and vices or sins are not.

Article 3

Whether the Gravity of Sins Varies According to Their Objects?

AD TERTIUM SIC PROCEDITUR. Videtur quod peccatorum gravitas non varietur secundum obiecta. Gravitas enim peccati pertinet ad modum vel qualitatem ipsius peccati. Sed obiectum est materia ipsius peccati. Ergo secundum diversa obiecta, peccatorum gravitas non variatur.

PRAETEREA, gravitas peccati est intensio malitiae ipsius. Peccatum autem non habet rationem malitiae ex parte conversionis ad proprium obiectum, quod est quoddam bonum appetibile; sed magis ex parte aversionis. Ergo gravitas peccatorum non variatur secundum diversa obiecta.

PRAETEREA, peccata quae habent diversa obiecta, sunt diversorum generum. Sed ea quae sunt diversorum generum, non sunt comparabilia, ut probatur in VII Physic. Ergo unum peccatum non est gravius altero secundum diversitatem obiectorum.

SED CONTRA, peccata recipiunt speciem ex obiectis, ut ex supradictis patet. Sed aliquorum peccatorum unum est gravius altero secundum suam speciem, sicut homicidium furto. Ergo gravitas peccatorum differt secundum obiecta.

RESPONDEO dicendum quod, sicut ex supradictis patet, gravitas peccatorum differt eo modo quo una aegritudo est alia gravior, sicut enim bonum sanitatis consistit in quadam commensuratione humorum per convenientiam ad naturam animalis, ita bonum virtutis consistit in quadam commensuratione humani actus secundum convenientiam ad regulam rationis. Manifestum est autem quod tanto est gravior aegritudo, quanto tollitur debita humorum commensuratio per commensurationem prioris principii, sicut aegritudo quae provenit in corpore humano ex corde, quod est principium vitae, vel ex aliquo quod appropinquat cordi, periculosior est. Unde oportet etiam quod peccatum sit tanto gravius, quanto deordinatio contingit circa aliquod principium quod est prius in ordine rationis. Ratio autem ordinat omnia in agibilibus ex fine. Et ideo quanto peccatum contingit in actibus humanis ex altiori fine, tanto peccatum est gravius. Obiecta autem actuum sunt fines eorum, ut ex supradictis patet. Et ideo secundum diversitatem obiectorum attenditur diversitas gravitatis in peccatis. Sicut patet quod res exteriores ordinantur ad hominem sicut ad finem; homo autem ordinatur ulterius in Deum sicut in finem. Unde peccatum quod est circa ipsam substantiam hominis, sicut homicidium est gravius peccato quod est circa res exteriores, sicut furtum; et adhuc est gravius peccatum quod immediate contra Deum committitur, sicut infidelitas, blasphemia et huiusmodi. Et in ordine quorumlibet horum peccatorum

OBJECTION 1: It would seem that the gravity of sins does not vary according to their objects. Because the gravity of a sin pertains to its mode or quality: whereas the object is the matter of the sin. Therefore the gravity of sins does not vary according to their various objects.

OBJ. 2: Further, the gravity of a sin is the intensity of its malice. Now sin does not derive its malice from its proper object to which it turns, and which is some appetible good, but rather from that which it turns away from. Therefore the gravity of sins does not vary according to their various objects.

OBJ. 3: Further, sins that have different objects are of different kinds. But things of different kinds cannot be compared with one another, as is proved in *Phys.* vii, text. 30, seqq. Therefore one sin is not graver than another by reason of the difference of objects.

ON THE CONTRARY, Sins take their species from their objects, as was shown above (Q72, A1). But some sins are graver than others in respect of their species, as murder is graver than theft. Therefore the gravity of sins varies according to their objects.

I ANSWER THAT, As is clear from what has been said (Q71, A5), the gravity of sins varies in the same way as one sickness is graver than another: for just as the good of health consists in a certain commensuration of the humors, in keeping with an animal's nature, so the good of virtue consists in a certain commensuration of the human act in accord with the rule of reason. Now it is evident that the higher the principle the disorder of which causes the disorder in the humors, the graver is the sickness: thus a sickness which comes on the human body from the heart, which is the principle of life, or from some neighboring part, is more dangerous. Wherefore a sin must needs be so much the graver, as the disorder occurs in a principle which is higher in the order of reason. Now in matters of action the reason directs all things in view of the end: wherefore the higher the end which attaches to sins in human acts, the graver the sin. Now the object of an act is its end, as stated above (Q72, A3, ad 2); and consequently the difference of gravity in sins depends on their objects. Thus it is clear that external things are directed to man as their end, while man is further directed to God as his end. Wherefore a sin which is about the very substance of man, e.g., murder, is graver than a sin which is about external things, e.g., theft; and graver still is a sin committed directly against God, e.g., unbelief, blasphemy, and the like: and in each of these grades of sin, one sin will be graver than another according as it is about a higher or lower principle. And forasmuch as sins take their species from their objects, the difference of

unum peccatum est gravius altero, secundum quod est circa aliquid principalius vel minus principale. Et quia peccata habent speciem ex obiectis, differentia gravitatis quae attenditur penes obiecta, est prima et principalis, quasi consequens speciem.

AD PRIMUM ergo dicendum quod obiectum, etsi sit materia circa quam terminatur actus, habet tamen rationem finis, secundum quod intentio agentis fertur in ipsum, ut supra dictum est. Forma autem actus moralis dependet ex fine, ut ex superioribus patet.

AD SECUNDUM dicendum quod ex ipsa indebita conversione ad aliquod bonum commutabile, sequitur aversio ab incommutabili bono, in qua perficitur ratio mali. Et ideo oportet quod secundum diversitatem eorum quae pertinent ad conversionem, sequatur diversa gravitas malitiae in peccatis.

AD TERTIUM dicendum quod omnia obiecta humanorum actuum habent ordinem ad invicem, et ideo omnes actus humani quodammodo conveniunt in uno genere, secundum quod ordinantur ad ultimum finem. Et ideo nihil prohibet omnia peccata esse comparabilia.

gravity which is derived from the objects is first and foremost, as resulting from the species.

REPLY OBJ. 1: Although the object is the matter about which an act is concerned, yet it has the character of an end, insofar as the intention of the agent is fixed on it, as stated above (Q72, A3, ad 2). Now the form of a moral act depends on the end, as was shown above (Q72, A6; Q18, A6).

REPLY OBJ. 2: From the very fact that man turns unduly to some mutable good, it follows that he turns away from the immutable Good, which aversion completes the nature of evil. Hence the various degrees of malice in sins must needs follow the diversity of those things to which man turns.

REPLY OBJ. 3: All the objects of human acts are related to one another, wherefore all human acts are somewhat of one kind, insofar as they are directed to the last end. Therefore nothing prevents all sins from being compared with one another.

Article 4

Whether the Gravity of Sins Depends on the Excellence of the Virtues to Which They Are Opposed?

AD QUARTUM SIC PROCEDITUR. Videtur quod gravitas peccatorum non differat secundum dignitatem virtutum quibus peccata opponuntur, ut scilicet maiori virtuti gravius peccatum opponatur. Quia ut dicitur Prov. XV, *in abundanti iustitia virtus maxima est*. Sed sicut dicit dominus, Matth. V, abundans iustitia cohibet iram; quae est minus peccatum quam homicidium, quod cohibet minor iustitia. Ergo maximae virtuti opponitur minimum peccatum.

PRAETEREA, in II Ethic. dicitur quod *virtus est circa difficile et bonum*, ex quo videtur quod maior virtus sit circa magis difficile. Sed minus est peccatum si homo deficiat in magis difficili, quam si deficiat in minus difficili. Ergo maiori virtuti minus peccatum opponitur.

PRAETEREA, caritas est maior virtus quam fides et spes, ut dicitur I ad Cor. XIII. Odium autem, quod opponitur caritati, est minus peccatum quam infidelitas vel desperatio, quae opponuntur fidei et spei. Ergo maiori virtuti opponitur minus peccatum.

SED CONTRA est quod philosophus dicit, in VIII Ethic., quod *pessimum optimo contrarium est*. Optimum autem in moralibus est maxima virtus; pessimum autem, gravissimum peccatum. Ergo maximae virtuti opponitur gravissimum peccatum.

OBJECTION 1: It would seem that the gravity of sins does not vary according to the excellence of the virtues to which they are opposed, so that, to wit, the graver the sin is opposed to the greater virtue. For, according to Prov. 15:5, *In abundant justice there is the greatest strength*. Now, as Our Lord says (Matt 5:20, seqq.) abundant justice restrains anger, which is a less grievous sin than murder, which less abundant justice restrains. Therefore the least grievous sin is opposed to the greatest virtue.

OBJ. 2: Further, it is stated in *Ethic.* ii, 3 that *virtue is about the difficult and the good*: whence it seems to follow that the greater virtue is about what is more difficult. But it is a less grievous sin to fail in what is more difficult, than in what is less difficult. Therefore the less grievous sin is opposed to the greater virtue.

OBJ. 3: Further, charity is a greater virtue than faith or hope (1 Cor 13:13). Now hatred which is opposed to charity is a less grievous sin than unbelief or despair which are opposed to faith and hope. Therefore the less grievous sin is opposed to the greater virtue.

ON THE CONTRARY, The Philosopher says (*Ethic.* 8:10) that the *worst is opposed to the best*. Now in morals the best is the greatest virtue; and the worst is the most grievous sin. Therefore the most grievous sin is opposed to the greatest virtue.

Respondeo dicendum quod virtuti opponitur aliquod peccatum, uno quidem modo principaliter et directe, quod scilicet est circa idem obiectum, nam contraria circa idem sunt. Et hoc modo oportet quod maiori virtuti opponatur gravius peccatum. Sicut enim ex parte obiecti attenditur maior gravitas peccati, ita etiam maior dignitas virtutis, utrumque enim ex obiecto speciem sortitur, ut ex supradictis patet. Unde oportet quod maximae virtuti directe contrarietur maximum peccatum, quasi maxime ab eo distans in eodem genere. Alio modo potest considerari oppositio virtutis ad peccatum, secundum quandam extensionem virtutis cohibentis peccatum, quanto enim fuerit virtus maior, tanto magis elongat hominem a peccato sibi contrario, ita quod non solum ipsum peccatum, sed etiam inducentia ad peccatum cohibet. Et sic manifestum est quod quanto aliqua virtus fuerit maior, tanto etiam minora peccata cohibet, sicut etiam sanitas, quanto fuerit maior, tanto etiam minores distemperantias excludit. Et per hunc modum maiori virtuti minus peccatum opponitur ex parte effectus.

Ad primum ergo dicendum quod ratio illa procedit de oppositione quae attenditur secundum cohibitionem peccati, sic enim abundans iustitia etiam minora peccata cohibet.

Ad secundum dicendum quod maiori virtuti, quae est circa bonum magis difficile, contrariatur directe peccatum quod est circa malum magis difficile. Utrobique enim invenitur quaedam eminentia, ex hoc quod ostenditur voluntas proclivior in bonum vel in malum, ex hoc quod difficultate non vincitur.

Ad tertium dicendum quod caritas non est quicumque amor, sed amor Dei. Unde non opponitur ei quodcumque odium directe, sed odium Dei, quod est gravissimum peccatorum.

I answer that, A sin is opposed to a virtue in two ways: first, principally and directly; that sin, to with, which is about the same object: because contraries are about the same thing. In this way, the more grievous sin must needs be opposed to the greater virtue: because, just as the degrees of gravity in a sin depend on the object, so also does the greatness of a virtue, since both sin and virtue take their species from the object, as shown above (Q60, A5; Q72, A1). Wherefore the greatest sin must needs be directly opposed to the greatest virtue, as being furthest removed from it in the same genus. Second, the opposition of virtue to sin may be considered in respect of a certain extension of the virtue in checking sin. For the greater a virtue is, the further it removes man from the contrary sin, so that it withdraws man not only from that sin, but also from whatever leads to it. And thus it is evident that the greater a virtue is, the more it withdraws man also from less grievous sins: even as the more perfect health is, the more does it ward off even minor ailments. And in this way the less grievous sin is opposed to the greater virtue, on the part of the latter's effect.

Reply Obj. 1: This argument considers the opposition which consists in restraining from sin; for thus abundant justice checks even minor sins.

Reply Obj. 2: The greater virtue that is about a more difficult good is opposed directly to the sin which is about a more difficult evil. For in each case there is a certain superiority, in that the will is shown to be more intent on good or evil, through not being overcome by the difficulty.

Reply Obj. 3: Charity is not any kind of love, but the love of God: hence not any kind of hatred is opposed to it directly, but the hatred of God, which is the most grievous of all sins.

Article 5

Whether Carnal Sins Are of Less Guilt Than Spiritual Sins?

Ad quintum sic proceditur. Videtur quod peccata carnalia non sint minoris culpae quam peccata spiritualia. Adulterium enim gravius peccatum est quam furtum, dicitur enim Prov. VI, *non grandis est culpae cum quis furatus fuerit. Qui autem adulter est, propter cordis inopiam perdet animam suam.* Sed furtum pertinet ad avaritiam, quae est peccatum spirituale; adulterium autem ad luxuriam, quae est peccatum carnale. Ergo peccata carnalia sunt maioris culpae.

Praeterea, Augustinus dicit, super Levit., quod *Diabolus maxime gaudet de peccato luxuriae et*

Objection 1: It would seem that carnal sins are not of less guilt than spiritual sins. Because adultery is a more grievous sin than theft: for it is written (Prov 6:30,32): *The fault is not so great when a man has stolen . . . but he that is an adulterer, for the folly of his heart shall destroy his own soul.* Now theft belongs to covetousness, which is a spiritual sin; while adultery pertains to lust, which is a carnal sin. Therefore carnal sins are of greater guilt than spiritual sins.

Obj. 2: Further, Augustine says in his commentary on Leviticus that *the devil rejoices chiefly in lust and idolatry.*

idololatriae. Sed de maiori culpa magis gaudet. Ergo, cum luxuria sit peccatum carnale, videtur quod peccata carnalia sint maximae culpae.

PRAETEREA, philosophus probat, in VII Ethic., quod *incontinens concupiscentiae est turpior quam incontinens irae.* Sed ira est peccatum spirituale, secundum Gregorium, XXXI Moral.; concupiscentia autem pertinet ad peccata carnalia. Ergo peccatum carnale est gravius quam peccatum spirituale.

SED CONTRA est quod Gregorius dicit, quod peccata carnalia sunt minoris culpae, et maioris infamiae.

RESPONDEO dicendum quod peccata spiritualia sunt maioris culpae quam peccata carnalia. Quod non est sic intelligendum quasi quodlibet peccatum spirituale sit maioris culpae quolibet peccato carnali, sed quia, considerata hac sola differentia spiritualitatis et carnalitatis, graviora sunt quam cetera peccata, ceteris paribus. Cuius ratio triplex potest assignari. Prima quidem ex parte subiecti. Nam peccata spiritualia pertinent ad spiritum, cuius est converti ad Deum et ab eo averti, peccata vero carnalia consummantur in delectatione carnalis appetitus, ad quem principaliter pertinet ad bonum corporale converti. Et ideo peccatum carnale, inquantum huiusmodi, plus habet de conversione, propter quod etiam est maioris adhaesionis, sed peccatum spirituale habet plus de aversione, ex qua procedit ratio culpae. Et ideo peccatum spirituale, inquantum huiusmodi, est maioris culpae. Secunda ratio potest sumi ex parte eius in quem peccatur. Nam peccatum carnale, inquantum huiusmodi, est in corpus proprium; quod est minus diligendum, secundum ordinem caritatis, quam Deus et proximus, in quos peccatur per peccata spiritualia. Et ideo peccata spiritualia, inquantum huiusmodi, sunt maioris culpae. Tertia ratio potest sumi ex parte motivi. Quia quanto est gravius impulsivum ad peccandum, tanto homo minus peccat, ut infra dicetur. Peccata autem carnalia habent vehementius impulsivum, idest ipsam concupiscentiam carnis nobis innatam. Et ideo peccata spiritualia, inquantum huiusmodi, sunt maioris culpae.

AD PRIMUM ergo dicendum quod adulterium non solum pertinet ad peccatum luxuriae, sed etiam pertinet ad peccatum iniustitiae. Et quantum ad hoc, potest ad avaritiam reduci; ut Glossa dicit, ad Ephes., super illud, *omnis fornicator, aut immundus, aut avarus.* Et tunc gravius est adulterium quam furtum, quanto homini carior est uxor quam res possessa.

AD SECUNDUM dicendum quod Diabolus dicitur maxime gaudere de peccato luxuriae, quia est maximae adhaerentiae, et difficile ab eo homo potest eripi, *insatiabilis est enim delectabilis appetitus* ut philosophus dicit, in III Ethic.

AD TERTIUM dicendum quod philosophus dicit, turpiorem esse incontinentem concupiscentiae quam

But he rejoices more in the greater sin. Therefore, since lust is a carnal sin, it seems that the carnal sins are of most guilt.

OBJ. 3: Further, the Philosopher proves (*Ethic.* vii, 6) that *it is more shameful to be incontinent in lust than in anger.* But anger is a spiritual sin, according to Gregory (*Moral.* xxxi, 17); while lust pertains to carnal sins. Therefore carnal sin is more grievous than spiritual sin.

ON THE CONTRARY, Gregory says (*Moral.* xxxiii, 11) that carnal sins are of less guilt, but of more shame than spiritual sins.

I ANSWER THAT, Spiritual sins are of greater guilt than carnal sins: yet this does not mean that each spiritual sin is of greater guilt than each carnal sin; but that, considering the sole difference between spiritual and carnal, spiritual sins are more grievous than carnal sins, other things being equal. Three reasons may be assigned for this. The first is on the part of the subject: because spiritual sins belong to the spirit, to which it is proper to turn to God, and to turn away from Him; whereas carnal sins are consummated in the carnal pleasure of the appetite, to which it chiefly belongs to turn to goods of the body; so that carnal sin, as such, denotes more a *turning to* something, and for that reason, implies a closer cleaving; whereas spiritual sin denotes more a *turning from* something, whence the notion of guilt arises; and for this reason it involves greater guilt. A second reason may be taken on the part of the person against whom sin is committed: because carnal sin, as such, is against the sinner's own body, which he ought to love less, in the order of charity, than God and his neighbor, against whom he commits spiritual sins, and consequently spiritual sins, as such, are of greater guilt. A third reason may be taken from the motive, since the stronger the impulse to sin, the less grievous the sin, as we shall state further on (A6). Now carnal sins have a stronger impulse, viz., our innate concupiscence of the flesh. Therefore spiritual sins, as such, are of greater guilt.

REPLY OBJ. 1: Adultery belongs not only to the sin of lust, but also to the sin of injustice, and in this respect may be brought under the head of covetousness, as a gloss observes on Eph. 5:5. *No fornicator, or unclean, or covetous person,* etc.; so that adultery is so much more grievous than theft, as a man loves his wife more than his chattels.

REPLY OBJ. 2: The devil is said to rejoice chiefly in the sin of lust, because it is of the greatest adhesion, and man can with difficulty be withdrawn from it. *For the desire of pleasure is insatiable,* as the Philosopher states (*Ethic.* iii, 12).

REPLY OBJ. 3: As the Philosopher himself says (*Ethic.* vii, 6), the reason why it is more shameful to be

incontinentem irae, quia minus participat de ratione. Et secundum hoc etiam dicit, in III Ethic., quod *peccata intemperantiae sunt maxime exprobrabilia, quia sunt circa illas delectationes quae sunt communes nobis et brutis*, unde quodammodo per ista peccata homo brutalis redditur. Et inde est quod, sicut Gregorius dicit, sunt maioris infamiae.

incontinent in lust than in anger, is that lust partakes less of reason; and in the same sense he says (*Ethic.* iii, 10) that *sins of intemperance are most worthy of reproach, because they are about those pleasures which are common to us and irrational minds*: hence, by these sins man is, so to speak, brutalized; for which same reason Gregory says (*Moral.* xxxi, 17) that they are more shameful.

Article 6

Whether the Gravity of a Sin Depends on Its Cause?

Ad sextum sic proceditur. Videtur quod gravitas peccatorum non attendatur secundum causam peccati. Quanto enim peccati causa fuerit maior, tanto vehementius movet ad peccandum, et ita difficilius potest ei resisti. Sed peccatum diminuitur ex hoc quod ei difficilius resistitur, hoc enim pertinet ad infirmitatem peccantis, ut non facile resistat peccato; peccatum autem quod est ex infirmitate, levius iudicatur. Non ergo peccatum habet gravitatem ex parte suae causae.

Praeterea, concupiscentia est generalis quaedam causa peccati, unde dicit Glossa, super illud Rom. VII, *nam concupiscentiam nesciebam etc., bona est lex, quae, dum concupiscentiam prohibet, omne malum prohibet*. Sed quanto homo fuerit victus maiori concupiscentia, tanto est minus peccatum. Gravitas ergo peccati diminuitur ex magnitudine causae.

Praeterea, sicut rectitudo rationis est causa virtuosi actus, ita defectus rationis videtur esse causa peccati. Sed defectus rationis, quanto fuerit maior, tanto est minus peccatum, intantum quod qui carent usu rationis, omnino excusentur a peccato; et qui ex ignorantia peccat, levius peccat. Ergo gravitas peccati non augetur ex magnitudine causae.

Sed contra, multiplicata causa, multiplicatur effectus. Ergo, si causa peccati maior fuerit, peccatum erit gravius.

Respondeo dicendum quod in genere peccati, sicut et in quolibet alio genere, potest accipi duplex causa. Una quae est propria et per se causa peccati, quae est ipsa voluntas peccandi, comparatur enim ad actum peccati sicut arbor ad fructum, ut dicitur in Glossa, super illud Matth. VII, *non potest arbor bona fructus malos facere*. Et huiusmodi causa quanto fuerit maior, tanto peccatum erit gravius, quanto enim voluntas fuerit maior ad peccandum, tanto homo gravius peccat.

Aliae vero causae peccati accipiuntur quasi extrinsecae et remotae, ex quibus scilicet voluntas inclinatur ad peccandum. Et in his causis est distinguendum. Quaedam enim harum inducunt voluntatem ad peccandum, secundum ipsam naturam voluntatis, sicut finis, quod

Objection 1: It would seem that the gravity of a sin does not depend on its cause. Because the greater a sin's cause, the more forcibly it moves to sin, and so the more difficult is it to resist. But sin is lessened by the fact that it is difficult to resist; for it denotes weakness in the sinner, if he cannot easily resist sin; and a sin that is due to weakness is deemed less grievous. Therefore sin does not derive its gravity from its cause.

Obj. 2: Further, concupiscence is a general cause of sin; wherefore a gloss on Rm. 7:7, *For I had not known concupiscence*, says: *The law is good, since by forbidding concupiscence, it forbids all evils*. Now the greater the concupiscence by which man is overcome, the less grievous his sin. Therefore the gravity of a sin is diminished by the greatness of its cause.

Obj. 3: Further, as rectitude of the reason is the cause of a virtuous act, so defect in the reason seems to be the cause of sin. Now the greater the defect in the reason, the less grievous the sin: so much so that he who lacks the use of reason, is altogether excused from sin, and he who sins through ignorance, sins less grievously. Therefore the gravity of a sin is not increased by the greatness of its cause.

On the contrary, If the cause be increased, the effect is increased. Therefore the greater the cause of sin, the more grievous the sin.

I answer that, In the genus of sin, as in every other genus, two causes may be observed. The first is the direct and proper cause of sin, and is the will to sin: for it is compared to the sinful act, as a tree to its fruit, as a gloss observes on Mt. 7:18, *A good tree cannot bring forth evil fruit*: and the greater this cause is, the more grievous will the sin be, since the greater the will to sin, the more grievously does man sin.

The other causes of sin are extrinsic and remote, as it were, being those whereby the will is inclined to sin. Among these causes we must make a distinction; for some of them induce the will to sin in accord with the very nature of the will: such is the end, which is the proper object of the will;

est proprium obiectum voluntatis. Et ex tali causa augetur peccatum, gravius enim peccat cuius voluntas ex intentione peioris finis inclinatur ad peccandum. Aliae vero causae sunt quae inclinant voluntatem ad peccandum, praeter naturam et ordinem ipsius voluntatis, quae nata est moveri libere ex seipsa secundum iudicium rationis. Unde causae quae diminuunt iudicium rationis, sicut ignorantia; vel quae diminuunt liberum motum voluntatis, sicut infirmitas vel violentia aut metus, aut aliquid huiusmodi, diminuunt peccatum, sicut et diminuunt voluntarium, intantum quod si actus sit omnino involuntarius, non habet rationem peccati.

AD PRIMUM ergo dicendum quod obiectio illa procedit de causa movente extrinseca, quae diminuit voluntarium, cuius quidem causae augmentum diminuit peccatum, ut dictum est.

AD SECUNDUM dicendum quod si sub concupiscentia includatur etiam ipse motus voluntatis, sic ubi est maior concupiscentia, est maius peccatum. Si vero concupiscentia dicatur passio quaedam, quae est motus vis concupiscibilis, sic maior concupiscentia praecedens iudicium rationis et motum voluntatis, diminuit peccatum, quia qui maiori concupiscentia stimulatus peccat, cadit ex graviori tentatione; unde minus ei imputatur. Si vero concupiscentia sic sumpta sequatur iudicium rationis et motum voluntatis, sic ubi est maior concupiscentia, est maius peccatum, insurgit enim interdum maior concupiscentiae motus ex hoc quod voluntas ineffrenate tendit in suum obiectum.

AD TERTIUM dicendum quod ratio illa procedit de causa quae causat involuntarium, et haec diminuit peccatum, ut dictum est.

and by a such like cause sin is made more grievous, because a man sins more grievously if his will is induced to sin by the intention of a more evil end. Other causes incline the will to sin, against the nature and order of the will, whose natural inclination is to be moved freely of itself in accord with the judgment of reason. Wherefore those causes which weaken the judgment of reason (e.g., ignorance), or which weaken the free movement of the will, (e.g., weakness, violence, fear, or the like), diminish the gravity of sin, even as they diminish its voluntariness; and so much so, that if the act be altogether involuntary, it is no longer sinful.

REPLY OBJ. 1: This argument considers the extrinsic moving cause, which diminishes voluntariness. The increase of such a cause diminishes the sin, as stated.

REPLY OBJ. 2: If concupiscence be understood to include the movement of the will, then, where there is greater concupiscence, there is a greater sin. But if by concupiscence we understand a passion, which is a movement of the concupiscible power, then a greater concupiscence, forestalling the judgment of reason and the movement of the will, diminishes the sin, because the man who sins, being stimulated by a greater concupiscence, falls through a more grievous temptation, wherefore he is less to be blamed. On the other hand, if concupiscence be taken in this sense follows the judgment of reason, and the movement of the will, then the greater concupiscence, the graver the sin: because sometimes the movement of concupiscence is redoubled by the will tending unrestrainedly to its object.

REPLY OBJ. 3: This argument considers the cause which renders the act involuntary, and such a cause diminishes the gravity of sin, as stated.

Article 7

Whether a Circumstance Aggravates a Sin?

AD SEPTIMUM SIC PROCEDITUR. Videtur quod circumstantia non aggravet peccatum. Peccatum enim habet gravitatem ex sua specie. Circumstantia autem non dat speciem peccato, cum sit quoddam accidens eius. Ergo gravitas peccati non consideratur ex circumstantia.

PRAETEREA, aut circumstantia est mala, aut non. Si circumstantia mala est, ipsa per se causat quandam speciem mali, si vero non sit mala, non habet unde augeat malum. Ergo circumstantia nullo modo auget peccatum.

PRAETEREA, malitia peccati est ex parte aversionis. Sed circumstantiae consequuntur peccatum ex parte conversionis. Ergo non augent malitiam peccati.

OBJECTION 1: It would seem that a circumstance does not aggravate a sin. Because sin takes its gravity from its species. Now a circumstance does not specify a sin, for it is an accident thereof. Therefore the gravity of a sin is not taken from a circumstance.

OBJ. 2: Further, a circumstance is either evil or not: if it is evil, it causes, of itself, a species of evil; and if it is not evil, it cannot make a thing worse. Therefore a circumstance nowise aggravates a sin.

OBJ. 3: Further, the malice of a sin is derived from its turning away (from God). But circumstances affect sin on the part of the object to which it turns. Therefore they do not add to the sin's malice.

Sed contra est quod ignorantia circumstantiae diminuit peccatum, qui enim peccat ex ignorantia circumstantiae, meretur veniam, ut dicitur in III Ethic. Hoc autem non esset, nisi circumstantia aggravaret peccatum. Ergo circumstantia peccatum aggravat.

Respondeo dicendum quod *unumquodque ex eodem natum est augeri, ex quo causatur*; sicut philosophus dicit de habitu virtutis, in II Ethic. Manifestum est autem quod peccatum causatur ex defectu alicuius circumstantiae, ex hoc enim receditur ab ordine rationis, quod aliquis in operando non observat debitas circumstantias. Unde manifestum est quod peccatum natum est aggravari per circumstantiam. Sed hoc quidem contingit tripliciter. Uno quidem modo, inquantum circumstantia transfert in aliud genus peccati. Sicut peccatum fornicationis consistit in hoc quod homo accedit ad non suam, si autem addatur haec circumstantia, ut illa ad quam accedit sit alterius uxor, transfertur iam in aliud genus peccati, scilicet in iniustitiam, inquantum homo usurpat rem alterius. Et secundum hoc, adulterium est gravius peccatum quam fornicatio. Aliquando vero circumstantia non aggravat peccatum quasi trahens in aliud genus peccati, sed solum quia multiplicat rationem peccati. Sicut si prodigus det quando non debet, et cui non debet, multiplicius peccat eodem genere peccati, quam si solum det cui non debet. Et ex hoc ipso peccatum fit gravius, sicut etiam aegritudo est gravior quae plures partes corporis inficit. Unde et Tullius dicit, in paradoxis, quod *in patris vita violanda, multa peccantur, violatur enim is qui procreavit, qui aluit, qui erudivit, qui in sede ac domo, atque in republica collocavit.* Tertio modo circumstantia aggravat peccatum ex eo quod auget deformitatem provenientem ex alia circumstantia. Sicut accipere alienum constituit peccatum furti, si autem addatur haec circumstantia, ut multum accipiat de alieno, est peccatum gravius; quamvis accipere multum vel parum, de se non dicat rationem boni vel mali.

Ad primum ergo dicendum quod aliqua circumstantia dat speciem actui morali, ut supra habitum est. Et tamen circumstantia quae non dat speciem, potest aggravare peccatum. Quia sicut bonitas rei non solum pensatur ex sua specie, sed etiam ex aliquo accidente; ita malitia actus non solum pensatur ex specie actus, sed etiam ex circumstantia.

Ad secundum dicendum quod utroque modo circumstantia potest aggravare peccatum. Si enim sit mala, non tamen propter hoc oportet quod semper constituat speciem peccati, potest enim addere rationem malitiae in eadem specie, ut dictum est. Si autem non sit mala, potest aggravare peccatum in ordine ad malitiam alterius circumstantiae.

On the contrary, Ignorance of a circumstance diminishes sin: for he who sins through ignorance of a circumstance, deserves to be forgiven (*Ethic.* iii, 1). Now this would not be the case unless a circumstance aggravated a sin. Therefore a circumstance makes a sin more grievous.

I answer that, As the Philosopher says in speaking of habits of virtue (*Ethic.* ii, 1,2), *it is natural for a thing to be increased by that which causes it.* Now it is evident that a sin is caused by a defect in some circumstance: because the fact that a man departs from the order of reason is due to his not observing the due circumstances in his action. Wherefore it is evident that it is natural for a sin to be aggravated by reason of its circumstances. This happens in three ways. First, insofar as a circumstance draws a sin from one kind to another: thus fornication is the intercourse of a man with one who is not his wife: but if to this be added the circumstance that the latter is the wife of another, the sin is drawn to another kind of sin, viz., injustice, insofar as he usurps another's property; and in this respect adultery is a more grievous sin than fornication. Second, a circumstance aggravates a sin, not by drawing it into another genus, but only by multiplying the ratio of sin: thus if a wasteful man gives both when he ought not, and to whom he ought not to give, he commits the same kind of sin in more ways than if he were to merely to give to whom he ought not, and for that very reason his sin is more grievous; even as that sickness is the graver which affects more parts of the body. Hence Cicero says (*Paradox.* iii) that *in taking his father's life a man commits many sins; for he outrages one who begot him, who fed him, who educated him, to whom he owes his lands, his house, his position in the republic.* Third, a circumstance aggravates a sin by adding to the deformity which the sin derives from another circumstance: thus, taking another's property constitutes the sin of theft; but if to this be added the circumstance that much is taken of another's property, the sin will be more grievous; although in itself, to take more or less has not the character of a good or of an evil act.

Reply Obj. 1: Some circumstances do specify a moral act, as stated above (Q18, A10). Nevertheless a circumstance which does not give the species, may aggravate a sin; because, even as the goodness of a thing is weighed, not only in reference to its species, but also in reference to an accident, so the malice of an act is measured, not only according to the species of that act, but also according to a circumstance.

Reply Obj. 2: A circumstance may aggravate a sin either way. For if it is evil, it does not follow that it constitutes the sin's species; because it may multiply the ratio of evil within the same species, as stated above. And if it be not evil, it may aggravate a sin in relation to the malice of another circumstance.

Ad tertium dicendum quod ratio debet ordinare actum non solum quantum ad obiectum, sed etiam quantum ad omnes circumstantias. Et ideo aversio quaedam a regula rationis attenditur secundum corruptionem cuiuslibet circumstantiae, puta si aliquis operetur quando non debet, vel ubi non debet. Et huiusmodi aversio sufficit ad rationem mali. Hanc autem aversionem a regula rationis, sequitur aversio a Deo, cui debet homo per rectam rationem coniungi.

Reply Obj. 3: Reason should direct the action not only as regards the object, but also as regards every circumstance. Therefore one may turn aside from the rule of reason through corruption of any single circumstance; for instance, by doing something when one ought not or where one ought not; and to depart thus from the rule of reason suffices to make the act evil. This turning aside from the rule of reason results from man's turning away from God, to Whom man ought to be united by right reason.

Article 8

Whether Sin Is Aggravated by Reason of Its Causing More Harm?

Ad octavum sic proceditur. Videtur quod gravitas peccati non augeatur secundum maius nocumentum. Nocumentum enim est quidam eventus consequens actum peccati. Sed eventus sequens non addit ad bonitatem vel malitiam actus, ut supra dictum est. Ergo peccatum non aggravatur propter maius nocumentum.

Praeterea, nocumentum maxime invenitur in peccatis quae sunt contra proximum, quia sibi ipsi nemo vult nocere; Deo autem nemo potest nocere, secundum illud Iob XXXV, *si multiplicatae fuerint iniquitates tuae, quid facies contra illum? Homini, qui similis tibi est, nocebit impietas tua.* Si ergo peccatum aggravaretur propter maius nocumentum, sequeretur quod peccatum quo quis peccat in proximum, esset gravius peccato quo quis peccat in Deum vel in seipsum.

Praeterea, maius nocumentum infertur alicui cum privatur vita gratiae, quam cum privatur vita naturae, quia vita gratiae est melior quam vita naturae, intantum quod homo debet vitam naturae contemnere ne amittat vitam gratiae. Sed ille qui inducit aliquam mulierem ad fornicandum, quantum est de se, privat eam vita gratiae, inducens eam ad peccatum mortale. Si ergo peccatum esset gravius propter maius nocumentum, sequeretur quod simplex fornicator gravius peccaret quam homicida, quod est manifeste falsum. Non ergo peccatum est gravius propter maius nocumentum.

Sed contra est quod Augustinus dicit, in III de Lib. Arb., *quia vitium naturae adversatur, tantum additur malitiae vitiorum, quantum integritati naturarum minuitur.* Sed diminutio integritatis naturae est nocumentum. Ergo tanto gravius est peccatum, quanto maius est nocumentum.

Respondeo dicendum quod nocumentum tripliciter se habere potest ad peccatum. Quandoque enim nocumentum quod provenit ex peccato, est praevisum et intentum, sicut cum aliquis aliquid operatur animo nocendi alteri, ut homicida vel fur. Et tunc directe quantitas

Objection 1: It would seem that a sin is not aggravated by reason of its causing more harm. Because the harm done is an issue consequent to the sinful act. But the issue of an act does not add to its goodness or malice, as stated above (Q20, A5). Therefore a sin is not aggravated on account of its causing more harm.

Obj. 2: Further, harm is inflicted by sins against our neighbor. Because no one wishes to harm himself: and no one can harm God, according to Job 35:6,8: *If thy iniquities be multiplied, what shalt thou do against Him? . . . Thy wickedness may hurt a man that is like thee.* If, therefore, sins were aggravated through causing more harm, it would follow that sins against our neighbor are more grievous than sins against God or oneself.

Obj. 3: Further, greater harm is inflicted on a man by depriving him of the life of grace, than by taking away his natural life; because the life of grace is better than the life of nature, so far that man ought to despise his natural life lest he lose the life of grace. Now, speaking absolutely, a man who leads a woman to commit fornication deprives her of the life of grace by leading her into mortal sin. If therefore a sin were more grievous on account of its causing a greater harm, it would follow that fornication, absolutely speaking, is a more grievous sin than murder, which is evidently untrue. Therefore a sin is not more grievous on account of its causing a greater harm.

On the contrary, Augustine says (*De Lib. Arb.* iii, 14): *Since vice is contrary to nature, a vice is the more grievous according as it diminishes the integrity of nature.* Now the diminution of the integrity of nature is a harm. Therefore a sin is graver according as it does more harm.

I answer that, Harm may bear a threefold relation to sin. Because sometimes the harm resulting from a sin is foreseen and intended, as when a man does something with a mind to harm another, e.g., a murderer or a thief. In this case the quantity of harm aggravates the sin directly,

nocumenti adauget gravitatem peccati, quia tunc nocumentum est per se obiectum peccati. Quandoque autem nocumentum est praevisum, sed non intentum, sicut cum aliquis transiens per agrum ut compendiosius vadat ad fornicandum, infert nocumentum his quae sunt seminata in agro, scienter, licet non animo nocendi. Et sic etiam quantitas nocumenti aggravat peccatum, sed indirecte, inquantum scilicet ex voluntate multum inclinata ad peccandum, procedit quod aliquis non praetermittat facere damnum sibi vel alii, quod simpliciter non vellet. Quandoque autem nocumentum nec est praevisum nec intentum. Et tunc si per accidens se habeat ad peccatum, non aggravat peccatum directe, sed propter negligentiam considerandi nocumenta quae consequi possent, imputantur homini ad poenam mala quae eveniunt praeter eius intentionem, si dabat operam rei illicitae. Si vero nocumentum per se sequatur ex actu peccati, licet non sit intentum nec praevisum, directe peccatum aggravat, quia quaecumque per se consequuntur ad peccatum, pertinent quodammodo ad ipsam peccati speciem. Puta si aliquis publice fornicetur, sequitur scandalum plurimorum, quod quamvis ipse non intendat, nec forte praevideat, directe per hoc aggravatur peccatum.

Aliter tamen videtur se habere circa nocumentum poenale, quod incurrit ipse qui peccat. Huiusmodi enim nocumentum, si per accidens se habeat ad actum peccati, et non sit praevisum nec intentum, non aggravat peccatum, neque sequitur maiorem gravitatem peccati, sicut si aliquis currens ad occidendum, impingat et laedat sibi pedem. Si vero tale nocumentum per se consequatur ad actum peccati, licet forte nec sit praevisum nec intentum, tunc maius nocumentum non facit gravius peccatum; sed e converso gravius peccatum inducit gravius nocumentum. Sicut aliquis infidelis, qui nihil audivit de poenis Inferni, graviorem poenam in Inferno patietur pro peccato homicidii quam pro peccato furti, quia enim hoc nec intendit nec praevidet, non aggravatur ex hoc peccatum (sicut contingit circa fidelem, qui ex hoc ipso videtur peccare gravius, quod maiores poenas contemnit ut impleat voluntatem peccati), sed gravitas huiusmodi nocumenti solum causatur ex gravitate peccati.

AD PRIMUM ergo dicendum quod, sicut etiam supra dictum est, cum de bonitate et malitia exteriorum actuum ageretur, eventus sequens, si sit praevisus et intentus, addit ad bonitatem vel malitiam actus.

AD SECUNDUM dicendum quod, quamvis nocumentum aggravet peccatum, non tamen sequitur quod ex solo nocumento peccatum aggravetur, quinimmo peccatum per se est gravius propter inordinationem, ut supra dictum est. Unde et ipsum nocumentum aggravat peccatum, inquantum facit actum esse magis inordinatum. Unde non sequitur quod, si nocumentum maxime habeat locum in peccatis quae sunt contra proximum, quod illa peccata sunt gravissima, quia multo

because then the harm is the direct object of the sin. Sometimes the harm is foreseen, but not intended; for instance, when a man takes a short cut through a field, the result being that he knowingly injures the growing crops, although his intention is not to do this harm, but to commit fornication. In this case again the quantity of the harm done aggravates the sin; indirectly, however, in so far, to wit, as it is owing to his will being strongly inclined to sin, that a man does not forbear from doing, to himself or to another, a harm which he would not wish simply. Sometimes, however, the harm is neither foreseen nor intended: and then if this harm is connected with the sin accidentally, it does not aggravate the sin directly; but, on account of his neglecting to consider the harm that might ensue, a man is deemed punishable for the evil results of his action if it be unlawful. If, on the other hand, the harm follow directly from the sinful act, although it be neither foreseen nor intended, it aggravates the sin directly, because whatever is directly consequent to a sin, belongs, in a manner, to the very species of that sin: for instance, if a man is a notorious fornicator, the result is that many are scandalized; and although such was not his intention, nor was it perhaps foreseen by him, yet it aggravates his sin directly.

But this does not seem to apply to penal harm, which the sinner himself incurs. Such like harm, if accidentally connected with the sinful act, and if neither foreseen nor intended, does not aggravate a sin, nor does it correspond with the gravity of the sin: for instance, if a man in running to slay, slips and hurts his foot. If, on the other hand, this harm is directly consequent to the sinful act, although perhaps it be neither foreseen nor intended, then greater harm does not make greater sin, but, on the contrary, a graver sin calls for the infliction of a greater harm. Thus, an unbeliever who has heard nothing about the pains of hell, would suffer greater pain in hell for a sin of murder than for a sin of theft: but his sin is not aggravated on account of his neither intending nor foreseeing this, as it would be in the case of a believer, who, seemingly, sins more grievously in the very fact that he despises a greater punishment, that he may satisfy his desire to sin; but the gravity of this harm is caused by the sole gravity of sin.

REPLY OBJ. 1: As we have already stated (Q20, A5), in treating of the goodness and malice of external actions, the result of an action if foreseen and intended adds to the goodness and malice of an act.

REPLY OBJ. 2: Although the harm done aggravates a sin, it does not follow that this alone renders a sin more grievous: in fact, it is inordinateness which of itself aggravates a sin. Wherefore the harm itself that ensues aggravates a sin, in so far only as it renders the act more inordinate. Hence it does not follow, supposing harm to be inflicted chiefly by sins against our neighbor, that such sins are the most grievous, since a much greater inordinateness is to be found against which man commits against God,

maior inordinatio invenitur in peccatis quae sunt contra Deum, et in quibusdam eorum quae sunt contra seipsum. Et tamen potest dici quod, etsi Deo nullus possit nocere quantum ad eius substantiam, potest tamen nocumentum attentare in his quae Dei sunt, sicut extirpando fidem, violando sacra, quae sunt peccata gravissima. Sibi etiam aliquis quandoque scienter et volenter infert nocumentum, sicut patet in his qui se interimunt, licet finaliter hoc referant ad aliquod bonum apparens, puta ad hoc quod liberentur ab aliqua angustia.

AD TERTIUM dicendum quod illa ratio non sequitur, propter duo. Primo quidem, quia homicida intendit directe nocumentum proximi, fornicator autem qui provocat mulierem, non intendit nocumentum, sed delectationem. Secundo, quia homicida est per se et sufficiens causa corporalis mortis, spiritualis autem mortis nullus potest esse alteri causa per se et sufficiens; quia nullus spiritualiter moritur nisi propria voluntate peccando.

and in some which he commits against himself. Moreover we might say that although no man can do God any harm in His substance, yet he can endeavor to do so in things concerning Him, e.g., by destroying faith, by outraging holy things, which are most grievous sins. Again, a man sometimes knowingly and freely inflicts harm on himself, as in the case of suicide, though this be referred finally to some apparent good, for example, delivery from some anxiety.

REPLY OBJ. 3: This argument does not prove, for two reasons: first, because the murderer intends directly to do harm to his neighbors; whereas the fornicator who solicits the woman intends not to harm but pleasure; second, because murder is the direct and sufficient cause of bodily death; whereas no man can of himself be the sufficient cause of another's spiritual death, because no man dies spiritually except by sinning of his own will.

Article 9

Whether a Sin Is Aggravated by Reason of the Condition of the Person Against Whom It Is Committed?

AD NONUM SIC PROCEDITUR. Videtur quod propter conditionem personae in quam peccatur, peccatum non aggravetur. Si enim hoc esset, maxime aggravaretur ex hoc quod aliquis peccat contra aliquem virum iustum et sanctum. Sed ex hoc non aggravatur peccatum, minus enim laeditur ex iniuria illata virtuosus, qui aequanimiter tolerat, quam alii, qui etiam interius scandalizati laeduntur. Ergo conditio personae in quam peccatur, non aggravat peccatum.

PRAETEREA, si conditio personae aggravaret peccatum, maxime aggravaretur ex propinquitate, quia sicut Tullius dicit in paradoxis, *in servo necando semel peccatur, in patris vita violanda multa peccantur.* Sed propinquitas personae in quam peccatur, non videtur aggravare peccatum, quia unusquisque sibi ipsi maxime est propinquus; et tamen minus peccat qui aliquod damnum sibi infert, quam si inferret alteri, puta si occideret equum suum, quam si occideret equum alterius, ut patet per philosophum, in V Ethic. Ergo propinquitas personae non aggravat peccatum.

PRAETEREA, conditio personae peccantis praecipue aggravat peccatum ratione dignitatis vel scientiae, secundum illud Sap. VI, *potentes potenter tormenta patientur;* et Luc. XII, *servus sciens voluntatem domini, et non faciens, plagis vapulabit multis.* Ergo, pari ratione, ex parte personae in quam peccatur, magis aggravaret peccatum dignitas aut scientia personae in quam peccatur. Sed non videtur gravius peccare qui facit iniuriam

OBJECTION 1: It would seem that sin is not aggravated by reason of the condition of the person against whom it is committed. For if this were the case a sin would be aggravated chiefly by being committed against a just and holy man. But this does not aggravate a sin: because a virtuous man who bears a wrong with equanimity is less harmed by the wrong done him, than others, who, through being scandalized, are also hurt inwardly. Therefore the condition of the person against whom a sin is committed does not aggravate the sin.

OBJ. 2: Further, if the condition of the person aggravated the sin, this would be still more the case if the person be near of kin, because, as Cicero says (*Paradox.* iii): *The man who kills his slave sins once: he that takes his father's life sins many times.* But the kinship of a person sinned against does not apparently aggravate a sin, because every man is most akin to himself; and yet it is less grievous to harm oneself than another, e.g., to kill one's own, than another's horse, as the Philosopher declares (*Ethic.* v, 11). Therefore kinship of the person sinned against does not aggravate the sin.

OBJ. 3: Further, the condition of the person who sins aggravates a sin chiefly on account of his position or knowledge, according to Wis. 6:7: *The mighty shall be mightily tormented,* and Lk. 12:47: *The servant who knew the will of his lord . . . and did it not . . . shall be beaten with many stripes.* Therefore, in like manner, on the part of the person sinned against, the sin is made more grievous by reason of his position and knowledge. But, apparently, it is not a

personae ditiori vel potentiori, quam alicui pauperi, quia non est personarum acceptio apud Deum, secundum cuius iudicium gravitas peccati pensatur. Ergo conditio personae in quam peccatur, non aggravat peccatum.

Sed contra est quod in sacra Scriptura specialiter vituperatur peccatum quod contra servos Dei committitur, sicut III Reg. XIX, *altaria tua destruxerunt, et prophetas tuos occiderunt gladio.* Vituperatur etiam specialiter peccatum commissum contra personas propinquas, secundum illud Mich. VII, *filius contumeliam facit patri, filia consurgit adversus matrem suam.* Vituperatur etiam specialiter peccatum quod committitur contra personas in dignitate constitutas, ut patet Iob XXXIV, *qui dicit regi, apostata; qui vocat duces impios.* Ergo conditio personae in quam peccatur, aggravat peccatum.

Respondeo dicendum quod persona in quam peccatur, est quodammodo obiectum peccati. Dictum est autem supra quod prima gravitas peccati attenditur ex parte obiecti. Ex quo quidem tanto attenditur maior gravitas in peccato, quanto obiectum eius est principalior finis. Fines autem principales humanorum actuum sunt Deus, ipse homo, et proximus, quidquid enim facimus, propter aliquod horum facimus; quamvis etiam horum trium unum sub altero ordinetur. Potest igitur ex parte horum trium considerari maior vel minor gravitas in peccato secundum conditionem personae in quam peccatur.

Primo quidem, ex parte Dei, cui tanto magis aliquis homo coniungitur, quanto est virtuosior vel Deo sacratior. Et ideo iniuria tali personae illata, magis redundat in Deum, secundum illud Zach. II, *qui vos tetigerit, tangit pupillam oculi mei.* Unde peccatum fit gravius ex hoc quod peccatur in personam magis Deo coniunctam, vel ratione virtutis vel ratione officii. Ex parte vero sui ipsius, manifestum est quod tanto aliquis gravius peccat, quanto in magis coniunctam personam, seu naturali necessitudine, seu beneficiis, seu quacumque coniunctione, peccaverit, quia videtur in seipsum magis peccare, et pro tanto gravius peccat, secundum illud Eccli. XIV, *qui sibi nequam est, cui bonus erit?* Ex parte vero proximi, tanto gravius peccatur, quanto peccatum plures tangit. Et ideo peccatum quod fit in personam publicam, puta regem vel principem, qui gerit personam totius multitudinis, est gravius quam peccatum quod committitur contra unam personam privatam, unde specialiter dicitur Exod. XXII, *principi populi tui non maledices.* Et similiter iniuria quae fit alicui famosae personae, videtur esse gravior, ex hoc quod in scandalum et in turbationem plurimorum redundat.

more grievous sin to inflict an injury on a rich and powerful person than on a poor man, since *there is no respect of persons with God* (Col 3:25), according to Whose judgment the gravity of a sin is measured. Therefore the condition of the person sinned against does not aggravate the sin.

On the contrary, Holy Writ censures especially those sins that are committed against the servants of God. Thus it is written (3 Kgs 19:14): *They have destroyed Thy altars, they have slain Thy prophets with the sword.* Moreover much blame is attached to the sin committed by a man against those who are akin to him, according to Micah 7:6: *the son dishonoreth the father, and the daughter riseth up against her mother.* Furthermore sins committed against persons of rank are expressly condemned: thus it is written (Job 34:18): *Who saith to the king: 'Thou art an apostate'; who calleth rulers ungodly.* Therefore the condition of the person sinned against aggravates the sin.

I answer that, The person sinned against is, in a manner, the object of the sin. Now it has been stated above (A3) that the primary gravity of a sin is derived from its object; so that a sin is deemed to be so much the more grave, as its object is a more principal end. But the principal ends of human acts are God, man himself, and his neighbor: for whatever we do, it is on account of one of these that we do it; although one of them is subordinate to the other. Therefore the greater or lesser gravity of a sin, in respect of the person sinned against, may be considered on the part of these three.

First, on the part of God, to Whom man is the more closely united, as he is more virtuous or more sacred to God: so that an injury inflicted on such a person redounds on to God according to Zach. 2:8: *He that toucheth you, toucheth the apple of My eye.* Wherefore a sin is the more grievous, according as it is committed against a person more closely united to God by reason of personal sanctity, or official station. On the part of man himself, it is evident that he sins all the more grievously, according as the person against whom he sins, is more united to him, either through natural affinity or kindness received or any other bond; because he seems to sin against himself rather than the other, and, for this very reason, sins all the more grievously, according to Ecclus. 14:5: *He that is evil to himself, to whom will he be good?* On the part of his neighbor, a man sins the more grievously, according as his sin affects more persons: so that a sin committed against a public personage, e.g., a sovereign prince who stands in the place of the whole people, is more grievous than a sin committed against a private person; hence it is expressly prohibited (Exod 22:28): *The prince of thy people thou shalt not curse.* In like manner it would seem that an injury done to a person of prominence, is all the more grave, on account of the scandal and the disturbance it would cause among many people.

AD PRIMUM ergo dicendum quod ille qui infert iniuriam virtuoso, quantum est in se, turbat eum et interius et exterius. Sed quod iste interius non turbetur, contingit ex eius bonitate, quae non diminuit peccatum iniuriantis.

AD SECUNDUM dicendum quod nocumentum quod quis sibi ipsi infert in his quae subsunt dominio propriae voluntatis, sicut in rebus possessis, habet minus de peccato quam si alteri inferatur, quia propria voluntate hoc agit. Sed in his quae non subduntur dominio voluntatis, sicut sunt naturalia et spiritualia bona, est gravius peccatum nocumentum sibi ipsi inferre, gravius enim peccat qui occidit seipsum, quam qui occidit alterum. Sed quia res propinquorum nostrorum non subduntur voluntatis nostrae dominio, non procedit ratio quantum ad nocumenta rebus illorum illata, quod circa ea minus peccetur; nisi forte velint, vel ratum habeant.

AD TERTIUM dicendum quod non est acceptio personarum si Deus gravius punit peccantem contra excellentiores personas, hoc enim fit propter hoc quod hoc redundat in plurium nocumentum.

REPLY OBJ. 1: He who inflicts an injury on a virtuous person, so far as he is concerned, disturbs him internally and externally; but that the latter is not disturbed internally is due to his goodness, which does not extenuate the sin of the injurer.

REPLY OBJ. 2: The injury which a man inflicts on himself in those things which are subject to the dominion of his will, for instance his possessions, is less sinful than if it were inflicted on another, because he does it of his own will; but in those things that are not subject to the dominion of his will, such as natural and spiritual goods, it is a graver sin to inflict an injury on oneself: for it is more grievous for a man to kill himself than another. Since, however, things belonging to our neighbor are not subject to the dominion of our will, the argument fails to prove, in respect of injuries done to such like things, that it is less grievous to sin in their regard, unless indeed our neighbor be willing, or give his approval.

REPLY OBJ. 3: There is no respect for persons if God punishes more severely those who sin against a person of higher rank; for this is done because such an injury redounds to the harm of many.

Article 10

Whether the Excellence of the Person Sinning Aggravates the Sin?

AD DECIMUM SIC PROCEDITUR. Videtur quod magnitudo personae peccantis non aggravet peccatum. Homo enim maxime redditur magnus ex hoc quod Deo adhaeret, secundum illud Eccli. XXV, *quam magnus est qui invenit sapientiam et scientiam. Sed non est super timentem Deum.* Sed quanto aliquis magis Deo adhaeret, tanto minus imputatur ei aliquid ad peccatum, dicitur enim II Paralip. XXX, *dominus bonus propitiabitur cunctis qui in toto corde requirunt dominum Deum patrum suorum, et non imputabitur eis quod minus sanctificati sunt.* Ergo peccatum non aggravatur ex magnitudine personae peccantis.

PRAETEREA, *non est personarum acceptio apud Deum*, ut dicitur Rom. II. Ergo non magis punit pro uno et eodem peccato, unum quam alium. Non ergo aggravatur ex magnitudine personae peccantis.

PRAETEREA, nullus debet ex bono incommodum reportare. Reportaret autem, si id quod agit, magis ei imputaretur ad culpam. Ergo propter magnitudinem personae peccantis non aggravatur peccatum.

SED CONTRA est quod Isidorus dicit, in II de summo bono, *tanto maius cognoscitur peccatum esse, quanto maior qui peccat habetur.*

RESPONDEO dicendum quod duplex est peccatum. Quoddam ex subreptione proveniens, propter

OBJECTION 1: It would seem that the excellence of the person sinning does not aggravate the sin. For man becomes great chiefly by cleaving to God, according to Ecclus. 25:13: *How great is he that findeth wisdom and knowledge! but there is none above him that feareth the Lord.* Now the more a man cleaves to God, the less is a sin imputed to him: for it is written (2 Chr 30: 18,19): *The Lord Who is good will show mercy to all them, who with their whole heart seek the Lord the God of their fathers; and will not impute it to them that they are not sanctified.* Therefore a sin is not aggravated by the excellence of the person sinning.

OBJ. 2: Further, *there is no respect of persons with God* (Rom 2:11). Therefore He does not punish one man more than another, for one and the same sin. Therefore a sin is not aggravated by the excellence of the person sinning.

OBJ. 3: Further, no one should reap disadvantage from good. But he would, if his action were the more blameworthy on account of his goodness. Therefore a sin is not aggravated by reason of the excellence of the person sinning.

ON THE CONTRARY, Isidore says (*De Summo Bono* ii, 18): *A sin is deemed so much the more grievous as the sinner is held to be a more excellent person.*

I ANSWER THAT, Sin is twofold. There is a sin which takes us unawares on account of the weakness of human

infirmitatem humanae naturae. Et tale peccatum minus imputatur ei qui est maior in virtute, eo quod minus negligit huiusmodi peccata reprimere, quae tamen omnino subterfugere infirmitas humana non sinit. Alia vero peccata sunt ex deliberatione procedentia. Et ista peccata tanto magis alicui imputantur, quanto maior est. Et hoc potest esse propter quatuor. Primo quidem, quia facilius possunt resistere peccato maiores, puta qui excedunt in scientia et virtute. Unde dominus dicit, Luc. XII, quod *servus sciens voluntatem domini sui, et non faciens, plagis vapulabit multis.* Secundo, propter ingratitudinem, quia omne bonum quo quis magnificatur, est Dei beneficium, cui homo fit ingratus peccando. Et quantum ad hoc, quaelibet maioritas, etiam in temporalibus bonis peccatum aggravat, secundum illud Sap. VI, *potentes potenter tormenta patientur.* Tertio, propter specialem repugnantiam actus peccati ad magnitudinem personae, sicut si princeps iustitiam violet, qui ponitur iustitiae custos; et si sacerdos fornicetur, qui castitatem vovit. Quarto, propter exemplum, sive scandalum, quia, ut Gregorius dicit in pastorali, *in exemplum culpa vehementer extenditur, quando pro reverentia gradus peccator honoratur.* Ad plurium etiam notitiam perveniunt peccata magnorum; et magis homines ea indigne ferunt.

AD PRIMUM ergo dicendum quod auctoritas illa loquitur de his quae per subreptionem infirmitatis humanae negligenter aguntur.

AD SECUNDUM dicendum quod Deus non accipit personas, si maiores plus punit, quia ipsorum maioritas facit ad gravitatem peccati, ut dictum est.

AD TERTIUM dicendum quod homo magnus non reportat incommodum ex bono quod habet, sed ex malo usu illius.

nature: and such like sins are less imputable to one who is more virtuous, because he is less negligent in checking those sins, which nevertheless human weakness does not allow us to escape altogether. But there are other sins which proceed from deliberation: and these sins are all the more imputed to man according as he is more excellent. Four reasons may be assigned for this. First, because a more excellent person, e.g., one who excels in knowledge and virtue, can more easily resist sin; hence Our Lord said (Luke 12:47) that the *servant who knew the will of his lord . . . and did it not . . . shall be beaten with many stripes.* Second, on account of ingratitude, because every good in which a man excels, is a gift of God, to Whom man is ungrateful when he sins: and in this respect any excellence, even in temporal goods, aggravates a sin, according to Wis. 6:7: *The mighty shall be mightily tormented.* Third, on account of the sinful act being specially inconsistent with the excellence of the person sinning: for instance, if a prince were to violate justice, whereas he is set up as the guardian of justice, or if a priest were to be a fornicator, whereas he has taken the vow of chastity. Fourth, on account of the example or scandal; because, as Gregory says (*Pastor.* i, 2): *Sin becomes much more scandalous, when the sinner is honored for his position*: and the sins of the great are much more notorious and men are wont to bear them with more indignation.

REPLY OBJ. 1: The passage quoted alludes to those things which are done negligently when we are taken unawares through human weakness.

REPLY OBJ. 2: God does not respect persons in punishing the great more severely, because their excellence conduces to the gravity of their sin, as stated.

REPLY OBJ. 3: The man who excels in anything reaps disadvantage, not from the good which he has, but from his abuse thereof.

QUESTION 74

OF THE SUBJECT OF SIN

Deinde considerandum est de subiecto vitiorum, sive peccatorum. Et circa hoc quaeruntur decem.

Primo, utrum voluntas possit esse subiectum peccati.

Secundo, utrum voluntas sola sit peccati subiectum.

Tertio, utrum sensualitas possit esse subiectum peccati.

Quarto, utrum possit esse subiectum peccati mortalis.

Quinto, utrum ratio possit esse subiectum peccati.

Sexto, utrum delectatio morosa, vel non morosa, sit in ratione inferiori sicut in subiecto.

Septimo, utrum peccatum consensus in actum sit in superiori ratione sicut in subiecto.

Octavo, utrum ratio inferior possit esse subiectum peccati mortalis.

Nono, utrum ratio superior possit esse subiectum peccati venialis.

Decimo, utrum in ratione superiori possit esse peccatum veniale circa proprium obiectum.

We must now consider the subject of vice or sin: under which head there are ten points of inquiry:

(1) Whether the will can be the subject of sin?

(2) Whether the will alone is the subject of sin?

(3) Whether the sensuality can be the subject of sin?

(4) Whether it can be the subject of mortal sin?

(5) Whether the reason can be the subject of sin?

(6) Whether morose delectation or non-morose delectation be subjected in the higher reason?

(7) Whether the sin of consent in the act of sin is subjected in the higher reason?

(8) Whether the lower reason can be the subject of mortal sin?

(9) Whether the higher reason can be the subject of venial sin?

(10) Whether there can be in the higher reason a venial sin directed to its proper object?

Article 1

Whether the Will Is a Subject of Sin?

AD PRIMUM SIC PROCEDITUR. Videtur quod voluntas non possit esse subiectum peccati. Dicit enim Dionysius, in IV cap. de Div. Nom., quod *malum est praeter voluntatem et intentionem.* Sed peccatum habet rationem mali. Ergo peccatum non potest esse in voluntate.

PRAETEREA, voluntas est boni, vel apparentis boni. Ex hoc autem quod voluntas vult bonum, non peccat, hoc autem quod vult apparens bonum quod non est vere bonum, magis pertinere videtur ad defectum virtutis apprehensivae quam ad defectum voluntatis. Ergo peccatum nullo modo est in voluntate.

PRAETEREA, non potest esse idem subiectum peccati, et causa efficiens, quia *causa efficiens et materialis non incidunt in idem,* ut dicitur in II Physic. Sed voluntas est causa efficiens peccati, prima enim causa peccandi est voluntas, ut Augustinus dicit, in libro de duabus animabus. Ergo non est subiectum peccati.

SED CONTRA est quod Augustinus dicit, in libro Retract., quod *voluntas est qua peccatur, et recte vivitur.*

RESPONDEO dicendum quod peccatum quidam actus est, sicut supra dictum est. Actuum autem quidam

OBJECTION 1: It would seem that the will cannot be a subject of sin. For Dionysius says (*Div. Nom.* iv) that *evil is outside the will and the intention.* But sin has the character of evil. Therefore sin cannot be in the will.

OBJ. 2: Further, the will is directed either to the good or to what seems good. Now from the fact that will wishes the good, it does not sin: and that it wishes what seems good but is not truly good, points to a defect in the apprehensive power rather than in the will. Therefore sin is nowise in the will.

OBJ. 3: Further, the same thing cannot be both subject and efficient cause of sin: because *the efficient and the material cause do not coincide* (*Phys.* 2, text. 70). Now the will is the efficient cause of sin: because the first cause of sinning is the will, as Augustine states (*De Duabus Anim.* x, 10,11). Therefore it is not the subject of sin.

ON THE CONTRARY, Augustine says (*Retract.* i, 9) that *it is by the will that we sin, and live righteously.*

I ANSWER THAT, Sin is an act, as stated above (Q71, AA1,6). Now some acts pass into external matter,

transeunt in exteriorem materiam, ut urere et secare, et huiusmodi actus habent pro materia et subiecto id in quod transit actio; sicut philosophus dicit, in III Physic., quod *motus est actus mobilis a movente*. Quidam vero actus sunt non transeuntes in exteriorem materiam, sed manentes in agente, sicut appetere et cognoscere, et tales actus sunt omnes actus morales, sive sint actus virtutum, sive peccatorum. Unde oportet quod proprium subiectum actus peccati sit potentia quae est principium actus. Cum autem proprium sit actuum moralium quod sint voluntarii, ut supra habitum est; sequitur quod voluntas, quae est principium actuum voluntariorum, sive bonorum sive malorum, quae sunt peccata, sit principium peccatorum. Et ideo sequitur quod peccatum sit in voluntate sicut in subiecto.

AD PRIMUM ergo dicendum quod malum dicitur esse praeter voluntatem, quia voluntas non tendit in ipsum sub ratione mali. Sed quia aliquod malum est apparens bonum, ideo voluntas aliquando appetit aliquod malum. Et secundum hoc peccatum est in voluntate.

AD SECUNDUM dicendum quod si defectus apprehensivae virtutis nullo modo subiaceret voluntati, non esset peccatum nec in voluntate nec in apprehensiva virtute, sicut patet in his qui habent ignorantiam invincibilem. Et ideo relinquitur quod etiam defectus apprehensivae virtutis subiacens voluntati, deputetur in peccatum.

AD TERTIUM dicendum quod ratio illa procedit in causis efficientibus quarum actiones transeunt in materiam exteriorem, et quae non movent se, sed alia. Cuius contrarium est in voluntate. Unde ratio non sequitur.

e.g., *to cut* and *to burn*: and such acts have for their matter and subject, the thing into which the action passes: thus the Philosopher states (*Phys.* iii, text. 18) that *movement is the act of the thing moved, caused by a mover*. On the other hand, there are acts which do not pass into external matter, but remain in the agent, e.g., *to desire* and *to know*: and such are all moral acts, whether virtuous or sinful. Consequently the proper subject of sin must needs be the power which is the principle of the act. Now since it is proper to moral acts that they are voluntary, as stated above (Q1, A1; Q18, A6), it follows that the will, which is the principle of voluntary acts, both of good acts, and of evil acts or sins, is the principle of sins. Therefore it follows that sin is in the will as its subject.

REPLY OBJ. 1: Evil is said to be outside the will, because the will does not tend to it under the aspect of evil. But since some evil is an apparent good, the will sometimes desires an evil, and in this sense is in the will.

REPLY OBJ. 2: If the defect in the apprehensive power were nowise subject to the will, there would be no sin, either in the will, or in the apprehensive power, as in the case of those whose ignorance is invincible. It remains therefore that when there is in the apprehensive power a defect that is subject to the will, this defect also is deemed a sin.

REPLY OBJ. 3: This argument applies to those efficient causes whose actions pass into external matter, and which do not move themselves, but move other things; the contrary of which is to be observed in the will; hence the argument does not prove.

Article 2

Whether the Will Alone Is the Subject of Sin?

AD SECUNDUM SIC PROCEDITUR. Videtur quod sola voluntas sit subiectum peccati. Dicit enim Augustinus, in libro de duabus animabus, quod *non nisi voluntate peccatur*. Sed peccatum est sicut in subiecto in potentia qua peccatur. Ergo sola voluntas est subiectum peccati.

PRAETEREA, peccatum est quoddam malum contra rationem. Sed bonum et malum ad rationem pertinens, est obiectum solius voluntatis. Ergo sola voluntas est subiectum peccati.

PRAETEREA, omne peccatum est actus voluntarius, quia, ut dicit Augustinus, in libro de Lib. Arb., *peccatum adeo est voluntarium, quod si non sit voluntarium, non est peccatum*. Sed actus aliarum virium non sunt voluntarii nisi inquantum illae vires moventur a voluntate. Hoc autem non sufficit ad hoc quod sint subiectum peccati, quia secundum hoc etiam membra exteriora, quae moventur

OBJECTION 1: It would seem that the will alone is the subject of sin. For Augustine says (*De Duabus Anim.* x, 10) that *no one sins except by the will*. Now the subject of sin is the power by which we sin. Therefore the will alone is the subject of sin.

OBJ. 2: Further, sin is an evil contrary to reason. Now good and evil pertaining to reason are the object of the will alone. Therefore the will alone is the subject of sin.

OBJ. 3: Further, every sin is a voluntary act, because, as Augustine states (*De Lib. Arb.* iii, 18), *so true is it that every sin is voluntary, that unless it be voluntary, it is no sin at all*. Now the acts of the other powers are not voluntary, except insofar as those powers are moved by the will; nor does this suffice for them to be the subject of sin, because then even the external members of the body, which are moved by

a voluntate, essent subiectum peccati; quod patet esse falsum. Ergo sola voluntas est subiectum peccati.

Sed contra, peccatum virtuti contrariatur. Contraria autem sunt circa idem. Sed aliae etiam vires animae praeter voluntatem, sunt subiecta virtutum, ut supra dictum est. Ergo non sola voluntas est subiectum peccati.

Respondeo dicendum quod, sicut ex praedictis patet, omne quod est principium voluntarii actus, est subiectum peccati. Actus autem voluntarii dicuntur non solum illi qui eliciuntur a voluntate, sed etiam illi qui a voluntate imperantur; ut supra dictum est, cum de voluntario ageretur. Unde non sola voluntas potest esse subiectum peccati, sed omnes illae potentiae quae possunt moveri ad suos actus, vel ab eis reprimi, per voluntatem. Et eaedem etiam potentiae sunt subiecta habituum moralium bonorum vel malorum, quia eiusdem est actus et habitus.

Ad primum ergo dicendum quod non peccatur nisi voluntate sicut primo movente, aliis autem potentiis peccatur sicut ab ea motis.

Ad secundum dicendum quod bonum et malum pertinent ad voluntatem sicut per se obiecta ipsius, sed aliae potentiae habent aliquod determinatum bonum et malum, ratione cuius potest in eis esse et virtus et vitium et peccatum, secundum quod participant voluntate et ratione.

Ad tertium dicendum quod membra corporis non sunt principia actuum, sed solum organa, unde et comparantur ad animam moventem sicut servus, qui agitur et non agit. Potentiae autem appetitivae interiores comparantur ad rationem quasi liberae, quia agunt quodammodo et aguntur, ut patet per id quod dicitur I Polit. Et praeterea actus exteriorum membrorum sunt actiones in exteriorem materiam transeuntes, sicut patet de percussione in peccato homicidii. Et propter hoc non est similis ratio.

the will, would be a subject of sin; which is clearly untrue. Therefore the will alone is the subject of sin.

On the contrary, Sin is contrary to virtue: and contraries are about one same thing. But the other powers of the soul, besides the will, are the subject of virtues, as stated above (Q56). Therefore the will is not the only subject of sin.

I answer that, As was shown above (A1), whatever is the a principle of a voluntary act is a subject of sin. Now voluntary acts are not only those which are elicited by the will, but also those which are commanded by the will, as we stated above (Q6, A4) in treating of voluntariness. Therefore not only the will can be a subject of sin, but also all those powers which can be moved to their acts, or restrained from their acts, by the will; and these same powers are the subjects of good and evil moral habits, because act and habit belong to the same subject.

Reply Obj. 1: We do not sin except by the will as first mover; but we sin by the other powers as moved by the will.

Reply Obj. 2: Good and evil pertain to the will as its proper objects; but the other powers have certain determinate goods and evils, by reason of which they can be the subject of virtue, vice, and sin, insofar as they partake of will and reason.

Reply Obj. 3: The members of the body are not principles but merely organs of action: wherefore they are compared to the soul which moves them, as a slave who is moved but moves no other. On the other hand, the internal appetitive powers are compared to reason as free agents, because they both act and are acted upon, as is made clear in *Polit*. i, 3. Moreover, the acts of the external members are actions that pass into external matter, as may be seen in the blow that is inflicted in the sin of murder. Consequently there is no comparison.

Article 3

Whether There Can Be Sin in the Sensuality?

Ad tertium sic proceditur. Videtur quod in sensualitate non possit esse peccatum. Peccatum enim est proprium homini, qui ex suis actibus laudatur vel vituperatur. Sed sensualitas est communis nobis et brutis. Ergo in sensualitate non potest esse peccatum.

Praeterea, *nullus peccat in eo quod vitare non potest*; sicut Augustinus dicit, in libro de Lib. Arb. Sed homo non potest vitare quin actus sensualitatis sit inordinatus, est enim *sensualitas perpetuae corruptionis, quandiu in hac mortali vita vivimus; unde et per serpentem*

Objection 1: It would seem that there cannot be sin in the sensuality. For sin is proper to man who is praised or blamed for his actions. Now sensuality is common to us and irrational animals. Therefore sin cannot be in the sensuality.

Obj. 2: Further, *no man sins in what he cannot avoid*, as Augustine states (*De Lib. Arb.* iii, 18). But man cannot prevent the movement of the sensuality from being inordinate, since *the sensuality ever remains corrupt, so long as we abide in this mortal life; wherefore it is signified by the serpent*, as

significatur, ut Augustinus dicit, XII de Trin. Ergo inordinatio motus sensualitatis non est peccatum.

Praeterea, illud quod homo ipse non facit, non imputatur ei ad peccatum. Sed *hoc solum videmur nos ipsi facere, quod cum deliberatione rationis facimus*; ut philosophus dicit, in IX Ethic. Ergo motus sensualitatis qui est sine deliberatione rationis, non imputatur homini ad peccatum.

Sed contra est quod dicitur Rom. VII, *non enim quod volo bonum, hoc ago; sed quod odi malum, illud facio*, quod exponit Augustinus de malo concupiscentiae, quam constat esse motum quendam sensualitatis. Ergo in sensualitate est aliquod peccatum.

Respondeo dicendum quod, sicut supra dictum est, peccatum potest inveniri in qualibet potentia cuius actus potest esse voluntarius et inordinatus, in quo consistit ratio peccati. Manifestum est autem quod actus sensualitatis potest esse voluntarius, inquantum sensualitas, idest appetitus sensitivus, nata est a voluntate moveri. Unde relinquitur quod in sensualitate possit esse peccatum.

Ad primum ergo dicendum quod aliquae vires sensitivae partis, etsi sint communes nobis et brutis, tamen in nobis habent aliquam excellentiam ex hoc quod rationi iunguntur, sicut nos, prae aliis animalibus, habemus in parte sensitiva cogitativam et reminiscentiam, ut in primo dictum est. Et per hunc modum etiam appetitus sensitivus in nobis prae aliis animalibus habet quandam excellentiam, scilicet quod natus est obedire rationi. Et quantum ad hoc, potest esse principium actus voluntarii; et per consequens subiectum peccati.

Ad secundum dicendum quod perpetua corruptio sensualitatis est intelligenda quantum ad fomitem, qui nunquam totaliter tollitur in hac vita, transit enim peccatum originale reatu, et remanet actu. Sed talis corruptio fomitis non impedit quin homo rationabili voluntate possit reprimere singulos motus inordinatos sensualitatis, si praesentiat, puta divertendo cogitationem ad alia. Sed dum homo ad aliud cogitationem divertit, potest etiam circa illud aliquis inordinatus motus insurgere, sicut cum aliquis transfert cogitationem suam a delectabilibus carnis, volens concupiscentiae motus vitare, ad speculationem scientiae, insurgit quandoque aliquis motus inanis gloriae impraemeditatus. Et ideo non potest homo vitare omnes huiusmodi motus, propter corruptionem praedictam, sed hoc solum sufficit ad rationem peccati voluntarii, quod possit vitare singulos.

Ad tertium dicendum quod illud quod homo facit sine deliberatione rationis, non perfecte ipse facit, quia nihil operatur ibi id quod est principale in homine. Unde non est perfecte actus humanus. Et per consequens non potest esse perfecte actus virtutis vel peccati, sed aliquid

Augustine declares (*De Trin.* xii, 12,13). Therefore the inordinate movement of the sensuality is not a sin.

Obj. 3: Further, that which man himself does not do is not imputed to him as a sin. Now *that alone do we seem to do ourselves, which we do with the deliberation of reason*, as the Philosopher says (*Ethic.* ix, 8). Therefore the movement of the sensuality, which is without the deliberation of reason, is not imputed to a man as a sin.

On the contrary, It is written (Rom 7:19): *The good which I will I do not; but the evil which I will not, that I do*: which words Augustine explains (*Contra Julian.* iii, 26; *De Verb. Apost.* xii, 2,3), as referring to the evil of concupiscence, which is clearly a movement of the sensuality. Therefore there can be sin in the sensuality.

I answer that, As stated above (AA2,3), sin may be found in any power whose act can be voluntary and inordinate, wherein consists the nature of sin. Now it is evident that the act of the sensuality, or sensitive appetite, is naturally inclined to be moved by the will. Wherefore it follows that sin can be in the sensuality.

Reply Obj. 1: Although some of the powers of the sensitive part are common to us and irrational animals, nevertheless, in us, they have a certain excellence through being united to the reason; thus we surpass other animals in the sensitive part for as much as we have the powers of cogitation and reminiscence, as stated in the FP, Q78, A4. In the same way our sensitive appetite surpasses that of other animals by reason of a certain excellence consisting in its natural aptitude to obey the reason; and in this respect it can be the principle of a voluntary action, and, consequently, the subject of sin.

Reply Obj. 2: The continual corruption of the sensuality is to be understood as referring to the *fomes*, which is never completely destroyed in this life, since, though the stain of original sin passes, its effect remains. However, this corruption of the *fomes* does not hinder man from using his rational will to check individual inordinate movements, if he be presentient to them, for instance by turning his thoughts to other things. Yet while he is turning his thoughts to something else, an inordinate movement may arise about this also: thus when a man, in order to avoid the movements of concupiscence, turns his thoughts away from carnal pleasures, to the considerations of science, sometimes an unpremeditated movement of vainglory will arise. Consequently, a man cannot avoid all such movements, on account of the aforesaid corruption: but it is enough, for the conditions of a voluntary sin, that he be able to avoid each single one.

Reply Obj. 3: Man does not do perfectly himself what he does without the deliberation of reason, since the principal part of man does nothing therein: wherefore such is not perfectly a human act; and consequently it cannot be a perfect act of virtue or of sin, but is something imperfect

imperfectum in genere horum. Unde talis motus sensualitatis rationem praeveniens, est peccatum veniale, quod est quiddam imperfectum in genere peccati.

of that kind. Therefore such movement of the sensuality as forestalls the reason, is a venial sin, which is something imperfect in the genus of sin.

Article 4

Whether Mortal Sin Can Be in the Sensuality?

AD QUARTUM SIC PROCEDITUR. Videtur quod in sensualitate possit esse peccatum mortale. Actus enim ex obiecto cognoscitur. Sed circa obiecta sensualitatis contingit peccare mortaliter, sicut circa delectabilia carnis. Ergo actus sensualitatis potest esse peccatum mortale. Et ita in sensualitate peccatum mortale invenitur.

PRAETEREA, peccatum mortale contrariatur virtuti. Sed virtus potest esse in sensualitate, temperantia enim et fortitudo sunt virtutes irrationabilium partium, ut philosophus dicit, in III Ethic. Ergo in sensualitate potest esse peccatum mortale, cum contraria sint nata fieri circa idem.

PRAETEREA, veniale peccatum est dispositio ad mortale. Sed dispositio et habitus sunt in eodem. Cum igitur veniale peccatum sit in sensualitate, ut dictum est; etiam mortale peccatum esse poterit in eadem.

SED CONTRA est quod Augustinus dicit, in libro Retract., et habetur in Glossa Rom. VII, *inordinatus concupiscentiae motus (qui est peccatum sensualitatis) potest etiam esse in his qui sunt in gratia*, in quibus tamen peccatum mortale non invenitur. Ergo inordinatus motus sensualitatis non est peccatum mortale.

RESPONDEO dicendum quod, sicut inordinatio corrumpens principium vitae corporalis, causat corporalem mortem; ita etiam inordinatio corrumpens principium spiritualis vitae, quod est finis ultimus, causat mortem spiritualem peccati mortalis, ut supra dictum est. Ordinare autem aliquid in finem non est sensualitatis, sed solum rationis. Inordinatio autem a fine non est nisi eius cuius est ordinare in finem. Unde peccatum mortale non potest esse in sensualitate, sed solum in ratione.

AD PRIMUM ergo dicendum quod actus sensualitatis potest concurrere ad peccatum mortale, sed tamen actus peccati mortalis non habet quod sit peccatum mortale, ex eo quod est sensualitatis; sed ex eo quod est rationis, cuius est ordinare in finem. Et ideo peccatum mortale non attribuitur sensualitati, sed rationi.

AD SECUNDUM dicendum quod etiam actus virtutis non perficitur per id quod est sensualitatis tantum, sed magis per id quod est rationis et voluntatis, cuius est eligere, nam actus virtutis moralis non est sine electione. Unde semper cum actu virtutis moralis, quae perficit vim appetitivam, est etiam actus prudentiae, quae

OBJECTION 1: It would seem that mortal sin can be in the sensuality. Because an act is discerned by its object. Now it is possible to commit a mortal sin about the objects of the sensuality, e.g., about carnal pleasures. Therefore the act of the sensuality can be a mortal sin, so that mortal sin can be found in the sensuality.

OBJ. 2: Further, mortal sin is opposed to virtue. But virtue can be in the sensuality; for temperance and fortitude are virtues of the irrational parts, as the Philosopher states (*Ethic*. iii, 10). Therefore, since it is natural to contraries to be about the same subject, sensuality can be the subject of mortal sin.

OBJ. 3: Further, venial sin is a disposition to mortal sin. Now disposition and habit are in the same subject. Since therefore venial sin may be in the sensuality, as stated above (A3, ad 3), mortal sin can be there also.

ON THE CONTRARY, Augustine says (*Retract.* i, 23): *The inordinate movement of concupiscence, which is the sin of the sensuality, can even be in those who are in a state of grace*, in whom, however, mortal sin is not to be found. Therefore the inordinate movement of the sensuality is not a mortal sin.

I ANSWER THAT, Just as a disorder which destroys the principle of the body's life causes the body's death, so too a disorder which destroys the principle of spiritual life, viz., the last end, causes spiritual death, which is mortal sin, as stated above (Q72, A5). Now it belongs to the reason alone, and not to the sensuality, to order anything to the end: and disorder in respect of the end can only belong to the power whose function it is to order others to the end. Wherefore mortal sin cannot be in the sensuality, but only in the reason.

REPLY OBJ. 1: The act of the sensuality can concur towards a mortal sin: yet the fact of its being a mortal sin is due, not to its being an act of the sensuality, but to its being an act of reason, to whom the ordering to the end belongs. Consequently mortal sin is imputed, not to the sensuality, but to reason.

REPLY OBJ. 2: An act of virtue is perfected not only in that it is an act of the sensuality, but still more in the fact of its being an act of reason and will, whose function is to choose: for the act of moral virtue is not without the exercise of choice: wherefore the act of moral virtue, which perfects the appetitive power, is always accompanied by an

perficit vim rationalem. Et idem est etiam de peccato mortali, sicut dictum est.

Ad tertium dicendum quod dispositio tripliciter se habet ad id ad quod disponit. Quandoque enim est idem et in eodem, sicut scientia inchoata dicitur esse dispositio ad scientiam perfectam. Quandoque autem est in eodem, sed non idem, sicut calor est dispositio ad formam ignis. Quandoque vero nec idem nec in eodem, sicut in his quae habent ordinem ad invicem ut ex uno perveniatur in aliud, sicut bonitas imaginationis est dispositio ad scientiam, quae est in intellectu. Et hoc modo veniale peccatum, quod est in sensualitate, potest esse dispositio ad peccatum mortale, quod est in ratione.

act of prudence, which perfects the rational power; and the same applies to mortal sin, as stated (ad 1).

Reply Obj. 3: A disposition may be related in three ways to that to which it disposes: for sometimes it is the same thing and is in the same subject; thus inchoate science is a disposition to perfect science: sometimes it is in the same subject, but is not the same thing; thus heat is a disposition to the form of fire: sometimes it is neither the same thing, nor in the same subject, as in those things which are subordinate to one another in such a way that we can arrive at one through the other, e.g., goodness of the imagination is a disposition to science which is in the intellect. In this way the venial sin that is in the sensuality, may be a disposition to mortal sin, which is in the reason.

Article 5

Whether Sin Can Be in the Reason?

Ad quintum sic proceditur. Videtur quod peccatum non possit esse in ratione. Cuiuslibet enim potentiae peccatum est aliquis defectus ipsius. Sed defectus rationis non est peccatum, sed magis excusat peccatum, excusatur enim aliquis a peccato propter ignorantiam. Ergo in ratione non potest esse peccatum.

Praeterea, primum subiectum peccati est voluntas, ut dictum est. Sed ratio praecedit voluntatem, cum sit directiva ipsius. Ergo peccatum esse non potest in ratione.

Praeterea, non potest esse peccatum nisi circa ea quae sunt in nobis. Sed perfectio et defectus rationis non est eorum quae sunt in nobis, quidam enim sunt naturaliter ratione deficientes, vel ratione solertes. Ergo in ratione non est peccatum.

Sed contra est quod Augustinus dicit, in libro XII de Trin., quod peccatum est in ratione inferiori et in ratione superiori.

Respondeo dicendum quod peccatum cuiuslibet potentiae consistit in actu ipsius, sicut ex dictis patet. Habet autem ratio duplicem actum, unum quidem secundum se, in comparatione ad proprium obiectum, quod est cognoscere aliquod verum; alius autem actus rationis est inquantum est directiva aliarum virium. Utroque igitur modo contingit esse peccatum in ratione. Et primo quidem, inquantum errat in cognitione veri, quod quidem tunc imputatur ei ad peccatum, quando habet ignorantiam vel errorem circa id quod potest et debet scire. Secundo, quando inordinatos actus inferiorum virium vel imperat, vel etiam post deliberationem non coercet.

Ad primum ergo dicendum quod ratio illa procedit de defectu rationis qui pertinet ad actum proprium

Objection 1: It would seem that sin cannot be in the reason. For the sin of any power is a defect thereof. But the fault of the reason is not a sin, on the contrary, it excuses sin: for a man is excused from sin on account of ignorance. Therefore sin cannot be in the reason.

Obj. 2: Further, the primary object of sin is the will, as stated above (A1). Now reason precedes the will, since it directs it. Therefore sin cannot be in the reason.

Obj. 3: Further, there can be no sin except about things which are under our control. Now perfection and defect of reason are not among those things which are under our control: since by nature some are mentally deficient, and some shrewd-minded. Therefore no sin is in the reason.

On the contrary, Augustine says (*De Trin.* xii, 12) that sin is in the lower and in the higher reason.

I answer that, The sin of any power is an act of that power, as we have clearly shown (AA1,2,3). Now reason has a twofold act: one is its proper act in respect of its proper object, and this is the act of knowing the truth; the other is the act of reason as directing the other powers. Now in both of these ways there may be sin in the reason. First, insofar as it errs in the knowledge of truth, which error is imputed to the reason as a sin, when it is in ignorance or error about what it is able and ought to know: second, when it either commands the inordinate movements of the lower powers, or deliberately fails to check them.

Reply Obj. 1: This argument considers the defect in the proper act of the reason in respect of its proper object,

respectu proprii obiecti, et hoc quando est defectus cognitionis eius quod quis non potest scire. Tunc enim talis defectus rationis non est peccatum, sed excusat a peccato, sicut patet in his quae per furiosos committuntur. Si vero sit defectus rationis circa id quod homo potest et debet scire, non omnino homo excusatur a peccato, sed ipse defectus imputatur ei ad peccatum. Defectus autem qui est solum in dirigendo alias vires, semper imputatur ei ad peccatum, quia huic defectui occurrere potest per proprium actum.

Ad secundum dicendum quod, sicut supra dictum est, cum de actibus voluntatis et rationis ageretur, voluntas quodammodo movet et praecedit rationem, et ratio quodammodo voluntatem, unde et motus voluntatis dici potest rationalis, et actus rationis potest dici voluntarius. Et secundum hoc in ratione invenitur peccatum, vel prout est defectus eius voluntarius, vel prout actus rationis est principium actus voluntatis.

Ad tertium patet responsio ex dictis.

and with regard to the case when it is a defect of knowledge about something which one is unable to know: for then this defect of reason is not a sin, and excuses from sin, as is evident with regard to the actions of madmen. If, however, the defect of reason be about something which a man is able and ought to know, he is not altogether excused from sin, and the defect is imputed to him as a sin. The defect which belongs only to the act of directing the other powers, is always imputed to reason as a sin, because it can always obviate this defect by means of its proper act.

Reply Obj. 2: As stated above (Q17, A1), when we were treating of the acts of the will and reason, the will moves and precedes the reason, in one way, and the reason moves and precedes the will in another: so that both the movement of the will can be called rational, and the act of the reason, voluntary. Accordingly sin is found in the reason, either through being a voluntary defect of the reason, or through the reason being the principle of the will's act.

The Reply to the Third Objection is evident from what has been said (ad 1).

Article 6

Whether the Sin of Morose Delectation Is in the Reason?

Ad sextum sic proceditur. Videtur quod peccatum morosae delectationis non sit in ratione. Delectatio enim importat motum appetitivae virtutis, ut supra dictum est. Sed vis appetitiva distinguitur a ratione, quae est vis apprehensiva. Ergo delectatio morosa non est in ratione.

Praeterea, ex obiectis cognosci potest ad quam potentiam actus pertineat, per quem potentia ordinatur ad obiectum. Sed quandoque est delectatio morosa circa bona sensibilia, et non circa bona rationis. Ergo peccatum delectationis morosae non est in ratione.

Praeterea, morosum dicitur aliquid propter diuturnitatem temporis. Sed diuturnitas temporis non est ratio quod aliquis actus pertineat ad aliquam potentiam. Ergo delectatio morosa non pertinet ad rationem.

Sed contra est quod Augustinus dicit, XII de Trin., quod *consensus illecebrae si sola cogitationis delectatione contentus est, sic habendum existimo velut cibum vetitum mulier sola comederit.* Per mulierem autem intelligitur ratio inferior, sicut ibidem ipse exponit. Ergo peccatum morosae delectationis est in ratione.

Respondeo dicendum quod, sicut iam dictum est, peccatum contingit esse in ratione quandoque quidem inquantum est directiva humanorum actuum. Manifestum est autem quod ratio non solum est directiva

Objection 1: It would seem that the sin of morose delectation is not in the reason. For delectation denotes a movement of the appetitive power, as stated above (Q31, A1). But the appetitive power is distinct from the reason, which is an apprehensive power. Therefore morose delectation is not in the reason.

Obj. 2: Further, the object shows to which power an act belongs, since it is through the act that the power is directed to its object. Now a morose delectation is sometimes about sensible goods, and not about the goods of the reason. Therefore the sin of morose delectation is not in the reason.

Obj. 3: Further, a thing is said to be morose through taking a length of time. But length of time is no reason why an act should belong to a particular power. Therefore morose delectation does not belong to the reason.

On the contrary, Augustine says (*De Trin*. xii, 12) that *if the consent to a sensual delectation goes no further than the mere thought of the pleasure, I deem this to be like as though the woman alone had partaken of the forbidden fruit.* Now *the woman* denotes the lower reason, as he himself explains (*De Trin*. xii, 12). Therefore the sin of morose delectation is in the reason.

I answer that, As stated (A5), sin may be in the reason, not only in respect of reason's proper act, but sometimes in respect of its directing human actions. Now it is evident that reason directs not only external acts, but also

exteriorum actuum, sed etiam interiorum passionum. Et ideo quando deficit ratio in directione interiorum passionum, dicitur esse peccatum in ratione, sicut etiam quando deficit in directione exteriorum actuum. Deficit autem in directione passionum interiorum dupliciter. Uno modo, quando imperat illicitas passiones, sicut quando homo ex deliberatione provocat sibi motum irae vel concupiscentiae. Alio modo, quando non reprimit illicitum passionis motum, sicut cum aliquis, postquam deliberavit quod motus passionis insurgens est inordinatus, nihilominus circa ipsum immoratur, et ipsum non expellit. Et secundum hoc dicitur peccatum delectationis morosae esse in ratione.

AD PRIMUM ergo dicendum quod delectatio quidem est in vi appetitiva sicut in proximo principio, sed in ratione est sicut in primo motivo, secundum hoc quod supra dictum est, quod actiones quae non transeunt in exteriorem materiam, sunt sicut in subiecto in suis principiis.

AD SECUNDUM dicendum quod ratio actum proprium illicitum habet circa proprium obiectum, sed directionem habet circa omnia obiecta inferiorum virium quae per rationem dirigi possunt. Et secundum hoc etiam delectatio circa sensibilia obiecta pertinet ad rationem.

AD TERTIUM dicendum quod delectatio dicitur morosa non ex mora temporis; sed ex eo quod ratio deliberans circa eam immoratur, nec tamen eam repellit, *tenens et volvens libenter quae statim ut attigerunt animum, respui debuerunt*, ut Augustinus dicit, XII de Trin.

internal passions. Consequently when the reason fails in directing the internal passions, sin is said to be in the reason, as also when it fails in directing external actions. Now it fails, in two ways, in directing internal passions: first, when it commands unlawful passions; for instance, when a man deliberately provokes himself to a movement of anger, or of lust: second, when it fails to check the unlawful movement of a passion; for instance, when a man, having deliberately considered that a rising movement of passion is inordinate, continues, notwithstanding, to dwell upon it, and fails to drive it away. And in this sense the sin of morose delectation is said to be in the reason.

REPLY OBJ. 1: Delectation is indeed in the appetitive power as its proximate principle; but it is in the reason as its first mover, in accordance with what has been stated above (A1), viz., that actions which do not pass into external matter are subjected in their principles.

REPLY OBJ. 2: Reason has its proper elicited act about its proper object; but it exercises the direction of all the objects of those lower powers that can be directed by the reason: and accordingly delectation about sensible objects comes also under the direction of reason.

REPLY OBJ. 3: Delectation is said to be morose not from a delay of time, but because the reason in deliberating dwells thereon, and fails to drive it away, *deliberately holding and turning over what should have been cast aside as soon as it touched the mind*, as Augustine says (*De Trin.* xii, 12).

Article 7

Whether the Sin of Consent to the Act Is in the Higher Reason?

AD SEPTIMUM SIC PROCEDITUR. Videtur quod peccatum consensus in actum non sit in ratione superiori. Consentire enim est actus appetitivae virtutis, ut supra habitum est. Sed ratio est vis apprehensiva. Ergo peccatum consensus in actum non est in ratione superiori.

PRAETEREA, *ratio superior intendit rationibus aeternis inspiciendis et consulendis*, ut Augustinus dicit, XII de Trin. Sed quandoque consentitur in actum non consultis rationibus aeternis, non enim semper homo cogitat de rebus divinis, quando consentit in aliquem actum. Ergo peccatum consensus in actum non semper est in ratione superiori.

PRAETEREA, sicut per rationes aeternas potest homo regulare actus exteriores, ita etiam interiores delectationes, vel alias passiones. *Sed consensus in delectationem absque hoc quod opere statuatur implendum, est rationis*

OBJECTION 1: It would seem that the sin of consent to the act is not in the higher reason. For consent is an act of the appetitive power, as stated above (Q15, A1): whereas the reason is an apprehensive power. Therefore the sin of consent to the act is not in the higher reason.

OBJ. 2: Further, *the higher reason is intent on contemplating and consulting the eternal law*, as Augustine states (*De Trin.* xii, 7). But sometimes consent is given to an act, without consulting the eternal law: since man does not always think about Divine things, whenever he consents to an act. Therefore the sin of consent to the act is not always in the higher reason.

OBJ. 3: Further, just as man can regulate his external actions according to the eternal law, so can he regulate his internal pleasures or other passions. But *consent to a pleasure without deciding to fulfill it by deed, belongs to the lower*

inferioris; ut dicit Augustinus, XII de Trin. Ergo etiam consensus in actum peccati debet interdum attribui rationi inferiori.

PRAETEREA, sicut ratio superior excedit inferiorem, ita ratio excedit vim imaginativam. Sed quandoque procedit homo in actum per apprehensionem virtutis imaginativae, absque omni deliberatione rationis, sicut cum aliquis ex impraemeditato movet manum aut pedem. Ergo etiam quandoque potest ratio inferior consentire in actum peccati, absque ratione superiori.

SED CONTRA est quod Augustinus dicit, XII de Trin., *si in consensione male utendi rebus quae per sensum corporis sentiuntur, ita decernitur quodcumque peccatum, ut, si potestas sit, etiam corpore compleatur, intelligenda est mulier cibum illicitum viro dedisse,* per quem superior ratio significatur. Ergo ad rationem superiorem pertinet consentire in actum peccati.

RESPONDEO dicendum quod consensus importat iudicium quoddam de eo in quod consentitur, sicut enim ratio speculativa iudicat et sententiat de rebus intelligibilibus, ita ratio practica iudicat et sententiat de agendis. Est autem considerandum quod in omni iudicio ultima sententia pertinet ad supremum iudicatorium, sicut videmus in speculativis quod ultima sententia de aliqua propositione datur per resolutionem ad prima principia. Quandiu enim remanet aliquod principium altius, adhuc per ipsum potest examinari id de quo quaeritur, unde adhuc est suspensum iudicium, quasi nondum data finali sententia. Manifestum est autem quod actus humani regulari possunt ex regula rationis humanae, quae sumitur ex rebus creatis, quas naturaliter homo cognoscit; et ulterius ex regula legis divinae, ut supra dictum est. Unde cum regula legis divinae sit superior, consequens est ut ultima sententia, per quam iudicium finaliter terminatur, pertineat ad rationem superiorem, quae intendit rationibus aeternis. Cum autem de pluribus occurrit iudicandum, finale iudicium est de eo quod ultimo occurrit. In actibus autem humanis ultimo occurrit ipse actus; praeambulum autem est delectatio, quae inducit ad actum. Et ideo ad rationem superiorem proprie pertinet consensus in actum; ad rationem vero inferiorem, quae habet inferius iudicium, pertinet iudicium praeambulum, quod est de delectatione. Quamvis etiam et de delectatione superior ratio iudicare possit, quia quidquid iudicio subditur inferioris, subditur etiam iudicio superioris, sed non convertitur.

AD PRIMUM ergo dicendum quod consentire est actus appetitivae virtutis non absolute, sed consequenter ad actum rationis deliberantis et iudicantis, ut supra dictum est, in hoc enim terminatur consensus, quod

reason, as Augustine states (*De Trin.* xii, 2). Therefore the consent to a sinful act should also be sometimes ascribed to the lower reason.

OBJ. 4: Further, just as the higher reason excels the lower, so does the reason excel the imagination. Now sometimes man proceeds to act through the apprehension of the power of imagination, without any deliberation of his reason, as when, without premeditation, he moves his hand, or foot. Therefore sometimes also the lower reason may consent to a sinful act, independently of the higher reason.

ON THE CONTRARY, Augustine says (*De Trin.* xii, 12): *If the consent to the evil use of things that can be perceived by the bodily senses, so far approves of any sin, as to point, if possible, to its consummation by deed, we are to understand that the woman has offered the forbidden fruit to her husband,* through which higher reason is signified. Therefore it pertains to higher reason to consent to the act of sin.

I ANSWER THAT, Consent implies a judgment about the thing to which consent is given. For just as the speculative reason judges and delivers its sentence about intelligible matters, so the practical reason judges and pronounces sentence on matters of action. Now we must observe that in every case brought up for judgment, the final sentence belongs to the supreme court, even as we see that in speculative matters the final sentence touching any proposition is delivered by referring it to the first principles; since, so long as there remains a yet higher principle, the question can yet be submitted to it: wherefore the judgment is still in suspense, the final sentence not being as yet pronounced. But it is evident that human acts can be regulated by the rule of human reason, which rule is derived from the created things that man knows naturally; and further still, from the rule of the Divine law, as stated above (Q19, A4). Consequently, since the rule of the Divine law is the higher rule, it follows that the ultimate sentence, whereby the judgment is finally pronounced, belongs to the higher reason which is intent on the eternal types. Now when judgment has to be pronounced on several points, the final judgment deals with that which comes last; and, in human acts, the action itself comes last, and the delectation which is the inducement to the action is a preamble thereto. Therefore the consent to an action belongs properly to the higher reason, while the preliminary judgment which is about the delectation belongs to the lower reason, which delivers judgment in a lower court: although the higher reason can also judge of the delectation, since whatever is subject to the judgment of the lower court, is subject also to the judgment of the higher court, but not conversely.

REPLY OBJ. 1: Consent is an act of the appetitive power, not absolutely, but in consequence of an act of reason deliberating and judging, as stated above (Q15, A3). Because the fact that the consent is finally given to a thing is due to the

voluntas tendit in id quod est ratione iudicatum. Unde consensus potest attribui et voluntati et rationi.

Ad secundum dicendum quod ex hoc ipso quod ratio superior non dirigit actus humanos secundum legem divinam, impediens actum peccati, dicitur ipsa consentire; sive cogitet de lege aeterna, sive non. Cum enim cogitat de lege Dei, actu eam contemnit, cum vero non cogitat, eam negligit per modum omissionis cuiusdam. Unde omnibus modis consensus in actum peccati procedit ex superiori ratione, quia, ut Augustinus dicit, XII de Trin., *non potest peccatum efficaciter perpetrandum mente decerni, nisi illa mentis intentio penes quam summa potestas est membra in opus movendi vel ab opere cohibendi, malae actioni cedat aut serviat.*

Ad tertium dicendum quod ratio superior, per considerationem legis aeternae, sicut potest dirigere vel cohibere actum exteriorem, ita etiam delectationem interiorem. Sed tamen antequam ad iudicium superioris rationis deveniatur, statim ut sensualitas proponit delectationem, inferior ratio, per rationes temporales deliberans, quandoque huiusmodi delectationem acceptat, et tunc consensus in delectationem pertinet ad inferiorem rationem. Si vero etiam consideratis rationibus aeternis, homo in eodem consensu perseveret, iam talis consensus ad superiorem rationem pertinebit.

Ad quartum dicendum quod apprehensio virtutis imaginativae est subita et sine deliberatione, et ideo potest aliquem actum causare antequam superior vel inferior ratio etiam habeat tempus deliberandi. Sed iudicium rationis inferioris est cum deliberatione, quae indiget tempore, in quo etiam ratio superior deliberare potest. Unde si non cohibeat ab actu peccati per suam deliberationem, ei imputatur.

fact that the will tends to that upon which the reason has already passed its judgment. Hence consent may be ascribed both to the will and to the reason.

Reply Obj. 2: The higher reason is said to consent, from the very fact that it fails to direct the human act according to the Divine law, whether or not it advert to the eternal law. For if it thinks of God's law, it holds it in actual contempt: and if not, it neglects it by a kind of omission. Therefore the consent to a sinful act always proceeds from the higher reason: because, as Augustine says (*De Trin.* xii, 12), *the mind cannot effectively decide on the commission of a sin, unless by its consent, whereby it wields its sovereign power of moving the members to action, or of restraining them from action, it become the servant or slave of the evil deed.*

Reply Obj. 3: The higher reason, by considering the eternal law, can direct or restrain the internal delectation, even as it can direct or restrain the external action: nevertheless, before the judgment of the higher reason is pronounced the lower reason, while deliberating the matter in reference to temporal principles, sometimes approves of this delectation: and then the consent to the delectation belongs to the lower reason. If, however, after considering the eternal law, man persists in giving the same consent, such consent will then belong to the higher reason.

Reply Obj. 4: The apprehension of the power of imagination is sudden and indeliberate: wherefore it can cause an act before the higher or lower reason has time to deliberate. But the judgment of the lower reason is deliberate, and so requires time, during which the higher reason can also deliberate; consequently, if by its deliberation it does not check the sinful act, this will deservedly by imputed to it.

Article 8

Whether Consent to Delectation Is a Mortal Sin?

Ad octavum sic proceditur. Videtur quod consensus in delectationem non sit peccatum mortale. Consentire enim in delectationem pertinet ad rationem inferiorem, cuius non est intendere rationibus aeternis vel legi divinae, et per consequens nec ab eis averti. Sed omne peccatum mortale est per aversionem a lege divina; ut patet per definitionem Augustini, de peccato mortali datam, quae supra posita est. Ergo consensus in delectationem non est peccatum mortale.

Praeterea, consentire in aliquid non est malum nisi quia illud est malum in quod consentitur. Sed propter quod unumquodque, et illud magis, vel saltem non minus. Non ergo illud in quod consentitur, potest esse

Objection 1: It would seem that consent to delectation is not a mortal sin, for consent to delectation belongs to the lower reason, which does not consider the eternal types, i.e., the eternal law, and consequently does not turn away from them. Now every mortal sin consists in turning away from Augustine's definition of mortal sin, which was quoted above (Q71, A6). Therefore consent to delectation is not a mortal sin.

Obj. 2: Further, consent to a thing is not evil, unless the thing to which consent is given be evil. Now *the cause of anything being such is yet more so*, or at any rate not less. Consequently the thing to which a man consents cannot be

minus malum quam consensus. Sed delectatio sine opere non est peccatum mortale, sed veniale tantum. Ergo nec consensus in delectationem est peccatum mortale.

Praeterea, delectationes differunt in bonitate et malitia secundum differentiam operationum, ut dicit philosophus, in X Ethic. Sed alia operatio est interior cogitatio, et alia actus exterior, puta fornicationis. Ergo et delectatio consequens actum interioris cogitationis, tantum differt a delectatione fornicationis in bonitate vel malitia, quantum differt cogitatio interior ab actu exteriori. Et per consequens etiam eodem modo differt consentire in utrumque. Sed cogitatio interior non est peccatum mortale; nec etiam consensus in cogitationem. Ergo per consequens nec consensus in delectationem.

Praeterea, exterior actus fornicationis vel adulterii non est peccatum mortale ratione delectationis, quae etiam invenitur in actu matrimoniali; sed ratione inordinationis ipsius actus. Sed ille qui consentit in delectationem, non propter hoc consentit in deordinationem actus. Ergo non videtur mortaliter peccare.

Praeterea, peccatum homicidii est gravius quam simplicis fornicationis. Sed consentire in delectationem quae consequitur cogitationem de homicidio, non est peccatum mortale. Ergo multo minus consentire in delectationem quae consequitur cogitationem de fornicatione, est peccatum mortale.

Praeterea, oratio dominica quotidie dicitur pro remissione venialium, ut Augustinus dicit. Sed consensum in delectationem Augustinus docet esse abolendum per orationem dominicam, dicit enim, in XII de Trin., quod *hoc est longe minus peccatum quam si opere statuatur implendum, et ideo de talibus quoque cogitationibus venia petenda est, pectusque percutiendum, atque dicendum, dimitte nobis debita nostra.* Ergo consensus in delectationem est peccatum veniale.

Sed contra est quod Augustinus post pauca subdit, *totus homo damnabitur, nisi haec quae, sine voluntate operandi, sed tamen cum voluntate animum talibus oblectandi, solius cogitationis sentiuntur esse peccata, per mediatoris gratiam remittantur.* Sed nullus damnatur nisi pro peccato mortali. Ergo consensus in delectationem est peccatum mortale.

Respondeo dicendum quod circa hoc aliqui diversimode opinati sunt. Quidam enim dixerunt quod consensus in delectationem non est peccatum mortale, sed veniale tantum. Alii vero dixerunt quod est peccatum mortale, et haec opinio est communior et verisimilior. Est enim considerandum quod, cum omnis delectatio consequatur aliquam operationem, ut dicitur in X Ethic.; et iterum cum omnis delectatio habeat aliquod obiectum, delectatio quaelibet potest comparari ad duo, scilicet ad operationem quam consequitur, et ad obiectum in quo quis delectatur. Contingit autem quod aliqua operatio sit obiectum delectationis, sicut et aliqua alia operatio est obiectum delectationis, sicut et aliqua alia

a lesser evil than his consent. But delectation without deed is not a mortal sin, but only a venial sin. Therefore neither is the consent to the delectation a mortal sin.

Obj. 3: Further, delectations differ in goodness and malice, according to the difference of the deeds, as the Philosopher states (*Ethic.* x, 3,5). Now the inward thought is one thing, and the outward deed, e.g., fornication, is another. Therefore the delectation consequent to the act of inward thought, differs in goodness and malice from the pleasure of fornication, as much as the inward thought differs from the outward deed; and consequently there is a like difference of consent on either hand. But the inward thought is not a mortal sin, nor is the consent to that thought: and therefore neither is the consent to the delectation.

Obj. 4: Further, the external act of fornication or adultery is a mortal sin, not by reason of the delectation, since this is found also in the marriage act, but by reason of an inordinateness in the act itself. Now he that consents to the delectation does not, for this reason, consent to the inordinateness of the act. Therefore he seems not to sin mortally.

Obj. 5: Further, the sin of murder is more grievous than simple fornication. Now it is not a mortal sin to consent to the delectation resulting from the thought of murder. Much less therefore is it a mortal sin to consent to the delectation resulting from the thought of fornication.

Obj. 6: Further, the Lord's prayer is recited every day for the remission of venial sins, as Augustine asserts (*Enchiridion* lxxviii). Now Augustine teaches that consent to delectation may be driven away by means of the Lord's Prayer: for he says (*De Trin.* xii, 12) that *this sin is much less grievous than if it be decided to fulfill it by deed: wherefore we ought to ask pardon for such thoughts also, and we should strike our breasts and say: 'Forgive us our trespasses.'* Therefore consent to delectation is a venial sin.

On the contrary, Augustine adds after a few words: *Man will be altogether lost unless, through the grace of the Mediator, he be forgiven those things which are deemed mere sins of thought, since without the will to do them, he desires nevertheless to enjoy them.* But no man is lost except through mortal sin. Therefore consent to delectation is a mortal sin.

I answer that, There have been various opinions on this point, for some have held that consent to delectation is not a mortal sin, but only a venial sin, while others have held it to be a mortal sin, and this opinion is more common and more probable. For we must take note that since every delectation results from some action, as stated in *Ethic.* x, 4, and again, that since every delectation may be compared to two things, viz., to the operation from which it results, and to the object in which a person takes delight. Now it happens that an action, just as a thing, is an object of delectation, because the action itself can be considered as a good and an end, in which the person who delights in it,

res, quia ipsa operatio potest accipi ut bonum et finis, in quo quis delectatus requiescit. Et quandoque quidem ipsamet operatio quam consequitur delectatio, est obiectum delectationis, inquantum scilicet vis appetitiva, cuius est delectari, reflectitur in ipsam operationem sicut in quoddam bonum; puta cum aliquis cogitat, et delectatur de hoc ipso quod cogitat, inquantum sua cogitatio placet. Quandoque vero delectatio consequens unam operationem, puta cogitationem aliquam, habet pro obiecto aliam operationem quasi rem cogitatam, et tunc talis delectatio procedit ex inclinatione appetitus non quidem in cogitationem, sed in operationem cogitatam. Sic igitur aliquis de fornicatione cogitans, de duobus potest delectari, uno modo, de ipsa cogitatione; alio modo, de fornicatione cogitata. Delectatio autem de cogitatione ipsa sequitur inclinationem affectus in cogitationem ipsam. Cogitatio autem ipsa secundum se non est peccatum mortale, immo quandoque est veniale tantum, puta cum aliquis inutiliter cogitat; quandoque autem sine peccato omnino, puta cum aliquis utiliter de ea cogitat, sicut cum vult de ea praedicare vel disputare. Et ideo per consequens affectio et delectatio quae sic est de cogitatione fornicationis, non est de genere peccati mortalis; sed quandoque est peccatum veniale, quandoque nullum. Unde nec consensus in talem delectationem est peccatum mortale. Et secundum hoc prima opinio habet veritatem.

Quod autem aliquis cogitans de fornicatione, delectetur de ipso actu cogitato, hoc contingit ex hoc quod affectio eius inclinata est in hunc actum. Unde quod aliquis consentiat in talem delectationem, hoc nihil aliud est quam quod ipse consentiat in hoc quod affectus suus sit inclinatus in fornicationem, nullus enim delectatur nisi in eo quod est conforme appetitui eius. Quod autem aliquis ex deliberatione eligat quod affectus suus conformetur his quae secundum se sunt peccata mortalia, est peccatum mortale. Unde talis consensus in delectationem peccati mortalis, est peccatum mortale; ut secunda opinio ponit.

AD PRIMUM ergo dicendum quod consensus in delectationem potest esse non solum rationis inferioris, sed etiam superioris, ut dictum est. Et tamen ipsa etiam ratio inferior potest averti a rationibus aeternis. Quia etsi non intendit eis ut secundum eas regulans, quod est proprium superioris rationis; intendit tamen eis ut secundum eas regulata. Et hoc modo, ab eis se avertens, potest peccare mortaliter. Nam et actus inferiorum virium, et etiam exteriorum membrorum, possunt esse peccata mortalia, secundum quod deficit ordinatio superioris rationis regulantis eos secundum rationes aeternas.

AD SECUNDUM dicendum quod consensus in peccatum quod est veniale ex genere, est veniale peccatum. Et secundum hoc potest concludi quod consensus in delectationem quae est de ipsa vana cogitatione fornicationis,

rests. Sometimes the action itself, which results in delectation, is the object of delectation, insofar as the appetitive power, to which it belongs to take delight in anything, is brought to bear on the action itself as a good: for instance, when a man thinks and delights in his thought, insofar as his thought pleases him; while at other times the delight consequent to an action, e.g., a thought, has for its object another action, as being the object of his thought; and then his thought proceeds from the inclination of the appetite, not indeed to the thought, but to the action thought of. Accordingly a man who is thinking of fornication, may delight in either of two things: first, in the thought itself, second, in the fornication thought of. Now the delectation in the thought itself results from the inclination of the appetite to the thought; and the thought itself is not in itself a mortal sin; sometimes indeed it is only a venial sin, as when a man thinks of such a thing for no purpose; and sometimes it is no sin at all, as when a man has a purpose in thinking of it; for instance, he may wish to preach or dispute about it. Consequently such affection or delectation in respect of the thought of fornication is not a mortal sin in virtue of its genus, but is sometimes a venial sin and sometimes no sin at all: wherefore neither is it a mortal sin to consent to such a thought. In this sense the first opinion is true.

But that a man in thinking of fornication takes pleasure in the act thought of, is due to his desire being inclined to this act. Wherefore the fact that a man consents to such a delectation, amounts to nothing less than a consent to the inclination of his appetite to fornication: for no man takes pleasure except in that which is in conformity with his appetite. Now it is a mortal sin, if a man deliberately chooses that his appetite be conformed to what is in itself a mortal sin. Wherefore such a consent to delectation in a mortal sin, is itself a mortal sin, as the second opinion maintains.

REPLY OBJ. 1: Consent to delectation may be not only in the lower reason, but also in the higher reason, as stated above (A7). Nevertheless the lower reason may turn away from the eternal types, for, though it is not intent on them, as regulating according to them, which is proper to the higher reason, yet, it is intent on them, as being regulated according to them: and by turning from them in this sense, it may sin mortally; since even the acts of the lower powers and of the external members may be mortal sins, insofar as the direction of the higher reason fails in directing them according to the eternal types.

REPLY OBJ. 2: Consent to a sin that is venial in its genus, is itself a venial sin, and accordingly one may conclude that the consent to take pleasure in a useless thought about fornication, is a venial sin. But delectation in the act itself of

est peccatum veniale. Sed delectatio quae est in ipso actu fornicationis, de genere suo est peccatum mortale. Sed quod ante consensum sit veniale peccatum tantum, hoc est per accidens, scilicet propter imperfectionem actus. Quae quidem imperfectio tollitur per consensum deliberatum supervenientem. Unde ex hoc adducitur in suam naturam, ut sit peccatum mortale.

AD TERTIUM dicendum quod ratio illa procedit de delectatione quae habet cogitationem pro obiecto.

AD QUARTUM dicendum quod delectatio quae habet actum exteriorem pro obiecto, non potest esse absque complacentia exterioris actus secundum se; etiam si non statuatur implendum, propter prohibitionem alicuius superioris. Unde actus fit inordinatus, et per consequens delectatio erit inordinata.

AD QUINTUM dicendum quod etiam consensus in delectationem quae procedit ex complacentia ipsius actus homicidii cogitati, est peccatum mortale. Non autem consensus in delectationem quae procedit ex complacentia cogitationis de homicidio.

AD SEXTUM dicendum quod oratio dominica non solum contra peccata venialia dicenda est, sed etiam contra mortalia.

fornication is, in its genus, a mortal sin: and that it be a venial sin before the consent is given, is accidental, viz., on account of the incompleteness of the act: which incompleteness ceases when the deliberate consent has been given, so that therefore it has its complete nature and is a mortal sin.

REPLY OBJ. 3: This argument considers the delectation which has the thought for its object.

REPLY OBJ. 4: The delectation which has an external act for its object, cannot be without complacency in the external act as such, even though there be no decision to fulfill it, on account of the prohibition of some higher authority: wherefore the act is inordinate, and consequently the delectation will be inordinate also.

REPLY OBJ. 5: The consent to delectation, resulting from complacency in an act of murder thought of, is a mortal sin also: but not the consent to delectation resulting from complacency in the thought of murder.

REPLY OBJ. 6: The Lord's Prayer is to be said in order that we may be preserved not only from venial sin, but also from mortal sin.

Article 9

Whether There Can Be Venial Sin in the Higher Reason As Directing the Lower Powers?

AD NONUM SIC PROCEDITUR. Videtur quod in superiori ratione non possit esse peccatum veniale, secundum quod est directiva inferiorum virium, idest secundum quod consentit in actum peccati. Dicit enim Augustinus, in XII de Trin., quod *ratio superior inhaeret rationibus aeternis*. Sed peccare mortaliter est per aversionem a rationibus aeternis. Ergo videtur quod in superiori ratione non possit esse peccatum nisi mortale.

PRAETEREA, superior ratio se habet in vita spirituali tanquam principium; sicut et cor in vita corporali. Sed infirmitates cordis sunt mortales. Ergo peccata superioris rationis sunt mortalia.

PRAETEREA, peccatum veniale fit mortale, si fiat ex contemptu. Sed hoc non videtur esse sine contemptu, quod aliquis ex deliberatione peccet etiam venialiter. Cum ergo consensus rationis superioris semper sit cum deliberatione legis divinae, videtur quod non possit esse sine peccato mortali, propter contemptum divinae legis.

SED CONTRA, consensus in actum peccati pertinet ad rationem superiorem, ut supra dictum est. Sed consensus in actum peccati venialis est peccatum veniale. Ergo in superiori ratione potest esse peccatum veniale.

OBJECTION 1: It would seem that there cannot be venial sin in the higher reason as directing the lower powers, i.e., as consenting to a sinful act. For Augustine says (*De Trin.* xii, 7) that the *higher reason is intent on considering and consulting the eternal law*. But mortal sin consists in turning away from the eternal law. Therefore it seems that there can be no other than mortal sin in the higher reason.

OBJ. 2: Further, the higher reason is the principle of the spiritual life, as the heart is of the body's life. But the diseases of the heart are deadly. Therefore the sins of the higher reason are mortal.

OBJ. 3: Further, a venial sin becomes a mortal sin if it be done out of contempt. But it would seem impossible to commit even a venial sin, deliberately, without contempt. Since then the consent of the higher reason is always accompanied by deliberate consideration of the eternal law, it seems that it cannot be without mortal sin, on account of the contempt of the Divine law.

ON THE CONTRARY, Consent to a sinful act belongs to the higher reason, as stated above (A7). But consent to an act of venial sin is itself a venial sin. Therefore a venial sin can be in the higher reason.

RESPONDEO dicendum quod, sicut Augustinus dicit, in XII de Trin., ratio superior *inhaeret rationibus aeternis conspiciendis aut consulendis*, conspiciendis quidem, secundum quod earum veritatem speculatur; consulendis autem, secundum quod per rationes aeternas de aliis iudicat et ordinat; ad quod pertinet quod, deliberando per rationes aeternas, consentit in aliquem actum, vel dissentit ab eo. Contingit autem quod inordinatio actus in quem consentit, non contrariatur rationibus aeternis, quia non est cum aversione a fine ultimo, sicut contrariatur actus peccati mortalis, sed est praeter eas, sicut actus peccati venialis. Unde quando ratio superior in actum peccati venialis consentit, non avertitur a rationibus aeternis. Unde non peccat mortaliter, sed venialiter.

ET PER HOC patet responsio ad primum.

AD SECUNDUM dicendum quod duplex est infirmitas cordis. Una quae est in ipsa substantia cordis, et immutat naturalem complexionem ipsius, et talis infirmitas semper est mortalis. Alia est autem infirmitas cordis propter aliquam inordinationem vel motus eius, vel alicuius eorum quae circumstant cor, et talis infirmitas non semper est mortalis. Et similiter in ratione superiori semper est peccatum mortale, quando tollitur ipsa ordinatio rationis superioris ad proprium obiectum, quod est rationes aeternae. Sed quando est inordinatio circa hoc, non est peccatum mortale, sed veniale.

AD TERTIUM dicendum quod deliberatus consensus in peccatum non semper pertinet ad contemptum legis divinae, sed solum quando peccatum legi divinae contrariatur.

I ANSWER THAT, As Augustine says (*De Trin.* xii, 7), the higher reason *is intent on contemplating or consulting the eternal law*; it contemplates it by considering its truth; it consults it by judging and directing other things according to it: and to this pertains the fact that by deliberating through the eternal types, it consents to an act or dissents from it. Now it may happen that the inordinateness of the act to which it consents, is not contrary to the eternal law, in the same way as mortal sin is, because it does not imply aversion from the last end, but is beside that law, as an act of venial sin is. Therefore when the higher reason consents to the act of a venial sin, it does not turn away from the eternal law: wherefore it sins, not mortally, but venially.

THIS SUFFICES for the Reply to the First Objection.

REPLY OBJ. 2: Disease of the heart is twofold: one which is in the very substance of the heart, and affects its natural consistency, and such a disease is always mortal: the other is a disease of the heart consisting in some disorder either of the movement or of the parts surrounding the heart, and such a disease is not always mortal. In like manner there is mortal sin in the higher reason whenever the order itself of the higher reason to its proper object which is the eternal law, is destroyed; but when the disorder leaves this untouched, the sin is not mortal but venial.

REPLY OBJ. 3: Deliberate consent to a sin does not always amount to contempt of the Divine law, but only when the sin is contrary to the Divine law.

Article 10

Whether Venial Sin Can Be in the Higher Reason As Such?

AD DECIMUM SIC PROCEDITUR. Videtur quod in superiori ratione non possit esse peccatum veniale secundum seipsam, idest secundum quod inspicit rationes aeternas. Actus enim potentiae non invenitur esse deficiens, nisi per hoc quod inordinate se habet circa suum obiectum. Sed obiectum superioris rationis sunt aeternae rationes, a quibus deordinari non est sine peccato mortali. Ergo in superiori ratione non potest esse peccatum veniale secundum seipsam.

PRAETEREA, cum ratio sit vis deliberativa, actus rationis semper est cum deliberatione. Sed omnis inordinatus motus in his quae Dei sunt, si sit cum deliberatione, est peccatum mortale. Ergo in ratione superiori secundum seipsam, nunquam est peccatum veniale.

PRAETEREA, contingit quandoque quod peccatum ex subreptione est peccatum veniale, peccatum autem ex deliberatione est peccatum mortale, per hoc quod ratio

OBJECTION 1: It would seem that venial sin cannot be in the higher reason as such, i.e., as considering the eternal law. For the act of a power is not found to fail except that power be inordinately disposed with regard to its object. Now the object of the higher reason is the eternal law, in respect of which there can be no disorder without mortal sin. Therefore there can be no venial sin in the higher reason as such.

OBJ. 2: Further, since the reason is a deliberative power, there can be no act of reason without deliberation. Now every inordinate movement in things concerning God, if it be deliberate, is a mortal sin. Therefore venial sin is never in the higher reason as such.

OBJ. 3: Further, it happens sometimes that a sin which takes us unawares, is a venial sin. Now a deliberate sin is a mortal sin, through the reason, in deliberating, having

deliberans recurrit ad aliquod maius bonum, contra quod homo agens gravius peccat, sicut cum de actu delectabili inordinato ratio deliberat quod est contra legem Dei, gravius peccat consentiendo, quam si solum consideraret quod est contra virtutem moralem. Sed ratio superior non potest recurrere ad aliquod altius quam sit suum obiectum. Ergo si motus ex subreptione non sit peccatum mortale, neque etiam deliberatio superveniens faciet ipsum esse peccatum mortale, quod patet esse falsum. Non ergo in ratione superiori secundum seipsam, potest esse peccatum veniale.

SED CONTRA, motus subreptitius infidelitatis est peccatum veniale. Sed pertinet ad superiorem rationem secundum seipsam. Ergo in ratione superiori potest esse peccatum veniale secundum seipsam.

RESPONDEO dicendum quod ratio superior aliter fertur in suum obiectum, atque aliter in obiecta inferiorum virium quae per ipsam diriguntur. In obiecta enim inferiorum virium non fertur nisi inquantum de eis consulit rationes aeternas. Unde non fertur in ea nisi per modum deliberationis. Deliberatus autem consensus in his quae ex genere suo sunt mortalia, est mortale peccatum. Et ideo ratio superior semper mortaliter peccat, si actus inferiorum virium in quos consentit, sint peccata mortalia.

Sed circa proprium obiectum habet duos actus, scilicet simplicem intuitum; et deliberationem, secundum quod etiam de proprio obiecto consulit rationes aeternas. Secundum autem simplicem intuitum, potest aliquem inordinatum motum habere circa divina, puta cum quis patitur subitum infidelitatis motum. Et quamvis infidelitas secundum suum genus sit peccatum mortale, tamen subitus motus infidelitatis est peccatum veniale. Quia peccatum mortale non est nisi sit contra legem Dei, potest autem aliquid eorum quae pertinent ad fidem, subito rationi occurrere sub quadam alia ratione, antequam super hoc consulatur, vel consuli possit, ratio aeterna, idest lex Dei; puta cum quis resurrectionem mortuorum subito apprehendit ut impossibilem secundum naturam, et simul apprehendendo renititur, antequam tempus habeat deliberandi quod hoc est nobis traditum ut credendum secundum legem divinam. Si vero post hanc deliberationem motus infidelitatis maneat, est peccatum mortale. Et ideo circa proprium obiectum, etsi sit peccatum mortale ex genere, potest ratio superior peccare venialiter in subitis motibus; vel etiam mortaliter per deliberatum consensum. In his autem quae pertinent ad inferiores vires, semper peccat mortaliter in his quae sunt peccata mortalia ex suo genere, non autem in his quae secundum suum genus sunt venialia peccata.

AD PRIMUM ergo dicendum quod peccatum quod est contra rationes aeternas, etsi sit peccatum mortale ex genere, potest tamen esse peccatum veniale propter imperfectionem actus subiti, ut dictum est.

recourse to some higher good, by acting against which, man sins more grievously; just as when the reason in deliberating about an inordinate pleasurable act, considers that it is contrary to the law of God, it sins more grievously in consenting, than if it only considered that it is contrary to moral virtue. But the higher reason cannot have recourse to any higher tribunal than its own object. Therefore if a movement that takes us unawares is not a mortal sin, neither will the subsequent deliberation make it a mortal sin; which is clearly false. Therefore there can be no venial sin in the higher reason as such.

ON THE CONTRARY, A sudden movement of unbelief is a venial sin. But it belongs to the higher reason as such. Therefore there can be a venial sin in the higher reason as such.

I ANSWER THAT, The higher reason regards its own object otherwise than the objects of the lower powers that are directed by the higher reason. For it does not regard the objects of the lower powers, except insofar as it consults the eternal law about them, and so it does not regard them save by way of deliberation. Now deliberate consent to what is a mortal sin in its genus, is itself a mortal sin; and consequently the higher reason always sins mortally, if the acts of the lower powers to which it consents are mortal sins.

With regard to its own object it has a twofold act, viz., simple *intuition*, and *deliberation*, in respect of which it again consults the eternal law about its own object. But in respect of simple intuition, it can have an inordinate movement about Divine things, as when a man suffers a sudden movement of unbelief. And although unbelief, in its genus, is a mortal sin, yet a sudden movement of unbelief is a venial sin, because there is no mortal sin unless it be contrary to the law of God. Now it is possible for one of the articles of faith to present itself to the reason suddenly under some other aspect, before the eternal law, i.e., the law of God, is consulted, or can be consulted, on the matter; as, for instance, when a man suddenly apprehends the resurrection of the dead as impossible naturally, and rejects it, as soon as he had thus apprehended it, before he has had time to deliberate and consider that this is proposed to our belief in accordance with the Divine law. If, however, the movement of unbelief remains after this deliberation, it is a mortal sin. Therefore, in sudden movements, the higher reason may sin venially in respect of its proper object, even if it be a mortal sin in its genus; or it may sin mortally in giving a deliberate consent; but in things pertaining to the lower powers, it always sins mortally, in things which are mortal sins in their genus, but not in those which are venial sins in their genus.

REPLY OBJ. 1: A sin which is against the eternal law, though it be mortal in its genus, may nevertheless be venial, on account of the incompleteness of a sudden action, as stated.

AD SECUNDUM dicendum quod in operativis ad rationem, ad quam pertinet deliberatio, pertinet etiam simplex intuitus eorum ex quibus deliberatio procedit, sicut etiam in speculativis ad rationem pertinet et syllogizare, et propositiones formare. Et ideo etiam ratio potest habere subitum motum.

AD TERTIUM dicendum quod una et eadem res potest diversas considerationes habere, quarum una est altera altior, sicut Deum esse potest considerari vel inquantum est cognoscibile ratione humana, vel inquantum creditur revelatione divina, quae est consideratio altior. Et ideo quamvis obiectum rationis superioris sit quiddam secundum naturam rei altissimum, tamen potest etiam reduci in quandam altiorem considerationem. Et hac ratione, quod in motu subito non erat peccatum mortale, per deliberationem reducentem in altiorem considerationem fit peccatum mortale, sicut supra expositum est.

REPLY OBJ. 2: In matters of action, the simple intuition of the principles from which deliberation proceeds, belongs to the reason, as well as the act of deliberation: even as in speculative matters it belongs to the reason both to syllogize and to form propositions: consequently the reason also can have a sudden movement.

REPLY OBJ. 3: One and the same thing may be the subject of different considerations, of which one is higher than the other; thus the existence of God may be considered, either as possible to be known by the human reason, or as delivered to us by Divine revelation, which is a higher consideration. And therefore, although the object of the higher reason is, in its nature, something sublime, yet it is reducible to some yet higher consideration: and in this way, that which in the sudden movement was not a mortal sin, becomes a mortal sin in virtue of the deliberation which brought it into the light of a higher consideration, as was explained above.

Question 75

Of the Causes of Sin, in General

Deinde considerandum est de causis peccatorum. Et primo, in generali; secundo, in speciali. Circa primum quaeruntur quatuor.

Primo, utrum peccatum habeat causam.

Secundo, utrum habeat causam interiorem.

Tertio, utrum habeat causam exteriorem.

Quarto, utrum peccatum sit causa peccati.

We must now consider the causes of sin: (1) in general; (2) in particular. Under the first head there are four points of inquiry:

(1) Whether sin has a cause?

(2) Whether it has an internal cause?

(3) Whether it has an external cause?

(4) Whether one sin is the cause of another?

Article 1

Whether Sin Has a Cause?

Ad primum sic proceditur. Videtur quod peccatum non habeat causam. Peccatum enim habet rationem mali, ut dictum est. Sed malum non habet causam, ut Dionysius dicit, IV cap. de Div. Nom. Ergo peccatum non habet causam.

Praeterea, causa est ad quam de necessitate sequitur aliud. Sed quod est ex necessitate, non videtur esse peccatum, eo quod omne peccatum est voluntarium. Ergo peccatum non habet causam.

Praeterea, si peccatum habet causam, aut habet pro causa bonum, aut malum. Non autem bonum, quia bonum non facit nisi bonum; *non enim potest arbor bona fructus malos facere,* ut dicitur Matth. VII similiter autem nec malum potest esse causa peccati, quia malum poenae sequitur ad peccatum; malum autem culpae est idem quod peccatum. Peccatum igitur non habet causam.

Sed contra, omne quod fit, habet causam, quia, ut dicitur Iob V, *nihil in terra sine causa fit.* Sed peccatum fit, est enim dictum vel factum vel concupitum contra legem Dei. Ergo peccatum habet causam.

Respondeo dicendum quod peccatum est quidam actus inordinatus. Ex parte igitur actus, potest habere per se causam, sicut et quilibet alius actus. Ex parte autem inordinationis, habet causam eo modo quo negatio vel privatio potest habere causam. Negationis autem alicuius potest duplex causa assignari. Primo quidem, defectus causae, idest ipsius causae negatio, est causa negationis secundum seipsam, ad remotionem enim causae sequitur remotio effectus; sicut obscuritatis causa est absentia solis. Alio modo, causa affirmationis ad quam sequitur negatio, est per accidens causa negationis consequentis, sicut ignis, causando calorem ex principali intentione, consequenter causat privationem frigiditatis.

Objection 1: It would seem that sin has no cause. For sin has the nature of evil, as stated above (Q71, A6). But evil has no cause, as Dionysius says (*Div. Nom.* iv). Therefore sin has no cause.

Obj. 2: Further, a cause is that from which something follows of necessity. Now that which is of necessity, seems to be no sin, for every sin is voluntary. Therefore sin has no cause.

Obj. 3: Further, if sin has a cause, this cause is either good or evil. It is not a good, because good produces nothing but good, for *a good tree cannot bring forth evil fruit* (Matt 7:18). Likewise neither can evil be the cause of sin, because the evil of punishment is a sequel to sin, and the evil of guilt is the same as sin. Therefore sin has no cause.

On the contrary, Whatever is done has a cause, for, according to Job 5:6, *nothing upon earth is done without a cause.* But sin is something done; since it a *word, deed, or desire contrary to the law of God.* Therefore sin has a cause.

I answer that, A sin is an inordinate act. Accordingly, so far as it is an act, it can have a direct cause, even as any other act; but, so far as it is inordinate, it has a cause, in the same way as a negation or privation can have a cause. Now two causes may be assigned to a negation: in the first place, absence of the cause of affirmation; i.e., the negation of the cause itself, is the cause of the negation in itself; since the result of the removing the cause is the removal of the effect: thus the absence of the sun is the cause of darkness. In the second place, the cause of an affirmation, of which a negation is a sequel, is the accidental cause of the resulting negation: thus fire by causing heat in virtue of its principal tendency, consequently causes a privation of cold. The

Quorum primum potest sufficere ad simplicem negationem. Sed cum inordinatio peccati, et quodlibet malum, non sit simplex negatio, sed privatio eius quod quid natum est et debet habere; necesse est quod talis inordinatio habeat causam agentem per accidens, quod enim natum est inesse et debet, nunquam abesset nisi propter causam aliquam impedientem. Et secundum hoc consuevit dici quod malum, quod in quadam privatione consistit, habet causam deficientem, vel agentem per accidens. Omnis autem causa per accidens reducitur ad causam per se. Cum igitur peccatum ex parte inordinationis habeat causam agentem per accidens, ex parte autem actus habeat causam agentem per se; sequitur quod inordinatio peccati consequatur ex ipsa causa actus. Sic igitur voluntas carens directione regulae rationis et legis divinae, intendens aliquod bonum commutabile, causat actum quidem peccati per se, sed inordinationem actus per accidens et praeter intentionem, provenit enim defectus ordinis in actu, ex defectu directionis in voluntate.

AD PRIMUM ergo dicendum quod peccatum non solum significat ipsam privationem boni, quae est inordinatio; sed significat actum sub tali privatione, quae habet rationem mali. Quod quidem qualiter habeat causam, dictum est.

AD SECUNDUM dicendum quod, si illa definitio causae universaliter debeat verificari, oportet ut intelligatur de causa sufficienti et non impedita. Contingit enim aliquid esse causam sufficientem alterius, et tamen non ex necessitate sequitur effectus, propter aliquod impedimentum superveniens, alioquin sequeretur quod omnia ex necessitate contingerent, ut patet in VI Metaphys. Sic igitur, etsi peccatum habeat causam, non tamen sequitur quod sit necessaria, quia effectus potest impediri.

AD TERTIUM dicendum quod, sicut dictum est, voluntas sine adhibitione regulae rationis vel legis divinae, est causa peccati. Hoc autem quod est non adhibere regulam rationis vel legis divinae, secundum se non habet rationem mali, nec poenae nec culpae, antequam applicetur ad actum. Unde secundum hoc, peccati primi non est causa aliquod malum, sed bonum aliquod cum absentia alicuius alterius boni.

first of these suffices to cause a simple negation. But, since the inordinateness of sin and of every evil is not a simple negation, but the privation of that which something ought naturally to have, such an inordinateness must needs have an accidental efficient cause. For that which naturally is and ought to be in a thing, is never lacking except on account of some impeding cause. And accordingly we are wont to say that evil, which consists in a certain privation, has a deficient cause, or an accidental efficient cause. Now every accidental cause is reducible to the direct cause. Since then sin, on the part of its inordinateness, has an accidental efficient cause, and on the part of the act, a direct efficient cause, it follows that the inordinateness of sin is a result of the cause of the act. Accordingly then, the will lacking the direction of the rule of reason and of the Divine law, and intent on some mutable good, causes the act of sin directly, and the inordinateness of the act, indirectly, and beside the intention: for the lack of order in the act results from the lack of direction in the will.

REPLY OBJ. 1: Sin signifies not only the privation of good, which privation is its inordinateness, but also the act which is the subject of that privation, which has the nature of evil: and how this evil has a cause, has been explained.

REPLY OBJ. 2: If this definition is to be verified in all cases, it must be understood as applying to a cause which is sufficient and not impeded. For it happens that a thing is the sufficient cause of something else, and that the effect does not follow of necessity, on account of some supervening impediment: else it would follow that all things happen of necessity, as is proved in *Metaph*. vi, text. 5. Accordingly, though sin has a cause, it does not follow that this is a necessary cause, since its effect can be impeded.

REPLY OBJ. 3: As stated above, the will in failing to apply the rule of reason or of the Divine law, is the cause of sin. Now the fact of not applying the rule of reason or of the Divine law, has not in itself the nature of evil, whether of punishment or of guilt, before it is applied to the act. Wherefore accordingly, evil is not the cause of the first sin, but some good lacking some other good.

Article 2

Whether Sin Has an Internal Cause?

AD SECUNDUM SIC PROCEDITUR. Videtur quod peccatum non habeat causam interiorem. Id enim quod est interius alicui rei, semper adest ei. Si igitur peccatum habeat causam interiorem, semper homo peccaret, cum, posita causa, ponatur effectus.

OBJECTION 1: It would seem that sin has no internal cause. For that which is within a thing is always in it. If therefore sin had an internal cause, man would always be sinning, since given the cause, the effect follows.

PRAETEREA, idem non est causa sui ipsius. Sed interiores motus hominis sunt peccatum. Ergo non sunt causa peccati.

PRAETEREA, quidquid est intra hominem, aut est naturale, aut voluntarium. Sed id quod est naturale, non potest esse peccati causa, quia peccatum est contra naturam, ut dicit Damascenus. Quod autem est voluntarium, si sit inordinatum, iam est peccatum. Non ergo aliquid intrinsecum potest esse causa primi peccati.

SED CONTRA est quod Augustinus dicit, quod *voluntas est causa peccati.*

RESPONDEO dicendum quod, sicut iam dictum est, per se causam peccati oportet accipere ex parte ipsius actus. Actus autem humani potest accipi causa interior et mediata, et immediata. Immediata quidem causa humani actus est ratio et voluntas, secundum quam homo est liber arbitrio. Causa autem remota est apprehensio sensitivae partis, et etiam appetitus sensitivus, sicut enim ex iudicio rationis voluntas movetur ad aliquid secundum rationem, ita etiam ex apprehensione sensus appetitus sensitivus in aliquid inclinatur. Quae quidem inclinatio interdum trahit voluntatem et rationem, sicut infra patebit. Sic igitur duplex causa peccati interior potest assignari, una proxima, ex parte rationis et voluntatis; alia vero remota, ex parte imaginationis vel appetitus sensitivi.

Sed quia supra dictum est quod causa peccati est aliquod bonum apparens motivum cum defectu debiti motivi, scilicet regulae rationis vel legis divinae; ipsum motivum quod est apparens bonum, pertinet ad apprehensionem sensus et appetitum. Ipsa autem absentia debitae regulae pertinet ad rationem, quae nata est huiusmodi regulam considerare. Sed ipsa perfectio voluntarii actus peccati pertinet ad voluntatem, ita quod ipse voluntatis actus, praemissis suppositis, iam est quoddam peccatum.

AD PRIMUM ergo dicendum quod id quod est intrinsecum sicut potentia naturalis, semper inest, id autem quod est intrinsecum sicut actus interior appetitivae vel apprehensivae virtutis, non semper inest. Ipsa autem potentia voluntatis est causa peccati in potentia, sed reducitur in actum per motus praecedentes et sensitivae partis primo, et rationis consequenter. Ex hoc enim quod aliquid proponitur ut appetibile secundum sensum et appetitus sensitivus inclinatur in illud, ratio interdum cessat a consideratione regulae debitae, et sic voluntas producit actum peccati. Quia igitur motus praecedentes non semper sunt in actu, neque peccatum semper est in actu.

AD SECUNDUM dicendum quod non omnes motus interiores sunt de substantia peccati, quod consistit

OBJ. 2: Further, a thing is not its own cause. But the internal movements of a man are sins. Therefore they are not the cause of sin.

OBJ. 3: Further, whatever is within man is either natural or voluntary. Now that which is natural cannot be the cause of sin, for sin is contrary to nature, as Damascene states (*De Fide Orth.* ii, 3; iv, 21); while that which is voluntary, if it be inordinate, is already a sin. Therefore nothing intrinsic can be the cause of the first sin.

ON THE CONTRARY, Augustine says (*De Duabus Anim.* x, 10,11; *Retract.* i, 9) that *the will is the cause of sin.*

I ANSWER THAT, As stated above (A1), the direct cause of sin must be considered on the part of the act. Now we may distinguish a twofold internal cause of human acts, one remote, the other proximate. The proximate internal cause of the human act is the reason and will, in respect of which man has a free-will; while the remote cause is the apprehension of the sensitive part, and also the sensitive appetite. For just as it is due to the judgment of reason, that the will is moved to something in accord with reason, so it is due to an apprehension of the senses that the sensitive appetite is inclined to something; which inclination sometimes influences the will and reason, as we shall explain further on (Q77, A1). Accordingly a double interior cause of sin may be assigned; one proximate, on the part of the reason and will; and the other remote, on the part of the imagination or sensitive appetite.

But since we have said above (A1, ad 3) that the cause of sin is some apparent good as motive, yet lacking the due motive, viz., the rule of reason or the Divine law, this motive which is an apparent good, appertains to the apprehension of the senses and to the appetite; while the lack of the due rule appertains to the reason, whose nature it is to consider this rule; and the completeness of the voluntary sinful act appertains to the will, so that the act of the will, given the conditions we have just mentioned, is already a sin.

REPLY OBJ. 1: That which is within a thing as its natural power, is always in it: but that which is within it, as the internal act of the appetitive or apprehensive power, is not always in it. Now the power of the will is the potential cause of sin, but is made actual by the preceding movements, both of the sensitive part, in the first place, and afterwards, of the reason. For it is because a thing is proposed as appetible to the senses, and because the appetite is inclined, that the reason sometimes fails to consider the due rule, so that the will produces the act of sin. Since therefore the movements that precede it are not always actual, neither is man always actually sinning.

REPLY OBJ. 2: It is not true that all the internal acts belong to the substance of sin, for this consists principally

principaliter in actu voluntatis, sed quidam praecedunt, et quidam consequuntur ipsum peccatum.

Ad tertium dicendum quod illud quod est causa peccati sicut potentia producens actum, est naturale. Motus etiam sensitivae partis, ex quo sequitur peccatum, interdum est naturalis, sicut cum propter appetitum cibi aliquis peccat. Sed efficitur peccatum innaturale ex hoc ipso quod deficit regula naturalis, quam homo secundum naturam suam debet attendere.

in the act of the will; but some precede and some follow the sin itself.

Reply Obj. 3: That which causes sin, as a power produces its act, is natural; and again, the movement of the sensitive part, from which sin follows, is natural sometimes, as, for instance, when anyone sins through appetite for food. Yet sin results in being unnatural from the very fact that the natural rule fails, which man, in accord with his nature, ought to observe.

Article 3

Whether Sin Has an External Cause?

Ad tertium sic proceditur. Videtur quod peccatum non habeat causam exteriorem. Peccatum enim est actus voluntarius. Voluntaria autem sunt eorum quae sunt in nobis; et ita non habent exteriorem causam. Ergo peccatum non habet exteriorem causam.

Praeterea, sicut natura est principium interius, ita etiam voluntas. Sed peccatum in rebus naturalibus nunquam accidit nisi ex aliqua interiori causa, ut puta monstruosi partus proveniunt ex corruptione alicuius principii interioris. Ergo neque in moralibus potest contingere peccatum nisi ex interiori causa. Non ergo habet peccatum causam exteriorem.

Praeterea, multiplicata causa, multiplicatur effectus. Sed quanto plura sunt et maiora exterius inducentia ad peccandum, tanto minus id quod quis inordinate agit, ei imputatur ad peccatum. Ergo nihil exterius est causa peccati.

Sed contra est quod dicitur Num. XXXI, *nonne istae sunt quae deceperunt filios Israel, et praevaricari vos fecerunt in domino super peccato Phogor?* Ergo aliquid exterius potest esse causa faciens peccare.

Respondeo dicendum quod, sicut supra dictum est, causa interior peccati est et voluntas, ut perficiens actum peccati; et ratio, quantum ad carentiam debitae regulae; et appetitus sensitivus inclinans. Sic ergo aliquid extrinsecum tripliciter posset esse causa peccati, vel quia moveret immediate ipsam voluntatem; vel quia moveret rationem; vel quia moveret appetitum sensitivum. Voluntatem autem, ut supra dictum est, interius movere non potest nisi Deus; qui non potest esse causa peccati, ut infra ostendetur. Unde relinquitur quod nihil exterius potest esse causa peccati, nisi vel inquantum movet rationem, sicut homo vel Daemon persuadens peccatum; vel sicut movens appetitum sensitivum, sicut aliqua sensibilia exteriora movent appetitum sensitivum. Sed neque persuasio exterior in rebus agendis ex necessitate movet rationem; neque etiam res exterius propositae

Objection 1: It would seem that sin has no external cause. For sin is a voluntary act. Now voluntary acts belong to principles that are within us, so that they have no external cause. Therefore sin has no external cause.

Obj. 2: Further, as nature is an internal principle, so is the will. Now in natural things sin can be due to no other than an internal cause; for instance, the birth of a monster is due to the corruption of some internal principle. Therefore in the moral order, sin can arise from no other than an internal cause. Therefore it has no external cause.

Obj. 3: Further, if the cause is multiplied, the effect is multiplied. Now the more numerous and weighty the external inducements to sin are, the less is a man's inordinate act imputed to him as a sin. Therefore nothing external is a cause of sin.

On the contrary, It is written (Num 21:16): *Are not these they, that deceived the children of Israel by the counsel of Balaam, and made you transgress against the Lord by the sin of Phogor?* Therefore something external can be a cause of sin.

I answer that, As stated above (A2), the internal cause of sin is both the will, as completing the sinful act, and the reason, as lacking the due rule, and the appetite, as inclining to sin. Accordingly something external might be a cause of sin in three ways, either by moving the will itself immediately, or by moving the reason, or by moving the sensitive appetite. Now, as stated above (Q9, A6; Q10, A4), none can move the will inwardly save God alone, who cannot be a cause of sin, as we shall prove further on (Q79, A1). Hence it follows that nothing external can be a cause of sin, except by moving the reason, as a man or devil by enticing to sin; or by moving the sensitive appetite, as certain external sensibles move it. Yet neither does external enticement move the reason, of necessity, in matters of action, nor do things proposed externally, of necessity move the sensitive appetite, except perhaps it be disposed thereto in a certain

ex necessitate movent appetitum sensitivum, nisi forte aliquo modo dispositum; et tamen etiam appetitus sensitivus non ex necessitate movet rationem et voluntatem. Unde aliquid exterius potest esse aliqua causa movens ad peccandum, non tamen sufficienter ad peccatum inducens, sed causa sufficienter complens peccatum est sola voluntas.

AD PRIMUM ergo dicendum quod ex hoc ipso quod exteriora moventia ad peccandum non sufficienter et ex necessitate inducunt, sequitur quod remaneat in nobis peccare et non peccare.

AD SECUNDUM dicendum quod per hoc quod ponitur interior causa peccati, non excluditur exterior, non enim id quod est exterius est causa peccati, nisi mediante causa interiori, ut dictum est.

AD TERTIUM dicendum quod, multiplicatis exterioribus causis inclinantibus ad peccandum, multiplicantur actus peccati, quia plures ex illis causis, et pluries, inclinantur ad actus peccati. Sed tamen minuitur ratio culpae, quae consistit in hoc quod aliquid sit voluntarium et in nobis.

way; and even the sensitive appetite does not, of necessity, move the reason and will. Therefore something external can be a cause moving to sin, but not so as to be a sufficient cause thereof: and the will alone is the sufficient completive cause of sin being accomplished.

REPLY OBJ. 1: From the very fact that the external motive causes of sin do not lead to sin sufficiently and necessarily, it follows that it remains in our power to sin or not to sin.

REPLY OBJ. 2: The fact that sin has an internal cause does not prevent its having an external cause; for nothing external is a cause of sin, except through the medium of the internal cause, as stated.

REPLY OBJ. 3: If the external causes inclining to sin be multiplied, the sinful acts are multiplied, because they incline to the sinful act in both greater numbers and greater frequency. Nevertheless the character of guilt is lessened, since this depends on the act being voluntary and in our power.

Article 4

Whether One Sin Is a Cause of Another?

AD QUARTUM SIC PROCEDITUR. Videtur quod peccatum non sit causa peccati. Sunt enim quatuor genera causarum, quorum nullum potest ad hoc congruere quod peccatum sit causa peccati. Finis enim habet rationem boni, quod non competit peccato, quod de sua ratione est malum. Et eadem ratione nec peccatum potest esse causa efficiens, quia *malum non est causa agens, sed est infirmum et impotens*, ut Dionysius dicit, IV cap. de Div. Nom. Causa autem materialis et formalis videntur habere solum locum in naturalibus corporibus quae sunt composita ex materia et forma. Ergo peccatum non potest habere causam materialem et formalem.

PRAETEREA, *agere sibi simile est rei perfectae*, ut dicitur in IV Meteor. Sed peccatum de sui ratione est imperfectum. Ergo peccatum non potest esse causa peccati.

PRAETEREA, si huius peccati sit causa aliud peccatum, eadem ratione et illius erit causa aliquod aliud peccatum, et sic procedetur in infinitum, quod est inconveniens. Non ergo peccatum est causa peccati.

SED CONTRA est quod Gregorius dicit, super Ezech., *peccatum quod per poenitentiam citius non deletur, peccatum est et causa peccati.*

RESPONDEO dicendum quod, cum peccatum habeat causam ex parte actus, hoc modo unum peccatum posset esse causa alterius, sicut unus actus humanus potest

OBJECTION 1: It would seem that one sin cannot be the cause of another. For there are four kinds of cause, none of which will fit in with one sin causing another. Because the end has the character of good; which is inconsistent with sin, which has the character of evil. In like manner neither can a sin be an efficient cause, since *evil is not an efficient cause, but is weak and powerless*, as Dionysius declares (*Div. Nom.* iv). The material and formal cause seems to have no place except in natural bodies, which are composed of matter and form. Therefore sin cannot have either a material or a formal cause.

OBJ. 2: Further, *to produce its like belongs to a perfect thing*, as stated in *Meteor.* iv, 2. But sin is essentially something imperfect. Therefore one sin cannot be a cause of another.

OBJ. 3: Further, if one sin is the cause of a second sin, in the same way, yet another sin will be the cause of the first, and thus we go on indefinitely, which is absurd. Therefore one sin is not the cause of another.

ON THE CONTRARY, Gregory says on Ezechiel (*Hom.* xi): *A sin is not quickly blotted out by repentance, is both a sin and a cause of sin.*

I ANSWER THAT, Forasmuch as a sin has a cause on the part of the act of sin, it is possible for one sin to be the cause of another, in the same way as one human act is the cause

esse causa alterius. Contingit igitur unum peccatum esse causam alterius secundum quatuor genera causarum. Primo quidem, secundum modum causae efficientis vel moventis, et per se et per accidens. Per accidens quidem, sicut removens prohibens dicitur movens per accidens, cum enim per unum actum peccati homo amittit gratiam, vel caritatem, vel verecundiam, vel quodcumque aliud retrahens a peccato, incidit ex hoc in aliud peccatum; et sic primum peccatum est causa secundi per accidens. Per se autem, sicut cum ex uno actu peccati homo disponitur ad hoc quod alium actum consimilem facilius committit, ex actibus enim causantur dispositiones et habitus inclinantes ad similes actus. Secundum vero genus causae materialis, unum peccatum est causa alterius, inquantum praeparat ei materiam, sicut avaritia praeparat materiam litigio, quod plerumque est de divitiis congregatis. Secundum vero genus causae finalis, unum peccatum est causa alterius, inquantum propter finem unius peccati aliquis committit aliud peccatum, sicut cum aliquis committit simoniam propter finem ambitionis, vel fornicationem propter furtum. Et quia finis dat formam in moralibus, ut supra habitum est, ex hoc etiam sequitur quod unum peccatum sit formalis causa alterius, in actu enim fornicationis quae propter furtum committitur, est quidem fornicatio sicut materiale, furtum vero sicut formale.

Ad primum ergo dicendum quod peccatum, inquantum est inordinatum, habet rationem mali, sed inquantum est actus quidam, habet aliquod bonum, saltem apparens, pro fine. Et ita ex parte actus potest esse causa et finalis et effectiva alterius peccati, licet non ex parte inordinationis. Materiam autem habet peccatum non ex qua, sed circa quam. Formam autem habet ex fine. Et ideo secundum quatuor genera causarum peccatum potest dici causa peccati, ut dictum est.

Ad secundum dicendum quod peccatum est imperfectum imperfectione morali ex parte inordinationis, sed ex parte actus potest habere perfectionem naturae. Et secundum hoc potest esse causa peccati.

Ad tertium dicendum quod non omnis causa peccati est peccatum. Unde non oportet quod procedatur in infinitum; sed potest perveniri ad aliquod primum peccatum, cuius causa non est aliud peccatum.

of another. Hence it happens that one sin may be the cause of another in respect of the four kinds of causes. First, after the manner of an efficient or moving cause, both directly and indirectly. Indirectly, as that which removes an impediment is called an indirect cause of movement: for when man, by one sinful act, loses grace, or charity, or shame, or anything else that withdraws him from sin, he thereby falls into another sin, so that the first sin is the accidental cause of the second. Directly, as when, by one sinful act, man is disposed to commit more readily another like act: because acts cause dispositions and habits inclining to like acts. Second, after the manner of a material cause, one sin is the cause of another, by preparing its matter: thus covetousness prepares the matter for strife, which is often about the wealth a man has amassed together. Third, after the manner of a final cause, one sin causes another, insofar as a man commits one sin for the sake of another which is his end; as when a man is guilty of simony for the end of ambition, or fornication for the purpose of theft. And since the end gives the form to moral matters, as stated above (Q1, A3; Q18, AA4,6), it follows that one sin is also the formal cause of another: because in the act of fornication committed for the purpose of theft, the former is material while the latter is formal.

Reply Obj. 1: Sin, insofar as it is inordinate, has the character of evil; but, insofar as it is an act, it has some good, at least apparent, for its end: so that, as an act, but not as being inordinate, it can be the cause, both final and efficient, of another sin. A sin has matter, not *of which* but *about which* it is: and it has its form from its end. Consequently one sin can be the cause of another, in respect of the four kinds of cause, as stated above.

Reply Obj. 2: Sin is something imperfect on account of its moral imperfection on the part of its inordinateness. Nevertheless, as an act it can have natural perfection: and thus it can be the cause of another sin.

Reply Obj. 3: Not every cause of one sin is another sin; so there is no need to go on indefinitely: for one may come to one sin which is not caused by another sin.

QUESTION 76

OF THE CAUSES OF SIN, IN PARTICULAR

Deinde considerandum est de causis peccati in speciali. Et primo, de causis interioribus peccati; secundo, de exterioribus; tertio, de peccatis quae sunt causa aliorum peccatorum. Prima autem consideratio, secundum praemissa, erit tripartita, nam primo, agetur de ignorantia, quae est causa peccati ex parte rationis; secundo, de infirmitate seu passione, quae est causa peccati ex parte appetitus sensitivi; tertio, de malitia, quae est causa peccati ex parte voluntatis.

Circa primum quaeruntur quatuor.

Primo, utrum ignorantia sit causa peccati.

Secundo, utrum ignorantia sit peccatum.

Tertio, utrum totaliter a peccato excuset.

Quarto, utrum diminuat peccatum.

We must now consider the causes of sin, in particular, and (1) The internal causes of sin; (2) its external causes; and (3) sins which are the causes of other sins. In view of what has been said above (A2), the first consideration will be threefold: so that in the first place we shall treat of ignorance, which is the cause of sin on the part of reason; second, of weakness or passion, which is the cause of sin on the part of the sensitive appetite; third, of malice, which is the cause of sin on the part of the will.

Under the first head, there are four points of inquiry:

(1) Whether ignorance is a cause of sin?

(2) Whether ignorance is a sin?

(3) Whether it excuses from sin altogether?

(4) Whether it diminishes sin?

Article 1

Whether Ignorance Can Be a Cause of Sin?

AD PRIMUM SIC PROCEDITUR. Videtur quod ignorantia non possit esse causa peccati. Quia quod non est, nullius est causa. Sed ignorantia est non ens, cum sit privatio quaedam scientiae. Ergo ignorantia non est causa peccati.

PRAETEREA, causae peccati sunt accipiendae ex parte conversionis, ut ex supradictis patet. Sed ignorantia videtur respicere aversionem. Ergo non debet poni causa peccati.

PRAETEREA, omne peccatum in voluntate consistit, ut supra dictum est. Sed voluntas non fertur nisi in aliquod cognitum, quia bonum apprehensum est obiectum voluntatis. Ergo ignorantia non potest esse causa peccati.

SED CONTRA est quod Augustinus dicit, in libro de natura et gratia, quod *quidam per ignorantiam peccant*.

RESPONDEO dicendum quod, secundum philosophum, in VIII Physic., causa movens est duplex, una per se, et alia per accidens. Per se quidem, quae propria virtute movet, sicut generans est causa movens gravia et levia. Per accidens autem, sicut removens prohibens, vel sicut ipsa remotio prohibentis. Et hoc modo ignorantia potest esse causa actus peccati, est enim privatio scientiae perficientis rationem, quae prohibet actum peccati, inquantum dirigit actus humanos.

Considerandum est autem quod ratio secundum duplicem scientiam est humanorum actuum directiva,

OBJECTION 1: It would seem that ignorance cannot be a cause of sin: because a non-being is not the cause of anything. Now ignorance is a non-being, since it is a privation of knowledge. Therefore ignorance is not a cause of sin.

OBJ. 2: Further, causes of sin should be reckoned in respect of sin being a *turning to* something, as was stated above (Q75, A1). Now ignorance seems to savor of *turning away* from something. Therefore it should not be reckoned a cause of sin.

OBJ. 3: Further, every sin is seated in the will. Now the will does not turn to that which is not known, because its object is the good apprehended. Therefore ignorance cannot be a cause of sin.

ON THE CONTRARY, Augustine says (*De Nat. et Grat.* lxvii) *that some sin through ignorance*.

I ANSWER THAT, According to the Philosopher (*Phys.* viii, 27) a moving cause is twofold, direct and indirect. A direct cause is one that moves by its own power, as the generator is the moving cause of heavy and light things. An indirect cause, is either one that removes an impediment, or the removal itself of an impediment: and it is in this way that ignorance can be the cause of a sinful act; because it is a privation of knowledge perfecting the reason that forbids the act of sin, insofar as it directs human acts.

Now we must observe that the reason directs human acts in accordance with a twofold knowledge, universal

scilicet secundum scientiam universalem, et particularem. Conferens enim de agendis, utitur quodam syllogismo, cuius conclusio est iudicium seu electio vel operatio. Actiones autem in singularibus sunt. Unde conclusio syllogismi operativi est singularis. Singularis autem propositio non concluditur ex universali nisi mediante aliqua propositione singulari, sicut homo prohibetur ab actu parricidii per hoc quod scit patrem non esse occidendum, et per hoc quod scit hunc esse patrem. Utriusque ergo ignorantia potest causare parricidii actum, scilicet et universalis principii, quod est quaedam regula rationis; et singularis circumstantiae. Unde patet quod non quaelibet ignorantia peccantis est causa peccati, sed illa tantum quae tollit scientiam prohibentem actum peccati. Unde si voluntas alicuius esset sic disposita quod non prohiberetur ab actu parricidii, etiam si patrem agnosceret; ignorantia patris non est huic causa peccati, sed concomitanter se habet ad peccatum. Et ideo talis non peccat propter ignorantiam, sed peccat ignorans, secundum philosophum, in III Ethic.

AD PRIMUM ergo dicendum quod non ens non potest esse alicuius causa per se, potest tamen esse causa per accidens, sicut remotio prohibentis.

AD SECUNDUM dicendum quod sicut scientia quam tollit ignorantia, respicit peccatum ex parte conversionis; ita etiam ignorantia ex parte conversionis est causa peccati ut removens prohibens.

AD TERTIUM dicendum quod in illud quod est quantum ad omnia ignotum, non potest ferri voluntas, sed si aliquid est secundum aliquid notum et secundum aliquid ignotum, potest voluntas illud velle. Et hoc modo ignorantia est causa peccati, sicut cum aliquis scit hunc quem occidit, esse hominem, sed nescit eum esse patrem; vel cum aliquis scit aliquem actum esse delectabilem, nescit tamen eum esse peccatum.

and particular: because in conferring about what is to be done, it employs a syllogism, the conclusion of which is an act of judgment, or of choice, or an operation. Now actions are about singulars: wherefore the conclusion of a practical syllogism is a singular proposition. But a singular proposition does not follow from a universal proposition, except through the medium of a particular proposition: thus a man is restrained from an act of parricide, by the knowledge that it is wrong to kill one's father, and that this man is his father. Hence ignorance about either of these two propositions, viz., of the universal principle which is a rule of reason, or of the particular circumstance, could cause an act of parricide. Hence it is clear that not every kind of ignorance is the cause of a sin, but that alone which removes the knowledge which would prevent the sinful act. Consequently if a man's will be so disposed that he would not be restrained from the act of parricide, even though he recognized his father, his ignorance about his father is not the cause of his committing the sin, but is concomitant with the sin: wherefore such a man sins, not *through ignorance* but *in ignorance*, as the Philosopher states (*Ethic.* iii, 1).

REPLY OBJ. 1: Non-being cannot be the direct cause of anything: but it can be an accidental cause, as being the removal of an impediment.

REPLY OBJ. 2: As knowledge, which is removed by ignorance, regards sin as turning towards something, so too, ignorance of this respect of a sin is the cause of that sin, as removing its impediment.

REPLY OBJ. 3: The will cannot turn to that which is absolutely unknown: but if something be known in one respect, and unknown in another, the will can will it. It is thus that ignorance is the cause of sin: for instance, when a man knows that what he is killing is a man, but not that it is his own father; or when one knows that a certain act is pleasurable, but not that it is a sin.

Article 2

Whether Ignorance Is a Sin?

AD SECUNDUM SIC PROCEDITUR. Videtur quod ignorantia non sit peccatum. Peccatum enim est dictum vel factum vel concupitum contra legem Dei, ut supra habitum est. Sed ignorantia non importat aliquem actum, neque interiorem neque exteriorem. Ergo ignorantia non est peccatum.

PRAETEREA, peccatum directius opponitur gratiae quam scientiae. Sed privatio gratiae non est peccatum, sed magis poena quaedam consequens peccatum. Ergo ignorantia, quae est privatio scientiae, non est peccatum.

OBJECTION 1: It would seem that ignorance is not a sin. For sin is *a word, deed or desire contrary to God's law*, as stated above (Q71, A5). Now ignorance does not denote an act, either internal or external. Therefore ignorance is not a sin.

OBJ. 2: Further, sin is more directly opposed to grace than to knowledge. Now privation of grace is not a sin, but a punishment resulting from sin. Therefore ignorance which is privation of knowledge is not a sin.

Praeterea, si ignorantia est peccatum, hoc non est nisi inquantum est voluntaria. Sed si ignorantia sit peccatum inquantum est voluntaria, videtur peccatum in ipso actu voluntatis consistere magis quam in ignorantia. Ergo ignorantia non erit peccatum, sed magis aliquid consequens ad peccatum.

Praeterea, omne peccatum per poenitentiam tollitur; nec aliquod peccatum transiens reatu remanet actu, nisi solum originale. Ignorantia autem non tollitur per poenitentiam, sed adhuc remanet actu, omni reatu per poenitentiam remoto. Ergo ignorantia non est peccatum, nisi forte sit originale.

Praeterea, si ipsa ignorantia sit peccatum, quandiu ignorantia remaneret in homine, tandiu actu peccaret. Sed continue manet ignorantia in ignorante. Ergo ignorans continue peccaret. Quod patet esse falsum, quia sic ignorantia esset gravissimum. Non ergo ignorantia est peccatum.

Sed contra, nihil meretur poenam nisi peccatum. Sed ignorantia meretur poenam, secundum illud I ad Cor. XIV, *si quis ignorat, ignorabitur*. Ergo ignorantia est peccatum.

Respondeo dicendum quod ignorantia in hoc a nescientia differt, quod nescientia dicit simplicem scientiae negationem, unde cuicumque deest aliquarum rerum scientia, potest dici nescire illas; secundum quem modum Dionysius in Angelis nescientiam ponit, VII cap. Cael. Hier. Ignorantia vero importat scientiae privationem, dum scilicet alicui deest scientia eorum quae aptus natus est scire. Horum autem quaedam aliquis scire tenetur, illa scilicet sine quorum scientia non potest debitum actum recte exercere. Unde omnes tenentur scire communiter ea quae sunt fidei, et universalia iuris praecepta, singuli autem ea quae ad eorum statum vel officium spectant. Quaedam vero sunt quae etsi aliquis natus est scire, non tamen ea scire tenetur, sicut theoremata geometriae, et contingentia particularia, nisi in casu. Manifestum est autem quod quicumque negligit habere vel facere id quod tenetur habere vel facere, peccat peccato omissionis. Unde propter negligentiam, ignorantia eorum quae aliquis scire tenetur, est peccatum. Non autem imputatur homini ad negligentiam, si nesciat ea quae scire non potest. Unde horum ignorantia invincibilis dicitur, quia scilicet studio superari non potest. Et propter hoc talis ignorantia, cum non sit voluntaria, eo quod non est in potestate nostra eam repellere, non est peccatum. Ex quo patet quod nulla ignorantia invincibilis est peccatum, ignorantia autem vincibilis est peccatum, si sit eorum quae aliquis scire tenetur; non autem si sit eorum quae quis scire non tenetur.

Ad primum ergo dicendum quod, sicut supra dictum est, in hoc quod dicitur dictum vel factum vel concupitum, sunt intelligendae etiam negationes oppositae,

Obj. 3: Further, if ignorance is a sin, this can only be insofar as it is voluntary. But if ignorance is a sin, through being voluntary, it seems that the sin will consist in the act itself of the will, rather than in the ignorance. Therefore the ignorance will not be a sin, but rather a result of sin.

Obj. 4: Further, every sin is taken away by repentance, nor does any sin, except only original sin, pass as to guilt, yet remain in act. Now ignorance is not removed by repentance, but remains in act, all its guilt being removed by repentance. Therefore ignorance is not a sin, unless perchance it be original sin.

Obj. 5: Further, if ignorance be a sin, then a man will be sinning, as long as he remains in ignorance. But ignorance is continual in the one who is ignorant. Therefore a person in ignorance would be continually sinning, which is clearly false, else ignorance would be a most grievous sin. Therefore ignorance is not a sin.

On the contrary, Nothing but sin deserves punishment. But ignorance deserves punishment, according to 1 Cor. 14:38: *If any man know not, he shall not be known*. Therefore ignorance is a sin.

I answer that, Ignorance differs from nescience, in that nescience denotes mere absence of knowledge; wherefore whoever lacks knowledge about anything, can be said to be nescient about it: in which sense Dionysius puts nescience in the angels (*Coel. Hier.* vii). On the other hand, ignorance denotes privation of knowledge, i.e., lack of knowledge of those things that one has a natural aptitude to know. Some of these we are under an obligation to know, those, to wit, without the knowledge of which we are unable to accomplish a due act rightly. Wherefore all are bound in common to know the articles of faith, and the universal principles of right, and each individual is bound to know matters regarding his duty or state. Meanwhile there are other things which a man may have a natural aptitude to know, yet he is not bound to know them, such as the geometrical theorems, and contingent particulars, except in some individual case. Now it is evident that whoever neglects to have or do what he ought to have or do, commits a sin of omission. Wherefore through negligence, ignorance of what one is bound to know, is a sin; whereas it is not imputed as a sin to man, if he fails to know what he is unable to know. Consequently ignorance of such like things is called *invincible*, because it cannot be overcome by study. For this reason such like ignorance, not being voluntary, since it is not in our power to be rid of it, is not a sin: wherefore it is evident that no invincible ignorance is a sin. On the other hand, vincible ignorance is a sin, if it be about matters one is bound to know; but not, if it be about things one is not bound to know.

Reply Obj. 1: As stated above (Q71, A6, ad 1), when we say that sin is a *word, deed or desire*, we include the opposite negations, by reason of which omissions have the character

secundum quod omissio habet rationem peccati. Et ita negligentia, secundum quam ignorantia est peccatum, continetur sub praedicta definitione peccati, inquantum praetermittitur aliquid quod debuit dici vel fieri vel concupisci, ad scientiam debitam acquirendam.

AD SECUNDUM dicendum quod privatio gratiae, etsi secundum se non sit peccatum, tamen ratione negligentiae praeparandi se ad gratiam, potest habere rationem peccati, sicut et ignorantia. Et tamen quantum ad hoc est dissimile, quia homo potest aliquam scientiam acquirere per suos actus, gratia vero non acquiritur ex nostris actibus, sed ex Dei munere.

AD TERTIUM dicendum quod, sicut in peccato transgressionis peccatum non consistit in solo actu voluntatis, sed etiam in actu volito qui est imperatus a voluntate; ita in peccato omissionis non solum actus voluntatis est peccatum, sed etiam ipsa omissio, inquantum est aliqualiter voluntaria. Et hoc modo ipsa negligentia sciendi, vel inconsideratio, est peccatum.

AD QUARTUM dicendum quod licet, transeunte reatu per poenitentiam, remaneat ignorantia secundum quod est privatio scientiae; non tamen remanet negligentia, secundum quam ignorantia peccatum dicitur.

AD QUINTUM dicendum quod, sicut in aliis peccatis omissionis solo illo tempore homo actu peccat, pro quo praeceptum affirmativum obligat; ita est etiam de peccato ignorantiae. Non enim continuo ignorans actu peccat, sed solum quando est tempus acquirendi scientiam quam habere tenetur.

of sin; so that negligence, in as much as ignorance is a sin, is comprised in the above definition of sin; insofar as one omits to say what one ought, or to do what one ought, or to desire what one ought, in order to acquire the knowledge which we ought to have.

REPLY OBJ. 2: Although privation of grace is not a sin in itself, yet by reason of negligence in preparing oneself for grace, it may have the character of sin, even as ignorance; nevertheless even here there is a difference, since man can acquire knowledge by his acts, whereas grace is not acquired by acts, but by God's favor.

REPLY OBJ. 3: Just as in a sin of transgression, the sin consists not only in the act of the will, but also in the act willed, which is commanded by the will; so in a sin of omission not only the act of the will is a sin, but also the omission, insofar as it is in some way voluntary; and accordingly, the neglect to know, or even lack of consideration is a sin.

REPLY OBJ. 4: Although when the guilt has passed away through repentance, the ignorance remains, according as it is a privation of knowledge, nevertheless the negligence does not remain, by reason of which the ignorance is said to be a sin.

REPLY OBJ. 5: Just as in other sins of omission, man sins actually only at the time at which the affirmative precept is binding, so is it with the sin of ignorance. For the ignorant man sins actually indeed, not continually, but only at the time for acquiring the knowledge that he ought to have.

Article 3

Whether Ignorance Excuses from Sin Altogether?

AD TERTIUM SIC PROCEDITUR. Videtur quod ignorantia, ex toto excuset a peccato. Quia, ut Augustinus dicit, omne peccatum voluntarium est. Sed ignorantia causat involuntarium ut supra habitum est. Ergo ignorantia totaliter excusat peccatum.

PRAETEREA, id quod aliquis facit praeter intentionem, per accidens agit. Sed intentio non potest esse de eo quod est ignotum. Ergo id quod per ignorantiam homo agit, per accidens se habet in actibus humanis. Sed quod est per accidens, non dat speciem. Nihil ergo quod est per ignorantiam factum, debet iudicari peccatum vel virtuosum in humanis actibus.

PRAETEREA, homo est subiectum virtutis et peccati inquantum est particeps rationis. Sed ignorantia excludit scientiam, per quam ratio perficitur. Ergo ignorantia totaliter excusat a peccato.

OBJECTION 1: It would seem that ignorance excuses from sin altogether. For as Augustine says (*Retract.* i, 9), every sin is voluntary. Now ignorance causes involuntariness, as stated above (Q6, A8). Therefore ignorance excuses from sin altogether.

OBJ. 2: Further, that which is done beside the intention, is done accidentally. Now the intention cannot be about what is unknown. Therefore what a man does through ignorance is accidental in human acts. But what is accidental does not give the species. Therefore nothing that is done through ignorance in human acts, should be deemed sinful or virtuous.

OBJ. 3: Further, man is the subject of virtue and sin, inasmuch as he is partaker of reason. Now ignorance excludes knowledge which perfects the reason. Therefore ignorance excuses from sin altogether.

SED CONTRA est quod Augustinus dicit, in libro de Lib. Arb., quod *quaedam per ignorantiam facta, recte improbantur.* Sed solum illa recte improbantur quae sunt peccata. Ergo quaedam per ignorantiam facta, sunt peccata. Non ergo ignorantia omnino excusat a peccato.

RESPONDEO dicendum quod ignorantia de se habet quod faciat actum quem causat, involuntarium esse. Iam autem dictum est quod ignorantia dicitur causare actum quem scientia opposita prohibebat. Et ita talis actus, si scientia adesset, esset contrarius voluntati, quod importat nomen involuntarii. Si vero scientia quae per ignorantiam privatur, non prohiberet actum, propter inclinationem voluntatis in ipsum; ignorantia huius scientiae non facit hominem involuntarium, sed non volentem, ut dicitur in III Ethic. Et talis ignorantia, quae non est causa actus peccati, ut dictum est, quia non causat involuntarium, non excusat a peccato. Et eadem ratio est de quacumque ignorantia non causante, sed consequente vel concomitante actum peccati.

Sed ignorantia quae est causa actus, quia causat involuntarium, de se habet quod excuset a peccato, eo quod voluntarium est de ratione peccati. Sed quod aliquando non totaliter excuset a peccato, potest contingere ex duobus. Uno modo, ex parte ipsius rei ignoratae. Intantum enim ignorantia excusat a peccato, inquantum ignoratur aliquid esse peccatum. Potest autem contingere quod aliquis ignoret quidem aliquam circumstantiam peccati, quam si sciret, retraheretur a peccando, sive illa circumstantia faciat ad rationem peccati sive non; et tamen adhuc remanet in eius scientia aliquid per quod cognoscit illud esse actum peccati. Puta si aliquis percutiens aliquem, sciat quidem ipsum esse hominem, quod sufficit ad rationem peccati; non tamen scit eum esse patrem, quod est circumstantia constituens novam speciem peccati; vel forte nescit quod ille se defendens repercutiat eum, quod si sciret, non percuteret, quod non pertinet ad rationem peccati. Unde licet talis propter ignorantiam peccet, non tamen totaliter excusatur a peccato, quia adhuc remanet ei cognitio peccati. Alio modo potest hoc contingere ex parte ipsius ignorantiae, quia scilicet ipsa ignorantia est voluntaria, vel directe, sicut cum aliquis studiose vult nescire aliqua, ut liberius peccet; vel indirecte, sicut cum aliquis propter laborem, vel propter alias occupationes, negligit addiscere id per quod a peccato retraheretur. Talis enim negligentia facit ignorantiam ipsam esse voluntariam et peccatum, dummodo sit eorum quae quis scire tenetur et potest. Et ideo talis ignorantia non totaliter excusat a peccato. Si vero sit talis ignorantia quae omnino sit involuntaria, sive quia

ON THE CONTRARY, Augustine says (*De Lib. Arb.* iii, 18) that *some things done through ignorance are rightly reproved.* Now those things alone are rightly reproved which are sins. Therefore some things done through ignorance are sins. Therefore ignorance does not altogether excuse from sin.

I ANSWER THAT, Ignorance, by its very nature, renders the act which it causes involuntary. Now it has already been stated (AA1,2) that ignorance is said to cause the act which the contrary knowledge would have prevented; so that this act, if knowledge were to hand, would be contrary to the will, which is the meaning of the word involuntary. If, however, the knowledge, which is removed by ignorance, would not have prevented the act, on account of the inclination of the will thereto, the lack of this knowledge does not make that man unwilling, but not willing, as stated in *Ethic.* iii, 1: and such like ignorance which is not the cause of the sinful act, as already stated, since it does not make the act to be involuntary, does not excuse from sin. The same applies to any ignorance that does not cause, but follows or accompanies the sinful act.

On the other hand, ignorance which is the cause of the act, since it makes it to be involuntary, of its very nature excuses from sin, because voluntariness is essential to sin. But it may fail to excuse altogether from sin, and this for two reasons. First, on the part of the thing itself which is not known. For ignorance excuses from sin, insofar as something is not known to be a sin. Now it may happen that a person ignores some circumstance of a sin, the knowledge of which circumstance would prevent him from sinning, whether it belong to the substance of the sin, or not; and nevertheless his knowledge is sufficient for him to be aware that the act is sinful; for instance, if a man strike someone, knowing that it is a man (which suffices for it to be sinful) and yet be ignorant of the fact that it is his father, (which is a circumstance constituting another species of sin); or, suppose that he is unaware that this man will defend himself and strike him back, and that if he had known this, he would not have struck him (which does not affect the sinfulness of the act). Wherefore, though this man sins through ignorance, yet he is not altogether excused, because, notwithstanding, he has knowledge of the sin. Second, this may happen on the part of the ignorance itself, because, to wit, this ignorance is voluntary, either directly, as when a man wishes of set purpose to be ignorant of certain things that he may sin the more freely; or indirectly, as when a man, through stress of work or other occupations, neglects to acquire the knowledge which would restrain him from sin. For such like negligence renders the ignorance itself voluntary and sinful, provided it be about matters one is bound and able to know. Consequently this ignorance does

est invincibilis, sive quia est eius quod quis scire non tenetur; talis ignorantia omnino excusat a peccato.

AD PRIMUM ergo dicendum quod non omnis ignorantia causat involuntarium, sicut supra dictum est. Unde non omnis ignorantia totaliter excusat a peccato.

AD SECUNDUM dicendum quod inquantum remanet in ignorante de voluntario, intantum remanet de intentione peccati. Et secundum hoc, non erit per accidens peccatum.

AD TERTIUM dicendum quod, si esset talis ignorantia quae totaliter usum rationis excluderet, omnino a peccato excusaret, sicut patet in furiosis et amentibus. Non autem semper ignorantia causans peccatum est talis. Et ideo non semper totaliter excusat a peccato.

not altogether excuse from sin. If, however, the ignorance be such as to be entirely involuntary, either through being invincible, or through being of matters one is not bound to know, then such like ignorance excuses from sin altogether.

REPLY OBJ. 1: Not every ignorance causes involuntariness, as stated above (Q6, A8). Hence not every ignorance excuses from sin altogether.

REPLY OBJ. 2: So far as voluntariness remains in the ignorant person, the intention of sin remains in him: so that, in this respect, his sin is not accidental.

REPLY OBJ. 3: If the ignorance be such as to exclude the use of reason entirely, it excuses from sin altogether, as is the case with madmen and imbeciles: but such is not always the ignorance that causes the sin; and so it does not always excuse from sin altogether.

Article 4

Whether Ignorance Diminishes a Sin?

AD QUARTUM SIC PROCEDITUR. Videtur quod ignorantia non diminuat peccatum. Illud enim quod est commune in omni peccato, non diminuit peccatum. Sed ignorantia est communis in omni peccato, dicit enim philosophus, in III Ethic., quod omnis malus est ignorans. Ergo ignorantia non diminuit peccatum.

PRAETEREA, peccatum additum peccato facit maius peccatum. Sed ipsa ignorantia est peccatum, ut dictum est. Ergo non diminuit peccatum.

PRAETEREA, non est eiusdem aggravare et diminuere peccatum. Sed ignorantia aggravat peccatum, quoniam super illud apostoli, *ignoras quoniam benignitas Dei*, etc., dicit Ambrosius, *gravissime peccas, si ignoras*. Ergo ignorantia non diminuit peccatum.

PRAETEREA, si aliqua ignorantia diminuit peccatum, hoc maxime videtur de illa quae totaliter tollit usum rationis. Sed huiusmodi ignorantia non minuit peccatum, sed magis auget, dicit enim philosophus, in III Ethic., quod *ebrius meretur duplices maledictiones*. Ergo ignorantia non minuit peccatum.

SED CONTRA, quidquid est ratio remissionis peccati, alleviat peccatum. Sed ignorantia est huiusmodi, ut patet I ad Tim. I, *misericordiam consecutus sum, quia ignorans feci*. Ergo ignorantia diminuit, vel alleviat peccatum.

RESPONDEO dicendum quod, quia omne peccatum est voluntarium, intantum ignorantia potest diminuere peccatum, inquantum diminuit voluntarium, si autem voluntarium non diminuat, nullo modo diminuet peccatum. Manifestum est autem quod ignorantia quae

OBJECTION 1: It would seem that ignorance does not diminish a sin. For that which is common to all sins does not diminish sin. Now ignorance is common to all sins, for the Philosopher says (*Ethic*. iii, 1) that *every evil man is ignorant*. Therefore ignorance does not diminish sin.

OBJ. 2: Further, one sin added to another makes a greater sin. But ignorance is itself a sin, as stated above (A2). Therefore it does not diminish a sin.

OBJ. 3: Further, the same thing does not both aggravate and diminish sin. Now ignorance aggravates sin; for Ambrose commenting on Rm. 2:4, *Knowest thou not that the benignity of God leadeth thee to penance?* says: *Thy sin is most grievous if thou knowest not*. Therefore ignorance does not diminish sin.

OBJ. 4: Further, if any kind of ignorance diminishes a sin, this would seem to be chiefly the case as regards the ignorance which removes the use of reason altogether. Now this kind of ignorance does not diminish sin, but increases it: for the Philosopher says (*Ethic*. iii, 5) that the *punishment is doubled for a drunken man*. Therefore ignorance does not diminish sin.

ON THE CONTRARY, Whatever is a reason for sin to be forgiven, diminishes sin. Now such is ignorance, as is clear from 1 Tim. 1:13: *I obtained . . . mercy . . . because I did it ignorantly*. Therefore ignorance diminishes or alleviates sin.

I ANSWER THAT, Since every sin is voluntary, ignorance can diminish sin, insofar as it diminishes its voluntariness; and if it does not render it less voluntary, it nowise alleviates the sin. Now it is evident that the ignorance which excuses from sin altogether (through making it altogether

totaliter a peccato excusat, quia totaliter voluntarium tollit, peccatum non minuit, sed omnino aufert. Ignorantia vero quae non est causa peccati, sed concomitanter se habet ad peccatum, nec minuit peccatum nec auget.

Illa igitur sola ignorantia potest peccatum minuere, quae est causa peccati, et tamen totaliter a peccato non excusat. Contingit autem quandoque quod talis ignorantia directe et per se est voluntaria, sicut cum aliquis sua sponte nescit aliquid, ut liberius peccet. Et talis ignorantia videtur augere voluntarium et peccatum, ex intensione enim voluntatis ad peccandum provenit quod aliquis vult subire ignorantiae damnum, propter libertatem peccandi. Quandoque vero ignorantia quae est causa peccati, non est directe voluntaria, sed indirecte vel per accidens, puta cum aliquis non vult laborare in studio, ex quo sequitur eum esse ignorantem; vel cum aliquis vult bibere vinum immoderate, ex quo sequitur eum inebriari et discretione carere. Et talis ignorantia diminuit voluntarium, et per consequens peccatum. Cum enim aliquid non cognoscitur esse peccatum, non potest dici quod voluntas directe et per se feratur in peccatum, sed per accidens, unde est ibi minor contemptus, et per consequens minus peccatum.

AD PRIMUM ergo dicendum quod ignorantia secundum quam omnis malus est ignorans, non est causa peccati; sed aliquid consequens ad causam, scilicet ad passionem vel habitum inclinantem in peccatum.

AD SECUNDUM dicendum quod peccatum peccato additum facit plura peccata, non tamen facit semper maius peccatum, quia forte non coincidunt in idem peccatum, sed sunt plura. Et potest contingere, si primum diminuat secundum, quod ambo simul non habeant tantam gravitatem quantam unum solum haberet. Sicut homicidium gravius peccatum est a sobrio homine factum, quam si fiat ab ebrio, quamvis haec sint duo peccata, quia ebrietas plus diminuit de ratione sequentis peccati, quam sit sua gravitas.

AD TERTIUM dicendum quod verbum Ambrosii potest intelligi de ignorantia simpliciter affectata. Vel potest intelligi in genere peccati ingratitudinis, in qua summus gradus est quod homo etiam beneficia non recognoscat. Vel potest intelligi de ignorantia infidelitatis, quae fundamentum spiritualis aedificii subvertit.

AD QUARTUM dicendum quod ebrius meretur quidem duplices maledictiones, propter duo peccata quae committit, scilicet ebrietatem et aliud peccatum quod ex ebrietate sequitur. Tamen ebrietas, ratione ignorantiae adiunctae, diminuit sequens peccatum, et forte plus quam sit gravitas ipsius ebrietatis, ut dictum est. Vel potest dici quod illud verbum inducitur secundum ordinationem cuiusdam Pittaci legislatoris, qui statuit *ebrios, si percusserint, amplius puniendos; non ad veniam*

involuntary) does not diminish a sin, but does away with it altogether. On the other hand, ignorance which is not the cause of the sin being committed, but is concomitant with it, neither diminishes nor increases the sin.

Therefore sin cannot be alleviated by any ignorance, but only by such as is a cause of the sin being committed, and yet does not excuse from the sin altogether. Now it happens sometimes that such like ignorance is directly and essentially voluntary, as when a man is purposely ignorant that he may sin more freely, and ignorance of this kind seems rather to make the act more voluntary and more sinful, since it is through the will's intention to sin that he is willing to bear the hurt of ignorance, for the sake of freedom in sinning. Sometimes, however, the ignorance which is the cause of a sin being committed, is not directly voluntary, but indirectly or accidentally, as when a man is unwilling to work hard at his studies, the result being that he is ignorant, or as when a man willfully drinks too much wine, the result being that he becomes drunk and indiscreet, and this ignorance diminishes voluntariness and consequently alleviates the sin. For when a thing is not known to be a sin, the will cannot be said to consent to the sin directly, but only accidentally; wherefore, in that case there is less contempt, and therefore less sin.

REPLY OBJ. 1: The ignorance whereby *every evil man is ignorant*, is not the cause of sin being committed, but something resulting from that cause, viz., of the passion or habit inclining to sin.

REPLY OBJ. 2: One sin is added to another makes more sins, but it does not always make a sin greater, since, perchance, the two sins do not coincide, but are separate. It may happen, if the first diminishes the second, that the two together have not the same gravity as one of them alone would have; thus murder is a more grievous sin if committed by a man when sober, than if committed by a man when drunk, although in the latter case there are two sins: because drunkenness diminishes the sinfulness of the resulting sin more than its own gravity implies.

REPLY OBJ. 3: The words of Ambrose may be understood as referring to simply affected ignorance; or they may have reference to a species of the sin of ingratitude, the highest degree of which is that man even ignores the benefits he has received; or again, they may be an allusion to the ignorance of unbelief, which undermines the foundation of the spiritual edifice.

REPLY OBJ. 4: The drunken man deserves a *double punishment* for the two sins which he commits, viz., drunkenness, and the sin which results from his drunkenness: and yet drunkenness, on account of the ignorance connected therewith, diminishes the resulting sin, and more, perhaps, than the gravity of the drunkenness implies, as stated above (ad 2). It might also be said that the words quoted refer to an ordinance of the legislator named Pittacus, who ordered *drunkards to be more severely punished*

respiciens, quam ebrii debent magis habere; sed ad utili-tatem, quia plures iniuriantur ebrii quam sobrii; ut patet per philosophum, in II politicorum.

if they assaulted anyone; having an eye, not to the indulgence which the drunkard might claim, but to expediency, since more harm is done by the drunk than by the sober, as the Philosopher observes (*Polit.* ii).

QUESTION 77

OF THE CAUSE OF SIN, ON THE PART OF THE SENSITIVE APPETITE

Deinde considerandum est de causa peccati ex parte appetitus sensitivi, utrum passio animae sit causa peccati. Et circa hoc quaeruntur octo.

Primo, utrum passio appetitus sensitivi possit movere vel inclinare voluntatem.

Secundo, utrum possit superare rationem contra eius scientiam.

Tertio, utrum peccatum quod ex passione provenit, sit peccatum ex infirmitate.

Quarto, utrum haec passio quae est amor sui, sit causa omnis peccati.

Quinto, de illis tribus causis quae ponuntur I Ioan. II, *concupiscentia oculorum, concupiscentia carnis, et superbia vitae.*

Sexto, utrum passio quae est causa peccati, diminuat ipsum.

Septimo, utrum totaliter excuset.

Octavo, utrum peccatum quod ex passione est, possit esse mortale.

We must now consider the cause of sin, on the part of the sensitive appetite, as to whether a passion of the soul may be a cause of sin: and under this head there are eight points of inquiry:

(1) Whether a passion of the sensitive appetite can move or incline the will?

(2) Whether it can overcome the reason against the latter's knowledge?

(3) Whether a sin resulting from a passion is a sin of weakness?

(4) Whether the passion of self-love is the cause of every sin?

(5) Of three causes mentioned in 1 Jn. 2:16: *Concupiscence of the eyes, Concupiscence of the flesh,* and *Pride of life.*

(6) Whether the passion which causes a sin diminishes it?

(7) Whether passion excuses from sin altogether?

(8) Whether a sin committed through passion can be mortal?

Article 1

Whether the Will Is Moved by a Passion of the Senstive Appetite?

AD PRIMUM SIC PROCEDITUR. Videtur quod voluntas non moveatur a passione appetitus sensitivi. Nulla enim potentia passiva movetur nisi a suo obiecto. Voluntas autem est potentia passiva et activa simul, inquantum est movens et mota, sicut in III de anima philosophus dicit universaliter de vi appetitiva. Cum ergo obiectum voluntatis non sit passio appetitus sensitivi, sed magis bonum rationis; videtur quod passio appetitus sensitivi non moveat voluntatem.

PRAETEREA, superior motor non movetur ab inferiori, sicut anima non movetur a corpore. Sed voluntas, quae est appetitus rationis, comparatur ad appetitum sensitivum sicut motor superior ad inferiorem, dicit enim philosophus, in III de anima, quod *appetitus rationis movet appetitum sensitivum, sicut in corporibus caelestibus sphaera movet sphaeram.* Ergo voluntas non potest moveri a passione appetitus sensitivi.

PRAETEREA, nullum immateriale potest moveri ab aliquo materiali. Sed voluntas est quaedam potentia immaterialis, non enim utitur organo corporali, cum sit in ratione, ut dicitur in III de anima. Appetitus autem

OBJECTION 1: It would seem that the will is not moved by a passion of the sensitive appetite. For no passive power is moved except by its object. Now the will is a power both passive and active, inasmuch as it is mover and moved, as the Philosopher says of the appetitive power in general (*De Anima* iii, text. 54). Since therefore the object of the will is not a passion of the sensitive appetite, but good defined by the reason, it seems that a passion of the sensitive appetite does not move the will.

OBJ. 2: Further, the higher mover is not moved by the lower; thus the soul is not moved by the body. Now the will, which is the rational appetite, is compared to the sensitive appetite, as a higher mover to a lower: for the Philosopher says (*De Anima* iii, text. 57) that *the rational appetite moves the sensitive appetite, even as, in the heavenly bodies, one sphere moves another.* Therefore the will cannot be moved by a passion of the sensitive appetite.

OBJ. 3: Further, nothing immaterial can be moved by that which is material. Now the will is an immaterial power, because it does not use a corporeal organ, since it is in the reason, as stated in *De Anima* iii, text. 42: whereas the

sensitivus est vis materialis, utpote fundata in organo corporali. Ergo passio appetitus sensitivi non potest movere appetitum intellectivum.

SED CONTRA est quod dicitur Dan. XIII, *concupiscentia subvertit cor tuum.*

RESPONDEO dicendum quod passio appetitus sensitivi non potest directe trahere aut movere voluntatem, sed indirecte potest. Et hoc dupliciter. Uno quidem modo, secundum quandam abstractionem. Cum enim omnes potentiae animae in una essentia animae radicentur, necesse est quod quando una potentia intenditur in suo actu, altera in suo actu remittatur, vel etiam totaliter impediatur. Tum quia omnis virtus ad plura dispersa fit minor, unde e contrario, quando intenditur circa unum, minus potest ad alia dispergi. Tum quia in operibus animae requiritur quaedam intentio, quae dum vehementer applicatur ad unum, non potest alteri vehementer attendere. Et secundum hunc modum, per quandam distractionem, quando motus appetitus sensitivi fortificatur secundum quamcumque passionem, necesse est quod remittatur, vel totaliter impediatur motus proprius appetitus rationalis, qui est voluntas.

Alio modo, ex parte obiecti voluntatis, quod est bonum ratione apprehensum. Impeditur enim iudicium et apprehensio rationis propter vehementem et inordinatam apprehensionem imaginationis, et iudicium virtutis aestimativae, ut patet in amentibus. Manifestum est autem quod passionem appetitus sensitivi sequitur imaginationis apprehensio, et iudicium aestimativae, sicut etiam dispositionem linguae sequitur iudicium gustus. Unde videmus quod homines in aliqua passione existentes, non facile imaginationem avertunt ab his circa quae afficiuntur. Unde per consequens iudicium rationis plerumque sequitur passionem appetitus sensitivi; et per consequens motus voluntatis, qui natus est sequi iudicium rationis.

AD PRIMUM ergo dicendum quod per passionem appetitus sensitivi fit aliqua immutatio circa iudicium de obiecto voluntatis, sicut dictum est; quamvis ipsa passio appetitus sensitivi non sit directe voluntatis obiectum.

AD SECUNDUM dicendum quod superius non movetur ab inferiori directe, sed indirecte quodammodo moveri potest, sicut dictum est.

ET SIMILITER dicendum est ad tertium.

sensitive appetite is a material force, since it is seated in an organ of the body. Therefore a passion of the sensitive appetite cannot move the intellective appetite.

ON THE CONTRARY, It is written (Dan 13:56): *Lust hath perverted thy heart.*

I ANSWER THAT, A passion of the sensitive appetite cannot draw or move the will directly; but it can do so indirectly, and this in two ways. First, by a kind of distraction: because, since all the soul's powers are rooted in the one essence of the soul, it follows of necessity that, when one power is intent in its act, another power becomes remiss, or is even altogether impeded, in its act, both because all energy is weakened through being divided, so that, on the contrary, through being centered on one thing, it is less able to be directed to several; and because, in the operations of the soul, a certain attention is requisite, and if this be closely fixed on one thing, less attention is given to another. In this way, by a kind of distraction, when the movement of the sensitive appetite is enforced in respect of any passion whatever, the proper movement of the rational appetite or will must, of necessity, become remiss or altogether impeded.

Second, this may happen on the part of the will's object, which is good apprehended by reason. Because the judgment and apprehension of reason is impeded on account of a vehement and inordinate apprehension of the imagination and judgment of the estimative power, as appears in those who are out of their mind. Now it is evident that the apprehension of the imagination and the judgment of the estimative power follow the passion of the sensitive appetite, even as the verdict of the taste follows the disposition of the tongue: for which reason we observe that those who are in some kind of passion, do not easily turn their imagination away from the object of their emotion, the result being that the judgment of the reason often follows the passion of the sensitive appetite, and consequently the will's movement follows it also, since it has a natural inclination always to follow the judgment of the reason.

REPLY OBJ. 1: Although the passion of the sensitive appetite is not the direct object of the will, yet it occasions a certain change in the judgment about the object of the will, as stated.

REPLY OBJ. 2: The higher mover is not directly moved by the lower; but, in a manner, it can be moved by it indirectly, as stated.

THE THIRD OBJECTION is solved in like manner.

Article 2

Whether the Reason Can Be Overcome by a Passion, Against Its Knowledge?

AD SECUNDUM SIC PROCEDITUR. Videtur quod ratio non possit superari a passione contra suam scientiam. Fortius enim non vincitur a debiliori. Sed scientia, propter suam certitudinem, est fortissimum eorum quae in nobis sunt. Ergo non potest superari a passione, quae est debilis et cito transiens.

PRAETEREA, voluntas non est nisi boni vel apparentis boni. Sed cum passio trahit voluntatem in id quod est vere bonum, non inclinat rationem contra scientiam. Cum autem trahit eam in id quod est apparens bonum et non existens, trahit eam in id quod rationi videtur, hoc autem est in scientia rationis, quod ei videtur. Ergo passio nunquam inclinat rationem contra suam scientiam.

SI DICATUR quod trahit rationem scientem aliquid in universali, ut contrarium iudicet in particulari, contra, universalis et particularis propositio, si opponantur, opponuntur secundum contradictionem, sicut omnis homo et non omnis homo. Sed duae opiniones quae sunt contradictoriarum, sunt contrariae, ut dicitur in II peri Herm. Si igitur aliquis sciens aliquid in universali, iudicaret oppositum in singulari, sequeretur quod haberet simul contrarias opiniones, quod est impossibile.

PRAETEREA, quicumque scit universale, scit etiam particulare quod novit sub universali contineri; sicut quicumque scit omnem mulam esse sterilem, scit hoc animal esse sterile, dummodo sciat quod sit mula; ut patet per id quod dicitur in I Poster. Sed ille qui scit aliquid in universali, puta nullam fornicationem esse faciendam, scit hoc particulare sub universali contineri, puta hunc actum esse fornicarium. Ergo videtur quod etiam in particulari sciat.

PRAETEREA, ea quae sunt in voce, sunt signa intellectus animae, secundum philosophum. Sed homo in passione existens frequenter confitetur id quod eligit esse malum etiam in particulari. Ergo etiam in particulari habet scientiam.

Sic igitur videtur quod passiones non possint trahere rationem contra scientiam universalem, quia non potest esse quod habeat scientiam universalem, et existimet oppositum in particulari.

SED CONTRA est quod dicit apostolus, Rom. VII, *video aliam legem in membris meis repugnantem legi mentis meae, et captivantem me in lege peccati.* Lex autem quae est in membris, est concupiscentia, de qua supra locutus fuerat. Cum igitur concupiscentia sit passio quaedam,

OBJECTION 1: It would seem that the reason cannot be overcome by a passion, against its knowledge. For the stronger is not overcome by the weaker. Now knowledge, on account of its certitude, is the strongest thing in us. Therefore it cannot be overcome by a passion, which is weak and soon passes away.

OBJ. 2: Further, the will is not directed save to the good or the apparent good. Now when a passion draws the will to that which is really good, it does not influence the reason against its knowledge; and when it draws it to that which is good apparently, but not really, it draws it to that which appears good to the reason. But what appears to the reason is in the knowledge of the reason. Therefore a passion never influences the reason against its knowledge.

OBJ. 3: Further, if it be said that it draws the reason from its knowledge of something in general, to form a contrary judgment about a particular matter—on the contrary, if a universal and a particular proposition be opposed, they are opposed by contradiction, e.g., *Every man*, and *Not every man*. Now if two opinions contradict one another, they are contrary to one another, as stated in Peri Herm. ii. If therefore anyone, while knowing something in general, were to pronounce an opposite judgment in a particular case, he would have two contrary opinions at the same time, which is impossible.

OBJ. 4: Further, whoever knows the universal, knows also the particular which he knows to be contained in the universal: thus who knows that every mule is sterile, knows that this particular animal is sterile, provided he knows it to be a mule, as is clear from *Poster.* i, text. 2. Now he who knows something in general, e.g., that *no fornication is lawful*, knows this general proposition to contain, for example, the particular proposition, *This is an act of fornication*. Therefore it seems that his knowledge extends to the particular.

OBJ. 5: Further, according to the Philosopher (*Peri Herm.* i), *words express the thoughts of the mind.* Now it often happens that man, while in a state of passion, confesses that what he has chosen is an evil, even in that particular case. Therefore he has knowledge, even in particular.

Therefore it seems that the passions cannot draw the reason against its universal knowledge; because it is impossible for it to have universal knowledge together with an opposite particular judgment.

ON THE CONTRARY, The Apostle says (Rom 7:23): *I see another law in my members, fighting against the law of my mind, and captivating me in the law of sin.* Now the law that is in the members is concupiscence, of which he had been speaking previously. Since then concupiscence is a

videtur quod passio trahat rationem etiam contra hoc quod scit.

RESPONDEO dicendum quod opinio Socratis fuit, ut philosophus dicit in VII Ethic., quod scientia nunquam posset superari a passione. Unde ponebat omnes virtutes esse scientias, et omnia peccata esse ignorantias. In quo quidem aliqualiter recte sapiebat. Quia cum voluntas sit boni vel apparentis boni, nunquam voluntas in malum moveretur, nisi id quod non est bonum, aliqualiter rationi bonum appareret, et propter hoc voluntas nunquam in malum tenderet, nisi cum aliqua ignorantia vel errore rationis. Unde dicitur Prov. XIV, *errant qui operantur malum.*

Sed quia experimento patet quod multi agunt contra ea quorum scientiam habent; et hoc etiam auctoritate divina confirmatur, secundum illud Luc. XII, *servus qui cognovit voluntatem domini sui et non fecit, plagis vapulabit multis*; et Iac. IV dicitur, *scienti bonum facere et non facienti, peccatum est illi*, non simpliciter verum dixit, sed oportet distinguere, ut philosophus tradit in VII Ethic. Cum enim ad recte agendum homo dirigatur duplici scientia, scilicet universali et particulari; utriusque defectus sufficit ad hoc quod impediatur rectitudo operis et voluntatis, ut supra dictum est. Contingit igitur quod aliquis habeat scientiam in universali, puta nullam fornicationem esse faciendam; sed tamen non cognoscat in particulari hunc actum qui est fornicatio, non esse faciendum. Et hoc sufficit ad hoc quod voluntas non sequatur universalem scientiam rationis. Iterum considerandum est quod nihil prohibet aliquid sciri in habitu, quod tamen actu non consideratur. Potest igitur contingere quod aliquis etiam rectam scientiam habeat in singulari, et non solum in universali, sed tamen in actu non consideret. Et tunc non videtur difficile quod praeter id quod actu non considerat, homo agat. Quod autem homo non consideret in particulari id quod habitualiter scit, quandoque quidem contingit ex solo defectu intentionis, puta cum homo sciens geometriam, non intendit ad considerandum geometriae conclusiones, quas statim in promptu habet considerare. Quandoque autem homo non considerat id quod habet in habitu propter aliquod impedimentum superveniens, puta propter aliquam occupationem exteriorem, vel propter aliquam infirmitatem corporalem. Et hoc modo ille qui est in passione constitutus, non considerat in particulari id quod scit in universali, inquantum passio impedit talem considerationem. Impedit autem tripliciter. Primo, per quandam distractionem, sicut supra expositum est. Secundo, per contrarietatem, quia plerumque passio inclinat ad contrarium huius quod scientia universalis habet. Tertio, per quandam immutationem corporalem, ex qua ratio quodammodo ligatur, ne libere in actum exeat, sicut etiam somnus vel ebrietas, quadam corporali transmutatione facta, ligant usum rationis. Et quod hoc

passion, it seems that a passion draws the reason counter to its knowledge.

I ANSWER THAT, As the Philosopher states (*Ethic.* vii, 2), the opinion of Socrates was that knowledge can never be overcome by passion; wherefore he held every virtue to be a kind of knowledge, and every sin a kind of ignorance. In this he was somewhat right, because, since the object of the will is a good or an apparent good, it is never moved to an evil, unless that which is not good appear good in some respect to the reason; so that the will would never tend to evil, unless there were ignorance or error in the reason. Hence it is written (Prov 14:22): *They err that work evil.*

Experience, however, shows that many act contrary to the knowledge that they have, and this is confirmed by Divine authority, according to the words of Lk. 12:47: *The servant who knew that the will of his lord . . . and did not . . . shall be beaten with many stripes*, and of James 4:17: *To him . . . who knoweth to do good, and doth it not, to him it is a sin.* Consequently he was not altogether right, and it is necessary, with the Philosopher (*Ethic.* vii, 3) to make a distinction. Because, since man is directed to right action by a twofold knowledge, viz., universal and particular, a defect in either of them suffices to hinder the rectitude of the will and of the deed, as stated above (Q76, A1). It may happen, then, that a man has some knowledge in general, e.g., that no fornication is lawful, and yet he does not know in particular that this act, which is fornication, must not be done; and this suffices for the will not to follow the universal knowledge of the reason. Again, it must be observed that nothing prevents a thing which is known habitually from not being considered actually: so that it is possible for a man to have correct knowledge not only in general but also in particular, and yet not to consider his knowledge actually: and in such a case it does not seem difficult for a man to act counter to what he does not actually consider. Now, that a man sometimes fails to consider in particular what he knows habitually, may happen through mere lack of attention: for instance, a man who knows geometry, may not attend to the consideration of geometrical conclusions, which he is ready to consider at any moment. Sometimes man fails to consider actually what he knows habitually, on account of some hindrance supervening, e.g., some external occupation, or some bodily infirmity; and, in this way, a man who is in a state of passion, fails to consider in particular what he knows in general, insofar as the passions hinder him from considering it. Now it hinders him in three ways. First, by way of distraction, as explained above (A1). Second, by way of opposition, because a passion often inclines to something contrary to what man knows in general. Third, by way of bodily transmutation, the result of which is that the reason is somehow fettered so as not to exercise its act freely; even as sleep or drunkenness, on account of some change wrought on the body, fetters the use of reason.

contingat in passionibus, patet ex hoc quod aliquando, cum passiones multum intenduntur, homo amittit totaliter usum rationis, multi enim propter abundantiam amoris et irae, sunt in insaniam conversi. Et per hunc modum passio trahit rationem ad iudicandum in particulari contra scientiam quam habet in universali.

AD PRIMUM ergo dicendum quod scientia universalis, quae est certissima, non habet principalitatem in operatione, sed magis scientia particularis, eo quod operationes sunt circa singularia. Unde non est mirum si in operabilibus passio agit contra scientiam universalem, absente consideratione in particulari.

AD SECUNDUM dicendum quod hoc ipsum quod rationi videatur in particulari aliquid bonum quod non est bonum, contingit ex aliqua passione. Et tamen hoc particulare iudicium est contra universalem scientiam rationis.

AD TERTIUM dicendum quod non posset contingere quod aliquis haberet simul in actu scientiam aut opinionem veram de universali affirmativo, et opinionem falsam de particulari negativo, aut e converso. Sed bene potest contingere quod aliquis habeat veram scientiam habitualiter de universali affirmativo, et falsam opinionem in actu de particulari negativo, actus enim directe non contrariatur habitui, sed actui.

AD QUARTUM dicendum quod ille qui habet scientiam in universali, propter passionem impeditur ne possit sub illa universali sumere, et ad conclusionem pervenire, sed assumit sub alia universali, quam suggerit inclinatio passionis, et sub ea concludit. Unde philosophus dicit, in VII Ethic., quod syllogismus incontinentis habet quatuor propositiones, duas universales, quarum una est rationis, puta nullam fornicationem esse committendam; alia est passionis, puta delectationem esse sectandam. Passio igitur ligat rationem ne assumat et concludat sub prima, unde, ea durante, assumit et concludit sub secunda.

AD QUINTUM dicendum quod, sicut ebrius quandoque proferre potest verba significantia profundas sententias, quas tamen mente diiudicare non potest, ebrietate prohibente; ita in passione existens, etsi ore proferat hoc non esse faciendum, tamen interius hoc animo sentit quod sit faciendum, ut dicitur in VII Ethic.

That this takes place in the passions is evident from the fact that sometimes, when the passions are very intense, man loses the use of reason altogether: for many have gone out of their minds through excess of love or anger. It is in this way that passion draws the reason to judge in particular, against the knowledge which it has in general.

REPLY OBJ. 1: Universal knowledge, which is most certain, does not hold the foremost place in action, but rather particular knowledge, since actions are about singulars: wherefore it is not astonishing that, in matters of action, passion acts counter to universal knowledge, if the consideration of particular knowledge be lacking.

REPLY OBJ. 2: The fact that something appears good in particular to the reason, whereas it is not good, is due to a passion: and yet this particular judgment is contrary to the universal knowledge of the reason.

REPLY OBJ. 3: It is impossible for anyone to have an actual knowledge or true opinion about a universal affirmative proposition, and at the same time a false opinion about a particular negative proposition, or vice versa: but it may well happen that a man has true habitual knowledge about a universal affirmative proposition, and actually a false opinion about a particular negative: because an act is directly opposed, not to a habit, but to an act.

REPLY OBJ. 4: He that has knowledge in a universal, is hindered, on account of a passion, from reasoning about that universal, so as to draw the conclusion: but he reasons about another universal proposition suggested by the inclination of the passion, and draws his conclusion accordingly. Hence the Philosopher says (*Ethic.* vii, 3) that the syllogism of an incontinent man has four propositions, two particular and two universal, of which one is of the reason, e.g., No fornication is lawful, and the other, of passion, e.g., Pleasure is to be pursued. Hence passion fetters the reason, and hinders it from arguing and concluding under the first proposition; so that while the passions lasts, the reason argues and concludes under the second.

REPLY OBJ. 5: Even as a drunken man sometimes gives utterance to words of deep signification, of which, however, he is incompetent to judge, his drunkenness hindering him; so that a man who is in a state of passion, may indeed say in words that he ought not to do so and so, yet his inner thought is that he must do it, as stated in *Ethic.* vii, 3.

Article 3

Whether a Sin Committed Through Passion, Should Be Called a Sin of Weakness?

AD TERTIUM SIC PROCEDITUR. Videtur quod peccatum quod est ex passione, non debeat dici ex infirmitate. Passio enim est quidam vehemens motus appetitus

OBJECTION 1: It would seem that a sin committed through passion should not be called a sin of weakness. For a passion is a vehement movement of the sensitive appetite,

sensitivi, ut dictum est. Vehementia autem motus magis attestatur fortitudini quam infirmitati. Ergo peccatum quod est ex passione, non debet dici ex infirmitate.

PRAETEREA, infirmitas hominis maxime attenditur secundum illud quod est in eo fragilius. Hoc autem est caro, unde dicitur in Psalmo LXXVII, *recordatus est quia caro sunt*. Ergo magis debet dici peccatum ex infirmitate quod est ex aliquo corporis defectu, quam quod est ex animae passione.

PRAETEREA, ad ea non videtur homo esse infirmus, quae eius voluntati subduntur. Sed facere vel non facere ea ad quae passio inclinat, hominis voluntati subditur, secundum illud Gen. IV, *sub te erit appetitus tuus, et tu dominaberis illius*. Ergo peccatum quod est ex passione, non est ex infirmitate.

SED CONTRA est quod Tullius, in IV libro de Tuscul. quaest., passiones animae aegritudines vocat. Aegritudines autem alio nomine infirmitates dicuntur. Ergo peccatum quod est ex passione, debet dici ex infirmitate.

RESPONDEO dicendum quod causa peccati propria est ex parte animae in qua principaliter est peccatum. Potest autem dici infirmitas in anima ad similitudinem infirmitatis corporis. Dicitur autem corpus hominis esse infirmum, quando debilitatur vel impeditur in executione propriae operationis, propter aliquam inordinationem partium corporis, ita scilicet quod humores et membra hominis non subduntur virtuti regitivae et motivae corporis. Unde et membrum dicitur esse infirmum, quando non potest perficere operationem membri sani, sicut oculus quando non potest clare videre, ut dicit philosophus, in X de historiis animalium. Unde et infirmitas animae dicitur quando impeditur anima in propria operatione, propter inordinationem partium ipsius. Sicut autem partes corporis dicuntur esse inordinatae, quando non sequuntur ordinem naturae; ita et partes animae dicuntur inordinatae, quando non subduntur ordini rationis, ratio enim est vis regitiva partium animae. Sic ergo quando extra ordinem rationis vis concupiscibilis aut irascibilis aliqua passione afficitur, et per hoc impedimentum praestatur modo praedicto debitae actioni hominis, dicitur peccatum esse ex infirmitate. Unde et philosophus, in I Ethic., comparat incontinentem paralytico, cuius partes moventur in contrarium eius quod ipse disponit.

AD PRIMUM ergo dicendum quod, sicut quanto fuerit motus fortior in corpore praeter ordinem naturae, tanto est maior infirmitas; ita quanto fuerit motus fortior passionis praeter ordinem rationis, tanto est maior infirmitas animae.

AD SECUNDUM dicendum quod peccatum principaliter consistit in actu voluntatis, qui non impeditur per corporis infirmitatem, potest enim qui est corpore

as stated above (A1). Now vehemence of movements is evidence of strength rather than of weakness. Therefore a sin committed through passion, should not be called a sin of weakness.

OBJ. 2: Further, weakness in man regards that which is most fragile in him. Now this is the flesh; whence it is written (Ps 77:39): *He remembered that they are flesh*. Therefore sins of weakness should be those which result from bodily defects, rather than those which are due to a passion.

OBJ. 3: Further, man does not seem to be weak in respect of things which are subject to his will. Now it is subject to man's will, whether he do or do not the things to which his passions incline him, according to Gn. 4:7: *Thy appetite shall be under thee, and thou shalt have dominion over it*. Therefore sin committed through passion is not a sin of weakness.

ON THE CONTRARY, Cicero (*De Quaest. Tusc.* iv) calls the passions diseases of the soul. Now weakness is another name for disease. Therefore a sin that arises from passion should be called a sin of weakness.

I ANSWER THAT, The cause of sin is on the part of the soul, in which, chiefly, sin resides. Now weakness may be applied to the soul by way of likeness to weakness of the body. Accordingly, man's body is said to be weak, when it is disabled or hindered in the execution of its proper action, through some disorder of the body's parts, so that the humors and members of the human body cease to be subject to its governing and motive power. Hence a member is said to be weak, when it cannot do the work of a healthy member, the eye, for instance, when it cannot see clearly, as the Philosopher states (*De Hist. Animal.* x, 1). Therefore weakness of the soul is when the soul is hindered from fulfilling its proper action on account of a disorder in its parts. Now as the parts of the body are said to be out of order, when they fail to comply with the order of nature, so too the parts of the soul are said to be inordinate, when they are not subject to the order of reason, for the reason is the ruling power of the soul's parts. Accordingly, when the concupiscible or irascible power is affected by any passion contrary to the order of reason, the result being that an impediment arises in the aforesaid manner to the due action of man, it is said to be a sin of weakness. Hence the Philosopher (*Ethic.* vii, 8) compares the incontinent man to an epileptic, whose limbs move in a manner contrary to his intention.

REPLY OBJ. 1: Just as in the body the stronger the movement against the order of nature, the greater the weakness, so likewise, the stronger the movement of passion against the order of reason, the greater the weakness of the soul.

REPLY OBJ. 2: Sin consists chiefly in an act of the will, which is not hindered by weakness of the body: for he that is weak in body may have a will ready for action, and yet be

infirmus, promptam habere voluntatem ad aliquid faciendum. Impeditur autem per passionem, ut supra dictum est. Unde cum dicitur peccatum esse ex infirmitate, magis est referendum ad infirmitatem animae quam ad infirmitatem corporis. Dicitur tamen etiam ipsa infirmitas animae infirmitas carnis, inquantum ex conditione carnis passiones animae insurgunt in nobis, eo quod appetitus sensitivus est virtus utens organo corporali.

AD TERTIUM dicendum quod in potestate quidem voluntatis est assentire vel non assentire his in quae passio inclinat, et pro tanto dicitur noster appetitus sub nobis esse. Sed tamen ipse assensus vel dissensus voluntatis impeditur per passionem, modo praedicto.

hindered by a passion, as stated above (A1). Hence when we speak of sins of weakness, we refer to weakness of soul rather than of body. And yet even weakness of soul is called weakness of the flesh, insofar as it is owing to a condition of the flesh that the passions of the soul arise in us through the sensitive appetite being a power using a corporeal organ.

REPLY OBJ. 3: It is in the will's power to give or refuse its consent to what passion inclines us to do, and it is in this sense that our appetite is said to be under us; and yet this consent or dissent of the will is hindered in the way already explained (A1).

Article 4

Whether Self-Love Is the Source of Every Sin?

AD QUARTUM SIC PROCEDITUR. Videtur quod amor sui non sit principium omnis peccati. Id enim quod est secundum se bonum et debitum, non est propria causa peccati. Sed amor sui est secundum se bonum et debitum, unde et praecipitur homini ut diligat proximum sicut seipsum, Levit. XIX. Ergo amor sui non potest esse propria causa peccati.

PRAETEREA, apostolus dicit, Rom. VII, *occasione accepta, peccatum per mandatum operatum est in me omnem concupiscentiam,* ubi Glossa dicit quod *bona est lex, quae, dum concupiscentiam prohibet, omne malum prohibet,* quod dicitur propter hoc, quia concupiscentia est causa omnis peccati. Sed concupiscentia est alia passio ab amore, ut supra habitum est. Ergo amor sui non est causa omnis peccati.

PRAETEREA, Augustinus, super illud Psalmi, incensa igni et suffossa, dicit quod omne peccatum est *ex amore male inflammante, vel ex timore male humiliante.* Non ergo solus amor sui est causa peccati.

PRAETEREA, sicut homo quandoque peccat propter inordinatum sui amorem, ita etiam interdum peccat propter inordinatum amorem proximi. Ergo amor sui non est causa omnis peccati.

SED CONTRA est quod Augustinus dicit, XIV de Civ. Dei, quod *amor sui usque ad contemptum Dei, facit civitatem Babylonis.* Sed per quodlibet peccatum pertinet homo ad civitatem Babylonis. Ergo amor sui est causa omnis peccati.

RESPONDEO dicendum quod, sicut supra dictum est, propria et per se causa peccati accipienda est ex parte conversionis ad commutabile bonum; ex qua quidem parte omnis actus peccati procedit ex aliquo inordinato appetitu alicuius temporalis boni. Quod autem aliquis

OBJECTION 1: It would seem that self-love is not the source of every sin. For that which is good and right in itself is not the proper cause of sin. Now love of self is a good and right thing in itself: wherefore man is commanded to love his neighbor as himself (Lev 19:18). Therefore self-love cannot be the proper cause of sin.

OBJ. 2: Further, the Apostle says (Rom 7:8): *Sin taking occasion by the commandment wrought in me all manner of concupiscence*; on which words a gloss says that *the law is good, since by forbidding concupiscence, it forbids all evils,* the reason for which is that concupiscence is the cause of every sin. Now concupiscence is a distinct passion from love, as stated above (Q3, A2; Q23, A4). Therefore self-love is not the cause of every sin.

OBJ. 3: Further, Augustine in commenting on Ps. 79:17, *Things set on fire and dug down,* says that *every sin is due either to love arousing us to undue ardor or to fear inducing false humility.* Therefore self-love is not the only cause of sin.

OBJ. 4: Further, as man sins at times through inordinate love of self, so does he sometimes through inordinate love of his neighbor. Therefore self-love is not the cause of every sin.

ON THE CONTRARY, Augustine says (*De Civ. Dei* xiv, 28) that *self-love, amounting to contempt of God, builds up the city of Babylon.* Now every sin makes man a citizen of Babylon. Therefore self-love is the cause of every sin.

I ANSWER THAT, As stated above (Q75, A1), the proper and direct cause of sin is to be considered on the part of the adherence to a mutable good; in which respect every sinful act proceeds from inordinate desire for some temporal good. Now the fact that anyone desires a temporal good

appetat inordinate aliquod temporale bonum, procedit ex hoc quod inordinate amat seipsum, hoc enim est amare aliquem, velle ei bonum. Unde manifestum est quod inordinatus amor sui est causa omnis peccati.

AD PRIMUM ergo dicendum quod amor sui ordinatus est debitus et naturalis, ita scilicet quod velit sibi bonum quod congruit. Sed amor sui inordinatus, qui perducit ad contemptum Dei, ponitur esse causa peccati secundum Augustinum.

AD SECUNDUM dicendum quod concupiscentia, qua aliquis appetit sibi bonum, reducitur ad amorem sui sicut ad causam, ut iam dictum est.

AD TERTIUM dicendum quod aliquis dicitur amare et illud bonum quod optat sibi, et se, cui bonum optat. Amor igitur secundum quod dicitur eius esse quod optatur, puta quod aliquis dicitur amare vinum vel pecuniam, recipit pro causa timorem, qui pertinet ad fugam mali. Omne enim peccatum provenit vel ex inordinato appetitu alicuius boni, vel ex inordinata fuga alicuius mali. Sed utrumque horum reducitur ad amorem sui. Propter hoc enim homo vel appetit bona vel fugit mala, quia amat seipsum.

AD QUARTUM dicendum quod amicus est quasi alter ipse. Et ideo quod peccatur propter amorem amici, videtur propter amorem sui peccari.

inordinately, is due to the fact that he loves himself inordinately; for to wish anyone some good is to love him. Therefore it is evident that inordinate love of self is the cause of every sin.

REPLY OBJ. 1: Well ordered self-love, whereby man desires a fitting good for himself, is right and natural; but it is inordinate self-love, leading to contempt of God, that Augustine (*De Civ. Dei* xiv, 28) reckons to be the cause of sin.

REPLY OBJ. 2: Concupiscence, whereby a man desires good for himself, is reduced to self-love as to its cause, as stated.

REPLY OBJ. 3: Man is said to love both the good he desires for himself, and himself to whom he desires it. Love, insofar as it is directed to the object of desire (e.g., a man is said to love wine or money) admits, as its cause, fear which pertains to avoidance of evil: for every sin arises either from inordinate desire for some good, or from inordinate avoidance of some evil. But each of these is reduced to self-love, since it is through loving himself that man either desires good things, or avoids evil things.

REPLY OBJ. 4: A friend is like another self (*Ethic.* ix): wherefore the sin which is committed through love for a friend, seems to be committed through self-love.

Article 5

*Whether Concupiscence of the Flesh, Concupiscence of the Eyes, and
Pride of Life Are Fittingly Described As Causes of Sin?*

AD QUINTUM SIC PROCEDITUR. Videtur quod inconvenienter ponantur causae peccatorum esse concupiscentia carnis, concupiscentia oculorum, et superbia vitae. Quia secundum apostolum, I ad Tim. ult., *radix omnium malorum est cupiditas*. Sed superbia vitae sub cupiditate non continetur. Ergo non oportet poni inter causas peccatorum.

PRAETEREA, concupiscentia carnis maxime ex visione oculorum excitatur, secundum illud Dan. XIII, *species decepit te*. Ergo non debet dividi concupiscentia oculorum contra concupiscentiam carnis.

PRAETEREA, concupiscentia est delectabilis appetitus, ut supra habitum est. Delectationes autem contingunt non solum secundum visum, sed etiam secundum alios sensus. Ergo deberet etiam poni concupiscentia auditus, et aliorum sensuum.

PRAETEREA, sicut homo inducitur ad peccandum ex inordinata concupiscentia boni, ita etiam ex inordinata fuga mali, ut dictum est. Sed nihil hic enumeratur

OBJECTION 1: It would seem that *concupiscence of the flesh, concupiscence of the eyes, and pride of life* are unfittingly described as causes of sin. Because, according to the Apostle (1 Tim 6:10), *covetousness is the root of all evils*. Now pride of life is not included in covetousness. Therefore it should not be reckoned among the causes of sin.

OBJ. 2: Further, concupiscence of the flesh is aroused chiefly by what is seen by the eyes, according to Dan. 13:56: *Beauty hath deceived thee*. Therefore concupiscence of the eyes should not be condivided with concupiscence of the flesh.

OBJ. 3: Further, concupiscence is desire for pleasure, as stated above (Q30, A2). Now objects of pleasure are perceived not only by the sight, but also by the other senses. Therefore *concupiscence of the hearing* and of the other senses should also have been mentioned.

OBJ. 4: Further, just as man is induced to sin, through inordinate desire of good things, so is he also, through inordinate avoidance of evil things, as stated above (A4, ad 3).

pertinens ad fugam mali. Ergo insufficienter causae peccatorum tanguntur.

SED CONTRA est quod dicitur I Ioan. II, *omne quod est in mundo, aut est concupiscentia carnis, aut concupiscentia oculorum, aut superbia vitae.* In mundo autem dicitur aliquid esse propter peccatum, unde et ibidem, dicit quod *totus mundus in maligno positus est.* Ergo praedicta tria sunt causae peccatorum.

RESPONDEO dicendum quod, sicut iam dictum est, inordinatus amor sui est causa omnis peccati. In amore autem sui includitur inordinatus appetitus boni, unusquisque enim appetit bonum ei quem amat. Unde manifestum est quod inordinatus appetitus boni est causa omnis peccati. Bonum autem dupliciter est obiectum sensibilis appetitus, in quo sunt animae passiones, quae sunt causa peccati, uno modo, absolute, secundum quod est obiectum concupiscibilis; alio modo, sub ratione ardui, prout est obiectum irascibilis, ut supra dictum est. Est autem duplex concupiscentia, sicut supra habitum est. Una quidem naturalis, quae est eorum quibus natura corporis sustentatur; sive quantum ad conservationem individui, sicut cibus et potus et alia huiusmodi; sive quantum ad conservationem speciei, sicut in venereis. Et horum inordinatus appetitus dicitur concupiscentia carnis. Alia est concupiscentia animalis, eorum scilicet quae per sensum carnis sustentationem aut delectationem non afferunt, sed sunt delectabilia secundum apprehensionem imaginationis, aut alicuius huiusmodi acceptionis, sicut sunt pecunia, ornatus vestium, et alia huiusmodi. Et haec quidem animalis concupiscentia vocatur concupiscentia oculorum, sive intelligatur concupiscentia oculorum, idest ipsius visionis, quae fit per oculos, ut referatur ad curiositatem, secundum quod Augustinus exponit, X Confess.; sive referatur ad concupiscentiam rerum quae exterius oculis proponuntur, ut referatur ad cupiditatem, secundum quod ab aliis exponitur.

Appetitus autem inordinatus boni ardui pertinet ad superbiam vitae, nam superbia est appetitus inordinatus excellentiae, ut inferius dicetur.

Et sic patet quod ad ista tria reduci possunt omnes passiones, quae sunt causa peccati. Nam ad duo prima reducuntur omnes passiones concupiscibilis, ad tertium autem omnes passiones irascibilis; quod ideo non dividitur in duo, quia omnes passiones irascibilis conformantur concupiscentiae animali.

AD PRIMUM ergo dicendum quod secundum quod cupiditas importat universaliter appetitum cuiuscumque boni, sic etiam superbia vitae continetur sub cupiditate. Quomodo autem cupiditas, secundum quod est speciale vitium, quod avaritia nominatur, sit radix omnium peccatorum, infra dicetur.

AD SECUNDUM dicendum quod concupiscentia oculorum non dicitur hic concupiscentia omnium rerum

But nothing is mentioned here pertaining to avoidance of evil. Therefore the causes of sin are insufficiently described.

ON THE CONTRARY, It is written (1 John 2:16): *All that is in the world is concupiscence of the flesh, or pride of life.* Now a thing is said to be *in the world* by reason of sin: wherefore it is written (1 John 5:19): *The whole world is seated in wickedness.* Therefore these three are causes of sin.

I ANSWER THAT, As stated above (A4), inordinate self-love is the cause of every sin. Now self-love includes inordinate desire of good: for a man desires good for the one he loves. Hence it is evident that inordinate desire of good is the cause of every sin. Now good is, in two ways, the object of the sensitive appetite, wherein are the passions which are the cause of sin: first, absolutely, according as it is the object of the concupiscible part; second, under the aspect of difficulty, according as it is the object of the irascible part, as stated above (Q23, A1). Again, concupiscence is twofold, as stated above (Q30, A3). One is natural, and is directed to those things which sustain the nature of the body, whether as regards the preservation of the individual, such as food, drink, and the like, or as regards the preservation of the species, such as sexual matters: and the inordinate appetite of such things is called *concupiscence of the flesh.* The other is spiritual concupiscence, and is directed to those things which do not afford sustentation or pleasure in respect of the fleshly senses, but are delectable in respect of the apprehension or imagination, or some similar mode of perception; such are money, apparel, and the like; and this spiritual concupiscence is called *concupiscence of the eyes,* whether this be taken as referring to the sight itself, of which the eyes are the organ, so as to denote curiosity according to Augustine's exposition (*Confess.* x); or to the concupiscence of things which are proposed outwardly to the eyes, so as to denote covetousness, according to the explanation of others.

The inordinate appetite of the arduous good pertains to the *pride of life;* for pride is the inordinate appetite of excellence, as we shall state further on (Q84, A2; SS, Q162, A1).

It is therefore evident that all passions that are a cause of sin can be reduced to these three: since all the passions of the concupiscible part can be reduced to the first two, and all the irascible passions to the third, which is not divided into two because all the irascible passions conform to spiritual concupiscence.

REPLY OBJ. 1: *Pride of life* is included in covetousness according as the latter denotes any kind of appetite for any kind of good. How covetousness, as a special vice, which goes by the name of *avarice,* is the root of all sins, shall be explained further on (Q84, A1).

REPLY OBJ. 2: *Concupiscence of the eyes* does not mean here the concupiscence for all things which can be seen by

quae oculis videri possunt, sed solum earum in quibus non quaeritur delectatio carnis, quae est secundum tactum, sed solum delectatio oculi, idest cuiuscumque apprehensivae virtutis.

AD TERTIUM dicendum quod sensus visus est excellentior inter omnes sensus, et ad plura se extendens, ut dicitur in I Metaphys. Et ideo nomen eius transfertur ad omnes alios sensus, et etiam ad omnes interiores apprehensiones, ut Augustinus dicit, in libro de verbis domini.

AD QUARTUM dicendum quod fuga mali causatur ex appetitu boni, ut supra dictum est. Et ideo ponuntur solum passiones inclinantes ad bonum, tanquam causae earum quae faciunt inordinate fugam mali.

the eyes, but only for such things as afford, not carnal pleasure in respect of touch, but in respect of the eyes, i.e., of any apprehensive power.

REPLY OBJ. 3: The sense of sight is the most excellent of all the senses, and covers a larger ground, as stated in *Metaph.* i: and so its name is transferred to all the other senses, and even to the inner apprehensions, as Augustine states (*De Verb. Dom.*, serm. xxxiii).

REPLY OBJ. 4: Avoidance of evil is caused by the appetite for good, as stated above (Q25, A2; Q39, A2); and so those passions alone are mentioned which incline to good, as being the causes of those which cause inordinately the avoidance of evil.

Article 6

Whether Sin Is Alleviated on Account of a Passion?

AD SEXTUM SIC PROCEDITUR. Videtur quod peccatum non allevietur propter passionem. Augmentum enim causae auget effectum, si enim calidum dissolvit, magis calidum magis dissolvit. Sed passio est causa peccati, ut habitum est. Ergo quanto est intensior passio, tanto est maius peccatum. Passio igitur non minuit peccatum, sed auget.

PRAETEREA, sicut se habet passio bona ad meritum, ita se habet mala passio ad peccatum. Sed bona passio auget meritum, tanto enim aliquis magis videtur mereri, quanto ex maiori misericordia pauperi subvenit. Ergo etiam mala passio magis aggravat peccatum quam alleviat.

PRAETEREA, quanto intensiori voluntate aliquis facit peccatum, tanto gravius videtur peccare. Sed passio impellens voluntatem, facit eam vehementius ferri in actum peccati. Ergo passio aggravat peccatum.

SED CONTRA, passio ipsa concupiscentiae vocatur tentatio carnis. Sed quanto aliquis maiori tentatione prosternitur, tanto minus peccat, ut patet per Augustinum. Ergo passio diminuit peccatum.

RESPONDEO dicendum quod peccatum essentialiter consistit in actu liberi arbitrii, quod est facultas voluntatis et rationis. Passio autem est motus appetitus sensitivi. Appetitus autem sensitivus potest se habere ad liberum arbitrium et antecedenter, et consequenter. Antecedenter quidem, secundum quod passio appetitus sensitivi trahit vel inclinat rationem et voluntatem, ut supra dictum est. Consequenter autem, secundum quod motus superiorum virium, si sint vehementes, redundant in inferiores, non enim potest voluntas intense moveri in aliquid, quin excitetur aliqua passio in appetitu sensitivo.

OBJECTION 1: It would seem that sin is not alleviated on account of passion. For increase of cause adds to the effect: thus if a hot thing causes something to melt, a hotter will do so yet more. Now passion is a cause of sin, as stated (A5). Therefore the more intense the passion, the greater the sin. Therefore passion does not diminish sin, but increases it.

OBJ. 2: Further, a good passion stands in the same relation to merit, as an evil passion does to sin. Now a good passion increases merit: for a man seems to merit the more, according as he is moved by a greater pity to help a poor man. Therefore an evil passion also increases rather than diminishes a sin.

OBJ. 3: Further, a man seems to sin the more grievously, according as he sins with a more intense will. But the passion that impels the will makes it tend with greater intensity to the sinful act. Therefore passion aggravates a sin.

ON THE CONTRARY, The passion of concupiscence is called a temptation of the flesh. But the greater the temptation that overcomes a man, the less grievous his sin, as Augustine states (*De Civ. Dei* iv, 12).

I ANSWER THAT, Sin consists essentially in an act of the free will, which is a faculty of the will and reason; while passion is a movement of the sensitive appetite. Now the sensitive appetite can be related to the free-will, antecedently and consequently: antecedently, according as a passion of the sensitive appetite draws or inclines the reason or will, as stated above (AA1,2; Q10, A3); and consequently, insofar as the movements of the higher powers redound on to the lower, since it is not possible for the will to be moved to anything intensely, without a passion being aroused in the sensitive appetite.

Si igitur accipiatur passio secundum quod praecedit actum peccati, sic necesse est quod diminuat peccatum. Actus enim intantum est peccatum, inquantum est voluntarium et in nobis existens. In nobis autem aliquid esse dicitur per rationem et voluntatem. Unde quanto ratio et voluntas ex se aliquid agunt, non ex impulsu passionis, magis est voluntarium et in nobis existens. Et secundum hoc passio minuit peccatum, inquantum minuit voluntarium.

Passio autem consequens non diminuit peccatum, sed magis auget, vel potius est signum magnitudinis eius, inquantum scilicet demonstrat intensionem voluntatis ad actum peccati. Et sic verum est quod quanto aliquis maiori libidine vel concupiscentia peccat, tanto magis peccat.

AD PRIMUM ergo dicendum quod passio est causa peccati ex parte conversionis. Gravitas autem peccati magis attenditur ex parte aversionis; quae quidem ex conversione sequitur per accidens, idest praeter intentionem peccantis. Causae autem per accidens augmentatae non augmentant effectus, sed solum causae per se.

AD SECUNDUM dicendum quod bona passio consequens iudicium rationis, augmentat meritum. Si autem praecedat, ut scilicet homo magis ex passione quam ex iudicio rationis moveatur ad bene agendum, talis passio diminuit bonitatem et laudem actus.

AD TERTIUM dicendum quod, etsi motus voluntatis sit intensior ex passione incitatus, non tamen ita est voluntatis proprius, sicut si sola ratione moveretur ad peccandum.

Accordingly if we take passion as preceding the sinful act, it must needs diminish the sin: because the act is a sin insofar as it is voluntary, and under our control. Now a thing is said to be under our control, through the reason and will: and therefore the more the reason and will do anything of their own accord, and not through the impulse of a passion, the more is it voluntary and under our control. In this respect passion diminishes sin, insofar as it diminishes its voluntariness.

On the other hand, a consequent passion does not diminish a sin, but increases it; or rather it is a sign of its gravity, in so far, to wit, as it shows the intensity of the will towards the sinful act; and so it is true that the greater the pleasure or the concupiscence with which anyone sins, the greater the sin.

REPLY OBJ. 1: Passion is the cause of sin on the part of that to which the sinner turns. But the gravity of a sin is measured on the part of that from which he turns, which results accidentally from his turning to something else—accidentally, i.e., beside his intention. Now an effect is increased by the increase, not of its accidental cause, but of its direct cause.

REPLY OBJ. 2: A good passion consequent to the judgment of reason increases merit; but if it precede, so that a man is moved to do well, rather by his passion than by the judgment of his reason, such a passion diminishes the goodness and praiseworthiness of his action.

REPLY OBJ. 3: Although the movement of the will incited by the passion is more intense, yet it is not so much the will's own movement, as if it were moved to sin by the reason alone.

Article 7

Whether Passion Excuses from Sin Altogether?

AD SEPTIMUM SIC PROCEDITUR. Videtur quod passio totaliter excuset a peccato. Quidquid enim causat involuntarium, excusat totaliter a peccato. Sed concupiscentia carnis, quae est quaedam passio, causat involuntarium, secundum illud Gal. V, *caro concupiscit adversus spiritum, ut non quaecumque vultis, illa faciatis.* Ergo passio totaliter excusat a peccato.

PRAETEREA, passio causat ignorantiam quandam in particulari, ut dictum est. Sed ignorantia particularis totaliter excusat a peccato, sicut supra habitum est. Ergo passio totaliter excusat a peccato.

PRAETEREA, infirmitas animae gravior est quam infirmitas corporis. Sed infirmitas corporis totaliter excusat a peccato, ut patet in phreneticis. Ergo multo magis passio, quae est infirmitas animae.

OBJECTION 1: It would seem that passion excuses from sin altogether. For whatever causes an act to be involuntary, excuses from sin altogether. But concupiscence of the flesh, which is a passion, makes an act to be involuntary, according to Gal. 5:17: *The flesh lusteth against the spirit . . . so that you do not the things that you would.* Therefore passion excuses from sin altogether.

OBJ. 2: Further, passion causes a certain ignorance of a particular matter, as stated above (A2; Q76, A3). But ignorance of a particular matter excuses from sin altogether, as stated above (Q6, A8). Therefore passion excuses from sin altogether.

OBJ. 3: Further, disease of the soul is graver than disease of the body. But bodily disease excuses from sin altogether, as in the case of mad people. Much more, therefore, does passion, which is a disease of the soul.

Sed contra est quod apostolus, Rom. VII, vocat passiones peccatorum, non nisi quia peccata causant. Quod non esset, si a peccato totaliter excusarent. Ergo passiones non totaliter a peccato excusant.

Respondeo dicendum quod secundum hoc solum actus aliquis qui de genere suo est malus, totaliter a peccato excusatur, quod totaliter involuntarius redditur. Unde si sit talis passio quae totaliter involuntarium reddat actum sequentem, totaliter a peccato excusat, alioquin, non totaliter. Circa quod duo consideranda videntur. Primo quidem, quod aliquid potest esse voluntarium vel secundum se, sicut quando voluntas directe in ipsum fertur, vel secundum suam causam, quando voluntas fertur in causam et non in effectum, ut patet in eo qui voluntarie inebriatur; ex hoc enim quasi voluntarium ei imputatur quod per ebrietatem committit. Secundo considerandum est quod aliquid dicitur voluntarium directe, vel indirecte, directe quidem, id in quod voluntas fertur; indirecte autem, illud quod voluntas potuit prohibere, sed non prohibet.

Secundum hoc igitur distinguendum est. Quia passio quandoque quidem est tanta quod totaliter aufert usum rationis, sicut patet in his qui propter amorem vel iram insaniunt. Et tunc si talis passio a principio fuit voluntaria, imputatur actus ad peccatum, quia est voluntarius in sua causa, sicut etiam de ebrietate dictum est. Si vero causa non fuit voluntaria, sed naturalis, puta cum aliquis ex aegritudine, vel aliqua huiusmodi causa, incidit in talem passionem quae totaliter aufert usum rationis; actus omnino redditur involuntarius, et per consequens totaliter a peccato excusatur. Quandoque vero passio non est tanta quod totaliter intercipiat usum rationis. Et tunc ratio potest passionem excludere, divertendo ad alias cogitationes; vel impedire ne suum consequatur effectum, quia membra non applicantur operi nisi per consensum rationis, ut supra dictum est. Unde talis passio non totaliter excusat a peccato.

Ad primum ergo dicendum quod hoc quod dicitur, *ut non quaecumque vultis, illa faciatis*, non est referendum ad ea quae fiunt per exteriorem actum, sed ad interiorem concupiscentiae motum, vellet enim homo nunquam concupiscere malum. Sicut etiam exponitur id quod dicitur Rom. VII, quod *odi malum, illud facio*. Vel potest referri ad voluntatem praecedentem passionem, ut patet in continentibus qui contra suum propositum agunt propter suam concupiscentiam.

Ad secundum dicendum quod ignorantia particularis quae totaliter excusat, est ignorantia circumstantiae quam quidem quis scire non potest, debita diligentia adhibita. Sed passio causat ignorantiam iuris in particulari, dum impedit applicationem communis scientiae ad particularem actum. Quam quidem passionem ratio repellere potest, ut dictum est.

On the contrary, The Apostle (Rom 7:5) speaks of the passions as *passions of sins*, for no other reason than that they cause sin: which would not be the case if they excused from sin altogether. Therefore passion does not excuse from sin altogether.

I answer that, An act which, in its genus, is evil, cannot be excused from sin altogether, unless it be rendered altogether involuntary. Consequently, if the passion be such that it renders the subsequent act wholly involuntary, it entirely excuses from sin; otherwise, it does not excuse entirely. In this matter two points apparently should be observed: first, that a thing may be voluntary either *in itself*, as when the will tends towards it directly; or *in its cause*, when the will tends towards that cause and not towards the effect; as is the case with one who wilfully gets drunk, for in that case he is considered to do voluntarily whatever he does through being drunk. Second, we must observe that a thing is said to be voluntary *directly* or *indirectly*; directly, if the will tends towards it; indirectly, if the will could have prevented it, but did not.

Accordingly therefore we must make a distinction: because a passion is sometimes so strong as to take away the use of reason altogether, as in the case of those who are mad through love or anger; and then if such a passion were voluntary from the beginning, the act is reckoned a sin, because it is voluntary in its cause, as we have stated with regard to drunkenness. If, however, the cause be not voluntary but natural, for instance, if anyone through sickness or some such cause fall into such a passion as deprives him of the use of reason, his act is rendered wholly involuntary, and he is entirely excused from sin. Sometimes, however, the passion is not such as to take away the use of reason altogether; and then reason can drive the passion away, by turning to other thoughts, or it can prevent it from having its full effect; since the members are not put to work, except by the consent of reason, as stated above (Q17, A9): wherefore such a passion does not excuse from sin altogether.

Reply Obj. 1: The words, *So that you do not the things that you would* are not to be referred to outward deeds, but to the inner movement of concupiscence; for a man would wish never to desire evil, in which sense we are to understand the words of Rm. 7:19: *The evil which I will not, that I do.* Or again they may be referred to the will as preceding the passion, as is the case with the incontinent, who act counter to their resolution on account of their concupiscence.

Reply Obj. 2: The particular ignorance which excuses altogether, is ignorance of a circumstance, which a man is unable to know even after taking due precautions. But passion causes ignorance of law in a particular case, by preventing universal knowledge from being applied to a particular act, which passion the reason is able to drive away, as stated.

AD TERTIUM dicendum quod infirmitas corporis est involuntaria. Esset autem simile, si esset voluntaria, sicut de ebrietate dictum est, quae est quaedam corporalis infirmitas.

REPLY OBJ. 3: Bodily disease is involuntary: there would be a comparison, however, if it were voluntary, as we have stated about drunkenness, which is a kind of bodily disease.

Article 8

Whether a Sin Committed Through Passion Can Be Mortal?

AD OCTAVUM SIC PROCEDITUR. Videtur quod peccatum quod est ex passione, non possit esse mortale. Veniale enim peccatum dividitur contra mortale. Sed peccatum quod est ex infirmitate, est veniale, cum habeat in se causam veniae. Cum igitur peccatum quod est ex passione, sit ex infirmitate, videtur quod non possit esse mortale.

PRAETEREA, causa non est potior effectu. Sed passio non potest esse peccatum mortale, non enim in sensualitate est peccatum mortale, ut supra habitum est. Ergo peccatum quod est ex passione, non potest esse mortale.

PRAETEREA, passio abducit a ratione, ut ex dictis patet. Sed rationis est converti ad Deum vel averti ab eo, in quo consistit ratio peccati mortalis. Peccatum ergo quod est ex passione, non potest esse mortale.

SED CONTRA est quod apostolus dicit, Rom. VII, quod *passiones peccatorum operantur in membris nostris ad fructificandum morti.* Hoc autem est proprium mortalis peccati, quod fructificet morti. Ergo peccatum quod est ex passione, potest esse mortale.

RESPONDEO dicendum quod peccatum mortale, ut supra dictum est, consistit in aversione ab ultimo fine, qui est Deus, quae quidem aversio pertinet ad rationem deliberantem, cuius etiam est ordinare in finem. Hoc igitur solo modo potest contingere quod inclinatio animae in aliquid quod contrariatur ultimo fini, non sit peccatum mortale quia ratio deliberans non potest occurrere, quod contingit in subitis motibus. Cum autem ex passione aliquis procedit ad actum peccati, vel ad consensum deliberatum, hoc non fit subito. Unde ratio deliberans potest hic occurrere, potest enim excludere, vel saltem impedire passionem, ut dictum est. Unde si non occurrat, est peccatum mortale, sicut videmus quod multa homicidia et adulteria per passionem committuntur.

AD PRIMUM ergo dicendum quod veniale dicitur tripliciter. Uno modo, ex causa, quia scilicet habet aliquam causam veniae, quae diminuit peccatum, et sic peccatum ex infirmitate et ignorantia dicitur veniale. Alio modo, ex eventu, sicut omne peccatum per poenitentiam fit veniale, idest veniam consecutum. Tertio modo dicitur veniale ex genere, sicut verbum otiosum. Et hoc solum

OBJECTION 1: It would seem that sin committed through passion cannot be mortal. Because venial sin is condivided with mortal sin. Now sin committed from weakness is venial, since it has in itself a motive for pardon. Since therefore sin committed through passion is a sin of weakness, it seems that it cannot be mortal.

OBJ. 2: Further, the cause is more powerful than its effect. But passion cannot be a mortal sin, for there is no mortal sin in the sensuality, as stated above (Q74, A4). Therefore a sin committed through passion cannot be mortal.

OBJ. 3: Further, passion is a hindrance to reason, as explained above (AA1,2). Now it belongs to the reason to turn to God, or to turn away from Him, which is the essence of a mortal sin. Therefore a sin committed through passion cannot be mortal.

ON THE CONTRARY, The Apostle says (Rom 7:5) that *the passions of the sins . . . work in our members to bring forth fruit unto death.* Now it is proper to mortal sin to bring forth fruit unto death. Therefore sin committed through passion may be mortal.

I ANSWER THAT, Mortal sin, as stated above (Q72, A5), consists in turning away from our last end which is God, which aversion pertains to the deliberating reason, whose function it is also to direct towards the end. Therefore that which is contrary to the last end can happen not to be a mortal sin, only when the deliberating reason is unable to come to the rescue, which is the case in sudden movements. Now when anyone proceeds from passion to a sinful act, or to a deliberate consent, this does not happen suddenly: and so the deliberating reason can come to the rescue here, since it can drive the passion away, or at least prevent it from having its effect, as stated above: wherefore if it does not come to the rescue, there is a mortal sin; and it is thus, as we see, that many murders and adulteries are committed through passion.

REPLY OBJ. 1: A sin may be venial in three ways. First, through its cause, i.e., through having cause to be forgiven, which cause lessens the sin; thus a sin that is committed through weakness or ignorance is said to be venial. Second, through its issue; thus every sin, through repentance, becomes venial, i.e., receives pardon. Third, by its genus, e.g., an idle word. This is the only kind of venial sin that is

veniale opponitur mortali, obiectio autem procedit de primo.

AD SECUNDUM dicendum quod passio est causa peccati ex parte conversionis. Quod autem sit mortale, est ex parte aversionis, quae per accidens sequitur ad conversionem, ut dictum est. Unde ratio non sequitur.

AD TERTIUM dicendum quod ratio non semper in suo actu totaliter a passione impeditur, unde remanet ei liberum arbitrium, ut possit averti vel converti ad Deum. Si autem totaliter tolleretur usus rationis, iam non esset peccatum nec mortale nec veniale.

opposed to mortal sin: whereas the objection regards the first kind.

REPLY OBJ. 2: Passion causes sin as regards the adherence to something. But that this be a mortal sin regards the aversion, which follows accidentally from the adherence, as stated above (A6, ad 1): hence the argument does not prove.

REPLY OBJ. 3: Passion does not always hinder the act of reason altogether: consequently the reason remains in possession of its free-will, so as to turn away from God, or turn to Him. If, however, the use of reason be taken away altogether, the sin is no longer either mortal or venial.

QUESTION 78

OF THAT CAUSE OF SIN WHICH IS MALICE

Deinde considerandum est de causa peccati quae est ex parte voluntatis, quae dicitur malitia. Et circa hoc quaeruntur quatuor.

Primo, utrum aliquis possit ex certa malitia, seu industria, peccare.

Secundo, utrum quicumque peccat ex habitu, peccet ex certa malitia.

Tertio, utrum quicumque peccat ex certa malitia, peccet ex habitu.

Quarto, utrum ille qui peccat ex certa malitia, gravius peccet quam ille qui peccat ex passione.

We must now consider the cause of sin on the part of the will, viz., malice: and under this head there are four points of inquiry:

(1) Whether it is possible for anyone to sin through certain malice, i.e., purposely?

(2) Whether everyone that sins through habit, sins through certain malice?

(3) Whether every one that sins through certain malice, sins through habit?

(4) Whether it is more grievous to sin through certain malice, than through passion?

Article 1

Whether Anyone Sins Through Certain Malice?

AD PRIMUM SIC PROCEDITUR. Videtur quod nullus peccet ex industria, sive ex certa malitia. Ignorantia enim opponitur industriae, seu certae malitiae. Sed omnis malus est ignorans, secundum philosophum. Et Prov. XIV, dicitur, *errant qui operantur malum*. Ergo nullus peccat ex certa malitia.

PRAETEREA, Dionysius dicit, IV cap. de Div. Nom., quod *nullus intendens ad malum operatur*. Sed hoc videtur esse peccare ex malitia, intendere malum in peccando, quod enim est praeter intentionem, est quasi per accidens, et non denominat actum. Ergo nullus ex malitia peccat.

PRAETEREA, malitia ipsa peccatum est. Si igitur malitia sit causa peccati, sequetur quod peccatum sit causa peccati in infinitum, quod est inconveniens. Nullus igitur ex malitia peccat.

SED CONTRA est quod dicitur Iob XXXIV, *quasi de industria recesserunt a Deo, et vias eius intelligere noluerunt*. Sed recedere a Deo est peccare. Ergo aliqui peccant ex industria, seu ex certa malitia.

RESPONDEO dicendum quod homo, sicut et quaelibet alia res, naturaliter habet appetitum boni. Unde quod ad malum eius appetitus declinet, contingit ex aliqua corruptione seu inordinatione in aliquo principiorum hominis, sic enim in actionibus rerum naturalium peccatum invenitur. Principia autem humanorum actuum sunt intellectus et appetitus, tam rationalis, qui dicitur voluntas, quam sensitivus. Peccatum igitur in humanis actibus contingit quandoque, sicut ex defectu intellectus, puta cum aliquis per ignorantiam peccat; et ex

OBJECTION 1: It would seem that no one sins purposely, or through certain malice. Because ignorance is opposed to purpose or certain malice. Now *every evil man is ignorant*, according to the Philosopher (*Ethic*. iii, 1); and it is written (Prov 14:22): *They err that work evil*. Therefore no one sins through certain malice.

OBJ. 2: Further, Dionysius says (*Div. Nom*. iv) that *no one works intending evil*. Now to sin through malice seems to denote the intention of doing evil in sinning, because an act is not denominated from that which is unintentional and accidental. Therefore no one sins through malice.

OBJ. 3: Further, malice itself is a sin. If therefore malice is a cause of sin, it follows that sin goes on causing sin indefinitely, which is absurd. Therefore no one sins through malice.

ON THE CONTRARY, It is written (Job 34:27): *[Who] as it were on purpose have revolted from God, and would not understand all His ways*. Now to revolt from God is to sin. Therefore some sin purposely or through certain malice.

I ANSWER THAT, Man like any other being has naturally an appetite for the good; and so if his appetite incline away to evil, this is due to corruption or disorder in some one of the principles of man: for it is thus that sin occurs in the actions of natural things. Now the principles of human acts are the intellect, and the appetite, both rational (i.e., the will) and sensitive. Therefore even as sin occurs in human acts, sometimes through a defect of the intellect, as when anyone sins through ignorance, and sometimes through a defect in the sensitive appetite, as when anyone

defectu appetitus sensitivi, sicut cum aliquis ex passione peccat; ita etiam ex defectu voluntatis, qui est inordinatio ipsius. Est autem voluntas inordinata, quando minus bonum magis amat. Consequens autem est ut aliquis eligat pati detrimentum in bono minus amato, ad hoc quod potiatur bono magis amato, sicut cum homo vult pati abscissionem membri etiam scienter, ut conservet vitam, quam magis amat. Et per hunc modum, quando aliqua inordinata voluntas aliquod bonum temporale plus amat, puta divitias vel voluptatem, quam ordinem rationis vel legis divinae, vel caritatem Dei, vel aliquid huiusmodi; sequitur quod velit dispendium pati in aliquo spiritualium bonorum, ut potiatur aliquo temporali bono. Nihil autem est aliud malum quam privatio alicuius boni. Et secundum hoc aliquis scienter vult aliquod malum spirituale, quod est malum simpliciter, per quod bonum spirituale privatur, ut bono temporali potiatur. Unde dicitur ex certa malitia, vel ex industria peccare, quasi scienter malum eligens.

AD PRIMUM ergo dicendum quod ignorantia quandoque quidem excludit scientiam qua aliquis simpliciter scit hoc esse malum quod agitur, et tunc dicitur ex ignorantia peccare. Quandoque autem excludit scientiam qua homo scit hoc nunc esse malum, sicut cum ex passione peccatur. Quandoque autem excludit scientiam qua aliquis scit hoc malum non sustinendum esse propter consecutionem illius boni, scit tamen simpliciter hoc esse malum, et sic dicitur ignorare qui ex certa malitia peccat.

AD SECUNDUM dicendum quod malum non potest esse secundum se intentum ab aliquo, potest tamen esse intentum ad vitandum aliud malum, vel ad consequendum aliud bonum, ut dictum est. Et in tali casu aliquis eligeret consequi bonum per se intentum, absque hoc quod pateretur detrimentum alterius boni. Sicut aliquis lascivus vellet frui delectatione absque offensa Dei, sed duobus propositis, magis vult peccando incurrere offensam Dei, quam delectatione privetur.

AD TERTIUM dicendum quod malitia ex qua aliquis dicitur peccare, potest intelligi malitia habitualis, secundum quod habitus malus a philosopho nominatur malitia, sicut habitus bonus nominatur virtus. Et secundum hoc aliquis dicitur ex malitia peccare, quia peccat ex inclinatione habitus. Potest etiam intelligi malitia actualis. Sive ipsa mali electio malitia nominetur, et sic dicitur aliquis ex malitia peccare, inquantum ex mali electione peccat. Sive etiam malitia dicatur aliqua praecedens culpa, ex qua oritur subsequens culpa, sicut cum aliquis impugnat fraternam gratiam ex invidia. Et tunc idem non est causa sui ipsius, sed actus interior est causa actus exterioris. Et unum peccatum est causa alterius, non tamen in infinitum, quia est devenire ad aliquod primum

sins through passion, so too does it occur through a defect consisting in a disorder of the will. Now the will is out of order when it loves more the lesser good. Again, the consequence of loving a thing less is that one chooses to suffer some hurt in its regard, in order to obtain a good that one loves more: as when a man, even knowingly, suffers the loss of a limb, that he may save his life which he loves more. Accordingly when an inordinate will loves some temporal good, e.g., riches or pleasure, more than the order of reason or Divine law, or Divine charity, or some such thing, it follows that it is willing to suffer the loss of some spiritual good, so that it may obtain possession of some temporal good. Now evil is merely the privation of some good; and so a man wishes knowingly a spiritual evil, which is evil simply, whereby he is deprived of a spiritual good, in order to possess a temporal good: wherefore he is said to sin through certain malice or on purpose, because he chooses evil knowingly.

REPLY OBJ. 1: Ignorance sometimes excludes the simple knowledge that a particular action is evil, and then man is said to sin through ignorance: sometimes it excludes the knowledge that a particular action is evil at this particular moment, as when he sins through passion: and sometimes it excludes the knowledge that a particular evil is not to be suffered for the sake of possessing a particular good, but not the simple knowledge that it is an evil: it is thus that a man is ignorant, when he sins through certain malice.

REPLY OBJ. 2: Evil cannot be intended by anyone for its own sake; but it can be intended for the sake of avoiding another evil, or obtaining another good, as stated above: and in this case anyone would choose to obtain a good intended for its own sake, without suffering loss of the other good; even as a lustful man would wish to enjoy a pleasure without offending God; but with the two set before him to choose from, he prefers sinning and thereby incurring God's anger, to being deprived of the pleasure.

REPLY OBJ. 3: The malice through which anyone sins, may be taken to denote habitual malice, in the sense in which the Philosopher (*Ethic.* v, 1) calls an evil habit by the name of malice, just as a good habit is called virtue: and in this way anyone is said to sin through malice when he sins through the inclination of a habit. It may also denote actual malice, whether by malice we mean the choice itself of evil (and thus anyone is said to sin through malice, insofar as he sins through making a choice of evil), or whether by malice we mean some previous fault that gives rise to a subsequent fault, as when anyone impugns the grace of his brother through envy. Nor does this imply that a thing is its own cause: for the interior act is the cause of the exterior act, and one sin is the cause of another; not indefinitely,

peccatum, quod non causatur ex aliquo priori peccato, ut ex supradictis patet.

however, since we can trace it back to some previous sin, which is not caused by any previous sin, as was explained above (Q75, A4, ad 3).

Article 2

Whether Everyone That Sins Through Habit, Sins Through Certain Malice?

AD SECUNDUM SIC PROCEDITUR. Videtur quod non omnis qui peccat ex habitu, peccet ex certa malitia. Peccatum enim quod est ex certa malitia, videtur esse gravissimum. Sed quandoque homo aliquod leve peccatum committit ex habitu, sicut cum dicit verbum otiosum. Non ergo omne peccatum quod est ex habitu, est ex certa malitia.

PRAETEREA, *actus ex habitu procedentes sunt similes actibus ex quibus habitus generantur*, ut dicitur in II Ethic. Sed actus praecedentes habitum vitiosum non sunt ex certa malitia. Ergo etiam peccata quae sunt ex habitu, non sunt ex certa malitia.

PRAETEREA, in his quae aliquis ex certa malitia committit, gaudet postquam commisit, secundum illud Prov. II, *qui laetantur cum male fecerint et exultant in rebus pessimis*. Et hoc ideo, quia unicuique est delectabile cum consequitur id quod intendit, et qui operatur quod est ei quodammodo connaturale secundum habitum. Sed illi qui peccant ex habitu, post peccatum commissum dolent, poenitudine enim replentur pravi, idest habentes habitum vitiosum, ut dicitur in IX Ethic. Ergo peccata quae sunt ex habitu, non sunt ex certa malitia.

SED CONTRA, peccatum ex certa malitia dicitur esse quod est ex electione mali. Sed unicuique est eligibile id ad quod inclinatur per proprium habitum; ut dicitur in VI Ethic. de habitu virtuoso. Ergo peccatum quod est ex habitu, est ex certa malitia.

RESPONDEO dicendum quod non est idem peccare habentem habitum, et peccare ex habitu. Uti enim habitu non est necessarium, sed subiacet voluntati habentis, unde et habitus definitur esse quo quis utitur cum voluerit. Et ideo sicut potest contingere quod aliquis habens habitum vitiosum, prorumpat in actum virtutis, eo quod ratio non totaliter corrumpitur per malum habitum, sed aliquid eius integrum manet, ex quo provenit quod peccator aliqua operatur de genere bonorum; ita etiam potest contingere quod aliquis habens habitum, interdum non ex habitu operetur, sed ex passione insurgente, vel etiam ex ignorantia. Sed quandocumque utitur habitu vitioso, necesse est quod ex certa malitia peccet. Quia unicuique habenti habitum, est per se diligibile id quod est ei conveniens secundum proprium habitum, quia fit ei quodammodo connaturale, secundum quod

OBJECTION 1: It would seem that not every one who sins through habit, sins through certain malice. Because sin committed through certain malice, seems to be most grievous. Now it happens sometimes that a man commits a slight sin through habit, as when he utters an idle word. Therefore sin committed from habit is not always committed through certain malice.

OBJ. 2: Further, *Acts proceeding from habits are like the acts by which those habits were formed* (*Ethic.* ii, 1,2). But the acts which precede a vicious habit are not committed through certain malice. Therefore the sins that arise from habit are not committed through certain malice.

OBJ. 3: Further, when a man commits a sin through certain malice, he is glad after having done it, according to Prov. 2:14: *Who are glad when they have done evil, and rejoice in most wicked things*: and this, because it is pleasant to obtain what we desire, and to do those actions which are connatural to us by reason of habit. But those who sin through habit, are sorrowful after committing a sin: because *bad men*, i.e., those who have a vicious habit, *are full of remorse* (*Ethic.* ix, 4). Therefore sins that arise from habit are not committed through certain malice.

ON THE CONTRARY, A sin committed through certain malice is one that is done through choice of evil. Now we make choice of those things to which we are inclined by habit, as stated in *Ethic.* vi, 2 with regard to virtuous habits. Therefore a sin that arises from habit is committed through certain malice.

I ANSWER THAT, There is a difference between a sin committed by one who has the habit, and a sin committed by habit: for it is not necessary to use a habit, since it is subject to the will of the person who has that habit. Hence habit is defined as being *something we use when we will*, as stated above (Q50, A1). And thus, even as it may happen that one who has a vicious habit may break forth into a virtuous act, because a bad habit does not corrupt reason altogether, something of which remains unimpaired, the result being that a sinner does some works which are generically good; so too it may happen sometimes that one who has a vicious habit, acts, not from that habit, but through the uprising of a passion, or again through ignorance. But whenever he uses the vicious habit he must needs sin through certain malice: because to anyone that has a habit, whatever is befitting to him in respect of that habit, has the aspect of

consuetudo et habitus vertitur in naturam. Hoc autem quod est alicui conveniens secundum habitum vitiosum, est id quod excludit bonum spirituale. Ex quo sequitur quod homo eligat malum spirituale, ut adipiscatur bonum quod est ei secundum habitum conveniens. Et hoc est ex certa malitia peccare. Unde manifestum est quod quicumque peccat ex habitu, peccet ex certa malitia.

AD PRIMUM ergo dicendum quod peccata venialia non excludunt bonum spirituale, quod est gratia Dei vel caritas. Unde non dicuntur mala simpliciter, sed secundum quid. Et propter hoc nec habitus ipsorum possunt dici simpliciter mali, sed solum secundum quid.

AD SECUNDUM dicendum quod actus qui procedunt ex habitibus, sunt similes secundum speciem actibus ex quibus habitus generantur, differunt tamen ab eis sicut perfectum ab imperfecto. Et talis est differentia peccati quod committitur ex certa malitia, ad peccatum quod committitur ex aliqua passione.

AD TERTIUM dicendum quod ille qui peccat ex habitu, semper gaudet de hoc quod ex habitu operatur, quandiu habitu utitur. Sed quia potest habitu non uti, sed per rationem, quae non est totaliter corrupta, aliquid aliud meditari; potest contingere quod, non utens habitu, doleat de hoc quod per habitum commisit. Plerumque tamen tales poenitent de peccato, non quia eis peccatum secundum se displiceat; sed propter aliquod incommodum quod ex peccato incurrunt.

something lovable, since it thereby becomes, in a way, connatural to him, according as custom and habit are a second nature. Now the very thing which befits a man in respect of a vicious habit, is something that excludes a spiritual good: the result being that a man chooses a spiritual evil, that he may obtain possession of what befits him in respect of that habit: and this is to sin through certain malice. Wherefore it is evident that whoever sins through habit, sins through certain malice.

REPLY OBJ. 1: Venial sin does not exclude spiritual good, consisting in the grace of God or charity. Wherefore it is an evil, not simply, but in a relative sense: and for that reason the habit thereof is not a simple but a relative evil.

REPLY OBJ. 2: Acts proceeding from habits are of like species as the acts from which those habits were formed: but they differ from them as perfect from imperfect. Such is the difference between sin committed through certain malice and sin committed through passion.

REPLY OBJ. 3: He that sins through habit is always glad for what he does through habit, as long as he uses the habit. But since he is able not to use the habit, and to think of something else, by means of his reason, which is not altogether corrupted, it may happen that while not using the habit he is sorry for what he has done through the habit. And so it often happens that such a man is sorry for his sin not because sin in itself is displeasing to him, but on account of his reaping some disadvantage from the sin.

Article 3

Whether One Who Sins Through Certain Malice, Sins Through Habit?

AD TERTIUM SIC PROCEDITUR. Videtur quod quicumque peccat ex certa malitia, peccet ex habitu. Dicit enim philosophus, in V Ethic., quod *non est cuiuslibet iniusta facere qualiter iniustus facit*, scilicet ex electione, *sed solum habentis habitum*. Sed peccare ex certa malitia est peccare ex electione mali, ut dictum est. Ergo peccare ex certa malitia non est nisi habentis habitum.

PRAETEREA, Origenes dicit, in I peri archon, quod *non ad subitum quis evacuatur aut deficit, sed paulatim per partes defluere necesse est*. Sed maximus defluxus esse videtur ut aliquis ex certa malitia peccet. Ergo non statim a principio, sed per multam consuetudinem, ex qua habitus generari potest, aliquis ad hoc devenit ut ex certa malitia peccet.

PRAETEREA, quandocumque aliquis ex certa malitia peccat, oportet quod ipsa voluntas de se inclinetur ad malum quod eligit. Sed ex natura potentiae non

OBJECTION 1: It would seem that whoever sins through certain malice, sins through habit. For the Philosopher says (*Ethic.* v, 9) that *an unjust action is not done as an unjust man does it*, i.e., through choice, *unless it be done through habit*. Now to sin through certain malice is to sin through making a choice of evil, as stated above (A1). Therefore no one sins through certain malice, unless he has the habit of sin.

OBJ. 2: Further, Origen says (*Peri Archon* iii) that *a man is not suddenly ruined and lost, but must needs fall away little by little*. But the greatest fall seems to be that of the man who sins through certain malice. Therefore a man comes to sin through certain malice, not from the outset, but from inveterate custom, which may engender a habit.

OBJ. 3: Further, whenever a man sins through certain malice, his will must needs be inclined of itself to the evil he chooses. But by the nature of that power man is inclined,

inclinatur homo ad malum, sed magis ad bonum. Ergo oportet, si eligit malum, quod hoc sit ex aliquo supervenienti, quod est passio vel habitus. Sed quando aliquis peccat ex passione, non peccat ex certa malitia, sed ex infirmitate, ut dictum est. Ergo quandocumque aliquis peccat ex certa malitia, oportet quod peccet ex habitu.

SED CONTRA, sicut se habet habitus bonus ad electionem boni, ita habitus malus ad electionem mali. Sed quandoque aliquis non habens habitum virtutis, eligit id quod est bonum secundum virtutem. Ergo etiam quandoque aliquis non habens habitum vitiosum, potest eligere malum, quod est ex certa malitia peccare.

RESPONDEO dicendum quod voluntas aliter se habet ad bonum, et aliter ad malum. Ex natura enim suae potentiae inclinatur ad bonum rationis, sicut ad proprium obiectum, unde et omne peccatum dicitur esse contra naturam. Quod ergo in aliquod malum voluntas eligendo inclinetur, oportet quod aliunde contingat. Et quandoque quidem contingit ex defectu rationis, sicut cum aliquis ex ignorantia peccat, quandoque autem ex impulsu appetitus sensitivi, sicut cum peccat ex passione. Sed neutrum horum est ex certa malitia peccare; sed tunc solum ex certa malitia aliquis peccat, quando ipsa voluntas ex seipsa movetur ad malum. Quod potest contingere dupliciter. Uno quidem modo, per hoc quod homo habet aliquam dispositionem corruptam inclinantem ad malum, ita quod secundum illam dispositionem fit homini quasi conveniens et simile aliquod malum, et in hoc, ratione convenientiae, tendit voluntas quasi in bonum, quia unumquodque secundum se tendit in id quod sibi est conveniens. Talis autem dispositio corrupta vel est aliquis habitus acquisitus ex consuetudine, quae vertitur in naturam, vel est aliqua aegritudinalis habitudo ex parte corporis, sicut aliquis habens quasdam naturales inclinationes ad aliqua peccata, propter corruptionem naturae in ipso. Alio modo contingit quod voluntas per se tendit in aliquod malum, per remotionem alicuius prohibentis. Puta si aliquis prohibeatur peccare non quia peccatum ei secundum se displiceat, sed propter spem vitae aeternae vel propter timorem Gehennae; remota spe per desperationem, vel timore per praesumptionem, sequitur quod ex certa malitia, quasi absque freno, peccet.

Sic igitur patet quod peccatum quod est ex certa malitia, semper praesupponit in homine aliquam inordinationem, quae tamen non semper est habitus. Unde non est necessarium quod quicumque peccat ex certa malitia, peccet ex habitu.

AD PRIMUM ergo dicendum quod operari qualiter iniustus operatur, non solum est operari iniusta ex certa malitia, sed etiam delectabiliter, et sine gravi renisu rationis. Quod non est nisi eius qui habet habitum.

not to evil but to good. Therefore if he chooses evil, this must be due to something supervening, which is passion or habit. Now when a man sins through passion, he sins not through certain malice, but through weakness, as stated (Q77, A3). Therefore whenever anyone sins through certain malice, he sins through habit.

ON THE CONTRARY, The good habit stands in the same relation to the choice of something good, as the bad habit to the choice of something evil. But it happens sometimes that a man, without having the habit of a virtue, chooses that which is good according to that virtue. Therefore sometimes also a man, without having the habit of a vice, may choose evil, which is to sin through certain malice.

I ANSWER THAT, The will is related differently to good and to evil. Because from the very nature of the power, it is inclined to the rational good, as its proper object; wherefore every sin is said to be contrary to nature. Hence, if a will be inclined, by its choice, to some evil, this must be occasioned by something else. Sometimes, in fact, this is occasioned through some defect in the reason, as when anyone sins through ignorance; and sometimes this arises through the impulse of the sensitive appetite, as when anyone sins through passion. Yet neither of these amounts to a sin through certain malice; for then alone does anyone sin through certain malice, when his will is moved to evil of its own accord. This may happen in two ways. First, through his having a corrupt disposition inclining him to evil, so that, in respect of that disposition, some evil is, as it were, suitable and similar to him; and to this thing, by reason of its suitableness, the will tends, as to something good, because everything tends, of its own accord, to that which is suitable to it. Moreover this corrupt disposition is either a habit acquired by custom, or a sickly condition on the part of the body, as in the case of a man who is naturally inclined to certain sins, by reason of some natural corruption in himself. Second, the will, of its own accord, may tend to an evil, through the removal of some obstacle: for instance, if a man be prevented from sinning, not through sin being in itself displeasing to him, but through hope of eternal life, or fear of hell, if hope give place to despair, or fear to presumption, he will end in sinning through certain malice, being freed from the bridle, as it were.

It is evident, therefore, that sin committed through certain malice, always presupposes some inordinateness in man, which, however, is not always a habit: so that it does not follow of necessity, if a man sins through certain malice, that he sins through habit.

REPLY OBJ. 1: To do an action as an unjust man does, may be not only to do unjust things through certain malice, but also to do them with pleasure, and without any notable resistance on the part of reason, and this occurs only in one who has a habit.

AD SECUNDUM dicendum quod non statim ad hoc aliquis labitur quod ex certa malitia peccet, sed praesupponitur aliquid, quod tamen non semper est habitus, ut dictum est.

AD TERTIUM dicendum quod illud propter quod voluntas inclinatur ad malum, non semper habitus est vel passio, sed quaedam alia, ut dictum est.

AD QUARTUM dicendum quod non est similis ratio de electione boni, et de electione mali. Quia malum numquam est sine bono naturae, sed bonum potest esse sine malo culpae perfecte.

REPLY OBJ. 2: It is true that a man does not fall suddenly into sin from certain malice, and that something is presupposed; but this something is not always a habit, as stated above.

REPLY OBJ. 3: That which inclines the will to evil, is not always a habit or a passion, but at times is something else.

MOREOVER, there is no comparison between choosing good and choosing evil: because evil is never without some good of nature, whereas good can be perfect without the evil of fault.

Article 4

Whether It Is More Grievous to Sin Through Certain Malice Than Through Passion?

AD QUARTUM SIC PROCEDITUR. Videtur quod ille qui peccat ex certa malitia, non peccet gravius quam ille qui peccat ex passione. Ignorantia enim excusat peccatum vel in toto vel in parte. Sed maior est ignorantia in eo qui peccat ex certa malitia, quam in eo qui peccat ex passione, nam ille qui peccat ex certa malitia, patitur ignorantiam principii, quae est maxima, ut philosophus dicit, in VII Ethic.; habet enim malam existimationem de fine, qui est principium in operativis. Ergo magis excusatur a peccato qui peccat ex certa malitia, quam ille qui peccat ex passione.

PRAETEREA, quanto aliquis habet maius impellens ad peccandum, tanto minus peccat, sicut patet de eo qui maiori impetu passionis deiicitur in peccatum. Sed ille qui peccat ex certa malitia, impellitur ab habitu, cuius est fortior impulsio quam passionis. Ergo ille qui peccat ex habitu, minus peccat quam ille qui peccat ex passione.

PRAETEREA, peccare ex certa malitia est peccare ex electione mali. Sed ille qui peccat ex passione, etiam eligit malum. Ergo non minus peccat quam ille qui peccat ex certa malitia.

SED CONTRA est quod peccatum quod ex industria committitur, ex hoc ipso graviorem poenam meretur, secundum illud Iob XXXIV, *quasi impios percussit eos in loco videntium, qui quasi de industria recesserunt ab eo.* Sed poena non augetur nisi propter gravitatem culpae. Ergo peccatum ex hoc aggravatur, quod est ex industria, seu certa malitia.

RESPONDEO dicendum quod peccatum quod est ex certa malitia, est gravius peccato quod est ex passione, triplici ratione. Primo quidem quia, cum peccatum principaliter in voluntate consistat, quanto motus peccati est magis proprius voluntati, tanto peccatum est gravius, ceteris paribus. Cum autem ex certa malitia peccatur,

OBJECTION 1: It would seem that it is not more grievous to sin through certain malice than through passion. Because ignorance excuses from sin either altogether or in part. Now ignorance is greater in one who sins through certain malice, than in one who sins through passion; since he that sins through certain malice suffers from the worst form of ignorance, which according to the Philosopher (*Ethic.* vii, 8) is ignorance of principle, for he has a false estimation of the end, which is the principle in matters of action. Therefore there is more excuse for one who sins through certain malice, than for one who sins through passion.

OBJ. 2: Further, the more a man is impelled to sin, the less grievous his sin, as is clear with regard to a man who is thrown headlong into sin by a more impetuous passion. Now he that sins through certain malice, is impelled by habit, the impulse of which is stronger than that of passion. Therefore to sin through habit is less grievous than to sin through passion.

OBJ. 3: Further, to sin through certain malice is to sin through choosing evil. Now he that sins through passion, also chooses evil. Therefore he does not sin less than the man who sins through certain malice.

ON THE CONTRARY, A sin that is committed on purpose, for this very reason deserves heavier punishment, according to Job 34:26: *He hath struck them as being wicked, in open sight, who, as it were, on purpose, have revolted from Him.* Now punishment is not increased except for a graver fault. Therefore a sin is aggravated through being done on purpose, i.e., through certain malice.

I ANSWER THAT, A sin committed through malice is more grievous than a sin committed through passion, for three reasons. First, because, as sin consists chiefly in an act of the will, it follows that, other things being equal, a sin is all the more grievous, according as the movement of the sin belongs more to the will. Now when a sin is committed

motus peccati est magis proprius voluntati, quae ex seipsa in malum movetur, quam quando ex passione peccatur, quasi ex quodam extrinseco impulsu ad peccandum. Unde peccatum ex hoc ipso quod est ex malitia, aggravatur, et tanto magis, quanto fuerit vehementior malitia. Ex eo vero quod est ex passione, diminuitur, et tanto magis, quanto passio fuerit magis vehemens. Secundo, quia passio quae inclinat voluntatem ad peccandum, cito transit, et sic homo cito redit ad bonum propositum, poenitens de peccato. Sed habitus, quo homo ex malitia peccat, est qualitas permanens, et ideo qui ex malitia peccat, diuturnius peccat. Unde philosophus, in VII Ethic., comparat intemperatum, qui peccat ex malitia, infirmo qui continue laborat; incontinentem autem, qui peccat ex passione, ei qui laborat interpolate. Tertio, quia ille qui peccat ex certa malitia, est male dispositus quantum ad ipsum finem, qui est principium in operabilibus. Et sic eius defectus est periculosior quam eius qui ex passione peccat, cuius propositum tendit in bonum finem, licet hoc propositum interrumpatur ad horam propter passionem. Semper autem defectus principii est pessimus. Unde manifestum est quod gravius est peccatum quod est ex malitia, quam quod est ex passione.

AD PRIMUM ergo dicendum quod ignorantia electionis, de qua obiectio procedit, neque excusat neque diminuit peccatum, ut supra dictum est. Unde neque maior ignorantia talis facit esse minus peccatum.

AD SECUNDUM dicendum quod impulsio quae est ex passione, est quasi ex exteriori respectu voluntatis, sed per habitum inclinatur voluntas quasi ab interiori. Unde non est similis ratio.

AD TERTIUM dicendum quod aliud est peccare eligentem, et aliud peccare ex electione. Ille enim qui peccat ex passione, peccat quidem eligens, non tamen ex electione, quia electio non est in eo primum peccati principium, sed inducitur ex passione ad eligendum id quod extra passionem existens non eligeret. Sed ille qui peccat ex certa malitia, secundum se eligit malum, eo modo quo dictum est. Et ideo electio in ipso est principium peccati; et propter hoc dicitur ex electione peccare.

through malice, the movement of sin belongs more to the will, which is then moved to evil of its own accord, than when a sin is committed through passion, when the will is impelled to sin by something extrinsic, as it were. Wherefore a sin is aggravated by the very fact that it is committed through certain malice, and so much the more, as the malice is greater; whereas it is diminished by being committed through passion, and so much the more, as the passion is stronger. Second, because the passion which incites the will to sin, soon passes away, so that man repents of his sin, and soon returns to his good intentions; whereas the habit, through which a man sins, is a permanent quality, so that he who sins through malice, abides longer in his sin. For this reason the Philosopher (*Ethic.* vii, 8) compares the intemperate man, who sins through malice, to a sick man who suffers from a chronic disease, while he compares the incontinent man, who sins through passion, to one who suffers intermittently. Third, because he who sins through certain malice is ill-disposed in respect of the end itself, which is the principle in matters of action; and so the defect is more dangerous than in the case of the man who sins through passion, whose purpose tends to a good end, although this purpose is interrupted on account of the passion, for the time being. Now the worst of all defects is defect of principle. Therefore it is evident that a sin committed through malice is more grievous than one committed through passion.

REPLY OBJ. 1: Ignorance of choice, to which the objection refers, neither excuses nor diminishes a sin, as stated above (Q76, A4). Therefore neither does a greater ignorance of the kind make a sin to be less grave.

REPLY OBJ. 2: The impulse due to passion, is, as it were, due to a defect which is outside the will: whereas, by a habit, the will is inclined from within. Hence the comparison fails.

REPLY OBJ. 3: It is one thing to sin while choosing, and another to sin through choosing. For he that sins through passion, sins while choosing, but not through choosing, because his choosing is not for him the first principle of his sin; for he is induced through the passion, to choose what he would not choose, were it not for the passion. On the other hand, he that sins through certain malice, chooses evil of his own accord, in the way already explained (AA2,3), so that his choosing, of which he has full control, is the principle of his sin: and for this reason he is said to sin *through* choosing.

QUESTION 79

OF THE EXTERNAL CAUSES OF SIN

Deinde considerandum est de causis exterioribus peccati. Et primo, ex parte Dei; secundo, ex parte Diaboli; tertio, ex parte hominis.

Circa primum quaeruntur quatuor.

Primo, utrum Deus sit causa peccati.

Secundo, utrum actus peccati sit a Deo.

Tertio, utrum Deus sit causa excaecationis et obdurationis.

Quarto, utrum haec ordinentur ad salutem eorum qui excaecantur vel obdurantur.

We must now consider the external causes of sin, and (1) on the part of God; (2) on the part of the devil; (3) on the part of man.

Under the first head there are four points of inquiry:

(1) Whether God is a cause of sin?

(2) Whether the act of sin is from God?

(3) Whether God is the cause of spiritual blindness and hardness of heart?

(4) Whether these things are directed to the salvation of those who are blinded or hardened?

Article 1

Whether God Is a Cause of Sin?

AD PRIMUM SIC PROCEDITUR. Videtur quod Deus sit causa peccati. Dicit enim apostolus, Rom. I, de quibusdam, *tradidit eos Deus in reprobum sensum, ut faciant ea quae non conveniunt*. Et Glossa ibidem dicit quod *Deus operatur in cordibus hominum, inclinando voluntates eorum in quodcumque voluerit, sive in bonum sive in malum*. Sed facere quae non conveniunt, et inclinari secundum voluntatem ad malum, est peccatum. Ergo Deus hominibus est causa peccati.

PRAETEREA, Sap. XIV, dicitur, *creaturae Dei in odium factae sunt, et in tentationem animae hominum*. Sed tentatio solet dici provocatio ad peccandum. Cum ergo creaturae non sint factae nisi a Deo, ut in primo habitum est, videtur quod Deus sit causa peccati provocans homines ad peccandum.

PRAETEREA, quidquid est causa causae, est causa effectus. Sed Deus est causa liberi arbitrii, quod est causa peccati. Ergo Deus est causa peccati.

PRAETEREA, omne malum opponitur bono. Sed non repugnat divinae bonitati quod ipse sit causa mali poenae, de isto enim malo dicitur Isaiae XLV, quod *Deus est creans malum*; et Amos III, *si est malum in civitate quod Deus non fecerit?* Ergo etiam divinae bonitati non repugnat quod Deus sit causa culpae.

SED CONTRA, Sap. XI, dicitur de Deo, *nihil odisti eorum quae fecisti*. Odit autem Deus peccatum, secundum illud Sap. XIV, *odio est Deo impius, et impietas eius*. Ergo Deus non est causa peccati.

RESPONDEO dicendum quod homo dupliciter est causa peccati vel sui vel alterius. Uno modo, directe,

OBJECTION 1: It would seem that God is a cause of sin. For the Apostle says of certain ones (Rom 1:28): *God delivered them up to a reprobate sense, to do those things which are not right*, and a gloss comments on this by saying that *God works in men's hearts, by inclining their wills to whatever He wills, whether to good or to evil*. Now sin consists in doing what is not right, and in having a will inclined to evil. Therefore God is to man a cause of sin.

OBJ. 2: Further, it is written (Wis 14:11): *The creatures of God are turned to an abomination; and a temptation to the souls of men*. But a temptation usually denotes a provocation to sin. Since therefore creatures were made by God alone, as was established in the FP, Q44, A1, it seems that God is a cause of sin, by provoking man to sin.

OBJ. 3: Further, the cause of the cause is the cause of the effect. Now God is the cause of the free-will, which itself is the cause of sin. Therefore God is the cause of sin.

OBJ. 4: Further, every evil is opposed to good. But it is not contrary to God's goodness that He should cause the evil of punishment; since of this evil it is written (Isa 45:7) that God creates evil, and (Amos 3:6): *Shall there be evil in the city which God hath not done?* Therefore it is not incompatible with God's goodness that He should cause the evil of fault.

ON THE CONTRARY, It is written (Wis 11:25): *Thou . . . hatest none of the things which Thou hast made*. Now God hates sin, according to Wis. 14:9: *To God the wicked and his wickedness are hateful*. Therefore God is not a cause of sin.

I ANSWER THAT, Man is, in two ways, a cause either of his own or of another's sin. First, directly, namely be

inclinando scilicet voluntatem suam vel alterius ad peccandum. Alio modo, indirecte, dum scilicet non retrahit aliquos a peccato, unde Ezech. III speculatori dicitur, *si non dixeris impio, morte morieris, sanguinem eius de manu tua requiram*. Deus autem non potest esse directe causa peccati vel sui vel alterius. Quia omne peccatum est per recessum ab ordine qui est in ipsum sicut in finem. Deus autem omnia inclinat et convertit in seipsum sicut in ultimum finem, sicut Dionysius dicit, I cap. de Div. Nom. Unde impossibile est quod sit sibi vel aliis causa discedendi ab ordine qui est in ipsum. Unde non potest directe esse causa peccati. Similiter etiam neque indirecte. Contingit enim quod Deus aliquibus non praebet auxilium ad vitandum peccata, quod si praeberet, non peccarent. Sed hoc totum facit secundum ordinem suae sapientiae et iustitiae, cum ipse sit sapientia et iustitia. Unde non imputatur ei quod alius peccat, sicut causae peccati, sicut gubernator non dicitur causa submersionis navis ex hoc quod non gubernat navem, nisi quando subtrahit gubernationem potens et debens gubernare. Et sic patet quod Deus nullo modo est causa peccati.

Ad primum ergo dicendum quod, quantum ad verba apostoli, ex ipso textu patet solutio. Si enim Deus tradit aliquos in reprobum sensum, iam ergo reprobum sensum habent ad faciendum ea quae non conveniunt. Dicitur ergo tradere eos in reprobum sensum, inquantum non prohibet eos quin suum sensum reprobum sequantur, sicut dicimur exponere illos quos non tuemur. Quod autem Augustinus dicit, in libro de gratia et libero arbitrio, unde sumpta est Glossa, quod *Deus inclinat voluntates hominum in bonum et malum*; sic intelligendum est quod in bonum quidem directe inclinat voluntatem, in malum autem inquantum non prohibet, sicut dictum est. Et tamen hoc etiam contingit ex merito praecedentis peccati.

Ad secundum dicendum quod, cum dicitur, *creaturae Dei factae sunt in odium et in tentationem animae hominum*, haec praepositio in non ponitur causaliter, sed consecutive, non enim Deus fecit creaturas ad malum hominum, sed hoc consecutum est propter insipientiam hominum. Unde subditur, *et in muscipulam pedibus insipientium*, qui scilicet per suam insipientiam utuntur creaturis ad aliud quam ad quod factae sunt.

Ad tertium dicendum quod effectus causae mediae procedens ab ea secundum quod subditur ordini causae primae, reducitur etiam in causam primam. Sed si procedat a causa media secundum quod exit ordinem causae primae, non reducitur in causam primam, sicut si minister faciat aliquid contra mandatum domini, hoc non reducitur in dominum sicut in causam. Et similiter peccatum quod liberum arbitrium committit contra praeceptum Dei, non reducitur in Deum sicut in causam.

inclining his or another's will to sin; second, indirectly, namely be not preventing someone from sinning. Hence (Ezek 3:18) it is said to the watchman: *If thou say not to the wicked, 'Thou shalt surely die,' I will require his blood at thy hand*. Now God cannot be directly the cause of sin, either in Himself or in another, since every sin is a departure from the order which is to God as the end: whereas God inclines and turns all things to Himself as to their last end, as Dionysius states (*Div. Nom.* i): so that it is impossible that He should be either to Himself or to another the cause of departing from the order which is to Himself. Therefore He cannot be directly the cause of sin. In like manner neither can He cause sin indirectly. For it happens that God does not give some the assistance, whereby they may avoid sin, which assistance were He to give, they would not sin. But He does all this according to the order of His wisdom and justice, since He Himself is Wisdom and Justice: so that if someone sin it is not imputable to Him as though He were the cause of that sin; even as a pilot is not said to cause the wrecking of the ship, through not steering the ship, unless he cease to steer while able and bound to steer. It is therefore evident that God is nowise a cause of sin.

Reply Obj. 1: As to the words of the Apostle, the solution is clear from the text. For if God delivered some up to a reprobate sense, it follows that they already had a reprobate sense, so as to do what was not right. Accordingly He is said to deliver them up to a reprobate sense, insofar as He does not hinder them from following that reprobate sense, even as we are said to expose a person to danger if we do not protect him. The saying of Augustine (*De Grat. et Lib. Arb.* xxi, whence the gloss quoted is taken) to the effect that *God inclines men's wills to good and evil*, is to be understood as meaning that He inclines the will directly to good; and to evil, insofar as He does not hinder it, as stated above. And yet even this is due as being deserved through a previous sin.

Reply Obj. 2: When it is said the *creatures of God are turned 'to' an abomination, and a temptation to the souls of men*, the preposition *to* does not denote causality but sequel; for God did not make the creatures that they might be an evil to man; this was the result of man's folly, wherefore the text goes on to say, *and a snare to the feet of the unwise*, who, to wit, in their folly, use creatures for a purpose other than that for which they were made.

Reply Obj. 3: The effect which proceeds from the middle cause, according as it is subordinate to the first cause, is reduced to that first cause; but if it proceed from the middle cause, according as it goes outside the order of the first cause, it is not reduced to that first cause: thus if a servant do anything contrary to his master's orders, it is not ascribed to the master as though he were the cause thereof. In like manner sin, which the free-will commits against the commandment of God, is not attributed to God as being its cause.

AD QUARTUM dicendum quod poena opponitur bono eius qui punitur, qui privatur quocumque bono. Sed culpa opponitur bono ordinis qui est in Deum, unde directe opponitur bonitati divinae. Et propter hoc non est similis ratio de culpa et poena.

REPLY OBJ. 4: Punishment is opposed to the good of the person punished, who is thereby deprived of some good or other: but fault is opposed to the good of subordination to God; and so it is directly opposed to the Divine goodness; consequently there is no comparison between fault and punishment.

Article 2

Whether the Act of Sin Is from God?

AD SECUNDUM SIC PROCEDITUR. Videtur quod actus peccati non sit a Deo. Dicit enim Augustinus, in libro de perfectione iustitiae, quod *actus peccati non est res aliqua*. Omne autem quod est a Deo, est res aliqua. Ergo actus peccati non est a Deo.

PRAETEREA, homo non dicitur esse causa peccati nisi quia homo est causa actus peccati, *nullus enim intendens ad malum operatur*, ut Dionysius dicit, IV cap. de Div. Nom. Sed Deus non est causa peccati, ut dictum est. Ergo Deus non est causa actus peccati.

PRAETEREA, aliqui actus secundum suam speciem sunt mali et peccata, ut ex supradictis patet. Sed quidquid est causa alicuius, est causa eius quod convenit ei secundum suam speciem. Si ergo Deus esset causa actus peccati, sequeretur quod esset causa peccati. Sed hoc non est verum, ut ostensum est. Ergo Deus non est causa actus peccati.

SED CONTRA, actus peccati est quidam motus liberi arbitrii. Sed *voluntas Dei est causa omnium motionum*, ut Augustinus dicit, III de Trin. Ergo voluntas Dei est causa actus peccati.

RESPONDEO dicendum quod actus peccati et est ens, et est actus; et ex utroque habet quod sit a Deo. Omne enim ens, quocumque modo sit, oportet quod derivetur a primo ente; ut patet per Dionysium, V cap. de Div. Nom. Omnis autem actio causatur ab aliquo existente in actu, quia nihil agit nisi secundum quod est actu, omne autem ens actu reducitur in primum actum, scilicet Deum, sicut in causam, qui est per suam essentiam actus. Unde relinquitur quod Deus sit causa omnis actionis, inquantum est actio. Sed peccatum nominat ens et actionem cum quodam defectu. Defectus autem ille est ex causa creata, scilicet libero arbitrio, inquantum deficit ab ordine primi agentis, scilicet Dei. Unde defectus iste non reducitur in Deum sicut in causam, sed in liberum arbitrium, sicut defectus claudicationis reducitur in tibiam curvam sicut in causam, non autem in virtutem motivam, a qua tamen causatur quidquid est motionis in claudicatione. Et secundum hoc, Deus est causa actus peccati, non tamen est causa peccati, quia non est causa huius, quod actus sit cum defectu.

OBJECTION 1: It would seem that the act of sin is not from God. For Augustine says (*De Perfect. Justit.* ii) that *the act of sin is not a thing*. Now whatever is from God is a thing. Therefore the act of sin is not from God.

OBJ. 2: Further, man is not said to be the cause of sin, except because he is the cause of the sinful act: for *no one works, intending evil*, as Dionysius states (*Div. Nom.* iv). Now God is not a cause of sin, as stated above (A1). Therefore God is not the cause of the act of sin.

OBJ. 3: Further, some actions are evil and sinful in their species, as was shown above (Q18, AA2,8). Now whatever is the cause of a thing, causes whatever belongs to it in respect of its species. If therefore God caused the act of sin, He would be the cause of sin, which is false, as was proved above (A1). Therefore God is not the cause of the act of sin.

ON THE CONTRARY, The act of sin is a movement of the free-will. Now *the will of God is the cause of every movement*, as Augustine declares (*De Trin.* iii, 4,9). Therefore God's will is the cause of the act of sin.

I ANSWER THAT, The act of sin is both a being and an act; and in both respects it is from God. Because every being, whatever the mode of its being, must be derived from the First Being, as Dionysius declares (*Div. Nom.* v). Again every action is caused by something existing in act, since nothing produces an action save insofar as it is in act; and every being in act is reduced to the First Act, viz., God, as to its cause, Who is act by His Essence. Therefore God is the cause of every action, insofar as it is an action. But sin denotes a being and an action with a defect: and this defect is from the created cause, viz., the free-will, as falling away from the order of the First Agent, viz., God. Consequently this defect is not reduced to God as its cause, but to the free-will: even as the defect of limping is reduced to a crooked leg as its cause, but not to the motive power, which nevertheless causes whatever there is of movement in the limping. Accordingly God is the cause of the act of sin: and yet He is not the cause of sin, because He does not cause the act to have a defect.

AD PRIMUM ergo dicendum quod Augustinus nominat ibi rem id quod est res simpliciter, scilicet substantiam. Sic enim actus peccati non est res.

AD SECUNDUM dicendum quod in hominem sicut in causam reducitur non solum actus, sed etiam ipse defectus, quia scilicet non subditur ei cui debet subdi, licet hoc ipse non intendat principaliter. Et ideo homo est causa peccati. Sed Deus sic est causa actus, quod nullo modo est causa defectus concomitantis actum. Et ideo non est causa peccati.

AD TERTIUM dicendum quod, sicut dictum est supra, actus et habitus non recipiunt speciem ex ipsa privatione, in qua consistit ratio mali; sed ex aliquo obiecto cui coniungitur talis privatio. Et sic ipse defectus, qui dicitur non esse a Deo, pertinet ad speciem actus consequenter, et non quasi differentia specifica.

REPLY OBJ. 1: In this passage Augustine calls by the name of *thing*, that which is a thing simply, viz., substance; for in this sense the act of sin is not a thing.

REPLY OBJ. 2: Not only the act, but also the defect, is reduced to man as its cause, which defect consists in man not being subject to Whom he ought to be, although he does not intend this principally. Wherefore man is the cause of the sin: while God is the cause of the act, in such a way, that nowise is He the cause of the defect accompanying the act, so that He is not the cause of the sin.

REPLY OBJ. 3: As stated above (Q72, A1), acts and habits do not take their species from the privation itself, wherein consists the nature of evil, but from some object, to which that privation is united: and so this defect which consists in not being from God, belongs to the species of the act consequently, and not as a specific difference.

Article 3

Whether God Is the Cause of Spiritual Blindness and Hardness of Heart?

AD TERTIUM SIC PROCEDITUR. Videtur quod Deus non sit causa excaecationis et indurationis. Dicit enim Augustinus, in libro octoginta trium quaest., quod *Deus non est causa eius quod homo sit deterior.* Sed per excaecationem et obdurationem fit homo deterior. Ergo Deus non est causa excaecationis et obdurationis.

PRAETEREA, Fulgentius dicit quod *Deus non est ultor illius rei cuius est auctor.* Sed Deus est ultor cordis obdurati, secundum illud Eccli. III, *cor durum male habebit in novissimo.* Ergo Deus non est causa obdurationis.

PRAETEREA, idem effectus non attribuitur causis contrariis. Sed causa excaecationis dicitur esse malitia hominis, secundum illud Sap. II, *excaecavit enim eos malitia eorum;* et etiam Diabolus, secundum illud II ad Cor. IV, *Deus huius saeculi excaecavit mentes infidelium;* quae quidem causae videntur esse contrariae Deo. Deus ergo non est causa excaecationis et obdurationis.

SED CONTRA est quod dicitur Isaiae VI, *excaeca cor populi huius, et aures eius aggrava.* Et Rom. IX dicitur, *cuius vult, miseretur; et quem vult, indurat.*

RESPONDEO dicendum quod excaecatio et obduratio duo important. Quorum unum est motus animi humani inhaerentis malo, et aversi a divino lumine. Et quantum ad hoc Deus non est causa excaecationis et obdurationis, sicut non est causa peccati. Aliud autem est subtractio gratiae, ex qua sequitur quod mens divinitus non illuminetur ad recte videndum, et cor hominis non

OBJECTION 1: It would seem that God is not the cause of spiritual blindness and hardness of heart. For Augustine says (Qq. lxxxiii, qu. 3) that *God is not the cause of that which makes man worse.* Now man is made worse by spiritual blindness and hardness of heart. Therefore God is not the cause of spiritual blindness and hardness of heart.

OBJ. 2: Further, Fulgentius says (*De Dupl. Praedest.* i, 19): *God does not punish what He causes.* Now God punishes the hardened heart, according to Ecclus. 3:27: *A hard heart shall fear evil at the last.* Therefore God is not the cause of hardness of heart.

OBJ. 3: Further, the same effect is not put down to contrary causes. But the cause of spiritual blindness is said to be the malice of man, according to Wis. 2:21: *For their own malice blinded them,* and again, according to 2 Cor. 4:4: *The god of this world hath blinded the minds of unbelievers:* which causes seem to be opposed to God. Therefore God is not the cause of spiritual blindness and hardness of heart.

ON THE CONTRARY, It is written (Isa 6:10): *Blind the heart of this people, and make their ears heavy,* and Rm. 9:18: *He hath mercy on whom He will, and whom He will He hardeneth.*

I ANSWER THAT, Spiritual blindness and hardness of heart imply two things. One is the movement of the human mind in cleaving to evil, and turning away from the Divine light; and as regards this, God is not the cause of spiritual blindness and hardness of heart, just as He is not the cause of sin. The other thing is the withdrawal of grace, the result of which is that the mind is not enlightened by God to see

emolliatur ad recte vivendum. Et quantum ad hoc Deus est causa excaecationis et obdurationis.

Est autem considerandum quod Deus est causa universalis illuminationis animarum, secundum illud Ioan. I, *erat lux vera quae illuminat omnem hominem venientem in hunc mundum*, sicut sol est universalis causa illuminationis corporum. Aliter tamen et aliter, nam sol agit illuminando per necessitatem naturae; Deus autem agit voluntarie, per ordinem suae sapientiae. Sol autem, licet quantum est de se omnia corpora illuminet, si quod tamen impedimentum inveniat in aliquo corpore, relinquit illud tenebrosum, sicut patet de domo cuius fenestrae sunt clausae. Sed tamen illius obscurationis nullo modo causa est sol, non enim suo iudicio agit ut lumen interius non immittat, sed causa eius est solum ille qui claudit fenestram. Deus autem proprio iudicio lumen gratiae non immittit illis in quibus obstaculum invenit. Unde causa subtractionis gratiae est non solum ille qui ponit obstaculum gratiae, sed etiam Deus, qui suo iudicio gratiam non apponit. Et per hunc modum Deus est causa excaecationis, et aggravationis aurium, et obdurationis cordis.

Quae quidem distinguuntur secundum effectus gratiae, quae et perficit intellectum dono sapientiae, et affectum emollit igne caritatis. Et quia ad cognitionem intellectus maxime deserviunt duo sensus, scilicet visus et auditus, quorum unus deservit inventioni, scilicet visus, alius disciplinae, scilicet auditus, ideo quantum ad visum, ponitur excaecatio; quantum ad auditum, aurium aggravatio; quantum ad affectum, obduratio.

AD PRIMUM ergo dicendum quod, cum excaecatio et induratio, ex parte subtractionis gratiae, sint quaedam poenae, ex hac parte eis homo non fit deterior, sed deterior factus per culpam, haec incurrit, sicut et ceteras poenas.

AD SECUNDUM dicendum quod obiectio illa procedit de obduratione secundum quod est culpa.

AD TERTIUM dicendum quod malitia est causa excaecationis meritoria, sicut culpa est causa poenae. Et hoc etiam modo Diabolus excaecare dicitur, inquantum inducit ad culpam.

aright, and man's heart is not softened to live aright; and as regards this God is the cause of spiritual blindness and hardness of heart.

Now we must consider that God is the universal cause of the enlightening of souls, according to Jn. 1:9: *That was the true light which enlighteneth every man that cometh into this world*, even as the sun is the universal cause of the enlightening of bodies, though not in the same way; for the sun enlightens by necessity of nature, whereas God works freely, through the order of His wisdom. Now although the sun, so far as it is concerned, enlightens all bodies, yet if it be encountered by an obstacle in a body, it leaves it in darkness, as happens to a house whose window-shutters are closed, although the sun is in no way the cause of the house being darkened, since it does not act of its own accord in failing to light up the interior of the house; and the cause of this is the person who closed the shutters. On the other hand, God, of His own accord, withholds His grace from those in whom He finds an obstacle: so that the cause of grace being withheld is not only the man who raises an obstacle to grace; but God, Who, of His own accord, withholds His grace. In this way, God is the cause of spiritual blindness, deafness of ear, and hardness of heart.

These differ from one another in respect of the effects of grace, which both perfects the intellect by the gift of wisdom, and softens the affections by the fire of charity. And since two of the senses excel in rendering service to the intellect, viz., sight and hearing, of which the former assists *discovery*, and the latter, *teaching*, hence it is that spiritual *blindness* corresponds to sight, *heaviness of the ears* to hearing, and *hardness of heart* to the affections.

REPLY OBJ. 1: Blindness and hardheartedness, as regards the withholding of grace, are punishments, and therefore, in this respect, they make man no worse. It is because he is already worsened by sin that he incurs them, even as other punishments.

REPLY OBJ. 2: This argument considers hardheartedness insofar as it is a sin.

REPLY OBJ. 3: Malice is the demeritorious cause of blindness, just as sin is the cause of punishment: and in this way too, the devil is said to blind, insofar as he induces man to sin.

Article 4

Whether Blindness and Hardness of Heart Are Directed to the Salvation of Those Who Are Blinded and Hardened?

AD QUARTUM SIC PROCEDITUR. Videtur quod excaecatio et obduratio semper ordinentur ad salutem eius qui excaecatur et obduratur. Dicit enim Augustinus, in Enchirid., quod *Deus, cum sit summe bonus, nullo modo*

OBJECTION 1: It would seem that blindness and hardness of heart are always directed to the salvation of those who are blinded and hardened. For Augustine says (*Enchiridion* xi) that *as God is supremely good, He would*

permitteret fieri aliquod malum, nisi posset ex quolibet malo elicere bonum. Multo igitur magis ordinat ad bonum illud malum cuius ipse est causa. Sed excaecationis et obdurationis Deus est causa, ut dictum est. Ergo haec ordinantur ad salutem eius qui excaecatur vel induratur.

PRAETEREA, Sap. I dicitur quod *Deus non delectatur in perditione impiorum.* Videretur autem in eorum perditione delectari, si eorum excaecationem in bonum eorum non converteret, sicut medicus videretur delectari in afflictione infirmi, si medicinam amaram, quam infirmo propinat, ad eius sanitatem non ordinaret. Ergo Deus excaecationem convertit in bonum excaecatorum.

PRAETEREA, *Deus non est personarum acceptor,* ut dicitur Act. X. Sed quorundam excaecationem ordinat ad eorum salutem, sicut quorundam Iudaeorum, qui excaecati sunt ut Christo non crederent, et non credentes occiderent, et postmodum compuncti converterentur, sicut de quibusdam legitur Act. II; ut patet per Augustinum, in libro de quaest. Evang. Ergo Deus omnium excaecationem convertit in eorum salutem.

SED CONTRA, non sunt facienda mala ut veniant bona, ut dicitur Rom. III. Sed excaecatio est malum. Ergo Deus non excaecat aliquos propter eorum bonum.

RESPONDEO dicendum quod excaecatio est quoddam praeambulum ad peccatum. Peccatum autem ad duo ordinatur, ad unum quidem per se, scilicet ad damnationem; ad aliud autem ex misericordi Dei providentia, scilicet ad sanationem, inquantum Deus permittit aliquos cadere in peccatum, ut peccatum suum agnoscentes, humilientur et convertantur, sicut Augustinus dicit, in libro de natura et gratia. Unde et excaecatio ex sui natura ordinatur ad damnationem eius qui excaecatur, propter quod etiam ponitur reprobationis effectus, sed ex divina misericordia excaecatio ad tempus ordinatur medicinaliter ad salutem eorum qui excaecantur. Sed haec misericordia non omnibus impenditur excaecatis, *sed praedestinatis solum, quibus omnia cooperantur in bonum,* sicut dicitur Rom. VIII. Unde quantum ad quosdam, excaecatio ordinatur ad sanationem, quantum autem ad alios, ad damnationem, ut Augustinus dicit, in III de quaest. Evang.

AD PRIMUM ergo dicendum quod omnia mala quae Deus facit vel permittit fieri, ordinantur in aliquod bonum, non tamen semper in bonum eius in quo est malum, sed quandoque ad bonum alterius, vel etiam totius universi. Sicut culpam tyrannorum ordinavit in bonum martyrum; et poenam damnatorum ordinat in gloriam suae iustitiae.

nowise allow evil to be done, unless He could draw some good from every evil. Much more, therefore, does He direct to some good, the evil of which He Himself is the cause. Now God is the cause of blindness and hardness of heart, as stated above (A3). Therefore they are directed to the salvation of those who are blinded and hardened.

OBJ. 2: Further, it is written (Wis 1:13) that *God hath no pleasure in the destruction of the ungodly.* Now He would seem to take pleasure in their destruction, if He did not turn their blindness to their profit: just as a physician would seem to take pleasure in torturing the invalid, if he did not intend to heal the invalid when he prescribes a bitter medicine for him. Therefore God turns blindness to the profit of those who are blinded.

OBJ. 3: Further, *God is not a respecter of persons* (Acts 10:34). Now He directs the blinding of some, to their salvation, as in the case of some of the Jews, who were blinded so as not to believe in Christ, and, through not believing, to slay Him, and afterwards were seized with compunction, and converted, as related by Augustine (*De Quaest. Evang.* iii). Therefore God turns all blindness to the spiritual welfare of those who are blinded.

OBJ. 4: On the other hand, according to Rm. 3:8, evil should not be done, that good may ensue. Now blindness is an evil. Therefore God does not blind some for the sake of their welfare.

I ANSWER THAT, Blindness is a kind of preamble to sin. Now sin has a twofold relation—to one thing directly, viz., to the sinner's damnation—to another, by reason of God's mercy or providence, viz., that the sinner may be healed, insofar as God permits some to fall into sin, that by acknowledging their sin, they may be humbled and converted, as Augustine states (*De Nat. et Grat.* xxii). Therefore blindness, of its very nature, is directed to the damnation of those who are blinded; for which reason it is accounted an effect of reprobation. But, through God's mercy, temporary blindness is directed medicinally to the spiritual welfare of those who are blinded. This mercy, however, is not vouchsafed to all those who are blinded, but only to the predestined, to whom *all things work together unto good* (Rom 8:28). Therefore as regards some, blindness is directed to their healing; but as regards others, to their damnation; as Augustine says (*De Quaest. Evang.* iii).

REPLY OBJ. 1: Every evil that God does, or permits to be done, is directed to some good; yet not always to the good of those in whom the evil is, but sometimes to the good of others, or of the whole universe: thus He directs the sin of tyrants to the good of the martyrs, and the punishment of the lost to the glory of His justice.

AD SECUNDUM dicendum quod Deus non delectatur in perditione hominum quantum ad ipsam perditionem, sed ratione suae iustitiae, vel propter bonum quod inde provenit.

AD TERTIUM dicendum quod hoc quod Deus aliquorum excaecationem ordinat in eorum salutem, misericordiae est, quod autem excaecatio aliorum ordinetur ad eorum damnationem, iustitiae est. Quod autem misericordiam quibusdam impendit et non omnibus, non facit personarum acceptionem in Deo, sicut in primo dictum est.

AD QUARTUM dicendum quod mala culpae non sunt facienda ut veniant bona, sed mala poenae sunt inferenda propter bonum.

REPLY OBJ. 2: God does not take pleasure in the loss of man, as regards the loss itself, but by reason of His justice, or of the good that ensues from the loss.

REPLY OBJ. 3: That God directs the blindness of some to their spiritual welfare, is due to His mercy; but that the blindness of others is directed to their loss is due to His justice: and that He vouchsafes His mercy to some, and not to all, does not make God a respecter of persons, as explained in the FP, Q23, A5, ad 3.

REPLY OBJ. 4: Evil of fault must not be done, that good may ensue; but evil of punishment must be inflicted for the sake of good.

QUESTION 80

OF THE CAUSE OF SIN, AS REGARDS THE DEVIL

Deinde considerandum est de causa peccati ex parte Diaboli. Et circa hoc quaeruntur quatuor.

Primo, utrum Diabolus sit directe causa peccati.

Secundo, utrum Diabolus inducat ad peccandum interius persuadendo.

Tertio, utrum possit necessitatem peccandi inducere.

Quarto, utrum omnia peccata ex Diaboli suggestione proveniant.

We must now consider the cause of sin, as regards the devil; and under this head there are four points of inquiry:

(1) Whether the devil is directly the cause of sin?

(2) Whether the devil induces us to sin, by persuading us inwardly?

(3) Whether he can make us sin of necessity?

(4) Whether all sins are due to the devil's suggestion?

Article 1

Whether the Devil Is Directly the Cause of Man's Sinning?

AD PRIMUM SIC PROCEDITUR. Videtur quod Diabolus sit homini directe causa peccandi. Peccatum enim directe in affectu consistit. Sed Augustinus dicit, IV de Trin., quod *Diabolus suae societati malignos affectus inspirat*. Et Beda, super Act., dicit quod *Diabolus animam in affectum malitiae trahit*. Et Isidorus dicit, in libro de summo bono, quod *Diabolus corda hominum occultis cupiditatibus replet*. Ergo Diabolus directe est causa peccati.

PRAETEREA, Hieronymus dicit quod *sicut Deus est perfector boni, ita Diabolus est perfector mali*. Sed Deus est directe causa bonorum nostrorum. Ergo Diabolus est directe causa peccatorum nostrorum.

PRAETEREA, philosophus probat, in quodam cap. Ethicae Eudemicae, quod oportet esse quoddam principium extrinsecum humani consilii. Consilium autem humanum non solum est de bonis, sed etiam de malis. Ergo sicut Deus movet ad consilium bonum, et per hoc directe est causa boni; ita Diabolus movet hominem ad consilium malum, et per hoc sequitur quod Diabolus directe sit causa peccati.

SED CONTRA est quod Augustinus probat, in I et III de Lib. Arb., *quod nulla alia re fit mens hominis serva libidinis, nisi propria voluntate*. Sed homo non fit servus libidinis nisi per peccatum. Ergo causa peccati non potest esse Diabolus, sed sola propria voluntas.

RESPONDEO dicendum quod peccatum actus quidam est. Unde hoc modo potest esse aliquid directe causa peccati, per quem modum aliquis directe est causa alicuius actus. Quod quidem non contingit nisi per hoc quod proprium principium illius actus movet ad agendum. Proprium autem principium actus peccati est

OBJECTION 1: It would seem that the devil is directly the cause of man's sinning. For sin consists directly in an act of the appetite. Now Augustine says (*De Trin.* iv, 12) that *the devil inspires his friends with evil desires*; and Bede, commenting on Acts 5:3, says that the devil *draws the mind to evil desires*; and Isidore says (*De Summo Bono* ii, 41; iii, 5) that the devil *fills men's hearts with secret lusts*. Therefore the devil is directly the cause of sin.

OBJ. 2: Further, Jerome says (*Contra Jovin.* ii, 2) that *as God is the perfecter of good, so is the devil the perfecter of evil*. But God is directly the cause of our good. Therefore the devil is directly the cause of our sins.

OBJ. 3: Further, the Philosopher says in a chapter of the *Eudemian Ethics* (vii, 18): *There must needs be some extrinsic principle of human counsel*. Now human counsel is not only about good things but also about evil things. Therefore, as God moves man to take good counsel, and so is the cause of good, so the devil moves him to take evil counsel, and consequently is directly the cause of sin.

ON THE CONTRARY, Augustine proves (*De Lib. Arb.* i, 11) that *nothing else than his own will makes man's mind the slave of his desire*. Now man does not become a slave to his desires, except through sin. Therefore the cause of sin cannot be the devil, but man's own will alone.

I ANSWER THAT, Sin is an action: so that a thing can be directly the cause of sin, in the same way as anyone is directly the cause of an action; and this can only happen by moving that action's proper principle to act. Now the proper principle of a sinful action is the will, since every sin is

voluntas, quia omne peccatum est voluntarium. Unde nihil potest directe esse causa peccati, nisi quod potest movere voluntatem ad agendum.

Voluntas autem, sicut supra dictum est, a duobus moveri potest, uno modo, ab obiecto, sicut dicitur quod appetibile apprehensum movet appetitum; alio modo, ab eo quod interius inclinat voluntatem ad volendum. Hoc autem non est nisi vel ipsa voluntas, vel Deus, ut supra ostensum est. Deus autem non potest esse causa peccati, ut dictum est. Relinquitur ergo quod ex hac parte sola voluntas hominis sit directe causa peccati eius.

Ex parte autem obiecti, potest intelligi quod aliquid moveat voluntatem tripliciter. Uno modo, ipsum obiectum propositum, sicut dicimus quod cibus excitat desiderium hominis ad comedendum. Alio modo, ille qui proponit vel offert huiusmodi obiectum. Tertio modo, ille qui persuadet obiectum propositum habere rationem boni, quia et hic aliqualiter proponit proprium obiectum voluntati, quod est rationis bonum verum vel apparens. Primo igitur modo, res sensibiles exterius apparentes movent voluntatem hominis ad peccandum, secundo autem et tertio modo, vel Diabolus, vel etiam homo, potest incitare ad peccandum, vel offerendo aliquid appetibile sensui, vel persuadendo rationi. Sed nullo istorum trium modorum potest aliquid esse directa causa peccati, quia voluntas non ex necessitate movetur ab aliquo obiecto nisi ab ultimo fine, ut supra dictum est; unde non est sufficiens causa peccati neque res exterius oblata, neque ille qui eam proponit, neque ille qui persuadet. Unde sequitur quod Diabolus non sit causa peccati directe et sufficienter; sed solum per modum persuadentis, vel proponentis appetibile.

AD PRIMUM ergo dicendum quod omnes illae auctoritates, et si quae similes inveniantur, sunt referendae ad hoc quod Diabolus suggerendo, vel aliqua appetibilia proponendo, inducit in affectum peccati.

AD SECUNDUM dicendum quod similitudo illa est attendenda quantum ad hoc, quod Diabolus quodammodo est causa peccatorum nostrorum, sicut Deus est aliquo modo causa bonorum nostrorum. Non tamen attenditur quantum ad modum causandi, nam Deus causat bona interius movendo voluntatem, quod Diabolo convenire non potest.

AD TERTIUM dicendum quod Deus est universale principium omnis interioris motus humani, sed quod determinetur ad malum consilium voluntas humana, hoc directe quidem est ex voluntate humana; et a Diabolo per modum persuadentis, vel appetibilia proponentis.

voluntary. Consequently nothing can be directly the cause of sin, except that which can move the will to act.

Now the will, as stated above (Q9, AA3,4,6), can be moved by two things: first by its object, inasmuch as the apprehended appetible is said to move the appetite: second by that agent which moves the will inwardly to will, and this is no other than the will itself, or God, as was shown above (Q9, AA3,4,6). Now God cannot be the cause of sin, as stated above (Q79, A1). Therefore it follows that in this respect, a man's will alone is directly the cause of his sin.

As regards the object, a thing may be understood as moving the will in three ways. First, the object itself which is proposed to the will: thus we say that food arouses man's desire to eat. Second, he that proposes or offers this object. Third, he that persuades the will that the object proposed has an aspect of good, because he also, in a fashion, offers the will its proper object, which is a real or apparent good of reason. Accordingly, in the first way the sensible things, which approach from without, move a man's will to sin. In the second and third ways, either the devil or a man may incite to sin, either by offering an object of appetite to the senses, or by persuading the reason. But in none of these three ways can anything be the direct cause of sin, because the will is not, of necessity, moved by any object except the last end, as stated above (Q10, AA1,2). Consequently neither the thing offered from without, nor he that proposes it, nor he that persuades, is the sufficient cause of sin. Therefore it follows that the devil is a cause of sin, neither directly nor sufficiently, but only by persuasion, or by proposing the object of appetite.

REPLY OBJ. 1: All these, and other like authorities, if we meet with them, are to be understood as denoting that the devil induces man to affection for a sin, either by suggesting to him, or by offering him objects of appetite.

REPLY OBJ. 2: This comparison is true insofar as the devil is somewhat the cause of our sins, even as God is in a certain way the cause of our good actions, but does not extend to the mode of causation: for God causes good things in us by moving the will inwardly, whereas the devil cannot move us in this way.

REPLY OBJ. 3: God is the universal principle of all inward movements of man; but that the human will be determined to an evil counsel, is directly due to the human will, and to the devil as persuading or offering the object of appetite.

Article 2

Whether the Devil Can Induce Man to Sin, by Internal Instigations?

AD SECUNDUM SIC PROCEDITUR. Videtur quod Diabolus non possit inducere ad peccandum interius instigando. Interiores enim motus animae sunt quaedam opera vitae. Sed nullum opus vitae potest esse nisi a principio intrinseco; nec etiam opus animae vegetabilis, quod est infimum inter opera vitae. Ergo Diabolus secundum interiores motus non potest hominem instigare ad malum.

PRAETEREA, omnes interiores motus, secundum ordinem naturae, a sensibus exterioribus oriuntur. Sed praeter ordinem naturae aliquid operari est solius Dei, ut in primo dictum est. Ergo Diabolus non potest in interioribus motibus hominis aliquid operari, nisi secundum ea quae exterioribus sensibus apparent.

PRAETEREA, interiores actus animae sunt intelligere et imaginari. Sed quantum ad neutrum horum potest Diabolus aliquid operari. Quia, ut in primo habitum est, Diabolus non imprimit in intellectum humanum. In phantasiam etiam videtur quod imprimere non possit, quia formae imaginatae, tanquam magis spirituales, sunt digniores quam formae quae sunt in materia sensibili; quas tamen Diabolus imprimere non potest, ut patet ex his quae in primo habita sunt. Ergo Diabolus non potest secundum interiores motus inducere hominem ad peccatum.

SED CONTRA est quia secundum hoc nunquam tentaret hominem nisi visibiliter apparendo. Quod patet esse falsum.

RESPONDEO dicendum quod interior pars animae est intellectiva et sensitiva. Intellectiva autem continet intellectum et voluntatem. Et de voluntate quidem iam dictum est quomodo ad eam Diabolus se habet. Intellectus autem per se quidem movetur ab aliquo illuminante ipsum ad cognitionem veritatis, quod Diabolus circa hominem non intendit, sed magis obtenebrare rationem ipsius ad consentiendum peccato. Quae quidem obtenebratio provenit ex phantasia et appetitu sensitivo. Unde tota interior operatio Diaboli esse videtur circa phantasiam et appetitum sensitivum. Quorum utrumque commovendo, potest inducere ad peccatum, potest enim operari ad hoc quod imaginationi aliquae formae imaginariae praesententur; potest etiam facere quod appetitus sensitivus concitetur ad aliquam passionem.

Dictum est enim in primo libro quod natura corporalis spirituali naturaliter obedit ad motum localem. Unde et Diabolus omnia illa causare potest quae ex motu locali corporum inferiorum provenire possunt, nisi virtute divina reprimatur. Quod autem aliquae formae repraesententur imaginationi, consequitur quandoque

OBJECTION 1: It would seem that the devil cannot induce man to sin, by internal instigations. Because the internal movements of the soul are vital functions. Now no vital functions can be exercised except by an intrinsic principle, not even those of the vegetal soul, which are the lowest of vital functions. Therefore the devil cannot instigate man to evil through his internal movements.

OBJ. 2: Further, all the internal movements arise from the external senses according to the order of nature. Now it belongs to God alone to do anything beside the order of nature, as was stated in the FP, Q110, A4. Therefore the devil cannot effect anything in man's internal movements, except in respect of things which are perceived by the external senses.

OBJ. 3: Further, the internal acts of the soul are to understand and to imagine. Now the devil can do nothing in connection with either of these, because, as stated in the FP, Q111, AA2,3, ad 2, the devil cannot impress species on the human intellect, nor does it seem possible for him to produce imaginary species, since imaginary forms, being more spiritual, are more excellent than those which are in sensible matter, which, nevertheless, the devil is unable to produce, as is clear from what we have said in the FP, Q110, A2; FP, Q111, AA2,3, ad 2. Therefore the devil cannot through man's internal movements induce him to sin.

ON THE CONTRARY, In that case, the devil would never tempt man, unless he appeared visibly; which is evidently false.

I ANSWER THAT, The interior part of the soul is intellective and sensitive; and the intellective part contains the intellect and the will. As regards the will, we have already stated (A1; FP, Q111, A1) what is the devil's relation thereto. Now the intellect, of its very nature, is moved by that which enlightens it in the knowledge of truth, which the devil has no intention of doing in man's regard; rather does he darken man's reason so that it may consent to sin, which darkness is due to the imagination and sensitive appetite. Consequently the operation of the devil seems to be confined to the imagination and sensitive appetite, by moving either of which he can induce man to sin. For his operation may result in presenting certain forms to the imagination; and he is able to incite the sensitive appetite to some passion or other.

The reason of this is, that as stated in the FP, Q110, A3, the corporeal nature has a natural aptitude to be moved locally by the spiritual nature: so that the devil can produce all those effects which can result from the local movement of bodies here below, except he be restrained by the Divine power. Now the representation of forms to the imagination

ad motum localem. Dicit enim philosophus, in libro de somno et vigilia, quod *cum animal dormierit, descendente plurimo sanguine ad principium sensitivum, simul descendunt motus, sive impressiones relictae ex sensibilium motionibus, quae in sensibilibus speciebus conservantur, et movent principium apprehensivum, ita quod apparent ac si tunc principium sensitivum a rebus ipsis exterioribus immutaretur.* Unde talis motus localis spirituum vel humorum potest procurari a Daemonibus, sive dormiant sive vigilent homines, et sic sequitur quod homo aliqua imaginetur.

Similiter etiam appetitus sensitivus concitatur ad aliquas passiones secundum quendam determinatum motum cordis et spirituum. Unde ad hoc etiam Diabolus potest cooperari. Et ex hoc quod passiones aliquae concitantur in appetitu sensitivo, sequitur quod et motum sive intentionem sensibilem praedicto modo reductam ad principium apprehensivum, magis homo percipiat, quia, ut philosophus in eodem libro dicit, *amantes modica similitudine in apprehensionem rei amatae moventur.* Contingit etiam ex hoc quod passio est concitata, ut id quod proponitur imaginationi, iudicetur prosequendum, quia ei qui a passione detinetur, videtur esse bonum id ad quod per passionem inclinatur. Et per hunc modum Diabolus interius inducit ad peccandum.

AD PRIMUM ergo dicendum quod opera vitae semper etsi sint ab aliquo principio intrinseco, tamen ad ea potest cooperari aliquod exterius agens, sicut etiam ad opera animae vegetabilis operatur calor exterior, ut facilius digeratur cibus.

AD SECUNDUM dicendum quod huiusmodi apparitio formarum imaginabilium non est omnino praeter ordinem naturae. Nec est per solum imperium, sed per motum localem, ut dictum est.

UNDE PATET responsio ad tertium, quia formae illae sunt a sensibus acceptae primordialiter.

is due, sometimes, to local movement: for the Philosopher says (*De Somno et Vigil.*) that *when an animal sleeps, the blood descends in abundance to the sensitive principle, and the movements descend with it, viz., the impressions left by the action of sensible objects, which impressions are preserved by means of sensible species, and continue to move the apprehensive principle, so that they appear just as though the sensitive principles were being affected by them at the time.* Hence such a local movement of the vital spirits or humors can be procured by the demons, whether man sleep or wake: and so it happens that man's imagination is brought into play.

In like manner, the sensitive appetite is incited to certain passions according to certain fixed movements of the heart and the vital spirits: wherefore the devil can cooperate in this also. And through certain passions being aroused in the sensitive appetite, the result is that man more easily perceives the movement or sensible image which is brought in the manner explained, before the apprehensive principle, since, as the Philosopher observes (*De Somno et Vigil.*: De Insomn. iii, iv), *lovers are moved, by even a slight likeness, to an apprehension of the beloved.* It also happens, through the rousing of a passion, that what is put before the imagination, is judged, as being something to be pursued, because, to him who is held by a passion, whatever the passion inclines him to, seems good. In this way the devil induces man inwardly to sin.

REPLY OBJ. 1: Although vital functions are always from an intrinsic principle, yet an extrinsic agent can cooperate with them, even as external heat cooperates with the functions of the vegetal soul, that food may be more easily digested.

REPLY OBJ. 2: This apparition of imaginary forms is not altogether outside the order of nature, nor is it due to a command alone, but according to local movement, as explained above.

CONSEQUENTLY the Reply to the Third Objection is clear, because these forms are received originally from the senses.

Article 3

Whether the Devil Can Induce Man to Sin of Necessity?

AD TERTIUM SIC PROCEDITUR. Videtur quod Diabolus possit necessitatem inferre ad peccandum. Potestas enim maior potest necessitatem inferre minori. Sed de Diabolo dicitur Iob XLI, *non est potestas super terram quae ei valeat comparari.* Ergo potest homini terreno necessitatem inferre ad peccandum.

PRAETEREA, ratio hominis non potest moveri nisi secundum ea quae exterius sensibus proponuntur et imaginationi repraesentantur, quia omnis nostra

OBJECTION 1: It would seem that the devil can induce man to sin of necessity. Because the greater can compel the lesser. Now it is said of the devil (Job 41:24) that *there is no power on earth that can compare with him.* Therefore he can compel man to sin, while he dwells on the earth.

OBJ. 2: Further, man's reason cannot be moved except in respect of things that are offered outwardly to the senses, or are represented to the imagination: because *all our*

cognitio ortum habet a sensu, *et non est intelligere sine phantasmate*, ut dicitur in libro de anima. Sed Diabolus potest movere imaginationem hominis, ut dictum est, et etiam exteriores sensus, dicit enim Augustinus, in libro octoginta trium quaest., quod *serpit hoc malum*, scilicet quod est a Diabolo, *per omnes aditus sensuales; dat se figuris, accommodat coloribus, adhaeret sonis, infundit saporibus*. Ergo potest rationem hominis ex necessitate inclinare ad peccandum.

PRAETEREA, secundum Augustinum, *nonnullum peccatum est, cum caro concupiscit adversus spiritum*. Sed concupiscentiam carnis Diabolus potest causare, sicut et ceteras passiones, eo modo quo supra dictum est. Ergo ex necessitate potest inducere ad peccandum.

SED CONTRA est quod dicitur I Petr. ult., *adversarius vester Diabolus tanquam leo rugiens circuit, quaerens quem devoret, cui resistite fortes in fide*. Frustra autem talis admonitio daretur, si homo ei ex necessitate succumberet. Non ergo potest homini necessitatem inducere ad peccandum.

RESPONDEO dicendum quod Diabolus propria virtute, nisi refraenetur a Deo, potest aliquem inducere ex necessitate ad faciendum aliquem actum qui de suo genere peccatum est, non autem potest inducere necessitatem peccandi. Quod patet ex hoc quod homo motivo ad peccandum non resistit nisi per rationem, cuius usum totaliter impedire potest movendo imaginationem et appetitum sensitivum, sicut in arreptitiis patet. Sed tunc, ratione sic ligata, quidquid homo agat, non imputatur ei ad peccatum. Sed si ratio non sit totaliter ligata, ex ea parte qua est libera, potest resistere peccato, sicut supra dictum est. Unde manifestum est quod Diabolus nullo modo potest necessitatem inducere homini ad peccandum.

AD PRIMUM ergo dicendum quod non quaelibet potestas maior homine, potest movere voluntatem hominis, sed solus Deus, ut supra habitum est.

AD SECUNDUM dicendum quod illud quod est apprehensum per sensum vel imaginationem, non ex necessitate movet voluntatem, si homo habeat usum rationis. Nec semper huiusmodi apprehensio ligat rationem.

AD TERTIUM dicendum quod concupiscentia carnis contra spiritum, quando ratio ei actualiter resistit, non est peccatum, sed materia exercendae virtutis. Quod autem ratio ei non resistat, non est in potestate Diaboli. Et ideo non potest inducere necessitatem peccati.

knowledge arises from the senses, and we cannot understand without a phantasm (*De Anima* iii, text. 30. 39). Now the devil can move man's imagination, as stated above (A2); and also the external senses, for Augustine says (*Qq. lxxxiii*, qu. 12) that *this evil*, of which, to wit, the devil is the cause, *extends gradually through all the approaches to the senses, it adapts itself to shapes, blends with colors, mingles with sounds, seasons every flavor*. Therefore it can incline man's reason to sin of necessity.

OBJ. 3: Further, Augustine says (*De Civ. Dei* xix, 4) that *there is some sin when the flesh lusteth against the spirit*. Now the devil can cause concupiscence of the flesh, even as other passions, in the way explained above (A2). Therefore he can induce man to sin of necessity.

ON THE CONTRARY, It is written (1 Pet 5:8): *Your adversary the devil, as a roaring lion, goeth about seeking whom he may devour*. Now it would be useless to admonish thus, if it were true that man were under the necessity of succumbing to the devil. Therefore he cannot induce man to sin of necessity.

I ANSWER THAT, The devil, by his own power, unless he be restrained by God, can compel anyone to do an act which, in its genus, is a sin; but he cannot bring about the necessity of sinning. This is evident from the fact that man does not resist that which moves him to sin, except by his reason; the use of which the devil is able to impede altogether, by moving the imagination and the sensitive appetite; as is the case with one who is possessed. But then, the reason being thus fettered, whatever man may do, it is not imputed to him as a sin. If, however, the reason is not altogether fettered, then, insofar as it is free, it can resist sin, as stated above (Q77, A7). It is consequently evident that the devil can nowise compel man to sin.

REPLY OBJ. 1: Not every power that is greater than man, can move man's will; God alone can do this, as stated above (Q9, A6).

REPLY OBJ. 2: That which is apprehended by the senses or the imagination does not move the will, of necessity, so long as man has the use of reason; nor does such an apprehension always fetter the reason.

REPLY OBJ. 3: The lusting of the flesh against the spirit, when the reason actually resists it, is not a sin, but is matter for the exercise of virtue. That reason does not resist, is not in the devil's power; wherefore he cannot bring about the necessity of sinning.

Article 4

Whether All the Sins of Men Are Due to the Devil's Suggestion?

AD QUARTUM SIC PROCEDITUR. Videtur quod omnia peccata hominum sint ex suggestione Diaboli. Dicit enim Dionysius, IV cap. de Div. Nom., quod *multitudo Daemonum causa est omnium malorum et sibi et aliis.*

PRAETEREA, quicumque peccat mortaliter, efficitur servus Diaboli; secundum illud Ioan. VIII, *qui facit peccatum, servus est peccati. Sed ei aliquis in servitutem addicitur, a quo superatus est*, ut dicitur II Petr. II. Ergo quicumque facit peccatum, superatus est a Diabolo.

PRAETEREA, Gregorius dicit quod peccatum Diaboli est irreparabile, quia cecidit nullo suggerente. Si igitur aliqui homines peccarent per liberum arbitrium, nullo suggerente, eorum peccatum esset irremediabile, quod patet esse falsum. Ergo omnia peccata humana a Diabolo suggeruntur.

SED CONTRA est quod dicitur in libro de ecclesiasticis dogmatibus, *non omnes cogitationes nostrae malae a Diabolo excitantur, sed aliquoties ex nostri arbitrii motu emergunt.*

RESPONDEO dicendum quod occasionaliter quidem et indirecte Diabolus est causa omnium peccatorum nostrorum, inquantum induxit primum hominem ad peccandum, ex cuius peccato intantum vitiata est humana natura, ut omnes simus ad peccandum proclives, sicut diceretur esse causa combustionis lignorum qui ligna siccaret, ex quo sequeretur quod facile incenderentur. Directe autem non est causa omnium peccatorum humanorum, ita quod singula peccata persuadeat. Quod Origenes probat ex hoc, quia etiam si Diabolus non esset, homines haberent appetitum cibi et venereorum et similium, qui posset esse inordinatus nisi ratione ordinaretur, quod subiacet libero arbitrio.

AD PRIMUM ergo dicendum quod multitudo Daemonum est causa omnium malorum nostrorum secundum primam originem, ut dictum est.

AD SECUNDUM dicendum quod non solum fit servus alicuius qui ab eo superatur, sed etiam qui se ei voluntarie subiicit. Et hoc modo fit servus Diaboli qui motu proprio peccat.

AD TERTIUM dicendum quod peccatum Diaboli fuit irremediabile, quia nec aliquo suggerente peccavit, nec habuit aliquam pronitatem ad peccandum ex praecedenti suggestione causatam. Quod de nullo hominis peccato dici potest.

OBJECTION 1: It would seem that all the sins of men are due to the devil's suggestion. For Dionysius says (*Div. Nom.* iv) that the *crowd of demons are the cause of all evils, both to themselves and to others.*

OBJ. 2: Further, whoever sins mortally, becomes the slave of the devil, according to Jn. 8:34: *Whosoever committeth sin is the slave of sin.* Now *by whom a man is overcome, of the same also he is the slave* (2 Pet 2:19). Therefore whoever commits a sin, has been overcome by the devil.

OBJ. 3: Further, Gregory says (*Moral.* iv, 10) the sin of the devil is irreparable, because he sinned at no other's suggestion. Therefore, if any men were to sin of their own free-will and without suggestion from any other, their sin would be irremediable: which is clearly false. Therefore all the sins of men are due to the devil's suggestion.

ON THE CONTRARY, It is written (*De Eccl. Dogm.* lxxxii): *Not all our evil thoughts are incited by the devil; sometimes they are due to a movement of the free-will.*

I ANSWER THAT, the devil is the occasional and indirect cause of all our sins, insofar as he induced the first man to sin, by reason of whose sin human nature is so infected, that we are all prone to sin: even as the burning of wood might be imputed to the man who dried the wood so as to make it easily inflammable. He is not, however, the direct cause of all the sins of men, as though each were the result of his suggestion. Origen proves this (*Peri Archon* iii, 2) from the fact that even if the devil were no more, men would still have the desire for food, sexual pleasures and the like; which desire might be inordinate, unless it were subordinate to reason, a matter that is subject to the free-will.

REPLY OBJ. 1: The crowd of demons are the cause of all our evils, as regards their original cause, as stated.

REPLY OBJ. 2: A man becomes another's slave not only by being overcome by him, but also by subjecting himself to him spontaneously: it is thus that one who sins of his own accord, becomes the slave of the devil.

REPLY OBJ. 3: The devil's sin was irremediable, not only because he sinned without another's suggestion; but also because he was not already prone to sin, on account of any previous sin; which can be said of no sin of man.

QUESTION 81

OF THE CAUSE OF SIN, ON THE PART OF MAN

Deinde considerandum est de causa peccati ex parte hominis. Cum autem homo sit causa peccati alteri homini exterius suggerendo, sicut et Diabolus, habet quendam specialem modum causandi peccatum in alterum per originem. Unde de peccato originali dicendum est. Circa quod tria consideranda occurrunt, primo, de eius traductione; secundo, de eius essentia; tertio, de eius subiecto.

    Circa primum quaeruntur quinque.

    Primo, utrum primum peccatum hominis derivetur per originem in posteros.

    Secundo, utrum omnia alia peccata primi parentis, vel etiam aliorum parentum, per originem in posteros deriventur.

    Tertio, utrum peccatum originale derivetur ad omnes qui ex Adam per viam seminis generantur.

    Quarto, utrum derivaretur ad illos qui miraculose ex aliqua parte humani corporis formarentur.

    Quinto, utrum si femina peccasset, viro non peccante, traduceretur originale peccatum.

We must now consider the cause of sin, on the part of man. Now, while man, like the devil, is the cause of another's sin, by outward suggestion, he has a certain special manner of causing sin, by way of origin. Wherefore we must speak about original sin, the consideration of which will be three-fold: (1) Of its transmission; (2) of its essence; (3) of its subject.

Under the first head there are five points of inquiry:

(1) Whether man's first sin is transmitted, by way of origin to his descendants?

(2) Whether all the other sins of our first parent, or of any other parents, are transmitted to their descendants, by way of origin?

(3) Whether original sin is contracted by all those who are begotten of Adam by way of seminal generation?

(4) Whether it would be contracted by anyone formed miraculously from some part of the human body?

(5) Whether original sin would have been contracted if the woman, and not the man, had sinned?

Article 1

Whether the First Sin of Our First Parent Is Contracted by His Descendants, by Way of Origin?

AD PRIMUM SIC PROCEDITUR. Videtur quod primum peccatum primi parentis non traducatur ad alios per originem. Dicitur enim Ezech. XVIII, *filius non portabit iniquitatem patris.* Portaret autem, si ab eo iniquitatem traheret. Ergo nullus trahit ab aliquo parentum per originem aliquod peccatum.

PRAETEREA, accidens non traducitur per originem, nisi traducto subiecto, eo quod accidens non transit de subiecto in subiectum. Sed anima rationalis, quae est subiectum culpae, non traducitur per originem, ut in primo ostensum est. Ergo neque aliqua culpa per originem traduci potest.

PRAETEREA, omne illud quod traducitur per originem humanam, causatur ex semine. Sed semen non potest causare peccatum, eo quod caret rationali parte animae, quae sola potest esse causa peccati. Ergo nullum peccatum potest trahi per originem.

PRAETEREA, quod est perfectius in natura, virtuosius est ad agendum. Sed caro perfecta non potest inficere animam sibi unitam, alioquin anima non posset

OBJECTION 1: It would seem that the first sin of our first parent is not contracted by others, by way of origin. For it is written (Ezek 18:20): *The son shall not bear the iniquity of the father.* But he would bear the iniquity if he contracted it from him. Therefore no one contracts any sin from one of his parents by way of origin.

OBJ. 2: Further, an accident is not transmitted by way of origin, unless its subject be also transmitted, since accidents do not pass from one subject to another. Now the rational soul which is the subject of sin, is not transmitted by way of origin, as was shown in the FP, Q118, A2. Therefore neither can any sin be transmitted by way of origin.

OBJ. 3: Further, whatever is transmitted by way of human origin, is caused by the semen. But the semen cannot cause sin, because it lacks the rational part of the soul, which alone can be a cause of sin. Therefore no sin can be contracted by way of origin.

OBJ. 4: Further, that which is more perfect in nature, is more powerful in action. Now perfect flesh cannot infect the soul united to it, else the soul could not be cleansed of

emundari a culpa originali dum est carni unita. Ergo multo minus semen potest inficere animam.

PRAETEREA, philosophus dicit, in III Ethic., quod *propter naturam turpes nullus increpat, sed eos qui propter desidiam et negligentiam.* Dicuntur autem natura turpes qui habent turpitudinem ex sua origine. Ergo nihil quod est per originem, est increpabile, neque peccatum.

SED CONTRA est quod apostolus dicit, Rom. V, *per unum hominem peccatum in hunc mundum intravit.* Quod non potest intelligi per modum imitationis, propter hoc quod dicitur Sap. II, *invidia Diaboli mors intravit in orbem terrarum.* Restat ergo quod per originem a primo homine peccatum in mundo intravit.

RESPONDEO dicendum quod secundum fidem Catholicam est tenendum quod primum peccatum primi hominis originaliter transit in posteros. Propter quod etiam pueri mox nati deferuntur ad Baptismum, tanquam ab aliqua infectione culpae abluendi. Contrarium autem est haeresis Pelagianae, ut patet per Augustinum in plurimis suis libris.

Ad investigandum autem qualiter peccatum primi parentis originaliter possit transire in posteros, diversi diversis viis processerunt. Quidam enim, considerantes quod peccati subiectum est anima rationalis, posuerunt quod cum semine rationalis anima traducatur, ut sic ex infecta anima animae infectae derivari videantur. Alii vero, hoc repudiantes tanquam erroneum, conati sunt ostendere quomodo culpa animae parentis traducitur in prolem, etiam si anima non traducatur, per hoc quod corporis defectus traducuntur a parente in prolem, sicut si leprosus generat leprosum, et podagricus podagricum, propter aliquam corruptionem seminis, licet talis corruptio non dicatur lepra vel podagra. Cum autem corpus sit proportionatum animae, et defectus animae redundent in corpus, et e converso; simili modo dicunt quod culpabilis defectus animae per traductionem seminis in prolem derivatur, quamvis semen actualiter non sit culpae subiectum.

Sed omnes huiusmodi viae insufficientes sunt. Quia dato quod aliqui defectus corporales a parente transeant in prolem per originem; et etiam aliqui defectus animae ex consequenti, propter corporis indispositionem, sicut interdum ex fatuis fatui generantur, tamen hoc ipsum quod est ex origine aliquem defectum habere, videtur excludere rationem culpae, de cuius ratione est quod sit voluntaria. Unde etiam posito quod anima rationalis traduceretur, ex hoc ipso quod infectio animae prolis non esset in eius voluntate, amitteret rationem culpae obligantis ad poenam, quia, ut philosophus dicit in III Ethic., *nullus improperabit caeco nato, sed magis miserebitur.*

original sin, so long as it is united to the body. Much less, therefore, can the semen infect the soul.

OBJ. 5: Further, the Philosopher says (*Ethic.* iii, 5): *No one finds fault with those who are ugly by nature, but only those who are so through want of exercise and through carelessness.* Now those are said to be *naturally ugly,* who are so from their origin. Therefore nothing which comes by way of origin is blameworthy or sinful.

ON THE CONTRARY, The Apostle says (Rom 5:12): *By one man sin entered into this world, and by sin death.* Nor can this be understood as denoting imitation or suggestion, since it is written (Wis 2:24): *By the envy of the devil, death came into this world.* It follows therefore that through origin from the first man sin entered into the world.

I ANSWER THAT, According to the Catholic Faith we are bound to hold that the first sin of the first man is transmitted to his descendants, by way of origin. For this reason children are taken to be baptized soon after their birth, to show that they have to be washed from some uncleanness. The contrary is part of the Pelagian heresy, as is clear from Augustine in many of his books

In endeavoring to explain how the sin of our first parent could be transmitted by way of origin to his descendants, various writers have gone about it in various ways. For some, considering that the subject of sin is the rational soul, maintained that the rational soul is transmitted with the semen, so that thus an infected soul would seem to produce other infected souls. Others, rejecting this as erroneous, endeavored to show how the guilt of the parent's soul can be transmitted to the children, even though the soul be not transmitted, from the fact that defects of the body are transmitted from parent to child—thus a leper may beget a leper, or a gouty man may be the father of a gouty son, on account of some seminal corruption, although this corruption is not leprosy or gout. Now since the body is proportionate to the soul, and since the soul's defects redound into the body, and vice versa, in like manner, say they, a culpable defect of the soul is passed on to the child, through the transmission of the semen, albeit the semen itself is not the subject of the guilt.

But all these explanations are insufficient. Because, granted that some bodily defects are transmitted by way of origin from parent to child, and granted that even some defects of the soul are transmitted in consequence, on account of a defect in the bodily habit, as in the case of idiots begetting idiots; nevertheless the fact of having a defect by the way of origin seems to exclude the notion of guilt, which is essentially something voluntary. Wherefore granted that the rational soul were transmitted, from the very fact that the stain on the child's soul is not in its will, it would cease to be a guilty stain binding its subject to punishment; for, as the Philosopher says (*Ethic.* iii, 5), *no one reproaches a man born blind; one rather takes pity on him.*

Et ideo alia via procedendum est, dicendo quod omnes homines qui nascuntur ex Adam, possunt considerari ut unus homo, inquantum conveniunt in natura, quam a primo parente accipiunt; secundum quod in civilibus omnes qui sunt unius communitatis, reputantur quasi unum corpus, et tota communitas quasi unus homo. Porphyrius etiam dicit quod *participatione speciei plures homines sunt unus homo*. Sic igitur multi homines ex Adam derivati, sunt tanquam multa membra unius corporis. Actus autem unius membri corporalis, puta manus, non est voluntarius voluntate ipsius manus, sed voluntate animae, quae primo movet membra. Unde homicidium quod manus committit, non imputaretur manui ad peccatum, si consideraretur manus secundum se ut divisa a corpore, sed imputatur ei inquantum est aliquid hominis quod movetur a primo principio motivo hominis. Sic igitur inordinatio quae est in isto homine, ex Adam generato, non est voluntaria voluntate ipsius sed voluntate primi parentis, qui movet motione generationis omnes qui ex eius origine derivantur, sicut voluntas animae movet omnia membra ad actum. Unde peccatum quod sic a primo parente in posteros derivatur, dicitur originale, sicut peccatum quod ab anima derivatur ad membra corporis, dicitur actuale. Et sicut peccatum actuale quod per membrum aliquod committitur, non est peccatum illius membri nisi inquantum illud membrum est aliquid ipsius hominis, propter quod vocatur peccatum humanum; ita peccatum originale non est peccatum huius personae, nisi inquantum haec persona recipit naturam a primo parente. Unde et vocatur peccatum naturae; secundum illud Ephes. II, *eramus natura filii irae*.

AD PRIMUM ergo dicendum quod filius dicitur non portare peccatum patris, quia non punitur pro peccato patris, nisi sit particeps culpae. Et sic est in proposito, derivatur enim per originem culpa a patre in filium, sicut et peccatum actuale per imitationem.

AD SECUNDUM dicendum quod, etsi anima non traducatur, quia virtus seminis non potest causare animam rationalem; movet tamen ad ipsam dispositive. Unde per virtutem seminis traducitur humana natura a parente in prolem, et simul cum natura naturae infectio, ex hoc enim fit iste qui nascitur consors culpae primi parentis, quod naturam ab eo sortitur per quandam generativam motionem.

AD TERTIUM dicendum quod, etsi culpa non sit actu in semine, est tamen ibi virtute humana natura, quam concomitatur talis culpa.

AD QUARTUM dicendum quod semen est principium generationis, quae est proprius actus naturae, eius propagationi deserviens. Et ideo magis inficitur anima

Therefore we must explain the matter otherwise by saying that all men born of Adam may be considered as one man, inasmuch as they have one common nature, which they receive from their first parents; even as in civil matters, all who are members of one community are reputed as one body, and the whole community as one man. Indeed Porphyry says (*Praedic., De Specie*) that *by sharing the same species, many men are one man*. Accordingly the multitude of men born of Adam, are as so many members of one body. Now the action of one member of the body, of the hand for instance, is voluntary not by the will of that hand, but by the will of the soul, the first mover of the members. Wherefore a murder which the hand commits would not be imputed as a sin to the hand, considered by itself as apart from the body, but is imputed to it as something belonging to man and moved by man's first moving principle. In this way, then, the disorder which is in this man born of Adam, is voluntary, not by his will, but by the will of his first parent, who, by the movement of generation, moves all who originate from him, even as the soul's will moves all the members to their actions. Hence the sin which is thus transmitted by the first parent to his descendants is called *original*, just as the sin which flows from the soul into the bodily members is called *actual*. And just as the actual sin that is committed by a member of the body, is not the sin of that member, except inasmuch as that member is a part of the man, for which reason it is called a *human sin*; so original sin is not the sin of this person, except inasmuch as this person receives his nature from his first parent, for which reason it is called the *sin of nature*, according to Eph. 2:3: *We . . . were by nature children of wrath.*

REPLY OBJ. 1: The son is said not to bear the iniquity of his father, because he is not punished for his father's sin, unless he share in his guilt. It is thus in the case before us: because guilt is transmitted by the way of origin from father to son, even as actual sin is transmitted through being imitated.

REPLY OBJ. 2: Although the soul is not transmitted, because the power in the semen is not able to cause the rational soul, nevertheless the motion of the semen is a disposition to the transmission of the rational soul: so that the semen by its own power transmits the human nature from parent to child, and with that nature, the stain which infects it: for he that is born is associated with his first parent in his guilt, through the fact that he inherits his nature from him by a kind of movement which is that of generation.

REPLY OBJ. 3: Although the guilt is not actually in the semen, yet human nature is there virtually accompanied by that guilt.

REPLY OBJ. 4: The semen is the principle of generation, which is an act proper to nature, by helping it to propagate itself. Hence the soul is more infected by the semen, than

per semen quam per carnem iam perfectam, quae iam determinata est ad personam.

AD QUINTUM dicendum quod illud quod est per originem, non est increpabile, si consideretur iste qui nascitur secundum se. Sed si consideretur prout refertur ad aliquod principium, sic potest esse ei increpabile, sicut aliquis qui nascitur patitur ignominiam generis ex culpa alicuius progenitorum causatam.

by the flesh which is already perfect, and already affixed to a certain person.

REPLY OBJ. 5: A man is not blamed for that which he has from his origin, if we consider the man born, in himself. But if we consider him as referred to a principle, then he may be reproached for it: thus a man may from his birth be under a family disgrace, on account of a crime committed by one of his forbears.

Article 2

Whether Also Other Sins of the First Parent or of Nearer Ancestors Are Transmitted to Their Descendants?

AD SECUNDUM SIC PROCEDITUR. Videtur quod etiam alia peccata vel ipsius primi parentis, vel proximorum parentum, traducantur in posteros. Poena enim nunquam debetur nisi culpae. Sed aliqui puniuntur iudicio divino pro peccato proximorum parentum; secundum illud Exod. XX, *ego sum Deus Zelotes, visitans iniquitatem patrum in filios, in tertiam et quartam generationem.* Iudicio etiam humano, in crimine laesae maiestatis, filii exheredantur pro peccato parentum. Ergo etiam culpa proximorum parentum transit ad posteros.

PRAETEREA, magis potest transferre in alterum id quod habet aliquis a seipso, quam id quod habet ex alio, sicut ignis magis potest calefacere quam aqua calefacta, sed homo transfert in prolem per originem peccatum quod habet ab Adam. Ergo multo magis peccatum quod ipse commisit.

PRAETEREA, ideo contrahimus a primo parente peccatum originale, quia in eo fuimus sicut in principio naturae, quam ipse corrupit. Sed similiter fuimus in proximis parentibus sicut in quibusdam principiis naturae, quae etsi sit corrupta, potest adhuc magis corrumpi per peccatum, secundum illud Apoc. ult., *qui in sordibus est, sordescat adhuc.* Ergo filii contrahunt peccata proximorum parentum per originem, sicut et primi parentis.

SED CONTRA, bonum est magis diffusivum sui quam malum. Sed merita proximorum parentum non traducuntur ad posteros. Ergo multo minus peccata.

RESPONDEO dicendum quod Augustinus hanc quaestionem movet in Enchiridio, et insolutam relinquit. Sed si quis diligenter attendit, impossibile est quod aliqua peccata proximorum parentum, vel etiam primi parentis praeter primum, per originem traducantur. Cuius ratio est quia homo generat sibi idem in specie, non autem secundum individuum. Et ideo ea quae directe pertinent ad individuum, sicut personales actus et quae ad eos pertinent, non traducuntur a parentibus in filios, non enim

OBJECTION 1: It would seem that also other sins, whether of the first parent or of nearer ancestors, are transmitted to their descendants. For punishment is never due unless for fault. Now some are punished by the judgment of God for the sin of their immediate parents, according to Ex. 20:5: *I am . . . God . . . jealous, visiting the iniquity of the fathers upon the children, unto the third and fourth generation.* Furthermore, according to human law, the children of those who are guilty of high treason are disinherited. Therefore the guilt of nearer ancestors is also transmitted to their descendants.

OBJ. 2: Further, a man can better transmit to another, that which he has of himself, than that which he has received from another: thus fire heats better than hot water does. Now a man transmits to his children, by the way, of origin, the sin which he has from Adam. Much more therefore should he transmit the sin which he has contracted of himself.

OBJ. 3: Further, the reason why we contract original sin from our first parent is because we were in him as in the principle of our nature, which he corrupted. But we were likewise in our nearer ancestors, as in principles of our nature, which however it be corrupt, can be corrupted yet more by sin, according to Apoc. 22:11: *He that is filthy, let him be filthier still.* Therefore children contract, by the way of origin, the sins of their nearer ancestors, even as they contract the sin of their first parent.

ON THE CONTRARY, Good is more self-diffusive than evil. But the merits of the nearer ancestors are not transmitted to their descendants. Much less therefore are their sins.

I ANSWER THAT, Augustine puts this question in the *Enchiridion* xlvi, xlvii, and leaves it unsolved. Yet if we look into the matter carefully we shall see that it is impossible for the sins of the nearer ancestors, or even any other but the first sin of our first parent to be transmitted by way of origin. The reason is that a man begets his like in species but not in individual. Consequently those things that pertain directly to the individual, such as personal actions and matters affecting them, are not transmitted by parents to

grammaticus traducit in filium scientiam grammaticae, quam proprio studio acquisivit. Sed ea quae pertinent ad naturam speciei, traducuntur a parentibus in filios, nisi sit defectus naturae, sicut oculatus generat oculatum, nisi natura deficiat. Et si natura sit fortis, etiam aliqua accidentia individualia propagantur in filios, pertinentia ad dispositionem naturae, sicut velocitas corporis, bonitas ingenii, et alia huiusmodi, nullo autem modo ea quae sunt pure personalia, ut dictum est.

Sicut autem ad personam pertinet aliquid secundum seipsam, et aliquid ex dono gratiae; ita etiam ad naturam potest aliquid pertinere secundum seipsam, scilicet quod causatur ex principiis eius, et aliquid ex dono gratiae. Et hoc modo iustitia originalis, sicut in primo dictum est, erat quoddam donum gratiae toti humanae naturae divinitus collatum in primo parente. Quod quidem primus homo amisit per primum peccatum. Unde sicut illa originalis iustitia traducta fuisset in posteros simul cum natura, ita etiam inordinatio opposita. Sed alia peccata actualia vel primi parentis vel aliorum, non corrumpunt naturam quantum ad id quod naturae est; sed solum quantum ad id quod personae est, idest secundum pronitatem ad actum. Unde alia peccata non traducuntur.

Ad primum ergo dicendum quod poena spirituali, sicut Augustinus dicit in epistola ad avitum, nunquam puniuntur filii pro parentibus, nisi communicent in culpa, vel per originem vel per imitationem, quia omnes animae immediate sunt Dei, ut dicitur Ezech. XVIII. Sed poena corporali interdum, iudicio divino vel humano, puniuntur filii pro parentibus, inquantum filius est aliquid patris secundum corpus.

Ad secundum dicendum quod illud quod habet aliquis ex se, magis potest traducere, dummodo sit traducibile. Sed peccata actualia proximorum parentum non sunt traducibilia, quia sunt pure personalia, ut dictum est.

Ad tertium dicendum quod primum peccatum corrumpit naturam humanam corruptione ad naturam pertinente, alia vero peccata corrumpunt eam corruptione pertinente ad solam personam.

their children: for a grammarian does not transmit to his son the knowledge of grammar that he has acquired by his own studies. On the other hand, those things that concern the nature of the species, are transmitted by parents to their children, unless there be a defect of nature: thus a man with eyes begets a son having eyes, unless nature fails. And if nature be strong, even certain accidents of the individual pertaining to natural disposition, are transmitted to the children, e.g., fleetness of body, acuteness of intellect, and so forth; but nowise those that are purely personal, as stated above.

Now just as something may belong to the person as such, and also something through the gift of grace, so may something belong to the nature as such, viz., whatever is caused by the principles of nature, and something too through the gift of grace. In this way original justice, as stated in the FP, Q100, A1, was a gift of grace, conferred by God on all human nature in our first parent. This gift the first man lost by his first sin. Wherefore as that original justice together with the nature was to have been transmitted to his posterity, so also was its disorder. Other actual sins, however, whether of the first parent or of others, do not corrupt the nature as nature, but only as the nature of that person, i.e., in respect of the proneness to sin: and consequently other sins are not transmitted.

Reply Obj. 1: According to Augustine in his letter to Avitus, children are never inflicted with spiritual punishment on account of their parents, unless they share in their guilt, either in their origin, or by imitation, because every soul is God's immediate property, as stated in Ezech. 18:4. Sometimes, however, by Divine or human judgment, children receive bodily punishment on their parents' account, inasmuch as the child, as to its body, is part of its father.

Reply Obj. 2: A man can more easily transmit that which he has of himself, provided it be transmissible. But the actual sins of our nearer ancestors are not transmissible, because they are purely personal, as stated above.

Reply Obj. 3: The first sin infects nature with a human corruption pertaining to nature; whereas other sins infect it with a corruption pertaining only to the person.

Article 3

Whether the Sin of the First Parent Is Transmitted, by the Way of Origin, to All Men?

Ad tertium sic proceditur. Videtur quod peccatum primi parentis non transeat per originem in omnes homines. Mors enim est poena consequens originale peccatum. Sed non omnes qui procedunt seminaliter ex

Objection 1: It would seem that the sin of the first parent is not transmitted, by the way of origin, to all men. Because death is a punishment consequent upon original sin. But not all those, who are born of the seed of Adam,

Adam, morientur, illi enim qui vivi reperientur in adventu domini, nunquam morientur, ut videtur per quod dicitur I Thessal. IV, *nos qui vivimus, non praeveniemus in adventu domini eos qui dormierunt.* Ergo illi non contrahunt originale peccatum.

PRAETEREA, nullus dat alteri quod ipse non habet. Sed homo baptizatus non habet peccatum originale. Ergo non traducit ipsum in prolem.

PRAETEREA, donum Christi est maius quam peccatum Adae, ut apostolus dicit, Rom. V. Sed donum Christi non transit in omnes homines. Ergo nec peccatum Adae.

SED CONTRA est quod apostolus dicit, Rom. V, *mors in omnes pertransiit, in quo omnes peccaverunt.*

RESPONDEO dicendum quod secundum fidem Catholicam firmiter est tenendum quod omnes homines, praeter solum Christum, ex Adam derivati, peccatum originale ex eo contrahunt, alioquin non omnes indigerent redemptione quae est per Christum; quod est erroneum. Ratio autem sumi potest ex hoc quod supra dictum est, quod sic ex peccato primi parentis traducitur culpa originalis in posteros, sicut a voluntate animae per motionem membrorum traducitur peccatum actuale ad membra corporis. Manifestum est autem quod peccatum actuale traduci potest ad omnia membra quae nata sunt moveri a voluntate. Unde et culpa originalis traducitur ad omnes illos qui moventur ab Adam motione generationis.

AD PRIMUM ergo dicendum quod probabilius et communius tenetur quod omnes illi qui in adventu domini reperientur, morientur, et post modicum resurgent, ut in tertio plenius dicetur. Si tamen hoc verum sit quod alii dicunt, quod illi nunquam morientur, sicut Hieronymus narrat diversorum opiniones in quadam epistola ad Minerium, de resurrectione carnis; dicendum est ad argumentum, quod illi etsi non moriantur, est tamen in eis reatus mortis, sed poena aufertur a Deo, qui etiam peccatorum actualium poenas condonare potest.

AD SECUNDUM dicendum quod peccatum originale per Baptismum aufertur reatu, inquantum anima recuperat gratiam quantum ad mentem. Remanet tamen peccatum originale actu quantum ad fomitem, qui est inordinatio inferiorum partium animae et ipsius corporis, secundum quod homo generat, et non secundum mentem. Et ideo baptizati traducunt peccatum originale, non enim generant inquantum sunt renovati per Baptismum, sed inquantum retinent adhuc aliquid de vetustate primi peccati.

AD TERTIUM dicendum quod, sicut peccatum Adae traducitur in omnes qui ab Adam corporaliter generantur, ita gratia Christi traducitur in omnes qui ab eo spiritualiter generantur per fidem et Baptismum, et non

will die: since those who will be still living at the coming of our Lord, will never die, as, seemingly, may be gathered from 1 Thess. 4:14: *We who are alive . . . unto the coming of the Lord, shall not prevent them who have slept.* Therefore they do not contract original sin.

OBJ. 2: Further, no one gives another what he has not himself. Now a man who has been baptized has not original sin. Therefore he does not transmit it to his children.

OBJ. 3: Further, the gift of Christ is greater than the sin of Adam, as the Apostle declares (Rom 5:15, seqq). But the gift of Christ is not transmitted to all men: neither, therefore, is the sin of Adam.

ON THE CONTRARY, The Apostle says (Rom 5:12): *Death passed upon all men in whom all have sinned.*

I ANSWER THAT, According to the Catholic Faith we must firmly believe that, Christ alone excepted, all men descended from Adam contract original sin from him; else all would not need redemption which is through Christ; and this is erroneous. The reason for this may be gathered from what has been stated (A1), viz., that original sin, in virtue of the sin of our first parent, is transmitted to his posterity, just as, from the soul's will, actual sin is transmitted to the members of the body, through their being moved by the will. Now it is evident that actual sin can be transmitted to all such members as have an inborn aptitude to be moved by the will. Therefore original sin is transmitted to all those who are moved by Adam by the movement of generation.

REPLY OBJ. 1: It is held with greater probability and more commonly that all those that are alive at the coming of our Lord, will die, and rise again shortly, as we shall state more fully in the TP (XP, Q78, A1, OBJ1). If, however, it be true, as others hold, that they will never die, (an opinion which Jerome mentions among others in a letter to Minerius, on the Resurrection of the Body—*Ep. cxix*), then we must say in reply to the objection, that although they are not to die, the debt of death is nonetheless in them, and that the punishment of death will be remitted by God, since He can also forgive the punishment due for actual sins.

REPLY OBJ. 2: Original sin is taken away by Baptism as to the guilt, insofar as the soul recovers grace as regards the mind. Nevertheless original sin remains in its effect as regards the *fomes*, which is the disorder of the lower parts of the soul and of the body itself, in respect of which, and not of the mind, man exercises his power of generation. Consequently those who are baptized transmit original sin: since they do not beget as being renewed in Baptism, but as still retaining something of the oldness of the first sin.

REPLY OBJ. 3: Just as Adam's sin is transmitted to all who are born of Adam corporally, so is the grace of Christ transmitted to all that are begotten of Him spiritually, by faith and Baptism: and this, not only unto the removal of

solum ad removendam culpam primi parentis, sed etiam ad removendum peccata actualia, et ad introducendum in gloriam.

Article 4

Whether Original Sin Would Be Contracted by a Person Formed Miraculously from Human Flesh?

Ad quartum sic proceditur. Videtur quod, si aliquis formaretur ex carne humana miraculose, contraheret originale peccatum. Dicit enim quaedam Glossa Gen. IV, quod *in lumbis Adae fuit tota posteritas corrupta, quia non est separata prius in loco vitae, sed postea in loco exilii.* Sed si aliquis homo sic formaretur sicut dictum est, caro eius separaretur in loco exilii. Ergo contraheret originale peccatum.

Praeterea, peccatum originale causatur in nobis inquantum anima inficitur ex carne. Sed caro tota hominis est infecta. Ergo ex quacumque parte carnis homo formaretur, anima eius inficeretur infectione originalis peccati.

Praeterea, peccatum originale a primo parente pervenit in omnes, inquantum omnes in eo peccante fuerunt. Sed illi qui ex carne humana formarentur, in Adam fuissent. Ergo peccatum originale contraherent.

Sed contra est quia non fuissent in Adam secundum seminalem rationem; quod solum causat traductionem peccati originalis, ut Augustinus dicit, X super Gen. ad Litt.

Respondeo dicendum quod, sicut iam dictum est, peccatum originale a primo parente traducitur in posteros, inquantum moventur ab ipso per generationem, sicut membra moventur ab anima ad peccatum actuale. Non autem est motio ad generationem nisi per virtutem activam in generatione. Unde illi soli peccatum originale contrahunt, qui ab Adam descendunt per virtutem activam in generatione originaliter ab Adam derivatam, quod est secundum seminalem rationem ab eo descendere, nam ratio seminalis nihil aliud est quam vis activa in generatione. Si autem aliquis formaretur virtute divina ex carne humana, manifestum est quod vis activa non derivaretur ab Adam. Unde non contraheret peccatum originale, sicut nec actus manus pertineret ad peccatum humanum, si manus non moveretur a voluntate hominis, sed ab aliquo extrinseco movente.

Ad primum ergo dicendum quod Adam non fuit in loco exilii nisi post peccatum. Unde non propter locum exilii, sed propter peccatum, traducitur originalis culpa ad eos ad quos activa eius generatio pervenit.

Objection 1: It would seem that original sin would be contracted by a person formed miraculously from human flesh. For a gloss on Gn. 4:1 says that *Adam's entire posterity was corrupted in his loins, because they were not severed from him in the place of life, before he sinned, but in the place of exile after he had sinned.* But if a man were to be formed in the aforesaid manner, his flesh would be severed in the place of exile. Therefore it would contract original sin.

Obj. 2: Further, original sin is caused in us by the soul being infected through the flesh. But man's flesh is entirely corrupted. Therefore a man's soul would contract the infection of original sin, from whatever part of the flesh it was formed.

Obj. 3: Further, original sin comes upon all from our first parent, insofar as we were all in him when he sinned. But those who might be formed out of human flesh, would have been in Adam. Therefore they would contract original sin.

On the contrary, They would not have been in Adam *according to seminal virtue,* which alone is the cause of the transmission of original sin, as Augustine states (*Gen ad lit.* x, 18, seqq.).

I answer that, As stated above (AA1,3), original sin is transmitted from the first parent to his posterity, inasmuch as they are moved by him through generation, even as the members are moved by the soul to actual sin. Now there is no movement to generation except by the active power of generation: so that those alone contract original sin, who are descended from Adam through the active power of generation originally derived from Adam, i.e., who are descended from him through seminal power; for the seminal power is nothing else than the active power of generation. But if anyone were to be formed by God out of human flesh, it is evident that the active power would not be derived from Adam. Consequently he would not contract original sin: even as a hand would have no part in a human sin, if it were moved, not by the man's will, but by some external power.

Reply Obj. 1: Adam was not in the place of exile until after his sin. Consequently it is not on account of the place of exile, but on account of the sin, that original sin is transmitted to those to whom his active generation extends.

Ad secundum dicendum quod caro non inficit animam nisi inquantum est principium activum in generatione, ut dictum est.

Ad tertium dicendum quod ille qui formaretur ex carne humana, fuisset in Adam secundum corpulentam substantiam; sed non secundum seminalem rationem, ut dictum est. Et ideo non contraheret originale peccatum.

Reply Obj. 2: The flesh does not corrupt the soul, except insofar as it is the active principle in generation, as we have stated.

Reply Obj. 3: If a man were to be formed from human flesh, he would have been in Adam, *by way of bodily substance*, but not according to seminal virtue, as stated above. Therefore he would not contract original sin.

Article 5

Whether If Eve, and Not Adam, Had Sinned, Their Children Would Have Contracted Original Sin?

Ad quintum sic proceditur. Videtur quod, si Adam non peccasset, Eva peccante, filii originale peccatum contraherent. Peccatum enim originale a parentibus contrahimus, inquantum in eis fuimus, secundum illud apostoli, Rom. V, *in quo omnes peccaverunt.* Sed sicut homo praeexistit in patre suo, ita in matre. Ergo ex peccato matris homo peccatum originale contraheret, sicut et ex peccato patris.

Praeterea, si Eva peccasset, Adam non peccante, filii passibiles et mortales nascerentur, mater enim dat materiam in generatione, ut dicit philosophus, in II de Generat. Animal.; mors autem, et omnis passibilitas, provenit ex necessitate materiae. Sed passibilitas et necessitas moriendi sunt poena peccati originalis. Ergo, si Eva peccasset, Adam non peccante, filii contraherent originale peccatum.

Praeterea, Damascenus dicit, in libro III, quod Spiritus Sanctus praevenit in virginem, de qua Christus erat absque peccato originali nasciturus, purgans eam. Sed illa purgatio non fuisset necessaria, si infectio originalis peccati non traheretur ex matre. Ergo infectio originalis peccati ex matre trahitur. Et sic, Eva peccante, eius filii peccatum originale contraherent, etiam si Adam non peccasset.

Sed contra est quod apostolus dicit, Rom. V, *per unum hominem peccatum in hunc mundum intravit.* Magis autem fuisset dicendum quod per duos intrasset, cum ambo peccaverint; vel potius per mulierem, quae primo peccavit; si femina peccatum originale in prolem transmitteret. Non ergo peccatum originale derivatur in filios a matre, sed a patre.

Respondeo dicendum quod huius dubitationis solutio ex praemissis apparet. Dictum est enim supra quod peccatum originale a primo parente traducitur inquantum ipse movet ad generationem natorum, unde dictum est quod, si materialiter tantum aliquis ex carne humana generaretur, originale peccatum non contraheret. Manifestum est autem secundum doctrinam philosophorum,

Objection 1: It would seem that if Eve, and not Adam, had sinned, their children would have contracted original sin. Because we contract original sin from our parents, insofar as we were once in them, according to the word of the Apostle (Rom 5:12): *In whom all have sinned.* Now a man pre-exist in his mother as well as in his father. Therefore a man would have contracted original sin from his mother's sin as well as from his father's.

Obj. 2: Further, if Eve, and not Adam, had sinned, their children would have been born liable to suffering and death, since it is *the mother* that *provides the matter in generation* as the Philosopher states (*De Gener. Animal.* ii, 1,4), when death and liability to suffering are the necessary results of matter. Now liability to suffering and the necessity of dying are punishments of original sin. Therefore if Eve, and not Adam, had sinned, their children would contract original sin.

Obj. 3: Further, Damascene says (*De Fide Orth.* iii, 3) that *the Holy Spirit came upon the Virgin,* (of whom Christ was to be born without original sin) *purifying her.* But this purification would not have been necessary, if the infection of original sin were not contracted from the mother. Therefore the infection of original sin is contracted from the mother: so that if Eve had sinned, her children would have contracted original sin, even if Adam had not sinned.

On the contrary, The Apostle says (Rom 5:12): *By one man sin entered into this world.* Now if the woman would have transmitted original sin to her children, he should have said that it entered by two, since both of them sinned, or rather that it entered by a woman, since she sinned first. Therefore original sin is transmitted to the children, not by the mother, but by the father.

I answer that, The solution of this question is made clear by what has been said. For it has been stated (A1) that original sin is transmitted by the first parent insofar as he is the mover in the begetting of his children: wherefore it has been said (A4) that if anyone were begotten materially only, of human flesh, they would not contract original sin. Now it is evident that in the opinion of philosophers, the

quod principium activum in generatione est a patre, materiam autem mater ministrat. Unde peccatum originale non contrahitur a matre, sed a patre. Et secundum hoc, si, Adam non peccante, Eva peccasset, filii originale peccatum non contraherent. E converso autem esset, si Adam peccasset, et Eva non peccasset.

AD PRIMUM ergo dicendum quod in patre praeexistit filius sicut in principio activo, sed in matre sicut in principio materiali et passivo. Unde non est similis ratio.

AD SECUNDUM dicendum quod quibusdam videtur quod, Eva peccante, si Adam non peccasset, filii essent immunes a culpa, paterentur tamen necessitatem moriendi, et alias passibilitates provenientes ex necessitate materiae, quam mater ministrat, non sub ratione poenae, sed sicut quosdam naturales defectus. Sed hoc non videtur conveniens. Immortalitas enim et impassibilitas primi status non erat ex conditione materiae, ut in primo dictum est; sed ex originali iustitiae, per quam corpus subdebatur animae, quandiu anima esset subiecta Deo. Defectus autem originalis iustitiae est peccatum originale. Si igitur, Adam non peccante, peccatum originale non transfunderetur in posteros propter peccatum Evae; manifestum est quod in filiis non esset defectus originalis iustitiae. Unde non esset in eis passibilitas vel necessitas moriendi.

AD TERTIUM dicendum quod illa purgatio praeveniens in beata virgine, non requirebatur ad auferendum transfusionem originalis peccati, sed quia oportebat ut mater Dei maxima puritate niteret. Non enim est aliquid digne receptaculum Dei, nisi sit mundum; secundum illud Psalmi XCII, *domum tuam, domine, decet sanctitudo.*

active principle of generation is from the father, while the mother provides the matter. Therefore original sin, is contracted, not from the mother, but from the father: so that, accordingly, if Eve, and not Adam, had sinned, their children would not contract original sin: whereas, if Adam, and not Eve, had sinned, they would contract it.

REPLY OBJ. 1: The child pre-exists in its father as in its active principle, and in its mother, as in its material and passive principle. Consequently the comparison fails.

REPLY OBJ. 2: Some hold that if Eve, and not Adam, had sinned, their children would be immune from the sin, but would have been subject to the necessity of dying and to other forms of suffering that are a necessary result of the matter which is provided by the mother, not as punishments, but as actual defects. This, however, seems unreasonable. Because, as stated in the FP, Q97, AA1, 2, ad 4, immortality and impassibility, in the original state, were a result, not of the condition of matter, but of original justice, whereby the body was subjected to the soul, so long as the soul remained subject to God. Now privation of original justice is original sin. If, therefore, supposing Adam had not sinned, original sin would not have been transmitted to posterity on account of Eve's sin; it is evident that the children would not have been deprived of original justice: and consequently they would not have been liable to suffer and subject to the necessity of dying.

REPLY OBJ. 3: This prevenient purification in the Blessed Virgin was not needed to hinder the transmission of original sin, but because it behooved the Mother of God *to shine with the greatest purity.* For nothing is worthy to receive God unless it be pure, according to Ps. 92:5: *Holiness becometh Thy House, O Lord.*

QUESTION 82

OF ORIGINAL SIN, AS TO ITS ESSENCE

Deinde considerandum est de peccato originali quantum ad suam essentiam. Et circa hoc quaeruntur quatuor.

Primo, utrum originale peccatum sit habitus.
Secundo, utrum sit unum tantum in uno homine.
Tertio, utrum sit concupiscentia.
Quarto, utrum sit aequaliter in omnibus.

We must now consider original sin as to its essence, and under this head there are four points of inquiry:

(1) Whether original sin is a habit?
(2) Whether there is but one original sin in each man?
(3) Whether original sin is concupiscence?
(4) Whether original sin is equally in all?

Article 1

Whether Original Sin Is a Habit?

AD PRIMUM SIC PROCEDITUR. Videtur quod originale peccatum non sit habitus. Originale enim peccatum est carentia originalis iustitiae, ut Anselmus dicit, in libro de concepto virginali, et sic originale peccatum est quaedam privatio. Sed privatio opponitur habitui. Ergo originale peccatum non est habitus.

PRAETEREA, actuale peccatum habet plus de ratione culpae quam originale, inquantum habet plus de ratione voluntarii. Sed habitus actualis peccati non habet rationem culpae, alioquin sequeretur quod homo dormiens culpabiliter, peccaret. Ergo nullus habitus originalis habet rationem culpae.

PRAETEREA, in malis actus semper praecedit habitum, nullus enim habitus malus est infusus, sed acquisitus. Sed originale peccatum non praecedit aliquis actus. Ergo originale peccatum non est habitus.

SED CONTRA est quod Augustinus dicit, in libro de Baptismo puerorum, quod secundum peccatum originale parvuli sunt concupiscibiles, etsi non sint actu concupiscentes. Sed habilitas dicitur secundum aliquem habitum. Ergo peccatum originale est habitus.

RESPONDEO dicendum quod, sicut supra dictum est, duplex est habitus. Unus quidem quo inclinatur potentia ad agendum, sicut scientiae et virtutes habitus dicuntur. Et hoc modo peccatum originale non est habitus. Alio modo dicitur habitus dispositio alicuius naturae ex multis compositae, secundum quam bene se habet vel male ad aliquid, et praecipue cum talis dispositio versa fuerit quasi in naturam, ut patet de aegritudine et sanitate. Et hoc modo peccatum originale est habitus. Est enim quaedam inordinata dispositio proveniens ex dissolutione illius harmoniae in qua consistebat ratio originalis iustitiae, sicut etiam aegritudo corporalis est quaedam inordinata dispositio corporis, secundum quam solvitur

OBJECTION 1: It would seem that original sin is not a habit. For original sin is the absence of original justice, as Anselm states (*De Concep. Virg.* ii, iii, xxvi), so that original sin is a privation. But privation is opposed to habit. Therefore original sin is not a habit.

OBJ. 2: Further, actual sin has the nature of fault more than original sin, insofar as it is more voluntary. Now the habit of actual sin has not the nature of a fault, else it would follow that a man while asleep, would be guilty of sin. Therefore no original habit has the nature of a fault.

OBJ. 3: Further, in wickedness act always precedes habit, because evil habits are not infused, but acquired. Now original sin is not preceded by an act. Therefore original sin is not a habit.

ON THE CONTRARY, Augustine says in his book on the Baptism of infants (*De Pecc. Merit. et Remiss.* i, 39) that on account of original sin little children have the aptitude of concupiscence though they have not the act. Now aptitude denotes some kind of habit. Therefore original sin is a habit.

I ANSWER THAT, As stated above (Q49, A4; Q50, A1), habit is twofold. The first is a habit whereby power is inclined to an act: thus science and virtue are called habits. In this way original sin is not a habit. The second kind of habit is the disposition of a complex nature, whereby that nature is well or ill disposed to something, chiefly when such a disposition has become like a second nature, as in the case of sickness or health. In this sense original sin is a habit. For it is an inordinate disposition, arising from the destruction of the harmony which was essential to original justice, even as bodily sickness is an inordinate disposition of the body, by reason of the destruction of that equilibrium which is

aequalitas in qua consistit ratio sanitatis. Unde peccatum originale languor naturae dicitur.

AD PRIMUM ergo dicendum quod, sicut aegritudo corporalis habet aliquid de privatione, inquantum tollitur aequalitas sanitatis; et aliquid habet positive, scilicet ipsos humores inordinate dispositos, ita etiam peccatum originale habet privationem originalis iustitiae, et cum hoc inordinatam dispositionem partium animae. Unde non est privatio pura, sed est quidam habitus corruptus.

AD SECUNDUM dicendum quod actuale peccatum est inordinatio quaedam actus, originale vero, cum sit peccatum naturae, est quaedam inordinata dispositio ipsius naturae, quae habet rationem culpae inquantum derivatur ex primo parente, ut dictum est. Huiusmodi autem dispositio naturae inordinata habet rationem habitus, sed inordinata dispositio actus non habet rationem habitus. Et propter hoc, peccatum originale potest esse habitus, non autem peccatum actuale.

AD TERTIUM dicendum quod obiectio illa procedit de habitu quo potentia inclinatur in actum, talis autem habitus non est peccatum originale. Quamvis etiam ex peccato originali sequatur aliqua inclinatio in actum inordinatum, non directe, sed indirecte, scilicet per remotionem prohibentis, idest originalis iustitiae, quae prohibebat inordinatos motus, sicut etiam ex aegritudine corporali indirecte sequitur inclinatio ad motus corporales inordinatos. Nec debet dici quod peccatum originale sit habitus infusus; aut acquisitus per actum nisi primi parentis, non autem huius personae; sed per vitiatam originem innatus.

essential to health. Hence it is that original sin is called the *languor of nature*.

REPLY OBJ. 1: As bodily sickness is partly a privation, insofar as it denotes the destruction of the equilibrium of health, and partly something positive, viz., the very humors that are inordinately disposed, so too original sin denotes the privation of original justice, and besides this, the inordinate disposition of the parts of the soul. Consequently it is not a pure privation, but a corrupt habit.

REPLY OBJ. 2: Actual sin is an inordinateness of an act: whereas original sin, being the sin of nature, is an inordinate disposition of nature, and has the character of fault through being transmitted from our first parent, as stated above (Q81, A1). Now this inordinate disposition of nature is a kind of habit, whereas the inordinate disposition of an act is not: and for this reason original sin can be a habit, whereas actual sin cannot.

REPLY OBJ. 3: This objection considers the habit which inclines a power to an act: but original sin is not this kind of habit. Nevertheless a certain inclination to an inordinate act does follow from original sin, not directly, but indirectly, viz., by the removal of the obstacle, i.e., original justice, which hindered inordinate movements: just as an inclination to inordinate bodily movements results indirectly from bodily sickness. Nor is it necessary to says that original sin is a habit *infused*, or a habit *acquired* (except by the act of our first parent, but not by our own act): but it is a habit *inborn* due to our corrupt origin.

Article 2

Whether There Are Several Original Sins in One Man?

AD SECUNDUM SIC PROCEDITUR. Videtur quod in uno homine sint multa originalia peccata. Dicitur enim in Psalmo l, *ecce enim in iniquitatibus conceptus sum, et in peccatis concepit me mater mea.* Sed peccatum in quo homo concipitur, est originale. Ergo plura peccata originalia sunt in uno homine.

PRAETEREA, unus et idem habitus non inclinat ad contraria, habitus enim inclinat per modum naturae, quae tendit in unum. Sed peccatum originale, etiam in uno homine, inclinat ad diversa peccata et contraria. Ergo peccatum originale non est unus habitus, sed plures.

PRAETEREA, peccatum originale inficit omnes animae partes. Sed diversae partes animae sunt diversa subiecta peccati, ut ex praemissis patet. Cum igitur unum peccatum non possit esse in diversis subiectis, videtur quod peccatum originale non sit unum, sed multa.

OBJECTION 1: It would seem that there are many original sins in one man. For it is written (Ps 1:7): *Behold I was conceived in iniquities, and in sins did my mother conceive me.* But the sin in which a man is conceived is original sin. Therefore there are several original sins in man.

OBJ. 2: Further, one and the same habit does not incline its subject to contraries: since the inclination of habit is like that of nature which tends to one thing. Now original sin, even in one man, inclines to various and contrary sins. Therefore original sin is not one habit; but several.

OBJ. 3: Further, original sin infects every part of the soul. Now the different parts of the soul are different subjects of sin, as shown above (Q74). Since then one sin cannot be in different subjects, it seems that original sin is not one but several.

SED CONTRA est quod dicitur Ioan. I, *ecce agnus Dei, ecce qui tollit peccatum mundi*. Quod singulariter dicitur, quia peccatum mundi, quod est peccatum originale, est unum; ut Glossa ibidem exponit.

RESPONDEO dicendum quod in uno homine est unum peccatum originale. Cuius ratio dupliciter accipi potest. Uno modo, ex parte causae peccati originalis. Dictum est enim supra quod solum primum peccatum primi parentis in posteros traducitur. Unde peccatum originale in uno homine est unum numero; et in omnibus hominibus est unum proportione, in respectu scilicet ad primum principium. Alio modo potest accipi ratio eius ex ipsa essentia originalis peccati. In omni enim inordinata dispositione unitas speciei consideratur ex parte causae; unitas autem secundum numerum, ex parte subiecti. Sicut patet in aegritudine corporali, sunt enim diversae aegritudines specie quae ex diversis causis procedunt, puta ex superabundantia calidi vel frigidi, vel ex laesione pulmonis vel hepatis; una autem aegritudo secundum speciem, in uno homine non est nisi una numero. Causa autem huius corruptae dispositionis quae dicitur originale peccatum, est una tantum, scilicet privatio originalis iustitiae, per quam sublata est subiectio humanae mentis ad Deum. Et ideo peccatum originale est unum specie. Et in uno homine non potest esse nisi unum numero, in diversis autem hominibus est unum specie et proportione, diversum autem numero.

AD PRIMUM ergo dicendum quod pluraliter dicitur in peccatis, secundum illum morem divinae Scripturae quo frequenter ponitur pluralis numerus pro singulari, sicut Matth. II, *defuncti sunt qui quaerebant animam pueri*. Vel quia in peccato originali virtualiter praeexistunt omnia peccata actualia, sicut in quodam principio, unde est multiplex virtute. Vel quia in peccato primi parentis quod per originem traducitur, fuerunt plures deformitates, scilicet superbiae, inobedientiae, gulae, et alia huiusmodi. Vel quia multae partes animae inficiuntur per peccatum originale.

AD SECUNDUM dicendum quod unus habitus non potest inclinare per se et directe, idest per propriam formam, ad contraria. Sed indirecte et per accidens, scilicet per remotionem prohibentis, nihil prohibet, sicut, soluta harmonia corporis mixti, elementa tendunt in loca contraria. Et similiter, soluta harmonia originalis iustitiae, diversae animae potentiae in diversa feruntur.

AD TERTIUM dicendum quod peccatum originale inficit diversas partes animae, secundum quod sunt partes unius totius, sicut et iustitia originalis continebat omnes animae partes in unum. Et ideo est unum tantum peccatum originale. Sicut etiam est una febris in uno homine, quamvis diversae partes corporis graventur.

ON THE CONTRARY, It is written (John 1:29): *Behold the Lamb of God, behold Him Who taketh away the sin of the world*: and the reason for the employment of the singular is that the *sin of the world* is original sin, as a gloss expounds this passage.

I ANSWER THAT, In one man there is one original sin. Two reasons may be assigned for this. The first is on the part of the cause of original sin. For it has been stated (Q81, A2), that the first sin alone of our first parent was transmitted to his posterity. Wherefore in one man original sin is one in number; and in all men, it is one in proportion, i.e., in relation to its first principle. The second reason may be taken from the very essence of original sin. Because in every inordinate disposition, unity of species depends on the cause, while the unity of number is derived from the subject. For example, take bodily sickness: various species of sickness proceed from different causes, e.g., from excessive heat or cold, or from a lesion in the lung or liver; while one specific sickness in one man will be one in number. Now the cause of this corrupt disposition that is called original sin, is one only, viz., the privation of original justice, removing the subjection of man's mind to God. Consequently original sin is specifically one, and, in one man, can be only one in number; while, in different men, it is one in species and in proportion, but is numerically many.

REPLY OBJ. 1: The employment of the plural—*in sins*—may be explained by the custom of the Divine Scriptures in the frequent use of the plural for the singular, e.g., *They are dead that sought the life of the child*; or by the fact that all actual sins virtually pre-exist in original sin, as in a principle so that it is virtually many; or by the fact of there being many deformities in the sin of our first parent, viz., pride, disobedience, gluttony, and so forth; or by several parts of the soul being infected by original sin.

REPLY OBJ. 2: Of itself and directly, i.e., by its own form, one habit cannot incline its subject to contraries. But there is no reason why it should not do so, indirectly and accidentally, i.e., by the removal of an obstacle: thus, when the harmony of a mixed body is destroyed, the elements have contrary local tendencies. In like manner, when the harmony of original justice is destroyed, the various powers of the soul have various opposite tendencies.

REPLY OBJ. 3: Original sin infects the different parts of the soul, insofar as they are the parts of one whole; even as original justice held all the soul's parts together in one. Consequently there is but one original sin: just as there is but one fever in one man, although the various parts of the body are affected.

Article 3

Whether Original Sin Is Concupiscence?

AD TERTIUM SIC PROCEDITUR. Videtur quod peccatum originale non sit concupiscentia. Omne enim peccatum est contra naturam, ut dicit Damascenus, in II libro. Sed concupiscentia est secundum naturam, est enim proprius actus virtutis concupiscibilis, quae est potentia naturalis. Ergo concupiscentia non est peccatum originale.

PRAETEREA, per peccatum originale sunt in nobis passiones peccatorum; ut patet per apostolum, Rom. VII. Sed multae aliae sunt passiones praeter concupiscentiam, ut supra habitum est. Ergo peccatum originale non magis est concupiscentia quam aliqua alia passio.

PRAETEREA, per peccatum originale deordinantur omnes animae partes, ut dictum est. Sed intellectus est suprema inter animae partes; ut patet per philosophum, in X Ethic. Ergo peccatum originale magis est ignorantia quam concupiscentia.

SED CONTRA est quod Augustinus dicit, in libro Retract., *concupiscentia est reatus originalis peccati.*

RESPONDEO dicendum quod unumquodque habet speciem a sua forma. Dictum est autem supra quod species peccati originalis sumitur ex sua causa. Unde oportet quod id quod est formale in originali peccato, accipiatur ex parte causae peccati originalis. Oppositorum autem oppositae sunt causae. Est igitur attendenda causa originalis peccati ex causa originalis iustitiae, quae ei opponitur. Tota autem ordinatio originalis iustitiae ex hoc est, quod voluntas hominis erat Deo subiecta. Quae quidem subiectio primo et principaliter erat per voluntatem, cuius est movere omnes alias partes in finem, ut supra dictum est. Unde ex aversione voluntatis a Deo, consecuta est inordinatio in omnibus aliis animae viribus. Sic ergo privatio originalis iustitiae, per quam voluntas subdebatur Deo, est formale in peccato originali, omnis autem alia inordinatio virium animae se habet in peccato originali sicut quiddam materiale. Inordinatio autem aliarum virium animae praecipue in hoc attenditur, quod inordinate convertuntur ad bonum commutabile, quae quidem inordinatio communi nomine potest dici concupiscentia. Et ita peccatum originale materialiter quidem est concupiscentia; formaliter vero, defectus originalis iustitiae.

AD PRIMUM ergo dicendum quod, quia in homine concupiscibilis naturaliter regitur ratione, intantum concupiscere est homini naturale, inquantum est secundum rationis ordinem, concupiscentia autem quae transcendit limites rationis, est homini contra naturam. Et talis est concupiscentia originalis peccati.

AD SECUNDUM dicendum quod, sicut supra dictum est, omnes passiones irascibilis ad passiones

OBJECTION 1: It would seem that original sin is not concupiscence. For every sin is contrary to nature, according to Damascene (*De Fide* Orth. ii, 4,30). But concupiscence is in accordance with nature, since it is the proper act of the concupiscible faculty which is a natural power. Therefore concupiscence is not original sin.

OBJ. 2: Further, through original sin *the passions of sins* are in us, according to the Apostle (Rom 7:5). Now there are several other passions besides concupiscence, as stated above (Q23, A4). Therefore original sin is not concupiscence any more than another passion.

OBJ. 3: Further, by original sin, all the parts of the soul are disordered, as stated above (A2, OBJ3). But the intellect is the highest of the soul's parts, as the Philosopher states (*Ethic.* x, 7). Therefore original sin is ignorance rather than concupiscence.

ON THE CONTRARY, Augustine says (*Retract.* i, 15): *Concupiscence is the guilt of original sin.*

I ANSWER THAT, Everything takes its species from its form: and it has been stated (A2) that the species of original sin is taken from its cause. Consequently the formal element of original sin must be considered in respect of the cause of original sin. But contraries have contrary causes. Therefore the cause of original sin must be considered with respect to the cause of original justice, which is opposed to it. Now the whole order of original justice consists in man's will being subject to God: which subjection, first and chiefly, was in the will, whose function it is to move all the other parts to the end, as stated above (Q9, A1), so that the will being turned away from God, all the other powers of the soul become inordinate. Accordingly the privation of original justice, whereby the will was made subject to God, is the formal element in original sin; while every other disorder of the soul's powers, is a kind of material element in respect of original sin. Now the inordinateness of the other powers of the soul consists chiefly in their turning inordinately to mutable good; which inordinateness may be called by the general name of concupiscence. Hence original sin is concupiscence, materially, but privation of original justice, formally.

REPLY OBJ. 1: Since, in man, the concupiscible power is naturally governed by reason, the act of concupiscence is so far natural to man, as it is in accord with the order of reason; while, insofar as it trespasses beyond the bounds of reason, it is, for a man, contrary to reason. Such is the concupiscence of original sin.

REPLY OBJ. 2: As stated above (Q25, A1), all the irascible passions are reducible to concupiscible passions, as

concupiscibilis reducuntur, sicut ad principaliores. Inter quas concupiscentia vehementius movet, et magis sentitur, ut supra habitum est. Et ideo concupiscentiae attribuitur, tanquam principaliori, et in qua quodammodo omnes aliae passiones includuntur.

AD TERTIUM dicendum quod, sicut in bonis intellectus et ratio principalitatem habent, ita e converso in malis inferior pars animae principalior invenitur, quae obnubilat et trahit rationem, ut supra dictum est. Et propter hoc peccatum originale magis dicitur esse concupiscentia quam ignorantia, licet etiam ignorantia inter defectus materiales peccati originalis contineatur.

holding the principle place: and of these, concupiscence is the most impetuous in moving, and is felt most, as stated above (Q25, A2, ad 1). Therefore original sin is ascribed to concupiscence, as being the chief passion, and as including all the others, in a fashion.

REPLY OBJ. 3: As, in good things, the intellect and reason stand first, so conversely in evil things, the lower part of the soul is found to take precedence, for it clouds and draws the reason, as stated above (Q77, AA1,2; Q80, A2). Hence original sin is called concupiscence rather than ignorance, although ignorance is comprised among the material defects of original sin.

Article 4

Whether Original Sin Is Equally in All?

AD QUARTUM SIC PROCEDITUR. Videtur quod peccatum originale non sit aequaliter in omnibus. Est enim peccatum originale concupiscentia inordinata, ut dictum est. Sed non omnes aequaliter sunt proni ad concupiscendum. Ergo peccatum originale non est aequaliter in omnibus.

PRAETEREA, peccatum originale est quaedam inordinata dispositio animae, sicut aegritudo est quaedam inordinata dispositio corporis. Sed aegritudo recipit magis et minus. Ergo peccatum originale recipit magis et minus.

PRAETEREA, Augustinus dicit, in libro de Nupt. et Concupisc., quod *libido transmittit originale peccatum in prolem*. Sed contingit esse maiorem libidinem unius in actu generationis, quam alterius. Ergo peccatum originale potest esse maius in uno quam in alio.

SED CONTRA est quia peccatum originale est peccatum naturae, ut dictum est. Sed natura aequaliter est in omnibus. Ergo et peccatum originale.

RESPONDEO dicendum quod in originali peccato sunt duo, quorum unum est defectus originalis iustitiae; aliud autem est relatio huius defectus ad peccatum primi parentis, a quo per vitiatam originem deducitur. Quantum autem ad primum, peccatum originale non recipit magis et minus, quia totum donum originalis iustitiae est sublatum; privationes autem totaliter aliquid privantes, ut mors et tenebrae, non recipiunt magis et minus, sicut supra dictum est. Similiter etiam nec quantum ad secundum, aequaliter enim omnes relationem habent ad primum principium vitiatae originis, ex quo peccatum originale recipit rationem culpae; relationes enim non recipiunt magis et minus. Unde manifestum est quod peccatum originale non potest esse magis in uno quam in alio.

OBJECTION 1: It would seem that original sin is not equally in all. Because original sin is inordinate concupiscence, as stated above (A3). Now all are not equally prone to acts of concupiscence. Therefore original sin is not equally in all.

OBJ. 2: Further, original sin is an inordinate disposition of the soul, just as sickness is an inordinate disposition of the body. But sickness is subject to degrees. Therefore original sin is subject to degrees.

OBJ. 3: Further, Augustine says (*De Nup. et Concep.* i, 23) that *lust transmits original sin to the child*. But the act of generation may be more lustful in one than in another. Therefore original sin may be greater in one than in another.

ON THE CONTRARY, Original sin is the sin of nature, as stated above (Q81, A1). But nature is equally in all. Therefore original sin is too.

I ANSWER THAT, There are two things in original sin: one is the privation of original justice; the other is the relation of this privation to the sin of our first parent, from whom it is transmitted to man through his corrupt origin. As to the first, original sin has no degrees, since the gift of original justice is taken away entirely; and privations that remove something entirely, such as death and darkness, cannot be more or less, as stated above (Q73, A2). In like manner, neither is this possible, as to the second: since all are related equally to the first principle of our corrupt origin, from which principle original sin takes the nature of guilt; for relations cannot be more or less. Consequently it is evident that original sin cannot be more in one than in another.

AD PRIMUM ergo dicendum quod, soluto vinculo originalis iustitiae, sub quo quodam ordine omnes vires animae continebantur, unaquaeque vis animae tendit in suum proprium motum; et tanto vehementius, quanto fuerit fortior. Contingit autem vires aliquas animae esse fortiores in uno quam in alio, propter diversas corporis complexiones. Quod ergo unus homo sit pronior ad concupiscendum quam alter, non est ratione peccati originalis, cum in omnibus aequaliter solvatur vinculum originalis iustitiae, et aequaliter in omnibus partes inferiores animae sibi relinquantur, sed accidit hoc ex diversa dispositione potentiarum, sicut dictum est.

AD SECUNDUM dicendum quod aegritudo corporalis non habet in omnibus aequalem causam, etiam si sit eiusdem speciei, puta, si sit febris ex cholera putrefacta, potest esse maior vel minor putrefactio, et propinquior vel remotior a principio vitae. Sed causa originalis peccati in omnibus est aequalis. Unde non est simile.

AD TERTIUM dicendum quod libido quae transmittit peccatum originale in prolem, non est libido actualis, quia dato quod virtute divina concederetur alicui quod nullam inordinatam libidinem in actu generationis sentiret, adhuc transmitteret in prolem originale peccatum. Sed libido illa est intelligenda habitualiter, secundum quod appetitus sensitivus non continetur sub ratione vinculo originalis iustitiae. Et talis libido in omnibus est aequalis.

REPLY OBJ. 1: Through the bond of original justice being broken, which held together all the powers of the soul in a certain order, each power of the soul tends to its own proper movement, and the more impetuously, as it is stronger. Now it happens that some of the soul's powers are stronger in one man than in another, on account of the different bodily temperaments. Consequently if one man is more prone than another to acts of concupiscence, this is not due to original sin, because the bond of original justice is equally broken in all, and the lower parts of the soul are, in all, left to themselves equally; but it is due to the various dispositions of the powers, as stated.

REPLY OBJ. 2: Sickness of the body, even sickness of the same species, has not an equal cause in all; for instance if a fever be caused by corruption of the bile, the corruption may be greater or less, and nearer to, or further from a vital principle. But the cause of original sin is equal to all, so that there is not comparison.

REPLY OBJ. 3: It is not the actual lust that transmits original sin: for, supposing God were to grant to a man to feel no inordinate lust in the act of generation, he would still transmit original sin; we must understand this to be habitual lust, whereby the sensitive appetite is not kept subject to reason by the bonds of original justice. This lust is equally in all.

QUESTION 83

OF THE SUBJECT OF ORIGINAL SIN

Deinde considerandum est de subiecto originalis peccati. Et circa hoc quaeruntur quatuor.

Primo, utrum subiectum originalis peccati per prius sit caro vel anima.

Secundo, si anima, utrum per essentiam aut per potentias suas.

Tertio, utrum voluntas per prius sit subiectum peccati originalis quam aliae potentiae.

Quarto, utrum aliquae potentiae animae sint specialiter infectae, scilicet generativa, vis concupiscibilis et sensus tactus.

We must now consider the subject of original sin, under which head there are four points of inquiry:

(1) Whether the subject of original sin is the flesh rather than the soul?

(2) If it be the soul, whether this be through its essence, or through its powers?

(3) Whether the will prior to the other powers is the subject of original sin?

(4) Whether certain powers of the soul are specially infected, viz., the generative power, the concupiscible part, and the sense of touch?

Article 1

Whether Original Sin Is More in the Flesh Than in the Soul?

AD PRIMUM SIC PROCEDITUR. Videtur quod peccatum originale magis sit in carne quam in anima. Repugnantia enim carnis ad mentem ex corruptione originalis peccati procedit. Sed radix huius repugnantiae in carne consistit, dicit enim apostolus ad Rom. VII, *video aliam legem in membris meis, repugnantem legi mentis meae.* Ergo originale peccatum in carne principaliter consistit.

PRAETEREA, unumquodque potius est in causa quam in effectu, sicut calor magis est in igne calefaciente quam in aqua calefacta. Sed anima inficitur infectione originalis peccati per semen carnale. Ergo peccatum originale magis est in carne quam in anima.

PRAETEREA, peccatum originale ex primo parente contrahimus, prout in eo fuimus secundum rationem seminalem. Sic autem non fuit ibi anima, sed sola caro. Ergo originale peccatum non est in anima, sed in carne.

PRAETEREA, anima rationalis creata a Deo corpori infunditur. Si igitur anima per peccatum originale inficeretur, consequens esset quod ex sua creatione vel infusione inquinaretur. Et sic Deus esset causa peccati, qui est auctor creationis et infusionis.

PRAETEREA, nullus sapiens liquorem pretiosum vasi infunderet ex quo sciret ipsum liquorem infici. Sed anima rationalis est pretiosior omni liquore. Si ergo anima ex corporis unione infici posset infectione originalis culpae, Deus, qui ipsa sapientia est, nunquam animam tali corpori infunderet. Infundit autem. Non ergo inquinatur ex carne. Sic igitur peccatum originale non est in anima, sed in carne.

OBJECTION 1: It would seem that original sin is more in the flesh than in the soul. Because the rebellion of the flesh against the mind arises from the corruption of original sin. Now the root of this rebellion is seated in the flesh: for the Apostle says (Rom 7:23): *I see another law in my members fighting against the law of my mind.* Therefore original sin is seated chiefly in the flesh.

OBJ. 2: Further, a thing is more in its cause than in its effect: thus heat is in the heating fire more than in the hot water. Now the soul is infected with the corruption of original sin by the carnal semen. Therefore original sin is in the flesh rather than in the soul.

OBJ. 3: Further, we contract original sin from our first parent, insofar as we were in him by reason of seminal virtue. Now our souls were not in him thus, but only our flesh. Therefore original sin is not in the soul, but in the flesh.

OBJ. 4: Further, the rational soul created by God is infused into the body. If therefore the soul were infected with original sin, it would follow that it is corrupted in its creation or infusion: and thus God would be the cause of sin, since He is the author of the soul's creation and fusion.

OBJ. 5: Further, no wise man pours a precious liquid into a vessel, knowing that the vessel will corrupt the liquid. But the rational soul is more precious than any liquid. If therefore the soul, by being united with the body, could be corrupted with the infection of original sin, God, Who is wisdom itself, would never infuse the soul into such a body. And yet He does; wherefore it is not corrupted by the flesh. Therefore original sin is not in the soul but in the flesh.

Sed contra est quod idem est subiectum virtutis et vitii sive peccati, quod contrariatur virtuti. Sed caro non potest esse subiectum virtutis, dicit enim apostolus, ad Rom. VII, *scio quod non habitat in me, hoc est in carne mea, bonum.* Ergo caro non potest esse subiectum originalis peccati, sed solum anima.

Respondeo dicendum quod aliquid potest esse in aliquo dupliciter, uno modo, sicut in causa, vel principali vel instrumentali; alio modo, sicut in subiecto. Peccatum ergo originale omnium hominum fuit quidem in ipso Adam sicut in prima causa principali; secundum illud apostoli, Rom. V, *in quo omnes peccaverunt.* In semine autem corporali est peccatum originale sicut in causa instrumentali, eo quod per virtutem activam seminis traducitur peccatum originale in prolem, simul cum natura humana. Sed sicut in subiecto, peccatum originale nullo modo potest esse in carne, sed solum in anima.

Cuius ratio est quia, sicut supra dictum est, hoc modo ex voluntate primi parentis peccatum originale traducitur in posteros per quandam generativam motionem, sicut a voluntate alicuius hominis derivatur peccatum actuale ad alias partes eius. In qua quidem derivatione hoc potest attendi, quod quidquid provenit ex motione voluntatis peccati ad quamcumque partem hominis quae quocumque modo potest esse particeps peccati, vel per modum subiecti vel per modum instrumenti, habet rationem culpae, sicut ex voluntate gulae provenit concupiscentia cibi ad concupiscibilem, et sumptio cibi ad manus et os, quae inquantum moventur a voluntate ad peccatum, sunt instrumenta peccati. Quod vero ulterius derivatur ad vim nutritivam et ad interiora membra, quae non sunt nata moveri a voluntate, non habet rationem culpae.

Sic igitur, cum anima possit esse subiectum culpae, caro autem de se non habeat quod sit subiectum culpae; quidquid provenit de corruptione primi peccati ad animam, habet rationem culpae; quod autem provenit ad carnem, non habet rationem culpae, sed poenae. Sic igitur anima est subiectum peccati originalis, non autem caro.

Ad primum ergo dicendum quod, sicut Augustinus dicit in libro Retract., apostolus loquitur ibi de homine iam redempto, qui liberatus est a culpa, sed subiacet poenae, ratione cuius peccatum dicitur habitare in carne. Unde ex hoc non sequitur quod caro sit subiectum culpae, sed solum poenae.

Ad secundum dicendum quod peccatum originale causatur ex semine sicut ex causa instrumentali. Non autem oportet quod aliquid sit principalius in causa instrumentali quam in effectu, sed solum in causa principali. Et hoc modo peccatum originale potiori modo fuit in Adam, in quo fuit secundum rationem actualis peccati.

Ad tertium dicendum quod anima huius hominis non fuit secundum seminalem rationem in Adam

On the contrary, The same is the subject of a virtue and of the vice or sin contrary to that virtue. But the flesh cannot be the subject of virtue: for the Apostle says (Rom 7:18): *I know that there dwelleth not in me, that is to say, in my flesh, that which is good.* Therefore the flesh cannot be the subject of original sin, but only the soul.

I answer that, One thing can be in another in two ways. First, as in its cause, either principal, or instrumental; second, as in its subject. Accordingly the original sin of all men was in Adam indeed, as in its principal cause, according to the words of the Apostle (Rom 5:12): *In whom all have sinned*: whereas it is in the bodily semen, as in its instrumental cause, since it is by the active power of the semen that original sin together with human nature is transmitted to the child. But original sin can nowise be in the flesh as its subject, but only in the soul.

The reason for this is that, as stated above (Q81, A1), original sin is transmitted from the will of our first parent to this posterity by a certain movement of generation, in the same way as actual sin is transmitted from any man's will to his other parts. Now in this transmission it is to be observed, that whatever accrues from the motion of the will consenting to sin, to any part of man that can in any way share in that guilt, either as its subject or as its instrument, has the character of sin. Thus from the will consenting to gluttony, concupiscence of food accrues to the concupiscible faculty, and partaking of food accrues to the hand and the mouth, which, insofar as they are moved by the will to sin, are the instruments of sin. But that further action is evoked in the nutritive power and the internal members, which have no natural aptitude for being moved by the will, does not bear the character of guilt.

Accordingly, since the soul can be the subject of guilt, while the flesh, of itself, cannot be the subject of guilt; whatever accrues to the soul from the corruption of the first sin, has the character of guilt, while whatever accrues to the flesh, has the character, not of guilt but of punishment: so that, therefore, the soul is the subject of original sin, and not the flesh.

Reply Obj. 1: As Augustine says (*Retract.* i, 27), the Apostle is speaking, in that passage, of man already redeemed, who is delivered from guilt, but is still liable to punishment, by reason of which sin is stated to dwell *in the flesh*. Consequently it follows that the flesh is the subject, not of guilt, but of punishment.

Reply Obj. 2: Original sin is caused by the semen as instrumental cause. Now there is no need for anything to be more in the instrumental cause than in the effect; but only in the principal cause: and, in this way, original sin was in Adam more fully, since in him it had the nature of actual sin.

Reply Obj. 3: The soul of any individual man was in Adam, in respect of its seminal power, not indeed as in its

peccante sicut in principio effectivo, sed sicut in principio dispositivo, eo quod semen corporale, quod ex Adam traducitur, sua virtute non efficit animam rationalem, sed ad eam disponit.

AD QUARTUM dicendum quod infectio originalis peccati nullo modo causatur a Deo, sed ex solo peccato primi parentis per carnalem generationem. Et ideo, cum creatio importet respectum animae ad solum Deum, non potest dici quod anima ex sua creatione inquinetur. Sed infusio importat respectum et ad Deum infundentem, et ad carnem cui infunditur anima. Et ideo, habito respectu ad Deum infundentem, non potest dici quod anima per infusionem maculetur; sed solum habito respectu ad corpus cui infunditur.

AD QUINTUM dicendum quod bonum commune praefertur bono singulari. Unde Deus, secundum suam sapientiam, non praetermittit universalem ordinem rerum, qui est ut tali corpori talis anima infundatur, ut videtur singularis infectio huius animae, praesertim cum natura animae hoc habeat, ut esse non incipiat nisi in corpore, ut in primo habitum est. Melius est autem ei sic esse secundum naturam, quam nullo modo esse, praesertim cum possit per gratiam damnationem evadere.

effective principle, but as in a dispositive principle: because the bodily semen, which is transmitted from Adam, does not of its own power produce the rational soul, but disposes the matter for it.

REPLY OBJ. 4: The corruption of original sin is nowise caused by God, but by the sin alone of our first parent through carnal generation. And so, since creation implies a relation in the soul to God alone, it cannot be said that the soul is tainted through being created. On the other hand, infusion implies relation both to God infusing and to the flesh into which the soul is infused. And so, with regard to God infusing, it cannot be said that the soul is stained through being infused; but only with regard to the body into which it is infused.

REPLY OBJ. 5: The common good takes precedence of private good. Wherefore God, according to His wisdom, does not overlook the general order of things (which is that such a soul be infused into such a body), lest this soul contract a singular corruption: all the more that the nature of the soul demands that it should not exist prior to its infusion into the body, as stated in the FP, Q90, A4; FP, Q118, A3. And it is better for the soul to be thus, according to its nature, than not to be at all, especially since it can avoid damnation, by means of grace.

Article 2

Whether Original Sin Is in the Essence of the Soul Rather Than in the Powers?

AD SECUNDUM SIC PROCEDITUR. Videtur quod peccatum originale non sit per prius in essentia animae quam in potentiis. Anima enim nata est esse subiectum peccati, quantum ad id quod potest a voluntate moveri. Sed anima non movetur a voluntate secundum suam essentiam, sed solum secundum potentias. Ergo peccatum originale non est in anima secundum suam essentiam, sed solum secundum potentias.

PRAETEREA, peccatum originale opponitur originali iustitiae. Sed originalis iustitia erat in aliqua potentia animae, quae est subiectum virtutis. Ergo et peccatum originale est magis in potentia animae quam in eius essentia.

PRAETEREA, sicut a carne peccatum originale derivatur ad animam, ita ab essentia animae derivatur ad potentias. Sed peccatum originale magis est in anima quam in carne. Ergo etiam magis est in potentiis animae quam in essentia.

PRAETEREA, peccatum originale dicitur esse concupiscentia, ut dictum est. Sed concupiscentia est in potentiis animae. Ergo et peccatum originale.

SED CONTRA est quod peccatum originale dicitur esse peccatum naturale, ut supra dictum est. Anima

OBJECTION 1: It would seem that original sin is not in the essence of the soul rather than in the powers. For the soul is naturally apt to be the subject of sin, in respect of those parts which can be moved by the will. Now the soul is moved by the will, not as to its essence but only as to the powers. Therefore original sin is in the soul, not according to its essence, but only according to the powers.

OBJ. 2: Further, original sin is opposed to original justice. Now original justice was in a power of the soul, because power is the subject of virtue. Therefore original sin also is in a power of the soul, rather than in its essence.

OBJ. 3: Further, just as original sin is derived from the soul as from the flesh, so is it derived by the powers from the essence. But original sin is more in the soul than in the flesh. Therefore it is more in the powers than in the essence of the soul.

OBJ. 4: Further, original sin is said to be concupiscence, as stated (Q82, A3). But concupiscence is in the powers of the soul. Therefore original sin is also.

ON THE CONTRARY, Original sin is called the sin of nature, as stated above (Q81, A1). Now the soul is the form

autem est forma et natura corporis secundum essentiam suam, et non secundum potentias, ut in primo habitum est. Ergo anima est subiectum originalis peccati principaliter secundum suam essentiam.

Respondeo dicendum quod illud animae est principaliter subiectum alicuius peccati, ad quod primo pertinet causa motiva illius peccati, sicut si causa motiva ad peccandum sit delectatio sensus, quae pertinet ad vim concupiscibilem sicut obiectum proprium eius, sequitur quod vis concupiscibilis sit proprium subiectum illius peccati. Manifestum est autem quod peccatum originale causatur per originem. Unde illud animae quod primo attingitur ab origine hominis, est primum subiectum originalis peccati. Attingit autem origo animam ut terminum generationis, secundum quod est forma corporis; quod quidem convenit ei secundum essentiam propriam, ut in primo habitum est. Unde anima secundum essentiam est primum subiectum originalis peccati.

Ad primum ergo dicendum quod, sicut motio voluntatis alicuius propriae pervenit ad potentias animae, non autem ad animae essentiam; ita motio voluntatis primi generantis, per viam generationis, pervenit primo ad animae essentiam, ut dictum est.

Ad secundum dicendum quod etiam originalis iustitia pertinebat primordialiter ad essentiam animae, erat enim donum divinitus datum humanae naturae, quam per prius respicit essentia animae quam potentiae. Potentiae enim magis videntur pertinere ad personam, inquantum sunt principia personalium actuum. Unde sunt propria subiecta peccatorum actualium, quae sunt peccata personalia.

Ad tertium dicendum quod corpus comparatur ad animam sicut materia ad formam, quae etsi sit posterior ordine generationis, est tamen prior ordine perfectionis et naturae. Essentia autem animae comparatur ad potentias sicut subiecta ad accidentia propria, quae sunt posteriora subiecto et ordine generationis et etiam perfectionis. Unde non est similis ratio.

Ad quartum dicendum quod concupiscentia se habet materialiter et ex consequenti in peccato originali, ut supra dictum est.

and nature of the body, in respect of its essence and not in respect of its powers, as stated in the FP, Q76, A6. Therefore the soul is the subject of original sin chiefly in respect of its essence.

I answer that, The subject of a sin is chiefly that part of the soul to which the motive cause of that sin primarily pertains: thus if the motive cause of a sin is sensual pleasure, which regards the concupiscible power through being its proper object, it follows that the concupiscible power is the proper subject of that sin. Now it is evident that original sin is caused through our origin. Consequently that part of the soul which is first reached by man's origin, is the primary subject of original sin. Now the origin reaches the soul as the term of generation, according as it is the form of the body: and this belongs to the soul in respect of its essence, as was proved in the FP, Q76, A6. Therefore the soul, in respect of its essence, is the primary subject of original sin.

Reply Obj. 1: As the motion of the will of an individual reaches to the soul's powers and not to its essence, so the motion of the will of the first generator, through the channel of generation, reaches first of all to the essence of the soul, as stated.

Reply Obj. 2: Even original justice pertained radically to the essence of the soul, because it was God's gift to human nature, to which the essence of the soul is related before the powers. For the powers seem to regard the person, in as much as they are the principles of personal acts. Hence they are the proper subjects of actual sins, which are the sins of the person.

Reply Obj. 3: The body is related to the soul as matter to form, which though it comes second in order of generation, nevertheless comes first in the order of perfection and nature. But the essence of the soul is related to the powers, as a subject to its proper accidents, which follow their subject both in the order of generation and in that of perfection. Consequently the comparison fails.

Reply Obj. 4: Concupiscence, in relation to original sin, holds the position of matter and effect, as stated above (Q82, A3).

Article 3

Whether Original Sin Infects the Will Before the Other Powers?

Ad tertium sic proceditur. Videtur quod peccatum originale non per prius inficiat voluntatem quam alias potentias. Omne enim peccatum principaliter pertinet ad potentiam per cuius actum causatur. Sed

Objection 1: It would seem that original sin does not infect the will before the other powers. For every sin belongs chiefly to that power by whose act it was caused. Now original sin is caused by an act of the generative power.

peccatum originale causatur per actum generativae potentiae. Ergo inter ceteras potentias animae, videtur magis pertinere ad generativam potentiam.

PRAETEREA, peccatum originale per semen carnale traducitur. Sed aliae vires animae propinquiores sunt carni quam voluntas, sicut patet de omnibus sensitivis, quae utuntur organo corporali. Ergo in eis magis est peccatum originale quam in voluntate.

PRAETEREA, intellectus est prior voluntate, non enim est voluntas nisi de bono intellecto. Si ergo peccatum originale inficit omnes potentias animae, videtur quod per prius inficiat intellectum, tanquam priorem.

SED CONTRA est quod iustitia originalis per prius respicit voluntatem, est enim rectitudo voluntatis, ut Anselmus dicit, in libro de conceptu virginali. Ergo et peccatum originale, quod ei opponitur, per prius respicit voluntatem.

RESPONDEO dicendum quod in infectione peccati originalis duo est considerare. Primo quidem, inhaerentiam eius ad subiectum, et secundum hoc primo respicit essentiam animae, ut dictum est. Deinde oportet considerare inclinationem eius ad actum, et hoc modo respicit potentias animae. Oportet ergo quod illam per prius respiciat, quae primam inclinationem habet ad peccandum. Haec autem est voluntas, ut ex supradictis patet. Unde peccatum originale per prius respicit voluntatem.

AD PRIMUM ergo dicendum quod peccatum originale non causatur in homine per potentiam generativam prolis, sed per actum potentiae generativae parentis. Unde non oportet quod sua potentia generativa sit primum subiectum originalis peccati.

AD SECUNDUM dicendum quod peccatum originale habet duplicem processum, unum quidem a carne ad animam; alium vero ab essentia animae ad potentias. Primus quidem processus est secundum ordinem generationis, secundus autem secundum ordinem perfectionis. Et ideo quamvis aliae potentiae, scilicet sensitivae, propinquiores sint carni; quia tamen voluntas est propinquior essentiae animae, tanquam superior potentia, primo pervenit ad ipsam infectio originalis peccati.

AD TERTIUM dicendum quod intellectus quodam modo praecedit voluntatem, inquantum proponit ei suum obiectum. Alio vero modo voluntas praecedit intellectum, secundum ordinem motionis ad actum, quae quidem motio pertinet ad peccatum.

Therefore it seems to belong to the generative power more than to the others.

OBJ. 2: Further, original sin is transmitted through the carnal semen. But the other powers of the soul are more akin to the flesh than the will is, as is evident with regard to all the sensitive powers, which use a bodily organ. Therefore original sin is in them more than in the will.

OBJ. 3: Further, the intellect precedes the will, for the object of the will is only the good understood. If therefore original sin infects all the powers of the soul, it seems that it must first of all infect the intellect, as preceding the others.

ON THE CONTRARY, Original justice has a prior relation to the will, because it is *rectitude of the will*, as Anselm states (*De Concep. Virg.* iii). Therefore original sin, which is opposed to it, also has a prior relation to the will.

I ANSWER THAT, Two things must be considered in the infection of original sin. First, its inherence to its subject; and in this respect it regards first the essence of the soul, as stated above (A2). In the second place we must consider its inclination to act; and in this way it regards the powers of the soul. It must therefore regard first of all that power in which is seated the first inclination to commit a sin, and this is the will, as stated above (Q74, AA1,2). Therefore original sin regards first of all the will.

REPLY OBJ. 1: Original sin, in man, is not caused by the generative power of the child, but by the act of the parental generative power. Consequently, it does not follow that the child's generative power is the subject of original sin.

REPLY OBJ. 2: Original sin spreads in two ways; from the flesh to the soul, and from the essence of the soul to the powers. The former follows the order of generation, the latter follows the order of perfection. Therefore, although the other, viz., the sensitive powers, are more akin to the flesh, yet, since the will, being the higher power, is more akin to the essence of the soul, the infection of original sin reaches it first.

REPLY OBJ. 3: The intellect precedes the will, in one way, by proposing its object to it. In another way, the will precedes the intellect, in the order of motion to act, which motion pertains to sin.

Article 4

Whether the Aforesaid Powers Are More Infected Than the Others?

AD QUARTUM SIC PROCEDITUR. Videtur quod praedictae potentiae non sint magis infectae quam aliae. Infectio enim originalis peccati magis videtur pertinere ad illam animae partem quae prius potest esse subiectum peccati. Haec autem est rationalis pars, et praecipue voluntas. Ergo ipsa est magis infecta per peccatum originale.

PRAETEREA, nulla vis animae inficitur per culpam, nisi inquantum potest obedire rationi. Generativa autem non potest obedire, ut dicitur in I Ethic. Ergo generativa non est maxime infecta per originale peccatum.

PRAETEREA, visus inter alios sensus est spiritualior et propinquior rationi, inquantum *plures differentias rerum ostendit*, ut dicitur in I Metaphys. Sed infectio culpae primo est in ratione. Ergo visus magis est infectus quam tactus.

SED CONTRA est quod Augustinus dicit, in XIV de Civ. Dei, quod infectio originalis culpae maxime apparet in motu genitalium membrorum, qui rationi non subditur. Sed illa membra deserviunt generativae virtuti in commixtione sexuum, in qua est delectatio secundum tactum, quae maxime concupiscentiam movet. Ergo infectio originalis peccati maxime pertinet ad ista tria, scilicet potentiam generativam, vim concupiscibilem et sensum tactus.

RESPONDEO dicendum quod illa corruptio praecipue infectio nominari solet, quae nata est in aliud transferri, unde et morbi contagiosi, sicut lepra et scabies et huiusmodi, infectiones dicuntur. Corruptio autem originalis peccati traducitur per actum generationis, sicut supra dictum est. Unde potentiae quae ad huiusmodi actum concurrunt, maxime dicuntur esse infectae. Huiusmodi autem actus deservit generativae, inquantum ad generationem ordinatur, habet autem in se delectationem tactus, quae est maximum obiectum concupiscibilis. Et ideo, cum omnes partes animae dicantur esse corruptae per peccatum originale, specialiter tres praedictae dicuntur esse corruptae et infectae.

AD PRIMUM ergo dicendum quod peccatum originale ex ea parte qua inclinat in peccata actualia, praecipue pertinet ad voluntatem, ut dictum est. Sed ex ea parte qua traducitur in prolem, pertinet propinque ad potentias praedictas, ad voluntatem autem remote.

AD SECUNDUM dicendum quod infectio actualis culpae non pertinet nisi ad potentias quae moventur a voluntate peccantis. Sed infectio originalis culpae non derivatur a voluntate eius qui ipsam contrahit, sed per originem naturae, cui deservit potentia generativa. Et ideo in ea est infectio originalis peccati.

OBJECTION 1: It would seem that the aforesaid powers are not more infected than the others. For the infection of original sin seems to pertain more to that part of the soul which can be first the subject of sin. Now this is the rational part, and chiefly the will. Therefore that power is most infected by original sin.

OBJ. 2: Further, no power of the soul is infected by guilt, except insofar as it can obey reason. Now the generative power cannot obey reason, as stated in *Ethic.* i, 13. Therefore the generative power is not the most infected by original sin.

OBJ. 3: Further, of all the senses the sight is the most spiritual and the nearest to reason, in so far *as it shows us how a number of things differ* (*Metaph.* i). But the infection of guilt is first of all in the reason. Therefore the sight is more infected than touch.

ON THE CONTRARY, Augustine says (*De Civ. Dei* xiv, 16, seqq., 24) that the infection of original sin is most apparent in the movements of the members of generation, which are not subject to reason. Now those members serve the generative power in the mingling of sexes, wherein there is the delectation of touch, which is the most powerful incentive to concupiscence. Therefore the infection of original sin regards these three chiefly, viz., the generative power, the concupiscible faculty and the sense of touch.

I ANSWER THAT, Those corruptions especially are said to be infectious, which are of such a nature as to be transmitted from one subject to another: hence contagious diseases, such as leprosy and murrain and the like, are said to be infectious. Now the corruption of original sin is transmitted by the act of generation, as stated above (Q81, A1). Therefore the powers which concur in this act, are chiefly said to be infected. Now this act serves the generative power, in as much as it is directed to generation; and it includes delectation of the touch, which is the most powerful object of the concupiscible faculty. Consequently, while all the parts of the soul are said to be corrupted by original sin, these three are said specially to be corrupted and infected.

REPLY OBJ. 1: Original sin, insofar as it inclines to actual sins, belongs chiefly to the will, as stated above (A3). But insofar as it is transmitted to the offspring, it belongs to the aforesaid powers proximately, and to the will, remotely.

REPLY OBJ. 2: The infection of actual sin belongs only to the powers which are moved by the will of the sinner. But the infection of original sin is not derived from the will of the contractor, but through his natural origin, which is effected by the generative power. Hence it is this power that is infected by original sin.

Ad tertium dicendum quod visus non pertinet ad actum generationis nisi secundum dispositionem remotam, prout scilicet per visum apparet species concupiscibilis. Sed delectatio perficitur in tactu. Et ideo talis infectio magis attribuitur tactui quam visui.

Reply Obj. 3: Sight is not related to the act of generation except in respect of remote disposition, insofar as the concupiscible species is seen through the sight. But the delectation is completed in the touch. Wherefore the aforesaid infection is ascribed to the touch rather than to the sight.

QUESTION 84

OF THE CAUSE OF SIN

Deinde considerandum est de causa peccati secundum quod unum peccatum est causa alterius. Et circa hoc quaeruntur quatuor.

Primo, utrum cupiditas sit radix omnium peccatorum.

Secundo, utrum superbia sit initium omnis peccati.

Tertio, utrum praeter superbiam et avaritiam, debeant dici capitalia vitia aliqua specialia peccata.

Quarto, quot et quae sint capitalia vitia.

We must now consider the cause of sin, insofar as one sin can be the cause of another. Under this head there are four points of inquiry:

(1) Whether covetousness is the root of all sins?

(2) Whether pride is the beginning of every sin?

(3) Whether other special sins should be called capital vices, besides pride and covetousness?

(4) How many capital vices there are, and which are they?

Article 1

Whether Covetousness Is the Root of All Sins?

AD PRIMUM SIC PROCEDITUR. Videtur quod cupiditas non sit radix omnium peccatorum. Cupiditas enim, quae est immoderatus appetitus divitiarum, opponitur virtuti liberalitatis. Sed liberalitas non est radix omnium virtutum. Ergo cupiditas non est radix omnium peccatorum.

PRAETEREA, appetitus eorum quae sunt ad finem, procedit ex appetitu finis. Sed divitiae, quarum appetitus est cupiditas, non appetuntur nisi ut utiles ad aliquem finem, sicut dicitur in I Ethic. Ergo cupiditas non est radix omnis peccati, sed procedit ex alia priori radice.

PRAETEREA, frequenter invenitur quod avaritia, quae cupiditas nominatur, oritur ex aliis peccatis, puta cum quis appetit pecuniam propter ambitionem, vel ut satisfaciat gulae. Non ergo est radix omnium peccatorum.

SED CONTRA est quod dicit apostolus, I ad Tim. ult., *radix omnium malorum est cupiditas.*

RESPONDEO dicendum quod secundum quosdam cupiditas multipliciter dicitur. Uno modo, prout est appetitus inordinatus divitiarum. Et sic est speciale peccatum. Alio modo, secundum quod significat inordinatum appetitum cuiuscumque boni temporalis. Et sic est genus omnis peccati, nam in omni peccato est inordinata conversio ad commutabile bonum, ut dictum est. Tertio modo sumitur prout significat quandam inclinationem naturae corruptae ad bona corruptibilia inordinate appetenda. Et sic dicunt cupiditatem esse radicem omnium peccatorum, ad similitudinem radicis arboris, quae ex

OBJECTION 1: It would seem that covetousness is not the root of all sins. For covetousness, which is immoderate desire for riches, is opposed to the virtue of liberality. But liberality is not the root of all virtues. Therefore covetousness is not the root of all sins.

OBJ. 2: Further, the desire for the means proceeds from desire for the end. Now riches, the desire for which is called covetousness, are not desired except as being useful for some end, as stated in *Ethic*. i, 5. Therefore covetousness is not the root of all sins, but proceeds from some deeper root.

OBJ. 3: Further, it often happens that avarice, which is another name for covetousness, arises from other sins; as when a man desires money through ambition, or in order to sate his gluttony. Therefore it is not the root of all sins.

ON THE CONTRARY, The Apostle says (1 Tim 6:10): *The desire of money is the root of all evil.*

I ANSWER THAT, According to some, covetousness may be understood in different ways. First, as denoting inordinate desire for riches: and thus it is a special sin. Second, as denoting inordinate desire for any temporal good: and thus it is a genus comprising all sins, because every sin includes an inordinate turning to a mutable good, as stated above (Q72, A2). Third, as denoting an inclination of a corrupt nature to desire corruptible goods inordinately: and they say that in this sense covetousness is the root of all sins, comparing it to the root of a tree, which draws its

terra trahit alimentum, sic enim ex amore rerum temporalium omne peccatum procedit.

Et haec quidem quamvis vera sint, non tamen videntur esse secundum intentionem apostoli, qui dixit cupiditatem esse radicem omnium peccatorum. Manifeste enim ibi loquitur contra eos qui, *cum velint divites fieri, incidunt in tentationes et in laqueum Diaboli, eo quod radix omnium malorum est cupiditas*, unde manifestum est quod loquitur de cupiditate secundum quod est appetitus inordinatus divitiarum. Et secundum hoc, dicendum est quod cupiditas, secundum quod est speciale peccatum, dicitur radix omnium peccatorum, ad similitudinem radicis arboris, quae alimentum praestat toti arbori. Videmus enim quod per divitias homo acquirit facultatem perpetrandi quodcumque peccatum, et adimplendi desiderium cuiuscumque peccati, eo quod ad habenda quaecumque temporalia bona, potest homo per pecuniam iuvari; secundum quod dicitur Eccle. X, *pecuniae obediunt omnia*. Et secundum hoc, patet quod cupiditas divitiarum est radix omnium peccatorum.

AD PRIMUM ergo dicendum quod non ab eodem oritur virtus et peccatum. Oritur enim peccatum ex appetitu commutabilis boni, et ideo appetitus illius boni quod iuvat ad consequenda omnia temporalia bona, radix peccatorum dicitur. Virtus autem oritur ex appetitu incommutabilis boni, et ideo caritas, quae est amor Dei, ponitur radix virtutum; secundum illud Ephes. III, *in caritate radicati et fundati*.

AD SECUNDUM dicendum quod appetitus pecuniarum dicitur esse radix peccatorum, non quia divitiae propter se quaerantur, tanquam ultimus finis, sed quia multum quaeruntur ut utiles ad omnem temporalem finem. Et quia universale bonum est appetibilius quam aliquod particulare bonum, ideo magis movent appetitum quam quaedam bona singularia, quae simul cum multis aliis per pecuniam haberi possunt.

AD TERTIUM dicendum quod, sicut in rebus naturalibus non quaeritur quid semper fiat, sed quid in pluribus accidit, eo quod natura corruptibilium rerum impediri potest, ut non semper eodem modo operetur; ita etiam in moralibus consideratur quod ut in pluribus est, non autem quod est semper, eo quod voluntas non ex necessitate operatur. Non igitur dicitur avaritia radix omnis mali, quin interdum aliquod aliud malum sit radix eius, sed quia ex ipsa frequentius alia mala oriuntur, ratione praedicta.

sustenance from earth, just as every sin grows out of the love of temporal things.

Now, though all this is true, it does not seem to explain the mind of the Apostle when he states that covetousness is the root of all sins. For in that passage he clearly speaks against those who, because they *will become rich, fall into temptation, and into the snare of the devil . . . for covetousness is the root of all evils*. Hence it is evident that he is speaking of covetousness as denoting the inordinate desire for riches. Accordingly, we must say that covetousness, as denoting a special sin, is called the root of all sins, in likeness to the root of a tree, in furnishing sustenance to the whole tree. For we see that by riches man acquires the means of committing any sin whatever, and of sating his desire for any sin whatever, since money helps man to obtain all manner of temporal goods, according to Eccles. 10:19: *All things obey money*: so that in this desire for riches is the root of all sins.

REPLY OBJ. 1: Virtue and sin do not arise from the same source. For sin arises from the desire of mutable good; and consequently the desire of that good which helps one to obtain all temporal goods, is called the root of all sins. But virtue arises from the desire for the immutable God; and consequently charity, which is the love of God, is called the root of the virtues, according to Eph. 3:17: *Rooted and founded in charity*.

REPLY OBJ. 2: The desire of money is said to be the root of sins, not as though riches were sought for their own sake, as being the last end; but because they are much sought after as useful for any temporal end. And since a universal good is more desirable than a particular good, they move the appetite more than any individual goods, which along with many others can be procured by means of money.

REPLY OBJ. 3: Just as in natural things we do not ask what always happens, but what happens most frequently, for the reason that the nature of corruptible things can be hindered, so as not always to act in the same way; so also in moral matters, we consider what happens in the majority of cases, not what happens invariably, for the reason that the will does not act of necessity. So when we say that covetousness is the root of all evils, we do not assert that no other evil can be its root, but that other evils more frequently arise therefrom, for the reason given.

Article 2

Whether Pride Is the Beginning of Every Sin?

AD SECUNDUM SIC PROCEDITUR. Videtur quod superbia non sit initium omnis peccati. Radix enim est quoddam principium arboris, et ita videtur idem esse radix peccati et initium peccati. Sed cupiditas est radix omnis peccati, ut dictum est. Ergo ipsa etiam est initium omnis peccati, non autem superbia.

PRAETEREA, Eccli. X dicitur, *initium superbiae hominis apostatare a Deo.* Sed apostasia a Deo est quoddam peccatum. Ergo aliquod peccatum est initium superbiae, et ipsa non est initium omnis peccati.

PRAETEREA, illud videtur esse initium omnis peccati, quod facit omnia peccata. Sed hoc est inordinatus amor sui, *qui facit civitatem Babylonis,* ut Augustinus dicit, in XIV de Civ. Dei. Ergo amor sui est initium omnis peccati, non autem superbia.

SED CONTRA est quod dicitur Eccli. X, *initium omnis peccati superbia.*

RESPONDEO dicendum quod quidam dicunt superbiam dici tripliciter. Uno modo, secundum quod superbia significat inordinatum appetitum propriae excellentiae. Et sic est speciale peccatum. Alio modo, secundum quod importat quendam actualem contemptum Dei, quantum ad hunc effectum qui est non subdi eius praecepto. Et sic dicunt quod est generale peccatum. Tertio modo, secundum quod importat quandam inclinationem ad huiusmodi contemptum, ex corruptione naturae. Et sic dicunt quod est initium omnis peccati. Et differt a cupiditate, quia cupiditas respicit peccatum ex parte conversionis ad bonum commutabile, ex quo peccatum quodammodo nutritur et fovetur, et propter hoc cupiditas dicitur radix, sed superbia respicit peccatum ex parte aversionis a Deo, cuius praecepto homo subdi recusat; et ideo vocatur initium, quia ex parte aversionis incipit ratio mali.

Et haec quidem quamvis vera sint, tamen non sunt secundum intentionem sapientis, qui dixit, initium omnis peccati est superbia. Manifeste enim loquitur de superbia secundum quod est inordinatus appetitus propriae excellentiae, ut patet per hoc quod subdit, *sedes ducum superborum destruxit Deus.* Et de hac materia fere loquitur in toto capitulo. Et ideo dicendum est quod superbia, etiam secundum quod est speciale peccatum, est initium omnis peccati. Considerandum est enim quod in actibus voluntariis, cuiusmodi sunt peccata, duplex ordo invenitur, scilicet intentionis, et executionis. In primo quidem ordine, habet rationem principii finis, ut supra multoties dictum est. Finis autem in omnibus bonis temporalibus acquirendis, est ut homo per illa quandam perfectionem et excellentiam habeat. Et ideo ex hac parte superbia, quae est appetitus excellentiae, ponitur initium omnis

OBJECTION 1: It would seem that pride is not the beginning of every sin. For the root is a beginning of a tree, so that the beginning of a sin seems to be the same as the root of sin. Now covetousness is the root of every sin, as stated above (A1). Therefore it is also the beginning of every sin, and not pride.

OBJ. 2: Further, it is written (Sir 10:14): *The beginning of the pride of man is apostasy from God.* But apostasy from God is a sin. Therefore another sin is the beginning of pride, so that the latter is not the beginning of every sin.

OBJ. 3: Further, the beginning of every sin would seem to be that which causes all sins. Now this is inordinate self-love, which, according to Augustine (*De Civ. Dei* xiv), *builds up the city of Babylon.* Therefore self-love and not pride, is the beginning of every sin.

ON THE CONTRARY, It is written (Sir 10:15): *Pride is the beginning of all sin.*

I ANSWER THAT, Some say pride is to be taken in three ways. First, as denoting inordinate desire to excel; and thus it is a special sin. Second, as denoting actual contempt of God, to the effect of not being subject to His commandment; and thus, they say, it is a generic sin. Third, as denoting an inclination to this contempt, owing to the corruption of nature; and in this sense they say that it is the beginning of every sin, and that it differs from covetousness, because covetousness regards sin as turning towards the mutable good by which sin is, as it were, nourished and fostered, for which reason covetousness is called the *root*; whereas pride regards sin as turning away from God, to Whose commandment man refuses to be subject, for which reason it is called the *beginning*, because the beginning of evil consists in turning away from God.

Now though all this is true, nevertheless it does not explain the mind of the wise man who said (Sir 10:15): *Pride is the beginning of all sin.* For it is evident that he is speaking of pride as denoting inordinate desire to excel, as is clear from what follows (verse 17): *God hath overturned the thrones of proud princes;* indeed this is the point of nearly the whole chapter. We must therefore say that pride, even as denoting a special sin, is the beginning of every sin. For we must take note that, in voluntary actions, such as sins, there is a twofold order, of intention, and of execution. In the former order, the principle is the end, as we have stated many times before (Q1, A1, ad 1; Q18, A7, ad 2; Q15, A1, ad 2; Q25, A2). Now man's end in acquiring all temporal goods is that, through their means, he may have some perfection and excellence. Therefore, from this point of view, pride, which is the desire to excel, is said to be the *beginning*

139

peccati. Sed ex parte executionis, est primum id quod praebet opportunitatem adimplendi omnia desideria peccati, quod habet rationem radicis, scilicet divitiae. Et ideo ex hac parte avaritia ponitur esse radix omnium malorum, ut dictum est.

ET PER HOC patet responsio ad primum.

AD SECUNDUM dicendum quod apostatare a Deo dicitur esse initium superbiae ex parte aversionis, ex hoc enim quod homo non vult subdi Deo, sequitur quod inordinate velit propriam excellentiam in rebus temporalibus. Et sic apostasia a Deo non sumitur ibi quasi speciale peccatum, sed magis ut quaedam conditio generalis omnis peccati, quae est aversio ab incommutabili bono. Vel potest dici quod apostatare a Deo dicitur esse initium superbiae, quia est prima superbiae species. Ad superbiam enim pertinet cuicumque superiori nolle subiici, et praecipue nolle subdi Deo; ex quo contingit quod homo supra seipsum indebite extollatur, quantum ad alias superbiae species.

AD TERTIUM dicendum quod in hoc homo se amat, quod sui excellentiam vult, idem enim est se amare quod sibi velle bonum. Unde ad idem pertinet quod ponatur initium omnis peccati superbia, vel amor proprius.

of every sin. On the other hand, in the order of execution, the first place belongs to that which by furnishing the opportunity of fulfilling all desires of sin, has the character of a root, and such are riches; so that, from this point of view, covetousness is said to be the *root* of all evils, as stated above (A1).

THIS SUFFICES for the Reply to the First Objection.

REPLY OBJ. 2: Apostasy from God is stated to be the beginning of pride, insofar as it denotes a turning away from God, because from the fact that man wishes not to be subject to God, it follows that he desires inordinately his own excellence in temporal things. Wherefore, in the passage quoted, apostasy from God does not denote the special sin, but rather that general condition of every sin, consisting in its turning away from God. It may also be said that apostasy from God is said to be the beginning of pride, because it is the first species of pride. For it is characteristic of pride to be unwilling to be subject to any superior, and especially to God; the result being that a man is unduly lifted up, in respect of the other species of pride.

REPLY OBJ. 3: In desiring to excel, man loves himself, for to love oneself is the same as to desire some good for oneself. Consequently it amounts to the same whether we reckon pride or self-love as the beginning of every evil.

Article 3

Whether Any Other Special Sins, Besides Pride and Avarice, Should Be Called Capital?

AD TERTIUM SIC PROCEDITUR. Videtur quod praeter superbiam et avaritiam, non sint quaedam alia peccata specialia quae dicantur capitalia. *Ita enim se videtur habere caput ad animalia, sicut radix ad plantas*, ut dicitur in II de anima, nam radices sunt ori similes. Si igitur cupiditas dicitur radix omnium malorum, videtur quod ipsa sola debeat dici vitium capitale, et nullum aliud peccatum.

PRAETEREA, caput habet quendam ordinem ad alia membra, inquantum a capite diffunditur quodammodo sensus et motus. Sed peccatum dicitur per privationem ordinis. Ergo peccatum non habet rationem capitis. Et ita non debent poni aliqua capitalia peccata.

PRAETEREA, capitalia crimina dicuntur quae capite plectuntur. Sed tali poena puniuntur quaedam peccata in singulis generibus. Ergo vitia capitalia non sunt aliqua determinata secundum speciem.

SED CONTRA est quod Gregorius, XXXI Moral., enumerat quaedam specialia vitia, quae dicit esse capitalia.

RESPONDEO dicendum quod capitale a capite dicitur. Caput autem proprie quidem est quoddam membrum animalis, quod est principium et directivum totius animalis. Unde metaphorice omne principium caput

OBJECTION 1: It would seem that no other special sins, besides pride and avarice, should be called capital. Because *the head seems to be to an animal, what the root is to a plant*, as stated in *De Anima* ii, text. 38: for the roots are like a mouth. If therefore covetousness is called the *root of all evils*, it seems that it alone, and no other sin, should be called a capital vice.

OBJ. 2: Further, the head bears a certain relation of order to the other members, insofar as sensation and movement follow from the head. But sin implies privation of order. Therefore sin has not the character of head: so that no sins should be called capital.

OBJ. 3: Further, capital crimes are those which receive capital punishment. But every kind of sin comprises some that are punished thus. Therefore the capital sins are not certain specific sins.

ON THE CONTRARY, Gregory (*Moral.* xxxi, 17) enumerates certain special vices under the name of capital.

I ANSWER THAT, The word capital is derived from *caput*. Now the head, properly speaking, is that part of an animal's body, which is the principle and director of the whole animal. Hence, metaphorically speaking, every principle is

vocatur, et etiam homines qui alios dirigunt et gubernant, capita aliorum dicuntur. Dicitur ergo vitium capitale uno modo a capite proprie dicto, et secundum hoc, peccatum capitale dicitur peccatum quod capitis poena punitur. Sed sic nunc non intendimus de capitalibus peccatis, sed secundum quod alio modo dicitur peccatum capitale a capite prout metaphorice significat principium vel directivum aliorum. Et sic dicitur vitium capitale ex quo alia vitia oriuntur, et praecipue secundum originem causae finalis, quae est formalis origo, ut supra dictum est. Et ideo vitium capitale non solum est principium aliorum, sed etiam est directivum et quodammodo ductivum aliorum, semper enim ars vel habitus ad quem pertinet finis, principatur et imperat circa ea quae sunt ad finem. Unde Gregorius, XXXI Moral., huiusmodi vitia capitalia ducibus exercituum comparat.

AD PRIMUM ergo dicendum quod capitale dicitur denominative a capite, quod quidem est per quandam derivationem vel participationem capitis, sicut habens aliquam proprietatem capitis, non sicut simpliciter caput. Et ideo capitalia vitia dicuntur non solum illa quae habent rationem primae originis, sicut avaritia, quae dicitur radix, et superbia, quae dicitur initium, sed etiam illa quae habent rationem originis propinquae respectu plurium peccatorum.

AD SECUNDUM dicendum quod peccatum caret ordine ex parte aversionis, ex hac enim parte habet rationem mali; *malum autem*, secundum Augustinum, in libro de natura boni, *est privatio modi, speciei et ordinis.* Sed ex parte conversionis, respicit quoddam bonum. Et ideo ex hac parte potest habere ordinem.

AD TERTIUM dicendum quod illa ratio procedit de capitali peccato secundum quod dicitur a reatu poenae. Sic autem hic non loquimur.

called a head, and even men who direct and govern others are called heads. Accordingly a capital vice is so called, in the first place, from *head* taken in the proper sense, and thus the name *capital* is given to a sin for which capital punishment is inflicted. It is not in this sense that we are now speaking of capital sins, but in another sense, in which the term *capital* is derived from head, taken metaphorically for a principle or director of others. In this way a capital vice is one from which other vices arise, chiefly by being their final cause, which origin is formal, as stated above (Q72, A6). Wherefore a capital vice is not only the principle of others, but is also their director and, in a way, their leader: because the art or habit, to which the end belongs, is always the principle and the commander in matters concerning the means. Hence Gregory (*Moral.* xxxi, 17) compares these capital vices to the *leaders of an army*.

REPLY OBJ. 1: The term *capital* is taken from *caput* and applied to something connected with, or partaking of the head, as having some property thereof, but not as being the head taken literally. And therefore the capital vices are not only those which have the character of primary origin, as covetousness which is called the *root*, and pride which is called the beginning, but also those which have the character of proximate origin in respect of several sins.

REPLY OBJ. 2: Sin lacks order insofar as it turns away from God, for in this respect it is an evil, and evil, according to Augustine (*De Natura Boni* iv), is *the privation of mode, species and order.* But insofar as sin implies a turning to something, it regards some good: wherefore, in this respect, there can be order in sin.

REPLY OBJ. 3: This objection considers capital sin as so called from the punishment it deserves, in which sense we are not taking it here.

Article 4

Whether the Seven Capital Vices Are Suitably Reckoned?

AD QUARTUM SIC PROCEDITUR. Videtur quod non sit dicendum septem esse vitia capitalia, quae sunt inanis gloria, invidia, ira, tristitia, avaritia, gula, luxuria. Peccata enim virtutibus opponuntur. Virtutes autem principales sunt quatuor, ut supra dictum est. Ergo et vitia principalia, sive capitalia, non sunt nisi quatuor.

PRAETEREA, passiones animae sunt quaedam causae peccati, ut supra dictum est. Sed passiones animae principales sunt quatuor. De quarum duabus nulla fit mentio inter praedicta peccata, scilicet de spe et timore. Enumerantur autem aliqua vitia ad quae pertinet delectatio et tristitia, nam delectatio pertinet ad gulam

OBJECTION 1: It would seem that we ought not to reckon seven capital vices, viz., vainglory, envy, anger, sloth, covetousness, gluttony, lust. For sins are opposed to virtues. But there are four principal virtues, as stated above (Q61, A2). Therefore there are only four principal or capital vices.

OBJ. 2: Further, the passions of the soul are causes of sin, as stated above (Q77). But there are four principal passions of the soul; two of which, viz., hope and fear, are not mentioned among the above sins, whereas certain vices are mentioned to which pleasure and sadness belong, since pleasure belongs to gluttony and lust, and sadness to sloth

et luxuriam, tristitia vero ad acediam et invidiam. Ergo inconvenienter enumerantur principalia peccata.

PRAETEREA, ira non est principalis passio. Non ergo debuit poni inter principalia vitia.

PRAETEREA, sicut cupiditas, sive avaritia, est radix peccati, ita superbia est peccati initium, ut supra dictum est. Sed avaritia ponitur unum de septem vitiis capitalibus. Ergo superbia inter vitia capitalia enumeranda esset.

PRAETEREA, quaedam peccata committuntur quae ex nullo horum causari possunt, sicut cum aliquis errat ex ignorantia; vel cum aliquis ex aliqua bona intentione committit aliquod peccatum, puta cum aliquis furatur ut det eleemosynam. Ergo insufficienter capitalia vitia enumerantur.

SED IN CONTRARIUM est auctoritas Gregorii sic enumerantis, XXXI Moralium.

RESPONDEO dicendum quod, sicut dictum est, vitia capitalia dicuntur ex quibus alia oriuntur, praecipue secundum rationem causae finalis. Huiusmodi autem origo potest attendi dupliciter. Uno quidem modo, secundum conditionem peccantis, qui sic dispositus est ut maxime afficiatur ad unum finem, ex quo ut plurimum in alia peccata procedat. Sed iste modus originis sub arte cadere non potest, eo quod infinitae sunt particulares hominum dispositiones. Alio modo, secundum naturalem habitudinem ipsorum finium ad invicem. Et secundum hoc, ut in pluribus unum vitium ex alio oritur. Unde iste modus originis sub arte cadere potest.

Secundum hoc ergo, illa vitia capitalia dicuntur, quorum fines habent quasdam primarias rationes movendi appetitum, et secundum harum rationum distinctionem, distinguuntur capitalia vitia. Movet autem aliquid appetitum dupliciter. Uno modo, directe et per se, et hoc modo bonum movet appetitum ad prosequendum, malum autem, secundum eandem rationem, ad fugiendum. Alio modo, indirecte et quasi per aliud, sicut aliquis aliquod malum prosequitur propter aliquod bonum adiunctum, vel aliquod bonum fugit propter aliquod malum adiunctum.

Bonum autem hominis est triplex. Est enim primo quoddam bonum animae, quod scilicet ex sola apprehensione rationem appetibilitatis habet, scilicet excellentia laudis vel honoris, et hoc bonum inordinate prosequitur inanis gloria. Aliud est bonum corporis, et hoc vel pertinet ad conservationem individui, sicut cibus et potus, et hoc bonum inordinate prosequitur gula; aut ad conservationem speciei, sicut coitus, et ad hoc ordinatur luxuria. Tertium bonum est exterius, scilicet divitiae, et ad hoc ordinatur avaritia. Et eadem quatuor vitia inordinate fugiunt mala contraria.

and envy. Therefore the principal sins are unfittingly enumerated.

OBJ. 3: Further, anger is not a principal passion. Therefore it should not be placed among the principal vices.

OBJ. 4: Further, just as covetousness or avarice is the root of sin, so is pride the beginning of sin, as stated above (A2). But avarice is reckoned to be one of the capital vices. Therefore pride also should be placed among the capital vices.

OBJ. 5: Further, some sins are committed which cannot be caused through any of these: as, for instance, when one sins through ignorance, or when one commits a sin with a good intention, e.g., steals in order to give an alms. Therefore the capital vices are insufficiently enumerated.

ON THE CONTRARY, stands the authority of Gregory who enumerates them in this way (*Moral.* xxxi, 17).

I ANSWER THAT, As stated above (A3), the capital vices are those which give rise to others, especially by way of final cause. Now this kind of origin may take place in two ways. First, on account of the condition of the sinner, who is disposed so as to have a strong inclination for one particular end, the result being that he frequently goes forward to other sins. But this kind of origin does not come under the consideration of art, because man's particular dispositions are infinite in number. Second, on account of a natural relationship of the ends to one another: and it is in this way that most frequently one vice arises from another, so that this kind of origin can come under the consideration of art.

Accordingly therefore, those vices are called capital, whose ends have certain fundamental reasons for moving the appetite; and it is in respect of these fundamental reasons that the capital vices are differentiated. Now a thing moves the appetite in two ways. First, directly and of its very nature: thus good moves the appetite to seek it, while evil, for the same reason, moves the appetite to avoid it. Second, indirectly and on account of something else, as it were: thus one seeks an evil on account of some attendant good, or avoids a good on account of some attendant evil.

Again, man's good is threefold. For, in the first place, there is a certain good of the soul, which derives its aspect of appetibility, merely through being apprehended, viz., the excellence of honor and praise, and this good is sought inordinately by *vainglory*. Second, there is the good of the body, and this regards either the preservation of the individual, e.g., meat and drink, which good is pursued inordinately by *gluttony*, or the preservation of the species, e.g., sexual intercourse, which good is sought inordinately by *lust*. Third, there is external good, viz., riches, to which *covetousness* is referred. These same four vices avoid inordinately the contrary evils.

Vel aliter, bonum praecipue movet appetitum ex hoc quod participat aliquid de proprietate felicitatis, quam naturaliter omnes appetunt. De cuius ratione est quidem primo quaedam perfectio, nam felicitas est perfectum bonum, ad quod pertinet excellentia vel claritas, quam appetit superbia vel inanis gloria. Secundo de ratione eius est sufficientia, quam appetit avaritia in divitiis eam promittentibus. Tertio est de conditione eius delectatio, sine qua felicitas esse non potest, ut dicitur in I et X Ethic., et hanc appetunt gula et luxuria.

Quod autem aliquis bonum fugiat propter aliquod malum coniunctum, hoc contingit dupliciter. Quia aut hoc est respectu boni proprii, et sic est acedia, quae tristatur de bono spirituali, propter laborem corporalem adiunctum. Aut est de bono alieno, et hoc, si sit sine insurrectione, pertinet ad invidiam, quae tristatur de bono alieno, inquantum est impeditivum propriae excellentiae; aut est cum quadam insurrectione ad vindictam, et sic est ira. Et ad eadem etiam vitia pertinet prosecutio mali oppositi.

AD PRIMUM ergo dicendum quod non est eadem ratio originis in virtutibus et vitiis, nam virtutes causantur per ordinem appetitus ad rationem, vel etiam ad bonum incommutabile, quod est Deus; vitia autem oriuntur ex appetitu boni commutabilis. Unde non oportet quod principalia vitia opponantur principalibus virtutibus.

AD SECUNDUM dicendum quod timor et spes sunt passiones irascibilis. Omnes autem passiones irascibilis oriuntur ex passionibus concupiscibilis, quae etiam omnes ordinantur quodammodo ad delectationem et tristitiam. Et ideo delectatio et tristitia principaliter connumerantur in peccatis capitalibus, tanquam principalissimae passiones, ut supra habitum est.

AD TERTIUM dicendum quod ira, licet non sit principalis passio, quia tamen habet specialem rationem appetitivi motus, prout aliquis impugnat bonum alterius sub ratione honesti, idest iusti vindicativi; ideo distinguitur ab aliis capitalibus vitiis.

AD QUARTUM dicendum quod superbia dicitur esse initium omnis peccati secundum rationem finis, ut dictum est. Et secundum eandem rationem accipitur principalitas vitiorum capitalium. Et ideo superbia, quasi universale vitium, non connumeratur, sed magis ponitur velut regina quaedam omnium vitiorum, sicut Gregorius dicit. Avaritia autem dicitur radix secundum aliam rationem, sicut supra dictum est.

AD QUINTUM dicendum quod ista vitia dicuntur capitalia, quia ex eis ut frequentius alia oriuntur. Unde nihil prohibet aliqua peccata interdum ex aliis causis oriri. Potest tamen dici quod omnia peccata quae ex ignorantia proveniunt, possunt reduci ad acediam, ad quam pertinet negligentia qua aliquis recusat bona spiritualia acquirere propter laborem, ignorantia enim quae potest esse causa peccati, ex negligentia provenit, ut supra

Or again, good moves the appetite chiefly through possessing some property of happiness, which all men seek naturally. Now in the first place happiness implies perfection, since happiness is a perfect good, to which belongs excellence or renown, which is desired by *pride* or *vainglory*. Second, it implies satiety, which *covetousness* seeks in riches that give promise thereof. Third, it implies pleasure, without which happiness is impossible, as stated in *Ethic.* i, 7; x, 6,7,8 and this *gluttony* and *lust* pursue.

On the other hand, avoidance of good on account of an attendant evil occurs in two ways. For this happens either in respect of one's own good, and thus we have *sloth*, which is sadness about one's spiritual good, on account of the attendant bodily labor: or else it happens in respect of another's good, and this, if it be without recrimination, belongs to *envy*, which is sadness about another's good as being a hindrance to one's own excellence, while if it be with recrimination with a view to vengeance, it is *anger*. Again, these same vices seek the contrary evils.

REPLY OBJ. 1: Virtue and vice do not originate in the same way: since virtue is caused by the subordination of the appetite to reason, or to the immutable good, which is God, whereas vice arises from the appetite for mutable good. Wherefore there is no need for the principal vices to be contrary to the principal virtues.

REPLY OBJ. 2: Fear and hope are irascible passions. Now all the passions of the irascible part arise from passions of the concupiscible part; and these are all, in a way, directed to pleasure or sorrow. Hence pleasure and sorrow have a prominent place among the capital sins, as being the most important of the passions, as stated above (Q25, A4).

REPLY OBJ. 3: Although anger is not a principal passion, yet it has a distinct place among the capital vices, because it implies a special kind of movement in the appetite, insofar as recrimination against another's good has the aspect of a virtuous good, i.e., of the right to vengeance.

REPLY OBJ. 4: Pride is said to be the beginning of every sin, in the order of the end, as stated above (A2): and it is in the same order that we are to consider the capital sin as being principal. Wherefore pride, like a universal vice, is not counted along with the others, but is reckoned as the *queen of them all*, as Gregory states (*Moral.* xxxi, 27). But covetousness is said to be the root from another point of view, as stated above (AA1,2).

REPLY OBJ. 5: These vices are called capital because others, most frequently, arise from them: so that nothing prevents some sins from arising out of other causes. Nevertheless we might say that all the sins which are due to ignorance, can be reduced to sloth, to which pertains the negligence of a man who declines to acquire spiritual goods on account of the attendant labor; for the ignorance that can cause sin, is due to negligence, as stated above (Q76, A2).

dictum est. Quod autem aliquis committat aliquod peccatum ex bona intentione, videtur ad ignorantiam pertinere, inquantum scilicet ignorat quod non sunt facienda mala ut veniant bona.

That a man commit a sin with a good intention, seems to point to ignorance, insofar as he knows not that evil should not be done that good may come of it.

QUESTION 85

OF THE EFFECTS OF SIN

Deinde considerandum est de effectibus peccati. Et primo quidem, de corruptione boni naturae; secundo, de macula animae; tertio, de reatu poenae.

Circa primum quaeruntur sex.

Primo, utrum bonum naturae diminuatur per peccatum.

Secundo, utrum totaliter tolli possit.

Tertio, de quatuor vulneribus quae Beda ponit, quibus natura humana vulnerata est propter peccatum.

Quarto, utrum privatio modi, speciei et ordinis, sit effectus peccati.

Quinto, utrum mors et alii defectus corporales sint effectus peccati.

Sexto, utrum sint aliquo modo homini naturales.

We must now consider the effects of sin; and (1) the corruption of the good of nature; (2) the stain on the soul; (3) the debt of punishment.

Under the first head there are six points of inquiry:

(1) Whether the good of nature is diminished by sin?

(2) Whether it can be taken away altogether?

(3) Of the four wounds, mentioned by Bede, with which human nature is stricken in consequence of sin.

(4) Whether privation of mode, species and order is an effect of sin?

(5) Whether death and other bodily defects are the result of sin?

(6) Whether they are, in any way, natural to man?

Article 1

Whether Sin Diminishes the Good of Nature?

AD PRIMUM SIC PROCEDITUR. Videtur quod peccatum non diminuat bonum naturae. Peccatum enim hominis non est gravius quam peccatum Daemonis. Sed bona naturalia in Daemonibus manent integra post peccatum, ut Dionysius dicit, IV cap. de Div. Nom. Ergo peccatum etiam bonum naturae humanae non diminuit.

PRAETEREA, transmutato posteriori, non transmutatur prius, manet enim substantia eadem, transmutatis accidentibus. Sed natura praeexistit actioni voluntariae. Ergo, facta deordinatione circa actionem voluntariam per peccatum, non transmutatur propter hoc natura, ita quod bonum naturae diminuatur.

PRAETEREA, peccatum est actus quidam, diminutio autem passio. Nullum autem agens, ex hoc ipso quod agit, patitur, potest autem contingere quod in unum agat, et ab alio patiatur. Ergo ille qui peccat, per peccatum non diminuit bonum suae naturae.

PRAETEREA, nullum accidens agit in suum subiectum, quia quod patitur, est potentia ens; quod autem subiicitur accidenti, iam est actu ens secundum accidens illud. Sed peccatum est in bono naturae sicut accidens in subiecto. Ergo peccatum non diminuit bonum naturae, diminuere enim quoddam agere est.

SED CONTRA est quod, sicut dicitur Luc. X, *homo descendens a Ierusalem in Iericho, idest in defectum peccati,*

OBJECTION 1: It would seem that sin does not diminish the good of nature. For man's sin is no worse than the devil's. But natural good remains unimpaired in devils after sin, as Dionysius states (*Div. Nom.* iv). Therefore neither does sin diminish the good of human nature.

OBJ. 2: Further, when that which follows is changed, that which precedes remains unchanged, since substance remains the same when its accidents are changed. But nature exists before the voluntary action. Therefore, when sin has caused a disorder in a voluntary act, nature is not changed on that account, so that the good of nature be diminished.

OBJ. 3: Further, sin is an action, while diminution is a passion. Now no agent is passive by the very reason of its acting, although it is possible for it to act on one thing, and to be passive as regards another. Therefore he who sins, does not, by his sin, diminish the good of his nature.

OBJ. 4: Further, no accident acts on its subject: because that which is patient is a potential being, while that which is subjected to an accident, is already an actual being as regards that accident. But sin is in the good of nature as an accident in a subject. Therefore sin does not diminish the good of nature, since to diminish is to act.

ON THE CONTRARY, *A certain man going down from Jerusalem to Jericho* (Luke 10:30), i.e., to the corruption of

145

expoliatur gratuitis et vulneratur in naturalibus, ut Beda exponit. Ergo peccatum diminuit bonum naturae.

RESPONDEO dicendum quod bonum naturae humanae potest tripliciter dici. Primo, ipsa principia naturae, ex quibus natura constituitur, et proprietates ex his causatae, sicut potentiae animae et alia huiusmodi. Secundo, quia homo a natura habet inclinationem ad virtutem, ut supra habitum est, ipsa inclinatio ad virtutem est quoddam bonum naturae. Tertio modo potest dici bonum naturae donum originalis iustitiae, quod fuit in primo homine collatum toti humanae naturae.

Primum igitur bonum naturae nec tollitur nec diminuitur per peccatum. Tertium vero bonum naturae totaliter est ablatum per peccatum primi parentis. Sed medium bonum naturae, scilicet ipsa naturalis inclinatio ad virtutem, diminuitur per peccatum. Per actus enim humanos fit quaedam inclinatio ad similes actus, ut supra habitum est. Oportet autem quod ex hoc quod aliquid inclinatur ad unum contrariorum, diminuatur inclinatio eius ad aliud. Unde cum peccatum sit contrarium virtuti, ex hoc ipso quod homo peccat, diminuitur bonum naturae quod est inclinatio ad virtutem.

AD PRIMUM ergo dicendum quod Dionysius loquitur de bono primo naturae, quod est esse, vivere et intelligere; ut patet eius verba intuenti.

AD SECUNDUM dicendum quod natura, etsi sit prior quam voluntaria actio, tamen habet inclinationem ad quandam voluntariam actionem. Unde ipsa natura secundum se non variatur propter variationem voluntariae actionis, sed ipsa inclinatio variatur ex illa parte qua ordinatur ad terminum.

AD TERTIUM dicendum quod actio voluntaria procedit ex diversis potentiis, quarum una est activa et alia passiva. Et ex hoc contingit quod per actiones voluntarias causatur aliquid, vel aufertur ab homine sic agente, ut supra dictum est, cum de generatione habituum ageretur.

AD QUARTUM dicendum quod accidens non agit effective in subiectum; agit tamen formaliter in ipsum, eo modo loquendi quo dicitur quod albedo facit album. Et sic nihil prohibet quod peccatum diminuat bonum naturae, eo tamen modo quo est ipsa diminutio boni naturae, inquantum pertinet ad inordinationem actus. Sed quantum ad inordinationem agentis, oportet dicere quod talis inordinatio causatur per hoc quod in actibus animae aliquid est activum et aliquid passivum, sicut sensibile movet appetitum sensitivum, et appetitus sensitivus inclinat rationem et voluntatem, ut supra dictum est. Et ex hoc causatur inordinatio, non quidem ita quod accidens agat in proprium subiectum; sed secundum quod obiectum agit in potentiam, et una potentia agit in aliam, et deordinat ipsam.

sin, was stripped of his gifts, and wounded in his nature, as Bede expounds the passage. Therefore sin diminishes the good of nature.

I ANSWER THAT, The good of human nature is threefold. First, there are the principles of which nature is constituted, and the properties that flow from them, such as the powers of the soul, and so forth. Second, since man has from nature an inclination to virtue, as stated above (Q60, A1; Q63, A1), this inclination to virtue is a good of nature. Third, the gift of original justice, conferred on the whole of human nature in the person of the first man, may be called a good of nature.

Accordingly, the first-mentioned good of nature is neither destroyed nor diminished by sin. The third good of nature was entirely destroyed through the sin of our first parent. But the second good of nature, viz., the natural inclination to virtue, is diminished by sin. Because human acts produce an inclination to like acts, as stated above (Q50, A1). Now from the very fact that thing becomes inclined to one of two contraries, its inclination to the other contrary must needs be diminished. Wherefore as sin is opposed to virtue, from the very fact that a man sins, there results a diminution of that good of nature, which is the inclination to virtue.

REPLY OBJ. 1: Dionysius is speaking of the first-mentioned good of nature, which consists in *being, living and understanding*, as anyone may see who reads the context.

REPLY OBJ. 2: Although nature precedes the voluntary action, it has an inclination to a certain voluntary action. Wherefore nature is not changed in itself, through a change in the voluntary action: it is the inclination that is changed insofar as it is directed to its term.

REPLY OBJ. 3: A voluntary action proceeds from various powers, active and passive. The result is that through voluntary actions something is caused or taken away in the man who acts, as we have stated when treating of the production of habits (Q51, A2).

REPLY OBJ. 4: An accident does not act effectively on its subject, but it acts on it formally, in the same sense as when we say that whiteness makes a thing white. In this way there is nothing to hinder sin from diminishing the good of nature; but only insofar as sin is itself a diminution of the good of nature, through being an inordinateness of action. But as regards the inordinateness of the agent, we must say that such like inordinateness is caused by the fact that in the acts of the soul, there is an active, and a passive element: thus the sensible object moves the sensitive appetite, and the sensitive appetite inclines the reason and will, as stated above (Q77, AA1, 2). The result of this is the inordinateness, not as though an accident acted on its own subject, but insofar as the object acts on the power, and one power acts on another and puts it out of order.

Article 2

Whether the Entire Good of Human Nature Can Be Destroyed by Sin?

AD SECUNDUM SIC PROCEDITUR. Videtur quod totum bonum humanae naturae possit per peccatum auferri. Bonum enim naturae humanae finitum est, cum et ipsa natura humana sit finita. Sed quodlibet finitum totaliter consumitur, facta continua ablatione. Cum ergo bonum naturae continue per peccatum diminui possit, videtur quod possit quandoque totaliter consumi.

PRAETEREA, eorum quae sunt unius naturae, similis est ratio de toto et de partibus, sicut patet in aere et in aqua et carne, et omnibus corporibus similium partium. Sed bonum naturae est totaliter uniforme. Cum igitur pars eius possit auferri per peccatum, totum etiam per peccatum auferri posse videtur.

PRAETEREA, bonum naturae quod per peccatum minuitur, est habilitas ad virtutem. Sed in quibusdam propter peccatum habilitas praedicta totaliter tollitur, ut patet in damnatis, qui reparari ad virtutem non possunt, sicut nec caecus ad visum. Ergo peccatum potest totaliter tollere bonum naturae.

SED CONTRA est quod Augustinus dicit, in Enchirid., quod *malum non est nisi in bono*. Sed malum culpae non potest esse in bono virtutis vel gratiae, quia est ei contrarium. Ergo oportet quod sit in bono naturae. Non ergo totaliter tollit ipsum.

RESPONDEO dicendum quod, sicut dictum est, bonum naturae quod per peccatum diminuitur, est naturalis inclinatio ad virtutem. Quae quidem convenit homini ex hoc ipso quod rationalis est, ex hoc enim habet quod secundum rationem operetur, quod est agere secundum virtutem. Per peccatum autem non potest totaliter ab homine tolli quod sit rationalis, quia iam non esset capax peccati. Unde non est possibile quod praedictum naturae bonum totaliter tollatur.

Cum autem inveniatur huiusmodi bonum continue diminui per peccatum, quidam ad huius manifestationem usi sunt quodam exemplo, in quo invenitur aliquod finitum in infinitum diminui, nunquam tamen totaliter consumi. Dicit enim philosophus, in III Physic., quod si ab aliqua magnitudine finita continue auferatur aliquid secundum eandem quantitatem, totaliter tandem consumetur, puta si a quacumque quantitate finita semper subtraxero mensuram palmi. Si vero fiat subtractio semper secundum eandem proportionem, et non secundum eandem quantitatem, poterit in infinitum subtrahi, puta, si quantitas dividatur in duas partes, et a dimidio subtrahatur dimidium, ita in infinitum poterit procedi; ita tamen quod semper quod posterius subtrahitur, erit minus eo quod prius subtrahebatur. Sed hoc in proposito

OBJECTION 1: It would seem that the entire good of human nature can be destroyed by sin. For the good of human nature is finite, since human nature itself is finite. Now any finite thing is entirely taken away, if the subtraction be continuous. Since therefore the good of nature can be continually diminished by sin, it seems that in the end it can be entirely taken away.

OBJ. 2: Further, in a thing of one nature, the whole and the parts are uniform, as is evidently the case with air, water, flesh and all bodies with similar parts. But the good of nature is wholly uniform. Since therefore a part thereof can be taken away by sin, it seems that the whole can also be taken away by sin.

OBJ. 3: Further, the good of nature, that is weakened by sin, is aptitude for virtue. Now this aptitude is destroyed entirely in some on account of sin: thus the lost cannot be restored to virtue any more than the blind can to sight. Therefore sin can take away the good of nature entirely.

ON THE CONTRARY, Augustine says (*Enchiridion* xiv) that *evil does not exist except in some good*. But the evil of sin cannot be in the good of virtue or of grace, because they are contrary to it. Therefore it must be in the good of nature, and consequently it does not destroy it entirely.

I ANSWER THAT, As stated above (A1), the good of nature, that is diminished by sin, is the natural inclination to virtue, which is befitting to man from the very fact that he is a rational being; for it is due to this that he performs actions in accord with reason, which is to act virtuously. Now sin cannot entirely take away from man the fact that he is a rational being, for then he would no longer be capable of sin. Wherefore it is not possible for this good of nature to be destroyed entirely.

Since, however, this same good of nature may be continually diminished by sin, some, in order to illustrate this, have made use of the example of a finite thing being diminished indefinitely, without being entirely destroyed. For the Philosopher says (*Phys.* i, text. 37) that if from a finite magnitude a continual subtraction be made in the same quantity, it will at last be entirely destroyed, for instance if from any finite length I continue to subtract the length of a span. If, however, the subtraction be made each time in the same proportion, and not in the same quantity, it may go on indefinitely, as, for instance, if a quantity be halved, and one half be diminished by half, it will be possible to go on thus indefinitely, provided that what is subtracted in each case be less than what was subtracted before. But this does not apply to the question at issue, since a subsequent sin does

non habet locum, non enim sequens peccatum minus diminuit bonum naturae quam praecedens, sed forte magis, si sit gravius.

Et ideo aliter est dicendum quod praedicta inclinatio intelligitur ut media inter duo, fundatur enim sicut in radice in natura rationali, et tendit in bonum virtutis sicut in terminum et finem. Dupliciter igitur potest intelligi eius diminutio, uno modo, ex parte radicis; alio modo, ex parte termini. Primo quidem modo non diminuitur per peccatum, eo quod peccatum non diminuit ipsam naturam, ut supra dictum est. Sed diminuitur secundo modo, inquantum scilicet ponitur impedimentum pertingendi ad terminum. Si autem primo modo diminueretur, oporteret quod quandoque totaliter consumeretur, natura rationali totaliter consumpta. Sed quia diminuitur ex parte impedimenti quod apponitur ne pertingat ad terminum, manifestum est quod diminui quidem potest in infinitum, quia in infinitum possunt impedimenta apponi, secundum quod homo potest in infinitum addere peccatum peccato, non tamen potest totaliter consumi, quia semper manet radix talis inclinationis. Sicut patet in diaphano corpore, quod quidem habet inclinationem ad susceptionem lucis ex hoc ipso quod est diaphanum, diminuitur autem haec inclinatio vel habilitas ex parte nebularum supervenientium, cum tamen semper maneat in radice naturae.

AD PRIMUM ergo dicendum quod obiectio illa procedit quando fit diminutio per subtractionem. Hic autem fit diminutio per appositionem impedimenti, quod neque tollit neque diminuit radicem inclinationis, ut dictum est.

AD SECUNDUM dicendum quod inclinatio naturalis est quidem tota uniformis, sed tamen habet respectum et ad principium et ad terminum, secundum quam diversitatem quodammodo diminuitur et quodammodo non diminuitur.

AD TERTIUM dicendum quod etiam in damnatis manet naturalis inclinatio ad virtutem, alioquin non esset in eis remorsus conscientiae. Sed quod non reducatur in actum, contingit quia deest gratia, secundum divinam iustitiam. Sicut etiam in caeco remanet aptitudo ad videndum in ipsa radice naturae, inquantum est animal naturaliter habens visum, sed non reducitur in actum, quia deest causa quae reducere possit formando organum quod requiritur ad videndum.

not diminish the good of nature less than a previous sin, but perhaps more, if it be a more grievous sin.

We must, therefore, explain the matter otherwise by saying that the aforesaid inclination is to be considered as a middle term between two others: for it is based on the rational nature as on its root, and tends to the good of virtue, as to its term and end. Consequently its diminution may be understood in two ways: first, on the part of its rood, second, on the part of its term. In the first way, it is not diminished by sin, because sin does not diminish nature, as stated above (A1). But it is diminished in the second way, insofar as an obstacle is placed against its attaining its term. Now if it were diminished in the first way, it would needs be entirely destroyed at last by the rational nature being entirely destroyed. Since, however, it is diminished on the part of the obstacle which is place against its attaining its term, it is evident that it can be diminished indefinitely, because obstacles can be placed indefinitely, inasmuch as man can go on indefinitely adding sin to sin: and yet it cannot be destroyed entirely, because the root of this inclination always remains. An example of this may be seen in a transparent body, which has an inclination to receive light, from the very fact that it is transparent; yet this inclination or aptitude is diminished on the part of supervening clouds, although it always remains rooted in the nature of the body.

REPLY OBJ. 1: This objection avails when diminution is made by subtraction. But here the diminution is made by raising obstacles, and this neither diminishes nor destroys the root of the inclination, as stated above.

REPLY OBJ. 2: The natural inclination is indeed wholly uniform: nevertheless it stands in relation both to its principle and to its term, in respect of which diversity of relation, it is diminished on the one hand, and not on the other.

REPLY OBJ. 3: Even in the lost the natural inclination to virtue remains, else they would have no remorse of conscience. That it is not reduced to act is owing to their being deprived of grace by Divine justice. Thus even in a blind man the aptitude to see remains in the very root of his nature, inasmuch as he is an animal naturally endowed with sight: yet this aptitude is not reduced to act, for the lack of a cause capable of reducing it, by forming the organ requisite for sight.

Article 3

*Whether Weakness, Ignorance, Malice and Concupiscence Are Suitably
Reckoned As the Wounds of Nature Consequent upon Sin?*

AD TERTIUM SIC PROCEDITUR. Videtur quod inconvenienter ponantur vulnera naturae esse, ex peccato consequentia, infirmitas, ignorantia, malitia et concupiscentia. Non enim idem est effectus et causa eiusdem. Sed ista ponuntur causae peccatorum, ut ex supradictis patet. Ergo non debent poni effectus peccati.

PRAETEREA, malitia nominat quoddam peccatum. Non ergo debet poni inter effectus peccati.

PRAETEREA, concupiscentia est quiddam naturale, cum sit actus virtutis concupiscibilis. Sed illud quod est naturale, non debet poni vulnus naturae. Ergo concupiscentia non debet poni vulnus naturae.

PRAETEREA, dictum est quod idem est peccare ex infirmitate, et ex passione. Sed concupiscentia passio quaedam est. Ergo non debet contra infirmitatem dividi.

PRAETEREA, Augustinus, in libro de natura et gratia, *ponit duo poenalia animae peccanti, scilicet ignorantiam et difficultatem, ex quibus oritur error et cruciatus,* quae quidem quatuor non concordant istis quatuor. Ergo videtur quod alterum eorum insufficienter ponatur.

IN CONTRARIUM est auctoritas Bedae.

RESPONDEO dicendum quod per iustitiam originalem perfecte ratio continebat inferiores animae vires, et ipsa ratio a Deo perficiebatur ei subiecta. Haec autem originalis iustitia subtracta est per peccatum primi parentis, sicut iam dictum est. Et ideo omnes vires animae remanent quodammodo destitutae proprio ordine, quo naturaliter ordinantur ad virtutem, et ipsa destitutio vulneratio naturae dicitur.

Sunt autem quatuor potentiae animae quae possunt esse subiecta virtutum, ut supra dictum est, scilicet ratio, in qua est prudentia; voluntas, in qua est iustitia; irascibilis, in qua est fortitudo; concupiscibilis, in qua est temperantia. Inquantum ergo ratio destituitur suo ordine ad verum, est vulnus ignorantiae; inquantum vero voluntas destituitur ordine ad bonum, est vulnus malitiae; inquantum vero irascibilis destituitur suo ordine ad arduum, est vulnus infirmitatis; inquantum vero concupiscentia destituitur ordine ad delectabile moderatum ratione, est vulnus concupiscentiae.

Sic igitur ita quatuor sunt vulnera inflicta toti humanae naturae ex peccato primi parentis. Sed quia inclinatio ad bonum virtutis in unoquoque diminuitur per

OBJECTION 1: It would seem that weakness, ignorance, malice and concupiscence are not suitably reckoned as the wounds of nature consequent upon sin. For one same thing is not both effect and cause of the same thing. But these are reckoned to be causes of sin, as appears from what has been said above (Q76, A1; Q77, AA3,5; Q78, A1). Therefore they should not be reckoned as effects of sin.

OBJ. 2: Further, malice is the name of a sin. Therefore it should have no place among the effects of sin.

OBJ. 3: Further, concupiscence is something natural, since it is an act of the concupiscible power. But that which is natural should not be reckoned a wound of nature. Therefore concupiscence should not be reckoned a wound of nature.

OBJ. 4: Further, it has been stated (Q77, A3) that to sin from weakness is the same as to sin from passion. But concupiscence is a passion. Therefore it should not be condivided with weakness.

OBJ. 5: Further, Augustine (*De Nat. et Grat.* lxvii, 67) reckons *two things to be punishments inflicted on the soul of the sinner, viz., ignorance and difficulty,* from which arise *error and vexation,* which four do not coincide with the four in question. Therefore it seems that one or the other reckoning is incomplete.

ON THE CONTRARY, The authority of Bede suffices.

I ANSWER THAT, As a result of original justice, the reason had perfect hold over the lower parts of the soul, while reason itself was perfected by God, and was subject to Him. Now this same original justice was forfeited through the sin of our first parent, as already stated (Q81, A2); so that all the powers of the soul are left, as it were, destitute of their proper order, whereby they are naturally directed to virtue; which destitution is called a wounding of nature.

Again, there are four of the soul's powers that can be subject of virtue, as stated above (Q61, A2), viz., the reason, where prudence resides, the will, where justice is, the irascible, the subject of fortitude, and the concupiscible, the subject of temperance. Therefore insofar as the reason is deprived of its order to the true, there is the wound of ignorance; insofar as the will is deprived of its order of good, there is the wound of malice; insofar as the irascible is deprived of its order to the arduous, there is the wound of weakness; and insofar as the concupiscible is deprived of its order to the delectable, moderated by reason, there is the wound of concupiscence.

Accordingly these are the four wounds inflicted on the whole of human nature as a result of our first parent's sin. But since the inclination to the good of virtue is

peccatum actuale, ut ex dictis patet, et ista sunt quatuor vulnera ex aliis peccatis consequentia, inquantum scilicet per peccatum et ratio hebetatur, praecipue in agendis; et voluntas induratur ad bonum; et maior difficultas bene agendi accrescit; et concupiscentia magis exardescit.

Ad primum ergo dicendum quod nihil prohibet id quod est effectus unius peccati, esse causam peccati alterius. Ex hoc enim quod anima deordinatur per peccatum praecedens, facilius inclinatur ad peccandum.

Ad secundum dicendum quod malitia non sumitur hic pro peccato, sed pro quadam pronitate voluntatis ad malum; secundum quod dicitur Gen. VIII, *proni sunt sensus hominis ad malum ab adolescentia sua.*

Ad tertium dicendum quod, sicut supra dictum est, concupiscentia intantum est naturalis homini, inquantum subditur rationi. Quod autem excedat limites rationis, hoc est homini contra naturam.

Ad quartum dicendum quod infirmitas communiter potest dici omnis passio, inquantum debilitat robur animae et impedit rationem. Sed Beda accepit infirmitatem stricte, secundum quod opponitur fortitudini, quae pertinet ad irascibilem.

Ad quintum dicendum quod difficultas quae ponitur in libro Augustini, includit ista tria quae pertinent ad appetitivas potentias, scilicet malitiam, infirmitatem et concupiscentiam, ex his enim tribus contingit quod aliquis non facile tendit in bonum. Error autem et dolor sunt vulnera consequentia, ex hoc enim aliquis dolet, quod infirmatur circa ea quae concupiscit.

diminished in each individual on account of actual sin, as was explained above (AA1, 2), these four wounds are also the result of other sins, insofar as, through sin, the reason is obscured, especially in practical matters, the will hardened to evil, good actions become more difficult and concupiscence more impetuous.

Reply Obj. 1: There is no reason why the effect of one sin should not be the cause of another: because the soul, through sinning once, is more easily inclined to sin again.

Reply Obj. 2: Malice is not to be taken here as a sin, but as a certain proneness of the will to evil, according to the words of Gn. 8:21: *Man's senses are prone to evil from his youth.*

Reply Obj. 3: As stated above (Q82, A3, ad 1), concupiscence is natural to man, insofar as it is subject to reason: whereas, insofar as it is goes beyond the bounds of reason, it is unnatural to man.

Reply Obj. 4: Speaking in a general way, every passion can be called a weakness, insofar as it weakens the soul's strength and clogs the reason. Bede, however, took weakness in the strict sense, as contrary to fortitude which pertains to the irascible.

Reply Obj. 5: The *difficulty* which is mentioned in this book of Augustine, includes the three wounds affecting the appetitive powers, viz., *malice, weakness* and *concupiscence,* for it is owing to these three that a man finds it difficult to tend to the good. *Error* and *vexation* are consequent wounds, since a man is vexed through being weakened in respect of the objects of his concupiscence.

Article 4

Whether Privation of Mode, Species and Order Is the Effect of Sin?

Ad quartum sic proceditur. Videtur quod privatio modi, speciei et ordinis, non sit effectus peccati. Dicit enim Augustinus, in libro de natura boni, quod *ubi haec tria magna sunt, magnum bonum est; ubi parva, parvum; ubi nulla, nullum.* Sed peccatum non annullat bonum naturae. Ergo non privat modum, speciem et ordinem.

Praeterea, nihil est causa sui ipsius. Sed ipsum peccatum est privatio modi, speciei et ordinis, ut Augustinus dicit, in libro de natura boni. Ergo privatio modi, speciei et ordinis, non est effectus peccati.

Praeterea, diversa peccata diversos habent effectus. Sed modus, species et ordo, cum sint quaedam diversa, diversas privationes habere videntur. Ergo per diversa peccata privantur. Non ergo est effectus cuiuslibet peccati privatio modi, speciei et ordinis.

Objection 1: It would seem that privation of mode, species and order is not the effect of sin. For Augustine says (*De Natura Boni* iii) that *where these three abound, the good is great; where they are less, there is less good; where they are not, there is no good at all.* But sin does not destroy the good of nature. Therefore it does not destroy mode, species and order.

Obj. 2: Further, nothing is its own cause. But sin itself is the *privation of mode, species and order,* as Augustine states (*De Natura Boni* iv). Therefore privation of mode, species and order is not the effect of sin.

Obj. 3: Further, different effects result from different sins. Now since mode, species and order are diverse, their corresponding privations must be diverse also, and, consequently, must be the result of different sins. Therefore privation of mode, species and order is not the effect of each sin.

SED CONTRA est quod peccatum est in anima sicut infirmitas in corpore; secundum illud Psalmi VI, *miserere mei, domine, quoniam infirmus sum.* Sed infirmitas privat modum, speciem et ordinem ipsius corporis. Ergo peccatum privat modum, speciem et ordinem animae.

RESPONDEO dicendum quod, sicut in primo dictum est, modus, species et ordo consequuntur unumquodque bonum creatum inquantum huiusmodi, et etiam unumquodque ens. Omne enim esse et bonum consideratur per aliquam formam, secundum quam sumitur species. Forma autem uniuscuiusque rei, qualiscumque sit, sive substantialis sive accidentalis, est secundum aliquam mensuram, unde et in VIII Metaphys. dicitur quod *formae rerum sunt sicut numeri.* Et ex hoc habet modum quendam, qui mensuram respicit. Ex forma vero sua unumquodque ordinatur ad aliud.

Sic igitur secundum diversos gradus bonorum, sunt diversi gradus modi, speciei et ordinis. Est ergo quoddam bonum pertinens ad ipsam substantiam naturae, quod habet suum modum, speciem et ordinem, et illud nec privatur nec diminuitur per peccatum. Est etiam quoddam bonum naturalis inclinationis, et hoc etiam habet suum modum, speciem et ordinem, et hoc diminuitur per peccatum, ut dictum est, sed non totaliter tollitur. Est etiam quoddam bonum virtutis et gratiae, quod etiam habet suum modum, speciem et ordinem, et hoc totaliter tollitur per peccatum mortale. Est etiam quoddam bonum quod est ipse actus ordinatus, quod etiam habet suum modum, speciem et ordinem, et huius privatio est essentialiter ipsum peccatum. Et sic patet qualiter peccatum et est privatio modi, speciei et ordinis; et privat vel diminuit modum, speciem et ordinem.

UNDE PATET responsio ad duo prima.

AD TERTIUM dicendum quod modus, species et ordo se consequuntur, sicut ex dictis patet. Unde simul privantur et diminuuntur.

ON THE CONTRARY, Sin is to the soul what weakness is to the body, according to Ps. 6:3, *Have mercy on me, O Lord, for I am weak.* Now weakness deprives the body of mode, species and order.

I ANSWER THAT, As stated in the FP, Q5, A5, mode, species and order are consequent upon every created good, as such, and also upon every being. Because every being and every good as such depends on its form from which it derives its *species.* Again, any kind of form, whether substantial or accidental, of anything whatever, is according to some measure, wherefore it is stated in *Metaph.* viii, that *the forms of things are like numbers,* so that a form has a certain *mode* corresponding to its measure. Lastly owing to its form, each thing has a relation of *order* to something else.

Accordingly there are different grades of mode, species and order, corresponding to the different degrees of good. For there is a good belonging to the very substance of nature, which good has its mode, species and order, and is neither destroyed nor diminished by sin. There is again the good of the natural inclination, which also has its mode, species and order; and this is diminished by sin, as stated above (AA1,2), but is not entirely destroyed. Again, there is the good of virtue and grace: this too has its mode, species and order, and is entirely taken away by sin. Lastly, there is a good consisting in the ordinate act itself, which also has its mode, species and order, the privation of which is essentially sin. Hence it is clear both how sin is privation of mode, species and order, and how it destroys or diminishes mode, species and order.

THIS SUFFICES for the Replies to the first two Objections.

REPLY OBJ. 3: Mode, species and order follow one from the other, as explained above: and so they are destroyed or diminished together.

Article 5

Whether Death and Other Bodily Defects Are the Result of Sin?

AD QUINTUM SIC PROCEDITUR. Videtur quod mors et alii corporales defectus non sint effectus peccati. Si enim causa fuerit aequalis, et effectus erit aequalis. Sed huiusmodi defectus non sunt aequales in omnibus, sed in quibusdam huiusmodi defectus magis abundant, cum tamen peccatum originale sit in omnibus aequale, sicut dictum est, cuius videntur huiusmodi defectus maxime esse effectus. Ergo mors et huiusmodi defectus non sunt effectus peccati.

OBJECTION 1: It would seem that death and other bodily defects are not the result of sin. Because equal causes have equal effects. Now these defects are not equal in all, but abound in some more than in others, whereas original sin, from which especially these defects seem to result, is equal in all, as stated above (Q82, A4). Therefore death and suchlike defects are not the result of sin.

PRAETEREA, remota causa, removetur effectus. Sed remoto omni peccato per Baptismum vel poenitentiam, non removentur huiusmodi defectus. Ergo non sunt effectus peccati.

PRAETEREA, peccatum actuale habet plus de ratione culpae quam originale. Sed peccatum actuale non transmutat naturam corporis ad aliquem defectum. Ergo multo minus peccatum originale. Non ergo mors et alii defectus corporales sunt effectus peccati.

SED CONTRA est quod apostolus dicit, Rom. V, *per unum hominem peccatum in hunc mundum intravit, et per peccatum mors.*

RESPONDEO dicendum quod aliquid est causa alterius dupliciter, uno quidem modo, per se; alio modo, per accidens. Per se quidem est causa alterius quod secundum virtutem suae naturae vel formae producit effectum, unde sequitur quod effectus sit per se intentus a causa. Unde cum mors et huiusmodi defectus sint praeter intentionem peccantis, manifestum est quod peccatum non est per se causa istorum defectuum. Per accidens autem aliquid est causa alterius, si sit causa removendo prohibens, sicut dicitur in VIII Physic. quod *divellens columnam, per accidens movet lapidem columnae superpositum.* Et hoc modo peccatum primi parentis est causa mortis et omnium huiusmodi defectuum in natura humana, inquantum per peccatum primi parentis sublata est originalis iustitia, per quam non solum inferiores animae vires continebantur sub ratione absque omni deordinatione, sed totum corpus continebatur sub anima absque omni defectu, ut in primo habitum est. Et ideo, subtracta hac originali iustitia per peccatum primi parentis, sicut vulnerata est humana natura quantum ad animam per deordinationem potentiarum, ut supra dictum est; ita etiam est corruptibilis effecta per deordinationem ipsius corporis.

Subtractio autem originalis iustitiae habet rationem poenae, sicut etiam subtractio gratiae. Unde etiam mors, et omnes defectus corporales consequentes, sunt quaedam poenae originalis peccati. Et quamvis huiusmodi defectus non sint intenti a peccante, sunt tamen ordinati secundum iustitiam Dei punientis.

AD PRIMUM ergo dicendum quod aequalitas causae per se, causat aequalem effectum, augmentata enim vel diminuta causa per se, augetur vel diminuitur effectus. Sed aequalitas causae removentis prohibens, non ostendit aequalitatem effectuum. Si quis enim aequali impulsu divellat duas columnas, non sequitur quod lapides superpositi aequaliter moveantur, sed ille velocius movebitur qui gravior erit secundum proprietatem suae naturae, cui relinquitur remoto prohibente. Sic igitur, remota originali iustitia, natura corporis humani relicta est sibi, et secundum hoc, secundum diversitatem naturalis complexionis, quorundam corpora pluribus defectibus

OBJ. 2: Further, if the cause is removed, the effect is removed. But these defects are not removed, when all sin is removed by Baptism or Penance. Therefore they are not the effect of sin.

OBJ. 3: Further, actual sin has more of the character of guilt than original sin has. But actual sin does not change the nature of the body by subjecting it to some defect. Much less, therefore, does original sin. Therefore death and other bodily defects are not the result of sin.

ON THE CONTRARY, The Apostle says (Rom 5:12), *By one man sin entered into this world, and by sin death.*

I ANSWER THAT, One thing causes another in two ways: first, by reason of itself; second, accidentally. By reason of itself, one thing is the cause of another, if it produces its effect by reason of the power of its nature or form, the result being that the effect is directly intended by the cause. Consequently, as death and such like defects are beside the intention of the sinner, it is evident that sin is not, of itself, the cause of these defects. Accidentally, one thing is the cause of another if it causes it by removing an obstacle: thus it is stated in *Phys.* viii, text. 32, that *by displacing a pillar a man moves accidentally the stone resting thereon.* In this way the sin of our first parent is the cause of death and all such like defects in human nature, insofar as by the sin of our first parent original justice was taken away, whereby not only were the lower powers of the soul held together under the control of reason, without any disorder whatever, but also the whole body was held together in subjection to the soul, without any defect, as stated in the FP, Q97, A1. Wherefore, original justice being forfeited through the sin of our first parent; just as human nature was stricken in the soul by the disorder among the powers, as stated above (A3; Q82, A3), so also it became subject to corruption, by reason of disorder in the body.

Now the withdrawal of original justice has the character of punishment, even as the withdrawal of grace has. Consequently, death and all consequent bodily defects are punishments of original sin. And although the defects are not intended by the sinner, nevertheless they are ordered according to the justice of God Who inflicts them as punishments.

REPLY OBJ. 1: Causes that produce their effects of themselves, if equal, produce equal effects: for if such causes be increased or diminished, the effect is increased or diminished. But equal causes of an obstacle being removed, do not point to equal effects. For supposing a man employs equal force in displacing two columns, it does not follow that the movements of the stones resting on them will be equal; but that one will move with greater velocity, which has the greater weight according to the property of its nature, to which it is left when the obstacle to its falling is removed. Accordingly, when original justice is removed, the nature of the human body is left to itself, so that according

subiacent, quorundam vero paucioribus, quamvis existente originali peccato aequali.

AD SECUNDUM dicendum quod culpa originalis et actualis removetur ab eodem a quo etiam removentur et huiusmodi defectus, secundum illud apostoli, Rom. VIII, *vivificabit mortalia corpora vestra per inhabitantem spiritum eius in vobis*, sed utrumque fit secundum ordinem divinae sapientiae, congruo tempore. Oportet enim quod ad immortalitatem et impassibilitatem gloriae, quae in Christo inchoata est, et per Christum nobis acquisita, perveniamus conformati prius passionibus eius. Unde oportet quod ad tempus passibilitas in nostris corporibus remaneat, ad impassibilitatem gloriae promerendam conformiter Christo.

AD TERTIUM dicendum quod in peccato actuali duo possumus considerare, scilicet ipsam substantiam actus, et rationem culpae. Ex parte quidem substantiae actus, potest peccatum actuale aliquem defectum corporalem causare, sicut ex superfluo cibo aliqui infirmantur et moriuntur. Sed ex parte culpae, privat gratiam quae datur homini ad rectificandum animae actus, non autem ad cohibendum defectus corporales, sicut originalis iustitia cohibebat. Et ideo peccatum actuale non causat huiusmodi defectus, sicut originale.

to diverse natural temperaments, some men's bodies are subject to more defects, some to fewer, although original sin is equal in all.

REPLY OBJ. 2: Both original and actual sin are removed by the same cause that removes these defects, according to the Apostle (Rom 8:11): *He . . . shall quicken . . . your mortal bodies, because of His Spirit that dwelleth in you*: but each is done according to the order of Divine wisdom, at a fitting time. Because it is right that we should first of all be conformed to Christ's sufferings, before attaining to the immortality and impassibility of glory, which was begun in Him, and by Him acquired for us. Hence it behooves that our bodies should remain, for a time, subject to suffering, in order that we may merit the impassibility of glory, in conformity with Christ.

REPLY OBJ. 3: Two things may be considered in actual sin, the substance of the act, and the aspect of fault. As regards the substance of the act, actual sin can cause a bodily defect: thus some sicken and die through eating too much. But as regards the fault, it deprives us of grace which is given to us that we may regulate the acts of the soul, but not that we may ward off defects of the body, as original justice did. Wherefore actual sin does not cause those defects, as original sin does.

Article 6

Whether Death and Other Defects Are Natural to Man?

AD SEXTUM SIC PROCEDITUR. Videtur quod mors et huiusmodi defectus sint homini naturales. *Corruptibile enim et incorruptibile differunt genere*, ut dicitur in X Metaphys. Sed homo est eiusdem generis cum aliis animalibus, quae sunt naturaliter corruptibilia. Ergo homo est naturaliter corruptibilis.

PRAETEREA, omne quod est compositum ex contrariis, est naturaliter corruptibile, quasi habens in se causam corruptionis suae. Sed corpus humanum est huiusmodi. Ergo est naturaliter corruptibile.

PRAETEREA, calidum naturaliter consumit humidum. Vita autem hominis conservatur per calidum et humidum. Cum igitur operationes vitae expleantur per actum caloris naturalis, ut dicitur in II de anima, videtur quod mors et huiusmodi defectus sint homini naturales.

SED CONTRA, quidquid est homini naturale, Deus in homine fecit. Sed *Deus mortem non fecit*, ut dicitur Sap. I. Ergo mors non est homini naturalis.

PRAETEREA, id quod est secundum naturam, non potest dici poena nec malum, quia unicuique rei est conveniens id quod est ei naturale. Sed mors et huiusmodi

OBJECTION 1: It would seem that death and such like defects are natural to man. For *the corruptible and the incorruptible differ generically* (*Metaph.* x, text. 26). But man is of the same genus as other animals which are naturally corruptible. Therefore man is naturally corruptible.

OBJ. 2: Further, whatever is composed of contraries is naturally corruptible, as having within itself the cause of corruption. But such is the human body. Therefore it is naturally corruptible.

OBJ. 3: Further, a hot thing naturally consumes moisture. Now human life is preserved by hot and moist elements. Since therefore the vital functions are fulfilled by the action of natural heat, as stated in *De Anima* ii, text. 50, it seems that death and such like defects are natural to man.

ON THE CONTRARY, God made in man whatever is natural to him. Now *God made not death* (Wis 1:13). Therefore death is not natural to man.

FURTHER, that which is natural cannot be called either a punishment or an evil: since what is natural to a thing is suitable to it. But death and such like defects are the

defectus sunt poena peccati originalis, ut supra dictum est. Ergo non sunt homini naturales.

PRAETEREA, materia proportionatur formae, et quaelibet res suo fini. Finis autem hominis est beatitudo perpetua, ut supra dictum est. Forma etiam humani corporis est anima rationalis, quae est incorruptibilis, ut in primo habitum est. Ergo corpus humanum est naturaliter incorruptibile.

RESPONDEO dicendum quod de unaquaque re corruptibili dupliciter loqui possumus, uno modo, secundum naturam universalem; alio modo, secundum naturam particularem. Natura quidem particularis est propria virtus activa et conservativa uniuscuiusque rei. Et secundum hanc, omnis corruptio et defectus est contra naturam, ut dicitur in II de caelo, quia huiusmodi virtus intendit esse et conservationem eius cuius est.

Natura vero universalis est virtus activa in aliquo universali principio naturae, puta in aliquo caelestium corporum; vel alicuius superioris substantiae, secundum quod etiam Deus a quibusdam dicitur natura naturans. Quae quidem virtus intendit bonum et conservationem universi, ad quod exigitur alternatio generationis et corruptionis in rebus. Et secundum hoc, corruptiones et defectus rerum sunt naturales, non quidem secundum inclinationem formae, quae est principium essendi et perfectionis; sed secundum inclinationem materiae, quae proportionaliter attribuitur tali formae secundum distributionem universalis agentis. Et quamvis omnis forma intendat perpetuum esse quantum potest, nulla tamen forma rei corruptibilis potest assequi perpetuitatem sui, praeter animam rationalem, eo quod ipsa non est subiecta omnino materiae corporali, sicut aliae formae; quinimmo habet propriam operationem immaterialem, ut in primo habitum est. Unde ex parte suae formae, naturalior est homini incorruptio quam aliis rebus corruptibilibus. Sed quia et ipsa habet materiam ex contrariis compositam, ex inclinatione materiae sequitur corruptibilitas in toto. Et secundum hoc, homo est naturaliter corruptibilis secundum naturam materiae sibi relictae, sed non secundum naturam formae.

Primae autem tres rationes procedunt ex parte materiae, aliae vero tres procedunt ex parte formae. Unde ad earum solutionem, considerandum est quod forma hominis, quae est anima rationalis, secundum suam incorruptibilitatem proportionata est suo fini, qui est beatitudo perpetua. Sed corpus humanum, quod est corruptibile secundum suam naturam consideratum, quodammodo proportionatum est suae formae, et quodammodo non. Duplex enim conditio potest attendi in aliqua materia, una scilicet quam agens eligit; alia quae non est ab agente electa, sed est secundum conditionem naturalem materiae. Sicut faber ad faciendum cultellum eligit materiam duram et ductilem, quae subtiliari possit ut sit apta incisioni, et secundum hanc conditionem

punishment of original sin, as stated above (A5). Therefore they are not natural to man.

FURTHER, matter is proportionate to form, and everything to its end. Now man's end is everlasting happiness, as stated above (Q2, A7; Q5, AA3,4): and the form of the human body is the rational soul, as was proved in the FP, Q75, A6. Therefore the human body is naturally incorruptible.

I ANSWER THAT, We may speak of any corruptible thing in two ways; first, in respect of its universal nature, second, as regards its particular nature. A thing's particular nature is its own power of action and self-preservation. And in respect of this nature, every corruption and defect is contrary to nature, as stated in *De Coelo* ii, text. 37, since this power tends to the being and preservation of the thing to which it belongs.

On the other hand, the universal nature is an active force in some universal principle of nature, for instance in some heavenly body; or again belonging to some superior substance, in which sense God is said by some to be *the Nature Who makes nature*. This force intends the good and the preservation of the universe, for which alternate generation and corruption in things are requisite: and in this respect corruption and defect in things are natural, not indeed as regards the inclination of the form which is the principle of being and perfection, but as regards the inclination of matter which is allotted proportionately to its particular form according to the discretion of the universal agent. And although every form intends perpetual being as far as it can, yet no form of a corruptible being can achieve its own perpetuity, except the rational soul; for the reason that the latter is not entirely subject to matter, as other forms are; indeed it has an immaterial operation of its own, as stated in the FP, Q75, A2. Consequently as regards his form, incorruption is more natural to man than to other corruptible things. But since that very form has a matter composed of contraries, from the inclination of that matter there results corruptibility in the whole. In this respect man is naturally corruptible as regards the nature of his matter left to itself, but not as regards the nature of his form.

The first three objections argue on the side of the matter; while the other three argue on the side of the form. Wherefore in order to solve them, we must observe that the form of man which is the rational soul, in respect of its incorruptibility is adapted to its end, which is everlasting happiness: whereas the human body, which is corruptible, considered in respect of its nature, is, in a way, adapted to its form, and, in another way, it is not. For we may note a twofold condition in any matter, one which the agent chooses, and another which is not chosen by the agent, and is a natural condition of matter. Thus, a smith in order to make a knife, chooses a matter both hard and flexible, which can be sharpened so as to be useful for cutting, and in respect of this condition iron is a matter adapted for a

ferrum est materia proportionata cultello, sed hoc quod ferrum sit frangibile et rubiginem contrahens, consequitur ex naturali dispositione ferri, nec hoc eligit artifex in ferro, sed magis repudiaret si posset. Unde haec dispositio materiae non est proportionata intentioni artificis, nec intentioni artis. Similiter corpus humanum est materia electa a natura quantum ad hoc, quod est temperatae complexionis, ut possit esse convenientissimum organum tactus et aliarum virtutum sensitivarum et motivarum. Sed quod sit corruptibile, hoc est ex conditione materiae, nec est electum a natura, quin potius natura eligeret materiam incorruptibilem, si posset. Sed Deus, cui subiacet omnis natura, in ipsa institutione hominis supplevit defectum naturae, et dono iustitiae originalis dedit corpori incorruptibilitatem quandam, ut in primo dictum est. Et secundum hoc dicitur quod Deus mortem non fecit, et quod mors est poena peccati.

UNDE PATET responsio ad obiecta.

knife: but that iron be breakable and inclined to rust, results from the natural disposition of iron, nor does the workman choose this in the iron, indeed he would do without it if he could: wherefore this disposition of matter is not adapted to the workman's intention, nor to the purpose of his art. In like manner the human body is the matter chosen by nature in respect of its being of a mixed temperament, in order that it may be most suitable as an organ of touch and of the other sensitive and motive powers. Whereas the fact that it is corruptible is due to a condition of matter, and is not chosen by nature: indeed nature would choose an incorruptible matter if it could. But God, to Whom every nature is subject, in forming man supplied the defect of nature, and by the gift of original justice, gave the body a certain incorruptibility, as was stated in the FP, Q97, A1. It is in this sense that it is said that *God made not death*, and that death is the punishment of sin.

THIS SUFFICES for the Replies to the Objections.

QUESTION 86

OF THE STAIN OF SIN

Deinde considerandum est de macula peccati. Et circa hoc quaeruntur duo.

Primo, utrum macula animae sit effectus peccati.

Secundo, utrum remaneat in anima post actum peccati.

We must now consider the stain of sin; under which head there are two points of inquiry:

(1) Whether an effect of sin is a stain on the soul?

(2) Whether it remains in the soul after the act of sin?

Article 1

Whether Sin Causes a Stain on the Soul?

AD PRIMUM SIC PROCEDITUR. Videtur quod peccatum non causet aliquam maculam in anima. Natura enim superior non potest inquinari ex contactu naturae inferioris, unde radius solaris non inquinatur per tactum corporum fetidorum, ut Augustinus dicit, in libro contra quinque haereses. Sed anima humana est multo superioris naturae quam res commutabiles, ad quas peccando convertitur. Ergo ex eis maculam non contrahit peccando.

PRAETEREA, peccatum est principaliter in voluntate, ut supra dictum est. Voluntas autem est in ratione, ut dicitur in III de anima. Sed ratio, sive intellectus, non maculatur ex consideratione quarumcumque rerum, sed magis perficitur. Ergo nec voluntas ex peccato maculatur.

PRAETEREA, si peccatum maculam causat, aut macula illa est aliquid positive, aut est privatio pura. Si sit aliquid positive, non potest esse nisi dispositio vel habitus, nihil enim aliud videtur ex actu causari. Dispositio autem et habitus non est, contingit enim, remota dispositione vel habitu, adhuc remanere maculam; ut patet in eo qui peccavit mortaliter prodigalitate, et postea transmutatur, mortaliter peccando, in habitum vitii oppositi. Non ergo macula ponit aliquid positive in anima. Similiter etiam nec est privatio pura. Quia omnia peccata conveniunt ex parte aversionis et privationis gratiae. Sequeretur ergo quod omnium peccatorum esset macula una. Ergo macula non est effectus peccati.

SED CONTRA est quod dicitur, Eccli. XLVII, Salomoni, *dedisti maculam in gloria tua*. Et Ephes. V, *ut exhiberet sibi gloriosam Ecclesiam non habentem maculam aut rugam*. Et utrobique loquitur de macula peccati. Ergo macula est effectus peccati.

RESPONDEO dicendum quod macula proprie dicitur in corporalibus, quando aliquod corpus nitidum perdit suum nitorem ex contactu alterius corporis, sicut vestis

OBJECTION 1: It would seem that sin causes no stain on the soul. For a higher nature cannot be defiled by contact with a lower nature: hence the sun's ray is not defiled by contact with tainted bodies, as Augustine says (*Contra Quinque Haereses* v). Now the human soul is of a much higher nature than mutable things, to which it turns by sinning. Therefore it does not contract a stain from them by sinning.

OBJ. 2: Further, sin is chiefly in the will, as stated above (Q74, AA1,2). Now the will is in the reason, as stated in *De Anima* iii, text. 42. But the reason or intellect is not stained by considering anything whatever; rather indeed is it perfected thereby. Therefore neither is the will stained by sin.

OBJ. 3: Further, if sin causes a stain, this stain is either something positive, or a pure privation. If it be something positive, it can only be either a disposition or a habit: for it seems that nothing else can be caused by an act. But it is neither disposition nor habit: for it happens that a stain remains even after the removal of a disposition or habit; for instance, in a man who after committing a mortal sin of prodigality, is so changed as to fall into a sin of the opposite vice. Therefore the stain does not denote anything positive in the soul. Again, neither is it a pure privation. Because all sins agree on the part of aversion and privation of grace: and so it would follow that there is but one stain caused by all sins. Therefore the stain is not the effect of sin.

ON THE CONTRARY, It was said to Solomon (Sir 47:22): *Thou hast stained thy glory*: and it is written (Eph 5:27): *That He might present it to Himself a glorious church not having spot or wrinkle*: and in each case it is question of the stain of sin. Therefore a stain is the effect of sin.

I ANSWER THAT, A stain is properly ascribed to corporeal things, when a comely body loses its comeliness through contact with another body, e.g., a garment, gold

et aurum et argentum, aut aliud huiusmodi. In rebus autem spiritualibus ad similitudinem huius oportet maculam dici. Habet autem anima hominis duplicem nitorem, unum quidem ex refulgentia luminis naturalis rationis, per quam dirigitur in suis actibus; alium vero ex refulgentia divini luminis, scilicet sapientiae et gratiae, per quam etiam homo perficitur ad bene et decenter agendum. Est autem quasi quidam animae tactus, quando inhaeret aliquibus rebus per amorem. Cum autem peccat, adhaeret rebus aliquibus contra lumen rationis et divinae legis, ut ex supradictis patet. Unde ipsum detrimentum nitoris ex tali contactu proveniens, macula animae metaphorice vocatur.

AD PRIMUM ergo dicendum quod anima non inquinatur ex rebus inferioribus virtute earum, quasi agentibus eis in animam, sed magis e converso anima sua actione se inquinat, inordinate eis inhaerendo, contra lumen rationis et divinae legis.

AD SECUNDUM dicendum quod actio intellectus perficitur secundum quod res intelligibiles sunt in intellectu per modum ipsius intellectus, et ideo intellectus ex eis non inficitur, sed magis perficitur. Sed actus voluntatis consistit in motu ad ipsas res, ita quod amor conglutinat animam rei amatae. Et ex hoc anima maculatur, quando in ordinate inhaeret; secundum illud Osee IX, *facti sunt abominabiles, sicut ea quae dilexerunt.*

AD TERTIUM dicendum quod macula non est aliquid positive in anima, nec significat privationem solam, sed significat privationem quandam nitoris animae in ordine ad suam causam, quae est peccatum. Et ideo diversa peccata diversas maculas inducunt. Et est simile de umbra, quae est privatio luminis ex obiecto alicuius corporis, et secundum diversitatem corporum obiectorum diversificantur umbrae.

or silver, or the like. Accordingly a stain is ascribed to spiritual things in like manner. Now man's soul has a twofold comeliness; one from the refulgence of the natural light of reason, whereby he is directed in his actions; the other, from the refulgence of the Divine light, viz., of wisdom and grace, whereby man is also perfected for the purpose of doing good and fitting actions. Now, when the soul cleaves to things by love, there is a kind of contact in the soul: and when man sins, he cleaves to certain things, against the light of reason and of the Divine law, as shown above (Q71, A6). Wherefore the loss of comeliness occasioned by this contact, is metaphorically called a stain on the soul.

REPLY OBJ. 1: The soul is not defiled by inferior things, by their own power, as though they acted on the soul: on the contrary, the soul, by its own action, defiles itself, through cleaving to them inordinately, against the light of reason and of the Divine law.

REPLY OBJ. 2: The action of the intellect is accomplished by the intelligible thing being in the intellect, according to the mode of the intellect, so that the intellect is not defiled, but perfected, by them. On the other hand, the act of the will consists in a movement towards things themselves, so that love attaches the soul to the thing loved. Thus it is that the soul is stained, when it cleaves inordinately, according to Osee 9:10: *They . . . became abominable as those things were which they loved.*

REPLY OBJ. 3: The stain is neither something positive in the soul, nor does it denote a pure privation: it denotes a privation of the soul's brightness in relation to its cause, which is sin; wherefore diverse sins occasion diverse stains. It is like a shadow, which is the privation of light through the interposition of a body, and which varies according to the diversity of the interposed bodies.

Article 2

Whether the Stain Remains in the Soul After the Act of Sin?

AD SECUNDUM SIC PROCEDITUR. Videtur quod macula non maneat in anima post actum peccati. Nihil enim manet in anima post actum, nisi habitus vel dispositio. Sed macula non est habitus vel dispositio, ut supra habitum est. Ergo macula non manet in anima post actum peccati.

PRAETEREA, hoc modo se habet macula ad peccatum, sicut umbra ad corpus, ut supra dictum est. Sed transeunte corpore, non manet umbra. Ergo, transeunte actu peccati, non manet macula.

OBJECTION 1: It would seem that the stain does not remain in the soul after the act of sin. For after an action, nothing remains in the soul except habit or disposition. But the stain is not a habit or disposition, as stated above (A1, OBJ3). Therefore the stain does not remain in the soul after the act of sin.

OBJ. 2: Further, the stain is to the sin what the shadow is to the body, as stated above (A1, ad 3). But the shadow does not remain when the body has passed by. Therefore the stain does not remain in the soul when the act of sin is past.

PRAETEREA, omnis effectus dependet ex sua causa. Causa autem maculae est actus peccati. Ergo, remoto actu peccati, non remanet macula in anima.

SED CONTRA est quod dicitur Iosue XXII, *an parum vobis est quod peccastis in Beelphegor, et usque in praesentem diem macula huius sceleris in vobis permanet?*

RESPONDEO dicendum quod macula peccati remanet in anima, etiam transeunte actu peccati. Cuius ratio est quia macula, sicut dictum est, importat quendam defectum nitoris propter recessum a lumine rationis vel divinae legis. Et ideo quandiu homo manet extra huiusmodi lumen, manet in eo macula peccati, sed postquam redit ad lumen divinum et ad lumen rationis, quod fit per gratiam, tunc macula cessat. Licet autem cesset actus peccati, quo homo discessit a lumine rationis vel legis divinae, non tamen statim homo ad illud redit in quo fuerat, sed requiritur aliquis motus voluntatis contrarius primo motui. Sicut si aliquis sit distans alicui per aliquem motum, non statim cessante motu fit ei propinquus, sed oportet quod appropinquet rediens per motum contrarium.

AD PRIMUM ergo dicendum quod post actum peccati nihil positive remanet in anima nisi dispositio vel habitus, remanet tamen aliquid privative, scilicet privatio coniunctionis ad divinum lumen.

AD SECUNDUM dicendum quod, transeunte obstaculo corporis, remanet corpus diaphanum in aequali propinquitate et habitudine ad corpus illuminans, et ideo statim umbra transit. Sed remoto actu peccati, non remanet anima in eadem habitudine ad Deum. Unde non est similis ratio.

AD TERTIUM dicendum quod actus peccati facit distantiam a Deo, quam quidem distantiam sequitur defectus nitoris, hoc modo sicut motus localis facit localem distantiam. Unde sicut, cessante motu, non tollitur distantia localis; ita nec, cessante actu peccati, tollitur macula.

OBJ. 3: Further, every effect depends on its cause. Now the cause of the stain is the act of sin. Therefore when the act of sin is no longer there, neither is the stain in the soul.

ON THE CONTRARY, It is written (Josh 22:17): *Is it a small thing to you that you sinned with Beelphegor, and the stain of that crime remaineth in you to this day?*

I ANSWER THAT, The stain of sin remains in the soul even when the act of sin is past. The reason for this is that the stain, as stated above (A1), denotes a blemish in the brightness of the soul, on account of its withdrawing from the light of reason or of the Divine law. And therefore so long as man remains out of this light, the stain of sin remains in him: but as soon as, moved by grace, he returns to the Divine light and to the light of reason, the stain is removed. For although the act of sin ceases, whereby man withdrew from the light of reason and of the Divine law, man does not at once return to the state in which he was before, and it is necessary that his will should have a movement contrary to the previous movement. Thus if one man be parted from another on account of some kind of movement, he is not reunited to him as soon as the movement ceases, but he needs to draw nigh to him and to return by a contrary movement.

REPLY OBJ. 1: Nothing positive remains in the soul after the act of sin, except the disposition or habit; but there does remain something private, viz., the privation of union with the Divine light.

REPLY OBJ. 2: After the interposed body has passed by, the transparent body remains in the same position and relation as regards the illuminating body, and so the shadow passes at once. But when the sin is past, the soul does not remain in the same relation to God: and so there is no comparison.

REPLY OBJ. 3: The act of sin parts man from God, which parting causes the defect of brightness, just as local movement causes local parting. Wherefore, just as when movement ceases, local distance is not removed, so neither, when the act of sin ceases, is the stain removed.

QUESTION 87

OF THE DEBT OF PUNISHMENT

Deinde considerandum est de reatu poenae. Et primo, de ipso reatu; secundo, de mortali et veniali peccato, quae distinguuntur secundum reatum.

Circa primum quaeruntur octo.

Primo, utrum reatus poenae sit effectus peccati.

Secundo, utrum peccatum possit esse poena alterius peccati.

Tertio, utrum aliquod peccatum faciat reum aeterna poena.

Quarto, utrum faciat reum poena infinita secundum quantitatem.

Quinto, utrum omne peccatum faciat reum aeterna et infinita poena.

Sexto, utrum reatus poenae possit remanere post peccatum.

Septimo, utrum omnis poena inferatur pro aliquo peccato.

Octavo, utrum unus sit reus poenae pro peccato alterius.

We must now consider the debt of punishment. We shall consider (1) the debt itself; (2) mortal and venial sin, which differ in respect of the punishment due to them.

Under the first head there are eight points of inquiry:

(1) Whether the debt of punishment is an effect of sin?

(2) Whether one sin can be the punishment of another?

(3) Whether any sin incurs a debt of eternal punishment?

(4) Whether sin incurs a debt of punishment that is infinite in quantity?

(5) Whether every sin incurs a debt of eternal and infinite punishment?

(6) Whether the debt of punishment can remain after sin?

(7) Whether every punishment is inflicted for a sin?

(8) Whether one person can incur punishment for another's sin?

Article 1

Whether the Debt of Punishment Is an Effect of Sin?

AD PRIMUM SIC PROCEDITUR. Videtur quod reatus poenae non sit effectus peccati. Quod enim per accidens se habet ad aliquid, non videtur esse proprius effectus eius. Sed reatus poenae per accidens se habet ad peccatum, cum sit praeter intentionem peccantis. Ergo reatus poenae non est effectus peccati.

PRAETEREA, malum non est causa boni. Sed poena bona est, cum sit iusta, et a Deo. Ergo non est effectus peccati, quod est malum.

PRAETEREA, Augustinus dicit, in I Confess., quod *omnis inordinatus animus sibi ipsi est poena.* Sed poena non causat reatum alterius poenae, quia sic iretur in infinitum. Ergo peccatum non causat reatum poenae.

SED CONTRA est quod dicitur Rom. II, *tribulatio et angustia in animam omnem operantis malum.* Sed operari malum est peccare. Ergo peccatum inducit poenam, quae nomine tribulationis et angustiae designatur.

RESPONDEO dicendum quod ex rebus naturalibus ad res humanas derivatur ut id quod contra aliquid insurgit, ab eo detrimentum patiatur. Videmus enim in rebus naturalibus quod unum contrarium vehementius agit,

OBJECTION 1: It would seem that the debt of punishment is not an effect of sin. For that which is accidentally related to a thing, does not seem to be its proper effect. Now the debt of punishment is accidentally related to sin, for it is beside the intention of the sinner. Therefore the debt of punishment is not an effect of sin.

OBJ. 2: Further, evil is not the cause of good. But punishment is good, since it is just, and is from God. Therefore it is not an effect of sin, which is evil.

OBJ. 3: Further, Augustine says (*Confess.* i) that *every inordinate affection is its own punishment.* But punishment does not incur a further debt of punishment, because then it would go on indefinitely. Therefore sin does not incur the debt of punishment.

ON THE CONTRARY, It is written (Rom 2:9): *Tribulation and anguish upon every soul of man that worketh evil.* But to work evil is to sin. Therefore sin incurs a punishment which is signified by the words *tribulation and anguish.*

I ANSWER THAT, It has passed from natural things to human affairs that whenever one thing rises up against another, it suffers some detriment therefrom. For we observe in natural things that when one contrary supervenes, the

altero contrario superveniente, propter quod aquae calefactae magis congelantur, ut dicitur in I Meteor. Unde in hominibus hoc ex naturali inclinatione invenitur, ut unusquisque deprimat eum qui contra ipsum insurgit. Manifestum est autem quod quaecumque continentur sub aliquo ordine, sunt quodammodo unum in ordine ad principium ordinis. Unde quidquid contra ordinem aliquem insurgit, consequens est ut ab ipso ordine, vel principe ordinis, deprimatur. Cum autem peccatum sit actus inordinatus, manifestum est quod quicumque peccat, contra aliquem ordinem agit. Et ideo ab ipso ordine consequens est quod deprimatur. Quae quidem depressio poena est.

Unde secundum tres ordines quibus subditur humana voluntas, triplici poena potest homo puniri. Primo quidem enim subditur humana natura ordini propriae rationis; secundo, ordini exterioris hominis gubernantis vel spiritualiter vel temporaliter, politice seu oeconomice; tertio, subditur universali ordini divini regiminis. Quilibet autem horum ordinum per peccatum pervertitur, dum ille qui peccat, agit et contra rationem, et contra legem humanam, et contra legem divinam. Unde triplicem poenam incurrit, unam quidem a seipso, quae est conscientiae remorsus, aliam vero ab homine, tertiam vero a Deo.

AD PRIMUM ergo dicendum quod poena consequitur peccatum inquantum malum est, ratione suae inordinationis. Unde sicut malum est per accidens in actu peccantis, praeter intentionem ipsius, ita et reatus poenae.

AD SECUNDUM dicendum quod poena quidem iusta esse potest et a Deo et ab homine inflicta, unde ipsa poena non est effectus peccati directe, sed solum dispositive. Sed peccatum facit hominem esse reum poenae, quod est malum, dicit enim Dionysius, IV cap. de Div. Nom., quod *puniri non est malum, sed fieri poena dignum.* Unde reatus poenae directe ponitur effectus peccati.

AD TERTIUM dicendum quod poena illa inordinati animi debetur peccato ex hoc quod ordinem rationis pervertit. Fit autem reus alterius poenae, per hoc quod pervertit ordinem legis divinae vel humanae.

other acts with greater energy, for which reason *hot water freezes more rapidly,* as stated in *Meteor.* i, 12. Wherefore we find that the natural inclination of man is to repress those who rise up against him. Now it is evident that all things contained in an order, are, in a manner, one, in relation to the principle of that order. Consequently, whatever rises up against an order, is put down by that order or by the principle thereof. And because sin is an inordinate act, it is evident that whoever sins, commits an offense against an order: wherefore he is put down, in consequence, by that same order, which repression is punishment.

Accordingly, man can be punished with a threefold punishment corresponding to the three orders to which the human will is subject. In the first place a man's nature is subjected to the order of his own reason; second, it is subjected to the order of another man who governs him either in spiritual or in temporal matters, as a member either of the state or of the household; third, it is subjected to the universal order of the Divine government. Now each of these orders is disturbed by sin, for the sinner acts against his reason, and against human and Divine law. Wherefore he incurs a threefold punishment; one, inflicted by himself, viz., remorse of conscience; another, inflicted by man; and a third, inflicted by God.

REPLY OBJ. 1: Punishment follows sin, inasmuch as this is an evil by reason of its being inordinate. Wherefore just as evil is accidental to the sinner's act, being beside his intention, so also is the debt of punishment.

REPLY OBJ. 2: Further, a just punishment may be inflicted either by God or by man: wherefore the punishment itself is the effect of sin, not directly but dispositively. Sin, however, makes man deserving of punishment, and that is an evil: for Dionysius says (*Div. Nom.* iv) that *punishment is not an evil, but to deserve punishment is.* Consequently the debt of punishment is considered to be directly the effect of sin.

REPLY OBJ. 3: This punishment of the *inordinate affection* is due to sin as overturning the order of reason. Nevertheless sin incurs a further punishment, through disturbing the order of the Divine or human law.

Article 2

Whether Sin Can Be the Punishment of Sin?

AD SECUNDUM SIC PROCEDITUR. Videtur quod peccatum non possit esse poena peccati. Poenae enim sunt inductae ut per eas homines reducantur ad bonum virtutis, ut patet per philosophum, in X Ethic. Sed per

OBJECTION 1: It would seem that sin cannot be the punishment of sin. For the purpose of punishment is to bring man back to the good of virtue, as the Philosopher declares (*Ethic.* x, 9). Now sin does not bring man back to

peccatum non reducitur homo in bonum virtutis, sed in oppositum. Ergo peccatum non est poena peccati.

PRAETEREA, poenae iustae sunt a Deo, ut patet per Augustinum, in libro octoginta trium quaest. Peccatum autem non est a Deo, et est iniustum. Non ergo peccatum potest esse poena peccati.

PRAETEREA, de ratione poenae est quod sit contra voluntatem. Sed peccatum est a voluntate, ut ex supradictis patet. Ergo peccatum non potest esse poena peccati.

SED CONTRA est quod Gregorius dicit, super Ezech., quod quaedam peccata sunt poenae peccati.

RESPONDEO dicendum quod de peccato dupliciter loqui possumus, per se, et per accidens. Per se quidem nullo modo peccatum potest esse poena peccati. Peccatum enim per se consideratur secundum quod egreditur a voluntate, sic enim habet rationem culpae. De ratione autem poenae est quod sit contra voluntatem, ut in primo habitum est. Unde manifestum est quod nullo modo, per se loquendo, peccatum potest esse poena peccati.

Per accidens autem peccatum potest esse poena peccati, tripliciter. Primo quidem, ex parte causae quae est remotio prohibentis. Sunt enim causae inclinantes ad peccatum passiones, tentatio Diaboli, et alia huiusmodi; quae quidem causae impediuntur per auxilium divinae gratiae, quae subtrahitur per peccatum. Unde cum ipsa subtractio gratiae sit quaedam poena, et a Deo, ut supra dictum est; sequitur quod per accidens etiam peccatum quod ex hoc sequitur, poena dicatur. Et hoc modo loquitur apostolus, Rom. I, dicens, *propter quod tradidit eos Deus in desideria cordis eorum*, quae sunt animae passiones, quia scilicet deserti homines ab auxilio divinae gratiae, vincuntur a passionibus. Et hoc modo semper peccatum dicitur esse poena praecedentis peccati. Alio modo ex parte substantiae actus, quae afflictionem inducit, sive sit actus interior, ut patet in ira et invidia; sive actus exterior, ut patet cum aliqui gravi labore opprimuntur et damno, ut expleant actum peccati, secundum illud Sap. V, *lassati sumus in via iniquitatis*. Tertio modo, ex parte effectus, ut scilicet aliquod peccatum dicatur poena respectu effectus consequentis. Et his duobus ultimis modis, unum peccatum non solum est poena praecedentis peccati, sed etiam sui.

AD PRIMUM ergo dicendum quod hoc etiam quod aliqui puniuntur a Deo, dum permittit eos in aliqua peccata profluere, ad bonum virtutis ordinatur. Quandoque quidem etiam ipsorum qui peccant, cum scilicet post peccatum humiliores et cautiores resurgunt. Semper autem est ad emendationem aliorum, qui videntes aliquos ruere de peccato in peccatum, magis reformidant peccare. In aliis autem duobus modis, manifestum est quod poena ordinatur ad emendationem quia hoc ipsum quod

the good of virtue, but leads him in the opposite direction. Therefore sin is not the punishment of sin.

OBJ. 2: Further, just punishments are from God, as Augustine says (*Qq. lxxxiii*, qu. 82). But sin is not from God, and is an injustice. Therefore sin cannot be the punishment of sin.

OBJ. 3: Further, the nature of punishment is to be something against the will. But sin is something from the will, as shown above (Q74, AA1,2). Therefore sin cannot be the punishment of sin.

ON THE CONTRARY, Gregory speaks (*Hom. xi in Ezech.*) that some sins are punishments of others.

I ANSWER THAT, We may speak of sin in two ways: first, in its essence, as such; second, as to that which is accidental thereto. Sin as such can nowise be the punishment of another. Because sin considered in its essence is something proceeding from the will, for it is from this that it derives the character of guilt. Whereas punishment is essentially something against the will, as stated in the FP, Q48, A5. Consequently it is evident that sin regarded in its essence can nowise be the punishment of sin.

On the other hand, sin can be the punishment of sin accidentally in three ways. First, when one sin is the cause of another, by removing an impediment thereto. For passions, temptations of the devil, and the like are causes of sin, but are impeded by the help of Divine grace which is withdrawn on account of sin. Wherefore since the withdrawal of grace is a punishment, and is from God, as stated above (Q79, A3), the result is that the sin which ensues from this is also a punishment accidentally. It is in this sense that the Apostle speaks (Rom 1:24) when he says: *Wherefore God gave them up to the desires of their heart*, i.e., to their passions; because, to wit, when men are deprived of the help of Divine grace, they are overcome by their passions. In this way sin is always said to be the punishment of a preceding sin. Second, by reason of the substance of the act, which is such as to cause pain, whether it be an interior act, as is clearly the case with anger or envy, or an exterior act, as is the case with one who endures considerable trouble and loss in order to achieve a sinful act, according to Wis. 5:7: *We wearied ourselves in the way of iniquity*. Third, on the part of the effect, so that one sin is said to be a punishment by reason of its effect. In the last two ways, a sin is a punishment not only in respect of a preceding sin, but also with regard to itself.

REPLY OBJ. 1: Even when God punishes men by permitting them to fall into sin, this is directed to the good of virtue. Sometimes indeed it is for the good of those who are punished, when, to wit, men arise from sin, more humble and more cautious. But it is always for the amendment of others, who seeing some men fall from sin to sin, are the more fearful of sinning. With regard to the other two ways, it is evident that the punishment is intended for the sinner's

homo laborem et detrimentum patitur in peccando, natum est retrahere homines a peccato.

Ad secundum dicendum quod ratio illa procedit de peccato secundum se.

Et similiter dicendum est ad tertium.

amendment, since the very fact that man endures toil and loss in sinning, is of a nature to withdraw man from sin.

Reply Obj. 2: This objection considers sin essentially as such.

And the same answer applies to the Third Objection.

Article 3

Whether Any Sin Incurs a Debt of Eternal Punishment?

Ad tertium sic proceditur. Videtur quod nullum peccatum inducat reatum aeternae poenae. Poena enim iusta adaequatur culpae, iustitia enim aequalitas est. Unde dicitur Isaiae XXVII, *in mensura contra mensuram, cum abiecta fuerit, iudicabit eam.* Sed peccatum est temporale. Ergo non inducit reatum poenae aeternae.

Praeterea, poenae medicinae quaedam sunt, ut dicitur in II Ethic. Sed nulla medicina debet esse infinita, quia ordinatur ad finem; *quod autem ordinatur ad finem, non est infinitum,* ut philosophus dicit, in I Polit. Ergo nulla poena debet esse infinita.

Praeterea, nullus semper facit aliquid, nisi propter se in ipso delectetur. *Sed Deus non delectatur in perditione hominum,* ut dicitur Sap. I. Ergo non puniet homines poena sempiterna.

Praeterea, nihil quod est per accidens, est infinitum. Sed poena est per accidens, non est enim secundum naturam eius qui punitur. Ergo non potest in infinitum durare.

Sed contra est quod dicitur Matth. XXV, *ibunt hi in supplicium aeternum.* Et Marc. III dicitur, *qui autem blasphemaverit in spiritum sanctum, non habebit remissionem in aeternum, sed erit reus aeterni delicti.*

Respondeo dicendum quod, sicut supra dictum est, peccatum ex hoc inducit reatum poenae, quod pervertit aliquem ordinem. Manente autem causa, manet effectus. Unde quandiu perversitas ordinis remanet, necesse est quod remaneat reatus poenae. Pervertit autem aliquis ordinem quandoque quidem reparabiliter, quandoque autem irreparabiliter. Semper enim defectus quo subtrahitur principium, irreparabilis est, si autem salvetur principium, eius virtute defectus reparari possunt. Sicut si corrumpatur principium visivum, non potest fieri visionis reparatio, nisi sola virtute divina, si vero, salvo principio visivo, aliqua impedimenta adveniant visioni, reparari possunt per naturam vel per artem. Cuiuslibet autem ordinis est aliquod principium, per quod aliquis fit particeps illius ordinis. Et ideo si per peccatum corrumpatur principium ordinis quo voluntas hominis subditur Deo, erit inordinatio, quantum est de se, irreparabilis, etsi reparari possit virtute divina. Principium autem huius ordinis est ultimus finis, cui homo inhaeret

Objection 1: It would seem that no sin incurs a debt of eternal punishment. For a just punishment is equal to the fault, since justice is equality: wherefore it is written (Isa 27:8): *In measure against measure, when it shall be cast off, thou shalt judge it.* Now sin is temporal. Therefore it does not incur a debt of eternal punishment.

Obj. 2: Further, *punishments are a kind of medicine* (*Ethic.* ii, 3). But no medicine should be infinite, because it is directed to an end, and *what is directed to an end, is not infinite,* as the Philosopher states (*Polit.* i, 6). Therefore no punishment should be infinite.

Obj. 3: Further, no one does a thing always unless he delights in it for its own sake. But *God hath not pleasure in the destruction of men.* Therefore He will not inflict eternal punishment on man.

Obj. 4: Further, nothing accidental is infinite. But punishment is accidental, for it is not natural to the one who is punished. Therefore it cannot be of infinite duration.

On the contrary, It is written (Matt 25:46): *These shall go into everlasting punishment*; and (Mark 3:29): *He that shall blaspheme against the Holy Spirit, shall never have forgiveness, but shall be guilty of an everlasting sin.*

I answer that, As stated above (A1), sin incurs a debt of punishment through disturbing an order. But the effect remains so long as the cause remains. Wherefore so long as the disturbance of the order remains the debt of punishment must needs remain also. Now disturbance of an order is sometimes reparable, sometimes irreparable: because a defect which destroys the principle is irreparable, whereas if the principle be saved, defects can be repaired by virtue of that principle. For instance, if the principle of sight be destroyed, sight cannot be restored except by Divine power; whereas, if the principle of sight be preserved, while there arise certain impediments to the use of sight, these can be remedied by nature or by art. Now in every order there is a principle whereby one takes part in that order. Consequently if a sin destroys the principle of the order whereby man's will is subject to God, the disorder will be such as to be considered in itself, irreparable, although it is possible to repair it by the power of God. Now the principle of this order is the last end, to which man adheres by charity.

per caritatem. Et ideo quaecumque peccata avertunt a Deo, caritatem auferentia, quantum est de se, inducunt reatum aeternae poenae.

AD PRIMUM ergo dicendum quod poena peccato proportionatur secundum acerbitatem, tam in iudicio divino quam in humano, sicut Augustinus dicit, XXI de Civ. Dei, in nullo iudicio requiritur ut poena adaequetur culpae secundum durationem. Non enim quia adulterium vel homicidium in momento committitur, propter hoc momentanea poena punitur, sed quandoque quidem perpetuo carcere vel exilio, quandoque etiam morte. In qua non consideratur occisionis mora, sed potius quod in perpetuum auferatur a societate viventium, et sic repraesentat suo modo aeternitatem poenae inflictae divinitus. Iustum autem est, secundum Gregorium, quod qui in suo aeterno peccavit contra Deum, in aeterno Dei puniatur. Dicitur autem aliquis in suo aeterno peccasse, non solum secundum continuationem actus in tota hominis vita durantis, sed quia ex hoc ipso quod finem in peccato constituit, voluntatem habet in aeternum peccandi. Unde dicit Gregorius, XXXIV Moral., quod *iniqui voluissent sine fine vivere, ut sine fine potuissent in iniquitatibus permanere.*

AD SECUNDUM dicendum quod poena etiam quae secundum leges humanas infligitur, non semper est medicinalis ei qui punitur, sed solum aliis, sicut cum latro suspenditur, non ut ipse emendetur, sed propter alios, ut saltem metu poenae peccare desistant; secundum illud Prov. XIX, *pestilente flagellato, stultus sapientior erit.* Sic igitur et aeternae poenae reproborum a Deo inflictae, sunt medicinales his qui consideratione poenarum abstinent a peccatis; secundum illud Psalmi LIX, *dedisti metuentibus te significationem, ut fugiant a facie arcus, ut liberentur dilecti tui.*

AD TERTIUM dicendum quod Deus non delectatur in poenis propter ipsas; sed delectatur in ordine suae iustitiae, quae haec requirit.

AD QUARTUM dicendum quod poena, etsi per accidens ordinetur ad naturam, per se tamen ordinatur ad privationem ordinis et ad Dei iustitiam. Et ideo, durante inordinatione, semper durat poena.

Therefore whatever sins turn man away from God, so as to destroy charity, considered in themselves, incur a debt of eternal punishment.

REPLY OBJ. 1: Punishment is proportionate to sin in point of severity, both in Divine and in human judgments. In no judgment, however, as Augustine says (*De Civ. Dei* xxi, 11) is it requisite for punishment to equal fault in point of duration. For the fact that adultery or murder is committed in a moment does not call for a momentary punishment: in fact they are punished sometimes by imprisonment or banishment for life—sometimes even by death; wherein account is not taken of the time occupied in killing, but rather of the expediency of removing the murderer from the fellowship of the living, so that this punishment, in its own way, represents the eternity of punishment inflicted by God. Now according to Gregory (*Dial.* iv, 44) it is just that he who has sinned against God in his own eternity should be punished in God's eternity. A man is said to have sinned in his own eternity, not only as regards continual sinning throughout his whole life, but also because, from the very fact that he fixes his end in sin, he has the will to sin, everlastingly. Wherefore Gregory says (*Dial.* iv, 44) that the *wicked would wish to live without end, that they might abide in their sins for ever.*

REPLY OBJ. 2: Even the punishment that is inflicted according to human laws, is not always intended as a medicine for the one who is punished, but sometimes only for others: thus when a thief is hanged, this is not for his own amendment, but for the sake of others, that at least they may be deterred from crime through fear of the punishment, according to Prov. 19:25: *The wicked man being scourged, the fool shall be wiser.* Accordingly the eternal punishments inflicted by God on the reprobate, are medicinal punishments for those who refrain from sin through the thought of those punishments, according to Ps. 59:6: *Thou hast given a warning to them that fear Thee, that they may flee from before the bow, that Thy beloved may be delivered.*

REPLY OBJ. 3: God does not delight in punishments for their own sake; but He does delight in the order of His justice, which requires them.

REPLY OBJ. 4: Although punishment is related indirectly to nature, nevertheless it is essentially related to the disturbance of the order, and to God's justice. Wherefore, so long as the disturbance lasts, the punishment endures.

Article 4

Whether Sin Incurs a Debt of Punishment Infinite in Quantity?

AD QUARTUM SIC PROCEDITUR. Videtur quod peccato debeatur poena infinita secundum quantitatem. Dicitur enim Ierem. X, *corripe me, domine, veruntamen*

OBJECTION 1: It would seem that sin incurs a debt of punishment infinite in quantity. For it is written (Jer 10:24): *Correct me, O Lord, but yet with judgment: and not in Thy*

in iudicio, et non in furore tuo, ne forte ad nihilum redigas me. Ira autem vel furor Dei metaphorice significat vindictam divinae iustitiae, redigi autem in nihilum est poena infinita, sicut et ex nihilo aliquid facere est virtutis infinitae. Ergo secundum vindictam divinam, peccatum punitur poena infinita secundum quantitatem.

PRAETEREA, quantitati culpae respondet quantitas poenae; secundum illud Deuteron. XXV, *pro mensura peccati erit et plagarum modus.* Sed peccatum quod contra Deum committitur, est infinitum, tanto enim gravius est peccatum, quanto maior est persona contra quam peccatur, sicut gravius peccatum est percutere principem quam percutere hominem privatum; Dei autem magnitudo est infinita. Ergo poena infinita debetur pro peccato quod contra Deum committitur.

PRAETEREA, dupliciter est aliquid infinitum, duratione scilicet, et quantitate. Sed duratione est poena infinita. Ergo et quantitate.

SED CONTRA est quia secundum hoc omnium mortalium peccatorum poenae essent aequales, non enim est infinitum infinito maius.

RESPONDEO dicendum quod poena proportionatur peccato. In peccato autem duo sunt. Quorum unum est aversio ab incommutabili bono, quod est infinitum, unde ex hac parte peccatum est infinitum. Aliud quod est in peccato, est inordinata conversio ad commutabile bonum. Et ex hac parte peccatum est finitum, tum quia ipsum bonum commutabile est finitum; tum quia ipsa conversio est finita, non enim possunt esse actus creaturae infiniti. Ex parte igitur aversionis, respondet peccato poena damni, quae etiam est infinita, est enim amissio infiniti boni, scilicet Dei. Ex parte autem inordinatae conversionis, respondet ei poena sensus, quae etiam est finita.

AD PRIMUM ergo dicendum quod omnino redigi in nihilum eum qui peccat, non convenit divinae iustitiae, quia repugnat perpetuitati poenae, quae est secundum divinam iustitiam, ut dictum est. Sed in nihilum redigi dicitur qui spiritualibus bonis privatur; secundum illud I Cor. XIII, *si non habuero caritatem, nihil sum.*

AD SECUNDUM dicendum quod ratio illa procedit de peccato ex parte aversionis, sic enim homo contra Deum peccat.

AD TERTIUM dicendum quod duratio poenae respondet durationi culpae, non quidem ex parte actus, sed ex parte maculae, qua durante manet reatus poenae. Sed acerbitas poenae respondet gravitati culpae. Culpa autem quae est irreparabilis, de se habet quod perpetuo duret, et ideo debetur ei poena aeterna. Non autem ex parte conversionis habet infinitatem, et ideo non debetur ei ex hac parte poena infinita secundum quantitatem.

fury, lest Thou bring me to nothing. Now God's anger or fury signifies metaphorically the vengeance of Divine justice: and to be brought to nothing is an infinite punishment, even as to make a thing out of nothing denotes infinite power. Therefore according to God's vengeance, sin is awarded a punishment infinite in quantity.

OBJ. 2: Further, quantity of punishment corresponds to quantity of fault, according to Dt. 25:2: *According to the measure of the sin shall the measure also of the stripes be.* Now a sin which is committed against God, is infinite: because the gravity of a sin increases according to the greatness of the person sinned against (thus it is a more grievous sin to strike the sovereign than a private individual), and God's greatness is infinite. Therefore an infinite punishment is due for a sin committed against God.

OBJ. 3: Further, a thing may be infinite in two ways, in duration, and in quantity. Now the punishment is infinite in duration. Therefore it is infinite in quantity also.

ON THE CONTRARY, If this were the case, the punishments of all mortal sins would be equal; because one infinite is not greater than another.

I ANSWER THAT, Punishment is proportionate to sin. Now sin comprises two things. First, there is the turning away from the immutable good, which is infinite, wherefore, in this respect, sin is infinite. Second, there is the inordinate turning to mutable good. In this respect sin is finite, both because the mutable good itself is finite, and because the movement of turning towards it is finite, since the acts of a creature cannot be infinite. Accordingly, insofar as sin consists in turning away from something, its corresponding punishment is the *pain of loss,* which also is infinite, because it is the loss of the infinite good, i.e., God. But insofar as sin turns inordinately to something, its corresponding punishment is the *pain of sense,* which is also finite.

REPLY OBJ. 1: It would be inconsistent with Divine justice for the sinner to be brought to nothing absolutely, because this would be incompatible with the perpetuity of punishment that Divine justice requires, as stated above (A3). The expression *to be brought to nothing* is applied to one who is deprived of spiritual goods, according to 1 Cor. 13:2: *If I . . . have not charity, I am nothing.*

REPLY OBJ. 2: This argument considers sin as turning away from something, for it is thus that man sins against God.

REPLY OBJ. 3: Duration of punishment corresponds to duration of fault, not indeed as regards the act, but on the part of the stain, for as long as this remains, the debt of punishment remains. But punishment corresponds to fault in the point of severity. And a fault which is irreparable, is such that, of itself, it lasts for ever; wherefore it incurs an everlasting punishment. But it is not infinite as regards the thing it turns to; wherefore, in this respect, it does not incur punishment of infinite quantity.

Article 5

Whether Every Sin Incurs a Debt of Eternal Punishment?

AD QUINTUM SIC PROCEDITUR. Videtur quod omne peccatum inducat reatum poenae aeternae. Poena enim, ut dictum est, proportionatur culpae. Sed poena aeterna differt a temporali in infinitum. Nullum autem peccatum differre videtur ab altero in infinitum, cum omne peccatum sit humanus actus, qui infinitus esse non potest. Cum ergo alicui peccato debeatur poena aeterna, sicut dictum est, videtur quod nulli peccato debeatur poena temporalis tantum.

PRAETEREA, peccatum originale est minimum peccatorum, unde et Augustinus dicit, in Enchirid., quod *mitissima poena est eorum qui pro solo peccato originali puniuntur.* Sed peccato originali debetur poena perpetua, nunquam enim videbunt regnum Dei pueri qui sine Baptismo decesserunt cum originali peccato; ut patet per id quod dominus dicit, Ioan. III, *nisi quis renatus fuerit denuo, non potest videre regnum Dei.* Ergo multo magis omnium aliorum peccatorum poena erit aeterna.

PRAETEREA, peccato non debetur maior poena ex hoc quod alteri peccato adiungitur, cum utrumque peccatum suam habeat poenam taxatam secundum divinam iustitiam. Sed peccato veniali debetur poena aeterna, si cum mortali peccato inveniatur in aliquo damnato, quia in Inferno nulla potest esse remissio. Ergo peccato veniali simpliciter debetur poena aeterna. Nulli ergo peccato debetur poena temporalis.

SED CONTRA est quod Gregorius dicit, in IV Dialog., quod quaedam leviores culpae post hanc vitam remittuntur. Non ergo omnia peccata aeterna poena puniuntur.

RESPONDEO dicendum quod, sicut supra dictum est, peccatum causat reatum poenae aeternae, inquantum irreparabiliter repugnat ordini divinae iustitiae, per hoc scilicet quod contrariatur ipsi principio ordinis, quod est ultimus finis. Manifestum est autem quod in quibusdam peccatis est quidem aliqua inordinatio, non tamen per contrarietatem ad ultimum finem, sed solum circa ea quae sunt ad finem, inquantum plus vel minus debite eis intenditur, salvato tamen ordine ad ultimum finem, puta cum homo, etsi nimis ad aliquam rem temporalem afficiatur, non tamen pro ea vellet Deum offendere, aliquid contra praeceptum eius faciendo. Unde huiusmodi peccatis non debetur aeterna poena, sed temporalis.

AD PRIMUM ergo dicendum quod peccata non differunt in infinitum ex parte conversionis ad bonum commutabile, in qua consistit substantia actus, differunt autem in infinitum ex parte aversionis. Nam quaedam peccata committuntur per aversionem ab ultimo fine, quaedam vero per inordinationem circa ea quae sunt ad

OBJECTION 1: It would seem that every sin incurs a debt of eternal punishment. Because punishment, as stated above (A4), is proportionate to the fault. Now eternal punishment differs infinitely from temporal punishment: whereas no sin, apparently, differs infinitely from another, since every sin is a human act, which cannot be infinite. Since therefore some sins incur a debt of everlasting punishment, as stated above (A4), it seems that no sin incurs a debt of mere temporal punishment.

OBJ. 2: Further, original sin is the least of all sins, wherefore Augustine says (*Enchiridion* xciii) that *the lightest punishment is incurred by those who are punished for original sin alone.* But original sin incurs everlasting punishment, since children who have died in original sin through not being baptized, will never see the kingdom of God, as shown by our Lord's words (John 3:3): *Unless a man be born again, he cannot see the kingdom of God.* Much more, therefore, will the punishments of all other sins be everlasting.

OBJ. 3: Further, a sin does not deserve greater punishment through being united to another sin; for Divine justice has allotted its punishment to each sin. Now a venial sin deserves eternal punishment if it be united to a mortal sin in a lost soul, because in hell there is no remission of sins. Therefore venial sin by itself deserves eternal punishment. Therefore temporal punishment is not due for any sin.

ON THE CONTRARY, Gregory says (*Dial.* iv, 39), that certain slighter sins are remitted after this life. Therefore all sins are not punished eternally.

I ANSWER THAT, As stated above (A3), a sin incurs a debt of eternal punishment, insofar as it causes an irreparable disorder in the order of Divine justice, through being contrary to the very principle of that order, viz., the last end. Now it is evident that in some sins there is disorder indeed, but such as not to involve contrariety in respect of the last end, but only in respect of things referable to the end, insofar as one is too much or too little intent on them without prejudicing the order to the last end: as, for instance, when a man is too fond of some temporal thing, yet would not offend God for its sake, by breaking one of His commandments. Consequently such sins do not incur everlasting, but only temporal punishment.

REPLY OBJ. 1: Sins do not differ infinitely from one another in respect of their turning towards mutable good, which constitutes the substance of the sinful act; but they do differ infinitely in respect of their turning away from something. Because some sins consist in turning away from the last end, and some in a disorder affecting things

finem. Finis autem ultimus ab his quae sunt ad finem, in infinitum differt.

Ad secundum dicendum quod peccato originali non debetur poena aeterna ratione suae gravitatis, sed ratione conditionis subiecti, scilicet hominis qui sine gratia invenitur, per quam solam fit remissio poenae.

Et similiter dicendum est ad tertium, de veniali peccato. Aeternitas enim poenae non respondet quantitati culpae, sed irremissibilitati ipsius, ut dictum est.

referable to the end: and the last end differs infinitely from the things that are referred to it.

Reply Obj. 2: Original sin incurs everlasting punishment, not on account of its gravity, but by reason of the condition of the subject, viz., a human being deprived of grace, without which there is no remission of sin.

The same answer applies to the Third Objection about venial sin. Because eternity of punishment does not correspond to the quantity of the sin, but to its irremissibility, as stated above (A3).

Article 6

Whether the Debt of Punishment Remains After Sin?

Ad sextum sic proceditur. Videtur quod reatus poenae non remaneat post peccatum. Remota enim causa, removetur effectus. Sed peccatum est causa reatus poenae. Ergo, remoto peccato, cessat reatus poenae.

Praeterea, peccatum removetur per hoc quod homo ad virtutem redit. Sed virtuoso non debetur poena, sed magis praemium. Ergo, remoto peccato, non remanet reatus poenae.

Praeterea, *poenae sunt medicinae*, ut dicitur in II Ethic. Sed postquam aliquis iam est ab infirmitate curatus, non adhibetur sibi medicina. Ergo, remoto peccato, non remanet debitum poenae.

Sed contra est quod dicitur II Reg. XII, quod *David dixit ad Nathan, peccavi domino. Dixitque Nathan ad David, dominus quoque transtulit peccatum tuum, non morieris. Veruntamen quia blasphemare fecisti inimicos nomen domini, filius qui natus est tibi, morte morietur.* Punitur ergo aliquis a Deo etiam postquam ei peccatum dimittitur. Et sic reatus poenae remanet, peccato remoto.

Respondeo dicendum quod in peccato duo possunt considerari, scilicet actus culpae, et macula sequens. Planum est autem quod, cessante actu peccati, remanet reatus, in omnibus peccatis actualibus. Actus enim peccati facit hominem reum poenae, inquantum transgreditur ordinem divinae iustitiae; ad quem non redit nisi per quandam recompensationem poenae, quae ad aequalitatem iustitiae reducit; ut scilicet qui plus voluntati suae indulsit quam debuit, contra mandatum Dei agens, secundum ordinem divinae iustitiae, aliquid contra illud quod vellet, spontaneus vel invitus patiatur. Quod etiam in iniuriis hominibus factis observatur, ut per recompensationem poenae reintegretur aequalitas iustitiae. Unde patet quod, cessante actu peccati vel iniuriae illatae, adhuc remanet debitum poenae.

Objection 1: It would seem that there remains no debt of punishment after sin. For if the cause be removed the effect is removed. But sin is the cause of the debt of punishment. Therefore, when the sin is removed, the debt of punishment ceases also.

Obj. 2: Further, sin is removed by man returning to virtue. Now a virtuous man deserves, not punishment, but reward. Therefore, when sin is removed, the debt of punishment no longer remains.

Obj. 3: Further, *Punishments are a kind of medicine* (*Ethic.* ii, 3). But a man is not given medicine after being cured of his disease. Therefore, when sin is removed the debt of punishment does not remain.

On the contrary, It is written (2 Kgs xii, 13,14): *David said to Nathan: I have sinned against the Lord. And Nathan said to David: The Lord also hath taken away thy sin; thou shalt not die. Nevertheless because thou hast given occasion to the enemies of the Lord to blaspheme . . . the child that is born to thee shall die.* Therefore a man is punished by God even after his sin is forgiven: and so the debt of punishment remains, when the sin has been removed.

I answer that, Two things may be considered in sin: the guilty act, and the consequent stain. Now it is evident that in all actual sins, when the act of sin has ceased, the guilt remains; because the act of sin makes man deserving of punishment, insofar as he transgresses the order of Divine justice, to which he cannot return except he pay some sort of penal compensation, which restores him to the equality of justice; so that, according to the order of Divine justice, he who has been too indulgent to his will, by transgressing God's commandments, suffers, either willingly or unwillingly, something contrary to what he would wish. This restoration of the equality of justice by penal compensation is also to be observed in injuries done to one's fellow men. Consequently it is evident that when the sinful or injurious act has ceased there still remains the debt of punishment.

Sed si loquamur de ablatione peccati quantum ad maculam, sic manifestum est quod macula peccati ab anima auferri non potest, nisi per hoc quod anima Deo coniungitur, per cuius distantiam detrimentum proprii nitoris incurrebat, quod est macula, ut supra dictum est. Coniungitur autem homo Deo per voluntatem. Unde macula peccati ab homine tolli non potest nisi voluntas hominis ordinem divinae iustitiae acceptet, ut scilicet vel ipse poenam sibi spontaneus assumat in recompensationem culpae praeteritae, vel etiam a Deo illatam patienter sustineat, utroque enim modo poena rationem satisfactionis habet. Poena autem satisfactoria diminuit aliquid de ratione poenae. Est enim de ratione poenae quod sit contra voluntatem. Poena autem satisfactoria, etsi secundum absolutam considerationem sit contra voluntatem, tamen tunc, et pro hoc, est voluntaria. Unde simpliciter est voluntaria, secundum quid autem involuntaria, sicut patet ex his quae supra de voluntario et involuntario dicta sunt. Dicendum est ergo quod, remota macula culpae, potest quidem remanere reatus non poenae simpliciter, sed satisfactoriae.

AD PRIMUM ergo dicendum quod sicut, cessante actu peccati, remanet macula, ut supra dictum est; ita etiam potest remanere reatus. Cessante vero macula, non remanet reatus secundum eandem rationem, ut dictum est.

AD SECUNDUM dicendum quod virtuoso non debetur poena simpliciter, potest tamen sibi deberi poena ut satisfactoria, quia hoc ipsum ad virtutem pertinet, ut satisfaciat pro his in quibus offendit vel Deum vel hominem.

AD TERTIUM dicendum quod, remota macula, sanatum est vulnus peccati quantum ad voluntatem. Requiritur autem adhuc poena ad sanationem aliarum virium animae, quae per peccatum praecedens deordinatae fuerunt, ut scilicet per contraria curentur. Requiritur etiam ad restituendum aequalitatem iustitiae; et ad amovendum scandalum aliorum, ut aedificentur in poena qui sunt scandalizati in culpa; ut patet ex exemplo de David inducto.

But if we speak of the removal of sin as to the stain, it is evident that the stain of sin cannot be removed from the soul, without the soul being united to God, since it was through being separated from Him that it suffered the loss of its brightness, in which the stain consists, as stated above (Q86, A1). Now man is united to God by his will. Wherefore the stain of sin cannot be removed from man, unless his will accept the order of Divine justice, that is to say, unless either of his own accord he take upon himself the punishment of his past sin, or bear patiently the punishment which God inflicts on him; and in both ways punishment avails for satisfaction. Now when punishment is satisfactory, it loses somewhat of the nature of punishment: for the nature of punishment is to be against the will; and although satisfactory punishment, absolutely speaking, is against the will, nevertheless in this particular case and for this particular purpose, it is voluntary. Consequently it is voluntary simply, but involuntary in a certain respect, as we have explained when speaking of the voluntary and the involuntary (Q6, A6). We must, therefore, say that, when the stain of sin has been removed, there may remain a debt of punishment, not indeed of punishment simply, but of satisfactory punishment.

REPLY OBJ. 1: Just as after the act of sin has ceased, the stain remains, as stated above (Q86, A2), so the debt of punishment also can remain. But when the stain has been removed, the debt of punishment does not remain in the same way, as stated.

REPLY OBJ. 2: The virtuous man does not deserve punishment simply, but he may deserve it as satisfactory: because his very virtue demands that he should do satisfaction for his offenses against God or man.

REPLY OBJ. 3: When the stain is removed, the wound of sin is healed as regards the will. But punishment is still requisite in order that the other powers of the soul be healed, since they were so disordered by the sin committed, so that, to wit, the disorder may be remedied by the contrary of that which caused it. Moreover punishment is requisite in order to restore the equality of justice, and to remove the scandal given to others, so that those who were scandalized at the sin may be edified by the punishment, as may be seen in the example of David quoted above.

Article 7

Whether Every Punishment Is Inflicted for a Sin?

AD SEPTIMUM SIC PROCEDITUR. Videtur quod non omnis poena sit propter aliquam culpam. Dicitur enim Ioan. IX, de caeco nato, *neque hic peccavit, neque parentes eius, ut nasceretur caecus.* Et similiter videmus quod

OBJECTION 1: It would seem that not every punishment is inflicted for a sin. For it is written (John 9:3,2) about the man born blind: *Neither hath this man sinned, nor his parents . . . that he should be born blind.* In like manner we

multi pueri, etiam baptizati, graves poenas patiuntur, ut puta febres, Daemonum oppressiones, et multa huiusmodi, cum tamen in eis non sit peccatum, postquam sunt baptizati. Et antequam sint baptizati, non est in eis plus de peccato quam in aliis pueris, qui haec non patiuntur. Non ergo omnis poena est pro peccato.

PRAETEREA, eiusdem rationis esse videtur quod peccatores prosperentur, et quod aliqui innocentes puniantur. Utrumque autem in rebus humanis frequenter invenimus, dicitur enim de iniquis in Psalmo LXXII, *in labore hominum non sunt, et cum hominibus non flagellabuntur*; et Iob XXI, *impii vivunt, sublevati sunt, confortatique divitiis*; et Habacuc I, dicitur, *quare respicis contemptores et taces, conculcante impio iustiorem se?* Non ergo omnis poena infligitur pro culpa.

PRAETEREA, de Christo dicitur I Pet. II, quod *peccatum non fecit, nec inventus est dolus in ore eius*. Et tamen ibidem dicitur quod *passus est pro nobis*. Ergo non semper poena a Deo dispensatur pro culpa.

SED CONTRA est quod dicitur Iob IV, *quis unquam innocens periit? Aut quando recti deleti sunt? Quin potius vidi eos qui operantur iniquitatem, flante Deo, periisse.* Et Augustinus dicit, in I Retract., quod *omnis poena iusta est, et pro peccato aliquo impenditur.*

RESPONDEO dicendum quod, sicut iam dictum est, poena potest dupliciter considerari, simpliciter, et inquantum est satisfactoria. Poena quidem satisfactoria est quodammodo voluntaria. Et quia contingit eos qui differunt in reatu poenae, esse unum secundum voluntatem unione amoris, inde est quod interdum aliquis qui non peccavit, poenam voluntarius pro alio portat, sicut etiam in rebus humanis videmus quod aliquis in se transfert alterius debitum. Si vero loquamur de poena simpliciter, secundum quod habet rationem poenae, sic semper habet ordinem ad culpam propriam, sed quandoque quidem ad culpam actualem, puta quando aliquis vel a Deo vel ab homine pro peccato commisso punitur; quandoque vero ad culpam originalem. Et hoc quidem vel principaliter, vel consequenter. Principaliter quidem poena originalis peccati est quod natura humana sibi relinquitur, destituta auxilio originalis iustitiae, sed ad hoc consequuntur omnes poenalitates quae ex defectu naturae in hominibus contingunt.

Sciendum tamen est quod quandoque aliquid videtur esse poenale, quod tamen non habet simpliciter rationem poenae. Poena enim est species mali, ut in primo dictum est. Malum autem est privatio boni. Cum autem sint plura hominis bona, scilicet animae, corporis, et exteriorum rerum; contingit interdum quod homo patiatur detrimentum in minori bono, ut augeatur in maiori, sicut cum patitur detrimentum pecuniae propter sanitatem corporis, vel in utroque horum propter salutem

see that many children, those also who have been baptized, suffer grievous punishments, fevers, for instance, diabolical possession, and so forth, and yet there is no sin in them after they have been baptized. Moreover before they are baptized, there is no more sin in them than in the other children who do not suffer such things. Therefore not every punishment is inflicted for a sin.

OBJ. 2: Further, that sinners should thrive and that the innocent should be punished seem to come under the same head. Now each of these is frequently observed in human affairs, for it is written about the wicked (Ps 72:5): *They are not in the labor of men: neither shall they be scourged like other men*; and (Job 21:7): *the wicked live, are advanced, and strengthened with riches*; and (Hab. 1:13): *Why lookest Thou upon the contemptuous, and holdest Thy peace, when the wicked man oppresseth, the man that is more just than himself?* Therefore not every punishment is inflicted for a sin.

OBJ. 3: Further, it is written of Christ (1 Pet 2:22) that *He did no sin, nor was guile found in His mouth*. And yet it is said (1 Pet 2:21) that *He suffered for us*. Therefore punishment is not always inflicted by God for sin.

ON THE CONTRARY, It is written (Job 4:7, seqq.): *Who ever perished innocent? Or when were the just destroyed? On the contrary, I have seen those who work iniquity . . . perishing by the blast of God*; and Augustine writes (*Retract.* i) that *all punishment is just, and is inflicted for a sin*.

I ANSWER THAT, As already stated (A6), punishment can be considered in two ways—simply, and as being satisfactory. A satisfactory punishment is, in a way, voluntary. And since those who differ as to the debt of punishment, may be one in will by the union of love, it happens that one who has not sinned, bears willingly the punishment for another: thus even in human affairs we see men take the debts of another upon themselves. If, however, we speak of punishment simply, in respect of its being something penal, it has always a relation to a sin in the one punished. Sometimes this is a relation to actual sin, as when a man is punished by God or man for a sin committed by him. Sometimes it is a relation to original sin: and this, either principally or consequently—principally, the punishment of original sin is that human nature is left to itself, and deprived of original justice: and consequently, all the penalties which result from this defect in human nature.

Nevertheless we must observe that sometimes a thing seems penal, and yet is not so simply. Because punishment is a species of evil, as stated in the FP, Q48, A5. Now evil is privation of good. And since man's good is manifold, viz., good of the soul, good of the body, and external goods, it happens sometimes that man suffers the loss of a lesser good, that he may profit in a greater good, as when he suffers loss of money for the sake of bodily health, or loss of both of these, for the sake of his soul's health and the glory

animae et propter gloriam Dei. Et tunc tale detrimentum non est simpliciter malum hominis, sed secundum quid. Unde non dicit simpliciter rationem poenae, sed medicinae, nam et medici austeras potiones propinant infirmis, ut conferant sanitatem. Et quia huiusmodi non proprie habent rationem poenae, non reducuntur ad culpam sicut ad causam, nisi pro tanto, quia hoc ipsum quod oportet humanae naturae medicinas poenales exhibere, est ex corruptione naturae, quae est poena originalis peccati. In statu enim innocentiae non oportuisset aliquem ad profectum virtutis inducere per poenalia exercitia. Unde hoc ipsum quod est poenale in talibus reducitur ad originalem culpam sicut ad causam.

AD PRIMUM ergo dicendum quod huiusmodi defectus eorum qui nascuntur, vel etiam puerorum, sunt effectus et poenae originalis peccati, ut dictum est. Et manent etiam post Baptismum, propter causam superius dictam. Et quod non sint aequaliter in omnibus, contingit propter naturae diversitatem, quae sibi relinquitur, ut supra dictum est. Ordinantur tamen huiusmodi defectus, secundum divinam providentiam, ad salutem hominum, vel eorum qui patiuntur, vel aliorum, qui poenis admonentur; et etiam ad gloriam Dei.

AD SECUNDUM dicendum quod bona temporalia et corporalia sunt quidem aliqua bona hominis, sed parva, bona vero spiritualia sunt magna hominis bona. Pertinet igitur ad divinam iustitiam ut virtuosis det spiritualia bona; et de temporalibus bonis vel malis tantum det eis, quantum sufficit ad virtutem, ut enim Dionysius dicit, VIII cap. de Div. Nom., *divinae iustitiae est non emollire optimorum fortitudinem materialium donationibus.* Aliis vero hoc ipsum quod temporalia dantur, in malum spiritualium cedit. Unde in Psalmo LXXII concluditur, *ideo tenuit eos superbia.*

AD TERTIUM dicendum quod Christus poenam sustinuit satisfactoriam non pro suis, sed pro nostris peccatis.

of God. In such cases the loss is an evil to man, not simply but relatively; wherefore it does not answer to the name of punishment simply, but of medicinal punishment, because a medical man prescribes bitter potions to his patients, that he may restore them to health. And since such like are not punishments properly speaking, they are not referred to sin as their cause, except in a restricted sense: because the very fact that human nature needs a treatment of penal medicines, is due to the corruption of nature which is itself the punishment of original sin. For there was no need, in the state of innocence, for penal exercises in order to make progress in virtue; so that whatever is penal in the exercise of virtue, is reduced to original sin as its cause.

REPLY OBJ. 1: Such like defects of those who are born with them, or which children suffer from, are the effects and the punishments of original sin, as stated above (Q85, A5); and they remain even after baptism, for the cause stated above (Q85, A5, ad 2): and that they are not equally in all, is due to the diversity of nature, which is left to itself, as stated above (Q85, A5, ad 1). Nevertheless, they are directed by Divine providence, to the salvation of men, either of those who suffer, or of others who are admonished by their means—and also to the glory of God.

REPLY OBJ. 2: Temporal and bodily goods are indeed goods of man, but they are of small account: whereas spiritual goods are man's chief goods. Consequently it belongs to Divine justice to give spiritual goods to the virtuous, and to award them as much temporal goods or evils, as suffices for virtue: for, as Dionysius says (*Div. Nom.* viii), *Divine justice does not enfeeble the fortitude of the virtuous man, by material gifts.* The very fact that others receive temporal goods, is detrimental to their spiritual good; wherefore the psalm quoted concludes (verse 6): *Therefore pride hath held them fast.*

REPLY OBJ. 3: Christ bore a satisfactory punishment, not for His, but for our sins.

Article 8

Whether Anyone Is Punished for Another's Sin?

AD OCTAVUM SIC PROCEDITUR. Videtur quod aliquis puniatur pro peccato alterius. Dicitur enim Exodi XX, *ego sum Deus Zelotes, visitans iniquitatem patrum in filios in tertiam et quartam generationem, his qui oderunt me.* Et Matth. XXIII dicitur, *ut veniat super vos omnis sanguis iustus qui effusus est super terram.*

PRAETEREA, iustitia humana derivatur a iustitia divina. Sed secundum iustitiam humanam aliquando filii puniuntur pro parentibus, sicut patet in crimine laesae

OBJECTION 1: It would seem that one may be punished for another's sin. For it is written (Exod 20:5): *I am . . . God . . . jealous, visiting the iniquity of the fathers upon the children, unto the third and fourth generation of them that hate Me*; and (Matt 23:35): *That upon you may come all the just blood that hath been shed upon the earth.*

OBJ. 2: Further, human justice springs from Divine justice. Now, according to human justice, children are sometimes punished for their parents, as in the case of high

maiestatis. Ergo etiam secundum divinam iustitiam, unus punitur pro peccato alterius.

PRAETEREA, si dicatur filius non puniri pro peccato patris, sed pro peccato proprio, inquantum imitatur malitiam paternam, non magis hoc diceretur de filiis quam de extraneis, qui simili poena puniuntur his quorum peccata imitantur. Non ergo videtur quod filii pro peccatis propriis puniantur, sed pro peccatis parentum.

SED CONTRA est quod dicitur Ezech. XVIII, *filius non portabit iniquitatem patris.*

RESPONDEO dicendum quod, si loquamur de poena satisfactoria, quae voluntarie assumitur, contingit quod unus portet poenam alterius inquantum sunt quodammodo unum, sicut iam dictum est. Si autem loquamur de poena pro peccato inflicta, inquantum habet rationem poenae, sic solum unusquisque pro peccato suo punitur, quia actus peccati aliquid personale est. Si autem loquamur de poena quae habet rationem medicinae, sic contingit quod unus punitur pro peccato alterius. Dictum est enim quod detrimenta corporalium rerum, vel etiam ipsius corporis, sunt quaedam poenales medicinae ordinatae ad salutem animae. Unde nihil prohibet talibus poenis aliquem puniri pro peccato alterius, vel a Deo vel ab homine, utpote filios pro patribus, et subditos pro dominis, inquantum sunt quaedam res eorum. Ita tamen quod, si filius vel subditus est particeps culpae, huiusmodi poenalis defectus habet rationem poenae quantum ad utrumque, scilicet eum qui punitur, et eum pro quo punitur. Si vero non sit particeps culpae, habet rationem poenae quantum ad eum pro quo punitur, quantum vero ad eum qui punitur, rationem medicinae tantum, nisi per accidens, inquantum peccato alterius consentit; ordinatur enim ei ad bonum animae, si patienter sustineat.

Poenae vero spirituales non sunt medicinales tantum, quia bonum animae non ordinatur ad aliud melius bonum. Unde in bonis animae nullus patitur detrimentum sine culpa propria. Et propter hoc etiam talibus poenis, ut dicit Augustinus in epistola ad avitum, unus non punitur pro alio, quia quantum ad animam, filius non est res patris. Unde et huius causam dominus assignans, dicit, Ezech. XVIII, *omnes animae meae sunt.*

AD PRIMUM ergo dicendum quod utrumque dictum videtur esse referendum ad poenas temporales vel corporales, inquantum filii sunt res quaedam parentum, et successores praedecessorum. Vel si referatur ad poenas spirituales, hoc dicitur propter imitationem culpae, unde in Exodo additur, *his qui oderunt me*; et in Matthaeo dicitur, *et vos implete mensuram patrum vestrorum*. Dicit autem puniri peccata patrum in filiis, quia filii, in peccatis parentum nutriti, proniores sunt ad peccandum, tum

treason. Therefore also according to Divine justice, one is punished for another's sin.

OBJ. 3: Further, if it be replied that the son is punished, not for the father's sin, but for his own, inasmuch as he imitates his father's wickedness; this would not be said of the children rather than of outsiders, who are punished in like manner as those whose crimes they imitate. It seems, therefore, that children are punished, not for their own sins, but for those of their parents.

ON THE CONTRARY, It is written (Ezek 18:20): *The son shall not bear the iniquity of the father.*

I ANSWER THAT, If we speak of that satisfactory punishment, which one takes upon oneself voluntarily, one may bear another's punishment, insofar as they are, in some way, one, as stated above (A7). If, however, we speak of punishment inflicted on account of sin, inasmuch as it is penal, then each one is punished for his own sin only, because the sinful act is something personal. But if we speak of a punishment that is medicinal, in this way it does happen that one is punished for another's sin. For it has been stated (A7) that ills sustained in bodily goods or even in the body itself, are medicinal punishments intended for the health of the soul. Wherefore there is no reason why one should not have such like punishments inflicted on one for another's sin, either by God or by man; e.g., on children for their parents, or on servants for their masters, inasmuch as they are their property so to speak; in such a way, however, that, if the children or the servants take part in the sin, this penal ill has the character of punishment in regard to both the one punished and the one he is punished for. But if they do not take part in the sin, it has the character of punishment in regard to the one for whom the punishment is borne, while, in regard to the one who is punished, it is merely medicinal (except accidentally, if he consent to the other's sin), since it is intended for the good of his soul, if he bears it patiently.

With regard to spiritual punishments, these are not merely medicinal, because the good of the soul is not directed to a yet higher good. Consequently no one suffers loss in the goods of the soul without some fault of his own. Wherefore Augustine says (*Ep. ad Avit.*), such like punishments are not inflicted on one for another's sin, because, as regards the soul, the son is not the father's property. Hence the Lord assigns the reason for this by saying (Ezek 18:4): *All souls are Mine.*

REPLY OBJ. 1: Both the passages quoted should, seemingly, be referred to temporal or bodily punishments, insofar as children are the property of their parents, and posterity, of their forefathers. Else, if they be referred to spiritual punishments, they must be understood in reference to the imitation of sin, wherefore in Exodus these words are added, *Of them that hate Me*, and in the chapter quoted from Matthew (verse 32) we read: *Fill ye up then the measure of your fathers*. The sins of the fathers are said to be punished

propter consuetudinem; tum etiam propter exemplum, patrum quasi auctoritatem sequentes. Sunt etiam maiori poena digni, si, poenas patrum videntes, correcti non sunt. Ideo autem addidit, in tertiam et quartam generationem, quia tantum consueverunt homines vivere, ut tertiam et quartam generationem videant; et sic mutuo videre possunt et filii peccata patrum ad imitandum, et patres poenas filiorum ad dolendum.

AD SECUNDUM dicendum quod poenae illae sunt corporales et temporales quas iustitia humana uni pro peccato alterius infligit. Et sunt remedia quaedam, vel medicinae, contra culpas sequentes, ut vel ipsi qui puniuntur, vel alii, cohibeantur a similibus culpis.

AD TERTIUM dicendum quod magis dicuntur puniri pro peccatis aliorum propinqui quam extranei, tum quia poena propinquorum quodammodo redundat in illos qui peccaverunt, ut dictum est, inquantum filius est quaedam res patris. Tum etiam quia et domestica exempla, et domesticae poenae, magis movent. Unde quando aliquis nutritus est in peccatis parentum, vehementius ea sequitur; et si ex eorum poenis non est deterritus, obstinatior videtur; unde et maiori poena dignus.

in their children, because the latter are the more prone to sin through being brought up amid their parents' crimes, both by becoming accustomed to them, and by imitating their parents' example, conforming to their authority as it were. Moreover they deserve heavier punishment if, seeing the punishment of their parents, they fail to mend their ways. The text adds, *to the third and fourth generation*, because men are wont to live long enough to see the third and fourth generation, so that both the children can witness their parents' sins so as to imitate them, and the parents can see their children's punishments so as to grieve for them.

REPLY OBJ. 2: The punishments which human justice inflicts on one for another's sin are bodily and temporal. They are also remedies or medicines against future sins, in order that either they who are punished, or others may be restrained from similar faults.

REPLY OBJ. 3: Those who are near of kin are said to be punished, rather than outsiders, for the sins of others, both because the punishment of kindred redounds somewhat upon those who sinned, as stated above, insofar as the child is the father's property, and because the examples and the punishments that occur in one's own household are more moving. Consequently when a man is brought up amid the sins of his parents, he is more eager to imitate them, and if he is not deterred by their punishments, he would seem to be the more obstinate, and, therefore, to deserve more severe punishment.

QUESTION 88

OF VENIAL AND MORTAL SIN

Deinde, quia peccatum veniale et mortale distinguuntur secundum reatum, considerandum est de eis. Et primo, considerandum est de veniali per comparationem ad mortale; secundo, de veniali secundum se.

Circa primum quaeruntur sex.

Primo, utrum veniale peccatum convenienter dividatur contra mortale.

Secundo, utrum distinguantur genere.

Tertio, utrum veniale peccatum sit dispositio ad mortale.

Quarto, utrum veniale peccatum possit fieri mortale.

Quinto, utrum circumstantia aggravans possit de veniali peccato facere mortale.

Sexto, utrum peccatum mortale possit fieri veniale.

In the next place, since venial and mortal sins differ in respect of the debt of punishment, we must consider them. First, we shall consider venial sin as compared with mortal sin; second, we shall consider venial sin in itself.

Under the first head there are six points of inquiry:

(1) Whether venial sin is fittingly condivided with mortal sin?

(2) Whether they differ generically?

(3) Whether venial sin is a disposition to mortal sin?

(4) Whether a venial sin can become mortal?

(5) Whether a venial sin can become mortal by reason of an aggravating circumstance?

(6) Whether a mortal sin can become venial?

Article 1

Whether Venial Sin Is Fittingly Condivided with Mortal Sin?

AD PRIMUM SIC PROCEDITUR. Videtur quod veniale peccatum non convenienter dividatur contra mortale. Dicit enim Augustinus, XXII libro contra Faustum, *peccatum est dictum vel factum vel concupitum contra legem aeternam.* Sed esse contra legem aeternam, dat peccato quod sit mortale. Ergo omne peccatum est mortale. Non ergo peccatum veniale dividitur contra mortale.

PRAETEREA, apostolus dicit, I Cor. X, *sive manducatis, sive bibitis, sive aliquid aliud facitis, omnia in gloriam Dei facite.* Sed contra hoc praeceptum facit quicumque peccat, non enim peccatum fit propter gloriam Dei. Cum ergo facere contra praeceptum sit peccatum mortale, videtur quod quicumque peccat, mortaliter peccet.

PRAETEREA, quicumque amore alicui rei inhaeret, inhaeret ei vel sicut fruens, vel sicut utens; ut patet per Augustinum, in I de Doctr. Christ. Sed nullus peccans inhaeret bono commutabili quasi utens, non enim refert ipsum ad bonum quod nos beatos facit, quod proprie est uti, ut Augustinus dicit ibidem. Ergo quicumque peccat, fruitur bono commutabili. *Sed frui rebus utendis est humana perversitas,* ut Augustinus dicit, in libro octoginta trium quaest. Cum ergo perversitas peccatum mortale nominet, videtur quod quicumque peccat, mortaliter peccet.

PRAETEREA, quicumque accedit ad unum terminum, ex hoc ipso recedit ab alio. Sed quicumque peccat,

OBJECTION 1: It would seem that venial sin is unfittingly condivided with mortal sin. For Augustine says (*Contra Faust.* xxii, 27): *Sin is a word, deed or desire contrary to the eternal law.* But the fact of being against the eternal law makes a sin to be mortal. Consequently every sin is mortal. Therefore venial sin is not condivided with mortal sin.

OBJ. 2: Further, the Apostle says (1 Cor 10:31): *Whether you eat or drink, or whatever else you do; do all to the glory of God.* Now whoever sins breaks this commandment, because sin is not done for God's glory. Consequently, since to break a commandment is to commit a mortal sin, it seems that whoever sins, sins mortally.

OBJ. 3: Further, whoever cleaves to a thing by love, cleaves either as enjoying it, or as using it, as Augustine states (*De Doctr. Christ.* i, 3,4). But no person, in sinning, cleaves to a mutable good as using it: because he does not refer it to that good which gives us happiness, which, properly speaking, is to use, according to Augustine (*De Doctr. Christ.* i, 3,4). Therefore whoever sins enjoys a mutable good. Now *to enjoy what we should use is human perverseness,* as Augustine again says (Qq. lxxxiii, qu. 30). Therefore, since *perverseness* denotes a mortal sin, it seems that whoever sins, sins mortally.

OBJ. 4: Further, whoever approaches one term, from that very fact turns away from the opposite. Now whoever

accedit ad bonum commutabile. Ergo recedit a bono incommutabili. Ergo peccat mortaliter. Non ergo convenienter peccatum veniale contra mortale dividitur.

SED CONTRA est quod Augustinus dicit, in Homil. XLI super Ioan., *quod crimen est quod damnationem meretur, veniale autem est quod non meretur damnationem.* Sed crimen nominat peccatum mortale. Ergo veniale peccatum convenienter dividitur contra mortale.

RESPONDEO dicendum quod aliqua, secundum quod proprie accipiuntur, non videntur esse opposita, quae si metaphorice accipiantur, opponi inveniuntur, sicut ridere non opponitur ei quod est arescere; sed secundum quod ridere metaphorice de prato dicitur propter eius floritionem et virorem, opponitur ei quod est arescere. Similiter si mortale proprie accipiatur, prout refertur ad mortem corporalem, non videtur oppositionem habere cum veniali, nec ad idem genus pertinere. Sed si mortale accipiatur metaphorice, secundum quod dicitur in peccatis, mortale opponitur ei quod est veniale.

Cum enim peccatum sit quaedam infirmitas animae, ut supra habitum est, peccatum aliquod mortale dicitur ad similitudinem morbi, qui dicitur mortalis ex eo quod inducit defectum irreparabilem per destitutionem alicuius principii, ut dictum est. Principium autem spiritualis vitae, quae est secundum virtutem, est ordo ad ultimum finem, ut supra dictum est. Qui quidem si destitutus fuerit, reparari non potest per aliquod principium intrinsecum, sed solum per virtutem divinam, ut supra dictum est, quia inordinationes eorum quae sunt ad finem, reparantur ex fine, sicut error qui accidit circa conclusiones, per veritatem principiorum. Defectus ergo ordinis ultimi finis non potest per aliquid aliud reparari quod sit principalius; sicut nec error qui est circa principia. Et ideo huiusmodi peccata dicuntur mortalia, quasi irreparabilia. Peccata autem quae habent inordinationem circa ea quae sunt ad finem, conservato ordine ad ultimum finem, reparabilia sunt. Et haec dicuntur venialia, tunc enim peccatum veniam habet, quando reatus poenae tollitur, qui cessat cessante peccato, ut dictum est.

Secundum hoc ergo, mortale et veniale opponuntur sicut reparabile et irreparabile. Et hoc dico per principium interius, non autem per comparationem ad virtutem divinam, quae omnem morbum et corporalem et spiritualem potest reparare. Et propter hoc veniale peccatum convenienter dividitur contra mortale.

AD PRIMUM ergo dicendum quod divisio peccati venialis et mortalis non est divisio generis in species, quae aequaliter participent rationem generis, sed analogi in ea de quibus praedicatur secundum prius et posterius. Et ideo perfecta ratio peccati, quam Augustinus ponit, convenit peccato mortali. Peccatum autem veniale dicitur

sins, approaches a mutable good, and, consequently turns away from the immutable good, so that he sins mortally. Therefore venial sin is unfittingly condivided with mortal sin.

ON THE CONTRARY, Augustine says (*Tract. xli in Joan.*), that *a crime is one that merits damnation, and a venial sin, one that does not.* But a crime denotes a mortal sin. Therefore venial sin is fittingly condivided with mortal sin.

I ANSWER THAT, Certain terms do not appear to be mutually opposed, if taken in their proper sense, whereas they are opposed if taken metaphorically: thus *to smile* is not opposed to *being dry*; but if we speak of the smiling meadows when they are decked with flowers and fresh with green hues this is opposed to drought. In like manner if mortal be taken literally as referring to the death of the body, it does not imply opposition to venial, nor belong to the same genus. But if mortal be taken metaphorically, as applied to sin, it is opposed to that which is venial.

For sin, being a sickness of the soul, as stated above (Q71, A1, ad 3; Q72, A5; Q74, A9, ad 2), is said to be mortal by comparison with a disease, which is said to be mortal, through causing an irreparable defect consisting in the corruption of a principle, as stated above (Q72, A5). Now the principle of the spiritual life, which is a life in accord with virtue, is the order to the last end, as stated above (Q72, A5; Q87, A3): and if this order be corrupted, it cannot be repaired by any intrinsic principle, but by the power of God alone, as stated above (Q87, A3), because disorders in things referred to the end, are repaired through the end, even as an error about conclusions can be repaired through the truth of the principles. Hence the defect of order to the last end cannot be repaired through something else as a higher principle, as neither can an error about principles. Wherefore such sins are called mortal, as being irreparable. On the other hand, sins which imply a disorder in things referred to the end, the order to the end itself being preserved, are reparable. These sins are called venial: because a sin receives its acquittal when the debt of punishment is taken away, and this ceases when the sin ceases, as explained above (Q87, A6).

Accordingly, mortal and venial are mutually opposed as reparable and irreparable: and I say this with reference to the intrinsic principle, but not to the Divine power, which can repair all diseases, whether of the body or of the soul. Therefore venial sin is fittingly condivided with mortal sin.

REPLY OBJ. 1: The division of sin into venial and mortal is not a division of a genus into its species which have an equal share of the generic nature: but it is the division of an analogous term into its parts, of which it is predicated, of the one first, and of the other afterwards. Consequently the perfect notion of sin, which Augustine gives, applies to

peccatum secundum rationem imperfectam, et in ordine ad peccatum mortale, sicut accidens dicitur ens in ordine ad substantiam, secundum imperfectam rationem entis. Non enim est contra legem, quia venialiter peccans non facit quod lex prohibet, nec praetermittit id ad quod lex per praeceptum obligat; sed facit praeter legem, quia non observat modum rationis quem lex intendit.

AD SECUNDUM dicendum quod illud praeceptum apostoli est affirmativum, unde non obligat ad semper. Et sic non facit contra hoc praeceptum quicumque non actu refert in gloriam Dei omne quod facit. Sufficit ergo quod aliquis habitualiter referat se et omnia sua in Deum, ad hoc quod non semper mortaliter peccet, cum aliquem actum non refert in gloriam Dei actualiter. Veniale autem peccatum non excludit habitualem ordinationem actus humani in gloriam Dei, sed solum actualem, quia non excludit caritatem, quae habitualiter ordinat in Deum. Unde non sequitur quod ille qui peccat venialiter, peccet mortaliter.

AD TERTIUM dicendum quod ille qui peccat venialiter, inhaeret bono temporali non ut fruens, quia non constituit in eo finem; sed ut utens, referens in Deum non actu, sed habitu.

AD QUARTUM dicendum quod bonum commutabile non accipitur ut terminus contrapositus incommutabili bono, nisi quando constituitur in eo finis. Quod enim est ad finem, non habet rationem termini.

mortal sin. On the other hand, venial sin is called a sin, in reference to an imperfect notion of sin, and in relation to mortal sin: even as an accident is called a being, in relation to substance, in reference to the imperfect notion of being. For it is not *against* the law, since he who sins venially neither does what the law forbids, nor omits what the law prescribes to be done; but he acts *beside* the law, through not observing the mode of reason, which the law intends.

REPLY OBJ. 2: This precept of the Apostle is affirmative, and so it does not bind for all times. Consequently everyone who does not actually refer all his actions to the glory of God, does not therefore act against this precept. In order, therefore, to avoid mortal sin each time that one fails actually to refer an action to God's glory, it is enough to refer oneself and all that one has to God habitually. Now venial sin excludes only actual reference of the human act to God's glory, and not habitual reference: because it does not exclude charity, which refers man to God habitually. Therefore it does not follow that he who sins venially, sins mortally.

REPLY OBJ. 3: He that sins venially, cleaves to temporal good, not as enjoying it, because he does not fix his end in it, but as using it, by referring it to God, not actually but habitually.

REPLY OBJ. 4: Mutable good is not considered to be a term in contraposition to the immutable good, unless one's end is fixed therein: because what is referred to the end has not the character of finality.

Article 2

Whether Mortal and Venial Sin Differ Generically?

AD SECUNDUM SIC PROCEDITUR. Videtur quod peccatum veniale et mortale non differant genere, ita scilicet quod aliquod sit peccatum mortale ex genere, et aliquod veniale ex genere. Bonum enim et malum ex genere in actibus humanis accipitur per comparationem ad materiam sive ad obiectum, ut supra dictum est. Sed secundum quodlibet obiectum vel materiam, contingit peccare mortaliter et venialiter, quodlibet enim bonum commutabile potest homo diligere vel infra Deum, quod est peccare venialiter, vel supra Deum quod est peccare mortaliter. Ergo peccatum veniale et mortale non differunt genere.

PRAETEREA, sicut dictum est supra, peccatum mortale dicitur quod est irreparabile, peccatum autem veniale quod est reparabile. Sed esse irreparabile convenit peccato quod fit ex malitia, quod secundum quosdam irremissibile dicitur, esse autem reparabile convenit peccato quod fit per infirmitatem vel ignorantiam, quod dicitur remissibile. Ergo peccatum mortale et veniale

OBJECTION 1: It would seem that venial and mortal sin do not differ generically, so that some sins be generically mortal, and some generically venial. Because human acts are considered to be generically good or evil according to their matter or object, as stated above (Q18, A2). Now either mortal or venial sin may be committed in regard to any object or matter: since man can love any mutable good, either less than God, which may be a venial sin, or more than God, which is a mortal sin. Therefore venial and mortal sin do not differ generically.

OBJ. 2: Further, as stated above (A1; Q72, A5; Q87, A3), a sin is called mortal when it is irreparable, venial when it can be repaired. Now irreparability belongs to sin committed out of malice, which, according to some, is irremissible: whereas reparability belongs to sins committed through weakness or ignorance, which are remissible. Therefore mortal and venial sin differ as sin committed through

differunt sicut peccatum quod est ex malitia commissum, vel ex infirmitate et ignorantia. Sed secundum hoc non differunt peccata genere, sed causa, ut supra dictum est. Ergo peccatum veniale et mortale non differunt genere.

PRAETEREA, supra dictum est quod subiti motus tam sensualitatis quam rationis, sunt peccata venialia. Sed subiti motus inveniuntur in quolibet peccati genere. Ergo non sunt aliqua peccata venialia ex genere.

SED CONTRA est quod Augustinus, in sermone de Purgatorio, enumerat quaedam genera peccatorum venialium, et quaedam genera peccatorum mortalium.

RESPONDEO dicendum quod peccatum veniale a venia dicitur. Potest igitur aliquod peccatum dici veniale uno modo, quia est veniam consecutum, et sic dicit Ambrosius quod *omne peccatum per poenitentiam fit veniale*. Et hoc dicitur veniale ex eventu. Alio modo dicitur veniale, quia non habet in se unde veniam non consequatur vel totaliter vel in parte. In parte quidem, sicut cum habet in se aliquid diminuens culpam, ut cum fit ex infirmitate vel ignorantia. Et hoc dicitur veniale ex causa. In toto autem, ex eo quod non tollit ordinem ad ultimum finem, unde non meretur poenam aeternam, sed temporalem. Et de hoc veniali ad praesens intendimus.

De primis enim duobus constat quod non habent genus aliquod determinatum. Sed veniale tertio modo dictum, potest habere genus determinatum, ita quod aliquod peccatum dicatur veniale ex genere, et aliquod mortale ex genere, secundum quod genus vel species actus determinantur ex obiecto. Cum enim voluntas fertur in aliquid quod secundum se repugnat caritati, per quam homo ordinatur in ultimum finem, peccatum ex suo obiecto habet quod sit mortale. Unde est mortale ex genere, sive sit contra dilectionem Dei, sicut blasphemia, periurium, et huiusmodi; sive contra dilectionem proximi, sicut homicidium, adulterium, et similia. Unde huiusmodi sunt peccata mortalia ex suo genere. Quandoque vero voluntas peccantis fertur in id quod in se continet quandam inordinationem, non tamen contrariatur dilectioni Dei et proximi, sicut verbum otiosum, risus superfluus, et alia huiusmodi. Et talia sunt peccata venialia ex suo genere.

Sed quia actus morales recipiunt rationem boni et mali non solum ex obiecto, sed etiam ex aliqua dispositione agentis, ut supra habitum est; contingit quandoque quod id quod est peccatum veniale ex genere ratione sui obiecti, fit mortale ex parte agentis, vel quia in eo constituit finem ultimum, vel quia ordinat ipsum ad aliquid quod est peccatum mortale ex genere, puta cum aliquis ordinat verbum otiosum ad adulterium committendum. Similiter etiam ex parte agentis contingit quod aliquod peccatum quod ex suo genere est mortale, fit veniale, propter hoc scilicet quod actus est imperfectus, idest

malice differs from sin committed through weakness or ignorance. But, in this respect, sins differ not in genus but in cause, as stated above (Q77, A8, ad 1). Therefore venial and mortal sin do not differ generically.

OBJ. 3: Further, it was stated above (Q74, A3, ad 3; A10) that sudden movements both of the sensuality and of the reason are venial sins. But sudden movements occur in every kind of sin. Therefore no sins are generically venial.

ON THE CONTRARY, Augustine, in a sermon on Purgatory (*De Sanctis*, serm. xli), enumerates certain generic venial sins, and certain generic mortal sins.

I ANSWER THAT, Venial sin is so called from *venia* (pardon). Consequently a sin may be called venial, first of all, because it has been pardoned: thus Ambrose says that *penance makes every sin venial*: and this is called venial *from the result*. Second, a sin is called venial because it does not contain anything either partially or totally, to prevent its being pardoned: partially, as when a sin contains something diminishing its guilt, e.g., a sin committed through weakness or ignorance: and this is called venial *from the cause*: totally, through not destroying the order to the last end, wherefore it deserves temporal, but not everlasting punishment. It is of this venial sin that we wish to speak now.

For as regards the first two, it is evident that they have no determinate genus: whereas venial sin, taken in the third sense, can have a determinate genus, so that one sin may be venial generically, and another generically mortal, according as the genus or species of an act is determined by its object. For, when the will is directed to a thing that is in itself contrary to charity, whereby man is directed to his last end, the sin is mortal by reason of its object. Consequently it is a mortal sin generically, whether it be contrary to the love of God, e.g., blasphemy, perjury, and the like, or against the love of one's neighbor, e.g., murder, adultery, and such like: wherefore such sins are mortal by reason of their genus. Sometimes, however, the sinner's will is directed to a thing containing a certain inordinateness, but which is not contrary to the love of God and one's neighbor, e.g., an idle word, excessive laughter, and so forth: and such sins are venial by reason of their genus.

Nevertheless, since moral acts derive their character of goodness and malice, not only from their objects, but also from some disposition of the agent, as stated above (Q18, AA4,6), it happens sometimes that a sin which is venial generically by reason of its object, becomes mortal on the part of the agent, either because he fixes his last end therein, or because he directs it to something that is a mortal sin in its own genus; for example, if a man direct an idle word to the commission of adultery. In like manner it may happen, on the part of the agent, that a sin generically mortal becomes venial, by reason of the act being imperfect,

non deliberatus ratione, quae est principium proprium mali actus, sicut supra dictum est de subitis motibus infidelitatis.

AD PRIMUM ergo dicendum quod ex hoc ipso quod aliquis eligit id quod repugnat divinae caritati, convincitur praeferre illud caritati divinae, et per consequens plus amare ipsum quam Deum. Et ideo aliqua peccata ex genere, quae de se repugnant caritati, habent quod aliquid diligatur supra Deum. Et sic sunt ex genere suo mortalia.

AD SECUNDUM dicendum quod ratio illa procedit de peccato veniali ex causa.

AD TERTIUM dicendum quod ratio illa procedit de peccato quod est veniale propter imperfectionem actus.

i.e., not deliberated by reason, which is the proper principle of an evil act, as we have said above in reference to sudden movements of unbelief.

REPLY OBJ. 1: The very fact that anyone chooses something that is contrary to divine charity, proves that he prefers it to the love of God, and consequently, that he loves it more than he loves God. Hence it belongs to the genus of some sins, which are of themselves contrary to charity, that something is loved more than God; so that they are mortal by reason of their genus.

REPLY OBJ. 2: This argument considers those sins which are venial from their cause.

REPLY OBJ. 3: This argument considers those sins which are venial by reason of the imperfection of the act.

Article 3

Whether Venial Sin Is a Disposition to Mortal Sin?

AD TERTIUM SIC PROCEDITUR. Videtur quod peccatum veniale non sit dispositio ad mortale. Unum enim oppositum non disponit ad aliud. Sed peccatum veniale et mortale ex opposito dividuntur, ut dictum est. Ergo peccatum veniale non est dispositio ad mortale.

PRAETEREA, actus disponit ad aliquid simile in specie sibi, unde in II Ethic. dicitur quod *ex similibus actibus generantur similes dispositiones et habitus*. Sed peccatum mortale et veniale differunt genere seu specie, ut dictum est. Ergo peccatum veniale non disponit ad mortale.

PRAETEREA, si peccatum dicatur veniale quia disponit ad mortale, oportebit quod quaecumque disponunt ad mortale peccatum, sint peccata venialia. Sed omnia bona opera disponunt ad peccatum mortale, dicit enim Augustinus, in regula, quod superbia bonis operibus insidiatur, ut pereant. Ergo etiam bona opera erunt peccata venialia, quod est inconveniens.

SED CONTRA est quod dicitur Eccli. XIX, *qui spernit minima, paulatim defluit*. Sed ille qui peccat venialiter, videtur minima spernere. Ergo paulatim disponitur ad hoc quod totaliter defluat per peccatum mortale.

RESPONDEO dicendum quod disponens est quodammodo causa. Unde secundum duplicem modum causae, est duplex dispositionis modus. Est enim causa quaedam movens directe ad effectum, sicut calidum calefacit. Est etiam causa indirecte movens, removendo prohibens, sicut removens columnam dicitur removere lapidem superpositum. Et secundum hoc, actus peccati dupliciter ad aliquid disponit. Uno quidem modo, directe, et sic disponit ad actum similem secundum speciem. Et hoc modo, primo et per se peccatum veniale ex genere non disponit ad mortale ex genere, cum differant

OBJECTION 1: It would seem that venial sin is not a disposition to mortal sin. For one contrary does not dispose to another. But venial and mortal sin are condivided as contrary to one another, as stated above (A1). Therefore venial sin is not a disposition to mortal sin.

OBJ. 2: Further, an act disposes to something of like species, wherefore it is stated in *Ethic.* ii, 1,2, that *from like acts like dispositions and habits are engendered*. But mortal and venial sin differ in genus or species, as stated above (A2). Therefore venial sin does not dispose to mortal sin.

OBJ. 3: Further, if a sin is called venial because it disposes to mortal sin, it follows that whatever disposes to mortal sin is a venial sin. Now every good work disposes to mortal sin; wherefore Augustine says in his *Rule* (*Ep. ccxi*) that *pride lies in wait for good works that it may destroy them*. Therefore even good works would be venial sins, which is absurd.

ON THE CONTRARY, It is written (Sir 19:1): *He that contemneth small things shall fall by little and little*. Now he that sins venially seems to contemn small things. Therefore by little and little he is disposed to fall away together into mortal sin.

I ANSWER THAT, A disposition is a kind of cause; wherefore as there is a twofold manner of cause, so is there a twofold manner of disposition. For there is a cause which moves directly to the production of the effect, as a hot thing heats: and there is a cause which moves indirectly, by removing an obstacle, as he who displaces a pillar is said to displace the stone that rests on it. Accordingly an act of sin disposes to something in two ways. First, directly, and thus it disposes to an act of like species. In this way, a sin generically venial does not, primarily and of its nature, dispose to a sin generically mortal, for they differ in species.

specie. Sed per hunc modum peccatum veniale potest disponere, per quandam consequentiam, ad peccatum quod est mortale ex parte agentis. Augmentata enim dispositione vel habitu per actus peccatorum venialium, intantum potest libido peccandi crescere, quod ille qui peccat, finem suum constituet in peccato veniali, nam unicuique habenti habitum, inquantum huiusmodi, finis est operatio secundum habitum. Et sic, multoties peccando venialiter, disponetur ad peccatum mortale. Alio modo actus humanus disponit ad aliquid removendo prohibens. Et hoc modo peccatum veniale ex genere potest disponere ad peccatum mortale ex genere. Qui enim peccat venialiter ex genere, praetermittit aliquem ordinem, et ex hoc quod consuescit voluntatem suam in minoribus debito ordini non subiicere, disponitur ad hoc quod etiam voluntatem suam non subiiciat ordini ultimi finis, eligendo id quod est peccatum mortale ex genere.

AD PRIMUM ergo dicendum quod peccatum veniale et mortale non dividuntur ex opposito, sicut duae species unius generis, ut dictum est, sed sicut accidens contra substantiam dividitur. Unde sicut accidens potest esse dispositio ad formam substantialem, ita et veniale peccatum ad mortale.

AD SECUNDUM dicendum quod peccatum veniale non est simile mortali in specie, est tamen simile ei in genere, inquantum utrumque importat defectum debiti ordinis, licet aliter et aliter, ut dictum est.

AD TERTIUM dicendum quod opus bonum non est per se dispositio ad mortale peccatum, potest tamen esse materia vel occasio peccati mortalis per accidens. Sed peccatum veniale per se disponit ad mortale, ut dictum est.

Nevertheless, in this same way, a venial sin can dispose, by way of consequence, to a sin which is mortal on the part of the agent: because the disposition or habit may be so far strengthened by acts of venial sin, that the lust of sinning increases, and the sinner fixes his end in that venial sin: since the end for one who has a habit, as such, is to work according to that habit; and the consequence will be that, by sinning often venially, he becomes disposed to a mortal sin. Second, a human act disposes to something by removing an obstacle thereto. In this way a sin generically venial can dispose to a sin generically mortal. Because he that commits a sin generically venial, turns aside from some particular order; and through accustoming his will not to be subject to the due order in lesser matters, is disposed not to subject his will even to the order of the last end, by choosing something that is a mortal sin in its genus.

REPLY OBJ. 1: Venial and mortal sin are not condivided in contrariety to one another, as though they were species of one genus, as stated above (A1, ad 1), but as an accident is condivided with substance. Wherefore an accident can be a disposition to a substantial form, so can a venial sin dispose to mortal.

REPLY OBJ. 2: Venial sin is not like mortal sin in species; but it is in genus, inasmuch as they both imply a defect of due order, albeit in different ways, as stated (AA1,2).

REPLY OBJ. 3: A good work is not, of itself, a disposition to mortal sin; but it can be the matter or occasion of mortal sin accidentally; whereas a venial sin, of its very nature, disposes to mortal sin, as stated.

Article 4

Whether a Venial Sin Can Become Mortal?

AD QUARTUM SIC PROCEDITUR. Videtur quod peccatum veniale possit fieri mortale. Dicit enim Augustinus, exponens illud Ioan. III, *qui incredulus est filio, non videbit vitam*, peccata minima (idest venialia), si negligantur, occidunt. Sed ex hoc dicitur peccatum mortale, quod spiritualiter occidit animam. Ergo peccatum veniale potest fieri mortale.

PRAETEREA, motus sensualitatis ante consensum rationis est peccatum veniale, post consensum vero est peccatum mortale, ut supra dictum est. Ergo peccatum veniale potest fieri mortale.

PRAETEREA, peccatum veniale et mortale differunt sicut morbus curabilis et incurabilis, ut dictum est. Sed morbus curabilis potest fieri incurabilis. Ergo peccatum veniale potest fieri mortale.

OBJECTION 1: It would seem that a venial sin can become a mortal sin. For Augustine in explaining the words of Jn. 3:36: *He that believeth not the Son, shall not see life*, says (*Tract. xii in Ioan.*): *The slightest*, i.e., venial, *sins kill if we make little of them*. Now a sin is called mortal through causing the spiritual death of the soul. Therefore a venial sin can become mortal.

OBJ. 2: Further, a movement in the sensuality before the consent of reason, is a venial sin, but after consent, is a mortal sin, as stated above (Q74, A8, ad 2). Therefore a venial sin can become mortal.

OBJ. 3: Further, venial and mortal sin differ as curable and incurable disease, as stated above (A1). But a curable disease may become incurable. Therefore a venial sin may become mortal.

PRAETEREA, dispositio potest fieri habitus. Sed peccatum veniale est dispositio ad mortale, ut dictum est. Ergo veniale peccatum potest fieri mortale.

SED CONTRA, ea quae differunt in infinitum, non transmutantur in invicem. Sed peccatum mortale et veniale differunt in infinitum, ut ex praedictis patet. Ergo veniale non potest fieri mortale.

RESPONDEO dicendum quod peccatum veniale fieri mortale, potest tripliciter intelligi. Uno modo sic quod idem actus numero, primo sit peccatum veniale, et postea mortale. Et hoc esse non potest. Quia peccatum principaliter consistit in actu voluntatis, sicut et quilibet actus moralis. Unde non dicitur unus actus moraliter, si voluntas mutetur, quamvis etiam actio secundum naturam sit continua. Si autem voluntas non mutetur, non potest esse quod de veniali fiat mortale.

Alio modo potest intelligi ut id quod est veniale ex genere, fiat mortale. Et hoc quidem possibile est, inquantum constituitur in eo finis, vel inquantum refertur ad mortale peccatum sicut ad finem, ut dictum est.

Tertio modo potest intelligi ita quod multa venialia peccata constituant unum peccatum mortale. Quod si sic intelligatur quod ex multis peccatis venialibus integraliter constituatur unum peccatum mortale, falsum est. Non enim omnia peccata venialia de mundo, possunt habere tantum de reatu, quantum unum peccatum mortale. Quod patet ex parte durationis, quia peccatum mortale habet reatum poenae aeternae, peccatum autem veniale reatum poenae temporalis, ut dictum est. Patet etiam ex parte poenae damni, quia peccatum mortale meretur carentiam visionis divinae, cui nulla alia poena comparari potest ut Chrysostomus dicit. Patet etiam ex parte poenae sensus, quantum ad vermem conscientiae, licet forte quantum ad poenam ignis, non sint improportionales poenae.

Si vero intelligatur quod multa peccata venialia faciunt unum mortale dispositive, sic verum est, sicut supra ostensum est, secundum duos modos dispositionis, quo peccatum veniale disponit ad mortale.

AD PRIMUM ergo dicendum quod Augustinus loquitur in illo sensu, quod multa peccata venialia dispositive causant mortale.

AD SECUNDUM dicendum quod ille idem motus sensualitatis qui praecessit consensum rationis nunquam fiet peccatum mortale, sed ipse actus rationis consentientis.

AD TERTIUM dicendum quod morbus corporalis non est actus, sed dispositio quaedam permanens, unde eadem manens, potest mutari. Sed peccatum veniale est actus transiens, qui resumi non potest. Et quantum ad hoc, non est simile.

OBJ. 4: Further, a disposition may become a habit. Now venial sin is a disposition to mortal, as stated (A3). Therefore a venial sin can become mortal.

ON THE CONTRARY, Things that differ infinitely are not changed into one another. Now venial and moral sin differ infinitely, as is evident from what has been said above (Q72, A5, ad 1; Q87, A5, ad 1). Therefore a venial sin cannot become mortal.

I ANSWER THAT, The fact of a venial sin becoming a mortal sin may be understood in three ways. First, so that the same identical act be at first a venial, and then a mortal sin. This is impossible: because a sin, like any moral act, consists chiefly in an act of the will: so that an act is not one morally, if the will be changed, although the act be continuous physically. If, however, the will be not changed, it is not possible for a venial sin to become mortal.

Second, this may be taken to mean that a sin generically venial, becomes mortal. This is possible, insofar as one may fix one's end in that venial sin, or direct it to some mortal sin as end, as stated above (A2).

Third, this may be understood in the sense of many venial sins constituting one mortal sin. If this be taken as meaning that many venial sins added together make one mortal sin, it is false, because all the venial sins in the world cannot incur a debt of punishment equal to that of one mortal sin. This is evident as regards the duration of the punishment, since mortal sin incurs a debt of eternal punishment, while venial sin incurs a debt of temporal punishment, as stated above (Q87, AA3,5). It is also evident as regards the pain of loss, because mortal sins deserve to be punished by the privation of seeing God, to which no other punishment is comparable, as Chrysostom states (*Hom. xxiv in Matth.*). It is also evident as regards the pain of sense, as to the remorse of conscience; although as to the pain of fire, the punishments may perhaps not be improportionate to one another.

If, however, this be taken as meaning that many venial sins make one mortal sin dispositively, it is true, as was shown above (A3) with regard to the two different manners of disposition, whereby venial sin disposes to mortal sin.

REPLY OBJ. 1: Augustine is referring to the fact of many venial sins making one mortal sin dispositively.

REPLY OBJ. 2: The same movement of the sensuality which preceded the consent of reason can never become a mortal sin; but the movement of the reason in consenting is a mortal sin.

REPLY OBJ. 3: Disease of the body is not an act, but an abiding disposition; wherefore, while remaining the same disease, it may undergo change. On the other hand, venial sin is a transient act, which cannot be taken up again: so that in this respect the comparison fails.

AD QUARTUM dicendum quod dispositio quae fit habitus, est sicut imperfectum in eadem specie, sicut imperfecta scientia, dum perficitur, fit habitus. Sed veniale peccatum est dispositio alterius generis, sicut accidens ad formam substantialem, in quam nunquam mutatur.

REPLY OBJ. 4: A disposition that becomes a habit, is like an imperfect thing in the same species; thus imperfect science, by being perfected, becomes a habit. On the other hand, venial sin is a disposition to something differing generically, even as an accident which disposes to a substantial form, into which it is never changed.

Article 5

Whether a Circumstance Can Make a Venial Sin to Be Mortal?

AD QUINTUM SIC PROCEDITUR. Videtur quod circumstantia possit de veniali peccato facere mortale. Dicit enim Augustinus, in sermone de Purgatorio, quod *si diu teneatur iracundia, et ebrietas si assidua sit, transeunt in numerum peccatorum mortalium.* Sed ira et ebrietas non sunt ex suo genere peccata mortalia, sed venialia, alioquin semper essent mortalia. Ergo circumstantia facit peccatum veniale esse mortale.

PRAETEREA, Magister dicit, XXIV dist. II libri Sent., quod delectatio, si sit morosa, est peccatum mortale; si autem non sit morosa, est peccatum veniale. Sed morositas est quaedam circumstantia. Ergo circumstantia facit de peccato veniali mortale.

PRAETEREA, plus differunt malum et bonum quam veniale peccatum et mortale, quorum utrumque est in genere mali. Sed circumstantia facit de actu bono malum, sicut patet cum quis dat eleemosynam propter inanem gloriam. Ergo multo magis potest facere de peccato veniali mortale.

SED CONTRA est quod, cum circumstantia sit accidens, quantitas eius non potest excedere quantitatem ipsius actus, quam habet ex suo genere, semper enim subiectum praeeminet accidenti. Si igitur actus ex suo genere sit peccatum veniale, non poterit per circumstantiam fieri peccatum mortale, cum peccatum mortale in infinitum quodammodo excedat quantitatem venialis, ut ex dictis patet.

RESPONDEO dicendum quod, sicut supra dictum est, cum de circumstantiis ageretur, circumstantia, inquantum huiusmodi, est accidens actus moralis, contingit tamen circumstantiam accipi ut differentiam specificam actus moralis, et tunc amittit rationem circumstantiae, et constituit speciem moralis actus. Hoc autem contingit in peccatis quando circumstantia addit deformitatem alterius generis sicut cum aliquis accedit ad non suam, est actus deformis deformitate opposita castitati; sed si accedat ad non suam quae est alterius uxor, additur deformitas opposita iustitiae, contra quam est ut aliquis usurpet rem alienam; et secundum hoc huiusmodi circumstantia constituit novam speciem peccati, quae dicitur adulterium.

OBJECTION 1: It would seem that a circumstance can make a venial sin mortal. For Augustine says in a sermon on Purgatory (*De Sanctis*, serm. xli) that *if anger continue for a long time, or if drunkenness be frequent, they become mortal sins.* But anger and drunkenness are not mortal but venial sins generically, else they would always be mortal sins. Therefore a circumstance makes a venial sin to be mortal.

OBJ. 2: Further, the Master says (*Sentent.* ii, D, 24) that delectation, if morose, is a mortal sin, but that if it be not morose, it is a venial sin. Now moroseness is a circumstance. Therefore a circumstance makes a venial sin to be mortal.

OBJ. 3: Further, evil and good differ more than venial and mortal sin, both of which are generically evil. But a circumstance makes a good act to be evil, as when a man gives an alms for vainglory. Much more, therefore, can it make a venial sin to be mortal.

ON THE CONTRARY, Since a circumstance is an accident, its quantity cannot exceed that of the act itself, derived from the act's genus, because the subject always excels its accident. If, therefore, an act be venial by reason of its genus, it cannot become mortal by reason of an accident: since, in a way, mortal sin infinitely surpasses the quantity of venial sin, as is evident from what has been said (Q72, A5, ad 1; Q87, A5, ad 1).

I ANSWER THAT, As stated above (Q7, A1; Q18, A5, ad 4; AA10,11), when we were treating of circumstances, a circumstance, as such, is an accident of the moral act: and yet a circumstance may happen to be taken as the specific difference of a moral act, and then it loses its nature of circumstance, and constitutes the species of the moral act. This happens in sins when a circumstance adds the deformity of another genus; thus when a man has knowledge of another woman than his wife, the deformity of his act is opposed to chastity; but if this other be another man's wife, there is an additional deformity opposed to justice which forbids one to take what belongs to another; and accordingly this circumstance constitutes a new species of sin known as adultery.

Impossibile est autem quod circumstantia de peccato veniali faciat mortale, nisi afferat deformitatem alterius generis. Dictum est enim quod peccatum veniale habet deformitatem per hoc quod importat deordinationem circa ea quae sunt ad finem, peccatum autem mortale habet deformitatem per hoc quod importat deordinationem respectu ultimi finis. Unde manifestum est quod circumstantia non potest de veniali peccato facere mortale, manens circumstantia, sed solum tunc quando transfert in aliam speciem, et fit quodammodo differentia specifica moralis actus.

Ad primum ergo dicendum quod diuturnitas non est circumstantia trahens in aliam speciem, similiter nec frequentia vel assiduitas, nisi forte per accidens ex aliquo supervenienti. Non enim aliquid acquirit novam speciem ex hoc quod multiplicatur vel protelatur, nisi forte in actu protelato vel multiplicato superveniat aliquid quod variet speciem, puta inobedientia vel contemptus, vel aliquid huiusmodi.

Dicendum est ergo quod, cum ira sit motus animi ad nocendum proximo, si sit tale nocumentum in quod tendit motus irae, quod ex genere suo sit peccatum mortale, sicut homicidium vel furtum, talis ira ex genere suo est peccatum mortale. Sed quod sit peccatum veniale, habet ex imperfectione actus, inquantum est motus subitus sensualitatis. Si vero sit diuturna, redit ad naturam sui generis per consensum rationis. Si vero nocumentum in quod tendit motus irae, esset veniale ex genere suo, puta cum aliquis in hoc irascitur contra aliquem, quod vult ei dicere aliquod verbum leve et iocosum, quod modicum ipsum contristet; non erit ira peccatum mortale, quantumcumque sit diuturna; nisi forte per accidens, puta si ex hoc grave scandalum oriatur, vel propter aliquid huiusmodi.

De ebrietate vero dicendum est quod secundum suam rationem habet quod sit peccatum mortale, quod enim homo absque necessitate reddat se impotentem ad utendum ratione, per quam homo in Deum ordinatur et multa peccata occurrentia vitat, ex sola voluptate vini, expresse contrariatur virtuti. Sed quod sit peccatum veniale, contingit propter ignorantiam quandam vel infirmitatem, puta cum homo nescit virtutem vini, aut propriam debilitatem, unde non putat se inebriari, tunc enim non imputatur ei ebrietas ad peccatum, sed solum superabundantia potus. Sed quando frequenter inebriatur, non potest per hanc ignorantiam excusari quin videatur voluntas eius eligere magis pati ebrietatem, quam abstinere a vino superfluo. Unde redit peccatum ad suam naturam.

Ad secundum dicendum quod delectatio morosa non dicitur esse peccatum mortale, nisi in his quae ex suo genere sunt peccata mortalia; in quibus si delectatio non morosa sit, peccatum veniale est ex imperfectione actus, sicut et de ira dictum est. Dicitur enim ira

It is, however, impossible for a circumstance to make a venial sin become mortal, unless it adds the deformity of another species. For it has been stated above (A1) that the deformity of a venial sin consists in a disorder affecting things that are referred to the end, whereas the deformity of a mortal sin consists in a disorder about the last end. Consequently it is evident that a circumstance cannot make a venial sin to be mortal, so long as it remains a circumstance, but only when it transfers the sin to another species, and becomes, as it were, the specific difference of the moral act.

Reply Obj. 1: Length of time is not a circumstance that draws a sin to another species, nor is frequency or custom, except perhaps by something accidental supervening. For an action does not acquire a new species through being repeated or prolonged, unless by chance something supervene in the repeated or prolonged act to change its species, e.g., disobedience, contempt, or the like.

We must therefore reply to the objection by saying that since anger is a movement of the soul tending to the hurt of one's neighbor, if the angry movement tend to a hurt which is a mortal sin generically, such as murder or robbery, that anger will be a mortal sin generically: and if it be a venial sin, this will be due to the imperfection of the act, insofar as it is a sudden movement of the sensuality: whereas, if it last a long time, it returns to its generic nature, through the consent of reason. If, on the other hand, the hurt to which the angry movement tends, is a sin generically venial, for instance, if a man be angry with someone, so as to wish to say some trifling word in jest that would hurt him a little, the anger will not be mortal sin, however long it last, unless perhaps accidentally; for instance, if it were to give rise to great scandal or something of the kind.

With regard to drunkenness we reply that it is a mortal sin by reason of its genus; for, that a man, without necessity, and through the mere lust of wine, make himself unable to use his reason, whereby he is directed to God and avoids committing many sins, is expressly contrary to virtue. That it be a venial sin, is due some sort of ignorance or weakness, as when a man is ignorant of the strength of the wine, or of his own unfitness, so that he has no thought of getting drunk, for in that case the drunkenness is not imputed to him as a sin, but only the excessive drink. If, however, he gets drunk frequently, this ignorance no longer avails as an excuse, for his will seems to choose to give way to drunkenness rather than to refrain from excess of wine: wherefore the sin returns to its specific nature.

Reply Obj. 2: Morose delectation is not a mortal sin except in those matters which are mortal sins generically. In such matters, if the delectation be not morose, there is a venial sin through imperfection of the act, as we have said with regard to anger (ad 1): because anger is said to

diuturna, et delectatio morosa, propter approbationem rationis deliberantis.

AD TERTIUM dicendum quod circumstantia non facit de bono actu malum, nisi constituens speciem peccati, ut supra etiam habitum est.

be lasting, and delectation to be morose, on account of the approval of the deliberating reason.

REPLY OBJ. 3: A circumstance does not make a good act to be evil, unless it constitute the species of a sin, as we have stated above (Q18, A5, ad 4).

Article 6

Whether a Mortal Sin Can Become Venial?

AD SEXTUM SIC PROCEDITUR. Videtur quod peccatum mortale possit fieri veniale. Aequaliter enim distat peccatum veniale a mortali, et e contrario. Sed peccatum veniale fit mortale, ut dictum est. Ergo etiam peccatum mortale potest fieri veniale.

PRAETEREA, peccatum veniale et mortale ponuntur differre secundum hoc, quod peccans mortaliter diligit creaturam plus quam Deum, peccans autem venialiter diligit creaturam infra Deum. Contingit autem quod aliquis committens id quod est ex genere suo peccatum mortale, diligat creaturam infra Deum, puta si aliquis, nesciens fornicationem simplicem esse peccatum mortale et contrariam divino amori, fornicetur, ita tamen quod propter divinum amorem paratus esset fornicationem praetermittere, si sciret fornicando se contra divinum amorem agere. Ergo peccabit venialiter. Et sic peccatum mortale potest fieri veniale.

PRAETEREA, sicut dictum est, plus differt bonum a malo quam veniale a mortali. Sed actus qui est de se malus, potest fieri bonus, sicut homicidium potest fieri actus iustitiae, sicut patet in iudice qui occidit latronem. Ergo multo magis peccatum mortale potest fieri veniale.

SED CONTRA est quod aeternum nunquam potest fieri temporale. Sed peccatum mortale meretur poenam aeternam, peccatum autem veniale poenam temporalem. Ergo peccatum mortale nunquam potest fieri veniale.

RESPONDEO dicendum quod veniale et mortale differunt sicut perfectum et imperfectum in genere peccati, ut dictum est. Imperfectum autem per aliquam additionem potest ad perfectionem venire. Unde et veniale, per hoc quod additur ei deformitas pertinens ad genus peccati mortalis, efficitur mortale, sicut cum quis dicit verbum otiosum ut fornicetur. Sed id quod est perfectum, non potest fieri imperfectum per additionem. Et ideo peccatum mortale non fit veniale per hoc quod additur ei aliqua deformitas pertinens ad genus peccati venialis, non enim diminuitur peccatum eius qui fornicatur ut dicat verbum otiosum, sed magis aggravatur propter deformitatem adiunctam.

OBJECTION 1: It would seem that a mortal sin can become venial. Because venial sin is equally distant from mortal, as mortal sin is from venial. But a venial sin can become mortal, as stated above (A5). Therefore also a mortal sin can become venial.

OBJ. 2: Further, venial and mortal sin are said to differ in this, that he who sins mortally loves a creature more than God, while he who sins venially loves the creature less than God. Now it may happen that a person in committing a sin generically mortal, loves a creature less than God; for instance, if anyone being ignorant that simple fornication is a mortal sin, and contrary to the love of God, commits the sin of fornication, yet so as to be ready, for the love of God, to refrain from that sin if he knew that by committing it he was acting counter to the love of God. Therefore his will be a venial sin; and accordingly a mortal sin can become venial.

OBJ. 3: Further, as stated above (A5, OBJ3), good is more distant from evil, than venial from mortal sin. But an act which is evil in itself, can become good; thus to kill a man may be an act of justice, as when a judge condemns a thief to death. Much more therefore can a mortal sin become venial.

ON THE CONTRARY, An eternal thing can never become temporal. But mortal sin deserves eternal punishment, whereas venial sin deserves temporal punishment. Therefore a mortal sin can never become venial.

I ANSWER THAT, Venial and mortal differ as perfect and imperfect in the genus of sin, as stated above (A1, ad 1). Now the imperfect can become perfect, by some sort of addition: and, consequently, a venial sin can become mortal, by the addition of some deformity pertaining to the genus of mortal sin, as when a man utters an idle word for the purpose of fornication. On the other hand, the perfect cannot become imperfect, by addition; and so a mortal sin cannot become venial, by the addition of a deformity pertaining to the genus of venial sin, for the sin is not diminished if a man commit fornication in order to utter an idle word; rather is it aggravated by the additional deformity.

Potest tamen id quod est ex genere mortale, esse veniale propter imperfectionem actus, quia non perfecte pertingit ad rationem actus moralis, cum non sit deliberatus sed subitus, ut ex dictis patet. Et hoc fit per subtractionem quandam, scilicet deliberatae rationis. Et quia a ratione deliberata habet speciem moralis actus, inde est quod per talem subtractionem solvitur species.

Ad primum ergo dicendum quod veniale differt a mortali sicut imperfectum a perfecto, ut puer a viro. Fit autem ex puero vir, sed non convertitur. Unde ratio non cogit.

Ad secundum dicendum quod, si sit talis ignorantia quae peccatum omnino excuset, sicut est furiosi vel amentis, tunc ex tali ignorantia fornicationem committens nec mortaliter nec venialiter peccat. Si vero sit ignorantia non invincibilis, tunc ignorantia ipsa est peccatum, et continet in se defectum divini amoris, inquantum negligit homo addiscere ea per quae potest se in divino amore conservare.

Ad tertium dicendum quod, sicut Augustinus dicit, in libro contra mendacium, *ea quae sunt secundum se mala, nullo fine bene fieri possunt.* Homicidium autem est occisio innocentis, et hoc nullo modo bene fieri potest. Sed iudex qui occidit latronem, vel miles qui occidit hostem reipublicae, non appellantur homicidae, ut Augustinus dicit, in libro de libero arbitrio.

Nevertheless a sin which is generically mortal, can become venial by reason of the imperfection of the act, because then it does not completely fulfill the conditions of a moral act, since it is not a deliberate, but a sudden act, as is evident from what we have said above (A2). This happens by a kind of subtraction, namely, of deliberate reason. And since a moral act takes its species from deliberate reason, the result is that by such a subtraction the species of the act is destroyed.

Reply Obj. 1: Venial differs from mortal as imperfect from perfect, even as a boy differs from a man. But the boy becomes a man and not vice versa. Hence the argument does not prove.

Reply Obj. 2: If the ignorance be such as to excuse sin altogether, as the ignorance of a madman or an imbecile, then he that commits fornication in a state of such ignorance, commits no sin either mortal or venial. But if the ignorance be not invincible, then the ignorance itself is a sin, and contains within itself the lack of the love of God, insofar as a man neglects to learn those things whereby he can safeguard himself in the love of God.

Reply Obj. 3: As Augustine says (*Contra Mendacium* vii), *those things which are evil in themselves, cannot be well done for any good end.* Now murder is the slaying of the innocent, and this can nowise be well done. But, as Augustine states (*De Lib. Arb.* i, 4,5), the judge who sentences a thief to death, or the soldier who slays the enemy of the common weal, are not murderers.

QUESTION 89

OF VENIAL SIN IN ITSELF

Deinde considerandum est de peccato veniali secundum se. Et circa hoc quaeruntur sex.

Primo, utrum peccatum veniale causet maculam in anima.

Secundo, de distinctione peccati venialis, prout figuratur per lignum, faenum et stipulam, I Cor. III.

Tertio, utrum homo in statu innocentiae potuerit peccare venialiter.

Quarto, utrum Angelus bonus vel malus possit peccare venialiter.

Quinto, utrum primi motus infidelium sint peccata venialia.

Sexto, utrum peccatum veniale possit esse in aliquo simul cum solo peccato originali.

We must now consider venial sin in itself, and under this head there are six points of inquiry:

(1) Whether venial sin causes a stain in the soul?

(2) Of the different kinds of venial sin, as denoted by *wood, hay, stubble* (1 Cor 3:12);

(3) Whether man could sin venially in the state of innocence?

(4) Whether a good or a wicked angel can sin venially?

(5) Whether the movements of unbelievers are venial sins?

(6) Whether venial sin can be in a man with original sin alone?

Article 1

Whether Venial Sin Causes a Stain on the Soul?

AD PRIMUM SIC PROCEDITUR. Videtur quod peccatum veniale causet maculam in anima. Dicit enim Augustinus, in libro de Poenit., quod peccata venialia, si multiplicentur, decorem nostrum ita exterminant, ut a caelestis sponsi amplexibus nos separent. Sed nihil aliud est macula quam detrimentum decoris. Ergo peccata venialia causant maculam in anima.

PRAETEREA, peccatum mortale causat maculam in anima propter inordinationem actus et affectus ipsius peccantis. Sed in peccato veniali est quaedam deordinatio actus et affectus. Ergo peccatum veniale causat maculam in anima.

PRAETEREA, macula animae causatur ex contactu rei temporalis per amorem, ut supra dictum est. Sed in peccato veniali anima inordinato amore contingit rem temporalem. Ergo peccatum veniale inducit maculam in anima.

SED CONTRA est quod dicitur Ephes. V, *ut exhiberet ipse sibi gloriosam Ecclesiam non habentem maculam;* Glossa, *idest aliquod peccatum criminale.* Ergo proprium peccati mortalis esse videtur quod maculam in anima causet.

RESPONDEO dicendum quod, sicut ex dictis patet, macula importat detrimentum nitoris ex aliquo contactu, sicut in corporalibus patet, ex quibus per similitudinem nomen maculae ad animam transfertur. Sicut

OBJECTION 1: It would seem that venial sin causes a stain in the soul. For Augustine says (*De Poenit.*), that if venial sins be multiplied, they destroy the beauty of our souls so as to deprive us of the embraces of our heavenly spouse. But the stain of sin is nothing else but the loss of the soul's beauty. Therefore venial sins cause a stain in the soul.

OBJ. 2: Further, mortal sin causes a stain in the soul, on account of the inordinateness of the act and of the sinner's affections. But, in venial sin, there is an inordinateness of the act and of the affections. Therefore venial sin causes a stain in the soul.

OBJ. 3: Further, the stain on the soul is caused by contact with a temporal thing, through love thereof as stated above (Q86, A1). But, in venial sin, the soul is in contact with a temporal thing through inordinate love. Therefore venial sin brings a stain on the soul.

ON THE CONTRARY, it is written, (Eph 5:27): *That He might present it to Himself a glorious church, not having spot or wrinkle*, on which the gloss says: *i.e., some grievous sin.* Therefore it seems proper to mortal sin to cause a stain on the soul.

I ANSWER THAT as stated above (Q86, A1), a stain denotes a loss of comeliness due to contact with something, as may be seen in corporeal matters, from which the term has been transferred to the soul, by way of similitude. Now, just

autem in corpore est duplex nitor, unus quidem ex intrinseca dispositione membrorum et coloris, alius autem ex exteriori claritate superveniente; ita etiam in anima est duplex nitor, unus quidem habitualis, quasi intrinsecus, alius autem actualis, quasi exterior fulgor. Peccatum autem veniale impedit quidem nitorem actualem, non tamen habitualem, quia non excludit neque diminuit habitum caritatis et aliarum virtutum, ut infra patebit, sed solum impedit earum actum. Macula autem importat aliquid manens in re maculata, unde magis videtur pertinere ad detrimentum habitualis nitoris quam actualis. Unde, proprie loquendo, peccatum veniale non causat maculam in anima. Et si alicubi dicatur maculam inducere, hoc est secundum quid, inquantum impedit nitorem qui est ex actibus virtutum.

AD PRIMUM ergo dicendum quod Augustinus loquitur in eo casu in quo multa peccata venialia dispositive inducunt ad mortale. Aliter enim non separarent ab amplexu caelestis sponsi.

AD SECUNDUM dicendum quod inordinatio actus in peccato mortali corrumpit habitum virtutis, non autem in peccato veniali.

AD TERTIUM dicendum quod in peccato mortali anima per amorem contingit rem temporalem quasi finem, et per hoc totaliter impeditur influxus splendoris gratiae, qui provenit in eos qui Deo adhaerent ut ultimo fini per caritatem. Sed in peccato veniali non adhaeret homo creaturae tanquam fini ultimo. Unde non est simile.

as in the body there is a twofold comeliness, one resulting from the inward disposition of the members and colors, the other resulting from outward refulgence supervening, so too, in the soul, there is a twofold comeliness, one habitual and, so to speak, intrinsic, the other actual like an outward flash of light. Now venial sin is a hindrance to actual comeliness, but not to habitual comeliness, because it neither destroys nor diminishes the habit of charity and of the other virtues, as we shall show further on (SS, Q24, A10; Q133, A1, ad 2), but only hinders their acts. On the other hand a stain denotes something permanent in the thing stained, wherefore it seems in the nature of a loss of habitual rather than of actual comeliness. Therefore, properly speaking, venial sin does not cause a stain in the soul. If, however, we find it stated anywhere that it does induce a stain, this is in a restricted sense, insofar as it hinders the comeliness that results from acts of virtue.

REPLY OBJ. 1: Augustine is speaking of the case in which many venial sins lead to mortal sin dispositively: because otherwise they would not sever the soul from its heavenly spouse.

REPLY OBJ. 2: In mortal sin the inordinateness of the act destroys the habit of virtue, but not in venial sin.

REPLY OBJ. 3: In mortal sin the soul comes into contact with a temporal thing as its end, so that the shedding of the light of grace, which accrues to those who, by charity, cleave to God as their last end, is entirely cut off. On the contrary, in venial sin, man does not cleave to a creature as his last end: hence there is no comparison.

Article 2

Whether Venial Sins Are Suitably Designated As Wood, Hay, and Stubble?

AD SECUNDUM SIC PROCEDITUR. Videtur quod inconvenienter peccata venialia per lignum, faenum et stipulam designentur. Lignum enim, faenum et stipula dicuntur superaedificari spirituali fundamento. Sed peccata venialia sunt praeter spirituale aedificium, sicut etiam quaelibet falsae opiniones sunt praeter scientiam. Ergo peccata venialia non convenienter designantur per lignum, faenum et stipulam.

PRAETEREA, ille qui aedificat lignum, faenum et stipulam, *sic salvus erit quasi per ignem*. Sed quandoque ille qui committit peccata venialia, non erit salvus etiam per ignem, puta cum peccata venialia inveniuntur in eo qui decedit cum peccato mortali. Ergo inconvenienter per lignum, faenum et stipulam peccata venialia designantur.

OBJECTION 1: It would seem that venial sins are unsuitably designated as *wood*, *hay*, and *stubble*. Because wood hay and stubble are said (1 Cor 3:12) to be built on a spiritual foundation. Now venial sins are something outside a spiritual foundation, even as false opinions are outside the pale of science. Therefore, venial sins are not suitably designated as wood, hay and stubble.

OBJ. 2: Further, he who builds wood, hay and stubble, *shall be saved yet so as by fire* (1 Cor 3:15). But sometimes the man who commits a venial sin, will not be saved, even by fire, e.g., when a man dies in mortal sin to which venial sins are attached. Therefore, venial sins are unsuitably designated by wood, hay, and stubble.

PRAETEREA, secundum apostolum, alii sunt qui aedificant aurum, argentum, lapides pretiosos, idest amorem Dei et proximi et bona opera; et alii qui aedificant lignum, faenum et stipulam. Sed peccata venialia committunt etiam illi qui diligunt Deum et proximum, et bona opera faciunt, dicitur enim I Ioan. I, *si dixerimus quia peccatum non habemus, nosipsos seducimus*. Ergo non convenienter designantur peccata venialia per ista tria.

PRAETEREA, multo plures differentiae et gradus sunt peccatorum venialium quam tres. Ergo inconvenienter sub his tribus comprehenduntur.

SED CONTRA est quod apostolus dicit de eo qui superaedificat lignum, faenum et stipulam, quod salvus erit quasi per ignem, et sic patietur poenam, sed non aeternam. Reatus autem poenae temporalis proprie pertinet ad peccatum veniale, ut dictum est. Ergo per illa tria significantur peccata venialia.

RESPONDEO dicendum quod quidam intellexerunt fundamentum esse fidem informem, super quam aliqui aedificant bona opera, quae significantur per aurum, argentum et lapides pretiosos; quidam vero peccata etiam mortalia, quae significantur, secundum eos, per lignum, faenum et stipulam. Sed hanc expositionem improbat Augustinus, in libro de fide et operibus, quia, ut apostolus dicit, ad Gal. V, qui opera carnis facit, regnum Dei non consequetur, quod est salvum fieri; apostolus autem dicit quod ille qui aedificat lignum, faenum et stipulam, salvus erit quasi per ignem. Unde non potest intelligi quod per lignum, faenum et stipulam peccata mortalia designentur.

Quidam vero dicunt quod per lignum, faenum et stipulam significantur opera bona, quae superaedificantur quidem spirituali aedificio, sed tamen commiscent se eis peccata venialia sicut, cum aliquis habet curam rei familiaris, quod bonum est, commiscet se superfluus amor vel uxoris vel filiorum vel possessionum, sub Deo tamen, ita scilicet quod pro his homo nihil vellet facere contra Deum. Sed hoc iterum non videtur convenienter dici. Manifestum est enim quod omnia opera bona referuntur ad caritatem Dei et proximi, unde pertinent ad aurum, argentum et lapides pretiosos. Non ergo ad lignum, faenum et stipulam.

Et ideo dicendum est quod ipsa peccata venialia quae admiscent se procurantibus terrena, significantur per lignum, faenum et stipulam. Sicut enim huiusmodi congregantur in domo, et non pertinent ad substantiam aedificii, et possunt comburi aedificio remanente; ita etiam peccata venialia multiplicantur in homine, manente spirituali aedificio; et pro istis patitur ignem vel temporalis tribulationis in hac vita, vel Purgatorii post hanc vitam; et tamen salutem consequitur aeternam.

AD PRIMUM ergo dicendum quod peccata venialia non dicuntur superaedificari spirituali fundamento

OBJ. 3: Further, according to the Apostle (1 Cor 3:12) those who build *gold, silver, precious stones*, i.e., love of God and our neighbor, and good works, are others from those who build wood, hay, and stubble. But those even who love God and their neighbor, and do good works, commit venial sins: for it is written (1 John 1:8): *If we say that we have no sin, we deceive ourselves*. Therefore venial sins are not suitably designated by these three.

OBJ. 4: Further, there are many more than three differences and degrees of venial sins. Therefore they are unsuitably comprised under these three.

ON THE CONTRARY, The Apostle says (1 Cor 3:15) that the man who builds up wood, hay and stubble, *shall be saved yet so as by fire*, so that he will suffer punishment, but not everlasting. Now the debt of temporal punishment belongs properly to venial sin, as stated above (Q87, A5). Therefore these three signify venial sins.

I ANSWER THAT, Some have understood the *foundation* to be dead faith, upon which some build good works, signified by gold, silver, and precious stones, while others build mortal sins, which according to them are designated by wood, hay and stubble. But Augustine disapproves of this explanation (De Fide et Oper. xv), because, as the Apostle says (Gal 5:21), he who does the works of the flesh, *shall not obtain the kingdom of God*, which signifies to be saved; whereas the Apostle says that he who builds wood, hay, and stubble *shall be saved yet so as by fire*. Consequently wood, hay, stubble cannot be understood to denote mortal sins.

Others say that wood, hay, stubble designate good works, which are indeed built upon the spiritual edifice, but are mixed with venial sins: as, when a man is charged with the care of a family, which is a good thing, excessive love of his wife or of his children or of his possessions insinuates itself into his life, under God however, so that, to wit, for the sake of these things he would be unwilling to do anything in opposition to God. But neither does this seem to be reasonable. For it is evident that all good works are referred to the love of God, and one's neighbor, wherefore they are designated by *gold*, *silver*, and *precious stones*, and consequently not by *wood*, *hay*, and *stubble*.

We must therefore say that the very venial sins that insinuate themselves into those who have a care for earthly things, are designated by wood, hay, and stubble. For just as these are stored in a house, without belonging to the substance of the house, and can be burnt, while the house is saved, so also venial sins are multiplied in a man, while the spiritual edifice remains, and for them, man suffers fire, either of temporal trials in this life, or of purgatory after this life, and yet he is saved for ever.

REPLY OBJ. 1: Venial sins are not said to be built upon the spiritual foundation, as though they were laid directly

quasi directe supra ipsum posita, sed quia ponuntur iuxta ipsum; sicut accipitur ibi, super flumina Babylonis, idest iuxta. Quia peccata venialia non destruunt spirituale aedificium, ut dictum est.

AD SECUNDUM dicendum quod non dicitur de quocumque aedificante lignum, faenum et stipulam, quod salvus sit quasi per ignem, sed solum de eo qui aedificat supra fundamentum. Quod quidem non est fides informis, ut quidam aestimabant, sed fides formata caritate, secundum illud Ephes. III, *in caritate radicati et fundati*. Ille ergo qui decedit cum peccato mortali et venialibus, habet quidem lignum, faenum et stipulam, sed non superaedificata supra fundamentum spirituale. Et ideo non erit salvus sic quasi per ignem.

AD TERTIUM dicendum quod illi qui sunt abstracti a cura temporalium rerum, etsi aliquando venialiter peccent, tamen levia peccata venialia committunt, et frequentissime per fervorem caritatis purgantur. Unde tales non superaedificant venialia, quia in eis modicum manent. Sed peccata venialia ipsorum qui circa terrena occupantur, diutius manent, quia non ita frequenter recurrere possunt ad huiusmodi peccata delenda per caritatis fervorem.

AD QUARTUM dicendum quod, sicut philosophus dicit, in I de caelo, *omnia tribus includuntur, scilicet principio, medio et fine*. Et secundum hoc, omnes gradus venialium peccatorum ad tria reducuntur, scilicet ad lignum, quod diutius manet in igne; ad stipulam, quae citissime expeditur; ad faenum, quod medio modo se habet. Secundum enim quod peccata venialia sunt maioris vel minoris adhaerentiae vel gravitatis, citius vel tardius per ignem purgantur.

upon it, but because they are laid beside it; in the same sense as it is written (Ps 136:1): *Upon the waters of Babylon*, i.e., *beside the waters*: because venial sins do not destroy the edifice.

REPLY OBJ. 2: It is not said that everyone who builds wood, hay and stubble, shall be saved as by fire, but only those who build *upon* the *foundation*. And this foundation is not dead faith, as some have esteemed, but faith quickened by charity, according to Eph. 3:17: *Rooted and founded in charity*. Accordingly, he that dies in mortal sin with venial sins, has indeed wood, hay, and stubble, but not built upon the spiritual edifice; and consequently he will not be saved so as by fire.

REPLY OBJ. 3: Although those who are withdrawn from the care of temporal things, sin venially sometimes, yet they commit but slight venial sins, and in most cases they are cleansed by the fervor of charity: wherefore they do not build up venial sins, because these do not remain long in them. But the venial sins of those who are busy about earthly remain longer, because they are unable to have such frequent recourse to the fervor of charity in order to remove them.

REPLY OBJ. 4: As the Philosopher says (*De Coelo* i, text. 2), *all things are comprised under three, the beginning, the middle, the end*. Accordingly all degrees of venial sins are reduced to three, viz., to *wood*, which remains longer in the fire; *stubble*, which is burnt up at once; and *hay*, which is between these two: because venial sins are removed by fire, quickly or slowly, according as man is more or less attached to them.

Article 3

Whether Man Could Commit a Venial Sin in the State of Innocence?

AD TERTIUM SIC PROCEDITUR. Videtur quod homo in statu innocentiae potuerit peccare venialiter. Quia super illud I ad Tim. II, *Adam non est seductus*, dicit Glossa, *inexpertus divinae severitatis, in eo falli potuit, ut crederet veniale esse commissum*. Sed hoc non credidisset, nisi venialiter peccare potuisset. Ergo venialiter peccare potuit, non peccando mortaliter.

PRAETEREA, Augustinus dicit, XI super Gen. ad Litt., *non est arbitrandum quod esset hominem deiecturus tentator, nisi praecessisset in anima hominis quaedam elatio comprimenda*. Elatio autem deiectionem praecedens, quae facta est per peccatum mortale, non potuit esse nisi peccatum veniale. Similiter etiam in eodem Augustinus dicit quod *virum sollicitavit aliqua experiendi cupiditas*,

OBJECTION 1: It would seem that man could commit a venial sin in the state of innocence. Because on 1 Tim. 2:14, *Adam was not seduced*, a gloss says: *Having had no experience of God's severity, it was possible for him to be so mistaken as to think that what he had done was a venial sin*. But he would not have thought this unless he could have committed a venial sin. Therefore he could commit a venial sin without sinning mortally.

OBJ. 2: Further Augustine says (*Gen ad lit.* xi, 5): *We must not suppose that the tempter would have overcome man, unless first of all there had arisen in man's soul a movement of vainglory which should have been checked*. Now the vainglory which preceded man's defeat, which was accomplished through his falling into mortal sin, could be nothing more than a venial sin. In like manner, Augustine says

cum mulierem videret, sumpto vetito pomo, non esse mortuam. Videtur etiam in Eva fuisse aliquis infidelitatis motus, in hoc quod de verbis domini dubitavit, ut patet per hoc quod dixit, *ne forte moriamur,* ut habetur Gen. III. Haec autem videntur esse venialia peccata. Ergo homo potuit venialiter peccare, antequam mortaliter peccaret.

Praeterea, peccatum mortale magis opponitur integritati primi status quam peccatum veniale. Sed homo potuit peccare mortaliter, non obstante integritate primi status. Ergo etiam potuit peccare venialiter.

Sed contra est quod cuilibet peccato debetur aliqua poena. Sed nihil poenale esse potuit in statu innocentiae, ut Augustinus dicit, XIV de Civ. Dei. Ergo non potuit peccare aliquo peccato quo non eiiceretur ab illo integritatis statu. Sed peccatum veniale non mutat statum hominis. Ergo non potuit peccare venialiter.

Respondeo dicendum quod communiter ponitur quod homo in statu innocentiae non potuit venialiter peccare. Hoc autem non est sic intelligendum, quasi id quod nobis est veniale, si ipse committeret, esset sibi mortale, propter altitudinem sui status. Dignitas enim personae est quaedam circumstantia aggravans peccatum, non tamen transfert in aliam speciem, nisi forte superveniente deformitate inobedientiae vel voti, vel alicuius huiusmodi, quod in proposito dici non potest. Unde id quod est de se veniale, non potuit transferri in mortale, propter dignitatem primi status. Sic ergo intelligendum est quod non potuit peccare venialiter, quia non potuit esse ut committeret aliquid quod esset de se veniale, antequam integritatem primi status amitteret peccando mortaliter.

Cuius ratio est quia peccatum veniale in nobis contingit vel propter imperfectionem actus, sicut subiti motus in genere peccatorum mortalium, vel propter inordinationem existentem circa ea quae sunt ad finem, servato debito ordine ad finem. Utrumque autem horum contingit propter quendam defectum ordinis, ex eo quod inferius non continetur firmiter sub superiori. Quod enim in nobis insurgat subitus motus sensualitatis, contingit ex hoc quod sensualitas non est omnino subdita rationi. Quod vero insurgat subitus motus in ratione ipsa, provenit in nobis ex hoc quod ipsa executio actus rationis non subditur deliberationi quae est ex altiori bono, ut supra dictum est. Quod vero humanus animus inordinetur circa ea quae sunt ad finem, servato debito ordine ad finem, provenit ex hoc quod ea quae sunt ad finem non ordinantur infallibiliter sub fine, qui tenet summum locum, quasi principium in appetibilibus, ut supra dictum est. In statu autem innocentiae, ut in primo habitum est, erat infallibilis ordinis firmitas, ut semper inferius contineretur sub superiori, quandiu summum hominis

(Gen ad lit. xi, 5) that *man was allured by a certain desire of making the experiment, when he saw that the woman did not die when she had taken the forbidden fruit.* Again there seems to have been a certain movement of unbelief in Eve, since she doubted what the Lord had said, as appears from her saying (Gen 3:3): *Lest perhaps we die.* Now these apparently were venial sins. Therefore man could commit a venial sin before he committed a mortal sin.

Obj. 3: Further, mortal sin is more opposed to the integrity of the original state, than venial sin is. Now man could sin mortally notwithstanding the integrity of the original state. Therefore he could also sin venially.

On the contrary, Every sin deserves some punishment. But nothing penal was possible in the state of innocence, as Augustine declares (*De Civ. Dei* xiv, 10). Therefore he could commit a sin that would not deprive him of that state of integrity. But venial sin does not change man's state. Therefore he could not sin venially.

I answer that, It is generally admitted that man could not commit a venial sin in the state of innocence. This, however, is not to be understood as though on account of the perfection of his state, the sin which is venial for us would have been mortal for him, if he had committed it. Because the dignity of a person is circumstance that aggravates a sin, but it does not transfer it to another species, unless there be an additional deformity by reason of disobedience, or vow or the like, which does not apply to the question in point. Consequently what is venial in itself could not be changed into mortal by reason of the excellence of the original state. We must therefore understand this to mean that he could not sin venially, because it was impossible for him to commit a sin which was venial in itself, before losing the integrity of the original state by sinning mortally.

The reason for this is because venial sin occurs in us, either through the imperfection of the act, as in the case of sudden movements, in a genus of mortal sin or through some inordinateness in respect of things referred to the end, the due order of the end being safeguarded. Now each of these happens on account of some defect of order, by reason of the lower powers not being checked by the higher. Because the sudden rising of a movement of the sensuality in us is due to the sensuality not being perfectly subject to reason: and the sudden rising of a movement of reason itself is due, in us, to the fact that the execution of the act of reason is not subject to the act of deliberation which proceeds from a higher good, as stated above (Q74, A10); and that the human mind be out of order as regards things directed to the end, the due order of the end being safeguarded, is due to the fact that the things referred to the end are not infallibly directed under the end, which holds the highest place, being the beginning, as it were, in matters concerning the appetite, as stated above (Q10, AA1,2, ad 3; Q72, A5). Now, in the state of innocence, as stated in the FP,

contineretur sub Deo, ut etiam Augustinus dicit, XIV de Civ. Dei. Et ideo oportebat quod inordinatio in homine non esset, nisi inciperet ab hoc quod summum hominis non subderetur Deo; quod fit per peccatum mortale. Ex quo patet quod homo in statu innocentiae non potuit peccare venialiter, antequam peccaret mortaliter.

Ad primum ergo dicendum quod veniale non sumitur ibi secundum quod nunc de veniali loquimur, sed dicitur veniale quod est facile remissibile.

Ad secundum dicendum quod illa elatio quae praecessit in animo hominis, fuit primum hominis peccatum mortale, dicitur autem praecessisse deiectionem eius in exteriorem actum peccati. Huiusmodi autem elationem subsecuta est et experiendi cupiditas in viro, et dubitatio in muliere; quae ex hoc solo in quandam elationem prorupit, quod praecepti mentionem a serpente audivit, quasi nollet sub praecepto contineri.

Ad tertium dicendum quod peccatum mortale intantum opponitur integritati primi status, quod corrumpit ipsum, quod peccatum veniale facere non potest. Et quia non potest simul esse quaecumque inordinatio cum integritate primi status, consequens est quod primus homo non potuerit peccare venialiter, antequam peccaret mortaliter.

Q95, A1, there was an unerring stability of order, so that the lower powers were always subjected to the higher, so long as man remained subject to God, as Augustine says (*De Civ. Dei* xiv, 13). Hence there can be no inordinateness in man, unless first of all the highest part of man were not subject to God, which constitutes a mortal sin. From this it is evident that, in the state of innocence, man could not commit a venial sin, before committing a mortal sin.

Reply Obj. 1: In the passage quoted, venial is not taken in the same sense as we take it now; but by venial sin we mean that which is easily forgiven.

Reply Obj. 2: This vainglory which preceded man's downfall, was his first mortal sin, for it is stated to have preceded his downfall into the outward act of sin. This vainglory was followed, in the man, by the desire to make and experiment, and in the woman, by doubt, for she gave way to vainglory, merely through hearing the serpent mention the precept, as though she refused to be held in check by the precept.

Reply Obj. 3: Mortal sin is opposed to the integrity of the original state in the fact of its destroying that state: this a venial sin cannot do. And because the integrity of the primitive state is incompatible with any inordinateness whatever, the result is that the first man could not sin venially, before committing a mortal sin.

Article 4

Whether a Good or a Wicked Angel Can Sin Venially?

Ad quartum sic proceditur. Videtur quod Angelus bonus vel malus possit peccare venialiter. Homo enim cum Angelis convenit in superiori animae parte, quae mens vocatur; secundum illud Gregorii, in Homil., *homo intelligit cum Angelis*. Sed homo secundum superiorem partem animae potest peccare venialiter. Ergo et Angelus.

Praeterea, quicumque potest quod est plus, potest etiam quod est minus. Sed Angelus potuit diligere bonum creatum plus quam Deum, quod fecit peccando mortaliter. Ergo etiam potuit bonum creatum diligere infra Deum inordinate, venialiter peccando.

Praeterea, Angeli mali videntur aliqua facere quae sunt ex genere suo venialia peccata, provocando homines ad risum, et ad alias huiusmodi levitates. Sed circumstantia personae non facit de veniali mortale, ut dictum est, nisi speciali prohibitione superveniente, quod non est in proposito. Ergo Angelus potest peccare venialiter.

Sed contra est quod maior est perfectio Angeli quam perfectio hominis in primo statu. Sed homo in

Objection 1: It seems that a good or wicked angel can sin venially. Because man agrees with the angels in the higher part of his soul which is called the mind, according to Gregory, who says (*Hom. xxix in Evang.*) that *man understands in common with the angels*. But man can commit a venial sin in the higher part of his soul. Therefore an angel can commit a venial sin also.

Obj. 2: Further, He that can do more can do less. But an angel could love a created good more than God, and he did, by sinning mortally. Therefore he could also love a creature less than God inordinately, by sinning venially.

Obj. 3: Further, wicked angels seem to do things which are venial sins generically, by provoking men to laughter, and other like frivolities. Now the circumstance of the person does not make a mortal sin to be venial as stated above (A3), unless there is a special prohibition, which is not the case in point. Therefore an angel can sin venially.

On the contrary, The perfection of an angel is greater than that of man in the primitive state. But man could

primo statu non potuit peccare venialiter. Ergo multo minus Angelus.

RESPONDEO dicendum quod intellectus Angeli, sicut in primo dictum est, non est discursivus, ut scilicet procedat a principiis in conclusiones, seorsum utrumque intelligens, sicut in nobis contingit. Unde oportet quod quandocumque considerat conclusiones, consideret eas prout sunt in principiis. In appetibilibus autem, sicut multoties dictum est, fines sunt sicut principia; ea vero quae sunt ad finem, sunt sicut conclusiones. Unde mens Angeli non fertur in ea quae sunt ad finem, nisi secundum quod constant sub ordine finis. Propter hoc ex natura sua habent quod non possit in eis esse deordinatio circa ea quae sunt ad finem, nisi simul sit deordinatio circa finem ipsum, quod est per peccatum mortale. Sed Angeli boni non moventur in ea quae sunt ad finem, nisi in ordine ad finem debitum, qui est Deus. Et propter hoc omnes eorum actus sunt actus caritatis. Et sic in eis non potest esse peccatum veniale. Angeli vero mali in nihil moventur nisi in ordine ad finem peccati superbiae ipsorum. Et ideo in omnibus peccant mortaliter, quaecumque propria voluntate agunt. Secus autem est de appetitu naturalis boni qui est in eis, ut in primo dictum est.

AD PRIMUM ergo dicendum quod homo convenit quidem cum Angelis in mente, sive in intellectu; sed differt in modo intelligendi, ut dictum est.

AD SECUNDUM dicendum quod Angelus non potuit minus diligere creaturam quam Deum, nisi simul referens eam in Deum, sicut in ultimum finem, vel aliquem finem inordinatum, ratione iam dicta.

AD TERTIUM dicendum quod omnia illa quae videntur esse venialia, Daemones procurant ut homines ad sui familiaritatem attrahant, et sic deducant eos in peccatum mortale. Unde in omnibus talibus mortaliter peccant, propter intentionem finis.

not sin venially in the primitive state, and much less, therefore, can an angel.

I ANSWER THAT, An angel's intellect, as stated above in the FP, Q58, A3; FP, Q79, A8, is not discursive, i.e., it does not proceed from principles to conclusions, so as to understand both separately, as we do. Consequently, whenever the angelic intellect considers a conclusion, it must, of necessity, consider it in its principles. Now in matters of appetite, as we have often stated (Q8, A2; Q10, A1; Q72, A5), ends are like principles, while the means are like conclusions. Wherefore, an angel's mind is not directed to the means, except as they stand under the order to the end. Consequently, from their very nature, they can have no inordinateness in respect of the means, unless at the same time they have an inordinateness in respect of the end, and this is a mortal sin. Now good angels are not moved to the means, except in subordination to the due end which is God: wherefore all their acts are acts of charity, so that no venial sin can be in them. On the other hand, wicked angels are moved to nothing except in subordination to the end which is their sin of pride. Therefore they sin mortally in everything that they do of their own will. This does not apply to the appetite for the natural good, which appetite we have stated to be in them (FP, Q63, A4; Q64, A2, ad 5).

REPLY OBJ. 1: Man does indeed agree with the angels in the mind or intellect, but he differs in his mode of understanding, as stated above.

REPLY OBJ. 2: An angel could not love a creature less than God, without, at the same time, either referring it to God, as the last end, or to some inordinate end, for the reason given above.

REPLY OBJ. 3: The demons incite man to all such things which seem venial, that he may become used to them, so as to lead him on to mortal sin. Consequently in all such things they sin mortally, on account of the end they have in view.

Article 5

Whether the First Movements of the Sensuality in Unbelievers Are Mortal Sin?

AD QUINTUM SIC PROCEDITUR. Videtur quod primi motus sensualitatis in infidelibus sint peccata mortalia. Dicit enim apostolus, ad Rom. VIII, quod *nihil est damnationis his qui sunt in Christo Iesu, qui non secundum carnem ambulant*, et loquitur ibi de concupiscentia sensualitatis, ut ex praemissis apparet. Haec ergo causa est quare concupiscere non sit damnabile his qui non secundum carnem ambulant, consentiendo scilicet concupiscentiae, quia sunt in Christo Iesu. Sed infideles non

OBJECTION 1: It would seem that the first movements of the sensuality in unbelievers are mortal sins. For the Apostle says (Rom 8:1) that *there is . . . no condemnation to them that are in Christ Jesus, who walk not according to the flesh*: and he is speaking there of the concupiscence of the sensuality, as appears from the context (Rom 7). Therefore the reason why concupiscence is not a matter of condemnation to those who walk not according to the flesh, i.e., by consenting to concupiscence, is because they are in Christ

sunt in Christo Iesu. Ergo in infidelibus est damnabile. Primi igitur motus infidelium sunt peccata mortalia.

PRAETEREA, Anselmus dicit, in libro de gratia et Lib. Arb., *qui non sunt in Christo, sentientes carnem, sequuntur damnationem, etiam si non secundum carnem ambulant.* Sed damnatio non debetur nisi peccato mortali. Ergo, cum homo sentiat carnem secundum primum motum concupiscentiae, videtur quod primus motus concupiscentiae in infidelibus sit peccatum mortale.

PRAETEREA, Anselmus dicit, in eodem libro, *sic factus est homo, ut concupiscentiam sentire non deberet.* Hoc autem debitum videtur homini remissum per gratiam baptismalem, quam infideles non habent. Ergo quandocumque infidelis concupiscit, etiam si non consentiat, peccat mortaliter, contra debitum faciens.

SED CONTRA est quod dicitur Act. X, *non est personarum acceptor Deus.* Quod ergo uni non imputat ad damnationem, nec alteri. Sed primos motus fidelibus non imputat ad damnationem. Ergo etiam nec infidelibus.

RESPONDEO dicendum quod irrationabiliter dicitur quod primi motus infidelium sint peccata mortalia, si eis non consentiatur. Et hoc patet dupliciter. Primo quidem, quia ipsa sensualitas non potest esse subiectum peccati mortalis, ut supra habitum est. Est autem eadem natura sensualitatis in infidelibus et fidelibus. Unde non potest esse quod solus motus sensualitatis in infidelibus sit peccatum mortale. Alio modo, ex statu ipsius peccantis. Nunquam enim dignitas personae diminuit peccatum, sed magis auget, ut ex supra dictis patet. Unde nec peccatum est minus in fideli quam in infideli, sed multo maius. Nam et infidelium peccata magis merentur veniam, propter ignorantiam, secundum illud I ad Tim. I, *misericordiam Dei consecutus sum, quia ignorans feci in incredulitate mea*; et peccata fidelium aggravantur propter gratiae sacramenta, secundum illud Heb. X, *quanto magis putatis deteriora mereri supplicia, qui sanguinem testamenti, in quo sanctificatus est, pollutum duxerit?*

AD PRIMUM ergo dicendum quod apostolus loquitur de damnatione debita peccato originali, quae aufertur per gratiam Iesu Christi, quamvis maneat concupiscentiae fomes. Unde hoc quod fideles concupiscunt, non est in eis signum damnationis originalis peccati, sicut est in infidelibus.

ET HOC ETIAM modo intelligendum est dictum Anselmi. Unde patet solutio ad secundum.

AD TERTIUM dicendum quod illud debitum non concupiscendi erat per originalem iustitiam. Unde id

Jesus. But unbelievers are not in Christ Jesus. Therefore in unbelievers this is a matter of condemnation. Therefore the first movements of unbelievers are mortal sins.

OBJ. 2: Further Anselm says (*De Gratia et Lib. Arb.* vii): *Those who are not in Christ, when they feel the sting of the flesh, follow the road of damnation, even if they walk not according to the flesh.* But damnation is not due save to mortal sin. Therefore, since man feels the sting of the flesh in the first movements of the concupiscence, it seems that the first movements of concupiscence in unbelievers are mortal sins.

OBJ. 3: Further, Anselm says (*De Gratia et Lib. Arb.* vii): *Man was so made that he was not liable to feel concupiscence.* Now this liability seems to be remitted to man by the grace of Baptism, which the unbeliever has not. Therefore every act of concupiscence in an unbeliever, even without his consent, is a mortal sin, because he acts against his duty.

ON THE CONTRARY, It is stated in Acts 10:34 that *God is not a respecter of persons.* Therefore he does not impute to one unto condemnation, what He does not impute to another. But he does not impute first movements to believers, unto condemnation. Neither therefore does He impute them to unbelievers.

I ANSWER THAT, It is unreasonable to say that the first movements of unbelievers are mortal sins, when they do not consent to them. This is evident for two reasons. First, because the sensuality itself could not be the subject of mortal sin, as stated above (Q79, A4). Now the sensuality has the same nature in unbelievers as in believers. Therefore it is not possible for the mere movements of the sensuality in unbelievers, to be mortal sins. Second, from the state of the sinner. Because excellence of the person never diminishes sin, but, on the contrary, increases it, as stated above (Q73, A10). Therefore a sin is not less grievous in a believer than in an unbeliever, but much more so. For the sins of an unbeliever are more deserving of forgiveness, on account of their ignorance, according to 1 Tim. 1:13: *I obtained the mercy of God, because I did it ignorantly in my unbelief*: whereas the sins of believers are more grievous on account of the sacraments of grace, according to Heb. 10:29: *How much more, do you think, he deserveth worse punishments . . . who hath esteemed the blood of the testament unclean, by which he was sanctified?*

REPLY OBJ. 1: The Apostle is speaking of the condemnation due to original sin, which condemnation is remitted by the grace of Jesus Christ, although the *fomes* of concupiscence remain. Wherefore the fact that believers are subject to concupiscence is not in them a sign of the condemnation due to original sin, as it is in unbelievers.

IN THIS WAY also is to be understood the saying of Anselm, wherefore the Reply to the Second Objection is evident.

REPLY OBJ. 3: This freedom from liability to concupiscence was a result of original justice. Wherefore that which

quod opponitur tali debito, non pertinet ad peccatum actuale, sed ad peccatum originale.

is opposed to such liability pertains, not to actual but to original sin.

Article 6

Whether Venial Sin Can Be in Anyone with Original Sin Alone?

AD SEXTUM SIC PROCEDITUR. Videtur quod peccatum veniale possit esse in aliquo cum solo originali. Dispositio enim praecedit habitum. Sed veniale est dispositio ad mortale, ut supra dictum est. Ergo veniale in infideli, cui non remittitur originale, invenitur ante mortale. Et sic quandoque infideles habent peccata venialia cum originali, sine mortalibus.

PRAETEREA, minus habet de connexione et convenientia veniale cum mortali, quam mortale peccatum cum mortali. Sed infidelis subiectus originali peccato, potest committere unum peccatum mortale et non aliud. Ergo etiam potest committere peccatum veniale, et non mortale.

PRAETEREA, determinari potest tempus in quo puer primo potest esse actor peccati actualis. Ad quod tempus cum pervenerit, potest ad minus per aliquod breve spatium stare, quin peccet mortaliter, quia hoc etiam in maximis sceleratis contingit. In illo autem spatio, quantumcumque brevi, potest peccare venialiter. Ergo peccatum veniale potest esse in aliquo cum originali peccato, absque mortali.

SED CONTRA est quia pro peccato originali puniuntur homines in Limbo puerorum, ubi non est poena sensus, ut infra dicetur. In Inferno autem detruduntur homines propter solum peccatum mortale. Ergo non erit locus in quo possit puniri ille qui habet peccatum veniale cum originali solo.

RESPONDEO dicendum quod impossibile est quod peccatum veniale sit in aliquo cum originali peccato, absque mortali. Cuius ratio est quia antequam ad annos discretionis perveniat, defectus aetatis, prohibens usum rationis, excusat eum a peccato mortali, unde multo magis excusat eum a peccato veniali, si committat aliquid quod sit ex genere suo tale. Cum vero usum rationis habere inceperit, non omnino excusatur a culpa venialis et mortalis peccati. Sed primum quod tunc homini cogitandum occurrit, est deliberare de seipso. Et si quidem seipsum ordinaverit ad debitum finem, per gratiam consequetur remissionem originalis peccati. Si vero non ordinet seipsum ad debitum finem, secundum quod in illa aetate est capax discretionis, peccabit mortaliter, non faciens quod in se est. Et ex tunc non erit in eo peccatum veniale sine mortali, nisi postquam totum fuerit sibi per gratiam remissum.

OBJECTION 1: It would seem that venial sin can be in a man with original sin alone. For disposition precedes habit. Now venial sin is a disposition to mortal sin, as stated above (Q88, A3). Therefore in an unbeliever, in whom original sin is not remitted, venial sin exists before mortal sin: and so sometimes unbelievers have venial together with original sin, and without mortal sins.

OBJ. 2: Further, venial sin has less in common, and less connection with mortal sin, than one mortal sin has with another. But an unbeliever in the state of original sin, can commit one mortal sin without committing another. Therefore he can also commit a venial sin without committing a mortal sin.

OBJ. 3: Further, it is possible to fix the time at which a child is first able to commit an actual sin: and when the child comes to that time, it can stay a short time at least, without committing a mortal sin, because this happens in the worst criminals. Now it is possible for the child to sin venially during that space of time, however short it may be. Therefore venial sin can be in anyone with original sin alone and without mortal sin.

ON THE CONTRARY, Man is punished for original sin in the children's limbo, where there is no pain of sense as we shall state further on (SS, Q69, A6): whereas men are punished in hell for no other than mortal sin. Therefore there will be no place where a man can be punished for venial sin with no other than original sin.

I ANSWER THAT, It is impossible for venial sin to be in anyone with original sin alone, and without mortal sin. The reason for this is because before a man comes to the age of discretion, the lack of years hinders the use of reason and excuses him from mortal sin, wherefore, much more does it excuse him from venial sin, if he does anything which is such generically. But when he begins to have the use of reason, he is not entirely excused from the guilt of venial or mortal sin. Now the first thing that occurs to a man to think about then, is to deliberate about himself. And if he then direct himself to the due end, he will, by means of grace, receive the remission of original sin: whereas if he does not then direct himself to the due end, and as far as he is capable of discretion at that particular age, he will sin mortally, for through not doing that which is in his power to do. Accordingly thenceforward there cannot be venial sin in him without mortal, until afterwards all sin shall have been remitted to him through grace.

AD PRIMUM ergo dicendum quod veniale non est dispositio ex necessitate praecedens mortale, sed contingenter, sicut labor disponit quandoque ad febrem, non autem sicut calor disponit ad formam ignis.

AD SECUNDUM dicendum quod non impeditur peccatum veniale esse simul cum solo originali propter distantiam eius vel convenientiam; sed propter defectum usus rationis, ut dictum est.

AD TERTIUM dicendum quod ab aliis peccatis mortalibus potest puer incipiens habere usum rationis, per aliquod tempus abstinere, sed a peccato omissionis praedictae non liberatur, nisi quam cito potest, se convertat ad Deum. Primum enim quod occurrit homini discretionem habenti est quod de seipso cogitet, ad quem alia ordinet sicut ad finem, finis enim est prior in intentione. Et ideo hoc est tempus pro quo obligatur ex Dei praecepto affirmativo, quo dominus dicit, *convertimini ad me, et ego convertar ad vos*, Zachariae I.

REPLY OBJ. 1: Venial sin always precedes mortal sin not as a necessary, but as a contingent disposition, just as work sometimes disposes to fever, but not as heat disposes to the form of fire.

REPLY OBJ. 2: Venial sin is prevented from being with original sin alone, not on account of its want of connection or likeness, but on account of the lack of use of reason, as stated above.

REPLY OBJ. 3: The child that is beginning to have the use of reason can refrain from other mortal sins for a time, but it is not free from the aforesaid sin of omission, unless it turns to God as soon as possible. For the first thing that occurs to a man who has discretion, is to think of himself, and to direct other things to himself as to their end, since the end is the first thing in the intention. Therefore this is the time when man is bound by God's affirmative precept, which the Lord expressed by saying (Zech 1:3): *Turn ye to Me . . . and I will turn to you.*

QUESTION 90

OF THE ESSENCE OF LAW

Consequenter considerandum est de principiis exterioribus actuum. Principium autem exterius ad malum inclinans est Diabolus, de cuius tentatione in primo dictum est. Principium autem exterius movens ad bonum est Deus, qui et nos instruit per legem, et iuvat per gratiam. Unde primo, de lege; secundo, de gratia dicendum est.

Circa legem autem, primo oportet considerare de ipsa lege in communi; secundo, de partibus eius. Circa legem autem in communi tria occurrunt consideranda, primo quidem, de essentia ipsius; secundo, de differentia legum; tertio, de effectibus legis.

Circa primum quaeruntur quatuor.

Primo, utrum lex sit aliquid rationis.

Secundo, de fine legis.

Tertio, de causa eius.

Quarto, de promulgatione ipsius.

We have now to consider the extrinsic principles of acts. Now the extrinsic principle inclining to evil is the devil, of whose temptations we have spoken in the FP, Q114. But the extrinsic principle moving to good is God, Who both instructs us by means of His Law, and assists us by His Grace: wherefore in the first place we must speak of law; in the second place, of grace.

Concerning law, we must consider: (1) Law itself in general; (2) its parts. Concerning law in general three points offer themselves for our consideration: (1) Its essence; (2) The different kinds of law; (3) The effects of law.

Under the first head there are four points of inquiry:

(1) Whether law is something pertaining to reason?

(2) Concerning the end of law;

(3) Its cause;

(4) The promulgation of law.

Article 1

Whether Law Is Something of Reason?

AD PRIMUM SIC PROCEDITUR. Videtur quod lex non sit aliquid rationis. Dicit enim apostolus, ad Rom. VII, *video aliam legem in membris meis,* et cetera. Sed nihil quod est rationis, est in membris, quia ratio non utitur organo corporali. Ergo lex non est aliquid rationis.

PRAETEREA, in ratione non est nisi potentia, habitus et actus. Sed lex non est ipsa potentia rationis. Similiter etiam non est aliquis habitus rationis, quia habitus rationis sunt virtutes intellectuales, de quibus supra dictum est. Nec etiam est actus rationis, quia cessante rationis actu, lex cessaret, puta in dormientibus. Ergo lex non est aliquid rationis.

PRAETEREA, lex movet eos qui subiiciuntur legi, ad recte agendum. Sed movere ad agendum proprie pertinet ad voluntatem, ut patet ex praemissis. Ergo lex non pertinet ad rationem, sed magis ad voluntatem, secundum quod etiam iurisperitus dicit, *quod placuit principi, legis habet vigorem.*

SED CONTRA est quod ad legem pertinet praecipere et prohibere. Sed imperare est rationis, ut supra habitum est. Ergo lex est aliquid rationis.

OBJECTION 1: It would seem that law is not something pertaining to reason. For the Apostle says (Rom 7:23): *I see another law in my members,* etc. But nothing pertaining to reason is in the members; since the reason does not make use of a bodily organ. Therefore law is not something pertaining to reason.

OBJ. 2: Further, in the reason there is nothing else but power, habit, and act. But law is not the power itself of reason. In like manner, neither is it a habit of reason: because the habits of reason are the intellectual virtues of which we have spoken above (Q57). Nor again is it an act of reason: because then law would cease, when the act of reason ceases, for instance, while we are asleep. Therefore law is nothing pertaining to reason.

OBJ. 3: Further, the law moves those who are subject to it to act aright. But it belongs properly to the will to move to act, as is evident from what has been said above (Q9, A1). Therefore law pertains, not to the reason, but to the will; according to the words of the Jurist (Lib. i, ff., *De Const. Prin.* leg. i): *Whatsoever pleaseth the sovereign, has force of law.*

ON THE CONTRARY, It belongs to the law to command and to forbid. But it belongs to reason to command, as stated above (Q17, A1). Therefore law is something pertaining to reason.

RESPONDEO dicendum quod lex quaedam regula est et mensura actuum, secundum quam inducitur aliquis ad agendum, vel ab agendo retrahitur, dicitur enim lex a ligando, quia obligat ad agendum. Regula autem et mensura humanorum actuum est ratio, quae est primum principium actuum humanorum, ut ex praedictis patet, rationis enim est ordinare ad finem, qui est primum principium in agendis, secundum philosophum. In unoquoque autem genere id quod est principium, est mensura et regula illius generis, sicut unitas in genere numeri, et motus primus in genere motuum. Unde relinquitur quod lex sit aliquid pertinens ad rationem.

AD PRIMUM ergo dicendum quod, cum lex sit regula quaedam et mensura, dicitur dupliciter esse in aliquo. Uno modo, sicut in mensurante et regulante. Et quia hoc est proprium rationis, ideo per hunc modum lex est in ratione sola. Alio modo, sicut in regulato et mensurato. Et sic lex est in omnibus quae inclinantur in aliquid ex aliqua lege, ita quod quaelibet inclinatio proveniens ex aliqua lege, potest dici lex, non essentialiter, sed quasi participative. Et hoc modo inclinatio ipsa membrorum ad concupiscendum lex membrorum vocatur.

AD SECUNDUM dicendum quod, sicut in actibus exterioribus est considerare operationem et operatum, puta aedificationem et aedificatum; ita in operibus rationis est considerare ipsum actum rationis, qui est intelligere et ratiocinari, et aliquid per huiusmodi actum constitutum. Quod quidem in speculativa ratione primo quidem est definitio; secundo, enunciatio; tertio vero, syllogismus vel argumentatio. Et quia ratio etiam practica utitur quodam syllogismo in operabilibus, ut supra habitum est, secundum quod philosophus docet in VII Ethic.; ideo est invenire aliquid in ratione practica quod ita se habeat ad operationes, sicut se habet propositio in ratione speculativa ad conclusiones. Et huiusmodi propositiones universales rationis practicae ordinatae ad actiones, habent rationem legis. Quae quidem propositiones aliquando actualiter considerantur, aliquando vero habitualiter a ratione tenentur.

AD TERTIUM dicendum quod ratio habet vim movendi a voluntate, ut supra dictum est, ex hoc enim quod aliquis vult finem, ratio imperat de his quae sunt ad finem. Sed voluntas de his quae imperantur, ad hoc quod legis rationem habeat, oportet quod sit aliqua ratione regulata. Et hoc modo intelligitur quod voluntas principis habet vigorem legis, alioquin voluntas principis magis esset iniquitas quam lex.

I ANSWER THAT, Law is a rule and measure of acts, whereby man is induced to act or is restrained from acting: for *lex* is derived from *ligare*, because it binds one to act. Now the rule and measure of human acts is the reason, which is the first principle of human acts, as is evident from what has been stated above (Q1, A1, ad 3); since it belongs to the reason to direct to the end, which is the first principle in all matters of action, according to the Philosopher (*Phys.* ii). Now that which is the principle in any genus, is the rule and measure of that genus: for instance, unity in the genus of numbers, and the first movement in the genus of movements. Consequently it follows that law is something pertaining to reason.

REPLY OBJ. 1: Since law is a kind of rule and measure, it may be in something in two ways. First, as in that which measures and rules: and since this is proper to reason, it follows that, in this way, law is in the reason alone. Second, as in that which is measured and ruled. In this way, law is in all those things that are inclined to something from some law: so that any inclination arising from a law, may be called a law, not essentially but by participation as it were. And thus the inclination of the members to concupiscence is called *the law of the members*.

REPLY OBJ. 2: Just as, in external action, we may consider the work and the work done, for instance the work of building and the house built; so in the acts of reason, we may consider the act itself of reason, i.e., to understand and to reason, and something produced by this act. With regard to the speculative reason, this is first of all the definition; second, the proposition; third, the syllogism or argument. And since also the practical reason makes use of a syllogism in respect of the work to be done, as stated above (Q13, A3; Q76, A1) and since as the Philosopher teaches (*Ethic.* vii, 3); hence we find in the practical reason something that holds the same position in regard to operations, as, in the speculative intellect, the proposition holds in regard to conclusions. Such like universal propositions of the practical intellect that are directed to actions have the nature of law. And these propositions are sometimes under our actual consideration, while sometimes they are retained in the reason by means of a habit.

REPLY OBJ. 3: Reason has its power of moving from the will, as stated above (Q17, A1): for it is due to the fact that one wills the end, that the reason issues its commands as regards things ordained to the end. But in order that the volition of what is commanded may have the nature of law, it needs to be in accord with some rule of reason. And in this sense is to be understood the saying that the will of the sovereign has the force of law; otherwise the sovereign's will would savor of lawlessness rather than of law.

Article 2

Whether the Law Is Always Something Directed to the Common Good?

AD SECUNDUM SIC PROCEDITUR. Videtur quod lex non ordinetur semper ad bonum commune sicut ad finem. Ad legem enim pertinet praecipere et prohibere. Sed praecepta ordinantur ad quaedam singularia bona. Non ergo semper finis legis est bonum commune.

PRAETEREA, lex dirigit hominem ad agendum. Sed actus humani sunt in particularibus. Ergo et lex ad aliquod particulare bonum ordinatur.

PRAETEREA, Isidorus dicit, in libro Etymol., *si ratione lex constat, lex erit omne quod ratione constiterit.* Sed ratione consistit non solum quod ordinatur ad bonum commune, sed etiam quod ordinatur ad bonum privatum. Ergo lex non ordinatur solum ad bonum commune, sed etiam ad bonum privatum unius.

SED CONTRA est quod Isidorus dicit, in V Etymol., quod *lex est nullo privato commodo, sed pro communi utilitate civium conscripta.*

RESPONDEO dicendum quod, sicut dictum est, lex pertinet ad id quod est principium humanorum actuum, ex eo quod est regula et mensura. Sicut autem ratio est principium humanorum actuum, ita etiam in ipsa ratione est aliquid quod est principium respectu omnium aliorum. Unde ad hoc oportet quod principaliter et maxime pertineat lex. Primum autem principium in operativis, quorum est ratio practica, est finis ultimus. Est autem ultimus finis humanae vitae felicitas vel beatitudo, ut supra habitum est. Unde oportet quod lex maxime respiciat ordinem qui est in beatitudinem. Rursus, cum omnis pars ordinetur ad totum sicut imperfectum ad perfectum; unus autem homo est pars communitatis perfectae, necesse est quod lex proprie respiciat ordinem ad felicitatem communem. Unde et philosophus, in praemissa definitione legalium, mentionem facit et de felicitate et communione politica. Dicit enim, in V Ethic., quod *legalia iusta dicimus factiva et conservativa felicitatis et particularum ipsius, politica communicatione*, perfecta enim communitas civitas est, ut dicitur in I Polit.

In quolibet autem genere id quod maxime dicitur, est principium aliorum, et alia dicuntur secundum ordinem ad ipsum, sicut ignis, qui est maxime calidus, est causa caliditatis in corporibus mixtis, quae intantum dicuntur calida, inquantum participant de igne. Unde oportet quod, cum lex maxime dicatur secundum ordinem ad bonum commune, quodcumque aliud praeceptum de particulari opere non habeat rationem legis nisi secundum ordinem ad bonum commune. Et ideo omnis lex ad bonum commune ordinatur.

AD PRIMUM ergo dicendum quod praeceptum importat applicationem legis ad ea quae ex lege regulantur.

OBJECTION 1: It would seem that the law is not always directed to the common good as to its end. For it belongs to law to command and to forbid. But commands are directed to certain individual goods. Therefore the end of the law is not always the common good.

OBJ. 2: Further, the law directs man in his actions. But human actions are concerned with particular matters. Therefore the law is directed to some particular good.

OBJ. 3: Further, Isidore says (*Etym.* v, 3): *If the law is based on reason, whatever is based on reason will be a law.* But reason is the foundation not only of what is ordained to the common good, but also of that which is directed to the private good. Therefore the law is not only directed to the good of all, but also to the private good of an individual.

ON THE CONTRARY, Isidore says (*Etym.* v, 21) that *laws are enacted for no private profit, but for the common benefit of the citizens.*

I ANSWER THAT, As stated above (A1), the law belongs to that which is a principle of human acts, because it is their rule and measure. Now as reason is a principle of human acts, so in reason itself there is something which is the principle in respect of all the rest: wherefore to this principle chiefly and mainly law must needs be referred. Now the first principle in practical matters, which are the object of the practical reason, is the last end: and the last end of human life is bliss or happiness, as stated above (Q2, A7; Q3, A1). Consequently the law must needs regard principally the relationship to happiness. Moreover, since every part is ordained to the whole, as imperfect to perfect; and since one man is a part of the perfect community, the law must needs regard properly the relationship to common happiness. Wherefore the Philosopher, in the above definition of legal matters mentions both happiness and the body politic: for he says (*Ethic.* v, 1) that we call those legal matters *just, which are adapted to produce and preserve happiness and its parts for the body politic*: since the state is a perfect community, as he says in *Polit.* i, 1.

Now in every genus, that which is said to be greatest is the principle of the others, and the others belong to that genus according to this order to that thing: thus fire, which is chief among hot things, is the cause of heat in mixed bodies, and these are said to be hot insofar as they have a share of fire. Consequently, since the law is chiefly ordained to the common good, any other precept in regard to some individual work, must needs be devoid of the nature of a law, save insofar as it regards the common good. Therefore every law is ordained to the common good.

REPLY OBJ. 1: A command denotes an application of a law to matters regulated by the law. Now the order to

Ordo autem ad bonum commune, qui pertinet ad legem, est applicabilis ad singulares fines. Et secundum hoc, etiam de particularibus quibusdam praecepta dantur.

AD SECUNDUM dicendum quod operationes quidem sunt in particularibus, sed illa particularia referri possunt ad bonum commune, non quidem communitate generis vel speciei, sed communitate causae finalis, secundum quod bonum commune dicitur finis communis.

AD TERTIUM dicendum quod, sicut nihil constat firmiter secundum rationem speculativam nisi per resolutionem ad prima principia indemonstrabilia, ita firmiter nihil constat per rationem practicam nisi per ordinationem ad ultimum finem, qui est bonum commune. Quod autem hoc modo ratione constat, legis rationem habet.

the common good, at which the law aims, is applicable to particular ends. And in this way commands are given even concerning particular matters.

REPLY OBJ. 2: Actions are indeed concerned with particular matters: but those particular matters are referable to the common good, not as to a common genus or species, but as to a common final cause, according as the common good is said to be the common end.

REPLY OBJ. 3: Just as nothing stands firm with regard to the speculative reason except that which is traced back to the first indemonstrable principles, so nothing stands firm with regard to the practical reason, unless it be directed to the last end which is the common good: and whatever stands to reason in this sense, has the nature of a law.

Article 3

Whether the Reason of Any Man Is Competent to Make Laws?

AD TERTIUM SIC PROCEDITUR. Videtur quod cuiuslibet ratio sit factiva legis. Dicit enim apostolus, ad Rom. II, quod *cum gentes, quae legem non habent, naturaliter ea quae legis sunt faciunt, ipsi sibi sunt lex.* Hoc autem communiter de omnibus dicit. Ergo quilibet potest facere sibi legem.

PRAETEREA, sicut philosophus dicit, in libro II Ethic., *intentio legislatoris est ut inducat hominem ad virtutem.* Sed quilibet homo potest alium inducere ad virtutem. Ergo cuiuslibet hominis ratio est factiva legis.

PRAETEREA, sicut princeps civitatis est civitatis gubernator, ita quilibet paterfamilias est gubernator domus. Sed princeps civitatis potest legem in civitate facere. Ergo quilibet paterfamilias potest in sua domo facere legem.

SED CONTRA est quod Isidorus dicit, in libro Etymol., et habetur in decretis, dist. II, *lex est constitutio populi, secundum quam maiores natu simul cum plebibus aliquid sanxerunt.* Non est ergo cuiuslibet facere legem.

RESPONDEO dicendum quod lex proprie, primo et principaliter respicit ordinem ad bonum commune. Ordinare autem aliquid in bonum commune est vel totius multitudinis, vel alicuius gerentis vicem totius multitudinis. Et ideo condere legem vel pertinet ad totam multitudinem, vel pertinet ad personam publicam quae totius multitudinis curam habet. Quia et in omnibus aliis ordinare in finem est eius cuius est proprius ille finis.

AD PRIMUM ergo dicendum quod, sicut supra dictum est, lex est in aliquo non solum sicut in regulante, sed etiam participative sicut in regulato. Et hoc modo unusquisque sibi est lex, inquantum participat ordinem

OBJECTION 1: It would seem that the reason of any man is competent to make laws. For the Apostle says (Rom 2:14) that *when the Gentiles, who have not the law, do by nature those things that are of the law . . . they are a law to themselves.* Now he says this of all in general. Therefore anyone can make a law for himself.

OBJ. 2: Further, as the Philosopher says (*Ethic.* ii, 1), *the intention of the lawgiver is to lead men to virtue.* But every man can lead another to virtue. Therefore the reason of any man is competent to make laws.

OBJ. 3: Further, just as the sovereign of a state governs the state, so every father of a family governs his household. But the sovereign of a state can make laws for the state. Therefore every father of a family can make laws for his household.

ON THE CONTRARY, Isidore says (*Etym.* v, 10): *A law is an ordinance of the people, whereby something is sanctioned by the Elders together with the Commonalty.*

I ANSWER THAT, A law, properly speaking, regards first and foremost the order to the common good. Now to order anything to the common good, belongs either to the whole people, or to someone who is the viceregent of the whole people. And therefore the making of a law belongs either to the whole people or to a public personage who has care of the whole people: since in all other matters the directing of anything to the end concerns him to whom the end belongs.

REPLY OBJ. 1: As stated above (A1, ad 1), a law is in a person not only as in one that rules, but also by participation as in one that is ruled. In the latter way each one is a law to himself, insofar as he shares the direction that he

alicuius regulantis. Unde et ibidem subditur, *qui ostendunt opus legis scriptum in cordibus suis.*

AD SECUNDUM dicendum quod persona privata non potest inducere efficaciter ad virtutem. Potest enim solum monere, sed si sua monitio non recipiatur, non habet vim coactivam; quam debet habere lex, ad hoc quod efficaciter inducat ad virtutem, ut philosophus dicit, in X Ethic. Hanc autem virtutem coactivam habet multitudo vel persona publica, ad quam pertinet poenas infligere, ut infra dicetur. Et ideo solius eius est leges facere.

AD TERTIUM dicendum quod, sicut homo est pars domus, ita domus est pars civitatis, civitas autem est communitas perfecta, ut dicitur in I Politic. Et ideo sicut bonum unius hominis non est ultimus finis, sed ordinatur ad commune bonum; ita etiam et bonum unius domus ordinatur ad bonum unius civitatis, quae est communitas perfecta. Unde ille qui gubernat aliquam familiam, potest quidem facere aliqua praecepta vel statuta; non tamen quae proprie habeant rationem legis.

receives from one who rules him. Hence the same text goes on: *Who show the work of the law written in their hearts.*

REPLY OBJ. 2: A private person cannot lead another to virtue efficaciously: for he can only advise, and if his advice be not taken, it has no coercive power, such as the law should have, in order to prove an efficacious inducement to virtue, as the Philosopher says (*Ethic.* x, 9). But this coercive power is vested in the whole people or in some public personage, to whom it belongs to inflict penalties, as we shall state further on (Q92, A2, ad 3; SS, Q64, A3). Wherefore the framing of laws belongs to him alone.

REPLY OBJ. 3: As one man is a part of the household, so a household is a part of the state: and the state is a perfect community, according to *Polit.* i, 1. And therefore, as the good of one man is not the last end, but is ordained to the common good; so too the good of one household is ordained to the good of a single state, which is a perfect community. Consequently he that governs a family, can indeed make certain commands or ordinances, but not such as to have properly the force of law.

Article 4

Whether Promulgation Is Essential to a Law?

AD QUARTUM SIC PROCEDITUR. Videtur quod promulgatio non sit de ratione legis. Lex enim naturalis maxime habet rationem legis. Sed lex naturalis non indiget promulgatione. Ergo non est de ratione legis quod promulgetur.

PRAETEREA, ad legem pertinet proprie obligare ad aliquid faciendum vel non faciendum. Sed non solum obligantur ad implendam legem illi coram quibus promulgatur lex, sed etiam alii. Ergo promulgatio non est de ratione legis.

PRAETEREA, obligatio legis extenditur etiam in futurum, quia leges futuris negotiis necessitatem imponunt, ut iura dicunt. Sed promulgatio fit ad praesentes. Ergo promulgatio non est de necessitate legis.

SED CONTRA est quod dicitur in decretis, IV dist., quod *leges instituuntur cum promulgantur.*

RESPONDEO dicendum quod, sicut dictum est, lex imponitur aliis per modum regulae et mensurae. Regula autem et mensura imponitur per hoc quod applicatur his quae regulantur et mensurantur. Unde ad hoc quod lex virtutem obligandi obtineat, quod est proprium legis, oportet quod applicetur hominibus qui secundum eam regulari debent. Talis autem applicatio fit per hoc quod in notitiam eorum deducitur ex ipsa promulgatione. Unde promulgatio necessaria est ad hoc quod lex habeat suam virtutem.

OBJECTION 1: It would seem that promulgation is not essential to a law. For the natural law above all has the character of law. But the natural law needs no promulgation. Therefore it is not essential to a law that it be promulgated.

OBJ. 2: Further, it belongs properly to a law to bind one to do or not to do something. But the obligation of fulfilling a law touches not only those in whose presence it is promulgated, but also others. Therefore promulgation is not essential to a law.

OBJ. 3: Further, the binding force of a law extends even to the future, since *laws are binding in matters of the future*, as the jurists say (Cod. 1, tit. *De lege et constit.* leg. vii). But promulgation concerns those who are present. Therefore it is not essential to a law.

ON THE CONTRARY, It is laid down in the *Decretals*, dist. 4, that *laws are established when they are promulgated.*

I ANSWER THAT, As stated above (A1), a law is imposed on others by way of a rule and measure. Now a rule or measure is imposed by being applied to those who are to be ruled and measured by it. Wherefore, in order that a law obtain the binding force which is proper to a law, it must needs be applied to the men who have to be ruled by it. Such application is made by its being notified to them by promulgation. Wherefore promulgation is necessary for the law to obtain its force.

Et sic ex quatuor praedictis potest colligi definitio legis, quae nihil est aliud quam quaedam rationis ordinatio ad bonum commune, ab eo qui curam communitatis habet, promulgata.

Ad primum ergo dicendum quod promulgatio legis naturae est ex hoc ipso quod Deus eam mentibus hominum inseruit naturaliter cognoscendam.

Ad secundum dicendum quod illi coram quibus lex non promulgatur, obligantur ad legem servandam, inquantum in eorum notitiam devenit per alios, vel devenire potest, promulgatione facta.

Ad tertium dicendum quod promulgatio praesens in futurum extenditur per firmitatem scripturae, quae quodammodo semper eam promulgat. Unde Isidorus dicit, in II Etymol., quod *lex a legendo vocata est, quia scripta est.*

Thus from the four preceding articles, the definition of law may be gathered; and it is nothing else than an ordinance of reason for the common good, made by him who has care of the community, and promulgated.

Reply Obj. 1: The natural law is promulgated by the very fact that God instilled it into man's mind so as to be known by him naturally.

Reply Obj. 2: Those who are not present when a law is promulgated, are bound to observe the law, insofar as it is notified or can be notified to them by others, after it has been promulgated.

Reply Obj. 3: The promulgation that takes place now, extends to future time by reason of the durability of written characters, by which means it is continually promulgated. Hence Isidore says (*Etym.* v, 3; ii, 10) that *lex is derived from legere because it is written.*

QUESTION 91

OF THE VARIOUS KINDS OF LAW

Deinde considerandum est de diversitate legum. Et circa hoc quaeruntur sex.

Primo, utrum sit aliqua lex aeterna.

Secundo, utrum sit aliqua lex naturalis.

Tertio, utrum sit aliqua lex humana.

Quarto, utrum sit aliqua lex divina.

Quinto, utrum sit una tantum, vel plures.

Sexto, utrum sit aliqua lex peccati.

We must now consider the various kinds of law: under which head there are six points of inquiry:

(1) Whether there is an eternal law?

(2) Whether there is a natural law?

(3) Whether there is a human law?

(4) Whether there is a Divine law?

(5) Whether there is one Divine law, or several?

(6) Whether there is a law of sin?

Article 1

Whether There Is an Eternal Law?

AD PRIMUM SIC PROCEDITUR. Videtur quod non sit aliqua lex aeterna. Omnis enim lex aliquibus imponitur. Sed non fuit ab aeterno aliquis cui lex posset imponi, solus enim Deus fuit ab aeterno. Ergo nulla lex est aeterna.

PRAETEREA, promulgatio est de ratione legis. Sed promulgatio non potuit esse ab aeterno, quia non erat ab aeterno cui promulgaretur. Ergo nulla lex potest esse aeterna.

PRAETEREA, lex importat ordinem ad finem. Sed nihil est aeternum quod ordinetur ad finem, solus enim ultimus finis est aeternus. Ergo nulla lex est aeterna.

SED CONTRA est quod Augustinus dicit, in I de Lib. Arb., *lex quae summa ratio nominatur, non potest cuipiam intelligenti non incommutabilis aeternaque videri.*

RESPONDEO dicendum quod, sicut supra dictum est, nihil est aliud lex quam quoddam dictamen practicae rationis in principe qui gubernat aliquam communitatem perfectam. Manifestum est autem, supposito quod mundus divina providentia regatur, ut in primo habitum est, quod tota communitas universi gubernatur ratione divina. Et ideo ipsa ratio gubernationis rerum in Deo sicut in principe universitatis existens, legis habet rationem. Et quia divina ratio nihil concipit ex tempore, sed habet aeternum conceptum, ut dicitur Prov. VIII; inde est quod huiusmodi legem oportet dicere aeternam.

AD PRIMUM ergo dicendum quod ea quae in seipsis non sunt, apud Deum existunt, inquantum sunt ab ipso praecognita et praeordinata; secundum illud Rom. IV, *qui vocat ea quae non sunt, tanquam ea quae sunt.* Sic igitur aeternus divinae legis conceptus habet rationem legis aeternae, secundum quod a Deo ordinatur ad gubernationem rerum ab ipso praecognitarum.

OBJECTION 1: It would seem that there is no eternal law. Because every law is imposed on someone. But there was not someone from eternity on whom a law could be imposed: since God alone was from eternity. Therefore no law is eternal.

OBJ. 2: Further, promulgation is essential to law. But promulgation could not be from eternity: because there was no one to whom it could be promulgated from eternity. Therefore no law can be eternal.

OBJ. 3: Further, a law implies order to an end. But nothing is eternal that is ordained to an end: for the last end alone is eternal. Therefore no law is eternal.

ON THE CONTRARY, Augustine says (*De Lib. Arb.* i, 6): *That Law which is the Supreme Reason cannot be understood to be otherwise than unchangeable and eternal.*

I ANSWER THAT, As stated above (Q90, A1, ad 2; AA3,4), a law is nothing else but a dictate of practical reason emanating from the ruler who governs a perfect community. Now it is evident, granted that the world is ruled by Divine Providence, as was stated in the FP, Q22, AA1,2, that the whole community of the universe is governed by Divine Reason. Wherefore the very Idea of the government of things in God the Ruler of the universe, has the nature of a law. And since the Divine Reason conceives nothing from time, but has an eternal concept, according to Prov. 8:23, therefore it is that this kind of law must be called eternal.

REPLY OBJ. 1: Those things that are not in themselves, exist with God, inasmuch as they are foreknown and preordained by Him, according to Rm. 4:17: *Who calls those things that are not, as those that are.* Accordingly the eternal concept of the Divine law bears the character of an eternal law, insofar as it is ordained by God to the government of things foreknown by Him.

AD SECUNDUM dicendum quod promulgatio fit et verbo et scripto; et utroque modo lex aeterna habet promulgationem ex parte Dei promulgantis, quia et verbum divinum est aeternum, et scriptura libri vitae est aeterna. Sed ex parte creaturae audientis aut inspicientis, non potest esse promulgatio aeterna.

AD TERTIUM dicendum quod lex importat ordinem ad finem active, inquantum scilicet per eam ordinantur aliqua in finem, non autem passive, idest quod ipsa lex ordinetur ad finem, nisi per accidens in gubernante cuius finis est extra ipsum, ad quem etiam necesse est ut lex eius ordinetur. Sed finis divinae gubernationis est ipse Deus, nec eius lex est aliud ab ipso. Unde lex aeterna non ordinatur in alium finem.

REPLY OBJ. 2: Promulgation is made by word of mouth or in writing; and in both ways the eternal law is promulgated: because both the Divine Word and the writing of the Book of Life are eternal. But the promulgation cannot be from eternity on the part of the creature that hears or reads.

REPLY OBJ. 3: The law implies order to the end actively, insofar as it directs certain things to the end; but not passively—that is to say, the law itself is not ordained to the end—except accidentally, in a governor whose end is extrinsic to him, and to which end his law must needs be ordained. But the end of the Divine government is God Himself, and His law is not distinct from Himself. Wherefore the eternal law is not ordained to another end.

Article 2

Whether There Is in Us a Natural Law?

AD SECUNDUM SIC PROCEDITUR. Videtur quod non sit in nobis aliqua lex naturalis. Sufficienter enim homo gubernatur per legem aeternam, dicit enim Augustinus, in I de Lib. Arb., quod *lex aeterna est qua iustum est ut omnia sint ordinatissima*. Sed natura non abundat in superfluis, sicut nec deficit in necessariis. Ergo non est aliqua lex homini naturalis.

PRAETEREA, per legem ordinatur homo in suis actibus ad finem, ut supra habitum est. Sed ordinatio humanorum actuum ad finem non est per naturam, sicut accidit in creaturis irrationabilibus, quae solo appetitu naturali agunt propter finem, sed agit homo propter finem per rationem et voluntatem. Ergo non est aliqua lex homini naturalis.

PRAETEREA, quanto aliquis est liberior, tanto minus est sub lege. Sed homo est liberior omnibus animalibus, propter liberum arbitrium, quod prae aliis animalibus habet. Cum igitur alia animalia non subdantur legi naturali, nec homo alicui legi naturali subditur.

SED CONTRA est quod, Rom. II, super illud, *cum gentes, quae legem non habent, naturaliter ea quae legis sunt faciunt*, dicit Glossa, *etsi non habent legem scriptam, habent tamen legem naturalem, qua quilibet intelligit et sibi conscius est quid sit bonum et quid malum.*

RESPONDEO dicendum quod, sicut supra dictum est, lex, cum sit regula et mensura, dupliciter potest esse in aliquo, uno modo, sicut in regulante et mensurante; alio modo, sicut in regulato et mensurato, quia inquantum participat aliquid de regula vel mensura, sic regulatur vel mensuratur. Unde cum omnia quae divinae providentiae subduntur, a lege aeterna regulentur et mensurentur, ut ex dictis patet; manifestum est quod omnia participant aliqualiter legem aeternam, inquantum scilicet ex

OBJECTION 1: It would seem that there is no natural law in us. Because man is governed sufficiently by the eternal law: for Augustine says (*De Lib. Arb.* i) that *the eternal law is that by which it is right that all things should be most orderly*. But nature does not abound in superfluities as neither does she fail in necessaries. Therefore no law is natural to man.

OBJ. 2: Further, by the law man is directed, in his acts, to the end, as stated above (Q90, A2). But the directing of human acts to their end is not a function of nature, as is the case in irrational creatures, which act for an end solely by their natural appetite; whereas man acts for an end by his reason and will. Therefore no law is natural to man.

OBJ. 3: Further, the more a man is free, the less is he under the law. But man is freer than all the animals, on account of his free-will, with which he is endowed above all other animals. Since therefore other animals are not subject to a natural law, neither is man subject to a natural law.

ON THE CONTRARY, A gloss on Rm. 2:14: *When the Gentiles, who have not the law, do by nature those things that are of the law*, comments as follows: *Although they have no written law, yet they have the natural law, whereby each one knows, and is conscious of, what is good and what is evil.*

I ANSWER THAT, As stated above (Q90, A1, ad 1), law, being a rule and measure, can be in a person in two ways: in one way, as in him that rules and measures; in another way, as in that which is ruled and measured, since a thing is ruled and measured, insofar as it partakes of the rule or measure. Wherefore, since all things subject to Divine providence are ruled and measured by the eternal law, as was stated above (A1); it is evident that all things partake somewhat of the eternal law, insofar as, namely, from its being imprinted

impressione eius habent inclinationes in proprios actus et fines. Inter cetera autem rationalis creatura excellentiori quodam modo divinae providentiae subiacet, inquantum et ipsa fit providentiae particeps, sibi ipsi et aliis providens. Unde et in ipsa participatur ratio aeterna, per quam habet naturalem inclinationem ad debitum actum et finem. Et talis participatio legis aeternae in rationali creatura lex naturalis dicitur. Unde cum Psalmista dixisset, sacrificate sacrificium iustitiae, quasi quibusdam quaerentibus quae sunt iustitiae opera, subiungit, multi dicunt, quis ostendit nobis bona? Cui quaestioni respondens, dicit, signatum est super nos lumen vultus tui, domine, quasi lumen rationis naturalis, quo discernimus quid sit bonum et malum, quod pertinet ad naturalem legem, nihil aliud sit quam impressio divini luminis in nobis. Unde patet quod lex naturalis nihil aliud est quam participatio legis aeternae in rationali creatura.

AD PRIMUM ergo dicendum quod ratio illa procederet, si lex naturalis esset aliquid diversum a lege aeterna. Non autem est nisi quaedam participatio eius, ut dictum est.

AD SECUNDUM dicendum quod omnis operatio, rationis et voluntatis derivatur in nobis ab eo quod est secundum naturam, ut supra habitum est, nam omnis ratiocinatio derivatur a principiis naturaliter notis, et omnis appetitus eorum quae sunt ad finem, derivatur a naturali appetitu ultimi finis. Et sic etiam oportet quod prima directio actuum nostrorum ad finem, fiat per legem naturalem.

AD TERTIUM dicendum quod etiam animalia irrationalia participant rationem aeternam suo modo, sicut et rationalis creatura. Sed quia rationalis creatura participat eam intellectualiter et rationaliter, ideo participatio legis aeternae in creatura rationali proprie lex vocatur, nam lex est aliquid rationis, ut supra dictum est. In creatura autem irrationali non participatur rationaliter, unde non potest dici lex nisi per similitudinem.

on them, they derive their respective inclinations to their proper acts and ends. Now among all others, the rational creature is subject to Divine providence in the most excellent way, insofar as it partakes of a share of providence, by being provident both for itself and for others. Wherefore it has a share of the Eternal Reason, whereby it has a natural inclination to its proper act and end: and this participation of the eternal law in the rational creature is called the natural law. Hence the Psalmist after saying (Ps 4:6): *Offer up the sacrifice of justice*, as though someone asked what the works of justice are, adds: *Many say, Who showeth us good things?* in answer to which question he says: *The light of Thy countenance, O Lord, is signed upon us*: thus implying that the light of natural reason, whereby we discern what is good and what is evil, which is the function of the natural law, is nothing else than an imprint on us of the Divine light. It is therefore evident that the natural law is nothing else than the rational creature's participation of the eternal law.

REPLY OBJ. 1: This argument would hold, if the natural law were something different from the eternal law: whereas it is nothing but a participation thereof, as stated above.

REPLY OBJ. 2: Every act of reason and will in us is based on that which is according to nature, as stated above (Q10, A1): for every act of reasoning is based on principles that are known naturally, and every act of appetite in respect of the means is derived from the natural appetite in respect of the last end. Accordingly the first direction of our acts to their end must needs be in virtue of the natural law.

REPLY OBJ. 3: Even irrational animals partake in their own way of the Eternal Reason, just as the rational creature does. But because the rational creature partakes thereof in an intellectual and rational manner, therefore the participation of the eternal law in the rational creature is properly called a law, since a law is something pertaining to reason, as stated above (Q90, A1). Irrational creatures, however, do not partake thereof in a rational manner, wherefore there is no participation of the eternal law in them, except by way of similitude.

Article 3

Whether There Is a Human Law?

AD TERTIUM SIC PROCEDITUR. Videtur quod non sit aliqua lex humana. Lex enim naturalis est participatio legis aeternae, ut dictum est. Sed per legem aeternam omnia sunt ordinatissima, ut Augustinus dicit, in I de Lib. Arb. Ergo lex naturalis sufficit ad omnia humana ordinanda. Non est ergo necessarium quod sit aliqua lex humana.

OBJECTION 1: It would seem that there is not a human law. For the natural law is a participation of the eternal law, as stated above (A2). Now through the eternal law *all things are most orderly*, as Augustine states (*De Lib. Arb.* i, 6). Therefore the natural law suffices for the ordering of all human affairs. Consequently there is no need for a human law.

PRAETEREA, lex habet rationem mensurae, ut dictum est. Sed ratio humana non est mensura rerum, sed potius e converso, ut in X Metaphys. dicitur. Ergo ex ratione humana nulla lex procedere potest.

PRAETEREA, mensura debet esse certissima, ut dicitur in X Metaphys. Sed dictamen humanae rationis de rebus gerendis est incertum; secundum illud Sap. IX, *cogitationes mortalium timidae, et incertae providentiae nostrae.* Ergo ex ratione humana nulla lex procedere potest.

SED CONTRA est quod Augustinus, in I de Lib. Arb., ponit duas leges, unam aeternam et aliam temporalem, quam dicit esse humanam.

RESPONDEO dicendum quod, sicut supra dictum est, lex est quoddam dictamen practicae rationis. Similis autem processus esse invenitur rationis practicae et speculativae, utraque enim ex quibusdam principiis ad quasdam conclusiones procedit, ut superius habitum est. Secundum hoc ergo dicendum est quod, sicut in ratione speculativa ex principiis indemonstrabilibus naturaliter cognitis producuntur conclusiones diversarum scientiarum, quarum cognitio non est nobis naturaliter indita, sed per industriam rationis inventa; ita etiam ex praeceptis legis naturalis, quasi ex quibusdam principiis communibus et indemonstrabilibus, necesse est quod ratio humana procedat ad aliqua magis particulariter disponenda. Et istae particulares dispositiones adinventae secundum rationem humanam, dicuntur leges humanae, servatis aliis conditionibus quae pertinent ad rationem legis, ut supra dictum est. Unde et Tullius dicit, in sua Rhetor., quod *initium iuris est a natura profectum; deinde quaedam in consuetudinem ex utilitate rationis venerunt; postea res et a natura profectas et a consuetudine probatas legum metus et religio sanxit.*

AD PRIMUM ergo dicendum quod ratio humana non potest participare ad plenum dictamen rationis divinae, sed suo modo et imperfecte. Et ideo sicut ex parte rationis speculativae, per naturalem participationem divinae sapientiae, inest nobis cognitio quorundam communium principiorum, non autem cuiuslibet veritatis propria cognitio, sicut in divina sapientia continetur; ita etiam ex parte rationis practicae naturaliter homo participat legem aeternam secundum quaedam communia principia, non autem secundum particulares directiones singulorum, quae tamen in aeterna lege continentur. Et ideo necesse est ulterius quod ratio humana procedat ad particulares quasdam legum sanctiones.

AD SECUNDUM dicendum quod ratio humana secundum se non est regula rerum, sed principia ei naturaliter indita, sunt quaedam regulae generales et mensurae omnium eorum quae sunt per hominem agenda, quorum ratio naturalis est regula et mensura, licet non sit mensura eorum quae sunt a natura.

OBJ. 2: Further, a law bears the character of a measure, as stated above (Q90, A1). But human reason is not a measure of things, but vice versa, as stated in *Metaph.* x, text. 5. Therefore no law can emanate from human reason.

OBJ. 3: Further, a measure should be most certain, as stated in *Metaph.* x, text. 3. But the dictates of human reason in matters of conduct are uncertain, according to Wis. 9:14: *The thoughts of mortal men are fearful, and our counsels uncertain.* Therefore no law can emanate from human reason.

ON THE CONTRARY, Augustine (*De Lib. Arb.* i, 6) distinguishes two kinds of law, the one eternal, the other temporal, which he calls human.

I ANSWER THAT, As stated above (Q90, A1, ad 2), a law is a dictate of the practical reason. Now it is to be observed that the same procedure takes place in the practical and in the speculative reason: for each proceeds from principles to conclusions, as stated above (*De Lib. Arb.* i, 6). Accordingly we conclude that just as, in the speculative reason, from naturally known indemonstrable principles, we draw the conclusions of the various sciences, the knowledge of which is not imparted to us by nature, but acquired by the efforts of reason, so too it is from the precepts of the natural law, as from general and indemonstrable principles, that the human reason needs to proceed to the more particular determination of certain matters. These particular determinations, devised by human reason, are called human laws, provided the other essential conditions of law be observed, as stated above (Q90, AA2,3,4). Wherefore Tully says in his Rhetoric (*De Invent. Rhet.* ii) that *justice has its source in nature; thence certain things came into custom by reason of their utility; afterwards these things which emanated from nature and were approved by custom, were sanctioned by fear and reverence for the law.*

REPLY OBJ. 1: The human reason cannot have a full participation of the dictate of the Divine Reason, but according to its own mode, and imperfectly. Consequently, as on the part of the speculative reason, by a natural participation of Divine Wisdom, there is in us the knowledge of certain general principles, but not proper knowledge of each single truth, such as that contained in the Divine Wisdom; so too, on the part of the practical reason, man has a natural participation of the eternal law, according to certain general principles, but not as regards the particular determinations of individual cases, which are, however, contained in the eternal law. Hence the need for human reason to proceed further to sanction them by law.

REPLY OBJ. 2: Human reason is not, of itself, the rule of things: but the principles impressed on it by nature, are general rules and measures of all things relating to human conduct, whereof the natural reason is the rule and measure, although it is not the measure of things that are from nature.

AD TERTIUM dicendum quod ratio practica est circa operabilia, quae sunt singularia et contingentia, non autem circa necessaria, sicut ratio speculativa. Et ideo leges humanae non possunt illam infallibilitatem habere quam habent conclusiones demonstrativae scientiarum. Nec oportet quod omnis mensura sit omni modo infallibilis et certa, sed secundum quod est possibile in genere suo.

REPLY OBJ. 3: The practical reason is concerned with practical matters, which are singular and contingent: but not with necessary things, with which the speculative reason is concerned. Wherefore human laws cannot have that inerrancy that belongs to the demonstrated conclusions of sciences. Nor is it necessary for every measure to be altogether unerring and certain, but according as it is possible in its own particular genus.

Article 4

Whether There Was Any Need for a Divine Law?

AD QUARTUM SIC PROCEDITUR. Videtur quod non fuerit necessarium esse aliquam legem divinam. Quia, ut dictum est, lex naturalis est quaedam participatio legis aeternae in nobis. Sed lex aeterna est lex divina, ut dictum est. Ergo non oportet quod praeter legem naturalem, et leges humanas ab ea derivatas, sit aliqua alia lex divina.

PRAETEREA, Eccli. XV dicitur quod *Deus dimisit hominem in manu consilii sui.* Consilium autem est actus rationis, ut supra habitum est. Ergo homo dimissus est gubernationi suae rationis. Sed dictamen rationis humanae est lex humana, ut dictum est. Ergo non oportet quod homo alia lege divina gubernetur.

PRAETEREA, natura humana est sufficientior irrationalibus creaturis. Sed irrationales creaturae non habent aliquam legem divinam praeter inclinationem naturalem eis inditam. Ergo multo minus creatura rationalis debet habere aliquam legem divinam praeter naturalem legem.

SED CONTRA est quod David expetit legem a Deo sibi poni, dicens, *legem pone mihi, domine, in via iustificationum tuarum.*

RESPONDEO dicendum quod praeter legem naturalem et legem humanam, necessarium fuit ad directionem humanae vitae habere legem divinam. Et hoc propter quatuor rationes. Primo quidem, quia per legem dirigitur homo ad actus proprios in ordine ad ultimum finem. Et si quidem homo ordinaretur tantum ad finem qui non excederet proportionem naturalis facultatis hominis, non oporteret quod homo haberet aliquid directivum ex parte rationis, supra legem naturalem et legem humanitus positam, quae ab ea derivatur. Sed quia homo ordinatur ad finem beatitudinis aeternae, quae excedit proportionem naturalis facultatis humanae, ut supra habitum est; ideo necessarium fuit ut supra legem naturalem et humanam, dirigeretur etiam ad suum finem lege divinitus data.

Secundo, quia propter incertitudinem humani iudicii, praecipue de rebus contingentibus et particularibus,

OBJECTION 1: It would seem that there was no need for a Divine law. Because, as stated above (A2), the natural law is a participation in us of the eternal law. But the eternal law is a Divine law, as stated above (A1). Therefore there was no need for a Divine law in addition to the natural law, and human laws derived therefrom.

OBJ. 2: Further, it is written (Sir 15:14) that *God left man in the hand of his own counsel.* Now counsel is an act of reason, as stated above (Q14, A1). Therefore man was left to the direction of his reason. But a dictate of human reason is a human law as stated above (A3). Therefore there is no need for man to be governed also by a Divine law.

OBJ. 3: Further, human nature is more self-sufficing than irrational creatures. But irrational creatures have no Divine law besides the natural inclination impressed on them. Much less, therefore, should the rational creature have a Divine law in addition to the natural law.

ON THE CONTRARY, David prayed God to set His law before him, saying (Ps 118:33): *Set before me for a law the way of Thy justifications, O Lord.*

I ANSWER THAT, Besides the natural and the human law it was necessary for the directing of human conduct to have a Divine law. And this for four reasons. First, because it is by law that man is directed how to perform his proper acts in view of his last end. And indeed if man were ordained to no other end than that which is proportionate to his natural faculty, there would be no need for man to have any further direction on the part of his reason, besides the natural law and human law which is derived from it. But since man is ordained to an end of eternal happiness which is inproportionate to man's natural faculty, as stated above (Q5, A5), therefore it was necessary that, besides the natural and the human law, man should be directed to his end by a law given by God.

Second, because, on account of the uncertainty of human judgment, especially on contingent and particular

contingit de actibus humanis diversorum esse diversa iudicia, ex quibus etiam diversae et contrariae leges procedunt. Ut ergo homo absque omni dubitatione scire possit quid ei sit agendum et quid vitandum, necessarium fuit ut in actibus propriis dirigeretur per legem divinitus datam, de qua constat quod non potest errare.

Tertio, quia de his potest homo legem ferre, de quibus potest iudicare. Iudicium autem hominis esse non potest de interioribus motibus, qui latent, sed solum de exterioribus actibus, qui apparent. Et tamen ad perfectionem virtutis requiritur quod in utrisque actibus homo rectus existat. Et ideo lex humana non potuit cohibere et ordinare sufficienter interiores actus, sed necessarium fuit quod ad hoc superveniret lex divina.

Quarto quia, sicut Augustinus dicit, in I de Lib. Arb., lex humana non potest omnia quae male fiunt, punire vel prohibere, quia dum auferre vellet omnia mala, sequeretur quod etiam multa bona tollerentur, et impediretur utilitas boni communis, quod est necessarium ad conversationem humanam. Ut ergo nullum malum improhibitum et impunitum remaneat, necessarium fuit supervenire legem divinam, per quam omnia peccata prohibentur.

Et istae quatuor causae tanguntur in Psalmo XVIII, ubi dicitur, lex domini immaculata, idest nullam peccati turpitudinem permittens; convertens animas, quia non solum exteriores actus, sed etiam interiores dirigit; testimonium domini fidele, propter certitudinem veritatis et rectitudinis; sapientiam praestans parvulis, inquantum ordinat hominem ad supernaturalem finem et divinum.

Ad primum ergo dicendum quod per naturalem legem participatur lex aeterna secundum proportionem capacitatis humanae naturae. Sed oportet ut altiori modo dirigatur homo in ultimum finem supernaturalem. Et ideo superadditur lex divinitus data, per quam lex aeterna participatur altiori modo.

Ad secundum dicendum quod consilium est inquisitio quaedam, unde oportet quod procedat ex aliquibus principiis. Nec sufficit quod procedat ex principiis naturaliter inditis, quae sunt praecepta legis naturae, propter praedicta, sed oportet quod superaddantur quaedam alia principia, scilicet praecepta legis divinae.

Ad tertium dicendum quod creaturae irrationales non ordinantur ad altiorem finem quam sit finis qui est proportionatus naturali virtuti ipsarum. Et ideo non est similis ratio.

matters, different people form different judgments on human acts; whence also different and contrary laws result. In order, therefore, that man may know without any doubt what he ought to do and what he ought to avoid, it was necessary for man to be directed in his proper acts by a law given by God, for it is certain that such a law cannot err.

Third, because man can make laws in those matters of which he is competent to judge. But man is not competent to judge of interior movements, that are hidden, but only of exterior acts which appear: and yet for the perfection of virtue it is necessary for man to conduct himself aright in both kinds of acts. Consequently human law could not sufficiently curb and direct interior acts; and it was necessary for this purpose that a Divine law should supervene.

Fourth, because, as Augustine says (*De Lib. Arb.* i, 5,6), human law cannot punish or forbid all evil deeds: since while aiming at doing away with all evils, it would do away with many good things, and would hinder the utility of the common good, which is necessary for human intercourse. In order, therefore, that no evil might remain unforbidden and unpunished, it was necessary for the Divine law to supervene, whereby all sins are forbidden.

And these four causes are touched upon in Ps. 118:8, where it is said: *The law of the Lord is unspotted*, i.e., allowing no foulness of sin; *converting souls*, because it directs not only exterior, but also interior acts; *the testimony of the Lord is faithful*, because of the certainty of what is true and right; *giving wisdom to little ones*, by directing man to an end supernatural and Divine.

Reply Obj. 1: By the natural law the eternal law is participated proportionately to the capacity of human nature. But to his supernatural end man needs to be directed in a yet higher way. Hence the additional law given by God, whereby man shares more perfectly in the eternal law.

Reply Obj. 2: Counsel is a kind of inquiry: hence it must proceed from some principles. Nor is it enough for it to proceed from principles imparted by nature, which are the precepts of the natural law, for the reasons given above: but there is need for certain additional principles, namely, the precepts of the Divine law.

Reply Obj. 3: Irrational creatures are not ordained to an end higher than that which is proportionate to their natural powers: consequently the comparison fails.

Article 5

Whether There Is But One Divine Law?

AD QUINTUM SIC PROCEDITUR. Videtur quod lex divina sit una tantum. Unius enim regis in uno regno est una lex. Sed totum humanum genus comparatur ad Deum sicut ad unum regem; secundum illud Psalmi XLVI, *rex omnis terrae Deus.* Ergo est una tantum lex divina.

PRAETEREA, omnis lex ordinatur ad finem quem legislator intendit in eis quibus legem fert. Sed unum et idem est quod Deus intendit in omnibus hominibus; secundum illud I ad Tim. II, *vult omnes homines salvos fieri, et ad agnitionem veritatis venire.* Ergo una tantum est lex divina.

PRAETEREA, lex divina propinquior esse videtur legi aeternae, quae est una, quam lex naturalis, quanto altior est revelatio gratiae quam cognitio naturae. Sed lex naturalis est una omnium hominum. Ergo multo magis lex divina.

SED CONTRA est quod apostolus dicit, ad Heb. VII, *translato sacerdotio, necesse est ut legis translatio fiat.* Sed sacerdotium est duplex, ut ibidem dicitur, scilicet sacerdotium leviticum, et sacerdotium Christi. Ergo etiam duplex est lex divina, scilicet lex vetus, et lex nova.

RESPONDEO dicendum quod, sicut in primo dictum est, distinctio est causa numeri. Dupliciter autem inveniuntur aliqua distingui. Uno modo, sicut ea quae sunt omnino specie diversa, ut equus et bos. Alio modo, sicut perfectum et imperfectum in eadem specie, sicut puer et vir. Et hoc modo lex divina distinguitur in legem veterem et legem novam. Unde apostolus, ad Gal. III, comparat statum veteris legis statui puerili existenti sub paedagogo, statum autem novae legis comparat statui viri perfecti, qui iam non est sub paedagogo.

Attenditur autem perfectio et imperfectio utriusque legis secundum tria quae ad legem pertinent, ut supra dictum est. Primo enim ad legem pertinet ut ordinetur ad bonum commune sicut ad finem, ut supra dictum est. Quod quidem potest esse duplex. Scilicet bonum sensibile et terrenum, et ad tale bonum ordinabat directe lex vetus; unde statim, Exodi III, in principio legis, invitatur populus ad regnum terrenum Chananaeorum. Et iterum bonum intelligibile et caeleste, et ad hoc ordinat lex nova. Unde statim Christus ad regnum caelorum in suae praedicationis principio invitavit, dicens, *poenitentiam agite, appropinquavit enim regnum caelorum,* Matth. IV. Et ideo Augustinus dicit, in IV contra Faustum, quod *temporalium rerum promissiones testamento veteri continentur, et ideo vetus appellatur, sed aeternae vitae promissio ad novum pertinet testamentum.*

OBJECTION 1: It would seem that there is but one Divine law. Because, where there is one king in one kingdom there is but one law. Now the whole of mankind is compared to God as to one king, according to Ps. 46:8: *God is the King of all the earth.* Therefore there is but one Divine law.

OBJ. 2: Further, every law is directed to the end which the lawgiver intends for those for whom he makes the law. But God intends one and the same thing for all men; since according to 1 Tim. 2:4: *He will have all men to be saved, and to come to the knowledge of the truth.* Therefore there is but one Divine law.

OBJ. 3: Further, the Divine law seems to be more akin to the eternal law, which is one, than the natural law, according as the revelation of grace is of a higher order than natural knowledge. Therefore much more is the Divine law but one.

ON THE CONTRARY, The Apostle says (Heb 7:12): *The priesthood being changed, it is necessary that a change also be made of the law.* But the priesthood is twofold, as stated in the same passage, viz., the levitical priesthood, and the priesthood of Christ. Therefore the Divine law is twofold, namely the Old Law and the New Law.

I ANSWER THAT, As stated in the FP, Q30, A3, distinction is the cause of number. Now things may be distinguished in two ways. First, as those things that are altogether specifically different, e.g., a horse and an ox. Second, as perfect and imperfect in the same species, e.g., a boy and a man: and in this way the Divine law is divided into Old and New. Hence the Apostle (Gal 3:24,25) compares the state of man under the Old Law to that of a child *under a pedagogue*; but the state under the New Law, to that of a full grown man, who is *no longer under a pedagogue.*

Now the perfection and imperfection of these two laws is to be taken in connection with the three conditions pertaining to law, as stated above. For, in the first place, it belongs to law to be directed to the common good as to its end, as stated above (Q90, A2). This good may be twofold. It may be a sensible and earthly good; and to this, man was directly ordained by the Old Law: wherefore, at the very outset of the law, the people were invited to the earthly kingdom of the Canaanites (Exod 3:8,17). Again it may be an intelligible and heavenly good: and to this, man is ordained by the New Law. Wherefore, at the very beginning of His preaching, Christ invited men to the kingdom of heaven, saying (Matt 4:17): *Do penance, for the kingdom of heaven is at hand.* Hence Augustine says (*Contra Faust.* iv) that *promises of temporal goods are contained in the Old Testament, for which reason it is called old; but the promise of eternal life belongs to the New Testament.*

Secundo ad legem pertinet dirigere humanos actus secundum ordinem iustitiae. In quo etiam superabundat lex nova legi veteri, interiores actus animi ordinando; secundum illud Matth. V, *nisi abundaverit iustitia vestra plus quam Scribarum et Pharisaeorum, non intrabitis in regnum caelorum.* Et ideo dicitur quod *lex vetus cohibet manum, lex nova animum.*

Tertio ad legem pertinet inducere homines ad observantias mandatorum. Et hoc quidem lex vetus faciebat timore poenarum, lex autem nova facit hoc per amorem, qui in cordibus nostris infunditur per gratiam Christi, quae in lege nova confertur, sed in lege veteri figurabatur. Et ideo dicit Augustinus, contra Adimantum Manichaei discipulum, *quod brevis differentia est legis et Evangelii, timor et amor.*

AD PRIMUM ergo dicendum quod, sicut paterfamilias in domo alia mandata proponit pueris et adultis, ita etiam unus rex Deus, in uno suo regno, aliam legem dedit hominibus adhuc imperfectis existentibus; et aliam perfectiorem iam manuductis per priorem legem ad maiorem capacitatem divinorum.

AD SECUNDUM dicendum quod salus hominum non poterat esse nisi per Christum; secundum illud Act. IV, *non est aliud nomen datum hominibus, in quo oporteat nos salvos fieri.* Et ideo lex perfecte ad salutem omnes inducens, dari non potuit nisi post Christi adventum. Antea vero dari oportuit populo ex quo Christus erat nasciturus, legem praeparatoriam ad Christi susceptionem, in qua quaedam rudimenta salutaris iustitiae continerentur.

AD TERTIUM dicendum quod lex naturalis dirigit hominem secundum quaedam praecepta communia, in quibus conveniunt tam perfecti quam imperfecti, et ideo est una omnium. Sed lex divina dirigit hominem etiam in quibusdam particularibus, ad quae non similiter se habent perfecti et imperfecti. Et ideo oportuit legem divinam esse duplicem, sicut iam dictum est.

Second, it belongs to the law to direct human acts according to the order of righteousness (Q90, A4): wherein also the New Law surpasses the Old Law, since it directs our internal acts, according to Mt. 5:20: *Unless your justice abound more than that of the Scribes and Pharisees, you shall not enter into the kingdom of heaven.* Hence the saying that *the Old Law restrains the hand, but the New Law controls the mind* (*Sentent.* iii, D, xl).

Third, it belongs to the law to induce men to observe its commandments. This the Old Law did by the fear of punishment: but the New Law, by love, which is poured into our hearts by the grace of Christ, bestowed in the New Law, but foreshadowed in the Old. Hence Augustine says (*Contra Adimant. Manich.* discip. xvii) that *there is a little difference between the Law and the Gospel—fear and love.*

REPLY OBJ. 1: As the father of a family issues different commands to the children and to the adults, so also the one King, God, in His one kingdom, gave one law to men, while they were yet imperfect, and another more perfect law, when, by the preceding law, they had been led to a greater capacity for Divine things.

REPLY OBJ. 2: The salvation of man could not be achieved otherwise than through Christ, according to Acts 4:12: *There is no other name . . . given to men, whereby we must be saved.* Consequently the law that brings all to salvation could not be given until after the coming of Christ. But before His coming it was necessary to give to the people, of whom Christ was to be born, a law containing certain rudiments of righteousness unto salvation, in order to prepare them to receive Him.

REPLY OBJ. 3: The natural law directs man by way of certain general precepts, common to both the perfect and the imperfect: wherefore it is one and the same for all. But the Divine law directs man also in certain particular matters, to which the perfect and imperfect do not stand in the same relation. Hence the necessity for the Divine law to be twofold, as already explained.

Article 6

Whether There Is a Law in the Fomes of Sin?

AD SEXTUM SIC PROCEDITUR. Videtur quod non sit aliqua lex fomitis. Dicit enim Isidorus, in V Etymol., quod *lex ratione consistit.* Fomes autem non consistit ratione, sed magis a ratione deviat. Ergo fomes non habet rationem legis.

PRAETEREA, omnis lex obligatoria est, ita quod qui ipsam non servant, transgressores dicuntur. Sed fomes non constituit aliquem transgressorem ex hoc quod

OBJECTION 1: It would seem that there is no law of the *fomes* of sin. For Isidore says (*Etym.* v) that the *law is based on reason.* But the *fomes* of sin is not based on reason, but deviates from it. Therefore the *fomes* has not the nature of a law.

OBJ. 2: Further, every law is binding, so that those who do not obey it are called transgressors. But man is not called a transgressor, from not following the instigations of the

ipsum non sequitur, sed magis transgressor redditur si quis ipsum sequatur. Ergo fomes non habet rationem legis.

PRAETEREA, lex ordinatur ad bonum commune, ut supra habitum est. Sed fomes non inclinat ad bonum commune, sed magis ad bonum privatum. Ergo fomes non habet rationem legis.

SED CONTRA est quod apostolus dicit, Rom. VII, *video aliam legem in membris meis, repugnantem legi mentis meae.*

RESPONDEO dicendum quod, sicut supra dictum est, lex essentialiter invenitur in regulante et mensurante, participative autem in eo quod mensuratur et regulatur; ita quod omnis inclinatio vel ordinatio quae invenitur in his quae subiecta sunt legi, participative dicitur lex, ut ex supradictis patet. Potest autem in his quae subduntur legi, aliqua inclinatio inveniri dupliciter a legislatore. Uno modo, inquantum directe inclinat suos subditos ad aliquid; et diversos interdum ad diversos actus; secundum quem modum potest dici quod alia est lex militum, et alia est lex mercatorum. Alio modo, indirecte, inquantum scilicet per hoc quod legislator destituit aliquem sibi subditum aliqua dignitate, sequitur quod transeat in alium ordinem et quasi in aliam legem, puta si miles ex militia destituatur, transibit in legem rusticorum vel mercatorum.

Sic igitur sub Deo legislatore diversae creaturae diversas habent naturales inclinationes, ita ut quod uni est quodammodo lex, alteri sit contra legem, ut si dicam quod furibundum esse est quodammodo lex canis, est autem contra legem ovis vel alterius mansueti animalis. Est ergo hominis lex, quam sortitur ex ordinatione divina secundum propriam conditionem, ut secundum rationem operetur. Quae quidem lex fuit tam valida in primo statu, ut nihil vel praeter rationem vel contra rationem posset subrepere homini. Sed dum homo a Deo recessit, incurrit in hoc quod feratur secundum impetum sensualitatis, et unicuique etiam particulariter hoc contingit, quanto magis a ratione recesserit, ut sic quodammodo bestiis assimiletur, quae sensualitatis impetu feruntur; secundum illud Psalmi XLVIII, *homo, cum in honore esset, non intellexit, comparatus est iumentis insipientibus, et similis factus est illis.*

Sic igitur ipsa sensualitatis inclinatio, quae fomes dicitur, in aliis quidem animalibus simpliciter habet rationem legis, illo tamen modo quo in talibus lex dici potest, secundum directam inclinationem. In hominibus autem secundum hoc non habet rationem legis, sed magis est deviatio a lege rationis. Sed inquantum per divinam iustitiam homo destituitur originali iustitia et vigore rationis, ipse impetus sensualitatis qui eum ducit, habet rationem legis, inquantum est poenalis et ex lege divina consequens, hominem destituente propria dignitate.

fomes; but rather from his following them. Therefore the *fomes* has not the nature of a law.

OBJ. 3: Further, the law is ordained to the common good, as stated above (Q90, A2). But the *fomes* inclines us, not to the common, but to our own private good. Therefore the *fomes* has not the nature of law.

ON THE CONTRARY, The Apostle says (Rom 7:23): *I see another law in my members, fighting against the law of my mind.*

I ANSWER THAT, As stated above (A2; Q90, A1, ad 1), the law, as to its essence, resides in him that rules and measures; but, by way of participation, in that which is ruled and measured; so that every inclination or ordination which may be found in things subject to the law, is called a law by participation, as stated above (A2; Q90, A1, ad 1). Now those who are subject to a law may receive a twofold inclination from the lawgiver. First, insofar as he directly inclines his subjects to something; sometimes indeed different subjects to different acts; in this way we may say that there is a military law and a mercantile law. Second, indirectly; thus by the very fact that a lawgiver deprives a subject of some dignity, the latter passes into another order, so as to be under another law, as it were: thus if a soldier be turned out of the army, he becomes a subject of rural or of mercantile legislation.

Accordingly under the Divine Lawgiver various creatures have various natural inclinations, so that what is, as it were, a law for one, is against the law for another: thus I might say that fierceness is, in a way, the law of a dog, but against the law of a sheep or another meek animal. And so the law of man, which, by the Divine ordinance, is allotted to him, according to his proper natural condition, is that he should act in accordance with reason: and this law was so effective in the primitive state, that nothing either beside or against reason could take man unawares. But when man turned his back on God, he fell under the influence of his sensual impulses: in fact this happens to each one individually, the more he deviates from the path of reason, so that, after a fashion, he is likened to the beasts that are led by the impulse of sensuality, according to Ps. 48:21: *Man, when he was in honor, did not understand: he hath been compared to senseless beasts, and made like to them.*

So, then, this very inclination of sensuality which is called the *fomes*, in other animals has simply the nature of a law (yet only insofar as a law may be said to be in such things), by reason of a direct inclination. But in man, it has not the nature of law in this way, rather is it a deviation from the law of reason. But since, by the just sentence of God, man is destitute of original justice, and his reason bereft of its vigor, this impulse of sensuality, whereby he is led, insofar as it is a penalty following from the Divine law depriving man of his proper dignity, has the nature of a law.

AD PRIMUM ergo dicendum quod ratio illa procedit de fomite secundum se considerato, prout inclinat ad malum. Sic enim non habet rationem legis, ut dictum est, sed secundum quod sequitur ex divinae legis iustitia, tanquam si diceretur lex esse quod aliquis nobilis, propter suam culpam, ad servilia opera induci permitteretur.

AD SECUNDUM dicendum quod obiectio illa procedit de eo quod est lex quasi regula et mensura, sic enim deviantes a lege transgressores constituuntur. Sic autem fomes non est lex, sed per quandam participationem, ut supra dictum est.

AD TERTIUM dicendum quod ratio illa procedit de fomite quantum ad inclinationem propriam, non autem quantum ad suam originem. Et tamen si consideretur inclinatio sensualitatis prout est in aliis animalibus, sic ordinatur ad bonum commune, idest ad conservationem naturae in specie vel in individuo. Et hoc est etiam in homine, prout sensualitas subditur rationi. Sed fomes dicitur secundum quod exit rationis ordinem.

REPLY OBJ. 1: This argument considers the *fomes* in itself, as an incentive to evil. It is not thus that it has the nature of a law, as stated above, but according as it results from the justice of the Divine law: it is as though we were to say that the law allows a nobleman to be condemned to hard labor for some misdeed.

REPLY OBJ. 2: This argument considers law in the light of a rule or measure: for it is in this sense that those who deviate from the law become transgressors. But the *fomes* is not a law in this respect, but by a kind of participation, as stated above.

REPLY OBJ. 3: This argument considers the *fomes* as to its proper inclination, and not as to its origin. And yet if the inclination of sensuality be considered as it is in other animals, thus it is ordained to the common good, namely, to the preservation of nature in the species or in the individual. And this is in man also, insofar as sensuality is subject to reason. But it is called *fomes* insofar as it strays from the order of reason.

QUESTION 92

OF THE EFFECTS OF LAW

Deinde considerandum est de effectibus legis. Et circa hoc quaeruntur duo.

Primo, utrum effectus legis sit homines facere bonos.

Secundo, utrum effectus legis sint imperare, vetare, permittere et punire, sicut legisperitus dicit.

We must now consider the effects of law; under which head there are two points of inquiry:

(1) Whether an effect of law is to make men good?

(2) Whether the effects of law are to command, to forbid, to permit, and to punish, as the Jurist states?

Article 1

Whether an Effect of Law Is to Make Men Good?

AD PRIMUM SIC PROCEDITUR. Videtur quod legis non sit facere homines bonos. Homines enim sunt boni per virtutem, *virtus enim est quae bonum facit habentem*, ut dicitur in II Ethic. Sed virtus est homini a solo Deo, ipse enim eam facit in nobis sine nobis, ut supra dictum est in definitione virtutis. Ergo legis non est facere homines bonos.

PRAETEREA, lex non prodest homini nisi legi obediat. Sed hoc ipsum quod homo obedit legi, est ex bonitate. Ergo bonitas praeexigitur in homine ad legem. Non igitur lex facit homines bonos.

PRAETEREA, lex ordinatur ad bonum commune, ut supra dictum est. Sed quidam bene se habent in his quae ad commune pertinent, qui tamen in propriis non bene se habent. Non ergo ad legem pertinet quod faciat homines bonos.

PRAETEREA, quaedam leges sunt tyrannicae, ut philosophus dicit, in sua politica. Sed tyrannus non intendit ad bonitatem subditorum, sed solum ad propriam utilitatem. Non ergo legis est facere homines bonos.

SED CONTRA est quod philosophus dicit, in II Ethic., quod *voluntas cuiuslibet legislatoris haec est, ut faciat cives bonos*.

RESPONDEO dicendum quod, sicut supra dictum est, lex nihil aliud est quam dictamen rationis in praesidente, quo subditi gubernantur. Cuiuslibet autem subditi virtus est ut bene subdatur ei a quo gubernatur, sicut videmus quod virtus irascibilis et concupiscibilis in hoc consistit quod sint bene obedientes rationi. Et per hunc modum *virtus cuiuslibet subiecti est ut bene subiiciatur principanti*, ut philosophus dicit, in I Polit. Ad hoc autem ordinatur unaquaeque lex, ut obediatur ei a subditis. Unde manifestum est quod hoc sit proprium legis, inducere subiectos ad propriam ipsorum virtutem. Cum igitur virtus sit quae bonum facit habentem, sequitur quod

OBJECTION 1: It seems that it is not an effect of law to make men good. For men are good through virtue, since virtue, as stated in *Ethic.* ii, 6 is *that which makes its subject good*. But virtue is in man from God alone, because He it is Who *works it in us without us*, as we stated above (Q55, A4) in giving the definition of virtue. Therefore the law does not make men good.

OBJ. 2: Further, law does not profit a man unless he obeys it. But the very fact that a man obeys a law is due to his being good. Therefore in man goodness is presupposed to the law. Therefore the law does not make men good.

OBJ. 3: Further, law is ordained to the common good, as stated above (Q90, A2). But some behave well in things regarding the community, who behave ill in things regarding themselves. Therefore it is not the business of the law to make men good.

OBJ. 4: Further, some laws are tyrannical, as the Philosopher says (*Polit.* iii, 6). But a tyrant does not intend the good of his subjects, but considers only his own profit. Therefore law does not make men good.

ON THE CONTRARY, The Philosopher says (*Ethic.* ii, 1) that the *intention of every lawgiver is to make good citizens*.

I ANSWER THAT, as stated above (Q90, A1, ad 2; AA3,4), a law is nothing else than a dictate of reason in the ruler by whom his subjects are governed. Now the virtue of any subordinate thing consists in its being well subordinated to that by which it is regulated: thus we see that the virtue of the irascible and concupiscible faculties consists in their being obedient to reason; and accordingly *the virtue of every subject consists in his being well subjected to his ruler*, as the Philosopher says (*Polit.* i). But every law aims at being obeyed by those who are subject to it. Consequently it is evident that the proper effect of law is to lead its subjects to their proper virtue: and since virtue is *that which makes*

proprius effectus legis sit bonos facere eos quibus datur, vel simpliciter vel secundum quid. Si enim intentio ferentis legem tendat in verum bonum, quod est bonum commune secundum iustitiam divinam regulatum, sequitur quod per legem homines fiant boni simpliciter. Si vero intentio legislatoris feratur ad id quod non est bonum simpliciter, sed utile vel delectabile sibi, vel repugnans iustitiae divinae; tunc lex non facit homines bonos simpliciter, sed secundum quid, scilicet in ordine ad tale regimen. Sic autem bonum invenitur etiam in per se malis, sicut aliquis dicitur bonus latro, quia operatur accommode ad finem.

AD PRIMUM ergo dicendum quod duplex est virtus, ut ex supradictis patet, scilicet acquisita, et infusa. Ad utramque autem aliquid operatur operum assuetudo, sed diversimode, nam virtutem quidem acquisitam causat; ad virtutem autem infusam disponit, et eam iam habitam conservat et promovet. Et quia lex ad hoc datur ut dirigat actus humanos, inquantum actus humani operantur ad virtutem, intantum lex facit homines bonos. Unde et philosophus dicit, II Polit., quod *legislatores assuefacientes faciunt bonos.*

AD SECUNDUM dicendum quod non semper aliquis obedit legi ex bonitate perfecta virtutis, sed quandoque quidem ex timore poenae; quandoque autem ex solo dictamine rationis, quod est quoddam principium virtutis, ut supra habitum est.

AD TERTIUM dicendum quod bonitas cuiuslibet partis consideratur in proportione ad suum totum, unde et Augustinus dicit, in III Confess., quod *turpis omnis pars est quae suo toti non congruit.* Cum igitur quilibet homo sit pars civitatis, impossibile est quod aliquis homo sit bonus, nisi sit bene proportionatus bono communi, nec totum potest bene consistere nisi ex partibus sibi proportionatis. Unde impossibile est quod bonum commune civitatis bene se habeat, nisi cives sint virtuosi, ad minus illi quibus convenit principari. Sufficit autem, quantum ad bonum communitatis, quod alii intantum sint virtuosi quod principum mandatis obediant. Et ideo philosophus dicit, in III Polit., quod *eadem est virtus principis et boni viri; non autem eadem est virtus cuiuscumque civis et boni viri.*

AD QUARTUM dicendum quod lex tyrannica, cum non sit secundum rationem, non est simpliciter lex, sed magis est quaedam perversitas legis. Et tamen inquantum habet aliquid de ratione legis, intendit ad hoc quod cives sint boni. Non enim habet de ratione legis nisi secundum hoc quod est dictamen alicuius praesidentis in subditis, et ad hoc tendit ut subditi legi sint bene obedientes; quod est eos esse bonos, non simpliciter, sed in ordine ad tale regimen.

its possessor good, it follows that the proper effect of law is to make those to whom it is given, good, either simply or in some particular respect. For if the intention of the lawgiver is fixed on true good, which is the common good regulated according to Divine justice, it follows that the effect of the law is to make men good simply. If, however, the intention of the lawgiver is fixed on that which is not simply good, but useful or pleasurable to himself, or in opposition to Divine justice; then the law does not make men good simply, but in respect to that particular government. In this way good is found even in things that are bad of themselves: thus a man is called a good robber, because he works in a way that is adapted to his end.

REPLY OBJ. 1: Virtue is twofold, as explained above (Q63, A2), viz., acquired and infused. Now the fact of being accustomed to an action contributes to both, but in different ways; for it causes the acquired virtue; while it disposes to infused virtue, and preserves and fosters it when it already exists. And since law is given for the purpose of directing human acts; as far as human acts conduce to virtue, so far does law make men good. Wherefore the Philosopher says in the second book of the Politics (*Ethic.* ii) that *lawgivers make men good by habituating them to good works.*

REPLY OBJ. 2: It is not always through perfect goodness of virtue that one obeys the law, but sometimes it is through fear of punishment, and sometimes from the mere dictates of reason, which is a beginning of virtue, as stated above (Q63, A1).

REPLY OBJ. 3: The goodness of any part is considered in comparison with its whole; hence Augustine says (*Confess.* iii) that *unseemly is every part that harmonizes not with its whole.* Since then every man is a part of the state, it is impossible that a man be good, unless he be well proportionate to the common good: nor can the whole be well established unless its parts be proportionate to it. Consequently the common good of the state cannot flourish, unless the citizens be virtuous, at least those whose business it is to govern. But it is enough for the good of the community, that the other citizens be so far virtuous that they obey the commands of their rulers. Hence the Philosopher says (*Polit.* ii, 2) that *the virtue of a sovereign is the same as that of a good man, but the virtue of any common citizen is not the same as that of a good man.*

REPLY OBJ. 4: A tyrannical law, through not being according to reason, is not a law, absolutely speaking, but rather a perversion of law; and yet insofar as it has something of the ratio of a law, it aims at the citizens' being good. For all it has in the nature of a law consists in its being an ordinance made by a superior to his subjects, and aims at being obeyed by them, which is to make them good, not simply, but with respect to that particular government.

Article 2

Whether the Acts of Law Are Suitably Assigned?

AD SECUNDUM SIC PROCEDITUR. Videtur quod legis actus non sint convenienter assignati in hoc quod dicitur quod legis actus est imperare, vetare, permittere et punire. Lex enim omnis praeceptum commune est, ut legisconsultus dicit. Sed idem est imperare quod praecipere. Ergo alia tria superfluunt.

PRAETEREA, effectus legis est ut inducat subditos ad bonum, sicut supra dictum est. Sed consilium est de meliori bono quam praeceptum. Ergo magis pertinet ad legem consulere quam praecipere.

PRAETEREA, sicut homo aliquis incitatur ad bonum per poenas, ita etiam et per praemia. Ergo sicut punire ponitur effectus legis, ita etiam et praemiare.

PRAETEREA, intentio legislatoris est ut homines faciat bonos, sicut supra dictum est. Sed ille qui solo metu poenarum obedit legi, non est bonus, nam *timore servili, qui est timor poenarum, etsi bonum aliquis faciat, non tamen bene aliquid fit,* ut Augustinus dicit. Non ergo videtur esse proprium legis quod puniat.

SED CONTRA est quod Isidorus dicit, in V Etymol., *omnis lex aut permittit aliquid, ut, vir fortis praemium petat. Aut vetat, ut, sacrarum virginum nuptias nulli liceat petere. Aut punit, ut, qui caedem fecerit, capite plectatur.*

RESPONDEO dicendum quod, sicut enuntiatio est rationis dictamen per modum enuntiandi, ita etiam lex per modum praecipiendi. Rationis autem proprium est ut ex aliquo ad aliquid inducat. Unde sicut in demonstrativis scientiis ratio inducit ut assentiatur conclusioni per quaedam principia, ita etiam inducit ut assentiatur legis praecepto per aliquid.

Praecepta autem legis sunt de actibus humanis, in quibus lex dirigit, ut supra dictum est. Sunt autem tres differentiae humanorum actuum. Nam sicut supra dictum est, quidam actus sunt boni ex genere, qui sunt actus virtutum, et respectu horum, ponitur legis actus praecipere vel imperare; *praecipit enim lex omnes actus virtutum,* ut dicitur in V Ethic. Quidam vero sunt actus mali ex genere, sicut actus vitiosi, et respectu horum, lex habet prohibere. Quidam vero ex genere suo sunt actus indifferentes, et respectu horum, lex habet permittere. Et possunt etiam indifferentes dici omnes illi actus qui sunt vel parum boni vel parum mali. Id autem per quod inducit lex ad hoc quod sibi obediatur, est timor poenae, et quantum ad hoc, ponitur legis effectus punire.

AD PRIMUM ergo dicendum quod, sicut cessare a malo habet quandam rationem boni, ita etiam prohibitio

OBJECTION 1: It would seem that the acts of law are not suitably assigned as consisting in *command, prohibition, permission* and *punishment.* For *every law is a general precept,* as the jurist states. But command and precept are the same. Therefore the other three are superfluous.

OBJ. 2: Further, the effect of a law is to induce its subjects to be good, as stated above (A1). But counsel aims at a higher good than a command does. Therefore it belongs to law to counsel rather than to command.

OBJ. 3: Further, just as punishment stirs a man to good deeds, so does reward. Therefore if to punish is reckoned an effect of law, so also is to reward.

OBJ. 4: Further, the intention of a lawgiver is to make men good, as stated above (A1). But he that obeys the law, merely through fear of being punished, is not good: because *although a good deed may be done through servile fear, i.e., fear of punishment, it is not done well,* as Augustine says (*Contra duas Epist. Pelag.* ii). Therefore punishment is not a proper effect of law.

ON THE CONTRARY, Isidore says (*Etym.* v, 19): *Every law either permits something, as: 'A brave man may demand his reward':* or forbids something, as: *No man may ask a consecrated virgin in marriage*: or punishes, as: *Let him that commits a murder be put to death.*

I ANSWER THAT, Just as an assertion is a dictate of reason asserting something, so is a law a dictate of reason, commanding something. Now it is proper to reason to lead from one thing to another. Wherefore just as, in demonstrative sciences, the reason leads us from certain principles to assent to the conclusion, so it induces us by some means to assent to the precept of the law.

Now the precepts of law are concerned with human acts, in which the law directs, as stated above (Q90, AA1,2; Q91, A4). Again there are three kinds of human acts: for, as stated above (Q18, A8), some acts are good generically, viz., acts of virtue; and in respect of these the act of the law is a precept or command, for *the law commands all acts of virtue* (*Ethic.* v, 1). Some acts are evil generically, viz., acts of vice, and in respect of these the law forbids. Some acts are generically indifferent, and in respect of these the law permits; and all acts that are either not distinctly good or not distinctly bad may be called indifferent. And it is the fear of punishment that law makes use of in order to ensure obedience: in which respect punishment is an effect of law.

REPLY OBJ. 1: Just as to cease from evil is a kind of good, so a prohibition is a kind of precept: and accordingly,

habet quandam rationem praecepti. Et secundum hoc, large accipiendo praeceptum, universaliter lex praeceptum dicitur.

AD SECUNDUM dicendum quod consulere non est proprius actus legis, sed potest pertinere etiam ad personam privatam, cuius non est condere legem. Unde etiam apostolus, I ad Cor. VII, cum consilium quoddam daret, dixit, *ego dico, non dominus.* Et ideo non ponitur inter effectus legis.

AD TERTIUM dicendum quod etiam praemiare potest ad quemlibet pertinere, sed punire non pertinet nisi ad ministrum legis, cuius auctoritate poena infertur. Et ideo praemiare non ponitur actus legis, sed solum punire.

AD QUARTUM dicendum quod per hoc quod aliquis incipit assuefieri ad vitandum mala et ad implendum bona propter metum poenae, perducitur quandoque ad hoc quod delectabiliter et ex propria voluntate hoc faciat. Et secundum hoc, lex etiam puniendo perducit ad hoc quod homines sint boni.

taking precept in a wide sense, every law is a kind of precept.

REPLY OBJ. 2: To advise is not a proper act of law, but may be within the competency even of a private person, who cannot make a law. Wherefore too the Apostle, after giving a certain counsel (1 Cor 7:12) says: *I speak, not the Lord.* Consequently it is not reckoned as an effect of law.

REPLY OBJ. 3: To reward may also pertain to anyone: but to punish pertains to none but the minister of the law, by whose authority the pain is inflicted. Wherefore to reward is not reckoned an effect of law, but only to punish.

REPLY OBJ. 4: From becoming accustomed to avoid evil and fulfill what is good, through fear of punishment, one is sometimes led on to do so likewise, with delight and of one's own accord. Accordingly, law, even by punishing, leads men on to being good.

QUESTION 93

OF THE ETERNAL LAW

Deinde considerandum est de singulis legibus. Et primo, de lege aeterna; secundo, de lege naturali; tertio, de lege humana; quarto, de lege veteri; quinto, de lege nova, quae est lex Evangelii. De sexta autem lege, quae est lex fomitis, sufficiat quod dictum est cum de peccato originali ageretur.

Circa primum quaeruntur sex.

Primo, quid sit lex aeterna.

Secundo, utrum sit omnibus nota.

Tertio, utrum omnis lex ab ea derivetur.

Quarto, utrum necessaria subiiciantur legi aeternae.

Quinto, utrum contingentia naturalia subiiciantur legi aeternae.

Sexto, utrum omnes res humanae ei subiiciantur.

We must now consider each law by itself; and (1) The eternal law; (2) The natural law; (3) The human law; (4) The old law; (5) The new law, which is the law of the Gospel. Of the sixth law which is the law of the *fomes*, suffice what we have said when treating of original sin.

Concerning the first there are six points of inquiry:

(1) What is the eternal law?

(2) Whether it is known to all?

(3) Whether every law is derived from it?

(4) Whether necessary things are subject to the eternal law?

(5) Whether natural contingencies are subject to the eternal law?

(6) Whether all human things are subject to it?

Article 1

Whether the Eternal Law Is a Sovereign Type Existing in God?

AD PRIMUM SIC PROCEDITUR. Videtur quod lex aeterna non sit ratio summa in Deo existens. Lex enim aeterna est una tantum. Sed rationes rerum in mente divina sunt plures, dicit enim Augustinus, in libro octoginta trium quaest., quod *Deus singula fecit propriis rationibus*. Ergo lex aeterna non videtur esse idem quod ratio in mente divina existens.

PRAETEREA, de ratione legis est quod verbo promulgetur, ut supra dictum est. Sed verbum in divinis dicitur personaliter, ut in primo habitum est, ratio autem dicitur essentialiter. Non igitur idem est lex aeterna quod ratio divina.

PRAETEREA, Augustinus dicit, in libro de vera Relig., *apparet supra mentem nostram legem esse, quae veritas dicitur*. Lex autem supra mentem nostram existens est lex aeterna. Ergo veritas est lex aeterna. Sed non est eadem ratio veritatis et rationis. Ergo lex aeterna non est idem quod ratio summa.

SED CONTRA est quod Augustinus dicit, in I de Lib. Arb., quod *lex aeterna est summa ratio, cui semper obtemperandum est.*

RESPONDEO dicendum quod, sicut in quolibet artifice praeexistit ratio eorum quae constituuntur per artem, ita etiam in quolibet gubernante oportet quod praeexistat ratio ordinis eorum quae agenda sunt per eos qui gubernationi subduntur. Et sicut ratio rerum fiendarum

OBJECTION 1: It would seem that the eternal law is not a sovereign type existing in God. For there is only one eternal law. But there are many types of things in the Divine mind; for Augustine says (*Qq. lxxxiii*, qu. 46) that God *made each thing according to its type*. Therefore the eternal law does not seem to be a type existing in the Divine mind.

OBJ. 2: Further, it is essential to a law that it be promulgated by word, as stated above (Q90, A4). But Word is a Personal name in God, as stated in the FP, Q34, A1: whereas type refers to the Essence. Therefore the eternal law is not the same as a Divine type.

OBJ. 3: Further, Augustine says (*De Vera Relig.* xxx): *We see a law above our minds, which is called truth*. But the law which is above our minds is the eternal law. Therefore truth is the eternal law. But the ratio of truth is not the same as that of idea. Therefore the eternal law is not the same as the sovereign type.

ON THE CONTRARY, Augustine says (*De Lib. Arb.* i, 6) that *the eternal law is the sovereign type, to which we must always conform.*

I ANSWER THAT, Just as in every artificer there pre-exists an idea of the things that are made by his art, so too in every governor there must pre-exist the type of the order of those things that are to be done by those who are subject to his government. And just as the type of the things yet

per artem vocatur ars vel exemplar rerum artificiatarum, ita etiam ratio gubernantis actus subditorum, rationem legis obtinet, servatis aliis quae supra esse diximus de legis ratione. Deus autem per suam sapientiam conditor est universarum rerum, ad quas comparatur sicut artifex ad artificiata, ut in primo habitum est. Est etiam gubernator omnium actuum et motionum quae inveniuntur in singulis creaturis, ut etiam in primo habitum est. Unde sicut ratio divinae sapientiae inquantum per eam cuncta sunt creata, rationem habet artis vel exemplaris vel ideae; ita ratio divinae sapientiae moventis omnia ad debitum finem, obtinet rationem legis. Et secundum hoc, lex aeterna nihil aliud est quam ratio divinae sapientiae, secundum quod est directiva omnium actuum et motionum.

AD PRIMUM ergo dicendum quod Augustinus loquitur ibi de rationibus idealibus, quae respiciunt proprias naturas singularum rerum, et ideo in eis invenitur quaedam distinctio et pluralitas, secundum diversos respectus ad res, ut in primo habitum est. Sed lex dicitur directiva actuum in ordine ad bonum commune, ut supra dictum est. Ea autem quae sunt in seipsis diversa, considerantur ut unum, secundum quod ordinantur ad aliquod commune. Et ideo lex aeterna est una, quae est ratio huius ordinis.

AD SECUNDUM dicendum quod circa verbum quodcumque duo possunt considerari, scilicet ipsum verbum, et ea quae verbo exprimuntur. Verbum enim vocale est quiddam ab ore hominis prolatum; sed hoc verbo exprimuntur quae verbis humanis significantur. Et eadem ratio est de verbo hominis mentali, quod nihil est aliud quam quiddam mente conceptum, quo homo exprimit mentaliter ea de quibus cogitat. Sic igitur in divinis ipsum verbum, quod est conceptio paterni intellectus, personaliter dicitur, sed omnia quaecumque sunt in scientia patris, sive essentialia sive personalia, sive etiam Dei opera exprimuntur hoc verbo, ut patet per Augustinum, in XV de Trin. Et inter cetera quae hoc verbo exprimuntur, etiam ipsa lex aeterna verbo ipso exprimitur. Nec tamen propter hoc sequitur quod lex aeterna personaliter in divinis dicatur. Appropriatur tamen filio, propter convenientiam quam habet ratio ad verbum.

AD TERTIUM dicendum quod ratio intellectus divini aliter se habet ad res quam ratio intellectus humani. Intellectus enim humanus est mensuratus a rebus, ut scilicet conceptus hominis non sit verus propter seipsum, sed dicitur verus ex hoc quod consonat rebus, ex hoc enim quod res est vel non est, opinio vera vel falsa est. Intellectus vero divinus est mensura rerum, quia unaquaeque res intantum habet de veritate, inquantum imitatur intellectum divinum, ut in primo dictum est. Et ideo intellectus divinus est verus secundum se. Unde ratio eius est ipsa veritas.

to be made by an art is called the art or exemplar of the products of that art, so too the type in him who governs the acts of his subjects, bears the character of a law, provided the other conditions be present which we have mentioned above (Q90). Now God, by His wisdom, is the Creator of all things in relation to which He stands as the artificer to the products of his art, as stated in the FP, Q14, A8. Moreover He governs all the acts and movements that are to be found in each single creature, as was also stated in the FP, Q103, A5. Wherefore as the type of the Divine Wisdom, inasmuch as by It all things are created, has the character of art, exemplar or idea; so the type of Divine Wisdom, as moving all things to their due end, bears the character of law. Accordingly the eternal law is nothing else than the type of Divine Wisdom, as directing all actions and movements.

REPLY OBJ. 1: Augustine is speaking in that passage of the ideal types which regard the proper nature of each single thing; and consequently in them there is a certain distinction and plurality, according to their different relations to things, as stated in the FP, Q15, A2. But law is said to direct acts by ordaining them to the common good, as stated above (Q90, A2). And things, which are in themselves different, may be considered as one, according as they are ordained to one common thing. Wherefore the eternal law is one since it is the type of this order.

REPLY OBJ. 2: With regard to any sort of word, two points may be considered: viz., the word itself, and that which is expressed by the word. For the spoken word is something uttered by the mouth of man, and expresses that which is signified by the human word. The same applies to the human mental word, which is nothing else that something conceived by the mind, by which man expresses his thoughts mentally. So then in God the Word conceived by the intellect of the Father is the name of a Person: but all things that are in the Father's knowledge, whether they refer to the Essence or to the Persons, or to the works of God, are expressed by this Word, as Augustine declares (*De Trin.* xv, 14). And among other things expressed by this Word, the eternal law itself is expressed thereby. Nor does it follow that the eternal law is a Personal name in God: yet it is appropriated to the Son, on account of the kinship between type and word.

REPLY OBJ. 3: The types of the Divine intellect do not stand in the same relation to things, as the types of the human intellect. For the human intellect is measured by things, so that a human concept is not true by reason of itself, but by reason of its being consonant with things, since *an opinion is true or false according as it answers to the reality*. But the Divine intellect is the measure of things: since each thing has so far truth in it, as it represents the Divine intellect, as was stated in the FP, Q16, A1. Consequently the Divine intellect is true in itself; and its type is truth itself.

Article 2

Whether the Eternal Law Is Known to All?

AD SECUNDUM SIC PROCEDITUR. Videtur quod lex aeterna non sit omnibus nota. Quia ut dicit apostolus, I ad Cor., *quae sunt Dei, nemo novit nisi spiritus Dei.* Sed lex aeterna est quaedam ratio in mente divina existens. Ergo omnibus est ignota nisi soli Deo.

PRAETEREA, sicut Augustinus dicit, in libro de Lib. Arb., *lex aeterna est qua iustum est ut omnia sint ordinatissima.* Sed non omnes cognoscunt qualiter omnia sint ordinatissima. Non ergo omnes cognoscunt legem aeternam.

PRAETEREA, Augustinus dicit, in libro de vera Relig., quod *lex aeterna est de qua homines iudicare non possunt.* Sed sicut in I Ethic. dicitur, *unusquisque bene iudicat quae cognoscit.* Ergo lex aeterna non est nobis nota.

SED CONTRA est quod Augustinus dicit, in libro de Lib. Arb., quod *aeternae legis notio nobis impressa est.*

RESPONDEO dicendum quod dupliciter aliquid cognosci potest, uno modo, in seipso; alio modo, in suo effectu, in quo aliqua similitudo eius invenitur; sicut aliquis non videns solem in sua substantia, cognoscit ipsum in sua irradiatione. Sic igitur dicendum est quod legem aeternam nullus potest cognoscere secundum quod in seipsa est, nisi solum beati, qui Deum per essentiam vident. Sed omnis creatura rationalis ipsam cognoscit secundum aliquam eius irradiationem, vel maiorem vel minorem. Omnis enim cognitio veritatis est quaedam irradiatio et participatio legis aeternae, quae est veritas incommutabilis, ut Augustinus dicit, in libro de vera Relig. Veritatem autem omnes aliqualiter cognoscunt, ad minus quantum ad principia communia legis naturalis. In aliis vero quidam plus et quidam minus participant de cognitione veritatis; et secundum hoc etiam plus vel minus cognoscunt legem aeternam.

AD PRIMUM ergo dicendum quod ea quae sunt Dei, in seipsis quidem cognosci a nobis non possunt, sed tamen in effectibus suis nobis manifestantur, secundum illud Rom. I, *invisibilia Dei per ea quae facta sunt, intellecta, conspiciuntur.*

AD SECUNDUM dicendum quod legem aeternam etsi unusquisque cognoscat pro sua capacitate, secundum modum praedictum, nullus tamen eam comprehendere potest, non enim totaliter manifestari potest per suos effectus. Et ideo non oportet quod quicumque cognoscit legem aeternam secundum modum praedictum, cognoscat totum ordinem rerum, quo omnia sunt ordinatissima.

AD TERTIUM dicendum quod iudicare de aliquo potest intelligi dupliciter. Uno modo, sicut vis cognitiva diiudicat de proprio obiecto; secundum illud Iob XII,

OBJECTION 1: It would seem that the eternal law is not known to all. Because, as the Apostle says (1 Cor 2:11), *the things that are of God no man knoweth, but the Spirit of God.* But the eternal law is a type existing in the Divine mind. Therefore it is unknown to all save God alone.

OBJ. 2: Further, as Augustine says (*De Lib. Arb.* i, 6) *the eternal law is that by which it is right that all things should be most orderly.* But all do not know how all things are most orderly. Therefore all do not know the eternal law.

OBJ. 3: Further, Augustine says (*De Vera Relig.* xxxi) that *the eternal law is not subject to the judgment of man.* But according to *Ethic.* i, *any man can judge well of what he knows.* Therefore the eternal law is not known to us.

ON THE CONTRARY, Augustine says (*De Lib. Arb.* i, 6) that *knowledge of the eternal law is imprinted on us.*

I ANSWER THAT, A thing may be known in two ways: first, in itself; second, in its effect, wherein some likeness of that thing is found: thus someone not seeing the sun in its substance, may know it by its rays. So then no one can know the eternal law, as it is in itself, except the blessed who see God in His Essence. But every rational creature knows it in its reflection, greater or less. For every knowledge of truth is a kind of reflection and participation of the eternal law, which is the unchangeable truth, as Augustine says (*De Vera Relig.* xxxi). Now all men know the truth to a certain extent, at least as to the common principles of the natural law: and as to the others, they partake of the knowledge of truth, some more, some less; and in this respect are more or less cognizant of the eternal law.

REPLY OBJ. 1: We cannot know the things that are of God, as they are in themselves; but they are made known to us in their effects, according to Rm. 1:20: *The invisible things of God . . . are clearly seen, being understood by the things that are made.*

REPLY OBJ. 2: Although each one knows the eternal law according to his own capacity, in the way explained above, yet none can comprehend it: for it cannot be made perfectly known by its effects. Therefore it does not follow that anyone who knows the eternal law in the way aforesaid, knows also the whole order of things, whereby they are most orderly.

REPLY OBJ. 3: To judge a thing may be understood in two ways. First, as when a cognitive power judges of its proper object, according to Job 12:11: *Doth not the ear*

nonne auris verba diiudicat, et fauces comedentis saporem? Et secundum istum modum iudicii, philosophus dicit quod unusquisque bene iudicat quae cognoscit, iudicando scilicet an sit verum quod proponitur. Alio modo, secundum quod superior iudicat de inferiori quodam practico iudicio, an scilicet ita debeat esse vel non ita. Et sic nullus potest iudicare de lege aeterna.

discern words, and the palate of him that eateth, the taste? It is to this kind of judgment that the Philosopher alludes when he says that *anyone can judge well of what he knows,* by judging, namely, whether what is put forward is true. In another way we speak of a superior judging of a subordinate by a kind of practical judgment, as to whether he should be such or not such. And thus none can judge of the eternal law.

Article 3

Whether Every Law Is Derived from the Eternal Law?

Ad tertium sic proceditur. Videtur quod non omnis lex a lege aeterna derivetur. Est enim quaedam lex fomitis, ut supra dictum est. Ipsa autem non derivatur a lege divina, quae est lex aeterna, ad ipsam enim pertinet prudentia carnis, de qua apostolus dicit, ad Rom. VIII, quod *legi Dei non potest esse subiecta.* Ergo non omnis lex procedit a lege aeterna.

Praeterea, a lege aeterna nihil iniquum procedere potest, quia sicut dictum est, lex aeterna est secundum quam iustum est ut omnia sint ordinatissima. Sed quaedam leges sunt iniquae; secundum illud Isaiae X, *vae qui condunt leges iniquas.* Ergo non omnis lex procedit a lege aeterna.

Praeterea, Augustinus dicit, in I de Lib. Arbit., quod *lex quae populo regendo scribitur, recte multa permittit quae per divinam providentiam vindicantur.* Sed ratio divinae providentiae est lex aeterna, ut dictum est. Ergo nec etiam omnis lex recta procedit a lege aeterna.

Sed contra est quod, Prov. VIII, divina sapientia dicit, *per me reges regnant, et legum conditores iusta decernunt.* Ratio autem divinae sapientiae est lex aeterna, ut supra dictum est. Ergo omnes leges a lege aeterna procedunt.

Respondeo dicendum quod, sicut supra dictum est, lex importat rationem quandam directivam actuum ad finem. In omnibus autem moventibus ordinatis oportet quod virtus secundi moventis derivetur a virtute moventis primi, quia movens secundum non movet nisi inquantum movetur a primo. Unde et in omnibus gubernantibus idem videmus, quod ratio gubernationis a primo gubernante ad secundos derivatur, sicut ratio eorum quae sunt agenda in civitate, derivatur a rege per praeceptum in inferiores administratores. Et in artificialibus etiam ratio artificialium actuum derivatur ab architectore ad inferiores artifices, qui manu operantur. Cum ergo lex aeterna sit ratio gubernationis in supremo gubernante, necesse est quod omnes rationes gubernationis quae sunt in inferioribus gubernantibus, a lege

Objection 1: It would seem that not every law is derived from the eternal law. For there is a law of the *fomes,* as stated above (Q91, A6), which is not derived from that Divine law which is the eternal law, since thereunto pertains the *prudence of the flesh,* of which the Apostle says (Rom 8:7), that *it cannot be subject to the law of God.* Therefore not every law is derived from the eternal law.

Obj. 2: Further, nothing unjust can be derived from the eternal law, because, as stated above (A2, OBJ2), *the eternal law is that, according to which it is right that all things should be most orderly.* But some laws are unjust, according to Is. 10:1: *Woe to them that make wicked laws.* Therefore not every law is derived from the eternal law.

Obj. 3: Further, Augustine says (*De Lib. Arb.* i, 5) that *the law which is framed for ruling the people, rightly permits many things which are punished by Divine providence.* But the type of Divine providence is the eternal law, as stated above (A1). Therefore not even every good law is derived from the eternal law.

On the contrary, Divine Wisdom says (Prov 8:15): *By Me kings reign, and lawgivers decree just things.* But the type of Divine Wisdom is the eternal law, as stated above (A1). Therefore all laws proceed from the eternal law.

I answer that, As stated above (Q90, AA1,2), law denotes a kind of plan directing acts towards an end. Now wherever there are movers ordained to one another, the power of the second mover must needs be derived from the power of the first mover; since the second mover does not move except insofar as it is moved by the first. Wherefore we observe the same in all those who govern, so that the plan of government is derived by secondary governors from the governor in chief; thus the plan of what is to be done in a state flows from the king's command to his inferior administrators: and again in things of art the plan of whatever is to be done by art flows from the chief craftsman to the under-crafts-men, who work with their hands. Since then the eternal law is the plan of government in the Chief Governor, all the plans of government in the inferior

aeterna deriventur. Huiusmodi autem rationes inferiorum gubernantium sunt quaecumque aliae leges praeter legem aeternam. Unde omnes leges, inquantum participant de ratione recta, intantum derivantur a lege aeterna. Et propter hoc Augustinus dicit, in I de Lib. Arb., quod *in temporali lege nihil est iustum ac legitimum, quod non ex lege aeterna homines sibi derivaverunt.*

Ad primum ergo dicendum quod fomes habet rationem legis in homine, inquantum est poena consequens divinam iustitiam, et secundum hoc manifestum est quod derivatur a lege aeterna. Inquantum vero inclinat ad peccatum, sic contrariatur legi Dei, et non habet rationem legis, ut ex supradictis patet.

Ad secundum dicendum quod lex humana intantum habet rationem legis, inquantum est secundum rationem rectam, et secundum hoc manifestum est quod a lege aeterna derivatur. Inquantum vero a ratione recedit, sic dicitur lex iniqua, et sic non habet rationem legis, sed magis violentiae cuiusdam. Et tamen in ipsa lege iniqua inquantum servatur aliquid de similitudine legis propter ordinem potestatis eius qui legem fert, secundum hoc etiam derivatur a lege aeterna, omnis enim potestas a domino Deo est, ut dicitur Rom. XIII.

Ad tertium dicendum quod lex humana dicitur aliqua permittere, non quasi ea approbans, sed quasi ea dirigere non potens. Multa autem diriguntur lege divina quae dirigi non possunt lege humana, plura enim subduntur causae superiori quam inferiori. Unde hoc ipsum quod lex humana non se intromittat de his quae dirigere non potest, ex ordine legis aeternae provenit. Secus autem esset si approbaret ea quae lex aeterna reprobat. Unde ex hoc non habetur quod lex humana non derivetur a lege aeterna, sed quod non perfecte eam assequi possit.

governors must be derived from the eternal law. But these plans of inferior governors are all other laws besides the eternal law. Therefore all laws, insofar as they partake of right reason, are derived from the eternal law. Hence Augustine says (*De Lib. Arb.* i, 6) that *in temporal law there is nothing just and lawful, but what man has drawn from the eternal law.*

Reply Obj. 1: The *fomes* has the nature of law in man, insofar as it is a punishment resulting from Divine justice; and in this respect it is evident that it is derived from the eternal law. But insofar as it denotes a proneness to sin, it is contrary to the Divine law, and has not the nature of law, as stated above (Q91, A6).

Reply Obj. 2: Human law has the nature of law insofar as it is according to right reason; and it is clear that, in this respect, it is derived from the eternal law. But insofar as it deviates from reason, it is called an unjust law, and has the nature, not of law but of violence. Nevertheless even an unjust law, insofar as it retains some appearance of law, through being framed by one who is in power, is derived from the eternal law; since all power is from the Lord God, according to Rm. 13:1.

Reply Obj. 3: Human law is said to permit certain things, not as approving them, but as being unable to direct them. And many things are directed by the Divine law, which human law is unable to direct, because more things are subject to a higher than to a lower cause. Hence the very fact that human law does not meddle with matters it cannot direct, comes under the ordination of the eternal law. It would be different, were human law to approve what the eternal law condemns. Consequently it does not follow that human law is not derived from the eternal law, but that it is not on a perfect equality with it.

Article 4

Whether Necessary and Eternal Things Are Subject to the Eternal Law?

Ad quartum sic proceditur. Videtur quod necessaria et aeterna subiiciantur legi aeternae. Omne enim quod rationabile est, rationi subditur. Sed voluntas divina est rationabilis, cum sit iusta. Ergo rationi subditur. Sed lex aeterna est ratio divina. Ergo voluntas Dei subditur legi aeternae. Voluntas autem Dei est aliquod aeternum. Ergo etiam aeterna et necessaria legi aeternae subduntur.

Praeterea, quidquid subiicitur regi, subiicitur legi regis. *Filius autem,* ut dicitur I ad Cor. XV, *subiectus erit Deo et patri, cum tradiderit ei regnum.* Ergo filius, qui est aeternus, subiicitur legi aeternae.

Objection 1: It would seem that necessary and eternal things are subject to the eternal law. For whatever is reasonable is subject to reason. But the Divine will is reasonable, for it is just. Therefore it is subject to (the Divine) reason. But the eternal law is the Divine reason. Therefore God's will is subject to the eternal law. But God's will is eternal. Therefore eternal and necessary things are subject to the eternal law.

Obj. 2: Further, whatever is subject to the King, is subject to the King's law. Now the Son, according to 1 Cor. 15:28,24, *shall be subject . . . to God and the Father . . . when He shall have delivered up the Kingdom to Him.* Therefore the Son, Who is eternal, is subject to the eternal law.

PRAETEREA, lex aeterna est ratio divinae providentiae. Sed multa necessaria subduntur divinae providentiae, sicut permanentia substantiarum incorporalium et corporum caelestium. Ergo legi aeternae subduntur etiam necessaria.

SED CONTRA, ea quae sunt necessaria, impossibile est aliter se habere, unde cohibitione non indigent. Sed imponitur hominibus lex ut cohibeantur a malis, ut ex supradictis patet. Ergo ea quae sunt necessaria, legi non subduntur.

RESPONDEO dicendum quod, sicut supra dictum est, lex aeterna est ratio divinae gubernationis. Quaecumque ergo divinae gubernationi subduntur, subiiciuntur etiam legi aeternae, quae vero gubernationi aeternae non subduntur, neque legi aeternae subduntur. Horum autem distinctio attendi potest ex his quae circa nos sunt. Humanae enim gubernationi subduntur ea quae per homines fieri possunt, quae vero ad naturam hominis pertinent, non subduntur gubernationi humanae, scilicet quod homo habeat animam, vel manus aut pedes. Sic igitur legi aeternae subduntur omnia quae sunt in rebus a Deo creatis, sive sint contingentia sive sint necessaria, ea vero quae pertinent ad naturam vel essentiam divinam, legi aeternae non subduntur, sed sunt realiter ipsa lex aeterna.

AD PRIMUM ergo dicendum quod de voluntate Dei dupliciter possumus loqui. Uno modo, quantum ad ipsam voluntatem, et sic, cum voluntas Dei sit ipsa eius essentia, non subditur gubernationi divinae neque legi aeternae, sed est idem quod lex aeterna. Alio modo possumus loqui de voluntate divina quantum ad ipsa quae Deus vult circa creaturas, quae quidem subiecta sunt legi aeternae, inquantum horum ratio est in divina sapientia. Et ratione horum, voluntas Dei dicitur rationabilis. Alioquin, ratione sui ipsius, magis est dicenda ipsa ratio.

AD SECUNDUM dicendum quod filius Dei non est a Deo factus, sed naturaliter ab ipso genitus. Et ideo non subditur divinae providentiae aut legi aeternae, sed magis ipse est lex aeterna per quandam appropriationem, ut patet per Augustinum, in libro de vera Relig. Dicitur autem esse subiectus patri ratione humanae naturae, secundum quam etiam pater dicitur esse maior eo.

TERTIUM concedimus, quia procedit de necessariis creatis.

AD QUARTUM dicendum quod, sicut philosophus dicit, in V Metaphys., quaedam necessaria habent causam suae necessitatis, et sic hoc ipsum quod impossibile est ea aliter esse, habent ab alio. Et hoc ipsum est cohibitio quaedam efficacissima, nam quaecumque cohibentur, intantum cohiberi dicuntur, inquantum non possunt aliter facere quam de eis disponatur.

OBJ. 3: Further, the eternal law is Divine providence as a type. But many necessary things are subject to Divine providence: for instance, the stability of incorporeal substances and of the heavenly bodies. Therefore even necessary things are subject to the eternal law.

ON THE CONTRARY, Things that are necessary cannot be otherwise, and consequently need no restraining. But laws are imposed on men, in order to restrain them from evil, as explained above (Q92, A2). Therefore necessary things are not subject to the eternal law.

I ANSWER THAT, As stated above (A1), the eternal law is the type of the Divine government. Consequently whatever is subject to the Divine government, is subject to the eternal law: while if anything is not subject to the Divine government, neither is it subject to the eternal law. The application of this distinction may be gathered by looking around us. For those things are subject to human government, which can be done by man; but what pertains to the nature of man is not subject to human government; for instance, that he should have a soul, hands, or feet. Accordingly all that is in things created by God, whether it be contingent or necessary, is subject to the eternal law: while things pertaining to the Divine Nature or Essence are not subject to the eternal law, but are the eternal law itself.

REPLY OBJ. 1: We may speak of God's will in two ways. First, as to the will itself: and thus, since God's will is His very Essence, it is subject neither to the Divine government, nor to the eternal law, but is the same thing as the eternal law. Second, we may speak of God's will, as to the things themselves that God wills about creatures; which things are subject to the eternal law, insofar as they are planned by Divine Wisdom. In reference to these things God's will is said to be reasonable: though regarded in itself it should rather be called their type.

REPLY OBJ. 2: God the Son was not made by God, but was naturally born of God. Consequently He is not subject to Divine providence or to the eternal law: but rather is Himself the eternal law by a kind of appropriation, as Augustine explains (*De Vera Relig.* xxxi). But He is said to be subject to the Father by reason of His human nature, in respect of which also the Father is said to be greater than He.

THE THIRD OBJECTION we grant, because it deals with those necessary things that are created.

REPLY OBJ. 4: As the Philosopher says (*Metaph.* v, text. 6), some necessary things have a cause of their necessity: and thus they derive from something else the fact that they cannot be otherwise. And this is in itself a most effective restraint; for whatever is restrained, is said to be restrained insofar as it cannot do otherwise than it is allowed to.

Article 5

Whether Natural Contingents Are Subject to the Eternal Law?

AD QUINTUM SIC PROCEDITUR. Videtur quod naturalia contingentia non subsint legi aeternae. Promulgatio enim est de ratione legis, ut supra dictum est. Sed promulgatio non potest fieri nisi ad creaturas rationales, quibus potest aliquid denuntiari. Ergo solae creaturae rationales subsunt legi aeternae. Non ergo naturalia contingentia.

PRAETEREA, *ea quae obediunt rationi, participant aliqualiter ratione*, ut dicitur in I Ethic. Lex autem aeterna est ratio summa, ut supra dictum est. Cum igitur naturalia contingentia non participent aliqualiter ratione, sed penitus sint irrationabilia, videtur quod non subsint legi aeternae.

PRAETEREA, lex aeterna est efficacissima. Sed in naturalibus contingentibus accidit defectus. Non ergo subsunt legi aeternae.

SED CONTRA est quod dicitur Prov. VIII, *quando circumdabat mari terminum suum, et legem ponebat aquis ne transirent fines suos.*

RESPONDEO dicendum quod aliter dicendum est de lege hominis, et aliter de lege aeterna, quae est lex Dei. Lex enim hominis non se extendit nisi ad creaturas rationales quae homini subiiciuntur. Cuius ratio est quia lex est directiva actuum qui conveniunt subiectis gubernationi alicuius, unde nullus, proprie loquendo, suis actibus legem imponit. Quaecumque autem aguntur circa usum rerum irrationalium homini subditarum, aguntur per actum ipsius hominis moventis huiusmodi res, nam huiusmodi irrationales creaturae non agunt seipsas, sed ab aliis aguntur, ut supra habitum est. Et ideo rebus irrationalibus homo legem imponere non potest, quantumcumque ei subiiciantur. Rebus autem rationalibus sibi subiectis potest imponere legem, inquantum suo praecepto, vel denuntiatione quacumque, imprimit menti earum quandam regulam quae est principium agendi.

Sicut autem homo imprimit, denuntiando, quoddam interius principium actuum homini sibi subiecto, ita etiam Deus imprimit toti naturae principia propriorum actuum. Et ideo per hunc modum dicitur Deus praecipere toti naturae; secundum illud Psalmi CXLVIII, *praeceptum posuit, et non praeteribit.* Et per hanc etiam rationem omnes motus et actiones totius naturae legi aeternae subduntur. Unde alio modo creaturae irrationales subduntur legi aeternae, inquantum moventur a divina providentia, non autem per intellectum divini praecepti, sicut creaturae rationales.

AD PRIMUM ergo dicendum quod hoc modo se habet impressio activi principii intrinseci, quantum ad res

OBJECTION 1: It would seem that natural contingents are not subject to the eternal law. Because promulgation is essential to law, as stated above (Q90, A4). But a law cannot be promulgated except to rational creatures, to whom it is possible to make an announcement. Therefore none but rational creatures are subject to the eternal law; and consequently natural contingents are not.

OBJ. 2: Further, *Whatever obeys ratio partakes somewhat of reason*, as stated in *Ethic.* i. But the eternal law, is the supreme ratio, as stated above (A1). Since then natural contingents do not partake of reason in any way, but are altogether void of reason, it seems that they are not subject to the eternal law.

OBJ. 3: Further, the eternal law is most efficatious. But in natural contingents defects occur. Therefore they are not subject to the eternal law.

ON THE CONTRARY, It is written (Prov 8:29): *When He compassed the sea with its bounds, and set a law to the waters, that they should not pass their limits.*

I ANSWER THAT, We must speak otherwise of the law of man, than of the eternal law which is the law of God. For the law of man extends only to rational creatures subject to man. The reason of this is because law directs the actions of those that are subject to the government of someone: wherefore, properly speaking, none imposes a law on his own actions. Now whatever is done regarding the use of irrational things subject to man, is done by the act of man himself moving those things, for these irrational creatures do not move themselves, but are moved by others, as stated above (Q1, A2). Consequently man cannot impose laws on irrational beings, however much they may be subject to him. But he can impose laws on rational beings subject to him, insofar as by his command or pronouncement of any kind, he imprints on their minds a rule which is a principle of action.

Now just as man, by such pronouncement, impresses a kind of inward principle of action on the man that is subject to him, so God imprints on the whole of nature the principles of its proper actions. And so, in this way, God is said to command the whole of nature, according to Ps. 148:6: *He hath made a decree, and it shall not pass away.* And thus all actions and movements of the whole of nature are subject to the eternal law. Consequently irrational creatures are subject to the eternal law, through being moved by Divine providence; but not, as rational creatures are, through understanding the Divine commandment.

REPLY OBJ. 1: The impression of an inward active principle is to natural things, what the promulgation of law is to

naturales, sicut se habet promulgatio legis quantum ad homines, quia per legis promulgationem imprimitur hominibus quoddam directivum principium humanorum actuum, ut dictum est.

AD SECUNDUM dicendum quod creaturae irrationales non participant ratione humana, nec ei obediunt, participant tamen, per modum obedientiae, ratione divina. Ad plura enim se extendit virtus rationis divinae quam virtus rationis humanae. Et sicut membra corporis humani moventur ad imperium rationis, non tamen participant ratione, quia non habent aliquam apprehensionem ordinatam ad rationem; ita etiam creaturae irrationales moventur a Deo, nec tamen propter hoc sunt rationales.

AD TERTIUM dicendum quod defectus qui accidunt in rebus naturalibus, quamvis sint praeter ordinem causarum particularium, non tamen sunt praeter ordinem causarum universalium; et praecipue causae primae, quae Deus est, cuius providentiam nihil subterfugere potest, ut in primo dictum est. Et quia lex aeterna est ratio divinae providentiae, ut dictum est, ideo defectus rerum naturalium legi aeternae subduntur.

men: because law, by being promulgated, imprints on man a directive principle of human actions, as stated above.

REPLY OBJ. 2: Irrational creatures neither partake of nor are obedient to human reason: whereas they do partake of the Divine Reason by obeying it; because the power of Divine Reason extends over more things than human reason does. And as the members of the human body are moved at the command of reason, and yet do not partake of reason, since they have no apprehension ordered to reason; so too irrational creatures are moved by God, without, on that account, being rational.

REPLY OBJ. 3: Although the defects which occur in natural things are outside the order of particular causes, they are not outside the order of universal causes, especially of the First Cause, i.e., God, from Whose providence nothing can escape, as stated in the FP, Q22, A2. And since the eternal law is the type of Divine providence, as stated above (A1), hence the defects of natural things are subject to the eternal law.

Article 6

Whether All Human Affairs Are Subject to the Eternal Law?

AD SEXTUM SIC PROCEDITUR. Videtur quod non omnes res humanae subiiciantur legi aeternae. Dicit enim apostolus, ad Gal. V, *si spiritu ducimini, non estis sub lege*. Sed viri iusti, qui sunt filii Dei per adoptionem, spiritu Dei aguntur; secundum illud Rom. VIII, *qui spiritu Dei aguntur, hi filii Dei sunt*. Ergo non omnes homines sunt sub lege aeterna.

PRAETEREA, apostolus dicit, ad Rom. VIII, *prudentia carnis inimica est Deo, legi enim Dei subiecta non est*. Sed multi homines sunt in quibus prudentia carnis dominatur. Ergo legi aeternae, quae est lex Dei, non subiiciuntur omnes homines.

PRAETEREA, Augustinus dicit, in I de Lib. Arb., quod *lex aeterna est qua mali miseriam, boni vitam beatam merentur*. Sed homines iam beati, vel iam damnati, non sunt in statu merendi. Ergo non subsunt legi aeternae.

SED CONTRA est quod Augustinus dicit, XIX de Civ. Dei, *nullo modo aliquid legibus summi creatoris ordinatorisque subtrahitur, a quo pax universitatis administratur*.

RESPONDEO dicendum quod duplex est modus quo aliquid subditur legi aeternae, ut ex supradictis patet, uno modo, inquantum participatur lex aeterna per modum cognitionis; alio modo, per modum actionis et

OBJECTION 1: It would seem that not all human affairs are subject to the eternal law. For the Apostle says (Gal 5:18): *If you are led by the spirit you are not under the law*. But the righteous who are the sons of God by adoption, are led by the spirit of God, according to Rm. 8:14: *Whosoever are led by the spirit of God, they are the sons of God*. Therefore not all men are under the eternal law.

OBJ. 2: Further, the Apostle says (Rom 8:7): *The prudence of the flesh is an enemy to God: for it is not subject to the law of God*. But many are those in whom the prudence of the flesh dominates. Therefore all men are not subject to the eternal law which is the law of God.

OBJ. 3: Further, Augustine says (*De Lib. Arb.* i, 6) that *the eternal law is that by which the wicked merit misery, the good, a life of blessedness*. But those who are already blessed, and those who are already damned, are not in the state of merit. Therefore they are not under the eternal law.

ON THE CONTRARY, Augustine says (*De Civ. Dei* xix, 12): *Nothing evades the laws of the most high Creator and Governor, for by Him the peace of the universe is administered*.

I ANSWER THAT, There are two ways in which a thing is subject to the eternal law, as explained above (A5): first, insofar as it participates in the eternal law by way of knowledge; second, by way of action and passion, i.e., by partaking

passionis, inquantum participatur per modum principii motivi. Et hoc secundo modo subduntur legi aeternae irrationales creaturae, ut dictum est. Sed quia rationalis natura, cum eo quod est commune omnibus creaturis, habet aliquid sibi proprium inquantum est rationalis, ideo secundum utrumque modum legi aeternae subditur, quia et notionem legis aeternae aliquo modo habet, ut supra dictum est; et iterum unicuique rationali creaturae inest naturalis inclinatio ad id quod est consonum legi aeternae; *sumus enim innati ad habendum virtutes*, ut dicitur in II Ethic.

Uterque tamen modus imperfectus quidem est, et quodammodo corruptus, in malis; in quibus et inclinatio naturalis ad virtutem depravatur per habitum vitiosum; et iterum ipsa naturalis cognitio boni in eis obtenebratur per passiones et habitus peccatorum. In bonis autem uterque modus invenitur perfectior, quia et supra cognitionem naturalem boni, superadditur eis cognitio fidei et sapientiae; et supra naturalem inclinationem ad bonum, superadditur eis interius motivum gratiae et virtutis.

Sic igitur boni perfecte subsunt legi aeternae, tanquam semper secundum eam agentes. Mali autem subsunt quidem legi aeternae, imperfecte quidem quantum ad actiones ipsorum, prout imperfecte cognoscunt et imperfecte inclinantur ad bonum, sed quantum deficit ex parte actionis, suppletur ex parte passionis, prout scilicet intantum patiuntur quod lex aeterna dictat de eis, inquantum deficiunt facere quod legi aeternae convenit. Unde Augustinus dicit, in I de Lib. Arb., *iustos sub aeterna lege agere existimo*. Et in libro de catechizandis rudibus, dicit quod *Deus ex iusta miseria animarum se deserentium, convenientissimis legibus inferiores partes creaturae suae novit ornare.*

AD PRIMUM ergo dicendum quod illud verbum apostoli potest intelligi dupliciter. Uno modo, ut esse sub lege intelligatur ille qui nolens obligationi legis subditur, quasi cuidam ponderi. Unde Glossa ibidem dicit quod *sub lege est qui timore supplicii quod lex minatur, non amore iustitiae, a malo opere abstinet.* Et hoc modo spirituales viri non sunt sub lege, quia per caritatem, quam Spiritus Sanctus cordibus eorum infundit, voluntarie id quod legis est, implent. Alio modo potest etiam intelligi inquantum hominis opera qui spiritu sancto agitur, magis dicuntur esse opera spiritus sancti quam ipsius hominis. Unde cum Spiritus Sanctus non sit sub lege, sicut nec filius, ut supra dictum est; sequitur quod huiusmodi opera, inquantum sunt spiritus sancti, non sint sub lege. Et huic attestatur quod apostolus dicit, II ad Cor. III, *ubi spiritus domini, ibi libertas.*

AD SECUNDUM dicendum quod prudentia carnis non potest subiici legi Dei ex parte actionis, quia inclinat ad actiones contrarias legi Dei. Subiicitur tamen legi Dei ex parte passionis, quia meretur pati poenam

of the eternal law by way of an inward motive principle: and in this second way, irrational creatures are subject to the eternal law, as stated above (A5). But since the rational nature, together with that which it has in common with all creatures, has something proper to itself inasmuch as it is rational, consequently it is subject to the eternal law in both ways; because while each rational creature has some knowledge of the eternal law, as stated above (A2), it also has a natural inclination to that which is in harmony with the eternal law; for *we are naturally adapted to be the recipients of virtue (Ethic.* ii, 1).

Both ways, however, are imperfect, and to a certain extent destroyed, in the wicked; because in them the natural inclination to virtue is corrupted by vicious habits, and, moreover, the natural knowledge of good is darkened by passions and habits of sin. But in the good both ways are found to be more perfect: because in them, besides the natural knowledge of good, there is the added knowledge of faith and wisdom; and again, besides the natural inclination to good, there is the added motive of grace and virtue.

Accordingly, the good are perfectly subject to the eternal law, as always acting according to it: whereas the wicked are subject to the eternal law, imperfectly as to their actions, indeed, since both their knowledge of good, and their inclination thereto, are imperfect; but this imperfection on the part of action is supplied on the part of passion, insofar as they suffer what the eternal law decrees concerning them, according as they fail to act in harmony with that law. Hence Augustine says (*De Lib. Arb.* i, 15): *I esteem that the righteous act according to the eternal law;* and (*De Catech. Rud.* xviii): *Out of the just misery of the souls which deserted Him, God knew how to furnish the inferior parts of His creation with most suitable laws.*

REPLY OBJ. 1: This saying of the Apostle may be understood in two ways. First, so that a man is said to be under the law, through being pinned down thereby, against his will, as by a load. Hence, on the same passage a gloss says that *he is under the law, who refrains from evil deeds, through fear of punishment threatened by the law, and not from love of virtue.* In this way the spiritual man is not under the law, because he fulfils the law willingly, through charity which is poured into his heart by the Holy Spirit. Second, it can be understood as meaning that the works of a man, who is led by the Holy Spirit, are the works of the Holy Spirit rather than his own. Therefore, since the Holy Spirit is not under the law, as neither is the Son, as stated above (A4, ad 2); it follows that such works, insofar as they are of the Holy Spirit, are not under the law. The Apostle witnesses to this when he says (2 Cor 3:17): *Where the Spirit of the Lord is, there is liberty.*

REPLY OBJ. 2: The prudence of the flesh cannot be subject to the law of God as regards action; since it inclines to actions contrary to the Divine law: yet it is subject to the law of God, as regards passion; since it deserves to suffer

secundum legem divinae iustitiae. Nihilominus tamen in nullo homine ita prudentia carnis dominatur, quod totum bonum naturae corrumpatur. Et ideo remanet in homine inclinatio ad agendum ea quae sunt legis aeternae. Habitum est enim supra quod peccatum non tollit totum bonum naturae.

AD TERTIUM dicendum quod idem est per quod aliquid conservatur in fine, et per quod movetur ad finem, sicut corpus grave gravitate quiescit in loco inferiori, per quam etiam ad locum ipsum movetur. Et sic dicendum est quod, sicut secundum legem aeternam aliqui merentur beatitudinem vel miseriam, ita per eandem legem in beatitudine vel miseria conservantur. Et secundum hoc, et beati et damnati subsunt legi aeternae.

punishment according to the law of Divine justice. Nevertheless in no man does the prudence of the flesh dominate so far as to destroy the whole good of his nature: and consequently there remains in man the inclination to act in accordance with the eternal law. For we have seen above (Q85, A2) that sin does not destroy entirely the good of nature.

REPLY OBJ. 3: A thing is maintained in the end and moved towards the end by one and the same cause: thus gravity which makes a heavy body rest in the lower place is also the cause of its being moved thither. We therefore reply that as it is according to the eternal law that some deserve happiness, others unhappiness, so is it by the eternal law that some are maintained in a happy state, others in an unhappy state. Accordingly both the blessed and the damned are under the eternal law.

Question 94

Of the natural Law

Deinde considerandum est de lege naturali. Et circa hoc quaeruntur sex.

Primo, quid sit lex naturalis.

Secundo, quae sint praecepta legis naturalis.

Tertio, utrum omnes actus virtutum sint de lege naturali.

Quarto, utrum lex naturalis sit una apud omnes.

Quinto, utrum sit mutabilis.

Sexto, utrum possit a mente hominis deleri.

We must now consider the natural law; concerning which there are six points of inquiry:

(1) What is the natural law?

(2) What are the precepts of the natural law?

(3) Whether all acts of virtue are prescribed by the natural law?

(4) Whether the natural law is the same in all?

(5) Whether it is changeable?

(6) Whether it can be abolished from the heart of man?

Article 1

Whether the Natural Law Is a Habit?

AD PRIMUM SIC PROCEDITUR. Videtur quod lex naturalis sit habitus. Quia ut philosophus dicit, in II Ethic., *tria sunt in anima, potentia, habitus et passio.* Sed naturalis lex non est aliqua potentiarum animae, nec aliqua passionum, ut patet enumerando per singula. Ergo lex naturalis est habitus.

PRAETEREA, Basilius dicit quod conscientia, sive synderesis, est lex intellectus nostri, quod non potest intelligi nisi de lege naturali. Sed synderesis est habitus quidam, ut in primo habitum est. Ergo lex naturalis est habitus.

PRAETEREA, lex naturalis semper in homine manet, ut infra patebit. Sed non semper ratio hominis, ad quam lex pertinet, cogitat de lege naturali. Ergo lex naturalis non est actus, sed habitus.

SED CONTRA est quod Augustinus dicit, in libro de bono coniugali, quod *habitus est quo aliquid agitur cum opus est.* Sed naturalis lex non est huiusmodi, est enim in parvulis et damnatis, qui per eam agere non possunt. Ergo lex naturalis non est habitus.

RESPONDEO dicendum quod aliquid potest dici esse habitus dupliciter. Uno modo, proprie et essentialiter, et sic lex naturalis non est habitus. Dictum est enim supra quod lex naturalis est aliquid per rationem constitutum, sicut etiam propositio est quoddam opus rationis. Non est autem idem quod quis agit, et quo quis agit, aliquis enim per habitum grammaticae agit orationem congruam. Cum igitur habitus sit quo quis agit, non potest esse quod lex aliqua sit habitus proprie et essentialiter.

Alio modo potest dici habitus id quod habitu tenetur, sicut dicitur fides id quod fide tenetur. Et hoc modo, quia praecepta legis naturalis quandoque considerantur

OBJECTION 1: It would seem that the natural law is a habit. Because, as the Philosopher says (*Ethic.* ii, 5), *there are three things in the soul: power, habit, and passion.* But the natural law is not one of the soul's powers: nor is it one of the passions; as we may see by going through them one by one. Therefore the natural law is a habit.

OBJ. 2: Further, Basil says that the conscience or *synderesis is the law of our mind*; which can only apply to the natural law. But the *synderesis* is a habit, as was shown in the Prima Pars, Q. 79 A. 12. Therefore the natural law is a habit.

OBJ. 3: Further, the natural law abides in man always, as will be shown further on (A6). But man's reason, which the law regards, does not always think about the natural law. Therefore the natural law is not an act, but a habit.

ON THE CONTRARY, Augustine says (*De Bono Conjug.* xxi) that *a habit is that whereby something is done when necessary.* But such is not the natural law: since it is in infants and in the damned who cannot act by it. Therefore the natural law is not a habit.

I ANSWER THAT, A thing may be called a habit in two ways. First, properly and essentially: and thus the natural law is not a habit. For it has been stated above (Q90, A1, ad 2) that the natural law is something appointed by reason, just as a proposition is a work of reason. Now that which a man does is not the same as that whereby he does it: for he makes a becoming speech by the habit of grammar. Since then a habit is that by which we act, a law cannot be a habit properly and essentially.

Second, the term habit may be applied to that which we hold by a habit: thus faith may mean that which we hold by faith. And accordingly, since the precepts of the natural law

227

in actu a ratione, quandoque autem sunt in ea habitualiter tantum, secundum hunc modum potest dici quod lex naturalis sit habitus. Sicut etiam principia indemonstrabilia in speculativis non sunt ipse habitus principiorum, sed sunt principia quorum est habitus.

AD PRIMUM ergo dicendum quod philosophus intendit ibi investigare genus virtutis, et cum manifestum sit quod virtus sit quoddam principium actus, illa tantum ponit quae sunt principia humanorum actuum, scilicet potentias, habitus et passiones. Praeter haec autem tria sunt quaedam alia in anima, sicut quidam actus, ut velle est in volente; et etiam cognita sunt in cognoscente; et proprietates naturales animae insunt ei, ut immortalitas et alia huiusmodi.

AD SECUNDUM dicendum quod synderesis dicitur lex intellectus nostri, inquantum est habitus continens praecepta legis naturalis, quae sunt prima principia operum humanorum.

AD TERTIUM dicendum quod ratio illa concludit quod lex naturalis habitualiter tenetur. Et hoc concedimus.

AD ID VERO quod in contrarium obiicitur, dicendum quod eo quod habitualiter inest, quandoque aliquis uti non potest propter aliquod impedimentum, sicut homo non potest uti habitu scientiae propter somnum. Et similiter puer non potest uti habitu intellectus principiorum, vel etiam lege naturali, quae ei habitualiter inest, propter defectum aetatis.

are sometimes considered by reason actually, while sometimes they are in the reason only habitually, in this way the natural law may be called a habit. Thus, in speculative matters, the indemonstrable principles are not the habit itself whereby we hold those principles, but are the principles the habit of which we possess.

REPLY OBJ. 1: The Philosopher proposes there to discover the genus of virtue; and since it is evident that virtue is a principle of action, he mentions only those things which are principles of human acts, viz., powers, habits and passions. But there are other things in the soul besides these three: there are acts; thus *to will* is in the one that wills; again, things known are in the knower; moreover its own natural properties are in the soul, such as immortality and the like.

REPLY OBJ. 2: *Synderesis* is said to be the law of our mind, because it is a habit containing the precepts of the natural law, which are the first principles of human actions.

REPLY OBJ. 3: This argument proves that the natural law is held habitually; and this is granted.

TO THE ARGUMENT advanced in the contrary sense we reply that sometimes a man is unable to make use of that which is in him habitually, on account of some impediment: thus, on account of sleep, a man is unable to use the habit of science. In like manner, through the deficiency of his age, a child cannot use the habit of understanding of principles, or the natural law, which is in him habitually.

Article 2

Whether the Natural Law Contains Several Precepts, or Only One?

AD SECUNDUM SIC PROCEDITUR. Videtur quod lex naturalis non contineat plura praecepta, sed unum tantum. Lex enim continetur in genere praecepti, ut supra habitum est. Si igitur essent multa praecepta legis naturalis, sequeretur quod etiam essent multae leges naturales.

PRAETEREA, lex naturalis consequitur hominis naturam. Sed humana natura est una secundum totum, licet sit multiplex secundum partes. Aut ergo est unum praeceptum tantum legis naturae, propter unitatem totius, aut sunt multa, secundum multitudinem partium humanae naturae. Et sic oportebit quod etiam ea quae sunt de inclinatione concupiscibilis, pertineant ad legem naturalem.

PRAETEREA, lex est aliquid ad rationem pertinens, ut supra dictum est. Sed ratio in homine est una tantum. Ergo solum unum praeceptum est legis naturalis.

OBJECTION 1: It would seem that the natural law contains, not several precepts, but one only. For law is a kind of precept, as stated above (Q92, A2). If therefore there were many precepts of the natural law, it would follow that there are also many natural laws.

OBJ. 2: Further, the natural law is consequent to human nature. But human nature, as a whole, is one; though, as to its parts, it is manifold. Therefore, either there is but one precept of the law of nature, on account of the unity of nature as a whole; or there are many, by reason of the number of parts of human nature. The result would be that even things relating to the inclination of the concupiscible faculty belong to the natural law.

OBJ. 3: Further, law is something pertaining to reason, as stated above (Q90, A1). Now reason is but one in man. Therefore there is only one precept of the natural law.

SED CONTRA est quia sic se habent praecepta legis naturalis in homine quantum ad operabilia, sicut se habent prima principia in demonstrativis. Sed prima principia indemonstrabilia sunt plura. Ergo etiam praecepta legis naturae sunt plura.

RESPONDEO dicendum quod, sicut supra dictum est, praecepta legis naturae hoc modo se habent ad rationem practicam, sicut principia prima demonstrationum se habent ad rationem speculativam, utraque enim sunt quaedam principia per se nota. Dicitur autem aliquid per se notum dupliciter, uno modo, secundum se; alio modo, quoad nos. Secundum se quidem quaelibet propositio dicitur per se nota, cuius praedicatum est de ratione subiecti, contingit tamen quod ignoranti definitionem subiecti, talis propositio non erit per se nota. Sicut ista propositio, homo est rationale, est per se nota secundum sui naturam, quia qui dicit hominem, dicit rationale, et tamen ignoranti quid sit homo, haec propositio non est per se nota. Et inde est quod, sicut dicit Boetius, in libro de Hebdomad., quaedam sunt dignitates vel propositiones per se notae communiter omnibus, et huiusmodi sunt illae propositiones quarum termini sunt omnibus noti, ut, omne totum est maius sua parte, et, quae uni et eidem sunt aequalia, sibi invicem sunt aequalia. Quaedam vero propositiones sunt per se notae solis sapientibus, qui terminos propositionum intelligunt quid significent, sicut intelligenti quod Angelus non est corpus, per se notum est quod non est circumscriptive in loco, quod non est manifestum rudibus, qui hoc non capiunt.

In his autem quae in apprehensione omnium cadunt, quidam ordo invenitur. Nam illud quod primo cadit in apprehensione, est ens, cuius intellectus includitur in omnibus quaecumque quis apprehendit. Et ideo primum principium indemonstrabile est quod non est simul affirmare et negare, quod fundatur supra rationem entis et non entis, et super hoc principio omnia alia fundantur, ut dicitur in IV Metaphys. Sicut autem ens est primum quod cadit in apprehensione simpliciter, ita bonum est primum quod cadit in apprehensione practicae rationis, quae ordinatur ad opus, omne enim agens agit propter finem, qui habet rationem boni. Et ideo primum principium in ratione practica est quod fundatur supra rationem boni, quae est, bonum est quod omnia appetunt. Hoc est ergo primum praeceptum legis, quod bonum est faciendum et prosequendum, et malum vitandum. Et super hoc fundantur omnia alia praecepta legis naturae, ut scilicet omnia illa facienda vel vitanda pertineant ad praecepta legis naturae, quae ratio practica naturaliter apprehendit esse bona humana.

Quia vero bonum habet rationem finis, malum autem rationem contrarii, inde est quod omnia illa ad quae homo habet naturalem inclinationem, ratio naturaliter apprehendit ut bona, et per consequens ut opere

ON THE CONTRARY, The precepts of the natural law in man stand in relation to practical matters, as the first principles to matters of demonstration. But there are several first indemonstrable principles. Therefore there are also several precepts of the natural law.

I ANSWER THAT, As stated above (Q91, A3), the precepts of the natural law are to the practical reason, what the first principles of demonstrations are to the speculative reason; because both are self-evident principles. Now a thing is said to be self-evident in two ways: first, in itself; second, in relation to us. Any proposition is said to be self-evident in itself, if its predicate is contained in the notion of the subject: although, to one who knows not the definition of the subject, it happens that such a proposition is not self-evident. For instance, this proposition, *Man is a rational being*, is, in its very nature, self-evident, since who says *man*, says *a rational being*: and yet to one who knows not what a man is, this proposition is not self-evident. Hence it is that, as Boethius says (*De Hebdom.*), certain axioms or propositions are universally self-evident to all; and such are those propositions whose terms are known to all, as, *Every whole is greater than its part*, and, *Things equal to one and the same are equal to one another*. But some propositions are self-evident only to the wise, who understand the meaning of the terms of such propositions: thus to one who understands that an angel is not a body, it is self-evident that an angel is not circumscriptively in a place: but this is not evident to the unlearned, for they cannot grasp it.

Now a certain order is to be found in those things that are apprehended universally. For that which, before aught else, falls under apprehension, is *being*, the notion of which is included in all things whatsoever a man apprehends. Wherefore the first indemonstrable principle is that *the same thing cannot be affirmed and denied at the same time*, which is based on the notion of *being* and *not-being*: and on this principle all others are based, as is stated in *Metaph.* iv, text. 9. Now as *being* is the first thing that falls under the apprehension simply, so *good* is the first thing that falls under the apprehension of the practical reason, which is directed to action: since every agent acts for an end under the aspect of good. Consequently the first principle of practical reason is one founded on the notion of good, viz., that *good is that which all things seek after*. Hence this is the first precept of law, that *good is to be done and pursued, and evil is to be avoided*. All other precepts of the natural law are based upon this: so that whatever the practical reason naturally apprehends as man's good (or evil) belongs to the precepts of the natural law as something to be done or avoided.

Since, however, good has the nature of an end, and evil, the nature of a contrary, hence it is that all those things to which man has a natural inclination, are naturally apprehended by reason as being good, and consequently as

prosequenda, et contraria eorum ut mala et vitanda. Secundum igitur ordinem inclinationum naturalium, est ordo praeceptorum legis naturae. Inest enim primo inclinatio homini ad bonum secundum naturam in qua communicat cum omnibus substantiis, prout scilicet quaelibet substantia appetit conservationem sui esse secundum suam naturam. Et secundum hanc inclinationem, pertinent ad legem naturalem ea per quae vita hominis conservatur, et contrarium impeditur. Secundo inest homini inclinatio ad aliqua magis specialia, secundum naturam in qua communicat cum ceteris animalibus. Et secundum hoc, dicuntur ea esse de lege naturali quae natura omnia animalia docuit, ut est coniunctio maris et feminae, et educatio liberorum, et similia. Tertio modo inest homini inclinatio ad bonum secundum naturam rationis, quae est sibi propria, sicut homo habet naturalem inclinationem ad hoc quod veritatem cognoscat de Deo, et ad hoc quod in societate vivat. Et secundum hoc, ad legem naturalem pertinent ea quae ad huiusmodi inclinationem spectant, utpote quod homo ignorantiam vitet, quod alios non offendat cum quibus debet conversari, et cetera huiusmodi quae ad hoc spectant.

AD PRIMUM ergo dicendum quod omnia ista praecepta legis naturae, inquantum referuntur ad unum primum praeceptum, habent rationem unius legis naturalis.

AD SECUNDUM dicendum quod omnes inclinationes quarumcumque partium humanae naturae, puta concupiscibilis et irascibilis, secundum quod regulantur ratione, pertinent ad legem naturalem, et reducuntur ad unum primum praeceptum, ut dictum est. Et secundum hoc, sunt multa praecepta legis naturae in seipsis, quae tamen communicant in una radice.

AD TERTIUM dicendum quod ratio, etsi in se una sit, tamen est ordinativa omnium quae ad homines spectant. Et secundum hoc, sub lege rationis continentur omnia ea quae ratione regulari possunt.

objects of pursuit, and their contraries as evil, and objects of avoidance. Wherefore according to the order of natural inclinations, is the order of the precepts of the natural law. Because in man there is first of all an inclination to good in accordance with the nature which he has in common with all substances: inasmuch as every substance seeks the preservation of its own being, according to its nature: and by reason of this inclination, whatever is a means of preserving human life, and of warding off its obstacles, belongs to the natural law. Second, there is in man an inclination to things that pertain to him more specially, according to that nature which he has in common with other animals: and in virtue of this inclination, those things are said to belong to the natural law, *which nature has taught to all animals*, such as sexual intercourse, education of offspring and so forth. Third, there is in man an inclination to good, according to the nature of his reason, which nature is proper to him: thus man has a natural inclination to know the truth about God, and to live in society: and in this respect, whatever pertains to this inclination belongs to the natural law; for instance, to shun ignorance, to avoid offending those among whom one has to live, and other such things regarding the above inclination.

REPLY OBJ. 1: All these precepts of the law of nature have the character of one natural law, inasmuch as they flow from one first precept.

REPLY OBJ. 2: All the inclinations of any parts whatsoever of human nature, e.g., of the concupiscible and irascible parts, insofar as they are ruled by reason, belong to the natural law, and are reduced to one first precept, as stated above: so that the precepts of the natural law are many in themselves, but they have one root in common.

REPLY OBJ. 3: Although reason is one in itself, yet it directs all things regarding man; so that whatever can be ruled by reason, is contained under the law of reason.

Article 3

Whether All Acts of Virtue Are Prescribed by the Natural Law?

AD TERTIUM SIC PROCEDITUR. Videtur quod non omnes actus virtutum sint de lege naturae. Quia, ut supra dictum est, de ratione legis est ut ordinetur ad bonum commune. Sed quidam virtutum actus ordinantur ad bonum privatum alicuius, ut patet praecipue in actibus temperantiae. Non ergo omnes actus virtutum legi subduntur naturali.

PRAETEREA, omnia peccata aliquibus virtuosis actibus opponuntur. Si igitur omnes actus virtutum sint de lege naturae, videtur ex consequenti quod omnia

OBJECTION 1: It would seem that not all acts of virtue are prescribed by the natural law. Because, as stated above (Q90, A2) it is essential to a law that it be ordained to the common good. But some acts of virtue are ordained to the private good of the individual, as is evident especially in regards to acts of temperance. Therefore not all acts of virtue are the subject of natural law.

OBJ. 2: Further, every sin is opposed to some virtuous act. If therefore all acts of virtue are prescribed by the

peccata sint contra naturam. Quod tamen specialiter de quibusdam peccatis dicitur.

PRAETEREA, in his quae sunt secundum naturam, omnes conveniunt. Sed in actibus virtutum non omnes conveniunt, aliquid enim est virtuosum uni, quod est alteri vitiosum. Ergo non omnes actus virtutum sunt de lege naturae.

SED CONTRA est quod Damascenus dicit, in III libro, quod *virtutes sunt naturales*. Ergo et actus virtuosi subiacent legi naturae.

RESPONDEO dicendum quod de actibus virtuosis dupliciter loqui possumus, uno modo, inquantum sunt virtuosi; alio modo, inquantum sunt tales actus in propriis speciebus considerati. Si igitur loquamur de actibus virtutum inquantum sunt virtuosi, sic omnes actus virtuosi pertinent ad legem naturae. Dictum est enim quod ad legem naturae pertinet omne illud ad quod homo inclinatur secundum suam naturam. Inclinatur autem unumquodque naturaliter ad operationem sibi convenientem secundum suam formam, sicut ignis ad calefaciendum. Unde cum anima rationalis sit propria forma hominis, naturalis inclinatio inest cuilibet homini ad hoc quod agat secundum rationem. Et hoc est agere secundum virtutem. Unde secundum hoc, omnes actus virtutum sunt de lege naturali, dictat enim hoc naturaliter unicuique propria ratio, ut virtuose agat. Sed si loquamur de actibus virtuosis secundum seipsos, prout scilicet in propriis speciebus considerantur, sic non omnes actus virtuosi sunt de lege naturae. Multa enim secundum virtutem fiunt, ad quae natura non primo inclinat; sed per rationis inquisitionem ea homines adinvenerunt, quasi utilia ad bene vivendum.

AD PRIMUM ergo dicendum quod temperantia est circa concupiscentias naturales cibi et potus et venereorum, quae quidem ordinantur ad bonum commune naturae, sicut et alia legalia ordinantur ad bonum commune morale.

AD SECUNDUM dicendum quod natura hominis potest dici vel illa quae est propria homini, et secundum hoc, omnia peccata, inquantum sunt contra rationem, sunt etiam contra naturam, ut patet per Damascenum, in II libro. Vel illa quae est communis homini et aliis animalibus, et secundum hoc, quaedam specialia peccata dicuntur esse contra naturam; sicut contra commixtionem maris et feminae, quae est naturalis omnibus animalibus, est concubitus masculorum, quod specialiter dicitur vitium contra naturam.

AD TERTIUM dicendum quod ratio illa procedit de actibus secundum seipsos consideratis. Sic enim, propter diversas hominum conditiones, contingit quod aliqui actus sunt aliquibus virtuosi, tanquam eis proportionati et convenientes, qui tamen sunt aliis vitiosi, tanquam eis non proportionati.

natural law, it seems to follow that all sins are against nature: whereas this applies to certain special sins.

OBJ. 3: Further, those things which are according to nature are common to all. But acts of virtue are not common to all: since a thing is virtuous in one, and vicious in another. Therefore not all acts of virtue are prescribed by the natural law.

ON THE CONTRARY, Damascene says (*De Fide Orth.* iii, 4) that *virtues are natural*. Therefore virtuous acts also are a subject of the natural law.

I ANSWER THAT, We may speak of virtuous acts in two ways: first, under the aspect of virtuous; second, as such and such acts considered in their proper species. If then we speak of acts of virtue, considered as virtuous, thus all virtuous acts belong to the natural law. For it has been stated (A2) that to the natural law belongs everything to which a man is inclined according to his nature. Now each thing is inclined naturally to an operation that is suitable to it according to its form: thus fire is inclined to give heat. Wherefore, since the rational soul is the proper form of man, there is in every man a natural inclination to act according to reason: and this is to act according to virtue. Consequently, considered thus, all acts of virtue are prescribed by the natural law: since each one's reason naturally dictates to him to act virtuously. But if we speak of virtuous acts, considered in themselves, i.e., in their proper species, thus not all virtuous acts are prescribed by the natural law: for many things are done virtuously, to which nature does not incline at first; but which, through the inquiry of reason, have been found by men to be conducive to well-living.

REPLY OBJ. 1: Temperance is about the natural concupiscences of food, drink and sexual matters, which are indeed ordained to the natural common good, just as other matters of law are ordained to the moral common good.

REPLY OBJ. 2: By human nature we may mean either that which is proper to man—and in this sense all sins, as being against reason, are also against nature, as Damascene states (*De Fide Orth.* ii, 30): or we may mean that nature which is common to man and other animals; and in this sense, certain special sins are said to be against nature; thus contrary to the commingling of male and female, which is natural to all animals, is the lying together of men, which has received the special name of the vice against nature.

REPLY OBJ. 3: This argument considers acts in themselves. For it is owing to the various conditions of men, that certain acts are virtuous for some, as being proportionate and becoming to them, while they are vicious for others, as being out of proportion to them.

Article 4

Whether the Natural Law Is the Same in All Men?

AD QUARTUM SIC PROCEDITUR. Videtur quod lex naturae non sit una apud omnes. Dicitur enim in decretis, dist. I, quod *ius naturale est quod in lege et in Evangelio continetur.* Sed hoc non est commune omnibus, quia, ut dicitur Rom. X, *non omnes obediunt Evangelio.* Ergo lex naturalis non est una apud omnes.

PRAETEREA, *ea quae sunt secundum legem, iusta esse dicuntur,* ut dicitur in V Ethic. Sed in eodem libro dicitur quod nihil est ita iustum apud omnes, quin apud aliquos diversificetur. Ergo lex etiam naturalis non est apud omnes eadem.

PRAETEREA, ad legem naturae pertinet id ad quod homo secundum naturam suam inclinatur, ut supra dictum est. Sed diversi homines naturaliter ad diversa inclinantur, alii quidem ad concupiscentiam voluptatum, alii ad desideria honorum, alii ad alia. Ergo non est una lex naturalis apud omnes.

SED CONTRA est quod Isidorus dicit, in libro Etymol., *ius naturale est commune omnium nationum.*

RESPONDEO dicendum quod, sicut supra dictum est, ad legem naturae pertinent ea ad quae homo naturaliter inclinatur; inter quae homini proprium est ut inclinetur ad agendum secundum rationem. Ad rationem autem pertinet ex communibus ad propria procedere, ut patet ex I Physic. Aliter tamen circa hoc se habet ratio speculativa, et aliter ratio practica. Quia enim ratio speculativa praecipue negotiatur circa necessaria, quae impossibile est aliter se habere, absque aliquo defectu invenitur veritas in conclusionibus propriis, sicut et in principiis communibus. Sed ratio practica negotiatur circa contingentia, in quibus sunt operationes humanae, et ideo, etsi in communibus sit aliqua necessitas, quanto magis ad propria descenditur, tanto magis invenitur defectus. Sic igitur in speculativis est eadem veritas apud omnes tam in principiis quam in conclusionibus, licet veritas non apud omnes cognoscatur in conclusionibus, sed solum in principiis, quae dicuntur communes conceptiones. In operativis autem non est eadem veritas vel rectitudo practica apud omnes quantum ad propria, sed solum quantum ad communia, et apud illos apud quos est eadem rectitudo in propriis, non est aequaliter omnibus nota.

Sic igitur patet quod, quantum ad communia principia rationis sive speculativae sive practicae, est eadem veritas seu rectitudo apud omnes, et aequaliter nota. Quantum vero ad proprias conclusiones rationis speculativae, est eadem veritas apud omnes, non tamen aequaliter omnibus nota, apud omnes enim verum est quod triangulus habet tres angulos aequales duobus rectis, quamvis hoc non sit omnibus notum. Sed quantum

OBJECTION 1: It would seem that the natural law is not the same in all. For it is stated in the *Decretals* (Dist. i) that *the natural law is that which is contained in the Law and the Gospel.* But this is not common to all men; because, as it is written (Rom 10:16), *all do not obey the gospel.* Therefore the natural law is not the same in all men.

OBJ. 2: Further, *Things which are according to the law are said to be just,* as stated in *Ethic.* v. But it is stated in the same book that nothing is so universally just as not to be subject to change in regard to some men. Therefore even the natural law is not the same in all men.

OBJ. 3: Further, as stated above (AA2,3), to the natural law belongs everything to which a man is inclined according to his nature. Now different men are naturally inclined to different things; some to the desire of pleasures, others to the desire of honors, and other men to other things. Therefore there is not one natural law for all.

ON THE CONTRARY, Isidore says (*Etym.* v, 4): *The natural law is common to all nations.*

I ANSWER THAT, As stated above (AA2,3), to the natural law belongs those things to which a man is inclined naturally: and among these it is proper to man to be inclined to act according to reason. Now the process of reason is from the common to the proper, as stated in *Phys.* i. The speculative reason, however, is differently situated in this matter, from the practical reason. For, since the speculative reason is busied chiefly with the necessary things, which cannot be otherwise than they are, its proper conclusions, like the universal principles, contain the truth without fail. The practical reason, on the other hand, is busied with contingent matters, about which human actions are concerned: and consequently, although there is necessity in the general principles, the more we descend to matters of detail, the more frequently we encounter defects. Accordingly then in speculative matters truth is the same in all men, both as to principles and as to conclusions: although the truth is not known to all as regards the conclusions, but only as regards the principles which are called common notions. But in matters of action, truth or practical rectitude is not the same for all, as to matters of detail, but only as to the general principles: and where there is the same rectitude in matters of detail, it is not equally known to all.

It is therefore evident that, as regards the general principles whether of speculative or of practical reason, truth or rectitude is the same for all, and is equally known by all. As to the proper conclusions of the speculative reason, the truth is the same for all, but is not equally known to all: thus it is true for all that the three angles of a triangle are together equal to two right angles, although it is not known to all. But as to the proper conclusions of the practical reason,

ad proprias conclusiones rationis practicae, nec est eadem veritas seu rectitudo apud omnes; nec etiam apud quos est eadem, est aequaliter nota. Apud omnes enim hoc rectum est et verum, ut secundum rationem agatur. Ex hoc autem principio sequitur quasi conclusio propria, quod deposita sint reddenda. Et hoc quidem ut in pluribus verum est, sed potest in aliquo casu contingere quod sit damnosum, et per consequens irrationabile, si deposita reddantur; puta si aliquis petat ad impugnandam patriam. Et hoc tanto magis invenitur deficere, quanto magis ad particularia descenditur, puta si dicatur quod deposita sunt reddenda cum tali cautione, vel tali modo, quanto enim plures conditiones particulares apponuntur, tanto pluribus modis poterit deficere, ut non sit rectum vel in reddendo vel in non reddendo.

Sic igitur dicendum est quod lex naturae, quantum ad prima principia communia, est eadem apud omnes et secundum rectitudinem, et secundum notitiam. Sed quantum ad quaedam propria, quae sunt quasi conclusiones principiorum communium, est eadem apud omnes ut in pluribus et secundum rectitudinem et secundum notitiam, sed ut in paucioribus potest deficere et quantum ad rectitudinem, propter aliqua particularia impedimenta (sicut etiam naturae generabiles et corruptibiles deficiunt ut in paucioribus, propter impedimenta), et etiam quantum ad notitiam; et hoc propter hoc quod aliqui habent depravatam rationem ex passione, seu ex mala consuetudine, seu ex mala habitudine naturae; sicut apud germanos olim latrocinium non reputabatur iniquum, cum tamen sit expresse contra legem naturae, ut refert Iulius Caesar, in libro de bello Gallico.

AD PRIMUM ergo dicendum quod verbum illud non est sic intelligendum quasi omnia quae in lege et in Evangelio continentur, sint de lege naturae, cum multa tradantur ibi supra naturam, sed quia ea quae sunt de lege naturae, plenarie ibi traduntur. Unde cum dixisset Gratianus quod *ius naturale est quod in lege et in Evangelio continetur*, statim, exemplificando, subiunxit, *quo quisque iubetur alii facere quod sibi vult fieri.*

AD SECUNDUM dicendum quod verbum philosophi est intelligendum de his quae sunt naturaliter iusta non sicut principia communia, sed sicut quaedam conclusiones ex his derivatae; quae ut in pluribus rectitudinem habent, et ut in paucioribus deficiunt.

AD TERTIUM dicendum quod, sicut ratio in homine dominatur et imperat aliis potentiis, ita oportet quod omnes inclinationes naturales ad alias potentias pertinentes ordinentur secundum rationem. Unde hoc est apud omnes communiter rectum, ut secundum rationem dirigantur omnes hominum inclinationes.

neither is the truth or rectitude the same for all, nor, where it is the same, is it equally known by all. Thus it is right and true for all to act according to reason: and from this principle it follows as a proper conclusion, that goods entrusted to another should be restored to their owner. Now this is true for the majority of cases: but it may happen in a particular case that it would be injurious, and therefore unreasonable, to restore goods held in trust; for instance, if they are claimed for the purpose of fighting against one's country. And this principle will be found to fail the more, according as we descend further into detail, e.g., if one were to say that goods held in trust should be restored with such and such a guarantee, or in such and such a way; because the greater the number of conditions added, the greater the number of ways in which the principle may fail, so that it be not right to restore or not to restore.

Consequently we must say that the natural law, as to common first principles, is the same for all, both as to rectitude and as to knowledge. But as to certain matters of detail, which are conclusions, as it were, of those general principles, it is the same for all in the majority of cases, both as to rectitude and as to knowledge; and yet in some few cases it may fail, both as to rectitude, by reason of certain obstacles (just as natures subject to generation and corruption fail in some few cases on account of some obstacle), and as to knowledge, since in some the reason is perverted by passion, or evil habit, or an evil disposition of nature; thus formerly, theft, although it is expressly contrary to the natural law, was not considered wrong among the Germans, as Julius Caesar relates (*De Bello Gall.* vi).

REPLY OBJ. 1: The meaning of the sentence quoted is not that whatever is contained in the Law and the Gospel belongs to the natural law, since they contain many things that are above nature; but that whatever belongs to the natural law is fully contained in them. Wherefore Gratian, after saying that *the natural law is what is contained in the Law and the Gospel*, adds at once, by way of example, *by which everyone is commanded to do to others as he would be done by.*

REPLY OBJ. 2: The saying of the Philosopher is to be understood of things that are naturally just, not as general principles, but as conclusions drawn from them, having rectitude in the majority of cases, but failing in a few.

REPLY OBJ. 3: As, in man, reason rules and commands the other powers, so all the natural inclinations belonging to the other powers must needs be directed according to reason. Wherefore it is universally right for all men, that all their inclinations should be directed according to reason.

Article 5

Whether the Natural Law Can Be Changed?

AD QUINTUM SIC PROCEDITUR. Videtur quod lex naturae mutari possit. Quia super illud Eccli. XVII, *addidit eis disciplinam et legem vitae*, dicit Glossa, *legem litterae, quantum ad correctionem legis naturalis, scribi voluit.* Sed illud quod corrigitur, mutatur. Ergo lex naturalis potest mutari.

PRAETEREA, contra legem naturalem est occisio innocentis, et etiam adulterium et furtum. Sed ista inveniuntur esse mutata a Deo, puta cum Deus praecepit Abrahae quod occideret filium innocentem, ut habetur Gen. XXII; et cum praecepit Iudaeis ut mutuata Aegyptiorum vasa subriperent, ut habetur Exod. XII; et cum praecepit Osee ut uxorem fornicariam acciperet, ut habetur Osee I. Ergo lex naturalis potest mutari.

PRAETEREA, Isidorus dicit, in libro Etymol., quod *communis omnium possessio, et una libertas, est de iure naturali.* Sed haec videmus esse commutata per leges humanas. Ergo videtur quod lex naturalis sit mutabilis.

SED CONTRA est quod dicitur in decretis, dist. V, *naturale ius ab exordio rationalis creaturae. Nec variatur tempore, sed immutabile permanet.*

RESPONDEO dicendum quod lex naturalis potest intelligi mutari dupliciter. Uno modo, per hoc quod aliquid ei addatur. Et sic nihil prohibet legem naturalem mutari, multa enim supra legem naturalem superaddita sunt, ad humanam vitam utilia, tam per legem divinam, quam etiam per leges humanas.

Alio modo intelligitur mutatio legis naturalis per modum subtractionis, ut scilicet aliquid desinat esse de lege naturali, quod prius fuit secundum legem naturalem. Et sic quantum ad prima principia legis naturae, lex naturae est omnino immutabilis. Quantum autem ad secunda praecepta, quae diximus esse quasi quasdam proprias conclusiones propinquas primis principiis, sic lex naturalis non immutatur quin ut in pluribus rectum sit semper quod lex naturalis habet. Potest tamen immutari in aliquo particulari, et in paucioribus, propter aliquas speciales causas impedientes observantiam talium praeceptorum, ut supra dictum est.

AD PRIMUM ergo dicendum quod lex scripta dicitur esse data ad correctionem legis naturae, vel quia per legem scriptam suppletum est quod legi naturae deerat, vel quia lex naturae in aliquorum cordibus, quantum ad aliqua, corrupta erat intantum ut existimarent esse bona quae naturaliter sunt mala; et talis corruptio correctione indigebat.

AD SECUNDUM dicendum quod naturali morte moriuntur omnes communiter, tam nocentes quam

OBJECTION 1: It would seem that the natural law can be changed. Because on Ecclus. 17:9, *He gave them instructions, and the law of life*, the gloss says: *He wished the law of the letter to be written, in order to correct the law of nature.* But that which is corrected is changed. Therefore the natural law can be changed.

OBJ. 2: Further, the slaying of the innocent, adultery, and theft are against the natural law. But we find these things changed by God: as when God commanded Abraham to slay his innocent son (Gen 22:2); and when he ordered the Jews to borrow and purloin the vessels of the Egyptians (Exod 12:35); and when He commanded Osee to take to himself *a wife of fornications* (Hos 1:2). Therefore the natural law can be changed.

OBJ. 3: Further, Isidore says (*Etym.* 5:4) that *the possession of all things in common, and universal freedom, are matters of natural law.* But these things are seen to be changed by human laws. Therefore it seems that the natural law is subject to change.

ON THE CONTRARY, It is said in the *Decretals* (Dist. v): *The natural law dates from the creation of the rational creature. It does not vary according to time, but remains unchangeable.*

I ANSWER THAT, A change in the natural law may be understood in two ways. First, by way of addition. In this sense nothing hinders the natural law from being changed: since many things for the benefit of human life have been added over and above the natural law, both by the Divine law and by human laws.

Second, a change in the natural law may be understood by way of subtraction, so that what previously was according to the natural law, ceases to be so. In this sense, the natural law is altogether unchangeable in its first principles: but in its secondary principles, which, as we have said (A4), are certain detailed proximate conclusions drawn from the first principles, the natural law is not changed so that what it prescribes be not right in most cases. But it may be changed in some particular cases of rare occurrence, through some special causes hindering the observance of such precepts, as stated above (A4).

REPLY OBJ. 1: The written law is said to be given for the correction of the natural law, either because it supplies what was wanting to the natural law; or because the natural law was perverted in the hearts of some men, as to certain matters, so that they esteemed those things good which are naturally evil; which perversion stood in need of correction.

REPLY OBJ. 2: All men alike, both guilty and innocent, die the death of nature: which death of nature is inflicted by

innocentes. Quae quidem naturalis mors divina potestate inducitur propter peccatum originale; secundum illud I Reg. II, *dominus mortificat et vivificat.* Et ideo absque aliqua iniustitia, secundum mandatum Dei, potest infligi mors cuicumque homini, vel nocenti vel innocenti. Similiter etiam adulterium est concubitus cum uxore aliena, quae quidem est ei deputata secundum legem divinitus traditam. Unde ad quamcumque mulierem aliquis accedat ex mandato divino, non est adulterium nec fornicatio. Et eadem ratio est de furto, quod est acceptio rei alienae. Quidquid enim accipit aliquis ex mandato Dei, qui est dominus universorum, non accipit absque voluntate domini, quod est furari. Nec solum in rebus humanis quidquid a Deo mandatur, hoc ipso est debitum, sed etiam in rebus naturalibus quidquid a Deo fit, est quodammodo naturale, ut in primo dictum est.

AD TERTIUM dicendum quod aliquid dicitur esse de iure naturali dupliciter. Uno modo, quia ad hoc natura inclinat, sicut non esse iniuriam alteri faciendam. Alio modo, quia natura non induxit contrarium, sicut possemus dicere quod hominem esse nudum est de iure naturali, quia natura non dedit ei vestitum, sed ars adinvenit. Et hoc modo communis omnium possessio, et omnium una libertas, dicitur esse de iure naturali, quia scilicet distinctio possessionum et servitus non sunt inductae a natura, sed per hominum rationem, ad utilitatem humanae vitae. Et sic in hoc lex naturae non est mutata nisi per additionem.

the power of God on account of original sin, according to 1 Kgs. 2:6: *The Lord killeth and maketh alive.* Consequently, by the command of God, death can be inflicted on any man, guilty or innocent, without any injustice whatever. In like manner adultery is intercourse with another's wife; who is allotted to him by the law emanating from God. Consequently intercourse with any woman, by the command of God, is neither adultery nor fornication. The same applies to theft, which is the taking of another's property. For whatever is taken by the command of God, to Whom all things belong, is not taken against the will of its owner, whereas it is in this that theft consists. Nor is it only in human things, that whatever is commanded by God is right; but also in natural things, whatever is done by God, is, in some way, natural, as stated in the FP, Q105, A6, ad 1.

REPLY OBJ. 3: A thing is said to belong to the natural law in two ways. First, because nature inclines thereto: e.g., that one should not do harm to another. Second, because nature did not bring in the contrary: thus we might say that for man to be naked is of the natural law, because nature did not give him clothes, but art invented them. In this sense, *the possession of all things in common and universal freedom* are said to be of the natural law, because, to wit, the distinction of possessions and slavery were not brought in by nature, but devised by human reason for the benefit of human life. Accordingly the law of nature was not changed in this respect, except by addition.

Article 6

Whether the Law of Nature Can Be Abolished from the Heart of Man?

AD SEXTUM SIC PROCEDITUR. Videtur quod lex naturae possit a corde hominis aboleri. Quia Rom. II, super illud, *cum gentes, quae legem non habent*, etc., dicit Glossa quod *in interiori homine per gratiam innovato, lex iustitiae inscribitur, quam deleverat culpa.* Sed lex iustitiae est lex naturae. Ergo lex naturae potest deleri.

PRAETEREA, lex gratiae est efficacior quam lex naturae. Sed lex gratiae deletur per culpam. Ergo multo magis lex naturae potest deleri.

PRAETEREA, illud quod lege statuitur, inducitur quasi iustum. Sed multa sunt ab hominibus statuta contra legem naturae. Ergo lex naturae potest a cordibus hominum aboleri.

SED CONTRA est quod Augustinus dicit, in II Confess., *lex tua scripta est in cordibus hominum, quam nec ulla quidem delet iniquitas.* Sed lex scripta in cordibus hominum est lex naturalis. Ergo lex naturalis deleri non potest.

OBJECTION 1: It would seem that the natural law can be abolished from the heart of man. Because on Rm. 2:14, *When the Gentiles who have not the law*, etc. a gloss says that *the law of righteousness, which sin had blotted out, is graven on the heart of man when he is restored by grace.* But the law of righteousness is the law of nature. Therefore the law of nature can be blotted out.

OBJ. 2: Further, the law of grace is more efficacious than the law of nature. But the law of grace is blotted out by sin. Much more therefore can the law of nature be blotted out.

OBJ. 3: Further, that which is established by law is made just. But many things are enacted by men, which are contrary to the law of nature. Therefore the law of nature can be abolished from the heart of man.

ON THE CONTRARY, Augustine says (*Confess.* ii): *Thy law is written in the hearts of men, which iniquity itself effaces not.* But the law which is written in men's hearts is the natural law. Therefore the natural law cannot be blotted out.

RESPONDEO dicendum quod, sicut supra dictum est, ad legem naturalem pertinent primo quidem quaedam praecepta communissima, quae sunt omnibus nota, quaedam autem secundaria praecepta magis propria, quae sunt quasi conclusiones propinquae principiis. Quantum ergo ad illa principia communia, lex naturalis nullo modo potest a cordibus hominum deleri in universali. Deletur tamen in particulari operabili, secundum quod ratio impeditur applicare commune principium ad particulare operabile, propter concupiscentiam vel aliquam aliam passionem, ut supra dictum est. Quantum vero ad alia praecepta secundaria, potest lex naturalis deleri de cordibus hominum, vel propter malas persuasiones, eo modo quo etiam in speculativis errores contingunt circa conclusiones necessarias; vel etiam propter pravas consuetudines et habitus corruptos; sicut apud quosdam non reputabantur latrocinia peccata, vel etiam vitia contra naturam, ut etiam apostolus dicit, ad Rom. I.

AD PRIMUM ergo dicendum quod culpa delet legem naturae in particulari, non autem in universali, nisi forte quantum ad secunda praecepta legis naturae, eo modo quo dictum est.

AD SECUNDUM dicendum quod gratia etsi sit efficacior quam natura, tamen natura essentialior est homini, et ideo magis permanens.

AD TERTIUM dicendum quod ratio illa procedit de secundis praeceptis legis naturae, contra quae aliqui legislatores statuta aliqua fecerunt, quae sunt iniqua.

I ANSWER THAT, As stated above (AA4,5), there belong to the natural law, first, certain most general precepts, that are known to all; and second, certain secondary and more detailed precepts, which are, as it were, conclusions following closely from first principles. As to those general principles, the natural law, in the universal, can nowise be blotted out from men's hearts. But it is blotted out in the case of a particular action, insofar as reason is hindered from applying the general principle to a particular point of practice, on account of concupiscence or some other passion, as stated above (Q77, A2). But as to the other, i.e., the secondary precepts, the natural law can be blotted out from the human heart, either by evil persuasions, just as in speculative matters errors occur in respect of necessary conclusions; or by vicious customs and corrupt habits, as among some men, theft, and even unnatural vices, as the Apostle states (Rom i), were not esteemed sinful.

REPLY OBJ. 1: Sin blots out the law of nature in particular cases, not universally, except perchance in regard to the secondary precepts of the natural law, in the way stated above.

REPLY OBJ. 2: Although grace is more efficacious than nature, yet nature is more essential to man, and therefore more enduring.

REPLY OBJ. 3: This argument is true of the secondary precepts of the natural law, against which some legislators have framed certain enactments which are unjust.

QUESTION 95

Of Human Law

Deinde considerandum est de lege humana. Et primo quidem, de ipsa lege secundum se; secundo, de potestate eius; tertio, de eius mutabilitate. Circa primum quaeruntur quatuor.

    Primo, de utilitate ipsius.
    Secundo, de origine eius.
    Tertio, de qualitate ipsius.
    Quarto, de divisione eiusdem.

We must now consider human law; and (1) this law considered in itself; (2) its power; (3) its mutability. Under the first head there are four points of inquiry:

    (1) Its utility.
    (2) Its origin.
    (3) Its quality.
    (4) Its division.

Article 1

Whether It Was Useful for Laws to Be Framed by Men?

Ad primum sic proceditur. Videtur quod non fuerit utile aliquas leges poni ab hominibus. Intentio enim cuiuslibet legis est ut per eam homines fiant boni, sicut supra dictum est. Sed homines magis inducuntur ad bonum voluntarii per monitiones, quam coacti per leges. Ergo non fuit necessarium leges ponere.

Praeterea, sicut dicit philosophus, in V Ethic., *ad iudicem confugiunt homines sicut ad iustum animatum.* Sed iustitia animata est melior quam inanimata, quae legibus continetur. Ergo melius fuisset ut executio iustitiae committeretur arbitrio iudicum, quam quod super hoc lex aliqua ederetur.

Praeterea, lex omnis directiva est actuum humanorum, ut ex supradictis patet. Sed cum humani actus consistant in singularibus, quae sunt infinita, non possunt ea quae ad directionem humanorum actuum pertinent, sufficienter considerari, nisi ab aliquo sapiente, qui inspiciat singula. Ergo melius fuisset arbitrio sapientum dirigi actus humanos, quam aliqua lege posita. Ergo non fuit necessarium leges humanas ponere.

Sed contra est quod Isidorus dicit, in libro Etymol., *factae sunt leges ut earum metu humana coerceretur audacia, tutaque sit inter improbos innocentia, et in ipsis improbis formidato supplicio refrenetur nocendi facultas.* Sed haec sunt maxime necessaria humano generi. Ergo necessarium fuit ponere leges humanas.

Respondeo dicendum quod, sicut ex supradictis patet, homini naturaliter inest quaedam aptitudo ad virtutem; sed ipsa virtutis perfectio necesse est quod homini adveniat per aliquam disciplinam. Sicut etiam

Objection 1: It would seem that it was not useful for laws to be framed by men. Because the purpose of every law is that man be made good thereby, as stated above (Q92, A1). But men are more to be induced to be good willingly by means of admonitions, than against their will, by means of laws. Therefore there was no need to frame laws.

Obj. 2: Further, as the Philosopher says (*Ethic.* v, 4), *men have recourse to a judge as to animate justice.* But animate justice is better than inanimate justice, which is contained in laws. Therefore it would have been better for the execution of justice to be entrusted to the decision of judges, than to frame laws in addition.

Obj. 3: Further, every law is framed for the direction of human actions, as is evident from what has been stated above (Q90, AA1,2). But since human actions are about singulars, which are infinite in number, matters pertaining to the direction of human actions cannot be taken into sufficient consideration except by a wise man, who looks into each one of them. Therefore it would have been better for human acts to be directed by the judgment of wise men, than by the framing of laws. Therefore there was no need of human laws.

On the contrary, Isidore says (*Etym.* v, 20): *Laws were made that in fear thereof human audacity might be held in check, that innocence might be safeguarded in the midst of wickedness, and that the dread of punishment might prevent the wicked from doing harm.* But these things are most necessary to mankind. Therefore it was necessary that human laws should be made.

I answer that, As stated above (Q63, A1; Q94, A3), man has a natural aptitude for virtue; but the perfection of virtue must be acquired by man by means of some kind of training. Thus we observe that man is helped by industry in

videmus quod per aliquam industriam subvenitur homini in suis necessitatibus, puta in cibo et vestitu, quorum initia quaedam habet a natura, scilicet rationem et manus, non autem ipsum complementum, sicut cetera animalia, quibus natura dedit sufficienter tegumentum et cibum. Ad hanc autem disciplinam non de facili invenitur homo sibi sufficiens. Quia perfectio virtutis praecipue consistit in retrahendo hominem ab indebitis delectationibus, ad quas praecipue homines sunt proni, et maxime iuvenes, circa quos efficacior est disciplina. Et ideo oportet quod huiusmodi disciplinam, per quam ad virtutem perveniatur, homines ab alio sortiantur. Et quidem quantum ad illos iuvenes qui sunt proni ad actus virtutum, ex bona dispositione naturae, vel consuetudine, vel magis divino munere, sufficit disciplina paterna, quae est per monitiones. Sed quia inveniuntur quidam protervi et ad vitia proni, qui verbis de facili moveri non possunt; necessarium fuit ut per vim et metum cohiberentur a malo, ut saltem sic male facere desistentes, et aliis quietam vitam redderent, et ipsi tandem per huiusmodi assuetudinem ad hoc perducerentur quod voluntarie facerent quae prius metu implebant, et sic fierent virtuosi. Huiusmodi autem disciplina cogens metu poenae, est disciplina legum. Unde necessarium fuit ad pacem hominum et virtutem, ut leges ponerentur, quia sicut philosophus dicit, in I Polit., *sicut homo, si sit perfectus virtute, est optimum animalium; sic, si sit separatus a lege et iustitia, est pessimum omnium*; quia homo habet arma rationis ad explendas concupiscentias et saevitias, quae non habent alia animalia.

AD PRIMUM ergo dicendum quod homines bene dispositi melius inducuntur ad virtutem monitionibus voluntariis quam coactione, sed quidam male dispositi non ducuntur ad virtutem nisi cogantur.

AD SECUNDUM dicendum quod, sicut philosophus dicit, I Rhetor., *melius est omnia ordinari lege, quam dimittere iudicum arbitrio*. Et hoc propter tria. Primo quidem, quia facilius est invenire paucos sapientes, qui sufficiant ad rectas leges ponendas, quam multos, qui requirerentur ad recte iudicandum de singulis. Secundo, quia illi qui leges ponunt, ex multo tempore considerant quid lege ferendum sit, sed iudicia de singularibus factis fiunt ex casibus subito exortis. Facilius autem ex multis consideratis potest homo videre quid rectum sit, quam solum ex aliquo uno facto. Tertio, quia legislatores iudicant in universali, et de futuris, sed homines iudiciis praesidentes iudicant de praesentibus, ad quae afficiuntur amore vel odio, aut aliqua cupiditate; et sic eorum depravatur iudicium.

Quia ergo iustitia animata iudicis non invenitur in multis; et quia flexibilis est; ideo necessarium fuit, in quibuscumque est possibile, legem determinare quid iudicandum sit, et paucissima arbitrio hominum committere.

his necessities, for instance, in food and clothing. Certain beginnings of these he has from nature, viz., his reason and his hands; but he has not the full complement, as other animals have, to whom nature has given sufficiency of clothing and food. Now it is difficult to see how man could suffice for himself in the matter of this training: since the perfection of virtue consists chiefly in withdrawing man from undue pleasures, to which above all man is inclined, and especially the young, who are more capable of being trained. Consequently a man needs to receive this training from another, whereby to arrive at the perfection of virtue. And as to those young people who are inclined to acts of virtue, by their good natural disposition, or by custom, or rather by the gift of God, paternal training suffices, which is by admonitions. But since some are found to be depraved, and prone to vice, and not easily amenable to words, it was necessary for such to be restrained from evil by force and fear, in order that, at least, they might desist from evil-doing, and leave others in peace, and that they themselves, by being habituated in this way, might be brought to do willingly what hitherto they did from fear, and thus become virtuous. Now this kind of training, which compels through fear of punishment, is the discipline of laws. Therefore in order that man might have peace and virtue, it was necessary for laws to be framed: for, as the Philosopher says (*Polit.* i, 2), *as man is the most noble of animals if he be perfect in virtue, so is he the worst of all, if he be severed from law and righteousness*; because man can use his reason to devise means of satisfying his lusts and evil passions, which other animals are unable to do.

REPLY OBJ. 1: Men who are well disposed are led willingly to virtue by being admonished better than by coercion: but men who are evilly disposed are not led to virtue unless they are compelled.

REPLY OBJ. 2: As the Philosopher says (*Rhet.* i, 1), *it is better that all things be regulated by law, than left to be decided by judges*: and this for three reasons. First, because it is easier to find a few wise men competent to frame right laws, than to find the many who would be necessary to judge aright of each single case. Second, because those who make laws consider long beforehand what laws to make; whereas judgment on each single case has to be pronounced as soon as it arises: and it is easier for man to see what is right, by taking many instances into consideration, than by considering one solitary fact. Third, because lawgivers judge in the abstract and of future events; whereas men presiding in judgment judge of things present, towards which they are affected by love, hatred, or some kind of cupidity; wherefore their judgment is perverted.

Since then the animated justice of the judge is not found in every man, and since it can be deflected, therefore it was necessary, whenever possible, for the law to determine how to judge, and for very few matters to be left to the decision of men.

AD TERTIUM dicendum quod quaedam singularia, quae non possunt lege comprehendi, necesse est committere iudicibus, ut ibidem philosophus dicit, puta de eo quod est factum esse vel non esse, et de aliis huiusmodi.

REPLY OBJ. 3: Certain individual facts which cannot be covered by the law *have necessarily to be committed to judges*, as the Philosopher says in the same passage: for instance, *concerning something that has happened or not happened*, and the like.

Article 2

Whether Every Human Law Is Derived from the Natural Law?

AD SECUNDUM SIC PROCEDITUR. Videtur quod non omnis lex humanitus posita a lege naturali derivetur. Dicit enim philosophus, in V Ethic., quod *iustum legale est quod ex principio quidem nihil differt utrum sic vel aliter fiat.* Sed in his quae oriuntur ex lege naturali, differt utrum sic vel aliter fiat. Ergo ea quae sunt legibus humanis statuta, non omnia derivantur a lege naturae.

PRAETEREA, ius positivum dividitur contra ius naturale, ut patet per Isidorum, in libro Etymol., et per philosophum, in V Ethic. Sed ea quae derivantur a principiis communibus legis naturae sicut conclusiones, pertinent ad legem naturae, ut supra dictum est. Ergo ea quae sunt de lege humana, non derivantur a lege naturae.

PRAETEREA, lex naturae est eadem apud omnes, dicit enim philosophus, in V Ethic., quod *naturale iustum est quod ubique habet eandem potentiam.* Si igitur leges humanae a naturali lege derivarentur, sequeretur quod etiam ipsae essent eaedem apud omnes. Quod patet esse falsum.

PRAETEREA, eorum quae a lege naturali derivantur, potest aliqua ratio assignari. Sed non omnium quae a maioribus lege statuta sunt, ratio reddi potest, ut iurisperitus dicit. Ergo non omnes leges humanae derivantur a lege naturali.

SED CONTRA est quod Tullius dicit, in sua Rhetor., *res a natura profectas, et a consuetudine probatas, legum metus et religio sanxit.*

RESPONDEO dicendum quod, sicut Augustinus dicit, in I de Lib. Arb., *non videtur esse lex, quae iusta non fuerit.* Unde inquantum habet de iustitia, intantum habet de virtute legis. In rebus autem humanis dicitur esse aliquid iustum ex eo quod est rectum secundum regulam rationis. Rationis autem prima regula est lex naturae, ut ex supradictis patet. Unde omnis lex humanitus posita intantum habet de ratione legis, inquantum a lege naturae derivatur. Si vero in aliquo, a lege naturali discordet, iam non erit lex sed legis corruptio.

Sed sciendum est quod a lege naturali dupliciter potest aliquid derivari, uno modo, sicut conclusiones ex principiis; alio modo, sicut determinationes quaedam aliquorum communium. Primus quidem modus est

OBJECTION 1: It would seem that not every human law is derived from the natural law. For the Philosopher says (*Ethic.* v, 7) that *the legal just is that which originally was a matter of indifference.* But those things which arise from the natural law are not matters of indifference. Therefore the enactments of human laws are not derived from the natural law.

OBJ. 2: Further, positive law is contrasted with natural law, as stated by Isidore (*Etym.* v, 4) and the Philosopher (*Ethic.* v, 7). But those things which flow as conclusions from the general principles of the natural law belong to the natural law, as stated above (Q94, A4). Therefore that which is established by human law does not belong to the natural law.

OBJ. 3: Further, the law of nature is the same for all; since the Philosopher says (*Ethic.* v, 7) that *the natural just is that which is equally valid everywhere.* If therefore human laws were derived from the natural law, it would follow that they too are the same for all: which is clearly false.

OBJ. 4: Further, it is possible to give a reason for things which are derived from the natural law. But *it is not possible to give the reason for all the legal enactments of the lawgivers,* as the jurist says. Therefore not all human laws are derived from the natural law.

ON THE CONTRARY, Tully says (*Rhet.* ii): *Things which emanated from nature and were approved by custom, were sanctioned by fear and reverence for the laws.*

I ANSWER THAT, As Augustine says (*De Lib. Arb.* i, 5) *that which is not just seems to be no law at all*: wherefore the force of a law depends on the extent of its justice. Now in human affairs a thing is said to be just, from being right, according to the rule of reason. But the first rule of reason is the law of nature, as is clear from what has been stated above (Q91, A2, ad 2). Consequently every human law has just so much of the nature of law, as it is derived from the law of nature. But if in any point it deflects from the law of nature, it is no longer a law but a perversion of law.

But it must be noted that something may be derived from the natural law in two ways: first, as a conclusion from premises, second, by way of determination of certain generalities. The first way is like to that by which, in sciences,

similis ei quo in scientiis ex principiis conclusiones demonstrativae producuntur. Secundo vero modo simile est quod in artibus formae communes determinantur ad aliquid speciale, sicut artifex formam communem domus necesse est quod determinet ad hanc vel illam domus figuram. Derivantur ergo quaedam a principiis communibus legis naturae per modum conclusionum, sicut hoc quod est non esse occidendum, ut conclusio quaedam derivari potest ab eo quod est nulli esse malum faciendum. Quaedam vero per modum determinationis, sicut lex naturae habet quod ille qui peccat, puniatur; sed quod tali poena puniatur, hoc est quaedam determinatio legis naturae.

Utraque igitur inveniuntur in lege humana posita. Sed ea quae sunt primi modi, continentur lege humana non tanquam sint solum lege posita, sed habent etiam aliquid vigoris ex lege naturali. Sed ea quae sunt secundi modi, ex sola lege humana vigorem habent.

AD PRIMUM ergo dicendum quod philosophus loquitur de illis quae sunt lege posita per determinationem vel specificationem quandam praeceptorum legis naturae.

AD SECUNDUM dicendum quod ratio illa procedit de his quae derivantur a lege naturae tanquam conclusiones.

AD TERTIUM dicendum quod principia communia legis naturae non possunt eodem modo applicari omnibus, propter multam varietatem rerum humanarum. Et exinde provenit diversitas legis positivae apud diversos.

AD QUARTUM dicendum quod verbum illud iurisperiti intelligendum est in his quae sunt introducta a maioribus circa particulares determinationes legis naturalis; ad quas quidem determinationes se habet expertorum et prudentum iudicium sicut ad quaedam principia; inquantum scilicet statim vident quid congruentius sit particulariter determinari.

Unde philosophus dicit, in VI Ethic., quod *in talibus oportet attendere expertorum et seniorum vel prudentum indemonstrabilibus enuntiationibus et opinionibus, non minus quam demonstrationibus.*

demonstrated conclusions are drawn from the principles: while the second mode is likened to that whereby, in the arts, general forms are particularized as to details: thus the craftsman needs to determine the general form of a house to some particular shape. Some things are therefore derived from the general principles of the natural law, by way of conclusions; e.g., that *one must not kill* may be derived as a conclusion from the principle that *one should do harm to no man*: while some are derived therefrom by way of determination; e.g., the law of nature has it that the evil-doer should be punished; but that he be punished in this or that way, is a determination of the law of nature.

Accordingly both modes of derivation are found in the human law. But those things which are derived in the first way, are contained in human law not as emanating therefrom exclusively, but have some force from the natural law also. But those things which are derived in the second way, have no other force than that of human law.

REPLY OBJ. 1: The Philosopher is speaking of those enactments which are by way of determination or specification of the precepts of the natural law.

REPLY OBJ. 2: This argument avails for those things that are derived from the natural law, by way of conclusions.

REPLY OBJ. 3: The general principles of the natural law cannot be applied to all men in the same way on account of the great variety of human affairs: and hence arises the diversity of positive laws among various people.

REPLY OBJ. 4: These words of the Jurist are to be understood as referring to decisions of rulers in determining particular points of the natural law: on which determinations the judgment of expert and prudent men is based as on its principles; in so far, to wit, as they see at once what is the best thing to decide.

Hence the Philosopher says (*Ethic.* vi, 11) that in such matters, *we ought to pay as much attention to the undemonstrated sayings and opinions of persons who surpass us in experience, age and prudence, as to their demonstrations.*

Article 3

Whether Isidore's Description of the Quality of Positive Law Is Appropriate?

AD TERTIUM SIC PROCEDITUR. Videtur quod Isidorus inconvenienter qualitatem legis positivae describat, dicens, *erit lex honesta, iusta, possibilis secundum naturam, secundum consuetudinem patriae, loco temporique conveniens, necessaria, utilis; manifesta quoque, ne aliquid per obscuritatem in captionem contineat; nullo*

OBJECTION 1: It would seem that Isidore's description of the quality of positive law is not appropriate, when he says (*Etym.* v, 21): *Law shall be virtuous, just, possible to nature, according to the custom of the country, suitable to place and time, necessary, useful; clearly expressed, lest by its obscurity it lead to misunderstanding; framed for no private*

privato commodo, sed pro communi utilitate civium scripta. Supra enim in tribus conditionibus qualitatem legis explicaverat, dicens, *lex erit omne quod ratione constiterit, dumtaxat quod religioni congruat, quod disciplinae conveniat, quod saluti proficiat.* Ergo superflue postmodum conditiones legis multiplicat.

PRAETEREA, iustitia pars est honestatis; ut Tullius dicit, in I de Offic. Ergo postquam dixerat honesta, superflue additur iusta.

PRAETEREA, lex scripta, secundum Isidorum, contra consuetudinem dividitur. Non ergo debuit in definitione legis poni quod esset secundum consuetudinem patriae.

PRAETEREA, necessarium dupliciter dicitur. Scilicet id quod est necessarium simpliciter, quod impossibile est aliter se habere, et huiusmodi necessarium non subiacet humano iudicio, unde talis necessitas ad legem humanam non pertinet. Est etiam aliquid necessarium propter finem, et talis necessitas idem est quod utilitas. Ergo superflue utrumque ponitur, necessaria et utilis.

SED CONTRA est auctoritas ipsius Isidori.

RESPONDEO dicendum quod uniuscuiusque rei quae est propter finem, necesse est quod forma determinetur secundum proportionem ad finem; sicut forma serrae talis est qualis convenit sectioni; ut patet in II Physic. Quaelibet etiam res recta et mensurata oportet quod habeat formam proportionalem suae regulae et mensurae. Lex autem humana utrumque habet, quia et est aliquid ordinatum ad finem; et est quaedam regula vel mensura regulata vel mensurata quadam superiori mensura; quae quidem est duplex, scilicet lex divina et lex naturae, ut ex supradictis patet. Finis autem humanae legis est utilitas hominum; sicut etiam iurisperitus dicit. Et ideo Isidorus in conditione legis, primo quidem tria posuit, scilicet quod religioni congruat, inquantum scilicet est proportionata legi divinae; quod disciplinae conveniat, inquantum est proportionata legi naturae; quod saluti proficiat, inquantum est proportionata utilitati humanae.

Et ad haec tria omnes aliae conditiones quas postea ponit, reducuntur. Nam quod dicitur honesta, refertur ad hoc quod religioni congruat. Quod autem subditur, *iusta, possibilis secundum naturam, secundum consuetudinem patriae, loco temporique conveniens*, additur ad hoc quod conveniat disciplinae. Attenditur enim humana disciplina primum quidem quantum ad ordinem rationis, qui importatur in hoc quod dicitur iusta. Secundo, quantum ad facultatem agentium. Debet enim esse disciplina conveniens unicuique secundum suam possibilitatem, observata etiam possibilitate naturae (non enim eadem sunt imponenda pueris, quae imponuntur viris perfectis); et secundum humanam consuetudinem; non enim potest homo solus in societate vivere, aliis morem non gerens. Tertio, quantum ad debitas circumstantias, dicit, loco temporique conveniens. Quod vero

benefit, but for the common good. Because he had previously expressed the quality of law in three conditions, saying that *law is anything founded on reason, provided that it foster religion, be helpful to discipline, and further the common weal.* Therefore it was needless to add any further conditions to these.

OBJ. 2: Further, Justice is included in honesty, as Tully says (*De Offic.* vii). Therefore after saying *honest* it was superfluous to add *just.*

OBJ. 3: Further, written law is condivided with custom, according to Isidore (*Etym.* ii, 10). Therefore it should not be stated in the definition of law that it is *according to the custom of the country.*

OBJ. 4: Further, a thing may be necessary in two ways. It may be necessary simply, because it cannot be otherwise: and that which is necessary in this way, is not subject to human judgment, wherefore human law is not concerned with necessity of this kind. Again a thing may be necessary for an end: and this necessity is the same as usefulness. Therefore it is superfluous to say both *necessary* and *useful.*

ON THE CONTRARY, stands the authority of Isidore.

I ANSWER THAT, Whenever a thing is for an end, its form must be determined proportionately to that end; as the form of a saw is such as to be suitable for cutting (*Phys.* ii, text. 88). Again, everything that is ruled and measured must have a form proportionate to its rule and measure. Now both these conditions are verified of human law: since it is both something ordained to an end; and is a rule or measure ruled or measured by a higher measure. And this higher measure is twofold, viz., the Divine law and the natural law, as explained above (A2; Q93, A3). Now the end of human law is to be useful to man, as the jurist states. Wherefore Isidore in determining the nature of law, lays down, at first, three conditions; viz., that it *foster religion*, inasmuch as it is proportionate to the Divine law; that it be *helpful to discipline*, inasmuch as it is proportionate to the nature law; and that it *further the common weal*, inasmuch as it is proportionate to the utility of mankind.

All the other conditions mentioned by him are reduced to these three. For it is called virtuous because it fosters religion. And when he goes on to say that it should be *just, possible to nature, according to the customs of the country, adapted to place and time*, he implies that it should be helpful to discipline. For human discipline depends first on the order of reason, to which he refers by saying *just*: second, it depends on the ability of the agent; because discipline should be adapted to each one according to his ability, taking also into account the ability of nature (for the same burdens should be not laid on children as adults); and should be according to human customs; since man cannot live alone in society, paying no heed to others: third, it depends on certain circumstances, in respect of which he says, *adapted to place and time*. The remaining words, *necessary, useful*, etc. mean that law should further the common weal: so

subditur, necessaria, utilis, etc., refertur ad hoc quod expediat saluti, ut necessitas referatur ad remotionem malorum; utilitas, ad consecutionem bonorum; manifestatio vero, ad cavendum nocumentum quod ex ipsa lege posset provenire. Et quia, sicut supra dictum est, lex ordinatur ad bonum commune, hoc ipsum in ultima parte determinationis ostenditur.

Et per hoc patet responsio ad obiecta.

that *necessity* refers to the removal of evils; *usefulness* to the attainment of good; *clearness of expression*, to the need of preventing any harm ensuing from the law itself. And since, as stated above (Q90, A2), law is ordained to the common good, this is expressed in the last part of the description.

This suffices for the Replies to the Objections.

Article 4

Whether Isidore's Division of Human Laws Is Appropriate?

Ad quartum sic proceditur. Videtur quod inconvenienter Isidorus divisionem legum humanarum ponat, sive iuris humani. Sub hoc enim iure comprehendit ius gentium, quod ideo sic nominatur, ut ipse dicit, quia eo omnes fere gentes utuntur. Sed sicut ipse dicit, *ius naturale est quod est commune omnium nationum*. Ergo ius gentium non continetur sub iure positivo humano, sed magis sub iure naturali.

Praeterea, ea quae habent eandem vim, non videntur formaliter differre, sed solum materialiter. Sed leges, plebiscita, senatusconsulta, et alia huiusmodi quae ponit, omnia habent eandem vim. Ergo videtur quod non differant nisi materialiter. Sed talis distinctio in arte non est curanda, cum possit esse in infinitum. Ergo inconvenienter huiusmodi divisio humanarum legum introducitur.

Praeterea, sicut in civitate sunt principes et sacerdotes et milites, ita etiam sunt et alia hominum officia. Ergo videtur quod, sicut ponitur quoddam ius militare, et ius publicum, quod consistit in sacerdotibus et magistratibus; ita etiam debeant poni alia iura, ad alia officia civitatis pertinentia.

Praeterea, ea quae sunt per accidens, sunt praetermittenda. Sed accidit legi ut ab hoc vel illo homine feratur. Ergo inconvenienter ponitur divisio legum humanarum ex nominibus legislatorum, ut scilicet quaedam dicatur Cornelia, quaedam Falcidia, et cetera.

In contrarium auctoritas Isidori sufficiat.

Respondeo dicendum quod unumquodque potest per se dividi secundum id quod in eius ratione continetur. Sicut in ratione animalis continetur anima, quae est rationalis vel irrationalis, et ideo animal proprie et per se dividitur secundum rationale et irrationale; non autem secundum album et nigrum, quae sunt omnino praeter rationem eius. Sunt autem multa de ratione legis humanae, secundum quorum quodlibet lex humana proprie et per se dividi potest. Est enim primo de ratione legis humanae quod sit derivata a lege naturae,

Objection 1: It would seem that Isidore wrongly divided human statutes or human law (*Etym*. v, 4, seqq.). For under this law he includes the *law of nations*, so called, because, as he says, *nearly all nations use it*. But as he says, *natural law is that which is common to all nations*. Therefore the law of nations is not contained under positive human law, but rather under natural law.

Obj. 2: Further, those laws which have the same force, seem to differ not formally but only materially. But *statutes, decrees of the commonalty, senatorial decrees*, and the like which he mentions (*Etym*. v, 9), all have the same force. Therefore they do not differ, except materially. But art takes no notice of such a distinction: since it may go on to infinity. Therefore this division of human laws is not appropriate.

Obj. 3: Further, just as, in the state, there are princes, priests and soldiers, so are there other human offices. Therefore it seems that, as this division includes *military law*, and *public law*, referring to priests and magistrates; so also it should include other laws pertaining to other offices of the state.

Obj. 4: Further, those things that are accidental should be passed over. But it is accidental to law that it be framed by this or that man. Therefore it is unreasonable to divide laws according to the names of lawgivers, so that one be called the *Cornelian* law, another the *Falcidian* law, etc.

On the contrary, The authority of Isidore (OBJ1) suffices.

I answer that, A thing can of itself be divided in respect of something contained in the notion of that thing. Thus a soul either rational or irrational is contained in the notion of animal: and therefore animal is divided properly and of itself in respect of its being rational or irrational; but not in the point of its being white or black, which are entirely beside the notion of animal. Now, in the notion of human law, many things are contained, in respect of any of which human law can be divided properly and of itself. For in the first place it belongs to the notion of human law,

ut ex dictis patet. Et secundum hoc dividitur ius positivum in ius gentium et ius civile, secundum duos modos quibus aliquid derivatur a lege naturae, ut supra dictum est. Nam ad ius gentium pertinent ea quae derivantur ex lege naturae sicut conclusiones ex principiis, ut iustae emptiones, venditiones, et alia huiusmodi, sine quibus homines ad invicem convivere non possent; quod est de lege naturae, quia homo est naturaliter animal sociale, ut probatur in I Polit. Quae vero derivantur a lege naturae per modum particularis determinationis, pertinent ad ius civile, secundum quod quaelibet civitas aliquid sibi accommodum determinat.

Secundo est de ratione legis humanae quod ordinetur ad bonum commune civitatis. Et secundum hoc lex humana dividi potest secundum diversitatem eorum qui specialiter dant operam ad bonum commune, sicut sacerdotes, pro populo Deum orantes; principes, populum gubernantes; et milites, pro salute populi pugnantes. Et ideo istis hominibus specialia quaedam iura aptantur.

Tertio est de ratione legis humanae ut instituatur a gubernante communitatem civitatis, sicut supra dictum est. Et secundum hoc distinguuntur leges humanae secundum diversa regimina civitatum. Quorum unum, secundum philosophum, in III Polit., est regnum, quando scilicet civitas gubernatur ab uno, et secundum hoc accipiuntur constitutiones principum. Aliud vero regimen est aristocratia, idest principatus optimorum, vel optimatum, et secundum hoc sumuntur responsa prudentum, et etiam senatusconsulta. Aliud regimen est oligarchia, idest principatus paucorum divitum et potentum, et secundum hoc sumitur ius praetorium, quod etiam honorarium dicitur. Aliud autem regimen est populi, quod nominatur democratia, et secundum hoc sumuntur plebiscita. Aliud autem est tyrannicum, quod est omnino corruptum, unde ex hoc non sumitur aliqua lex. Est etiam aliquod regimen ex istis commixtum, quod est optimum, et secundum hoc sumitur lex, *quam maiores natu simul cum plebibus sanxerunt*, ut Isidorus dicit.

Quarto vero de ratione legis humanae est quod sit directiva humanorum actuum. Et secundum hoc, secundum diversa de quibus leges feruntur, distinguuntur leges, quae interdum ab auctoribus nominantur, sicut distinguitur lex Iulia de adulteriis, lex Cornelia de sicariis, et sic de aliis, non propter auctores, sed propter res de quibus sunt.

AD PRIMUM ergo dicendum quod ius gentium est quidem aliquo modo naturale homini, secundum quod est rationalis, inquantum derivatur a lege naturali per modum conclusionis quae non est multum remota a principiis. Unde de facili in huiusmodi homines

to be derived from the law of nature, as explained above (A2). In this respect positive law is divided into the *law of nations* and *civil law*, according to the two ways in which something may be derived from the law of nature, as stated above (A2). Because, to the law of nations belong those things which are derived from the law of nature, as conclusions from premises, e.g., just buyings and sellings, and the like, without which men cannot live together, which is a point of the law of nature, since man is by nature a social animal, as is proved in *Polit.* i, 2. But those things which are derived from the law of nature by way of particular determination, belong to the civil law, according as each state decides on what is best for itself.

Second, it belongs to the notion of human law, to be ordained to the common good of the state. In this respect human law may be divided according to the different kinds of men who work in a special way for the common good: e.g., priests, by praying to God for the people; princes, by governing the people; soldiers, by fighting for the safety of the people. Wherefore certain special kinds of law are adapted to these men.

Third, it belongs to the notion of human law, to be framed by that one who governs the community of the state, as shown above (Q90, A3). In this respect, there are various human laws according to the various forms of government. Of these, according to the Philosopher (*Polit.* iii, 10) one is *monarchy*, i.e., when the state is governed by one; and then we have *Royal Ordinances*. Another form is *aristocracy*, i.e., government by the best men or men of highest rank; and then we have the *Authoritative legal opinions* and *Decrees of the Senate*. Another form is *oligarchy*, i.e., government by a few rich and powerful men; and then we have *Praetorian*, also called *Honorary*, law. Another form of government is that of the people, which is called *democracy*, and there we have *Decrees of the commonalty*. There is also tyrannical government, which is altogether corrupt, which, therefore, has no corresponding law. Finally, there is a form of government made up of all these, and which is the best: and in this respect we have law sanctioned by the *Lords and Commons*, as stated by Isidore (*Etym.* v, 4, seqq.).

Fourth, it belongs to the notion of human law to direct human actions. In this respect, according to the various matters of which the law treats, there are various kinds of laws, which are sometimes named after their authors: thus we have the *Lex Julia* about adultery, the *Lex Cornelia* concerning assassins, and so on, differentiated in this way, not on account of the authors, but on account of the matters to which they refer.

REPLY OBJ. 1: The law of nations is indeed, in some way, natural to man, insofar as he is a reasonable being, because it is derived from the natural law by way of a conclusion that is not very remote from its premises. Wherefore men easily agreed thereto. Nevertheless it is distinct from

consenserunt. Distinguitur tamen a lege naturali, maxime ab eo quod est omnibus animalibus communis.

AD ALIA patet responsio ex his quae dicta sunt.

the natural law, especially it is distinct from that which is common to all animals.

THE REPLIES to the other Objections are evident from what has been said.

QUESTION 96

OF THE POWER OF HUMAN LAW

Deinde considerandum est de potestate legis humanae. Et circa hoc quaeruntur sex.

Primo, utrum lex humana debeat poni in communi.

Secundo, utrum lex humana debeat omnia vitia cohibere.

Tertio, utrum omnium virtutum actus habeat ordinare.

Quarto, utrum imponat homini necessitatem quantum ad forum conscientiae.

Quinto, utrum omnes homines legi humanae subdantur.

Sexto, utrum his qui sunt sub lege, liceat agere praeter verba legis.

We must now consider the power of human law. Under this head there are six points of inquiry:

(1) Whether human law should be framed for the community?

(2) Whether human law should repress all vices?

(3) Whether human law is competent to direct all acts of virtue?

(4) Whether it binds man in conscience?

(5) Whether all men are subject to human law?

(6) Whether those who are under the law may act beside the letter of the law?

Article 1

Whether Human Law Should Be Framed for the Community Rather Than for the Individual?

AD PRIMUM SIC PROCEDITUR. Videtur quod lex humana non debeat poni in communi, sed magis in particulari. Dicit enim philosophus, in V Ethic., quod *legalia sunt quaecumque in singularibus lege ponunt; et etiam sententialia*, quae sunt etiam singularia, quia de singularibus actibus sententiae feruntur. Ergo lex non solum ponitur in communi, sed etiam in singulari.

PRAETEREA, lex est directiva humanorum actuum, ut supra dictum est. Sed humani actus in singularibus consistunt. Ergo leges humanae non debent in universali ferri, sed magis in singulari.

PRAETEREA, lex est regula et mensura humanorum actuum, ut supra dictum est. Sed mensura debet esse certissima, ut dicitur in X Metaphys. Cum ergo in actibus humanis non possit esse aliquod universale certum, quin in particularibus deficiat; videtur quod necesse sit leges non in universali, sed in singulari poni.

SED CONTRA est quod iurisperitus dicit, quod *iura constitui oportet in his quae saepius accidunt, ex his autem quae forte uno casu accidere possunt, iura non constituuntur.*

RESPONDEO dicendum quod unumquodque quod est propter finem, necesse est quod sit fini proportionatum. Finis autem legis est bonum commune, quia, ut Isidorus dicit, in libro Etymol., *nullo privato commodo, sed pro communi utilitate civium lex debet esse conscripta.*

OBJECTION 1: It would seem that human law should be framed not for the community, but rather for the individual. For the Philosopher says (*Ethic.* v, 7) that *the legal just . . . includes all particular acts of legislation . . . and all those matters which are the subject of decrees*, which are also individual matters, since decrees are framed about individual actions. Therefore law is framed not only for the community, but also for the individual.

OBJ. 2: Further, law is the director of human acts, as stated above (Q90, AA1,2). But human acts are about individual matters. Therefore human laws should be framed, not for the community, but rather for the individual.

OBJ. 3: Further, law is a rule and measure of human acts, as stated above (Q. 90, AA. 1, 2). But a measure should be most certain, as stated in *Metaph.* x. Since therefore in human acts no general proposition can be so certain as not to fail in some individual cases, it seems that laws should be framed not in general but for individual cases.

ON THE CONTRARY, The Jurist says (*Pandect. Justin.* lib. i, tit. iii, art. ii; De legibus, etc.) that *laws should be made to suit the majority of instances; and they are not framed according to what may possibly happen in an individual case.*

I ANSWER THAT, Whatever is for an end should be proportionate to that end. Now the end of law is the common good; because, as Isidore says (*Etym.* v, 21) that *law should be framed, not for any private benefit, but for the common good of all the citizens.* Hence human laws should

Unde oportet leges humanas esse proportionatas ad bonum commune. Bonum autem commune constat ex multis. Et ideo oportet quod lex ad multa respiciat, et secundum personas, et secundum negotia, et secundum tempora. Constituitur enim communitas civitatis ex multis personis; et eius bonum per multiplices actiones procuratur; nec ad hoc solum instituitur quod aliquo modico tempore duret, sed quod omni tempore perseveret per civium successionem, ut Augustinus dicit, in XXII de Civ. Dei.

AD PRIMUM ergo dicendum quod philosophus in V Ethic. ponit tres partes iusti legalis, quod est ius positivum. Sunt enim quaedam quae simpliciter in communi ponuntur. Et haec sunt leges communes. Et quantum ad huiusmodi, dicit quod *legale est quod ex principio quidem nihil differt sic vel aliter, quando autem ponitur, differt*, puta quod captivi statuto pretio redimantur. Quaedam vero sunt quae sunt communia quantum ad aliquid, et singularia quantum ad aliquid. Et huiusmodi dicuntur privilegia, quasi leges privatae, quia respiciunt singulares personas, et tamen potestas eorum extenditur ad multa negotia. Et quantum ad hoc, subdit, *adhuc quaecumque in singularibus lege ponunt*. Dicuntur etiam quaedam legalia, non quia sint leges, sed propter applicationem legum communium ad aliqua particularia facta; sicut sunt sententiae, quae pro iure habentur. Et quantum ad hoc, subdit, et sententialia.

AD SECUNDUM dicendum quod illud quod est directivum, oportet esse plurium directivum, unde in X Metaphys., philosophus dicit quod omnia quae sunt unius generis, mensurantur aliquo uno, quod est primum in genere illo. Si enim essent tot regulae vel mensurae quot sunt mensurata vel regulata, cessaret utilitas regulae vel mensurae, quae est ut ex uno multa possint cognosci. Et ita nulla esset utilitas legis, si non se extenderet nisi ad unum singularem actum. Ad singulares enim actus dirigendos dantur singularia praecepta prudentium, sed lex est praeceptum commune, ut supra dictum est.

AD TERTIUM dicendum quod non est eadem certitudo quaerenda in omnibus, ut in I Ethic. dicitur. Unde in rebus contingentibus, sicut sunt naturalia et res humanae, sufficit talis certitudo ut aliquid sit verum ut in pluribus, licet interdum deficiat in paucioribus.

REPLY OBJ. 1: The Philosopher (*Ethic.* v, 7) divides the legal just, i.e., positive law, into three parts. For some things are laid down simply in a general way: and these are the general laws. Of these he says that *the legal is that which originally was a matter of indifference, but which, when enacted, is so no longer*: as the fixing of the ransom of a captive. Some things affect the community in one respect, and individuals in another. These are called *privileges*, i.e., *private laws*, as it were, because they regard private persons, although their power extends to many matters; and in regard to these, he adds, *and further, all particular acts of legislation*. Other matters are legal, not through being laws, but through being applications of general laws to particular cases: such are decrees which have the force of law; and in regard to these, he adds *all matters subject to decrees*.

REPLY OBJ. 2: A principle of direction should be applicable to many; wherefore (*Metaph.* x, text. 4) the Philosopher says that all things belonging to one genus, are measured by one, which is the principle in that genus. For if there were as many rules or measures as there are things measured or ruled, they would cease to be of use, since their use consists in being applicable to many things. Hence law would be of no use, if it did not extend further than to one single act. Because the decrees of prudent men are made for the purpose of directing individual actions; whereas law is a general precept, as stated above (Q. 92, A. 2, Obj. 2).

REPLY OBJ. 3: *We must not seek the same degree of certainty in all things* (*Ethic.* i, 3). Consequently in contingent matters, such as natural and human things, it is enough for a thing to be certain, as being true in the greater number of instances, though at times and less frequently it fail.

Article 2

Whether It Belongs to the Human Law to Repress All Vices?

AD SECUNDUM SIC PROCEDITUR. Videtur quod ad legem humanam pertineat omnia vitia cohibere. Dicit enim Isidorus, in libro Etymol., quod *leges sunt factae ut earum metu coerceatur audacia*. Non autem sufficienter

OBJECTION 1: It would seem that it belongs to human law to repress all vices. For Isidore says (*Etym.* v, 20) that *laws were made in order that, in fear thereof, man's audacity might be held in check*. But it would not be held in check

coerceretur, nisi quaelibet mala cohiberentur per legem. Ergo lex humana debet quaelibet mala cohibere.

Praeterea, intentio legislatoris est cives facere virtuosos. Sed non potest esse aliquis virtuosus, nisi ab omnibus vitiis compescatur. Ergo ad legem humanam pertinet omnia vitia compescere.

Praeterea, lex humana a lege naturali derivatur, ut supra dictum est. Sed omnia vitia repugnant legi naturae. Ergo lex humana omnia vitia debet cohibere.

Sed contra est quod dicitur in I de Lib. Arb., *videtur mihi legem istam quae populo regendo scribitur, recte ista permittere, et divinam providentiam vindicare.* Sed divina providentia non vindicat nisi vitia. Ergo recte lex humana permittit aliqua vitia, non cohibendo ipsa.

Respondeo dicendum quod, sicut iam dictum est, lex ponitur ut quaedam regula vel mensura humanorum actuum. Mensura autem debet esse homogenea mensurato, ut dicitur in X Metaphys., diversa enim diversis mensuris mensurantur. Unde oportet quod etiam leges imponantur hominibus secundum eorum conditionem, quia, ut Isidorus dicit. *Lex debet esse possibilis et secundum naturam, et secundum consuetudinem patriae.* Potestas autem sive facultas operandi ex interiori habitu seu dispositione procedit, non enim idem est possibile ei qui non habet habitum virtutis, et virtuoso; sicut etiam non est idem possibile puero et viro perfecto. Et propter hoc non ponitur eadem lex pueris quae ponitur adultis, multa enim pueris permittuntur quae in adultis lege puniuntur, vel etiam vituperantur. Et similiter multa sunt permittenda hominibus non perfectis virtute, quae non essent toleranda in hominibus virtuosis.

Lex autem humana ponitur multitudini hominum, in qua maior pars est hominum non perfectorum virtute. Et ideo lege humana non prohibentur omnia vitia, a quibus virtuosi abstinent; sed solum graviora, a quibus possibile est maiorem partem multitudinis abstinere; et praecipue quae sunt in nocumentum aliorum, sine quorum prohibitione societas humana conservari non posset, sicut prohibentur lege humana homicidia et furta et huiusmodi.

Ad primum ergo dicendum quod audacia pertinere videtur ad invasionem aliorum. Unde praecipue pertinet ad illa peccata quibus iniuria proximis irrogatur; quae lege humana prohibentur, ut dictum est.

Ad secundum dicendum quod lex humana intendit homines inducere ad virtutem, non subito, sed gradatim. Et ideo non statim multitudini imperfectorum imponit ea quae sunt iam virtuosorum, ut scilicet ab omnibus malis abstineant. Alioquin imperfecti, huiusmodi praecepta ferre non valentes, in deteriora mala

sufficiently, unless all evils were repressed by law. Therefore human laws should repress all evils.

Obj. 2: Further, the intention of the lawgiver is to make the citizens virtuous. But a man cannot be virtuous unless he forbear from all kinds of vice. Therefore it belongs to human law to repress all vices.

Obj. 3: Further, human law is derived from the natural law, as stated above (Q. 95, A. 2). But all vices are contrary to the law of nature. Therefore human law should repress all vices.

On the contrary, We read in De Lib. Arb. i, 5: *It seems to me that the law which is written for the governing of the people rightly permits these things, and that Divine providence punishes them.* But Divine providence punishes nothing but vices. Therefore human law rightly allows some vices, by not repressing them.

I answer that, As stated above (Q. 90, AA. 1, 2), law is framed as a rule or measure of human acts. Now a measure should be homogeneous with that which it measures, as stated in *Metaph.* x, text. 3, 4, since different things are measured by different measures. Wherefore laws imposed on men should also be in keeping with their condition, for, as Isidore says (*Etym.* v, 21), law should be *possible both according to nature, and according to the customs of the country.* Now power or faculty of action is due to an interior habit or disposition: since the same thing is not possible to one who has not a virtuous habit, as is possible to one who has. Thus the same is not possible to a child as to a full-grown man: for which reason the law for children is not the same as for adults, since many things are permitted to children, which in an adult are punished by law or at any rate are open to blame. In like manner many things are permissible to men not perfect in virtue, which would be intolerable in a virtuous man.

Now human law is framed for a multitude of human beings, the majority of whom are not perfect in virtue. Wherefore human laws do not forbid all vices, from which the virtuous abstain, but only the more grievous vices, from which it is possible for the majority to abstain; and chiefly those that are to the hurt of others, without the prohibition of which human society could not be maintained: thus human law prohibits murder, theft and such like.

Reply Obj. 1: Audacity seems to refer to the assailing of others. Consequently it belongs to those sins chiefly whereby one's neighbor is injured: and these sins are forbidden by human law, as stated.

Reply Obj. 2: The purpose of human law is to lead men to virtue, not suddenly, but gradually. Wherefore it does not lay upon the multitude of imperfect men the burdens of those who are already virtuous, viz., that they should abstain from all evil. Otherwise these imperfect ones, being unable to bear such precepts, would break out into yet

prorumperent, sicut dicitur Prov. XXX, *qui nimis emungit, elicit sanguinem*; et Matth. IX dicitur quod, si vinum novum, idest praecepta perfectae vitae, mittatur in utres veteres, idest in homines imperfectos, utres rumpuntur, et vinum effunditur, idest, praecepta contemnuntur, et homines ex contemptu ad peiora mala prorumpunt.

AD TERTIUM dicendum quod lex naturalis est quaedam participatio legis aeternae in nobis, lex autem humana deficit a lege aeterna. Dicit enim Augustinus, in I de Lib. Arb., *lex ista quae regendis civitatibus fertur, multa concedit atque impunita relinquit, quae per divinam providentiam vindicantur. Neque enim quia non omnia facit, ideo quae facit, improbanda sunt.* Unde etiam lex humana non omnia potest prohibere quae prohibet lex naturae.

greater evils: thus it is written (Ps 30:33): *He that violently bloweth his nose, bringeth out blood*; and (Matt 9:17) that if *new wine*, i.e., precepts of a perfect life, *is put into old bottles*, i.e., into imperfect men, *the bottles break, and the wine runneth out*, i.e., the precepts are despised, and those men, from contempt, break into evils worse still.

REPLY OBJ. 3: The natural law is a participation in us of the eternal law: while human law falls short of the eternal law. Now Augustine says (*De Lib. Arb.* i, 5): *The law which is framed for the government of states, allows and leaves unpunished many things that are punished by Divine providence. Nor, if this law does not attempt to do everything, is this a reason why it should be blamed for what it does.* Wherefore, too, human law does not prohibit everything that is forbidden by the natural law.

Article 3

Whether Human Law Prescribes Acts of All the Virtues?

AD TERTIUM SIC PROCEDITUR. Videtur quod lex humana non praecipiat actus omnium virtutum. Actibus enim virtutum opponuntur actus vitiosi. Sed lex humana non prohibet omnia vitia, ut dictum est. Ergo etiam non praecipit actus omnium virtutum.

PRAETEREA, actus virtutis a virtute procedit. Sed virtus est finis legis, et ita quod est ex virtute, sub praecepto legis cadere non potest. Ergo lex humana non praecipit actus omnium virtutum.

PRAETEREA, lex ordinatur ad bonum commune, ut dictum est. Sed quidam actus virtutum non ordinantur ad bonum commune, sed ad bonum privatum. Ergo lex non praecipit actus omnium virtutum.

SED CONTRA est quod philosophus dicit, in V Ethic., quod *praecipit lex fortis opera facere, et quae temperati, et quae mansueti; similiter autem secundum alias virtutes et malitias, haec quidem iubens, haec autem prohibens.*

RESPONDEO dicendum quod species virtutum distinguuntur secundum obiecta, ut ex supradictis patet. Omnia autem obiecta virtutum referri possunt vel ad bonum privatum alicuius personae, vel ad bonum commune multitudinis, sicut ea quae sunt fortitudinis potest aliquis exequi vel propter conservationem civitatis, vel ad conservandum ius amici sui; et simile est in aliis. Lex autem, ut dictum est, ordinatur ad bonum commune. Et ideo nulla virtus est de cuius actibus lex praecipere non possit. Non tamen de omnibus actibus omnium virtutum lex humana praecipit, sed solum de illis qui sunt ordinabiles ad bonum commune, vel immediate, sicut cum aliqua directe propter bonum commune fiunt; vel mediate, sicut cum aliqua ordinantur a legislatore pertinentia

OBJECTION 1: It would seem that human law does not prescribe acts of all the virtues. For vicious acts are contrary to acts of virtue. But human law does not prohibit all vices, as stated above (A. 2). Therefore neither does it prescribe all acts of virtue.

OBJ. 2: Further, a virtuous act proceeds from a virtue. But virtue is the end of law; so that whatever is from a virtue, cannot come under a precept of law. Therefore human law does not prescribe all acts of virtue.

OBJ. 3: Further, law is ordained to the common good, as stated above (Q. 90, A. 2). But some acts of virtue are ordained, not to the common good, but to private good. Therefore the law does not prescribe all acts of virtue.

ON THE CONTRARY, The Philosopher says (*Ethic.* v, 1) that the law *prescribes the performance of the acts of a brave man . . . and the acts of the temperate man . . . and the acts of the meek man: and in like manner as regards the other virtues and vices, prescribing the former, forbidding the latter.*

I ANSWER THAT, The species of virtues are distinguished by their objects, as explained above (Q. 54, A. 2; Q. 60, A. 1; Q. 62, A. 2). Now all the objects of virtues can be referred either to the private good of an individual, or to the common good of the multitude: thus matters of fortitude may be achieved either for the safety of the state, or for upholding the rights of a friend, and in like manner with the other virtues. But law, as stated above (Q. 90, A. 2) is ordained to the common good. Wherefore there is no virtue whose acts cannot be prescribed by the law. Nevertheless human law does not prescribe concerning all the acts of every virtue: but only in regard to those that are ordainable to the common good—either immediately, as when certain things are done directly for the common good—or mediately, as when

ad bonam disciplinam, per quam cives informantur ut commune bonum iustitiae et pacis conservent.

AD PRIMUM ergo dicendum quod lex humana non prohibet omnes actus vitiosos, secundum obligationem praecepti, sicut nec praecipit omnes actus virtuosos. Prohibet tamen aliquos actus singulorum vitiorum, sicut etiam praecipit quosdam actus singularum virtutum.

AD SECUNDUM dicendum quod aliquis actus dicitur esse virtutis dupliciter. Uno modo, ex eo quod homo operatur virtuosa, sicut actus iustitiae est facere recta, et actus fortitudinis facere fortia. Et sic lex praecipit aliquos actus virtutum. Alio modo dicitur actus virtutis, quia aliquis operatur virtuosa eo modo quo virtuosus operatur. Et talis actus semper procedit a virtute, nec cadit sub praecepto legis, sed est finis ad quem legislator ducere intendit.

AD TERTIUM dicendum quod non est aliqua virtus cuius actus non sint ordinabiles ad bonum commune, ut dictum est, vel mediate vel immediate.

a lawgiver prescribes certain things pertaining to good order, whereby the citizens are directed in the upholding of the common good of justice and peace.

REPLY OBJ. 1: Human law does not forbid all vicious acts, by the obligation of a precept, as neither does it prescribe all acts of virtue. But it forbids certain acts of each vice, just as it prescribes some acts of each virtue.

REPLY OBJ. 2: An act is said to be an act of virtue in two ways. In one way, from the fact that a man does something virtuous; thus the act of justice is to do what is right, and an act of fortitude is to do brave things: and in this way law prescribes certain acts of virtue. In another way an act of virtue is when a man does a virtuous thing in a way in which a virtuous man does it. Such an act always proceeds from virtue: and it does not come under a precept of law, but is the end at which every lawgiver aims.

REPLY OBJ. 3: There is no virtue whose act is not ordainable to the common good, as stated above, either mediately or immediately.

Article 4

Whether Human Law Binds a Man in Conscience?

AD QUARTUM SIC PROCEDITUR. Videtur quod lex humana non imponat homini necessitatem in foro conscientiae. Inferior enim potestas non potest imponere legem in iudicio superioris potestatis. Sed potestas hominis, quae fert legem humanam, est infra potestatem divinam. Ergo lex humana non potest imponere legem quantum ad iudicium divinum, quod est iudicium conscientiae.

PRAETEREA, iudicium conscientiae maxime dependet ex divinis mandatis. Sed quandoque divina mandata evacuantur per leges humanas; secundum illud Matth. XV, *irritum fecistis mandatum Dei propter traditiones vestras.* Ergo lex humana non imponit necessitatem homini quantum ad conscientiam.

PRAETEREA, leges humanae frequenter ingerunt calumniam et iniuriam hominibus; secundum illud Isaiae X, *vae qui condunt leges iniquas, et scribentes iniustitias scripserunt, ut opprimerent in iudicio pauperes, et vim facerent causae humilium populi mei.* Sed licitum est unicuique oppressionem et violentiam evitare. Ergo leges humanae non imponunt necessitatem homini quantum ad conscientiam.

SED CONTRA est quod dicitur I Petr. II, *haec est gratia, si propter conscientiam sustineat quis tristitias, patiens iniuste.*

RESPONDEO dicendum quod leges positae humanitus vel sunt iustae, vel iniustae. Si quidem iustae sint,

OBJECTION 1: It would seem that human law does not bind man in conscience. For an inferior power has no jurisdiction in a court of higher power. But the power of man, which frames human law, is beneath the Divine power. Therefore human law cannot impose its precept in a Divine court, such as is the court of conscience.

OBJ. 2: Further, the judgment of conscience depends chiefly on the commandments of God. But sometimes God's commandments are made void by human laws, according to Matt. 15:6: *You have made void the commandment of God for your tradition.* Therefore human law does not bind a man in conscience.

OBJ. 3: Further, human laws often bring loss of character and injury on man, according to Isa. 10:1 et seqq.: *Woe to them that make wicked laws, and when they write, write injustice; to oppress the poor in judgment, and do violence to the cause of the humble of My people.* But it is lawful for anyone to avoid oppression and violence. Therefore human laws do not bind man in conscience.

ON THE CONTRARY, It is written (1 Pet 2:19): *This is thankworthy, if for the sake of conscience a man endure sorrows, suffering wrongfully.*

I ANSWER THAT, Laws framed by man are either just or unjust. If they be just, they have the power of binding in

habent vim obligandi in foro conscientiae a lege aeterna, a qua derivantur; secundum illud Prov. VIII, *per me reges regnant, et legum conditores iusta decernunt.* Dicuntur autem leges iustae et ex fine, quando scilicet ordinantur ad bonum commune; et ex auctore, quando scilicet lex lata non excedit potestatem ferentis; et ex forma, quando scilicet secundum aequalitatem proportionis imponuntur subditis onera in ordine ad bonum commune. Cum enim unus homo sit pars multitudinis, quilibet homo hoc ipsum quod est et quod habet, est multitudinis, sicut et quaelibet pars id quod est, est totius. Unde et natura aliquod detrimentum infert parti, ut salvet totum. Et secundum hoc, leges huiusmodi, onera proportionabiliter inferentes, iustae sunt, et obligant in foro conscientiae, et sunt leges legales.

Iniustae autem sunt leges dupliciter. Uno modo, per contrarietatem ad bonum humanum, e contrario praedictis, vel ex fine, sicut cum aliquis praesidens leges imponit onerosas subditis non pertinentes ad utilitatem communem, sed magis ad propriam cupiditatem vel gloriam; vel etiam ex auctore, sicut cum aliquis legem fert ultra sibi commissam potestatem; vel etiam ex forma, puta cum inaequaliter onera multitudini dispensantur, etiam si ordinentur ad bonum commune. Et huiusmodi magis sunt violentiae quam leges, quia, sicut Augustinus dicit, in libro de Lib. Arb., *lex esse non videtur, quae iusta non fuerit.* Unde tales leges non obligant in foro conscientiae, nisi forte propter vitandum scandalum vel turbationem, propter quod etiam homo iuri suo debet cedere, secundum illud Matth. V, *qui angariaverit te mille passus, vade cum eo alia duo; et qui abstulerit tibi tunicam, da ei et pallium.*

Alio modo leges possunt esse iniustae per contrarietatem ad bonum divinum, sicut leges tyrannorum inducentes ad idololatriam, vel ad quodcumque aliud quod sit contra legem divinam. Et tales leges nullo modo licet observare, quia sicut dicitur Act. V, *obedire oportet Deo magis quam hominibus.*

AD PRIMUM ergo dicendum quod, sicut apostolus dicit, ad Rom. XIII, *omnis potestas humana a Deo est, et ideo qui potestati resistit, in his quae ad ordinem potestatis pertinent, Dei ordinationi resistit.* Et secundum hoc efficitur reus quantum ad conscientiam.

AD SECUNDUM dicendum quod ratio illa procedit de legibus humanis quae ordinantur contra Dei mandatum. Et ad hoc ordo potestatis non se extendit. Unde in talibus legi humanae non est parendum.

AD TERTIUM dicendum quod ratio illa procedit de lege quae infert gravamen iniustum subditis, ad quod etiam ordo potestatis divinitus concessus non se extendit. Unde nec in talibus homo obligatur ut obediat legi, si sine scandalo vel maiori detrimento resistere possit.

conscience, from the eternal law whence they are derived, according to Prov. 8:15: *By Me kings reign, and lawgivers decree just things.* Now laws are said to be just, both from the end, when, to wit, they are ordained to the common good—and from their author, that is to say, when the law that is made does not exceed the power of the lawgiver—and from their form, when, to wit, burdens are laid on the subjects, according to an equality of proportion and with a view to the common good. For, since one man is a part of the community, each man in all that he is and has, belongs to the community; just as a part, in all that it is, belongs to the whole; wherefore nature inflicts a loss on the part, in order to save the whole: so that on this account, such laws as these, which impose proportionate burdens, are just and binding in conscience, and are legal laws.

On the other hand laws may be unjust in two ways: first, by being contrary to human good, through being opposed to the things mentioned above—either in respect of the end, as when an authority imposes on his subjects burdensome laws, conducive, not to the common good, but rather to his own cupidity or vainglory—or in respect of the author, as when a man makes a law that goes beyond the power committed to him—or in respect of the form, as when burdens are imposed unequally on the community, although with a view to the common good. The like are acts of violence rather than laws; because, as Augustine says (*De Lib. Arb.* i, 5), *a law that is not just, seems to be no law at all.* Wherefore such laws do not bind in conscience, except perhaps in order to avoid scandal or disturbance, for which cause a man should even yield his right, according to Matt. 5:40, 41: *If a man . . . take away thy coat, let go thy cloak also unto him; and whosoever will force thee one mile, go with him another two.*

Second, laws may be unjust through being opposed to the Divine good: such are the laws of tyrants inducing to idolatry, or to anything else contrary to the Divine law: and laws of this kind must nowise be observed, because, as stated in Acts 5:29, *we ought to obey God rather than man.*

REPLY OBJ. 1: As the Apostle says (Rom 13:1, 2), all human power is from God; *therefore he that resisteth the power,* in matters that are within its scope, *resisteth the ordinance of God*; so that he becomes guilty according to his conscience.

REPLY OBJ. 2: This argument is true of laws that are contrary to the commandments of God, which is beyond the scope of (human) power. Wherefore in such matters human law should not be obeyed.

REPLY OBJ. 3: This argument is true of a law that inflicts unjust hurt on its subjects. The power that man holds from God does not extend to this: wherefore neither in such matters is man bound to obey the law, provided he avoid giving scandal or inflicting a more grievous hurt.

Article 5

Whether All Are Subject to the Law?

AD QUINTUM SIC PROCEDITUR. Videtur quod non omnes legi subiiciantur. Illi enim soli subiiciuntur legi, quibus lex ponitur. Sed apostolus dicit, I ad Tim. I, quod *iusto non est lex posita*. Ergo iusti non subiiciuntur legi humanae.

PRAETEREA, Urbanus Papa dicit, et habetur in decretis, XIX qu. II, *qui lege privata ducitur, nulla ratio exigit ut publica constringatur*. Lege autem privata Spiritus Sancti ducuntur omnes viri spirituales, qui sunt filii Dei; secundum illud Rom. VIII, *qui spiritu Dei aguntur, hi filii Dei sunt*. Ergo non omnes homines legi humanae subiiciuntur.

PRAETEREA, iurisperitus dicit quod princeps legibus solutus est. Qui autem est solutus a lege, non subditur legi. Ergo non omnes subiecti sunt legi.

SED CONTRA est quod apostolus dicit, Rom. XIII, *omnis anima potestatibus sublimioribus subdita sit*. Sed non videtur esse subditus potestati, qui non subiicitur legi quam fert potestas. Ergo omnes homines debent esse legi humanae subiecti.

RESPONDEO dicendum quod, sicut ex supradictis patet, lex de sui ratione duo habet, primo quidem, quod est regula humanorum actuum; secundo, quod habet vim coactivam. Dupliciter ergo aliquis homo potest esse legi subiectus. Uno modo, sicut regulatum regulae. Et hoc modo omnes illi qui subduntur potestati, subduntur legi quam fert potestas. Quod autem aliquis potestati non subdatur, potest contingere dupliciter. Uno modo, quia est simpliciter absolutus ab eius subiectione. Unde illi qui sunt de una civitate vel regno, non subduntur legibus principis alterius civitatis vel regni, sicut nec eius dominio. Alio modo, secundum quod regitur superiori lege. Puta si aliquis subiectus sit proconsuli, regulari debet eius mandato, non tamen in his quae dispensantur ei ab imperatore, quantum enim ad illa, non adstringitur mandato inferioris, cum superiori mandato dirigatur. Et secundum hoc contingit quod aliquis simpliciter subiectus legi, secundum aliqua legi non adstringitur, secundum quae regitur superiori lege.

Alio vero modo dicitur aliquis subdi legi sicut coactum cogenti. Et hoc modo homines virtuosi et iusti non subduntur legi, sed soli mali. Quod enim est coactum et violentum, est contrarium voluntati. Voluntas autem bonorum consonat legi, a qua malorum voluntas discordat. Et ideo secundum hoc boni non sunt sub lege, sed solum mali.

AD PRIMUM ergo dicendum quod ratio illa procedit de subiectione quae est per modum coactionis. Sic enim iusto non est lex posita, quia ipsi sibi sunt lex, dum

OBJECTION 1: It would seem that not all are subject to the law. For those alone are subject to a law for whom a law is made. But the Apostle says (1 Tim 1:9): *The law is not made for the just man*. Therefore the just are not subject to the law.

OBJ. 2: Further, Pope Urban says: *He that is guided by a private law need not for any reason be bound by the public law*. Now all spiritual men are led by the private law of the Holy Spirit, for they are the sons of God, of whom it is said (Rom 8:14): *Whosoever are led by the Spirit of God, they are the sons of God*. Therefore not all men are subject to human law.

OBJ. 3: Further, the jurist says that *the sovereign is exempt from the laws*. But he that is exempt from the law is not bound thereby. Therefore not all are subject to the law.

ON THE CONTRARY, The Apostle says (Rom 13:1): *Let every soul be subject to the higher powers*. But subjection to a power seems to imply subjection to the laws framed by that power. Therefore all men should be subject to human law.

I ANSWER THAT, As stated above (Q. 90, AA. 1, 2; A. 3, ad 2), the notion of law contains two things: first, that it is a rule of human acts; second, that it has coercive power. Wherefore a man may be subject to law in two ways. First, as the regulated is subject to the regulator: and, in this way, whoever is subject to a power, is subject to the law framed by that power. But it may happen in two ways that one is not subject to a power. In one way, by being altogether free from its authority: hence the subjects of one city or kingdom are not bound by the laws of the sovereign of another city or kingdom, since they are not subject to his authority. In another way, by being under a yet higher law; thus the subject of a proconsul should be ruled by his command, but not in those matters in which the subject receives his orders from the emperor: for in these matters, he is not bound by the mandate of the lower authority, since he is directed by that of a higher. In this way, one who is simply subject to a law, may not be subject thereto in certain matters, in respect of which he is ruled by a higher law.

Second, a man is said to be subject to a law as the coerced is subject to the coercer. In this way the virtuous and righteous are not subject to the law, but only the wicked. Because coercion and violence are contrary to the will: but the will of the good is in harmony with the law, whereas the will of the wicked is discordant from it. Wherefore in this sense the good are not subject to the law, but only the wicked.

REPLY OBJ. 1: This argument is true of subjection by way of coercion: for, in this way, *the law is not made for the just men*: because *they are a law to themselves*, since

ostendunt opus legis scriptum in cordibus suis, sicut apostolus, ad Rom. II, dicit. Unde in eos non habet lex vim coactivam, sicut habet in iniustos.

AD SECUNDUM dicendum quod lex spiritus sancti est superior omni lege humanitus posita. Et ideo viri spirituales, secundum hoc quod lege spiritus sancti ducuntur, non subduntur legi, quantum ad ea quae repugnant ductioni spiritus sancti. Sed tamen hoc ipsum est de ductu spiritus sancti, quod homines spirituales legibus humanis subdantur; secundum illud I Petr. II, *subiecti estote omni humanae creaturae, propter Deum.*

AD TERTIUM dicendum quod princeps dicitur esse solutus a lege, quantum ad vim coactivam legis, nullus enim proprie cogitur a seipso; lex autem non habet vim coactivam nisi ex principis potestate. Sic igitur princeps dicitur esse solutus a lege, quia nullus in ipsum potest iudicium condemnationis ferre, si contra legem agat. Unde super illud Psalmi l, *tibi soli peccavi* etc., dicit Glossa quod *lex non habet hominem qui sua facta diiudicet.* Sed quantum ad vim directivam legis, princeps subditur legi propria voluntate; secundum quod dicitur extra, de constitutionibus, cap. cum omnes, *quod quisque iuris in alterum statuit, ipse eodem iure uti debet. Et sapientis dicit auctoritas, patere legem quam ipse tuleris.* Improperatur etiam his a domino qui dicunt et non faciunt; et qui aliis onera gravia imponunt, et ipsi nec digito volunt ea movere; ut habetur Matth. XXIII. Unde quantum ad Dei iudicium, princeps non est solutus a lege, quantum ad vim directivam eius; sed debet voluntarius, non coactus, legem implere. Est etiam princeps supra legem, inquantum, si expediens fuerit, potest legem mutare, et in ea dispensare, pro loco et tempore.

they *show the work of the law written in their hearts*, as the Apostle says (Rom 2:14, 15). Consequently the law does not enforce itself upon them as it does on the wicked.

REPLY OBJ. 2: The law of the Holy Spirit is above all law framed by man: and therefore spiritual men, insofar as they are led by the law of the Holy Spirit, are not subject to the law in those matters that are inconsistent with the guidance of the Holy Spirit. Nevertheless the very fact that spiritual men are subject to law, is due to the leading of the Holy Spirit, according to 1 Pet. 2:13: *Be ye subject . . . to every human creature for God's sake.*

REPLY OBJ. 3: The sovereign is said to be *exempt from the law*, as to its coercive power; since, properly speaking, no man is coerced by himself, and law has no coercive power save from the authority of the sovereign. Thus then is the sovereign said to be exempt from the law, because none is competent to pass sentence on him, if he acts against the law. Wherefore on Ps. 50:6: *To Thee only have I sinned*, a gloss says that *there is no man who can judge the deeds of a king.* But as to the directive force of law, the sovereign is subject to the law by his own will, according to the statement (Extra, *De Constit.* cap. Cum omnes) that *whatever law a man makes for another, he should keep himself. And a wise authority says: 'Obey the law that thou makest thyself.'* Moreover the Lord reproaches those who *say and do not*; and who *bind heavy burdens and lay them on men's shoulders, but with a finger of their own they will not move them* (Matt 23:3, 4). Hence, in the judgment of God, the sovereign is not exempt from the law, as to its directive force; but he should fulfill of to his own free-will and not by constraint. Again the sovereign is above the law, insofar as, when it is expedient, he can change the law, and dispense in it according to time and place.

Article 6

Whether He Who Is Under a Law May Act Beside the Letter of the Law?

AD SEXTUM SIC PROCEDITUR. Videtur quod non liceat ei qui subditur legi, praeter verba legis agere. Dicit enim Augustinus, in libro de vera Relig., *in temporalibus legibus, quamvis homines iudicent de his cum eas instituunt, tamen quando fuerint institutae et firmatae, non licebit de ipsis iudicare, sed secundum ipsas.* Sed si aliquis praetermittat verba legis, dicens se intentionem legislatoris servare, videtur iudicare de lege. Ergo non licet ei qui subditur legi, ut praetermittat verba legis, ut intentionem legislatoris servet.

PRAETEREA, ad eum solum pertinet leges interpretari, cuius est condere leges. Sed hominum subditorum legi non est leges condere. Ergo eorum non est

OBJECTION 1: It seems that he who is subject to a law may not act beside the letter of the law. For Augustine says (*De Vera Relig.* 31): *Although men judge about temporal laws when they make them, yet when once they are made they must pass judgment not on them, but according to them.* But if anyone disregard the letter of the law, saying that he observes the intention of the lawgiver, he seems to pass judgment on the law. Therefore it is not right for one who is under the law to disregard the letter of the law, in order to observe the intention of the lawgiver.

OBJ. 2: Further, he alone is competent to interpret the law who can make the law. But those who are subject to the law cannot make the law. Therefore they have no right to

interpretari legislatoris intentionem, sed semper secundum verba legis agere debent.

PRAETEREA, omnis sapiens intentionem suam verbis novit explicare. Sed illi qui leges condiderunt, reputari debent sapientes, dicit enim sapientia, Prov. VIII, *per me reges regnant, et legum conditores iusta decernunt.* Ergo de intentione legislatoris non est iudicandum nisi per verba legis.

SED CONTRA est quod Hilarius dicit, in IV de Trin., *intelligentia dictorum ex causis est assumenda dicendi, quia non sermoni res, sed rei debet esse sermo subiectus.* Ergo magis est attendendum ad causam quae movit legislatorem, quam ad ipsa verba legis.

RESPONDEO dicendum quod, sicut supra dictum est, omnis lex ordinatur ad communem hominum salutem, et intantum obtinet vim et rationem legis; secundum vero quod ab hoc deficit, virtutem obligandi non habet. Unde iurisperitus dicit quod *nulla iuris ratio aut aequitatis benignitas patitur ut quae salubriter pro utilitate hominum introducuntur, ea nos duriori interpretatione, contra ipsorum commodum, perducamus ad severitatem.* Contingit autem multoties quod aliquid observari communi saluti est utile ut in pluribus, quod tamen in aliquibus casibus est maxime nocivum. Quia igitur legislator non potest omnes singulares casus intueri, proponit legem secundum ea quae in pluribus accidunt, ferens intentionem suam ad communem utilitatem. Unde si emergat casus in quo observatio talis legis sit damnosa communi saluti, non est observanda. Sicut si in civitate obsessa statuatur lex quod portae civitatis maneant clausae, hoc est utile communi saluti ut in pluribus, si tamen contingat casus quod hostes insequantur aliquos cives, per quos civitas conservatur, damnosissimum esset civitati nisi eis portae aperirentur, et ideo in tali casu essent portae aperiendae, contra verba legis, ut servaretur utilitas communis, quam legislator intendit.

Sed tamen hoc est considerandum, quod si observatio legis secundum verba non habeat subitum periculum, cui oportet statim occurri, non pertinet ad quemlibet ut interpretetur quid sit utile civitati et quid inutile, sed hoc solum pertinet ad principes, qui propter huiusmodi casus habent auctoritatem in legibus dispensandi. Si vero sit subitum periculum, non patiens tantam moram ut ad superiorem recurri possit, ipsa necessitas dispensationem habet annexam, quia necessitas non subditur legi.

AD PRIMUM ergo dicendum quod ille qui in casu necessitatis agit praeter verba legis, non iudicat de ipsa lege, sed iudicat de casu singulari, in quo videt verba legis observanda non esse.

AD SECUNDUM dicendum quod ille qui sequitur intentionem legislatoris, non interpretatur legem simpliciter; sed in casu in quo manifestum est per evidentiam nocumenti, legislatorem aliud intendisse. Si enim

interpret the intention of the lawgiver, but should always act according to the letter of the law.

OBJ. 3: Further, every wise man knows how to explain his intention by words. But those who framed the laws should be reckoned wise: for Wisdom says (Prov 8:15): *By Me kings reign, and lawgivers decree just things.* Therefore we should not judge of the intention of the lawgiver otherwise than by the words of the law.

ON THE CONTRARY, Hilary says (*De Trin.* iv): *The meaning of what is said is according to the motive for saying it: because things are not subject to speech, but speech to things.* Therefore we should take account of the motive of the lawgiver, rather than of his very words.

I ANSWER THAT, As stated above (A. 4), every law is directed to the common weal of men, and derives the force and nature of law accordingly. Hence the jurist says: *By no reason of law, or favor of equity, is it allowable for us to interpret harshly, and render burdensome, those useful measures which have been enacted for the welfare of man.* Now it happens often that the observance of some point of law conduces to the common weal in the majority of instances, and yet, in some cases, is very hurtful. Since then the lawgiver cannot have in view every single case, he shapes the law according to what happens most frequently, by directing his attention to the common good. Wherefore if a case arise wherein the observance of that law would be hurtful to the general welfare, it should not be observed. For instance, suppose that in a besieged city it be an established law that the gates of the city are to be kept closed, this is good for public welfare as a general rule: but, if it were to happen that the enemy are in pursuit of certain citizens, who are defenders of the city, it would be a great loss to the city, if the gates were not opened to them: and so in that case the gates ought to be opened, contrary to the letter of the law, in order to maintain the common weal, which the lawgiver had in view.

Nevertheless it must be noted, that if the observance of the law according to the letter does not involve any sudden risk needing instant remedy, it is not competent for everyone to expound what is useful and what is not useful to the state: those alone can do this who are in authority, and who, on account of such like cases, have the power to dispense from the laws. If, however, the peril be so sudden as not to allow of the delay involved by referring the matter to authority, the mere necessity brings with it a dispensation, since necessity knows no law.

REPLY OBJ. 1: He who in a case of necessity acts beside the letter of the law, does not judge the law; but judges a particular case in which he sees that the letter of the law is not to be observed.

REPLY OBJ. 2: He who follows the intention of the lawgiver, does not interpret the law simply; but in a case in which it is evident, by reason of the manifest harm, that the lawgiver intended otherwise. For if it be a matter of doubt,

dubium sit, debet vel secundum verba legis agere, vel superiores consulere.

AD TERTIUM dicendum quod nullius hominis sapientia tanta est ut possit omnes singulares casus excogitare, et ideo non potest sufficienter per verba sua exprimere ea quae conveniunt ad finem intentum. Et si posset legislator omnes casus considerare, non oporteret ut omnes exprimeret, propter confusionem vitandam, sed legem ferre deberet secundum ea quae in pluribus accidunt.

he must either act according to the letter of the law, or consult those in power.

REPLY OBJ. 3: No man is so wise as to be able to take account of every single case; wherefore he is not able sufficiently to express in words all those things that are suitable for the end he has in view. And even if a lawgiver were able to take all the cases into consideration, he ought not to mention them all, in order to avoid confusion: but should frame the law according to that which is of most common occurrence.

QUESTION 97

OF CHANGE IN LAWS

Deinde considerandum est de mutatione legum. Et circa hoc quaeruntur quatuor.

Primo, utrum lex humana sit mutabilis.

Secundo, utrum semper debeat mutari, quando aliquid melius occurrerit.

Tertio, utrum per consuetudinem aboleatur; et utrum consuetudo obtineat vim legis.

Quarto, utrum usus legis humanae per dispensationem rectorum immutari debeat.

We must now consider change in laws: under which head there are four points of inquiry:

(1) Whether human law is changeable?

(2) Whether it should be always changed, whenever anything better occurs?

(3) Whether it is abolished by custom, and whether custom obtains the force of law?

(4) Whether the application of human law should be changed by dispensation of those in authority?

Article 1

Whether Human Law Should Be Changed in Any Way?

AD PRIMUM SIC PROCEDITUR. Videtur quod lex humana nullo modo debeat mutari. Lex enim humana derivatur a lege naturali, ut supra dictum est. Sed lex naturalis immobilis perseverat. Ergo et lex humana debet immobilis permanere.

PRAETEREA, sicut philosophus dicit, in V Ethic., mensura maxime debet esse permanens. Sed lex humana est mensura humanorum actuum, ut supra dictum est. Ergo debet immobiliter permanere.

PRAETEREA, de ratione legis est quod sit iusta et recta, ut supra dictum est. Sed illud quod semel est rectum, semper est rectum. Ergo illud quod semel est lex, semper debet esse lex.

SED CONTRA est quod Augustinus dicit, in I de Lib. Arb., *lex temporalis quamvis iusta sit, commutari tamen per tempora iuste potest.*

RESPONDEO dicendum quod sicut supra dictum est, lex humana est quoddam dictamen rationis, quo diriguntur humani actus. Et secundum hoc duplex causa potest esse quod lex humana iuste mutetur, una quidem ex parte rationis; alia vero ex parte hominum, quorum actus lege regulantur. Ex parte quidem rationis, quia humanae rationi naturale esse videtur ut gradatim ab imperfecto ad perfectum perveniat. Unde videmus in scientiis speculativis quod qui primo philosophati sunt, quaedam imperfecta tradiderunt, quae postmodum per posteriores sunt magis perfecta. Ita etiam est in operabilibus. Nam primi qui intenderunt invenire aliquid utile communitati hominum, non valentes omnia ex seipsis considerare, instituerunt quaedam imperfecta in multis deficientia quae posteriores mutaverunt, instituentes

OBJECTION 1: It would seem that human law should not be changed in any way at all. Because human law is derived from the natural law, as stated above (Q. 95, A. 2). But the natural law endures unchangeably. Therefore human law should also remain without any change.

OBJ. 2: Further, as the Philosopher says (*Ethic.* v, 5), a measure should be absolutely stable. But human law is the measure of human acts, as stated above (Q. 90, AA. 1, 2). Therefore it should remain without change.

OBJ. 3: Further, it is of the essence of law to be just and right, as stated above (Q. 95, A. 2). But that which is right once is right always. Therefore that which is law once, should be always law.

ON THE CONTRARY, Augustine says (*De Lib. Arb.* i, 6): *A temporal law, however just, may be justly changed in course of time.*

I ANSWER THAT, As stated above (Q. 91, A. 3), human law is a dictate of reason, whereby human acts are directed. Thus there may be two causes for the just change of human law: one on the part of reason; the other on the part of man whose acts are regulated by law. The cause on the part of reason is that it seems natural to human reason to advance gradually from the imperfect to the perfect. Hence, in speculative sciences, we see that the teaching of the early philosophers was imperfect, and that it was afterwards perfected by those who succeeded them. So also in practical matters: for those who first endeavored to discover something useful for the human community, not being able by themselves to take everything into consideration, set up certain institutions which were deficient in many ways; and these were changed by subsequent lawgivers who made institutions

aliqua quae in paucioribus deficere possent a communi utilitate.

Ex parte vero hominum, quorum actus lege regulantur, lex recte mutari potest propter mutationem conditionum hominum, quibus secundum diversas eorum conditiones diversa expediunt. Sicut Augustinus ponit exemplum, in I de Lib. Arb., quod *si populus sit bene moderatus et gravis, communisque utilitatis diligentissimus custos, recte lex fertur qua tali populo liceat creare sibi magistratus, per quos respublica administretur. Porro si paulatim idem populus depravatus habeat venale suffragium, et regimen flagitiosis sceleratisque committat; recte adimitur tali populo potestas dandi honores, et ad paucorum bonorum redit arbitrium.*

AD PRIMUM ergo dicendum quod naturalis lex est participatio quaedam legis aeternae, ut supra dictum est, et ideo immobilis perseverat, quod habet ex immobilitate et perfectione divinae rationis instituentis naturam. Sed ratio humana mutabilis est et imperfecta. Et ideo eius lex mutabilis est. Et praeterea lex naturalis continet quaedam universalia praecepta, quae semper manent, lex vero posita ab homine continet praecepta quaedam particularia, secundum diversos casus qui emergunt.

AD SECUNDUM dicendum quod mensura debet esse permanens quantum est possibile. Sed in rebus mutabilibus non potest esse aliquid omnino immutabiliter permanens. Et ideo lex humana non potest esse omnino immutabilis.

AD TERTIUM dicendum quod rectum in rebus corporalibus dicitur absolute, et ideo semper, quantum est de se, manet rectum. Sed rectitudo legis dicitur in ordine ad utilitatem communem, cui non semper proportionatur una eademque res, sicut supra dictum est. Et ideo talis rectitudo mutatur.

that might prove less frequently deficient in respect of the common weal.

On the part of man, whose acts are regulated by law, the law can be rightly changed on account of the changed condition of man, to whom different things are expedient according to the difference of his condition. An example is proposed by Augustine (*De Lib. Arb.* i, 6): *If the people have a sense of moderation and responsibility, and are most careful guardians of the common weal, it is right to enact a law allowing such a people to choose their own magistrates for the government of the commonwealth. But if, as time goes on, the same people become so corrupt as to sell their votes, and entrust the government to scoundrels and criminals; then the right of appointing their public officials is rightly forfeit to such a people, and the choice devolves to a few good men.*

REPLY OBJ. 1: The natural law is a participation of the eternal law, as stated above (Q91, A2), and therefore endures without change, owing to the unchangeableness and perfection of the Divine Reason, the Author of nature. But the reason of man is changeable and imperfect: wherefore his law is subject to change. Moreover the natural law contains certain universal precepts, which are everlasting: whereas human law contains certain particular precepts, according to different cases that emerge.

REPLY OBJ. 2: A measure should be as enduring as possible. But nothing can be absolutely unchangeable in things that are subject to change. And therefore human law cannot be altogether unchangeable.

REPLY OBJ. 3: In corporeal things, right is predicated absolutely: and therefore, as far as itself is concerned, always remains right. But right is predicated of law with reference to the common weal, to which one and the same thing is not always adapted, as stated above: wherefore rectitude of this kind is subject to change.

Article 2

Whether Human Law Should Always Be Changed, Whenever Something Better Occurs?

AD SECUNDUM SIC PROCEDITUR. Videtur quod semper lex humana, quando aliquid melius occurrit, sit mutanda. Leges enim humanae sunt adinventae per rationem humanam, sicut etiam aliae artes. Sed in aliis artibus mutatur id quod prius tenebatur, si aliquid melius occurrat. Ergo idem est etiam faciendum in legibus humanis.

PRAETEREA, ex his quae praeterita sunt, providere possumus de futuris. Sed nisi leges humanae mutatae fuissent supervenientibus melioribus adinventionibus, multa inconvenientia sequerentur, eo quod leges antiquae inveniuntur multas ruditates continere. Ergo

OBJECTION 1: It would seem that human law should be changed, whenever something better occurs. Because human laws are devised by human reason, like other arts. But in the other arts, the tenets of former times give place to others, if something better occurs. Therefore the same should apply to human laws.

OBJ. 2: Further, by taking note of the past we can provide for the future. Now unless human laws had been changed when it was found possible to improve them, considerable inconvenience would have ensued; because the laws of old were crude in many points. Therefore it seems

videtur quod leges sint mutandae, quotiescumque aliquid melius occurrit statuendum.

PRAETEREA, leges humanae circa singulares actus hominum statuuntur. In singularibus autem perfectam cognitionem adipisci non possumus nisi per experientiam, quae tempore indiget, ut dicitur in II Ethic. Ergo videtur quod per successionem temporis possit aliquid melius occurrere statuendum.

SED CONTRA est quod dicitur in decretis, dist. XII, *ridiculum est et satis abominabile dedecus, ut traditiones quas antiquitus a patribus suscepimus, infringi patiamur.*

RESPONDEO dicendum quod, sicut dictum est, lex humana intantum recte mutatur, inquantum per eius mutationem communi utilitati providetur. Habet autem ipsa legis mutatio, quantum in se est, detrimentum quoddam communis salutis. Quia ad observantiam legum plurimum valet consuetudo, intantum quod ea quae contra communem consuetudinem fiunt, etiam si sint leviora de se, graviora videantur. Unde quando mutatur lex, diminuitur vis constrictiva legis, inquantum tollitur consuetudo. Et ideo nunquam debet mutari lex humana, nisi ex aliqua parte tantum recompensetur communi saluti, quantum ex ista parte derogatur. Quod quidem contingit vel ex hoc quod aliqua maxima et evidentissima utilitas ex novo statuto provenit, vel ex eo quod est maxima necessitas, ex eo quod lex consueta aut manifestam iniquitatem continet, aut eius observatio est plurimum nociva. Unde dicitur a iurisperito quod *in rebus novis constituendis, evidens debet esse utilitas, ut recedatur ab eo iure quod diu aequum visum est.*

AD PRIMUM ergo dicendum quod ea quae sunt artis, habent efficaciam ex sola ratione, et ideo ubicumque melior ratio occurrat, est mutandum quod prius tenebatur. *Sed leges habent maximam virtutem ex consuetudine,* ut philosophus dicit, in II Polit. Et inde non sunt de facili mutandae.

AD SECUNDUM dicendum quod ratio illa concludit quod leges sunt mutandae, non tamen pro quacumque melioratione, sed pro magna utilitate vel necessitate, ut dictum est.

ET SIMILITER dicendum est ad tertium.

that laws should be changed, whenever anything better occurs to be enacted.

OBJ. 3: Further, human laws are enacted about single acts of man. But we cannot acquire perfect knowledge in singular matters, except by experience, which *requires time*, as stated in *Ethic.* ii. Therefore it seems that as time goes on it is possible for something better to occur for legislation.

ON THE CONTRARY, It is stated in the *Decretals* (Dist. xii, 5): *It is absurd, and a detestable shame, that we should suffer those traditions to be changed which we have received from the fathers of old.*

I ANSWER THAT, As stated above (A1), human law is rightly changed, insofar as such change is conducive to the common weal. But, to a certain extent, the mere change of law is of itself prejudicial to the common good: because custom avails much for the observance of laws, seeing that what is done contrary to general custom, even in slight matters, is looked upon as grave. Consequently, when a law is changed, the binding power of the law is diminished, insofar as custom is abolished. Wherefore human law should never be changed, unless, in some way or other, the common weal be compensated according to the extent of the harm done in this respect. Such compensation may arise either from some very great and every evident benefit conferred by the new enactment; or from the extreme urgency of the case, due to the fact that either the existing law is clearly unjust, or its observance extremely harmful. Wherefore the jurist says that *in establishing new laws, there should be evidence of the benefit to be derived, before departing from a law which has long been considered just.*

REPLY OBJ. 1: Rules of art derive their force from reason alone: and therefore whenever something better occurs, the rule followed hitherto should be changed. But *laws derive very great force from custom,* as the Philosopher states (*Polit.* ii, 5): consequently they should not be quickly changed.

REPLY OBJ. 2: This argument proves that laws ought to be changed: not in view of any improvement, but for the sake of a great benefit or in a case of great urgency, as stated above.

THIS ANSWER applies also to the Third Objection.

Article 3

Whether Custom Can Obtain Force of Law?

AD TERTIUM SIC PROCEDITUR. Videtur quod consuetudo non possit obtinere vim legis, nec legem amovere. Lex enim humana derivatur a lege naturae et a lege divina, ut ex supradictis patet. Sed consuetudo hominum

OBJECTION 1: It would seem that custom cannot obtain force of law, nor abolish a law. Because human law is derived from the natural law and from the Divine law, as stated above (Q93, A3; Q95, A2). But human custom cannot

non potest immutare legem naturae, nec legem divinam. Ergo etiam nec legem humanam immutare potest.

Praeterea, ex multis malis non potest fieri unum bonum. Sed ille qui incipit primo contra legem agere, male facit. Ergo, multiplicatis similibus actibus, non efficietur aliquod bonum. Lex autem est quoddam bonum, cum sit regula humanorum actuum. Ergo per consuetudinem non potest removeri lex, ut ipsa consuetudo vim legis obtineat.

Praeterea, ferre legem pertinet ad publicas personas, ad quas pertinet regere communitatem, unde privatae personae legem facere non possunt. Sed consuetudo invalescit per actus privatarum personarum. Ergo consuetudo non potest obtinere vim legis, per quam lex removeatur.

Sed contra est quod Augustinus dicit, in Epist. ad Casulan., *mos populi Dei et instituta maiorum pro lege sunt tenenda. Et sicut praevaricatores legum divinarum, ita et contemptores consuetudinum ecclesiasticarum coercendi sunt.*

Respondeo dicendum quod omnis lex proficiscitur a ratione et voluntate legislatoris, lex quidem divina et naturalis a rationabili Dei voluntate; lex autem humana a voluntate hominis ratione regulata. Sicut autem ratio et voluntas hominis manifestantur verbo in rebus agendis, ita etiam manifestantur facto, hoc enim unusquisque eligere videtur ut bonum, quod opere implet. Manifestum est autem quod verbo humano potest et mutari lex, et etiam exponi, inquantum manifestat interiorem motum et conceptum rationis humanae. Unde etiam et per actus, maxime multiplicatos, qui consuetudinem efficiunt, mutari potest lex, et exponi, et etiam aliquid causari quod legis virtutem obtineat, inquantum scilicet per exteriores actus multiplicatos interior voluntatis motus, et rationis conceptus, efficacissime declaratur; cum enim aliquid multoties fit, videtur ex deliberato rationis iudicio provenire. Et secundum hoc, consuetudo et habet vim legis, et legem abolet, et est legum interpretatrix.

Ad primum ergo dicendum quod lex naturalis et divina procedit a voluntate divina, ut dictum est. Unde non potest mutari per consuetudinem procedentem a voluntate hominis, sed solum per auctoritatem divinam mutari posset. Et inde est quod nulla consuetudo vim obtinere potest contra legem divinam vel legem naturalem, dicit enim Isidorus, in Synonym., *usus auctoritati cedat, pravum usum lex et ratio vincat.*

Ad secundum dicendum quod, sicut supra dictum est, leges humanae in aliquibus casibus deficiunt, unde possibile est quandoque praeter legem agere, in casu scilicet in quo deficit lex, et tamen actus non erit malus. Et cum tales casus multiplicantur, propter aliquam mutationem hominum, tunc manifestatur per consuetudinem quod lex ulterius utilis non est, sicut etiam

change either the law of nature or the Divine law. Therefore neither can it change human law.

Obj. 2: Further, many evils cannot make one good. But he who first acted against the law, did evil. Therefore by multiplying such acts, nothing good is the result. Now a law is something good; since it is a rule of human acts. Therefore law is not abolished by custom, so that the mere custom should obtain force of law.

Obj. 3: Further, the framing of laws belongs to those public men whose business it is to govern the community; wherefore private individuals cannot make laws. But custom grows by the acts of private individuals. Therefore custom cannot obtain force of law, so as to abolish the law.

On the contrary, Augustine says (*Ep. ad Casulan. xxxvi*): *The customs of God's people and the institutions of our ancestors are to be considered as laws. And those who throw contempt on the customs of the Church ought to be punished as those who disobey the law of God.*

I answer that, All law proceeds from the reason and will of the lawgiver; the Divine and natural laws from the reasonable will of God; the human law from the will of man, regulated by reason. Now just as human reason and will, in practical matters, may be made manifest by speech, so may they be made known by deeds: since seemingly a man chooses as good that which he carries into execution. But it is evident that by human speech, law can be both changed and expounded, insofar as it manifests the interior movement and thought of human reason. Wherefore by actions also, especially if they be repeated, so as to make a custom, law can be changed and expounded; and also something can be established which obtains force of law, insofar as by repeated external actions, the inward movement of the will, and concepts of reason are most effectually declared; for when a thing is done again and again, it seems to proceed from a deliberate judgment of reason. Accordingly, custom has the force of a law, abolishes law, and is the interpreter of law.

Reply Obj. 1: The natural and Divine laws proceed from the Divine will, as stated above. Wherefore they cannot be changed by a custom proceeding from the will of man, but only by Divine authority. Hence it is that no custom can prevail over the Divine or natural laws: for Isidore says (*Synon.* ii, 16): *Let custom yield to authority: evil customs should be eradicated by law and reason.*

Reply Obj. 2: As stated above (Q96, A6), human laws fail in some cases: wherefore it is possible sometimes to act beside the law; namely, in a case where the law fails; yet the act will not be evil. And when such cases are multiplied, by reason of some change in man, then custom shows that the law is no longer useful: just as it might be declared by the verbal promulgation of a law to the contrary. If, however,

manifestaretur si lex contraria verbo promulgaretur. Si autem adhuc maneat ratio eadem propter quam prima lex utilis erat, non consuetudo legem, sed lex consuetudinem vincit, nisi forte propter hoc solum inutilis lex videatur, quia non est possibilis secundum consuetudinem patriae, quae erat una de conditionibus legis. Difficile enim est consuetudinem multitudinis removere.

Ad tertium dicendum quod multitudo in qua consuetudo introducitur duplicis conditionis esse potest. Si enim sit libera multitudo, quae possit sibi legem facere, plus est consensus totius multitudinis ad aliquid observandum, quem consuetudo manifestat, quam auctoritas principis, qui non habet potestatem condendi legem, nisi inquantum gerit personam multitudinis. Unde licet singulae personae non possint condere legem, tamen totus populus legem condere potest. Si vero multitudo non habeat liberam potestatem condendi sibi legem, vel legem a superiori potestate positam removendi; tamen ipsa consuetudo in tali multitudine praevalens obtinet vim legis, inquantum per eos toleratur ad quos pertinet multitudini legem imponere, ex hoc enim ipso videntur approbare quod consuetudo induxit.

the same reason remains, for which the law was useful hitherto, then it is not the custom that prevails against the law, but the law that overcomes the custom: unless perhaps the sole reason for the law seeming useless, be that it is not *possible according to the custom of the country*, which has been stated to be one of the conditions of law. For it is not easy to set aside the custom of a whole people.

Reply Obj. 3: The people among whom a custom is introduced may be of two conditions. For if they are free, and able to make their own laws, the consent of the whole people expressed by a custom counts far more in favor of a particular observance, than does the authority of the sovereign, who has not the power to frame laws, except as representing the people. Wherefore although each individual cannot make laws, yet the whole people can. If however the people have not the free power to make their own laws, or to abolish a law made by a higher authority; nevertheless with such a people a prevailing custom obtains force of law, insofar as it is tolerated by those to whom it belongs to make laws for that people: because by the very fact that they tolerate it they seem to approve of that which is introduced by custom.

Article 4

Whether the Rulers of the People Can Dispense from Human Laws?

Ad quartum sic proceditur. Videtur quod rectores multitudinis non possint in legibus humanis dispensare. Lex enim statuta est pro communi utilitate, ut Isidorus dicit. Sed bonum commune non debet intermitti pro privato commodo alicuius personae, quia, ut dicit philosophus, in I Ethic., *bonum gentis divinius est quam bonum unius hominis.* Ergo videtur quod non debeat dispensari cum aliquo ut contra legem communem agat.

Praeterea, illis qui super alios constituuntur, praecipitur Deut. I, *ita parvum audietis ut magnum, nec accipietis cuiusquam personam, quia Dei iudicium est.* Sed concedere alicui quod communiter denegatur omnibus, videtur esse acceptio personarum. Ergo huiusmodi dispensationes facere rectores multitudinis non possunt, cum hoc sit contra praeceptum legis divinae.

Praeterea, lex humana, si sit recta, oportet quod consonet legi naturali et legi divinae, aliter enim non congrueret religioni, nec conveniret disciplinae, quod requiritur ad legem, ut Isidorus dicit. Sed in lege divina et naturali nullus homo potest dispensare. Ergo nec etiam in lege humana.

Sed contra est quod dicit apostolus, I ad Cor. IX, *dispensatio mihi credita est.*

Objection 1: It would seem that the rulers of the people cannot dispense from human laws. For the law is established for the *common weal*, as Isidore says (*Etym.* v, 21). But the common good should not be set aside for the private convenience of an individual: because, as the Philosopher says (*Ethic.* i, 2), *the good of the nation is more godlike than the good of one man.* Therefore it seems that a man should not be dispensed from acting in compliance with the general law.

Obj. 2: Further, those who are placed over others are commanded as follows (Deut 1:17): *You shall hear the little as well as the great; neither shall you respect any man's person, because it is the judgment of God.* But to allow one man to do that which is equally forbidden to all, seems to be respect of persons. Therefore the rulers of a community cannot grant such dispensations, since this is against a precept of the Divine law.

Obj. 3: Further, human law, in order to be just, should accord with the natural and Divine laws: else it would not *foster religion*, nor be *helpful to discipline*, which is requisite to the nature of law, as laid down by Isidore (*Etym.* v, 3). But no man can dispense from the Divine and natural laws. Neither, therefore, can he dispense from the human law.

On the contrary, The Apostle says (1 Cor 9:17): *A dispensation is committed to me.*

RESPONDEO dicendum quod dispensatio proprie importat commensurationem alicuius communis ad singula, unde etiam gubernator familiae dicitur dispensator, inquantum unicuique de familia cum pondere et mensura distribuit et operationes et necessaria vitae. Sic igitur et in quacumque multitudine ex eo dicitur aliquis dispensare, quod ordinat qualiter aliquod commune praeceptum sit a singulis adimplendum. Contingit autem quandoque quod aliquod praeceptum quod est ad commodum multitudinis ut in pluribus, non est conveniens huic personae, vel in hoc casu, quia vel per hoc impediretur aliquid melius, vel etiam induceretur aliquod malum, sicut ex supradictis patet. Periculosum autem esset ut hoc iudicio cuiuslibet committeretur, nisi forte propter evidens et subitum periculum, ut supra dictum est. Et ideo ille qui habet regere multitudinem, habet potestatem dispensandi in lege humana quae suae auctoritati innititur, ut scilicet in personis vel casibus in quibus lex deficit, licentiam tribuat ut praeceptum legis non servetur. Si autem absque hac ratione, pro sola voluntate, licentiam tribuat, non erit fidelis in dispensatione, aut erit imprudens, infidelis quidem, si non habeat intentionem ad bonum commune; imprudens autem, si rationem dispensandi ignoret. Propter quod dominus dicit, Lucae XII, *quis, putas, est fidelis dispensator et prudens, quem constituit dominus super familiam suam?*

AD PRIMUM ergo dicendum quod, quando cum aliquo dispensatur ut legem communem non servet, non debet fieri in praeiudicium boni communis; sed ea intentione ut ad bonum commune proficiat.

AD SECUNDUM dicendum quod non est acceptio personarum si non serventur aequalia in personis inaequalibus. Unde quando conditio alicuius personae requirit ut rationabiliter in ea aliquid specialiter observetur, non est personarum acceptio si sibi aliqua specialis gratia fiat.

AD TERTIUM dicendum quod lex naturalis inquantum continet praecepta communia, quae nunquam fallunt, dispensationem recipere non potest. In aliis vero praeceptis, quae sunt quasi conclusiones praeceptorum communium, quandoque per hominem dispensatur, puta quod mutuum non reddatur proditori patriae, vel aliquid huiusmodi. Ad legem autem divinam ita se habet quilibet homo, sicut persona privata ad legem publicam cui subiicitur. Unde sicut in lege humana publica non potest dispensare nisi ille a quo lex auctoritatem habet, vel is cui ipse commiserit; ita in praeceptis iuris divini, quae sunt a Deo, nullus potest dispensare nisi Deus, vel si cui ipse specialiter committeret.

I ANSWER THAT, Dispensation, properly speaking, denotes a measuring out to individuals of some thing common: thus the head of a household is called a dispenser, because to each member of the household he distributes work and necessaries of life in due weight and measure. Accordingly in every community a man is said to dispense, from the very fact that he directs how some general precept is to be fulfilled by each individual. Now it happens at times that a precept, which is conducive to the common weal as a general rule, is not good for a particular individual, or in some particular case, either because it would hinder some greater good, or because it would be the occasion of some evil, as explained above (Q96, A6). But it would be dangerous to leave this to the discretion of each individual, except perhaps by reason of an evident and sudden emergency, as stated above (Q96, A6). Consequently he who is placed over a community is empowered to dispense in a human law that rests upon his authority, so that, when the law fails in its application to persons or circumstances, he may allow the precept of the law not to be observed. If however he grant this permission without any such reason, and of his mere will, he will be an unfaithful or an imprudent dispenser: unfaithful, if he has not the common good in view; imprudent, if he ignores the reasons for granting dispensations. Hence Our Lord says (Luke 12:42): *Who, thinkest thou, is the faithful and wise steward, whom his lord setteth over his family?*

REPLY OBJ. 1: When a person is dispensed from observing the general law, this should not be done to the prejudice of, but with the intention of benefiting, the common good.

REPLY OBJ. 2: It is not respect of persons if unequal measures are served out to those who are themselves unequal. Wherefore when the condition of any person requires that he should reasonably receive special treatment, it is not respect of persons if he be the object of special favor.

REPLY OBJ. 3: Natural law, so far as it contains general precepts, which never fail, does not allow of dispensations. In other precepts, however, which are as conclusions of the general precepts, man sometimes grants a dispensation: for instance, that a loan should not be paid back to the betrayer of his country, or something similar. But to the Divine law each man stands as a private person to the public law to which he is subject. Wherefore just as none can dispense from public human law, except the man from whom the law derives its authority, or his delegate; so, in the precepts of the Divine law, which are from God, none can dispense but God, or the man to whom He may give special power for that purpose.

QUESTION 98

OF THE OLD LAW

Consequenter considerandum est de lege veteri. Et primo, de ipsa lege; secundo, de praeceptis eius. Circa primum quaeruntur sex.

Primo, utrum lex vetus sit bona.

Secundo, utrum sit a Deo.

Tertio, utrum sit ab eo mediantibus Angelis.

Quarto, utrum data sit omnibus.

Quinto, utrum omnes obliget.

Sexto, utrum congruo tempore fuerit data.

In due sequence we must now consider the Old Law; and (1) The Law itself; (2) Its precepts. Under the first head there are six points of inquiry:

(1) Whether the Old Law was good?

(2) Whether it was from God?

(3) Whether it came from Him through the angels?

(4) Whether it was given to all?

(5) Whether it was binding on all?

(6) Whether it was given at a suitable time?

Article 1

Whether the Old Law Was Good?

AD PRIMUM SIC PROCEDITUR. Videtur quod lex vetus non fuerit bona. Dicitur enim Ezech. XX *dedi eis praecepta non bona, et iudicia in quibus non vivent.* Sed lex non dicitur bona nisi propter bonitatem praeceptorum quae continet. Ergo lex vetus non fuit bona.

PRAETEREA, ad bonitatem legis pertinet ut communi saluti proficiat sicut Isidorus dicit. Sed lex vetus non fuit salutifera, sed magis mortifera et nociva. Dicit enim apostolus, Rom. VII, *sine lege peccatum mortuum erat. Ego autem vivebam sine lege aliquando, sed cum venisset mandatum, peccatum revixit, ego autem mortuus sum*; et Rom. V, *lex subintravit ut abundaret delictum.* Ergo lex vetus non fuit bona.

PRAETEREA, ad bonitatem legis pertinet quod sit possibilis ad observandum et secundum naturam, et secundum humanam consuetudinem. Sed hoc non habuit lex vetus, dicit enim Petrus, Act. XV, *quid tentatis imponere iugum super cervicem discipulorum, quod neque nos, neque patres nostri, portare potuimus?* Ergo videtur quod lex vetus non fuerit bona.

SED CONTRA est quod apostolus dicit, Rom. VII, itaque *lex quidem sancta est, et mandatum sanctum et iustum et bonum.*

RESPONDEO dicendum quod absque omni dubio lex vetus bona fuit. Sicut enim doctrina ostenditur esse vera ex hoc quod consonat rationi rectae, ita etiam lex aliqua ostenditur esse bona ex eo quod consonat rationi. Lex autem vetus rationi consonabat. Quia concupiscentiam reprimebat, quae rationi adversatur; ut patet in illo mandato, *non concupisces rem proximi tui*, quod ponitur Exod. XX. Ipsa etiam omnia peccata prohibebat, quae

OBJECTION 1: It would seem that the Old Law was not good. For it is written (Ezek 20:25): *I gave them statutes that were not good, and judgments in which they shall not live.* But a law is not said to be good except on account of the goodness of the precepts that it contains. Therefore the Old Law was not good.

OBJ. 2: Further, it belongs to the goodness of a law that it conduce to the common welfare, as Isidore says (*Etym.* v, 3). But the Old Law was not salutary; rather was it deadly and hurtful. For the Apostle says (Rom 7:8, seqq.): *Without the law sin was dead. And I lived some time without the law. But when the commandment came sin revived; and I died.* Again he says (Rom 5:20): *Law entered in that sin might abound.* Therefore the Old Law was not good.

OBJ. 3: Further, it belongs to the goodness of the law that it should be possible to obey it, both according to nature, and according to human custom. But such the Old Law was not: since Peter said (Acts 15:10): *Why tempt you (God) to put a yoke on the necks of the disciples, which neither our fathers nor we have been able to bear?* Therefore it seems that the Old Law was not good.

ON THE CONTRARY, The Apostle says (Rom 7:12): *Wherefore the law indeed is holy, and the commandment holy, and just, and good.*

I ANSWER THAT, Without any doubt, the Old Law was good. For just as a doctrine is shown to be good by the fact that it accords with right reason, so is a law proved to be good if it accords with reason. Now the Old Law was in accordance with reason. Because it repressed concupiscence which is in conflict with reason, as evidenced by the commandment, *Thou shalt not covet thy neighbor's goods* (Exod 20:17). Moreover the same law forbade all kinds of

sunt contra rationem. Unde manifestum est quod bona erat. Et haec est ratio apostoli, Rom. VII, condelector, inquit, legi Dei secundum interiorem hominem; et iterum, consentio legi, quoniam bona est.

Sed notandum est quod bonum diversos gradus habet, ut Dionysius dicit, IV cap. de Div. Nom., est enim aliquod bonum perfectum, et aliquod bonum imperfectum. Perfecta quidem bonitas est, in his quae ad finem ordinantur, quando aliquid est tale quod per se sufficiens est inducere ad finem, imperfectum autem bonum est quod operatur aliquid ad hoc quod perveniatur ad finem, non tamen sufficit ad hoc quod ad finem perducat. Sicut medicina perfecte bona est quae hominem sanat, imperfecta autem est quae hominem adiuvat, sed tamen sanare non potest. Est autem sciendum quod est alius finis legis humanae, et alius legis divinae. Legis enim humanae finis est temporalis tranquillitas civitatis, ad quem finem pervenit lex cohibendo exteriores actus, quantum ad illa mala quae possunt perturbare pacificum statum civitatis. Finis autem legis divinae est perducere hominem ad finem felicitatis aeternae; qui quidem finis impeditur per quodcumque peccatum, et non solum per actus exteriores, sed etiam per interiores. Et ideo illud quod sufficit ad perfectionem legis humanae, ut scilicet peccata prohibeat et poenam apponat, non sufficit ad perfectionem legis divinae, sed oportet quod hominem totaliter faciat idoneum ad participationem felicitatis aeternae. Quod quidem fieri non potest nisi per gratiam spiritus sancti, per quam diffunditur caritas in cordibus nostris, quae legem adimplet, gratia enim Dei vita aeterna, ut dicitur Rom. VI. Hanc autem gratiam lex vetus conferre non potuit, reservabatur enim hoc Christo, quia, ut dicitur Ioan. I, *lex per Moysen data est; gratia et veritas per Iesum Christum facta est.* Et inde est quod lex vetus bona quidem est, sed imperfecta; secundum illud Heb. VII, *nihil ad perfectum adduxit lex.*

Ad primum ergo dicendum quod dominus loquitur ibi de praeceptis caeremonialibus; quae quidem dicuntur non bona, quia gratiam non conferebant, per quam homines a peccato mundarentur, cum tamen per huiusmodi se peccatores ostenderent. Unde signanter dicitur, et iudicia in quibus non vivent, idest per quae vitam gratiae obtinere non possunt; et postea subditur, et pollui eos in muneribus suis, idest pollutos ostendi, *cum offerrent omne quod aperit vulvam, propter delicta sua.*

Ad secundum dicendum quod lex dicitur occidisse, non quidem effective, sed occasionaliter, ex sua imperfectione, inquantum scilicet gratiam non conferebat, per quam homines implere possent quod mandabat, vel vitare quod vetabat. Et sic occasio ista non erat data, sed sumpta ab hominibus. Unde et apostolus ibidem dicit, *occasione accepta peccatum per mandatum seduxit me, et per illud occidit.* Et ex hac etiam ratione dicitur quod

sin; and these too are contrary to reason. Consequently it is evident that it was a good law. The Apostle argues in the same way (Rom 7): *I am delighted,* says he (verse 22), *with the law of God, according to the inward man:* and again (verse 16): *I consent to the law, that is good.*

But it must be noted that the good has various degrees, as Dionysius states (*Div. Nom.* iv): for there is a perfect good, and an imperfect good. In things ordained to an end, there is perfect goodness when a thing is such that it is sufficient in itself to conduce to the end: while there is imperfect goodness when a thing is of some assistance in attaining the end, but is not sufficient for the realization thereof. Thus a medicine is perfectly good, if it gives health to a man; but it is imperfect, if it helps to cure him, without being able to bring him back to health. Again it must be observed that the end of human law is different from the end of Divine law. For the end of human law is the temporal tranquillity of the state, which end law effects by directing external actions, as regards those evils which might disturb the peaceful condition of the state. On the other hand, the end of the Divine law is to bring man to that end which is everlasting happiness; which end is hindered by any sin, not only of external, but also of internal action. Consequently that which suffices for the perfection of human law, viz., the prohibition and punishment of sin, does not suffice for the perfection of the Divine law: but it is requisite that it should make man altogether fit to partake of everlasting happiness. Now this cannot be done save by the grace of the Holy Spirit, whereby *charity* which fulfilleth the law . . . *is spread abroad in our hearts* (Rom 5:5): since *the grace of God is life everlasting* (Rom 6:23). But the Old Law could not confer this grace, for this was reserved to Christ; because, as it is written (John 1:17), the law was given *by Moses, grace and truth came by Jesus Christ.* Consequently the Old Law was good indeed, but imperfect, according to Heb. 7:19: *The law brought nothing to perfection.*

Reply Obj. 1: The Lord refers there to the ceremonial precepts; which are said not to be good, because they did not confer grace unto the remission of sins, although by fulfilling these precepts man confessed himself a sinner. Hence it is said pointedly, *and judgments in which they shall not live;* i.e., whereby they are unable to obtain life; and so the text goes on: *And I polluted them,* i.e., showed them to be polluted, *in their own gifts, when they offered all that opened the womb, for their offenses.*

Reply Obj. 2: The law is said to have been deadly, as being not the cause, but the occasion of death, on account of its imperfection: insofar as it did not confer grace enabling man to fulfill what is prescribed, and to avoid what it forbade. Hence this occasion was not given to men, but taken by them. Wherefore the Apostle says (Rom 5:11): *Sin, taking occasion by the commandment, seduced me, and by it killed me.* In the same sense when it is said that *the law*

lex subintravit ut abundaret delictum, ut ly ut teneatur consecutive, non causaliter, inquantum scilicet homines, accipientes occasionem a lege, abundantius peccaverunt; tum quia gravius fuit peccatum post legis prohibitionem; tum etiam quia concupiscentia crevit, magis enim concupiscimus quod nobis prohibetur.

Ad tertium dicendum quod iugum legis servari non poterat sine gratia adiuvante, quam lex non dabat, dicitur enim Rom. IX, *non est volentis neque currentis*, scilicet velle et currere in praeceptis Dei, sed miserentis Dei. Unde et in Psalmo CXVIII dicitur, *viam mandatorum tuorum cucurri, cum dilatasti cor meum*, scilicet per donum gratiae et caritatis.

entered in that sin might abound, the conjunction *that* must be taken as consecutive and not final: insofar as men, taking occasion from the law, sinned all the more, both because a sin became more grievous after law had forbidden it, and because concupiscence increased, since we desire a thing the more from its being forbidden.

Reply Obj. 3: The yoke of the law could not be borne without the help of grace, which the law did not confer: for it is written (Rom 9:16): *It is not him that willeth, nor of him that runneth*, viz., that he wills and runs in the commandments of God, *but of God that showeth mercy*. Wherefore it is written (Ps 118:32): *I have run the way of Thy commandments, when Thou didst enlarge my heart*, i.e., by giving me grace and charity.

Article 2

Whether the Old Law Was from God?

Ad secundum sic proceditur. Videtur quod lex vetus non fuerit a Deo. Dicitur enim Deut. XXXII, *Dei perfecta sunt opera*. Sed lex fuit imperfecta, ut supra dictum est. Ergo lex vetus non fuit a Deo.

Praeterea, Eccle. III dicitur, *didici quod omnia opera quae fecit Deus, perseverent in aeternum*. Sed lex vetus non perseverat in aeternum, dicit enim apostolus, ad Heb. VII, *reprobatio fit quidem praecedentis mandati, propter infirmitatem eius et inutilitatem*. Ergo lex vetus non fuit a Deo.

Praeterea, ad sapientem legislatorem pertinet non solum mala auferre, sed etiam occasiones malorum. Sed vetus lex fuit occasio peccati, ut supra dictum est. Ergo ad Deum, cui nullus est similis in legislatoribus, ut dicitur Iob XXXVI, non pertinebat legem talem dare.

Praeterea, I ad Tim. II, dicitur quod *Deus vult omnes homines salvos fieri*. Sed lex vetus non sufficiebat ad salutem hominum, ut supra dictum est. Ergo ad Deum non pertinebat talem legem dare. Lex ergo vetus non est a Deo.

Sed contra est quod dominus dicit, Matth. XV, loquens Iudaeis, quibus erat lex vetus data, *irritum fecistis mandatum Dei propter traditiones vestras*. Et paulo ante praemittitur, *honora patrem tuum et matrem tuam*, quod manifeste in lege veteri continetur. Ergo lex vetus est a Deo.

Respondeo dicendum quod lex vetus a bono Deo data est, qui est pater domini nostri Iesu Christi. Lex enim vetus homines ordinabat ad Christum dupliciter. Uno quidem modo, testimonium Christo perhibendo, unde ipse dicit, Lucae ult., *oportet impleri omnia quae scripta sunt in lege et Psalmis et prophetis de me*; et Ioan. V, *si crederetis Moysi, crederetis forsitan et mihi, de me*

Objection 1: It would seem that the Old Law was not from God. For it is written (Deut 32:4): *The works of God are perfect*. But the Law was imperfect, as stated above (A1). Therefore the Old Law was not from God.

Obj. 2: Further, it is written (Eccl 3:14): *I have learned that all the works which God hath made continue for ever*. But the Old Law does not continue for ever: since the Apostle says (Heb 7:18): *There is indeed a setting aside of the former commandment, because of the weakness and unprofitableness thereof*. Therefore the Old Law was not from God.

Obj. 3: Further, a wise lawgiver should remove, not only evil, but also the occasions of evil. But the Old Law was an occasion of sin, as stated above (A1, ad 2). Therefore the giving of such a law does not pertain to God, to Whom *none is like among the lawgivers* (Job 36:22).

Obj. 4: Further, it is written (1 Tim 2:4) that God *will have all men to be saved*. But the Old Law did not suffice to save man, as stated above (A1). Therefore the giving of such a law did not appertain to God. Therefore the Old Law was not from God.

On the contrary, Our Lord said (Matt 15:6) while speaking to the Jews, to whom the Law was given: *You have made void the commandment of God for your tradition*. And shortly before (verse 4) He had said: *Honor thy father and mother*, which is contained expressly in the Old Law (Exod 20:12; Dt. 5:16). Therefore the Old Law was from God.

I answer that, The Old Law was given by the good God, Who is the Father of Our Lord Jesus Christ. For the Old Law ordained men to Christ in two ways. First by bearing witness to Christ; wherefore He Himself says (Luke 24:44): *All things must needs be fulfilled, which are written in the law . . . and in the prophets, and in the psalms, concerning Me*: and (John 5:46): *If you did believe Moses,*

enim ille scripsit. Alio modo, per modum cuiusdam dispositionis, dum, retrahens homines a cultu idololatriae, concludebat eos sub cultu unius Dei, a quo salvandum erat humanum genus per Christum, unde apostolus dicit, ad Gal. III, *priusquam veniret fides, sub lege custodiebamur conclusi in eam fidem quae revelanda erat.* Manifestum est autem quod eiusdem est disponere ad finem et ad finem perducere, et dico eiusdem per se vel per suos subiectos. Non enim Diabolus legem tulisset per quam homines adducerentur ad Christum, per quem erat eiiciendus; secundum illud Matth. XII, *si Satanas Satanam eiicit, divisum est regnum eius.* Et ideo ab eodem Deo a quo facta est salus hominum per gratiam Christi, lex vetus data est.

AD PRIMUM ergo dicendum quod nihil prohibet aliquid non esse perfectum simpliciter, quod tamen est perfectum secundum tempus, sicut dicitur aliquis puer perfectus non simpliciter, sed secundum temporis conditionem. Ita etiam praecepta quae pueris dantur, sunt quidem perfecta secundum conditionem eorum quibus dantur, etsi non sint perfecta simpliciter. Et talia fuerunt praecepta legis. Unde apostolus dicit, ad Gal. III, *lex paedagogus noster fuit in Christo.*

AD SECUNDUM dicendum quod opera Dei perseverant in aeternum, quae sic Deus fecit ut in aeternum perseverent, et haec sunt ea quae sunt perfecta. Lex autem vetus reprobatur tempore perfectionis gratiae, non tanquam mala, sed tanquam infirma et inutilis pro isto tempore, quia, ut subditur, nihil ad perfectum adduxit lex. Unde ad Gal. III, dicit apostolus, *ubi venit fides, iam non sumus sub paedagogo.*

AD TERTIUM dicendum quod, sicut supra dictum est, Deus aliquando permittit aliquos cadere in peccatum, ut exinde humilientur. Ita etiam voluit talem legem dare quam suis viribus homines implere non possent, ut sic dum homines de se praesumentes peccatores se invenirent, humiliati recurrerent ad auxilium gratiae.

AD QUARTUM dicendum quod, quamvis lex vetus non sufficeret ad salvandum hominem, tamen aderat aliud auxilium a Deo hominibus simul cum lege, per quod salvari poterant, scilicet fides mediatoris, per quam iustificati sunt antiqui patres, sicut etiam nos iustificamur. Et sic Deus non deficiebat hominibus quin daret eis salutis auxilia.

you would perhaps believe Me also; for he wrote of Me. Second, as a kind of disposition, since by withdrawing men from idolatrous worship, it enclosed them in the worship of one God, by Whom the human race was to be saved through Christ. Wherefore the Apostle says (Gal 3:23): *Before the faith came, we were kept under the law shut up, unto that faith which was to be revealed.* Now it is evident that the same thing it is, which gives a disposition to the end, and which brings to the end; and when I say *the same*, I mean that it does so either by itself or through its subjects. For the devil would not make a law whereby men would be led to Christ, Who was to cast him out, according to Mt. 12:26: *If Satan cast out Satan, his kingdom is divided.* Therefore the Old Law was given by the same God, from Whom came salvation to man, through the grace of Christ.

REPLY OBJ. 1: Nothing prevents a thing being not perfect simply, and yet perfect in respect of time: thus a boy is said to be perfect, not simply, but with regard to the condition of time. So, too, precepts that are given to children are perfect in comparison with the condition of those to whom they are given, although they are not perfect simply. Hence the Apostle says (Gal 3:24): *The law was our pedagogue in Christ.*

REPLY OBJ. 2: Those works of God endure for ever which God so made that they would endure for ever; and these are His perfect works. But the Old Law was set aside when there came the perfection of grace; not as though it were evil, but as being weak and useless for this time; because, as the Apostle goes on to say, *the law brought nothing to perfection*: hence he says (Gal 3:25): *After the faith is come, we are no longer under a pedagogue.*

REPLY OBJ. 3: As stated above (Q79, A4), God sometimes permits certain ones to fall into sin, that they may thereby be humbled. So also did He wish to give such a law as men by their own forces could not fulfill, so that, while presuming on their own powers, they might find themselves to be sinners, and being humbled might have recourse to the help of grace.

REPLY OBJ. 4: Although the Old Law did not suffice to save man, yet another help from God besides the Law was available for man, viz., faith in the Mediator, by which the fathers of old were justified even as we were. Accordingly God did not fail man by giving him insufficient aids to salvation.

Article 3

Whether the Old Law Was Given Through the Angels?

AD TERTIUM SIC PROCEDITUR. Videtur quod lex vetus non fuerit data per Angelos, sed immediate a Deo. Angelus enim nuntius dicitur, et sic nomen Angeli ministerium importat, non dominium; secundum illud Psalmi CII, *benedicite domino, omnes Angeli eius, ministri eius.* Sed vetus lex a domino tradita esse perhibetur, dicitur enim Exod. XX, *locutusque est dominus sermones hos*, et postea subditur, *ego enim sum dominus Deus tuus.* Et idem modus loquendi frequenter repetitur in Exodo, et in libris consequentibus legis. Ergo lex est immediate data a Deo.

PRAETEREA, sicut dicitur Ioan. I, lex per Moysen data est. Sed Moyses immediate accepit a Deo, dicitur enim Exod. XXXIII, *loquebatur dominus ad Moysen facie ad faciem, sicut loqui solet homo ad amicum suum.* Ergo lex vetus immediate data est a Deo.

PRAETEREA, ad solum principem pertinet legem ferre, ut supra dictum est. Sed solus Deus est princeps salutis animarum, *Angeli vero sunt administratorii spiritus*, ut dicitur ad Heb. I. Ergo lex vetus per Angelos dari non debuit, cum ordinaretur ad animarum salutem.

SED CONTRA est quod dicit apostolus, ad Gal. III, *lex data est per Angelos in manu mediatoris.* Et Act. VII, dicit Stephanus, *accepistis legem in dispositione Angelorum.*

RESPONDEO dicendum quod lex data est a Deo per Angelos. Et praeter generalem rationem, quam Dionysius assignat, in IV cap. Cael. Hier., quod *divina debent deferri ad homines mediantibus Angelis*, specialis ratio est quare legem veterem per Angelos dari oportuit. Dictum est enim quod lex vetus imperfecta erat, sed disponebat ad salutem perfectam generis humani, quae futura erat per Christum. Sic autem videtur in omnibus potestatibus et artibus ordinatis, quod ille qui est superior, principalem et perfectum actum operatur per seipsum; ea vero quae disponunt ad perfectionem ultimam, operatur per suos ministros; sicut navifactor compaginat navem per seipsum, sed praeparat materiam per artifices subministrantes. Et ideo conveniens fuit ut lex perfecta novi testamenti daretur immediate per ipsum Deum hominem factum; lex autem vetus per ministros Dei, scilicet per Angelos, daretur hominibus. Et per hunc modum apostolus, in principio ad Heb., probat eminentiam novae legis ad veterem, quia in novo testamento locutus est nobis Deus in filio suo, in veteri autem testamento est sermo factus per Angelos.

OBJECTION 1: It seems that the Old Law was not given through the angels, but immediately by God. For an angel means a *messenger*; so that the word *angel* denotes ministry, not lordship, according to Ps. 102:20,21: *Bless the Lord, all ye His Angels . . . you ministers of His.* But the Old Law is related to have been given by the Lord: for it is written (Exod 20:1): *And the Lord spoke . . . these words*, and further on: *I am the Lord Thy God.* Moreover the same expression is often repeated in Exodus, and the later books of the Law. Therefore the Law was given by God immediately.

OBJ. 2: Further, according to Jn. 1:17, *the Law was given by Moses.* But Moses received it from God immediately: for it is written (Exod 33:11): *The Lord spoke to Moses face to face, as a man is wont to speak to his friend.* Therefore the Old Law was given by God immediately.

OBJ. 3: Further, it belongs to the sovereign alone to make a law, as stated above (Q90, A3). But God alone is Sovereign as regards the salvation of souls: while the angels are the *ministering spirits*, as stated in Heb. 1:14. Therefore it was not meet for the Law to be given through the angels, since it is ordained to the salvation of souls.

ON THE CONTRARY, The Apostle said (Gal 3:19) that the Law was *given by angels in the hand of a Mediator.* And Stephen said (Acts 7:53): *(Who) have received the Law by the disposition of angels.*

I ANSWER THAT, The Law was given by God through the angels. And besides the general reason given by Dionysius (*Coel. Hier.* iv), viz., that *the gifts of God should be brought to men by means of the angels*, there is a special reason why the Old Law should have been given through them. For it has been stated (AA1,2) that the Old Law was imperfect, and yet disposed man to that perfect salvation of the human race, which was to come through Christ. Now it is to be observed that wherever there is an order of powers or arts, he that holds the highest place, himself exercises the principal and perfect acts; while those things which dispose to the ultimate perfection are effected by him through his subordinates: thus the ship-builder himself rivets the planks together, but prepares the material by means of the workmen who assist him under his direction. Consequently it was fitting that the perfect law of the New Testament should be given by the incarnate God immediately; but that the Old Law should be given to men by the ministers of God, i.e., by the angels. It is thus that the Apostle at the beginning of his epistle to the Hebrews (1:2) proves the excellence of the New Law over the Old; because in the New Testament *God . . . hath spoken to us by His Son*, whereas in the Old Testament *the word was spoken by angels* (Heb 2:2).

AD PRIMUM ergo dicendum quod, sicut Gregorius dicit, in principio Moral., *Angelus qui Moysi apparuisse describitur, modo Angelus, modo dominus memoratur. Angelus videlicet, propter hoc quod exterius loquendo serviebat; dominus autem dicitur, quia interius praesidens loquendi efficaciam ministrabat.* Et inde est etiam quod quasi ex persona domini Angelus loquebatur.

AD SECUNDUM dicendum quod, sicut Augustinus dicit, XII super Gen. ad Litt., in Exodo dicitur, *locutus est dominus Moysi facie ad faciem*; et paulo post subditur, *ostende mihi gloriam tuam. Sentiebat ergo quid videbat; et quod non videbat, desiderabat.* Non ergo videbat ipsam Dei essentiam, et ita non immediate ab eo instruebatur. Quod ergo dicitur quod loquebatur ei facie ad faciem, secundum opinionem populi loquitur Scriptura, qui putabat Moysen ore ad os loqui cum Deo, cum per subiectam creaturam, idest per Angelum et nubem, ei loqueretur et appareret. Vel per visionem faciei intelligitur quaedam eminens contemplatio et familiaris, infra essentiae divinae visionem.

AD TERTIUM dicendum quod solius principis est sua auctoritate legem instituere, sed quandoque legem institutam per alios promulgat. Et ita Deus sua auctoritate instituit legem, sed per Angelos promulgavit.

REPLY OBJ. 1: As Gregory says at the beginning of his Morals (*Praef.* chap. i), *the angel who is described to have appeared to Moses, is sometimes mentioned as an angel, sometimes as the Lord: an angel, in truth, in respect of that which was subservient to the external delivery; and the Lord, because He was the Director within, Who supported the effectual power of speaking.* Hence also it is that the angel spoke as personating the Lord.

REPLY OBJ. 2: As Augustine says (*Gen ad lit.* xii, 27), it is stated in Exodus that *the Lord spoke to Moses face to face*; and shortly afterwards we read, *Show me Thy glory.* Therefore He perceived what he saw and he desired what he saw not. Hence he did not see the very Essence of God; and consequently he was not taught by Him immediately. Accordingly when Scripture states that *He spoke to him face to face*, this is to be understood as expressing the opinion of the people, who thought that Moses was speaking with God mouth to mouth, when God spoke and appeared to him, by means of a subordinate creature, i.e., an angel and a cloud. Again we may say that this vision *face to face* means some kind of sublime and familiar contemplation, inferior to the vision of the Divine Essence.

REPLY OBJ. 3: It is for the sovereign alone to make a law by his own authority; but sometimes after making a law, he promulgates it through others. Thus God made the Law by His own authority, but He promulgated it through the angels.

Article 4

Whether the Old Law Should Have Been Given to the Jews Alone?

AD QUARTUM SIC PROCEDITUR. Videtur quod lex vetus non debuerit dari soli populo Iudaeorum. Lex enim vetus disponebat ad salutem quae futura erat per Christum, ut dictum est. Sed salus illa non erat futura solum in Iudaeis, sed in omnibus gentibus; secundum illud Isaiae XLIX, *parum est ut sis mihi servus ad suscitandas tribus Iacob et faeces Israel convertendas, dedi te in lucem gentium, ut sis salus mea usque ad extremum terrae.* Ergo lex vetus dari debuit omnibus gentibus, et non uni populo tantum.

PRAETEREA, sicut dicitur Act. X, *non est personarum acceptor Deus, sed in omni gente qui timet Deum et facit iustitiam, acceptus est illi.* Non ergo magis uni populo quam aliis viam salutis debuit aperire.

PRAETEREA, lex data est per Angelos, sicut iam dictum est. Sed ministeria Angelorum Deus non solum Iudaeis, sed omnibus gentibus semper exhibuit, dicitur enim Eccli. XVII, *in unamquamque gentem praeposuit*

OBJECTION 1: It would seem that the Old Law should not have been given to the Jews alone. For the Old Law disposed men for the salvation which was to come through Christ, as stated above (AA2,3). But that salvation was to come not to the Jews alone but to all nations, according to Is. 49:6: *It is a small thing that thou shouldst be my servant to raise up the tribes of Jacob, and to convert the dregs of Israel. Behold I have given thee to be the light of the Gentiles, that thou mayest be My salvation, even to the farthest part of the earth.* Therefore the Old Law should have been given to all nations, and not to one people only.

OBJ. 2: Further, according to Acts 10:34,35, *God is not a respecter of persons: but in every nation, he that feareth Him, and worketh justice, is acceptable to Him.* Therefore the way of salvation should not have been opened to one people more than to another.

OBJ. 3: Further, the law was given through the angels, as stated above (A3). But God always vouchsafed the ministrations of the angels not to the Jews alone, but to all nations: for it is written (Sir 17:14): *Over every nation He set*

rectorem. Omnibus etiam gentibus temporalia bona largitur, quae minus sunt curae Deo quam spiritualia bona. Ergo etiam legem omnibus populis dare debuit.

SED CONTRA est quod dicitur Rom. III, *quid ergo amplius est Iudaeo? Multum quidem per omnem modum. Primum quidem, quia credita sunt illis eloquia Dei.* Et in Psalmo CXLVII dicitur, *non fecit taliter omni nationi, et iudicia sua non manifestavit eis.*

RESPONDEO dicendum quod posset una ratio assignari quare potius populo Iudaeorum data sit lex quam aliis populis, quia, aliis ad idololatriam declinantibus, solus populus Iudaeorum in cultu unius Dei remansit; et ideo alii populi indigni erant legem recipere, ne sanctum canibus daretur.

Sed ista ratio conveniens non videtur, quia populus ille etiam post legem latam, ad idololatriam declinavit, quod gravius fuit, ut patet Exod. XXXII; et Amos V, *numquid hostias et sacrificium obtulistis mihi in deserto quadraginta annis, domus Israel? Et portastis tabernaculum Moloch vestro, et imaginem idolorum vestrorum, sidus Dei vestri, quae fecistis vobis.* Expresse etiam dicitur Deut. IX, *scito quod non propter iustitias tuas dominus Deus tuus dedit tibi terram hanc in possessionem, cum durissimae cervici sis populus.* Sed ratio ibi praemittitur, *ut compleret verbum suum dominus, quod sub iuramento pollicitus est patribus tuis, Abraham, Isaac et Iacob.*

Quae autem promissio eis sit facta, ostendit apostolus, ad Galat. III, dicens, *Abrahae dictae sunt promissiones, et semini eius. Non dicit, seminibus, quasi in multis, sed quasi in uno, et semini tuo, qui est Christus.* Deus igitur et legem et alia beneficia specialia illi populo exhibuit propter promissionem eorum patribus factam ut ex eis Christus nasceretur. Decebat enim ut ille populus ex quo Christus nasciturus erat, quadam speciali sanctificatione polleret; secundum illud quod dicitur Levit. XIX, *sancti eritis, quia ego sanctus sum.* Nec etiam fuit propter meritum ipsius Abrahae ut talis promissio ei fieret, ut scilicet Christus ex eius semine nasceretur, sed ex gratuita electione et vocatione. Unde dicitur Isaiae XLI, *quis suscitavit ab oriente iustum, vocavit eum ut sequeretur se?*

Sic ergo patet quod ex sola gratuita electione patres promissionem acceperunt, et populus ex eis progenitus legem accepit; secundum illud Deut. IV, *audistis verba illius de medio ignis, quia dilexit patres, et elegit semen eorum post illos.* Si autem rursus quaeratur quare hunc populum elegit ut ex eo Christus nasceretur, et non alium, conveniet responsio Augustini, quam dicit super Ioan., *quare hunc trahat et illum non trahat, noli velle diiudicare, si non vis errare.*

AD PRIMUM ergo dicendum quod, quamvis salus futura per Christum, esset omnibus gentibus praeparata;

a ruler. Also on all nations He bestows temporal goods, which are of less account with God than spiritual goods. Therefore He should have given the Law also to all peoples.

ON THE CONTRARY, It is written (Rom 3:1,2): *What advantage then hath the Jew? . . . Much every way. First indeed, because the words of God were committed to them*: and (Ps 147:9): *He hath not done in like manner to every nation: and His judgments He hath not made manifest unto them.*

I ANSWER THAT, It might be assigned as a reason for the Law being given to the Jews rather than to other peoples, that the Jewish people alone remained faithful to the worship of one God, while the others turned away to idolatry; wherefore the latter were unworthy to receive the Law, lest a holy thing should be given to dogs.

But this reason does not seem fitting: because that people turned to idolatry, even after the Law had been made, which was more grievous, as is clear from Ex. 32 and from Amos 5:25,26: *Did you offer victims and sacrifices to Me in the desert for forty years, O house of Israel? But you carried a tabernacle for your Moloch, and the image of your idols, the star of your god, which you made to yourselves.* Moreover it is stated expressly (Deut 9:6): *Know therefore that the Lord thy God giveth thee not this excellent land in possession for thy justices, for thou art a very stiff-necked people*: but the real reason is given in the preceding verse: *That the Lord might accomplish His word, which He promised by oath to thy fathers Abraham, Isaac, and Jacob.*

What this promise was is shown by the Apostle, who says (Gal 3:16) that *to Abraham were the promises made and to his seed. He saith not, 'And to his seeds,' as of many: but as of one, 'And to thy seed,' which is Christ.* And so God vouchsafed both the Law and other special boons to that people, on account of the promised made to their fathers that Christ should be born of them. For it was fitting that the people, of whom Christ was to be born, should be signalized by a special sanctification, according to the words of Lev. 19:2: *Be ye holy, because I . . . am holy.* Nor again was it on account of the merit of Abraham himself that this promise was made to him, viz., that Christ should be born of his seed: but of gratuitous election and vocation. Hence it is written (Isa 41:2): *Who hath raised up the just one form the east, hath called him to follow him?*

It is therefore evident that it was merely from gratuitous election that the patriarchs received the promise, and that the people sprung from them received the law; according to Dt. 4:36, 37: *Ye did hear His words out of the midst of the fire, because He loved thy fathers, and chose their seed after them.* And if again it asked why He chose this people, and not another, that Christ might be born thereof; a fitting answer is given by Augustine (*Tract. super Joan. xxvi*): *Why He draweth one and draweth not another, seek not thou to judge, if thou wish not to err.*

REPLY OBJ. 1: Although the salvation, which was to come through Christ, was prepared for all nations, yet it

tamen oportebat ex uno populo Christum nasci, qui propter hoc prae aliis praerogativas habuit; secundum illud Rom. IX, quorum, scilicet Iudaeorum, *est adoptio filiorum Dei, et testamentum et legislatio; quorum patres; ex quibus Christus est secundum carnem.*

AD SECUNDUM dicendum quod acceptio personarum locum habet in his quae ex debito dantur, in his vero quae ex gratuita voluntate conferuntur, acceptio personarum locum non habet. Non enim est personarum acceptor qui ex liberalitate de suo dat uni et non alteri, sed si esset dispensator bonorum communium, et non distribueret aequaliter secundum merita personarum, esset personarum acceptor. Salutaria autem beneficia Deus humano generi confert ex sua gratia. Unde non est personarum acceptor si quibusdam prae aliis conferat. Unde Augustinus dicit, in libro de Praedest. Sanct., *omnes quos Deus docet, misericordia docet, quos autem non docet, iudicio non docet.* Hoc enim venit ex damnatione humani generis pro peccato primi parentis.

AD TERTIUM dicendum quod beneficia gratiae subtrahuntur homini propter culpam, sed beneficia naturalia non subtrahuntur. Inter quae sunt ministeria Angelorum, quae ipse naturarum ordo requirit, ut scilicet per media gubernentur infima; et etiam corporalia subsidia, quae non solum hominibus, sed etiam iumentis Deus administrat, secundum illud Psalmi XXXV, *homines et iumenta salvabis, domine.*

was necessary that Christ should be born of one people, which, for this reason, was privileged above other peoples; according to Rm. 9:4: *To whom*, namely the Jews, *belongeth the adoption as of children (of God) . . . and the testament, and the giving of the Law . . . whose are the fathers, and of whom is Christ according to the flesh.*

REPLY OBJ. 2: Respect of persons takes place in those things which are given according to due; but it has no place in those things which are bestowed gratuitously. Because he who, out of generosity, gives of his own to one and not to another, is not a respecter of persons: but if he were a dispenser of goods held in common, and were not to distribute them according to personal merits, he would be a respecter of persons. Now God bestows the benefits of salvation on the human race gratuitously: wherefore He is not a respecter of persons, if He gives them to some rather than to others. Hence Augustine says (*De Praedest. Sanct.* viii): *All whom God teaches, he teaches out of pity; but whom He teaches not, out of justice He teaches not*: for this is due to the condemnation of the human race for the sin of the first parent.

REPLY OBJ. 3: The benefits of grace are forfeited by man on account of sin: but not the benefits of nature. Among the latter are the ministries of the angels, which the very order of various natures demands, viz., that the lowest beings be governed through the intermediate beings: and also bodily aids, which God vouchsafes not only to men, but also to beasts, according to Ps. 35:7: *Men and beasts Thou wilt preserve, O Lord.*

Article 5

Whether All Men Were Bound to Observe the Old Law?

AD QUINTUM SIC PROCEDITUR. Videtur quod omnes homines obligarentur ad observandam veterem legem. Quicumque enim subditur regi, oportet quod subdatur legi ipsius. Sed vetus lex est data a Deo, qui est rex omnis terrae, ut in Psalmo XLVI dicitur. Ergo omnes habitantes terram tenebantur ad observantiam legis.

PRAETEREA, Iudaei salvari non poterant nisi legem veterem observarent, dicitur enim Deut. XXVII, *maledictus qui non permanet in sermonibus legis huius, nec eos opere perfecit.* Si igitur alii homines sine observantia legis veteris potuissent salvari, peior fuisset conditio Iudaeorum quam aliorum hominum.

PRAETEREA, gentiles ad ritum Iudaicum et ad observantias legis admittebantur, dicitur enim Exod. XII, *si quis peregrinorum in vestram voluerit transire coloniam, et facere phase domini, circumcidetur prius omne masculinum eius, et tunc rite celebrabit, eritque simul sicut indigena terrae.* Frustra autem ad observantias legales

OBJECTION 1: It would seem that all men were bound to observe the Old Law. Because whoever is subject to the king, must needs be subject to his law. But the Old Law was given by God, Who is *King of all the earth* (Ps 46:8). Therefore all the inhabitants of the earth were bound to observe the Law.

OBJ. 2: Further, the Jews could not be saved without observing the Old Law: for it is written (Deut 27:26): *Cursed be he that abideth not in the words of this law, and fulfilleth them not in work.* If therefore other men could be saved without the observance of the Old Law, the Jews would be in a worse plight than other men.

OBJ. 3: Further, the Gentiles were admitted to the Jewish ritual and to the observances of the Law: for it is written (Exod 12:48): *If any stranger be willing to dwell among you, and to keep the Phase of the Lord, all his males shall first be circumcised, and then shall he celebrate it according to the manner; and he shall be as he that is born in the land.* But it

fuissent extranei admissi ex ordinatione divina, si absque legalibus observantiis salvari potuissent. Ergo nullus salvari poterat nisi legem observaret.

SED CONTRA est quod Dionysius dicit, IX cap. Cael. Hier., quod multi gentilium per Angelos sunt reducti in Deum. Sed constat quod gentiles legem non observabant. Ergo absque observantia legis poterant aliqui salvari.

RESPONDEO dicendum quod lex vetus manifestabat praecepta legis naturae, et superaddebat quaedam propria praecepta. Quantum igitur ad illa quae lex vetus continebat de lege naturae, omnes tenebantur ad observantiam veteris legis, non quia erant de veteri lege, sed quia erant de lege naturae. Sed quantum ad illa quae lex vetus superaddebat, non tenebantur aliqui ad observantiam veteris legis nisi solus populus Iudaeorum.

Cuius ratio est quia lex vetus, sicut dictum est, data est populo Iudaeorum ut quandam praerogativam sanctitatis obtineret, propter reverentiam Christi, qui ex illo populo nasciturus erat. Quaecumque autem statuuntur ad specialem aliquorum sanctificationem, non obligant nisi illos, sicut ad quaedam obligantur clerici, qui mancipantur divino ministerio, ad quae laici non obligantur; similiter et religiosi ad quaedam perfectionis opera obligantur ex sua professione, ad quae saeculares non obligantur. Et similiter ad quaedam specialia obligabatur populus ille, ad quae alii populi non obligabantur. Unde dicitur Deut. XVIII, *perfectus eris, et absque macula, cum domino Deo tuo*. Et propter hoc etiam quadam professione utebantur; ut patet Deut. XXVI, *profiteor hodie coram domino Deo tuo* et cetera.

AD PRIMUM ergo dicendum quod quicumque subduntur regi, obligantur ad legem eius observandam quam omnibus communiter proponit. Sed si instituat aliqua observanda a suis familiaribus ministris, ad haec ceteri non obligantur.

AD SECUNDUM dicendum quod homo quanto Deo magis coniungitur, tanto efficitur melioris conditionis. Et ideo quanto populus Iudaeorum erat adstrictus magis ad divinum cultum, dignior aliis populis erat. Unde dicitur Deut. IV, *quae est alia gens sic inclyta, ut habeat caeremonias, iustaque iudicia, et universam legem?* Et similiter etiam quantum ad hoc sunt melioris conditionis clerici quam laici, et religiosi quam saeculares.

AD TERTIUM dicendum quod gentiles perfectius et securius salutem consequebantur sub observantiis legis quam sub sola lege naturali, et ideo ad eas admittebantur. Sicut etiam nunc laici transeunt ad clericatum, et saeculares ad religionem, quamvis absque hoc possint salvari.

would have been useless to admit strangers to the legal observances according to Divine ordinance, if they could have been saved without the observance of the Law. Therefore none could be saved without observing the Law.

ON THE CONTRARY, Dionysius says (*Coel. Hier.* ix) that many of the Gentiles were brought back to God by the angels. But it is clear that the Gentiles did not observe the Law. Therefore some could be saved without observing the Law.

I ANSWER THAT, The Old Law showed forth the precepts of the natural law, and added certain precepts of its own. Accordingly, as to those precepts of the natural law contained in the Old Law, all were bound to observe the Old Law; not because they belonged to the Old Law, but because they belonged to the natural law. But as to those precepts which were added by the Old Law, they were not binding on any save the Jewish people alone.

The reason of this is because the Old Law, as stated above (A4), was given to the Jewish people, that it might receive a prerogative of holiness, in reverence for Christ Who was to be born of that people. Now whatever laws are enacted for the special sanctification of certain ones, are binding on them alone: thus clerics who are set aside for the service of God are bound to certain obligations to which the laity are not bound; likewise religious are bound by their profession to certain works of perfection, to which people living in the world are not bound. In like manner this people was bound to certain special observances, to which other peoples were not bound. Wherefore it is written (Deut 18:13): *Thou shalt be perfect and without spot before the Lord thy God*: and for this reason they used a kind of form of profession, as appears from Dt. 26:3: *I profess this day before the Lord thy God*, etc.

REPLY OBJ. 1: Whoever are subject to a king, are bound to observe his law which he makes for all in general. But if he orders certain things to be observed by the servants of his household, others are not bound thereto.

REPLY OBJ. 2: The more a man is united to God, the better his state becomes: wherefore the more the Jewish people were bound to the worship of God, the greater their excellence over other peoples. Hence it is written (Deut 4:8): *What other nation is there so renowned that hath ceremonies and just judgments, and all the law?* In like manner, from this point of view, the state of clerics is better than that of the laity, and the state of religious than that of folk living in the world.

REPLY OBJ. 3: The Gentiles obtained salvation more perfectly and more securely under the observances of the Law than under the mere natural law: and for this reason they were admitted to them. So too the laity are now admitted to the ranks of the clergy, and secular persons to those of the religious, although they can be saved without this.

Article 6

Whether the Old Law Was Suitably Given at the Time of Moses?

AD SEXTUM SIC PROCEDITUR. Videtur quod lex vetus non convenienter fuerit data tempore Moysi. Lex enim vetus disponebat ad salutem quae erat futura per Christum, sicut dictum est. Sed statim homo post peccatum indiguit huiusmodi salutis remedio. Ergo statim post peccatum lex vetus debuit dari.

PRAETEREA, lex vetus data est propter sanctificationem eorum ex quibus Christus nasciturus erat. Sed Abrahae incoepit fieri promissio de semine, quod est Christus, ut habetur Gen. XII. Ergo statim tempore Abrahae debuit lex dari.

PRAETEREA, sicut Christus non est natus ex aliis descendentibus ex Noe nisi ex Abraham, cui facta est promissio; ita etiam non est natus ex aliis filiis Abrahae nisi ex David, cui est promissio renovata, secundum illud II Reg. XXIII, *dixit vir cui constitutum est de Christo Dei Iacob*. Ergo lex vetus debuit dari post David, sicut data est post Abraham.

SED CONTRA est quod apostolus dicit, ad Gal. III, quod *lex propter transgressionem posita est, donec veniret semen cui promiserat, ordinata per Angelos in manu mediatoris*, idest ordinabiliter data, ut Glossa dicit. Ergo congruum fuit ut lex vetus illo temporis ordine traderetur.

RESPONDEO dicendum quod convenientissime lex vetus data fuit tempore Moysi. Cuius ratio potest accipi ex duobus, secundum quod quaelibet lex duobus generibus hominum imponitur. Imponitur enim quibusdam duris et superbis, qui per legem compescuntur et domantur, imponitur etiam bonis, qui, per legem instructi, adiuvantur ad implendum quod intendunt. Conveniens igitur fuit tali tempore legem veterem dari, ad superbiam hominum convincendam. De duobus enim homo superbiebat, scilicet de scientia, et de potentia. De scientia quidem, quasi ratio naturalis ei posset sufficere ad salutem. Et ideo ut de hoc eius superbia convinceretur permissus est homo regimini suae rationis absque adminiculo legis scriptae, et experimento homo discere potuit quod patiebatur rationis defectum, per hoc quod homines usque ad idololatriam et turpissima vitia circa tempora Abrahae sunt prolapsi. Et ideo post haec tempora fuit necessarium legem scriptam dari in remedium humanae ignorantiae, quia per legem est cognitio peccati, ut dicitur Rom. III. Sed postquam homo est instructus per legem, convicta est eius superbia de infirmitate, dum implere non poterat quod cognoscebat. Et ideo, sicut apostolus concludit, ad Rom. VIII, *quod impossibile erat*

OBJECTION 1: It would seem that the Old Law was not suitably given at the time of Moses. Because the Old Law disposed man for the salvation which was to come through Christ, as stated above (AA2,3). But man needed this salutary remedy immediately after he had sinned. Therefore the Law should have been given immediately after sin.

OBJ. 2: Further, the Old Law was given for the sanctification of those from whom Christ was to be born. Now the promise concerning the *seed, which is Christ* (Gal 3:16) was first made to Abraham, as related in Gn. 12:7. Therefore the Law should have been given at once at the time of Abraham.

OBJ. 3: Further, as Christ was born of those alone who descended from Noah through Abraham, to whom the promise was made; so was He born of no other of the descendants of Abraham but David, to whom the promise was renewed, according to 2 Kgs. 23:1: *The man to whom it was appointed concerning the Christ of the God of Jacob . . . said*. Therefore the Old Law should have been given after David, just as it was given after Abraham.

ON THE CONTRARY, The Apostle says (Gal 3:19) that the Law *was set because of transgressions, until the seed should come, to whom He made the promise, being ordained by angels in the hand of a Mediator*: ordained, i.e., *given in orderly fashion*, as the gloss explains. Therefore it was fitting that the Old Law should be given in this order of time.

I ANSWER THAT, It was most fitting for the Law to be given at the time of Moses. The reason for this may be taken from two things in respect of which every law is imposed on two kinds of men. Because it is imposed on some men who are hard-hearted and proud, whom the law restrains and tames: and it is imposed on good men, who, through being instructed by the law, are helped to fulfill what they desire to do. Hence it was fitting that the Law should be given at such a time as would be appropriate for the overcoming of man's pride. For man was proud of two things, viz., of knowledge and of power. He was proud of his knowledge, as though his natural reason could suffice him for salvation: and accordingly, in order that his pride might be overcome in this matter, man was left to the guidance of his reason without the help of a written law: and man was able to learn from experience that his reason was deficient, since about the time of Abraham man had fallen headlong into idolatry and the most shameful vices. Wherefore, after those times, it was necessary for a written law to be given as a remedy for human ignorance: because *by the Law is the knowledge of sin* (Rom 3:20). But, after man had been instructed by the Law, his pride was convinced of his weakness, through his being unable to fulfill what he knew. Hence, as the Apostle concludes (Rom 8:3,4), *what the Law could not do in that it*

legi, in qua infirmabatur per carnem, misit Deus filium suum, ut iustificatio legis impleretur in nobis.

Ex parte vero bonorum, lex data est in auxilium. Quod quidem tunc maxime populo necessarium fuit, quando lex naturalis obscurari incipiebat propter exuberantiam peccatorum. Oportebat autem huiusmodi auxilium quodam ordine dari, ut per imperfecta ad perfectionem manuducerentur. Et ideo inter legem naturae et legem gratiae, oportuit legem veterem dari.

AD PRIMUM ergo dicendum quod statim post peccatum primi hominis non competebat legem veterem dari, tum quia nondum homo recognoscebat se ea indigere, de sua ratione confisus. Tum quia adhuc dictamen legis naturae nondum erat obtenebratum per consuetudinem peccandi.

AD SECUNDUM dicendum quod lex non debet dari nisi populo, est enim praeceptum commune, ut dictum est. Et ideo tempore Abrahae data sunt quaedam familiaria praecepta, et quasi domestica, Dei ad homines. Sed postmodum, multiplicatis eius posteris intantum quod populus esset, et liberatis eis a servitute, lex convenienter potuit dari, nam servi non sunt pars populi vel civitatis, cui legem dari competit, ut philosophus dicit, in III Polit.

AD TERTIUM dicendum quod, quia legem oportebat alicui populo dari, non solum illi ex quibus Christus natus est, legem acceperunt; sed totus populus consignatus signaculo circumcisionis, quae fuit signum promissionis Abrahae factae et ab eo creditae, ut dicit apostolus, Rom. IV. Et ideo etiam ante David oportuit legem dari tali populo iam collecto.

was weak through the flesh, God sent His own Son . . . that the justification of the Law might be fulfilled in us.

With regard to good men, the Law was given to them as a help; which was most needed by the people, at the time when the natural law began to be obscured on account of the exuberance of sin: for it was fitting that this help should be bestowed on men in an orderly manner, so that they might be led from imperfection to perfection; wherefore it was becoming that the Old Law should be given between the law of nature and the law of grace.

REPLY OBJ. 1: It was not fitting for the Old Law to be given at once after the sin of the first man: both because man was so confident in his own reason, that he did not acknowledge his need of the Old Law; because as yet the dictate of the natural law was not darkened by habitual sinning.

REPLY OBJ. 2: A law should not be given save to the people, since it is a general precept, as stated above (Q90, AA2,3); wherefore at the time of Abraham God gave men certain familiar, and, as it were, household precepts: but when Abraham's descendants had multiplied, so as to form a people, and when they had been freed from slavery, it was fitting that they should be given a law; for *slaves are not that part of the people or state to which it is fitting for the law to be directed*, as the Philosopher says (*Polit.* iii, 2,4,5).

REPLY OBJ. 3: Since the Law had to be given to the people, not only those, of whom Christ was born, received the Law, but the whole people, who were marked with the seal of circumcision, which was the sign of the promise made to Abraham, and in which he believed, according to Rm. 4:11: hence even before David, the Law had to be given to that people as soon as they were collected together.

QUESTION 99

OF THE PRECEPTS OF THE OLD LAW

Deinde considerandum est de praeceptis veteris legis. Et primo, de distinctione ipsorum; secundo, de singulis generibus distinctis. Circa primum quaeruntur sex.

Primo, utrum legis veteris sint plura praecepta, vel unum tantum.

Secundo, utrum lex vetus contineat aliqua praecepta moralia.

Tertio, utrum praeter moralia contineat caeremonialia.

Quarto, utrum contineat, praeter haec, iudicialia.

Quinto, utrum praeter ista tria contineat aliqua alia.

Sexto, de modo quo lex inducebat ad observantiam praedictorum.

We must now consider the precepts of the Old Law; and (1) how they are distinguished from one another; (2) each kind of precept. Under the first head there are six points of inquiry:

(1) Whether the Old Law contains several precepts or only one?

(2) Whether the Old Law contains any moral precepts?

(3) Whether it contains ceremonial precepts in addition to the moral precepts?

(4) Whether besides these it contains judicial precepts?

(5) Whether it contains any others besides these?

(6) How the Old Law induced men to keep its precepts.

Article 1

Whether the Old Law Contains Only One Precept?

AD PRIMUM SIC PROCEDITUR. Videtur quod in lege veteri non contineatur nisi unum praeceptum. Lex enim est nihil aliud quam praeceptum, ut supra habitum est. Sed lex vetus est una. Ergo non continet nisi unum praeceptum.

PRAETEREA, apostolus dicit, Rom. XIII, *si quod est aliud mandatum, in hoc verbo instauratur, diliges proximum tuum sicut teipsum.* Sed istud mandatum est unum. Ergo lex vetus non continet nisi unum mandatum.

PRAETEREA, Matth. VII, dicitur, *omnia quaecumque vultis ut faciant vobis homines, et vos facite illis, haec est enim lex et prophetae.* Sed tota lex vetus continetur in lege et prophetis. Ergo tota lex vetus non habet nisi unum praeceptum.

SED CONTRA est quod apostolus dicit, ad Ephes. II, *legem mandatorum decretis evacuans.* Et loquitur de lege veteri, ut patet per Glossam ibidem. Ergo lex vetus continet in se multa mandata.

RESPONDEO dicendum quod praeceptum legis, cum sit obligatorium, est de aliquo quod fieri debet. Quod autem aliquid debeat fieri, hoc provenit ex necessitate alicuius finis. Unde manifestum est quod de ratione praecepti est quod importet ordinem ad finem, inquantum scilicet illud praecipitur quod est necessarium vel

OBJECTION 1: It would seem that the Old Law contains but one precept. Because a law is nothing else than a precept, as stated above (Q90, AA2,3). Now there is but one Old Law. Therefore it contains but one precept.

OBJ. 2: Further, the Apostle says (Rom 13:9): *If there be any other commandment, it is comprised in this word: Thou shalt love thy neighbor as thyself.* But this is only one commandment. Therefore the Old Law contained but one commandment.

OBJ. 3: Further, it is written (Matt 7:12): *All things . . . whatsoever you would that men should do to you, do you also to them. For this is the Law and the prophets.* But the whole of the Old Law is comprised in the Law and the prophets. Therefore the whole of the Old Law contains but one commandment.

ON THE CONTRARY, The Apostle says (Eph 2:15): *Making void the Law of commandments contained in decrees:* where he is referring to the Old Law, as the gloss comments, on the passage. Therefore the Old Law comprises many commandments.

I ANSWER THAT, Since a precept of law is binding, it is about something which must be done: and, that a thing must be done, arises from the necessity of some end. Hence it is evident that a precept implies, in its very idea, relation to an end, insofar as a thing is commanded as being necessary or expedient to an end. Now many things may happen

expediens ad finem. Contingit autem ad unum finem multa esse necessaria vel expedientia. Et secundum hoc possunt de diversis rebus dari praecepta inquantum ordinantur ad unum finem. Unde dicendum est quod omnia praecepta legis veteris sunt unum secundum ordinem ad unum finem, sunt tamen multa secundum diversitatem eorum quae ordinantur ad finem illum.

AD PRIMUM ergo dicendum quod lex vetus dicitur esse una secundum ordinem ad finem unum, et tamen continet diversa praecepta, secundum distinctionem eorum quae ordinat ad finem. Sicut etiam ars aedificativa est una secundum unitatem finis, quia tendit ad aedificationem domus, tamen continet diversa praecepta, secundum diversos actus ad hoc ordinatos.

AD SECUNDUM dicendum quod, sicut apostolus dicit, I ad Tim. I, *finis praecepti caritas est*, ad hoc enim omnis lex tendit, ut amicitiam constituat vel hominum ad invicem, vel hominis ad Deum. Et ideo tota lex impletur in hoc uno mandato, *diliges proximum tuum sicut teipsum*, sicut in quodam fine mandatorum omnium, in dilectione enim proximi includitur etiam Dei dilectio, quando proximus diligitur propter Deum. Unde apostolus hoc unum praeceptum posuit pro duobus quae sunt de dilectione Dei et proximi, de quibus dicit dominus, Matth. XXII, *in his duobus mandatis pendet omnis lex et prophetae.*

AD TERTIUM dicendum quod, sicut dicitur in IX Ethic., *amicabilia quae sunt ad alterum, venerunt ex amicabilibus quae sunt homini ad seipsum*, dum scilicet homo ita se habet ad alterum sicut ad se. Et ideo in hoc quod dicitur, *omnia quaecumque vultis ut faciant vobis homines, et vos facite illis*, explicatur quaedam regula dilectionis proximi, quae etiam implicite continetur in hoc quod dicitur, *diliges proximum tuum sicut teipsum*. Unde est quaedam explicatio istius mandati.

to be necessary or expedient to an end; and, accordingly, precepts may be given about various things as being ordained to one end. Consequently we must say that all the precepts of the Old Law are one in respect of their relation to one end: and yet they are many in respect of the diversity of those things that are ordained to that end.

REPLY OBJ. 1: The Old Law is said to be one as being ordained to one end: yet it comprises various precepts, according to the diversity of the things which it directs to the end. Thus also the art of building is one according to the unity of its end, because it aims at the building of a house: and yet it contains various rules, according to the variety of acts ordained thereto.

REPLY OBJ. 2: As the Apostle says (1 Tim 1:5), *the end of the commandment is charity*; since every law aims at establishing friendship, either between man and man, or between man and God. Wherefore the whole Law is comprised in this one commandment, *Thou shalt love thy neighbor as thyself*, as expressing the end of all commandments: because love of one's neighbor includes love of God, when we love our neighbor for God's sake. Hence the Apostle put this commandment in place of the two which are about the love of God and of one's neighbor, and of which Our Lord said (Matt 22:40): *On these two commandments dependeth the whole Law and the prophets.*

REPLY OBJ. 3: As stated in *Ethic.* ix, 8, *friendship towards another arises from friendship towards oneself*, insofar as man looks on another as on himself. Hence when it is said, *All things whatsoever you would that men should do to you, do you also to them*, this is an explanation of the rule of neighborly love contained implicitly in the words, *Thou shalt love thy neighbor as thyself*: so that it is an explanation of this commandment.

Article 2

Whether the Old Law Contains Moral Precepts?

AD SECUNDUM SIC PROCEDITUR. Videtur quod lex vetus non contineat praecepta moralia. Lex enim vetus distinguitur a lege naturae, ut supra habitum est. Sed praecepta moralia pertinent ad legem naturae. Ergo non pertinent ad legem veterem.

PRAETEREA, ibi subvenire debuit homini lex divina, ubi deficit ratio humana, sicut patet in his quae ad fidem pertinent, quae sunt supra rationem. Sed ad praecepta moralia ratio hominis sufficere videtur. Ergo praecepta moralia non sunt de lege veteri, quae est lex divina.

OBJECTION 1: It would seem that the Old Law contains no moral precepts. For the Old Law is distinct from the law of nature, as stated above (Q91, AA4,5; Q98, A5). But the moral precepts belong to the law of nature. Therefore they do not belong to the Old Law.

OBJ. 2: Further, the Divine Law should have come to man's assistance where human reason fails him: as is evident in regard to things that are of faith, which are above reason. But man's reason seems to suffice for the moral precepts. Therefore the moral precepts do not belong to the Old Law, which is a Divine law.

PRAETEREA, lex vetus dicitur littera occidens, ut patet II ad Cor. III. Sed praecepta moralia non occidunt, sed vivificant; secundum illud Psalmi CXVIII, *in aeternum non obliviscar iustificationes tuas, quia in ipsis vivificasti me.* Ergo praecepta moralia non pertinent ad veterem legem.

SED CONTRA est quod dicitur Eccli. XVII, *addidit illis disciplinam, et legem vitae haereditavit eos.* Disciplina autem pertinet ad mores, dicit enim Glossa ad Heb. XII, super illud, omnis disciplina etc., *disciplina est eruditio morum per difficilia.* Ergo lex a Deo data, praecepta moralia continebat.

RESPONDEO dicendum quod lex vetus continebat praecepta quaedam moralia, ut patet Exod. XX, *non occides, non furtum facies.* Et hoc rationabiliter. Nam sicut intentio principalis legis humanae est ut faciat amicitiam hominum ad invicem; ita intentio legis divinae est ut constituat principaliter amicitiam hominis ad Deum. Cum autem similitudo sit ratio amoris, secundum illud Eccli. XIII, *omne animal diligit simile sibi;* impossibile est esse amicitiam hominis ad Deum, qui est optimus, nisi homines boni efficiantur, unde dicitur Levit. XIX, *sancti eritis, quoniam ego sanctus sum.* Bonitas autem hominis est virtus, quae facit bonum habentem. Et ideo oportuit praecepta legis veteris etiam de actibus virtutum dari. Et haec sunt moralia legis praecepta.

AD PRIMUM ergo dicendum quod lex vetus distinguitur a lege naturae non tanquam ab ea omnino aliena, sed tanquam aliquid ei superaddens. Sicut enim gratia praesupponit naturam, ita oportet quod lex divina praesupponat legem naturalem.

AD SECUNDUM dicendum quod legi divinae conveniens erat ut non solum provideret homini in his ad quae ratio non potest, sed etiam in his circa quae contingit rationem hominis impediri. Ratio autem hominis circa praecepta moralia, quantum ad ipsa communissima praecepta legis naturae, non poterat errare in universali, sed tamen, propter consuetudinem peccandi, obscurabatur in particularibus agendis. Circa alia vero praecepta moralia, quae sunt quasi conclusiones deductae ex communibus principiis legis naturae, multorum ratio oberrabat, ita ut quaedam quae secundum se sunt mala, ratio multorum licita iudicaret. Unde oportuit contra utrumque defectum homini subveniri per auctoritatem legis divinae. Sicut etiam inter credenda nobis proponuntur non solum ea ad quae ratio attingere non potest, ut Deum esse trinum; sed etiam ea ad quae ratio recta pertingere potest, ut Deum esse unum; ad excludendum rationis humanae errorem, qui accidebat in multis.

AD TERTIUM dicendum quod, sicut Augustinus probat in libro de spiritu et littera, etiam littera legis quantum ad praecepta moralia, occidere dicitur occasionaliter, inquantum scilicet praecipit quod bonum est, non praebens auxilium gratiae ad implendum.

OBJ. 3: Further, the Old Law is said to be *the letter that killeth* (2 Cor 3:6). But the moral precepts do not kill, but quicken, according to Ps. 118:93: *Thy justifications I will never forget, for by them Thou hast given me life.* Therefore the moral precepts do not belong to the Old Law.

ON THE CONTRARY, It is written (Sir 17:9): *Moreover, He gave them discipline and the law of life for an inheritance.* Now discipline belongs to morals; for this gloss on Heb. 12:11: *Now all chastisement*, etc., says: *Discipline is an exercise in morals by means of difficulties.* Therefore the Law which was given by God comprised moral precepts.

I ANSWER THAT, The Old Law contained some moral precepts; as is evident from Ex. 20:13,15: *Thou shalt not kill, Thou shalt not steal.* This was reasonable: because, just as the principal intention of human law is to create friendship between man and man; so the chief intention of the Divine law is to establish man in friendship with God. Now since likeness is the reason of love, according to Ecclus. 13:19: *Every beast loveth its like;* there cannot possibly be any friendship of man to God, Who is supremely good, unless man become good: wherefore it is written (Lev 19:2; 11:45): *You shall be holy, for I am holy.* But the goodness of man is virtue, which *makes its possessor good* (*Ethic.* ii, 6). Therefore it was necessary for the Old Law to include precepts about acts of virtue: and these are the moral precepts of the Law.

REPLY OBJ. 1: The Old Law is distinct from the natural law, not as being altogether different from it, but as something added thereto. For just as grace presupposes nature, so must the Divine law presuppose the natural law.

REPLY OBJ. 2: It was fitting that the Divine law should come to man's assistance not only in those things for which reason is insufficient, but also in those things in which human reason may happen to be impeded. Now human reason could not go astray in the abstract, as to the universal principles of the natural law; but through being habituated to sin, it became obscured in the point of things to be done in detail. But with regard to the other moral precepts, which are like conclusions drawn from the universal principles of the natural law, the reason of many men went astray, to the extent of judging to be lawful, things that are evil in themselves. Hence there was need for the authority of the Divine law to rescue man from both these defects. Thus among the articles of faith not only are those things set forth to which reason cannot reach, such as the Trinity of the Godhead; but also those to which right reason can attain, such as the Unity of the Godhead; in order to remove the manifold errors to which reason is liable.

REPLY OBJ. 3: As Augustine proves (*De Spiritu et Litera* xiv), even the letter of the law is said to be the occasion of death, as to the moral precepts; insofar as, to wit, it prescribes what is good, without furnishing the aid of grace for its fulfilment.

Article 3

Whether the Old Law Comprises Ceremonial, Besides Moral, Precepts?

AD TERTIUM SIC PROCEDITUR. Videtur quod lex vetus non contineat praecepta caeremonialia, praeter moralia. Omnis enim lex quae hominibus datur, est directiva humanorum actuum. Actus autem humani morales dicuntur, ut supra dictum est. Ergo videtur quod in lege veteri hominibus data, non debeant contineri nisi praecepta moralia.

PRAETEREA, praecepta quae dicuntur caeremonialia, videntur ad divinum cultum pertinere. Sed divinus cultus est actus virtutis, scilicet religionis, quae, ut Tullius dicit in sua Rhetoric., *divinae naturae cultum caeremoniamque affert*. Cum igitur praecepta moralia sint de actibus virtutum, ut dictum est, videtur quod praecepta caeremonialia non sint distinguenda a moralibus.

PRAETEREA, praecepta caeremonialia esse videntur quae figurative aliquid significant. Sed sicut Augustinus dicit, in II de Doctr. Christ., *verba inter homines obtinuerunt principatum significandi*. Ergo nulla necessitas fuit ut in lege continerentur praecepta caeremonialia de aliquibus actibus figurativis.

SED CONTRA est quod dicitur Deut. IV, *decem verba scripsit in duabus tabulis lapideis, mihique mandavit in illo tempore ut docerem vos caeremonias et iudicia quae facere deberetis*. Sed decem praecepta legis sunt moralia. Ergo praeter praecepta moralia sunt etiam alia praecepta caeremonialia.

RESPONDEO dicendum quod, sicut dictum est, lex divina principaliter instituitur ad ordinandum homines ad Deum; lex autem humana principaliter ad ordinandum homines ad invicem. Et ideo leges humanae non curaverunt aliquid instituere de cultu divino nisi in ordine ad bonum commune hominum, et propter hoc etiam multa confinxerunt circa res divinas, secundum quod videbatur eis expediens ad informandos mores hominum; sicut patet in ritu gentilium. Sed lex divina e converso homines ad invicem ordinavit secundum quod conveniebat ordini qui est in Deum, quem principaliter intendebat. Ordinatur autem homo in Deum non solum per interiores actus mentis, qui sunt credere, sperare et amare; sed etiam per quaedam exteriora opera, quibus homo divinam servitutem profitetur. Et ista opera dicuntur ad cultum Dei pertinere. Qui quidem cultus caeremonia vocatur, quasi munia, idest dona, Caereris, quae dicebatur dea frugum, ut quidam dicunt, eo quod primo ex frugibus oblationes Deo offerebantur. Sive, ut maximus Valerius refert, nomen caeremoniae introductum est ad significandum cultum divinum apud Latinos, a quodam oppido iuxta Romam, quod Caere vocabatur, eo quod, Roma capta a gallis, illuc sacra Romanorum ablata sunt, et reverentissime habita. Sic igitur illa praecepta quae in

OBJECTION 1: It would seem that the Old Law does not comprise ceremonial, besides moral, precepts. For every law that is given to man is for the purpose of directing human actions. Now human actions are called moral, as stated above (Q1, A3). Therefore it seems that the Old Law given to men should not comprise other than moral precepts.

OBJ. 2: Further, those precepts that are styled ceremonial seem to refer to the Divine worship. But Divine worship is the act of a virtue, viz., religion, which, as Tully says (*De Invent.* ii) *offers worship and ceremony to the Godhead*. Since, then, the moral precepts are about acts of virtue, as stated above (A2), it seems that the ceremonial precepts should not be distinct from the moral.

OBJ. 3: Further, the ceremonial precepts seem to be those which signify something figuratively. But, as Augustine observes (*De Doctr. Christ.* ii, 3,4), *of all signs employed by men words hold the first place*. Therefore there is no need for the Law to contain ceremonial precepts about certain figurative actions.

ON THE CONTRARY, It is written (Deut 4:13,14): *Ten words . . . He wrote in two tables of stone; and He commanded me at that time that I should teach you the ceremonies and judgments which you shall do*. But the ten commandments of the Law are moral precepts. Therefore besides the moral precepts there are others which are ceremonial.

I ANSWER THAT, As stated above (A2), the Divine law is instituted chiefly in order to direct men to God; while human law is instituted chiefly in order to direct men in relation to one another. Hence human laws have not concerned themselves with the institution of anything relating to Divine worship except as affecting the common good of mankind: and for this reason they have devised many institutions relating to Divine matters, according as it seemed expedient for the formation of human morals; as may be seen in the rites of the Gentiles. On the other hand the Divine law directed men to one another according to the demands of that order whereby man is directed to God, which order was the chief aim of that law. Now man is directed to God not only by the interior acts of the mind, which are faith, hope, and love, but also by certain external works, whereby man makes profession of his subjection to God: and it is these works that are said to belong to the Divine worship. This worship is called *ceremony* of Ceres (who was the goddess of fruits), as some say: because, at first, offerings were made to God from the fruits: or because, as Valerius Maximus states, the word *ceremony* was introduced among the Latins, to signify the Divine worship, being derived from a town near Rome called *Caere*: since, when Rome was taken by the Gauls, the sacred chattels of the

lege pertinent ad cultum Dei, specialiter caeremonialia dicuntur.

AD PRIMUM ergo dicendum quod humani actus se extendunt etiam ad cultum divinum. Et ideo etiam de his continet praecepta lex vetus hominibus data.

AD SECUNDUM dicendum quod, sicut supra dictum est, praecepta legis naturae communia sunt, et indigent determinatione. Determinantur autem et per legem humanam, et per legem divinam. Et sicut ipsae determinationes quae fiunt per legem humanam, non dicuntur esse de lege naturae, sed de iure positivo; ita ipsae determinationes praeceptorum legis naturae quae fiunt per legem divinam, distinguuntur a praeceptis moralibus, quae pertinent ad legem naturae. Colere ergo Deum, cum sit actus virtutis, pertinet ad praeceptum morale, sed determinatio huius praecepti, ut scilicet colatur talibus hostiis et talibus muneribus, hoc pertinet ad praecepta caeremonialia. Et ideo praecepta caeremonialia distinguuntur a praeceptis moralibus.

AD TERTIUM dicendum quod, sicut Dionysius dicit, I cap. Cael. Hier., divina hominibus manifestari non possunt nisi sub aliquibus similitudinibus sensibilibus. Ipsae autem similitudines magis movent animum quando non solum verbo exprimuntur, sed etiam sensui offeruntur. Et ideo divina traduntur in Scripturis non solum per similitudines verbo expressas, sicut patet in metaphoricis locutionibus; sed etiam per similitudines rerum quae visui proponuntur, quod pertinet ad praecepta caeremonialia.

Romans were taken thither and most carefully preserved. Accordingly those precepts of the Law which refer to the Divine worship are specially called ceremonial.

REPLY OBJ. 1: Human acts extend also to the Divine worship: and therefore the Old Law given to man contains precepts about these matters also.

REPLY OBJ. 2: As stated above (Q91, A3), the precepts of the natural law are general, and require to be determined: and they are determined both by human law and by Divine law. And just as these very determinations which are made by human law are said to be, not of natural, but of positive law; so the determinations of the precepts of the natural law, effected by the Divine law, are distinct from the moral precepts which belong to the natural law. Wherefore to worship God, since it is an act of virtue, belongs to a moral precept; but the determination of this precept, namely that He is to be worshipped by such and such sacrifices, and such and such offerings, belongs to the ceremonial precepts. Consequently the ceremonial precepts are distinct from the moral precepts.

REPLY OBJ. 3: As Dionysius says (*Coel. Hier.* i), the things of God cannot be manifested to men except by means of sensible similitudes. Now these similitudes move the soul more when they are not only expressed in words, but also offered to the senses. Wherefore the things of God are set forth in the Scriptures not only by similitudes expressed in words, as in the case of metaphorical expressions; but also by similitudes of things set before the eyes, which pertains to the ceremonial precepts.

Article 4

Whether, Besides the Moral and Ceremonial Precepts, There Are Also Judicial Precepts?

AD QUARTUM SIC PROCEDITUR. Videtur quod praeter praecepta moralia et caeremonialia, non sint aliqua praecepta iudicialia in veteri lege. Dicit enim Augustinus, contra Faustum, quod in lege veteri sunt praecepta vitae agendae, et praecepta vitae significandae. Sed praecepta vitae agendae sunt moralia; praecepta autem vitae significandae sunt caeremonialia. Ergo praeter haec duo genera praeceptorum, non sunt ponenda in lege alia praecepta iudicialia.

PRAETEREA, super illud Psalmi CXVIII, *a iudiciis tuis non declinavi*, dicit Glossa, *idest ab his quae constituisti regulam vivendi*. Sed regula vivendi pertinet ad praecepta moralia. Ergo praecepta iudicialia non sunt distinguenda a moralibus.

PRAETEREA, iudicium videtur esse actus iustitiae; secundum illud Psalmi XCIII, *quoadusque iustitia convertatur in iudicium*. Sed actus iustitiae, sicut et actus

OBJECTION 1: It would seem that there are no judicial precepts in addition to the moral and ceremonial precepts in the Old Law. For Augustine says (*Contra Faust.* vi, 2) that in the Old Law there are *precepts concerning the life we have to lead, and precepts regarding the life that is foreshadowed.* Now the precepts of the life we have to lead are moral precepts; and the precepts of the life that is foreshadowed are ceremonial. Therefore besides these two kinds of precepts we should not put any judicial precepts in the Law.

OBJ. 2: Further, a gloss on Ps. 118:102, *I have not declined from Thy judgments*, says, i.e., *from the rule of life Thou hast set for me.* But a rule of life belongs to the moral precepts. Therefore the judicial precepts should not be considered as distinct from the moral precepts.

OBJ. 3: Further, judgment seems to be an act of justice, according to Ps. 93:15: *Until justice be turned into judgment.* But acts of justice, like the acts of other virtues, belong to

ceterarum virtutum, pertinet ad praecepta moralia. Ergo praecepta moralia includunt in se iudicialia, et sic non debent ab eis distingui.

Sed contra est quod dicitur Deut. VI, *haec sunt praecepta et caeremoniae atque iudicia*. Praecepta autem antonomastice dicuntur moralia. Ergo praeter praecepta moralia et caeremonialia, sunt etiam iudicialia.

Respondeo dicendum quod, sicut dictum est, ad legem divinam pertinet ut ordinet homines ad invicem et ad Deum. Utrumque autem horum in communi quidem pertinet ad dictamen legis naturae, ad quod referuntur moralia praecepta, sed oportet quod determinetur utrumque per legem divinam vel humanam, quia principia naturaliter nota sunt communia tam in speculativis quam in activis. Sicut igitur determinatio communis praecepti de cultu divino fit per praecepta caeremonialia, sic et determinatio communis praecepti de iustitia observanda inter homines, determinatur per praecepta iudicialia.

Et secundum hoc, oportet tria praecepta legis veteris ponere; scilicet moralia, quae sunt de dictamine legis naturae; caeremonialia, quae sunt determinationes cultus divini; et iudicialia, quae sunt determinationes iustitiae inter homines observandae. Unde cum apostolus, Rom. VII, dixisset quod lex est sancta, subiungit quod mandatum est iustum et sanctum et bonum, iustum quidem, quantum ad iudicialia; sanctum, quantum ad caeremonialia (nam sanctum dicitur quod est Deo dicatum); bonum, idest honestum, quantum ad moralia.

Ad primum ergo dicendum quod tam praecepta moralia, quam etiam iudicialia, pertinent ad directionem vitae humanae. Et ideo utraque continentur sub uno membro illorum quae ponit Augustinus, scilicet sub praeceptis vitae agendae.

Ad secundum dicendum quod iudicium significat executionem iustitiae, quae quidem est secundum applicationem rationis ad aliqua particularia determinate. Unde praecepta iudicialia communicant in aliquo cum moralibus, inquantum scilicet a ratione derivantur; et in aliquo cum caeremonialibus, inquantum scilicet sunt quaedam determinationes communium praeceptorum. Et ideo quandoque sub iudiciis comprehenduntur praecepta iudicialia et moralia, sicut Deut. V, audi, Israel, caeremonias atque iudicia; quandoque vero iudicialia et caeremonialia, sicut Levit. XVIII, facietis iudicia mea, et praecepta mea servabitis, ubi praecepta ad moralia referuntur, iudicia vero ad iudicialia et caeremonialia.

Ad tertium dicendum quod actus iustitiae in generali pertinet ad praecepta moralia, sed determinatio eius in speciali pertinet ad praecepta iudicialia.

the moral precepts. Therefore the moral precepts include the judicial precepts, and consequently should not be held as distinct from them.

On the contrary, It is written (Deut 6:1): *These are the precepts and ceremonies, and judgments*: where *precepts* stands for *moral precepts* antonomastically. Therefore there are judicial precepts besides moral and ceremonial precepts.

I answer that, As stated above (AA2,3), it belongs to the Divine law to direct men to one another and to God. Now each of these belongs in the abstract to the dictates of the natural law, to which dictates the moral precepts are to be referred: yet each of them has to be determined by Divine or human law, because naturally known principles are universal, both in speculative and in practical matters. Accordingly just as the determination of the universal principle about Divine worship is effected by the ceremonial precepts, so the determination of the general precepts of that justice which is to be observed among men is effected by the judicial precepts.

We must therefore distinguish three kinds of precept in the Old Law; viz., *moral* precepts, which are dictated by the natural law; *ceremonial* precepts, which are determinations of the Divine worship; and *judicial* precepts, which are determinations of the justice to be maintained among men. Wherefore the Apostle (Rom 7:12) after saying that the *Law is holy*, adds that *the commandment is just, and holy, and good*: *just*, in respect of the judicial precepts; *holy*, with regard to the ceremonial precepts (since the word *sanctus— holy—*is applied to that which is consecrated to God); and *good*, i.e., conducive to virtue, as to the moral precepts.

Reply Obj. 1: Both the moral and the judicial precepts aim at the ordering of human life: and consequently they are both comprised under one of the heads mentioned by Augustine, viz., under the precepts of the life we have to lead.

Reply Obj. 2: Judgment denotes execution of justice, by an application of the reason to individual cases in a determinate way. Hence the judicial precepts have something in common with the moral precepts, in that they are derived from reason; and something in common with the ceremonial precepts, in that they are determinations of general precepts. This explains why sometimes *judgments* comprise both judicial and moral precepts, as in Dt. 5:1: *Hear, O Israel, the ceremonies and judgments*; and sometimes judicial and ceremonial precepts, as in Lev. 18:4: *You shall do My judgments, and shall observe My precepts*, where *precepts* denotes moral precepts, while *judgments* refers to judicial and ceremonial precepts.

Reply Obj. 3: The act of justice, in general, belongs to the moral precepts; but its determination to some special kind of act belongs to the judicial precepts.

Article 5

Whether the Old Law Contains Any Others Besides the Moral, Judicial, and Ceremonial Precepts?

Ad quintum sic proceditur. Videtur quod aliqua alia praecepta contineantur in lege veteri praeter moralia, iudicialia et caeremonialia. Iudicialia enim praecepta pertinent ad actum iustitiae, quae est hominis ad hominem; caeremonialia vero pertinent ad actum religionis, qua Deus colitur. Sed praeter has sunt multae aliae virtutes, scilicet temperantia, fortitudo, liberalitas, et aliae plures, ut supra dictum est. Ergo praeter praedicta oportet plura alia in lege veteri contineri.

Praeterea, Deut. XI dicitur, *ama dominum Deum tuum, et observa eius praecepta et caeremonias et iudicia atque mandata*. Sed praecepta pertinent ad moralia, ut dictum est. Ergo praeter moralia, iudicialia et caeremonialia, adhuc alia continentur in lege, quae dicuntur mandata.

Praeterea, Deut. VI dicitur, *custodi praecepta domini Dei tui, ac testimonia et caeremonias quas tibi praecepi*. Ergo praeter omnia praedicta adhuc in lege testimonia continentur.

Praeterea, in Psalmo CXVIII dicitur, *in aeternum non obliviscar iustificationes tuas*, Glossa, *idest legem*. Ergo praecepta legis veteris non solum sunt moralia, caeremonialia et iudicialia, sed etiam iustificationes.

Sed contra est quod dicitur Deut. VI, *haec sunt praecepta et caeremoniae atque iudicia quae mandavit dominus Deus vobis*. Et haec ponuntur in principio legis. Ergo omnia praecepta legis sub his comprehenduntur.

Respondeo dicendum quod in lege ponuntur aliqua tanquam praecepta; aliqua vero tanquam ad praeceptorum adimpletionem ordinata. Praecepta quidem sunt de his quae sunt agenda. Ad quorum impletionem ex duobus homo inducitur, scilicet ex auctoritate praecipientis; et ex utilitate impletionis, quae quidem est consecutio alicuius boni utilis, delectabilis vel honesti, aut fuga alicuius mali contrarii. Oportuit igitur in veteri lege proponi quaedam quae auctoritatem Dei praecipientis indicarent, sicut illud Deut. VI, *audi, Israel, dominus Deus tuus Deus unus est*; et illud Gen. I, *in principio creavit Deus caelum et terram*. Et huiusmodi dicuntur testimonia. Oportuit etiam quod in lege proponerentur quaedam praemia observantium legem, et poenae transgredientium, ut patet Deut. XXVIII, *si audieris vocem domini Dei tui, faciet te excelsiorem cunctis gentibus*, et cetera. Et huiusmodi dicuntur iustificationes, secundum quod Deus aliquos iuste punit vel praemiat.

Objection 1: It would seem that the Old Law contains others besides the moral, judicial, and ceremonial precepts. Because the judicial precepts belong to the act of justice, which is between man and man; while the ceremonial precepts belong to the act of religion, whereby God is worshipped. Now besides these there are many other virtues, viz., temperance, fortitude, liberality, and several others, as stated above (Q60, A5). Therefore besides the aforesaid precepts, the Old Law should comprise others.

Obj. 2: Further, it is written (Deut 11:1): *Love the Lord thy God, and observe His precepts and ceremonies, His judgments and commandments*. Now precepts concern moral matters, as stated above (A4). Therefore besides the moral, judicial and ceremonial precepts, the Law contains others which are called *commandments*.

Obj. 3: Further, it is written (Deut 6:17): *Keep the precepts of the Lord thy God, and the testimonies and ceremonies which I have commanded thee*. Therefore in addition to the above, the Law comprises *testimonies*.

Obj. 4: Further, it is written (Ps 118:93): *Thy justifications (i.e., the Law, according to a gloss) I will never forget*. Therefore in the Old Law there are not only moral, ceremonial and judicial precepts, but also others, called *justifications*.

On the contrary, It is written (Deut 6:1): *These are the precepts and ceremonies and judgments which the Lord your God commanded . . . you*. And these words are placed at the beginning of the Law. Therefore all the precepts of the Law are included under them.

I answer that, Some things are included in the Law by way of precept; other things, as being ordained to the fulfilment of the precepts. Now the precepts refer to things which have to be done: and to their fulfilment man is induced by two considerations, viz., the authority of the lawgiver, and the benefit derived from the fulfilment, which benefit consists in the attainment of some good, useful, pleasurable or virtuous, or in the avoidance of some contrary evil. Hence it was necessary that in the Old Law certain things should be set forth to indicate the authority of God the lawgiver: e.g., Dt. 6:4: *Hear, O Israel, the Lord our God is one Lord*; and Gn. 1:1: *In the beginning God created heaven and earth*: and these are called *testimonies*. Again it was necessary that in the Law certain rewards should be appointed for those who observe the Law, and punishments for those who transgress; as it may be seen in Dt. 28: *If thou wilt hear the voice of the Lord thy God . . . He will make thee higher than all the nations*, etc.: and these are called *justifications*, according as God punishes or rewards certain ones justly.

Ipsa autem agenda sub praecepto non cadunt nisi inquantum habent aliquam debiti rationem. Est autem duplex debitum, unum quidem secundum regulam rationis, aliud autem secundum regulam legis determinantis; sicut philosophus, in V Ethic., distinguit duplex iustum, scilicet morale et legale.

Debitum autem morale est duplex, dictat enim ratio aliquid faciendum vel tanquam necessarium, sine quo non potest esse ordo virtutis; vel tanquam utile ad hoc quod ordo virtutis melius conservetur. Et secundum hoc, quaedam moralium praecise praecipiuntur vel prohibentur in lege, sicut, non occides, non furtum facies. Et haec proprie dicuntur praecepta. Quaedam vero praecipiuntur vel prohibentur, non quasi praecise debita, sed propter melius. Et ista possunt dici mandata, quia quandam inductionem habent et persuasionem. Sicut illud Exod. XXII, *si pignus acceperis vestimentum a proximo tuo, ante solis occasum reddas ei*; et aliqua similia. Unde Hieronymus dicit quod *in praeceptis est iustitia, in mandatis vero caritas*. Debitum autem ex determinatione legis, in rebus quidem humanis pertinet ad iudicialia; in rebus autem divinis, ad caeremonialia.

Quamvis etiam ea quae pertinent ad poenam vel praemia, dici possint testimonia, inquantum sunt protestationes quaedam divinae iustitiae. Omnia vero praecepta legis possunt dici iustificationes, inquantum sunt quaedam executiones legalis iustitiae. Possunt etiam aliter mandata a praeceptis distingui, ut praecepta dicantur quae Deus per seipsum iussit; mandata autem, quae per alios mandavit, ut ipsum nomen sonare videtur.

Ex quibus omnibus apparet quod omnia legis praecepta continentur sub moralibus, caeremonialibus et iudicialibus, alia vero non habent rationem praeceptorum, sed ordinantur ad praeceptorum observationem, ut dictum est.

Ad primum ergo dicendum quod sola iustitia, inter alias virtutes, importat rationem debiti. Et ideo moralia intantum sunt lege determinabilia, inquantum pertinent ad iustitiam, cuius etiam quaedam pars est religio, ut Tullius dicit. Unde iustum legale non potest esse aliquod praeter caeremonialia et iudicialia praecepta.

Ad alia patet responsio per ea quae dicta sunt.

The things that have to be done do not come under the precept except insofar as they have the character of a duty. Now a duty is twofold: one according to the rule of reason; the other according to the rule of a law which prescribes that duty: thus the Philosopher distinguishes a twofold just—moral and legal (*Ethic.* v, 7).

Moral duty is twofold: because reason dictates that something must be done, either as being so necessary that without it the order of virtue would be destroyed; or as being useful for the better maintaining of the order of virtue. And in this sense some of the moral precepts are expressed by way of absolute command or prohibition, as *Thou shalt not kill, Thou shalt not steal*: and these are properly called *precepts*. Other things are prescribed or forbidden, not as an absolute duty, but as something better to be done. These may be called *commandments*; because they are expressed by way of inducement and persuasion: an example whereof is seen in Ex. 22:26: *If thou take of thy neighbor a garment in pledge, thou shalt give it him again before sunset*; and in other like cases. Wherefore Jerome (*Praefat. in Comment. super Marc.*) says that *justice is in the precepts, charity in the commandments*. Duty as fixed by the Law, belongs to the judicial precepts, as regards human affairs; to the *ceremonial* precepts, as regards Divine matters.

Nevertheless those ordinances also which refer to punishments and rewards may be called *testimonies*, insofar as they testify to the Divine justice. Again all the precepts of the Law may be styled *justifications*, as being executions of legal justice. Furthermore the commandments may be distinguished from the precepts, so that those things be called *precepts* which God Himself prescribed; and those things *commandments* which He enjoined through others, as the very word seems to denote.

From this it is clear that all the precepts of the Law are either moral, ceremonial, or judicial; and that other ordinances have not the character of a precept, but are directed to the observance of the precepts, as stated above.

Reply Obj. 1: Justice alone, of all the virtues, implies the notion of duty. Consequently moral matters are determinable by law insofar as they belong to justice: of which virtue religion is a part, as Tully says (*De Invent.* ii). Wherefore the legal just cannot be anything foreign to the ceremonial and judicial precepts.

The Replies to the other Objections are clear from what has been said.

Article 6

Whether the Old Law Should Have Induced Men to the Observance of Its Precepts, by Means of Temporal Promises and Threats?

AD SEXTUM SIC PROCEDITUR. Videtur quod lex vetus non debuerit inducere ad observantiam praeceptorum per temporales promissiones et comminationes. Intentio enim legis divinae est ut homines Deo subdat per timorem et amorem, unde dicitur Deut. X, *et nunc, Israel, quid dominus Deus tuus petit a te, nisi ut timeas dominum Deum tuum, et ambules in viis eius, et diligas eum?* Sed cupiditas rerum temporalium abducit a Deo, dicit enim Augustinus, in libro octoginta trium quaest., quod *venenum caritatis est cupiditas.* Ergo promissiones et comminationes temporales videntur contrariari intentioni legislatoris, quod facit legem reprobabilem, ut patet per philosophum, in II Polit.

PRAETEREA, lex divina est excellentior quam lex humana. Videmus autem in scientiis quod quanto aliqua est altior, tanto per altiora media procedit. Ergo cum lex humana procedat ad inducendum homines per temporales comminationes et promissiones, lex divina non debuit ex his procedere, sed per aliqua maiora.

PRAETEREA, illud non potest esse praemium iustitiae vel poena culpae, quod aequaliter evenit et bonis et malis. Sed sicut dicitur Eccle. IX, *universa, temporalia, aeque eveniunt iusto et impio, bono et malo, mundo et immundo, immolanti victimas et sacrificia contemnenti.* Ergo temporalia bona vel mala non convenienter ponuntur ut poenae vel praemia mandatorum legis divinae.

SED CONTRA est quod dicitur Isaiae I, *si volueritis, et audieritis me, bona terrae comedetis. Quod si nolueritis, et me ad iracundiam provocaveritis, gladius devorabit vos.*

RESPONDEO dicendum quod, sicut in scientiis speculativis inducuntur homines ad assentiendum conclusionibus per media syllogistica, ita etiam in quibuslibet legibus homines inducuntur ad observantias praeceptorum per poenas et praemia. Videmus autem in scientiis speculativis quod media proponuntur auditori secundum eius conditionem, unde oportet ordinate in scientiis procedere, ut ex notioribus disciplina incipiat. Ita etiam oportet eum qui vult inducere hominem ad observantiam praeceptorum, ut ex illis eum movere incipiat quae sunt in eius affectu, sicut pueri provocantur ad aliquid faciendum aliquibus puerilibus munusculis. Dictum est autem supra quod lex vetus disponebat ad Christum sicut imperfectum ad perfectum, unde dabatur populo adhuc imperfecto in comparatione ad perfectionem quae erat futura per Christum, et ideo populus

OBJECTION 1: It would seem that the Old Law should not have induced men to the observance of its precepts, by means of temporal promises and threats. For the purpose of the Divine law is to subject man to God by fear and love: hence it is written (Deut 10:12): *And now, Israel, what doth the Lord thy God require of thee, but that thou fear the Lord thy God, and walk in His ways, and love Him?* But the desire for temporal goods leads man away from God: for Augustine says (Qq. lxxxiii, qu. 36), that *covetousness is the bane of charity.* Therefore temporal promises and threats seem to be contrary to the intention of a lawgiver: and this makes a law worthy of rejection, as the Philosopher declares (*Polit.* ii, 6).

OBJ. 2: Further, the Divine law is more excellent than human law. Now, in sciences, we notice that the loftier the science, the higher the means of persuasion that it employs. Therefore, since human law employs temporal threats and promises, as means of persuading man, the Divine law should have used, not these, but more lofty means.

OBJ. 3: Further, the reward of righteousness and the punishment of guilt cannot be that which befalls equally the good and the wicked. But as stated in Eccles. 9:2, *all* temporal *things equally happen to the just and to the wicked, to the good and the evil, to the clean and to the unclean, to him that offereth victims, and to him that despiseth sacrifices.* Therefore temporal goods or evils are not suitably set forth as punishments or rewards of the commandments of the Divine law.

ON THE CONTRARY, It is written (Isa 1:19,20): *If you be willing, and will hearken to Me, you shall eat the good things of the land. But if you will not, and will provoke Me to wrath: the sword shall devour you.*

I ANSWER THAT, As in speculative sciences men are persuaded to assent to the conclusions by means of syllogistic arguments, so too in every law, men are persuaded to observe its precepts by means of punishments and rewards. Now it is to be observed that, in speculative sciences, the means of persuasion are adapted to the conditions of the pupil: wherefore the process of argument in sciences should be ordered becomingly, so that the instruction is based on principles more generally known. And thus also he who would persuade a man to the observance of any precepts, needs to move him at first by things for which he has an affection; just as children are induced to do something, by means of little childish gifts. Now it has been said above (Q98, AA1,2,3) that the Old Law disposed men to (the coming of) Christ, as the imperfect in comparison disposes to the perfect, wherefore it was given to a people as

ille comparatur puero sub paedagogo existenti, ut patet Galat. III. Perfectio autem hominis est ut, contemptis temporalibus, spiritualibus inhaereat, ut patet per illud quod apostolus dicit, Philipp. III, *quae quidem retro sunt obliviscens, ad ea quae priora sunt me extendo. Quicumque ergo perfecti sumus, hoc sentiamus.* Imperfectorum autem est quod temporalia bona desiderent, in ordine tamen ad Deum. Perversorum autem est quod in temporalibus bonis finem constituant. Unde legi veteri conveniebat ut per temporalia, quae erant in affectu hominum imperfectorum, manuduceret homines ad Deum.

AD PRIMUM ergo dicendum quod cupiditas, qua homo constituit finem in temporalibus bonis, est caritatis venenum. Sed consecutio temporalium bonorum quae homo desiderat in ordine ad Deum, est quaedam via inducens imperfectos ad Dei amorem; secundum illud Psalmi XLVIII, *confitebitur tibi cum benefeceris illi.*

AD SECUNDUM dicendum quod lex humana inducit homines ex temporalibus praemiis vel poenis per homines inducendis, lex vero divina ex praemiis vel poenis exhibendis per Deum. Et in hoc procedit per media altiora.

AD TERTIUM dicendum quod, sicut patet historias veteris testamenti revolventi, communis status populi semper sub lege in prosperitate fuit, quandiu legem observabant; et statim declinantes a praeceptis legis, in multas adversitates incidebant. Sed aliquae personae particulares etiam iustitiam legis observantes, in aliquas adversitates incidebant, vel quia iam erant spirituales effecti, ut per hoc magis ab affectu temporalium abstraherentur, et eorum virtus probata redderetur; aut quia, opera legis exterius implentes, cor totum habebant in temporalibus defixum et a Deo elongatum, secundum quod dicitur Isaiae XXIX, *populus hic labiis me honorat, cor autem eorum longe est a me.*

yet imperfect in comparison to the perfection which was to result from Christ's coming: and for this reason, that people is compared to a child that is still under a pedagogue (Gal 3:24). But the perfection of man consists in his despising temporal things and cleaving to things spiritual, as is clear from the words of the Apostle (Phil 3:13,15): *Forgetting the things that are behind, I stretch forth myself to those that are before . . . Let us therefore, as many as are perfect, be thus minded.* Those who are yet imperfect desire temporal goods, albeit in subordination to God: whereas the perverse place their end in temporalities. It was therefore fitting that the Old Law should conduct men to God by means of temporal goods for which the imperfect have an affection.

REPLY OBJ. 1: Covetousness whereby man places his end in temporalities, is the bane of charity. But the attainment of temporal goods which man desires in subordination to God is a road leading the imperfect to the love of God, according to Ps. 48:19: *He will praise Thee, when Thou shalt do well to him.*

REPLY OBJ. 2: Human law persuades men by means of temporal rewards or punishments to be inflicted by men: whereas the Divine law persuades men by means of rewards or punishments to be received from God. In this respect it employs higher means.

REPLY OBJ. 3: As any one can see, who reads carefully the story of the Old Testament, the common weal of the people prospered under the Law as long as they obeyed it; and as soon as they departed from the precepts of the Law they were overtaken by many calamities. But certain individuals, although they observed the justice of the Law, met with misfortunes—either because they had already become spiritual (so that misfortune might withdraw them all the more from attachment to temporal things, and that their virtue might be tried)—or because, while outwardly fulfilling the works of the Law, their heart was altogether fixed on temporal goods, and far removed from God, according to Is. 29:13 (Matt 15:8): *This people honoreth Me with their lips; but their hearts is far from Me.*

QUESTION 100

OF THE MORAL PRECEPTS OF THE OLD LAW

Deinde considerandum est de singulis generibus praeceptorum veteris legis. Et primo, de praeceptis moralibus; secundo, de caeremonialibus; tertio, de iudicialibus. Circa primum quaeruntur duodecim.

Primo, utrum omnia praecepta moralia veteris legis sint de lege naturae.

Secundo, utrum praecepta moralia veteris legis sint de actibus omnium virtutum.

Tertio, utrum omnia praecepta moralia veteris legis reducantur ad decem praecepta Decalogi.

Quarto, de distinctione praeceptorum Decalogi.

Quinto, de numero eorum.

Sexto, de ordine.

Septimo, de modo tradendi ipsa.

Octavo, utrum sint dispensabilia.

Nono, utrum modus observandi virtutem cadat sub praecepto.

Decimo, utrum modus caritatis cadat sub praecepto.

Undecimo, de distinctione aliorum praeceptorum moralium.

Duodecimo, utrum praecepta moralia veteris legis iustificent.

We must now consider each kind of precept of the Old Law: and (1) the moral precepts, (2) the ceremonial precepts, (3) the judicial precepts. Under the first head there are twelve points of inquiry:

(1) Whether all the moral precepts of the Old Law belong to the law of nature?

(2) Whether the moral precepts of the Old Law are about the acts of all the virtues?

(3) Whether all the moral precepts of the Old Law are reducible to the ten precepts of the decalogue?

(4) How the precepts of the decalogue are distinguished from one another?

(5) Their number;

(6) Their order;

(7) The manner in which they were given;

(8) Whether they are dispensable?

(9) Whether the mode of observing a virtue comes under the precept of the Law?

(10) Whether the mode of charity comes under the precept?

(11) The distinction of other moral precepts;

(12) Whether the moral precepts of the Old Law justified man?

Article 1

Whether All the Moral Precepts of the Old Law Belong to the Law of Nature?

AD PRIMUM SIC PROCEDITUR. Videtur quod non omnia praecepta moralia pertineant ad legem naturae. Dicitur enim Eccli. XVII, *addidit illis disciplinam, et legem vitae haereditavit illos.* Sed disciplina dividitur contra legem naturae, eo quod lex naturalis non addiscitur, sed ex naturali instinctu habetur. Ergo non omnia praecepta moralia sunt de lege naturae.

PRAETEREA, lex divina perfectior est quam lex humana. Sed lex humana superaddit aliqua ad bonos mores pertinentia his quae sunt de lege naturae, quod patet ex hoc quod lex naturae est eadem apud omnes, huiusmodi autem morum instituta sunt diversa apud diversos. Ergo multo fortius divina lex aliqua ad bonos mores pertinentia debuit addere supra legem naturae.

PRAETEREA, sicut ratio naturalis inducit ad aliquos bonos mores, ita et fides, unde etiam dicitur ad Galat.

OBJECTION 1: It would seem that not all the moral precepts belong to the law of nature. For it is written (Sir 17:9): *Moreover He gave them instructions, and the law of life for an inheritance.* But instruction is in contradistinction to the law of nature; since the law of nature is not learnt, but instilled by natural instinct. Therefore not all the moral precepts belong to the natural law.

OBJ. 2: Further, the Divine law is more perfect than human law. But human law adds certain things concerning good morals, to those that belong to the law of nature: as is evidenced by the fact that the natural law is the same in all men, while these moral institutions are various for various people. Much more reason therefore was there why the Divine law should add to the law of nature, ordinances pertaining to good morals.

OBJ. 3: Further, just as natural reason leads to good morals in certain matters, so does faith: hence it is written

V, quod fides per dilectionem operatur. Sed fides non continetur sub lege naturae, quia ea quae sunt fidei, sunt supra rationem naturalem. Ergo non omnia praecepta moralia legis divinae pertinent ad legem naturae.

Sed contra est quod dicit apostolus, Rom. II, quod *gentes, quae legem non habent, naturaliter ea quae legis sunt, faciunt*, quod oportet intelligi de his quae pertinent ad bonos mores. Ergo omnia moralia praecepta legis sunt de lege naturae.

Respondeo dicendum quod praecepta moralia, a caeremonialibus et iudicialibus distincta, sunt de illis quae secundum se ad bonos mores pertinent. Cum autem humani mores dicantur in ordine ad rationem, quae est proprium principium humanorum actuum, illi mores dicuntur boni qui rationi congruunt, mali autem qui a ratione discordant. Sicut autem omne iudicium rationis speculativae procedit a naturali cognitione primorum principiorum, ita etiam omne iudicium rationis practicae procedit ex quibusdam principiis naturaliter cognitis, ut supra dictum est. Ex quibus diversimode procedi potest ad iudicandum de diversis. Quaedam enim sunt in humanis actibus adeo explicita quod statim, cum modica consideratione, possunt approbari vel reprobari per illa communia et prima principia. Quaedam vero sunt ad quorum iudicium requiritur multa consideratio diversarum circumstantiarum, quas considerare diligenter non est cuiuslibet, sed sapientum, sicut considerare particulares conclusiones scientiarum non pertinet ad omnes, sed ad solos philosophos. Quaedam vero sunt ad quae diiudicanda indiget homo adiuvari per instructionem divinam, sicut est circa credenda.

Sic igitur patet quod, cum moralia praecepta sint de his quae pertinent ad bonos mores; haec autem sunt quae rationi congruunt; omne autem rationis humanae iudicium aliqualiter a naturali ratione derivatur, necesse est quod omnia praecepta moralia pertineant ad legem naturae, sed diversimode. Quaedam enim sunt quae statim per se ratio naturalis cuiuslibet hominis diiudicat esse facienda vel non facienda, sicut *honora patrem tuum et matrem tuam, et, non occides, non furtum facies*. Et huiusmodi sunt absolute de lege naturae. Quaedam vero sunt quae subtiliori consideratione rationis a sapientibus iudicantur esse observanda. Et ista sic sunt de lege naturae, ut tamen indigeant disciplina, qua minores a sapientioribus instruantur, sicut illud, *coram cano capite consurge, et honora personam senis*, et alia huiusmodi. Quaedam vero sunt ad quae iudicanda ratio humana indiget instructione divina, per quam erudimur de divinis, sicut est illud, *non facies tibi sculptile neque omnem similitudinem; non assumes nomen Dei tui in vanum*.

Et per hoc patet responsio ad obiecta.

(Gal 5:6) that faith *worketh by charity*. But faith is not included in the law of nature; since that which is of faith is above nature. Therefore not all the moral precepts of the Divine law belong to the law of nature.

On the contrary, The Apostle says (Rom 2:14) that *the Gentiles, who have not the Law, do by nature those things that are of the Law*: which must be understood of things pertaining to good morals. Therefore all the moral precepts of the Law belong to the law of nature.

I answer that, The moral precepts, distinct from the ceremonial and judicial precepts, are about things pertaining of their very nature to good morals. Now since human morals depend on their relation to reason, which is the proper principle of human acts, those morals are called good which accord with reason, and those are called bad which are discordant from reason. And as every judgment of speculative reason proceeds from the natural knowledge of first principles, so every judgment of practical reason proceeds from principles known naturally, as stated above (Q94, AA2,4): from which principles one may proceed in various ways to judge of various matters. For some matters connected with human actions are so evident, that after very little consideration one is able at once to approve or disapprove of them by means of these general first principles: while some matters cannot be the subject of judgment without much consideration of the various circumstances, which all are not competent to do carefully, but only those who are wise: just as it is not possible for all to consider the particular conclusions of sciences, but only for those who are versed in philosophy: and lastly there are some matters of which man cannot judge unless he be helped by Divine instruction; such as the articles of faith.

It is therefore evident that since the moral precepts are about matters which concern good morals; and since good morals are those which are in accord with reason; and since also every judgment of human reason must needs by derived in some way from natural reason; it follows, of necessity, that all the moral precepts belong to the law of nature; but not all in the same way. For there are certain things which the natural reason of every man, of its own accord and at once, judges to be done or not to be done: e.g., *Honor thy father and thy mother*, and *Thou shalt not kill, Thou shalt not steal*: and these belong to the law of nature absolutely. And there are certain things which, after a more careful consideration, wise men deem obligatory. Such belong to the law of nature, yet so that they need to be inculcated, the wiser teaching the less wise: e.g., *Rise up before the hoary head, and honor the person of the aged man*, and the like. And there are some things, to judge of which, human reason needs Divine instruction, whereby we are taught about the things of God: e.g., *Thou shalt not make to thyself a graven thing, nor the likeness of anything; Thou shalt not take the name of the Lord thy God in vain*.

This suffices for the Replies to the Objections.

Article 2

Whether the Moral Precepts of the Law Are About All the Acts of Virtue?

AD SECUNDUM SIC PROCEDITUR. Videtur quod praecepta moralia legis non sint de omnibus actibus virtutum. Observatio enim praeceptorum veteris legis iustificatio nominatur, secundum illud Psalmi CXVIII, *iustificationes tuas custodiam*. Sed iustificatio est executio iustitiae. Ergo praecepta moralia non sunt nisi de actibus iustitiae.

PRAETEREA, id quod cadit sub praecepto, habet rationem debiti. Sed ratio debiti non pertinet ad alias virtutes nisi ad solam iustitiam, cuius proprius actus est reddere unicuique debitum. Ergo praecepta legis moralia non sunt de actibus aliarum virtutum, sed solum de actibus iustitiae.

PRAETEREA, omnis lex ponitur propter bonum commune, ut dicit Isidorus. Sed inter virtutes sola iustitia respicit bonum commune, ut philosophus dicit, in V Ethic. Ergo praecepta moralia sunt solum de actibus iustitiae.

SED CONTRA est quod Ambrosius dicit, quod *peccatum est transgressio legis divinae, et caelestium inobedientia mandatorum*. Sed peccata contrariantur omnibus actibus virtutum. Ergo lex divina habet ordinare de actibus omnium virtutum.

RESPONDEO dicendum quod, cum praecepta legis ordinentur ad bonum commune, sicut supra habitum est, necesse est quod praecepta legis diversificentur secundum diversos modos communitatum, unde et philosophus, in sua politica, docet quod alias leges oportet statuere in civitate quae regitur rege, et alias in ea quae regitur per populum, vel per aliquos potentes de civitate. Est autem alius modus communitatis ad quam ordinatur lex humana, et ad quam ordinatur lex divina. Lex enim humana ordinatur ad communitatem civilem, quae est hominum ad invicem. Homines autem ordinantur ad invicem per exteriores actus, quibus homines sibi invicem communicant. Huiusmodi autem communicatio pertinet ad rationem iustitiae, quae est proprie directiva communitatis humanae. Et ideo lex humana non proponit praecepta nisi de actibus iustitiae; et si praecipiat actus aliarum virtutum, hoc non est nisi inquantum assumunt rationem iustitiae; ut patet per philosophum, in V Ethic.

Sed communitas ad quam ordinat lex divina, est hominum ad Deum, vel in praesenti vel in futura vita. Et ideo lex divina praecepta proponit de omnibus illis per quae homines bene ordinentur ad communicationem cum Deo. Homo autem Deo coniungitur ratione, sive mente, in qua est Dei imago. Et ideo lex divina praecepta proponit de omnibus illis per quae ratio hominis est bene ordinata. Hoc autem contingit per actus omnium

OBJECTION 1: It would seem that the moral precepts of the Law are not about all the acts of virtue. For observance of the precepts of the Old Law is called justification, according to Ps. 118:8: *I will keep Thy justifications*. But justification is the execution of justice. Therefore the moral precepts are only about acts of justice.

OBJ. 2: Further, that which comes under a precept has the character of a duty. But the character of duty belongs to justice alone and to none of the other virtues, for the proper act of justice consists in rendering to each one his due. Therefore the precepts of the moral law are not about the acts of the other virtues, but only about the acts of justice.

OBJ. 3: Further, every law is made for the common good, as Isidore says (*Etym.* v, 21). But of all the virtues justice alone regards the common good, as the Philosopher says (*Ethic.* v, 1). Therefore the moral precepts are only about the acts of justice.

ON THE CONTRARY, Ambrose says (*De Paradiso* viii) that *a sin is a transgression of the Divine law, and a disobedience to the commandments of heaven*. But there are sins contrary to all the acts of virtue. Therefore it belongs to Divine law to direct all the acts of virtue.

I ANSWER THAT, Since the precepts of the Law are ordained to the common good, as stated above (Q90, A2), the precepts of the Law must needs be diversified according to the various kinds of community: hence the Philosopher (*Polit.* iv, 1) teaches that the laws which are made in a state which is ruled by a king must be different from the laws of a state which is ruled by the people, or by a few powerful men in the state. Now human law is ordained for one kind of community, and the Divine law for another kind. Because human law is ordained for the civil community, implying mutual duties of man and his fellows: and men are ordained to one another by outward acts, whereby men live in communion with one another. This life in common of man with man pertains to justice, whose proper function consists in directing the human community. Wherefore human law makes precepts only about acts of justice; and if it commands acts of other virtues, this is only insofar as they assume the nature of justice, as the Philosopher explains (*Ethic.* v, 1).

But the community for which the Divine law is ordained, is that of men in relation to God, either in this life or in the life to come. And therefore the Divine law proposes precepts about all those matters whereby men are well ordered in their relations to God. Now man is united to God by his reason or mind, in which is God's image. Wherefore the Divine law proposes precepts about all those matters whereby human reason is well ordered. But

virtutum, nam virtutes intellectuales ordinant bene actus rationis in seipsis; virtutes autem morales ordinant bene actus rationis circa interiores passiones et exteriores operationes. Et ideo manifestum est quod lex divina convenienter proponit praecepta de actibus omnium virtutum, ita tamen quod quaedam, sine quibus ordo virtutis, qui est ordo rationis, observari non potest, cadunt sub obligatione praecepti; quaedam vero, quae pertinent ad bene esse virtutis perfectae, cadunt sub admonitione consilii.

AD PRIMUM ergo dicendum quod adimpletio mandatorum legis etiam quae sunt de actibus aliarum virtutum, habet rationem iustificationis, inquantum iustum est ut homo obediat Deo. Vel etiam inquantum iustum est quod omnia quae sunt hominis, rationi subdantur.

AD SECUNDUM dicendum quod iustitia proprie dicta attendit debitum unius hominis ad alium, sed in omnibus aliis virtutibus attenditur debitum inferiorum virium ad rationem. Et secundum rationem huius debiti, philosophus assignat, in V Ethic., quandam iustitiam metaphoricam.

AD TERTIUM patet responsio per ea quae dicta sunt de diversitate communitatis.

this is effected by the acts of all the virtues: since the intellectual virtues set in good order the acts of the reason in themselves: while the moral virtues set in good order the acts of the reason in reference to the interior passions and exterior actions. It is therefore evident that the Divine law fittingly proposes precepts about the acts of all the virtues: yet so that certain matters, without which the order of virtue, which is the order of reason, cannot even exist, come under an obligation of precept; while other matters, which pertain to the well-being of perfect virtue, come under an admonition of counsel.

REPLY OBJ. 1: The fulfilment of the commandments of the Law, even of those which are about the acts of the other virtues, has the character of justification, inasmuch as it is just that man should obey God: or again, inasmuch as it is just that all that belongs to man should be subject to reason.

REPLY OBJ. 2: Justice properly so called regards the duty of one man to another: but all the other virtues regard the duty of the lower powers to reason. It is in relation to this latter duty that the Philosopher speaks (*Ethic.* v, 11) of a kind of metaphorical justice.

THE REPLY to the Third Objection is clear from what has been said about the different kinds of community.

Article 3

Whether All the Moral Precepts of the Old Law Are Reducible to the Ten Precepts of the Decalogue?

AD TERTIUM SIC PROCEDITUR. Videtur quod non omnia praecepta moralia veteris legis reducantur ad decem praecepta Decalogi. Prima enim et principalia legis praecepta sunt, *diliges dominum Deum tuum, et, diliges proximum tuum*, ut habetur Matth. XXII. Sed ista duo non continentur in praeceptis Decalogi. Ergo non omnia praecepta moralia continentur in praeceptis Decalogi.

PRAETEREA, praecepta moralia non reducuntur ad praecepta caeremonialia, sed potius e converso. Sed inter praecepta Decalogi est unum caeremoniale, scilicet, *memento ut diem sabbati sanctifices*. Ergo praecepta moralia non reducuntur ad omnia praecepta Decalogi.

PRAETEREA, praecepta moralia sunt de omnibus actibus virtutum. Sed inter praecepta Decalogi ponuntur sola praecepta pertinentia ad actus iustitiae; ut patet discurrenti per singula. Ergo praecepta Decalogi non continent omnia praecepta moralia.

SED CONTRA est quod, Matth. V, super illud, *beati estis cum maledixerint* etc., dicit Glossa quod *Moyses, decem praecepta proponens, postea per partes explicat*. Ergo

OBJECTION 1: It would seem that not all the moral precepts of the Old Law are reducible to the ten precepts of the decalogue. For the first and principal precepts of the Law are, *Thou shalt love the Lord thy God*, and *Thou shalt love thy neighbor*, as stated in Mt. 22:37,39. But these two are not contained in the precepts of the decalogue. Therefore not all the moral precepts are contained in the precepts of the decalogue.

OBJ. 2: Further, the moral precepts are not reducible to the ceremonial precepts, but rather vice versa. But among the precepts of the decalogue, one is ceremonial, viz., *Remember that thou keep holy the Sabbath-day*. Therefore the moral precepts are not reducible to all the precepts of the decalogue.

OBJ. 3: Further, the moral precepts are about all the acts of virtue. But among the precepts of the decalogue are only such as regard acts of justice; as may be seen by going through them all. Therefore the precepts of the decalogue do not include all the moral precepts.

ON THE CONTRARY, The gloss on Mt. 5:11: *Blessed are ye when they shall revile you*, etc. says that *Moses, after propounding the ten precepts, set them out in detail*. Therefore

omnia praecepta legis sunt quaedam partes praeceptorum Decalogi.

RESPONDEO dicendum quod praecepta Decalogi ab aliis praeceptis legis differunt in hoc, quod praecepta Decalogi per seipsum Deus dicitur populo proposuisse; alia vero praecepta proposuit populo per Moysen. Illa ergo praecepta ad Decalogum pertinent, quorum notitiam homo habet per seipsum a Deo. Huiusmodi vero sunt illa quae statim ex principiis communibus primis cognosci possunt modica consideratione, et iterum illa quae statim ex fide divinitus infusa innotescunt. Inter praecepta ergo Decalogi non computantur duo genera praeceptorum, illa scilicet quae sunt prima et communia, quorum non oportet aliam editionem esse nisi quod sunt scripta in ratione naturali quasi per se nota, sicut quod nulli debet homo malefacere, et alia huiusmodi; et iterum illa quae per diligentem inquisitionem sapientum inveniuntur rationi convenire, haec enim proveniunt a Deo ad populum mediante disciplina sapientum. Utraque tamen horum praeceptorum continentur in praeceptis Decalogi, sed diversimode. Nam illa quae sunt prima et communia, continentur in eis sicut principia in conclusionibus proximis, illa vero quae per sapientes cognoscuntur, continentur in eis, e converso, sicut conclusiones in principiis.

AD PRIMUM ergo dicendum quod illa duo praecepta sunt prima et communia praecepta legis naturae, quae sunt per se nota rationi humanae, vel per naturam vel per fidem. Et ideo omnia praecepta Decalogi ad illa duo referuntur sicut conclusiones ad principia communia.

AD SECUNDUM dicendum quod praeceptum de observatione sabbati est secundum aliquid morale, inquantum scilicet per hoc praecipitur quod homo aliquo tempore vacet rebus divinis; secundum illud Psalmi XLV, *vacate, et videte quoniam ego sum Deus*. Et secundum hoc, inter praecepta Decalogi computatur. Non autem quantum ad taxationem temporis, quia secundum hoc est caeremoniale.

AD TERTIUM dicendum quod ratio debiti in aliis virtutibus est magis latens quam in iustitia. Et ideo praecepta de actibus aliarum virtutum non sunt ita nota populo sicut praecepta de actibus iustitiae. Et propter hoc actus iustitiae specialiter cadunt sub praeceptis Decalogi, quae sunt prima legis elementa.

all the precepts of the Law are so many parts of the precepts of the decalogue.

I ANSWER THAT, The precepts of the decalogue differ from the other precepts of the Law, in the fact that God Himself is said to have given the precepts of the decalogue; whereas He gave the other precepts to the people through Moses. Wherefore the decalogue includes those precepts the knowledge of which man has immediately from God. Such are those which with but slight reflection can be gathered at once from the first general principles: and those also which become known to man immediately through divinely infused faith. Consequently two kinds of precepts are not reckoned among the precepts of the decalogue: viz., first general principles, for they need no further promulgation after being once imprinted on the natural reason to which they are self-evident; as, for instance, that one should do evil to no man, and other similar principles: and again those which the careful reflection of wise men shows to be in accord with reason; since the people receive these principles from God, through being taught by wise men. Nevertheless both kinds of precepts are contained in the precepts of the decalogue; yet in different ways. For the first general principles are contained in them, as principles in their proximate conclusions; while those which are known through wise men are contained, conversely, as conclusions in their principles.

REPLY OBJ. 1: Those two principles are the first general principles of the natural law, and are self-evident to human reason, either through nature or through faith. Wherefore all the precepts of the decalogue are referred to these, as conclusions to general principles.

REPLY OBJ. 2: The precept of the Sabbath observance is moral in one respect, insofar as it commands man to give some time to the things of God, according to Ps. 45:11: *Be still and see that I am God*. In this respect it is placed among the precepts of the decalogue: but not as to the fixing of the time, in which respect it is a ceremonial precept.

REPLY OBJ. 3: The notion of duty is not so patent in the other virtues as it is in justice. Hence the precepts about the acts of the other virtues are not so well known to the people as are the precepts about acts of justice. Wherefore the acts of justice especially come under the precepts of the decalogue, which are the primary elements of the Law.

Article 4

Whether the Precepts of the Decalogue Are Suitably Distinguished from One Another?

AD QUARTUM SIC PROCEDITUR. Videtur quod inconvenienter praecepta Decalogi distinguantur. Latria enim est alia virtus a fide. Sed praecepta dantur de actibus virtutum. Sed hoc quod dicitur in principio Decalogi, non habebis deos alienos coram me, pertinet ad fidem, quod autem subditur, non facies sculptile etc., pertinet ad latriam. Ergo sunt duo praecepta, et non unum, sicut Augustinus dicit.

PRAETEREA, praecepta affirmativa in lege distinguuntur a negativis, sicut, honora patrem et matrem, et, non occides. Sed hoc quod dicitur, ego sum dominus Deus tuus, est affirmativum, quod autem subditur, non habebis deos alienos coram me, est negativum. Ergo sunt duo praecepta, et non continentur sub uno, ut Augustinus ponit.

PRAETEREA, apostolus, ad Rom. VII, dicit, *concupiscentiam nesciebam, nisi lex diceret, non concupisces.* Et sic videtur quod hoc praeceptum, non concupisces, sit unum praeceptum. Non ergo debet distingui in duo.

SED CONTRA est auctoritas Augustini, in Glossa super Exod., ubi ponit tria praecepta pertinentia ad Deum, et septem ad proximum.

RESPONDEO dicendum quod praecepta Decalogi diversimode a diversis distinguuntur. Hesychius enim, Levit. XXVI, super illud, *decem mulieres in uno clibano coquunt panes*, dicit praeceptum de observatione sabbati non esse de decem praeceptis, quia non est observandum, secundum litteram, secundum omne tempus. Distinguit tamen quatuor praecepta pertinentia ad Deum, ut primum sit, ego sum dominus Deus tuus; secundum sit, non habebis deos alienos coram me (et sic etiam distinguit haec duo Hieronymus, Osee X, super illud, propter duas iniquitates tuas); tertium vero praeceptum esse dicit, non facies tibi sculptile; quartum vero, non assumes nomen Dei tui in vanum. Pertinentia vero ad proximum dicit esse sex, ut primum sit, honora patrem tuum et matrem tuam; secundum, non occides; tertium, non moechaberis; quartum, non furtum facies; quintum, non falsum testimonium dices; sextum, non concupisces.

Sed primo hoc videtur inconveniens, quod praeceptum de observatione sabbati praeceptis Decalogi interponatur, si nullo modo ad Decalogum pertineat. Secundo quia, cum scriptum sit Matth. VI, nemo potest duobus dominis servire, eiusdem rationis esse videtur, et sub eodem praecepto cadere, ego sum dominus Deus tuus, et, non habebis deos alienos. Unde Origenes, distinguens

OBJECTION 1: It would seem that the precepts of the decalogue are unsuitably distinguished from one another. For worship is a virtue distinct from faith. Now the precepts are about acts of virtue. But that which is said at the beginning of the decalogue, *Thou shalt not have strange gods before Me*, belongs to faith: and that which is added, *Thou shalt not make . . . any graven thing*, etc. belongs to worship. Therefore these are not one precept, as Augustine asserts (*Qq. in Exod.* qu. lxxi), but two.

OBJ. 2: Further, the affirmative precepts in the Law are distinct from the negative precepts; e.g., *Honor thy father and thy mother*, and, *Thou shalt not kill*. But this, *I am the Lord thy God*, is affirmative: and that which follows, *Thou shalt not have strange gods before Me*, is negative. Therefore these are two precepts, and do not, as Augustine says (*Qq. in Exod.* qu. lxxi), make one.

OBJ. 3: Further, the Apostle says (Rom 7:7): *I had not known concupiscence, if the Law did not say: 'Thou shalt not covet.'* Hence it seems that this precept, *Thou shalt not covet*, is one precept; and, therefore, should not be divided into two.

ON THE CONTRARY, stands the authority of Augustine who, in commenting on Exodus (*Qq. in Exod.* qu. lxxi) distinguishes three precepts as referring to God, and seven as referring to our neighbor.

I ANSWER THAT, The precepts of the decalogue are differently divided by different authorities. For Hesychius commenting on Lev. 26:26, *Ten women shall bake your bread in one oven*, says that the precept of the Sabbath-day observance is not one of the ten precepts, because its observance, in the letter, is not binding for all time. But he distinguishes four precepts pertaining to God, the first being, *I am the Lord thy God*; the second, *Thou shalt not have strange gods before Me*, (thus also Jerome distinguishes these two precepts, in his commentary on Osee 10:10, *On thy two iniquities*); the third precept according to him is, *Thou shalt not make to thyself any graven thing*; and the fourth, *Thou shalt not take the name of the Lord thy God in vain*. He states that there are six precepts pertaining to our neighbor; the first, *Honor thy father and thy mother*; the second, *Thou shalt not kill*; the third, *Thou shalt not commit adultery*; the fourth, *Thou shalt not steal*; the fifth, *Thou shalt not bear false witness*; the sixth, *Thou shalt not covet.*

But, in the first place, it seems unbecoming for the precept of the Sabbath-day observance to be put among the precepts of the decalogue, if it nowise belonged to the decalogue. Second, because, since it is written (Matt 6:24), *No man can serve two masters*, the two statements, *I am the Lord thy God*, and, *Thou shalt not have strange gods before Me* seem to be of the same nature and to form one precept.

etiam quatuor praecepta ordinantia ad Deum, ponit ista duo pro uno praecepto; secundum vero ponit, non facies sculptile; tertium, non assumes nomen Dei tui in vanum; quartum, memento ut diem sabbati sanctifices. Alia vero sex ponit sicut Hesychius.

Sed quia facere sculptile vel similitudinem non est prohibitum nisi secundum hoc, ut non colantur pro diis (nam et in tabernaculo Deus praecepit fieri imaginem Seraphim, ut habetur Exod. XXV); convenientius Augustinus ponit sub uno praecepto, non habebis deos alienos, et, non facies sculptile. Similiter etiam concupiscentia uxoris alienae ad commixtionem, pertinet ad concupiscentiam carnis; concupiscentiae autem aliarum rerum, quae desiderantur ad possidendum, pertinent ad concupiscentiam oculorum; unde etiam Augustinus ponit duo praecepta de non concupiscendo rem alienam, et uxorem alienam. Et sic ponit tria praecepta in ordine ad Deum, et septem in ordine ad proximum. Et hoc melius est.

AD PRIMUM ergo dicendum quod latria non est nisi quaedam protestatio fidei, unde non sunt alia praecepta danda de latria, et alia de fide. Potius tamen sunt danda de latria quam de fide, quia praeceptum fidei praesupponitur ad praecepta Decalogi, sicut praeceptum dilectionis. Sicut enim prima praecepta communia legis naturae sunt per se nota habenti rationem naturalem, et promulgatione non indigent; ita etiam et hoc quod est credere in Deum, est primum et per se notum ei qui habet fidem, *accedentem enim ad Deum oportet credere quia est*, ut dicitur ad Heb. XI. Et ideo non indiget alia promulgatione nisi infusione fidei.

AD SECUNDUM dicendum quod praecepta affirmativa distinguuntur a negativis, quando unum non comprehenditur in alio, sicut in honoratione parentum non includitur quod nullus homo occidatur, nec e converso. Sed quando affirmativum comprehenditur in negativo vel e converso, non dantur super hoc diversa praecepta, sicut non datur aliud praeceptum de hoc quod est, non furtum facies, et de hoc quod est conservare rem alienam, vel restituere eam. Et eadem ratione non sunt diversa praecepta de credendo in Deum, et de hoc quod non credatur in alienos deos.

AD TERTIUM dicendum quod omnis concupiscentia convenit in una communi ratione, et ideo apostolus singulariter de mandato concupiscendi loquitur. Quia tamen in speciali diversae sunt rationes concupiscendi, ideo Augustinus distinguit diversa praecepta de non concupiscendo, differunt enim specie concupiscentiae secundum diversitatem actionum vel concupiscibilium, ut philosophus dicit, in X Ethic.

Hence Origen (*Hom. viii in Exod.*) who also distinguishes four precepts as referring to God, unites these two under one precept; and reckons in the second place, *Thou shalt not make . . . any graven thing*; as third, *Thou shalt not take the name of the Lord thy God in vain*; and as fourth, *Remember that thou keep holy the Sabbath-day*. The other six he reckons in the same way as Hesychius.

Since, however, the making of graven things or the likeness of anything is not forbidden except as to the point of their being worshipped as gods—for God commanded an image of the Seraphim to be made and placed in the tabernacle, as related in Ex. 25:18—Augustine more fittingly unites these two, *Thou shalt not have strange gods before Me*, and, *Thou shalt not make . . . any graven thing*, into one precept. Likewise to covet another's wife, for the purpose of carnal knowledge, belongs to the concupiscence of the flesh; whereas, to covet other things, which are desired for the purpose of possession, belongs to the concupiscence of the eyes; wherefore Augustine reckons as distinct precepts, that which forbids the coveting of another's goods, and that which prohibits the coveting of another's wife. Thus he distinguishes three precepts as referring to God, and seven as referring to our neighbor. And this is better.

REPLY OBJ. 1: Worship is merely a declaration of faith: wherefore the precepts about worship should not be reckoned as distinct from those about faith. Nevertheless precepts should be given about worship rather than about faith, because the precept about faith is presupposed to the precepts of the decalogue, as is also the precept of charity. For just as the first general principles of the natural law are self-evident to a subject having natural reason, and need no promulgation; so also to believe in God is a first and self-evident principle to a subject possessed of faith: *for he that cometh to God, must believe that He is* (Heb 11:6). Hence it needs no other promulgation that the infusion of faith.

REPLY OBJ. 2: The affirmative precepts are distinct from the negative, when one is not comprised in the other: thus that man should honor his parents does not include that he should not kill another man; nor does the latter include the former. But when an affirmative precept is included in a negative, or vice versa, we do not find that two distinct precepts are given: thus there is not one precept saying that *Thou shalt not steal*, and another binding one to keep another's property intact, or to give it back to its owner. In the same way there are not different precepts about believing in God, and about not believing in strange gods.

REPLY OBJ. 3: All covetousness has one common ratio: and therefore the Apostle speaks of the commandment about covetousness as though it were one. But because there are various special kinds of covetousness, therefore Augustine distinguishes different prohibitions against coveting: for covetousness differs specifically in respect of the diversity of actions or things coveted, as the Philosopher says (*Ethic.* x, 5).

Article 5

Whether the Precepts of the Decalogue Are Suitably Set Forth?

AD QUINTUM SIC PROCEDITUR. Videtur quod inconvenienter praecepta Decalogi enumerentur. Peccatum enim, ut Ambrosius dicit, est *transgressio legis divinae, et caelestium inobedientia mandatorum.* Sed peccata distinguuntur per hoc quod homo peccat vel in Deum, vel in proximum, vel in seipsum. Cum igitur in praeceptis Decalogi non ponantur aliqua praecepta ordinantia hominem ad seipsum, sed solum ordinantia ipsum ad Deum et proximum; videtur quod insufficiens sit enumeratio praeceptorum Decalogi.

PRAETEREA, sicut ad cultum Dei pertinebat observatio sabbati, ita etiam observatio aliarum solemnitatum, et immolatio sacrificiorum. Sed inter praecepta Decalogi est unum pertinens ad observantiam sabbati. Ergo etiam debent esse aliqua pertinentia ad alias solemnitates, et ad ritum sacrificiorum.

PRAETEREA, sicut contra Deum peccare contingit periurando, ita etiam blasphemando, vel alias contra doctrinam divinam mentiendo. Sed ponitur unum praeceptum prohibens periurium, cum dicitur, *non assumes nomen Dei tui in vanum.* Ergo peccatum blasphemiae, et falsae doctrinae, debent aliquo praecepto Decalogi prohiberi.

PRAETEREA, sicut homo naturalem dilectionem habet ad parentes, ita etiam ad filios. Mandatum etiam caritatis ad omnes proximos extenditur. Sed praecepta Decalogi ordinantur ad caritatem; secundum illud I Tim. I, *finis praecepti caritas est.* Ergo sicut ponitur quoddam praeceptum pertinens ad parentes, ita etiam debuerunt poni aliqua praecepta pertinentia ad filios et ad alios proximos.

PRAETEREA, in quolibet genere peccati contingit peccare corde et opere. Sed in quibusdam generibus peccatorum, scilicet in furto et adulterio, seorsum prohibetur peccatum operis, cum dicitur, *non moechaberis, non furtum facies*; et seorsum peccatum cordis, cum dicitur, *non concupisces rem proximi tui*, et, *non concupisces uxorem proximi tui.* Ergo etiam idem debuit poni in peccato homicidii et falsi testimonii.

PRAETEREA, sicut contingit peccatum provenire ex inordinatione concupiscibilis, ita etiam ex inordinatione irascibilis. Sed quibusdam praeceptis prohibetur inordinata concupiscentia, cum dicitur, *non concupisces.* Ergo etiam aliqua praecepta in Decalogo debuerunt poni per quae prohiberetur inordinatio irascibilis. Non ergo videtur quod convenienter decem praecepta Decalogi enumerentur.

OBJECTION 1: It would seem that the precepts of the decalogue are unsuitably set forth. Because sin, as stated by Ambrose (*De Paradiso* viii), is *a transgression of the Divine law and a disobedience to the commandments of heaven.* But sins are distinguished according as man sins against God, or his neighbor, or himself. Since, then, the decalogue does not include any precepts directing man in his relations to himself, but only such as direct him in his relations to God and himself, it seems that the precepts of the decalogue are insufficiently enumerated.

OBJ. 2: Further, just as the Sabbath-day observance pertained to the worship of God, so also did the observance of other solemnities, and the offering of sacrifices. But the decalogue contains a precept about the Sabbath-day observance. Therefore it should contain others also, pertaining to the other solemnities, and to the sacrificial rite.

OBJ. 3: Further, as sins against God include the sin of perjury, so also do they include blasphemy, or other ways of lying against the teaching of God. But there is a precept forbidding perjury, *Thou shalt not take the name of the Lord thy God in vain.* Therefore there should be also a precept of the decalogue forbidding blasphemy and false doctrine.

OBJ. 4: Further, just as man has a natural affection for his parents, so has he also for his children. Moreover the commandment of charity extends to all our neighbors. Now the precepts of the decalogue are ordained unto charity, according to 1 Tim. 1:5: *The end of the commandment is charity.* Therefore as there is a precept referring to parents, so should there have been some precepts referring to children and other neighbors.

OBJ. 5: Further, in every kind of sin, it is possible to sin in thought or in deed. But in some kinds of sin, namely in theft and adultery, the prohibition of sins of deed, when it is said, *Thou shalt not commit adultery, Thou shalt not steal,* is distinct from the prohibition of the sin of thought, when it is said, *Thou shalt not covet thy neighbor's goods,* and, *Thou shalt not covet thy neighbor's wife.* Therefore the same should have been done in regard to the sins of homicide and false witness.

OBJ. 6: Further, just as sin happens through disorder of the concupiscible faculty, so does it arise through disorder of the irascible part. But some precepts forbid inordinate concupiscence, when it is said, *Thou shalt not covet.* Therefore the decalogue should have included some precepts forbidding the disorders of the irascible faculty. Therefore it seems that the ten precepts of the decalogue are unfittingly enumerated.

Sed contra est quod dicitur Deut. IV, *ostendit vobis pactum suum, quod praecepit ut faceretis; et decem verba quae scripsit in duabus tabulis lapideis.*

Respondeo dicendum quod, sicut supra dictum est, sicut praecepta legis humanae ordinant hominem ad communitatem humanam, ita praecepta legis divinae ordinant hominem ad quandam communitatem seu rempublicam hominum sub Deo. Ad hoc autem quod aliquis in aliqua communitate bene commoretur, duo requiruntur, quorum primum est ut bene se habeat ad eum qui praeest communitati; aliud autem est ut homo bene se habeat ad alios communitatis consocios et comparticipes. Oportet igitur quod in lege divina primo ferantur quaedam praecepta ordinantia hominem ad Deum; et deinde alia praecepta ordinantia hominem ad alios proximos simul conviventes sub Deo.

Principi autem communitatis tria debet homo, primo quidem, fidelitatem; secundo, reverentiam; tertio, famulatum. Fidelitas quidem ad dominum in hoc consistit, ut honorem principatus ad alium non deferat. Et quantum ad hoc accipitur primum praeceptum, cum dicitur, non habebis deos alienos. Reverentia autem ad dominum requiritur ut nihil iniuriosum in eum committatur. Et quantum ad hoc accipitur secundum praeceptum, quod est, non assumes nomen domini Dei tui in vanum. Famulatus autem debetur domino in recompensationem beneficiorum quae ab ipso percipiunt subditi. Et ad hoc pertinet tertium praeceptum, de sanctificatione sabbati in memoriam creationis rerum.

Ad proximos autem aliquis bene se habet et specialiter, et generaliter. Specialiter quidem, quantum ad illos quorum est debitor, ut eis debitum reddat. Et quantum ad hoc accipitur praeceptum de honoratione parentum. Generaliter autem, quantum ad omnes, ut nulli nocumentum inferatur, neque opere neque ore neque corde. Opere quidem infertur nocumentum proximo, quandoque quidem in personam propriam, quantum ad consistentiam scilicet personae. Et hoc prohibetur per hoc quod dicitur, non occides. Quandoque autem in personam coniunctam quantum ad propagationem prolis. Et hoc prohibetur cum dicitur, non moechaberis. Quandoque autem in rem possessam, quae ordinatur ad utrumque. Et quantum ad hoc dicitur, non furtum facies. Nocumentum autem oris prohibetur cum dicitur, *non loqueris contra proximum tuum falsum testimonium.* Nocumentum autem cordis prohibetur cum dicitur, non concupisces.

Et secundum hanc etiam differentiam possent distingui tria praecepta ordinantia in Deum. Quorum primum pertinet ad opus, unde ibi dicitur, non facies sculptile. Secundum ad os, unde dicitur, non assumes nomen Dei tui in vanum. Tertium pertinet ad cor, quia in sanctificatione sabbati, secundum quod est morale praeceptum, praecipitur quies cordis in Deum. Vel, secundum

On the contrary, It is written (Deut 4:13): *He showed you His covenant, which He commanded you to do, and the ten words that He wrote in two tablets of stone.*

I answer that, As stated above (A2), just as the precepts of human law direct man in his relations to the human community, so the precepts of the Divine law direct man in his relations to a community or commonwealth of men under God. Now in order that any man may dwell aright in a community, two things are required: the first is that he behave well to the head of the community; the other is that he behave well to those who are his fellows and partners in the community. It is therefore necessary that the Divine law should contain in the first place precepts ordering man in his relations to God; and in the second place, other precepts ordering man in his relations to other men who are his neighbors and live with him under God.

Now man owes three things to the head of the community: first, fidelity; second, reverence; third, service. Fidelity to his master consists in his not giving sovereign honor to another: and this is the sense of the first commandment, in the words *Thou shalt not have strange gods.* Reverence to his master requires that he should do nothing injurious to him: and this is conveyed by the second commandment, *Thou shalt not take the name of the Lord thy God in vain.* Service is due to the master in return for the benefits which his subjects receive from him: and to this belongs the third commandment of the sanctification of the Sabbath in memory of the creation of all things.

To his neighbors a man behaves himself well both in particular and in general. In particular, as to those to whom he is indebted, by paying his debts: and in this sense is to be taken the commandment about honoring one's parents. In general, as to all men, by doing harm to none, either by deed, or by word, or by thought. By deed, harm is done to one's neighbor—sometimes in his person, i.e., as to his personal existence; and this is forbidden by the words, *Thou shalt not kill:* sometimes in a person united to him, as to the propagation of offspring; and this is prohibited by the words, *Thou shalt not commit adultery:* sometimes in his possessions, which are directed to both the aforesaid; and with this regard to this it is said, *Thou shalt not steal.* Harm done by word is forbidden when it is said, *Thou shalt not bear false witness against thy neighbor:* harm done by thought is forbidden in the words, *Thou shalt not covet.*

The three precepts that direct man in his behavior towards God may also be differentiated in this same way. For the first refers to deeds; wherefore it is said, *Thou shalt not make . . . a graven thing:* the second, to words; wherefore it is said, *Thou shalt not take the name of the Lord thy God in vain:* the third, to thoughts; because the sanctification of the Sabbath, as the subject of a moral precept, requires

Augustinum, per primum praeceptum reveremur unitatem primi principii; per secundum, veritatem divinam; per tertium, eius bonitatem, qua sanctificamur, et in qua quiescimus sicut in fine.

AD PRIMUM ergo potest responderi dupliciter. Primo quidem, quia praecepta Decalogi referuntur ad praecepta dilectionis. Fuit autem dandum praeceptum homini de dilectione Dei et proximi, quia quantum ad hoc lex naturalis obscurata erat propter peccatum, non autem quantum ad dilectionem sui ipsius, quia quantum ad hoc lex naturalis vigebat. Vel quia etiam dilectio sui ipsius includitur in dilectione Dei et proximi, in hoc enim homo vere se diligit, quod se ordinat in Deum. Et ideo etiam in praeceptis Decalogi ponuntur solum praecepta pertinentia ad proximum et ad Deum.

Aliter potest dici quod praecepta Decalogi sunt illa quae immediate populus recepit a Deo, unde dicitur Deut. X, *scripsit in tabulis, iuxta id quod prius scripserat, verba decem, quae locutus est ad vos dominus.* Unde oportet praecepta Decalogi talia esse quae statim in mente populi cadere possunt. Praeceptum autem habet rationem debiti. Quod autem homo ex necessitate debeat aliquid Deo vel proximo, hoc de facili cadit in conceptione hominis, et praecipue fidelis. Sed quod aliquid ex necessitate sit debitum homini de his quae pertinent ad seipsum et non ad alium, hoc non ita in promptu apparet, videtur enim primo aspectu quod quilibet sit liber in his quae ad ipsum pertinent. Et ideo praecepta quibus prohibentur inordinationes hominis ad seipsum, perveniunt ad populum mediante instructione sapientum. Unde non pertinent ad Decalogum.

AD SECUNDUM dicendum quod omnes solemnitates legis veteris sunt institutae in commemorationem alicuius divini beneficii vel praeteriti commemorati, vel futuri praefigurati. Et similiter propter hoc omnia sacrificia offerebantur. Inter omnia autem beneficia Dei commemoranda, primum et praecipuum erat beneficium creationis, quod commemoratur in sanctificatione sabbati, unde Exod. XX pro ratione huius praecepti ponitur, *sex enim diebus fecit Deus caelum et terram et* cetera. Inter omnia autem futura beneficia, quae erant praefiguranda, praecipuum et finale erat quies mentis in Deo, vel in praesenti per gratiam, vel in futuro per gloriam, quae etiam figurabatur per observantiam sabbati; unde dicitur Isaiae LVIII, *si averteris a sabbato pedem tuum, facere voluntatem tuam in die sancto meo, et vocaveris sabbatum delicatum, et sanctum domini gloriosum.* Haec enim beneficia primo et principaliter sunt in mente hominum, maxime fidelium. Aliae vero solemnitates celebrantur propter aliqua particularia beneficia

repose of the heart in God. Or, according to Augustine (*In Ps. 32:* Conc. 1), by the first commandment we reverence the unity of the First Principle; by the second, the Divine truth; by the third, His goodness whereby we are sanctified, and wherein we rest as in our last end.

REPLY OBJ. 1: This objection may be answered in two ways. First, because the precepts of the decalogue can be reduced to the precepts of charity. Now there was need for man to receive a precept about loving God and his neighbor, because in this respect the natural law had become obscured on account of sin: but not about the duty of loving oneself, because in this respect the natural law retained its vigor: or again, because love of oneself is contained in the love of God and of one's neighbor: since true self-love consists in directing oneself to God. And for this reason the decalogue includes those precepts only which refer to our neighbor and to God.

Second, it may be answered that the precepts of the decalogue are those which the people received from God immediately; wherefore it is written (Deut 10:4): *He wrote in the tables, according as He had written before, the ten words, which the Lord spoke to you.* Hence the precepts of the decalogue need to be such as the people can understand at once. Now a precept implies the notion of duty. But it is easy for a man, especially for a believer, to understand that, of necessity, he owes certain duties to God and to his neighbor. But that, in matters which regard himself and not another, man has, of necessity, certain duties to himself, is not so evident: for, at the first glance, it seems that everyone is free in matters that concern himself. And therefore the precepts which prohibit disorders of a man with regard to himself, reach the people through the instruction of men who are versed through the instruction of men who are versed in such matters; and, consequently, they are not contained in the decalogue.

REPLY OBJ. 2: All the solemnities of the Old Law were instituted in celebration of some Divine favor, either in memory of past favors, or in sign of some favor to come: in like manner all the sacrifices were offered up with the same purpose. Now of all the Divine favors to be commemorated the chief was that of the Creation, which was called to mind by the sanctification of the Sabbath; wherefore the reason for this precept is given in Ex. 20:11: *In six days the Lord made heaven and earth*, etc. And of all future blessings, the chief and final was the repose of the mind in God, either, in the present life, by grace, or, in the future life, by glory; which repose was also foreshadowed in the Sabbath-day observance: wherefore it is written (Isa 58:13): *If thou turn away thy foot from the Sabbath, from doing thy own will in My holy day, and call the Sabbath delightful, and the holy of the Lord glorious.* Because these favors first and chiefly are borne in mind by men, especially by the faithful. But other solemnities were celebrated on account of certain particular favors temporal and transitory, such as the celebration

temporaliter transeuntia, sicut celebratio phase propter beneficium praeteritae liberationis ex Aegypto, et propter futuram passionem Christi, quae temporaliter transivit, inducens nos in quietem sabbati spiritualis. Et ideo, praetermissis omnibus aliis solemnitatibus et sacrificiis, de solo sabbato fiebat mentio inter praecepta Decalogi.

AD TERTIUM dicendum quod, sicut apostolus dicit, ad Heb. VI, *homines per maiorem sui iurant, et omnis controversiae eorum finis ad confirmationem est iuramentum*. Et ideo, quia iuramentum est omnibus commune, propter hoc prohibitio inordinationis circa iuramentum, specialiter praecepto Decalogi prohibetur. Peccatum vero falsae doctrinae non pertinet nisi ad paucos, unde non oportebat ut de hoc fieret mentio inter praecepta Decalogi. Quamvis etiam, quantum ad aliquem intellectum, in hoc quod dicitur, non assumes nomen Dei tui in vanum, prohibeatur falsitas doctrinae, una enim Glossa exponit, non dices Christum esse creaturam.

AD QUARTUM dicendum quod statim ratio naturalis homini dictat quod nulli iniuriam faciat, et ideo praecepta prohibentia nocumentum, extendunt se ad omnes. Sed ratio naturalis non statim dictat quod aliquid sit pro alio faciendum, nisi cui homo aliquid debet. Debitum autem filii ad patrem adeo est manifestum quod nulla tergiversatione potest negari, eo quod pater est principium generationis et esse, et insuper educationis et doctrinae. Et ideo non ponitur sub praecepto Decalogi ut aliquod beneficium vel obsequium alicui impendatur nisi parentibus. Parentes autem non videntur esse debitores filiis propter aliqua beneficia suscepta, sed potius e converso. Filius etiam est aliquid patris; et patres amant filios ut aliquid ipsorum, sicut dicit philosophus, in VIII Ethic. Unde eisdem rationibus non ponuntur aliqua praecepta Decalogi pertinentia ad amorem filiorum, sicut neque etiam aliqua ordinantia hominem ad seipsum.

AD QUINTUM dicendum quod delectatio adulterii, et utilitas divitiarum, sunt propter seipsa appetibilia, inquantum habent rationem boni delectabilis vel utilis. Et propter hoc oportuit in eis prohiberi non solum opus, sed etiam concupiscentiam. Sed homicidium et falsitas sunt secundum seipsa horribilia, quia proximus et veritas naturaliter amantur, et non desiderantur nisi propter aliud. Et ideo non oportuit circa peccatum homicidii et falsi testimonii prohibere peccatum cordis, sed solum operis.

AD SEXTUM dicendum quod, sicut supra dictum est, omnes passiones irascibilis derivantur a passionibus concupiscibilis. Et ideo in praeceptis Decalogi, quae sunt quasi prima elementa legis, non erat mentio facienda de passionibus irascibilis, sed solum de passionibus concupiscibilis.

of the Passover in memory of the past favor of the delivery from Egypt, and as a sign of the future Passion of Christ, which though temporal and transitory, brought us to the repose of the spiritual Sabbath. Consequently, the Sabbath alone, and none of the other solemnities and sacrifices, is mentioned in the precepts of the decalogue.

REPLY OBJ. 3: As the Apostle says (Heb 6:16), *men swear by one greater than themselves; and an oath for confirmation is the end of all their controversy*. Hence, since oaths are common to all, inordinate swearing is the matter of a special prohibition by a precept of the decalogue. According to one interpretation, however, the words, *Thou shalt not take the name of the Lord thy God in vain*, are a prohibition of false doctrine, for one gloss expounds them thus: *Thou shalt not say that Christ is a creature*.

REPLY OBJ. 4: That a man should not do harm to anyone is an immediate dictate of his natural reason: and therefore the precepts that forbid the doing of harm are binding on all men. But it is not an immediate dictate of natural reason that a man should do one thing in return for another, unless he happen to be indebted to someone. Now a son's debt to his father is so evident that one cannot get away from it by denying it: since the father is the principle of generation and being, and also of upbringing and teaching. Wherefore the decalogue does not prescribe deeds of kindness or service to be done to anyone except to one's parents. On the other hand parents do not seem to be indebted to their children for any favors received, but rather the reverse is the case. Again, a child is a part of his father; and *parents love their children as being a part of themselves*, as the Philosopher states (*Ethic.* viii, 12). Hence, just as the decalogue contains no ordinance as to man's behavior towards himself, so, for the same reason, it includes no precept about loving one's children.

REPLY OBJ. 5: The pleasure of adultery and the usefulness of wealth, insofar as they have the character of pleasurable or useful good, are of themselves, objects of appetite: and for this reason they needed to be forbidden not only in the deed but also in the desire. But murder and falsehood are, of themselves, objects of repulsion (since it is natural for man to love his neighbor and the truth): and are desired only for the sake of something else. Consequently with regard to sins of murder and false witness, it was necessary to proscribe, not sins of thought, but only sins of deed.

REPLY OBJ. 6: As stated above (Q25, A1), all the passions of the irascible faculty arise from the passions of the concupiscible part. Hence, as the precepts of the decalogue are, as it were, the first elements of the Law, there was no need for mention of the irascible passions, but only of the concupiscible passions.

Article 6

Whether the Ten Precepts of the Decalogue Are Set in Proper Order?

AD SEXTUM SIC PROCEDITUR. Videtur quod inconvenienter ordinentur decem praecepta Decalogi. Dilectio enim proximi videtur esse praevia ad dilectionem Dei, quia proximus est nobis magis notus quam Deus; secundum illud I Ioan. IV, *qui fratrem suum, quem videt, non diligit, Deum, quem non videt, quomodo potest diligere?* Sed tria prima praecepta pertinent ad dilectionem Dei, septem vero alia ad dilectionem proximi. Ergo inconvenienter praecepta Decalogi ordinantur.

PRAETEREA, per praecepta affirmativa imperantur actus virtutum, per praecepta vero negativa prohibentur actus vitiorum. Sed secundum Boetium, in commento praedicamentorum, prius sunt extirpanda vitia quam inserantur virtutes. Ergo inter praecepta pertinentia ad proximum, primo ponenda fuerunt praecepta negativa quam affirmativa.

PRAETEREA, praecepta legis dantur de actibus hominum. Sed prior est actus cordis quam oris vel exterioris operis. Ergo inconvenienti ordine praecepta de non concupiscendo, quae pertinent ad cor, ultimo ponuntur.

SED CONTRA est quod apostolus dicit, Rom. XIII, *quae a Deo sunt, ordinata sunt*. Sed praecepta Decalogi sunt immediate data a Deo, ut dictum est. Ergo convenientem ordinem habent.

RESPONDEO dicendum quod, sicut dictum est, praecepta Decalogi dantur de his quae statim in promptu mens hominis suscipit. Manifestum est autem quod tanto aliquid magis a ratione suscipitur, quanto contrarium est gravius et magis rationi repugnans. Manifestum est autem quod, cum rationis ordo a fine incipiat, maxime est contra rationem ut homo inordinate se habeat circa finem. Finis autem humanae vitae et societatis est Deus. Et ideo primo oportuit per praecepta Decalogi hominem ordinare ad Deum, cum eius contrarium sit gravissimum. Sicut etiam in exercitu, qui ordinatur ad ducem sicut ad finem, primum est quod miles subdatur duci, et huius contrarium est gravissimum; secundum vero est ut aliis coordinetur.

Inter ipsa autem per quae ordinamur in Deum, primum occurrit quod homo fideliter ei subdatur, nullam participationem cum inimicis habens. Secundum autem est quod ei reverentiam exhibeat. Tertium autem est quod etiam famulatum impendat. Maiusque peccatum est in exercitu si miles, infideliter agens, cum hoste pactum habeat, quam si aliquam irreverentiam faciat duci, et hoc est etiam gravius quam si in aliquo obsequio ducis deficiens inveniatur.

OBJECTION 1: It would seem that the ten precepts of the decalogue are not set in proper order. Because love of one's neighbor is seemingly previous to love of God, since our neighbor is better known to us than God is; according to 1 Jn. 4:20: *He that loveth not his brother, whom he seeth, how can he love God, Whom he seeth not?* But the first three precepts belong to the love of God, while the other seven pertain to the love of our neighbor. Therefore the precepts of the decalogue are not set in proper order.

OBJ. 2: Further, the acts of virtue are prescribed by the affirmative precepts, and acts of vice are forbidden by the negative precepts. But according to Boethius in his commentary on the Categories, vices should be uprooted before virtues are sown. Therefore among the precepts concerning our neighbor, the negative precepts should have preceded the affirmative.

OBJ. 3: Further, the precepts of the Law are about men's actions. But actions of thought precede actions of word or outward deed. Therefore the precepts about not coveting, which regard our thoughts, are unsuitably placed last in order.

ON THE CONTRARY, The Apostle says (Rom 13:1): *The things that are of God, are well ordered*. But the precepts of the decalogue were given immediately by God, as stated above (A3). Therefore they are arranged in becoming order.

I ANSWER THAT, As stated above (AA3,5, ad 1), the precepts of the decalogue are such as the mind of man is ready to grasp at once. Now it is evident that a thing is so much the more easily grasped by the reason, as its contrary is more grievous and repugnant to reason. Moreover, it is clear, since the order of reason begins with the end, that, for a man to be inordinately disposed towards his end, is supremely contrary to reason. Now the end of human life and society is God. Consequently it was necessary for the precepts of the decalogue, first of all, to direct man to God; since the contrary to this is most grievous. Thus also, in an army, which is ordained to the commander as to its end, it is requisite first that the soldier should be subject to the commander, and the opposite of this is most grievous; and second it is requisite that he should be in coordination with the other soldiers.

Now among those things whereby we are ordained to God, the first is that man should be subjected to Him faithfully, by having nothing in common with His enemies. The second is that he should show Him reverence: the third that he should offer Him service. Thus, in an army, it is a greater sin for a soldier to act treacherously and make a compact with the foe, than to be insolent to his commander: and this last is more grievous than if he be found wanting in some point of service to him.

In praeceptis autem ordinantibus ad proximum, manifestum est quod magis repugnat rationi, et gravius peccatum est, si homo non servet ordinem debitum ad personas quibus magis est debitor. Et ideo inter praecepta ordinantia ad proximum, primo ponitur praeceptum pertinens ad parentes. Inter alia vero praecepta etiam apparet ordo secundum ordinem gravitatis peccatorum. Gravius est enim, et magis rationi repugnans, peccare opere quam ore, et ore quam corde. Et inter peccata operis, gravius est homicidium, per quod tollitur vita hominis iam existentis, quam adulterium, per quod impeditur certitudo prolis nasciturae; et adulterium gravius quam furtum, quod pertinet ad bona exteriora.

Ad primum ergo dicendum quod, quamvis secundum viam sensus proximus sit magis notus quam Deus, tamen dilectio Dei est ratio dilectionis proximi, ut infra patebit. Et ideo praecepta ordinantia ad Deum, fuerunt praeordinanda.

Ad secundum dicendum quod, sicut Deus est universale principium essendi omnibus, ita etiam pater est principium quoddam essendi filio. Et ideo convenienter post praecepta pertinentia ad Deum, ponitur praeceptum pertinens ad parentes. Ratio autem procedit quando affirmativa et negativa pertinent ad idem genus operis. Quamvis etiam et in hoc non habeat omnimodam efficaciam. Etsi enim in executione operis, prius extirpanda sint vitia quam inserendae virtutes, secundum illud Psalmi XXXIII, *declina a malo, et fac bonum*, et Isaiae I, *quiescite agere perverse, discite benefacere*; tamen in cognitione prior est virtus quam peccatum, quia *per rectum cognoscitur obliquum*, ut dicitur in I de anima. *Per legem autem cognitio peccati*, ut Rom. III dicitur. Et secundum hoc, praeceptum affirmativum debuisset primo poni. Sed non est ista ratio ordinis, sed quae supra posita est. Quia in praeceptis pertinentibus ad Deum, quae sunt primae tabulae, ultimo ponitur praeceptum affirmativum, quia eius transgressio minorem reatum inducit.

Ad tertium dicendum quod peccatum cordis etsi sit prius in executione, tamen eius prohibitio posterius cadit in ratione.

As to the precepts that direct man in his behavior towards his neighbor, it is evident that it is more repugnant to reason, and a more grievous sin, if man does not observe the due order as to those persons to whom he is most indebted. Consequently, among those precepts that direct man in his relations to his neighbor, the first place is given to that one which regards his parents. Among the other precepts we again find the order to be according to the gravity of sin. For it is more grave and more repugnant to reason, to sin by deed than by word; and by word than by thought. And among sins of deed, murder which destroys life in one already living is more grievous than adultery, which imperils the life of the unborn child; and adultery is more grave than theft, which regards external goods.

Reply Obj. 1: Although our neighbor is better known than God by the way of the senses, nevertheless the love of God is the reason for the love of our neighbor, as shall be declared later on (SS, Q25, A1; SS, Q26, A2). Hence the precepts ordaining man to God demanded precedence of the others.

Reply Obj. 2: Just as God is the universal principle of being in respect of all things, so is a father a principle of being in respect of his son. Therefore the precept regarding parents was fittingly placed after the precepts regarding God. This argument holds in respect of affirmative and negative precepts about the same kind of deed: although even then it is not altogether cogent. For although in the order of execution, vices should be uprooted before virtues are sown, according to Ps. 33:15: *Turn away from evil, and do good*, and Is. 1:16,17: *Cease to do perversely; learn to do well*; yet, in the order of knowledge, virtue precedes vice, because *the crooked line is known by the straight* (De Anima i): and *by the law is the knowledge of sin* (Rom 3:20). Wherefore the affirmation precept demanded the first place. However, this is not the reason for the order, but that which is given above. Because in the precepts regarding God, which belongs to the first table, an affirmative precept is placed last, since its transgression implies a less grievous sin.

Reply Obj. 3: Although sin of thought stands first in the order of execution, yet its prohibition holds a later position in the order of reason.

Article 7

Whether the Precepts of the Decalogue Are Suitably Formulated?

Ad septimum sic proceditur. Videtur quod praecepta Decalogi inconvenienter tradantur. Praecepta enim affirmativa ordinant ad actus virtutum, praecepta autem negativa abstrahunt ab actibus vitiorum. Sed

Objection 1: It would seem that the precepts of the decalogue are unsuitably formulated. Because the affirmative precepts direct man to acts of virtue, while the negative precepts withdraw him from acts of vice. But in every

circa quamlibet materiam opponuntur sibi virtutes et vitia. Ergo in qualibet materia de qua ordinat praeceptum Decalogi, debuit poni praeceptum affirmativum et negativum. Inconvenienter igitur ponuntur quaedam affirmativa et quaedam negativa.

Praeterea, Isidorus dicit quod omnis lex ratione constat. Sed omnia praecepta Decalogi pertinent ad legem divinam. Ergo in omnibus debuit ratio assignari, et non solum in primo et tertio praecepto.

Praeterea, per observantiam praeceptorum meretur aliquis praemia a Deo. Sed divinae promissiones sunt de praemiis praeceptorum. Ergo promissio debuit poni in omnibus praeceptis, et non solum in primo et quarto.

Praeterea, lex vetus dicitur lex timoris, inquantum per comminationes poenarum inducebat ad observationes praeceptorum. Sed omnia praecepta Decalogi pertinent ad legem veterem. Ergo in omnibus debuit poni comminatio poenae, et non solum in primo et secundo.

Praeterea, omnia praecepta Dei sunt in memoria retinenda, dicitur enim Prov. III, *describe ea in tabulis cordis tui*. Inconvenienter ergo in solo tertio praecepto fit mentio de memoria. Et ita videntur praecepta Decalogi inconvenienter tradita esse.

Sed contra est quod dicitur Sap. XI, quod *Deus omnia fecit in numero, pondere et mensura*. Multo magis ergo in praeceptis suae legis congruum modum tradendi servavit.

Respondeo dicendum quod in praeceptis divinae legis maxima sapientia continetur, unde dicitur Deut. IV, *haec est vestra sapientia et intellectus coram populis*. Sapientis autem est omnia debito modo et ordine disponere. Et ideo manifestum esse debet quod praecepta legis convenienti modo sunt tradita.

Ad primum ergo dicendum quod semper ad affirmationem sequitur negatio oppositi, non autem semper ad negationem unius oppositi sequitur affirmatio alterius. Sequitur enim, si est album, non est nigrum, non tamen sequitur, si non est nigrum, ergo est album, quia ad plura sese extendit negatio quam affirmatio. Et inde est etiam quod non esse faciendum iniuriam, quod pertinet ad praecepta negativa, ad plures personas se extendit, secundum primum dictamen rationis, quam esse debitum ut alicui obsequium vel beneficium impendatur. Inest autem primo dictamen rationis quod homo debitor est beneficii vel obsequii exhibendi illis a quibus beneficia accepit, si nondum recompensavit. Duo autem sunt quorum beneficiis sufficienter nullus recompensare potest, scilicet Deus et pater, ut dicitur in VIII Ethic. Et ideo sola duo praecepta affirmativa ponuntur, unum de

matter there are virtues and vices opposed to one another. Therefore in whatever matter there is an ordinance of a precept of the decalogue, there should have been an affirmative and a negative precept. Therefore it was unfitting that affirmative precepts should be framed in some matters, and negative precepts in others.

Obj. 2: Further, Isidore says (*Etym.* ii, 10) that every law is based on reason. But all the precepts of the decalogue belong to the Divine law. Therefore the reason should have been pointed out in each precept, and not only in the first and third.

Obj. 3: Further, by observing the precepts man deserves to be rewarded by God. But the Divine promises concern the rewards of the precepts. Therefore the promise should have been included in each precept, and not only in the second and fourth.

Obj. 4: Further, the Old Law is called *the law of fear*, insofar as it induced men to observe the precepts, by means of the threat of punishments. But all the precepts of the decalogue belong to the Old Law. Therefore a threat of punishment should have been included in each, and not only in the first and second.

Obj. 5: Further, all the commandments of God should be retained in the memory: for it is written (Prov 3:3): *Write them in the tables of thy heart*. Therefore it was not fitting that mention of the memory should be made in the third commandment only. Consequently it seems that the precepts of the decalogue are unsuitably formulated.

On the contrary, It is written (Wis 11:21) that *God made all things, in measure, number and weight*. Much more therefore did He observe a suitable manner in formulating His Law.

I answer that, The highest wisdom is contained in the precepts of the Divine law: wherefore it is written (Deut 4:6): *This is your wisdom and understanding in the sight of nations*. Now it belongs to wisdom to arrange all things in due manner and order. Therefore it must be evident that the precepts of the Law are suitably set forth.

Reply Obj. 1: Affirmation of one thing always leads to the denial of its opposite: but the denial of one opposite does not always lead to the affirmation of the other. For it follows that if a thing is white, it is not black: but it does not follow that if it is not black, it is white: because negation extends further than affirmation. And hence too, that one ought not to do harm to another, which pertains to the negative precepts, extends to more persons, as a primary dictate of reason, than that one ought to do someone a service or kindness. Nevertheless it is a primary dictate of reason that man is a debtor in the point of rendering a service or kindness to those from whom he has received kindness, if he has not yet repaid the debt. Now there are two whose favors no man can sufficiently repay, viz., God and man's father, as stated in *Ethic.* viii, 14. Therefore it is that there are only two affirmative precepts; one about the honor due

honoratione parentum; aliud de celebratione sabbati in commemorationem divini beneficii.

AD SECUNDUM dicendum quod illa praecepta quae sunt pure moralia, habent manifestam rationem, unde non oportuit quod in eis aliqua ratio adderetur. Sed quibusdam praeceptis additur caeremoniale, vel determinativum praecepti moralis communis, sicut in primo praecepto, non facies sculptile; et in tertio praecepto determinatur dies sabbati. Et ideo utrobique oportuit rationem assignari.

AD TERTIUM dicendum quod homines ut plurimum actus suos ad aliquam utilitatem ordinant. Et ideo in illis praeceptis necesse fuit promissionem praemii apponere, ex quibus videbatur nulla utilitas sequi, vel aliqua utilitas impediri. Quia vero parentes sunt iam in recedendo, ab eis non expectatur utilitas. Et ideo praecepto de honore parentum additur promissio. Similiter etiam praecepto de prohibitione idololatriae, quia per hoc videbatur impediri apparens utilitas quam homines credunt se posse consequi per pactum cum Daemonibus initum.

AD QUARTUM dicendum quod poenae praecipue necessariae sunt contra illos qui sunt proni ad malum, ut dicitur in X Ethic. Et ideo illis solis praeceptis legis additur comminatio poenarum, in quibus erat pronitas ad malum. Erant autem homines proni ad idololatriam, propter generalem consuetudinem gentium. Et similiter sunt etiam homines proni ad periurium, propter frequentiam iuramenti. Et ideo primis duobus praeceptis adiungitur comminatio.

AD QUINTUM dicendum quod praeceptum de sabbato ponitur ut commemorativum beneficii praeteriti. Et ideo specialiter in eo fit mentio de memoria. Vel quia praeceptum de sabbato habet determinationem adiunctam quae non est de lege naturae; et ideo hoc praeceptum speciali admonitione indiguit.

to parents, the other about the celebration of the Sabbath in memory of the Divine favor.

REPLY OBJ. 2: The reasons for the purely moral precepts are manifest; hence there was no need to add the reason. But some of the precepts include ceremonial matter, or a determination of a general moral precept; thus the first precept includes the determination, *Thou shalt not make a graven thing*; and in the third precept the Sabbath-day is fixed. Consequently there was need to state the reason in each case.

REPLY OBJ. 3: Generally speaking, men direct their actions to some point of utility. Consequently in those precepts in which it seemed that there would be no useful result, or that some utility might be hindered, it was necessary to add a promise of reward. And since parents are already on the way to depart from us, no benefit is expected from them: wherefore a promise of reward is added to the precept about honoring one's parents. The same applies to the precept forbidding idolatry: since thereby it seemed that men were hindered from receiving the apparent benefit which they think they can get by entering into a compact with the demons.

REPLY OBJ. 4: Punishments are necessary against those who are prone to evil, as stated in *Ethic.* x, 9. Wherefore a threat of punishment is only affixed to those precepts of the law which forbade evils to which men were prone. Now men were prone to idolatry by reason of the general custom of the nations. Likewise men are prone to perjury on account of the frequent use of oaths. Hence it is that a threat is affixed to the first two precepts.

REPLY OBJ. 5: The commandment about the Sabbath was made in memory of a past blessing. Wherefore special mention of the memory is made therein. Or again, the commandment about the Sabbath has a determination affixed to it that does not belong to the natural law, wherefore this precept needed a special admonition.

Article 8

Whether the Precepts of the Decalogue Are Dispensable?

AD OCTAVUM SIC PROCEDITUR. Videtur quod praecepta Decalogi sint dispensabilia. Praecepta enim Decalogi sunt de iure naturali. Sed iustum naturale in aliquibus deficit, et mutabile est, sicut et natura humana, ut philosophus dicit, in V Ethic. Defectus autem legis in aliquibus particularibus casibus est ratio dispensandi, ut supra dictum est. Ergo in praeceptis Decalogi potest fieri dispensatio.

PRAETEREA, sicut se habet homo ad legem humanam, ita se habet Deus ad legem datam divinitus. Sed

OBJECTION 1: It would seem that the precepts of the decalogue are dispensable. For the precepts of the decalogue belong to the natural law. But the natural law fails in some cases and is changeable, like human nature, as the Philosopher says (*Ethic.* v, 7). Now the failure of law to apply in certain particular cases is a reason for dispensation, as stated above (Q96, A6; Q97, A4). Therefore a dispensation can be granted in the precepts of the decalogue.

OBJ. 2: Further, man stands in the same relation to human law as God does to Divine law. But man can dispense

homo potest dispensare in praeceptis legis quae homo statuit. Ergo, cum praecepta Decalogi sint instituta a Deo, videtur quod Deus in eis possit dispensare. Sed praelati vice Dei funguntur in terris, dicit enim apostolus, II ad Cor. II, *nam et ego, si quid donavi, propter vos donavi in persona Christi.* Ergo etiam praelati possunt in praeceptis Decalogi dispensare.

PRAETEREA, inter praecepta Decalogi continetur prohibitio homicidii. Sed in isto praecepto videtur dispensari per homines, puta cum, secundum praeceptum legis humanae, homines licite occiduntur, puta malefactores vel hostes. Ergo praecepta Decalogi sunt dispensabilia.

PRAETEREA, observatio sabbati continetur inter praecepta Decalogi. Sed in hoc praecepto fuit dispensatum, dicitur enim I Machab. II, *et cogitaverunt in die illa dicentes, omnis homo quicumque venerit ad nos in bello die sabbatorum, pugnemus adversus eum.* Ergo praecepta Decalogi sunt dispensabilia.

SED CONTRA est quod dicitur Isaiae XXIV, quidam reprehenduntur de hoc quod mutaverunt ius, dissipaverunt foedus sempiternum, quod maxime videtur intelligendum de praeceptis Decalogi. Ergo praecepta Decalogi mutari per dispensationem non possunt.

RESPONDEO dicendum quod, sicut supra dictum est, tunc in praeceptis debet fieri dispensatio, quando occurrit aliquis particularis casus in quo, si verbum legis observetur, contrariatur intentioni legislatoris. Intentio autem legislatoris cuiuslibet ordinatur primo quidem et principaliter ad bonum commune; secundo autem, ad ordinem iustitiae et virtutis, secundum quem bonum commune conservatur, et ad ipsum pervenitur. Si qua ergo praecepta dentur quae contineant ipsam conservationem boni communis, vel ipsum ordinem iustitiae et virtutis; huiusmodi praecepta continent intentionem legislatoris, et ideo indispensabilia sunt. Puta si poneretur hoc praeceptum in aliqua communitate, quod nullus destrueret rempublicam, neque proderet civitatem hostibus, sive quod nullus faceret aliquid iniuste vel male; huiusmodi praecepta essent indispensabilia. Sed si aliqua alia praecepta traderentur ordinata ad ista praecepta, quibus determinantur aliqui speciales modi, in talibus praeceptis dispensatio posset fieri; inquantum per omissionem huiusmodi praeceptorum in aliquibus casibus, non fieret praeiudicium primis praeceptis, quae continent intentionem legislatoris. Puta si, ad conservationem reipublicae, statueretur in aliqua civitate quod de singulis vicis aliqui vigilarent ad custodiam civitatis obsessae; posset cum aliquibus dispensari propter aliquam maiorem utilitatem.

Praecepta autem Decalogi continent ipsam intentionem legislatoris, scilicet Dei. Nam praecepta primae

with the precepts of a law made by man. Therefore, since the precepts of the decalogue are ordained by God, it seems that God can dispense with them. Now our superiors are God's viceregents on earth; for the Apostle says (2 Cor 2:10): *For what I have pardoned, if I have pardoned anything, for your sakes have I done it in the person of Christ.* Therefore superiors can dispense with the precepts of the decalogue.

OBJ. 3: Further, among the precepts of the decalogue is one forbidding murder. But it seems that a dispensation is given by men in this precept: for instance, when according to the prescription of human law, such as evil-doers or enemies are lawfully slain. Therefore the precepts of the decalogue are dispensable.

OBJ. 4: Further, the observance of the Sabbath is ordained by a precept of the decalogue. But a dispensation was granted in this precept; for it is written (1 Macc 2:4): *And they determined in that day, saying: Whosoever shall come up to fight against us on the Sabbath-day, we will fight against him.* Therefore the precepts of the decalogue are dispensable.

ON THE CONTRARY, are the words of Is. 24:5, where some are reproved for that *they have changed the ordinance, they have broken the everlasting covenant*; which, seemingly, apply principally to the precepts of the decalogue. Therefore the precepts of the decalogue cannot be changed by dispensation.

I ANSWER THAT, As stated above (Q96, A6; Q97, A4), precepts admit of dispensation, when there occurs a particular case in which, if the letter of the law be observed, the intention of the lawgiver is frustrated. Now the intention of every lawgiver is directed first and chiefly to the common good; second, to the order of justice and virtue, whereby the common good is preserved and attained. If therefore there be any precepts which contain the very preservation of the common good, or the very order of justice and virtue, such precepts contain the intention of the lawgiver, and therefore are indispensable. For instance, if in some community a law were enacted, such as this—that no man should work for the destruction of the commonwealth, or betray the state to its enemies, or that no man should do anything unjust or evil, such precepts would not admit of dispensation. But if other precepts were enacted, subordinate to the above, and determining certain special modes of procedure, these latter precepts would admit of dispensation, insofar as the omission of these precepts in certain cases would not be prejudicial to the former precepts which contain the intention of the lawgiver. For instance if, for the safeguarding of the commonwealth, it were enacted in some city that from each ward some men should keep watch as sentries in case of siege, some might be dispensed from this on account of some greater utility.

Now the precepts of the decalogue contain the very intention of the lawgiver, who is God. For the precepts of

tabulae, quae ordinant ad Deum, continent ipsum ordinem ad bonum commune et finale, quod Deus est; praecepta autem secundae tabulae continent ipsum ordinem iustitiae inter homines observandae, ut scilicet nulli fiat indebitum, et cuilibet reddatur debitum; secundum hanc enim rationem sunt intelligenda praecepta Decalogi. Et ideo praecepta Decalogi sunt omnino indispensabilia.

AD PRIMUM ergo dicendum quod philosophus non loquitur de iusto naturali quod continet ipsum ordinem iustitiae, hoc enim nunquam deficit, iustitiam esse servandam. Sed loquitur quantum ad determinatos modos observationis iustitiae, qui in aliquibus fallunt.

AD SECUNDUM dicendum quod, sicut apostolus dicit, II ad Tim. II, *Deus fidelis permanet, negare seipsum non potest*. Negaret autem seipsum, si ipsum ordinem suae iustitiae auferret, cum ipse sit ipsa iustitia. Et ideo in hoc Deus dispensare non potest, ut homini liceat non ordinate se habere ad Deum, vel non subdi ordini iustitiae eius, etiam in his secundum quae homines ad invicem ordinantur.

AD TERTIUM dicendum quod occisio hominis prohibetur in Decalogo secundum quod habet rationem indebiti, sic enim praeceptum continet ipsam rationem iustitiae. Lex autem humana hoc concedere non potest, quod licite homo indebite occidatur. Sed malefactores occidi, vel hostes reipublicae, hoc non est indebitum. Unde hoc non contrariatur praecepto Decalogi, nec talis occisio est homicidium, quod praecepto Decalogi prohibetur, ut Augustinus dicit, in I de Lib. Arb. Et similiter si alicui auferatur quod suum erat, si debitum est quod ipsum amittat, hoc non est furtum vel rapina, quae praecepto Decalogi prohibentur.

Et ideo quando filii Israel praecepto Dei tulerunt Aegyptiorum spolia, non fuit furtum, quia hoc eis debebatur ex sententia Dei. Similiter etiam Abraham, cum consensit occidere filium, non consensit in homicidium, quia debitum erat eum occidi per mandatum Dei, qui est dominus vitae et mortis. Ipse enim est qui poenam mortis infligit omnibus hominibus, iustis et iniustis, pro peccato primi parentis, cuius sententiae si homo sit executor auctoritate divina, non erit homicida, sicut nec Deus. Et similiter etiam Osee, accedens ad uxorem fornicariam, vel ad mulierem adulteram, non est moechatus nec fornicatus, quia accessit ad eam quae sua erat secundum mandatum divinum, qui est auctor institutionis matrimonii.

Sic igitur praecepta ipsa Decalogi, quantum ad rationem iustitiae quam continent, immutabilia sunt. Sed quantum ad aliquam determinationem per applicationem ad singulares actus, ut scilicet hoc vel illud sit homicidium, furtum vel adulterium, aut non, hoc quidem est mutabile, quandoque sola auctoritate divina, in his

the first table, which direct us to God, contain the very order to the common and final good, which is God; while the precepts of the second table contain the order of justice to be observed among men, that nothing undue be done to anyone, and that each one be given his due; for it is in this sense that we are to take the precepts of the decalogue. Consequently the precepts of the decalogue admit of no dispensation whatever.

REPLY OBJ. 1: The Philosopher is not speaking of the natural law which contains the very order of justice: for it is a never-failing principle that *justice should be preserved*. But he is speaking in reference to certain fixed modes of observing justice, which fail to apply in certain cases.

REPLY OBJ. 2: As the Apostle says (2 Tim 2:13), *God continueth faithful, He cannot deny Himself*. But He would deny Himself if He were to do away with the very order of His own justice, since He is justice itself. Wherefore God cannot dispense a man so that it be lawful for him not to direct himself to God, or not to be subject to His justice, even in those matters in which men are directed to one another.

REPLY OBJ. 3: The slaying of a man is forbidden in the decalogue, insofar as it bears the character of something undue: for in this sense the precept contains the very essence of justice. Human law cannot make it lawful for a man to be slain unduly. But it is not undue for evil-doers or foes of the common weal to be slain: hence this is not contrary to the precept of the decalogue; and such a killing is no murder as forbidden by that precept, as Augustine observes (*De Lib. Arb.* i, 4). In like manner when a man's property is taken from him, if it be due that he should lose it, this is not theft or robbery as forbidden by the decalogue.

Consequently when the children of Israel, by God's command, took away the spoils of the Egyptians, this was not theft; since it was due to them by the sentence of God. Likewise when Abraham consented to slay his son, he did not consent to murder, because his son was due to be slain by the command of God, Who is Lord of life and death: for He it is Who inflicts the punishment of death on all men, both godly and ungodly, on account of the sin of our first parent, and if a man be the executor of that sentence by Divine authority, he will be no murderer any more than God would be. Again Osee, by taking unto himself a wife of fornications, or an adulterous woman, was not guilty either of adultery or of fornication: because he took unto himself one who was his by command of God, Who is the Author of the institution of marriage.

Accordingly, therefore, the precepts of the decalogue, as to the essence of justice which they contain, are unchangeable: but as to any determination by application to individual actions—for instance, that this or that be murder, theft or adultery, or not—in this point they admit of change; sometimes by Divine authority alone, namely, in such

scilicet quae a solo Deo sunt instituta, sicut in matrimonio, et in aliis huiusmodi; quandoque etiam auctoritate humana, sicut in his quae sunt commissa hominum iurisdictioni. Quantum enim ad hoc, homines gerunt vicem Dei, non autem quantum ad omnia.

AD QUARTUM dicendum quod illa excogitatio magis fuit interpretatio praecepti quam dispensatio. Non enim intelligitur violare sabbatum qui facit opus quod est necessarium ad salutem humanam; sicut dominus probat, Matth. XII.

matters as are exclusively of Divine institution, as marriage and the like; sometimes also by human authority, namely in such matters as are subject to human jurisdiction: for in this respect men stand in the place of God: and yet not in all respects.

REPLY OBJ. 4: This determination was an interpretation rather than a dispensation. For a man is not taken to break the Sabbath, if he does something necessary for human welfare; as Our Lord proves (Matt 12:3, seqq.).

Article 9

Whether the Mode of Virtue Falls Under the Precept of the Law?

AD NONUM SIC PROCEDITUR. Videtur quod modus virtutis cadat sub praecepto legis. Est enim modus virtutis ut aliquis iuste operetur iusta, et fortiter fortia, et similiter de aliis virtutibus. Sed Deut. XVI praecipitur, *iuste quod iustum est exequeris*. Ergo modus virtutis cadit sub praecepto.

PRAETEREA, illud maxime cadit sub praecepto quod est de intentione legislatoris. Sed intentio legislatoris ad hoc principaliter fertur ut homines faciat virtuosos, sicut dicitur in II Ethic. Virtuosi autem est virtuose agere. Ergo modus virtutis cadit sub praecepto.

PRAETEREA, modus virtutis proprie esse videtur ut aliquis voluntarie et delectabiliter operetur. Sed hoc cadit sub praecepto legis divinae, dicitur enim in Psalmo XCIX, *servite domino in laetitia*; et II ad Cor. IX, *non ex tristitia aut ex necessitate, hilarem enim datorem diligit Deus*; ubi Glossa dicit, *quidquid boni facis, cum hilaritate fac, et tunc bene facis, si autem cum tristitia facis, fit de te, non tu facis*. Ergo modus virtutis cadit sub praecepto legis.

SED CONTRA, nullus potest operari eo modo quo operatur virtuosus, nisi habeat habitum virtutis; ut patet per philosophum, in II et V Ethic. Quicumque autem transgreditur praeceptum legis, meretur poenam. Sequeretur ergo quod ille qui non habet habitum virtutis, quidquid faceret, mereretur poenam. Hoc autem est contra intentionem legis, quae intendit hominem, assuefaciendo ad bona opera, inducere ad virtutem. Non ergo modus virtutis cadit sub praecepto.

RESPONDEO dicendum quod, sicut supra dictum est, praeceptum legis habet vim coactivam. Illud ergo directe cadit sub praecepto legis, ad quod lex cogit. Coactio autem legis est per metum poenae, ut dicitur X Ethic., nam illud proprie cadit sub praecepto legis, pro quo poena legis infligitur. Ad instituendam autem poenam aliter

OBJECTION 1: It would seem that the mode of virtue falls under the precept of the law. For the mode of virtue is that deeds of justice should be done justly, that deeds of fortitude should be done bravely, and in like manner as to the other virtues. But it is commanded (Deut 26:20) that *thou shalt follow justly after that which is just*. Therefore the mode of virtue falls under the precept.

OBJ. 2: Further, that which belongs to the intention of the lawgiver comes chiefly under the precept. But the intention of the lawgiver is directed chiefly to make men virtuous, as stated in *Ethic*. ii: and it belongs to a virtuous man to act virtuously. Therefore the mode of virtue falls under the precept.

OBJ. 3: Further, the mode of virtue seems to consist properly in working willingly and with pleasure. But this falls under a precept of the Divine law, for it is written (Ps 99:2): *Serve ye the Lord with gladness*; and (2 Cor 9:7): *Not with sadness or necessity: for God loveth a cheerful giver*; whereupon the gloss says: *Whatever ye do, do gladly; and then you will do it well; whereas if you do it sorrowfully, it is done in thee, not by thee*. Therefore the mode of virtue falls under the precept of the law.

ON THE CONTRARY, No man can act as a virtuous man acts unless he has the habit of virtue, as the Philosopher explains (*Ethic*. ii, 4; v, 8). Now whoever transgresses a precept of the law, deserves to be punished. Hence it would follow that a man who has not the habit of virtue, would deserve to be punished, whatever he does. But this is contrary to the intention of the law, which aims at leading man to virtue, by habituating him to good works. Therefore the mode of virtue does not fall under the precept.

I ANSWER THAT, As stated above (Q90, A3, ad 2), a precept of law has compulsory power. Hence that on which the compulsion of the law is brought to bear, falls directly under the precept of the law. Now the law compels through fear of punishment, as stated in *Ethic*. x, 9, because that properly falls under the precept of the law, for which the

se habet lex divina, et lex humana. Non enim poena legis infligitur nisi pro illis de quibus legislator habet iudicare, quia ex iudicio lex punit. Homo autem, qui est legis lator humanae, non habet iudicare nisi de exterioribus actibus, quia *homines vident ea quae parent*, ut dicitur I Reg. XVI. Sed solius Dei, qui est lator legis divinae est iudicare de interioribus motibus voluntatum; secundum illud Psalmi VII, *scrutans corda et renes Deus*.

Secundum hoc igitur dicendum est quod modus virtutis quantum ad aliquid respicitur a lege humana et divina; quantum ad aliquid autem, a lege divina sed non a lege humana; quantum ad aliquid vero, nec a lege humana nec a lege divina. Modus autem virtutis in tribus consistit, secundum philosophum, in II Ethic. Quorum primum est, si aliquis operetur sciens. Hoc autem diiudicatur et a lege divina et a lege humana. Quod enim aliquis facit ignorans, per accidens facit. Unde secundum ignorantiam aliqua diiudicantur ad poenam vel ad veniam, tam secundum legem humanam quam secundum legem divinam.

Secundum autem est ut aliquis operetur volens, vel eligens et propter hoc eligens; in quo importatur duplex motus interior, scilicet voluntatis et intentionis, de quibus supra dictum est. Et ista duo non diiudicat lex humana, sed solum lex divina. Lex enim humana non punit eum qui vult occidere et non occidit, punit autem eum lex divina, secundum illud Matth. V, *qui irascitur fratri suo, reus erit iudicio*.

Tertium autem est ut firme et immobiliter habeat et operetur. Et ista firmitas proprie pertinet ad habitum, ut scilicet aliquis ex habitu radicato operetur. Et quantum ad hoc, modus virtutis non cadit sub praecepto neque legis divinae neque legis humanae, neque enim ab homine neque a Deo punitur tanquam praecepti transgressor, qui debitum honorem impendit parentibus, quamvis non habeat habitum pietatis.

AD PRIMUM ergo dicendum quod modus faciendi actum iustitiae qui cadit sub praecepto, est ut fiat aliquid secundum ordinem iuris, non autem quod fiat ex habitu iustitiae.

AD SECUNDUM dicendum quod intentio legislatoris est de duobus. De uno quidem, ad quod intendit per praecepta legis inducere, et hoc est virtus. Aliud autem est de quo intendit praeceptum ferre, et hoc est id quod ducit vel disponit ad virtutem, scilicet actus virtutis. Non enim idem est finis praecepti et id de quo praeceptum datur, sicut neque in aliis rebus idem est finis et quod est ad finem.

penalty of the law is inflicted. But Divine law and human law are differently situated as to the appointment of penalties; since the penalty of the law is inflicted only for those things which come under the judgment of the lawgiver; for the law punishes in accordance with the verdict given. Now man, the framer of human law, is competent to judge only of outward acts; because *man seeth those things that appear*, according to 1 Kgs. 16:7: while God alone, the framer of the Divine law, is competent to judge of the inward movements of wills, according to Ps. 7:10: *The searcher of hearts and reins is God*.

Accordingly, therefore, we must say that the mode of virtue is in some sort regarded both by human and by Divine law; in some respect it is regarded by the Divine, but not by the human law; and in another way, it is regarded neither by the human nor by the Divine law. Now the mode of virtue consists in three things, as the Philosopher states in *Ethic*. ii. The first is that man should act *knowingly*: and this is subject to the judgment of both Divine and human law; because what a man does in ignorance, he does accidentally. Hence according to both human and Divine law, certain things are judged in respect of ignorance to be punishable or pardonable.

The second point is that a man should act *deliberately*, i.e., *from choice, choosing that particular action for its own sake*; wherein a twofold internal movement is implied, of volition and of intention, about which we have spoken above (QQ8, 12): and concerning these two, Divine law alone, and not human law, is competent to judge. For human law does not punish the man who wishes to slay, and slays not: whereas the Divine law does, according to Mt. 5:22: *Whosoever is angry with his brother, shall be in danger of the judgment*.

The third point is that he should *act from a firm and immovable principle*: which firmness belongs properly to a habit, and implies that the action proceeds from a rooted habit. In this respect, the mode of virtue does not fall under the precept either of Divine or of human law, since neither by man nor by God is he punished as breaking the law, who gives due honor to his parents and yet has not the habit of filial piety.

REPLY OBJ. 1: The mode of doing acts of justice, which falls under the precept, is that they be done in accordance with right; but not that they be done from the habit of justice.

REPLY OBJ. 2: The intention of the lawgiver is twofold. His aim, in the first place, is to lead men to something by the precepts of the law: and this is virtue. Second, his intention is brought to bear on the matter itself of the precept: and this is something leading or disposing to virtue, viz., an act of virtue. For the end of the precept and the matter of the precept are not the same: just as neither in other things is the end the same as that which conduces to the end.

AD TERTIUM dicendum quod operari sine tristitia opus virtutis, cadit sub praecepto legis divinae, quia quicumque cum tristitia operatur, non volens operatur. Sed delectabiliter operari, sive cum laetitia vel hilaritate, quodammodo cadit sub praecepto, scilicet secundum quod sequitur delectatio ex dilectione Dei et proximi, quae cadit sub praecepto, cum amor sit causa delectationis, et quodammodo non, secundum quod delectatio consequitur habitum; *delectatio enim operis est signum habitus generati*, ut dicitur in II Ethic. Potest enim aliquis actus esse delectabilis vel propter finem, vel propter convenientiam habitus.

REPLY OBJ. 3: That works of virtue should be done without sadness, falls under the precept of the Divine law; for whoever works with sadness works unwillingly. But to work with pleasure, i.e., joyfully or cheerfully, in one respect falls under the precept, viz., insofar as pleasure ensues from the love of God and one's neighbor (which love falls under the precept), and love causes pleasure: and in another respect does not fall under the precept, insofar as pleasure ensues from a habit; for *pleasure taken in a work proves the existence of a habit*, as stated in *Ethic.* ii, 3. For an act may give pleasure either on account of its end, or through its proceeding from a becoming habit.

Article 10

Whether the Mode of Charity Falls Under the Precept of the Divine Law?

AD DECIMUM SIC PROCEDITUR. Videtur quod modus caritatis cadat sub praecepto divinae legis. Dicitur enim Matth. XIX, *si vis ad vitam ingredi, serva mandata*, ex quo videtur quod observatio mandatorum sufficiat ad introducendum in vitam. Sed opera bona non sufficiunt ad introducendum in vitam, nisi ex caritate fiant, dicitur enim I ad Cor. XIII, *si distribuero in cibos pauperum omnes facultates meas, et si tradidero corpus meum ita ut ardeam, caritatem autem non habuero, nihil mihi prodest*. Ergo modus caritatis est in praecepto.

PRAETEREA, ad modum caritatis proprie pertinet ut omnia fiant propter Deum. Sed istud cadit sub praecepto, dicit enim apostolus, I ad Cor. X, *omnia in gloriam Dei facite*. Ergo modus caritatis cadit sub praecepto.

PRAETEREA, si modus caritatis non cadit sub praecepto, ergo aliquis potest implere praecepta legis non habens caritatem. Sed quod potest fieri sine caritate, potest fieri sine gratia, quae semper adiuncta est caritati. Ergo aliquis potest implere praecepta legis sine gratia. Hoc autem est Pelagiani erroris; ut patet per Augustinum, in libro de haeresibus. Ergo modus caritatis est in praecepto.

SED CONTRA est quia quicumque non servat praeceptum, peccat mortaliter. Si igitur modus caritatis cadat sub praecepto, sequitur quod quicumque operatur aliquid et non ex caritate, peccet mortaliter. Sed quicumque non habet caritatem, operatur non ex caritate. Ergo sequitur quod quicumque non habet caritatem, peccet mortaliter in omni opere quod facit, quantumcumque sit de genere bonorum. Quod est inconveniens.

RESPONDEO dicendum quod circa hoc fuerunt contrariae opiniones. Quidam enim dixerunt absolute modum caritatis esse sub praecepto. Nec est impossibile

OBJECTION 1: It would seem that the mode of charity falls under the precept of the Divine law. For it is written (Matt 19:17): *If thou wilt enter into life, keep the commandments*: whence it seems to follow that the observance of the commandments suffices for entrance into life. But good works do not suffice for entrance into life, except they be done from charity: for it is written (1 Cor 13:3): *If I should distribute all my goods to feed the poor, and if I should deliver my body to be burned, and have not charity, it profiteth me nothing*. Therefore the mode of charity is included in the commandment.

OBJ. 2: Further, the mode of charity consists properly speaking in doing all things for God. But this falls under the precept; for the Apostle says (1 Cor 10:31): *Do all to the glory of God*. Therefore the mode of charity falls under the precept.

OBJ. 3: Further, if the mode of charity does not fall under the precept, it follows that one can fulfill the precepts of the law without having charity. Now what can be done without charity can be done without grace, which is always united to charity. Therefore one can fulfill the precepts of the law without grace. But this is the error of Pelagius, as Augustine declares (*De Haeres*. lxxxviii). Therefore the mode of charity is included in the commandment.

ON THE CONTRARY, Whoever breaks a commandment sins mortally. If therefore the mode of charity falls under the precept, it follows that whoever acts otherwise than from charity sins mortally. But whoever has not charity, acts otherwise than from charity. Therefore it follows that whoever has not charity, sins mortally in whatever he does, however good this may be in itself: which is absurd.

I ANSWER THAT, Opinions have been contrary on this question. For some have said absolutely that the mode of charity comes under the precept; and yet that it is possible

observare hoc praeceptum caritatem non habenti, quia potest se disponere ad hoc quod caritas ei infundatur a Deo. Nec quandocumque aliquis non habens caritatem facit aliquid de genere bonorum, peccat mortaliter, quia hoc est praeceptum affirmativum, ut ex caritate operetur, et non obligat ad semper, sed pro tempore illo quo aliquis habet caritatem. Alii vero dixerunt quod omnino modus caritatis non cadit sub praecepto.

Utrique autem quantum ad aliquid, verum dixerunt. Actus enim caritatis dupliciter considerari potest. Uno modo, secundum quod est quidam actus per se. Et hoc modo cadit sub praecepto legis quod de hoc specialiter datur, scilicet, *diliges dominum Deum tuum, et, diliges proximum tuum*. Et quantum ad hoc, primi verum dixerunt. Non enim est impossibile hoc praeceptum observare, quod est de actu caritatis, quia homo potest se disponere ad caritatem habendam, et quando habuerit eam, potest ea uti. Alio modo potest considerari actus caritatis secundum quod est modus actuum aliarum virtutum, hoc est secundum quod actus aliarum virtutum ordinantur ad caritatem, quae est finis praecepti, ut dicitur I ad Tim. I, dictum est enim supra quod intentio finis est quidam modus formalis actus ordinati in finem. Et hoc modo verum est quod secundi dixerunt, quod modus caritatis non cadit sub praecepto, hoc est dictu, quod in hoc praecepto, honora patrem, non includitur quod honoretur pater ex caritate, sed solum quod honoretur pater. Unde qui honorat patrem, licet non habens caritatem, non efficitur transgressor huius praecepti, etsi sit transgressor praecepti quod est de actu caritatis, propter quam transgressionem meretur poenam.

AD PRIMUM ergo dicendum quod dominus non dixit, si vis ad vitam ingredi, serva unum mandatum, sed, serva omnia mandata. Inter quae etiam continetur mandatum de dilectione Dei et proximi.

AD SECUNDUM dicendum quod sub mandato caritatis continetur ut diligatur Deus ex toto corde, ad quod pertinet ut omnia referantur in Deum. Et ideo praeceptum caritatis implere homo non potest, nisi etiam omnia referantur in Deum. Sic ergo qui honorat parentes, tenetur ex caritate honorare, non ex vi huius praecepti quod est, honora parentes, sed ex vi huius praecepti, diliges dominum Deum tuum ex toto corde tuo. Et cum ista sint duo praecepta affirmativa non obligantia ad semper, possunt pro diversis temporibus obligare. Et ita potest contingere quod aliquis implens praeceptum de honoratione parentum, non tunc transgrediatur praeceptum de omissione modi caritatis.

AD TERTIUM dicendum quod observare omnia praecepta legis homo non potest, nisi impleat praeceptum caritatis, quod non fit sine gratia. Et ideo impossibile est quod Pelagius dixit, hominem implere legem sine gratia.

for one not having charity to fulfill this precept: because he can dispose himself to receive charity from God. Nor (say they) does it follow that a man not having charity sins mortally whenever he does something good of its kind: because it is an affirmative precept that binds one to act from charity, and is binding not for all time, but only for such time as one is in a state of charity. On the other hand, some have said that the mode of charity is altogether outside the precept.

Both these opinions are true up to a certain point. Because the act of charity can be considered in two ways. First, as an act by itself: and thus it falls under the precept of the law which specially prescribes it, viz., *Thou shalt love the Lord thy God*, and *Thou shalt love thy neighbor*. In this sense, the first opinion is true. Because it is not impossible to observe this precept which regards the act of charity; since man can dispose himself to possess charity, and when he possesses it, he can use it. Second, the act of charity can be considered as being the mode of the acts of the other virtues, i.e., inasmuch as the acts of the other virtues are ordained to charity, which is *the end of the commandment*, as stated in 1 Tim. i, 5: for it has been said above (Q12, A4) that the intention of the end is a formal mode of the act ordained to that end. In this sense the second opinion is true in saying that the mode of charity does not fall under the precept, that is to say that this commandment, *Honor thy father*, does not mean that a man must honor his father from charity, but merely that he must honor him. Wherefore he that honors his father, yet has not charity, does not break this precept: although he does break the precept concerning the act of charity, for which reason he deserves to be punished.

REPLY OBJ. 1: Our Lord did not say, *If thou wilt enter into life, keep one commandment*; but *keep all the commandments*: among which is included the commandment concerning the love of God and our neighbor.

REPLY OBJ. 2: The precept of charity contains the injunction that God should be loved from our whole heart, which means that all things would be referred to God. Consequently man cannot fulfill the precept of charity, unless he also refer all things to God. Wherefore he that honors his father and mother, is bound to honor them from charity, not in virtue of the precept, *Honor thy father and mother*, but in virtue of the precept, *Thou shalt love the Lord thy God with thy whole heart*. And since these are two affirmative precepts, not binding for all times, they can be binding, each one at a different time: so that it may happen that a man fulfils the precept of honoring his father and mother, without at the same time breaking the precept concerning the omission of the mode of charity.

REPLY OBJ. 3: Man cannot fulfill all the precepts of the law, unless he fulfill the precept of charity, which is impossible without charity. Consequently it is not possible, as Pelagius maintained, for man to fulfill the law without grace.

Article 11

Whether It Is Right to Distinguish Other Moral Precepts of the Law Besides the Decalogue?

AD UNDECIMUM SIC PROCEDITUR. Videtur quod inconvenienter distinguantur alia moralia praecepta legis praeter Decalogum. Quia ut dominus dicit, Matth. XXII, *in duobus praeceptis caritatis pendet omnis lex et prophetae.* Sed haec duo praecepta explicantur per decem praecepta Decalogi. Ergo non oportet alia praecepta moralia esse.

PRAETEREA, praecepta moralia a iudicialibus et caeremonialibus distinguuntur, ut dictum est. Sed determinationes communium praeceptorum moralium pertinent ad iudicialia et caeremonialia praecepta, communia autem praecepta moralia sub Decalogo continentur, vel etiam Decalogo praesupponuntur, ut dictum est. Ergo inconvenienter traduntur alia praecepta moralia praeter Decalogum.

PRAETEREA, praecepta moralia sunt de actibus omnium virtutum, ut supra dictum est. Sicut igitur in lege ponuntur praecepta moralia praeter Decalogum pertinentia ad latriam, liberalitatem et misericordiam, et castitatem; ita etiam deberent poni aliqua praecepta pertinentia ad alias virtutes, puta ad fortitudinem, sobrietatem, et alia huiusmodi. Quod tamen non invenitur. Non ergo convenienter distinguuntur in lege alia praecepta moralia quae sunt praeter Decalogum.

SED CONTRA est quod in Psalmo XVIII dicitur, *lex domini immaculata, convertens animas.* Sed per alia etiam moralia quae Decalogo superadduntur, homo conservatur absque macula peccati, et anima eius ad Deum convertitur. Ergo ad legem pertinebat etiam alia praecepta moralia tradere.

RESPONDEO dicendum quod, sicut ex dictis patet, praecepta iudicialia et caeremonialia ex sola institutione vim habent, quia antequam instituerentur, non videbatur differre utrum sic vel aliter fieret. Sed praecepta moralia ex ipso dictamine naturalis rationis efficaciam habent, etiam si nunquam in lege statuantur. Horum autem triplex est gradus. Nam quaedam sunt certissima, et adeo manifesta quod editione non indigent; sicut mandata de dilectione Dei et proximi, et alia huiusmodi, ut supra dictum est, quae sunt quasi fines praeceptorum, unde in eis nullus potest errare secundum iudicium rationis. Quaedam vero sunt magis determinata, quorum rationem statim quilibet, etiam popularis, potest de facili videre; et tamen quia in paucioribus circa huiusmodi contingit iudicium humanum perverti, huiusmodi editione indigent, et haec sunt praecepta Decalogi. Quaedam vero sunt quorum ratio non est adeo cuilibet manifesta, sed solum sapientibus, et ista sunt praecepta

OBJECTION 1: It would seem that it is wrong to distinguish other moral precepts of the law besides the decalogue. Because, as Our Lord declared (Matt 22:40), *on these two commandments* of charity *dependeth the whole law and the prophets.* But these two commandments are explained by the ten commandments of the decalogue. Therefore there is no need for other moral precepts.

OBJ. 2: Further, the moral precepts are distinct from the judicial and ceremonial precepts, as stated above (Q99, AA3,4). But the determinations of the general moral precepts belong to the judicial and ceremonial precepts: and the general moral precepts are contained in the decalogue, or are even presupposed to the decalogue, as stated above (A3). Therefore it was unsuitable to lay down other moral precepts besides the decalogue.

OBJ. 3: Further, the moral precepts are about the acts of all the virtues, as stated above (A2). Therefore, as the Law contains, besides the decalogue, moral precepts pertaining to religion, liberality, mercy, and chastity; so there should have been added some precepts pertaining to the other virtues, for instance, fortitude, sobriety, and so forth. And yet such is not the case. It is therefore unbecoming to distinguish other moral precepts in the Law besides those of the decalogue.

ON THE CONTRARY, It is written (Ps 18:8): *The law of the Lord is unspotted, converting souls.* But man is preserved from the stain of sin, and his soul is converted to God by other moral precepts besides those of the decalogue. Therefore it was right for the Law to include other moral precepts.

I ANSWER THAT, As is evident from what has been stated (Q99, AA3,4), the judicial and ceremonial precepts derive their force from their institution alone: since before they were instituted, it seemed of no consequence whether things were done in this or that way. But the moral precepts derive their efficacy from the very dictate of natural reason, even if they were never included in the Law. Now of these there are three grades: for some are most certain, and so evident as to need no promulgation; such as the commandments of the love of God and our neighbor, and others like these, as stated above (A3), which are, as it were, the ends of the commandments; wherefore no man can have an erroneous judgment about them. Some precepts are more detailed, the reason of which even an uneducated man can easily grasp; and yet they need to be promulgated, because human judgment, in a few instances, happens to be led astray concerning them: these are the precepts of the decalogue. Again, there are some precepts the reason of which

moralia superaddita Decalogo, tradita a Deo populo per Moysen et Aaron.

Sed quia ea quae sunt manifesta, sunt principia cognoscendi eorum quae non sunt manifesta; alia praecepta moralia superaddita Decalogo reducuntur ad praecepta Decalogi, per modum cuiusdam additionis ad ipsa. Nam in primo praecepto Decalogi prohibetur cultus alienorum deorum, cui superadduntur alia praecepta prohibitiva eorum quae ordinantur in cultum idolorum; sicut habetur Deut. XVIII, *non inveniatur in te qui lustret filium suum aut filiam, ducens per ignem, nec sit maleficus atque incantator, nec Pythones consulat neque divinos, et quaerat a mortuis veritatem.* Secundum autem praeceptum prohibet periurium. Superadditur autem ei prohibitio blasphemiae, Levit. XXIV; et prohibitio falsae doctrinae, Deut. XIII. Tertio vero praecepto superadduntur omnia caeremonialia. Quarto autem praecepto, de honore parentum, superadditur praeceptum de honoratione senum, secundum illud Levit. XIX, *coram cano capite consurge, et honora personam senis*; et universaliter omnia praecepta inducentia ad reverentiam exhibendam maioribus, vel ad beneficia exhibenda vel aequalibus vel minoribus. Quinto autem praecepto, quod est de prohibitione homicidii, additur prohibitio odii et cuiuslibet violationis contra proximum, sicut illud Levit. XIX, *non stabis contra sanguinem proximi tui*; et etiam prohibitio odii fratris, secundum illud, *ne oderis fratrem tuum in corde tuo.* Praecepto autem sexto, quod est de prohibitione adulterii, superadditur praeceptum de prohibitione meretricii, secundum illud Deut. XXIII, *non erit meretrix de filiabus Israel, neque fornicator de filiis Israel*; et iterum prohibitio vitii contra naturam, secundum illud Levit. XVIII, *cum masculo non commisceberis, cum omni pecore non coibis.* Septimo autem praecepto, de prohibitione furti adiungitur praeceptum de prohibitione usurae, secundum illud Deut. XXIII, *non foenerabis fratri tuo ad usuram*; et prohibitio fraudis, secundum illud Deut. XXV, *non habebis in sacculo diversa pondera*; et universaliter omnia quae ad prohibitionem calumniae et rapinae pertinent. Octavo vero praecepto, quod est de prohibitione falsi testimonii, additur prohibitio falsi iudicii, secundum illud Exod. XXIII, *nec in iudicio plurimorum acquiesces sententiae, ut a veritate devies*; et prohibitio mendacii, sicut ibi subditur, *mendacium fugies*; et prohibitio detractionis, secundum illud Levit. XIX, *non eris criminator et susurro in populis.* Aliis autem duobus praeceptis nulla alia adiunguntur, quia per ea universaliter omnis mala concupiscentia prohibetur.

AD PRIMUM ergo dicendum quod ad dilectionem Dei et proximi ordinantur quidem praecepta Decalogi

is not so evident to everyone, but only the wise; these are moral precepts added to the decalogue, and given to the people by God through Moses and Aaron.

But since the things that are evident are the principles whereby we know those that are not evident, these other moral precepts added to the decalogue are reducible to the precepts of the decalogue, as so many corollaries. Thus the first commandment of the decalogue forbids the worship of strange gods: and to this are added other precepts forbidding things relating to worship of idols: thus it is written (Deut 18:10,11): *Neither let there be found among you anyone that shall expiate his son or daughter, making them to pass through the fire: . . . neither let there by any wizard nor charmer, nor anyone that consulteth pythonic spirits, or fortune-tellers, or that seeketh the truth from the dead.* The second commandment forbids perjury. To this is added the prohibition of blasphemy (Lev 24:15, seqq) and the prohibition of false doctrine (Deut 13). To the third commandment are added all the ceremonial precepts. To the fourth commandment prescribing the honor due to parents, is added the precept about honoring the aged, according to Lev. 19:32: *Rise up before the hoary head, and honor the person of the aged man*; and likewise all the precepts prescribing the reverence to be observed towards our betters, or kindliness towards our equals or inferiors. To the fifth commandment, which forbids murder, is added the prohibition of hatred and of any kind of violence inflicted on our neighbor, according to Lev. 19:16: *Thou shalt not stand against the blood of thy neighbor*: likewise the prohibition against hating one's brother (Lev 19:17): *Thou shalt not hate thy brother in thy heart.* To the sixth commandment which forbids adultery, is added the prohibition about whoredom, according to Dt. 23:17: *There shall be no whore among the daughters of Israel, nor whoremonger among the sons of Israel*; and the prohibition against unnatural sins, according to Lev. 28:22,23: *Thou shalt not lie with mankind . . . thou shalt not copulate with any beast.* To the seventh commandment which prohibits theft, is added the precept forbidding usury, according to Dt. 23:19: *Thou shalt not lend to thy brother money to usury*; and the prohibition against fraud, according to Dt. 25:13: *Thou shalt not have diverse weights in thy bag*; and universally all prohibitions relating to peculations and larceny. To the eighth commandment, forbidding false testimony, is added the prohibition against false judgment, according to Ex. 23:2: *Neither shalt thou yield in judgment, to the opinion of the most part, to stray from the truth*; and the prohibition against lying (Exod 23:7): *Thou shalt fly lying*, and the prohibition against detraction, according to Lev. 19:16: *Thou shalt not be a detractor, nor a whisperer among the people.* To the other two commandments no further precepts are added, because thereby are forbidden all kinds of evil desires.

REPLY OBJ. 1: The precepts of the decalogue are ordained to the love of God and our neighbor as pertaining

secundum manifestam rationem debiti, alia vero secundum rationem magis occultam.

AD SECUNDUM dicendum quod praecepta caeremonialia et iudicialia sunt determinativa praeceptorum Decalogi ex vi institutionis, non autem ex vi naturalis instinctus, sicut praecepta moralia superaddita.

AD TERTIUM dicendum quod praecepta legis ordinantur ad bonum commune, ut supra dictum est. Et quia virtutes ordinantes ad alium directe pertinent ad bonum commune; et similiter virtus castitatis, inquantum actus generationis deservit bono communi speciei; ideo de istis virtutibus directe dantur praecepta et Decalogi et superaddita. De actu autem fortitudinis datur praeceptum proponendum per duces exhortantes in bello, quod pro bono communi suscipitur, ut patet Deut. XX, ubi mandatur sacerdoti, *nolite metuere, nolite cedere*. Similiter etiam actus gulae prohibendus committitur monitioni paternae, quia contrariatur bono domestico, unde dicitur Deut. XXI, ex persona parentum, *monita nostra audire contemnit, comessationibus vacat et luxuriae atque conviviis*.

evidently to our duty towards them; but the other precepts are so ordained as pertaining thereto less evidently.

REPLY OBJ. 2: It is in virtue of their institution that the ceremonial and judicial precepts *are determinations of the precepts of the decalogue*, not by reason of a natural instinct, as in the case of the superadded moral precepts.

REPLY OBJ. 3: The precepts of a law are ordained for the common good, as stated above (Q90, A2). And since those virtues which direct our conduct towards others pertain directly to the common good, as also does the virtue of chastity, insofar as the generative act conduces to the common good of the species; hence precepts bearing directly on these virtues are given, both in the decalogue and in addition thereto. As to the act of fortitude there are the order to be given by the commanders in the war, which is undertaken for the common good: as is clear from Dt. 20:3, where the priest is commanded (to speak thus): *Be not afraid, do not give back*. In like manner the prohibition of acts of gluttony is left to paternal admonition, since it is contrary to the good of the household; hence it is said (Deut 21:20) in the person of parents: *He slighteth hearing our admonitions, he giveth himself to revelling, and to debauchery and banquetings*.

Article 12

Whether the Moral Precepts of the Old Law Justified Man?

AD DUODECIMUM SIC PROCEDITUR. Videtur quod praecepta moralia veteris legis iustificarent. Dicit enim apostolus, Rom. II, *non enim auditores legis iusti sunt apud Deum, sed factores legis iustificabuntur*. Sed factores legis dicuntur qui implent praecepta legis. Ergo praecepta legis adimpleta iustificabant.

PRAETEREA, Levit. XVIII dicitur, *custodite leges meas atque iudicia, quae faciens homo vivet in eis*. Sed vita spiritualis hominis est per iustitiam. Ergo praecepta legis adimpleta iustificabant.

PRAETEREA, lex divina efficacior est quam lex humana. Sed lex humana iustificat, est enim quaedam iustitia in hoc quod praecepta legis adimplentur. Ergo praecepta legis iustificabant.

SED CONTRA est quod apostolus dicit, II ad Cor. III, *littera occidit*. Quod secundum Augustinum, in libro de spiritu et littera, intelligitur etiam de praeceptis moralibus. Ergo praecepta moralia non iustificabant.

RESPONDEO dicendum quod, sicut sanum proprie et primo dicitur quod habet sanitatem, per posterius autem quod significat sanitatem, vel quod conservat sanitatem; ita iustificatio primo et proprie dicitur ipsa factio

OBJECTION 1: It would seem that the moral precepts of the Old Law justified man. Because the Apostle says (Rom 2:13): *For not the hearers of the Law are justified before God, but the doers of the Law shall be justified*. But the doers of the Law are those who fulfill the precepts of the Law. Therefore the fulfilling of the precepts of the Law was a cause of justification.

OBJ. 2: Further, it is written (Lev 18:5): *Keep My laws and My judgments, which if a man do, he shall live in them*. But the spiritual life of man is through justice. Therefore the fulfilling of the precepts of the Law was a cause of justification.

OBJ. 3: Further, the Divine law is more efficacious than human law. But human law justifies man; since there is a kind of justice consisting in fulfilling the precepts of law. Therefore the precepts of the Law justified man.

ON THE CONTRARY, The Apostle says (2 Cor 3:6): *The letter killeth*: which, according to Augustine (*De Spir. et Lit.* xiv), refers even to the moral precepts. Therefore the moral precepts did not cause justice.

I ANSWER THAT, Just as *healthy* is said properly and first of that which is possessed of health, and secondarily of that which is a sign or a safeguard of health; so justification means first and properly the causing of justice; while

iustitiae; secundario vero, et quasi improprie, potest dici iustificatio significatio iustitiae, vel dispositio ad iustitiam. Quibus duobus modis manifestum est quod praecepta legis iustificabant, inquantum scilicet disponebant homines ad gratiam Christi iustificantem, quam etiam significabant; quia sicut dicit Augustinus, contra Faustum, *etiam vita illius populi prophetica erat, et Christi figurativa.*

Sed si loquamur de iustificatione proprie dicta, sic considerandum est quod iustitia potest accipi prout est in habitu, vel prout est in actu, et secundum hoc, iustificatio dupliciter dicitur. Uno quidem modo, secundum quod homo fit iustus adipiscens habitum iustitiae. Alio vero modo, secundum quod opera iustitiae operatur, ut secundum hoc iustificatio nihil aliud sit quam iustitiae executio. Iustitia autem, sicut et aliae virtutes potest accipi et acquisita et infusa, ut ex supradictis patet. Acquisita quidem causatur ex operibus, sed infusa causatur ab ipso Deo per eius gratiam. Et haec est vera iustitia, de qua nunc loquimur, secundum quam aliquis dicitur iustus apud Deum; secundum illud Rom. IV, *si Abraham ex operibus legis iustificatus est, habet gloriam, sed non apud Deum.* Haec igitur iustitia causari non poterat per praecepta moralia, quae sunt de actibus humanis. Et secundum hoc, praecepta moralia iustificare non poterant iustitiam causando.

Si vero accipiatur iustificatio pro executione iustitiae, sic omnia praecepta legis iustificabant, aliter tamen et aliter. Nam praecepta caeremonialia continebant quidem iustitiam secundum se in generali, prout scilicet exhibebantur in cultum Dei, in speciali vero non continebant secundum se iustitiam, nisi ex sola determinatione legis divinae. Et ideo de huiusmodi praeceptis dicitur quod non iustificabant nisi ex devotione et obedientia facientium. Praecepta vero moralia et iudicialia continebant id quod erat secundum se iustum vel in generali, vel etiam in speciali. Sed moralia praecepta continebant id quod est secundum se iustum secundum iustitiam generalem quae est omnis virtus, ut dicitur in V Ethic. Praecepta vero iudicialia pertinebant ad iustitiam specialem, quae consistit circa contractus humanae vitae, qui sunt inter homines ad invicem.

AD PRIMUM ergo dicendum quod apostolus accipit ibi iustificationem pro executione iustitiae.

AD SECUNDUM dicendum quod homo faciens praecepta legis dicitur vivere in eis, quia non incurrebat poenam mortis, quam lex transgressoribus infligebat. In quo sensu inducit hoc apostolus, Gal. III.

AD TERTIUM dicendum quod praecepta legis humanae iustificant iustitia acquisita, de qua non quaeritur ad praesens, sed solum de iustitia quae est apud Deum.

secondarily and improperly, as it were, it may denote a sign of justice or a disposition thereto. If justice be taken in the last two ways, it is evident that it was conferred by the precepts of the Law; in so far, to wit, as they disposed men to the justifying grace of Christ, which they also signified, because as Augustine says (*Contra Faust.* xxii, 24), *even the life of that people foretold and foreshadowed Christ.*

But if we speak of justification properly so called, then we must notice that it can be considered as in the habit or as in the act: so that accordingly justification may be taken in two ways. First, according as man is made just, by becoming possessed of the habit of justice: second, according as he does works of justice, so that in this sense justification is nothing else than the execution of justice. Now justice, like the other virtues, may denote either the acquired or the infused virtue, as is clear from what has been stated (Q63, A4). The acquired virtue is caused by works; but the infused virtue is caused by God Himself through His grace. The latter is true justice, of which we are speaking now, and in this respect of which a man is said to be just before God, according to Rm. 4:2: *If Abraham were justified by works, he hath whereof to glory, but not before God.* Hence this justice could not be caused by moral precepts, which are about human actions: wherefore the moral precepts could not justify man by causing justice.

If, on the other hand, by justification we understand the execution of justice, thus all the precepts of the Law justified man, but in various ways. Because the ceremonial precepts taken as a whole contained something just in itself, insofar as they aimed at offering worship to God; whereas taken individually they contained that which is just, not in itself, but by being a determination of the Divine law. Hence it is said of these precepts that they did not justify man save through the devotion and obedience of those who complied with them. On the other hand the moral and judicial precepts, either in general or also in particular, contained that which is just in itself: but the moral precepts contained that which is just in itself according to that *general justice* which is *every virtue* according to *Ethic.* v, 1: whereas the judicial precepts belonged to *special justice*, which is about contracts connected with the human mode of life, between one man and another.

REPLY OBJ. 1: The Apostle takes justification for the execution of justice.

REPLY OBJ. 2: The man who fulfilled the precepts of the Law is said to live in them, because he did not incur the penalty of death, which the Law inflicted on its transgressors: in this sense the Apostle quotes this passage (Gal 3:12).

REPLY OBJ. 3: The precepts of human law justify man by acquired justice: it is not about this that we are inquiring now, but only about that justice which is before God.

QUESTION 101

OF THE CEREMONIAL PRECEPTS IN THEMSELVES

Consequenter considerandum est de praeceptis cae-remonialibus. Et primo, de ipsis secundum se; secundo, de causa eorum; tertio, de duratione ipsorum. Circa primum quaeruntur quatuor.

Primo, quae sit ratio praeceptorum caeremonialium.

Secundo, utrum sint figuralia.

Tertio, utrum debuerint esse multa.

Quarto, de distinctione ipsorum.

We must now consider the ceremonial precepts: and first we must consider them in themselves; second, their cause; third, their duration. Under the first head there are four points of inquiry:

(1) The nature of the ceremonial precepts;

(2) Whether they are figurative?

(3) Whether there should have been many of them?

(4) Of their various kinds.

Article 1

Whether the Nature of the Ceremonial Precepts Consists in Their Pertaining to the Worship of God?

AD PRIMUM SIC PROCEDITUR. Videtur quod ratio praeceptorum caeremonialium non in hoc consistat quod pertinent ad cultum Dei. In lege enim veteri dantur Iudaeis quaedam praecepta de abstinentia ciborum, ut patet Levit. XI; et etiam de abstinendo ab aliquibus vestimentis, sicut illud Levit. XIX, *vestem quae ex duobus texta est, non indueris*; et iterum quod praecipitur Num. XV, *ut faciant sibi fimbrias per angulos palliorum.* Sed huiusmodi non sunt praecepta moralia, quia non manent in nova lege. Nec etiam iudicialia, quia non pertinent ad iudicium faciendum inter homines. Ergo sunt caeremonialia. Sed in nullo pertinere videntur ad cultum Dei. Ergo non est ratio caeremonialium praeceptorum quod pertineant ad cultum Dei.

PRAETEREA, dicunt quidam quod praecepta caeremonialia dicuntur illa quae pertinent ad solemnitates, quasi dicerentur a cereis, qui in solemnitatibus accenduntur. Sed multa alia sunt pertinentia ad cultum Dei praeter solemnitates. Ergo non videtur quod praecepta caeremonialia ea ratione dicantur, quia pertinent ad cultum Dei.

PRAETEREA, secundum quosdam praecepta caeremonialia dicuntur quasi normae, idest regulae, salutis, nam chaire in Graeco idem est quod salve. Sed omnia praecepta legis sunt regulae salutis, et non solum illa quae pertinent ad Dei cultum. Ergo non solum illa praecepta dicuntur caeremonialia quae pertinent ad cultum Dei.

PRAETEREA, Rabbi Moyses dicit quod praecepta caeremonialia dicuntur quorum ratio non est manifesta. Sed multa pertinentia ad cultum Dei habent rationem manifestam, sicut observatio sabbati, et celebratio phase

OBJECTION 1: It would seem that the nature of the ceremonial precepts does not consist in their pertaining to the worship of God. Because, in the Old Law, the Jews were given certain precepts about abstinence from food (Lev 11); and about refraining from certain kinds of clothes, e.g., (Lev 19:19): *Thou shalt not wear a garment that is woven of two sorts*; and again (Num 15:38): *To make to themselves fringes in the corners of their garments.* But these are not moral precepts; since they do not remain in the New Law. Nor are they judicial precepts; since they do not pertain to the pronouncing of judgment between man and man. Therefore they are ceremonial precepts. Yet they seem in no way to pertain to the worship of God. Therefore the nature of the ceremonial precepts does not consist in their pertaining to Divine worship.

OBJ. 2: Further, some state that the ceremonial precepts are those which pertain to solemnities; as though they were so called from the *cerei* (candles) which are lit up on those occasions. But many other things besides solemnities pertain to the worship of God. Therefore it does not seem that the ceremonial precepts are so called from their pertaining to the Divine worship.

OBJ. 3: Further, some say that the ceremonial precepts are patterns, i.e., rules, of salvation: because the Greek {chaire} is the same as the Latin *salve*. But all the precepts of the Law are rules of salvation, and not only those that pertain to the worship of God. Therefore not only those precepts which pertain to Divine worship are called ceremonial.

OBJ. 4: Further, Rabbi Moses says (*Doct. Perplex.* iii) that the ceremonial precepts are those for which there is no evident reason. But there is evident reason for many things pertaining to the worship of God; such as the observance

et Scenopegiae, et multorum aliorum, quorum ratio assignatur in lege. Ergo caeremonialia non sunt quae pertinent ad cultum Dei.

SED CONTRA est quod dicitur Exod. XVIII, *esto populo in his quae ad Deum pertinent, ostendasque populo caeremonias et ritum colendi.*

RESPONDEO dicendum quod, sicut supra dictum est, caeremonialia praecepta determinant praecepta moralia in ordine ad Deum, sicut iudicialia determinant praecepta moralia in ordine ad proximum. Homo autem ordinatur ad Deum per debitum cultum. Et ideo caeremonialia proprie dicuntur quae ad cultum Dei pertinent. Ratio autem huius nominis posita est supra, ubi praecepta caeremonialia ab aliis sunt distincta.

AD PRIMUM ergo dicendum quod ad cultum Dei pertinent non solum sacrificia et alia huiusmodi, quae immediate ad Deum ordinari videntur, sed etiam debita praeparatio colentium Deum ad cultum ipsius, sicut etiam in aliis quaecumque sunt praeparatoria ad finem, cadunt sub scientia quae est de fine. Huiusmodi autem praecepta quae dantur in lege de vestibus et cibis colentium Deum, et aliis huiusmodi, pertinent ad quandam praeparationem ipsorum ministrantium, ut sint idonei ad cultum Dei, sicut etiam specialibus observantiis aliqui utuntur qui sunt in ministerio regis. Unde etiam sub praeceptis caeremonialibus continentur.

AD SECUNDUM dicendum quod illa expositio nominis non videtur esse multum conveniens, praesertim cum non multum inveniatur in lege quod in solemnitatibus cerei accenderentur, sed in ipso etiam candelabro lucernae cum oleo olivarum praeparabantur, ut patet Lev. XXIV. Nihilominus tamen potest dici quod in solemnitatibus omnia illa quae pertinebant ad cultum Dei, diligentius observabantur, et secundum hoc, in observatione solemnitatum omnia caeremonialia includuntur.

AD TERTIUM dicendum quod nec illa expositio nominis videtur esse multum conveniens, nomen enim caeremoniae non est Graecum, sed Latinum. Potest tamen dici quod, cum salus hominis sit a Deo, praecipue illa praecepta videntur esse salutis regulae, quae hominem ordinant ad Deum. Et sic caeremonialia dicuntur quae ad cultum Dei pertinent.

AD QUARTUM dicendum quod illa ratio caeremonialium est quodammodo probabilis, non quod ex eo dicuntur caeremonialia quia eorum ratio non est manifesta; sed hoc est quoddam consequens. Quia enim praecepta ad cultum Dei pertinentia oportet esse figuralia, ut infra dicetur, inde est quod eorum ratio non est adeo manifesta.

of the Sabbath, the feasts of the Passover and of the Tabernacles, and many other things, the reason for which is set down in the Law. Therefore the ceremonial precepts are not those which pertain to the worship of God.

ON THE CONTRARY, It is written (Exod 18:19,20): *Be thou to the people in those things that pertain to God . . . and . . . show the people the ceremonies and the manner of worshipping.*

I ANSWER THAT, As stated above (Q99, A4), the ceremonial precepts are determinations of the moral precepts whereby man is directed to God, just as the judicial precepts are determinations of the moral precepts whereby he is directed to his neighbor. Now man is directed to God by the worship due to Him. Wherefore those precepts are properly called ceremonial, which pertain to the Divine worship. The reason for their being so called was given above (Q99, A3), when we established the distinction between the ceremonial and the other precepts.

REPLY OBJ. 1: The Divine worship includes not only sacrifices and the like, which seem to be directed to God immediately, but also those things whereby His worshippers are duly prepared to worship Him: thus too in other matters, whatever is preparatory to the end comes under the science whose object is the end. Accordingly those precepts of the Law which regard the clothing and food of God's worshippers, and other such matters, pertain to a certain preparation of the ministers, with the view of fitting them for the Divine worship: just as those who administer to a king make use of certain special observances. Consequently such are contained under the ceremonial precepts.

REPLY OBJ. 2: The alleged explanation of the name does not seem very probable: especially as the Law does not contain many instances of the lighting of candles in solemnities; since, even the lamps of the Candlestick were furnished with *oil of olives*, as stated in Lev. 24:2. Nevertheless we may say that all things pertaining to the Divine worship were more carefully observed on solemn festivals: so that all ceremonial precepts may be included under the observance of solemnities.

REPLY OBJ. 3: Neither does this explanation of the name appear to be very much to the point, since the word *ceremony* is not Greek but Latin. We may say, however, that, since man's salvation is from God, those precepts above all seem to be rules of salvation, which direct man to God: and accordingly those which refer to Divine worship are called ceremonial precepts.

REPLY OBJ. 4: This explanation of the ceremonial precepts has a certain amount of probability: not that they are called ceremonial precisely because there is no evident reason for them; this is a kind of consequence. For, since the precepts referring to the Divine worship must needs be figurative, as we shall state further on (A2), the consequence is that the reason for them is not so very evident.

Article 2

Whether the Ceremonial Precepts Are Figurative?

Ad secundum sic proceditur. Videtur quod praecepta caeremonialia non sint figuralia. Pertinet enim ad officium cuiuslibet doctoris ut sic pronunciet ut de facili intelligi possit, sicut Augustinus dicit, in IV de Doctr. Christ. Et hoc maxime videtur esse necessarium in legis latione, quia praecepta legis populo proponuntur. Unde lex debet esse manifesta, ut Isidorus dicit. Si igitur praecepta caeremonialia data sunt in alicuius rei figuram, videtur inconvenienter tradidisse huiusmodi praecepta Moyses, non exponens quid figurarent.

Praeterea, ea quae in cultum Dei aguntur, maxime debent honestatem habere. Sed facere aliqua facta ad alia repraesentanda, videtur esse theatricum, sive poeticum, in theatris enim repraesentabantur olim per aliqua quae ibi gerebantur, quaedam aliorum facta. Ergo videtur quod huiusmodi non debeant fieri ad cultum Dei. Sed caeremonialia ordinantur ad cultum Dei, ut dictum est. Ergo caeremonialia non debent esse figuralia.

Praeterea, Augustinus dicit, in Enchirid., quod *Deus maxime colitur fide, spe et caritate.* Sed praecepta quae dantur de fide, spe et caritate, non sunt figuralia. Ergo praecepta caeremonialia non debent esse figuralia.

Praeterea, dominus dicit, Ioan. IV, *spiritus est Deus, et eos qui adorant eum, in spiritu et veritate adorare oportet.* Sed figura non est ipsa veritas, immo contra se invicem dividuntur. Ergo caeremonialia, quae pertinent ad cultum Dei, non debent esse figuralia.

Sed contra est quod apostolus dicit, ad Colos. II, *nemo vos iudicet in cibo aut in potu, aut in parte diei festi aut Neomeniae aut sabbatorum, quae sunt umbra futurorum.*

Respondeo dicendum quod, sicut iam dictum est, praecepta caeremonialia dicuntur quae ordinantur ad cultum Dei. Est autem duplex cultus Dei, interior, et exterior. Cum enim homo sit compositus ex anima et corpore, utrumque debet applicari ad colendum Deum, ut scilicet anima colat interiori cultu, et corpus exteriori, unde dicitur in Psalmo LXXXIII, *cor meum et caro mea exultaverunt in Deum vivum.* Et sicut corpus ordinatur in Deum per animam, ita cultus exterior ordinatur ad interiorem cultum. Consistit autem interior cultus in hoc quod anima coniungatur Deo per intellectum et affectum. Et ideo secundum quod diversimode intellectus et affectus colentis Deum Deo recte coniungitur, secundum hoc diversimode exteriores actus hominis ad cultum Dei applicantur.

Objection 1: It would seem that the ceremonial precepts are not figurative. For it is the duty of every teacher to express himself in such a way as to be easily understood, as Augustine states (*De Doctr. Christ.* iv, 4,10) and this seems very necessary in the framing of a law: because precepts of law are proposed to the populace; for which reason a law should be manifest, as Isidore declares (*Etym.* v, 21). If therefore the precepts of the Law were given as figures of something, it seems unbecoming that Moses should have delivered these precepts without explaining what they signified.

Obj. 2: Further, whatever is done for the worship of God, should be entirely free from unfittingness. But the performance of actions in representation of others, seems to savor of the theatre or of the drama: because formerly the actions performed in theatres were done to represent the actions of others. Therefore it seems that such things should not be done for the worship of God. But the ceremonial precepts are ordained to the Divine worship, as stated above (A1). Therefore they should not be figurative.

Obj. 3: Further, Augustine says (*Enchiridion* iii, iv) that *God is worshipped chiefly by faith, hope, and charity.* But the precepts of faith, hope, and charity are not figurative. Therefore the ceremonial precepts should not be figurative.

Obj. 4: Further, Our Lord said (John 4:24): *God is a spirit, and they that adore Him, must adore Him in spirit and in truth.* But a figure is not the very truth: in fact one is condivided with the other. Therefore the ceremonial precepts, which refer to the Divine worship, should not be figurative.

On the contrary, The Apostle says (Col 2:16,17): *Let no man . . . judge you in meat or in drink, or in respect of a festival day, or of the new moon, or of the sabbaths, which are a shadow of things to come.*

I answer that, As stated above (A1; Q99, AA3,4), the ceremonial precepts are those which refer to the worship of God. Now the Divine worship is twofold: internal, and external. For since man is composed of soul and body, each of these should be applied to the worship of God; the soul by an interior worship; the body by an outward worship: hence it is written (Ps 83:3): *My heart and my flesh have rejoiced in the living God.* And as the body is ordained to God through the soul, so the outward worship is ordained to the internal worship. Now interior worship consists in the soul being united to God by the intellect and affections. Wherefore according to the various ways in which the intellect and affections of the man who worships God are rightly united to God, his external actions are applied in various ways to the Divine worship.

In statu enim futurae beatitudinis, intellectus humanus ipsam divinam veritatem in seipsa intuebitur. Et ideo exterior cultus non consistet in aliqua figura, sed solum in laude Dei, quae procedit ex interiori cognitione et affectione; secundum illud Isaiae li, *gaudium et laetitia invenietur in ea, gratiarum actio et vox laudis.*

In statu autem praesentis vitae, non possumus divinam veritatem in seipsa intueri, sed oportet quod radius divinae veritatis nobis illucescat sub aliquibus sensibilibus figuris, sicut Dionysius dicit, I cap. Cael. Hier., diversimode tamen, secundum diversum statum cognitionis humanae. In veteri enim lege neque ipsa divina veritas in seipsa manifesta erat, neque etiam adhuc propalata erat via ad hoc perveniendi, sicut apostolus dicit, ad Heb. IX. Et ideo oportebat exteriorem cultum veteris legis non solum esse figurativum futurae veritatis manifestandae in patria; sed etiam esse figurativum Christi, qui est via ducens ad illam patriae veritatem. Sed in statu novae legis, haec via iam est revelata. Unde hanc praefigurari non oportet sicut futuram, sed commemorari oportet per modum praeteriti vel praesentis, sed solum oportet praefigurari futuram veritatem gloriae nondum revelatam. Et hoc est quod apostolus dicit, ad Heb. X, *umbram habet lex futurorum bonorum, non ipsam imaginem rerum*, umbra enim minus est quam imago; tanquam imago pertineat ad novam legem, umbra vero ad veterem.

AD PRIMUM ergo dicendum quod divina non sunt revelanda hominibus nisi secundum eorum capacitatem, alioquin daretur eis praecipitii materia, dum contemnerent quae capere non possent. Et ideo utilius fuit ut sub quodam figurarum velamine divina mysteria rudi populo traderentur, ut sic saltem ea implicite cognoscerent, dum illis figuris deservirent ad honorem Dei.

AD SECUNDUM dicendum quod, sicut poetica non capiuntur a ratione humana propter defectum veritatis qui est in eis, ita etiam ratio humana perfecte capere non potest divina propter excedentem ipsorum veritatem. Et ideo utrobique opus est repraesentatione per sensibiles figuras.

AD TERTIUM dicendum quod Augustinus ibi loquitur de cultu interiore; ad quem tamen ordinari oportet exteriorem cultum, ut dictum est.

ET SIMILITER dicendum est ad quartum, quia per Christum homines plenius ad spiritualem Dei cultum sunt introducti.

For in the state of future bliss, the human intellect will gaze on the Divine Truth in Itself. Wherefore the external worship will not consist in anything figurative, but solely in the praise of God, proceeding from the inward knowledge and affection, according to Is. 51:3: *Joy and gladness shall be found therein, thanksgiving and the voice of praise.*

But in the present state of life, we are unable to gaze on the Divine Truth in Itself, and we need the ray of Divine light to shine upon us under the form of certain sensible figures, as Dionysius states (*Coel. Hier.* i); in various ways, however, according to the various states of human knowledge. For under the Old Law, neither was the Divine Truth manifest in Itself, nor was the way leading to that manifestation as yet opened out, as the Apostle declares (Heb 9:8). Hence the external worship of the Old Law needed to be figurative not only of the future truth to be manifested in our heavenly country, but also of Christ, Who is the way leading to that heavenly manifestation. But under the New Law this way is already revealed: and therefore it needs no longer to be foreshadowed as something future, but to be brought to our minds as something past or present: and the truth of the glory to come, which is not yet revealed, alone needs to be foreshadowed. This is what the Apostle says (Heb 11:1): *The Law has a shadow of the good things to come, not the very image of the things*: for a shadow is less than an image; so that the image belongs to the New Law, but the shadow to the Old.

REPLY OBJ. 1: The things of God are not to be revealed to man except in proportion to his capacity: else he would be in danger of downfall, were he to despise what he cannot grasp. Hence it was more beneficial that the Divine mysteries should be revealed to uncultured people under a veil of figures, that thus they might know them at least implicitly by using those figures to the honor of God.

REPLY OBJ. 2: Just as human reason fails to grasp poetical expressions on account of their being lacking in truth, so does it fail to grasp Divine things perfectly, on account of the sublimity of the truth they contain: and therefore in both cases there is need of signs by means of sensible figures.

REPLY OBJ. 3: Augustine is speaking there of internal worship; to which, however, external worship should be ordained, as stated above.

THE SAME ANSWER applies to the Fourth Objection: because men were taught by Him to practice more perfectly the spiritual worship of God.

Article 3

Whether There Should Have Been Many Ceremonial Precepts?

AD TERTIUM SIC PROCEDITUR. Videtur quod non debuerint esse multa caeremonialia praecepta. Ea enim quae sunt ad finem, debent esse fini proportionata. Sed caeremonialia praecepta, sicut dictum est, ordinantur ad cultum Dei et in figuram Christi. Est autem *unus Deus, a quo omnia; et unus dominus Iesus Christus, per quem omnia*, ut dicitur I ad Cor. VIII. Ergo caeremonialia non debuerunt multiplicari.

PRAETEREA, multitudo caeremonialium praeceptorum transgressionis erat occasio; secundum illud quod dicit Petrus, Act. XV, *quid tentatis Deum, imponere iugum super cervicem discipulorum, quod neque nos, neque patres nostri, portare potuimus?* Sed transgressio divinorum praeceptorum contrariatur humanae saluti. Cum igitur lex omnis debeat saluti congruere hominum, ut Isidorus dicit, videtur quod non debuerint multa praecepta caeremonialia dari.

PRAETEREA, praecepta caeremonialia pertinebant ad cultum Dei exteriorem et corporalem, ut dictum est. Sed huiusmodi cultum corporalem lex debebat diminuere, quia ordinabat ad Christum, qui docuit homines Deum colere *in spiritu et veritate*, ut habetur Ioan. IV. Non ergo debuerunt multa praecepta caeremonialia dari.

SED CONTRA est quod dicitur Osee VIII, *scribam eis multiplices leges intus;* et Iob XI, ut *ostenderet tibi secreta sapientiae, quod multiplex sit lex eius.*

RESPONDEO dicendum quod, sicut supra dictum est, omnis lex alicui populo datur. In populo autem duo genera hominum continentur, quidam proni ad malum, qui sunt per praecepta legis coercendi, ut supra dictum est; quidam habentes inclinationem ad bonum, vel ex natura vel ex consuetudine, vel magis ex gratia; et tales sunt per legis praeceptum instruendi et in melius promovendi. Quantum igitur ad utrumque genus hominum, expediebat praecepta caeremonialia in veteri lege multiplicari. Erant enim in illo populo aliqui ad idololatriam proni, et ideo necesse erat ut ab idololatriae cultu per praecepta caeremonialia revocarentur ad cultum Dei. Et quia multipliciter homines idololatriae deserviebant, oportebat e contrario multa institui ad singula reprimenda, et iterum multa talibus imponi, ut, quasi oneratis ex his quae ad cultum Dei impenderent, non vacaret idololatriae deservire. Ex parte vero eorum qui erant prompti ad bonum, etiam necessaria fuit multiplicatio caeremonialium praeceptorum. Tum quia per hoc diversimode mens eorum referebatur in Deum, et magis assidue. Tum etiam quia mysterium Christi, quod per huiusmodi caeremonialia figurabatur, multiplices utilitates attulit

OBJECTION 1: It would seem that there should not have been many ceremonial precepts. For those things which conduce to an end should be proportionate to that end. But the ceremonial precepts, as stated above (AA1,2), are ordained to the worship of God, and to the foreshadowing of Christ. Now *there is but one God, of Whom are all things . . . and one Lord Jesus Christ, by Whom are all things* (1 Cor 8:6). Therefore there should not have been many ceremonial precepts.

OBJ. 2: Further, the great number of the ceremonial precepts was an occasion of transgression, according to the words of Peter (Acts 15:10): *Why tempt you God, to put a yoke upon the necks of the disciples, which neither our fathers nor we have been able to bear?* Now the transgression of the Divine precepts is an obstacle to man's salvation. Since, therefore, every law should conduce to man's salvation, as Isidore says (*Etym.* v, 3), it seems that the ceremonial precepts should not have been given in great number.

OBJ. 3: Further, the ceremonial precepts referred to the outward and bodily worship of God, as stated above (A2). But the Law should have lessened this bodily worship: since it directed men to Christ, Who taught them to worship God *in spirit and in truth*, as stated in Jn. 4:23. Therefore there should not have been many ceremonial precepts.

ON THE CONTRARY, (Hos 8:12): *I shall write to them My manifold laws;* and (Job 11:6): *That He might show thee the secrets of His wisdom, and that His Law is manifold.*

I ANSWER THAT, As stated above (Q96, A1), every law is given to a people. Now a people contains two kinds of men: some, prone to evil, who have to be coerced by the precepts of the law, as stated above (Q95, A1); some, inclined to good, either from nature or from custom, or rather from grace; and the like have to be taught and improved by means of the precepts of the law. Accordingly, with regard to both kinds of the law. Accordingly, with regard to both kinds of men it was expedient that the Old Law should contain many ceremonial precepts. For in that people there were many prone to idolatry; wherefore it was necessary to recall them by means of ceremonial precepts from the worship of idols to the worship of God. And since men served idols in many ways, it was necessary on the other hand to devise many means of repressing every single one: and again, to lay many obligations on such like men, in order that being burdened, as it were, by their duties to the Divine worship, they might have no time for the service of idols. As to those who were inclined to good, it was again necessary that there should be many ceremonial precepts; both because thus their mind turned to God in many ways, and more continually; and because the mystery of Christ,

mundo, et multa circa ipsum consideranda erant, quae oportuit per diversa caeremonialia figurari.

AD PRIMUM ergo dicendum quod, quando id quod ordinatur ad finem, est sufficiens ad ducendum in finem, tunc sufficit unum ad unum finem, sicut una medicina, si sit efficax, sufficit quandoque ad sanitatem inducendam, et tunc non oportet multiplicari medicinam. Sed propter debilitatem et imperfectionem eius quod est ad finem, oportet eam multiplicari, sicut multa remedia adhibentur infirmo, quando unum non sufficit ad sanandum. Caeremoniae autem veteris legis invalidae et imperfectae erant et ad repraesentandum Christi mysterium, quod est superexcellens; et ad subiugandum mentes hominum Deo. Unde apostolus dicit, ad Heb. VII, *reprobatio fit praecedentis mandati, propter infirmitatem et inutilitatem, nihil enim ad perfectum adduxit lex.* Et ideo oportuit huiusmodi caeremonias multiplicari.

AD SECUNDUM dicendum quod sapientis legislatoris est minores transgressiones permittere, ut maiores caveantur. Et ideo, ut caveretur transgressio idololatriae, et superbiae quae in Iudaeorum cordibus nasceretur si omnia praecepta legis implerent, non propter hoc praetermisit Deus multa caeremonialia praecepta tradere, quia de facili sumebant ex hoc transgrediendi occasionem.

AD TERTIUM dicendum quod vetus lex in multis diminuit corporalem cultum. Propter quod statuit quod non in omni loco sacrificia offerrentur, neque a quibuslibet. Et multa huiusmodi statuit ad diminutionem exterioris cultus; sicut etiam Rabbi Moyses Aegyptius dicit. Oportebat tamen non ita attenuare corporalem cultum Dei, ut homines ad cultum Daemonum declinarent.

which was foreshadowed by these ceremonial precepts, brought many boons to the world, and afforded men many considerations, which needed to be signified by various ceremonies.

REPLY OBJ. 1: When that which conduces to an end is sufficient to conduce thereto, then one such thing suffices for one end: thus one remedy, if it be efficacious, suffices sometimes to restore men to health, and then the remedy needs not to be repeated. But when that which conduces to an end is weak and imperfect, it needs to be multiplied: thus many remedies are given to a sick man, when one is not enough to heal him. Now the ceremonies of the Old Law were weak and imperfect, both for representing the mystery of Christ, on account of its surpassing excellence; and for subjugating men's minds to God. Hence the Apostle says (Heb 7:18,19): *There is a setting aside of the former commandment because of the weakness and unprofitableness thereof, for the law brought nothing to perfection.* Consequently these ceremonies needed to be in great number.

REPLY OBJ. 2: A wise lawgiver should suffer lesser transgressions, that the greater may be avoided. And therefore, in order to avoid the sin of idolatry, and the pride which would arise in the hearts of the Jews, were they to fulfill all the precepts of the Law, the fact that they would in consequence find many occasions of disobedience did not prevent God from giving them many ceremonial precepts.

REPLY OBJ. 3: The Old Law lessened bodily worship in many ways. Thus it forbade sacrifices to be offered in every place and by any person. Many such like things did it enact for the lessening of bodily worship; as Rabbi Moses, the Egyptian testifies (*Doct. Perplex.* iii). Nevertheless it behooved not to attenuate the bodily worship of God so much as to allow men to fall away into the worship of idols.

Article 4

Whether the Ceremonies of the Old Law Are Suitably Divided into Sacrifices, Sacred Things, Sacraments, and Observances?

AD QUARTUM SIC PROCEDITUR. Videtur quod caeremoniae veteris legis inconvenienter dividantur in sacrificia, sacra, sacramenta et observantias. Caeremoniae enim veteris legis figurabant Christum. Sed hoc solum fiebat per sacrificia, per quae figurabatur sacrificium quo Christus *se obtulit oblationem et hostiam Deo*, ut dicitur ad Ephes. V. Ergo sola sacrificia erant caeremonialia.

PRAETEREA, vetus lex ordinabatur ad novam. Sed in nova lege ipsum sacrificium est sacramentum altaris. Ergo in veteri lege non debuerunt distingui sacramenta contra sacrificia.

OBJECTION 1: It would seem that the ceremonies of the Old Law are unsuitably divided into *sacrifices, sacred things, sacraments, and observances*. For the ceremonies of the Old Law foreshadowed Christ. But this was done only by the sacrifices, which foreshadowed the sacrifice in which Christ *delivered Himself an oblation and a sacrifice to God* (Eph 5:2). Therefore none but the sacrifices were ceremonies.

OBJ. 2: Further, the Old Law was ordained to the New. But in the New Law the sacrifice is the Sacrament of the Altar. Therefore in the Old Law there should be no distinction between *sacrifices* and *sacraments*.

PRAETEREA, sacrum dicitur quod est Deo dicatum, secundum quem modum tabernaculum et vasa eius sacrificari dicebantur. Sed omnia caeremonialia erant ordinata ad cultum Dei, ut dictum est. Ergo caeremonialia omnia sacra erant. Non ergo una pars caeremonialium debet sacra nominari.

PRAETEREA, observantiae ab observando dicuntur. Sed omnia praecepta legis observari debebant, dicitur enim Deut. VIII, *observa et cave ne quando obliviscaris domini Dei tui, et negligas mandata eius atque iudicia et caeremonias*. Non ergo observantiae debent poni una pars caeremonialium.

PRAETEREA, solemnitates inter caeremonialia computantur, cum sint in umbram futuri, ut patet ad Colos. II. Similiter etiam oblationes et munera; ut patet per apostolum, ad Heb. IX. Quae tamen sub nullo horum contineri videntur. Ergo inconveniens est praedicta distinctio caeremonialium.

SED CONTRA est quod in veteri lege singula praedicta caeremoniae vocantur. Sacrificia enim dicuntur caeremoniae Num. XV, *offerat vitulum et sacrificia eius ac libamenta, ut caeremoniae eius postulant*. De sacramento etiam ordinis dicitur Levit. VII, *haec est unctio Aaron et filiorum eius in caeremoniis*. De sacris etiam dicitur Exod. XXXVIII, haec sunt *instrumenta tabernaculi testimonii in caeremoniis Levitarum*. De observantiis etiam dicitur III Reg. IX, *si aversi fueritis, non sequentes me, nec observantes caeremonias quas proposui vobis*.

RESPONDEO dicendum quod, sicut supra dictum est, caeremonialia praecepta ordinantur ad cultum Dei. In quo quidem cultu considerari possunt et ipse cultus, et colentes, et instrumenta colendi. Ipse autem cultus specialiter consistit in sacrificiis, quae in Dei reverentiam offeruntur. Instrumenta autem colendi pertinent ad sacra, sicut est tabernaculum, et vasa, et alia huiusmodi. Ex parte autem colentium duo possunt considerari. Scilicet et eorum institutio ad cultum divinum, quod fit per quandam consecrationem vel populi, vel ministrorum, et ad hoc pertinent sacramenta. Et iterum eorum singularis conversatio, per quam distinguuntur ab his qui Deum non colunt, et ad hoc pertinent observantiae, puta in cibis et vestimentis et aliis huiusmodi.

AD PRIMUM ergo dicendum quod sacrificia oportebat offerri et in aliquibus locis, et per aliquos homines, et totum hoc ad cultum Dei pertinet. Unde sicut per sacrificia significatur Christus immolatus, ita etiam per sacramenta et sacra illorum figurabantur sacramenta et sacra novae legis; et per eorum observantias figurabatur conversatio populi novae legis. Quae omnia ad Christum pertinent.

OBJ. 3: Further, a *sacred thing* is something dedicated to God: in which sense the tabernacle and its vessels were said to be consecrated. But all the ceremonial precepts were ordained to the worship of God, as stated above (A1). Therefore all ceremonies were sacred things. Therefore *sacred things* should not be taken as a part of the ceremonies.

OBJ. 4: Further, *observances* are so called from having to be observed. But all the precepts of the Law had to be observed: for it is written (Deut 8:11): *Observe and beware lest at any time thou forget the Lord thy God, and neglect His commandments and judgments and ceremonies*. Therefore the *observances* should not be considered as a part of the ceremonies.

OBJ. 5: Further, the solemn festivals are reckoned as part of the ceremonial: since they were a shadow of things to come (Col 2:16,17): and the same may be said of the oblations and gifts, as appears from the words of the Apostle (Heb 9:9): and yet these do not seem to be inclined in any of those mentioned above. Therefore the above division of ceremonies is unsuitable.

ON THE CONTRARY, In the Old Law each of the above is called a ceremony. For the sacrifices are called ceremonies (Num 15:24): *They shall offer a calf... and the sacrifices and libations thereof, as the ceremonies require*. Of the sacrament of Order it is written (Lev 7:35): *This is the anointing of Aaron and his sons in the ceremonies*. Of sacred things also it is written (Exod 38:21): *These are the instruments of the tabernacle of the testimony ... in the ceremonies of the Levites*. And again of the observances it is written (3 Kgs 9:6): *If you ... shall turn away from following Me, and will not observe My ... ceremonies which I have set before you*.

I ANSWER THAT, As stated above (AA1,2), the ceremonial precepts are ordained to the Divine worship. Now in this worship we may consider the worship itself, the worshippers, and the instruments of worship. The worship consists specially in *sacrifices*, which are offered up in honor of God. The instruments of worship refer to the *sacred things*, such as the tabernacle, the vessels and so forth. With regard to the worshippers two points may be considered. The first point is their preparation for Divine worship, which is effected by a sort of consecration either of the people or of the ministers; and to this the *sacraments* refer. The second point is their particular mode of life, whereby they are distinguished from those who do not worship God: and to this pertain the *observances*, for instance, in matters of food, clothing, and so forth.

REPLY OBJ. 1: It was necessary for the sacrifices to be offered both in some certain place and by some certain men: and all this pertained to the worship of God. Wherefore just as their sacrifices signified Christ the victim, so too their sacraments and sacred things of the New Law; while their observances foreshadowed the mode of life of the people under the New Law: all of which things pertain to Christ.

AD SECUNDUM dicendum quod sacrificium novae legis, idest Eucharistia, continet ipsum Christum, qui est sanctificationis auctor, sanctificavit enim per suum sanguinem populum, ut dicitur ad Heb. ult. Et ideo hoc sacrificium etiam est sacramentum. Sed sacrificia veteris legis non continebant Christum, sed ipsum figurabant, et ideo non dicuntur sacramenta. Sed ad hoc designandum seorsum erant quaedam sacramenta in veteri lege, quae erant figurae futurae consecrationis. Quamvis etiam quibusdam consecrationibus quaedam sacrificia adiungerentur.

AD TERTIUM dicendum quod etiam sacrificia et sacramenta erant sacra. Sed quaedam erant quae erant sacra, utpote ad cultum Dei dicata, nec tamen erant sacrificia nec sacramenta, et ideo retinebant sibi commune nomen sacrorum.

AD QUARTUM dicendum quod ea quae pertinebant ad conversationem populi colentis Deum, retinebant sibi commune nomen observantiarum, inquantum a praemissis deficiebant. Non enim dicebantur sacra, quia non habebant immediatum respectum ad cultum Dei, sicut tabernaculum et vasa eius. Sed per quandam consequentiam erant caeremonialia, inquantum pertinebant ad quandam idoneitatem populi colentis Deum.

AD QUINTUM dicendum quod, sicut sacrificia offerebantur in determinato loco ita etiam offerebantur in determinatis temporibus, unde etiam solemnitates inter sacra computari videntur. Oblationes autem et munera computantur cum sacrificiis, quia Deo offerebantur, unde apostolus dicit, ad Heb. V, *omnis pontifex ex hominibus assumptus, pro hominibus constituitur in his quae sunt ad Deum, ut offerat dona et sacrificia.*

REPLY OBJ. 2: The sacrifice of the New Law, viz., the Eucharist, contains Christ Himself, the Author of our Sanctification: for He sanctified *the people by His own blood* (Heb 13:12). Hence this Sacrifice is also a sacrament. But the sacrifices of the Old Law did not contain Christ, but foreshadowed Him; hence they are not called sacraments. In order to signify this there were certain sacraments apart from the sacrifices of the Old Law, which sacraments were figures of the sanctification to come. Nevertheless to certain consecrations certain sacrifices were united.

REPLY OBJ. 3: The sacrifices and sacraments were of course sacred things. But certain things were sacred, through being dedicated to the Divine worship, and yet were not sacrifices or sacraments: wherefore they retained the common designation of sacred things.

REPLY OBJ. 4: Those things which pertained to the mode of life of the people who worshipped God, retained the common designation of observances, insofar as they fell short of the above. For they were not called sacred things, because they had no immediate connection with the worship of God, such as the tabernacle and its vessels had. But by a sort of consequence they were matters of ceremony, insofar as they affected the fitness of the people who worshipped God.

REPLY OBJ. 5: Just as the sacrifices were offered in a fixed place, so were they offered at fixed times: for which reason the solemn festivals seem to be reckoned among the sacred things. The oblations and gifts are counted together with the sacrifices; hence the Apostle says (Heb 5:1): *Every high-priest taken from among men, is ordained for men in things that appertain to God, that he may offer up gifts and sacrifices.*

QUESTION 102

OF THE CAUSES OF THE CEREMONIAL PRECEPTS

Deinde considerandum est de causis caeremonialium praeceptorum. Et circa hoc quaeruntur sex.

Primo, utrum praecepta caeremonialia habeant causam.

Secundo, utrum habeant causam litteralem, vel solum figuralem.

Tertio, de causis sacrificiorum.

Quarto, de causis sacramentorum.

Quinto, de causis sacrorum.

Sexto, de causis observantiarum.

We must now consider the causes of the ceremonial precepts: under which head there are six points of inquiry:

(1) Whether there was any cause for the ceremonial precepts?

(2) Whether the cause of the ceremonial precepts was literal or figurative?

(3) The causes of the sacrifices;

(4) The causes of the sacraments;

(5) The causes of the sacred things;

(6) The causes of the observances.

Article 1

Whether There Was Any Cause for the Ceremonial Precepts?

AD PRIMUM SIC PROCEDITUR. Videtur quod caeremonialia praecepta non habeant causam. Quia super illud Ephes. II, *legem mandatorum decretis evacuans*, dicit Glossa, *idest, evacuans legem veterem quantum ad carnales observantias, decretis, idest praeceptis evangelicis, quae ex ratione sunt.* Sed si observantiae veteris legis ex ratione erant, frustra evacuarentur per rationabilia decreta novae legis. Non ergo caeremoniales observantiae veteris legis habebant aliquam rationem.

PRAETEREA, vetus lex successit legi naturae. Sed in lege naturae fuit aliquod praeceptum quod nullam rationem habebat nisi ut hominis obedientia probaretur; sicut Augustinus dicit, VIII super Gen. ad Litt., de prohibitione ligni vitae. Ergo etiam in veteri lege aliqua praecepta danda erant in quibus hominis obedientia probaretur, quae de se nullam rationem haberent.

PRAETEREA, opera hominis dicuntur moralia secundum quod sunt a ratione. Si igitur caeremonialium praeceptorum sit aliqua ratio, non different a moralibus praeceptis. Videtur ergo quod caeremonialia praecepta non habeant aliquam causam, ratio enim praecepti ex aliqua causa sumitur.

SED CONTRA est quod dicitur in Psalmo XVIII, *praeceptum domini lucidum, illuminans oculos.* Sed caeremonialia sunt praecepta Dei. Ergo sunt lucida. Quod non esset nisi haberent rationabilem causam. Ergo praecepta caeremonialia habent rationabilem causam.

RESPONDEO dicendum quod, cum *sapientis sit ordinare*, secundum philosophum, in I Metaphys., ea quae ex divina sapientia procedunt, oportet esse ordinata, ut

OBJECTION 1: It would seem that there was no cause for the ceremonial precepts. Because on Eph. 2:15, *Making void the law of the commandments*, the gloss says, (i.e.) *making void the Old Law as to the carnal observances, by substituting decrees, i.e., evangelical precepts, which are based on reason.* But if the observances of the Old Law were based on reason, it would have been useless to void them by the reasonable decrees of the New Law. Therefore there was no reason for the ceremonial observances of the Old Law.

OBJ. 2: Further, the Old Law succeeded the law of nature. But in the law of nature there was a precept for which there was no reason save that man's obedience might be tested; as Augustine says (*Gen ad lit.* viii, 6,13), concerning the prohibition about the tree of life. Therefore in the Old Law there should have been some precepts for the purpose of testing man's obedience, having no reason in themselves.

OBJ. 3: Further, man's works are called moral according as they proceed from reason. If therefore there is any reason for the ceremonial precepts, they would not differ from the moral precepts. It seems therefore that there was no cause for the ceremonial precepts: for the reason of a precept is taken from some cause.

ON THE CONTRARY, It is written (Ps 18:9): *The commandment of the Lord is lightsome, enlightening the eyes.* But the ceremonial precepts are commandments of God. Therefore they are lightsome: and yet they would not be so, if they had no reasonable cause. Therefore the ceremonial precepts have a reasonable cause.

I ANSWER THAT, Since, according to the Philosopher (*Metaph.* i, 2), it is the function of a *wise man to do everything in order*, those things which proceed from the Divine

apostolus dicit, ad Rom. XIII. Ad hoc autem quod aliqua sint ordinata, duo requiruntur. Primo quidem, quod aliqua ordinentur ad debitum finem, qui est principium totius ordinis in rebus agendis, ea enim quae casu eveniunt praeter intentionem finis, vel quae non serio fiunt sed ludo, dicimus esse inordinata. Secundo oportet quod id quod est ad finem, sit proportionatum fini. Et ex hoc sequitur quod ratio eorum quae sunt ad finem, sumitur ex fine, sicut ratio dispositionis serrae sumitur ex sectione, quae est finis eius, ut dicitur in II Physic. Manifestum est autem quod praecepta caeremonialia, sicut et omnia alia praecepta legis, sunt ex divina sapientia instituta, unde dicitur Deut. IV, *haec est sapientia vestra et intellectus coram populis.* Unde necesse est dicere quod praecepta caeremonialia sint ordinata ad aliquem finem, ex quo eorum rationabiles causae assignari possunt.

AD PRIMUM ergo dicendum quod observantiae veteris legis possunt dici sine ratione quantum ad hoc, quod ipsa facta in sui natura rationem non habebant, puta quod vestis non conficeretur ex lana et lino. Poterant tamen habere rationem ex ordine ad aliud, inquantum scilicet vel aliquid per hoc figurabatur, vel aliquid excludebatur. Sed decreta novae legis, quae praecipue consistunt in fide et dilectione Dei, ex ipsa natura actus rationabilia sunt.

AD SECUNDUM dicendum quod prohibitio ligni scientiae boni et mali non fuit propter hoc quod illud lignum esset naturaliter malum, sed tamen ipsa prohibitio habuit aliquam rationem ex ordine ad aliud, inquantum scilicet per hoc aliquid figurabatur. Et sic etiam caeremonialia praecepta veteris legis habent rationem in ordine ad aliud.

AD TERTIUM dicendum quod praecepta moralia secundum suam naturam habent rationabiles causas, sicut, non occides, non furtum facies. Sed praecepta caeremonialia habent rationabiles causas ex ordine ad aliud, ut dictum est.

wisdom must needs be well ordered, as the Apostle states (Rom 13:1). Now there are two conditions required for things to be well ordered. First, that they be ordained to their due end, which is the principle of the whole order in matters of action: since those things that happen by chance outside the intention of the end, or which are not done seriously but for fun, are said to be inordinate. Second, that which is done in view of the end should be proportionate to the end. From this it follows that the reason for whatever conduces to the end is taken from the end: thus the reason for the disposition of a saw is taken from cutting, which is its end, as stated in *Phys.* ii, 9. Now it is evident that the ceremonial precepts, like all the other precepts of the Law, were institutions of Divine wisdom: hence it is written (Deut 4:6): *This is your wisdom and understanding in the sight of nations.* Consequently we must needs say that the ceremonial precepts were ordained to a certain end, wherefrom their reasonable causes can be gathered.

REPLY OBJ. 1: It may be said there was no reason for the observances of the Old Law, in the sense that there was no reason in the very nature of the thing done: for instance that a garment should not be made of wool and linen. But there could be a reason for them in relation to something else: namely, insofar as something was signified or excluded thereby. On the other hand, the decrees of the New Law, which refer chiefly to faith and the love of God, are reasonable from the very nature of the act.

REPLY OBJ. 2: The reason for the prohibition concerning the tree of knowledge of good and evil was not that this tree was naturally evil: and yet this prohibition was reasonable in its relation to something else, in as much as it signified something. And so also the ceremonial precepts of the Old Law were reasonable on account of their relation to something else.

REPLY OBJ. 3: The moral precepts in their very nature have reasonable causes: as for instance, *Thou shalt not kill, Thou shalt not steal.* But the ceremonial precepts have a reasonable cause in their relation to something else, as stated above.

Article 2

Whether the Ceremonial Precepts Have a Literal Cause or Merely a Figurative Cause?

AD SECUNDUM SIC PROCEDITUR. Videtur quod praecepta caeremonialia non habeant causam litteralem, sed figuralem tantum. Inter praecepta enim caeremonialia praecipua erant circumcisio, et immolatio agni paschalis. Sed utrumque istorum non habebat nisi causam figuralem, quia utrumque istorum datum est in signum. Dicitur enim Gen. XVII, *circumcidetis carnem praeputii vestri, ut sit in signum foederis inter me et vos.*

OBJECTION 1: It would seem that the ceremonial precepts have not a literal, but merely a figurative cause. For among the ceremonial precepts, the chief was circumcision and the sacrifice of the paschal lamb. But neither of these had any but a figurative cause: because each was given as a sign. For it is written (Gen 17:11): *You shall circumcise the flesh of your foreskin, that it may be a sign of the covenant between Me and you*: and of the celebration of the Passover

Et de celebratione phase dicitur Exod. XIII, *erit quasi signum in manu tua, et quasi monumentum ante oculos tuos*. Ergo multo magis alia caeremonialia non habent nisi causam figuralem.

Praeterea, effectus proportionatur suae causae. Sed omnia caeremonialia sunt figuralia, ut supra dictum est. Ergo non habent nisi causam figuralem.

Praeterea, illud quod de se est indifferens utrum sic vel non sic fiat, non videtur habere aliquam litteralem causam. Sed quaedam sunt in praeceptis caeremonialibus quae non videntur differre utrum sic vel sic fiant, sicut est de numero animalium offerendorum, et aliis huiusmodi particularibus circumstantiis. Ergo praecepta veteris legis non habent rationem litteralem.

Sed contra, sicut praecepta caeremonialia figurabant Christum, ita etiam historiae veteris testamenti, dicitur enim I ad Cor. X, quod omnia in figuram contingebant illis. Sed in historiis veteris testamenti, praeter intellectum mysticum seu figuralem, est etiam intellectus litteralis. Ergo etiam praecepta caeremonialia, praeter causas figurales, habebant etiam causas litterales.

Respondeo dicendum quod, sicut supra dictum est, ratio eorum quae sunt ad finem, oportet quod a fine sumatur. Finis autem praeceptorum caeremonialium est duplex, ordinabatur enim ad cultum Dei pro tempore illo, et ad figurandum Christum; sicut etiam verba prophetarum sic respiciebant praesens tempus, quod etiam in figuram futuri dicebantur, ut Hieronymus dicit, super Osee. Sic igitur rationes praeceptorum caeremonialium veteris legis dupliciter accipi possunt. Uno modo, ex ratione cultus divini qui erat pro tempore illo observandus. Et rationes istae sunt litterales, sive pertineant ad vitandum idololatriae cultum; sive ad rememoranda aliqua Dei beneficia; sive ad insinuandam excellentiam divinam; vel etiam ad designandam dispositionem mentis quae tunc requirebatur in colentibus Deum. Alio modo possunt eorum rationes assignari secundum quod ordinantur ad figurandum Christum. Et sic habent rationes figurales et mysticas, sive accipiantur ex ipso Christo et Ecclesia, quod pertinet ad allegoriam; sive ad mores populi Christiani, quod pertinet ad moralitatem; sive ad statum futurae gloriae, prout in eam introducimur per Christum, quod pertinet ad anagogiam.

Ad primum ergo dicendum quod, sicut intellectus metaphoricae locutionis in Scripturis est litteralis, quia verba ad hoc proferuntur ut hoc significent; ita etiam significationes caeremoniarum legis quae sunt commemorativae beneficiorum Dei propter quae instituta sunt, vel aliorum huiusmodi quae ad illum statum pertinebant, non transcendunt ordinem litteralium causarum.

it is written (Exod 13:9): *It shall be as a sign in thy hand, and as a memorial before thy eyes*. Therefore much more did the other ceremonial precepts have none but a figurative reason.

Obj. 2: Further, an effect is proportionate to its cause. But all the ceremonial precepts are figurative, as stated above (Q101, A2). Therefore they have no other than a figurative cause.

Obj. 3: Further, if it be a matter of indifference whether a certain thing, considered in itself, be done in a particular way or not, it seems that it has not a literal cause. Now there are certain points in the ceremonial precepts, which appear to be a matter of indifference, as to whether they be done in one way or in another: for instance, the number of animals to be offered, and other such particular circumstances. Therefore there is no literal cause for the precepts of the Old Law.

On the contrary, Just as the ceremonial precepts foreshadowed Christ, so did the stories of the Old Testament: for it is written (1 Cor 10:11) that *all (these things) happened to them in figure*. Now in the stories of the Old Testament, besides the mystical or figurative, there is the literal sense. Therefore the ceremonial precepts had also literal, besides their figurative causes.

I answer that, As stated above (A1), the reason for whatever conduces to an end must be taken from that end. Now the end of the ceremonial precepts was twofold: for they were ordained to the Divine worship, for that particular time, and to the foreshadowing of Christ; just as the words of the prophets regarded the time being in such a way as to be utterances figurative of the time to come, as Jerome says on Osee 1:3. Accordingly the reasons for the ceremonial precepts of the Old Law can be taken in two ways. First, in respect of the Divine worship which was to be observed for that particular time: and these reasons are literal: whether they refer to the shunning of idolatry; or recall certain Divine benefits; or remind men of the Divine excellence; or point out the disposition of mind which was then required in those who worshipped God. Second, their reasons can be gathered from the point of view of their being ordained to foreshadow Christ: and thus their reasons are figurative and mystical: whether they be taken from Christ Himself and the Church, which pertains to the allegorical sense; or to the morals of the Christian people, which pertains to the moral sense; or to the state of future glory, in as much as we are brought thereto by Christ, which refers to the anagogical sense.

Reply Obj. 1: Just as the use of metaphorical expressions in Scripture belongs to the literal sense, because the words are employed in order to convey that particular meaning; so also the meaning of those legal ceremonies which commemorated certain Divine benefits, on account of which they were instituted, and of others similar which belonged to that time, does not go beyond the order of

Unde quod assignetur causa celebrationis phase quia est signum liberationis ex Aegypto, et quod circumcisio est signum pacti quod Deus habuit cum Abraham, pertinet ad causam litteralem.

AD SECUNDUM dicendum quod ratio illa procederet, si caeremonialia praecepta essent data solum ad figurandum futurum, non autem ad praesentialiter Deum colendum.

AD TERTIUM dicendum quod, sicut in legibus humanis dictum est quod in universali habent rationem, non autem quantum ad particulares conditiones, sed haec sunt ex arbitrio instituentium; ita etiam multae particulares determinationes in caeremoniis veteris legis non habent aliquam causam litteralem, sed solam figuralem; in communi vero habent etiam causam litteralem.

literal causes. Consequently when we assert that the cause of the celebration of the Passover was its signification of the delivery from Egypt, or that circumcision was a sign of God's covenant with Abraham, we assign the literal cause.

REPLY OBJ. 2: This argument would avail if the ceremonial precepts had been given merely as figures of things to come, and not for the purpose of worshipping God then and there.

REPLY OBJ. 3: As we have stated when speaking of human laws (Q96, AA1,6), there is a reason for them in the abstract, but not in regard to particular conditions, which depend on the judgment of those who frame them; so also many particular determinations in the ceremonies of the Old Law have no literal cause, but only a figurative cause; whereas in the abstract they have a literal cause.

Article 3

Whether a Suitable Cause Can Be Assigned for the Ceremonies Which Pertained to Sacrifices?

AD TERTIUM SIC PROCEDITUR. Videtur quod non possit conveniens ratio assignari caeremoniarum quae ad sacrificia pertinent. Ea enim quae in sacrificium offerebantur, sunt illa quae sunt necessaria ad sustentandam humanam vitam, sicut animalia quaedam, et panes quidam. Sed tali sustentamento Deus non indiget; secundum illud Psalmi XLIX, *numquid manducabo carnes taurorum, aut sanguinem hircorum potabo?* Ergo inconvenienter huiusmodi sacrificia Deo offerebantur.

PRAETEREA, in sacrificium divinum non offerebantur nisi de tribus generibus animalium quadrupedum, scilicet de genere bovum, ovium et caprarum; et de avibus, communiter quidem turtur et columba; specialiter autem in emundatione leprosi fiebat sacrificium de passeribus. Multa autem alia animalia sunt eis nobiliora. Cum igitur omne quod est optimum Deo sit exhibendum, videtur quod non solum de istis rebus fuerint Deo sacrificia offerenda.

PRAETEREA, sicut homo a Deo habet dominium volatilium et bestiarum, ita etiam piscium. Inconvenienter igitur pisces a divino sacrificio excludebantur.

PRAETEREA, indifferenter offerri mandantur turtures et columbae. Sicut igitur mandantur offerri pulli columbarum, ita etiam pulli turturum.

PRAETEREA, Deus est auctor vitae non solum hominum, sed etiam animalium; ut patet per id quod dicitur Gen. I. Mors autem opponitur vitae. Non ergo debuerunt Deo offerri animalia occisa, sed magis animalia viventia. Praecipue quia etiam apostolus monet, Rom. XII,

OBJECTION 1: It would seem that no suitable cause can be assigned for the ceremonies pertaining to sacrifices. For those things which were offered in sacrifice, are those which are necessary for sustaining human life: such as certain animals and certain loaves. But God needs no such sustenance; according to Ps. 49:13: *Shall I eat the flesh of bullocks? Or shall I drink the blood of goats?* Therefore such sacrifices were unfittingly offered to God.

OBJ. 2: Further, only three kinds of quadrupeds were offered in sacrifice to God, viz., oxen, sheep and goats; of birds, generally the turtledove and the dove; but specially, in the cleansing of a leper, an offering was made of sparrows. Now many other animals are more noble than these. Since therefore whatever is best should be offered to God, it seems that not only of these three should sacrifices have been offered to Him.

OBJ. 3: Further, just as man has received from God the dominion over birds and beasts, so also has he received dominion over fishes. Consequently it was unfitting for fishes to be excluded from the divine sacrifices.

OBJ. 4: Further, turtledoves and doves indifferently are commanded to be offered up. Since then the young of the dove are commanded to be offered, so also should the young of the turtledove.

OBJ. 5: Further, God is the Author of life, not only of men, but also of animals, as is clear from Gn. 1:20, seqq. Now death is opposed to life. Therefore it was fitting that living animals rather than slain animals should be offered to God, especially as the Apostle admonishes us (Rom 12:1),

ut exhibeamus nostra corpora hostiam viventem, sanctam, Deo placentem.

Praeterea, si animalia Deo in sacrificium non offerebantur nisi occisa, nulla videtur esse differentia qualiter occidantur. Inconvenienter igitur determinatur modus immolationis, praecipue in avibus, ut patet Levit. I.

Praeterea, omnis defectus animalis via est ad corruptionem et mortem. Si igitur animalia occisa Deo offerebantur, inconveniens fuit prohibere oblationem animalis imperfecti, puta claudi aut caeci, aut aliter maculosi.

Praeterea, illi qui offerunt hostias Deo, debent de his participare; secundum illud apostoli, I Cor. X, *nonne qui edunt hostias, participes sunt altaris?* Inconvenienter igitur quaedam partes hostiarum offerentibus subtrahebantur, scilicet sanguis et adeps, et pectusculum et armus dexter.

Praeterea, sicut holocausta offerebantur in honorem Dei, ita etiam hostiae pacificae et hostiae pro peccato. Sed nullum animal feminini sexus offerebatur Deo in holocaustum, fiebant tamen holocausta tam de quadrupedibus quam de avibus. Ergo inconvenienter in hostiis pacificis et pro peccato offerebantur animalia feminini sexus; et tamen in hostiis pacificis non offerebantur aves.

Praeterea, omnes hostiae pacificae unius generis esse videntur. Non ergo debuit poni ista differentia, quod quorundam pacificorum carnes non possent vesci in crastino, quorundam autem possent, ut mandatur Levit. VII.

Praeterea, omnia peccata in hoc conveniunt quod a Deo avertunt. Ergo pro omnibus peccatis, in Dei reconciliationem, unum genus sacrificii debuit offerri.

Praeterea, omnia animalia quae offerebantur in sacrificium, uno modo offerebantur, scilicet occisa. Non videtur ergo conveniens quod de terrae nascentibus diversimode fiebat oblatio, nunc enim offerebantur spicae, nunc simila, nunc panis, quandoque quidem coctus in clibano, quandoque in sartagine, quandoque in craticula.

Praeterea, omnia quae in usum nostrum veniunt, a Deo recognoscere debemus. Inconvenienter ergo praeter animalia, solum haec Deo offerebantur, panis, vinum, oleum, thus et sal.

Praeterea, sacrificia corporalia exprimunt interius sacrificium cordis, quo homo spiritum suum offert Deo. Sed in interiori sacrificio plus est de dulcedine, quam repraesentat mel, quam de mordacitate, quam repraesentat sal, dicitur enim Eccli. XXIV, *spiritus meus super mel dulcis.* Ergo inconvenienter prohibebatur in sacrificio apponi mel et fermentum, quod etiam facit panem

to present our bodies *a living sacrifice, holy, pleasing unto God.*

Obj. 6: Further, if none but slain animals were offered in sacrifice to God, it seems that it mattered not how they were slain. Therefore it was unfitting that the manner of immolation should be determined, especially as regards birds (Lev 1:15, seqq.).

Obj. 7: Further, every defect in an animal is a step towards corruption and death. If therefore slain animals were offered to God, it was unreasonable to forbid the offering of an imperfect animal, e.g., a lame, or a blind, or otherwise defective animal.

Obj. 8: Further, those who offer victims to God should partake thereof, according to the words of the Apostle (1 Cor 10:18): *Are not they that eat of the sacrifices partakers of the altar?* It was therefore unbecoming for the offerers to be denied certain parts of the victims, namely, the blood, the fat, the breastbone and the right shoulder.

Obj. 9: Further, just as holocausts were offered up in honor of God, so also were the peace-offerings and sin-offerings. But no female animals was offered up to God as a holocaust, although holocausts were offered of both quadrupeds and birds. Therefore it was inconsistent that female animals should be offered up in peace-offerings and sin-offerings, and that nevertheless birds should not be offered up in peace-offerings.

Obj. 10: Further, all the peace-offerings seem to be of one kind. Therefore it was unfitting to make a distinction among them, so that it was forbidden to eat the flesh of certain peace-offerings on the following day, while it was allowed to eat the flesh of other peace-offerings, as laid down in Lev. 7:15, seqq.

Obj. 11: Further, all sins agree in turning us from God. Therefore, in order to reconcile us to God, one kind of sacrifice should have been offered up for all sins.

Obj. 12: Further, all animals that were offered up in sacrifice, were offered up in one way, viz., slain. Therefore it does not seem to be suitable that products of the soil should be offered up in various ways; for sometimes an offering was made of ears of corn, sometimes of flour, sometimes of bread, this being baked sometimes in an oven, sometimes in a pan, sometimes on a gridiron.

Obj. 13: Further, whatever things are serviceable to us should be recognized as coming from God. It was therefore unbecoming that besides animals, nothing but bread, wine, oil, incense, and salt should be offered to God.

Obj. 14: Further, bodily sacrifices denote the inward sacrifice of the heart, whereby man offers his soul to God. But in the inward sacrifice, the sweetness, which is denoted by honey, surpasses the pungency which salt represents; for it is written (Sir 24:27): *My spirit is sweet above honey.* Therefore it was unbecoming that the use of honey, and of leaven which makes bread savory, should be forbidden in a

sapidum; et praecipiebatur ibi apponi sal, quod est mordicativum, et thus, quod habet saporem amarum. Videtur ergo quod ea quae pertinent ad caeremonias sacrificiorum, non habeant rationabilem causam.

Sed contra est quod dicitur Levit. I, *oblata omnia adolebit sacerdos super altare in holocaustum et odorem suavissimum domino.* Sed sicut dicitur Sap. VII, *neminem diligit Deus nisi qui cum sapientia inhabitat,* ex quo potest accipi quod quidquid est Deo acceptum, est cum sapientia. Ergo illae caeremoniae sacrificiorum cum sapientia erant, velut habentes rationabiles causas.

Respondeo dicendum quod, sicut supra dictum est, caeremoniae veteris legis duplicem causam habebant, unam scilicet litteralem, secundum quod ordinabantur ad cultum Dei; aliam vero figuralem, sive mysticam, secundum quod ordinabantur ad figurandum Christum. Et ex utraque parte potest convenienter assignari causa caeremoniarum quae ad sacrificia pertinebant.

Secundum enim quod sacrificia ordinabantur ad cultum Dei, causa sacrificiorum dupliciter accipi potest. Uno modo, secundum quod per sacrificia repraesentabatur ordinatio mentis in Deum, ad quam excitabatur sacrificium offerens. Ad rectam autem ordinationem mentis in Deum pertinet quod omnia quae homo habet, recognoscat a Deo tanquam a primo principio, et ordinet in Deum tanquam in ultimum finem. Et hoc repraesentabatur in oblationibus et sacrificiis, secundum quod homo ex rebus suis, quasi in recognitionem quod haberet ea a Deo, in honorem Dei ea offerebat; secundum quod dixit David, I Paral. XXIX, *tua sunt omnia; et quae de manu tua accepimus, dedimus tibi.* Et ideo in oblatione sacrificiorum protestabatur homo quod Deus esset primum principium creationis rerum et ultimus finis, ad quem essent omnia referenda. Et quia pertinet ad rectam ordinationem mentis in Deum ut mens humana non recognoscat alium primum auctorem rerum nisi solum Deum, neque in aliquo alio finem suum constituat; propter hoc prohibebatur in lege offerre sacrificium alicui alteri nisi Deo, secundum illud Exod. XXII, *qui immolat diis, occidetur, praeter domino soli.* Et ideo de causa caeremoniarum circa sacrificia potest assignari ratio alio modo, ex hoc quod per huiusmodi homines retrahebantur a sacrificiis idolorum. Unde etiam praecepta de sacrificiis non fuerunt data populo Iudaeorum nisi postquam declinavit ad idololatriam, adorando vitulum conflatilem, quasi huiusmodi sacrificia sint instituta ut populus ad sacrificandum promptus, huiusmodi sacrificia magis Deo quam idolis offerret. Unde dicitur Ierem. VII, *non sum locutus cum patribus vestris, et non praecepi eis, in die qua eduxi eos de terra Aegypti, de verbo holocautomatum et victimarum.*

Inter omnia autem dona quae Deus humano generi iam per peccatum lapso dedit, praecipuum est quod dedit filium suum, unde dicitur Ioan. III, *sic Deus dilexit*

sacrifice; while the use was prescribed, of salt which is pungent, and of incense which has a bitter taste. Consequently it seems that things pertaining to the ceremonies of the sacrifices have no reasonable cause.

On the contrary, It is written (Lev 1:13): *The priest shall offer it all and burn it all upon the altar, for a holocaust, and most sweet savor to the Lord.* Now according to Wis. 7:28, *God loveth none but him that dwelleth with wisdom*: whence it seems to follow that whatever is acceptable to God is wisely done. Therefore these ceremonies of the sacrifices were wisely done, as having reasonable causes.

I answer that, As stated above (A2), the ceremonies of the Old Law had a twofold cause, viz., a literal cause, according as they were intended for Divine worship; and a figurative or mystical cause, according as they were intended to foreshadow Christ: and on either hand the ceremonies pertaining to the sacrifices can be assigned to a fitting cause.

For, according as the ceremonies of the sacrifices were intended for the divine worship, the causes of the sacrifices can be taken in two ways. First, insofar as the sacrifice represented the directing of the mind to God, to which the offerer of the sacrifice was stimulated. Now in order to direct his mind to God aright, man must recognize that whatever he has is from God as from its first principle, and direct it to God as its last end. This was denoted in the offerings and sacrifices, by the fact that man offered some of his own belongings in honor of God, as though in recognition of his having received them from God, according to the saying of David (1 Chr 29:14): *All things are Thine: and we have given Thee what we received of Thy hand.* Wherefore in offering up sacrifices man made protestation that God is the first principle of the creation of all things, and their last end, to which all things must be directed. And since, for the human mind to be directed to God aright, it must recognize no first author of things other than God, nor place its end in any other; for this reason it was forbidden in the Law to offer sacrifice to any other but God, according to Ex. 22:20: *He that sacrificeth to gods, shall be put to death, save only to the Lord.* Wherefore another reasonable cause may be assigned to the ceremonies of the sacrifices, from the fact that thereby men were withdrawn from offering sacrifices to idols. Hence too it is that the precepts about the sacrifices were not given to the Jewish people until after they had fallen into idolatry, by worshipping the molten calf: as though those sacrifices were instituted, that the people, being ready to offer sacrifices, might offer those sacrifices to God rather than to idols. Thus it is written (Jer 7:22): *I spake not to your fathers and I commanded them not, in the day that I brought them out of the land of Egypt, concerning the matter of burnt-offerings and sacrifices.*

Now of all the gifts which God vouchsafed to mankind after they had fallen away by sin, the chief is that He gave His Son; wherefore it is written (John 3:16): *God so loved*

mundum ut filium suum unigenitum daret, ut omnis qui credit in ipsum non pereat, sed habeat vitam aeternam. Et ideo potissimum sacrificium est quo ipse Christus seipsum obtulit Deo in odorem suavitatis, ut dicitur ad Ephes. V. Et propter hoc omnia alia sacrificia offerebantur in veteri lege ut hoc unum singulare et praecipuum sacrificium figuraretur, tanquam perfectum per imperfecta. Unde apostolus dicit, ad Heb. X, quod *sacerdos veteris legis easdem saepe offerebat hostias, quae nunquam possunt auferre peccata, Christus autem pro peccatis obtulit unam in sempiternum.* Et quia ex figurato sumitur ratio figurae, ideo rationes sacrificiorum figuralium veteris legis sunt sumendae ex vero sacrificio Christi.

AD PRIMUM ergo dicendum quod Deus non volebat huiusmodi sacrificia sibi offerri propter ipsas res quae offerebantur, quasi eis indigeret, unde dicitur Isaiae I, *holocausta arietum, et adipem pinguium, et sanguinem vitulorum et hircorum et agnorum, nolui.* Sed volebat ea sibi offerri, ut supra dictum est, tum ad excludendam idololatriam; tum ad significandum debitum ordinem mentis humanae in Deum; tum etiam ad figurandum mysterium redemptionis humanae factae per Christum.

AD SECUNDUM dicendum quod quantum ad omnia praedicta, conveniens ratio fuit quare ista animalia offerebantur Deo in sacrificium, et non alia. Primo quidem, ad excludendum idololatriam. Quia omnia alia animalia offerebant idololatrae diis suis, vel eis ad maleficia utebantur, ista autem animalia apud Aegyptios, cum quibus conversati erant, abominabilia erant ad occidendum, unde ea non offerebant in sacrificium diis suis; unde dicitur Exod. VIII, *abominationes Aegyptiorum immolabimus domino Deo nostro.* Oves enim colebant; hircos venerabantur, quia in eorum figura Daemones apparebant; bobus autem utebantur ad agriculturam, quam inter res sacras habebant.

Secundo, hoc conveniens erat ad praedictam ordinationem mentis in Deum. Et hoc dupliciter. Primo quidem, quia huiusmodi animalia maxime sunt per quae sustentatur humana vita, et cum hoc mundissima sunt, et mundissimum habent nutrimentum. Alia vero animalia vel sunt silvestria, et non sunt communiter hominum usui deputata, vel, si sunt domestica, immundum habent nutrimentum, ut porcus et gallina; solum autem id quod est purum, Deo est attribuendum. Huiusmodi autem aves specialiter offerebantur, quia habentur in copia in terra promissionis. Secundo, quia per immolationem huiusmodi animalium puritas mentis designatur. Quia, ut dicitur in Glossa Levit. I, *vitulum offerimus, cum carnis superbiam vincimus; agnum, cum irrationales motus corrigimus; haedum, cum lasciviam superamus; turturem,*

the world, as to give His only-begotten Son; that whosoever believeth in Him, may not perish, but may have life everlasting.* Consequently the chief sacrifice is that whereby Christ Himself *delivered Himself . . . to God for an odor of sweetness* (Eph 5:2). And for this reason all the other sacrifices of the Old Law were offered up in order to foreshadow this one individual and paramount sacrifice—the imperfect forecasting the perfect. Hence the Apostle says (Heb 10:11) that the priest of the Old Law *often* offered *the same sacrifices, which can never take away sins: but* Christ offered *one sacrifice for sins, for ever.* And since the reason of the figure is taken from that which the figure represents, therefore the reasons of the figurative sacrifices of the Old Law should be taken from the true sacrifice of Christ.

REPLY OBJ. 1: God did not wish these sacrifices to be offered to Him on account of the things themselves that were offered, as though He stood in need of them: wherefore it is written (Isa 1:11): *I desire not holocausts of rams, and fat of fatlings, and blood of calves and lambs and buckgoats.* But, as stated above, He wished them to be offered to Him, in order to prevent idolatry; in order to signify the right ordering of man's mind to God; and in order to represent the mystery of the Redemption of man by Christ.

REPLY OBJ. 2: In all the respects mentioned above (ad 1), there was a suitable reason for these animals, rather than others, being offered in sacrifice to God. First, in order to prevent idolatry. Because idolaters offered all other animals to their gods, or made use of them in their sorceries: while the Egyptians (among whom the people had been dwelling) considered it abominable to slay these animals, wherefore they used not to offer them in sacrifice to their gods. Hence it is written (Exod 8:26): *We shall sacrifice the abominations of the Egyptians to the Lord our God.* For they worshipped the sheep; they reverenced the ram (because demons appeared under the form thereof); while they employed oxen for agriculture, which was reckoned by them as something sacred.

Second, this was suitable for the aforesaid right ordering of man's mind to God: and in two ways. First, because it is chiefly by means of these animals that human life is sustained: and moreover they are most clean, and partake of a most clean food: whereas other animals are either wild, and not deputed to ordinary use among men: or, if they be tame, they have unclean food, as pigs and geese: and nothing but what is clean should be offered to God. These birds especially were offered in sacrifice because there were plenty of them in the land of promise. Second, because the sacrificing of these animals represented purity of heart. Because as the gloss says on Lev. 1, *We offer a calf, when we overcome the pride of the flesh; a lamb, when we restrain our unreasonable motions; a goat, when we conquer wantonness; a turtledove, when we keep chaste; unleavened bread, when*

dum castitatem servamus; panes azymos, cum in azymis sinceritatis epulamur. In columba vero manifestum est quod significatur caritas et simplicitas mentis.

Tertio vero, conveniens fuit haec animalia offerri in figuram Christi. Quia, ut in eadem Glossa dicitur, *Christus in vitulo offertur, propter virtutem crucis; in agno, propter innocentiam; in ariete, propter principatum; in hirco, propter similitudinem carnis peccati. In turture et columba duarum naturarum coniunctio monstrabatur, vel in turture castitas, in columba caritas significatur. In similagine aspersio credentium per aquam Baptismi figurabatur.*

AD TERTIUM dicendum quod pisces, quia in aquis vivunt, magis sunt alieni ab homine quam alia animalia, quae vivunt in aere, sicut et homo. Et iterum pisces, ex aqua extracti, statim moriuntur, unde non poterant in templo offerri, sicut alia animalia.

AD QUARTUM dicendum quod in turturibus meliores sunt maiores quam pulli; in columbis autem e converso. Et ideo, ut Rabbi Moyses dicit, mandantur offerri turtures et pulli columbarum, quia omne quod est optimum, Deo est attribuendum.

AD QUINTUM dicendum quod animalia in sacrificium oblata occidebantur, quia veniunt in usum hominis occisa, secundum quod a Deo dantur homini ad esum. Et ideo etiam igni cremabantur, quia per ignem decocta fiunt apta humano usui. Similiter etiam per occisionem animalium significatur destructio peccatorum. Et quod homines erant digni occisione pro peccatis suis, ac si illa animalia loco eorum occiderentur, ad significandum expiationem peccatorum. Per occisionem etiam huiusmodi animalium significabatur occisio Christi.

AD SEXTUM dicendum quod specialis modus occidendi animalia immolata determinabatur in lege ad excludendum alios modos, quibus idololatrae animalia idolis immolabant. Vel etiam, ut Rabbi Moyses dicit, *lex elegit genus occisionis quo animalia minus affligebantur occisa.* Per quod excludebatur etiam immisericordia offerentium, et deterioratio animalium occisorum.

AD SEPTIMUM dicendum quod, quia animalia maculosa solent haberi contemptui etiam apud homines, ideo prohibitum est ne Deo in sacrificium offerrentur, propter quod etiam prohibitum erat *ne mercedem prostibuli, aut pretium canis, in domum Dei offerrent.* Et eadem etiam ratione non offerebant animalia ante septimum diem, quia talia animalia erant quasi abortiva, nondum plene consistentia, propter teneritudinem.

AD OCTAVUM dicendum quod triplex erat sacrificiorum genus. Quoddam erat quod totum comburebatur, et hoc dicebatur holocaustum, quasi totum incensum. Huiusmodi enim sacrificium offerebatur Deo specialiter

we feast on the unleavened bread of sincerity. And it is evident that the dove denotes charity and simplicity of heart.

Third, it was fitting that these animals should be offered, that they might foreshadow Christ. Because, as the gloss observes, *Christ is offered in the calf, to denote the strength of the cross; in the lamb, to signify His innocence; in the ram, to foreshadow His headship; and in the goat, to signify the likeness of 'sinful flesh.' The turtledove and dove denoted the union of the two natures;* or else the turtledove signified chastity; while the dove was a figure of charity. *The wheat-flour foreshadowed the sprinkling of believers with the water of Baptism.*

REPLY OBJ. 3: Fish through living in water are further removed from man than other animals, which, like man, live in the air. Again, fish die as soon as they are taken out of water; hence they could not be offered in the temple like other animals.

REPLY OBJ. 4: Among turtledoves the older ones are better than the young; while with doves the case is the reverse. Wherefore, as Rabbi Moses observes (*Doct. Perplex.* iii), turtledoves and young doves are commanded to be offered, because nothing should be offered to God but what is best.

REPLY OBJ. 5: The animals which were offered in sacrifice were slain, because it is by being killed that they become useful to man, forasmuch as God gave them to man for food. Wherefore also they were burnt with fire: because it is by being cooked that they are made fit for human consumption. Moreover the slaying of the animals signified the destruction of sins: and also that man deserved death on account of his sins; as though those animals were slain in man's stead, in order to betoken the expiation of sins. Again the slaying of these animals signified the slaying of Christ.

REPLY OBJ. 6: The Law fixed the special manner of slaying the sacrificial animals in order to exclude other ways of killing, whereby idolaters sacrificed animals to idols. Or again, as Rabbi Moses says (*Doct. Perplex.* iii), *the Law chose that manner of slaying which was least painful to the slain animal.* This excluded cruelty on the part of the offerers, and any mangling of the animals slain.

REPLY OBJ. 7: It is because unclean animals are wont to be held in contempt among men, that it was forbidden to offer them in sacrifice to God: and for this reason too they were forbidden (Deut 23:18) to offer *the hire of a strumpet or the price of a dog in the house of . . . God.* For the same reason they did not offer animals before the seventh day, because such were abortive as it were, the flesh being not yet firm on account of its exceeding softness.

REPLY OBJ. 8: There were three kinds of sacrifices. There was one in which the victim was entirely consumed by fire: this was called *a holocaust, i.e., all burnt.* For this kind of sacrifice was offered to God specially to show

ad reverentiam maiestatis ipsius, et amorem bonitatis eius, et conveniebat perfectionis statui in impletione consiliorum. Et ideo totum comburebatur, ut sicut totum animal, resolutum in vaporem, sursum ascendebat, ita etiam significaretur totum hominem, et omnia quae ipsius sunt, Dei dominio esse subiecta, et ei esse offerenda.

Aliud autem erat sacrificium pro peccato, quod offerebatur Deo ex necessitate remissionis peccati, et conveniebat statui poenitentium in satisfactione peccatorum. Quod dividebatur in duas partes, nam una pars eius comburebatur, alia vero cedebat in usum sacerdotum; ad significandum quod expiatio peccatorum fit a Deo per ministerium sacerdotum. Nisi quando offerebatur sacrificium pro peccato totius populi, vel specialiter pro peccato sacerdotis, tunc enim totum comburebatur. Non enim debebant in usum sacerdotum venire ea quae pro peccato eorum offerebantur, ut nihil peccati in eis remaneret. Et quia hoc non esset satisfactio pro peccato, si enim cederet in usum eorum pro quorum peccatis offerebatur, idem esse videretur ac si non offerrent.

Tertium vero sacrificium vocabatur hostia pacifica, quae offerebatur Deo vel pro gratiarum actione, vel pro salute et prosperitate offerentium, ex debito beneficii vel accepti vel accipiendi, et convenit statui proficientium in impletione mandatorum. Et ista dividebantur in tres partes, nam una pars incendebatur ad honorem Dei, alia pars cedebat in usum sacerdotum, tertia vero pars in usum offerentium; ad significandum quod salus hominis procedit a Deo, dirigentibus ministris Dei, et cooperantibus ipsis hominibus qui salvantur.

Hoc autem generaliter observabatur, quod sanguis et adeps non veniebant neque in usum sacerdotum, neque in usum offerentium, sed sanguis effundebatur ad crepidinem altaris, in honorem Dei; adeps vero adurebatur in igne. Cuius ratio una quidem fuit ad excludendam idololatriam. Idololatrae enim bibebant de sanguine victimarum, et comedebant adipes; secundum illud Deut. XXXII, *de quorum victimis comedebant adipes, et bibebant vinum libaminum.* Secunda ratio est ad informationem humanae vitae. Prohibebatur enim eis usus sanguinis, ad hoc quod horrerent humani sanguinis effusionem, unde dicitur Gen. IX, *carnem cum sanguine non comedetis, sanguinem enim animarum vestrarum requiram.* Esus vero adipum prohibebatur eis ad vitandam lasciviam, unde dicitur Ezech. XXXIV, *quod crassum erat, occidebatis.* Tertia ratio est propter reverentiam divinam. Quia sanguis est maxime necessarius ad vitam, ratione cuius dicitur anima esse in sanguine, adeps autem abundantiam nutrimenti demonstrat. Et ideo ut ostenderetur quod a Deo nobis est et vita et omnis bonorum sufficientia, ad honorem Dei effundebatur sanguis, et adurebatur

reverence to His majesty, and love of His goodness: and typified the state of perfection as regards the fulfilment of the counsels. Wherefore the whole was burnt up: so that as the whole animal by being dissolved into vapor soared aloft, so it might denote that the whole man, and whatever belongs to him, are subject to the authority of God, and should be offered to Him.

Another sacrifice was the *sin-offering,* which was offered to God on account of man's need for the forgiveness of sin: and this typifies the state of penitents in satisfying for sins. It was divided into two parts: for one part was burnt; while the other was granted to the use of the priests to signify that remission of sins is granted by God through the ministry of His priests. When, however, this sacrifice was offered for the sins of the whole people, or specially for the sin of the priest, the whole victim was burnt up. For it was not fitting that the priests should have the use of that which was offered for their own sins, to signify that nothing sinful should remain in them. Moreover, this would not be satisfaction for sin: for if the offering were granted to the use of those for whose sins it was offered, it would seem to be the same as if it had not been offered.

The third kind of sacrifice was called the *peace-offering,* which was offered to God, either in thanksgiving, or for the welfare and prosperity of the offerers, in acknowledgment of benefits already received or yet to be received: and this typifies the state of those who are proficient in the observance of the commandments. These sacrifices were divided into three parts: for one part was burnt in honor of God; another part was allotted to the use of the priests; and the third part to the use of the offerers; in order to signify that man's salvation is from God, by the direction of God's ministers, and through the cooperation of those who are saved.

But it was the universal rule that the blood and fat were not allotted to the use either of the priests or of the offerers: the blood being poured out at the foot of the altar, in honor of God, while the fat was burnt upon the altar (Lev 9:9,10). The reason for this was, first, in order to prevent idolatry: because idolaters used to drink the blood and eat the fat of the victims, according to Dt. 32:38: *Of whose victims they eat the fat, and drank the wine of their drink-offerings.* Second, in order to form them to a right way of living. For they were forbidden the use of the blood that they might abhor the shedding of human blood; wherefore it is written (Gen 9:4,5): *Flesh with blood you shall not eat: for I will require the blood of your lives:* and they were forbidden to eat the fat, in order to withdraw them from lasciviousness; hence it is written (Ezek 34:3): *You have killed that which was fat.* Third, on account of the reverence due to God: because blood is most necessary for life, for which reason *life* is said to be *in the blood* (Lev 17:11,14): while fat is a sign of abundant nourishment. Wherefore, in order to show that to God we owe both life and a sufficiency of all good things, the blood was poured out, and the fat burnt up in

adeps. Quarta ratio est quia per hoc figurabatur effusio sanguinis Christi, et pinguedo caritatis eius, per quam se obtulit Deo pro nobis.

De hostiis autem pacificis in usum sacerdotis cedebat pectusculum et armus dexter, ad excludendum quandam divinationis speciem quae vocatur spatulamantia, quia scilicet in spatulis animalium immolatorum divinabant, et similiter in osse pectoris. Et ideo ista offerentibus subtrahebantur. Per hoc etiam significabatur quod sacerdoti erat necessaria sapientia cordis ad instruendum populum, quod significabatur per pectus, quod est tegumentum cordis; et etiam fortitudo ad sustentandum defectus, quae significatur per armum dextrum.

AD NONUM dicendum quod, quia holocaustum erat perfectissimum inter sacrificia, ideo non offerebatur in holocaustum nisi masculus, nam femina est animal imperfectum. Oblatio autem turturum et columbarum erat propter paupertatem offerentium, qui maiora animalia offerre non poterant. Et quia hostiae pacificae gratis offerebantur, et nullus eas offerre cogebatur nisi spontaneus; ideo huiusmodi aves non offerebantur inter hostias pacificas, sed inter holocausta et hostias pro peccato, quas quandoque oportebat offerre. Aves etiam huiusmodi, propter altitudinem volatus, congruunt perfectioni holocaustorum, et etiam hostiis pro peccato, quia habent gemitum pro cantu.

AD DECIMUM dicendum quod inter omnia sacrificia holocaustum erat praecipuum, quia totum comburebatur in honorem Dei, et nihil ex eo comedebatur. Secundum vero locum in sanctitate tenebat hostia pro peccato, quae comedebatur solum in atrio a sacerdotibus, et in ipsa die sacrificii. Tertium vero gradum tenebant hostiae pacificae pro gratiarum actione, quae comedebantur ipso die, sed ubique in Ierusalem. Quartum vero locum tenebant hostiae pacificae ex voto, quarum carnes poterant etiam in crastino comedi. Et est ratio huius ordinis quia maxime obligatur homo Deo propter eius maiestatem, secundo, propter offensam commissam; tertio, propter beneficia iam suscepta; quarto, propter beneficia sperata.

AD UNDECIMUM dicendum quod peccata aggravantur ex statu peccantis, ut supra dictum est. Et ideo alia hostia mandatur offerri pro peccato sacerdotis et principis, vel alterius privatae personae. Est autem attendendum, ut Rabbi Moyses dicit, quod *quanto gravius erat peccatum, tanto vilior species animalis offerebatur pro eo. Unde capra, quod est vilissimum animal, offerebatur pro idololatria, quod est gravissimum peccatum; pro ignorantia vero sacerdotis offerebatur vitulus; pro negligentia autem principis, hircus.*

AD DUODECIMUM dicendum quod lex in sacrificiis providere voluit paupertati offerentium, ut qui non posset habere animal quadrupes, saltem offerret avem;

His honor. Fourth, in order to foreshadow the shedding of Christ's blood, and the abundance of His charity, whereby He offered Himself to God for us.

In the peace-offerings, the breast-bone and the right shoulder were allotted to the use of the priest, in order to prevent a certain kind of divination which is known as *spatulamantia*, so called because it was customary in divining to use the shoulder-blade, and the breast-bone of the animals offered in sacrifice; wherefore these things were taken away from the offerers. This also denoted the priest's need of wisdom in the heart, to instruct the people—this was signified by the breast-bone, which covers the heart; and his need of fortitude, in order to bear with human frailty—and this was signified by the right shoulder.

REPLY OBJ. 9: Because the holocaust was the most perfect kind of sacrifice, therefore none but a male was offered for a holocaust: because the female is an imperfect animal. The offering of turtledoves and doves was on account of the poverty of the offerers, who were unable to offer bigger animals. And since peace-victims were offered freely, and no one was bound to offer them against his will, hence these birds were offered not among the peace-victims, but among the holocausts and victims for sin, which man was obliged to offer at times. Moreover these birds, on account of their lofty flight, while befitting the perfection of the holocausts: and were suitable for sin-offerings because their song is doleful.

REPLY OBJ. 10: The holocaust was the chief of all the sacrifices: because all was burnt in honor of God, and nothing of it was eaten. The second place in holiness, belongs to the sacrifice for sins, which was eaten in the court only, and on the very day of the sacrifice (Lev 7:6,15). The third place must be given to the peace-offerings of thanksgiving, which were eaten on the same day, but anywhere in Jerusalem. Fourth in order were the *ex-voto* peace-offerings, the flesh of which could be eaten even on the morrow. The reason for this order is that man is bound to God, chiefly on account of His majesty; second, on account of the sins he has committed; third, because of the benefits he has already received from Him; fourth, by reason of the benefits he hopes to receive from Him.

REPLY OBJ. 11: Sins are more grievous by reason of the state of the sinner, as stated above (Q73, A10): wherefore different victims are commanded to be offered for the sin of a priest, or of a prince, or of some other private individual. *But*, as Rabbi Moses says (*Doct. Perplex.* iii), *we must take note that the more grievous the sin, the lower the species of animals offered for it. Wherefore the goat, which is a very base animal, was offered for idolatry; while a calf was offered for a priest's ignorance, and a ram for the negligence of a prince.*

REPLY OBJ. 12: In the matter of sacrifices the Law had in view the poverty of the offerers; so that those who could not have a four-footed animal at their disposal, might at

quam qui habere non posset, saltem offerret panem; et si hunc habere non posset, saltem offerret farinam vel spicas.

Causa vero figuralis est quia panis significat Christum, qui est *panis vivus*, ut dicitur Ioan. VI. Qui quidem erat sicut in spica, pro statu legis naturae, in fide patrum; erat autem sicut simila in doctrina legis prophetarum; erat autem sicut panis formatus post humanitatem assumptam; coctus igne, idest formatus spiritu sancto in clibano uteri virginalis; qui etiam fuit coctus in sartagine, per labores quos in mundo sustinebat; in cruce vero quasi in craticula adustus.

AD DECIMUMTERTIUM dicendum quod ea quae in usum hominis veniunt de terrae nascentibus, vel sunt in cibum, et de eis offerebatur panis. Vel sunt in potum, et de his offerebatur vinum. Vel sunt in condimentum, et de his offerebatur oleum et sal. Vel sunt in medicamentum, et de his offerebatur thus, quod est aromaticum et consolidativum.

Per panem autem figuratur caro Christi; per vinum autem sanguis eius, per quem redempti sumus; oleum figurat gratiam Christi; sal scientiam; thus orationem.

AD DECIMUMQUARTUM dicendum quod mel non offerebatur in sacrificiis Dei, tum quia consueverat offerri in sacrificiis idolorum. Tum etiam ad excludendam omnem carnalem dulcedinem et voluptatem ab his qui Deo sacrificare intendunt. Fermentum vero non offerebatur, ad excludendam corruptionem. Et forte etiam in sacrificiis idolorum solitum erat offerri.

Sal autem offerebatur, quia impedit corruptionem putredinis, sacrificia autem Dei debent esse incorrupta. Et etiam quia in sale significatur discretio sapientiae; vel etiam mortificatio carnis.

Thus autem offerebatur ad designandam devotionem mentis, quae est necessaria offerentibus; et etiam ad designandum odorem bonae famae, nam thus et pingue est, et odoriferum. Et quia sacrificium zelotypiae non procedebat ex devotione, sed magis ex suspicione, ideo in eo non offerebatur thus.

least offer a bird; and that he who could not have a bird might at least offer bread; and that if a man had not even bread he might offer flour or ears of corn.

The figurative cause is that the bread signifies Christ Who is the *living bread* (John 6:41,51). He was indeed an ear of corn, as it were, during the state of the law of nature, in the faith of the patriarchs; He was like flour in the doctrine of the Law of the prophets; and He was like perfect bread after He had taken human nature; baked in the fire, i.e., formed by the Holy Spirit in the oven of the virginal womb; baked again in a pan by the toils which He suffered in the world; and consumed by fire on the cross as on a gridiron.

REPLY OBJ. 13: The products of the soil are useful to man, either as food, and of these bread was offered; or as drink, and of these wine was offered; or as seasoning, and of these oil and salt were offered; or as healing, and of these they offered incense, which both smells sweetly and binds easily together.

Now the bread foreshadowed the flesh of Christ; and the wine, His blood, whereby we were redeemed; oil betokens the grace of Christ; salt, His knowledge; incense, His prayer.

REPLY OBJ. 14: Honey was not offered in the sacrifices to God, both because it was wont to be offered in the sacrifices to idols; and in order to denote the absence of all carnal sweetness and pleasure from those who intend to sacrifice to God. Leaven was not offered, to denote the exclusion of corruption. Perhaps too, it was wont to be offered in the sacrifices to idols.

Salt, however, was offered, because it wards off the corruption of putrefaction: for sacrifices offered to God should be incorrupt. Moreover, salt signifies the discretion of wisdom, or again, mortification of the flesh.

Incense was offered to denote devotion of the heart, which is necessary in the offerer; and again, to signify the odor of a good name: for incense is composed of matter, both rich and fragrant. And since the sacrifice *of jealousy* did not proceed from devotion, but rather from suspicion, therefore incense was not offered therein (Num 5:15).

Article 4

Whether Sufficient Reason Can Be Assigned for the Ceremonies Pertaining to Holy Things?

AD QUARTUM SIC PROCEDITUR. Videtur quod caeremoniarum veteris legis quae ad sacra pertinent sufficiens ratio assignari non possit. Dicit enim Paulus, Act. XVII, *Deus, qui fecit mundum et omnia quae in eo sunt, hic, caeli et terrae cum sit dominus, non in manufactis*

OBJECTION 1: It would seem that no sufficient reason can be assigned for the ceremonies of the Old Law that pertain to holy things. For Paul said (Acts 17:24): *God Who made the world and all things therein; He being Lord of heaven and earth, dwelleth not in temples made by hands*. It

templis habitat. Inconvenienter igitur ad cultum Dei tabernaculum, vel templum, in lege veteri est institutum.

PRAETEREA, status veteris legis non fuit immutatus nisi per Christum. Sed tabernaculum designabat statum veteris legis. Non ergo debuit mutari per aedificationem alicuius templi.

PRAETEREA, divina lex praecipue etiam debet homines inducere ad divinum cultum. Sed ad augmentum divini cultus pertinet quod fiant multa altaria et multa templa, sicut patet in nova lege. Ergo videtur quod etiam in veteri lege non debuit esse solum unum templum aut unum tabernaculum sed multa.

PRAETEREA, tabernaculum, seu templum, ad cultum Dei ordinabatur. Sed in Deo praecipue oportet venerari unitatem et simplicitatem. Non videtur igitur fuisse conveniens ut tabernaculum, seu templum, per quaedam vela distingueretur.

PRAETEREA, virtus primi moventis, qui est Deus, primo apparet in parte orientis, a qua parte incipit primus motus. Sed tabernaculum fuit institutum ad Dei adorationem. Ergo debebat esse dispositum magis versus orientem quam versus occidentem.

PRAETEREA, Exod. XX, dominus praecepit ut *non facerent sculptile, neque aliquam similitudinem.* Inconvenienter igitur in tabernaculo, vel in templo, fuerunt sculptae imagines Cherubim. Similiter etiam et arca, et propitiatorium, et candelabrum, et mensa, et duplex altare, sine rationabili causa ibi fuisse videntur.

PRAETEREA, dominus praecepit, Exod. XX, *altare de terra facietis mihi.* Et iterum, *non ascendes ad altare meum per gradus.* Inconvenienter igitur mandatur postmodum altare fieri de lignis auro vel aere contextis; et tantae altitudinis ut ad illud nisi per gradus ascendi non posset. Dicitur enim Exod. XXVII, *facies et altare de lignis setim, quod habebit quinque cubitos in longitudine, et totidem in latitudine, et tres cubitos in altitudine; et operies illud aere.* Et Exod. XXX dicitur, *facies altare ad adolendum thymiamata, de lignis setim, vestiesque illud auro purissimo.*

PRAETEREA, in operibus Dei nihil debet esse superfluum, quia nec in operibus naturae aliquid superfluum invenitur. Sed uni tabernaculo, vel domui, sufficit unum operimentum. Inconvenienter igitur tabernaculo fuerunt apposita multa tegumenta, scilicet cortinae, saga cilicina, pelles arietum rubricatae, et pelles hyacintinae.

PRAETEREA, consecratio exterior interiorem sanctitatem significat, cuius subiectum est anima. Inconvenienter igitur tabernaculum et eius vasa consecrabantur, cum essent quaedam corpora inanimata.

was therefore unfitting that in the Old Law a tabernacle or temple should be set up for the worship of God.

OBJ. 2: Further, the state of the Old Law was not changed except by Christ. But the tabernacle denoted the state of the Old Law. Therefore it should not have been changed by the building of a temple.

OBJ. 3: Further, the Divine Law, more than any other indeed, should lead man to the worship of God. But an increase of divine worship requires multiplication of altars and temples; as is evident in regard to the New Law. Therefore it seems that also under the Old Law there should have been not only one tabernacle or temple, but many.

OBJ. 4: Further, the tabernacle or temple was ordained to the worship of God. But in God we should worship above all His unity and simplicity. Therefore it seems unbecoming for the tabernacle or temple to be divided by means of veils.

OBJ. 5: Further, the power of the First Mover, i.e., God, appears first of all in the east, for it is in that quarter that the first movement begins. But the tabernacle was set up for the worship of God. Therefore it should have been built so as to point to the east rather than the west.

OBJ. 6: Further, the Lord commanded (Exod 20:4) that they should *not make . . . a graven thing, nor the likeness of anything.* It was therefore unfitting for graven images of the cherubim to be set up in the tabernacle or temple. In like manner, the ark, the propitiatory, the candlestick, the table, the two altars, seem to have been placed there without reasonable cause.

OBJ. 7: Further, the Lord commanded (Exod 20:24): *You shall make an altar of earth unto Me*: and again (Exod 20:26): *Thou shalt not go up by steps unto My altar.* It was therefore unfitting that subsequently they should be commanded to make an altar of wood laid over with gold or brass; and of such a height that it was impossible to go up to it except by steps. For it is written (Exod 27:1,2): *Thou shalt make also an altar of setim wood, which shall be five cubits long, and as many broad . . . and three cubits high . . . and thou shalt cover it with brass*: and (Exod 30:1,3): *Thou shalt make . . . an altar to burn incense, of setim wood . . . and thou shalt overlay it with the purest gold.*

OBJ. 8: Further, in God's works nothing should be superfluous; for not even in the works of nature is anything superfluous to be found. But one cover suffices for one tabernacle or house. Therefore it was unbecoming to furnish the tabernacle with many coverings, viz., curtains, curtains of goats' hair, rams' skins dyed red, and violet-colored skins (Exod 26).

OBJ. 9: Further, exterior consecration signifies interior holiness, the subject of which is the soul. It was therefore unsuitable for the tabernacle and its vessels to be consecrated, since they were inanimate things.

PRAETEREA, in Psalmo XXXIII dicitur, *benedicam dominum in omni tempore, semper laus eius in ore meo.* Sed solemnitates instituuntur ad laudandum Deum. Non ergo fuit conveniens ut aliqui certi dies statuerentur ad solemnitates peragendas. Sic igitur videtur quod caeremoniae sacrorum convenientes causas non haberent.

SED CONTRA est quod apostolus dicit, ad Heb. VIII, quod *illi qui offerunt secundum legem munera, exemplari et umbrae deserviunt caelestium, sicut responsum est Moysi, cum consummaret tabernaculum, vide, inquit, omnia facito secundum exemplar quod tibi in monte monstratum est.* Sed valde rationabile est quod imaginem caelestium repraesentat. Ergo caeremoniae sacrorum rationabilem causam habebant.

RESPONDEO dicendum quod totus exterior cultus Dei ad hoc praecipue ordinatur ut homines Deum in reverentia habeant. Habet autem hoc humanus affectus, ut ea quae communia sunt, et non distincta ab aliis, minus revereatur; ea vero quae habent aliquam excellentiae discretionem ab aliis, magis admiretur et revereatur. Et inde etiam hominum consuetudo inolevit ut reges et principes, quos oportet in reverentia haberi a subditis, et pretiosioribus vestibus ornentur, et etiam ampliores et pulchriores habitationes possideant. Et propter hoc oportuit ut aliqua specialia tempora, et speciale habitaculum, et specialia vasa, et speciales ministri ad cultum Dei ordinarentur, ut per hoc animi hominum ad maiorem Dei reverentiam adducerentur.

Similiter etiam status veteris legis, sicut dictum est, institutus erat ad figurandum mysterium Christi. Oportet autem esse aliquid determinatum id per quod aliud figurari debet, ut scilicet eius aliquam similitudinem repraesentet. Et ideo etiam oportuit aliqua specialia observari in his quae pertinent ad cultum Dei.

AD PRIMUM ergo dicendum quod cultus Dei duo respicit, scilicet Deum, qui colitur; et homines colentes. Ipse igitur Deus, qui colitur, nullo corporali loco clauditur, unde propter ipsum non oportuit tabernaculum fieri, aut templum. Sed homines ipsum colentes corporales sunt, et propter eos oportuit speciale tabernaculum, vel templum, institui ad cultum Dei, propter duo. Primo quidem, ut ad huiusmodi locum convenientes cum hac cogitatione quod deputaretur ad colendum Deum, cum maiori reverentia accederent. Secundo, ut per dispositionem talis templi, vel tabernaculi, significarentur aliqua pertinentia ad excellentiam divinitatis vel humanitatis Christi.

Et hoc est quod Salomon dicit, III Reg. VIII, *si caelum et caeli caelorum te capere non possunt, quanto magis domus haec, quam aedificavi tibi? Et* postea subdit, *sint oculi tui aperti super domum hanc, de qua dixisti, erit nomen meum ibi; ut exaudias deprecationem servi tui*

OBJ. 10: Further, it is written (Ps 33:2): *I will bless the Lord at all times, His praise shall always be in my mouth.* But the solemn festivals were instituted for the praise of God. Therefore it was not fitting that certain days should be fixed for keeping solemn festivals; so that it seems that there was no suitable cause for the ceremonies relating to holy things.

ON THE CONTRARY, The Apostle says (Heb 8:4) that those who *offer gifts according to the law . . . serve unto the example and shadow of heavenly things. As it was answered to Moses, when he was to finish the tabernacle: See, says He, that thou make all things according to the pattern which was shown thee on the mount.* But that is most reasonable, which presents a likeness to heavenly things. Therefore the ceremonies relating to holy things had a reasonable cause.

I ANSWER THAT, The chief purpose of the whole external worship is that man may give worship to God. Now man's tendency is to reverence less those things which are common, and indistinct from other things; whereas he admires and reveres those things which are distinct from others in some point of excellence. Hence too it is customary among men for kings and princes, who ought to be reverenced by their subjects, to be clothed in more precious garments, and to possess vaster and more beautiful abodes. And for this reason it behooved special times, a special abode, special vessels, and special ministers to be appointed for the divine worship, so that thereby the soul of man might be brought to greater reverence for God.

In like manner the state of the Old Law, as observed above (A2; Q100, A12; Q101, A2), was instituted that it might foreshadow the mystery of Christ. Now that which foreshadows something should be determinate, so that it may present some likeness thereto. Consequently, certain special points had to be observed in matters pertaining to the worship of God.

REPLY OBJ. 1: The divine worship regards two things: namely, God Who is worshipped; and men, who worship Him. Accordingly God, Who is worshipped, is confined to no bodily place: wherefore there was no need, on His part, for a tabernacle or temple to be set up. But men, who worship Him, are corporeal beings: and for their sake there was need for a special tabernacle or temple to be set up for the worship of God, for two reasons. First, that through coming together with the thought that the place was set aside for the worship of God, they might approach thither with greater reverence. Second, that certain things relating to the excellence of Christ's Divine or human nature might be signified by the arrangement of various details in such temple or tabernacle.

To this Solomon refers (3 Kgs 8:27) when he says: *If heaven and the heavens of heavens cannot contain Thee, how much less this house which I have built* for Thee? And further on (3 Kgs 8:29,20) he adds: *That Thy eyes may be open upon this house . . . of which Thou hast said: My name shall*

et populi tui Israel. Ex quo patet quod domus sanctuarii non est instituta ad hoc quod Deum capiat, quasi localiter inhabitantem; sed ad hoc quod nomen Dei habitet ibi, idest ut notitia Dei ibi manifestetur per aliqua quae ibi fiebant vel dicebantur; et quod, propter reverentiam loci, orationes fierent ibi magis exaudibiles ex devotione orantium.

AD SECUNDUM dicendum quod status veteris legis non fuit immutatus ante Christum quantum ad impletionem legis, quae facta est solum per Christum, est tamen immutatus quantum ad conditionem populi qui erat sub lege. Nam primo populus fuit in deserto, non habens certam mansionem; postmodum autem habuerunt varia bella cum finitimis gentibus; ultimo autem, tempore David et Salomonis, populus ille habuit quietissimum statum. Et tunc primo aedificatum fuit templum, in loco quem designaverat Abraham, ex divina demonstratione, ad immolandum. Dicitur enim Gen. XXII, quod dominus mandavit Abrahae ut offerret filium suum *in holocaustum super unum montium quem monstravero tibi.* Et postea dicit quod appellavit nomen illius loci, *dominus videt,* quasi secundum Dei praevisionem esset locus ille electus ad cultum divinum. Propter quod dicitur Deut. XII, *ad locum quem elegerit dominus Deus vester, venietis, et offeretis holocausta et victimas vestras.*

Locus autem ille designari non debuit per aedificationem templi ante tempus praedictum, propter tres rationes, quas Rabbi Moyses assignat. Prima est ne gentes appropriarent sibi locum illum. Secunda est ne gentes ipsum destruerent. Tertia vero ratio est ne quaelibet tribus vellet habere locum illum in sorte sua, et propter hoc orirentur lites et iurgia. Et ideo non fuit aedificatum templum donec haberent regem, per quem posset huiusmodi iurgium compesci. Antea vero ad cultum Dei erat ordinatum tabernaculum portatile per diversa loca, quasi nondum existente determinato loco divini cultus. Et haec est ratio litteralis diversitatis tabernaculi et templi.

Ratio autem figuralis esse potest quia per haec duo significatur duplex status. Per tabernaculum enim, quod est mutabile, significatur status praesentis vitae mutabilis. Per templum vero, quod erat fixum et stans, significatur status futurae vitae, quae omnino invariabilis est. Et propter hoc in aedificatione templi dicitur quod non est auditus sonitus mallei vel securis, ad significandum quod omnis perturbationis tumultus longe erit a statu futuro. Vel per tabernaculum significatur status veteris legis, per templum autem a Salomone constructum, status novae legis. Unde ad constructionem tabernaculi soli Iudaei sunt operati, ad aedificationem vero templi cooperati sunt etiam gentiles, scilicet Tyrii et Sidonii.

be there; . . . that Thou mayest hearken to the supplication of Thy servant and of Thy people Israel. From this it is evident that the house of the sanctuary was set up, not in order to contain God, as abiding therein locally, but that God might be made known there by means of things done and said there; and that those who prayed there might, through reverence for the place, pray more devoutly, so as to be heard more readily.

REPLY OBJ. 2: Before the coming of Christ, the state of the Old Law was not changed as regards the fulfilment of the Law, which was effected in Christ alone: but it was changed as regards the condition of the people that were under the Law. Because, at first, the people were in the desert, having no fixed abode: afterwards they were engaged in various wars with the neighboring nations; and lastly, at the time of David and Solomon, the state of that people was one of great peace. And then for the first time the temple was built in the place which Abraham, instructed by God, had chosen for the purpose of sacrifice. For it is written (Gen 22:2) that the Lord commanded Abraham to *offer* his son *for a holocaust upon one of the mountains which I will show thee*: and it is related further on (Gen 22:14) that *he calleth the name of that place, The Lord seeth,* as though, according to the Divine prevision, that place were chosen for the worship of God. Hence it is written (Deut 12:5,6): *You shall come to the place which the Lord your God shall choose . . . and you shall offer . . . your holocausts and victims.*

Now it was not meet for that place to be pointed out by the building of the temple before the aforesaid time; for three reasons assigned by Rabbi Moses. First, lest the Gentiles might seize hold of that place. Second, lest the Gentiles might destroy it. The third reason is lest each tribe might wish that place to fall to their lot, and strifes and quarrels be the result. Hence the temple was not built until they had a king who would be able to quell such quarrels. Until that time a portable tabernacle was employed for divine worship, no place being as yet fixed for the worship of God. This is the literal reason for the distinction between the tabernacle and the temple.

The figurative reason may be assigned to the fact that they signify a twofold state. For the tabernacle, which was changeable, signifies the state of the present changeable life: whereas the temple, which was fixed and stable, signifies the state of future life which is altogether unchangeable. For this reason it is said that in the building of the temple no sound was heard of hammer or saw, to signify that all movements of disturbance will be far removed from the future state. Or else the tabernacle signifies the state of the Old Law; while the temple built by Solomon betokens the state of the New Law. Hence the Jews alone worked at the building of the tabernacle; whereas the temple was built with the cooperation of the Gentiles, viz., the Tyrians and Sidonians.

AD TERTIUM dicendum quod ratio unitatis templi, vel tabernaculi, potest esse et litteralis, et figuralis. Litteralis quidem est ratio ad exclusionem idololatriae. Quia gentiles diversis diis diversa templa constituebant, et ideo, ut firmaretur in animis hominum fides unitatis divinae, voluit Deus ut in uno loco tantum sibi sacrificium offerretur. Et iterum ut per hoc ostenderet quod corporalis cultus non propter se erat ei acceptus. Et ideo compescebantur ne passim et ubique sacrificia offerrent. Sed cultus novae legis, in cuius sacrificio spiritualis gratia continetur, est secundum se Deo acceptus. Et ideo multiplicatio altarium et templorum acceptatur in nova lege.

Quantum vero ad ea quae pertinebant ad spiritualem cultum Dei, qui consistit in doctrina legis et prophetarum, erant etiam in veteri lege diversa loca deputata in quibus conveniebant ad laudem Dei, quae dicebantur synagogae, sicut et nunc dicuntur Ecclesiae, in quibus populus Christianus ad laudem Dei congregatur. Et sic Ecclesia nostra succedit in locum et templi et synagogae, quia ipsum sacrificium Ecclesiae spirituale est; unde non distinguitur apud nos locus sacrificii a loco doctrinae. Ratio autem figuralis esse potest quia per hoc significatur unitas Ecclesiae, vel militantis vel triumphantis.

AD QUARTUM dicendum quod, sicut in unitate templi, vel tabernaculi, repraesentabatur unitas Dei, vel unitas Ecclesiae; ita etiam in distinctione tabernaculi, vel templi, repraesentabatur distinctio eorum quae Deo sunt subiecta, ex quibus in Dei venerationem consurgimus. Distinguebatur autem tabernaculum in duas partes, in unam quae vocabatur sancta sanctorum, quae erat Occidentalis; et aliam quae vocabatur sancta, quae erat ad orientem. Et iterum ante tabernaculum erat atrium. Haec igitur distinctio duplicem habet rationem. Unam quidem, secundum quod tabernaculum ordinatur ad cultum Dei. Sic enim diversae partes mundi in distinctione tabernaculi figurantur. Nam pars illa quae sancta sanctorum dicitur, figurabat saeculum altius, quod est spiritualium substantiarum, pars vero illa quae dicitur sancta, exprimebat mundum corporalem. Et ideo sancta a sanctis sanctorum distinguebantur quodam velo, quod quatuor coloribus erat distinctum, per quos quatuor elementa designantur, scilicet bysso, per quod designatur terra, quia byssus, idest linum, de terra nascitur; purpura, per quam significatur aqua, fiebat enim purpureus color ex quibusdam conchis quae inveniuntur in mari; hyacintho, per quem significatur aer, quia habet aereum colorem; et cocco bis tincto, per quem designatur ignis. Et hoc ideo quia materia quatuor elementorum est impedimentum per quod velantur nobis incorporales substantiae. Et ideo in interius tabernaculum, idest in sancta sanctorum, solus summus sacerdos, et semel in anno, introibat, ut designaretur quod haec est finalis

REPLY OBJ. 3: The reason for the unity of the temple or tabernacle may be either literal or figurative. The literal reason was the exclusion of idolatry. For the Gentiles put up various times to various gods: and so, to strengthen in the minds of men their belief in the unity of the Godhead, God wished sacrifices to be offered to Him in one place only. Another reason was in order to show that bodily worship is not acceptable of itself: and so they restrained from offering sacrifices anywhere and everywhere. But the worship of the New Law, in the sacrifice whereof spiritual grace is contained, is of itself acceptable to God; and consequently the multiplication of altars and temples is permitted in the New Law.

As to those matters that regarded the spiritual worship of God, consisting in the teaching of the Law and the Prophets, there were, even under the Old Law, various places, called synagogues, appointed for the people to gather together for the praise of God; just as now there are places called churches in which the Christian people gather together for the divine worship. Thus our church takes the place of both temple and synagogue: since the very sacrifice of the Church is spiritual; wherefore with us the place of sacrifice is not distinct from the place of teaching. The figurative reason may be that hereby is signified the unity of the Church, whether militant or triumphant.

REPLY OBJ. 4: Just as the unity of the temple or tabernacle betokened the unity of God, or the unity of the Church, so also the division of the tabernacle or temple signified the distinction of those things that are subject to God, and from which we arise to the worship of God. Now the tabernacle was divided into two parts: one was called the *Holy of Holies*, and was placed to the west; the other was called the *Holy Place*, which was situated to the east. Moreover there was a court facing the tabernacle. Accordingly there are two reasons for this distinction. One is in respect of the tabernacle being ordained to the worship of God. Because the different parts of the world are thus betokened by the division of the tabernacle. For that part which was called the Holy of Holies signified the higher world, which is that of spiritual substances: while that part which is called the Holy Place signified the corporeal world. Hence the Holy Place was separated from the Holy of Holies by a veil, which was of four different colors (denoting the four elements), viz., of linen, signifying earth, because linen, i.e., flax, grows out of the earth; purple, signifying water, because the purple tint was made from certain shells found in the sea; violet, signifying air, because it has the color of the air; and scarlet twice dyed, signifying fire: and this because matter composed of the four elements is a veil between us and incorporeal substances. Hence the high-priest alone, and that once a year, entered into the inner tabernacle, i.e., the Holy of Holies: whereby we are taught that man's final perfection consists in his entering into that (higher) world: whereas into the outward tabernacle, i.e., the Holy Place,

perfectio hominis, ut ad illud saeculum introducatur. In tabernaculum vero exterius, idest in sancta, introibant sacerdotes quotidie, non autem populus, qui solum ad atrium accedebat, quia ipsa corpora populus percipere potest; ad interiores autem eorum rationes soli sapientes per considerationem attingere possunt.

Secundum vero rationem figuralem, per exterius tabernaculum, quod dicitur sancta, significatur status veteris legis, ut apostolus dicit, ad Heb. IX, quia ad illud tabernaculum *semper introibant sacerdotes sacrificiorum officia consummantes*. Per interius vero tabernaculum, quod dicitur sancta sanctorum, significatur vel caelestis gloria, vel etiam status spiritualis novae legis, qui est quaedam inchoatio futurae gloriae. In quem statum nos Christus introduxit, quod figurabatur per hoc quod summus sacerdos, semel in anno, solus in sancta sanctorum intrabat. Velum autem figurabat spiritualium occultationem sacrificiorum in veteribus sacrificiis. Quod velum quatuor coloribus erat ornatum, bysso quidem, ad designandam carnis puritatem; purpura autem, ad figurandum passiones quas sancti sustinuerunt pro Deo; cocco bis tincto, ad significandum caritatem geminam Dei et proximi; hyacintho autem significabatur caelestis meditatio. Ad statum autem veteris legis aliter se habebat populus, et aliter sacerdotes. Nam populus ipsa corporalia sacrificia considerabat, quae in atrio offerebantur. Sacerdotes vero rationem sacrificiorum considerabant, habentes fidem magis explicitam de mysteriis Christi. Et ideo intrabant in exterius tabernaculum. Quod etiam quodam velo distinguebatur ab atrio, quia quaedam erant velata populo circa mysterium Christi, quae sacerdotibus erant nota. Non tamen erant eis plene revelata, sicut postea in novo testamento, ut habetur Ephes. III.

AD QUINTUM dicendum quod adoratio ad occidentem fuit introducta in lege ad excludendam idololatriam, nam omnes gentiles, in reverentiam solis, adorabant ad orientem; unde dicitur Ezech. VIII, quod *quidam habebant dorsa contra templum domini et facies ad orientem, et adorabant ad ortum solis*. Unde ad hoc excludendum, tabernaculum habebat sancta sanctorum ad occidentem, ut versus occidentem adorarent. Ratio etiam figuralis esse potest quia totus status prioris tabernaculi ordinabatur ad figurandum mortem Christi, quae significatur per occasum; secundum illud Psalmi LXVII, *qui ascendit super occasum, dominus nomen illi*.

AD SEXTUM dicendum quod eorum quae in tabernaculo continebantur, ratio reddi potest et litteralis et figuralis. Litteralis quidem, per relationem ad cultum divinum. Et quia dictum est quod per tabernaculum interius, quod dicebatur sancta sanctorum, significabatur saeculum altius spiritualium substantiarum, ideo in illo tabernaculo tria continebantur. Scilicet arca testamenti, in qua erat urna aurea habens manna, et virga Aaron

the priests entered every day: whereas the people were only admitted to the court; because the people were able to perceive material things, the inner nature of which only wise men by dint of study are able to discover.

But regard to the figurative reason, the outward tabernacle, which was called the Holy Place, betokened the state of the Old Law, as the Apostle says (Heb 9:6, seqq.): because into that tabernacle *the priests always entered accomplishing the offices of sacrifices*. But the inner tabernacle, which was called the Holy of Holies, signified either the glory of heaven or the spiritual state of the New Law to come. To the latter state Christ brought us; and this was signified by the high-priest entering alone, once a year, into the Holy of Holies. The veil betokened the concealing of the spiritual sacrifices under the sacrifices of old. This veil was adorned with four colors: viz., that of linen, to designate purity of the flesh; purple, to denote the sufferings which the saints underwent for God; scarlet twice dyed, signifying the twofold love of God and our neighbor; and violet, in token of heavenly contemplation. With regard to the state of the Old Law the people and the priests were situated differently from one another. For the people saw the mere corporeal sacrifices which were offered in the court: whereas the priests were intent on the inner meaning of the sacrifices, because their faith in the mysteries of Christ was more explicit. Hence they entered into the outer tabernacle. This outer tabernacle was divided from the court by a veil; because some matters relating to the mystery of Christ were hidden from the people, while they were known to the priests: though they were not fully revealed to them, as they were subsequently in the New Testament (cf. Eph. 3:5).

REPLY OBJ. 5: Worship towards the west was introduced in the Law to the exclusion of idolatry: because all the Gentiles, in reverence to the sun, worshipped towards the east; hence it is written (Ezek 8:16) that certain men *had their backs towards the temple of the Lord, and their faces to the east, and they adored towards the rising of the sun*. Accordingly, in order to prevent this, the tabernacle had the Holy of Holies to westward, that they might adore toward the west. A figurative reason may also be found in the fact that the whole state of the first tabernacle was ordained to foreshadow the death of Christ, which is signified by the west, according to Ps. 67:5: *Who ascendeth unto the west; the Lord is His name*.

REPLY OBJ. 6: Both literal and figurative reasons may be assigned for the things contained in the tabernacle. The literal reason is in connection with the divine worship. And because, as already observed (ad 4), the inner tabernacle, called the Holy of Holies, signified the higher world of spiritual substances, hence that tabernacle contained three things, viz., *the ark of the testament in which was a golden pot that had manna, and the rod of Aaron that had*

quae fronduerat, et tabulae in quibus erant scripta decem praecepta legis. Haec autem arca sita erat inter duos Cherubim, qui se mutuis vultibus respiciebant. Et super arcam erat quaedam tabula, quae dicebatur propitiatorium, super alas Cherubim, quasi ab ipsis Cherubim portaretur, ac si imaginaretur quod illa tabula esset sedes Dei. Unde et propitiatorium dicebatur, quasi exinde populo propitiaretur, ad preces summi sacerdotis. Et ideo quasi portabatur a Cherubim, quasi Deo obsequentibus, arca vero testamenti erat quasi scabellum sedentis supra propitiatorium. Per haec autem tria designantur tria quae sunt in illo altiori saeculo. Scilicet Deus, qui super omnia est, et incomprehensibilis omni creaturae. Et propter hoc nulla similitudo eius ponebatur, ad repraesentandam eius invisibilitatem. Sed ponebatur quaedam figura sedis eius, quia scilicet creatura comprehensibilis est, quae est subiecta Deo, sicut sedes sedenti. Sunt etiam in illo altiori saeculo spirituales substantiae, quae Angeli dicuntur. Et hi significantur per duos Cherubim; mutuo se respicientes, ad designandam concordiam eorum ad invicem, secundum illud Iob XXV, qui facit concordiam in sublimibus. Et propter hoc etiam non fuit unus tantum Cherubim, ut designaretur multitudo caelestium spirituum, et excluderetur cultus eorum ab his quibus praeceptum erat ut solum unum Deum colerent. Sunt etiam in illo intelligibili saeculo rationes omnium eorum quae in hoc saeculo perficiuntur quodammodo clausae, sicut rationes effectuum clauduntur in suis causis, et rationes artificiatorum in artifice. Et hoc significabatur per arcam, in qua repraesentabantur, per tria ibi contenta, tria quae sunt potissima in rebus humanis, scilicet sapientia, quae repraesentabatur per tabulas testamenti; potestas regiminis, quae repraesentabatur per virgam Aaron; vita, quae repraesentabatur per manna, quod fuit sustentamentum vitae. Vel per haec tria significabantur tria Dei attributa, scilicet sapientia, in tabulis; potentia, in virga; bonitas, in manna, tum propter dulcedinem, tum quia ex Dei misericordia est populo datum, et ideo in memoriam divinae misericordiae conservabatur. Et haec tria etiam figurata sunt in visione Isaiae. Vidit enim dominum sedentem super solium excelsum et elevatum; et Seraphim assistentes; et domum impleri a gloria Dei. Unde et Seraphim dicebant, plena est omnis terra gloria eius. Et sic similitudines Seraphim non ponebantur ad cultum, quod prohibebatur primo legis praecepto, sed in signum ministerii, ut dictum est.

In exteriori vero tabernaculo, quod significat praesens saeculum, continebantur etiam tria, scilicet altare thymiamatis, quod erat directe contra arcam; mensa propositionis, super quam duodecim panes apponebantur, erat posita ex parte aquilonari; candelabrum vero ex parte Australi. Quae tria videntur respondere tribus

blossomed, and the tables (Heb 9:4) on which were written the ten commandments of the Law. Now the ark stood between two *cherubim* that looked one towards the other: and over the ark was a table, called the *propitiatory*, raised above the wings of the cherubim, as though it were held up by them; and appearing, to the imagination, to be the very seat of God. For this reason it was called the *propitiatory*, as though the people received propitiation thence at the prayers of the high-priest. And so it was held up, so to speak, by the cherubim, in obedience, as it were, to God: while the ark of the testament was like the foot-stool to Him that sat on the propitiatory. These three things denote three things in that higher world: namely, God Who is above all, and incomprehensible to any creature. Hence no likeness of Him was set up; to denote His invisibility. But there was something to represent his seat; since, to wit, the creature, which is beneath God, as the seat under the sitter, is comprehensible. Again in that higher world there are spiritual substances called angels. These are signified by the two cherubim, looking one towards the other, to show that they are at peace with one another, according to Job 25:2: *Who maketh peace in . . . high places.* For this reason, too, there was more than one cherub, to betoken the multitude of heavenly spirits, and to prevent their receiving worship from those who had been commanded to worship but one God. Moreover there are, enclosed as it were in that spiritual world, the intelligible types of whatsoever takes place in this world, just as in every cause are enclosed the types of its effects, and in the craftsman the types of the works of his craft. This was betokened by the ark, which represented, by means of the three things it contained, the three things of greatest import in human affairs. These are wisdom, signified by the tables of the testament; the power of governing, betokened by the rod of Aaron; and life, betokened by the manna which was the means of sustenance. Or else these three things signified the three Divine attributes, viz., wisdom, in the tables; power, in the rod; goodness, in the manna—both by reason of its sweetness, and because it was through the goodness of God that it was granted to man, wherefore it was preserved as a memorial of the Divine mercy. Again, these three things were represented in Isaias' vision. For he *saw the Lord sitting upon a throne high and elevated*; and the seraphim standing by; and that the house was filled with the glory of the Lord; wherefrom the seraphim cried out: *All the earth is full of His glory* (Isa 6:1,3). And so the images of the seraphim were set up, not to be worshipped, for this was forbidden by the first commandment; but as a sign of their function, as stated above.

The outer tabernacle, which denotes this present world, also contained three things, viz., the *altar of incense*, which was directly opposite the ark; the *table of proposition*, with the twelve loaves of proposition on it, which stood on the northern side; and the *candlestick*, which was placed towards the south. These three things seem to correspond to

quae erant in arca clausa, sed magis manifeste eadem repraesentabant, oportet enim rationes rerum ad manifestiorem demonstrationem perduci quam sint in mente divina et Angelorum, ad hoc quod homines sapientes eas cognoscere possint qui significantur per sacerdotes ingredientes tabernaculum. In candelabro igitur designabatur, sicut in signo sensibili, sapientia quae intelligibilibus verbis exprimebatur in tabulis. Per altare vero thymiamatis significabatur officium sacerdotum, quorum erat populum ad Deum reducere, et hoc etiam significabatur per virgam. Nam in illo altari incedebatur thymiama boni odoris, per quod significabatur sanctitas populi acceptabilis Deo, dicitur enim Apoc. VIII, quod per fumum aromatum significantur iustificationes sanctorum. Convenienter autem sacerdotalis dignitas in arca significabatur per virgam, in exteriori vero tabernaculo per altare thymiamatis, quia sacerdos mediator est inter Deum et populum, regens populum per potestatem divinam, quam virga significat; et fructum sui regiminis, scilicet sanctitatem populi, Deo offert, quasi in altari thymiamatis. Per mensam autem significatur nutrimentum vitae, sicut et per manna. Sed hoc est communius et grossius nutrimentum, illud autem suavius et subtilius. Convenienter autem candelabrum ponebatur ex parte Australi, mensa autem ex parte aquilonari, quia Australis pars est dextera pars mundi, aquilonaris autem sinistra, ut dicitur in II de caelo et mundo; sapientia autem pertinet ad dextram, sicut et cetera spiritualia bona; temporale autem nutrimentum ad sinistram, secundum illud Prov. III, *in sinistra illius divitiae et gloria*. Potestas autem sacerdotalis media est inter temporalia et spiritualem sapientiam, quia per eam et spiritualis sapientia et temporalia dispensantur.

Potest autem et horum alia ratio assignari magis litteralis. In arca enim continebantur tabulae legis, ad tollendam legis oblivionem, unde dicitur Exod. XXIV, *dabo tibi duas tabulas lapideas et legem ac mandata quae scripsi, ut doceas filios Israel*. Virga vero Aaron ponebatur ibi ad comprimendam dissensionem populi de sacerdotio Aaron, unde dicitur Num. XVII, *refer virgam Aaron in tabernaculum testimonii, ut servetur in signum rebellium filiorum Israel*. Manna autem conservabatur in arca, ad commemorandum beneficium quod dominus praestitit filiis Israel in deserto, unde dicitur Exod. XVI, *imple gomor ex eo, et custodiatur in futuras retro generationes, ut noverint panes de quibus alui vos in solitudine*. Candelabrum vero erat institutum ad honorificentiam tabernaculi, pertinet enim ad magnificentiam domus quod sit bene luminosa. Habebat autem candelabrum septem calamos, ut Iosephus dicit, ad significandum septem planetas, quibus totus mundus illuminatur. Et ideo ponebatur candelabrum ex parte Australi, quia ex illa parte est nobis planetarum cursus. Altare vero thymiamatis

the three which were enclosed in the ark; and they represented the same things as the latter, but more clearly: because, in order that wise men, denoted by the priests entering the temple, might grasp the meaning of these types, it was necessary to express them more manifestly than they are in the Divine or angelic mind. Accordingly the candlestick betokened, as a sensible sign thereof, the wisdom which was expressed on the tables (of the Law) in intelligible words. The altar of incense signified the office of the priest, whose duty it was to bring the people to God: and this was signified also by the rod: because on that altar the sweet-smelling incense was burnt, signifying the holiness of the people acceptable to God: for it is written (Rev 8:3) that the smoke of the sweet-smelling spices signifies the *justifications of the saints* (cf. Apoc. 19:8). Moreover it was fitting that the dignity of the priesthood should be denoted, in the ark, by the rod, and, in the outer tabernacle, by the altar of incense: because the priest is the mediator between God and the people, governing the people by Divine power, denoted by the rod; and offering to God the fruit of His government, i.e., the holiness of the people, on the altar of incense, so to speak. The table signified the sustenance of life, just as the manna did: but the former, a more general and a coarser kind of nourishment; the latter, a sweeter and more delicate. Again, the candlestick was fittingly placed on the southern side, while the table was placed to the north: because the south is the right-hand side of the world, while the north is the left-hand side, as stated in *De Coelo et Mundo* ii; and wisdom, like other spiritual goods, belongs to the right hand, while temporal nourishment belongs on the left, according to Prov. 3:16: *In her left hand (are) riches and glory*. And the priestly power is midway between temporal goods and spiritual wisdom; because thereby both spiritual wisdom and temporal goods are dispensed.

Another literal signification may be assigned. For the ark contained the tables of the Law, in order to prevent forgetfulness of the Law, wherefore it is written (Exod 24:12): *I will give thee two tables of stone, and the Law, and the commandments which I have written: that thou mayest teach them* to the children of Israel. The rod of Aaron was placed there to restrain the people from insubordination to the priesthood of Aaron; wherefore it is written (Num 17:10): *Carry back the rod of Aaron into the tabernacle of the testimony, that it may be kept there for a token of the rebellious children of Israel*. The manna was kept in the ark to remind them of the benefit conferred by God on the children of Israel in the desert; wherefore it is written (Exod 16:32): *Fill a gomor of it, and let it be kept unto generations to come hereafter, that they may know the bread wherewith I fed you in the wilderness*. The candlestick was set up to enhance the beauty of the temple, for the magnificence of a house depends on its being well lighted. Now the candlestick had seven branches, as Josephus observes (*Antiquit*. iii, 7,8), to signify the seven planets, wherewith the whole world

erat institutum ut iugiter in tabernaculo esset fumus boni odoris, tum propter venerationem tabernaculi; tum etiam in remedium fetoris quem oportebat accidere ex effusione sanguinis et occisione animalium. Ea enim quae sunt fetida, despiciuntur quasi vilia, quae vero sunt boni odoris, homines magis appretiant. Mensa autem apponebatur ad significandum quod sacerdotes templo servientes, in templo victum habere debebant, unde duodecim panes superpositos mensae, in memoriam duodecim tribuum, solis sacerdotibus edere licitum erat, ut habetur Matth. XII. Mensa autem non ponebatur directe in medio ante propitiatorium, ad excludendum ritum idololatriae, nam gentiles in sacris lunae proponebant mensam coram idolo lunae; unde dicitur Ierem. VII, *mulieres conspergunt adipem ut faciant placentas reginae caeli.*

In atrio vero extra tabernaculum continebatur altare holocaustorum, in quo offerebantur Deo sacrificia de his quae erant a populo possessa. Et ideo in atrio poterat esse populus, qui huiusmodi Deo offerebat per manus sacerdotum. Sed ad altare interius, in quo ipsa devotio et sanctitas populi Deo offerebatur, non poterant accedere nisi sacerdotes, quorum erat Deo offerre populum. Est autem hoc altare extra tabernaculum in atrio constitutum, ad removendum cultum idololatriae, nam gentiles infra templa altaria constituebant ad immolandum idolis.

Figuralis vero ratio omnium horum assignari potest ex relatione tabernaculi ad Christum, qui figurabatur. Est autem considerandum quod ad designandum imperfectionem legalium figurarum, diversae figurae fuerunt institutae in templo ad significandum Christum. Ipse enim significatur per propitiatorium, quia ipse est propitiatio pro peccatis nostris, ut dicitur I Ioan. II. Et convenienter hoc propitiatorium a Cherubim portatur, quia de eo scriptum est, adorent eum omnes Angeli Dei, ut habetur Heb. I. Ipse etiam significatur per arcam, quia sicut arca erat constructa de lignis setim, ita corpus Christi de membris purissimis constabat. Erat autem deaurata, quia Christus fuit plenus sapientia et caritate, quae per aurum significantur. Intra arcam autem erat urna aurea, idest sancta anima; habens manna, idest omnem plenitudinem divinitatis. Erat etiam in arca virga, idest potestas sacerdotalis, quia ipse est factus sacerdos in aeternum. Erant etiam ibi tabulae testamenti, ad designandum quod ipse Christus est legis dator. Ipse etiam Christus significatur per candelabrum, quia ipse dicit, ego sum lux mundi, per septem lucernas, septem dona spiritus sancti. Ipse est spiritualis cibus, secundum illud Ioan. VI, ego sum panis vivus, duodecim autem panes significant duodecim apostolos, vel doctrinam eorum. Sive per candelabrum et mensam potest significari

is illuminated. Hence the candlestick was placed towards the south; because for us the course of the planets is from that quarter. The altar of incense was instituted that there might always be in the tabernacle a sweet-smelling smoke; both through respect for the tabernacle, and as a remedy for the stenches arising from the shedding of blood and the slaying of animals. For men despise evil-smelling things as being vile, whereas sweet-smelling things are much appreciated. The table was place there to signify that the priests who served the temple should take their food in the temple: wherefore, as stated in Mt. 12:4, it was lawful for none but the priests to eat the twelve loaves which were put on the table in memory of the twelve tribes. And the table was not placed in the middle directly in front of the propitiatory, in order to exclude an idolatrous rite: for the Gentiles, on the feasts of the moon, set up a table in front of the idol of the moon, wherefore it is written (Jer 7:18): *The women knead the dough, to make cakes to the queen of heaven.*

In the court outside the tabernacle was the altar of holocausts, on which sacrifices of those things which the people possessed were offered to God: and consequently the people who offered these sacrifices to God by the hands of the priest could be present in the court. But the priests alone, whose function it was to offer the people to God, could approach the inner altar, whereon the very devotion and holiness of the people was offered to God. And this altar was put up outside the tabernacle and in the court, to the exclusion of idolatrous worship: for the Gentiles placed altars inside the temples to offer up sacrifices thereon to idols.

The figurative reason for all these things may be taken from the relation of the tabernacle to Christ, who was foreshadowed therein. Now it must be observed that to show the imperfection of the figures of the Law, various figures were instituted in the temple to betoken Christ. For He was foreshadowed by the *propitiatory*, since He is *a propitiation for our sins* (1 John 2:2). This propitiatory was fittingly carried by cherubim, since of Him it is written (Heb 1:6): *Let all the angels of God adore Him.* He is also signified by the ark: because just as the ark was made of setim-wood, so was Christ's body composed of most pure members. Moreover it was gilded: for Christ was full of wisdom and charity, which are betokened by gold. And in the ark was a golden pot, i.e., His holy soul, having manna, i.e., *all the fullness of the Godhead* (Col 2:9). Also there was a rod in the ark, i.e., His priestly power: for *He was made a . . . priest for ever* (Heb 6:20). And therein were the tables of the Testament, to denote that Christ Himself is a lawgiver. Again, Christ was signified by the candlestick, for He said Himself (John 8:12): *I am the Light of the world;* while the seven lamps denoted the seven gifts of the Holy Spirit. He is also betokened in the table, because He is our spiritual food, according to Jn. 6:41,51: *I am the living bread:* and the twelve loaves signified the twelve apostles, or their teaching. Or again, the candlestick and table may signify the Church's

doctrina et fides Ecclesiae, quae etiam illuminat et spiritualiter reficit. Ipse etiam Christus significatur per duplex altare holocaustorum et thymiamatis. Quia per ipsum oportet nos Deo offerre omnia virtutum opera, sive illa quibus carnem affligimus, quae offeruntur quasi in altari holocaustorum; sive illa quae, maiore mentis perfectione, per spiritualia perfectorum desideria, Deo offeruntur in Christo, quasi in altari thymiamatis, secundum illud ad Heb. ult., *per ipsum ergo offeramus hostiam laudis semper Deo.*

Ad septimum dicendum quod dominus praecepit altare construi ad sacrificia et munera offerenda, in honorem Dei et sustentationem ministrorum qui tabernaculo deserviebant. De constructione autem altaris datur a domino duplex praeceptum. Unum quidem in principio legis, Exod. XX, ubi dominus mandavit quod facerent altare de terra, vel saltem de lapidibus non sectis; et iterum quod non facerent altare excelsum, ad quod oporteret per gradus ascendere. Et hoc, ad detestandum idololatriae cultum, gentiles enim idolis construebant altaria ornata et sublimia, in quibus credebant aliquid sanctitatis et numinis esse. Propter quod etiam dominus mandavit, Deut. XVI, *non plantabis lucum, et omnem arborem, iuxta altare domini Dei tui*, idololatrae enim consueverunt sub arboribus sacrificare, propter amoenitatem et umbrositatem. Quorum etiam praeceptorum ratio figuralis fuit. Quia in Christo, qui est nostrum altare, debemus confiteri veram carnis naturam, quantum ad humanitatem, quod est altare de terra facere, et quantum ad divinitatem, debemus in eo confiteri patris aequalitatem, quod est non ascendere per gradus ad altare. Nec etiam iuxta Christum debemus admittere doctrinam gentilium, ad lasciviam provocantem.

Sed facto tabernaculo ad honorem Dei, non erant timendae huiusmodi occasiones idololatriae. Et ideo dominus mandavit quod fieret altare holocaustorum de aere, quod esset omni populo conspicuum; et altare thymiamatis de auro, quod soli sacerdotes videbant. Nec erat tanta pretiositas aeris ut per hoc populus ad aliquam idololatriam provocaretur.

Sed quia Exod. XX ponitur pro ratione huius praecepti, *non ascendes per gradus ad altare meum*, id quod subditur, ne reveletur turpitudo tua; considerandum est quod hoc etiam fuit institutum ad excludendam idololatriam, nam in sacris Priapi sua pudenda gentiles populo denudabant. Postmodum autem indictus est sacerdotibus feminalium usus ad tegimen pudendorum. Et ideo sine periculo institui potuit tanta altaris altitudo ut per aliquos gradus ligneos, non stantes sed portatiles, in hora sacrificii, sacerdotes ad altare ascenderent sacrificia offerentes.

Ad octavum dicendum quod corpus tabernaculi constabat ex quibusdam tabulis in longitudinem erectis,

teaching, and faith, which also enlightens and refreshes. Again, Christ is signified by the two altars of holocausts and incense. Because all works of virtue must be offered to us to God through Him; both those whereby we afflict the body, which are offered, as it were, on the altar of holocausts; and those which, with greater perfection of mind, are offered to God in Christ, by the spiritual desires of the perfect, on the altar of incense, as it were, according to Heb. 13:15: *By Him therefore let us offer the sacrifice of praise always to God.*

Reply Obj. 7: The Lord commanded an altar to be made for the offering of sacrifices and gifts, in honor of God, and for the upkeep of the ministers who served the tabernacle. Now concerning the construction of the altar the Lord issued a twofold precept. One was at the beginning of the Law (Exod 20:24, seqq.) when the Lord commanded them to make *an altar of earth*, or at least *not of hewn stones*; and again, not to make the altar high, so as to make it necessary to *go up* to it *by steps*. This was in detestation of idolatrous worship: for the Gentiles made their altars ornate and high, thinking that there was something holy and divine in such things. For this reason, too, the Lord commanded (Deut 16:21): *Thou shalt plant no grove, nor any tree near the altar of the Lord thy God*: since idolaters were wont to offer sacrifices beneath trees, on account of the pleasantness and shade afforded by them. There was also a figurative reason for these precepts. Because we must confess that in Christ, Who is our altar, there is the true nature of flesh, as regards His humanity—and this is to make an altar of earth; and again, in regard to His Godhead, we must confess His equality with the Father—and this is *not to go up* to the altar by steps. Moreover we should not couple the doctrine of Christ to that of the Gentiles, which provokes men to lewdness.

But when once the tabernacle had been constructed to the honor of God, there was no longer reason to fear these occasions of idolatry. Wherefore the Lord commanded the altar of holocausts to be made of brass, and to be conspicuous to all the people; and the altar of incense, which was visible to none but the priests. Nor was brass so precious as to give the people an occasion for idolatry.

Since, however, the reason for the precept, *Thou shalt not go up by steps unto My altar* (Exod 20:26) is stated to have been *lest thy nakedness be discovered*, it should be observed that this too was instituted with the purpose of preventing idolatry, for in the feasts of Priapus the Gentiles uncovered their nakedness before the people. But later on the priests were prescribed the use of loin-cloths for the sake of decency: so that without any danger the altar could be placed so high that the priests when offering sacrifices would go up by steps of wood, not fixed but movable.

Reply Obj. 8: The body of the tabernacle consisted of boards placed on end, and covered on the inside with

quae quidem interius tegebantur quibusdam cortinis ex quatuor coloribus variatis, scilicet de bysso retorta, et hyacintho, ac purpura, coccoque bis tincto. Sed huiusmodi cortinae tegebant solum latera tabernaculi, in tecto autem tabernaculi erat operimentum unum de pellibus hyacinthinis; et super hoc aliud de pellibus arietum rubricatis; et desuper tertium de quibusdam sagis cilicinis, quae non tantum operiebant tectum tabernaculi, sed etiam descendebant usque terram, et tegebant tabulas tabernaculi exterius. Horum autem operimentorum ratio litteralis in communi erat ornatus et protectio tabernaculi, ut in reverentia haberetur. In speciali vero, secundum quosdam, per cortinas designabatur caelum sydereum, quod est diversis stellis variatum; per saga, aquae quae sunt supra firmamentum; per pelles rubricatas, caelum Empyreum, in quo sunt Angeli; per pelles hyacinthinas, caelum sanctae Trinitatis.

Figuralis autem ratio horum est quia per tabulas ex quibus construebatur tabernaculum, significantur Christi fideles, ex quibus construitur Ecclesia. Tegebantur autem interius tabulae cortinis quadricoloribus, quia fideles interius ornantur quatuor virtutibus; *nam in bysso retorta*, ut Glossa dicit, *significatur caro castitate renitens; in hyacintho, mens superna cupiens; in purpura, caro passionibus subiacens; in cocco bis tincto, mens inter passiones Dei et proximi dilectione praefulgens*. Per operimenta vero tecti designantur praelati et doctores, in quibus debet renitere caelestis conversatio, quod significatur per pelles hyacinthinas; promptitudo ad martyrium, quod significant pelles rubricatae; austeritas vitae et tolerantia adversorum, quae significantur per saga cilicina, quae erant exposita ventis et pluviis, ut Glossa dicit.

AD NONUM dicendum quod sanctificatio tabernaculi et vasorum eius habebat causam litteralem ut in maiori reverentia haberetur, quasi per huiusmodi consecrationem divino cultui deputatum. Figuralis autem ratio est quia per huiusmodi sanctificationem significatur spiritualis sanctificatio viventis tabernaculi, scilicet fidelium, ex quibus constituitur Ecclesia Christi.

AD DECIMUM dicendum quod in veteri lege erant septem solemnitates temporales, et una continua, ut potest colligi Num. XXVIII et XXIX. Erat enim quasi continuum festum, quia quotidie mane et vespere immolabatur agnus. Et per illud continuum festum iugis sacrificii repraesentabatur perpetuitas divinae beatitudinis. Festorum autem temporalium primum erat quod iterabatur qualibet septimana. Et haec erat solemnitas sabbati, quod celebrabatur in memoriam creationis rerum, ut supra dictum est. Alia autem solemnitas iterabatur quolibet mense, scilicet festum Neomeniae, quod celebrabatur ad commemorandum opus divinae gubernationis. Nam haec inferiora praecipue variantur

curtains of four different colors, viz., twisted linen, violet, purple, and scarlet twice dyed. These curtains, however, covered the sides only of the tabernacle; and the roof of the tabernacle was covered with violet-colored skins; and over this there was another covering of rams' skins dyed red; and over this there was a third curtain made of goats' hair, which covered not only the roof of the tabernacle, but also reached to the ground and covered the boards of the tabernacle on the outside. The literal reason of these coverings taken altogether was the adornment and protection of the tabernacle, that it might be an object of respect. Taken singly, according to some, the curtains denoted the starry heaven, which is adorned with various stars; the curtain (of goats' skin) signified the waters which are above the firmament; the skins dyed red denoted the empyrean heaven, where the angels are; the violet skins, the heaven of the Blessed Trinity.

The figurative meaning of these things is that the boards of which the tabernacle was constructed signify the faithful of Christ, who compose the Church. The boards were covered on the inner side by curtains of four colors: because the faithful are inwardly adorned with the four virtues: for *the twisted linen*, as the gloss observes, *signifies the flesh refulgent with purity; violet signifies the mind desirous of heavenly things; purple denotes the flesh subject to passions; the twice dyed scarlet betokens the mind in the midst of the passions enlightened by the love of God and our neighbor*. The coverings of the building designate prelates and doctors, who ought to be conspicuous for their heavenly manner of life, signified by the violet colored skins: and who should also be ready to suffer martyrdom, denoted by the skins dyed red; and austere of life and patient in adversity, betokened by the curtains of goats' hair, which were exposed to wind and rain, as the gloss observes.

REPLY OBJ. 9: The literal reason for the sanctification of the tabernacle and vessels was that they might be treated with greater reverence, being deputed, as it were, to the divine worship by this consecration. The figurative reason is that this sanctification signified the sanctification of the living tabernacle, i.e., the faithful of whom the Church of Christ is composed.

REPLY OBJ. 10: Under the Old Law there were seven temporal solemnities, and one continual solemnity, as may be gathered from Num. 28,29. There was a continual feast, since the lamb was sacrificed every day, morning and evening: and this continual feast of an abiding sacrifice signified the perpetuity of Divine bliss. Of the temporal feasts the first was that which was repeated every week. This was the solemnity of the *Sabbath*, celebrated in memory of the work of the creation of the universe. Another solemnity, viz., the *New Moon*, was repeated every month, and was observed in memory of the work of the Divine government. For the things of this lower world owe their variety chiefly to the movement of the moon; wherefore this feast was

secundum motum lunae, et ideo celebrabatur hoc festum in novitate lunae. Non autem in eius plenitudine, ad evitandum idololatrarum cultum, qui in tali tempore lunae sacrificabant. Haec autem duo beneficia sunt communia toti humano generi, et ideo frequentius iterabantur.

Alia vero quinque festa celebrabantur semel in anno, et recolebantur in eis beneficia specialiter illi populo exhibita. Celebrabatur enim festum phase primo mense, ad commemorandum beneficium liberationis ex Aegypto. Celebrabatur autem festum Pentecostes post quinquaginta dies, ad recolendum beneficium legis datae. Alia vero tria festa celebrabantur in mense septimo, qui quasi totus apud eos erat solemnis, sicut et septimus dies. In prima enim die mensis septimi erat festum tubarum, in memoriam liberationis Isaac, quando Abraham invenit arietem haerentem cornibus, quem repraesentabant per cornua quibus buccinabant. Erat autem festum tubarum quasi quaedam invitatio ut praepararent se ad sequens festum, quod celebrabatur decimo die. Et hoc erat festum expiationis, in memoriam illius beneficii quo Deus propitiatus est peccato populi de adoratione vituli, ad preces Moysi. Post hoc autem celebrabatur festum Scenopegiae, idest tabernaculorum, septem diebus, ad commemorandum beneficium divinae protectionis et deductionis per desertum, ubi in tabernaculis habitaverunt. Unde in hoc festo debebant habere fructum arboris pulcherrimae, idest citrum, et lignum densarum frondium, idest myrtum, quae sunt odorifera; et spatulas palmarum, et salices de torrente, quae diu retinent suum virorem; et haec inveniuntur in terra promissionis; ad significandum quod per aridam terram deserti eos duxerat Deus ad terram deliciosam. Octavo autem die celebrabatur aliud festum, scilicet coetus atque collectae, in quo colligebantur a populo ea quae erant necessaria ad expensas cultus divini. Et significabatur adunatio populi et pax praestita in terra promissionis.

Figuralis autem ratio horum festorum est quia per iuge sacrificium agni figuratur perpetuitas Christi, qui est agnus Dei; secundum illud Heb. ult., *Iesus Christus heri et hodie, ipse et in saecula.* Per sabbatum autem significatur spiritualis requies nobis data per Christum, ut habetur ad Heb. IV. Per Neomeniam autem, quae est incoeptio novae lunae, significatur illuminatio primitivae Ecclesiae per Christum, eo praedicante et miracula faciente. Per festum autem Pentecostes significatur descensus spiritus sancti in apostolos. Per festum autem tubarum significatur praedicatio apostolorum. Per festum autem expiationis significatur emundatio a peccatis populi Christiani. Per festum autem tabernaculorum, peregrinatio eorum in hoc mundo, in quo ambulant in virtutibus proficiendo. Per festum autem coetus atque collectae significatur congregatio fidelium in regno

kept at the new moon: and not at the full moon, to avoid the worship of idolaters who used to offer sacrifices to the moon at that particular time. And these two blessings are bestowed in common on the whole human race; and hence they were repeated more frequently.

The other five feasts were celebrated once a year: and they commemorated the benefits which had been conferred especially on that people. For there was the feast of the *Passover* in the first month to commemorate the blessing of being delivered out of Egypt. The feast of *Pentecost* was celebrated fifty days later, to recall the blessing of the giving of the Law. The other three feasts were kept in the seventh month, nearly the whole of which was solemnized by them, just as the seventh day. For on the first of the seventh month was the feast of *Trumpets*, in memory of the delivery of Isaac, when Abraham found the ram caught by its horns, which they represented by the horns which they blew. The feast of Trumpets was a kind of invitation whereby they prepared themselves to keep the following feast which was kept on the tenth day. This was the feast of *Expiation*, in memory of the blessing whereby, at the prayer of Moses, God forgave the people's sin of worshipping the calf. After this was the feast of *Scenopegia* or of *Tents*, which was kept for seven days, to commemorate the blessing of being protected and led by God through the desert, where they lived in tents. Hence during this feast they had to take *the fruits of the fairest tree,* i.e., the citron, *and the trees of dense foliage,* i.e., the myrtle, which is fragrant, *and the branches of palm-trees, and willows of the brook,* which retain their greenness a long time; and these are to be found in the Land of promise; to signify that God had brought them through the arid land of the wilderness to a land of delights. On the eighth day another feast was observed, of *Assembly and Congregation,* on which the people collected the expenses necessary for the divine worship: and it signified the uniting of the people and the peace granted to them in the Land of promise.

The figurative reason for these feasts was that the continual sacrifice of the lamb foreshadowed the perpetuity of Christ, Who is the *Lamb of God,* according to Heb. 13:8: *Jesus Christ yesterday and today, and the same for ever.* The Sabbath signified the spiritual rest bestowed by Christ, as stated in Heb. 4. The Neomenia, which is the beginning of the new moon, signified the enlightening of the primitive Church by Christ's preaching and miracles. The feast of Pentecost signified the Descent of the Holy Spirit on the apostles. The feast of Trumpets signified the preaching of the apostles. The feast of Expiation signified the cleansing of the Christian people from sins: and the feast of Tabernacles signified their pilgrimage in this world, wherein they walk by advancing in virtue. The feast of Assembly or Congregation foreshadowed the assembly of the faithful in the kingdom of heaven: wherefore this feast is described

caelorum, et ideo istud festum dicebatur sanctissimum esse. Et haec tria festa erant continua ad invicem, quia oportet expiatos a vitiis proficere in virtute, quousque perveniant ad Dei visionem, ut dicitur in Psalmo LXXXIII.

as *most holy* (Lev 23:36). These three feasts followed immediately on one another, because those who expiate their vices should advance in virtue, until they come to see God, as stated in Ps. 83:8.

Article 5

Whether There Can Be Any Suitable Cause for the Sacraments of the Old Law?

AD QUINTUM SIC PROCEDITUR. Videtur quod sacramentorum veteris legis conveniens causa esse non possit. Ea enim quae ad cultum divinum fiunt, non debent esse similia his quae idololatrae observabant, dicitur enim Deut. XII, *non facies similiter domino Deo tuo, omnes enim abominationes quas aversatur dominus, fecerunt diis suis.* Sed cultores idolorum in eorum cultu se incidebant usque ad effusionem sanguinis, dicitur enim III Reg. XVIII, quod *incidebant se, iuxta ritum suum, cultris et lanceolis, donec perfunderentur sanguine.* Propter quod dominus mandavit, Deut. XIV, *non vos incidetis, nec facietis calvitium super mortuo.* Inconvenienter igitur circumcisio erat instituta in lege.

PRAETEREA, ea quae in cultum divinum fiunt, debent honestatem et gravitatem habere; secundum illud Psalmi XXXIV, *in populo gravi laudabo te.* Sed ad levitatem quandam pertinere videtur ut homines festinanter comedant. Inconvenienter igitur praeceptum est, Exod. XII, ut comederent festinanter agnum paschalem. Et alia etiam circa eius comestionem sunt instituta, quae videntur omnino irrationabilia esse.

PRAETEREA, sacramenta veteris legis figurae fuerunt sacramentorum novae legis. Sed per agnum paschalem significatur sacramentum Eucharistiae; secundum illud I ad Cor. V, *Pascha nostrum immolatus est Christus.* Ergo etiam debuerunt esse aliqua sacramenta in lege quae praefigurarent alia sacramenta novae legis, sicut confirmationem et extremam unctionem et matrimonium, et alia sacramenta.

PRAETEREA, purificatio non potest convenienter fieri nisi ab aliquibus immunditiis. Sed quantum ad Deum, nullum corporale reputatur immundum, quia omne corpus creatura Dei est; *et omnis creatura Dei bona, et nihil reiiciendum quod cum gratiarum actione percipitur,* ut dicitur I ad Tim. IV. Inconvenienter igitur purificabantur propter contactum hominis mortui, vel alicuius huiusmodi corporalis infectionis.

PRAETEREA, Eccli. XXXIV dicitur, *ab immundo quid mundabitur?* Sed cinis vitulae rufae quae comburebatur, immundus erat, quia immundum reddebat, dicitur enim Num. XIX, quod sacerdos qui immolabat eam,

OBJECTION 1: It would seem that there can be no suitable cause for the sacraments of the Old Law. Because those things that are done for the purpose of divine worship should not be like the observances of idolaters: since it is written (Deut 12:31): *Thou shalt not do in like manner to the Lord thy God: for they have done to their gods all the abominations which the Lord abhorreth.* Now worshippers of idols used to knive themselves to the shedding of blood: for it is related (3 Kgs 18:28) that they *cut themselves after their manner with knives and lancets, till they were all covered with blood.* For this reason the Lord commanded (Deut 14:1): *You shall not cut yourselves nor make any baldness for the dead.* Therefore it was unfitting for circumcision to be prescribed by the Law (Lev 12:3).

OBJ. 2: Further, those things which are done for the worship of God should be marked with decorum and gravity; according to Ps. 34:18: *I will praise Thee in a grave people.* But it seems to savor of levity for a man to eat with haste. Therefore it was unfittingly commanded (Exod 12:11) that they should eat the Paschal lamb *in haste.* Other things too relative to the eating of the lamb were prescribed, which seem altogether unreasonable.

OBJ. 3: Further, the sacraments of the Old Law were figures of the sacraments of the New Law. Now the Paschal lamb signified the sacrament of the Eucharist, according to 1 Cor. 5:7: *Christ our Pasch is sacrificed.* Therefore there should also have been some sacraments of the Old Law to foreshadow the other sacraments of the New Law, such as Confirmation, Extreme Unction, and Matrimony, and so forth.

OBJ. 4: Further, purification can scarcely be done except by removing something impure. But as far as God is concerned, no bodily thing is reputed impure, because all bodies are God's creatures; and *every creature of God is good, and nothing to be rejected that is received with thanksgiving* (1 Tim 4:4). It was therefore unfitting for them to be purified after contact with a corpse, or any similar corporeal infection.

OBJ. 5: Further, it is written (Sir 34:4): *What can be made clean by the unclean?* But the ashes of the red heifer which was burnt, were unclean, since they made a man unclean: for it is stated (Num 19:7, seqq.) that the priest who

commaculatus erat usque ad vesperum; similiter et ille qui eam comburebat; et etiam ille qui eius cineres colligebat. Ergo inconvenienter praeceptum ibi fuit ut per huiusmodi cinerem aspersum immundi purificarentur.

PRAETEREA, peccata non sunt aliquid corporale, quod possit deferri de loco ad locum, neque etiam per aliquid immundum potest homo a peccato mundari. Inconvenienter igitur ad expiationem peccatorum populi, sacerdos super unum hircorum confitebatur peccata filiorum Israel, ut portaret ea in desertum, per alium autem, quo utebantur ad purificationes, simul cum vitulo comburentes extra castra, immundi reddebantur, ita quod oportebat eos lavare vestimenta et carnem aqua.

PRAETEREA, illud quod iam est mundatum, non oportet iterum mundari. Inconvenienter igitur, mundata lepra hominis, vel etiam domus, alia purificatio adhibebatur; ut habetur Levit. XIV.

PRAETEREA, spiritualis immunditia non potest per corporalem aquam, vel pilorum rasuram, emundari. Irrationabile igitur videtur quod dominus praecepit Exod. XXX, ut fieret labium aeneum cum basi sua ad lavandum manus et pedes sacerdotum qui ingressuri erant tabernaculum; et quod praecipitur Num. VIII, quod Levitae abstergerentur aqua lustrationis, et raderent omnes pilos carnis suae.

PRAETEREA, quod maius est, non potest sanctificari per illud quod minus est. Inconvenienter igitur per quandam unctionem corporalem, et corporalia sacrificia, et oblationes corporales, fiebat in lege consecratio maiorum et minorum sacerdotum, ut habetur Levit. VIII; et Levitarum, ut habetur Num. VIII.

PRAETEREA, sicut dicitur I Reg. XVI, *homines vident ea quae parent, Deus autem intuetur cor*. Sed ea quae exterius parent in homine, est corporalis dispositio, et etiam indumenta. Inconvenienter igitur sacerdotibus maioribus et minoribus quaedam specialia vestimenta deputabantur, de quibus habetur Exod. XXVIII. Et sine ratione videtur quod prohiberetur aliquis a sacerdotio propter corporales defectus, secundum quod dicitur Levit. XXI, *homo de semine tuo per familias qui habuerit maculam, non offeret panes Deo suo, si caecus fuerit, vel claudus*, et cetera. Sic igitur videtur quod sacramenta veteris legis irrationabilia fuerint.

SED CONTRA est quod dicitur Levit. XX, *ego sum dominus, qui sanctifico vos*. Sed a Deo nihil sine ratione fit, dicitur enim in Psalmo CIII, *omnia in sapientia fecisti*. Ergo in sacramentis veteris legis, quae ordinabantur ad hominum sanctificationem, nihil erat sine rationabili causa.

RESPONDEO dicendum quod, sicut supra dictum est, sacramenta proprie dicuntur illa quae adhibebantur Dei

immolated her was rendered unclean *until the evening*; likewise he that burnt her; and he that gathered up her ashes. Therefore it was unfittingly prescribed there that the unclean should be purified by being sprinkled with those cinders.

OBJ. 6: Further, sins are not something corporeal that can be carried from one place to another: nor can man be cleansed from sin by means of something unclean. It was therefore unfitting for the purpose of expiating the sins of the people that the priest should confess the sins of the children of Israel on one of the buck-goats, that it might carry them away into the wilderness: while they were rendered unclean by the other, which they used for the purpose of purification, by burning it together with the calf outside the camp; so that they had to wash their clothes and their bodies with water (Lev 16).

OBJ. 7: Further, what is already cleansed should not be cleansed again. It was therefore unfitting to apply a second purification to a man cleansed from leprosy, or to a house; as laid down in Lev. 14.

OBJ. 8: Further, spiritual uncleanness cannot be cleansed by material water or by shaving the hair. Therefore it seems unreasonable that the Lord ordered (Exod 30:18, seqq.) the making of a brazen laver with its foot, that the priests might wash their hands and feet before entering the temple; and that He commanded (Num 8:7) the Levites to be sprinkled with the water of purification, and to shave all the hairs of their flesh.

OBJ. 9: Further, that which is greater cannot be cleansed by that which is less. Therefore it was unfitting that, in the Law, the higher and lower priests, as stated in Lev. 8, and the Levites, according to Num. 8, should be consecrated with any bodily anointing, bodily sacrifices, and bodily oblations.

OBJ. 10: Further, as stated in 1 Kgs. 16:7, *Man seeth those things that appear, but the Lord beholdeth the heart*. But those things that appear outwardly in man are the dispositions of his body and his clothes. Therefore it was unfitting for certain special garments to be appointed to the higher and lower priests, as related in Ex. 28. It seems, moreover, unreasonable that anyone should be debarred from the priesthood on account of defects in the body, as stated in Lev. 21:17, seqq.: *Whosoever of thy seed throughout their families, hath a blemish, he shall not offer bread to his God . . . if he be blind, if he be lame*, etc. It seems, therefore, that the sacraments of the Old Law were unreasonable.

ON THE CONTRARY, It is written (Lev 20:8): *I am the Lord that sanctify you*. But nothing unreasonable is done by God, for it is written (Ps 103:24): *Thou hast made all things in wisdom*. Therefore there was nothing without a reasonable cause in the sacraments of the Old Law, which were ordained to the sanctification of man.

I ANSWER THAT, As stated above (Q101, A4), the sacraments are, properly speaking, things applied to the

cultoribus ad quandam consecrationem, per quam scilicet deputabantur quodammodo ad cultum Dei. Cultus autem Dei generali quidem modo pertinebat ad totum populum; sed speciali modo pertinebat ad sacerdotes et Levitas, qui erant ministri cultus divini. Et ideo in istis sacramentis veteris legis quaedam pertinebant communiter ad totum populum; quaedam autem specialiter ad ministros.

Et circa utrosque tria erant necessaria. Quorum primum est institutio in statu colendi Deum. Et haec quidem institutio communiter quantum ad omnes, fiebat per circumcisionem, sine qua nullus admittebatur ad aliquid legalium, quantum vero ad sacerdotes, per sacerdotum consecrationem. Secundo requirebatur usus eorum quae pertinent ad divinum cultum. Et sic quantum ad populum, erat esus paschalis convivii, ad quem nullus incircumcisus admittebatur, ut patet Exod. XII, et quantum ad sacerdotes, oblatio victimarum, et esus panum propositionis et aliorum quae erant sacerdotum usibus deputata. Tertio requirebatur remotio eorum per quae aliqui impediebantur a cultu divino, scilicet immunditiarum. Et sic quantum ad populum, erant institutae quaedam purificationes a quibusdam exterioribus immunditiis, et etiam expiationes a peccatis, quantum vero ad sacerdotes et Levitas, erat instituta ablutio manuum et pedum, et rasio pilorum.

Et haec omnia habebant rationabiles causas et litterales, secundum quod ordinabantur ad cultum Dei pro tempore illo; et figurales, secundum quod ordinabantur ad figurandum Christum; ut patebit per singula.

AD PRIMUM ergo dicendum quod litteralis ratio circumcisionis principalis quidem fuit ad protestationem fidei unius Dei. Et quia Abraham fuit primus qui se ab infidelibus separavit, exiens de domo sua et de cognatione sua, ideo ipse primus circumcisionem accepit. Et hanc causam assignat apostolus, ad Rom. IV, *signum accepit circumcisionis, signaculum iustitiae fidei quae est in praeputio*, quia scilicet in hoc legitur Abrahae fides reputata ad iustitiam, quod contra spem in spem credidit, scilicet contra spem naturae in spem gratiae, ut fieret pater multarum gentium, cum ipse esset senex, et uxor sua esset anus et sterilis. Et ut haec protestatio, et imitatio fidei Abrahae, firmaretur in cordibus Iudaeorum, acceperunt signum in carne sua, cuius oblivisci non possent, unde dicitur Gen. XVII, *erit pactum meum in carne vestra in foedus aeternum*. Ideo autem fiebat octava die, quia antea puer est valde tenellus, et posset ex hoc graviter laedi, et reputatur adhuc quasi quiddam non solidatum, unde etiam nec animalia offerebantur ante octavum diem. Ideo vero non magis tardabatur, ne propter dolorem aliqui signum circumcisionis refugerent, et ne parentes etiam, quorum amor increscit ad filios post frequentem conversationem et eorum augmentum, eos

worshippers of God for their consecration so as, in some way, to depute them to the worship of God. Now the worship of God belonged in a general way to the whole people; but in a special way, it belonged to the priests and Levites, who were the ministers of divine worship. Consequently, in these sacraments of the Old Law, certain things concerned the whole people in general; while others belonged to the ministers.

In regard to both, three things were necessary. The first was to be established in the state of worshipping God: and this institution was brought about—for all in general, by circumcision, without which no one was admitted to any of the legal observances—and for the priests, by their consecration. The second thing required was the use of those things that pertain to divine worship. And thus, as to the people, there was the partaking of the paschal banquet, to which no uncircumcised man was admitted, as is clear from Ex. 12:43, seqq.: and, as to the priests, the offering of the victims, and the eating of the loaves of proposition and of other things that were allotted to the use of the priests. The third thing required was the removal of all impediments to divine worship, viz., of uncleannesses. And then, as to the people, certain purifications were instituted for the removal of certain external uncleannesses; and also expiations from sins; while, as to the priests and Levites, the washing of hands and feet and the shaving of the hair were instituted.

And all these things had reasonable causes, both literal, insofar as they were ordained to the worship of God for the time being, and figurative, insofar as they were ordained to foreshadow Christ: as we shall see by taking them one by one.

REPLY OBJ. 1: The chief literal reason for circumcision was in order that man might profess his belief in one God. And because Abraham was the first to sever himself from the infidels, by going out from his house and kindred, for this reason he was the first to receive circumcision. This reason is set forth by the Apostle (Rom 4:9, seqq.) thus: *He received the sign of circumcision, a seal of the justice of the faith which he had, being uncircumcised*; because, to wit, we are told that *unto Abraham faith was reputed to justice*, for the reason that *against hope he believed in hope*, i.e., against the hope that is of nature he believed in the hope that is of grace, *that he might be made the father of many nations*, when he was an old man, and his wife an old and barren woman. And in order that this declaration, and imitation of Abraham's faith, might be fixed firmly in the hearts of the Jews, they received in their flesh such a sign as they could not forget, wherefore it is written (Gen 17:13): *My covenant shall be in your flesh for a perpetual covenant*. This was done on the eighth day, because until then a child is very tender, and so might be seriously injured; and is considered as something not yet consolidated: wherefore neither are animals offered before the eighth day. And it was not delayed after that time, lest some might refuse the sign

circumcisioni subtraherent. Secunda ratio esse potuit ad debilitationem concupiscentiae in membro illo. Tertia ratio, in sugillationem sacrorum Veneris et Priapi, in quibus illa pars corporis honorabatur. Dominus autem non prohibuit nisi incisionem quae in cultum idolorum fiebat, cui non erat similis praedicta circumcisio.

Figuralis vero ratio circumcisionis erat quia figurabatur ablatio corruptionis fienda per Christum, quae perfecte complebitur in octava aetate, quae est aetas resurgentium. Et quia omnis corruptio culpae et poenae provenit in nos per carnalem originem ex peccato primi parentis, ideo talis circumcisio fiebat in membro generationis. Unde apostolus dicit, ad Colos. II, *circumcisi estis in Christo circumcisione non manu facta in expoliatione corporis carnis, sed in circumcisione domini nostri Iesu Christi.*

AD SECUNDUM dicendum quod litteralis ratio paschalis convivii fuit in commemorationem beneficii quo Deus eduxit eos de Aegypto. Unde per huiusmodi convivii celebrationem profitebantur se ad illum populum pertinere quem Deus sibi assumpserat ex Aegypto. Quando enim sunt ex Aegypto liberati, praeceptum est eis ut sanguine agni linirent superliminaria domorum, quasi protestantes se recedere a ritibus Aegyptiorum, qui arietem colebant. Unde et liberati sunt per sanguinis agni aspersionem vel linitionem in postibus domorum, a periculo exterminii quod imminebat Aegyptiis.

In illo autem exitu eorum de Aegypto duo fuerunt, scilicet festinantia ad egrediendum, impellebant enim eos Aegyptii ut exirent velociter, ut habetur Exod. XII; imminebatque periculum ei qui non festinaret exire cum multitudine, ne remanens occideretur ab Aegyptiis. Festinantia autem designabatur dupliciter. Uno quidem modo per ea quae comedebant. Praeceptum enim erat eis quod comederent panes azymos, in huius signum, quod non poterant fermentari, cogentibus exire Aegyptiis; et quod comederent assum igni, sic enim velocius praeparabatur; et quod os non comminuerent ex eo, quia in festinantia non vacat ossa frangere. Alio modo, quantum ad modum comedendi. Dicitur enim, *renes vestros accingetis, calceamenta habebitis in pedibus, tenentes baculos in manibus, et comedetis festinanter,* quod manifeste designat homines existentes in promptu itineris. Ad idem etiam pertinet quod eis praecipitur, *in una domo comedetis, neque feretis de carnibus eius foras,* quia scilicet, propter festinantiam, non vacabat invicem mittere exennia.

of circumcision on account of the pain: and also lest the parents, whose love for their children increases as they become used to their presence and as they grow older, should withdraw their children from circumcision. A second reason may have been the weakening of concupiscence in that member. A third motive may have been to revile the worship of Venus and Priapus, which gave honor to that part of the body. The Lord's prohibition extended only to the cutting of oneself in honor of idols: and such was not the circumcision of which we have been speaking.

The figurative reason for circumcision was that it foreshadowed the removal of corruption, which was to be brought about by Christ, and will be perfectly fulfilled in the eighth age, which is the age of those who rise from the dead. And since all corruption of guilt and punishment comes to us through our carnal origin, from the sin of our first parent, therefore circumcision was applied to the generative member. Hence the Apostle says (Col 2:11): *You are circumcised* in Christ *with circumcision not made by hand in despoiling of the body of the flesh, but in the circumcision of* Our Lord Jesus *Christ.*

REPLY OBJ. 2: The literal reason of the paschal banquet was to commemorate the blessing of being led by God out of Egypt. Hence by celebrating this banquet they declared that they belonged to that people which God had taken to Himself out of Egypt. For when they were delivered from Egypt, they were commanded to sprinkle the lamb's blood on the transoms of their house doors, as though declaring that they were averse to the rites of the Egyptians who worshipped the ram. Wherefore they were delivered by the sprinkling or rubbing of the blood of the lamb on the doorposts, from the danger of extermination which threatened the Egyptians.

Now two things are to be observed in their departure from Egypt: namely, their haste in going, for the Egyptians pressed them to go forth speedily, as related in Ex. 12:33; and there was danger that anyone who did not hasten to go with the crowd might be slain by the Egyptians. Their haste was shown in two ways. First by what they ate. For they were commanded to eat unleavened bread, as a sign *that it could not be leavened, the Egyptians pressing them to depart*; and to eat roast meat, for this took less time to prepare; and that they should not break a bone thereof, because in their haste there was no time to break bones. Second, as to the manner of eating. For it is written: *You shall gird your reins, and you shall have shoes on your feet, holding staves in your hands, and you shall eat in haste*: which clearly designates men at the point of starting on a journey. To this also is to be referred the command: *In one house shall it be eaten, neither shall you carry forth of the flesh thereof out of the house*: because, to wit, on account of their haste, they could not send any gifts of it.

Amaritudo autem quam passi fuerant in Aegypto, significabatur per lactucas agrestes. Figuralis autem ratio patet. Quia per immolationem agni paschalis significabatur immolatio Christi; secundum illud I ad Cor. V, *Pascha nostrum immolatus est Christus.* Sanguis vero agni liberans ab exterminatore, linitis superliminaribus domorum, significat fidem passionis Christi in corde et ore fidelium, per quam liberamur a peccato et a morte; secundum illud I Petr. I, *redempti estis pretioso sanguine agni immaculati.* Comedebantur autem carnes illae, ad significandum esum corporis Christi in sacramento. Erant autem assae igni, ad significandum passionem, vel caritatem Christi. Comedebantur autem cum azymis panibus, ad significandam puram conversationem fidelium sumentium corpus Christi, secundum illud I ad Cor. V, *epulemur in azymis sinceritatis et veritatis.* Lactucae autem agrestes addebantur, in signum poenitentiae peccatorum, quae necessaria est sumentibus corpus Christi. Renes autem accingendi sunt cingulo castitatis. Calceamenta autem pedum sunt exempla mortuorum patrum. Baculi autem habendi in manibus, significant pastoralem custodiam. Praecipitur autem quod in una domo agnus paschalis comedatur, idest in Ecclesia Catholicorum, non in conventiculis haereticorum.

Ad tertium dicendum quod quaedam sacramenta novae legis habuerunt in veteri lege sacramenta figuralia sibi correspondentia. Nam circumcisioni respondet Baptismus, qui est fidei sacramentum, unde dicitur ad Col. II, *circumcisi estis in circumcisione domini nostri Iesu Christi, consepulti ei in Baptismo.* Convivio vero agni paschalis respondet in nova lege sacramentum Eucharistiae. Omnibus autem purificationibus veteris legis respondet in nova lege sacramentum poenitentiae. Consecrationi autem pontificum et sacerdotum respondet sacramentum ordinis. Sacramento autem confirmationis, quod est sacramentum plenitudinis gratiae, non potest respondere in veteri lege aliquod sacramentum, quia nondum advenerat tempus plenitudinis, eo quod neminem ad perfectum adduxit lex. Similiter autem et sacramento extremae unctionis, quod est quaedam immediata praeparatio ad introitum gloriae, cuius aditus nondum patebat in veteri lege, pretio nondum soluto. Matrimonium autem fuit quidem in veteri lege prout erat in officium naturae; non autem prout est sacramentum coniunctionis Christi et Ecclesiae, quae nondum erat facta. Unde et in veteri lege dabatur libellus repudii, quod est contra sacramenti rationem.

Ad quartum dicendum quod, sicut dictum est, purificationes veteris legis ordinabantur ad removendum impedimenta cultus divini. Qui quidem est duplex, scilicet spiritualis, qui consistit in devotione mentis ad Deum; et corporalis, qui consistit in sacrificiis et oblationibus et aliis huiusmodi. A cultu autem spirituali

The stress they suffered while in Egypt was denoted by the wild lettuces. The figurative reason is evident, because the sacrifice of the paschal lamb signified the sacrifice of Christ according to 1 Cor. 5:7: *Christ our pasch is sacrificed.* The blood of the lamb, which ensured deliverance from the destroyer, by being sprinkled on the transoms, signified faith in Christ's Passion, in the hearts and on the lips of the faithful, by which same Passion we are delivered from sin and death, according to 1 Pt. 1:18: *You were . . . redeemed . . . with the precious blood . . . of a lamb unspotted.* The partaking of its flesh signified the eating of Christ's body in the Sacrament; and the flesh was roasted at the fire to signify Christ's Passion or charity. And it was eaten with unleavened bread to signify the blameless life of the faithful who partake of Christ's body, according to 1 Cor. 5:8: *Let us feast . . . with the unleavened bread of sincerity and truth.* The wild lettuces were added to denote repentance for sins, which is required of those who receive the body of Christ. Their loins were girt in sign of chastity: and the shoes of their feet are the examples of our dead ancestors. The staves they were to hold in their hands denoted pastoral authority: and it was commanded that the paschal lamb should be eaten in one house, i.e., in a catholic church, and not in the conventicles of heretics.

Reply Obj. 3: Some of the sacraments of the New Law had corresponding figurative sacraments in the Old Law. For Baptism, which is the sacrament of Faith, corresponds to circumcision. Hence it is written (Col 2:11,12): *You are circumcised . . . in the circumcision of* Our Lord Jesus *Christ: buried with Him in Baptism.* In the New Law the sacrament of the Eucharist corresponds to the banquet of the paschal lamb. The sacrament of Penance in the New Law corresponds to all the purifications of the Old Law. The sacrament of Orders corresponds to the consecration of the pontiff and of the priests. To the sacrament of Confirmation, which is the sacrament of the fullness of grace, there would be no corresponding sacrament of the Old Law, because the time of fullness had not yet come, since *the Law brought no man to perfection* (Heb 7:19). The same applies to the sacrament of Extreme Unction, which is an immediate preparation for entrance into glory, to which the way was not yet opened out in the Old Law, since the price had not yet been paid. Matrimony did indeed exist under the Old Law, as a function of nature, but not as the sacrament of the union of Christ with the Church, for that union was not as yet brought about. Hence under the Old Law it was allowable to give a bill of divorce, which is contrary to the nature of the sacrament.

Reply Obj. 4: As already stated, the purifications of the Old Law were ordained for the removal of impediments to the divine worship: which worship is twofold; viz., spiritual, consisting in devotion of the mind to God; and corporal, consisting in sacrifices, oblations, and so forth. Now men are hindered in the spiritual worship by sins, whereby men

impediuntur homines per peccata, quibus homines pollui dicebantur, sicut per idololatriam et homicidium, per adulteria et incestus. Et ab istis pollutionibus purificabantur homines per aliqua sacrificia vel communiter oblata pro tota multitudine, vel etiam pro peccatis singulorum. Non quod sacrificia illa carnalia haberent ex seipsis virtutem expiandi peccatum, sed quia significabant expiationem peccatorum futuram per Christum, cuius participes erant etiam antiqui, protestantes fidem redemptoris in figuris sacrificiorum.

A cultu vero exteriori impediebantur homines per quasdam immunditias corporales, quae quidem primo considerabantur in hominibus; consequenter etiam in aliis animalibus, et in vestimentis et domibus et vasis. In hominibus quidem immunditia reputabatur partim quidem ex ipsis hominibus; partim autem ex contactu rerum immundarum. Ex ipsis autem hominibus immundum reputabatur omne illud quod corruptionem aliquam iam habebat, vel erat corruptioni expositum. Et ideo, quia mors est corruptio quaedam, cadaver hominis reputabatur immundum. Similiter etiam, quia lepra ex corruptione humorum contingit, qui etiam exterius erumpunt et alios inficiunt, leprosi etiam reputabantur immundi. Similiter etiam mulieres patientes sanguinis fluxum, sive per infirmitatem, sive etiam per naturam vel temporibus menstruis vel etiam tempore conceptionis. Et eadem ratione viri reputabantur immundi fluxum seminis patientes, vel per infirmitatem, vel per pollutionem nocturnam, vel etiam per coitum. Nam omnis humiditas praedictis modis ab homine egrediens, quandam immundam infectionem habet. Inerat etiam hominibus immunditia quaedam ex contactu quarumcumque rerum immundarum.

Istarum autem immunditiarum ratio erat et litteralis, et figuralis. Litteralis quidem, propter reverentiam eorum quae ad divinum cultum pertinent. Tum quia homines pretiosas res contingere non solent cum fuerint immundi. Tum etiam ut ex raro accessu ad sacra, ea magis venerarentur. Cum enim omnes huiusmodi immunditias raro aliquis cavere possit, contingebat quod raro poterant homines accedere ad attingendum ea quae pertinebant ad divinum cultum, et sic quando accedebant, cum maiori reverentia et humilitate mentis accedebant. Erat autem in quibusdam horum ratio litteralis ut homines non reformidarent accedere ad divinum cultum, quasi refugientes consortium leprosorum et similium infirmorum, quorum morbus abominabilis erat et contagiosus. In quibusdam etiam ratio erat ad vitandum idololatriae cultum, quia gentiles in ritu suorum sacrificiorum utebantur quandoque humano sanguine et semine. Omnes autem huiusmodi immunditiae corporales purificabantur vel per solam aspersionem aquae, vel quae maiores erant, per aliquod sacrificium ad expiandum peccatum, ex quo tales infirmitates contingebant.

were said to be polluted, for instance, by idolatry, murder, adultery, or incest. From such pollutions men were purified by certain sacrifices, offered either for the whole community in general, or also for the sins of individuals; not that those carnal sacrifices had of themselves the power of expiating sin; but that they signified that expiation of sins which was to be effected by Christ, and of which those of old became partakers by protesting their faith in the Redeemer, while taking part in the figurative sacrifices.

The impediments to external worship consisted in certain bodily uncleannesses; which were considered in the first place as existing in man, and consequently in other animals also, and in man's clothes, dwelling-place, and vessels. In man himself uncleanness was considered as arising partly from himself and partly from contact with unclean things. Anything proceeding from man was reputed unclean that was already subject to corruption, or exposed thereto: and consequently since death is a kind of corruption, the human corpse was considered unclean. In like manner, since leprosy arises from corruption of the humors, which break out externally and infect other persons, therefore were lepers also considered unclean; and, again, women suffering from a flow of blood, whether from weakness, or from nature (either at the monthly course or at the time of conception); and, for the same reason, men were reputed unclean if they suffered from a flow of seed, whether due to weakness, to nocturnal pollution, or to sexual intercourse. Because every humor issuing from man in the aforesaid ways involves some unclean infection. Again, man contracted uncleanness by touching any unclean thing whatever.

Now there was both a literal and a figurative reason for these uncleannesses. The literal reason was taken from the reverence due to those things that belong to the divine worship: both because men are not wont, when unclean, to touch precious things: and in order that by rarely approaching sacred things they might have greater respect for them. For since man could seldom avoid all the aforesaid uncleannesses, the result was that men could seldom approach to touch things belonging to the worship of God, so that when they did approach, they did so with greater reverence and humility. Moreover, in some of these the literal reason was that men should not be kept away from worshipping God through fear of coming in contact with lepers and others similarly afflicted with loathsome and contagious diseases. In others, again, the reason was to avoid idolatrous worship: because in their sacrificial rites the Gentiles sometimes employed human blood and seed. All these bodily uncleannesses were purified either by the mere sprinkling of water, or, in the case of those which were more grievous, by some sacrifice of expiation for the sin which was the occasion of the uncleanness in question.

Ratio autem figuralis harum immunditiarum fuit quia per huiusmodi exteriores immunditias figurabantur diversa peccata. Nam immunditia cadaveris cuiuscumque significat immunditiam peccati, quod est mors animae. Immunditia autem leprae significat immunditiam haereticae doctrinae, tum quia haeretica doctrina contagiosa est, sicut et lepra; tum etiam quia nulla falsa doctrina est quae vera falsis non admisceat, sicut etiam in superficie corporis leprosi apparet quaedam distinctio quarundam macularum ab alia carne integra. Per immunditiam vero mulieris sanguinifluae, designatur immunditia idololatriae, propter immolatitium cruorem. Per immunditiam vero viri seminiflui, designatur immunditia vanae locutionis, eo quod semen est verbum Dei. Per immunditiam vero coitus, et mulieris parientis, designatur immunditia peccati originalis. Per immunditiam vero mulieris menstruatae, designatur immunditia mentis per voluptates emollitae. Universaliter vero per immunditiam contactus rei immundae designatur immunditia consensus in peccatum alterius; secundum illud II ad Cor. VI, *exite de medio eorum et separamini, et immundum ne tetigeritis.*

Huiusmodi autem immunditia contactus derivabatur etiam ad res inanimatas, quidquid enim quocumque modo tangebat immundus, immundum erat. In quo lex attenuavit superstitionem gentilium, qui non solum per contactum immundi dicebant immunditiam contrahi, sed etiam per collocutionem aut per aspectum, ut Rabbi Moyses dicit de muliere menstruata. Per hoc autem mystice significabatur id quod dicitur Sap. XIV, *similiter odio sunt Deo impius et impietas eius.*

Erat autem et immunditia quaedam ipsarum rerum inanimatarum secundum se, sicut erat immunditia leprae in domo et in vestimentis. Sicut enim morbus leprae accidit in hominibus ex humore corrupto putrefaciente carnem et corrumpente, ita etiam propter aliquam corruptionem et excessum humiditatis vel siccitatis, fit quandoque aliqua corrosio in lapidibus domus, vel etiam in vestimento. Et ideo hanc corruptionem vocabat lex lepram, ex qua domus vel vestis immunda iudicaretur. Tum quia omnis corruptio ad immunditiam pertinebat, ut dictum est. Tum etiam quia contra huiusmodi corruptionem gentiles deos Penates colebant, et ideo lex praecepit huiusmodi domus, in quibus fuerit talis corruptio perseverans, destrui, et vestes comburi, ad tollendam idololatriae occasionem. Erat etiam et quaedam immunditia vasorum, de qua dicitur Num. XIX, vas quod *non habuerit cooperculum et ligaturam desuper, immundum erit.* Cuius immunditiae causa est quia in talia vasa de facili poterat aliquid immundum cadere, unde poterant immundari. Erat etiam hoc praeceptum ad declinandam idololatriam, credebant enim idololatrae quod, si mures aut lacertae, vel aliquid huiusmodi, quae immolabant idolis, cito caderent in vasa vel in aquas, quod essent diis

The figurative reason for these uncleannesses was that they were figures of various sins. For the uncleanness of any corpse signifies the uncleanness of sin, which is the death of the soul. The uncleanness of leprosy betokened the uncleanness of heretical doctrine: both because heretical doctrine is contagious just as leprosy is, and because no doctrine is so false as not to have some truth mingled with error, just as on the surface of a leprous body one may distinguish the healthy parts from those that are infected. The uncleanness of a woman suffering from a flow of blood denotes the uncleanness of idolatry, on account of the blood which is offered up. The uncleanness of the man who has suffered seminal loss signifies the uncleanness of empty words, for *the seed is the word of God.* The uncleanness of sexual intercourse and of the woman in child-birth signifies the uncleanness of original sin. The uncleanness of the woman in her periods signifies the uncleanness of a mind that is sensualized by pleasure. Speaking generally, the uncleanness contracted by touching an unclean thing denotes the uncleanness arising from consent in another's sin, according to 2 Cor. 6:17: *Go out from among them, and be ye separate . . . and touch not the unclean thing.*

Moreover, this uncleanness arising from the touch was contracted even by inanimate objects; for whatever was touched in any way by an unclean man, became itself unclean. Wherein the Law attenuated the superstition of the Gentiles, who held that uncleanness was contracted not only by touch, but also by speech or looks, as Rabbi Moses states (*Doct. Perplex.* iii) of a woman in her periods. The mystical sense of this was that *to God the wicked and his wickedness are hateful alike* (Wis 14:9).

There was also an uncleanness of inanimate things considered in themselves, such as the uncleanness of leprosy in a house or in clothes. For just as leprosy occurs in men through a corrupt humor causing putrefaction and corruption in the flesh; so, too, through some corruption and excess of humidity or dryness, there arises sometimes a kind of corruption in the stones with which a house is built, or in clothes. Hence the Law called this corruption by the name of leprosy, whereby a house or a garment was deemed to be unclean: both because all corruption savored of uncleanness, as stated above, and because the Gentiles worshiped their household gods as a preservative against this corruption. Hence the Law prescribed such houses, where this kind of corruption was of a lasting nature, to be destroyed; and such garments to be burnt, in order to avoid all occasion of idolatry. There was also an uncleanness of vessels, of which it is written (Num 19:15): *The vessel that hath no cover, and binding over it, shall be unclean.* The cause of this uncleanness was that anything unclean might easily drop into such vessels, so as to render them unclean. Moreover, this command aimed at the prevention of idolatry. For idolaters believed that if mice, lizards, or the like, which they used to sacrifice to the idols, fell into the vessels or into the

gratiosa. Adhuc etiam aliquae mulierculae vasa dimittunt discooperta in obsequium nocturnorum numinum, quae ianas vocant.

Harum autem immunditiarum ratio est figuralis quia per lepram domus significatur immunditia congregationis haereticorum. Per lepram vero in veste linea significatur perversitas morum ex amaritudine mentis. Per lepram vero vestis laneae significatur perversitas adulatorum. Per lepram in stamine significantur vitia animae, per lepram vero in subtegmine significantur peccata carnalia, sicut enim stamen est in subtegmine, ita anima in corpore. Per vas autem quod non habet operculum nec ligaturam, significatur homo qui non habet aliquod velamen taciturnitatis, et qui non constringitur aliqua censura disciplinae.

AD QUINTUM dicendum quod, sicut dictum est, duplex erat immunditia in lege. Una quidem per aliquam corruptionem mentis vel corporis, et haec immunditia maior erat. Alia vero erat immunditia ex solo contactu rei immundae, et haec minor erat, et faciliori ritu expiabatur. Nam immunditia prima expiabatur sacrificio pro peccato, quia omnis corruptio ex peccato procedit et peccatum significat, sed secunda immunditia expiabatur per solam aspersionem aquae cuiusdam, de qua quidem aqua expiationis habetur Num. XIX. Mandatur enim ibi a domino quod accipiant vaccam rufam, in memoriam peccati quod commiserunt in adoratione vituli. Et dicitur vacca magis quam vitulus, quia sic dominus synagogam vocare consuevit; secundum illud Osee IV, *sicut vacca lasciviens declinavit Israel.* Et hoc forte ideo quia vaccas in morem Aegyptii, coluerunt; secundum illud Osee X, vaccas Bethaven coluerunt. Et in detestationem peccati idololatriae, immolabatur extra castra. Et ubicumque sacrificium fiebat pro expiatione multitudinis peccatorum, cremabatur extra castra totum. Et ut significaretur per hoc sacrificium emundari populus ab universitate peccatorum, intingebat sacerdos digitum in sanguine eius, et aspergebat contra fores sanctuarii septem vicibus, quia septenarius universitatem significat. Et ipsa etiam aspersio sanguinis pertinebat ad detestationem idololatriae, in qua sanguis immolatitius non effundebatur, sed congregabatur, et circa ipsum homines comedebant in honorem idolorum. Comburebatur autem in igne. Vel quia Deus Moysi in igne apparuit, et in igne data est lex. Vel quia per hoc significabatur quod idololatria totaliter erat extirpanda, et omne quod ad idololatriam pertinebat, sicut vacca cremabatur, tam pelle et carnibus, quam sanguine et fimo, flammae traditis. Adiungebatur etiam in combustione lignum cedrinum, hyssopus, coccusque bis tinctus, ad significandum quod, sicut ligna cedrina non de facili putrescunt, et coccus bis tinctus non amittit colorem, et hyssopus retinet odorem etiam postquam fuerit desiccatus; ita etiam hoc sacrificium erat in conservationem ipsius populi, et honestatis

water, these became more pleasing to the gods. Even now some women let down uncovered vessels in honor of the nocturnal deities which they call *Janae.*

The figurative reason of these uncleannesses is that the leprosy of a house signified the uncleanness of the assembly of heretics; the leprosy of a linen garment signified an evil life arising from bitterness of mind; the leprosy of a woolen garment denoted the wickedness of flatterers; leprosy in the warp signified the vices of the soul; leprosy on the woof denoted sins of the flesh, for as the warp is in the woof, so is the soul in the body. The vessel that has neither cover nor binding, betokens a man who lacks the veil of taciturnity, and who is unrestrained by any severity of discipline.

REPLY OBJ. 5: As stated above (ad 4), there was a twofold uncleanness in the Law; one by way of corruption in the mind or in the body; and this was the graver uncleanness; the other was by mere contact with an unclean thing, and this was less grave, and was more easily expiated. Because the former uncleanness was expiated by sacrifices for sins, since all corruption is due to sin, and signifies sin: whereas the latter uncleanness was expiated by the mere sprinkling of a certain water, of which water we read in Num. 19. For there God commanded them to take a red cow in memory of the sin they had committed in worshipping a calf. And a cow is mentioned rather than a calf, because it was thus that the Lord was wont to designate the synagogue, according to Osee 4:16: *Israel hath gone astray like a wanton heifer*: and this was, perhaps, because they worshipped heifers after the custom of Egypt, according to Osee 10:5: *(They) have worshipped the kine of Bethaven*. And in detestation of the sin of idolatry it was sacrificed outside the camp; in fact, whenever sacrifice was offered up in expiation of the multitude of sins, it was all burnt outside the camp. Moreover, in order to show that this sacrifice cleansed the people from all their sins, *the priest* dipped *his finger in her blood*, and sprinkled *it over against the door of the tabernacle seven times*; for the number seven signified universality. Further, the very sprinkling of blood pertained to the detestation of idolatry, in which the blood that was offered up was not poured out, but was collected together, and men gathered round it to eat in honor of the idols. Likewise it was burnt by fire, either because God appeared to Moses in a fire, and the Law was given from the midst of fire; or to denote that idolatry, together with all that was connected therewith, was to be extirpated altogether; just as the cow was burnt *with her skin and her flesh, her blood and dung being delivered to the flames*. To this burning were added *cedar-wood, and hyssop, and scarlet twice dyed*, to signify that just as cedar-wood is not liable to putrefaction, and scarlet twice dyed does not easily lose its color, and hyssop retains its odor after it has been dried; so also was this sacrifice for the preservation of the whole people, and for their good behavior and

et devotionis ipsius. Unde dicitur de cineribus vaccae, *ut sint multitudini filiorum Israel in custodiam*. Vel, secundum Iosephum, quatuor elementa significata sunt, igni enim apponebatur cedrus, significans terram, propter sui terrestreitatem; hyssopus, significans aerem, propter odorem; coccus, significans aquam, eadem ratione qua et purpura, propter tincturas, quae ex aquis sumuntur, ut per hoc exprimeretur quod illud sacrificium offerebatur creatori quatuor elementorum. Et quia huiusmodi sacrificium offerebatur pro peccato idololatriae, in eius detestationem et comburens, et cineres colligens, et ille qui aspergit aquas in quibus cinis ponebatur, immundi reputabantur, ut per hoc ostenderetur quod quidquid quocumque modo ad idololatriam pertinet, quasi immundum est abiiciendum. Ab hac autem immunditia purificabantur per solam ablutionem vestimentorum, nec indigebant aqua aspergi propter huiusmodi immunditiam, quia sic esset processus in infinitum. Ille enim qui aspergebat aquam, immundus fiebat, et sic si ipse seipsum aspergeret, immundus remaneret; si autem alius eum aspergeret, ille immundus esset; et similiter ille qui illum aspergeret, et sic in infinitum.

Figuralis autem ratio huius sacrificii est quia per vaccam rufam significatur Christus secundum infirmitatem assumptam, quam femininus sexus designat. Sanguinem passionis eius designat vaccae color. Erat autem vacca rufa aetatis integrae, quia omnis operatio Christi est perfecta. In qua nulla erat macula, nec portavit iugum, quia non portavit iugum peccati. Praecipitur autem adduci ad Moysen, quia imputabant ei transgressionem Mosaicae legis in violatione sabbati. Praecipitur etiam tradi Eleazaro sacerdoti, quia Christus occidendus in manus sacerdotum traditus est. Immolatur autem extra castra, quia extra portam Christus passus est. Intingit autem sacerdos digitum in sanguine eius, quia per discretionem, quam digitus significat, mysterium passionis Christi est considerandum et imitandum.

Aspergitur autem contra tabernaculum, per quod synagoga designatur, vel ad condemnationem Iudaeorum non credentium; vel ad purificationem credentium. Et hoc septem vicibus, vel propter septem dona spiritus sancti; vel propter septem dies, in quibus omne tempus intelligitur. Sunt autem omnia quae ad Christi incarnationem pertinent, igne cremanda, idest spiritualiter intelligenda, nam per pellem et carnem exterior Christi operatio significatur; per sanguinem, subtilis et interna virtus exteriora vivificans; per fimum, lassitudo, sitis, et omnia huiusmodi ad infirmitatem pertinentia. Adduntur autem tria, cedrus, quod significat altitudinem spei, vel contemplationis; hyssopus, quod significat humilitatem, vel fidem; coccus bis tinctus, quod significat geminam caritatem; per haec enim debemus Christo passo

devotion. Hence it is said of the ashes of the cow: *That they may be reserved for the multitude of the children of Israel*. Or, according to Josephus (*Antiq.* iii, 8,9,10), the four elements are indicated here: for *cedar-wood* was added to the fire, to signify the earth, on account of its earthiness; *hyssop*, to signify the air, on account of its smell; *scarlet twice dyed*, to signify water, for the same reason as purple, on account of the dyes which are taken out of the water: thus denoting the fact that this sacrifice was offered to the Creator of the four elements. And since this sacrifice was offered for the sin of idolatry, both *he that burned her*, and *he that gathered up the ashes*, and *he that sprinkled the water* in which the ashes were placed, were deemed unclean in detestation of that sin, in order to show that whatever was in any way connected with idolatry should be cast aside as being unclean. From this uncleanness they were purified by the mere washing of their clothes; nor did they need to be sprinkled with the water on account of this kind of uncleanness, because otherwise the process would have been unending, since he that sprinkled the water became unclean, so that if he were to sprinkle himself he would remain unclean; and if another were to sprinkle him, that one would have become unclean, and in like manner, whoever might sprinkle him, and so on indefinitely.

The figurative reason of this sacrifice was that the red cow signified Christ in respect his assumed weakness, denoted by the female sex; while the color of the cow designated the blood of His Passion. And the *red cow was of full age*, because all Christ's works are perfect, *in which there* was *no blemish*; *and which* had *not carried the yoke*, because Christ was innocent, nor did He carry the yoke of sin. It was commanded to be taken to Moses, because they blamed Him for transgressing the law of Moses by breaking the Sabbath. And it was commanded to be delivered *to Eleazar the priest*, because Christ was delivered into the hands of the priests to be slain. It was immolated *without the camp*, because Christ *suffered outside the gate* (Heb 13:12). And the priest dipped *his finger in her blood*, because the mystery of Christ's Passion should be considered and imitated.

It was sprinkled *over against . . . the tabernacle*, which denotes the synagogue, to signify either the condemnation of the unbelieving Jews, or the purification of believers; and this *seven times*, in token either of the seven gifts of the Holy Spirit, or of the seven days wherein all time is comprised. Again, all things that pertain to the Incarnation of Christ should be burnt with fire, i.e., they should be understood spiritually; for the *skin* and *flesh* signified Christ's outward works; the *blood* denoted the subtle inward force which quickened His external deeds; the *dung* betokened His weariness, His thirst, and all such like things pertaining to His weakness. Three things were added, viz., *cedar-wood*, which denotes the height of hope or contemplation; *hyssop*, in token of humility or faith; *scarlet twice dyed*, which denotes twofold charity; for it is by these three that

adhaerere. Iste autem cinis combustionis colligitur a viro mundo, quia reliquiae passionis pervenerunt ad gentiles, qui non fuerunt culpabiles in Christi morte. Apponuntur autem cineres in aqua ad expiandum, quia ex passione Christi Baptismus sortitur virtutem emundandi peccata. Sacerdos autem qui immolabat et comburebat vaccam, et ille qui comburebat, et qui colligebat cineres, immundus erat, et etiam qui aspergebat aquam, vel quia Iudaei facti sunt immundi ex occisione Christi, per quam nostra peccata expiantur; et hoc usque ad vesperum, idest usque ad finem mundi, quando reliquiae Israel convertentur. Vel quia illi qui tractant sancta intendentes ad emundationem aliorum, ipsi etiam aliquas immunditias contrahunt, ut Gregorius dicit, in pastorali; et hoc usque ad vesperum, idest usque ad finem praesentis vitae.

AD SEXTUM dicendum quod, sicut dictum est, immunditia quae ex corruptione proveniebat vel mentis vel corporis, expiabatur per sacrificia pro peccato. Offerebantur autem specialia sacrificia pro peccatis singulorum, sed quia aliqui negligentes erant circa expiationem huiusmodi peccatorum et immunditiarum; vel etiam propter ignorantiam ab expiatione huiusmodi desistebant; institutum fuit ut semel in anno, decima die septimi mensis, fieret sacrificium expiationis pro toto populo. Et quia, sicut apostolus dicit, ad Heb. VII, *lex constituit homines sacerdotes infirmitatem habentes*, oportebat quod sacerdos prius offerret pro seipso vitulum pro peccato, in commemorationem peccati quod Aaron fecerat in conflatione vituli aurei; et arietem in holocaustum, per quod significabatur quod sacerdotis praelatio, quam aries designat, qui est dux gregis, erat ordinanda ad honorem Dei. Deinde autem offerebat pro populo duos hircos. Quorum unus immolabatur, ad expiandum peccatum multitudinis. Hircus enim animal fetidum est, et de pilis eius fiunt vestimenta pungentia, ut per hoc significaretur fetor et immunditia et aculei peccatorum. Huius autem hirci immolati sanguis inferebatur, simul etiam cum sanguine vituli, in sancta sanctorum, et aspergebatur ex eo totum sanctuarium, ad significandum quod tabernaculum emundabatur ab immunditiis filiorum Israel. Corpus vero hirci et vituli quae immolata sunt pro peccato, oportebat comburi, ad ostendendum consumptionem peccatorum. Non autem in altari, quia ibi non comburebantur totaliter nisi holocausta. Unde mandatum erat ut comburerentur extra castra, in detestationem peccati, hoc enim fiebat quandocumque immolabatur sacrificium pro aliquo gravi peccato, vel pro multitudine peccatorum. Alter vero hircus emittebatur in desertum, non quidem ut offerretur Daemonibus, quos colebant gentiles in desertis, quia eis nihil licebat immolari; sed ad designandum effectum illius sacrificii immolati. Et ideo sacerdos imponebat manum super caput eius, confitens peccata filiorum Israel,

we should cling to Christ suffering. The ashes of this burning were gathered by *a man that is clean*, because the relics of the Passion came into the possession of the Gentiles, who were not guilty of Christ's death. The ashes were put into water for the purpose of expiation, because Baptism receives from Christ's Passion the power of washing away sins. The priest who immolated and burned the cow, and he who burned, and he who gathered together the ashes, were unclean, as also he that sprinkled the water: either because the Jews became unclean through putting Christ to death, whereby our sins are expiated; and this, until the evening, i.e., until the end of the world, when the remnants of Israel will be converted; or else because they who handle sacred things with a view to the cleansing of others contract certain uncleannesses, as Gregory says (*Pastor.* ii, 5); and this until the evening, i.e., until the end of this life.

REPLY OBJ. 6: As stated above (ad 5), an uncleanness which was caused by corruption either of mind or of body was expiated by sin-offerings. Now special sacrifices were wont to be offered for the sins of individuals: but since some were neglectful about expiating such sins and uncleannesses; or, through ignorance, failed to offer this expiation; it was laid down that once a year, on the tenth day of the seventh month, a sacrifice of expiation should be offered for the whole people. And because, as the Apostle says (Heb 7:28), *the Law maketh men priests, who have infirmity*, it behooved the priest first of all to offer a calf for his own sins, in memory of Aaron's sin in fashioning the molten calf; and besides, to offer a ram for a holocaust, which signified that the priestly sovereignty denoted by the ram, who is the head of the flock, was to be ordained to the glory of God. Then he offered two he-goats for the people: one of which was offered in expiation of the sins of the multitude. For the he-goat is an evil-smelling animal; and from its skin clothes are made having a pungent odor; to signify the stench, uncleanness and the sting of sin. After this he-goat had been immolated, its blood was taken, together with the blood of the calf, into the Holy of Holies, and the entire sanctuary was sprinkled with it; to signify that the tabernacle was cleansed from the uncleanness of the children of Israel. But the corpses of the he-goat and calf which had been offered up for sin had to be burnt, to denote the destruction of sins. They were not, however, burnt on the altar: since none but holocausts were burnt thereon; but it was prescribed that they should be burnt without the camp, in detestation of sin: for this was done whenever sacrifice was offered for a grievous sin, or for the multitude of sins. The other goat was let loose into the wilderness: not indeed to offer it to the demons, whom the Gentiles worshipped in desert places, because it was unlawful to offer aught to them; but in order to point out the effect of the sacrifice which had been offered up. Hence the priest put his hand on its head, while confessing the sins of the children of Israel: as though that goat were to carry them away into the wilderness, where it

ac si ille hircus deportaret ea in desertum, ubi a bestiis comederetur, quasi portans poenam pro peccatis populi. Dicebatur autem portare peccata populi, vel quia in eius emissione significabatur remissio peccatorum populi, vel quia colligabatur super caput eius aliqua schedula ubi erant scripta peccata.

Ratio autem figuralis horum erat quia Christus significatur et per vitulum, propter virtutem; et per arietem, quia ipse est dux fidelium; et per hircum, propter similitudinem carnis peccati. Et ipse Christus est immolatus pro peccatis et sacerdotum et populi, quia per eius passionem et maiores et minores a peccato mundantur. Sanguis autem vituli et hirci infertur in sancta per pontificem, quia per sanguinem passionis Christi patet nobis introitus in regnum caelorum. Comburuntur autem eorum corpora extra castra, quia extra portam Christus passus est, ut apostolus dicit, ad Heb. ult. Per hircum autem qui emittebatur, potest significari vel ipsa divinitas Christi, quae in solitudinem abiit, homine Christo patiente, non quidem locum mutans, sed virtutem cohibens, vel significatur concupiscentia mala, quam debemus a nobis abiicere, virtuosos autem motus domino immolare.

De immunditia vero eorum qui huiusmodi sacrificia comburebant, eadem ratio est quae in sacrificio vitulae rufae dicta est.

Ad septimum dicendum quod per ritum legis leprosus non emundabatur a macula leprae, sed emundatus ostendebatur. Et hoc significatur Lev. XIV, cum dicitur de sacerdote, *cum invenerit lepram esse emundatam, praecipiet ei qui purificatur.* Iam ergo lepra mundata erat, sed purificari dicebatur, inquantum iudicio sacerdotis restituebatur consortio hominum et cultui divino. Contingebat tamen quandoque ut divino miraculo per ritum legis corporalis mundaretur lepra, quando sacerdos decipiebatur in iudicio.

Huiusmodi autem purificatio leprosi dupliciter fiebat, nam primo, iudicabatur esse mundus; secundo autem, restituebatur tanquam mundus consortio hominum et cultui divino, scilicet post septem dies. In prima autem purificatione offerebat pro se leprosus mundandus duos passeres vivos, et lignum cedrinum, et vermiculum, et hyssopum; hoc modo ut filo coccineo ligarentur passer et hyssopus simul cum ligno cedrino, ita scilicet quod lignum cedrinum esset quasi manubrium aspersorii. Hyssopus vero et passer erant id quod de aspersorio tingebatur in sanguine alterius passeris immolati in aquis vivis. Haec autem quatuor offerebat contra quatuor defectus leprae, nam contra putredinem, offerebatur cedrus, quae est arbor imputribilis; contra fetorem, hyssopus, quae est herba odorifera; contra insensibilitatem, passer vivus; contra turpitudinem coloris, vermiculus, qui habet

would be devoured by wild beasts, because it bore the punishment of the people's sins. And it was said to bear the sins of the people, either because the forgiveness of the people's sins was signified by its being let loose, or because on its head written lists of sins were fastened.

The figurative reason of these things was that Christ was foreshadowed both by the calf, on account of His power; and by the ram, because He is the Head of the faithful; and by the he-goat, on account of *the likeness of sinful flesh* (Rom 8:3). Moreover, Christ was sacrificed for the sins of both priests and people: since both those of high and those of low degree are cleansed from sin by His Passion. The blood of the calf and of the goat was brought into the Holies by the priest, because the entrance to the kingdom of heaven was opened to us by the blood of Christ's Passion. Their bodies were burnt without the camp, because *Christ suffered without the gate,* as the Apostle declares (Heb 13:12). The scape-goat may denote either Christ's Godhead Which went away into solitude when the Man Christ suffered, not by going to another place, but by restraining His power: or it may signify the base concupiscence which we ought to cast away from ourselves, while we offer up to Our Lord acts of virtue.

With regard to the uncleanness contracted by those who burnt these sacrifices, the reason is the same as that which we assigned (ad 5) to the sacrifice of the red heifer.

Reply Obj. 7: The legal rite did not cleanse the leper of his deformity, but declared him to be cleansed. This is shown by the words of Lev. 14:3, seqq., where it was said that the priest, *when he shall find that the leprosy is cleansed,* shall command *him that is to be purified*: consequently, the leper was already healed: but he was said to be purified insofar as the verdict of the priest restored him to the society of men and to the worship of God. It happened sometimes, however, that bodily leprosy was miraculously cured by the legal rite, when the priest erred in his judgment.

Now this purification of a leper was twofold: for, in the first place, he was declared to be clean; and, second, he was restored, as clean, to the society of men and to the worship of God, to wit, after seven days. At the first purification the leper who sought to be cleansed offered for himself *two living sparrows . . . cedar-wood, and scarlet, and hyssop,* in such wise that a sparrow and the hyssop should be tied to the cedar-wood with a scarlet thread, so that the cedar-wood was like the handle of an aspersory: while the hyssop and sparrow were that part of the aspersory which was dipped into the blood of the other sparrow which was *immolated . . . over living waters.* These things he offered as an antidote to the four defects of leprosy: for cedar-wood, which is not subject to putrefaction, was offered against the putrefaction; hyssop, which is a sweet-smelling herb, was offered up against the stench; a living sparrow was offered up against numbness; and scarlet, which has a vivid color, was offered

vivum colorem. Passer vero vivus avolare dimittebatur in agrum, quia leprosus restituebatur pristinae libertati.

In octavo vero die admittebatur ad cultum divinum, et restituebatur consortio hominum. Primo tamen rasis pilis totius corporis et vestimentis, eo quod lepra pilos corrodit, et vestimenta inquinat et fetida reddit. Et postmodum sacrificium offerebatur pro delicto eius, quia lepra plerumque inducitur pro peccato. De sanguine autem sacrificii tingebatur extremum auriculae eius qui erat mundandus, et pollices manus dextrae et pedis, quia in istis partibus primum lepra dignoscitur et sentitur. Adhibebantur etiam huic ritui tres liquores, scilicet sanguis, contra sanguinis corruptionem; oleum, ad designandam sanationem morbi; aqua viva, ad emundandum spurcitiem.

Figuralis autem ratio erat quia per duos passeres significantur divinitas et humanitas Christi. Quorum unus, scilicet humanitas, immolatur in vase fictili super aquas viventes, quia per passionem Christi aquae Baptismi consecrantur. Alius autem, scilicet impassibilis divinitas, vivus remanebat, quia divinitas mori non potest. Unde et avolabat, quia passione astringi non poterat. Hic autem passer vivus, simul cum ligno cedrino et cocco, vel vermiculo, et hyssopo, idest fide, spe et caritate, ut supra dictum est, mittitur in aquam ad aspergendum, quia in fide Dei et hominis baptizamur. Lavat autem homo, per aquam Baptismi vel lacrymarum, vestimenta sua, idest opera, et omnes pilos, idest cogitationes. Tingitur autem extremum auriculae dextrae eius qui mundatur, de sanguine et de oleo, ut eius auditum muniat contra corrumpentia verba, pollices autem manus dextrae et pedis tinguntur, ut sit eius actio sancta. Alia vero quae ad hanc purificationem pertinent, vel etiam aliarum immunditiarum, non habent aliquid speciale praeter alia sacrificia pro peccatis vel pro delictis.

AD OCTAVUM ET NONUM dicendum quod, sicut populus instituebatur ad cultum Dei per circumcisionem, ita ministri per aliquam specialem purificationem vel consecrationem, unde et separari ab aliis praecipiuntur, quasi specialiter ad ministerium cultus divini prae aliis deputati. Et totum quod circa eos fiebat in eorum consecratione vel institutione ad hoc pertinebat ut ostenderetur eos habere quandam praerogativam puritatis et virtutis et dignitatis. Et ideo in institutione ministrorum tria fiebant, primo enim, purificabantur; secundo, ornabantur et consecrabantur; tertio, applicabantur ad usum ministerii. Purificabantur quidem communiter omnes per ablutionem aquae, et per quaedam sacrificia; specialiter autem Levitae radebant omnes pilos carnis suae; ut habetur Lev. VIII.

up against the repulsive color of leprosy. The living sparrow was let loose to fly away into the plain, because the leper was restored to his former liberty.

On the eighth day he was admitted to divine worship, and was restored to the society of men; but only after having shaved all the hair of his body, and washed his clothes, because leprosy rots the hair, infects the clothes, and gives them an evil smell. Afterwards a sacrifice was offered for his sin, since leprosy was frequently a result of sin: and some of the blood of the sacrifice was put on the tip of the ear of the man that was to be cleansed, *and on the thumb of his right hand, and the great toe of his right foot*; because it is in these parts that leprosy is first diagnosed and felt. In this rite, moreover, three liquids were employed: viz., blood, against the corruption of the blood; oil, to denote the healing of the disease; and living waters, to wash away the filth.

The figurative reason was that the Divine and human natures in Christ were denoted by the two sparrows, one of which, in likeness of His human nature, was offered up in an earthen vessel over living waters, because the waters of Baptism are sanctified by Christ's Passion. The other sparrow, in token of His impassible Godhead, remained living, because the Godhead cannot die: hence it flew away, for the Godhead could not be encompassed by the Passion. Now this living sparrow, together with the cedar-wood and scarlet or cochineal, and hyssop, i.e., faith, hope and charity, as stated above (ad 5), was put into the water for the purpose of sprinkling, because we are baptized in the faith of the God-Man. By the waters of Baptism or of his tears man washes his clothes, i.e., his works, and all his hair, i.e., his thoughts. The tip of the right ear of the man to be cleansed is moistened with some of the blood and oil, in order to strengthen his hearing against harmful words; and the thumb and toe of his right hand and foot are moistened that his deeds may be holy. Other matters pertaining to this purification, or to that also of any other uncleannesses, call for no special remark, beyond what applies to other sacrifices, whether for sins or for trespasses.

REPLY OBJ. 8 AND 9: Just as the people were initiated by circumcision to the divine worship, so were the ministers by some special purification or consecration: wherefore they are commanded to be separated from other men, as being specially deputed, rather than others, to the ministry of the divine worship. And all that was done touching them in their consecration or institution, was with a view to show that they were in possession of a prerogative of purity, power and dignity. Hence three things were done in the institution of ministers: for first, they were purified; second, they were adorned and consecrated; third, they were employed in the ministry. All in general used to be purified by washing in water, and by certain sacrifices; but the Levites in particular shaved all the hair of their bodies, as stated in Lev. 8 (cf. Num. 8).

Consecratio vero circa pontifices et sacerdotes hoc ordine fiebat. Primo enim, postquam abluti erant, induebantur quibusdam vestimentis specialibus pertinentibus ad designandum dignitatem ipsorum. Specialiter autem pontifex oleo unctionis in capite ungebatur, ut designaretur quod ab ipso diffundebatur potestas consecrandi ad alios, sicut oleum a capite derivatur ad inferiora; ut habetur in Psalmo CXXXII, *sicut unguentum in capite, quod descendit in barbam, barbam Aaron.* Levitae vero non habebant aliam consecrationem, nisi quod offerebantur domino a filiis Israel per manus pontificis, qui orabat pro eis. Minorum vero sacerdotum solae manus consecrabantur, quae erant applicandae ad sacrificia. Et de sanguine animalis immolatitii tingebatur extremum auriculae dextrae ipsorum, et pollices pedis ac manus dextrae, ut scilicet essent obedientes legi Dei in oblatione sacrificiorum, quod significatur in intinctione auris dextrae; et quod essent solliciti et prompti in executione sacrificiorum, quod significatur in intinctione pedis et manus dextrae. Aspergebantur etiam ipsi, et vestimenta eorum, sanguine animalis immolati, in memoriam sanguinis agni per quem fuerunt liberati in Aegypto. Offerebantur autem in eorum consecratione huiusmodi sacrificia, vitulus pro peccato, in memoriam remissionis peccati Aaron circa conflationem vituli; aries in holocaustum, in memoriam oblationis Abrahae, cuius obedientiam pontifex imitari debebat; aries etiam consecrationis, qui erat quasi hostia pacifica, in memoriam liberationis de Aegypto per sanguinem agni; canistrum panum, in memoriam mannae praestiti populo.

Pertinebat autem ad applicationem ministerii quod imponebantur super manus eorum adeps arietis, et torta panis unius, et armus dexter, ut ostenderetur quod accipiebant potestatem huiusmodi offerendi domino. Levitae vero applicabantur ad ministerium per hoc quod intromittebantur in tabernaculum foederis, quasi ad ministrandum circa vasa sanctuarii.

Figuralis vero horum ratio erat quia illi qui sunt consecrandi ad spirituale ministerium Christi, debent primo purificari per aquam Baptismi et lacrymarum in fide passionis Christi, quod est expiativum et purgativum sacrificium. Et debent radere omnes pilos carnis, idest omnes pravas cogitationes. Debent etiam ornari virtutibus; et consecrari oleo spiritus sancti; et aspersione sanguinis Christi. Et sic debent esse intenti ad exequenda spiritualia ministeria.

Ad decimum dicendum quod, sicut iam dictum est, intentio legis erat inducere ad reverentiam divini cultus. Et hoc dupliciter, uno modo, excludendo a cultu divino omne id quod poterat esse contemptibile; alio modo, apponendo ad cultum divinum omne illud quod videbatur

With regard to the high-priests and priests the consecration was performed as follows. First, when they had been washed, they were clothed with certain special garments in designation of their dignity. In particular, the high-priest was anointed on the head with the oil of unction: to denote that the power of consecration was poured forth by him on to others, just as oil flows from the head on to the lower parts of the body; according to Ps. 132:2: *Like the precious ointment on the head that ran down upon the beard, the beard of Aaron.* But the Levites received no other consecration besides being offered to the Lord by the children of Israel through the hands of the high-priest, who prayed for them. The lesser priests were consecrated on the hands only, which were to be employed in the sacrifices. The tip of their right ear and the thumb of their right hand, and the great toe of their right foot were tinged with the blood of the sacrificial animal, to denote that they should be obedient to God's law in offering the sacrifices (this is denoted by touching their right ear); and that they should be careful and ready in performing the sacrifices (this is signified by the moistening of the right foot and hand). They themselves and their garments were sprinkled with the blood of the animal that had been sacrificed, in memory of the blood of the lamb by which they had been delivered in Egypt. At their consecration the following sacrifices were offered: a calf, for sin, in memory of Aaron's sin in fashioning the molten calf; a ram, for a holocaust, in memory of the sacrifice of Abraham, whose obedience it behooved the high-priest to imitate; again, a ram of consecration, which was a peace-offering, in memory of the delivery form Egypt through the blood of the lamb; and a basket of bread, in memory of the manna vouchsafed to the people.

In reference to their being destined to the ministry, the fat of the ram, one roll of bread, and the right shoulder were placed on their hands, to show that they received the power of offering these things to the Lord: while the Levites were initiated to the ministry by being brought into the tabernacle of the covenant, as being destined to the ministry touching the vessels of the sanctuary.

The figurative reason of these things was that those who are to be consecrated to the spiritual ministry of Christ, should be first of all purified by the waters of Baptism, and by the waters of tears, in their faith in Christ's Passion, which is a sacrifice both of expiation and of purification. They have also to shave all the hair of their body, i.e., all evil thoughts. They should, moreover, be decked with virtues, and be consecrated with the oil of the Holy Spirit, and with the sprinkling of Christ's blood. And thus they should be intent on the fulfilment of their spiritual ministry.

Reply Obj. 10: As already stated (A4), the purpose of the Law was to induce men to have reverence for the divine worship: and this in two ways; first, by excluding from the worship of God whatever might be an object of contempt; second, by introducing into the divine worship all that

ad honorificentiam pertinere. Et si hoc quidem observabatur in tabernaculo et vasis eius, et animalibus immolandis, multo magis hoc observandum erat in ipsis ministris. Et ideo ad removendum contemptum ministrorum, praeceptum fuit ut non haberent maculam vel defectum corporalem, quia huiusmodi homines solent apud alios in contemptu haberi. Propter quod etiam institutum fuit ut non sparsim ex quolibet genere ad Dei ministerium applicarentur, sed ex certa prosapia secundum generis successionem, ut ex hoc clariores et nobiliores haberentur.

Ad hoc autem quod in reverentia haberentur, adhibebatur eis specialis ornatus vestium, et specialis consecratio. Et haec est in communi causa ornatus vestium. In speciali autem sciendum est quod pontifex habebat octo ornamenta. Primo enim, habebat vestem lineam. Secundo, habebat tunicam hyacinthinam; in cuius extremitate versus pedes, ponebantur per circuitum tintinabula quaedam, et mala Punica facta ex hyacintho et purpura coccoque bis tincto. Tertio, habebat superhumerale, quod tegebat humeros et anteriorem partem usque ad cingulum; quod erat ex auro et hyacintho et purpura, coccoque bis tincto, et bysso retorta. Et super humeros habebat duos onychinos, in quibus erant sculpta nomina filiorum Israel. Quartum erat rationale, ex eadem materia factum; quod erat quadratum, et ponebatur in pectore, et coniungebatur superhumerali. Et in hoc rationali erant duodecim lapides pretiosi distincti per quatuor ordines, in quibus etiam sculpta erant nomina filiorum Israel, quasi ad designandum quod ferret onus totius populi, per hoc quod habebat nomina eorum in humeris; et quod iugiter debebat de eorum salute cogitare, per hoc quod portabat eos in pectore, quasi in corde habens. In quo etiam rationali mandavit dominus poni doctrinam et veritatem, quia quaedam pertinentia ad veritatem iustitiae et doctrinae, scribebantur in illo rationali. Iudaei tamen fabulantur quod in rationali erat lapis qui secundum diversos colores mutabatur, secundum diversa quae debebant accidere filiis Israel, et hoc vocant veritatem et doctrinam. Quintum erat balteus, idest cingulus quidam, factus ex praedictis quatuor coloribus. Sextum erat tiara, idest mitra quaedam, de bysso. Septimum autem erat lamina aurea, pendens in fronte eius, in qua erat nomen domini. Octavum autem erant femoralia linea, ut operirent carnem turpitudinis suae, quando accederent ad sanctuarium vel ad altare. Ex istis autem octo ornamentis minores sacerdotes habebant quatuor, scilicet tunicam lineam, femoralia, balteum et tiaram.

Horum autem ornamentorum quidam rationem litteralem assignant, dicentes quod in istis ornamentis designatur dispositio orbis terrarum, quasi pontifex protestaretur se esse ministrum creatoris mundi, unde etiam Sap. XVIII dicitur quod in veste Aaron erat descriptus

seemed to savor of reverence. And, indeed, if this was observed in regard to the tabernacle and its vessels, and in the animals to be sacrificed, much more was it to be observed in the very ministers. Wherefore, in order to obviate contempt for the ministers, it was prescribed that they should have no bodily stain or defect: since men so deformed are wont to be despised by others. For the same reason it was also commanded that the choice of those who were to be destined to the service of God was not to be made in a broadcast manner from any family, but according to their descent from one particular stock, thus giving them distinction and nobility.

In order that they might be revered, special ornate vestments were appointed for their use, and a special form of consecration. This indeed is the general reason of ornate garments. But the high-priest in particular had eight vestments. First, he had a linen tunic. Second, he had a purple tunic; round the bottom of which were placed *little bells* and *pomegranates of violet, and purple, and scarlet twice dyed*. Third, he had the ephod, which covered his shoulders and his breast down to the girdle; and it was made of gold, and violet and purple, and scarlet twice dyed and twisted linen: and on his shoulders he bore two onyx stones, on which were graven the names of the children of Israel. Fourth, he had the rational, made of the same material; it was square in shape, and was worn on the breast, and was fastened to the ephod. On this rational there were twelve precious stones set in four rows, on which also were graven the names of the children of Israel, in token that the priest bore the burden of the whole people, since he bore their names on his shoulders; and that it was his duty ever to think of their welfare, since he wore them on his breast, bearing them in his heart, so to speak. And the Lord commanded the *Doctrine and Truth* to be put in the rational: for certain matters regarding moral and dogmatic truth were written on it. The Jews indeed pretend that on the rational was placed a stone which changed color according to the various things which were about to happen to the children of Israel: and this they call the *Truth and Doctrine*. Fifth, he wore a belt or girdle made of the four colors mentioned above. Sixth, there was the tiara or mitre which was made of linen. Seventh, there was the golden plate which hung over his forehead; on it was inscribed the Lord's name. Eighthly, there were *the linen breeches to cover the flesh of their nakedness*, when they went up to the sanctuary or altar. Of these eight vestments the lesser priests had four, viz., the linen tunic and breeches, the belt and the tiara.

According to some, the literal reason for these vestments was that they denoted the disposition of the terrestrial globe; as though the high-priest confessed himself to be the minister of the Creator of the world, wherefore it is written (Wis 18:24): *In the robe* of Aaron *was the whole*

orbis terrarum. Nam femoralia linea figurabant terram, ex qua linum nascitur. Baltei circumvolutio significabat Oceanum, qui circumcingit terram. Tunica hyacinthina suo colore significabat aerem, per cuius tintinabula significabantur tonitrua; per mala granata, coruscationes. Superhumerale vero significabat sua varietate caelum sidereum, duo onychini, duo hemisphaeria, vel solem et lunam. Duodecim gemmae in pectore, duodecim signa in zodiaco, quae dicebantur posita in rationali, quia in caelestibus sunt rationes terrenorum, secundum illud Iob XXXVIII, *numquid nosti ordinem caeli, et ponis rationem eius in terra?* Cidaris autem, vel tiara, significabat caelum Empyreum. Lamina aurea, Deum omnibus praesidentem.

Figuralis vero ratio manifesta est. Nam maculae vel defectus corporales a quibus debebant sacerdotes esse immunes, significant diversa vitia et peccata quibus debent carere. Prohibetur enim esse caecus, idest, ne sit ignorans. Ne sit claudus, idest instabilis, et ad diversa se inclinans. Ne sit parvo, vel grandi, vel torto naso, idest ne per defectum discretionis, vel in plus vel in minus excedat, aut etiam aliqua prava exerceat; per nasum enim discretio designatur, quia est discretivus odoris. Ne sit fracto pede vel manus, idest ne amittat virtutem bene operandi, vel procedendi in virtutem. Repudiatur etiam si habeat gibbum vel ante vel retro, per quem significatur superfluus amor terrenorum. Si est lippus, idest per carnalem affectum eius ingenium obscuratur, contingit enim lippitudo ex fluxu humoris. Repudiatur etiam si habeat albuginem in oculo, idest praesumptionem candoris iustitiae in sua cogitatione. Repudiatur etiam si habuerit iugem scabiem, idest petulantiam carnis. Et si habuerit impetiginem, quae sine dolore corpus occupat, et membrorum decorem foedat, per quam avaritia designatur. Et etiam si sit herniosus vel ponderosus, qui scilicet gestat pondus turpitudinis in corde, licet non exerceat in opere.

Per ornamenta vero designantur virtutes ministrorum Dei. Sunt autem quatuor quae sunt necessariae omnibus ministris, scilicet castitas, quae significatur per femoralia; puritas vero vitae, quae significatur per lineam tunicam; moderatio discretionis quae significatur per cingulum; rectitudo intentionis, quae significatur per tiaram protegentem caput. Sed prae his pontifices debent quatuor habere. Primo quidem, iugem Dei memoriam in contemplatione, et hoc significat lamina aurea habens nomen Dei, in fronte. Secundo, quod supportent infirmitates populi, quod significat superhumerale. Tertio, quod habeant populum in corde et in visceribus per sollicitudinem caritatis, quod significatur per rationale. Quarto, quod habeant conversationem caelestem per opera perfectionis, quod significatur per tunicam

world described. For the linen breeches signified the earth out of which the flax grows. The surrounding belt signified the ocean which surrounds the earth. The violet tunic denoted the air by its color: its little bells betoken the thunder; the pomegranates, the lightning. The ephod, by its many colors, signified the starry heaven; the two onyx stones denoted the two hemispheres, or the sun and moon. The twelve precious stones on the breast are the twelve signs of the zodiac: and they are said to have been placed on the rational because in heaven, are the types of earthly things, according to Job 38:33: *Dost thou know the order of heaven, and canst thou set down the reason thereof on the earth?* The turban or tiara signified the empyrean: the golden plate was a token of God, the governor of the universe.

The figurative reason is evident. Because bodily stains or defects wherefrom the priests had to be immune, signify the various vices and sins from which they should be free. Thus it is forbidden that he should be blind, i.e., he ought not to be ignorant: he must not be lame, i.e., vacillating and uncertain of purpose: that he must have *a little, or a great, or a crooked nose*, i.e., that he should not, from lack of discretion, exceed in one direction or in another, or even exercise some base occupation: for the nose signifies discretion, because it discerns odors. It is forbidden that he should have *a broken foot* or *hand*, i.e., he should not lose the power of doing good works or of advancing in virtue. He is rejected, too, if he have a swelling either in front or behind: by which is signified too much love of earthly things: if he be blear-eyed, i.e., if his mind is darkened by carnal affections: for running of the eyes is caused by a flow of matter. He is also rejected if he had *a pearl in his eye*, i.e., if he presumes in his own estimation that he is clothed in the white robe of righteousness. Again, he is rejected *if he have a continued scab*, i.e., lustfulness of the flesh: also, if he have *a dry scurf*, which covers the body without giving pain, and is a blemish on the comeliness of the members; which denotes avarice. Lastly, he is rejected *if he have a rupture* or hernia; through baseness rending his heart, though it appear not in his deeds.

The vestments denote the virtues of God's ministers. Now there are four things that are necessary to all His ministers, viz., chastity denoted by the breeches; a pure life, signified by the linen tunic; the moderation of discretion, betokened by the girdle; and rectitude of purpose, denoted by the mitre covering the head. But the high-priests needed four other things in addition to these. First, a continual recollection of God in their thoughts; and this was signified by the golden plate worn over the forehead, with the name of God engraved thereon. Second, they had to bear with the shortcomings of the people: this was denoted by the ephod which they bore on their shoulders. Third, they had to carry the people in their mind and heart by the solicitude of charity, in token of which they wore the rational. Fourth, they had to lead a godly life by performing works of

hyacinthinam. Unde et tunicae hyacinthinae adiunguntur in extremitate tintinabula aurea, per quae significatur doctrina divinorum, quae debet coniungi caelesti conversationi pontificis. Adiunguntur autem mala Punica, per quae significatur unitas fidei et concordia in bonis moribus, quia sic coniuncta debet esse eius doctrina, ut per eam fidei et pacis unitas non rumpatur.

perfection; and this was signified by the violet tunic. Hence little golden bells were fixed to the bottom of the violet tunic, which bells signified the teaching of divine things united in the high-priest to his godly mode of life. In addition to these were the pomegranates, signifying unity of faith and concord in good morals: because his doctrine should hold together in such a way that it should not rend asunder the unity of faith and peace.

Article 6

Whether There Was Any Reasonable Cause for the Ceremonial Observances?

Ad sextum sic proceditur. Videtur quod observantiarum caeremonialium nulla fuerit rationabilis causa. Quia ut apostolus dicit, I ad Tim. IV, *omnis creatura Dei est bona, et nihil reiiciendum quod cum gratiarum actione percipitur.* Inconvenienter igitur prohibiti sunt ab esu quorundam ciborum tanquam immundorum, ut patet Lev. XI.

Praeterea, sicut animalia dantur in cibum hominis, ita etiam et herbae, unde dicitur Gen. IX, *quasi olera virentia dedi vobis omnem carnem.* Sed in herbis lex non distinxit aliquas immundas, cum tamen aliquae illarum sint maxime nocivae, ut puta venenosae. Ergo videtur quod nec de animalibus aliqua debuerint prohiberi tanquam immunda.

Praeterea, si materia est immunda ex qua aliquid generatur, pari ratione videtur quod id quod generatur ex ea, sit immundum. Sed ex sanguine generatur caro. Cum igitur non omnes carnes prohiberentur tanquam immundae, pari ratione nec sanguis debuit prohiberi quasi immundus; aut adeps, qui ex sanguine generatur.

Praeterea, dominus dicit, Matth. X, eos non esse timendos qui occidunt corpus, quia post mortem non habent quid faciant, quod non esset verum, si in nocumentum homini cederet quid ex eo fieret. Multo igitur minus pertinet ad animal iam occisum qualiter eius carnes decoquantur. Irrationabile igitur videtur esse quod dicitur Exod. XXIII, *non coques haedum in lacte matris suae.*

Praeterea, ea quae sunt primitiva in hominibus et animalibus, tanquam perfectiora, praecipiuntur domino offerri. Inconvenienter igitur praecipitur Lev. XIX, *quando ingressi fueritis terram, et plantaveritis in ea ligna pomifera, auferetis praeputia eorum,* idest prima germina, et immunda erunt vobis, nec edetis ex eis.

Praeterea, vestimentum extra corpus hominis est. Non igitur debuerunt quaedam specialia vestimenta Iudaeis interdici, puta quod dicitur Lev. XIX, *vestem*

Objection 1: It would seem that there was no reasonable cause for the ceremonial observances. Because, as the Apostle says (1 Tim 4:4), *every creature of God is good, and nothing to be rejected that is received with thanksgiving.* It was therefore unfitting that they should be forbidden to eat certain foods, as being unclean according to Lev. 11.

Obj. 2: Further, just as animals are given to man for food, so also are herbs: wherefore it is written (Gen 9:3): *As the green herbs have I delivered all* flesh *to you.* But the Law did not distinguish any herbs from the rest as being unclean, although some are most harmful, for instance, those that are poisonous. Therefore it seems that neither should any animals have been prohibited as being unclean.

Obj. 3: Further, if the matter from which a thing is generated be unclean, it seems that likewise the thing generated therefrom is unclean. But flesh is generated from blood. Since therefore all flesh was not prohibited as unclean, it seems that in like manner neither should blood have been forbidden as unclean; nor the fat which is engendered from blood.

Obj. 4: Further, Our Lord said (Matt 10:28; cf. Lk. 12:4), that those should not be feared *that kill the body,* since after death they *have no more that they can do*: which would not be true if after death harm might come to man through anything done with his body. Much less therefore does it matter to an animal already dead how its flesh be cooked. Consequently there seems to be no reason in what is said, Ex. 23:19: *Thou shalt not boil a kid in the milk of its dam.*

Obj. 5: Further, all that is first brought forth of man and beast, as being most perfect, is commanded to be offered to the Lord (Exod 13). Therefore it is an unfitting command that is set forth in Lev. 19:23: *when you shall be come into the land, and shall have planted in it fruit trees, you shall take away the uncircumcision of them,* i.e., the first crops, and they *shall be unclean to you, neither shall you eat of them.*

Obj. 6: Further, clothing is something extraneous to man's body. Therefore certain kinds of garments should not have been forbidden to the Jews: for instance (Lev 19:19):

quae ex duobus texta est, non indueris; et Deut. XXII, *non induetur mulier veste virili, et vir non induetur veste feminea*; et infra, *non indueris vestimento quod ex lana linoque contextum est.*

Praeterea, memoria mandatorum Dei non pertinet ad corpus, sed ad cor. Inconvenienter igitur praecipitur Deut. VI, quod *ligarent praecepta Dei quasi signum in manu sua, et quod scriberentur in limine ostiorum; et quod per angulos palliorum facerent fimbrias, in quibus ponerent vittas hyacinthinas, in memoriam mandatorum Dei*, ut habetur Num. XV.

Praeterea, apostolus dicit, I ad Cor. IX, quod non est cura Deo de bobus, et per consequens neque de aliis animalibus irrationalibus. Inconvenienter igitur praecipitur Deut. XXII, *si ambulaveris per viam, et inveneris nidum avis, non tenebis matrem cum filiis*; et Deut. XXV, *non alligabis os bovis triturantis*; et Lev. XIX, *iumenta tua non facies coire cum alterius generis animantibus.*

Praeterea, inter plantas non fiebat discretio mundorum ab immundis. Ergo multo minus circa culturam plantarum debuit aliqua discretio adhiberi. Ergo inconvenienter praecipitur Lev. XIX, *agrum non seres diverso semine*; et Deut. XXII, *non seres vineam tuam altero semine*; et, *non arabis in bove simul et asino.*

Praeterea, ea quae sunt inanimata, maxime videmus hominum potestati esse subiecta. Inconvenienter igitur arcetur homo ab argento et auro ex quibus fabricata sunt idola, et ab aliis quae in idolorum domibus inveniuntur, praecepto legis quod habetur Deut. VII. Ridiculum etiam videtur esse praeceptum quod habetur Deut. XXIII, ut *egestiones humo operirent, fodientes in terra.*

Praeterea, pietas maxime in sacerdotibus requiritur. Sed ad pietatem pertinere videtur quod aliquis funeribus amicorum intersit, unde etiam de hac Tobias laudatur, ut habetur Tob. I. Similiter etiam quandoque ad pietatem pertinet quod aliquis in uxorem accipiat meretricem, quia per hoc eam a peccato et infamia liberat. Ergo videtur quod haec inconvenienter prohibeantur sacerdotibus, Lev. XXI.

Sed contra est quod dicitur Deut. XVIII, *tu autem a domino Deo tuo aliter institutus es*, ex quo potest accipi quod huiusmodi observantiae sunt institutae a Deo ad quandam specialem illius populi praerogativam. Non ergo sunt irrationabiles, aut sine causa.

Respondeo dicendum quod populus Iudaeorum, ut supra dictum est, specialiter erat deputatus ad cultum divinum; et inter eos, specialiter sacerdotes. Et sicut aliae res quae applicantur ad cultum divinum, aliquam specialitatem debent habere, quod pertinet ad honorificentiam

Thou shalt not wear a garment that is woven of two sorts: and (Deut 22:5): *A woman shall not be clothed with man's apparel, neither shall a man use woman's apparel*: and further on (Deut 22:11): *Thou shalt not wear a garment that is woven of woolen and linen together.*

Obj. 7: Further, to be mindful of God's commandments concerns not the body but the heart. Therefore it is unsuitably prescribed (Deut 6:8, seqq.) that they should *bind* the commandments of God *as a sign* on their hands; and that they should *write them in the entry*; and (Num 15:38, seqq.) that they should *make to themselves fringes in the corners of their garments, putting in them ribands of blue . . . they may remember . . . the commandments of the Lord.*

Obj. 8: Further, the Apostle says (1 Cor 9:9) that God does not *take care for oxen*, and, therefore, neither of other irrational animals. Therefore without reason is it commanded (Deut 22:6): *If thou find, as thou walkest by the way, a bird's nest in a tree . . . thou shalt not take the dam with her young*; and (Deut 25:4): *Thou shalt not muzzle the ox that treadeth out thy corn*; and (Lev 19:19): *Thou shalt not make thy cattle to gender with beasts of any other kind.*

Obj. 9: Further, no distinction was made between clean and unclean plants. Much less therefore should any distinction have been made about the cultivation of plants. Therefore it was unfittingly prescribed (Lev 19:19): *Thou shalt not sow thy field with different seeds*; and (Deut 22:9, seqq.): *Thou shalt sow thy vineyard with diverse seeds*; and: *Thou shalt not plough with an ox and an ass together.*

Obj. 10: Further, it is apparent that inanimate things are most of all subject to the power of man. Therefore it was unfitting to debar man from taking silver and gold of which idols were made, or anything they found in the houses of idols, as expressed in the commandment of the Law (Deut 7:25, seqq.). It also seems an absurd commandment set forth in Dt. 23:13, that they should *dig round about and . . . cover with earth that which they were eased of.*

Obj. 11: Further, piety is required especially in priests. But it seems to be an act of piety to assist at the burial of one's friends: wherefore Tobias is commended for so doing (Tob 1:20, seqq.). In like manner it is sometimes an act of piety to marry a loose woman, because she is thereby delivered from sin and infamy. Therefore it seems inconsistent for these things to be forbidden to priests (Lev 21).

On the contrary, It is written (Deut 18:14): *But thou art otherwise instructed by the Lord thy God*: from which words we may gather that these observances were instituted by God to be a special prerogative of that people. Therefore they are not without reason or cause.

I answer that, The Jewish people, as stated above (A5), were specially chosen for the worship of God, and among them the priests themselves were specially set apart for that purpose. And just as other things that are applied to the divine worship, need to be marked in some particular

divini cultus; ita etiam et in conversatione illius populi, et praecipue sacerdotum, debuerunt esse aliqua specialia congruentia ad cultum divinum, vel spiritualem vel corporalem. Cultus autem legis figurabat mysterium Christi, unde omnia eorum gesta figurabant ea quae ad Christum pertinent; secundum illud I Cor. X, *omnia in figuram contingebant illis*. Et ideo rationes harum observantiarum dupliciter assignari possunt, uno modo, secundum congruentiam ad divinum cultum; alio modo, secundum quod figurant aliquid circa Christianorum vitam.

AD PRIMUM ergo dicendum quod, sicut supra dictum est, duplex pollutio, vel immunditia, observabatur in lege, una quidem culpae, per quam polluebatur anima; alia autem corruptionis cuiusdam, per quam quodammodo inquinatur corpus. Loquendo igitur de prima immunditia, nulla genera ciborum immunda sunt, vel hominem inquinare possunt, secundum suam naturam, unde dicitur Matth. XV, *non quod intrat in os, coinquinat hominem; sed quae procedunt de ore, haec coinquinant hominem*; et exponitur hoc de peccatis. Possunt tamen aliqui cibi per accidens inquinare animam, inquantum scilicet contra obedientiam vel votum, vel nimia concupiscentia comeduntur; vel inquantum praebent fomentum luxuriae, propter quod aliqui a vino et carnibus abstinent.

Secundum autem corporalem immunditiam, quae est corruptionis cuiusdam, aliquae animalium carnes immunditiam habent, vel quia ex rebus immundis nutriuntur, sicut porcus; aut immunde conversantur, sicut quaedam animalia sub terra habitantia, sicut talpae et mures et alia huiusmodi, unde etiam quendam fetorem contrahunt; vel quia eorum carnes, propter superfluam umiditatem vel siccitatem, corruptos humores in corporibus humanis generant. Et ideo prohibitae sunt eis carnes animalium habentium soleas, idest ungulam unam non fissam, propter eorum terrestreitatem. Et similiter sunt eis prohibitae carnes animalium habentium multas fissuras in pedibus, quia sunt nimis cholerica et adusta, sicut carnes leonis et huiusmodi. Et eadem ratione prohibitae sunt eis aves quaedam rapaces, quae sunt nimiae siccitatis; et quaedam aves aquaticae, propter excessum humiditatis. Similiter etiam quidam pisces non habentes pinnulas et squamas, ut anguillae et huiusmodi, propter excessum humiditatis. Sunt autem eis concessa ad esum animalia ruminantia et findentia ungulam, quia habent humores bene digestos, et sunt medie complexionata, quia nec sunt nimis humida, quod significant ungulae; neque sunt nimis terrestria, cum non habeant ungulam continuam, sed fissam. In piscibus etiam concessi sunt eis pisces sicciores, quod significatur per hoc quod habent squamas et pinnulas, per hoc enim efficitur temperata complexio humida piscium. In avibus etiam sunt eis concessae magis temperatae, sicut gallinae, perdices,

way so that they be worthy of the worship of God; so too in that people's, and especially the priests', mode of life, there needed to be certain special things befitting the divine worship, whether spiritual or corporal. Now the worship prescribed by the Law foreshadowed the mystery of Christ: so that whatever they did was a figure of things pertaining to Christ, according to 1 Cor. 10:11: *All these things happened to them in figures*. Consequently the reasons for these observances may be taken in two ways, first according to their fittingness to the worship of God; second, according as they foreshadow something touching the Christian mode of life.

REPLY OBJ. 1: As stated above (A5, ad 4,5), the Law distinguished a twofold pollution or uncleanness; one, that of sin, whereby the soul was defiled; and another consisting in some kind of corruption, whereby the body was in some way infected. Speaking then of the first-mentioned uncleanness, no kind of food is unclean, or can defile a man, by reason of its nature; wherefore we read (Matt 15:11): *Not that which goeth into the mouth defileth a man; but what cometh out of the mouth, this defileth a man*: which words are explained (Matt 15:17) as referring to sins. Yet certain foods can defile the soul accidentally; insofar as man partakes of them against obedience or a vow, or from excessive concupiscence; or through their being an incentive to lust, for which reason some refrain from wine and flesh-meat.

If, however, we speak of bodily uncleanness, consisting in some kind of corruption, the flesh of certain animals is unclean, either because like the pig they feed on unclean things; or because their life is among unclean surroundings: thus certain animals, like moles and mice and such like, live underground, whence they contract a certain unpleasant smell; or because their flesh, through being too moist or too dry, engenders corrupt humors in the human body. Hence they were forbidden to eat the flesh of flat-footed animals, i.e., animals having an uncloven hoof, on account of their earthiness; and in like manner they were forbidden to eat the flesh of animals that have many clefts in their feet, because such are very fierce and their flesh is very dry, such as the flesh of lions and the like. For the same reason they were forbidden to eat certain birds of prey the flesh of which is very dry, and certain water-fowl on account of their exceeding humidity. In like manner certain fish lacking fins and scales were prohibited on account of their excessive moisture; such as eels and the like. They were, however, allowed to eat ruminants and animals with a divided hoof, because in such animals the humors are well absorbed, and their nature well balanced: for neither are they too moist, as is indicated by the hoof; nor are they too earthly, which is shown by their having not a flat but a cloven hoof. Of fishes they were allowed to partake of the drier kinds, of which the fins and scales are an indication, because thereby the moist nature of the fish is tempered. Of birds they were allowed to eat the tamer kinds, such as hens, partridges, and the

et aliae huiusmodi. Alia ratio fuit in detestationem idololatriae. Nam gentiles, et praecipue Aegyptii, inter quos erant nutriti, huiusmodi animalia prohibita idolis immolabant, vel eis ad maleficia utebantur. Animalia vero quae Iudaeis sunt concessa ad esum non comedebant, sed ea tanquam deos colebant; vel propter aliam causam ab eis abstinebant, ut supra dictum est. Tertia ratio est ad tollendam nimiam diligentiam circa cibaria. Et ideo conceduntur illa animalia quae de facili et in promptu haberi possunt.

Generaliter tamen prohibitus est eis esus sanguinis et adipis cuiuslibet animalis. Sanguinis quidem tum ad vitandam crudelitatem, ut detestarentur humanum sanguinem effundere, sicut supra dictum est. Tum etiam ad vitandum idololatriae ritum, quia eorum consuetudo erat ut circa sanguinem congregatum adunarentur ad comedendum in honorem idolorum, quibus reputabant sanguinem acceptissimum esse. Et ideo dominus mandavit quod sanguis effunderetur, et quod pulvere operiretur. Et propter hoc etiam prohibitum est eis comedere animalia suffocata vel strangulata, quia sanguis eorum non separaretur a carne. Vel quia in tali morte animalia multum affliguntur; et dominus voluit eos a crudelitate prohibere etiam circa animalia bruta, ut per hoc magis recederent a crudelitate hominis, habentes exercitium pietatis etiam circa bestias. Adipis etiam esus prohibitus est eis, tum quia idololatrae comedebant illum in honorem deorum suorum. Tum etiam quia cremabatur in honorem Dei. Tum etiam quia sanguis et adeps non generant bonum nutrimentum, quod pro causa inducit Rabbi Moyses. Causa autem prohibitionis esus nervorum exprimitur Gen. XXXII, ubi dicitur quod *non comedunt filii Israel nervum, eo quod tetigerit nervum femoris Iacob, et obstupuerit.*

Figuralis autem ratio horum est quia per omnia huiusmodi animalia prohibita designantur aliqua peccata, in quorum figuram illa animalia prohibentur. Unde dicit Augustinus, in libro contra Faustum, *si de porco et agno requiratur, utrumque natura mundum est, quia omnis creatura Dei bona est, quadam vero significatione, agnus mundus, porcus immundus est. Tanquam, si stultum et sapientem diceres, utrumque hoc verbum natura vocis et litterarum et syllabarum ex quibus constat, mundum est, significatione autem unum est mundum, et aliud immundum.* Animal enim quod ruminat et ungulam findit, mundum est significatione. Quia fissio ungulae significat distinctionem duorum testamentorum; vel patris et filii; vel duarum naturarum in Christo; vel discretionem boni et mali. Ruminatio autem significat meditationem Scripturarum, et sanum intellectum earum. Cuicumque autem horum alterum deest, spiritualiter immundus est. Similiter etiam in piscibus illi qui habent squamas et pinnulas, significatione mundi sunt. Quia

like. Another reason was detestation of idolatry: because the Gentiles, and especially the Egyptians, among whom they had grown up, offered up these forbidden animals to their idols, or employed them for the purpose of sorcery: whereas they did not eat those animals which the Jews were allowed to eat, but worshipped them as gods, or abstained, for some other motive, from eating them, as stated above (A3, ad 2). The third reason was to prevent excessive care about food: wherefore they were allowed to eat those animals which could be procured easily and promptly.

With regard to blood and fat, they were forbidden to partake of those of any animals whatever without exception. Blood was forbidden, both in order to avoid cruelty, that they might abhor the shedding of human blood, as stated above (A3, ad 8); and in order to shun idolatrous rite whereby it was customary for men to collect the blood and to gather together around it for a banquet in honor of the idols, to whom they held the blood to be most acceptable. Hence the Lord commanded the blood to be poured out and to be covered with earth (Lev 17:13). For the same reason they were forbidden to eat animals that had been suffocated or strangled: because the blood of these animals would not be separated from the body: or because this form of death is very painful to the victim; and the Lord wished to withdraw them from cruelty even in regard to irrational animals, so as to be less inclined to be cruel to other men, through being used to be kind to beasts. They were forbidden to eat the fat: both because idolaters ate it in honor of their gods; and because it used to be burnt in honor of God; and, again, because blood and fat are not nutritious, which is the cause assigned by Rabbi Moses (*Doct. Perplex.* iii). The reason why they were forbidden to eat the sinews is given in Gn. 32:32, where it is stated that *the children of Israel . . . eat not the sinew . . . because he touched the sinew of* Jacob's *thigh and it shrank.*

The figurative reason for these things is that all these animals signified certain sins, in token of which those animals were prohibited. Hence Augustine says (*Contra Faustum* iv, 7): *If the swine and lamb be called in question, both are clean by nature, because all God's creatures are good: yet the lamb is clean, and the pig is unclean in a certain signification. Thus if you speak of a foolish, and of a wise man, each of these expressions is clean considered in the nature of the sound, letters and syllables of which it is composed: but in signification, the one is clean, the other unclean.* The animal that chews the cud and has a divided hoof, is clean in signification. Because division of the hoof is a figure of the two Testaments: or of the Father and Son: or of the two natures in Christ: of the distinction of good and evil. While chewing the cud signifies meditation on the Scriptures and a sound understanding thereof; and whoever lacks either of these is spiritually unclean. In like manner those fish that have scales and fins are clean in signification. Because fins signify the heavenly or contemplative life; while scales

per pinnulas significatur vita sublimis, vel contemplatio; per squamas autem significatur aspera vita; quorum utrumque necessarium est ad munditiam spiritualem. In avibus autem specialia quaedam genera prohibentur. In aquila enim, quae alte volat, prohibetur superbia. In gryphe autem, qui equis et hominibus infestus est, crudelitas potentum prohibetur. In haliaeeto autem, qui pascitur minutis avibus, significantur illi qui sunt pauperibus molesti. In milvo autem, qui maxime insidiis utitur, designantur fraudulenti. In vulture autem, qui sequitur exercitum expectans comedere cadavera mortuorum, significantur illi qui mortes et seditiones hominum affectant ut inde lucrentur. Per animalia corvini generis significantur illi qui sunt voluptatibus denigrati, vel qui sunt expertes bonae affectionis, quia corvus, semel emissus ab arca, non est reversus. Per struthionem, qui, cum sit avis, volare non potest, sed semper est circa terram, significantur Deo militantes et se negotiis saecularibus implicantes. Nycticorax, quae in nocte acuti est visus, in die autem non videt, significat eos qui in temporalibus sunt astuti, in spiritualibus hebetes. Larus autem, qui et volat in aere et natat in aqua, significat eos qui et circumcisionem et Baptismum venerantur, vel significat eos qui per contemplationem volare volunt, et tamen vivunt in aquis voluptatum. Accipiter vero, qui deservit hominibus ad praedam, significat eos qui ministrant potentibus ad depraedandum pauperes. Per bubonem, qui in nocte pastum quaerit, de die autem latet, significantur luxuriosi, qui occultari quaerunt in nocturnis operibus quae agunt. Mergulus autem, cuius natura est ut sub undis diutius immoretur, significat gulosos, qui aquis deliciarum se immergunt. Ibis vero avis est in Africa habens longum rostrum, quae serpentibus pascitur, et forte est idem quod ciconia, et significat invidos, qui de malis aliorum, quasi de serpentibus, reficiuntur. Cygnus autem est coloris candidi, et longo collo quod habet, ex profunditate terrae vel aquae cibum trahit, et potest significare homines qui per exteriorem iustitiae candorem lucra terrena quaerunt. Onocrotalus autem avis est in partibus orientis, longo rostro, quae in faucibus habet quosdam folliculos, in quibus primo cibum reponit, et post horam in ventrem mittit, et significat avaros, qui immoderata sollicitudine vitae necessaria congregant. Porphyrio autem, praeter modum aliarum avium, habet unum pedem latum ad natandum, alium fissum ad ambulandum, quia et in aqua natat ut anates, et in terra ambulat ut perdices, solo morsu bibit, omnem cibum aqua tingens, et significat eos qui nihil ad alterius arbitrium facere volunt, sed solum quod fuerit tinctum aqua propriae voluntatis. Per Herodionem qui vulgariter falco dicitur, significantur illi quorum pedes sunt veloces ad effundendum sanguinem. Charadrius autem, quae est avis garrula, significat loquaces. Upupa autem, quae nidificat in stercoribus et fetenti pascitur fimo, et

signify a life of trials, each of which is required for spiritual cleanness. Of birds certain kinds were forbidden. In the eagle which flies at a great height, pride is forbidden: in the griffon which is hostile to horses and men, cruelty of powerful men is prohibited. The osprey, which feeds on very small birds, signifies those who oppress the poor. The kite, which is full of cunning, denotes those who are fraudulent in their dealings. The vulture, which follows an army, expecting to feed on the carcases of the slain, signifies those who like others to die or to fight among themselves that they may gain thereby. Birds of the raven kind signify those who are blackened by their lusts; or those who lack kindly feelings, for the raven did not return when once it had been let loose from the ark. The ostrich which, though a bird, cannot fly, and is always on the ground, signifies those who fight God's cause, and at the same time are taken up with worldly business. The owl, which sees clearly at night, but cannot see in the daytime, denotes those who are clever in temporal affairs, but dull in spiritual matters. The gull, which flies both in the air and swims in the water, signifies those who are partial both to Circumcision and to Baptism: or else it denotes those who would fly by contemplation, yet dwell in the waters of sensual delights. The hawk, which helps men to seize the prey, is a figure of those who assist the strong to prey on the poor. The screech-owl, which seeks its food by night but hides by day, signifies the lustful man who seeks to lie hidden in his deeds of darkness. The cormorant, so constituted that it can stay a long time under water, denotes the glutton who plunges into the waters of pleasure. The ibis is an African bird with a long beak, and feeds on snakes; and perhaps it is the same as the stork: it signifies the envious man, who refreshes himself with the ills of others, as with snakes. The swan is bright in color, and by the aid of its long neck extracts its food from deep places on land or water: it may denote those who seek earthly profit though an external brightness of virtue. The bittern is a bird of the East: it has a long beak, and its jaws are furnished with follicules, wherein it stores its food at first, after a time proceeding to digest it: it is a figure of the miser, who is excessively careful in hoarding up the necessaries of life. The coot has this peculiarity apart from other birds, that it has a webbed foot for swimming, and a cloven foot for walking: for it swims like a duck in the water, and walks like a partridge on land: it drinks only when it bites, since it dips all its food in water: it is a figure of a man who will not take advice, and does nothing but what is soaked in the water of his own will. The heron, commonly called a falcon, signifies those whose *feet are swift to shed blood* (Ps 13:3). The plover, which is a garrulous bird, signifies the gossip. The hoopoe, which builds its nest on dung, feeds on foetid ordure, and whose song is like a groan, denotes worldly grief which works death in those who are unclean. The bat, which flies near the ground, signifies those who being gifted with worldly knowledge, seek none but earthly

gemitum in cantu simulat, significat tristitiam saeculi, quae in hominibus immundis mortem operatur. Per vespertilionem autem, quae circa terram volitat, significantur illi qui, saeculari scientia praediti, sola terrena sapiunt. Circa volatilia autem et quadrupedia, illa sola conceduntur eis quae posteriora crura habent longiora, ut salire possint. Alia vero, quae terrae magis adhaerent, prohibentur, quia illi qui abutuntur doctrina quatuor Evangelistarum, ut per eam in altum non subleventur, immundi reputantur. In sanguine vero et adipe et nervo, intelligitur prohiberi crudelitas, et voluptas, et fortitudo ad peccandum.

AD SECUNDUM dicendum quod esus plantarum et aliorum terrae nascentium adfuit apud homines etiam ante diluvium, sed esus carnium videtur esse post diluvium introductus; dicitur enim Gen. IX, *quasi olera virentia dedi vobis omnem carnem.* Et hoc ideo, quia esus terrae nascentium magis pertinet ad quandam simplicitatem vitae; esus autem carnium ad quasdam delicias et curiositatem vivendi. Sponte enim terra herbam germinat, vel cum modico studio huiusmodi terrae nascentia in magna copia procurantur, oportet autem cum magno studio animalia vel nutrire, vel etiam capere. Et ideo volens dominus populum suum reducere ad simpliciorem victum, multa in genere animalium eis prohibuit, non autem in genere terrae nascentium. Vel etiam quia animalia immolabantur idolis, non autem terrae nascentia.

AD TERTIUM patet responsio ex dictis.

AD QUARTUM dicendum quod, etsi haedus occisus non sentiat qualiter carnes eius coquantur, tamen in animo decoquentis ad quandam crudelitatem pertinere videtur si lac matris, quod datum est ei pro nutrimento, adhibeatur ad consumptionem carnium ipsius. Vel potest dici quod gentiles in solemnitatibus idolorum taliter carnes haedi coquebant, ad immolandum vel ad comedendum. Et ideo Exod. XXIII, postquam praedictum fuerat de solemnitatibus celebrandis in lege, subditur, *non coques haedum in lacte matris suae.* Figuralis autem ratio huius prohibitionis est quia praefigurabatur quod Christus, qui est haedus propter similitudinem carnis peccati, non erat a Iudaeis coquendus, idest occidendus, in lacte matris, idest tempore infantiae. Vel significatur quod haedus idest peccator, non est coquendus in lacte matris, idest non est blanditiis deliniendus.

AD QUINTUM dicendum quod gentiles fructus primitivos, quos fortunatos aestimabant, diis suis offerebant, vel etiam comburebant eos ad quaedam magica facienda. Et ideo praeceptum est eis ut fructus trium primorum annorum immundos reputarent. In tribus enim annis fere omnes arbores terrae illius fructum producunt, quae scilicet vel seminando, vel inserendo, vel plantando coluntur. Raro autem contingit quod ossa

things. Of fowls and quadrupeds those alone were permitted which have the hind-legs longer than the forelegs, so that they can leap: whereas those were forbidden which cling rather to the earth: because those who abuse the doctrine of the four Evangelists, so that they are not lifted up thereby, are reputed unclean. By the prohibition of blood, fat and nerves, we are to understand the forbidding of cruelty, lust, and bravery in committing sin.

REPLY OBJ. 2: Men were wont to eat plants and other products of the soil even before the deluge: but the eating of flesh seems to have been introduced after the deluge; for it is written (Gen 9:3): *Even as the green herbs have I delivered . . . all* flesh *to you.* The reason for this was that the eating of the products of the soil savors rather of a simple life; whereas the eating of flesh savors of delicate and over-careful living. For the soil gives birth to the herb of its own accord; and such like products of the earth may be had in great quantities with very little effort: whereas no small trouble is necessary either to rear or to catch an animal. Consequently God being wishful to bring His people back to a more simple way of living, forbade them to eat many kinds of animals, but not those things that are produced by the soil. Another reason may be that animals were offered to idols, while the products of the soil were not.

THE REPLY to the Third Objection is clear from what has been said (ad 1).

REPLY OBJ. 4: Although the kid that is slain has no perception of the manner in which its flesh is cooked, yet it would seem to savor of heartlessness if the dam's milk, which was intended for the nourishment of her offspring, were served up on the same dish. It might also be said that the Gentiles in celebrating the feasts of their idols prepared the flesh of kids in this manner, for the purpose of sacrifice or banquet: hence (Exod 23) after the solemnities to be celebrated under the Law had been foretold, it is added: *Thou shalt not boil a kid in the milk of its dam.* The figurative reason for this prohibition is this: the kid, signifying Christ, on account of *the likeness of sinful flesh* (Rom 8:3), was not to be seethed, i.e., slain, by the Jews, *in the milk of its dam,* i.e., during His infancy. Or else it signifies that the kid, i.e., the sinner, should not be boiled in the milk of its dam, i.e., should not be cajoled by flattery.

REPLY OBJ. 5: The Gentiles offered their gods the first-fruits, which they held to bring them good luck: or they burnt them for the purpose of secrecy. Consequently (the Israelites) were commanded to look upon the fruits of the first three years as unclean: for in that country nearly all the trees bear fruit in three years' time; those trees, to wit, that are cultivated either from seed, or from a graft, or from a cutting: but it seldom happens that the fruit-stones

fructuum arboris, vel semina latentia, seminentur, haec enim tardius facerent fructum, sed lex respexit ad id quod frequentius fit. Poma autem quarti anni, tanquam primitiae mundorum fructuum, Deo offerebantur, a quinto autem anno, et deinceps, comedebantur.

Figuralis autem ratio est quia per hoc praefiguratur quod post tres status legis, quorum unus est ab Abraham usque ad David, secundus usque ad transmigrationem Babylonis, tertius usque ad Christum, erat Christus Deo offerendus, qui est fructus legis. Vel quia primordia nostrorum operum debent esse nobis suspecta, propter imperfectionem.

AD SEXTUM dicendum quod sicut dicitur Eccli. XIX, *amictus corporis enuntiat de homine.* Et ideo voluit dominus ut populus eius distingueretur ab aliis populis non solum signo circumcisionis, quod erat in carne, sed etiam certa habitus distinctione. Et ideo prohibitum fuit eis ne induerentur vestimento ex lana et lino contexto, et ne mulier indueretur veste virili, aut e converso, propter duo. Primo quidem, ad vitandum idololatriae cultum. Huiusmodi enim variis vestibus ex diversis confectis gentiles in cultu suorum deorum utebantur. Et etiam in cultu Martis mulieres utebantur armis virorum; in cultu autem Veneris e converso viri utebantur vestibus mulierum. Alia ratio est ad declinandam luxuriam. Nam per commixtiones varias in vestimentis omnis inordinata commixtio coitus excluditur. Quod autem mulier induatur veste virili, aut e converso, incentivum est concupiscentiae, et occasionem libidini praestat. Figuralis autem ratio est quia in vestimento contexto ex lana et lino interdicitur coniunctio simplicitatis innocentiae, quae figuratur per lanam, et subtilitatis malitiae, quae figuratur per linum. Prohibetur etiam quod mulier non usurpet sibi doctrinam, vel alia virorum officia; vel vir declinet ad mollities mulierum.

AD SEPTIMUM dicendum quod, sicut Hieronymus dicit, super Matth., *dominus iussit ut in quatuor angulis palliorum hyacinthinas fimbrias facerent, ad populum Israel dignoscendum ab aliis populis.* Unde per hoc se esse Iudaeos profitebantur, et ideo per aspectum huius signi inducebantur in memoriam suae legis.

Quod autem dicitur, *ligabis ea in manu tua, et erunt semper ante oculos tuos, Pharisaei male interpretabantur, scribentes in membranis Decalogum Moysi, et ligabant in fronte, quasi coronam, ut ante oculos moverentur,* cum tamen intentio domini mandantis fuerit ut ligarentur in manu, idest in operatione; et essent ante oculos, idest in meditatione. In hyacinthinis etiam vittis, quae palliis inserebantur, significatur caelestis intentio, quae omnibus operibus nostris debet adiungi. Potest tamen dici quod, quia populus ille carnalis erat et durae cervicis, oportuit

or seeds encased in a pod are sown: since it would take a longer time for these to bear fruit: and the Law considered what happened most frequently. The fruits, however, of the fourth year, as being the firstlings of clean fruits, were offered to God: and from the fifth year onward they were eaten.

The figurative reason was that this foreshadowed the fact that after the three states of the Law (the first lasting from Abraham to David, the second, until they were carried away to Babylon, the third until the time of Christ), the Fruit of the Law, i.e., Christ, was to be offered to God. Or again, that we must mistrust our first efforts, on account of their imperfection.

REPLY OBJ. 6: It is said of a man in Ecclus. 19:27, that *the attire of the body . . . shows what he is.* Hence the Lord wished His people to be distinguished from other nations, not only by the sign of the circumcision, which was in the flesh, but also by a certain difference of attire. Wherefore they were forbidden to wear garments woven of woolen and linen together, and for a woman to be clothed with man's apparel, or vice versa, for two reasons. First, to avoid idolatrous worship. Because the Gentiles, in their religious rites, used garments of this sort, made of various materials. Moreover in the worship of Mars, women put on men's armor; while, conversely, in the worship of Venus men donned women's attire. The second reason was to preserve them from lust: because the employment of various materials in the making of garments signified inordinate union of sexes, while the use of male attire by a woman, or vice versa, has an incentive to evil desires, and offers an occasion of lust. The figurative reason is that the prohibition of wearing a garment woven of woolen and linen signified that it was forbidden to unite the simplicity of innocence, denoted by wool, with the duplicity of malice, betokened by linen. It also signifies that woman is forbidden to presume to teach, or perform other duties of men: or that man should not adopt the effeminate manners of a woman.

REPLY OBJ. 7: As Jerome says on Mt. 23:6, *the Lord commanded them to make violet-colored fringes in the four corners of their garments, so that the Israelites might be distinguished from other nations.* Hence, in this way, they professed to be Jews: and consequently the very sight of this sign reminded them of their law.

When we read: *Thou shalt bind them on thy hand, and they shall be ever before thy eyes,* the Pharisees gave a false interpretation to these words, and wrote the decalogue of Moses on a parchment, and tied it on their foreheads like a wreath, so that it moved in front of their eyes: whereas the intention of the Lord in giving this commandment was that they should be bound in their hands, i.e., in their works; and that they should be before their eyes, i.e., in their thoughts. The violet-colored fillets which were inserted in their cloaks signify the godly intention which should accompany our every deed. It may, however, be said that, because they were

etiam per huiusmodi sensibilia eos ad legis observantiam excitari.

Ad octavum dicendum quod affectus hominis est duplex, unus quidem secundum rationem; alius vero secundum passionem. Secundum igitur affectum rationis, non refert quid homo circa bruta animalia agat, quia omnia sunt subiecta eius potestati a Deo, secundum illud Psalmi VIII, *omnia subiecisti sub pedibus eius.* Et secundum hoc apostolus dicit quod non est cura Deo de bobus, quia Deus non requirit ab homine quid circa boves agat, vel circa alia animalia.

Quantum vero ad affectum passionis, movetur affectus hominis etiam circa alia animalia, quia enim passio misericordiae consurgit ex afflictionibus aliorum, contingit autem etiam bruta animalia poenas sentire, potest in homine consurgere misericordiae affectus etiam circa afflictiones animalium. Proximum autem est ut qui exercetur in affectu misericordiae circa animalia, magis ex hoc disponatur ad affectum misericordiae circa homines, unde dicitur Prov. XII, *novit iustus animas iumentorum suorum; viscera autem impiorum crudelia.* Et ideo ut dominus populum Iudaicum, ad crudelitatem pronum, ad misericordiam revocaret, voluit eos exerceri ad misericordiam etiam circa bruta animalia, prohibens quaedam circa animalia fieri quae ad crudelitatem quandam pertinere videntur. Et ideo prohibuit ne coqueretur haedus in lacte matris; et quod non alligaretur os bovi trituranti; et quod non occideretur mater cum filiis. Quamvis etiam dici possit quod haec prohibita sunt eis in detestationem idololatriae. Nam Aegyptii nefarium reputabant ut boves triturantes de frugibus comederent. Aliqui etiam malefici utebantur matre avis incubante et pullis eius simul captis, ad fecunditatem et fortunam circa nutritionem filiorum. Et etiam quia in auguriis reputabatur hoc esse fortunatum, quod inveniretur mater incubans filiis.

Circa commixtionem vero animalium diversae speciei, ratio litteralis potuit esse triplex. Una quidem, ad detestationem idololatriae Aegyptiorum, qui diversis commixtionibus utebantur in servitium planetarum, qui secundum diversas coniunctiones habent diversos effectus, et super diversas species rerum. Alia ratio est ad excludendum concubitus contra naturam. Tertia ratio est ad tollendam universaliter occasionem concupiscentiae. Animalia enim diversarum specierum non commiscentur de facili ad invicem, nisi hoc per homines procuretur; et in aspectu coitus animalium excitatur homini concupiscentiae motus. Unde etiam in traditionibus Iudaeorum praeceptum invenitur, ut Rabbi Moyses dicit, ut homines avertant oculos ab animalibus coeuntibus.

Figuralis autem horum ratio est quia bovi trituranti, idest praedicatori deferenti segetes doctrinae, non sunt necessaria victus subtrahenda; ut apostolus dicit, I ad

a carnal-minded and stiff-necked people, it was necessary for them to be stirred by these sensible things to the observance of the Law.

Reply Obj. 8: Affection in man is twofold: it may be an affection of reason, or it may be an affection of passion. If a man's affection be one of reason, it matters not how man behaves to animals, because God has subjected all things to man's power, according to Ps. 8:8: *Thou hast subjected all things under his feet*: and it is in this sense that the Apostle says that *God has no care for oxen*; because God does not ask of man what he does with oxen or other animals.

But if man's affection be one of passion, then it is moved also in regard to other animals: for since the passion of pity is caused by the afflictions of others; and since it happens that even irrational animals are sensible to pain, it is possible for the affection of pity to arise in a man with regard to the sufferings of animals. Now it is evident that if a man practice a pitiful affection for animals, he is all the more disposed to take pity on his fellow-men: wherefore it is written (Prov 11:10): *The just regardeth the lives of his beasts: but the bowels of the wicked are cruel.* Consequently the Lord, in order to inculcate pity to the Jewish people, who were prone to cruelty, wished them to practice pity even with regard to dumb animals, and forbade them to do certain things savoring of cruelty to animals. Hence He prohibited them to *boil a kid in the milk of its dam*; and to *muzzle the ox that treadeth out the corn*; and to slay *the dam with her young*. It may, nevertheless, be also said that these prohibitions were made in hatred of idolatry. For the Egyptians held it to be wicked to allow the ox to eat of the grain while threshing the corn. Moreover certain sorcerers were wont to ensnare the mother bird with her young during incubation, and to employ them for the purpose of securing fruitfulness and good luck in bringing up children: also because it was held to be a good omen to find the mother sitting on her young.

As to the mingling of animals of diverse species, the literal reason may have been threefold. The first was to show detestation for the idolatry of the Egyptians, who employed various mixtures in worshipping the planets, which produce various effects, and on various kinds of things according to their various conjunctions. The second reason was in condemnation of unnatural sins. The third reason was the entire removal of all occasions of concupiscence. Because animals of different species do not easily breed, unless this be brought about by man; and movements of lust are aroused by seeing such things. Wherefore in the Jewish traditions we find it prescribed as stated by Rabbi Moses that men shall turn away their eyes from such sights.

The figurative reason for these things is that the necessities of life should not be withdrawn from the ox that treadeth the corn, i.e., from the preacher bearing the

Cor. IX. Matrem etiam non simul debemus tenere cum filiis, quia in quibusdam retinendi sunt spirituales sensus, quasi filii, et dimittenda est litteralis observantia, quasi mater; sicut in omnibus caeremoniis legis. Prohibetur etiam quod iumenta, idest populares homines, non faciamus coire, idest coniunctionem habere, cum alterius generis animantibus, idest cum gentilibus vel Iudaeis.

AD NONUM dicendum quod omnes illae commixtiones in agricultura sunt prohibitae, ad litteram, in detestationem idololatriae. Quia Aegyptii, in venerationem stellarum, diversas commixtiones faciebant et in seminibus et in animalibus et in vestibus, repraesentantes diversas coniunctiones stellarum. Vel omnes huiusmodi commixtiones variae prohibentur ad detestationem coitus contra naturam.

Habent tamen figuralem rationem. Quia quod dicitur, non seres vineam tuam altero semine, est spiritualiter intelligendum, quod in Ecclesia, quae est spiritualis vinea, non est seminanda aliena doctrina. Et similiter ager, idest Ecclesia, non est seminandus diverso semine, idest Catholica doctrina et haeretica. Non est etiam simul arandum in bove et asino, quia fatuus sapienti in praedicatione non est sociandus, quia unus impedit alium.

AD UNDECIMUM dicendum quod malefici et sacerdotes idolorum utebantur in suis ritibus ossibus vel carnibus hominum mortuorum. Et ideo, ad extirpandum idololatriae cultum, praecepit dominus ut sacerdotes minores, qui per tempora certa ministrabant in sanctuario, non inquinarentur in mortibus nisi valde propinquorum, scilicet patris et matris et huiusmodi coniunctarum personarum. Pontifex autem semper debebat esse paratus ad ministerium sanctuarii, et ideo totaliter prohibitus erat ei accessus ad mortuos, quantumcumque propinquos. Praeceptum etiam est eis ne ducerent uxorem meretricem ac repudiatam, sed virginem. Tum propter reverentiam sacerdotum, quorum dignitas quodammodo ex tali coniugio diminui videretur. Tum etiam propter filios, quibus esset ad ignominiam turpitudo matris, quod maxime tunc erat vitandum, quando sacerdotii dignitas secundum successionem generis conferebatur. Praeceptum etiam erat eis ut non raderent caput nec barbam, nec in carnibus suis facerent incisuram, ad removendum idololatriae ritum. Nam sacerdotes gentilium radebant caput et barbam, unde dicitur Baruch VI, *sacerdotes sedent habentes tunicas scissas, et capita et barbam rasam*. Et etiam in cultu idolorum incidebant se cultris et lanceolis, ut dicitur III regum XVIII. Unde contraria praecepta sunt sacerdotibus veteris legis.

Spiritualis autem ratio horum est quia sacerdotes omnino debent esse immunes ab operibus mortuis, quae

sheaves of doctrine, as the Apostle states (1 Cor 9:4, seqq.). Again, we should not take the dam with her young: because in certain things we have to keep the spiritual senses, i.e., the offspring, and set aside the observance of the letter, i.e., the mother, for instance, in all the ceremonies of the Law. It is also forbidden that beasts of burden, i.e., any of the common people, should be allowed to engender, i.e., to have any connection, with animals of another kind, i.e., with Gentiles or Jews.

REPLY OBJ. 9: All these minglings were forbidden in agriculture; literally, in detestation of idolatry. For the Egyptians in worshipping the stars employed various combinations of seeds, animals and garments, in order to represent the various connections of the stars. Or else all these minglings were forbidden in detestation of the unnatural vice.

They have, however, a figurative reason. For the prohibition: *Thou shalt not sow thy field with different seeds*, is to be understood, in the spiritual sense, of the prohibition to sow strange doctrine in the Church, which is a spiritual vineyard. Likewise *the field*, i.e., the Church, must not be sown *with different seeds*, i.e., with Catholic and heretical doctrines. Neither is it allowed to plough *with an ox and an ass together*; thus a fool should not accompany a wise man in preaching, for one would hinder the other.

REPLY OBJ. 11: Sorcerers and idolatrous priests made use, in their rites, of the bones and flesh of dead men. Wherefore, in order to extirpate the customs of idolatrous worship, the Lord commanded that the priests of inferior degree, who at fixed times served in the temple, should not *incur an uncleanness at the death* of anyone except of those who were closely related to them, viz., their father or mother, and others thus near of kin to them. But the high-priest had always to be ready for the service of the sanctuary; wherefore he was absolutely forbidden to approach the dead, however nearly related to him. They were also forbidden to marry a *harlot* or *one that has been put away*, or any other than a virgin: both on account of the reverence due to the priesthood, the honor of which would seem to be tarnished by such a marriage: and for the sake of the children who would be disgraced by the mother's shame: which was most of all to be avoided when the priestly dignity was passed on from father to son. Again, they were commanded to shave neither head nor beard, and not to make incisions in their flesh, in order to exclude the rites of idolatry. For the priests of the Gentiles shaved both head and beard, wherefore it is written (Bar 6:30): *Priests sit in their temples having their garments rent, and their heads and beards shaven*. Moreover, in worshipping their idols *they cut themselves with knives and lancets* (3 Kgs 18:28). For this reason the priests of the Old Law were commanded to do the contrary.

The spiritual reason for these things is that priests should be entirely free from dead works, i.e., sins. And they

sunt opera peccati. Et etiam non debent radere caput, idest deponere sapientiam; neque deponere barbam, idest sapientiae perfectionem; neque etiam scindere vestimenta aut incidere carnes, ut scilicet vitium schismatis non incurrant.

should not shave their heads, i.e., set wisdom aside; nor should they shave their beards, i.e., set aside the perfection of wisdom; nor rend their garments or cut their flesh, i.e., they should not incur the sin of schism.

QUESTION 103

OF THE DURATION OF THE CEREMONIAL PRECEPTS

Deinde considerandum est de duratione caeremonialium praeceptorum. Et circa hoc quaeruntur quatuor.

Primo, utrum praecepta caeremonialia fuerint ante legem.

Secundo, utrum in lege aliquam virtutem habuerint iustificandi.

Tertio, utrum cessaverint Christo veniente.

Quarto, utrum sit peccatum mortale observare ea post Christum.

We must now consider the duration of the ceremonial precepts: under which head there are four points of inquiry:

(1) Whether the ceremonial precepts were in existence before the Law?

(2) Whether at the time of the Law the ceremonies of the Old Law had any power of justification?

(3) Whether they ceased at the coming of Christ?

(4) Whether it is a mortal sin to observe them after the coming of Christ?

Article 1

Whether the Ceremonies of the Law Were in Existence Before the Law?

AD PRIMUM SIC PROCEDITUR. Videtur quod caeremoniae legis fuerint ante legem. Sacrificia enim et holocausta pertinent ad caeremonias veteris legis, ut supra dictum est. Sed sacrificia et holocausta fuerunt ante legem. Dicitur enim Gen. IV, quod *Cain obtulit de fructibus terrae munera domino; Abel autem obtulit de primogenitis gregis sui, et de adipibus eorum.* Noe etiam obtulit holocausta domino, ut dicitur Gen. VIII; et Abraham similiter, ut dicitur Gen. XXII. Ergo caeremoniae veteris legis fuerunt ante legem.

PRAETEREA, ad caeremonias sacrorum pertinet constructio altaris, et eius inunctio. Sed ista fuerunt ante legem. Legitur enim Gen. XIII, quod Abraham aedificavit altare domino; et de Iacob dicitur Gen. XXVIII, quod *tulit lapidem et erexit in titulum fundens oleum desuper.* Ergo caeremoniae legales fuerunt ante legem.

PRAETEREA, inter sacramenta legalia primum videtur fuisse circumcisio. Sed circumcisio fuit ante legem, ut patet Gen. XVII. Similiter etiam sacerdotium fuit ante legem, dicitur enim Gen. XIV, quod *Melchisedech erat sacerdos Dei summi.* Ergo caeremoniae sacramentorum fuerunt ante legem.

PRAETEREA, discretio mundorum animalium ab immundis pertinet ad caeremonias observantiarum, ut supra dictum est. Sed talis discretio fuit ante legem, dicitur enim Gen. VII, *ex omnibus mundis animalibus tolle septena et septena; de animantibus vero immundis, duo et duo.* Ergo caeremoniae legales fuerunt ante legem.

SED CONTRA est quod dicitur Deut. VI, *haec sunt praecepta et caeremoniae quae mandavit dominus Deus vester ut docerem vos.* Non autem indiguissent super his

OBJECTION 1: It would seem that the ceremonies of the Law were in existence before the Law. For sacrifices and holocausts were ceremonies of the Old Law, as stated above (Q101, A4). But sacrifices and holocausts preceded the Law: for it is written (Gen 4:3,4) that *Cain offered, of the fruits of the earth, gifts to the Lord*, and that *Abel offered of the firstlings of his flock, and of their fat.* Noah also *offered holocausts* to the Lord (Gen 18:20), and Abraham did in like manner (Gen 22:13). Therefore the ceremonies of the Old Law preceded the Law.

OBJ. 2: Further, the erecting and consecrating of the altar were part of the ceremonies relating to holy things. But these preceded the Law. For we read (Gen 13:18) that *Abraham . . . built . . . an altar to the Lord*; and (Gen 28:18) that *Jacob . . . took the stone . . . and set it up for a title, pouring oil upon the top of it.* Therefore the legal ceremonies preceded the Law.

OBJ. 3: Further, the first of the legal sacraments seems to have been circumcision. But circumcision preceded the Law, as appears from Gn. 17. In like manner the priesthood preceded the Law; for it is written (Gen 14:18) that *Melchisedech . . . was the priest of the most high God.* Therefore the sacramental ceremonies preceded the Law.

OBJ. 4: Further, the distinction of clean from unclean animals belongs to the ceremonies of observances, as stated above (Q100, 2, A6, ad 1). But this distinction preceded the Law; for it is written (Gen 7:2,3): *Of all clean beasts take seven and seven . . . but of the beasts that are unclean, two and two.* Therefore the legal ceremonies preceded the Law.

ON THE CONTRARY, It is written (Deut 6:1): *These are the precepts and ceremonies . . . which the Lord your God commanded that I should teach you.* But they would not

doceri, si prius praedictae caeremoniae fuissent. Ergo caeremoniae legis non fuerunt ante legem.

RESPONDEO dicendum quod, sicut ex dictis patet, caeremoniae legis ad duo ordinabantur, scilicet ad cultum Dei, et ad figurandum Christum. Quicumque autem colit Deum, oportet quod per aliqua determinata eum colat, quae ad exteriorem cultum pertinent. Determinatio autem divini cultus ad caeremonias pertinet; sicut etiam determinatio eorum per quae ordinamur ad proximum, pertinet ad praecepta iudicialia; ut supra dictum est. Et ideo sicut inter homines communiter erant aliqua iudicialia, non tamen ex auctoritate legis divinae instituta, sed ratione hominum ordinata; ita etiam erant quaedam caeremoniae, non quidem ex auctoritate alicuius legis determinatae, sed solum secundum voluntatem et devotionem hominum Deum colentium. Sed quia etiam ante legem fuerunt quidam viri praecipui prophetico spiritu pollentes, credendum est quod ex instinctu divino, quasi ex quadam privata lege, inducerentur ad aliquem certum modum colendi Deum, qui et conveniens esset interiori cultui, et etiam congrueret ad significandum Christi mysteria, quae figurabantur etiam per alia eorum gesta, secundum illud I ad Cor. X, *omnia in figuram contingebant illis.* Fuerunt igitur ante legem quaedam caeremoniae, non tamen caeremoniae legis, quia non erant per aliquam legislationem institutae.

AD PRIMUM ergo dicendum quod huiusmodi oblationes et sacrificia et holocausta offerebant antiqui ante legem ex quadam devotione propriae voluntatis, secundum quod eis videbatur conveniens ut in rebus quas a Deo acceperant, quas in reverentiam divinam offerrent, protestarentur se colere Deum, qui est omnium principium et finis.

AD SECUNDUM dicendum quod etiam sacra quaedam instituerunt, quia videbatur eis conveniens ut in reverentiam divinam essent aliqua loca ab aliis discreta, divino cultui mancipata.

AD TERTIUM dicendum quod sacramentum circumcisionis praecepto divino fuit statutum ante legem. Unde non potest dici sacramentum legis quasi in lege institutum, sed solum quasi in lege observatum. Et hoc est quod dominus dicit, Ioan. VII, *circumcisio non ex Moyse est, sed ex patribus eius.* Sacerdotium etiam erat ante legem apud colentes Deum, secundum humanam determinationem, quia hanc dignitatem primogenitis attribuebant.

AD QUARTUM dicendum quod distinctio mundorum animalium et immundorum non fuit ante legem quantum ad esum, cum dictum sit Gen. IX, *omne quod movetur et vivit, erit vobis in cibum,* sed solum quantum ad sacrificiorum oblationem, quia de quibusdam determinatis animalibus sacrificia offerebant. Si tamen quantum ad esum erat aliqua discretio animalium, hoc

have needed to be taught about these things, if the aforesaid ceremonies had been already in existence. Therefore the legal ceremonies did not precede the Law.

I ANSWER THAT, As is clear from what has been said (Q101, A2; Q102, A2), the legal ceremonies were ordained for a double purpose; the worship of God, and the foreshadowing of Christ. Now whoever worships God must needs worship Him by means of certain fixed things pertaining to external worship. But the fixing of the divine worship belongs to the ceremonies; just as the determining of our relations with our neighbor is a matter determined by the judicial precepts, as stated above (Q99, A4). Consequently, as among men in general there were certain judicial precepts, not indeed established by Divine authority, but ordained by human reason; so also there were some ceremonies fixed, not by the authority of any law, but according to the will and devotion of those that worship God. Since, however, even before the Law some of the leading men were gifted with the spirit of prophecy, it is to be believed that a heavenly instinct, like a private law, prompted them to worship God in a certain definite way, which would be both in keeping with the interior worship, and a suitable token of Christ's mysteries, which were foreshadowed also by other things that they did, according to 1 Cor. 10:11: *All . . . things happened to them in figure.* Therefore there were some ceremonies before the Law, but they were not legal ceremonies, because they were not as yet established by legislation.

REPLY OBJ. 1: The patriarchs offered up these oblations, sacrifices and holocausts previously to the Law, out of a certain devotion of their own will, according as it seemed proper to them to offer up in honor of God those things which they had received from Him, and thus to testify that they worshipped God Who is the beginning and end of all.

REPLY OBJ. 2: They also established certain sacred things, because they thought that the honor due to God demanded that certain places should be set apart from others for the purpose of divine worship.

REPLY OBJ. 3: The sacrament of circumcision was established by command of God before the Law. Hence it cannot be called a sacrament of the Law as though it were an institution of the Law, but only as an observance included in the Law. Hence Our Lord said (John 7:20) that circumcision was *not of Moses, but of his fathers.* Again, among those who worshipped God, the priesthood was in existence before the Law by human appointment, for the Law allotted the priestly dignity to the firstborn.

REPLY OBJ. 4: The distinction of clean from unclean animals was in vogue before the Law, not with regard to eating them, since it is written (Gen 9:3): *Everything that moveth and liveth shall be meat for you*: but only as to the offering of sacrifices because they used only certain animals for that purpose. If, however, they did make any distinction in regard to eating; it was not that it was considered illegal

non erat quia esus illorum reputaretur illicitus, cum nulla lege esset prohibitus, sed propter abominationem vel consuetudinem, sicut et nunc videmus quod aliqua cibaria sunt in aliquibus terris abominabilia, quae in aliis comeduntur.

to eat such animals, since this was not forbidden by any law, but from dislike or custom: thus even now we see that certain foods are looked upon with disgust in some countries, while people partake of them in others.

Article 2

Whether, at the Time of the Law, the Ceremonies of the Old Law Had Any Power of Justification?

AD SECUNDUM SIC PROCEDITUR. Videtur quod caeremoniae veteris legis habuerint virtutem iustificandi tempore legis. Expiatio enim a peccato, et consecratio hominis, ad iustificationem pertinent, sed Exod. XXIX, dicitur quod per aspersionem sanguinis et inunctionem olei consecrabantur sacerdotes et vestes eorum; et Levit. XVI, dicitur quod sacerdos per aspersionem sanguinis vituli *expiabat sanctuarium ab immunditiis filiorum Israel, et a praevaricationibus eorum atque peccatis.* Ergo caeremoniae veteris legis habebant virtutem iustificandi.

PRAETEREA, id per quod homo placet Deo, ad iustitiam pertinet; secundum illud Psalmi X, *iustus dominus, et iustitias dilexit,* sed per caeremonias aliqui Deo placebant, secundum illud Levit. X, *quomodo potui placere domino in caeremoniis mente lugubri?* Ergo caeremoniae veteris legis habebant virtutem iustificandi.

PRAETEREA, ea quae sunt divini cultus magis pertinent ad animam quam ad corpus; secundum illud Psalmi XVIII, *lex domini immaculata, convertens animas.* Sed per caeremonias veteris legis mundabatur leprosus, ut dicitur Levit. XIV. Ergo multo magis caeremoniae veteris legis poterant mundare animam, iustificando.

SED CONTRA est quod apostolus dicit, Galat. II, *si data esset lex quae posset iustificare, Christus gratis mortuus esset,* idest sine causa. Sed hoc est inconveniens. Ergo caeremoniae veteris legis non iustificabant.

RESPONDEO dicendum quod, sicut supra dictum est, in veteri lege duplex immunditia observabatur. Una quidem spiritualis, quae est immunditia culpae. Alia vero corporalis, quae tollebat idoneitatem ad cultum divinum, sicut leprosus dicebatur immundus, vel ille qui tangebat aliquod morticinum, et sic immunditia nihil aliud erat quam irregularitas quaedam. Ab hac igitur immunditia caeremoniae veteris legis habebant virtutem emundandi, quia huiusmodi caeremoniae erant quaedam remedia adhibita ex ordinatione legis ad tollendas praedictas immunditias ex statuto legis inductas. Et ideo apostolus dicit, ad Heb. IX, quod *sanguis hircorum et taurorum, et cinis vitulae aspersus, inquinatos sanctificat ad emundationem carnis.* Et sicut ista immunditia quae per huiusmodi caeremonias emundabatur, erat magis

OBJECTION 1: It would seem that the ceremonies of the Old Law had the power of justification at the time of the Law. Because expiation from sin and consecration pertains to justification. But it is written (Exod 39:21) that the priests and their apparel were consecrated by the sprinkling of blood and the anointing of oil; and (Lev 16:16) that, by sprinkling the blood of the calf, the priest expiated *the sanctuary from the uncleanness of the children of Israel, and from their transgressions and . . . their sins.* Therefore the ceremonies of the Old Law had the power of justification.

OBJ. 2: Further, that by which man pleases God pertains to justification, according to Ps. 10:8: *The Lord is just and hath loved justice.* But some pleased God by means of ceremonies, according to Lev. 10:19: *How could I . . . please the Lord in the ceremonies, having a sorrowful heart?* Therefore the ceremonies of the Old Law had the power of justification.

OBJ. 3: Further, things relating to the divine worship regard the soul rather than the body, according to Ps. 18:8: *The Law of the Lord is unspotted, converting souls.* But the leper was cleansed by means of the ceremonies of the Old Law, as stated in Lev. 14. Much more therefore could the ceremonies of the Old Law cleanse the soul by justifying it.

ON THE CONTRARY, The Apostle says (Gal 2): *If there had been a law given which could justify, Christ died in vain,* i.e., without cause. But this is inadmissible. Therefore the ceremonies of the Old Law did not confer justice.

I ANSWER THAT, As stated above (Q102, A5, ad 4), a twofold uncleanness was distinguished in the Old Law. One was spiritual and is the uncleanness of sin. The other was corporal, which rendered a man unfit for divine worship; thus a leper, or anyone that touched carrion, was said to be unclean: and thus uncleanness was nothing but a kind of irregularity. From this uncleanness, then, the ceremonies of the Old Law had the power to cleanse: because they were ordered by the Law to be employed as remedies for the removal of the aforesaid uncleannesses which were contracted in consequence of the prescription of the Law. Hence the Apostle says (Heb 9:13) that *the blood of goats and of oxen, and the ashes of a heifer, being sprinkled, sanctify such as are defiled, to the cleansing of the flesh.* And just as this uncleanness which was washed away by such like

carnis quam mentis; ita etiam ipsae caeremoniae iustitiae carnis dicuntur ab ipso apostolo, parum supra, *iustitiis, inquit, carnis usque ad tempus correctionis impositis.*

Ab immunditia vero mentis, quae est immunditia culpae, non habebant virtutem expiandi. Et hoc ideo quia expiatio a peccatis nunquam fieri potuit nisi per Christum, *qui tollit peccata mundi*, ut dicitur Ioan. I, et quia mysterium incarnationis et passionis Christi nondum erat realiter peractum, illae veteris legis caeremoniae non poterant in se continere realiter virtutem profluentem a Christo incarnato et passo, sicut continent sacramenta novae legis. Et ideo non poterant a peccato mundare, sicut apostolus dicit, ad Heb. X, quod *impossibile est sanguine taurorum aut hircorum auferri peccata.* Et hoc est quod, Gal. IV, apostolus vocat ea egena et infirma elementa, infirma quidem, quia non possunt a peccato mundare; sed haec infirmitas provenit ex eo quod sunt egena, idest eo quod non continent in se gratiam.

Poterat autem mens fidelium, tempore legis, per fidem coniungi Christo incarnato et passo, et ita ex fide Christi iustificabantur. Cuius fidei quaedam protestatio erat huiusmodi caeremoniarum observatio, inquantum erant figura Christi. Et ideo pro peccatis offerebantur sacrificia quaedam in veteri lege, non quia ipsa sacrificia a peccato emundarent, sed quia erant quaedam protestationes fidei, quae a peccato mundabat. Et hoc etiam ipsa lex innuit ex modo loquendi, dicitur enim Levit. IV et V, quod *in oblatione hostiarum pro peccato orabit pro eo sacerdos, et dimittetur ei*; quasi peccatum dimittatur non ex vi sacrificiorum, sed ex fide et devotione offerentium. Sciendum est tamen quod hoc ipsum quod veteris legis caeremoniae a corporalibus immunditiis expiabant, erat in figura expiationis a peccatis quae fit per Christum.

Sic igitur patet quod caeremoniae in statu veteris legis non habebant virtutem iustificandi.

AD PRIMUM ergo dicendum quod illa sanctificatio sacerdotum et filiorum eius, et vestium ipsorum, vel quorumcumque aliorum, per aspersionem sanguinis, nihil aliud erat quam deputatio ad divinum cultum, et remotio impedimentorum ad emundationem carnis, ut apostolus dicit; in praefigurationem illius sanctificationis qua Iesus per suum sanguinem sanctificavit populum. Expiatio etiam ad remotionem huiusmodi corporalium immunditiarum referenda est, non ad remotionem culpae. Unde etiam sanctuarium expiari dicitur, quod culpae subiectum esse non poterat.

AD SECUNDUM dicendum quod sacerdotes placebant Deo in caeremoniis propter obedientiam et devotionem

ceremonies, affected the flesh rather than the soul, so also the ceremonies themselves are called by the Apostle shortly before (Heb 9:10) justices of the flesh: *justices of the flesh*, says he, *being laid on them until the time of correction.*

On the other hand, they had no power of cleansing from uncleanness of the soul, i.e., from the uncleanness of sin. The reason of this was that at no time could there be expiation from sin, except through Christ, *Who taketh away the sins of the world* (John 1:29). And since the mystery of Christ's Incarnation and Passion had not yet really taken place, those ceremonies of the Old Law could not really contain in themselves a power flowing from Christ already incarnate and crucified, such as the sacraments of the New Law contain. Consequently they could not cleanse from sin: thus the Apostle says (Heb 10:4) that *it is impossible that with the blood of oxen and goats sin should be taken away*; and for this reason he calls them (Gal 4:9) *weak and needy elements*: weak indeed, because they cannot take away sin; but this weakness results from their being needy, i.e., from the fact that they do not contain grace within themselves.

However, it was possible at the time of the Law, for the minds of the faithful, to be united by faith to Christ incarnate and crucified; so that they were justified by faith in Christ: of which faith the observance of these ceremonies was a sort of profession, inasmuch as they foreshadowed Christ. Hence in the Old Law certain sacrifices were offered up for sins, not as though the sacrifices themselves washed sins away, but because they were professions of faith which cleansed from sin. In fact, the Law itself implies this in the terms employed: for it is written (Lev 4:26; 5:16) that in offering the sacrifice for sin *the priest shall pray for him . . . and it shall be forgiven him*, as though the sin were forgiven, not in virtue of the sacrifices, but through the faith and devotion of those who offered them. It must be observed, however, that the very fact that the ceremonies of the Old Law washed away uncleanness of the body, was a figure of that expiation from sins which was effected by Christ.

It is therefore evident that under the state of the Old Law the ceremonies had no power of justification.

REPLY OBJ. 1: That sanctification of priests and their sons, and of their apparel or of anything else belonging to them, by sprinkling them with blood, had no other effect but to appoint them to the divine worship, and to remove impediments from them, *to the cleansing of the flesh*, as the Apostle states (Heb 9:13) in token of that sanctification whereby *Jesus* sanctified *the people by His own blood* (Heb 13:12). Moreover, the expiation must be understood as referring to the removal of these bodily uncleannesses, not to the forgiveness of sin. Hence even the sanctuary which could not be the subject of sin is stated to be expiated.

REPLY OBJ. 2: The priests pleased God in the ceremonies by their obedience and devotion, and by their faith in

et fidem rei praefiguratae, non autem propter ipsas res secundum se consideratas.

AD TERTIUM dicendum quod caeremoniae illae quae erant institutae in emundatione leprosi, non ordinabantur ad tollendam immunditiam infirmitatis leprae. Quod patet ex hoc quod non adhibebantur huiusmodi caeremoniae nisi iam emundato, unde dicitur Levit. XIV, quod *sacerdos, egressus de castris, cum invenerit lepram esse mundatam, praecipiet ei qui purificatur ut offerat,* etc.; ex quo patet quod sacerdos constituebatur iudex leprae emundatae, non autem emundandae. Adhibebantur autem huiusmodi caeremoniae ad tollendam immunditiam irregularitatis. Dicunt tamen quod quandoque, si contingeret sacerdotem errare in iudicando, miraculose leprosus mundabatur a Deo virtute divina, non autem virtute sacrificiorum. Sicut etiam miraculose mulieris adulterae computrescebat femur, bibitis aquis in quibus sacerdos maledicta congesserat, ut habetur Num. V.

REPLY OBJ. 3: Those ceremonies which were prescribed in the cleansing of a leper, were not ordained for the purpose of taking away the defilement of leprosy. This is clear from the fact that these ceremonies were not applied to a man until he was already healed: hence it is written (Lev 14:3,4) that the priest, *going out of the camp, when he shall find that the leprosy is cleansed, shall command him that is to be purified to offer,* etc.; whence it is evident that the priest was appointed the judge of leprosy, not before, but after cleansing. But these ceremonies were employed for the purpose of taking away the uncleanness of irregularity. They do say, however, that if a priest were to err in his judgment, the leper would be cleansed miraculously by the power of God, but not in virtue of the sacrifice. Thus also it was by miracle that the thigh of the adulterous woman rotted, when she had drunk the water *on which* the priest had *heaped curses,* as stated in Num. 5:19–27.

Article 3

Whether the Ceremonies of the Old Law Ceased at the Coming of Christ?

AD TERTIUM SIC PROCEDITUR. Videtur quod caeremoniae veteris legis non cessaverint in Christi adventu. Dicitur enim Baruch IV, *hic est liber mandatorum Dei, et lex quae est in aeternum.* Sed ad legem pertinebant legis caeremoniae. Ergo legis caeremoniae in aeternum duraturae erant.

PRAETEREA, oblatio leprosi mundati ad legis caeremonias pertinebat. Sed etiam in Evangelio praecipitur leproso emundato ut huiusmodi oblationes offerat. Ergo caeremoniae veteris legis non cessaverunt Christo veniente.

PRAETEREA, manente causa, manet effectus. Sed caeremoniae veteris legis habebant quasdam rationabiles causas, inquantum ordinabantur ad divinum cultum; etiam praeter hoc quod ordinabantur in figuram Christi. Ergo caeremoniae veteris legis cessare non debuerunt.

PRAETEREA, circumcisio erat instituta in signum fidei Abrahae; observatio autem sabbati ad recolendum beneficium creationis; et aliae solemnitates legis ad recolendum alia beneficia Dei; ut supra dictum est. Sed fides Abrahae est semper imitanda etiam a nobis; et beneficium creationis, et alia Dei beneficia, semper sunt recolenda. Ergo ad minus circumcisio et solemnitates legis cessare non debuerunt.

SED CONTRA est quod apostolus dicit, ad Coloss. II, *nemo vos iudicet in cibo aut in potu, aut in parte diei festi aut Neomeniae aut sabbatorum, quae sunt umbra*

OBJECTION 1: It would seem that the ceremonies of the Old Law did not cease at the coming of Christ. For it is written (Bar 4:1): *This is the book of the commandments of God, and the law that is for ever.* But the legal ceremonies were part of the Law. Therefore the legal ceremonies were to last for ever.

OBJ. 2: Further, the offering made by a leper after being cleansed was a ceremony of the Law. But the Gospel commands the leper, who has been cleansed, to make this offering (Matt 8:4). Therefore the ceremonies of the Old Law did not cease at Christ's coming.

OBJ. 3: Further, as long as the cause remains, the effect remains. But the ceremonies of the Old Law had certain reasonable causes, inasmuch as they were ordained to the worship of God, besides the fact that they were intended to be figures of Christ. Therefore the ceremonies of the Old Law should not have ceased.

OBJ. 4: Further, circumcision was instituted as a sign of Abraham's faith: the observance of the sabbath, to recall the blessing of creation: and other solemnities, in memory of other Divine favors, as state above (Q102, A4, ad 10; A5, ad 1). But Abraham's faith is ever to be imitated even by us: and the blessing of creation and other Divine favors should never be forgotten. Therefore at least circumcision and the other legal solemnities should not have ceased.

ON THE CONTRARY, The Apostle says (Col 2:16,17): *Let no man . . . judge you in meat or in drink, or in respect of a festival day, or of the new moon, or of the sabbaths, which are*

futurorum. Et ad Heb. VIII dicitur quod, *dicendo novum testamentum, veteravit prius, quod autem antiquatur et senescit, prope interitum est.*

RESPONDEO dicendum quod omnia praecepta caeremonialia veteris legis ad cultum Dei sunt ordinata, ut supra dictum est. Exterior autem cultus proportionari debet interiori cultui, qui consistit in fide, spe et caritate. Unde secundum diversitatem interioris cultus, debuit diversificari cultus exterior. Potest autem triplex status distingui interioris cultus. Unus quidem secundum quem habetur fides et spes et de bonis caelestibus, et de his per quae in caelestia introducimur, de utrisque quidem sicut de quibusdam futuris. Et talis fuit status fidei et spei in veteri lege. Alius autem est status interioris cultus in quo habetur fides et spes de caelestibus bonis sicut de quibusdam futuris, sed de his per quae introducimur in caelestia, sicut de praesentibus vel praeteritis. Et iste est status novae legis. Tertius autem status est in quo utraque habentur ut praesentia, et nihil creditur ut absens, neque speratur ut futurum. Et iste est status beatorum.

In illo ergo statu beatorum nihil erit figurale ad divinum cultum pertinens, sed solum gratiarum actio et vox laudis. Et ideo dicitur Apoc. XXI, de civitate beatorum, *templum non vidi in ea, dominus enim Deus omnipotens templum illius est, et agnus.* Pari igitur ratione, caeremoniae primi status, per quas figurabatur et secundus et tertius, veniente secundo statu, cessare debuerunt; et aliae caeremoniae induci, quae convenirent statui cultus divini pro tempore illo, in quo bona caelestia sunt futura, beneficia autem Dei per quae ad caelestia introducimur, sunt praesentia.

AD PRIMUM ergo dicendum quod lex vetus dicitur esse in aeternum, secundum moralia quidem, simpliciter et absolute, secundum caeremonialia vero, quantum ad veritatem per ea figuratam.

AD SECUNDUM dicendum quod mysterium redemptionis humani generis completum fuit in passione Christi, unde tunc dominus *dixit, consummatum est,* ut habetur Ioan. XIX. Et ideo tunc totaliter debuerunt cessare legalia, quasi iam veritate eorum consummata. In cuius signum, in passione Christi *velum templi legitur esse scissum,* Matth. XXVII. Et ideo ante passionem Christi, Christo praedicante et miracula faciente, currebant simul lex et Evangelium, quia iam mysterium Christi erat inchoatum, sed nondum consummatum. Et propter hoc mandavit dominus, ante passionem suam, leproso, ut legales caeremonias observaret.

AD TERTIUM dicendum quod rationes litterales caeremoniarum supra assignatae referuntur ad divinum cultum, qui quidem cultus erat in fide venturi. Et ideo,

a shadow of things to come: and (Heb 8:13): *In saying a new (testament), he hath made the former old: and that which decayeth and groweth old, is near its end.*

I ANSWER THAT, All the ceremonial precepts of the Old Law were ordained to the worship of God as stated above (Q101, AA1,2). Now external worship should be in proportion to the internal worship, which consists in faith, hope and charity. Consequently exterior worship had to be subject to variations according to the variations in the internal worship, in which a threefold state may be distinguished. One state was in respect of faith and hope, both in heavenly goods, and in the means of obtaining them—in both of these considered as things to come. Such was the state of faith and hope in the Old Law. Another state of interior worship is that in which we have faith and hope in heavenly goods as things to come; but in the means of obtaining heavenly goods, as in things present or past. Such is the state of the New Law. The third state is that in which both are possessed as present; wherein nothing is believed in as lacking, nothing hoped for as being yet to come. Such is the state of the Blessed.

In this state of the Blessed, then, nothing in regard to worship of God will be figurative; there will be naught but *thanksgiving and voice of praise* (Isa 51:3). Hence it is written concerning the city of the Blessed (Rev 21:22): *I saw no temple therein: for the Lord God Almighty is the temple thereof, and the Lamb.* Proportionately, therefore, the ceremonies of the first-mentioned state which foreshadowed the second and third states, had need to cease at the advent of the second state; and other ceremonies had to be introduced which would be in keeping with the state of divine worship for that particular time, wherein heavenly goods are a thing of the future, but the Divine favors whereby we obtain the heavenly boons are a thing of the present.

REPLY OBJ. 1: The Old Law is said to be *for ever* simply and absolutely, as regards its moral precepts; but as regards the ceremonial precepts it lasts for even in respect of the reality which those ceremonies foreshadowed.

REPLY OBJ. 2: The mystery of the redemption of the human race was fulfilled in Christ's Passion: hence Our Lord said then: *It is consummated* (John 19:30). Consequently the prescriptions of the Law must have ceased then altogether through their reality being fulfilled. As a sign of this, we read that at the Passion of Christ *the veil of the temple was rent* (Matt 27:51). Hence, before Christ's Passion, while Christ was preaching and working miracles, the Law and the Gospel were concurrent, since the mystery of Christ had already begun, but was not as yet consummated. And for this reason Our Lord, before His Passion, commanded the leper to observe the legal ceremonies.

REPLY OBJ. 3: The literal reasons already given (Q102) for the ceremonies refer to the divine worship, which was founded on faith in that which was to come. Hence, at the

iam veniente eo qui venturus erat, et cultus ille cessat, et omnes rationes ad hunc cultum ordinatae.

Ad quartum dicendum quod fides Abrahae fuit commendata in hoc quod credidit divinae promissioni de futuro semine, in quo benedicerentur omnes gentes. Et ideo quandiu hoc erat futurum, oportebat protestari fidem Abrahae in circumcisione. Sed postquam iam hoc est perfectum, oportet idem alio signo declarari, scilicet Baptismo, qui in hoc circumcisioni succedit; secundum illud apostoli, ad Coloss. II, *circumcisi estis circumcisione non manu facta in expoliatione corporis carnis, sed in circumcisione domini nostri Iesu Christi, consepulti ei in Baptismo.*

Sabbatum autem, quod significabat primam creationem, mutatur in diem dominicum, in quo commemoratur nova creatura inchoata in resurrectione Christi. Et similiter aliis solemnitatibus veteris legis novae solemnitates succedunt, quia beneficia illi populo exhibita, significant beneficia nobis concessa per Christum. Unde festo phase succedit festum passionis Christi et resurrectionis. Festo Pentecostes, in quo fuit data lex vetus, succedit festum Pentecostes in quo fuit data lex spiritus vitae. Festo Neomeniae succedit festum beatae virginis, in qua primo apparuit illuminatio solis, idest Christi, per copiam gratiae. Festo tubarum succedunt festa apostolorum. Festo expiationis succedunt festa martyrum et confessorum. Festo tabernaculorum succedit festum consecrationis Ecclesiae. Festo coetus atque collectae succedit festum Angelorum; vel etiam festum omnium sanctorum.

advent of Him Who was to come, both that worship ceased, and all the reasons referring thereto.

Reply Obj. 4: The faith of Abraham was commended in that he believed in God's promise concerning his seed to come, in which all nations were to blessed. Wherefore, as long as this seed was yet to come, it was necessary to make profession of Abraham's faith by means of circumcision. But now that it is consummated, the same thing needs to be declared by means of another sign, viz., Baptism, which, in this respect, took the place of circumcision, according to the saying of the Apostle (Col 2:11, 12): *You are circumcised with circumcision not made by hand, in despoiling of the body of the flesh, but in the circumcision of Christ, buried with Him in Baptism.*

As to the sabbath, which was a sign recalling the first creation, its place is taken by the *Lord's Day*, which recalls the beginning of the new creature in the Resurrection of Christ. In like manner other solemnities of the Old Law are supplanted by new solemnities: because the blessings vouchsafed to that people, foreshadowed the favors granted us by Christ. Hence the feast of the Passover gave place to the feast of Christ's Passion and Resurrection: the feast of Pentecost when the Old Law was given, to the feast of Pentecost on which was given the Law of the living spirit: the feast of the New Moon, to Lady Day, when appeared the first rays of the sun, i.e., Christ, by the fullness of grace: the feast of Trumpets, to the feasts of the Apostles: the feast of Expiation, to the feasts of Martyrs and Confessors: the feast of Tabernacles, to the feast of the Church Dedication: the feast of the Assembly and Collection, to feast of the Angels, or else to the feast of All Hallows.

Article 4

Whether Since Christ's Passion the Legal Ceremonies Can Be Observed Without Committing Mortal Sin?

Ad quartum sic proceditur. Videtur quod post passionem Christi legalia possint sine peccato mortali observari. Non est enim credendum quod apostoli, post acceptum spiritum sanctum, mortaliter peccaverint, eius enim plenitudine sunt induti virtute ex alto, ut dicitur Lucae ult. Sed apostoli post adventum spiritus sancti legalia observaverunt, dicitur enim Act. XVI, quod Paulus circumcidit Timotheum; et Act. XXI, dicitur quod Paulus, secundum consilium Iacobi, *assumptis viris, purificatus cum eis intravit in templum, annuntians expletionem dierum purificationis, donec offerretur pro unoquoque eorum oblatio.* Ergo sine peccato mortali possunt post Christi passionem legalia observari.

Praeterea, vitare consortia gentilium ad caeremonias legis pertinebat. Sed hoc observavit primus pastor

Objection 1: It would seem that since Christ's Passion the legal ceremonies can be observed without committing mortal sin. For we must not believe that the apostles committed mortal sin after receiving the Holy Spirit: since by His fullness they were *endued with power from on high* (Luke 24:49). But the apostles observed the legal ceremonies after the coming of the Holy Spirit: for it is stated (Acts 16:3) that Paul circumcised Timothy: and (Acts 21:26) that Paul, at the advice of James, *took the men, and . . . being purified with them, entered into the temple, giving notice of the accomplishment of the days of purification, until an oblation should be offered for every one of them.* Therefore the legal ceremonies can be observed since the Passion of Christ without mortal sin.

Obj. 2: Further, one of the legal ceremonies consisted in shunning the fellowship of Gentiles. But the first Pastor of

Ecclesiae, dicitur enim ad Gal. II, quod, cum venissent quidam Antiochiam, *subtrahebat et segregabat se Petrus a gentilibus.* Ergo absque peccato post passionem Christi legis caeremoniae observari possunt.

PRAETEREA, praecepta apostolorum non induxerunt homines ad peccatum. Sed ex decreto apostolorum statutum fuit quod gentiles quaedam de caeremoniis legis observarent, dicitur enim Act. XV, *visum est spiritui sancto et nobis nihil ultra imponere oneris vobis quam haec necessaria, ut abstineatis vos ab immolatis simulacrorum, et sanguine, et suffocato, et fornicatione.* Ergo absque peccato caeremoniae legales possunt post Christi passionem observari.

SED CONTRA est quod apostolus dicit, ad Gal. V, *si circumcidimini, Christus nihil vobis proderit.* Sed nihil excludit fructum Christi nisi peccatum mortale. Ergo circumcidi, et alias caeremonias observare, post passionem Christi est peccatum mortale.

RESPONDEO dicendum quod omnes caeremoniae sunt quaedam protestationes fidei, in qua consistit interior Dei cultus. Sic autem fidem interiorem potest homo protestari factis, sicut et verbis, et in utraque protestatione, si aliquid homo falsum protestatur, peccat mortaliter. Quamvis autem sit eadem fides quam habemus de Christo, et quam antiqui patres habuerunt; tamen quia ipsi praecesserunt Christum, nos autem sequimur, eadem fides diversis verbis significatur a nobis et ab eis. Nam ab eis dicebatur, ecce virgo concipiet et pariet filium, quae sunt verba futuri temporis, nos autem idem repraesentamus per verba praeteriti temporis, dicentes quod concepit et peperit. Et similiter caeremoniae veteris legis significabant Christum ut nasciturum et passurum, nostra autem sacramenta significant ipsum ut natum et passum. Sicut igitur peccaret mortaliter qui nunc, suam fidem protestando, diceret Christum nasciturum, quod antiqui pie et veraciter dicebant; ita etiam peccaret mortaliter, si quis nunc caeremonias observaret, quas antiqui pie et fideliter observabant. Et hoc est quod Augustinus dicit, contra Faustum, *iam non promittitur nasciturus, passurus, resurrecturus, quod illa sacramenta quodammodo personabant, sed annuntiatur quod natus sit, passus sit, resurrexerit; quod haec sacramenta quae a Christianis aguntur, iam personant.*

AD PRIMUM ergo dicendum quod circa hoc diversimode sensisse videntur Hieronymus et Augustinus. Hieronymus enim distinxit duo tempora. Unum tempus ante passionem Christi, in quo legalia nec erant mortua, quasi non habentia vim obligatoriam, aut expiativam pro suo modo; nec etiam mortifera, quia non peccabant ea observantes. Statim autem post passionem Christi incoeperunt esse non solum mortua, idest non habentia

the Church complied with this observance; for it is stated (Gal 2:12) that, *when* certain men *had come* to Antioch, Peter *withdrew and separated himself* from the Gentiles. Therefore the legal ceremonies can be observed since Christ's Passion without committing mortal sin.

OBJ. 3: Further, the commands of the apostles did not lead men into sin. But it was commanded by apostolic decree that the Gentiles should observe certain ceremonies of the Law: for it is written (Acts 15:28,29): *It hath seemed good to the Holy Spirit and to us, to lay no further burden upon you than these necessary things: that you abstain from things sacrificed to idols, and from blood, and from things strangled, and from fornication.* Therefore the legal ceremonies can be observed since Christ's Passion without committing mortal sin.

ON THE CONTRARY, The Apostle says (Gal 5:2): *If you be circumcised, Christ shall profit you nothing.* But nothing save mortal sin hinders us from receiving Christ's fruit. Therefore since Christ's Passion it is a mortal sin to be circumcised, or to observe the other legal ceremonies.

I ANSWER THAT, All ceremonies are professions of faith, in which the interior worship of God consists. Now man can make profession of his inward faith, by deeds as well as by words: and in either profession, if he make a false declaration, he sins mortally. Now, though our faith in Christ is the same as that of the fathers of old; yet, since they came before Christ, whereas we come after Him, the same faith is expressed in different words, by us and by them. For by them was it said: *Behold a virgin shall conceive and bear a son*, where the verbs are in the future tense: whereas we express the same by means of verbs in the past tense, and say that she *conceived and bore*. In like manner the ceremonies of the Old Law betokened Christ as having yet to be born and to suffer: whereas our sacraments signify Him as already born and having suffered. Consequently, just as it would be a mortal sin now for anyone, in making a profession of faith, to say that Christ is yet to be born, which the fathers of old said devoutly and truthfully; so too it would be a mortal sin now to observe those ceremonies which the fathers of old fulfilled with devotion and fidelity. Such is the teaching Augustine (*Contra Faust.* xix, 16), who says: *It is no longer promised that He shall be born, shall suffer and rise again, truths of which their sacraments were a kind of image: but it is declared that He is already born, has suffered and risen again; of which our sacraments, in which Christians share, are the actual representation.*

REPLY OBJ. 1: On this point there seems to have been a difference of opinion between Jerome and Augustine. For Jerome (*Super Galat.* ii, 11, seqq.) distinguished two periods of time. One was the time previous to Christ's Passion, during which the legal ceremonies were neither dead, since they were obligatory, and did expiate in their own fashion; nor deadly, because it was not sinful to observe them. But immediately after Christ's Passion they began to be not

virtutem et obligationem; sed etiam mortifera, ita scilicet quod peccabant mortaliter quicumque ea observabant. Unde dicebat quod apostoli nunquam legalia observaverunt post passionem secundum veritatem; sed solum quadam pia simulatione, ne scilicet scandalizarent Iudaeos et eorum conversionem impedirent. Quae quidem simulatio sic intelligenda est, non quidem ita quod illos actus secundum rei veritatem non facerent, sed quia non faciebant tanquam legis caeremonias observantes; sicut si quis pelliculam virilis membri abscinderet propter sanitatem, non causa legalis circumcisionis observandae.

Sed quia indecens videtur quod apostoli ea occultarent propter scandalum quae pertinent ad veritatem vitae et doctrinae, et quod simulatione uterentur in his quae pertinent ad salutem fidelium; ideo convenientius Augustinus distinxit tria tempora. Unum quidem ante Christi passionem, in quo legalia non erant neque mortifera neque mortua. Aliud autem post tempus Evangelii divulgati, in quo legalia sunt et mortua et mortifera. Tertium autem est tempus medium, scilicet a passione Christi usque ad divulgationem Evangelii, in quo legalia fuerunt quidem mortua, quia neque vim aliquam habebant, neque aliquis ea observare tenebatur; non tamen fuerunt mortifera, quia illi qui conversi erant ad Christum ex Iudaeis, poterant illa legalia licite observare, dummodo non sic ponerent spem in eis quod ea reputarent sibi necessaria ad salutem, quasi sine legalibus fides Christi iustificare non posset. His autem qui convertebantur ex gentilitate ad Christum, non inerat causa ut ea observarent. Et ideo Paulus circumcidit Timotheum, qui ex matre Iudaea genitus erat; Titum autem, qui ex gentilibus natus erat, circumcidere noluit.

Ideo autem noluit Spiritus Sanctus ut statim inhiberetur his qui ex Iudaeis convertebantur observatio legalium, sicut inhibebatur his qui ex gentilibus convertebantur gentilitatis ritus, ut quaedam differentia inter hos ritus ostenderetur. Nam gentilitatis ritus repudiabatur tanquam omnino illicitus, et a Deo semper prohibitus, ritus autem legis cessabat tanquam impletus per Christi passionem, utpote a Deo in figuram Christi institutus.

AD SECUNDUM dicendum quod, secundum Hieronymum, Petrus simulatorie se a gentilibus subtrahebat, ut vitaret Iudaeorum scandalum, quorum erat apostolus. Unde in hoc nullo modo peccavit, sed Paulus eum similiter simulatorie reprehendit, ut vitaret scandalum gentilium, quorum erat apostolus. Sed Augustinus hoc improbat, quia Paulus in canonica Scriptura, scilicet Gal. II, in qua nefas est credere aliquid esse falsum, dicit quod Petrus reprehensibilis erat. Unde verum est quod Petrus peccavit, et Paulus vere eum, non simulatorie,

only dead, so as no longer to be either effectual or binding; but also deadly, so that whoever observed them was guilty of mortal sin. Hence he maintained that after the Passion the apostles never observed the legal ceremonies in real earnest; but only by a kind of pious pretense, lest, to wit, they should scandalize the Jews and hinder their conversion. This pretense, however, is to be understood, not as though they did not in reality perform those actions, but in the sense that they performed them without the mind to observe the ceremonies of the Law: thus a man might cut away his foreskin for health's sake, not with the intention of observing legal circumcision.

But since it seems unbecoming that the apostles, in order to avoid scandal, should have hidden things pertaining to the truth of life and doctrine, and that they should have made use of pretense, in things pertaining to the salvation of the faithful; therefore Augustine (*Epist. lxxxii*) more fittingly distinguished three periods of time. One was the time that preceded the Passion of Christ, during which the legal ceremonies were neither deadly nor dead: another period was after the publication of the Gospel, during which the legal ceremonies are both dead and deadly. The third is a middle period, viz., from the Passion of Christ until the publication of the Gospel, during which the legal ceremonies were dead indeed, because they had neither effect nor binding force; but were not deadly, because it was lawful for the Jewish converts to Christianity to observe them, provided they did not put their trust in them so as to hold them to be necessary unto salvation, as though faith in Christ could not justify without the legal observances. On the other hand, there was no reason why those who were converted from heathendom to Christianity should observe them. Hence Paul circumcised Timothy, who was born of a Jewish mother; but was unwilling to circumcise Titus, who was of heathen nationality.

The reason why the Holy Spirit did not wish the converted Jews to be debarred at once from observing the legal ceremonies, while converted heathens were forbidden to observe the rites of heathendom, was in order to show that there is a difference between these rites. For heathenish ceremonial was rejected as absolutely unlawful, and as prohibited by God for all time; whereas the legal ceremonial ceased as being fulfilled through Christ's Passion, being instituted by God as a figure of Christ.

REPLY OBJ. 2: According to Jerome, Peter withdrew himself from the Gentiles by pretense, in order to avoid giving scandal to the Jews, of whom he was the Apostle. Hence he did not sin at all in acting thus. On the other hand, Paul in like manner made a pretense of blaming him, in order to avoid scandalizing the Gentiles, whose Apostle he was. But Augustine disapproves of this solution: because in the canonical Scripture (viz., Gal. 2:11), wherein we must not hold anything to be false, Paul says that Peter *was to be blamed.* Consequently it is true that Peter was at fault: and

reprehendit. Non autem peccavit Petrus in hoc quod ad tempus legalia observabat, quia hoc sibi licebat, tanquam ex Iudaeis converso. Sed peccabat in hoc quod circa legalium observantiam nimiam diligentiam adhibebat ne scandalizaret Iudaeos, ita quod ex hoc sequebatur gentilium scandalum.

AD TERTIUM dicendum quod quidam dixerunt quod illa prohibitio apostolorum non est intelligenda ad litteram, sed secundum spiritualem intellectum, ut scilicet in prohibitione sanguinis, intelligatur prohibitio homicidii; in prohibitione suffocati, intelligatur prohibitio violentiae et rapinae; in prohibitione immolatorum, intelligatur prohibitio idololatriae; fornicatio autem prohibetur tanquam per se malum. Et hanc opinionem accipiunt ex quibusdam Glossis, quae huiusmodi praecepta mystice exponunt. Sed quia homicidium et rapina etiam apud gentiles reputabantur illicita, non oportuisset super hoc speciale mandatum dari his qui erant ex gentilitate conversi ad Christum. Unde alii dicunt quod ad litteram illa comestibilia fuerunt prohibita, non propter observantiam legalium, sed propter gulam comprimendam. Unde dicit Hieronymus, super illud Ezech. XLIV, *omne morticinum etc., condemnat sacerdotes qui in turdis et ceteris huiusmodi, haec, cupiditate gulae, non custodiunt.*

Sed quia sunt quaedam cibaria magis delicata et gulam provocantia, non videtur ratio quare fuerunt haec magis quam alia prohibita.

Et ideo dicendum, secundum tertiam opinionem, quod ad litteram ista sunt prohibita, non ad observandum caeremonias legis, sed ad hoc quod posset coalescere unio gentilium et Iudaeorum insimul habitantium. Iudaeis enim, propter antiquam consuetudinem, sanguis et suffocatum erant abominabilia, comestio autem immolatorum simulacris, poterat in Iudaeis aggenerare circa gentiles suspicionem reditus ad idolatriam. Et ideo ista fuerunt prohibita pro tempore illo, in quo de novo oportebat convenire in unum gentiles et Iudaeos. Procedente autem tempore, cessante causa, cessat effectus; manifestata evangelicae doctrinae veritate, in qua dominus docet quod nihil quod per os intrat, coinquinat hominem, ut dicitur Matth. XV; *et quod nihil est reiiciendum quod cum gratiarum actione percipitur,* ut I ad Tim. IV dicitur. Fornicatio autem prohibetur specialiter, quia gentiles eam non reputabant esse peccatum.

Paul blamed him in very truth and not with pretense. Peter, however, did not sin, by observing the legal ceremonial for the time being; because this was lawful for him who was a converted Jew. But he did sin by excessive minuteness in the observance of the legal rites lest he should scandalize the Jews, the result being that he gave scandal to the Gentiles.

REPLY OBJ. 3: Some have held that this prohibition of the apostles is not to be taken literally, but spiritually: namely, that the prohibition of blood signifies the prohibition of murder; the prohibition of things strangled, that of violence and rapine; the prohibition of things offered to idols, that of idolatry; while fornication is forbidden as being evil in itself: which opinion they gathered from certain glosses, which expound these prohibitions in a mystical sense. Since, however, murder and rapine were held to be unlawful even by the Gentiles, there would have been no need to give this special commandment to those who were converted to Christ from heathendom. Hence others maintain that those foods were forbidden literally, not to prevent the observance of legal ceremonies, but in order to prevent gluttony. Thus Jerome says on Ezech. 44:31 (*The priest shall not eat of anything that is dead*): *He condemns those priests who from gluttony did not keep these precepts.*

But since certain foods are more delicate than these and more conducive to gluttony, there seems no reason why these should have been forbidden more than the others.

We must therefore follow the third opinion, and hold that these foods were forbidden literally, not with the purpose of enforcing compliance with the legal ceremonies, but in order to further the union of Gentiles and Jews living side by side. Because blood and things strangled were loathsome to the Jews by ancient custom; while the Jews might have suspected the Gentiles of relapse into idolatry if the latter had partaken of things offered to idols. Hence these things were prohibited for the time being, during which the Gentiles and Jews were to become united together. But as time went on, with the lapse of the cause, the effect lapsed also, when the truth of the Gospel teaching was divulged, wherein Our Lord taught that *not that which entereth into the mouth defileth a man* (Matt 15:11); and that *nothing is to be rejected that is received with thanksgiving* (1 Tim 4:4). With regard to fornication a special prohibition was made, because the Gentiles did not hold it to be sinful.

QUESTION 104

OF THE JUDICIAL PRECEPTS

Consequenter considerandum est de praeceptis iudicialibus. Et primo, considerandum est de ipsis in communi; secundo, de rationibus eorum. Circa primum quaeruntur quatuor.

Primo, quae sint iudicialia praecepta.

Secundo, utrum sint figuralia.

Tertio, de duratione eorum.

Quarto, de distinctione eorum.

We must now consider the judicial precepts: and first of all we shall consider them in general; in the second place we shall consider their reasons. Under the first head there are four points of inquiry:

(1) What is meant by the judicial precepts?

(2) Whether they are figurative?

(3) Their duration;

(4) Their division.

Article 1

Whether the Judicial Precepts Were Those Which Directed Man in Relation to His Neighbor?

AD PRIMUM SIC PROCEDITUR. Videtur quod ratio praeceptorum iudicialium non consistat in hoc quod sunt ordinantia ad proximum. Iudicialia enim praecepta a iudicio dicuntur. Sed multa sunt alia quibus homo ad proximum ordinatur, quae non pertinent ad ordinem iudiciorum. Non ergo praecepta iudicialia dicuntur quibus homo ordinatur ad proximum.

PRAETEREA, praecepta iudicialia a moralibus distinguuntur, ut supra dictum est. Sed multa praecepta moralia sunt quibus homo ordinatur ad proximum, sicut patet in septem praeceptis secundae tabulae. Non ergo praecepta iudicialia dicuntur ex hoc quod ad proximum ordinant.

PRAETEREA, sicut se habent praecepta caeremonialia ad Deum, ita se habent iudicialia praecepta ad proximum, ut supra dictum est. Sed inter praecepta caeremonialia sunt quaedam quae pertinent ad seipsum, sicut observantiae ciborum et vestimentorum, de quibus supra dictum est. Ergo praecepta iudicialia non ex hoc dicuntur quod ordinent hominem ad proximum.

SED CONTRA est quod dicitur Ezech. XVIII, inter cetera bona opera viri iusti, *si iudicium verum fecerit inter virum et virum*. Sed iudicialia praecepta a iudicio dicuntur. Ergo praecepta iudicialia videntur dici illa quae pertinent ad ordinationem hominum ad invicem.

RESPONDEO dicendum quod, sicut ex supradictis patet, praeceptorum cuiuscumque legis quaedam habent vim obligandi ex ipso dictamine rationis, quia naturalis ratio dictat hoc esse debitum fieri vel vitari. Et huiusmodi praecepta dicuntur moralia, eo quod a ratione dicuntur mores humani. Alia vero praecepta sunt quae non

OBJECTION 1: It would seem that the judicial precepts were not those which directed man in his relations to his neighbor. For judicial precepts take their name from *judgment*. But there are many things that direct man as to his neighbor, which are not subordinate to judgment. Therefore the judicial precepts were not those which directed man in his relations to his neighbor.

OBJ. 2: Further, the judicial precepts are distinct from the moral precepts, as stated above (Q99, A4). But there are many moral precepts which direct man as to his neighbor: as is evidently the case with the seven precepts of the second table. Therefore the judicial precepts are not so called from directing man as to his neighbor.

OBJ. 3: Further, as the ceremonial precepts relate to God, so do the judicial precepts relate to one's neighbor, as stated above (Q99, A4; Q101, A1). But among the ceremonial precepts there are some which concern man himself, such as observances in matter of food and apparel, of which we have already spoken (Q102, A6, ad 1,6). Therefore the judicial precepts are not so called from directing man as to his neighbor.

ON THE CONTRARY, It is reckoned (Ezek 18:8) among other works of a good and just man, that *he hath executed true judgment between man and man*. But judicial precepts are so called from *judgment*. Therefore it seems that the judicial precepts were those which directed the relations between man and man.

I ANSWER THAT, As is evident from what we have stated above (Q95, A2; Q99, A4), in every law, some precepts derive their binding force from the dictate of reason itself, because natural reason dictates that something ought to be done or to be avoided. These are called *moral* precepts: since human morals are based on reason. At the same time

habent vim obligandi ex ipso dictamine rationis, quia scilicet in se considerata non habent absolute rationem debiti vel indebiti; sed habent vim obligandi ex aliqua institutione divina vel humana. Et huiusmodi sunt determinationes quaedam moralium praeceptorum. Si igitur determinentur moralia praecepta per institutionem divinam in his per quae ordinatur homo ad Deum, talia dicentur praecepta caeremonialia. Si autem in his quae pertinent ad ordinationem hominum ad invicem, talia dicentur praecepta iudicialia. In duobus ergo consistit ratio iudicialium praeceptorum, scilicet ut pertineant ad ordinationem hominum ad invicem; et ut non habeant vim obligandi ex sola ratione, sed ex institutione.

AD PRIMUM ergo dicendum quod iudicia exercentur officio aliquorum principum, qui habent potestatem iudicandi. Ad principem autem pertinet non solum ordinare de his quae veniunt in litigium, sed etiam de voluntariis contractibus qui inter homines fiunt, et de omnibus pertinentibus ad populi communitatem et regimen. Unde praecepta iudicialia non solum sunt illa quae pertinent ad lites iudiciorum; sed etiam quaecumque pertinent ad ordinationem hominum ad invicem, quae subest ordinationi principis tanquam supremi iudicis.

AD SECUNDUM dicendum quod ratio illa procedit de illis praeceptis ordinantibus ad proximum, quae habent vim obligandi ex solo dictamine rationis.

AD TERTIUM dicendum quod etiam in his quae ordinant ad Deum, quaedam sunt moralia, quae ipsa ratio fide informata dictat, sicut Deum esse amandum et colendum. Quaedam vero sunt caeremonialia, quae non habent vim obligationis nisi ex institutione divina. Ad Deum autem pertinet non solum sacrificia oblata Deo, sed etiam quaecumque pertinent ad idoneitatem offerentium et Deum colentium. Homines enim ordinantur in Deum sicut in finem, et ideo ad cultum Dei pertinet, et per consequens ad caeremonialia praecepta, quod homo habeat quandam idoneitatem respectu cultus divini. Sed homo non ordinatur ad proximum sicut in finem, ut oporteat eum disponi in seipso in ordine ad proximum, haec enim est comparatio servorum ad dominos, *qui id quod sunt, dominorum sunt*, secundum philosophum, in I Polit. Et ideo non sunt aliqua praecepta iudicialia ordinantia hominem in seipso, sed omnia talia sunt moralia, quia ratio, quae est principium moralium, se habet in homine respectu eorum quae ad ipsum pertinent, sicut princeps vel iudex in civitate. Sciendum tamen quod, quia ordo hominis ad proximum magis subiacet rationi quam ordo hominis ad Deum, plura praecepta moralia inveniuntur per quae ordinatur homo ad proximum, quam per quae ordinatur ad Deum. Et

there are other precepts which derive their binding force, not from the very dictate of reason (because, considered in themselves, they do not imply an obligation of something due or undue); but from some institution, Divine or human: and such are certain determinations of the moral precepts. When therefore the moral precepts are fixed by Divine institution in matters relating to man's subordination to God, they are called *ceremonial* precepts: but when they refer to man's relations to other men, they are called *judicial* precepts. Hence there are two conditions attached to the judicial precepts: viz., first, that they refer to man's relations to other men; second, that they derive their binding force not from reason alone, but in virtue of their institution.

REPLY OBJ. 1: Judgments emanate through the official pronouncement of certain men who are at the head of affairs, and in whom the judicial power is vested. Now it belongs to those who are at the head of affairs to regulate not only litigious matters, but also voluntary contracts which are concluded between man and man, and whatever matters concern the community at large and the government thereof. Consequently the judicial precepts are not only those which concern actions at law; but also all those that are directed to the ordering of one man in relation to another, which ordering is subject to the direction of the sovereign as supreme judge.

REPLY OBJ. 2: This argument holds in respect of those precepts which direct man in his relations to his neighbor, and derive their binding force from the mere dictate of reason.

REPLY OBJ. 3: Even in those precepts which direct us to God, some are moral precepts, which the reason itself dictates when it is quickened by faith; such as that God is to be loved and worshipped. There are also ceremonial precepts, which have no binding force except in virtue of their Divine institution. Now God is concerned not only with the sacrifices that are offered to Him, but also with whatever relates to the fitness of those who offer sacrifices to Him and worship Him. Because men are ordained to God as to their end; wherefore it concerns God and, consequently, is a matter of ceremonial precept, that man should show some fitness for the divine worship. On the other hand, man is not ordained to his neighbor as to his end, so as to need to be disposed in himself with regard to his neighbor, for such is the relationship of a slave to his master, since a slave *is his master's in all that he is*, as the Philosopher says (*Polit.* i, 2). Hence there are no judicial precepts ordaining man in himself; all such precepts are moral: because the reason, which is the principal in moral matters, holds the same position, in man, with regard to things that concern him, as a prince or judge holds in the state. Nevertheless we must take note that, since the relations of man to his neighbor are more subject to reason than the relations of man to God, there are more precepts whereby man is directed in his relations to his neighbor, than whereby he is directed to God. For the

propter hoc etiam oportuit plura esse caeremonialia in lege quam iudicialia.

same reason there had to be more ceremonial than judicial precepts in the Law.

Article 2

Whether the Judicial Precepts Were Figurative?

AD SECUNDUM SIC PROCEDITUR. Videtur quod praecepta iudicialia non figurent aliquid. Hoc enim videtur esse proprium caeremonialium praeceptorum, quod sint in figuram alicuius rei instituta. Si igitur etiam praecepta iudicialia aliquid figurent, non erit differentia inter iudicialia et caeremonialia praecepta.

PRAETEREA, sicuti illi populo Iudaeorum data sunt quaedam iudicialia praecepta, ita etiam aliis populis gentilium. Sed iudicialia praecepta aliorum populorum non figurant aliquid, sed ordinant quid fieri debeat. Ergo videtur quod neque praecepta iudicialia veteris legis aliquid figurarent.

PRAETEREA, ea quae ad cultum divinum pertinent, figuris quibusdam tradi oportuit, quia ea quae Dei sunt, supra nostram rationem sunt, ut supra dictum est. Sed ea quae sunt proximorum, non excedunt nostram rationem. Ergo per iudicialia, quae ad proximum nos ordinant, non oportuit aliquid figurari.

SED CONTRA est quod Exod. XXI iudicialia praecepta allegorice et moraliter exponuntur.

RESPONDEO dicendum quod dupliciter contingit aliquod praeceptum esse figurale. Uno modo, primo et per se, quia scilicet principaliter est institutum ad aliquid figurandum. Et hoc modo praecepta caeremonialia sunt figuralia, ad hoc enim sunt instituta, ut aliquid figurent pertinens ad cultum Dei et ad mysterium Christi. Quaedam vero praecepta sunt figuralia non primo et per se, sed ex consequenti. Et hoc modo praecepta iudicialia veteris legis sunt figuralia. Non enim sunt instituta ad aliquid figurandum; sed ad ordinandum statum illius populi secundum iustitiam et aequitatem. Sed ex consequenti aliquid figurabant, inquantum scilicet totus status illius populi, qui per huiusmodi praecepta disponebatur, figuralis erat; secundum illud I ad Cor. X, *omnia in figuram contingebant illis.*

AD PRIMUM ergo dicendum quod praecepta caeremonialia alio modo sunt figuralia quam iudicialia, ut dictum est.

AD SECUNDUM dicendum quod populus Iudaeorum ad hoc electus erat a Deo, quod ex eo Christus nasceretur. Et ideo oportuit totum illius populi statum esse propheticum et figuralem, ut Augustinus dicit, contra Faustum. Et propter hoc etiam iudicialia illi populo tradita,

OBJECTION 1: It would seem that the judicial precepts were not figurative. Because it seems proper to the ceremonial precepts to be instituted as figures of something else. Therefore, if the judicial precepts are figurative, there will be no difference between the judicial and ceremonial precepts.

OBJ. 2: Further, just as certain judicial precepts were given to the Jewish people, so also were some given to other heathen peoples. But the judicial precepts given to other peoples were not figurative, but stated what had to be done. Therefore it seems that neither were the judicial precepts of the Old Law figures of anything.

OBJ. 3: Further, those things which relate to the divine worship had to be taught under certain figures, because the things of God are above our reason, as stated above (Q101, A2, ad 2). But things concerning our neighbor are not above our reason. Therefore the judicial precepts which direct us in relation to our neighbor should not have been figurative.

ON THE CONTRARY, The judicial precepts are expounded both in the allegorical and in the moral sense (Exod 21).

I ANSWER THAT, A precept may be figurative in two ways. First, primarily and in itself: because, to wit, it is instituted principally that it may be the figure of something. In this way the ceremonial precepts are figurative; since they were instituted for the very purpose that they might foreshadow something relating to the worship of God and the mystery of Christ. But some precepts are figurative, not primarily and in themselves, but consequently. In this way the judicial precepts of the Old Law are figurative. For they were not instituted for the purpose of being figurative, but in order that they might regulate the state of that people according to justice and equity. Nevertheless they did foreshadow something consequently: since, to wit, the entire state of that people, who were directed by these precepts, was figurative, according to 1 Cor. 10:11: *All . . . things happened to them in figure.*

REPLY OBJ. 1: The ceremonial precepts are not figurative in the same way as the judicial precepts, as explained above.

REPLY OBJ. 2: The Jewish people were chosen by God that Christ might be born of them. Consequently the entire state of that people had to be prophetic and figurative, as Augustine states (*Contra Faust.* xxii, 24). For this reason even the judicial precepts that were given to this people

magis sunt figuralia quam iudicialia aliis populis tradita. Sicut etiam bella et gesta illius populi exponuntur mystice; non autem bella vel gesta Assyriorum vel Romanorum, quamvis longe clariora secundum homines.

AD TERTIUM dicendum quod ordo ad proximum in populo illo, secundum se consideratus, pervius erat rationi. Sed secundum quod referebatur ad cultum Dei, superabat rationem. Et ex hac parte erat figuralis.

were more figurative that those which were given to other nations. Thus, too, the wars and deeds of this people are expounded in the mystical sense: but not the wars and deeds of the Assyrians or Romans, although the latter are more famous in the eyes of men.

REPLY OBJ. 3: In this people the direction of man in regard to his neighbor, considered in itself, was subject to reason. But insofar as it was referred to the worship of God, it was above reason: and in this respect it was figurative.

Article 3

Whether the Judicial Precepts of the Old Law Bind for Ever?

AD TERTIUM SIC PROCEDITUR. Videtur quod praecepta iudicialia veteris legis perpetuam obligationem habeant. Praecepta enim iudicialia pertinent ad virtutem iustitiae, nam iudicium dicitur iustitiae executio. *Iustitia autem est perpetua et immortalis*, ut dicitur Sap. I. Ergo obligatio praeceptorum iudicialium est perpetua.

PRAETEREA, institutio divina est stabilior quam institutio humana. Sed praecepta iudicialia humanarum legum habent perpetuam obligationem. Ergo multo magis praecepta iudicialia legis divinae.

PRAETEREA, apostolus dicit, ad Heb. VII, quod *reprobatio fit praecedentis mandati propter infirmitatem ipsius et inutilitatem*. Quod quidem verum est de mandato caeremoniali quod *non poterat facere perfectum iuxta conscientiam servientem solummodo in cibis et in potibus et variis Baptismatibus et iustitiis carnis*, ut apostolus dicit, ad Heb. IX. Sed praecepta iudicialia utilia erant et efficacia ad id ad quod ordinabantur, scilicet ad iustitiam et aequitatem inter homines constituendam. Ergo praecepta iudicialia veteris legis non reprobantur, sed adhuc efficaciam habent.

SED CONTRA est quod apostolus dicit, ad Heb. VII, quod *translato sacerdotio, necesse est ut legis translatio fiat*. Sed sacerdotium est translatum ab Aaron ad Christum. Ergo etiam et tota lex est translata. Non ergo iudicialia praecepta adhuc obligationem habent.

RESPONDEO dicendum quod iudicialia praecepta non habuerunt perpetuam obligationem, sed sunt evacuata per adventum Christi, aliter tamen quam caeremonialia. Nam caeremonialia adeo sunt evacuata ut non solum sint mortua, sed etiam mortifera observantibus post Christum, maxime post Evangelium divulgatum. Praecepta autem iudicialia sunt quidem mortua, quia non habent vim obligandi, non tamen sunt mortifera. Quia si quis princeps ordinaret in regno suo illa iudicialia observari, non peccaret, nisi forte hoc modo

OBJECTION 1: It would seem that the judicial precepts of the Old Law bind for ever. Because the judicial precepts relate to the virtue of justice: since a judgment is an execution of the virtue of justice. Now *justice is perpetual and immortal* (Wis 1:15). Therefore the judicial precepts bind for ever.

OBJ. 2: Further, Divine institutions are more enduring than human institutions. But the judicial precepts of human laws bind for ever. Therefore much more do the judicial precepts of the Divine Law.

OBJ. 3: Further, the Apostle says (Heb 7:18) that *there is a setting aside of the former commandment, because of the weakness and unprofitableness thereof*. Now this is true of the ceremonial precept, which *could not, as to the conscience, make him perfect that serveth only in meats and in drinks, and diverse washings and justices of the flesh*, as the Apostle declares (Heb 9:9,10). On the other hand, the judicial precepts were useful and efficacious in respect of the purpose for which they were instituted, viz., to establish justice and equity among men. Therefore the judicial precepts of the Old Law are not set aside, but still retain their efficacy.

ON THE CONTRARY, The Apostle says (Heb 7:12) that *the priesthood being translated it is necessary that a translation also be made of the Law*. But the priesthood was transferred from Aaron to Christ. Therefore the entire Law was also transferred. Therefore the judicial precepts are no longer in force.

I ANSWER THAT, The judicial precepts did not bind for ever, but were annulled by the coming of Christ: yet not in the same way as the ceremonial precepts. For the ceremonial precepts were annulled so far as to be not only *dead*, but also deadly to those who observe them since the coming of Christ, especially since the promulgation of the Gospel. On the other hand, the judicial precepts are dead indeed, because they have no binding force: but they are not deadly. For if a sovereign were to order these judicial precepts to be observed in his kingdom, he would not sin:

observarentur, vel observari mandarentur, tanquam habentia vim obligandi ex veteris legis institutione. Talis enim intentio observandi esset mortifera.

Et huius differentiae ratio potest accipi ex praemissis. Dictum est enim quod praecepta caeremonialia sunt figuralia primo et per se, tanquam instituta principaliter ad figurandum Christi mysteria ut futura. Et ideo ipsa observatio eorum praeiudicat fidei veritati, secundum quam confitemur illa mysteria iam esse completa. Praecepta autem iudicialia non sunt instituta ad figurandum, sed ad disponendum statum illius populi, qui ordinabatur ad Christum. Et ideo, mutato statu illius populi, Christo iam veniente, iudicialia praecepta obligationem amiserunt, lex enim fuit paedagogus ducens ad Christum, ut dicitur ad Gal. III. Quia tamen huiusmodi iudicialia praecepta non ordinantur ad figurandum, sed ad aliquid fiendum, ipsa eorum observatio absolute non praeiudicat fidei veritati. Sed intentio observandi tanquam ex obligatione legis, praeiudicat veritati fidei, quia per hoc haberetur quod status prioris populi adhuc duraret, et quod Christus nondum venisset.

Ad primum ergo dicendum quod iustitia quidem perpetuo est observanda. Sed determinatio eorum quae sunt iusta secundum institutionem humanam vel divinam, oportet quod varietur secundum diversum hominum statum.

Ad secundum dicendum quod praecepta iudicialia ab hominibus instituta habent perpetuam obligationem, manente illo statu regiminis. Sed si civitas vel gens ad aliud regimen deveniat, oportet leges mutari. Non enim eaedem leges conveniunt in democratia, quae est potestas populi, et in oligarchia, quae est potestas divitum; ut patet per philosophum, in sua politica. Et ideo etiam, mutato statu illius populi, oportuit praecepta iudicialia mutari.

Ad tertium dicendum quod illa praecepta iudicialia disponebant populum ad iustitiam et aequitatem secundum quod conveniebat illi statui. Sed post Christum, statum illius populi oportuit mutari, ut iam in Christo non esset discretio gentilis et Iudaei, sicut antea erat. Et propter hoc oportuit etiam praecepta iudicialia mutari.

unless perchance they were observed, or ordered to be observed, as though they derived their binding force through being institutions of the Old Law: for it would be a deadly sin to intend to observe them thus.

The reason for this difference may be gathered from what has been said above (A2). For it has been stated that the ceremonial precepts are figurative primarily and in themselves, as being instituted chiefly for the purpose of foreshadowing the mysteries of Christ to come. On the other hand, the judicial precepts were not instituted that they might be figures, but that they might shape the state of that people who were directed to Christ. Consequently, when the state of that people changed with the coming of Christ, the judicial precepts lost their binding force: for the Law was a pedagogue, leading men to Christ, as stated in Gal. 3:24. Since, however, these judicial precepts are instituted, not for the purpose of being figures, but for the performance of certain deeds, the observance thereof is not prejudicial to the truth of faith. But the intention of observing them, as though one were bound by the Law, is prejudicial to the truth of faith: because it would follow that the former state of the people still lasts, and that Christ has not yet come.

Reply Obj. 1: The obligation of observing justice is indeed perpetual. But the determination of those things that are just, according to human or Divine institution, must needs be different, according to the different states of mankind.

Reply Obj. 2: The judicial precepts established by men retain their binding force for ever, so long as the state of government remains the same. But if the state or nation pass to another form of government, the laws must needs be changed. For democracy, which is government by the people, demands different laws from those of oligarchy, which is government by the rich, as the Philosopher shows (*Polit.* iv, 1). Consequently when the state of that people changed, the judicial precepts had to be changed also.

Reply Obj. 3: Those judicial precepts directed the people to justice and equity, in keeping with the demands of that state. But after the coming of Christ, there had to be a change in the state of that people, so that in Christ there was no distinction between Gentile and Jew, as there had been before. For this reason the judicial precepts needed to be changed also.

Article 4

Whether It Is Possible to Assign a Distinct Division of the Judicial Precepts?

Ad quartum sic proceditur. Videtur quod praecepta iudicialia non possint habere aliquam certam divisionem. Praecepta enim iudicialia ordinant homines

Objection 1: It would seem that it is impossible to assign a distinct division of the judicial precepts. Because the judicial precepts direct men in their relations to one

ad invicem. Sed ea quae inter homines ordinari oportet, in usum eorum venientia, non cadunt sub certa distinctione, cum sint infinita. Ergo praecepta iudicialia non possunt habere certam distinctionem.

PRAETEREA, praecepta iudicialia sunt determinationes moralium. Sed moralia praecepta non videntur habere aliquam distinctionem, nisi secundum quod reducuntur ad praecepta Decalogi. Ergo praecepta iudicialia non habent aliquam certam distinctionem.

PRAETEREA, praecepta caeremonialia quia certam distinctionem habent, eorum distinctio in lege innuitur, dum quaedam vocantur sacrificia, quaedam observantiae. Sed nulla distinctio innuitur in lege praeceptorum iudicialium. Ergo videtur quod non habeant certam distinctionem.

SED CONTRA, ubi est ordo, oportet quod sit distinctio. Sed ratio ordinis maxime pertinet ad praecepta iudicialia, per quae populus ille ordinabatur. Ergo maxime debent habere distinctionem certam.

RESPONDEO dicendum quod, cum lex sit quasi quaedam ars humanae vitae instituendae vel ordinandae, sicut in unaquaque arte est certa distinctio regularum artis, ita oportet in qualibet lege esse certam distinctionem praeceptorum, aliter enim ipsa confusio utilitatem legis auferret. Et ideo dicendum est quod praecepta iudicialia veteris legis, per quae homines ad invicem ordinabantur, distinctionem habent secundum distinctionem ordinationis humanae.

Quadruplex autem ordo in aliquo populo inveniri potest, unus quidem, principum populi ad subditos; alius autem, subditorum ad invicem; tertius autem, eorum qui sunt de populo ad extraneos; quartus autem, ad domesticos, sicut patris ad filium, uxoris ad virum, et domini ad servum. Et secundum istos quatuor ordines distingui possunt praecepta iudicialia veteris legis. Dantur enim quaedam praecepta de institutione principum et officio eorum, et de reverentia eis exhibenda, et haec est una pars iudicialium praeceptorum. Dantur etiam quaedam praecepta pertinentia ad concives ad invicem, puta circa emptiones et venditiones, et iudicia et poenas. Et haec est secunda pars iudicialium praeceptorum. Dantur etiam quaedam praecepta pertinentia ad extraneos, puta de bellis contra hostes, et de susceptione peregrinorum et advenarum. Et haec est tertia pars iudicialium praeceptorum. Dantur etiam in lege quaedam praecepta pertinentia ad domesticam conversationem, sicut de servis, et uxoribus, et filiis. Et haec est quarta pars iudicialium praeceptorum.

AD PRIMUM ergo dicendum quod ea quae pertinent ad ordinationem hominum ad invicem, sunt quidem numero infinita; sed tamen reduci possunt ad aliqua

another. But those things which need to be directed, as pertaining to the relationship between man and man, and which are made use of by men, are not subject to division, since they are infinite in number. Therefore it is not possible to assign a distinct division of the judicial precepts.

OBJ. 2: Further, the judicial precepts are decisions on moral matters. But moral precepts do not seem to be capable of division, except insofar as they are reducible to the precepts of the decalogue. Therefore there is no distinct division of the judicial precepts.

OBJ. 3: Further, because there is a distinct division of the ceremonial precepts, the Law alludes to this division, by describing some as *sacrifices*, others as *observances*. But the Law contains no allusion to a division of the judicial precepts. Therefore it seems that they have no distinct division.

ON THE CONTRARY, Wherever there is order there must needs be division. But the notion of order is chiefly applicable to the judicial precepts, since thereby that people was ordained. Therefore it is most necessary that they should have a distinct division.

I ANSWER THAT, Since law is the art, as it were, of directing or ordering the life of man, as in every art there is a distinct division in the rules of art, so, in every law, there must be a distinct division of precepts: else the law would be rendered useless by confusion. We must therefore say that the judicial precepts of the Old Law, whereby men were directed in their relations to one another, are subject to division according to the diverse ways in which man is directed.

Now in every people a fourfold order is to be found: one, of the people's sovereign to his subjects; a second of the subjects among themselves; a third, of the citizens to foreigners; a fourth, of members of the same household, such as the order of the father to his son; of the wife to her husband; of the master to his servant: and according to these four orders we may distinguish different kinds of judicial precepts in the Old Law. For certain precepts are laid down concerning the institution of the sovereign and relating to his office, and about the respect due to him: this is one part of the judicial precepts. Again, certain precepts are given in respect of a man to his fellow citizens: for instance, about buying and selling, judgments and penalties: this is the second part of the judicial precepts. Again, certain precepts are enjoined with regard to foreigners: for instance, about wars waged against their foes, and about the way to receive travelers and strangers: this is the third part of the judicial precepts. Lastly, certain precepts are given relating to home life: for instance, about servants, wives and children: this is the fourth part of the judicial precepts.

REPLY OBJ. 1: Things pertaining to the ordering of relations between one man and another are indeed infinite in number: yet they are reducible to certain distinct heads,

certa, secundum differentiam ordinationis humanae, ut dictum est.

AD SECUNDUM dicendum quod praecepta Decalogi sunt prima in genere moralium, ut supra dictum est, et ideo convenienter alia praecepta moralia secundum ea distinguuntur. Sed praecepta iudicialia et caeremonialia habent aliam rationem obligationis non quidem ex ratione naturali sed ex sola institutione. Et ideo distinctionis eorum est alia ratio.

AD TERTIUM dicendum quod ex ipsis rebus quae per praecepta iudicialia ordinantur in lege, innuit lex distinctionem iudicialium praeceptorum.

according to the different relations in which one man stands to another, as stated above.

REPLY OBJ. 2: The precepts of the decalogue held the first place in the moral order, as stated above (Q100, A3): and consequently it is fitting that other moral precepts should be distinguished in relation to them. But the judicial and ceremonial precepts have a different binding force, derived, not from natural reason, but from their institution alone. Hence there is a distinct reason for distinguishing them.

REPLY OBJ. 3: The Law alludes to the division of the judicial precepts in the very things themselves which are prescribed by the judicial precepts of the Law.

QUESTION 105

OF THE REASON FOR THE JUDICIAL PRECEPTS

Deinde considerandum est de ratione iudicialium praeceptorum. Et circa hoc quaeruntur quatuor.

Primo, de ratione praeceptorum iudicialium quae pertinent ad principes.

Secundo, de his quae pertinent ad convictum hominum ad invicem.

Tertio, de his quae pertinent ad extraneos.

Quarto, de his quae pertinent ad domesticam conversationem.

We must now consider the reason for the judicial precepts: under which head there are four points of inquiry:

(1) Concerning the reason for the judicial precepts relating to the rulers;

(2) Concerning the fellowship of one man with another;

(3) Concerning matters relating to foreigners;

(4) Concerning things relating to domestic matters.

Article 1

Whether the Old Law Enjoined Fitting Precepts Concerning Rulers?

AD PRIMUM SIC PROCEDITUR. Videtur quod inconvenienter lex vetus de principibus ordinaverit. Quia, ut philosophus dicit, in III Polit., *ordinatio populi praecipue dependet ex maximo principatu*. Sed in lege non invenitur qualiter debeat institui supremus princeps. Invenitur autem de inferioribus principibus, primo quidem, Exod. XVIII, *provide de omni plebe viros sapientes*, etc.; et Num. XI, *congrega mihi septuaginta viros de senioribus Israel*; et Deut. I, *date ex vobis viros sapientes et gnaros*, et cetera. Ergo insufficienter lex vetus principes populi ordinavit.

PRAETEREA, optimi est optima adducere, ut Plato dicit. Sed optima ordinatio civitatis vel populi cuiuscumque est ut gubernetur per regem, quia huiusmodi regimen maxime repraesentat divinum regimen, quo unus Deus mundum gubernat. A principio igitur lex debuit regem populo instituere; et non permittere hoc eorum arbitrio, sicut permittitur Deut. XVII, *cum dixeris, constituam super me regem, eum constitues*, et cetera.

PRAETEREA, sicut dicitur Matth. XII, *omne regnum in se divisum desolabitur*, quod etiam experimento patuit in populo Iudaeorum, in quo divisio regni fuit destructionis causa. Sed lex praecipue debet intendere ea quae pertinent ad communem salutem populi. Ergo debuit in lege prohiberi divisio regni in duos reges. Nec etiam debuit hoc auctoritate divina introduci; sicut legitur introductum auctoritate domini per Ahiam Silonitem prophetam, III Reg. XI.

OBJECTION 1: It would seem that the Old Law made unfitting precepts concerning rulers. Because, as the Philosopher says (*Polit.* iii, 4), *the ordering of the people depends mostly on the chief ruler*. But the Law contains no precept relating to the institution of the chief ruler; and yet we find therein prescriptions concerning the inferior rulers: first (Exod 18:21): *Provide out of all the people wise men*, etc.; again (Num 11:16): *Gather unto Me seventy men of the ancients of Israel*; and again (Deut 1:13): *Let Me have from among you wise and understanding men*, etc. Therefore the Law provided insufficiently in regard to the rulers of the people.

OBJ. 2: Further, *The best gives of the best*, as Plato states (Tim. ii). Now the best ordering of a state or of any nation is to be ruled by a king: because this kind of government approaches nearest in resemblance to the Divine government, whereby God rules the world from the beginning. Therefore the Law should have set a king over the people, and they should not have been allowed a choice in the matter, as indeed they were allowed (Deut 17:14,15): *When thou . . . shalt say: I will set a king over me . . . thou shalt set him*, etc.

OBJ. 3: Further, according to Mt. 12:25: *Every kingdom divided against itself shall be made desolate*: a saying which was verified in the Jewish people, whose destruction was brought about by the division of the kingdom. But the Law should aim chiefly at things pertaining to the general well-being of the people. Therefore it should have forbidden the kingdom to be divided under two kings: nor should this have been introduced even by Divine authority; as we read of its being introduced by the authority of the prophet Ahias the Silonite (3 Kgs 11:29, seqq.).

PRAETEREA, sicut sacerdotes instituuntur ad utilitatem populi in his quae ad Deum pertinent, ut patet Heb. V; ita etiam principes instituuntur ad utilitatem populi in rebus humanis. Sed sacerdotibus et Levitis qui sunt in lege, deputantur aliqua ex quibus vivere debeant, sicut decimae et primitiae, et multa alia huiusmodi. Ergo similiter principibus populi debuerunt aliqua ordinari unde sustentarentur, et praecipue cum inhibita sit eis munerum acceptio, ut patet Exod. XXIII, *non accipietis munera, quae excaecant etiam prudentes, et subvertunt verba iustorum.*

PRAETEREA, sicut regnum est optimum regimen, ita tyrannis est pessima corruptio regiminis. Sed dominus regi instituendo instituit ius tyrannicum, dicitur enim I Reg. VIII, *hoc erit ius regis qui imperaturus est vobis, filios vestros tollet*, et cetera. Ergo inconvenienter fuit provisum per legem circa principum ordinationem.

SED CONTRA est quod populus Israel de pulchritudine ordinationis commendatur, Num. XXIV, *quam pulchra tabernacula tua, Iacob; et tentoria tua, Israel.* Sed pulchritudo ordinationis populi dependet ex principibus bene institutis. Ergo per legem populus fuit circa principes bene institutus.

RESPONDEO dicendum quod circa bonam ordinationem principum in aliqua civitate vel gente, duo sunt attendenda. Quorum unum est ut omnes aliquam partem habeant in principatu, per hoc enim conservatur pax populi, et omnes talem ordinationem amant et custodiunt, ut dicitur in II Polit. Aliud est quod attenditur secundum speciem regiminis, vel ordinationis principatuum. Cuius cum sint diversae species, ut philosophus tradit, in III Polit., praecipuae tamen sunt regnum, in quo unus principatur secundum virtutem; et aristocratia, idest potestas optimorum, in qua aliqui pauci principantur secundum virtutem. Unde optima ordinatio principum est in aliqua civitate vel regno, in qua unus praeficitur secundum virtutem qui omnibus praesit; et sub ipso sunt aliqui principantes secundum virtutem; et tamen talis principatus ad omnes pertinet, tum quia ex omnibus eligi possunt, tum quia etiam ab omnibus eliguntur. Talis enim est optima politia, bene commixta ex regno, inquantum unus praeest; et aristocratia, inquantum multi principantur secundum virtutem; et ex democratia, idest potestate populi, inquantum ex popularibus possunt eligi principes, et ad populum pertinet electio principum.

Et hoc fuit institutum secundum legem divinam. Nam Moyses et eius successores gubernabant populum quasi singulariter omnibus principantes, quod est quaedam species regni. Eligebantur autem septuaginta duo seniores secundum virtutem, dicitur enim Deut. I, *tuli de vestris tribubus viros sapientes et nobiles, et constitui eos principes*, et hoc erat aristocraticum. Sed democraticum

OBJ. 4: Further, just as priests are instituted for the benefit of the people in things concerning God, as stated in Heb. 5:1; so are rulers set up for the benefit of the people in human affairs. But certain things were allotted as a means of livelihood for the priests and Levites of the Law: such as the tithes and first-fruits, and many like things. Therefore in like manner certain things should have been determined for the livelihood of the rulers of the people: the more that they were forbidden to accept presents, as is clearly stated in Ex. 23:8: *You shall not take bribes, which even blind the wise, and pervert the words of the just.*

OBJ. 5: Further, as a kingdom is the best form of government, so is tyranny the most corrupt. But when the Lord appointed the king, He established a tyrannical law; for it is written (1 Kgs 8:11): *This will be the right of the king, that shall reign over you: He will take your sons,* etc. Therefore the Law made unfitting provision with regard to the institution of rulers.

ON THE CONTRARY, The people of Israel is commended for the beauty of its order (Num 24:5): *How beautiful are thy tabernacles, O Jacob, and thy tents.* But the beautiful ordering of a people depends on the right establishment of its rulers. Therefore the Law made right provision for the people with regard to its rulers.

I ANSWER THAT, Two points are to be observed concerning the right ordering of rulers in a state or nation. One is that all should take some share in the government: for this form of constitution ensures peace among the people, commends itself to all, and is most enduring, as stated in *Polit.* ii, 6. The other point is to be observed in respect of the kinds of government, or the different ways in which the constitutions are established. For whereas these differ in kind, as the Philosopher states (*Polit.* iii, 5), nevertheless the first place is held by the *kingdom*, where the power of government is vested in one; and *aristocracy*, which signifies government by the best, where the power of government is vested in a few. Accordingly, the best form of government is in a state or kingdom, where one is given the power to preside over all; while under him are others having governing powers: and yet a government of this kind is shared by all, both because all are eligible to govern, and because the rules are chosen by all. For this is the best form of polity, being partly kingdom, since there is one at the head of all; partly aristocracy, insofar as a number of persons are set in authority; partly democracy, i.e., government by the people, insofar as the rulers can be chosen from the people, and the people have the right to choose their rulers.

Such was the form of government established by the Divine Law. For Moses and his successors governed the people in such a way that each of them was ruler over all; so that there was a kind of kingdom. Moreover, seventy-two men were chosen, who were elders in virtue: for it is written (Deut 1:15): *I took out of your tribes wise and honorable, and appointed them rulers*: so that there was an element of

erat quod isti de omni populo eligebantur; dicitur enim Exod. XVIII, *provide de omni plebe viros sapientes*, etc., et etiam quod populus eos eligebat; unde dicitur Deut. I, *date ex vobis viros sapientes*, et cetera. Unde patet quod optima fuit ordinatio principum quam lex instituit.

AD PRIMUM ergo dicendum quod populus ille sub speciali cura Dei regebatur, unde dicitur Deut. VII, *te elegit dominus Deus tuus ut sis ei populus peculiaris*. Et ideo institutionem summi principis dominus sibi reservavit. Et hoc est quod Moyses petivit, Num. XXVII, *provideat dominus Deus spirituum omnis carnis, hominem qui sit super multitudinem hanc*. Et sic ex Dei ordinatione institutus est Iosue in principatu post Moysen, et de singulis iudicibus qui post Iosue fuerunt, legitur quod Deus suscitavit populo salvatorem, et quod spiritus domini fuit in eis, ut patet Iudic. III. Et ideo etiam electionem regis non commisit dominus populo, sed sibi reservavit; ut patet Deut. XVII, *eum constitues regem, quem dominus Deus tuus elegerit*.

AD SECUNDUM dicendum quod regnum est optimum regimen populi, si non corrumpatur. Sed propter magnam potestatem quae regi conceditur, de facili regnum degenerat in tyrannidem, nisi sit perfecta virtus eius cui talis potestas conceditur, quia non est nisi virtuosi bene ferre bonas fortunas, ut philosophus dicit, in IV Ethic. Perfecta autem virtus in paucis invenitur, et praecipue Iudaei crudeles erant et ad avaritiam proni, per quae vitia maxime homines in tyrannidem decidunt. Et ideo dominus a principio eis regem non instituit cum plena potestate, sed iudicem et gubernatorem in eorum custodiam. Sed postea regem ad petitionem populi, quasi indignatus, concessit, ut patet per hoc quod dixit ad Samuelem, I Reg. VIII, *non te abiecerunt, sed me, ne regnem super eos*.

Instituit tamen a principio circa regem instituendum, primo quidem, modum eligendi. In quo duo determinavit, ut scilicet in eius electione expectarent iudicium domini; et ut non facerent regem alterius gentis, quia tales reges solent parum affici ad gentem cui praeficiuntur, et per consequens non curare de eis. Secundo, ordinavit circa reges institutos qualiter deberent se habere quantum ad seipsos, ut scilicet non multiplicarent currus et equos, neque uxores, neque etiam immensas divitias; quia ex cupiditate horum principes ad tyrannidem declinant, et iustitiam derelinquunt. Instituit etiam qualiter se deberent habere ad Deum, ut scilicet semper legerent et cogitarent de lege Dei, et semper essent in Dei timore et obedientia. Instituit etiam qualiter se haberent ad

aristocracy. But it was a democratical government insofar as the rulers were chosen from all the people; for it is written (Exod 18:21): *Provide out of all the people wise men*, etc.; and, again, insofar as they were chosen by the people; wherefore it is written (Deut 1:13): *Let me have from among you wise men*, etc. Consequently it is evident that the ordering of the rulers was well provided for by the Law.

REPLY OBJ. 1: This people was governed under the special care of God: wherefore it is written (Deut 7:6): *The Lord thy God hath chosen thee to be His peculiar people*: and this is why the Lord reserved to Himself the institution of the chief ruler. For this too did Moses pray (Num 27:16): *May the Lord the God of the spirits of all the flesh provide a man, that may be over this multitude*. Thus by God's orders Josue was set at the head in place of Moses; and we read about each of the judges who succeeded Josue that God *raised . . . up a savior* for the people, and that *the spirit of the Lord was* in them (Judg 3:9,10,15). Hence the Lord did not leave the choice of a king to the people; but reserved this to Himself, as appears from Dt. 17:15: *Thou shalt set him whom the Lord thy God shall choose*.

REPLY OBJ. 2: A kingdom is the best form of government of the people, so long as it is not corrupt. But since the power granted to a king is so great, it easily degenerates into tyranny, unless he to whom this power is given be a very virtuous man: for it is only the virtuous man that conducts himself well in the midst of prosperity, as the Philosopher observes (*Ethic.* iv, 3). Now perfect virtue is to be found in few: and especially were the Jews inclined to cruelty and avarice, which vices above all turn men into tyrants. Hence from the very first the Lord did not set up the kingly authority with full power, but gave them judges and governors to rule them. But afterwards when the people asked Him to do so, being indignant with them, so to speak, He granted them a king, as is clear from His words to Samuel (1 Kgs 8:7): *They have not rejected thee, but Me, that I should not reign over them*.

Nevertheless, as regards the appointment of a king, He did establish the manner of election from the very beginning (Deut 17:14, seqq.): and then He determined two points: first, that in choosing a king they should wait for the Lord's decision; and that they should not make a man of another nation king, because such kings are wont to take little interest in the people they are set over, and consequently to have no care for their welfare: second, He prescribed how the king after his appointment should behave, in regard to himself; namely, that he should not accumulate chariots and horses, nor wives, nor immense wealth: because through craving for such things princes become tyrants and forsake justice. He also appointed the manner in which they were to conduct themselves towards God: namely, that

subditos suos, ut scilicet non superbe eos contemnerent, aut opprimerent, neque etiam a iustitia declinarent.

AD TERTIUM dicendum quod divisio regni, et multitudo regum, magis est populo illi data in poenam pro multis dissensionibus eorum, quas maxime contra regnum David iustum moverant, quam ad eorum profectum. Unde dicitur Osee XIII, *dabo tibi regem in furore meo*; et Osee VIII, *ipsi regnaverunt, et non ex me, principes extiterunt, et non cognovi.*

AD QUARTUM dicendum quod sacerdotes per successionem originis sacris deputabantur. Et hoc ideo ut in maiori reverentia haberentur, si non quilibet ex populo posset sacerdos fieri, quorum honor cedebat in reverentiam divini cultus. Et ideo oportuit ut eis specialia quaedam deputarentur, tam in decimis quam in primitiis, quam etiam in oblationibus et sacrificiis, ex quibus viverent. Sed principes, sicut dictum est, assumebantur ex toto populo, et ideo habebant certas possessiones proprias, ex quibus vivere poterant. Et praecipue cum dominus prohiberet etiam in rege ne superabundaret divitiis aut magnifico apparatu, tum quia non erat facile quin ex his in superbiam et tyrannidem erigeretur; tum etiam quia, si principes non erant multum divites, et erat laboriosus principatus et sollicitudine plenus, non multum affectabatur a popularibus, et sic tollebatur seditionis materia.

AD QUINTUM dicendum quod illud ius non dabatur regi ex institutione divina; sed magis praenuntiatur usurpatio regum, qui sibi ius iniquum constituunt in tyrannidem degenerantes, et subditos depraedantes. Et hoc patet per hoc quod in fine subdit, *vosque eritis ei servi*, quod proprie pertinet ad tyrannidem, quia tyranni suis subditis principantur ut servis. Unde hoc dicebat Samuel ad deterrendum eos ne regem peterent, sequitur enim, *noluit autem audire populus vocem Samuelis.* Potest tamen contingere quod etiam bonus rex, absque tyrannide, filios tollat, et constituat tribunos et centuriones, et multa accipiat a subditis, propter commune bonum procurandum.

they should continually read and ponder on God's Law, and should ever fear and obey God. Moreover, He decided how they should behave towards their subjects: namely, that they should not proudly despise them, or ill-treat them, and that they should not depart from the paths of justice.

REPLY OBJ. 3: The division of the kingdom, and a number of kings, was rather a punishment inflicted on that people for their many dissensions, specially against the just rule of David, than a benefit conferred on them for their profit. Hence it is written (Hos 13:11): *I will give thee a king in My wrath*; and (Hos 8:4): *They have reigned, but not by Me: they have been princes, and I knew not.*

REPLY OBJ. 4: The priestly office was bequeathed by succession from father to son: and this, in order that it might be held in greater respect, if not any man from the people could become a priest: since honor was given to them out of reverence for the divine worship. Hence it was necessary to put aside certain things for them both as to tithes and as to first-fruits, and, again, as to oblations and sacrifices, that they might be afforded a means of livelihood. On the other hand, the rulers, as stated above, were chosen from the whole people; wherefore they had their own possessions, from which to derive a living: and so much the more, since the Lord forbade even a king to have superabundant wealth to make too much show of magnificence: both because he could scarcely avoid the excesses of pride and tyranny, arising from such things, and because, if the rulers were not very rich, and if their office involved much work and anxiety, it would not tempt the ambition of the common people; and would not become an occasion of sedition.

REPLY OBJ. 5: That right was not given to the king by Divine institution: rather was it foretold that kings would usurp that right, by framing unjust laws, and by degenerating into tyrants who preyed on their subjects. This is clear from the context that follows: *And you shall be his slaves*: which is significative of tyranny, since a tyrant rules is subjects as though they were his slaves. Hence Samuel spoke these words to deter them from asking for a king; since the narrative continues: *But the people would not hear the voice of Samuel*. It may happen, however, that even a good king, without being a tyrant, may take away the sons, and make them tribunes and centurions; and may take many things from his subjects in order to secure the common weal.

Article 2

Whether the Judicial Precepts Were Suitably Framed As to the Relations of One Man with Another?

AD SECUNDUM SIC PROCEDITUR. Videtur quod inconvenienter fuerint tradita praecepta iudicialia quantum ad popularium convictum. Non enim possunt homines pacifice vivere ad invicem, si unus accipiat ea quae

OBJECTION 1: It would seem that the judicial precepts were not suitably framed as regards the relations of one man with another. Because men cannot live together in peace, if one man takes what belongs to another. But this

sunt alterius. Sed hoc videtur esse inductum in lege, dicitur enim Deut. XXIII, *ingressus vineam proximi tui, comede uvas quantum tibi placuerit.* Ergo lex vetus non convenienter providebat hominum paci.

Praeterea, ex hoc maxime multae civitates et regna destruuntur, quod possessiones ad mulieres perveniunt, ut philosophus dicit, in II Polit. Sed hoc fuit introductum in veteri lege, dicitur enim Num. XXVII, *homo cum mortuus fuerit absque filio, ad filiam eius transibit hereditas.* Ergo non convenienter providit lex saluti populi.

Praeterea, societas hominum maxime per hoc conservatur, quod homines emendo et vendendo sibi invicem res suas commutant quibus indigent, ut dicitur in I Polit. Sed lex vetus abstulit virtutem venditionis, mandavit enim quod possessio vendita reverteretur ad venditorem in quinquagesimo anno iubilaei, ut patet Levit. XXV. Inconvenienter igitur lex populum illum circa hoc instituit.

Praeterea, necessitatibus hominum maxime expedit ut homines sint prompti ad mutuum concedendum. Quae quidem promptitudo tollitur per hoc quod creditores accepta non reddunt, unde dicitur Eccli. XXIX, *multi non causa nequitiae non faenerati sunt, sed fraudari gratis timuerunt.* Hoc autem induxit lex. Primo quidem, quia mandavit Deut. XV, *cui debetur aliquid ab amico vel proximo ac fratre suo, repetere non poterit, quia annus remissionis est domini;* et Exod. XXII dicitur quod si praesente domino animal mutuatum mortuum fuerit, reddere non tenetur. Secundo, quia aufertur ei securitas quae habetur per pignus, dicitur enim Deut. XXIV, *cum repetes a proximo tuo rem aliquam quam debet tibi, non ingredieris domum eius ut pignus auferas;* et iterum, *non pernoctabit apud te pignus, sed statim reddes ei.* Ergo insufficienter fuit ordinatum in lege de mutuis.

Praeterea, ex defraudatione depositi maximum periculum imminet, et ideo est maxima cautela adhibenda, unde etiam dicitur II Mach. III, quod *sacerdotes invocabant de caelo eum qui de depositis legem posuit, ut his qui deposuerant ea, salva custodiret.* Sed in praeceptis veteris legis parva cautela circa deposita adhibetur, dicitur enim Exod. XXII quod in amissione depositi statur iuramento eius apud quem fuit depositum. Ergo non fuit circa hoc legis ordinatio conveniens.

Praeterea, sicut aliquis mercenarius locat operas suas, ita etiam aliqui locant domum, vel quaecumque alia huiusmodi. Sed non est necessarium ut statim pretium locatae domus conductor exhibeat. Ergo etiam nimis durum fuit quod praecipitur Levit. XIX, *non morabitur opus mercenarii tui apud te usque mane.*

seems to have been approved by the Law: since it is written (Deut 23:24): *Going into thy neighbor's vineyard, thou mayest eat as many grapes as thou pleasest.* Therefore the Old Law did not make suitable provisions for man's peace.

Obj. 2: Further, one of the chief causes of the downfall of states has been the holding of property by women, as the Philosopher says (*Polit.* ii, 6). But this was introduced by the Old Law; for it is written (Num 27:8): *When a man dieth without a son, his inheritance shall pass to his daughter.* Therefore the Law made unsuitable provision for the welfare of the people.

Obj. 3: Further, it is most conducive to the preservation of human society that men may provide themselves with necessaries by buying and selling, as stated in *Polit.* i. But the Old Law took away the force of sales; since it prescribes that in the 50th year of the jubilee all that is sold shall return to the vendor (Lev 25:28). Therefore in this matter the Law gave the people an unfitting command.

Obj. 4: Further, man's needs require that men should be ready to lend: which readiness ceases if the creditors do not return the pledges: hence it is written (Sir 29:10): *Many have refused to lend, not out of wickedness, but they were afraid to be defrauded without cause.* And yet this was encouraged by the Law. First, because it prescribed (Deut 15:2): *He to whom any thing is owing from his friend or neighbor or brother, cannot demand it again, because it is the year of remission of the Lord;* and (Exod 22:15) it is stated that if a borrowed animal should die while the owner is present, the borrower is not bound to make restitution. Second, because the security acquired through the pledge is lost: for it is written (Deut 24:10): *When thou shalt demand of thy neighbor any thing that he oweth thee, thou shalt not go into his house to take away a pledge;* and again (Deut 24:12,13): *The pledge shall not lodge with thee that night, but thou shalt restore it to him presently.* Therefore the Law made insufficient provision in the matter of loans.

Obj. 5: Further, considerable risk attaches to goods deposited with a fraudulent depositary: wherefore great caution should be observed in such matters: hence it is stated in 2 Mach 3:15 that *the priests . . . called upon Him from heaven, Who made the law concerning things given to be kept, that He would preserve them safe, for them that had deposited them.* But the precepts of the Old Law observed little caution in regard to deposits: since it is prescribed (Exod 22:10,11) that when goods deposited are lost, the owner is to stand by the oath of the depositary. Therefore the Law made unsuitable provision in this matter.

Obj. 6: Further, just as a workman offers his work for hire, so do men let houses and so forth. But there is no need for the tenant to pay his rent as soon as he takes a house. Therefore it seems an unnecessarily hard prescription (Lev 19:13) that *the wages of him that hath been hired by thee shall not abide with thee until morning.*

PRAETEREA, cum frequenter immineat iudiciorum necessitas, facilis debet esse accessus ad iudicem. Inconvenienter igitur statuit lex, Deut. XVII, ut irent ad unum locum expetituri iudicium de suis dubiis.

PRAETEREA, possibile est non solum duos, sed etiam tres vel plures concordare ad mentiendum. Inconvenienter igitur dicitur Deut. XIX, *in ore duorum vel trium testium stabit omne verbum.*

PRAETEREA, poena debet taxari secundum quantitatem culpae, unde dicitur etiam Deut. XXV, *pro mensura peccati erit et plagarum modus.* Sed quibusdam aequalibus culpis lex statuit inaequales poenas, dicitur enim Exod. XXII, quod *restituet fur quinque boves pro uno bove, et quatuor oves pro una ove.* Quaedam etiam non multum gravia peccata gravi poena puniuntur, sicut Num. XV, lapidatus est qui collegerat ligna in sabbato. Filius etiam protervus propter parva delicta, quia scilicet comessationibus vacabat et conviviis, mandatur lapidari, Deut. XXI. Igitur inconvenienter in lege sunt institutae poenae.

PRAETEREA, sicut Augustinus dicit, XXI de Civ. Dei, *octo genera poenarum in legibus esse scribit Tullius, damnum, vincula, verbera, talionem, ignominiam, exilium, mortem, servitutem.* Ex quibus aliqua sunt in lege statuta. Damnum quidem, sicut cum fur condemnabatur ad quintuplum vel quadruplum. Vincula vero, sicut Num. XV, mandatur de quodam quod in carcerem includatur. Verbera vero, sicut Deut. XXV, *si eum qui peccavit dignum viderint plagis, prosternent, et coram se facient verberari.* Ignominiam etiam inferebat illi qui nolebat accipere uxorem fratris sui defuncti, quae tollebat calceamentum illius, et spuebat in faciem illius. Mortem etiam inferebat, ut patet Levit. XX, *qui maledixerit patri suo aut matri, morte moriatur.* Poenam etiam talionis lex induxit, dicens Exod. XXI, *oculum pro oculo, dentem pro dente.* Inconveniens igitur videtur quod alias duas poenas, scilicet exilium et servitutem, lex vetus non inflixit.

PRAETEREA, poena non debetur nisi culpae. Sed bruta animalia non possunt habere culpam. Ergo inconvenienter eis infligitur poena, Exod. XXI, *bos lapidibus obruetur qui occiderit virum aut mulierem.* Et Levit. XX dicitur, *mulier quae succubuerit cuilibet iumento, simul interficiatur cum eo.* Sic igitur videtur quod inconvenienter ea quae pertinent ad convictum hominum ad invicem, fuerint in lege veteri ordinata.

PRAETEREA, dominus mandavit Exod. XXI, quod homicidium morte hominis puniretur. Sed mors bruti animalis multo minus reputatur quam occisio hominis. Ergo non potest sufficienter recompensari poena homicidii per occisionem bruti animalis. Inconvenienter

OBJ. 7: Further, since there is often pressing need for a judge, it should be easy to gain access to one. It was therefore unfitting that the Law (Deut 17:8,9) should command them to go to a fixed place to ask for judgment on doubtful matters.

OBJ. 8: Further, it is possible that not only two, but three or more, should agree to tell a lie. Therefore it is unreasonably stated (Deut 19:15) that *in the mouth of two or three witnesses every word shall stand.*

OBJ. 9: Further, punishment should be fixed according to the gravity of the fault: for which reason also it is written (Deut 25:2): *According to the measure of the sin, shall the measure also of the stripes be.* Yet the Law fixed unequal punishments for certain faults: for it is written (Exod 22:1) that the thief *shall restore five oxen for one ox, and four sheep for one sheep.* Moreover, certain slight offenses are severely punished: thus (Num 15:32, seqq.) a man is stoned for gathering sticks on the sabbath day: and (Deut 21:18, seqq.) the unruly son is commanded to be stoned on account of certain small transgressions, viz., because *he gave himself to revelling . . . and banquetings.* Therefore the Law prescribed punishments in an unreasonable manner.

OBJ. 10: Further, as Augustine says (*De Civ. Dei* xxi, 11), Tully writes that the laws recognize eight forms of punishment, indemnity, prison, stripes, retaliation, public disgrace, exile, death, slavery. Now some of these were prescribed by the Law. *Indemnity*, as when a thief was condemned to make restitution fivefold or fourfold. *Prison*, as when (Num 15:34) a certain man is ordered to be imprisoned. *Stripes*; thus (Deut 25:2), *if they see that the offender be worthy of stripes; they shall lay him down, and shall cause him to be beaten before them. Public disgrace* was brought on to him who refused to take to himself the wife of his deceased brother, for she took *off his shoe from his foot, and* did *spit in his face* (Deut 25:9). It prescribed the *death* penalty, as is clear from (Lev 20:9): *He that curseth his father, or mother, dying let him die.* The Law also recognized the *lex talionis*, by prescribing (Exod 21:24): *Eye for eye, tooth for tooth.* Therefore it seems unreasonable that the Law should not have inflicted the two other punishments, viz., *exile* and *slavery.*

OBJ. 11: Further, no punishment is due except for a fault. But dumb animals cannot commit a fault. Therefore the Law is unreasonable in punishing them (Exod 21:29): *If the ox . . . shall kill a man or a woman, it shall be stoned*: and (Lev 20:16): *The woman that shall lie under any beast, shall be killed together with the same.* Therefore it seems that matters pertaining to the relations of one man with another were unsuitably regulated by the Law.

OBJ. 12: Further, the Lord commanded (Exod 21:12) a murderer to be punished with death. But the death of a dumb animal is reckoned of much less account than the slaying of a man. Hence murder cannot be sufficiently punished by the slaying of a dumb animal. Therefore it is

igitur mandatur Deut. XXI quod *quando inventum fuerit cadaver occisi hominis, et ignorabitur caedis reus, seniores propinquioris civitatis tollant vitulam de armento quae non traxit iugum nec terram scidit vomere, et ducent eam ad vallem asperam atque saxosam quae numquam arata est nec sementa recepit, et caedent in ea cervices vitulae.*

Sed contra est quod pro speciali beneficio commemoratur in Psalmo CXLVII, *non fecit taliter omni nationi, et iudicia sua non manifestavit eis.*

Respondeo dicendum quod, sicut Augustinus in II de Civ. Dei introducit a Tullio dictum, *populus est coetus multitudinis iuris consensu et utilitatis communione sociatus.* Unde ad rationem populi pertinet ut communicatio hominum ad invicem iustis praeceptis legis ordinetur. Est autem duplex communicatio hominum ad invicem, una quidem quae fit auctoritate principum; alia autem fit propria voluntate privatarum personarum. Et quia voluntate uniuscuiusque disponi potest quod eius subditur potestati, ideo auctoritate principum, quibus subiecti sunt homines, oportet quod iudicia inter homines exerceantur, et poenae malefactoribus inferantur. Potestati vero privatarum personarum subduntur res possessae, et ideo propria voluntate in his possunt sibi invicem communicare, puta emendo, vendendo, donando, et aliis huiusmodi modis. Circa utramque autem communicationem lex sufficienter ordinavit. Statuit enim iudices, ut patet Deut. XVI, *iudices et magistros constitues in omnibus portis eius, ut iudicent populum iusto iudicio.* Instituit etiam iustum iudicii ordinem, ut dicitur Deut. I, *quod iustum est iudicate, sive civis ille sit sive peregrinus, nulla erit personarum distantia.* Sustulit etiam occasionem iniusti iudicii, acceptionem munerum iudicibus prohibendo; ut patet Exod. XXIII, et Deut. XVI. Instituit etiam numerum testium duorum vel trium; ut patet Deut. XVII, et XIX. Instituit etiam certas poenas pro diversis delictis, ut post dicetur.

Sed circa res possessas optimum est, sicut dicit philosophus, in II Polit., quod possessiones sint distinctae, et usus sit partim communis, partim autem per voluntatem possessorum communicetur. Et haec tria fuerunt in lege statuta. Primo enim, ipsae possessiones divisae erant in singulos, dicitur enim Num. XXXIII, *ego dedi vobis terram in possessionem, quam sorte dividetis vobis.* Et quia per possessionum irregularitatem plures civitates destruuntur, ut philosophus dicit, in II Polit.; ideo circa possessiones regulandas triplex remedium lex adhibuit. Unum quidem, ut secundum numerum hominum aequaliter dividerentur, unde dicitur Num. XXXIII, *pluribus dabitis latiorem, et paucioribus angustiorem.* Aliud

unfittingly prescribed (Deut 21:1,4) that *when there shall be found . . . the corpse of a man slain, and it is not known who is guilty of the murder . . . the ancients of the nearest city shall take a heifer of the herd, that hath not drawn in the yoke, nor ploughed the ground, and they shall bring her into a rough and stony valley, that never was ploughed, nor sown; and there they shall strike off the head of the heifer.*

On the contrary, It is recalled as a special blessing (Ps 147:20) that *He hath not done in like manner to every nation; and His judgments He hath not made manifest to them.*

I answer that, As Augustine says (*De Civ. Dei* ii, 21), quoting Tully, *a nation is a body of men united together by consent to the law and by community of welfare.* Consequently it is of the essence of a nation that the mutual relations of the citizens be ordered by just laws. Now the relations of one man with another are twofold: some are effected under the guidance of those in authority: others are effected by the will of private individuals. And since whatever is subject to the power of an individual can be disposed of according to his will, hence it is that the decision of matters between one man and another, and the punishment of evildoers, depend on the direction of those in authority, to whom men are subject. On the other hand, the power of private persons is exercised over the things they possess: and consequently their dealings with one another, as regards such things, depend on their own will, for instance in buying, selling, giving, and so forth. Now the Law provided sufficiently in respect of each of these relations between one man and another. For it established judges, as is clearly indicated in Dt. 16:18: *Thou shalt appoint judges and magistrates in all its gates . . . that they may judge the people with just judgment.* It is also directed the manner of pronouncing just judgments, according to Dt. 1:16,17: *Judge that which is just, whether he be one of your own country or a stranger: there shall be no difference of persons.* It also removed an occasion of pronouncing unjust judgment, by forbidding judges to accept bribes (Exod 23:8; Dt. 16:19). It prescribed the number of witnesses, viz., two or three: and it appointed certain punishments to certain crimes, as we shall state farther on (ad 10).

But with regard to possessions, it is a very good thing, says the Philosopher (*Polit.* ii, 2) that the things possessed should be distinct, and the use thereof should be partly common, and partly granted to others by the will of the possessors. These three points were provided for by the Law. Because, in the first place, the possessions themselves were divided among individuals: for it is written (Num 33:53,54): *I have given you the land for a possession: and you shall divide it among you by lot.* And since many states have been ruined through want of regulations in the matter of possessions, as the Philosopher observes (*Polit.* ii, 6); therefore the Law provided a threefold remedy against the regularity of possessions. The first was that they should be divided

remedium est ut possessiones non in perpetuum alienentur, sed certo tempore ad suos possessores revertantur, ut non confundantur sortes possessionum. Tertium remedium est ad huiusmodi confusionem tollendam, ut proximi succedant morientibus, primo quidem gradu, filius; secundo autem, filia; tertio, fratres; quarto, patrui; quinto, quicumque propinqui. Et ad distinctionem sortium conservandam, ulterius lex statuit ut mulieres quae sunt haeredes, nuberent suae tribus hominibus, ut habetur Num. XXXVI.

Secundo vero, instituit lex ut quantum ad aliqua usus rerum esset communis. Et primo, quantum ad curam, praeceptum est enim Deut. XXII, *non videbis bovem et ovem fratris tui errantem, et praeteribis, sed reduces fratri tuo*; et similiter de aliis. Secundo, quantum ad fructum. Concedebatur enim communiter quantum ad omnes, ut ingressus in vineam amici posset licite comedere, dum tamen extra non auferret. Quantum ad pauperes vero specialiter, ut eis relinquerentur manipuli obliti, et fructus et racemi remanentes, ut habetur Lev. XIX, et Deut. XXIV. Et etiam communicabantur ea quae nascebantur in septimo anno; ut habetur Exod. XXIII, et Lev. XXV.

Tertio vero, statuit lex communicationem factam per eos qui sunt domini rerum. Unam pure gratuitam, unde dicitur Deut. XIV, *anno tertio separabis aliam decimam, venientque Levites et peregrinus et pupillus et vidua, et comedent et saturabuntur.* Aliam vero cum recompensatione utilitatis, sicut per venditionem et emptionem, et locationem et conductionem, et per mutuum, et iterum per depositum, de quibus omnibus inveniuntur ordinationes certae in lege. Unde patet quod lex vetus sufficienter ordinavit convictum illius populi.

AD PRIMUM ergo dicendum quod, sicut apostolus dicit, Rom. XIII, *qui diligit proximum, legem implevit,* quia scilicet omnia praecepta legis, praecipue ordinata ad proximum, ad hunc finem ordinari videntur, ut homines se invicem diligant. Ex dilectione autem procedit quod homines sibi invicem bona sua communicent, quia ut dicitur I Ioan. III, *qui viderit fratrem suum necessitatem patientem, et clauserit viscera sua ab eo, quomodo caritas Dei manet in illo?* Et ideo intendebat lex homines assuefacere ut facile sibi invicem sua communicarent, sicut et apostolus, I ad Tim. VI, divitibus mandat facile tribuere et communicare. Non autem facile communicativus est qui non sustinet quod proximus aliquid modicum de suo accipiat, absque magno sui detrimento. Et ideo lex ordinavit ut liceret intrantem in vineam proximi, racemos ibi comedere, non autem extra deferre, ne ex hoc daretur occasio gravis damni inferendi, ex quo

equally, wherefore it is written (Num 33:54): *To the more you shall give a larger part, and to the fewer, a lesser.* A second remedy was that possessions could not be alienated for ever, but after a certain lapse of time should return to their former owner, so as to avoid confusion of possessions (cf. ad 3). The third remedy aimed at the removal of this confusion, and provided that the dead should be succeeded by their next of kin: in the first place, the son; second, the daughter; third, the brother; fourth, the father's brother; fifth, any other next of kin. Furthermore, in order to preserve the distinction of property, the Law enacted that heiresses should marry within their own tribe, as recorded in Num. 36:6.

Second, the Law commanded that, in some respects, the use of things should belong to all in common. First, as regards the care of them; for it was prescribed (Deut 22:1–4): *Thou shalt not pass by, if thou seest thy brother's ox or his sheep go astray; but thou shalt bring them back to thy brother,* and in like manner as to other things. Second, as regards fruits. For all alike were allowed on entering a friend's vineyard to eat of the fruit, but not to take any away. And, specially, with respect to the poor, it was prescribed that the forgotten sheaves, and the bunches of grapes and fruit, should be left behind for them (Lev 19:9; Dt. 24:19). Moreover, whatever grew in the seventh year was common property, as stated in Ex. 23:11 and Lev. 25:4.

Third, the law recognized the transference of goods by the owner. There was a purely gratuitous transfer: thus it is written (Deut 14:28,29): *The third day thou shalt separate another tithe . . . and the Levite . . . and the stranger, and the fatherless, and the widow . . . shall come and shall eat and be filled.* And there was a transfer for a consideration, for instance, by selling and buying, by letting out and hiring, by loan and also by deposit, concerning all of which we find that the Law made ample provision. Consequently it is clear that the Old Law provided sufficiently concerning the mutual relations of one man with another.

REPLY OBJ. 1: As the Apostle says (Rom 13:8), *he that loveth his neighbor hath fulfilled the Law*: because, to wit, all the precepts of the Law, chiefly those concerning our neighbor, seem to aim at the end that men should love one another. Now it is an effect of love that men give their own goods to others: because, as stated in 1 Jn. 3:17: *He that . . . shall see his brother in need, and shall shut up his bowels from him: how doth the charity of God abide in him?* Hence the purpose of the Law was to accustom men to give of their own to others readily: thus the Apostle (1 Tim 6:18) commands the rich *to give easily and to communicate to others.* Now a man does not give easily to others if he will not suffer another man to take some little thing from him without any great injury to him. And so the Law laid down that it should be lawful for a man, on entering his neighbor's vineyard, to eat of the fruit there: but not to carry any away, lest this should lead to the infliction of a grievous harm, and

pax perturbaretur. Quae inter disciplinatos non perturbatur ex modicorum acceptione, sed magis amicitia confirmatur, et assuefiunt homines ad facile communicandum.

AD SECUNDUM dicendum quod lex non statuit quod mulieres succederent in bonis paternis, nisi in defectu filiorum masculorum. Tunc autem necessarium erat ut successio mulieribus concederetur in consolationem patris, cui grave fuisset si eius hereditas omnino ad extraneos transiret. Adhibuit tamen circa hoc lex cautelam debitam, praecipiens ut mulieres succedentes in haereditate paterna, nuberent suae tribus hominibus, ad hoc quod sortes tribuum non confunderentur, ut habetur Num. ult.

AD TERTIUM dicendum quod, sicut philosophus dicit, in II Polit., regulatio possessionum multum confert ad conservationem civitatis vel gentis. Unde, sicut ipse dicit, apud quasdam gentilium civitates statutum fuit *ut nullus possessionem vendere posset, nisi pro manifesto detrimento.* Si enim passim possessiones vendantur, potest contingere quod omnes possessiones ad paucos deveniant, et ita necesse erit civitatem vel regionem habitatoribus evacuari. Et ideo lex vetus, ad huiusmodi periculum amovendum, sic ordinavit quod et necessitatibus hominum subveniretur, concedens possessionum venditionem usque ad certum tempus; et tamen periculum removit, praecipiens ut certo tempore possessio vendita ad vendentem rediret. Et hoc instituit ut sortes non confunderentur, sed semper remaneret eadem distinctio determinata in tribubus.

Quia vero domus urbanae non erant sorte distinctae, ideo concessit quod in perpetuum vendi possent, sicut et mobilia bona. Non enim erat statutus numerus domorum civitatis, sicut erat certa mensura possessionis, ad quam non addebatur, poterat autem aliquid addi ad numerum domorum civitatis. Domus vero quae non erant in urbe, sed in villa muros non habente, in perpetuum vendi non poterant, quia huiusmodi domus non construuntur nisi ad cultum et ad custodiam possessionum; et ideo lex congrue statuit idem ius circa utrumque.

AD QUARTUM dicendum quod, sicut dictum est, intentio legis erat assuefacere homines suis praeceptis ad hoc quod sibi invicem de facili in necessitatibus subvenirent, quia hoc maxime est amicitiae fomentum. Et hanc quidem facilitatem subveniendi non solum statuit in his quae gratis et absolute donantur, sed etiam in his quae mutuo conceduntur, quia huiusmodi subventio frequentior est, et pluribus necessaria. Huiusmodi autem subventionis facilitatem multipliciter instituit. Primo quidem, ut faciles se praeberent ad mutuum exhibendum, nec ab hoc retraherentur anno remissionis appropinquante, ut habetur Deut. XV. Secundo, ne eum

cause a disturbance of the peace: for among well-behaved people, the taking of a little does not disturb the peace; in fact, it rather strengthens friendship and accustoms men to give things to one another.

REPLY OBJ. 2: The Law did not prescribe that women should succeed to their father's estate except in default of male issue: failing which it was necessary that succession should be granted to the female line in order to comfort the father, who would have been sad to think that his estate would pass to strangers. Nevertheless the Law observed due caution in the matter, by providing that those women who succeeded to their father's estate, should marry within their own tribe, in order to avoid confusion of tribal possessions, as stated in Num. 36:7,8.

REPLY OBJ. 3: As the Philosopher says (*Polit.* ii, 4), the regulation of possessions conduces much to the preservation of a state or nation. Consequently, as he himself observes, it was forbidden by the law in some of the heathen states, *that anyone should sell his possessions, except to avoid a manifest loss.* For if possessions were to be sold indiscriminately, they might happen to come into the hands of a few: so that it might become necessary for a state or country to become void of inhabitants. Hence the Old Law, in order to remove this danger, ordered things in such a way that while provision was made for men's needs, by allowing the sale of possessions to avail for a certain period, at the same time the said danger was removed, by prescribing the return of those possessions after that period had elapsed. The reason for this law was to prevent confusion of possessions, and to ensure the continuance of a definite distinction among the tribes.

But as the town houses were not allotted to distinct estates, therefore the Law allowed them to be sold in perpetuity, like movable goods. Because the number of houses in a town was not fixed, whereas there was a fixed limit to the amount of estates, which could not be exceeded, while the number of houses in a town could be increased. On the other hand, houses situated not in a town, but *in a village that hath no walls*, could not be sold in perpetuity: because such houses are built merely with a view to the cultivation and care of possessions; wherefore the Law rightly made the same prescription in regard to both (Lev 25).

REPLY OBJ. 4: As stated above (ad 1), the purpose of the Law was to accustom men to its precepts, so as to be ready to come to one another's assistance: because this is a very great incentive to friendship. The Law granted these facilities for helping others in the matter not only of gratuitous and absolute donations, but also of mutual transfers: because the latter kind of succor is more frequent and benefits the greater number: and it granted facilities for this purpose in many ways. First of all by prescribing that men should be ready to lend, and that they should not be less inclined to do so as the year of remission drew nigh, as stated in Dt. 15:7, seqq. Second, by forbidding them to burden a

cui mutuum concederent, gravarent vel usuris, vel etiam aliqua pignora omnino vitae necessaria accipiendo, et si accepta fuerint, quod statim restituerentur. Dicitur enim Deut. XXIII, *non faeneraberis fratri tuo ad usuram*; et XXIV, *non accipies loco pignoris inferiorem et superiorem molam, quia animam suam apposuit tibi*; et Exod. XXII dicitur, *si pignus a proximo tuo acceperis vestimentum, ante solis occasum reddes ei*. Tertio, ut non importune exigerent. Unde dicitur Exod. XXII, *si pecuniam mutuam dederis populo meo pauperi qui habitat tecum, non urgebis eum quasi exactor*. Et propter hoc etiam mandatur Deut. XXIV, *cum repetes a proximo tuo rem aliquam quam debet tibi, non ingredieris in domum eius ut pignus auferas; sed stabis foris, et ille tibi proferet quod habuerit*, tum quia domus est tutissimum uniuscuiusque receptaculum, unde molestum homini est ut in domo sua invadatur; tum etiam quia non concedit creditori ut accipiat pignus quod voluerit, sed magis debitori ut det quo minus indiguerit. Quarto, instituit quod in septimo anno debita penitus remitterentur. Probabile enim erat ut illi qui commode reddere possent, ante septimum annum redderent, et gratis mutuantem non defraudarent. Si autem omnino impotentes essent, eadem ratione eis erat debitum remittendum ex dilectione, qua etiam erat eis de novo dandum propter indigentiam.

Circa animalia vero mutuata haec lex statuit, ut propter negligentiam eius cui mutuata sunt, si in ipsius absentia moriantur vel debilitentur, reddere ea compellatur. Si vero eo praesente et diligenter custodiente, mortua fuerint vel debilitata, non cogebatur restituere, et maxime si erant mercede conducta, quia ita etiam potuissent mori et debilitari apud mutuantem; et ita, si conservationem animalis consequeretur, iam aliquod lucrum reportaret ex mutuo, et non esset gratuitum mutuum. Et maxime hoc observandum erat quando animalia erant mercede conducta, quia tunc habebat certum pretium pro usu animalium; unde nihil accrescere debebat per restitutionem animalium, nisi propter negligentiam custodientis. Si autem non essent mercede conducta, potuisset habere aliquam aequitatem ut saltem tantum restitueret quantum usus animalis mortui vel debilitati conduci potuisset.

AD QUINTUM dicendum quod haec differentia est inter mutuum et depositum, quia mutuum traditur in utilitatem eius cui traditur; sed depositum traditur in utilitatem deponentis. Et ideo magis arctabatur aliquis in aliquibus casibus ad restituendum mutuum, quam ad

man to whom they might grant a loan, either by exacting usury, or by accepting necessities of life in security; and by prescribing that when this had been done they should be restored at once. For it is written (Deut 23:19): *Thou shalt not lend to thy brother money to usury*: and (Deut 24:6): *Thou shalt not take the nether nor the upper millstone to pledge; for he hath pledged his life to thee*: and (Exod 22:26): *If thou take of thy neighbor a garment in pledge, thou shalt give it him again before sunset*. Third, by forbidding them to be importunate in exacting payment. Hence it is written (Exod 22:25): *If thou lend money to any of my people that is poor that dwelleth with thee, thou shalt not be hard upon them as an extortioner*. For this reason, too, it is enacted (Deut 24:10,11): *When thou shalt demand of thy neighbor anything that he oweth thee, thou shalt not go into his house to take away a pledge, but thou shalt stand without, and he shall bring out to thee what he hath*: both because a man's house is his surest refuge, wherefore it is offensive to a man to be set upon in his own house; and because the Law does not allow the creditor to take away whatever he likes in security, but rather permits the debtor to give what he needs least. Fourth, the Law prescribed that debts should cease together after the lapse of seven years. For it was probable that those who could conveniently pay their debts, would do so before the seventh year, and would not defraud the lender without cause. But if they were altogether insolvent, there was the same reason for remitting the debt from love for them, as there was for renewing the loan on account of their need.

As regards animals granted in loan, the Law enacted that if, through the neglect of the person to whom they were lent, they perished or deteriorated in his absence, he was bound to make restitution. But if they perished or deteriorated while he was present and taking proper care of them, he was not bound to make restitution, especially if they were hired for a consideration: because they might have died or deteriorated in the same way if they had remained in possession of the lender, so that if the animal had been saved through being lent, the lender would have gained something by the loan which would no longer have been gratuitous. And especially was this to be observed when animals were hired for a consideration: because then the owner received a certain price for the use of the animals; wherefore he had no right to any profit, by receiving indemnity for the animal, unless the person who had charge of it were negligent. In the case, however, of animals not hired for a consideration, equity demanded that he should receive something by way of restitution at least to the value of the hire of the animal that had perished or deteriorated.

REPLY OBJ. 5: The difference between a loan and a deposit is that a loan is in respect of goods transferred for the use of the person to whom they are transferred, whereas a deposit is for the benefit of the depositor. Hence in certain cases there was a stricter obligation of returning a loan than

restituendum depositum. Depositum enim perdi poterat dupliciter. Uno modo, ex causa inevitabili, vel naturali, puta si esset mortuum vel debilitatum animal depositum; vel extrinseca, puta si esset captum ab hostibus, vel si esset comestum a bestia; in quo tamen casu tenebatur deferre ad dominum animalis id quod de animali occiso supererat. In aliis autem praedictis casibus nihil reddere tenebatur, sed solum, ad expurgandam suspicionem fraudis, tenebatur iuramentum praestare. Alio modo poterat perdi ex causa evitabili, puta per furtum. Et tunc, propter negligentiam custodis, reddere tenebatur. Sed, sicut dictum est, ille qui mutuo accipiebat animal, tenebatur reddere, etiam si debilitatum aut mortuum fuisset in eius absentia. De minori enim negligentia tenebatur quam depositarius, qui non tenebatur nisi de furto.

AD SEXTUM dicendum quod mercenarii qui locant operas suas, pauperes sunt, de laboribus suis victum quaerentes quotidianum, et ideo lex provide ordinavit ut statim eis merces solveretur, ne victus eis deficeret. Sed illi qui locant alias res, divites esse consueverunt, nec ita indigent locationis pretio ad suum victum quotidianum. Et ideo non est eadem ratio in utroque.

AD SEPTIMUM dicendum quod iudices ad hoc inter homines constituuntur, quod determinent quod ambiguum inter homines circa iustitiam esse potest. Dupliciter autem aliquid potest esse ambiguum. Uno modo, apud simplices. Et ad hoc dubium tollendum, mandatur Deut. XVI, ut *iudices et magistri constituerentur per singulas tribus, ut iudicarent populum iusto iudicio.* Alio modo contingit aliquid esse dubium etiam apud peritos. Et ideo ad hoc dubium tollendum, constituit lex ut omnes recurrerent ad locum principalem a Deo electum, in quo et summus sacerdos esset, qui determinaret dubia circa caeremonias divini cultus; et summus iudex populi, qui determinaret quae pertinent ad iudicia hominum, sicut etiam nunc per appellationem, vel per consultationem, causae ab inferioribus iudicibus ad superiores deferuntur. Unde dicitur Deut. XVII, *si difficile et ambiguum apud te iudicium perspexeris, et iudicum intra portas tuas videris verba variari; ascende ad locum quem elegerit dominus, veniesque ad sacerdotes levitici generis, et ad iudicem qui fuerit illo tempore.* Huiusmodi autem ambigua iudicia non frequenter emergebant. Unde ex hoc populus non gravabatur.

AD OCTAVUM dicendum quod in negotiis humanis non potest haberi probatio demonstrativa et infallibilis, sed sufficit aliqua coniecturalis probabilitas, secundum quam rhetor persuadet. Et ideo, licet sit possibile duos aut tres testes in mendacium convenire, non tamen est facile nec probabile quod conveniant; et ideo accipitur

of restoring goods held in deposit. Because the latter might be lost in two ways. First, unavoidably: i.e., either through a natural cause, for instance if an animal held in deposit were to die or depreciate in value; or through an extrinsic cause, for instance, if it were taken by an enemy, or devoured by a beast (in which case, however, a man was bound to restore to the owner what was left of the animal thus slain): whereas in the other cases mentioned above, he was not bound to make restitution; but only to take an oath in order to clear himself of suspicion. Second, the goods deposited might be lost through an avoidable cause, for instance by theft: and then the depositary was bound to restitution on account of his neglect. But, as stated above (ad 4), he who held an animal on loan, was bound to restitution, even if he were absent when it depreciated or died: because he was held responsible for less negligence than a depositary, who was only held responsible in case of theft.

REPLY OBJ. 6: Workmen who offer their labor for hire, are poor men who toil for their daily bread: and therefore the Law commanded wisely that they should be paid at once, lest they should lack food. But they who offer other commodities for hire, are wont to be rich: nor are they in such need of their price in order to gain a livelihood: and consequently the comparison does not hold.

REPLY OBJ. 7: The purpose for which judges are appointed among men, is that they may decide doubtful points in matters of justice. Now a matter may be doubtful in two ways. First, among simple-minded people: and in order to remove doubts of this kind, it was prescribed (Deut 16:18) that *judges and magistrates* should be appointed in each tribe, *to judge the people with just judgment.* Second, a matter may be doubtful even among experts: and therefore, in order to remove doubts of this kind, the Law prescribed that all should foregather in some chief place chosen by God, where there would be both the high-priest, who would decide doubtful matters relating to the ceremonies of divine worship; and the chief judge of the people, who would decide matters relating to the judgments of men: just as even now cases are taken from a lower to a higher court either by appeal or by consultation. Hence it is written (Deut 17:8,9): *If thou perceive that there be among you a hard and doubtful matter in judgment . . . and thou see that the words of the judges within thy gates do vary; arise and go up to the place, which the Lord thy God shall choose; and thou shalt come to the priests of the Levitical race, and to the judge that shall be at that time.* But such like doubtful matters did not often occur for judgment: wherefore the people were not burdened on this account.

REPLY OBJ. 8: In the business affairs of men, there is no such thing as demonstrative and infallible proof, and we must be content with a certain conjectural probability, such as that which an orator employs to persuade. Consequently, although it is quite possible for two or three witnesses to agree to a falsehood, yet it is neither easy nor probable

eorum testimonium tanquam verum; et praecipue si in suo testimonio non vacillent, vel alias suspecti non fuerint. Et ad hoc etiam quod non de facili a veritate testes declinarent, instituit lex ut testes diligentissime examinarentur, et graviter punirentur qui invenirentur mendaces, ut habetur Deut. XIX.

Fuit tamen aliqua ratio huiusmodi numeri determinandi, ad significandam infallibilem veritatem personarum divinarum, quae quandoque numerantur duae, quia Spiritus Sanctus est nexus duorum, quandoque exprimuntur tres; ut Augustinus dicit, super illud Ioan. VIII, *in lege vestra scriptum est quia duorum hominum testimonium verum est.*

AD NONUM dicendum quod non solum propter gravitatem culpae, sed etiam propter alias causas gravis poena infligitur. Primo quidem, propter quantitatem peccati, quia maiori peccato, ceteris paribus, gravior poena debetur. Secundo, propter peccati consuetudinem, quia a peccatis consuetis non faciliter homines abstrahuntur nisi per graves poenas. Tertio, propter multam concupiscentiam vel delectationem in peccato, ab his enim non de facili homines abstrahuntur nisi per graves poenas. Quarto, propter facilitatem committendi peccatum, et latendi in ipso, huiusmodi enim peccata, quando manifestantur, sunt magis punienda, ad terrorem aliorum.

Circa ipsam etiam quantitatem peccati quadruplex gradus est attendendus, etiam circa unum et idem factum. Quorum primus est quando involuntarius peccatum committit. Tunc enim, si omnino est involuntarius, totaliter excusatur a poena, dicitur enim Deut. XXII, quod puella quae opprimitur in agro, *non est rea mortis, quia clamavit, et nullus affuit qui liberaret eam.* Si vero aliquo modo fuerit voluntarius, sed tamen ex infirmitate peccat, puta cum quis peccat ex passione, minuitur peccatum, et poena, secundum veritatem iudicii, diminui debet; nisi forte, propter communem utilitatem, poena aggravetur, ad abstrahendum homines ab huiusmodi peccatis, sicut dictum est. Secundus gradus est quando quis per ignorantiam peccavit. Et tunc aliquo modo reus reputabatur, propter negligentiam addiscendi; sed tamen non puniebatur per iudices, sed expiabat peccatum suum per sacrificia. Unde dicitur Levit. IV, *anima quae peccaverit per ignorantiam,* et cetera. Sed hoc intelligendum est de ignorantia facti, non autem de ignorantia praecepti divini, quod omnes scire tenebantur. Tertius gradus est quando aliquis ex superbia peccabat, idest ex certa electione vel ex certa malitia. Et tunc puniebatur secundum quantitatem delicti. Quartus autem gradus est quando peccabat per proterviam et pertinaciam. Et tunc, quasi rebellis et destructor ordinationis legis, omnino occidendus erat.

that they succeed in so doing: wherefore their testimony is taken as being true, especially if they do not waver in giving it, or are not otherwise suspect. Moreover, in order that witnesses might not easily depart from the truth, the Law commanded that they should be most carefully examined, and that those who were found untruthful should be severely punished, as stated in Dt. 19:16, seqq.

There was, however, a reason for fixing on this particular number, in token of the unerring truth of the Divine Persons, Who are sometimes mentioned as two, because the Holy Spirit is the bond of the other two Persons; and sometimes as three: as Augustine observes on Jn. 8:17: *In your law it is written that the testimony of two men is true.*

REPLY OBJ. 9: A severe punishment is inflicted not only on account of the gravity of a fault, but also for other reasons. First, on account of the greatness of the sin, because a greater sin, other things being equal, deserves a greater punishment. Second, on account of a habitual sin, since men are not easily cured of habitual sin except by severe punishments. Third, on account of a great desire for or a great pleasure in the sin: for men are not easily deterred from such sins unless they be severely punished. Fourth, on account of the facility of committing a sin and of concealing it: for such like sins, when discovered, should be more severely punished in order to deter others from committing them.

Again, with regard to the greatness of a sin, four degrees may be observed, even in respect of one single deed. The first is when a sin is committed unwillingly; because then, if the sin be altogether involuntary, man is altogether excused from punishment; for it is written (Deut 22:25, seqq.) that a damsel who suffers violence in a field is not guilty of death, because *she cried, and there was no man to help her.* But if a man sinned in any way voluntarily, and yet through weakness, as for instance when a man sins from passion, the sin is diminished: and the punishment, according to true judgment, should be diminished also; unless perchance the common weal requires that the sin be severely punished in order to deter others from committing such sins, as stated above. The second degree is when a man sins through ignorance: and then he was held to be guilty to a certain extent, on account of his negligence in acquiring knowledge: yet he was not punished by the judges but expiated his sin by sacrifices. Hence it is written (Lev 4:2): *The soul that sinneth through ignorance,* etc. This is, however, to be taken as applying to ignorance of fact; and not to ignorance of the Divine precept, which all were bound to know. The third degree was when a man sinned from pride, i.e., through deliberate choice or malice: and then he was punished according to the greatness of the sin. The fourth degree was when a man sinned from stubbornness or obstinacy: and then he was to be utterly cut off as a rebel and a destroyer of the commandment of the Law.

Secundum hoc, dicendum est quod in poena furti considerabatur secundum legem id quod frequenter accidere poterat. Et ideo pro furto aliarum rerum, quae de facili custodiri possunt a furibus, non reddebat fur nisi duplum. Oves autem non de facili possunt custodiri a furto, quia pascuntur in agris, et ideo frequentius contingebat quod oves furto subtraherentur. Unde lex maiorem poenam apposuit, ut scilicet quatuor oves pro una ove redderentur. Adhuc autem boves difficilius custodiuntur, quia habentur in agris, et non ita pascuntur gregatim sicut oves. Et ideo adhuc hic maiorem poenam apposuit, ut scilicet quinque boves pro uno bove redderentur. Et hoc dico, nisi forte idem animal inventum fuerit vivens apud eum, quia tunc solum duplum restituebat, sicut et in ceteris furtis; poterat enim haberi praesumptio quod cogitaret restituere, ex quo vivum servasset. Vel potest dici, secundum Glossam, quod *bos habet quinque utilitates, quia immolatur, arat, pascit carnibus, lactat, et corium etiam diversis usibus ministrat*, et ideo pro uno bove quinque boves reddebantur. Ovis autem habet quatuor utilitates, quia immolatur, pascit, lac dat, et lanam ministrat. Filius autem contumax, non quia comedebat et bibebat, occidebatur, sed propter contumaciam et rebellionem, quae semper morte puniebatur, ut dictum est. Ille vero qui colligebat ligna in sabbato, lapidatus fuit tanquam legis violator, quae sabbatum observari praecipiebat in commemorationem fidei novitatis mundi, sicut supra dictum est. Unde occisus fuit tanquam infidelis.

AD DECIMUM dicendum quod lex vetus poenam mortis inflixit in gravioribus criminibus, scilicet in his quae contra Deum peccantur, et in homicidio, et in furto hominum, et in irreverentia ad parentes, et in adulterio, et in incestibus. In furto autem aliarum rerum adhibuit poenam damni. In percussuris autem et mutilationibus induxit poenam talionis; et similiter in peccato falsi testimonii. In aliis autem minoribus culpis induxit poenam flagellationis vel ignominiae.

Poenam autem servitutis induxit in duobus casibus. In uno quidem, quando, septimo anno remissionis, ille qui erat servus, nolebat beneficio legis uti ut liber exiret. Unde pro poena ei infligebatur ut in perpetuum servus remaneret. Secundo, infligebatur furi, quando non habebat quod posset restituere, sicut habetur Exod. XXII.

Poenam autem exilii universaliter lex non statuit. Quia in solo populo illo Deus colebatur, omnibus aliis populis per idololatriam corruptis, unde si quis a populo illo universaliter exclusus esset, daretur ei occasio idololatriae. Et ideo I Reg. XXVI dicitur quod David dixit ad Saul, *maledicti sunt qui eiecerunt me hodie, ut non habitem in hereditate domini, dicentes, vade, servi diis alienis.*

Accordingly we must say that, in appointing the punishment for theft, the Law considered what would be likely to happen most frequently (Exod 22:1–9): wherefore, as regards theft of other things which can easily be safeguarded from a thief, the thief restored only twice their value. But sheep cannot be easily safeguarded from a thief, because they graze in the fields: wherefore it happened more frequently that sheep were stolen in the fields. Consequently the Law inflicted a heavier penalty, by ordering four sheep to be restored for the theft of one. As to cattle, they were yet more difficult to safeguard, because they are kept in the fields, and do not graze in flocks as sheep do; wherefore a yet more heavy penalty was inflicted in their regard, so that five oxen were to be restored for one ox. And this I say, unless perchance the animal itself were discovered in the thief's possession: because in that case he had to restore only twice the number, as in the case of other thefts: for there was reason to presume that he intended to restore the animal, since he kept it alive. Again, we might say, according to a gloss, that *a cow is useful in five ways: it may be used for sacrifice, for ploughing, for food, for milk, and its hide is employed for various purposes*: and therefore for one cow five had to be restored. But the sheep was useful in four ways: *for sacrifice, for meat, for milk, and for its wool*. The unruly son was slain, not because he ate and drank: but on account of his stubbornness and rebellion, which was always punished by death, as stated above. As to the man who gathered sticks on the sabbath, he was stoned as a breaker of the Law, which commanded the sabbath to be observed, to testify the belief in the newness of the world, as stated above (Q100, A5): wherefore he was slain as an unbeliever.

REPLY OBJ. 10: The Old Law inflicted the death penalty for the more grievous crimes, viz., for those which are committed against God, and for murder, for stealing a man, irreverence towards one's parents, adultery and incest. In the case of thief of other things it inflicted punishment by indemnification: while in the case of blows and mutilation it authorized punishment by retaliation; and likewise for the sin of bearing false witness. In other faults of less degree it prescribed the punishment of stripes or of public disgrace.

The punishment of slavery was prescribed by the Law in two cases. First, in the case of a slave who was unwilling to avail himself of the privilege granted by the Law, whereby he was free to depart in the seventh year of remission: wherefore he was punished by remaining a slave for ever. Second, in the case of a thief, who had not wherewith to make restitution, as stated in Ex. 22:3.

The punishment of absolute exile was not prescribed by the Law: because God was worshipped by that people alone, whereas all other nations were given to idolatry: wherefore if any man were exiled from that people absolutely, he would be in danger of falling into idolatry. For this reason it is related (1 Kgs 26:19) that David said to Saul: *They are cursed in the sight of the Lord, who have cast me*

Erat tamen aliquod particulare exilium. Dicitur enim Deut. XIX quod *qui percusserit proximum suum nesciens, et qui nullum contra ipsum habuisse odium comprobatur,* ad unam urbium refugii confugiebat, et ibi manebat usque ad mortem summi sacerdotis. Tunc enim licebat ei redire ad domum suam, quia in universali damno populi consueverunt particulares irae sedari, et ita proximi defuncti non sic proni erant ad eius occisionem.

AD UNDECIMUM dicendum quod animalia bruta mandabantur occidi, non propter aliquam ipsorum culpam; sed in poenam dominorum, qui talia animalia non custodierant ab huiusmodi peccatis. Et ideo magis puniebatur dominus si bos cornupeta fuerat ab heri et nudiustertius, in quo casu poterat occurri periculo; quam si subito cornupeta efficeretur. Vel occidebantur animalia in detestationem peccati; et ne ex eorum aspectu aliquis horror hominibus incuteretur.

AD DUODECIMUM dicendum quod ratio litteralis illius mandati fuit, ut Rabbi Moyses dicit, quia frequenter interfector est de civitate propinquiori. Unde occisio vitulae fiebat ad explorandum homicidium occultum. Quod quidem fiebat per tria. Quorum unum est quod seniores civitatis iurabant nihil se praetermisisse in custodia viarum. Aliud est quia ille cuius erat vitula damnificabatur in occisione animalis, et si prius manifestaretur homicidium, animal non occideretur. Tertium est quia locus in quo occidebatur vitula, remanebat incultus. Et ideo, ad evitandum utrumque damnum, homines civitatis de facili manifestarent homicidam, si scirent, et raro poterat esse quin aliqua verba vel iudicia super hoc facta essent. Vel hoc fiebat ad terrorem, in detestationem homicidii. Per occisionem enim vitulae, quae est animal utile et fortitudine plenum, praecipue antequam laboret sub iugo, significabatur quod quicumque homicidium fecisset, quamvis esset utilis et fortis, occidendus erat; et morte crudeli, quod cervicis concisio significabat; et quod tanquam vilis et abiectus a consortio hominum excludendus erat, quod significabatur per hoc quod vitula occisa in loco aspero et inculto relinquebatur, in putredinem convertenda.

Mystice autem per vitulam de armento significatur caro Christi; quae non traxit iugum, quia non fecit peccatum; nec terram scidit vomere, idest seditionis maculam non admisit. Per hoc autem quod in valle inculta occidebatur, significabatur despecta mors Christi; per quam purgantur omnia peccata, et Diabolus esse homicidii auctor ostenditur.

out this day, that I should not dwell in the inheritance of the Lord, saying: Go, serve strange gods.* There was, however, a restricted sort of exile: for it is written in Dt. 19:4 that *he that striketh his neighbor ignorantly, and is proved to have had no hatred against him, shall flee to one of the cities* of refuge and *abide there until the death of the high-priest.* For then it became lawful for him to return home, because when the whole people thus suffered a loss they forgot their private quarrels, so that the next of kin of the slain were not so eager to kill the slayer.

REPLY OBJ. 11: Dumb animals were ordered to be slain, not on account of any fault of theirs; but as a punishment to their owners, who had not safeguarded their beasts from these offenses. Hence the owner was more severely punished if his ox had butted anyone *yesterday or the day before* (in which case steps might have been taken to butting suddenly). Or again, the animal was slain in detestation of the sin; and lest men should be horrified at the sight thereof.

REPLY OBJ. 12: The literal reason for this commandment, as Rabbi Moses declares (*Doct. Perplex.* iii), was because the slayer was frequently from the nearest city: wherefore the slaying of the calf was a means of investigating the hidden murder. This was brought about in three ways. In the first place the elders of the city swore that they had taken every measure for safeguarding the roads. Second, the owner of the heifer was indemnified for the slaying of his beast, and if the murder was previously discovered, the beast was not slain. Third, the place, where the heifer was slain, remained uncultivated. Wherefore, in order to avoid this twofold loss, the men of the city would readily make known the murderer, if they knew who he was: and it would seldom happen but that some word or sign would escape about the matter. Or again, this was done in order to frighten people, in detestation of murder. Because the slaying of a heifer, which is a useful animal and full of strength, especially before it has been put under the yoke, signified that whoever committed murder, however useful and strong he might be, was to forfeit his life; and that, by a cruel death, which was implied by the striking off of its head; and that the murderer, as vile and abject, was to be cut off from the fellowship of men, which was betokened by the fact that the heifer after being slain was left to rot in a rough and uncultivated place.

Mystically, the heifer taken from the herd signifies the flesh of Christ; which had not drawn a yoke, since it had done no sin; nor did it plough the ground, i.e., it never knew the stain of revolt. The fact of the heifer being killed in an uncultivated valley signified the despised death of Christ, whereby all sins are washed away, and the devil is shown to be the arch-murderer.

Article 3

Whether the Judicial Precepts Regarding Foreigners Were Framed in a Suitable Manner?

AD TERTIUM SIC PROCEDITUR. Videtur quod iudicialia praecepta non sint convenienter tradita quantum ad extraneos. Dicit enim Petrus, Act. X, *in veritate comperi quoniam non est acceptor personarum Deus; sed in omni gente qui timet Deum et operatur iustitiam, acceptus est illi.* Sed illi qui sunt Deo accepti, non sunt ab Ecclesia Dei excludendi. Inconvenienter igitur mandatur Deut. XXIII, quod *Ammonites et Moabites, etiam post decimam generationem, non intrabunt Ecclesiam domini in aeternum*; e contrario autem ibidem praecipitur de quibusdam gentibus, *non abominaberis Idumaeum, quia frater tuus est; nec Aegyptium, quia advena fuisti in terra eius.*

PRAETEREA, ea quae non sunt in potestate nostra, non merentur aliquam poenam. Sed quod homo sit eunuchus, vel ex scorto natus, non est in potestate eius. Ergo inconvenienter mandatur Deut. XXIII, quod *eunuchus, et ex scorto natus, non ingrediatur Ecclesiam domini.*

PRAETEREA, lex vetus misericorditer mandavit ut advenae non affligantur, dicitur enim Exod. XXII, *advenam non contristabis, neque affliges eum, advenae enim et ipsi fuistis in terra Aegypti*; et XXIII, *peregrino molestus non eris, scitis enim advenarum animas, quia et ipsi peregrini fuistis in terra Aegypti.* Sed ad afflictionem alicuius pertinet quod usuris opprimatur. Inconvenienter igitur lex permisit, Deut. XXIII, ut alienis ad usuram pecuniam mutuarent.

PRAETEREA, multo magis appropinquant nobis homines quam arbores. Sed his quae sunt nobis magis propinqua, magis debemus affectum et effectum dilectionis impendere; secundum illud Eccli. XIII, *omne animal diligit simile sibi, sic et omnis homo proximum sibi.* Inconvenienter igitur dominus, Deut. XX, mandavit quod de civitatibus hostium captis omnes interficerent, et tamen arbores fructiferas non succiderent.

PRAETEREA, bonum commune secundum virtutem est bono privato praeferendum ab unoquoque. Sed in bello quod committitur contra hostes, quaeritur bonum commune. Inconvenienter igitur mandatur Deut. XX, quod, imminente proelio, aliqui domum remittantur, puta qui aedificavit domum novam, qui plantavit vineam, vel qui despondit uxorem.

PRAETEREA, ex culpa non debet quis commodum reportare. Sed quod homo sit formidolosus et corde pavido, culpabile est, contrariatur enim virtuti fortitudinis. Inconvenienter igitur a labore proelii excusabantur formidolosi et pavidum cor habentes.

OBJECTION 1: It would seem that the judicial precepts regarding foreigners were not suitably framed. For Peter said (Acts 10:34,35): *In very deed I perceive that God is not a respecter of persons, but in every nation, he that feareth Him and worketh justice is acceptable to Him.* But those who are acceptable to God should not be excluded from the Church of God. Therefore it is unsuitably commanded (Deut 23:3) that *the Ammonite and the Moabite, even after the tenth generation, shall not enter into the church of the Lord for ever*: whereas, on the other hand, it is prescribed (Deut 23:7) to be observed with regard to certain other nations: *Thou shalt not abhor the Edomite, because he is thy brother; nor the Egyptian because thou wast a stranger in his land.*

OBJ. 2: Further, we do not deserve to be punished for those things which are not in our power. But it is not in man's power to be an eunuch, or born of a prostitute. Therefore it is unsuitably commanded (Deut 23:1,2) that *an eunuch and one born of a prostitute shalt not enter into the church of the Lord.*

OBJ. 3: Further, the Old Law mercifully forbade strangers to be molested: for it is written (Exod 22:21): *Thou shalt not molest a stranger, nor afflict him; for yourselves also were strangers in the land of Egypt*: and (Exod 23:9): *Thou shalt not molest a stranger, for you know the hearts of strangers, for you also were strangers in the land of Egypt.* But it is an affliction to be burdened with usury. Therefore the Law unsuitably permitted them (Deut 23:19,20) to lend money to the stranger for usury.

OBJ. 4: Further, men are much more akin to us than trees. But we should show greater care and love for these things that are nearest to us, according to Ecclus. 13:19: *Every beast loveth its like: so also every man him that is nearest to himself.* Therefore the Lord unsuitably commanded (Deut 20:13–19) that all the inhabitants of a captured hostile city were to be slain, but that the fruit-trees should not be cut down.

OBJ. 5: Further, every one should prefer the common good of virtue to the good of the individual. But the common good is sought in a war which men fight against their enemies. Therefore it is unsuitably commanded (Deut 20:5–7) that certain men should be sent home, for instance a man that had built a new house, or who had planted a vineyard, or who had married a wife.

OBJ. 6: Further, no man should profit by his own fault. But it is a man's fault if he be timid or faint-hearted: since this is contrary to the virtue of fortitude. Therefore the timid and faint-hearted are unfittingly excused from the toil of battle (Deut 20:8).

SED CONTRA est quod sapientia divina dicit, Prov. VIII, *recti sunt omnes sermones mei, non est in eis pravum quid neque perversum.*

RESPONDEO dicendum quod cum extraneis potest esse hominum conversatio dupliciter, uno modo, pacifice; alio modo, hostiliter. Et quantum ad utrumque modum ordinandum, lex convenientia praecepta continebat. Tripliciter enim offerebatur Iudaeis occasio ut cum extraneis pacifice communicarent. Primo quidem, quando extranei per terram eorum transitum faciebant quasi peregrini. Alio modo, quando in terram eorum adveniebant ad inhabitandum sicut advenae. Et quantum ad utrumque, lex misericordiae praecepta proposuit, nam Exod. XXII dicitur, *advenam non contristabis*; et XXIII dicitur, *peregrino molestus non eris.* Tertio vero, quando aliqui extranei totaliter in eorum consortium et ritum admitti volebant. Et in his quidam ordo attendebatur. Non enim statim recipiebantur quasi cives, sicut etiam apud quosdam gentilium statutum erat ut non reputarentur cives nisi qui ex avo, vel abavo, cives existerent, ut philosophus dicit, in III Polit. Et hoc ideo quia, si statim extranei advenientes reciperentur ad tractandum ea quae sunt populi, possent multa pericula contingere; dum extranei, non habentes adhuc amorem firmatum ad bonum publicum, aliqua contra populum attentarent. Et ideo lex statuit ut de quibusdam gentibus habentibus aliquam affinitatem ad Iudaeos, scilicet de Aegyptiis, apud quos nati fuerant et nutriti, et de Idumaeis, filiis Esau fratris Iacob, in tertia generatione reciperentur in consortium populi; quidam vero, quia hostiliter se ad eos habuerant, sicut Ammonitae et Moabitae, nunquam in consortium populi admitterentur; Amalecitae autem, qui magis eis fuerant adversati, et cum eis nullum cognationis habebant consortium, quasi hostes perpetui haberentur; dicitur enim Exod. XVII, *bellum Dei erit contra Amalec a generatione in generationem.*

Similiter etiam quantum ad hostilem communicationem cum extraneis, lex convenientia praecepta tradidit. Nam primo quidem, instituit ut bellum iuste iniretur, mandatur enim Deut. XX, quod quando accederent ad expugnandum civitatem, offerrent ei primum pacem. Secundo, instituit ut fortiter bellum susceptum exequerentur, habentes de Deo fiduciam. Et ad hoc melius observandum, instituit quod, imminente proelio, sacerdos eos confortaret, promittendo auxilium Dei. Tertio, mandavit ut impedimenta proelii removerentur, remittendo quosdam ad domum, qui possent impedimenta praestare. Quarto, instituit ut victoria moderate uterentur, parcendo mulieribus et parvulis, et etiam ligna fructifera regionis non incidendo.

AD PRIMUM ergo dicendum quod homines nullius gentis exclusit lex a cultu Dei et ab his quae pertinent

ON THE CONTRARY, Divine Wisdom declares (Prov 8:8): *All my words are just, there is nothing wicked nor perverse in them.*

I ANSWER THAT, Man's relations with foreigners are twofold: peaceful, and hostile: and in directing both kinds of relation the Law contained suitable precepts. For the Jews were offered three opportunities of peaceful relations with foreigners. First, when foreigners passed through their land as travelers. Second, when they came to dwell in their land as newcomers. And in both these respects the Law made kind provision in its precepts: for it is written (Exod 22:21): *Thou shalt not molest a stranger*; and again (Exod 22:9): *Thou shalt not molest a stranger.* Third, when any foreigners wished to be admitted entirely to their fellowship and mode of worship. With regard to these a certain order was observed. For they were not at once admitted to citizenship: just as it was law with some nations that no one was deemed a citizen except after two or three generations, as the Philosopher says (*Polit.* iii, 1). The reason for this was that if foreigners were allowed to meddle with the affairs of a nation as soon as they settled down in its midst, many dangers might occur, since the foreigners not yet having the common good firmly at heart might attempt something hurtful to the people. Hence it was that the Law prescribed in respect of certain nations that had close relations with the Jews (viz., the Egyptians among whom they were born and educated, and the Idumeans, the children of Esau, Jacob's brother), that they should be admitted to the fellowship of the people after the third generation; whereas others (with whom their relations had been hostile, such as the Ammonites and Moabites) were never to be admitted to citizenship; while the Amalekites, who were yet more hostile to them, and had no fellowship of kindred with them, were to be held as foes in perpetuity: for it is written (Exod 17:16): *The war of the Lord shall be against Amalec from generation to generation.*

In like manner with regard to hostile relations with foreigners, the Law contained suitable precepts. For, in the first place, it commanded that war should be declared for a just cause: thus it is commanded (Deut 20:10) that when they advanced to besiege a city, they should at first make an offer of peace. Second, it enjoined that when once they had entered on a war they should undauntedly persevere in it, putting their trust in God. And in order that they might be the more heedful of this command, it ordered that on the approach of battle the priest should hearten them by promising them God's aid. Third, it prescribed the removal of whatever might prove an obstacle to the fight, and that certain men, who might be in the way, should be sent home. Fourth, it enjoined that they should use moderation in pursuing the advantage of victory, by sparing women and children, and by not cutting down fruit-trees of that country.

REPLY OBJ. 1: The Law excluded the men of no nation from the worship of God and from things pertaining

ad animae salutem, dicitur enim Exod. XII, *si quis peregrinorum in vestram voluerit transire coloniam, et facere phase domini; circumcidetur prius omne masculinum eius, et tunc rite celebrabit, eritque simul sicut indigena terrae.* Sed in temporalibus, quantum ad ea quae pertinebant ad communitatem populi, non statim quilibet admittebatur, ratione supra dicta, sed quidam in tertia generatione, scilicet Aegyptii et Idumaei; alii vero perpetuo excludebantur, in detestationem culpae praeteritae, sicut Moabitae et Ammonitae et Amalecitae. Sicut enim punitur unus homo propter peccatum quod commisit, ut alii videntes timeant et peccare desistant; ita etiam propter aliquod peccatum gens vel civitas potest puniri, ut alii a simili peccato abstineant.

Poterat tamen dispensative aliquis in collegium populi admitti propter aliquem virtutis actum, sicut Iudith XIV dicitur quod Achior, dux filiorum Ammon, *appositus est ad populum Israel, et omnis successio generis eius.* Et similiter Ruth Moabitis, quae mulier virtutis erat. Licet possit dici quod illa prohibitio extendebatur ad viros, non ad mulieres, quibus non competit simpliciter esse cives.

Ad secundum dicendum quod, sicut philosophus dicit, in III Polit., dupliciter aliquis dicitur esse civis, uno modo, simpliciter; et alio modo, secundum quid. Simpliciter quidem civis est qui potest agere ea quae sunt civium, puta dare consilium vel iudicium in populo. Secundum quid autem civis dici potest quicumque civitatem inhabitat, etiam viles personae et pueri et senes, qui non sunt idonei ad hoc quod habeant potestatem in his quae pertinent ad commune. Ideo ergo spurii, propter vilitatem originis, excludebantur ab Ecclesia, idest a collegio populi, usque ad decimam generationem. Et similiter eunuchi, quibus non poterat competere honor qui patribus debebatur, et praecipue in populo Iudaeorum, in quo Dei cultus conservabatur per carnis generationem, nam etiam apud gentiles, qui multos filios genuerant, aliquo insigni honore donabantur, sicut philosophus dicit, in II Polit. Tamen quantum ad ea quae ad gratiam Dei pertinent, eunuchi ab aliis non separabantur, sicut nec advenae, ut dictum est, dicitur enim Isaiae LVI, *non dicat filius advenae qui adhaeret domino, dicens, separatione dividet me dominus a populo suo. Et non dicat eunuchus, ecce ego lignum aridum.*

Ad tertium dicendum quod accipere usuras ab alienis non erat secundum intentionem legis, sed ex quadam permissione, propter pronitatem Iudaeorum ad avaritiam; et ut magis pacifice se haberent ad extraneos, a quibus lucrabantur.

Ad quartum dicendum quod circa civitates hostium quaedam distinctio adhibebatur. Quaedam enim

to the welfare of the soul: for it is written (Exod 12:48): *If any stranger be willing to dwell among you, and to keep the Phase of the Lord; all his males shall first be circumcised, and then shall he celebrate it according to the manner, and he shall be as that which is born in the land.* But in temporal matters concerning the public life of the people, admission was not granted to everyone at once, for the reason given above: but to some, i.e., the Egyptians and Idumeans, in the third generation; while others were excluded in perpetuity, in detestation of their past offense, i.e., the peoples of Moab, Ammon, and Amalec. For just as one man is punished for a sin committed by him, in order that others seeing this may be deterred and refrain from sinning; so too may one nation or city be punished for a crime, that others may refrain from similar crimes.

Nevertheless it was possible by dispensation for a man to be admitted to citizenship on account of some act of virtue: thus it is related (Jdt 14:6) that Achior, the captain of the children of Ammon, *was joined to the people of Israel, with all the succession of his kindred.* The same applies to Ruth the Moabite who was *a virtuous woman* (Ruth 3:11): although it may be said that this prohibition regarded men and not women, who are not competent to be citizens absolutely speaking.

Reply Obj. 2: As the Philosopher says (*Polit.* iii, 3), a man is said to be a citizen in two ways: first, simply; second, in a restricted sense. A man is a citizen simply if he has all the rights of citizenship, for instance, the right of debating or voting in the popular assembly. On the other hand, any man may be called citizen, only in a restricted sense, if he dwells within the state, even common people or children or old men, who are not fit to enjoy power in matters pertaining to the common weal. For this reason bastards, by reason of their base origin, were excluded from the *ecclesia*, i.e., from the popular assembly, down to the tenth generation. The same applies to eunuchs, who were not competent to receive the honor due to a father, especially among the Jews, where the divine worship was continued through carnal generation: for even among the heathens, those who had many children were marked with special honor, as the Philosopher remarks (*Polit.* ii, 6). Nevertheless, in matters pertaining to the grace of God, eunuchs were not discriminated from others, as neither were strangers, as already stated: for it is written (Iss 56:3): *Let not the son of the stranger that adhereth to the Lord speak, saying: The Lord will divide and separate me from His people. And let not the eunuch say: Behold I am a dry tree.*

Reply Obj. 3: It was not the intention of the Law to sanction the acceptance of usury from strangers, but only to tolerate it on account of the proneness of the Jews to avarice; and in order to promote an amicable feeling towards those out of whom they made a profit.

Reply Obj. 4: A distinction was observed with regard to hostile cities. For some of them were far distant, and

erant remotae, non de numero illarum urbium quae eis erant repromissae, et in talibus urbibus expugnatis occidebantur masculi, qui pugnaverant contra populum Dei; mulieribus autem et infantibus parcebatur. Sed in civitatibus vicinis, quae erant eis repromissae omnes mandabantur interfici, propter iniquitates eorum priores, ad quas puniendas dominus populum Israel quasi divinae iustitiae executorem mittebat, dicitur enim Deut. IX, *quia illae egerunt impie, introeunte te deletae sunt.* Ligna autem fructifera mandabantur reservari propter utilitatem ipsius populi, cuius ditioni civitas et eius territorium erat subiiciendum.

AD QUINTUM dicendum quod novus aedificator domus, aut plantator vineae, vel desponsator uxoris, excludebatur a proelio propter duo. Primo quidem, quia ea quae homo de novo habet, vel statim paratus est ad habendum, magis solet amare, et per consequens eorum amissionem timere. Unde probabile erat quod ex tali amore magis mortem timerent, et sic minus fortes essent ad pugnandum. Secundo quia, sicut philosophus dicit, in II Physic., *infortunium videtur quando aliquis appropinquat ad aliquod bonum habendum, si postea impediatur ab illo.* Et ideo ne propinqui remanentes magis contristarentur de morte talium, qui bonis sibi paratis potiti non fuerunt; et etiam populus, considerans hoc, horreret; huiusmodi homines a mortis periculo sunt sequestrati per subtractionem a proelio.

AD SEXTUM dicendum quod timidi remittebantur ad domum, non ut ipsi ex hoc commodum consequerentur; sed ne populus ex eorum praesentia incommodum consequeretur, dum per eorum timorem et fugam etiam alii ad timendum et fugiendum provocarentur.

were not among those which had been promised to them. When they had taken these cities, they killed all the men who had fought against God's people; whereas the women and children were spared. But in the neighboring cities which had been promised to them, all were ordered to be slain, on account of their former crimes, to punish which God sent the Israelites as executor of Divine justice: for it is written (Deut 9:5) *because they have done wickedly, they are destroyed at thy coming in.* The fruit-trees were commanded to be left untouched, for the use of the people themselves, to whom the city with its territory was destined to be subjected.

REPLY OBJ. 5: The builder of a new house, the planter of a vineyard, the newly married husband, were excluded from fighting, for two reasons. First, because man is wont to give all his affection to those things which he has lately acquired, or is on the point of having, and consequently he is apt to dread the loss of these above other things. Wherefore it was likely enough that on account of this affection they would fear death all the more, and be so much the less brave in battle. Second, because, as the Philosopher says (*Phys.* ii, 5), *it is a misfortune for a man if he is prevented from obtaining something good when it is within his grasp.* And so lest the surviving relations should be the more grieved at the death of these men who had not entered into the possession of the good things prepared for them; and also lest the people should be horror-stricken at the sight of their misfortune: these men were taken away from the danger of death by being removed from the battle.

REPLY OBJ. 6: The timid were sent back home, not that they might be the gainers thereby; but lest the people might be the losers by their presence, since their timidity and flight might cause others to be afraid and run away.

Article 4

Whether the Old Law Set Forth Suitable Precepts about the Members of the Household?

AD QUARTUM SIC PROCEDITUR. Videtur quod inconvenienter lex vetus praecepta ediderit circa personas domesticas. Servus enim id quod est, domini est, ut philosophus dicit, in I Polit. Sed id quod est alicuius, perpetuo eius esse debet. Ergo inconvenienter lex mandavit Exod. XXI, quod servi septimo anno liberi abscederent.

PRAETEREA, sicut animal aliquod, ut asinus aut bos, est possessio domini, ita etiam servus. Sed de animalibus praecipitur Deut. XXII, quod restituantur dominis suis, si errare inveniantur. Inconvenienter ergo mandatur

OBJECTION 1: It would seem that the Old Law set forth unsuitable precepts about the members of the household. For a slave *is in every respect his master's property*, as the Philosopher states (*Polit.* i, 2). But that which is a man's property should be his always. Therefore it was unfitting for the Law to command (Exod 21:2) that slaves should *go out free* in the seventh year.

OBJ. 2: Further, a slave is his master's property, just as an animal, e.g., an ass or an ox. But it is commanded (Deut 22:1–3) with regard to animals, that they should be brought back to the owner if they be found going astray.

Deut. XXIII, *non tradas servum domino suo, qui ad te confugerit.*

PRAETEREA, lex divina debet magis ad misericordiam provocare quam etiam lex humana. Sed secundum leges humanas graviter puniuntur qui nimis aspere affligunt servos aut ancillas. Asperrima autem videtur esse afflictio ex qua sequitur mors. Inconvenienter igitur statuitur Exod. XXI, quod *qui percusserit servum suum vel ancillam virga, si uno die supervixerit, non subiacebit poenae, quia pecunia illius est.*

PRAETEREA, alius est principatus domini ad servum, et patris ad filium, ut dicitur in I et III Polit. Sed hoc ad principatum domini ad servum pertinet, ut aliquis servum vel ancillam vendere possit. Inconvenienter igitur lex permisit quod aliquis venderet filiam suam in famulam vel ancillam.

PRAETEREA, pater habet sui filii potestatem. Sed eius est punire excessus, qui habet potestatem super peccantem. Inconvenienter igitur mandatur Deut. XXI, quod pater ducat filium ad seniores civitatis puniendum.

PRAETEREA, dominus prohibuit, Deut. VII, ut cum alienigenis non sociarent coniugia; et coniuncta etiam separarentur, ut patet I Esdrae X. Inconvenienter igitur Deut. XXI conceditur eis ut captivas alienigenarum ducere possint uxores.

PRAETEREA, dominus in uxoribus ducendis quosdam consanguinitatis et affinitatis gradus praecepit esse vitandos, ut patet Lev. XVIII. Inconvenienter igitur mandatur Deut. XXV, quod si aliquis esset mortuus absque liberis, uxorem ipsius frater eius acciperet.

PRAETEREA, inter virum et uxorem, sicut est maxima familiaritas, ita debet esse firmissima fides. Sed hoc non potest esse, si matrimonium dissolubile fuerit. Inconvenienter igitur dominus permisit, Deut. XXIV, quod aliquis posset uxorem dimittere, scripto libello repudii; et quod etiam ulterius eam recuperare non posset.

PRAETEREA, sicut uxor potest frangere fidem marito, ita etiam servus domino, et filius patri. Sed ad investigandam iniuriam servi in dominum, vel filii in patrem, non est institutum in lege aliquod sacrificium. Superflue igitur videtur institui sacrificium zelotypiae ad investigandum uxoris adulterium, Num. V. Sic igitur inconvenienter videntur esse tradita in lege praecepta iudicialia circa personas domesticas.

SED CONTRA est quod dicitur in Psalmo XVIII, *iudicia domini vera, iustificata in semetipsa.*

RESPONDEO dicendum quod communio domesticarum personarum ad invicem, ut philosophus dicit, in I Polit., est secundum quotidianos actus qui ordinantur

Therefore it was unsuitably commanded (Deut 23:15): *Thou shalt not deliver to his master the servant that is fled to thee.*

OBJ. 3: Further, the Divine Law should encourage mercy more even than the human law. But according to human laws those who ill-treat their servants and maidservants are severely punished: and the worse treatment of all seems to be that which results in death. Therefore it is unfittingly commanded (Exod 21:20,21) that *he that striketh his bondman or bondwoman with a rod, and they die under his hands . . . if the party remain alive a day . . . he shall not be subject to the punishment, because it is his money.*

OBJ. 4: Further, the dominion of a master over his slave differs from that of the father over his son (*Polit.* i, 3). But the dominion of master over slave gives the former the right to sell his servant or maidservant. Therefore it was unfitting for the Law to allow a man to sell his daughter to be a servant or handmaid (Exod 21:7).

OBJ. 5: Further, a father has power over his son. But he who has power over the sinner has the right to punish him for his offenses. Therefore it is unfittingly commanded (Deut 21:18, seqq.) that a father should bring his son to the ancients of the city for punishment.

OBJ. 6: Further, the Lord forbade them (Deut 7:3, seqq.) to make marriages with strange nations; and commanded the dissolution of such as had been contracted (1 Esdras 10). Therefore it was unfitting to allow them to marry captive women from strange nations (Deut 21:10, seqq.).

OBJ. 7: Further, the Lord forbade them to marry within certain degrees of consanguinity and affinity, according to Lev. 18. Therefore it was unsuitably commanded (Deut 25:5) that if any man died without issue, his brother should marry his wife.

OBJ. 8: Further, as there is the greatest familiarity between man and wife, so should there be the staunchest fidelity. But this is impossible if the marriage bond can be sundered. Therefore it was unfitting for the Lord to allow (Deut 24:1–4) a man to put his wife away, by writing a bill of divorce; and besides, that he could not take her again to wife.

OBJ. 9: Further, just as a wife can be faithless to her husband, so can a slave be to his master, and a son to his father. But the Law did not command any sacrifice to be offered in order to investigate the injury done by a servant to his master, or by a son to his father. Therefore it seems to have been superfluous for the Law to prescribe the *sacrifice of jealousy* in order to investigate a wife's adultery (Num 5:12, seqq.). Consequently it seems that the Law put forth unsuitable judicial precepts about the members of the household.

ON THE CONTRARY, It is written (Ps 18:10): *The judgments of the Lord are true, justified in themselves.*

I ANSWER THAT, The mutual relations of the members of a household regard everyday actions directed to the necessities of life, as the Philosopher states (*Polit.* i, 1). Now

401

ad necessitatem vitae. Vita autem hominis conservatur dupliciter. Uno modo, quantum ad individuum, prout scilicet homo idem numero vivit, et ad talem vitae conservationem opitulantur homini exteriora bona, ex quibus homo habet victum et vestitum et alia huiusmodi necessaria vitae; in quibus administrandis indiget homo servis. Alio modo conservatur vita hominis secundum speciem per generationem, ad quam indiget homo uxore, ut ex ea generet filium. Sic igitur in domestica communione sunt tres combinationes, scilicet domini ad servum, viri ad uxorem, patris ad filium. Et quantum ad omnia ista lex vetus convenientia praecepta tradidit. Nam quantum ad servos, instituit ut modeste tractarentur et quantum ad labores, ne scilicet immoderatis laboribus affligerentur, unde Deut. V, dominus mandavit ut in die sabbati requiesceret servus et ancilla tua sicut et tu, et iterum quantum ad poenas infligendas, imposuit enim poenam mutilatoribus servorum ut dimitterent eos liberos, sicut habetur Exod. XXI. Et simile etiam statuit in ancilla quam in uxorem aliquis duxerit. Statuit etiam specialiter circa servos qui erant ex populo, ut septimo anno liberi egrederentur cum omnibus quae apportaverant, etiam vestimentis, ut habetur Exod. XXI. Mandatur etiam insuper Deut. XV, ut ei detur viaticum.

Circa uxores vero, statuitur in lege quantum ad uxores ducendas. Ut scilicet ducant uxores suae tribus, sicut habetur Num. ult., et hoc ideo, ne sortes tribuum confundantur. Et quod aliquis in uxorem ducat uxorem fratris defuncti sine liberis, ut habetur Deut. XXV, et hoc ideo, ut ille qui non potuit habere successores secundum carnis originem, saltem habeat per quandam adoptionem, et sic non totaliter memoria defuncti deleretur. Prohibuit etiam quasdam personas ne in coniugium ducerentur, scilicet alienigenas, propter periculum seductionis; et propinquas, propter reverentiam naturalem quae eis debetur. Statuit etiam qualiter uxores iam ductae tractari deberent. Ut scilicet non leviter infamarentur, unde mandatur puniri ille qui falso crimen imponit uxori, ut habetur Deut. XXII. Et quod etiam propter uxoris odium filius detrimentum non pateretur, ut habetur Deut. XXI. Et etiam quod, propter odium uxorem non affligeret, sed potius, scripto libello, eam dimitteret, ut patet Deut. XXIV. Et ut etiam maior dilectio inter coniuges a principio contrahatur, praecipitur quod, cum aliquis nuper

the preservation of man's life may be considered from two points of view. First, from the point of view of the individual, i.e., insofar as man preserves his individuality: and for the purpose of the preservation of life, considered from this standpoint, man has at his service external goods, by means of which he provides himself with food and clothing and other such necessaries of life: in the handling of which he has need of servants. Second man's life is preserved from the point of view of the species, by means of generation, for which purpose man needs a wife, that she may bear him children. Accordingly the mutual relations of the members of a household admit of a threefold combination: viz., those of master and servant, those of husband and wife, and those of father and son: and in respect of all these relationships the Old Law contained fitting precepts. Thus, with regard to servants, it commanded them to be treated with moderation—both as to their work, lest, to wit, they should be burdened with excessive labor, wherefore the Lord commanded (Deut 5:14) that on the Sabbath day *thy manservant and thy maidservant* should *rest even as thyself*—and also as to the infliction of punishment, for it ordered those who maimed their servants, to set them free (Exod 21:26,27). Similar provision was made in favor of a maidservant when married to anyone (Exod 21:7, seqq.). Moreover, with regard to those servants in particular who were taken from among the people, the Law prescribed that they should go out free in the seventh year taking whatever they brought with them, even their clothes (Exod 21:2, seqq.): and furthermore it was commanded (Deut 15:13) that they should be given provision for the journey.

With regard to wives the Law made certain prescriptions as to those who were to be taken in marriage: for instance, that they should marry a wife from their own tribe (Num 36:6): and this lest confusion should ensue in the property of various tribes. Also that a man should marry the wife of his deceased brother when the latter died without issue, as prescribed in Dt. 25:5,6: and this in order that he who could not have successors according to carnal origin, might at least have them by a kind of adoption, and that thus the deceased might not be entirely forgotten. It also forbade them to marry certain women; to wit, women of strange nations, through fear of their losing their faith; and those of their near kindred, on account of the natural respect due to them. Furthermore it prescribed in what way wives were to be treated after marriage. To wit, that they should not be slandered without grave reason: wherefore it ordered punishment to be inflicted on the man who falsely accused his wife of a crime (Deut 22:13, seqq.). Also that a man's hatred of his wife should not be detrimental to his son (Deut 21:15, seqq.). Again, that a man should not ill-use his

uxorem acceperit, nihil ei publicae necessitatis iniungatur, ut libere possit laetari cum uxore sua.

Circa filios autem, instituit ut patres eis disciplinam adhiberent, instruendo eos in fide, unde habetur Exod. XII, *cum dixerint vobis filii vestri, quae est ista religio? Dicetis eis, victima transitus domini est.* Et quod etiam instruerent eos in moribus, unde dicitur Deut. XXI, quod patres dicere debent, *monita nostra audire contemnit, commessationibus vacat et luxuriae atque conviviis.*

Ad primum ergo dicendum quod, quia filii Israel erant a domino de servitute liberati, et per hoc divinae servituti addicti, noluit dominus ut in perpetuum servi essent. Unde dicitur Lev. XXV, *si paupertate compulsus vendiderit se tibi frater tuus, non eum opprimes servitute famulorum, sed quasi mercenarius et colonus erit. Mei enim sunt servi, et ego eduxi eos de terra Aegypti, non veneant conditione servorum.* Et ideo, quia simpliciter servi non erant, sed secundum quid, finito tempore, dimittebantur liberi.

Ad secundum dicendum quod mandatum illud intelligitur de servo qui a domino quaeritur ad occidendum, vel ad aliquod peccati ministerium.

Ad tertium dicendum quod circa laesiones servis illatas, lex considerasse videtur utrum sit certa vel incerta. Si enim laesio certa esset, lex poenam adhibuit, pro mutilatione quidem, amissionem servi qui mandabatur libertati donandus; pro morte autem, homicidii poenam, cum servus in manu domini verberantis moreretur. Si vero laesio non esset certa, sed aliquam apparentiam haberet, lex nullam poenam infligebat in proprio servo, puta cum percussus servus non statim moriebatur, sed post aliquos dies. Incertum enim erat utrum ex percussione mortuus esset. Quia si percussisset liberum hominem, ita tamen quod statim non moreretur, sed super baculum suum ambularet, non erat homicidii reus qui percusserat, etiam si postea moreretur. Tenebatur tamen ad impensas solvendas quas percussus in medicos fecerat. Sed hoc in servo proprio locum non habebat, quia quidquid servus habebat, et etiam ipsa persona servi, erat quaedam possessio domini. Et ideo pro causa assignatur quare non subiaceat poenae pecuniariae, quia pecunia illius est.

Ad quartum dicendum quod, sicut dictum est, nullus Iudaeus poterat possidere Iudaeum quasi simpliciter servum; sed erat servus secundum quid, quasi mercenarius, usque ad tempus. Et per hunc modum

wife through hatred of her, but rather that he should write a bill of divorce and send her away (Deut 24:1). Furthermore, in order to foster conjugal love from the very outset, it was prescribed that no public duties should be laid on a recently married man, so that he might be free to rejoice with his wife.

With regard to children, the Law commanded parents to educate them by instructing them in the faith: hence it is written (Exod 12:26, seqq.): *When your children shall say to you: What is the meaning of this service? You shall say to them: It is the victim of the passage of the Lord.* Moreover, they are commanded to teach them the rules of right conduct: wherefore it is written (Deut 21:20) that the parents had to say: *He slighteth hearing our admonitions, he giveth himself to revelling and to debauchery.*

Reply Obj. 1: As the children of Israel had been delivered by the Lord from slavery, and for this reason were bound to the service of God, He did not wish them to be slaves in perpetuity. Hence it is written (Lev 25:39, seqq.): *If thy brother, constrained by poverty, sell himself to thee, thou shalt not oppress him with the service of bondservants: but he shall be as a hireling and a sojourner . . . for they are My servants, and I brought them out of the land of Egypt: let them not be sold as bondmen*: and consequently, since they were slaves, not absolutely but in a restricted sense, after a lapse of time they were set free.

Reply Obj. 2: This commandment is to be understood as referring to a servant whom his master seeks to kill, or to help him in committing some sin.

Reply Obj. 3: With regard to the ill-treatment of servants, the Law seems to have taken into consideration whether it was certain or not: since if it were certain, the Law fixed a penalty: for maiming, the penalty was forfeiture of the servant, who was ordered to be given his liberty: while for slaying, the punishment was that of a murderer, when the slave died under the blow of his master. If, however, the hurt was not certain, but only probable, the Law did not impose any penalty as regards a man's own servant: for instance if the servant did not die at once after being struck, but after some days: for it would be uncertain whether he died as a result of the blows he received. For when a man struck a free man, yet so that he did not die at once, but *walked abroad again upon his staff*, he that struck him was quit of murder, even though afterwards he died. Nevertheless he was bound to pay the doctor's fees incurred by the victim of his assault. But this was not the case if a man killed his own servant: because whatever the servant had, even his very person, was the property of his master. Hence the reason for his not being subject to a pecuniary penalty is set down as being *because it is his money.*

Reply Obj. 4: As stated above (ad 1), no Jew could own a Jew as a slave absolutely: but only in a restricted sense, as a hireling for a fixed time. And in this way the Law permitted that through stress of poverty a man might sell his son or

permittebat lex quod, paupertate cogente, aliquis filium aut filiam venderet. Et hoc etiam verba ipsius legis ostendunt, dicit enim, *si quis vendiderit filiam suam in famulam, non egredietur sicut ancillae exire consueverunt.* Per hunc etiam modum non solum filium, sed etiam seipsum aliquis vendere poterat, magis quasi mercenarium quam quasi servum; secundum illud Levit. XXV, *si paupertate compulsus vendiderit se tibi frater tuus, non eum opprimes servitute famulorum, sed quasi mercenarius et colonus erit.*

AD QUINTUM dicendum quod, sicut philosophus dicit, in X Ethic., principatus paternus habet solam admonendi potestatem; non autem habet vim coactivam, per quam rebelles et contumaces comprimi possunt. Et ideo in hoc casu lex mandabat ut filius contumax a principibus civitatis puniretur.

AD SEXTUM dicendum quod dominus alienigenas prohibuit in matrimonium duci propter periculum seductionis, ne inducerentur in idololatriam. Et specialiter hoc prohibuit de illis gentibus quae in vicino habitabant, de quibus erat magis probabile quod suos ritus retinerent. Si qua vero idololatriae cultum dimittere vellet, et ad legis cultum se transferre, poterat in matrimonium duci, sicut patet de Ruth, quam duxit Booz in uxorem. Unde ipsa dixerat socrui suae, *populus tuus populus meus, Deus tuus Deus meus,* ut habetur Ruth I. Et ideo captiva non aliter permittebatur in uxorem duci nisi prius rasa caesarie, et circumcisis unguibus, et deposita veste in qua capta est, et fleret patrem et matrem, per quae significatur idololatriae perpetua abiectio.

AD SEPTIMUM dicendum quod, sicut Chrysostomus dicit, super Matth., *quia immitigabile malum mors erat apud Iudaeos, qui omnia pro praesenti vita faciebant, statutum fuit ut defuncto filius nasceretur ex fratre, quod erat quaedam mortis mitigatio. Non autem alius quam frater vel propinquus iubebatur accipere uxorem defuncti, quia non ita crederetur* (qui ex tali coniunctione erat nasciturus) *esse filius eius qui obiit; et iterum extraneus non ita haberet necessitatem statuere domum eius qui obierat, sicut frater, cui etiam ex cognatione hoc facere iustum erat.* Ex quo patet quod frater in accipiendo uxorem fratris sui, persona fratris defuncti fungebatur.

AD OCTAVUM dicendum quod lex permisit repudium uxoris, non quia simpliciter iustum esset, sed propter duritiam Iudaeorum; ut dominus dicit, Matth. XIX. Sed de hoc oportet plenius tractari cum de matrimonio agetur.

AD NONUM dicendum quod uxores fidem matrimonii frangunt per adulterium et de facili, propter delectationem; et latenter, *quia oculus adulteri observat caliginem,* ut dicitur Iob XXIV. Non autem est similis ratio

daughter. This is shown by the very words of the Law, where we read: *If any man sell his daughter to be a servant, she shall not go out as bondwomen are wont to go out.* Moreover, in this way a man might sell not only his son, but even himself, rather as a hireling than as a slave, according to Lev. 25:39,40: *If thy brother, constrained by poverty, sell himself to thee, thou shalt not oppress him with the service of bondservants: but he shall be as a hireling and a sojourner.*

REPLY OBJ. 5: As the Philosopher says (*Ethic.* x, 9), the paternal authority has the power only of admonition; but not that of coercion, whereby rebellious and headstrong persons can be compelled. Hence in this case the Lord commanded the stubborn son to be punished by the rulers of the city.

REPLY OBJ. 6: The Lord forbade them to marry strange women on account of the danger of seduction, lest they should be led astray into idolatry. And specially did this prohibition apply with respect to those nations who dwelt near them, because it was more probable that they would adopt their religious practices. When, however, the woman was willing to renounce idolatry, and become an adherent of the Law, it was lawful to take her in marriage: as was the case with Ruth whom Booz married. Wherefore she said to her mother-in-law (Ruth 1:16): *Thy people shall be my people, and thy God my God.* Accordingly it was not permitted to marry a captive woman unless she first shaved her hair, and pared her nails, and put off the raiment wherein she was taken, and mourned for her father and mother, in token that she renounced idolatry for ever.

REPLY OBJ. 7: As Chrysostom says (*Hom. xlviii super Matth.*), *because death was an unmitigated evil for the Jews, who did everything with a view to the present life, it was ordained that children should be born to the dead man through his brother: thus affording a certain mitigation to his death. It was not, however, ordained that any other than his brother or one next of kin should marry the wife of the deceased, because the offspring of this union would not be looked upon as that of the deceased: and moreover, a stranger would not be under the obligation to support the household of the deceased, as his brother would be bound to do from motives of justice on account of his relationship.* Hence it is evident that in marrying the wife of his dead brother, he took his dead brother's place.

REPLY OBJ. 8: The Law permitted a wife to be divorced, not as though it were just absolutely speaking, but on account of the Jews' hardness of heart, as Our Lord declared (Matt 19:8). Of this, however, we must speak more fully in the treatise on Matrimony (SP, Q67).

REPLY OBJ. 9: Wives break their conjugal faith by adultery, both easily, for motives of pleasure, and hiddenly, since *the eye of the adulterer observeth darkness* (Job 24:15). But this does not apply to a son in respect of his father, or

de filio ad patrem, vel de servo ad dominum, quia talis infidelitas non procedit ex concupiscentia delectationis, sed magis ex malitia; nec potest ita latere sicut infidelitas mulieris adulterae.

to a servant in respect of his master: because the latter infidelity is not the result of the lust of pleasure, but rather of malice: nor can it remain hidden like the infidelity of an adulterous woman.

QUESTION 106

OF THE LAW OF THE GOSPEL, CALLED THE NEW LAW

Consequenter considerandum est de lege Evangelii, quod dicitur lex nova. Et primo, de ipsa secundum se; secundo, de ipsa per comparationem ad legem veterem; tertio, de his quae in lege nova continentur. Circa primum quaeruntur quatuor.

Primo, qualis sit, utrum scilicet scripta vel indita.

Secundo, de virtute eius, utrum iustificet.
Tertio, de principio eius, utrum debuerit
dari a principio mundi.
Quarto, de termino eius utrum scilicet sit duratura
usque ad finem, an debeat ei alia lex succedere.

In proper sequence we have to consider now the Law of the Gospel which is called the New Law: and in the first place we must consider it in itself; second, in comparison with the Old Law; third, we shall treat of those things that are contained in the New Law. Under the first head there are four points of inquiry:
(1) What kind of law is it? i.e., Is it a written law or is it instilled in the heart?
(2) Of its efficacy, i.e., does it justify?
(3) Of its beginning: should it have been given at the beginning of the world?
(4) Of its end: i.e., whether it will last until the end, or will another law take its place?

Article 1

Whether the New Law Is a Written Law?

AD PRIMUM SIC PROCEDITUR. Videtur quod lex nova sit lex scripta. Lex enim nova est ipsum Evangelium. Sed Evangelium est descriptum, Ioan. XX, *haec autem scripta sunt ut credatis.* Ergo lex nova est lex scripta.

PRAETEREA, lex indita est lex naturae; secundum illud Rom. II, *naturaliter ea quae legis sunt faciunt, qui habent opus legis scriptum in cordibus suis.* Si igitur lex Evangelii esset lex indita, non differret a lege naturae.

PRAETEREA, lex Evangelii propria est eorum qui sunt in statu novi testamenti. Sed lex indita communis est et eis qui sunt in novo testamento, et eis qui sunt in veteri testamento, dicitur enim Sap. VII, quod *divina sapientia per nationes in animas sanctas se transfert, amicos Dei et prophetas constituit.* Ergo lex nova non est lex indita.

SED CONTRA est quod lex nova est lex novi testamenti. Sed lex novi testamenti est indita in corde. Apostolus enim, ad Heb. VIII, dicit, inducens auctoritatem quae habetur Ierem. XXXI, *ecce dies venient, dicit dominus, et consummabo super domum Israel et super domum Iuda testamentum novum,* et exponens quid sit hoc testamentum, dicit, *quia hoc est testamentum quod disponam domui Israel, dando leges meas in mentem eorum, et in*

OBJECTION 1: It would seem that the New Law is a written law. For the New Law is just the same as the Gospel. But the Gospel is set forth in writing, according to Jn. 20:31: *But these are written that you may believe.* Therefore the New Law is a written law.

OBJ. 2: Further, the law that is instilled in the heart is the natural law, according to Rm. 2:14,15: *(The Gentiles) do by nature those things that are of the law . . . who have the work of the law written in their hearts.* If therefore the law of the Gospel were instilled in our hearts, it would not be distinct from the law of nature.

OBJ. 3: Further, the law of the Gospel is proper to those who are in the state of the New Testament. But the law that is instilled in the heart is common to those who are in the New Testament and to those who are in the Old Testament: for it is written (Wis 7:27) that Divine Wisdom *through nations conveyeth herself into holy souls, she maketh the friends of God and prophets.* Therefore the New Law is not instilled in our hearts.

ON THE CONTRARY, The New Law is the law of the New Testament. But the law of the New Testament is instilled in our hearts. For the Apostle, quoting the authority of Jeremias 31:31,33: *Behold the days shall come, saith the Lord; and I will perfect unto the house of Israel, and unto the house of Judah, a new testament,* says, explaining what this statement is (Heb 8:8,10): *For this is the testament which I will make to the house of Israel . . . by giving My laws into*

corde eorum superscribam eas. Ergo lex nova est lex indita.

RESPONDEO dicendum quod *unaquaeque res illud videtur esse quod in ea est potissimum*, ut philosophus dicit, in IX Ethic.

Id autem quod est potissimum in lege novi testamenti, et in quo tota virtus eius consistit, est gratia spiritus sancti, quae datur per fidem Christi. Et ideo principaliter lex nova est ipsa gratia spiritus sancti, quae datur Christi fidelibus.

Et hoc manifeste apparet per apostolum, qui, ad Rom. III, dicit, *ubi est ergo gloriatio tua? Exclusa est. Per quam legem? Factorum? Non, sed per legem fidei*, ipsam enim fidei gratiam legem appellat. Et expressius ad Rom. VIII dicitur, *lex spiritus vitae in Christo Iesu liberavit me a lege peccati et mortis.* Unde et Augustinus dicit, in libro de spiritu et littera, quod *sicut lex factorum scripta fuit in tabulis lapideis, ita lex fidei scripta est in cordibus fidelium.* Et alibi dicit in eodem libro, *quae sunt leges Dei ab ipso Deo scriptae in cordibus, nisi ipsa praesentia spiritus sancti?* Habet tamen lex nova quaedam sicut dispositiva ad gratiam spiritus sancti, et ad usum huius gratiae pertinentia, quae sunt quasi secundaria in lege nova, de quibus oportuit instrui fideles Christi et verbis et scriptis, tam circa credenda quam circa agenda. Et ideo dicendum est quod principaliter nova lex est lex indita, secundario autem est lex scripta.

AD PRIMUM ergo dicendum quod in Scriptura Evangelii non continentur nisi ea quae pertinent ad gratiam spiritus sancti vel sicut dispositiva, vel sicut ordinativa ad usum huius gratiae. Sicut dispositiva quidem quantum ad intellectum per fidem, per quam datur spiritus sancti gratia, continentur in Evangelio ea quae pertinent ad manifestandam divinitatem vel humanitatem Christi. Secundum affectum vero, continentur in Evangelio ea quae pertinent ad contemptum mundi, per quem homo fit capax gratiae spiritus sancti, mundus enim, idest amatores mundi, non potest capere spiritum sanctum, ut habetur Ioan. XIV. Usus vero spiritualis gratiae est in operibus virtutum, ad quae multipliciter Scriptura novi testamenti homines exhortatur.

AD SECUNDUM dicendum quod dupliciter est aliquid inditum homini. Uno modo, pertinens ad naturam humanam, et sic lex naturalis est lex indita homini. Alio modo est aliquid inditum homini quasi naturae superadditum per gratiae donum. Et hoc modo lex nova est indita homini, non solum indicans quid sit faciendum, sed etiam adiuvans ad implendum.

AD TERTIUM dicendum quod nullus unquam habuit gratiam spiritus sancti nisi per fidem Christi explicitam vel implicitam. Per fidem autem Christi pertinet homo

their mind, and in their heart will I write them. Therefore the New Law is instilled in our hearts.

I ANSWER THAT, *Each thing appears to be that which preponderates in it*, as the Philosopher states (*Ethic.* ix, 8).

Now that which is preponderant in the law of the New Testament, and whereon all its efficacy is based, is the grace of the Holy Spirit, which is given through faith in Christ. Consequently the New Law is chiefly the grace itself of the Holy Spirit, which is given to those who believe in Christ.

This is manifestly stated by the Apostle who says (Rom 3:27): *Where is . . . thy boasting? It is excluded. By what law? Of works? No, but by the law of faith*: for he calls the grace itself of faith *a law*. And still more clearly it is written (Rom 8:2): *The law of the spirit of life, in Christ Jesus, hath delivered me from the law of sin and of death.* Hence Augustine says (*De Spir. et Lit.* xxiv) that *as the law of deeds was written on tables of stone, so is the law of faith inscribed on the hearts of the faithful*: and elsewhere, in the same book (xxi): *What else are the Divine laws written by God Himself on our hearts, but the very presence of His Holy Spirit?* Nevertheless the New Law contains certain things that dispose us to receive the grace of the Holy Spirit, and pertaining to the use of that grace: such things are of secondary importance, so to speak, in the New Law; and the faithful need to be instructed concerning them, both by word and writing, both as to what they should believe and as to what they should do. Consequently we must say that the New Law is in the first place a law that is inscribed on our hearts, but that secondarily it is a written law.

REPLY OBJ. 1: The Gospel writings contain only such things as pertain to the grace of the Holy Spirit, either by disposing us thereto, or by directing us to the use thereof. Thus with regard to the intellect, the Gospel contains certain matters pertaining to the manifestation of Christ's Godhead or humanity, which dispose us by means of faith through which we receive the grace of the Holy Spirit: and with regard to the affections, it contains matters touching the contempt of the world, whereby man is rendered fit to receive the grace of the Holy Spirit: for *the world*, i.e., worldly men, *cannot receive* the Holy Spirit (John 14:17). As to the use of spiritual grace, this consists in works of virtue to which the writings of the New Testament exhort men in diverse ways.

REPLY OBJ. 2: There are two ways in which a thing may be instilled into man. First, through being part of his nature, and thus the natural law is instilled into man. Second, a thing is instilled into man by being, as it were, added on to his nature by a gift of grace. In this way the New Law is instilled into man, not only by indicating to him what he should do, but also by helping him to accomplish it.

REPLY OBJ. 3: No man ever had the grace of the Holy Spirit except through faith in Christ either explicit or implicit: and by faith in Christ man belongs to the New

ad novum testamentum. Unde quibuscumque fuit lex gratiae indita, secundum hoc ad novum testamentum pertinebant.

Testament. Consequently whoever had the law of grace instilled into them belonged to the New Testament.

Article 2

Whether the New Law Justifies?

Ad secundum sic proceditur. Videtur quod lex nova non iustificet. Nullus enim iustificatur nisi legi Dei obediat; secundum illud ad Heb. V, *factus est*, scilicet Christus, *omnibus obtemperantibus sibi causa salutis aeternae*. Sed Evangelium non semper hoc operatur quod homines ei obediant, dicitur enim Rom. X, *non omnes obediunt Evangelio*. Ergo lex nova non iustificat.

Praeterea, apostolus probat, ad Rom., quod lex vetus non iustificabat, quia ea adveniente praevaricatio crevit, habetur enim ad Rom. IV, *lex iram operatur, ubi enim non est lex, nec praevaricatio*. Sed multo magis lex nova praevaricationem addidit, maiori enim poena est dignus qui post legem novam datam adhuc peccat; secundum illud Heb. X, *irritam quis faciens legem Moysi, sine ulla miseratione, duobus vel tribus testibus, moritur. Quanto magis putatis deteriora mereri supplicia, qui filium Dei conculcaverit, et cetera?* Ergo lex nova non iustificat, sicut nec vetus.

Praeterea, iustificare est proprius effectus Dei; secundum illud ad Rom. VIII, Deus qui iustificat. Sed lex vetus fuit a Deo, sicut et lex nova. Ergo lex nova non magis iustificat quam lex vetus.

Sed contra est quod apostolus dicit, ad Rom. I, *non erubesco Evangelium, virtus enim Dei est in salutem omni credenti*. Non autem est salus nisi iustificatis. Ergo lex Evangelii iustificat.

Respondeo dicendum quod, sicut dictum est, ad legem Evangelii duo pertinent. Unum quidem principaliter, scilicet ipsa gratia spiritus sancti interius data. Et quantum ad hoc, nova lex iustificat. Unde Augustinus dicit, in libro de spiritu et littera, *ibi*, scilicet in veteri testamento, *lex extrinsecus posita est, qua iniusti terrerentur; hic*, scilicet in novo testamento, *intrinsecus data est, qua iustificarentur*. Aliud pertinet ad legem Evangelii secundario, scilicet documenta fidei, et praecepta ordinantia affectum humanum et humanos actus. Et quantum ad hoc, lex nova non iustificat. Unde apostolus dicit, II ad Cor. III, *littera occidit, spiritus autem vivificat*. Et Augustinus exponit, in libro de spiritu et littera, quod per litteram intelligitur quaelibet Scriptura extra homines existens, etiam moralium praeceptorum qualia

Objection 1: It would seem that the New Law does not justify. For no man is justified unless he obeys God's law, according to Heb. 5:9: *He*, i.e., Christ, *became to all that obey Him the cause of eternal salvation*. But the Gospel does not always cause men to believe in it: for it is written (Rom 10:16): *All do not obey the Gospel*. Therefore the New Law does not justify.

Obj. 2: Further, the Apostle proves in his epistle to the Romans that the Old Law did not justify, because transgression increased at its advent: for it is stated (Rom 4:15): *The Law worketh wrath: for where there is no law, neither is there transgression*. But much more did the New Law increase transgression: since he who sins after the giving of the New Law deserves greater punishment, according to Heb. 10:28,29: *A man making void the Law of Moses dieth without any mercy under two or three witnesses. How much more, do you think, he deserveth worse punishments, who hath trodden underfoot the Son of God*, etc.? Therefore the New Law, like the Old Law, does not justify.

Obj. 3: Further, justification is an effect proper to God, according to Rm. 8:33: *God that justifieth*. But the Old Law was from God just as the New Law. Therefore the New Law does not justify any more than the Old Law.

On the contrary, The Apostle says (Rom 1:16): *I am not ashamed of the Gospel: for it is in the power of God unto salvation to everyone that believeth*. But there is no salvation but to those who are justified. Therefore the Law of the Gospel justifies.

I answer that, As stated above (A1), there is a twofold element in the Law of the Gospel. There is the chief element, viz., the grace of the Holy Spirit bestowed inwardly. And as to this, the New Law justifies. Hence Augustine says (*De Spir. et Lit.* xvii): *There*, i.e., in the Old Testament, *the Law was set forth in an outward fashion, that the ungodly might be afraid*; *here*, i.e., in the New Testament, *it is given in an inward manner, that they may be justified*. The other element of the Evangelical Law is secondary: namely, the teachings of faith, and those commandments which direct human affections and human actions. And as to this, the New Law does not justify. Hence the Apostle says (2 Cor 3:6) *The letter killeth, but the spirit quickeneth*: and Augustine explains this (*De Spir. et Lit*. xiv, xvii) by saying that the letter denotes any writing external to man, even that of the moral precepts such as are contained in the

continentur in Evangelio. Unde etiam littera Evangelii occideret, nisi adesset interius gratia fidei sanans.

Ad primum ergo dicendum quod illa obiectio procedit de lege nova non quantum ad id quod est principale in ipsa, sed quantum ad id quod est secundarium in ipsa, scilicet quantum ad documenta et praecepta exterius homini proposita vel verbo vel scripto.

Ad secundum dicendum quod gratia novi testamenti, etsi adiuvet hominem ad non peccandum, non tamen ita confirmat in bono ut homo peccare non possit, hoc enim pertinet ad statum gloriae. Et ideo si quis post acceptam gratiam novi testamenti peccaverit, maiori poena est dignus, tanquam maioribus beneficiis ingratus, et auxilio sibi dato non utens. Nec tamen propter hoc dicitur quod lex nova iram operatur, quia quantum est de se, sufficiens auxilium dat ad non peccandum.

Ad tertium dicendum quod legem novam et veterem unus Deus dedit, sed aliter et aliter. Nam legem veterem dedit scriptam in tabulis lapideis, legem autem novam dedit scriptam in tabulis cordis carnalibus, ut apostolus dicit, II ad Cor. III. Proinde sicut Augustinus dicit, in libro de spiritu et littera, *litteram istam extra hominem scriptam, et ministrationem mortis et ministrationem damnationis apostolus appellat. Hanc autem, scilicet novi testamenti legem, ministrationem spiritus et ministrationem iustitiae dicit, quia per donum spiritus operamur iustitiam, et a praevaricationis damnatione liberamur.*

Gospel. Wherefore the letter, even of the Gospel would kill, unless there were the inward presence of the healing grace of faith.

Reply Obj. 1: This argument holds true of the New Law, not as to its principal, but as to its secondary element: i.e., as to the dogmas and precepts outwardly put before man either in words or in writing.

Reply Obj. 2: Although the grace of the New Testament helps man to avoid sin, yet it does not so confirm man in good that he cannot sin: for this belongs to the state of glory. Hence if a man sin after receiving the grace of the New Testament, he deserves greater punishment, as being ungrateful for greater benefits, and as not using the help given to him. And this is why the New Law is not said to *work wrath*: because as far as it is concerned it gives man sufficient help to avoid sin.

Reply Obj. 3: The same God gave both the New and the Old Law, but in different ways. For He gave the Old Law written on tables of stone: whereas He gave the New Law written *in the fleshly tables of the heart*, as the Apostle expresses it (2 Cor 3:3). Wherefore, as Augustine says (*De Spir. et Lit.* xviii), *the Apostle calls this letter which is written outside man, a ministration of death and a ministration of condemnation: whereas he calls the other letter, i.e., the Law of the New Testament, the ministration of the spirit and the ministration of justice: because through the gift of the Spirit we work justice, and are delivered from the condemnation due to transgression.*

Article 3

Whether the New Law Should Have Been Given from the Beginning of the World?

Ad tertium sic proceditur. Videtur quod lex nova debuerit dari a principio mundi. *Non enim est personarum acceptio apud Deum,* ut dicitur ad Rom. II. Sed omnes homines peccaverunt, et egent gloria Dei, ut dicitur ad Rom. III. Ergo a principio mundi lex Evangelii dari debuit, ut omnibus per eam subveniretur.

Praeterea, sicut in diversis locis sunt diversi homines, ita etiam in diversis temporibus. Sed Deus, *qui vult omnes homines salvos fieri,* ut dicitur I ad Tim. II, mandavit Evangelium praedicari in omnibus locis; ut patet Matth. ult., et Marc. ult. Ergo omnibus temporibus debuit adesse lex Evangelii, ita quod a principio mundi daretur.

Praeterea, magis est necessaria homini salus spiritualis, quae est aeterna, quam salus corporalis, quae est temporalis. Sed Deus ab initio mundi providit homini ea quae sunt necessaria ad salutem corporalem, tradens

Objection 1: It would seem that the New Law should have been given from the beginning of the world. *For there is no respect of persons with God* (Rom 2:11). But *all men have sinned and do need the glory of God* (Rom 3:23). Therefore the Law of the Gospel should have been given from the beginning of the world, in order that it might bring succor to all.

Obj. 2: Further, as men dwell in various places, so do they live in various times. But God, *Who will have all men to be saved* (1 Tim 2:4), commanded the Gospel to be preached in all places, as may be seen in the last chapters of Matthew and Mark. Therefore the Law of the Gospel should have been at hand for all times, so as to be given from the beginning of the world.

Obj. 3: Further, man needs to save his soul, which is for all eternity, more than to save his body, which is a temporal matter. But God provided man from the beginning of the world with things that are necessary for the health

eius potestati omnia quae erant propter hominem creata, ut patet Gen. I. Ergo etiam lex nova, quae maxime est necessaria ad salutem spiritualem, debuit hominibus a principio mundi dari.

SED CONTRA est quod apostolus dicit, I ad Cor. XV, *non prius quod spirituale est, sed quod animale.* Sed lex nova est maxime spiritualis. Ergo lex nova non debuit dari a principio mundi.

RESPONDEO dicendum quod triplex ratio potest assignari quare lex nova non debuit dari a principio mundi. Quarum prima est quia lex nova, sicut dictum est, principaliter est gratia spiritus sancti; quae abundanter dari non debuit antequam impedimentum peccati ab humano genere tolleretur, consummata redemptione per Christum; unde dicitur Ioan. VII, *nondum erat spiritus datus, quia Iesus nondum erat glorificatus.* Et hanc rationem manifeste assignat apostolus ad Rom. VIII, ubi, postquam praemiserat de lege spiritus vitae, subiungit, *Deus, filium suum mittens in similitudinem carnis peccati, de peccato damnavit peccatum in carne, ut iustificatio legis impleretur in nobis.*

Secunda ratio potest assignari ex perfectione legis novae. Non enim aliquid ad perfectum adducitur statim a principio, sed quodam temporali successionis ordine, sicut aliquis prius fit puer, et postmodum vir. Et hanc rationem assignat apostolus ad Gal. III, *lex paedagogus noster fuit in Christo, ut ex fide iustificemur. At ubi venit fides, iam non sumus sub paedagogo.*

Tertia ratio sumitur ex hoc quod lex nova est lex gratiae, et ideo primo oportuit quod homo relinqueretur sibi in statu veteris legis, ut, in peccatum cadendo, suam infirmitatem cognoscens, recognosceret se gratia indigere. Et hanc rationem assignat apostolus ad Rom. V, dicens, *lex subintravit ut abundaret delictum, ubi autem abundavit delictum, superabundavit et gratia.*

AD PRIMUM ergo dicendum quod humanum genus propter peccatum primi parentis meruit privari auxilio gratiae. *Et ideo quibuscumque non datur, hoc est ex iustitia, quibuscumque autem datur, hoc est ex gratia,* ut Augustinus dicit, in libro de Perfect. Iustit. Unde non est acceptio personarum apud Deum ex hoc quod non omnibus a principio mundi legem gratiae proposuit, quae erat debito ordine proponenda, ut dictum est.

AD SECUNDUM dicendum quod diversitas locorum non variat diversum statum humani generis, qui variatur per temporis successionem. Et ideo omnibus locis proponitur lex nova, non autem omnibus temporibus, licet omni tempore fuerint aliqui ad novum testamentum pertinentes, ut supra dictum est.

of his body, by subjecting to his power whatever was created for the sake of man (Gen 1:26–29). Therefore the New Law also, which is very necessary for the health of the soul, should have been given to man from the beginning of the world.

ON THE CONTRARY, The Apostle says (1 Cor 15:46): *That was not first which is spiritual, but that which is natural.* But the New Law is highly spiritual. Therefore it was not fitting for it to be given from the beginning of the world.

I ANSWER THAT, Three reasons may be assigned why it was not fitting for the New Law to be given from the beginning of the world. The first is because the New Law, as stated above (A1), consists chiefly in the grace of the Holy Spirit: which it behoved not to be given abundantly until sin, which is an obstacle to grace, had been cast out of man through the accomplishment of his redemption by Christ: wherefore it is written (John 7:39): *As yet the Spirit was not given, because Jesus was not yet glorified.* This reason the Apostle states clearly (Rom 8:2, seqq.) where, after speaking of *the Law of the Spirit of life,* he adds: *God sending His own Son, in the likeness of sinful flesh, of sin hath condemned sin in the flesh, that the justification of the Law might be fulfilled in us.*

A second reason may be taken from the perfection of the New Law. Because a thing is not brought to perfection at once from the outset, but through an orderly succession of time; thus one is at first a boy, and then a man. And this reason is stated by the Apostle (Gal 3:24,25): *The Law was our pedagogue in Christ that we might be justified by faith. But after the faith is come, we are no longer under a pedagogue.*

The third reason is found in the fact that the New Law is the law of grace: wherefore it behoved man first of all to be left to himself under the state of the Old Law, so that through falling into sin, he might realize his weakness, and acknowledge his need of grace. This reason is set down by the Apostle (Rom 5:20): *The Law entered in, that sin might abound: and when sin abounded grace did more abound.*

REPLY OBJ. 1: Mankind on account of the sin of our first parents deserved to be deprived of the aid of grace: and so *from whom it is withheld it is justly withheld, and to whom it is given, it is mercifully given,* as Augustine states (*De Perfect. Justit.* iv). Consequently it does not follow that there is respect of persons with God, from the fact that He did not offer the Law of grace to all from the beginning of the world, which Law was to be published in due course of time, as stated above.

REPLY OBJ. 2: The state of mankind does not vary according to diversity of place, but according to succession of time. Hence the New Law avails for all places, but not for all times: although at all times there have been some persons belonging to the New Testament, as stated above (A1, ad 3).

AD TERTIUM dicendum quod ea quae pertinent ad salutem corporalem, deserviunt homini quantum ad naturam, quae non tollitur per peccatum. Sed ea quae pertinent ad spiritualem salutem, ordinantur ad gratiam, quae amittitur per peccatum. Et ideo non est similis ratio de utrisque.

REPLY OBJ. 3: Things pertaining to the health of the body are of service to man as regards his nature, which sin does not destroy: whereas things pertaining to the health of the soul are ordained to grace, which is forfeit through sin. Consequently the comparison will not hold.

Article 4

Whether the New Law Will Last Till the End of the World?

AD QUARTUM SIC PROCEDITUR. Videtur quod lex nova non sit duratura usque ad finem mundi. Quia ut apostolus dicit, I ad Cor. XIII, *cum venerit quod perfectum est, evacuabitur quod ex parte est.* Sed lex nova ex parte est, dicit enim apostolus ibidem, *ex parte cognoscimus, et ex parte prophetamus.* Ergo lex nova evacuanda est, alio perfectiori statu succedente.

PRAETEREA, dominus, Ioan. XVI, promisit discipulis suis in adventu spiritus sancti Paracleti cognitionem omnis veritatis. Sed nondum Ecclesia omnem veritatem cognoscit, in statu novi testamenti. Ergo expectandus est alius status, in quo per spiritum sanctum omnis veritas manifestetur.

PRAETEREA, sicut pater est alius a filio et filius a patre, ita Spiritus Sanctus a patre et filio. Sed fuit quidam status conveniens personae patris, scilicet status veteris legis, in quo homines generationi intendebant. Similiter etiam est alius status conveniens personae filii, scilicet status novae legis, in quo clerici, intendentes sapientiae, quae appropriatur filio, principantur. Ergo erit status tertius spiritus sancti, in quo spirituales viri principabuntur.

PRAETEREA, dominus dicit, Matth. XXIV, praedicabitur hoc *Evangelium regni in universo orbe, et tunc veniet consummatio.* Sed Evangelium Christi iamdiu est praedicatum in universo orbe; nec tamen adhuc venit consummatio. Ergo Evangelium Christi non est Evangelium regni, sed futurum est aliud Evangelium spiritus sancti, quasi alia lex.

SED CONTRA est quod dominus dicit, Matth. XXIV, *dico vobis quia non praeteribit generatio haec donec omnia fiant*, quod Chrysostomus exponit de generatione fidelium Christi. Ergo status fidelium Christi manebit usque ad consummationem saeculi.

RESPONDEO dicendum quod status mundi variari potest dupliciter. Uno modo, secundum diversitatem legis. Et sic huic statui novae legis nullus alius status

OBJECTION 1: It would seem that the New Law will not last until the end of the world. Because, as the Apostle says (1 Cor 13:10), *when that which is perfect is come, that which is in part shall be done away.* But the New Law is *in part*, since the Apostle says (1 Cor 13:9): *We know in part and we prophesy in part.* Therefore the New Law is to be done away, and will be succeeded by a more perfect state.

OBJ. 2: Further, Our Lord (John 16:13) promised His disciples the knowledge of all truth when the Holy Spirit, the Comforter, should come. But the Church knows not yet all truth in the state of the New Testament. Therefore we must look forward to another state, wherein all truth will be revealed by the Holy Spirit.

OBJ. 3: Further, just as the Father is distinct from the Son and the Son from the Father, so is the Holy Spirit distinct from the Father and the Son. But there was a state corresponding with the Person of the Father, viz., the state of the Old Law, wherein men were intent on begetting children: and likewise there is a state corresponding to the Person of the Son: viz., the state of the New Law, wherein the clergy who are intent on wisdom (which is appropriated to the Son) hold a prominent place. Therefore there will be a third state corresponding to the Holy Spirit, wherein spiritual men will hold the first place.

OBJ. 4: Further, Our Lord said (Matt 24:14): *This Gospel of the kingdom shall be preached in the whole world . . . and then shall the consummation come.* But the Gospel of Christ is already preached throughout the whole world: and yet the consummation has not yet come. Therefore the Gospel of Christ is not the Gospel of the kingdom, but another Gospel, that of the Holy Spirit, is to come yet, like unto another Law.

ON THE CONTRARY, Our Lord said (Matt 24:34): *I say to you that this generation shall not pass till all (these) things be done*: which passage Chrysostom (*Hom.* lxxvii) explains as referring to *the generation of those that believe in Christ.* Therefore the state of those who believe in Christ will last until the consummation of the world.

I ANSWER THAT, The state of the world may change in two ways. In one way, according to a change of law: and thus no other state will succeed this state of the New Law.

succedet. Successit enim status novae legis statui veteris legis tanquam perfectior imperfectiori. Nullus autem status praesentis vitae potest esse perfectior quam status novae legis. Nihil enim potest esse propinquius fini ultimo quam quod immediate in finem ultimum introducit. Hoc autem facit nova lex, unde apostolus dicit, ad Heb. X, *habentes itaque, fratres, fiduciam in introitu sanctorum in sanguine Christi, quam initiavit nobis viam novam, accedamus ad eum.* Unde non potest esse aliquis perfectior status praesentis vitae quam status novae legis, quia tanto est unumquodque perfectius, quanto ultimo fini propinquius.

Alio modo status hominum variari potest secundum quod homines diversimode se habent ad eandem legem, vel perfectius vel minus perfecte. Et sic status veteris legis frequenter fuit mutatus, cum quandoque leges optime custodirentur, quandoque omnino praetermitterentur. Sic etiam status novae legis diversificatur, secundum diversa loca et tempora et personas, inquantum gratia spiritus sancti perfectius vel minus perfecte ab aliquibus habetur. Non est tamen expectandum quod sit aliquis status futurus in quo perfectius gratia spiritus sancti habeatur quam hactenus habita fuerit, maxime ab apostolis, qui primitias spiritus acceperunt, *idest et tempore prius et ceteris abundantius,* ut Glossa dicit Rom. VIII.

AD PRIMUM ergo dicendum quod, sicut Dionysius dicit, in Eccl. Hier., triplex est hominum status, primus quidem veteris legis; secundus novae legis; tertius status succedit non in hac vita, sed in patria. Sed sicut primus status est figuralis et imperfectus respectu status evangelici, ita hic status est figuralis et imperfectus respectu status patriae; quo veniente, iste status evacuatur, sicut ibi dicitur, *videmus nunc per speculum in aenigmate, tunc autem facie ad faciem.*

AD SECUNDUM dicendum quod, sicut Augustinus dicit in libro contra Faustum, Montanus et Priscilla posuerunt quod promissio domini de spiritu sancto dando non fuit completa in apostolis, sed in eis. Et similiter Manichaei posuerunt quod fuit completa in Manichaeo, quem dicebant esse spiritum Paracletum. Et ideo utrique non recipiebant actus apostolorum, in quibus manifeste ostenditur quod illa promissio fuit in apostolis completa, sicut dominus iterato eis promisit, Act. I, *baptizamini in spiritu sancto non post multos hos dies*; quod impletum legitur Act. II. Sed istae vanitates excluduntur per hoc quod dicitur Ioan. VII, *nondum erat spiritus datus, quia Iesus nondum erat glorificatus,* ex quo datur intelligi quod statim glorificato Christo in resurrectione et ascensione, fuit Spiritus Sanctus datus. Et per hoc etiam excluditur quorumcumque vanitas qui dicerent esse expectandum aliud tempus spiritus sancti.

Because the state of the New Law succeeded the state of the Old Law, as a more perfect law a less perfect one. Now no state of the present life can be more perfect than the state of the New Law: since nothing can approach nearer to the last end than that which is the immediate cause of our being brought to the last end. But the New Law does this: wherefore the Apostle says (Heb 10:19–22): *Having therefore, brethren, a confidence in the entering into the Holies by the blood of Christ, a new . . . way which He hath dedicated for us . . . let us draw near.* Therefore no state of the present life can be more perfect than that of the New Law, since the nearer a thing is to the last end the more perfect it is.

In another way the state of mankind may change according as man stands in relation to one and the same law more or less perfectly. And thus the state of the Old Law underwent frequent changes, since at times the laws were very well kept, and at other times were altogether unheeded. Thus, too, the state of the New Law is subject to change with regard to various places, times, and persons, according as the grace of the Holy Spirit dwells in man more or less perfectly. Nevertheless we are not to look forward to a state wherein man is to possess the grace of the Holy Spirit more perfectly than he has possessed it hitherto, especially the apostles who *received the firstfruits of the Spirit, i.e., sooner and more abundantly than others,* as a gloss expounds on Rm. 8:23.

REPLY OBJ. 1: As Dionysius says (*Eccl. Hier.* v), there is a threefold state of mankind; the first was under the Old Law; the second is that of the New Law; the third will take place not in this life, but in heaven. But as the first state is figurative and imperfect in comparison with the state of the Gospel; so is the present state figurative and imperfect in comparison with the heavenly state, with the advent of which the present state will be done away as expressed in that very passage (1 Cor 13:12): *We see now through a glass in a dark manner; but then face to face.*

REPLY OBJ. 2: As Augustine says (*Contra Faust.* xix, 31), Montanus and Priscilla pretended that Our Lord's promise to give the Holy Spirit was fulfilled, not in the apostles, but in themselves. In like manner the Manicheans maintained that it was fulfilled in Manes whom they held to be the Paraclete. Hence none of the above received the Acts of the Apostles, where it is clearly shown that the aforesaid promise was fulfilled in the apostles: just as Our Lord promised them a second time (Acts 1:5): *You shall be baptized with the Holy Spirit, not many days hence*: which we read as having been fulfilled in Acts 2. However, these foolish notions are refuted by the statement (John 7:39) that *as yet the Spirit was not given, because Jesus was not yet glorified*; from which we gather that the Holy Spirit was given as soon as Christ was glorified in His Resurrection and Ascension. Moreover, this puts out of court the senseless idea that the Holy Spirit is to be expected to come at some other time.

Docuit autem Spiritus Sanctus apostolos omnem veritatem de his quae pertinent ad necessitatem salutis, scilicet de credendis et agendis. Non tamen docuit eos de omnibus futuris eventibus, hoc enim ad eos non pertinebat, secundum illud Act. I, *non est vestrum nosse tempora vel momenta, quae pater posuit in sua potestate.*

AD TERTIUM dicendum quod lex vetus non solum fuit patris, sed etiam filii, quia Christus in veteri lege figurabatur. Unde dominus dicit, Ioan. V, *si crederetis Moysi, crederetis forsitan et mihi, de me enim ille scripsit.* Similiter etiam lex nova non solum est Christi, sed etiam spiritus sancti; secundum illud Rom. VIII, *lex spiritus vitae in Christo Iesu*, et cetera. Unde non est expectanda alia lex, quae sit spiritus sancti.

AD QUARTUM dicendum quod, cum Christus statim in principio evangelicae praedicationis dixerit, appropinquavit regnum caelorum, stultissimum est dicere quod Evangelium Christi non sit Evangelium regni. Sed praedicatio Evangelii Christi potest intelligi dupliciter. Uno modo, quantum ad divulgationem notitiae Christi, et sic praedicatum fuit Evangelium in universo orbe etiam tempore apostolorum, ut Chrysostomus dicit. Et secundum hoc, quod additur, et tunc erit consummatio, intelligitur de destructione Ierusalem, de qua tunc ad litteram loquebatur. Alio modo potest intelligi praedicatio Evangelii in universo orbe cum pleno effectu, ita scilicet quod in qualibet gente fundetur Ecclesia. Et ita, sicut dicit Augustinus, in epistola ad Hesych., nondum est praedicatum Evangelium in universo orbe, sed, hoc facto, veniet consummatio mundi.

Now the Holy Spirit taught the apostles all truth in respect of matters necessary for salvation; those things, to wit, that we are bound to believe and to do. But He did not teach them about all future events: for this did not regard them according to Acts 1:7: *It is not for you to know the times or moments which the Father hath put in His own power.*

REPLY OBJ. 3: The Old Law corresponded not only to the Father, but also to the Son: because Christ was foreshadowed in the Old Law. Hence Our Lord said (John 5:46): *If you did believe Moses, you would perhaps believe me also; for he wrote of Me.* In like manner the New Law corresponds not only to Christ, but also to the Holy Spirit; according to Rm. 8:2: *The Law of the Spirit of life in Christ Jesus*, etc. Hence we are not to look forward to another law corresponding to the Holy Spirit.

REPLY OBJ. 4: Since Christ said at the very outset of the preaching of the Gospel: *The kingdom of heaven is at hand* (Matt 4:17), it is most absurd to say that the Gospel of Christ is not the Gospel of the kingdom. But the preaching of the Gospel of Christ may be understood in two ways. First, as denoting the spreading abroad of the knowledge of Christ: and thus the Gospel was preached throughout the world even at the time of the apostles, as Chrysostom states (*Hom. lxxv in Matth.*). And in this sense the words that follow—*and then shall the consummation come*, refer to the destruction of Jerusalem, of which He was speaking literally. Second, the preaching of the Gospel may be understood as extending throughout the world and producing its full effect, so that, to wit, the Church would be founded in every nation. And in these sense, as Augustine writes to Hesychius (*Epist. cxcix*), the Gospel is not preached to the whole world yet, but, when it is, the consummation of the world will come.

QUESTION 107

OF THE NEW LAW AS COMPARED WITH THE OLD

Deinde considerandum est de comparatione legis novae ad legem veterem. Et circa hoc quaeruntur quatuor.

Primo, utrum lex nova sit alia lex a lege veteri.

Secundo, utrum lex nova impleat veterem.

Tertio, utrum lex nova contineatur in veteri.

Quarto, quae sit gravior, utrum lex nova vel vetus.

We must now consider the New Law as compared with the Old: under which head there are four points of inquiry:

(1) Whether the New Law is distinct from the Old Law?
(2) Whether the New Law fulfils the Old?
(3) Whether the New Law is contained in the Old?
(4) Which is the more burdensome, the New or the Old Law?

Article 1

Whether the New Law Is Distinct from the Old Law?

AD PRIMUM SIC PROCEDITUR. Videtur quod lex nova non sit alia a lege veteri. Utraque enim lex datur fidem Dei habentibus, quia *sine fide impossibile est placere Deo*, ut dicitur Heb. XI. Sed eadem fides est antiquorum et modernorum, ut dicitur in Glossa Matth. XXI. Ergo etiam est eadem lex.

PRAETEREA, Augustinus dicit, in libro contra Adamantum Manich. Discip., quod *brevis differentia legis et Evangelii est timor et amor.* Sed secundum haec duo nova lex et vetus diversificari non possunt, quia etiam in veteri lege proponuntur praecepta caritatis; Lev. XIX, *diliges proximum tuum*; et Deut. VI, *diliges dominum Deum tuum.* Similiter etiam diversificari non possunt per aliam differentiam quam Augustinus assignat, contra Faustum, quod *vetus testamentum habuit promissa temporalia, novum testamentum habet promissa spiritualia et aeterna.* Quia etiam in novo testamento promittuntur aliqua promissa temporalia; secundum illud Marc. X, *accipiet centies tantum in tempore hoc, domos et fratres,* et cetera. Et in veteri testamento sperabantur promissa spiritualia et aeterna; secundum illud ad Heb. XI, *nunc autem meliorem patriam appetunt, idest caelestem,* quod dicitur de antiquis patribus. Ergo videtur quod nova lex non sit alia a veteri.

PRAETEREA, apostolus videtur distinguere utramque legem, ad Rom. III, veterem legem appellans legem factorum, legem vero novam appellans legem fidei. Sed lex vetus fuit etiam fidei; secundum illud Heb. XI, *omnes testimonio fidei probati sunt,* quod dicit de patribus veteris testamenti. Similiter etiam lex nova est lex factorum, dicitur enim Matth. V, *benefacite his qui oderunt vos*; et

OBJECTION 1: It would seem that the New Law is not distinct from the Old. Because both these laws were given to those who believe in God: since *without faith it is impossible to please God*, according to Heb. 11:6. But the faith of olden times and of nowadays is the same, as the gloss says on Mt. 21:9. Therefore the law is the same also.

OBJ. 2: Further, Augustine says (*Contra Adamant. Manich. discip.* xvii) that *there is little difference between the Law and Gospel—fear and love.* But the New and Old Laws cannot be differentiated in respect of these two things: since even the Old Law comprised precepts of charity: *Thou shalt love thy neighbor* (Lev 19:18), and: *Thou shalt love the Lord thy God* (Deut 6:5). In like manner neither can they differ according to the other difference which Augustine assigns (*Contra Faust.* iv, 2), viz., that the Old Testament contained temporal promises, whereas the New Testament contains spiritual and eternal promises: since even the New Testament contains temporal promises, according to Mk. 10:30: He shall receive *a hundred times as much . . . in this time, houses and brethren*, etc.: while in the Old Testament they hoped in promises spiritual and eternal, according to Heb. 11:16: *But now they desire a better, that is to say, a heavenly country,* which is said of the patriarchs. Therefore it seems that the New Law is not distinct from the Old.

OBJ. 3: Further, the Apostle seems to distinguish both laws by calling the Old Law *a law of works,* and the New Law *a law of faith* (Rom 3:27). But the Old Law was also a law of faith, according to Heb. 11:39: *All were approved by the testimony of faith,* which he says of the fathers of the Old Testament. In like manner the New Law is a law of works: since it is written (Matt 5:44): *Do good to them that hate*

Luc. XXII, *hoc facite in meam commemorationem*. Ergo lex nova non est alia a lege veteri.

SED CONTRA est quod apostolus dicit, ad Heb. VII, *translato sacerdotio, necesse est ut legis translatio fiat*. Sed aliud est sacerdotium novi et veteris testamenti, ut ibidem apostolus probat. Ergo est etiam alia lex.

RESPONDEO dicendum quod, sicut supra dictum est, omnis lex ordinat conversationem humanam in ordine ad aliquem finem. Ea autem quae ordinantur ad finem, secundum rationem finis dupliciter diversificari possunt. Uno modo, quia ordinantur ad diversos fines, et haec est diversitas speciei, maxime si sit finis proximus. Alio modo, secundum propinquitatem ad finem vel distantiam ab ipso. Sicut patet quod motus differunt specie secundum quod ordinantur ad diversos terminos, secundum vero quod una pars motus est propinquior termino quam alia, attenditur differentia in motu secundum perfectum et imperfectum.

Sic ergo duae leges distingui possunt dupliciter. Uno modo, quasi omnino diversae, utpote ordinatae ad diversos fines, sicut lex civitatis quae esset ordinata ad hoc quod populus dominaretur, esset specie differens ab illa lege quae esset ad hoc ordinata quod optimates civitatis dominarentur. Alio modo duae leges distingui possunt secundum quod una propinquius ordinat ad finem, alia vero remotius. Puta in una et eadem civitate dicitur alia lex quae imponitur viris perfectis, qui statim possunt exequi ea quae pertinent ad bonum commune; et alia lex de disciplina puerorum, qui sunt instruendi qualiter postmodum opera virorum exequantur.

Dicendum est ergo quod secundum primum modum, lex nova non est alia a lege veteri, quia utriusque est unus finis, scilicet ut homines subdantur Deo; est autem unus Deus et novi et veteris testamenti, secundum illud Rom. III, *unus Deus est qui iustificat circumcisionem ex fide, et praeputium per fidem*. Alio modo, lex nova est alia a veteri. Quia lex vetus est quasi paedagogus puerorum, ut apostolus dicit, ad Gal. III, lex autem nova est lex perfectionis, quia est lex caritatis, de qua apostolus dicit, ad Colos. III, quod est vinculum perfectionis.

AD PRIMUM ergo dicendum quod unitas fidei utriusque testamenti attestatur unitati finis, dictum est enim supra quod obiectum theologicarum virtutum, inter quas est fides, est finis ultimus. Sed tamen fides habuit alium statum in veteri et in nova lege, nam quod illi credebant futurum, nos credimus factum.

AD SECUNDUM dicendum quod omnes differentiae quae assignantur inter novam legem et veterem, accipiuntur secundum perfectum et imperfectum. Praecepta enim legis cuiuslibet dantur de actibus virtutum. Ad

you; and (Luke 22:19): *Do this for a commemoration of Me*. Therefore the New Law is not distinct from the Old.

ON THE CONTRARY, the Apostle says (Heb 7:12): *The priesthood being translated it is necessary that a translation also be made of the Law*. But the priesthood of the New Testament is distinct from that of the Old, as the Apostle shows in the same place. Therefore the Law is also distinct.

I ANSWER THAT, As stated above (Q90, A2; Q91, A4), every law ordains human conduct to some end. Now things ordained to an end may be divided in two ways, considered from the point of view of the end. First, through being ordained to different ends: and this difference will be specific, especially if such ends are proximate. Second, by reason of being closely or remotely connected with the end. Thus it is clear that movements differ in species through being directed to different terms: while according as one part of a movement is nearer to the term than another part, the difference of perfect and imperfect movement is assessed.

Accordingly then two laws may be distinguished from one another in two ways. First, through being altogether diverse, from the fact that they are ordained to diverse ends: thus a state-law ordained to democratic government, would differ specifically from a law ordained to government by the aristocracy. Second, two laws may be distinguished from one another, through one of them being more closely connected with the end, and the other more remotely: thus in one and the same state there is one law enjoined on men of mature age, who can forthwith accomplish that which pertains to the common good; and another law regulating the education of children who need to be taught how they are to achieve manly deeds later on.

We must therefore say that, according to the first way, the New Law is not distinct from the Old Law: because they both have the same end, namely, man's subjection to God; and there is but one God of the New and of the Old Testament, according to Rm. 3:30: *It is one God that justifieth circumcision by faith, and uncircumcision through faith*. According to the second way, the New Law is distinct from the Old Law: because the Old Law is like a pedagogue of children, as the Apostle says (Gal 3:24), whereas the New Law is the law of perfection, since it is the law of charity, of which the Apostle says (Col 3:14) that it is *the bond of perfection*.

REPLY OBJ. 1: The unity of faith under both Testaments witnesses to the unity of end: for it has been stated above (Q62, A2) that the object of the theological virtues, among which is faith, is the last end. Yet faith had a different state in the Old and in the New Law: since what they believed as future, we believe as fact.

REPLY OBJ. 2: All the differences assigned between the Old and New Laws are gathered from their relative perfection and imperfection. For the precepts of every law prescribe acts of virtue. Now the imperfect, who as yet are not

operanda autem virtutum opera aliter inclinantur imperfecti, qui nondum habent virtutis habitum; et aliter illi qui sunt per habitum virtutis perfecti. Illi enim qui nondum habent habitum virtutis, inclinantur ad agendum virtutis opera ex aliqua causa extrinseca, puta ex comminatione poenarum, vel ex promissione aliquarum extrinsecarum remunerationum, puta honoris vel divitiarum vel alicuius huiusmodi. Et ideo lex vetus, quae dabatur imperfectis, idest nondum consecutis gratiam spiritualem, dicebatur lex timoris, inquantum inducebat ad observantiam praeceptorum per comminationem quarundam poenarum. Et dicitur habere temporalia quaedam promissa. Illi autem qui habent virtutem, inclinantur ad virtutis opera agenda propter amorem virtutis, non propter aliquam poenam aut remunerationem extrinsecam. Et ideo lex nova, cuius principalitas consistit in ipsa spirituali gratia indita cordibus, dicitur lex amoris. Et dicitur habere promissa spiritualia et aeterna, quae sunt obiecta virtutis, praecipue caritatis. Et ita per se in ea inclinantur, non quasi in extranea, sed quasi in propria. Et propter hoc etiam lex vetus dicitur cohibere manum, non animum, quia qui timore poenae ab aliquo peccato abstinet, non simpliciter eius voluntas a peccato recedit, sicut recedit voluntas eius qui amore iustitiae abstinet a peccato. Et propter hoc lex nova, quae est lex amoris, dicitur animum cohibere.

Fuerunt tamen aliqui in statu veteris testamenti habentes caritatem et gratiam spiritus sancti, qui principaliter expectabant promissiones spirituales et aeternas. Et secundum hoc pertinebant ad legem novam. Similiter etiam in novo testamento sunt aliqui carnales nondum pertingentes ad perfectionem novae legis, quos oportuit etiam in novo testamento induci ad virtutis opera per timorem poenarum, et per aliqua temporalia promissa.

Lex autem vetus etsi praecepta caritatis daret, non tamen per eam dabatur Spiritus Sanctus, per quem diffunditur caritas in cordibus nostris, ut dicitur Rom. V.

AD TERTIUM dicendum quod, sicut supra dictum est, lex nova dicitur lex fidei, inquantum eius principalitas consistit in ipsa gratia quae interius datur credentibus, unde dicitur gratia fidei. Habet autem secundario aliqua facta et moralia et sacramentalia, sed in his non consistit principalitas legis novae, sicut principalitas veteris legis in eis consistebat. Illi autem qui in veteri testamento Deo fuerunt accepti per fidem, secundum hoc ad novum testamentum pertinebant, non enim iustificabantur nisi per fidem Christi, qui est auctor novi testamenti. Unde et de Moyse dicit apostolus, ad Heb. XI, quod *maiores divitias aestimabat thesauro Aegyptiorum, improperium Christi.*

possessed of a virtuous habit, are directed in one way to perform virtuous acts, while those who are perfected by the possession of virtuous habits are directed in another way. For those who as yet are not endowed with virtuous habits, are directed to the performance of virtuous acts by reason of some outward cause: for instance, by the threat of punishment, or the promise of some extrinsic rewards, such as honor, riches, or the like. Hence the Old Law, which was given to men who were imperfect, that is, who had not yet received spiritual grace, was called the *law of fear*, inasmuch as it induced men to observe its commandments by threatening them with penalties; and is spoken of as containing temporal promises. On the other hand, those who are possessed of virtue, are inclined to do virtuous deeds through love of virtue, not on account of some extrinsic punishment or reward. Hence the New Law which derives its pre-eminence from the spiritual grace instilled into our hearts, is called the *Law of love*: and it is described as containing spiritual and eternal promises, which are objects of the virtues, chiefly of charity. Accordingly such persons are inclined of themselves to those objects, not as to something foreign but as to something of their own. For this reason, too, the Old Law is described as *restraining the hand, not the will*; since when a man refrains from some sins through fear of being punished, his will does not shrink simply from sin, as does the will of a man who refrains from sin through love of righteousness: and hence the New Law, which is the Law of love, is said to restrain the will.

Nevertheless there were some in the state of the Old Testament who, having charity and the grace of the Holy Spirit, looked chiefly to spiritual and eternal promises: and in this respect they belonged to the New Law. In like manner in the New Testament there are some carnal men who have not yet attained to the perfection of the New Law; and these it was necessary, even under the New Testament, to lead to virtuous action by the fear of punishment and by temporal promises.

But although the Old Law contained precepts of charity, nevertheless it did not confer the Holy Spirit by Whom charity . . . *is spread abroad in our hearts* (Rom 5:5).

REPLY OBJ. 3: As stated above (Q106, AA1,2), the New Law is called the law of faith, insofar as its pre-eminence is derived from that very grace which is given inwardly to believers, and for this reason is called the grace of faith. Nevertheless it consists secondarily in certain deeds, moral and sacramental: but the New Law does not consist chiefly in these latter things, as did the Old Law. As to those under the Old Testament who through faith were acceptable to God, in this respect they belonged to the New Testament: for they were not justified except through faith in Christ, Who is the Author of the New Testament. Hence of Moses the Apostle says (Heb 11:26) that he esteemed *the reproach of Christ greater riches than the treasure of the Egyptians.*

Article 2

Whether the New Law Fulfils the Old?

AD SECUNDUM SIC PROCEDITUR. Videtur quod lex nova legem veterem non impleat. Impletio enim contrariatur evacuationi. Sed lex nova evacuat, vel excludit observantias legis veteris, dicit enim apostolus, ad Gal. V, *si circumcidimini, Christus nihil vobis proderit*. Ergo lex nova non est impletiva veteris legis.

PRAETEREA, contrarium non est impletivum sui contrarii. Sed dominus in lege nova proposuit quaedam praecepta contraria praeceptis veteris legis. Dicitur enim Matth. V, *audistis quia dictum est antiquis, quicumque dimiserit uxorem suam, det ei libellum repudii. Ego autem dico vobis, quicumque dimiserit uxorem suam, facit eam moechari*. Et idem consequenter patet in prohibitione iuramenti, et etiam in prohibitione talionis, et in odio inimicorum. Similiter etiam videtur dominus exclusisse praecepta veteris legis de discretione ciborum, Matth. XV, *non quod intrat in os, coinquinat hominem*. Ergo lex nova non est impletiva veteris.

PRAETEREA, quicumque contra legem agit, non implet legem. Sed Christus in aliquibus contra legem fecit. Tetigit enim leprosum, ut dicitur Matth. VIII, quod erat contra legem. Similiter etiam videtur sabbatum pluries violasse, unde de eo dicebant Iudaei, Ioan. IX, *non est hic homo a Deo, qui sabbatum non custodit*. Ergo Christus non implevit legem. Et ita lex nova data a Christo, non est veteris impletiva.

PRAETEREA, in veteri lege continebantur praecepta moralia, caeremonialia et iudicialia, ut supra dictum est. Sed dominus, Matth. V, ubi quantum ad aliqua legem implevit, nullam mentionem videtur facere de iudicialibus et caeremonialibus. Ergo videtur quod lex nova non sit totaliter veteris impletiva.

SED CONTRA est quod dominus dicit, Matth. V, *non veni solvere legem, sed adimplere*. Et postea, subdit, *iota unum, aut unus apex, non praeteribit a lege, donec omnia fiant*.

RESPONDEO dicendum quod, sicut dictum est, lex nova comparatur ad veterem sicut perfectum ad imperfectum. Omne autem perfectum adimplet id quod imperfecto deest. Et secundum hoc lex nova adimplet veterem legem, inquantum supplet illud quod veteri legi deerat.

In veteri autem lege duo possunt considerari, scilicet finis; et praecepta contenta in lege.

Finis vero cuiuslibet legis est ut homines efficiantur iusti et virtuosi, ut supra dictum est. Unde et finis veteris

OBJECTION 1: It would seem that the New Law does not fulfill the Old. Because to fulfill and to void are contrary. But the New Law voids or excludes the observances of the Old Law: for the Apostle says (Gal 5:2): *If you be circumcised, Christ shall profit you nothing*. Therefore the New Law is not a fulfilment of the Old.

OBJ. 2: Further, one contrary is not the fulfilment of another. But Our Lord propounded in the New Law precepts that were contrary to precepts of the Old Law. For we read (Matt 5:27–32): You have heard that it was said to them of old: . . . *Whosoever shall put away his wife, let him give her a bill of divorce. But I say to you that whosoever shall put away his wife . . . maketh her to commit adultery*. Furthermore, the same evidently applies to the prohibition against swearing, against retaliation, and against hating one's enemies. In like manner Our Lord seems to have done away with the precepts of the Old Law relating to the different kinds of foods (Matt 15:11): *Not that which goeth into the mouth defileth the man: but what cometh out of the mouth, this defileth a man*. Therefore the New Law is not a fulfilment of the Old.

OBJ. 3: Further, whoever acts against a law does not fulfill the law. But Christ in certain cases acted against the Law. For He touched the leper (Matt 8:3), which was contrary to the Law. Likewise He seems to have frequently broken the sabbath; since the Jews used to say of Him (John 9:16): *This man is not of God, who keepeth not the sabbath*. Therefore Christ did not fulfill the Law: and so the New Law given by Christ is not a fulfilment of the Old.

OBJ. 4: Further, the Old Law contained precepts, moral, ceremonial, and judicial, as stated above (Q99, A4). But Our Lord (Matt 5) fulfilled the Law in some respects, but without mentioning the judicial and ceremonial precepts. Therefore it seems that the New Law is not a complete fulfilment of the Old.

ON THE CONTRARY, Our Lord said (Matt 5:17): *I am not come to destroy, but to fulfill*: and went on to say (Matt 5:18): *One jot or one tittle shall not pass of the Law till all be fulfilled*.

I ANSWER THAT, As stated above (A1), the New Law is compared to the Old as the perfect to the imperfect. Now everything perfect fulfils that which is lacking in the imperfect. And accordingly the New Law fulfils the Old by supplying that which was lacking in the Old Law.

Now two things in the Old Law offer themselves to our consideration: viz., the end, and the precepts contained in the Law.

Now the end of every law is to make men righteous and virtuous, as was stated above (Q92, A1): and consequently

legis erat iustificatio hominum. Quam quidem lex efficere non poterat, sed figurabat quibusdam caeremonialibus factis, et promittebat verbis. Et quantum ad hoc, lex nova implet veterem legem iustificando virtute passionis Christi. Et hoc est quod apostolus dicit, ad Rom. VIII, *quod impossibile erat legi, Deus, filium suum mittens in similitudinem carnis peccati, damnavit peccatum in carne, ut iustificatio legis impleretur in nobis.* Et quantum ad hoc, lex nova exhibet quod lex vetus promittebat; secundum illud II ad Cor. I, quotquot promissiones Dei sunt, in illo est, idest in Christo. Et iterum quantum ad hoc etiam complet quod vetus lex figurabat. Unde ad Colos. II dicitur de caeremonialibus quod erant umbra futurorum, corpus autem Christi, idest, veritas pertinet ad Christum. Unde lex nova dicitur lex veritatis, lex autem vetus umbrae vel figurae.

Praecepta vero veteris legis adimplevit Christus et opere, et doctrina. Opere quidem, quia circumcidi voluit, et alia legalia observare, quae erant illo tempore observanda; secundum illud Gal. IV, *factum sub lege.* Sua autem doctrina adimplevit praecepta legis tripliciter. Primo quidem, verum intellectum legis exprimendo. Sicut patet in homicidio et adulterio, in quorum prohibitione Scribae et Pharisaei non intelligebant nisi exteriorem actum prohibitum, unde dominus legem adimplevit, ostendendo etiam interiores actus peccatorum cadere sub prohibitione. Secundo, adimplevit dominus praecepta legis, ordinando quomodo tutius observaretur quod lex vetus statuerat. Sicut lex vetus statuerat ut homo non peiuraret, et hoc tutius observatur si omnino a iuramento abstineat, nisi in casu necessitatis. Tertio, adimplevit dominus praecepta legis, superaddendo quaedam perfectionis consilia, ut patet Matth. XIX, ubi dominus dicenti se observasse praecepta veteris legis, dicit, unum tibi deest. *Si vis perfectus esse, vade et vende omnia quae habes,* et cetera.

Ad primum ergo dicendum quod lex nova non evacuat observantiam veteris legis nisi quantum ad caeremonialia, ut supra habitum est. Haec autem erant in figuram futuri. Unde ex hoc ipso quod caeremonialia praecepta sunt impleta, perfectis his quae figurabantur, non sunt ulterius observanda, quia si observarentur, adhuc significaretur aliquid ut futurum et non impletum. Sicut etiam promissio futuri doni locum iam non habet, promissione iam impleta per doni exhibitionem et per hunc modum, caeremoniae legis tolluntur cum implentur.

Ad secundum dicendum quod, sicut Augustinus dicit, contra Faustum, praecepta illa domini non sunt contraria praeceptis veteris legis *quod enim dominus*

the end of the Old Law was the justification of men. The Law, however, could not accomplish this: but foreshadowed it by certain ceremonial actions, and promised it in words. And in this respect, the New Law fulfils the Old by justifying men through the power of Christ's Passion. This is what the Apostle says (Rom 8:3,4): *What the Law could not do . . . God sending His own Son in the likeness of sinful flesh . . . hath condemned sin in the flesh, that the justification of the Law might be fulfilled in us.* And in this respect, the New Law gives what the Old Law promised, according to 2 Cor. 1:20: *Whatever are the promises of God, in Him,* i.e., in Christ, *they are 'Yea'.* Again, in this respect, it also fulfils what the Old Law foreshadowed. Hence it is written (Col 2:17) concerning the ceremonial precepts that they were *a shadow of things to come, but the body is of Christ;* in other words, the reality is found in Christ. Wherefore the New Law is called the law of reality; whereas the Old Law is called the law of shadow or of figure.

Now Christ fulfilled the precepts of the Old Law both in His works and in His doctrine. In His works, because He was willing to be circumcised and to fulfill the other legal observances, which were binding for the time being; according to Gal. 4:4: *Made under the Law.* In His doctrine He fulfilled the precepts of the Law in three ways. First, by explaining the true sense of the Law. This is clear in the case of murder and adultery, the prohibition of which the Scribes and Pharisees thought to refer only to the exterior act: wherefore Our Lord fulfilled the Law by showing that the prohibition extended also to the interior acts of sins. Second, Our Lord fulfilled the precepts of the Law by prescribing the safest way of complying with the statutes of the Old Law. Thus the Old Law forbade perjury: and this is more safely avoided, by abstaining altogether from swearing, save in cases of urgency. Third, Our Lord fulfilled the precepts of the Law, by adding some counsels of perfection: this is clearly seen in Mt. 19:21, where Our Lord said to the man who affirmed that he had kept all the precepts of the Old Law: *One thing is wanting to thee: If thou wilt be perfect, go, sell whatsoever thou hast,* etc..

Reply Obj. 1: The New Law does not void observance of the Old Law except in the point of ceremonial precepts, as stated above (Q103, AA3,4). Now the latter were figurative of something to come. Wherefore from the very fact that the ceremonial precepts were fulfilled when those things were accomplished which they foreshadowed, it follows that they are no longer to be observed: for if they were to be observed, this would mean that something is still to be accomplished and is not yet fulfilled. Thus the promise of a future gift holds no longer when it has been fulfilled by the presentation of the gift. In this way the legal ceremonies are abolished by being fulfilled.

Reply Obj. 2: As Augustine says (*Contra Faust.* xix, 26), those precepts of Our Lord are not contrary to the precepts of the Old Law. For what Our Lord commanded about

praecepit de uxore non dimittenda, non est contrarium ei quod lex praecepit. Neque enim ait lex, qui voluerit, dimittat uxorem; cui esset contrarium non dimittere. Sed utique nolebat dimitti uxorem a viro, qui hanc interposuit moram, ut in dissidium animus praeceps libelli conscriptione refractus absisteret. Unde dominus, ad hoc confirmandum ut non facile uxor dimittatur, solam causam fornicationis excepit. Et idem etiam dicendum est in prohibitione iuramenti, sicut dictum est. Et idem etiam patet in prohibitione talionis. Taxavit enim modum vindictae lex, ut non procederetur ad immoderatam vindictam, a qua dominus perfectius removit eum quem monuit omnino a vindicta abstinere. Circa odium vero inimicorum, removit falsum Pharisaeorum intellectum, nos monens ut persona odio non haberetur, sed culpa. Circa discretionem vero ciborum, quae caeremonialis erat, dominus non mandavit ut tunc non observaretur, sed ostendit quod nulli cibi secundum suam naturam erant immundi, sed solum secundum figuram, ut supra dictum est.

AD TERTIUM dicendum quod tactus leprosi erat prohibitus in lege, quia ex hoc incurrebat homo quandam irregularitatis immunditiam, sicut et ex tactu mortui, ut supra dictum est. Sed dominus, qui erat mundator leprosi, immunditiam incurrere non poterat. Per ea autem quae fecit in sabbato, sabbatum non solvit secundum rei veritatem, sicut ipse magister in Evangelio ostendit, tum quia operabatur miracula virtute divina, quae semper operatur in rebus; tum quia salutis humanae opera faciebat, cum Pharisaei etiam saluti animalium in die sabbati providerent; tum quia etiam ratione necessitatis discipulos excusavit in sabbato spicas colligentes. Sed videbatur solvere secundum superstitiosum intellectum Pharisaeorum, qui credebant etiam a salubribus operibus esse in die sabbati abstinendum, quod erat contra intentionem legis.

AD QUARTUM dicendum quod caeremonialia praecepta legis non commemorantur Matth. V, quia eorum observantia totaliter excluditur per impletionem, ut dictum est. De iudicialibus vero praeceptis commemoravit praeceptum talionis, ut quod de hoc diceretur, de omnibus aliis esset intelligendum. In quo quidem praecepto docuit legis intentionem non esse ad hoc quod poena talionis quaereretur propter livorem vindictae, quem ipse excludit, monens quod homo debet esse paratus etiam maiores iniurias sufferre, sed solum propter amorem iustitiae. Quod adhuc in nova lege remanet.

a man not putting away his wife, is not contrary to what the Law prescribed. *For the Law did not say: 'Let him that wills, put his wife away': the contrary of which would be not to put her away. On the contrary, the Law was unwilling that a man should put away his wife, since it prescribed a delay, so that excessive eagerness for divorce might cease through being weakened during the writing of the bill. Hence Our Lord, in order to impress the fact that a wife ought not easily to be put away, allowed no exception save in the case of fornication.* The same applies to the prohibition about swearing, as stated above. The same is also clear with respect to the prohibition of retaliation. For the Law fixed a limit to revenge, by forbidding men to seek vengeance unreasonably: whereas Our Lord deprived them of vengeance more completely by commanding them to abstain from it altogether. With regard to the hatred of one's enemies, He dispelled the false interpretation of the Pharisees, by admonishing us to hate, not the person, but his sin. As to discriminating between various foods, which was a ceremonial matter, Our Lord did not forbid this to be observed: but He showed that no foods are naturally unclean, but only in token of something else, as stated above (Q102, A6, ad 1).

REPLY OBJ. 3: It was forbidden by the Law to touch a leper; because by doing so, man incurred a certain uncleanness of irregularity, as also by touching the dead, as stated above (Q102, A5, ad 4). But Our Lord, Who healed the leper, could not contract an uncleanness. By those things which He did on the sabbath, He did not break the sabbath in reality, as the Master Himself shows in the Gospel: both because He worked miracles by His Divine power, which is ever active among things; and because His works were concerned with the salvation of man, while the Pharisees were concerned for the well-being of animals even on the sabbath; and again because on account of urgency He excused His disciples for gathering the ears of corn on the sabbath. But He did seem to break the sabbath according to the superstitious interpretation of the Pharisees, who thought that man ought to abstain from doing even works of kindness on the sabbath; which was contrary to the intention of the Law.

REPLY OBJ. 4: The reason why the ceremonial precepts of the Law are not mentioned in Mt. 5 is because, as stated above (ad 1), their observance was abolished by their fulfilment. But of the judicial precepts He mentioned that of retaliation: so that what He said about it should refer to all the others. With regard to this precept, He taught that the intention of the Law was that retaliation should be sought out of love of justice, and not as a punishment out of revengeful spite, which He forbade, admonishing man to be ready to suffer yet greater insults; and this remains still in the New Law.

Article 3

Whether the New Law Is Contained in the Old?

AD TERTIUM SIC PROCEDITUR. Videtur quod lex nova in lege veteri non contineatur. Lex enim nova praecipue in fide consistit, unde dicitur lex fidei, ut patet Rom. III. Sed multa credenda traduntur in nova lege quae in veteri non continentur. Ergo lex nova non continetur in veteri.

PRAETEREA, quaedam Glossa dicit, Matth. V, super illud, *qui solverit unum de mandatis istis minimis*, quod mandata legis sunt minora, in Evangelio vero sunt mandata maiora. Maius autem non potest contineri in minori. Ergo lex nova non continetur in veteri.

PRAETEREA, quod continetur in altero, simul habetur habito illo. Si igitur lex nova contineretur in veteri, sequeretur quod, habita veteri lege, habeatur et nova. Superfluum igitur fuit, habita veteri lege, iterum dari novam. Non ergo nova lex continetur in veteri.

SED CONTRA est quod, sicut dicitur Ezech. I, *rota erat in rota*, idest *novum testamentum in veteri*, ut Gregorius exponit.

RESPONDEO dicendum quod aliquid continetur in alio dupliciter. Uno modo, in actu, sicut locatum in loco. Alio modo, virtute, sicut effectus in causa, vel complementum in incompleto, sicut genus continet species potestate, et sicut tota arbor continetur in semine. Et per hunc modum nova lex continetur in veteri, dictum est enim quod nova lex comparatur ad veterem sicut perfectum ad imperfectum. Unde Chrysostomus exponens illud quod habetur Marc. IV, *ultro terra fructificat primum herbam, deinde spicam, deinde plenum frumentum in spica*, sic dicit, *primo herbam fructificat in lege naturae; postmodum spicas in lege Moysi; postea plenum frumentum, in Evangelio*. Sic igitur est lex nova in veteri sicut fructus in spica.

AD PRIMUM ergo dicendum quod omnia quae credenda traduntur in novo testamento explicite et aperte, traduntur credenda in veteri testamento, sed implicite sub figura. Et secundum hoc etiam quantum ad credenda lex nova continetur in veteri.

AD SECUNDUM dicendum quod praecepta novae legis dicuntur esse maiora quam praecepta veteris legis, quantum ad explicitam manifestationem. Sed quantum ad ipsam substantiam praeceptorum novi testamenti, omnia continentur in veteri testamento. Unde Augustinus dicit, contra Faustum, quod *pene omnia quae monuit vel praecepit dominus, ubi adiungebat, ego autem dico vobis, inveniuntur etiam in illis veteribus libris. Sed quia non intelligebant homicidium nisi peremptionem corporis*

OBJECTION 1: It would seem that the New Law is not contained in the Old. Because the New Law consists chiefly in faith: wherefore it is called the *law of faith* (Rom 3:27). But many points of faith are set forth in the New Law, which are not contained in the Old. Therefore the New Law is not contained in the Old.

OBJ. 2: Further, a gloss says on Mt. 5:19, *He that shall break one of these least commandments*, that the lesser commandments are those of the Law, and the greater commandments, those contained in the Gospel. Now the greater cannot be contained in the lesser. Therefore the New Law is not contained in the Old.

OBJ. 3: Further, who holds the container holds the contents. If, therefore, the New Law is contained in the Old, it follows that whoever had the Old Law had the New: so that it was superfluous to give men a New Law when once they had the Old. Therefore the New Law is not contained in the Old.

ON THE CONTRARY, As expressed in Ezech. 1:16, there was *a wheel in the midst of a wheel*, i.e., *the New Testament within the Old*, according to Gregory's exposition.

I ANSWER THAT, One thing may be contained in another in two ways. First, actually; as a located thing is in a place. Second, virtually; as an effect in its cause, or as the complement in that which is incomplete; thus a genus contains its species, and a seed contains the whole tree, virtually. It is in this way that the New Law is contained in the Old: for it has been stated (A1) that the New Law is compared to the Old as perfect to imperfect. Hence Chrysostom, expounding Mk. 4:28, *The earth of itself bringeth forth fruit, first the blade, then the ear, afterwards the full corn in the ear*, expresses himself as follows: *He brought forth first the blade, i.e., the Law of Nature; then the ear, i.e., the Law of Moses; lastly, the full corn, i.e., the Law of the Gospel*. Hence then the New Law is in the Old as the corn in the ear.

REPLY OBJ. 1: Whatsoever is set down in the New Testament explicitly and openly as a point of faith, is contained in the Old Testament as a matter of belief, but implicitly, under a figure. And accordingly, even as to those things which we are bound to believe, the New Law is contained in the Old.

REPLY OBJ. 2: The precepts of the New Law are said to be greater than those of the Old Law, in the point of their being set forth explicitly. But as to the substance itself of the precepts of the New Testament, they are all contained in the Old. Hence Augustine says (*Contra Faust.* xix, 23,28) that *nearly all Our Lord's admonitions or precepts, where He expressed Himself by saying: 'But I say unto you,' are to be found also in those ancient books. Yet, since they thought that murder was only the slaying of the human body, Our*

humani, aperuit dominus omnem iniquum motum ad nocendum fratri, in homicidii genere deputari. Et quantum ad huiusmodi manifestationes, praecepta novae legis dicuntur maiora praeceptis veteris legis. Nihil tamen prohibet maius in minori virtute contineri, sicut arbor continetur in semine.

AD TERTIUM dicendum quod illud quod implicite datum est, oportet explicari. Et ideo post veterem legem latam, oportuit etiam novam legem dari.

Lord declared to them that every wicked impulse to hurt our brother is to be looked on as a kind of murder. And it is in the point of declarations of this kind that the precepts of the New Law are said to be greater than those of the Old. Nothing, however, prevents the greater from being contained in the lesser virtually; just as a tree is contained in the seed.

REPLY OBJ. 3: What is set forth implicitly needs to be declared explicitly. Hence after the publishing of the Old Law, a New Law also had to be given.

Article 4

Whether the New Law Is More Burdensome Than the Old?

AD QUARTUM SIC PROCEDITUR. Videtur quod lex nova sit gravior quam lex vetus. Matth. enim V, super illud, *qui solverit unum de mandatis his minimis*, dicit Chrysostomus, *mandata Moysi in actu facilia sunt, non occides, non adulterabis. Mandata autem Christi, idest, non irascaris, non concupiscas, in actu difficilia sunt.* Ergo lex nova est gravior quam vetus.

PRAETEREA, facilius est terrena prosperitate uti quam tribulationes perpeti. Sed in veteri testamento observationem veteris legis consequebatur prosperitas temporalis, ut patet Deut. XXVIII. Observatores autem novae legis consequitur multiplex adversitas, prout dicitur II ad Cor. VI, *exhibeamus nosmetipsos sicut Dei ministros in multa patientia, in tribulationibus, in necessitatibus, in angustiis,* et cetera. Ergo lex nova est gravior quam lex vetus.

PRAETEREA, quod se habet ex additione ad alterum, videtur esse difficilius. Sed lex nova se habet ex additione ad veterem. Nam lex vetus prohibuit periurium, lex nova etiam iuramentum, lex vetus prohibuit discidium uxoris sine libello repudii, lex autem nova omnino discidium prohibuit, ut patet Matth. V, secundum expositionem Augustini. Ergo lex nova est gravior quam vetus.

SED CONTRA est quod dicitur Matth. XI, *venite ad me omnes qui laboratis et onerati estis.* Quod exponens Hilarius dicit, *legis difficultatibus laborantes, et peccatis saeculi oneratos, ad se advocat.* Et postmodum de iugo Evangelii subdit, *iugum enim meum suave est, et onus meum leve.* Ergo lex nova est levior quam vetus.

RESPONDEO dicendum quod circa opera virtutis, de quibus praecepta legis dantur, duplex difficultas attendi potest. Una quidem ex parte exteriorum operum, quae ex seipsis quandam difficultatem habent et gravitatem. Et quantum ad hoc, lex vetus est multo gravior quam

OBJECTION 1: It would seem that the New Law is more burdensome than the Old. For Chrysostom (*Opus Imp. in Matth.*, Hom. x) says: *The commandments given to Moses are easy to obey: Thou shalt not kill; Thou shalt not commit adultery: but the commandments of Christ are difficult to accomplish, for instance: Thou shalt not give way to anger, or to lust.* Therefore the New Law is more burdensome than the Old.

OBJ. 2: Further, it is easier to make use of earthly prosperity than to suffer tribulations. But in the Old Testament observance of the Law was followed by temporal prosperity, as may be gathered from Dt. 28:1–14; whereas many kinds of trouble ensue to those who observe the New Law, as stated in 2 Cor. 6:4–10: *Let us exhibit ourselves as the ministers of God, in much patience, in tribulation, in necessities, in distresses,* etc. Therefore the New Law is more burdensome than the Old.

OBJ. 3: The more one has to do, the more difficult it is. But the New Law is something added to the Old. For the Old Law forbade perjury, while the New Law proscribed even swearing: the Old Law forbade a man to cast off his wife without a bill of divorce, while the New Law forbade divorce altogether; as is clearly stated in Mt. 5:31, seqq., according to Augustine's expounding. Therefore the New Law is more burdensome than the Old.

ON THE CONTRARY, It is written (Matt 11:28): *Come to Me, all you that labor and are burdened*: which words are expounded by Hilary thus: *He calls to Himself all those that labor under the difficulty of observing the Law, and are burdened with the sins of this world.* And further on He says of the yoke of the Gospel: *For My yoke is sweet and My burden light.* Therefore the New Law is a lighter burden than the Old.

I ANSWER THAT, A twofold difficult may attach to works of virtue with which the precepts of the Law are concerned. One is on the part of the outward works, which of themselves are, in a way, difficult and burdensome. And in this respect the Old Law is a much heavier burden than the

nova, quia ad plures actus exteriores obligabat lex vetus in multiplicibus caeremoniis, quam lex nova, quae praeter praecepta legis naturae, paucissima superaddidit in doctrina Christi et apostolorum; licet aliqua sint postmodum superaddita ex institutione sanctorum patrum. In quibus etiam Augustinus dicit esse moderationem attendendam, ne conversatio fidelium onerosa reddatur. Dicit enim, ad inquisitiones Ianuarii, de quibusdam, quod *ipsam religionem nostram, quam in manifestissimis et paucissimis celebrationum sacramentis Dei misericordia voluit esse liberam, servilibus premunt oneribus, adeo ut tolerabilior sit conditio Iudaeorum, qui legalibus sacramentis, non humanis praesumptionibus subiiciuntur.*

Alia autem difficultas est circa opera virtutum in interioribus actibus, puta quod aliquis opus virtutis exerceat prompte et delectabiliter. Et circa hoc difficile est virtus, hoc enim non habenti virtutem est valde difficile; sed per virtutem redditur facile. Et quantum ad hoc, praecepta novae legis sunt graviora praeceptis veteris legis, quia in nova lege prohibentur interiores motus animi, qui expresse in veteri lege non prohibebantur in omnibus, etsi in aliquibus prohiberentur; in quibus tamen prohibendis poena non apponebatur. Hoc autem est difficillimum non habenti virtutem, sicut etiam philosophus dicit, in V Ethic., quod operari ea quae iustus operatur, facile est; sed operari ea eo modo quo iustus operatur, scilicet delectabiliter et prompte, est difficile non habenti iustitiam. Et sic etiam dicitur I Ioan. V, quod mandata eius gravia non sunt, quod exponens Augustinus dicit quod *non sunt gravia amanti, sed non amanti sunt gravia.*

AD PRIMUM ergo dicendum quod auctoritas illa expresse loquitur de difficultate novae legis quantum ad expressam cohibitionem interiorum motuum.

AD SECUNDUM dicendum quod adversitates quas patiuntur observatores novae legis, non sunt ab ipsa lege impositae. Sed tamen propter amorem, in quo ipsa lex consistit, faciliter tollerantur, quia sicut Augustinus dicit, in libro de verbis domini, *omnia saeva et immania facilia et prope nulla efficit amor.*

AD TERTIUM dicendum quod illae additiones ad praecepta veteris legis, ad hoc ordinantur ut facilius impleatur quod vetus lex mandabat, sicut Augustinus dicit. Et ideo per hoc non ostenditur quod lex nova sit gravior, sed magis quod sit facilior.

New: since the Old Law by its numerous ceremonies prescribed many more outward acts than the New Law, which, in the teaching of Christ and the apostles, added very few precepts to those of the natural law; although afterwards some were added, through being instituted by the holy Fathers. Even in these Augustine says that moderation should be observed, lest good conduct should become a burden to the faithful. For he says in reply to the queries of Januarius (*Ep. lv*) that, *whereas God in His mercy wished religion to be a free service rendered by the public solemnization of a small number of most manifest sacraments, certain persons make it a slave's burden; so much so that the state of the Jews who were subject to the sacraments of the Law, and not to the presumptuous devices of man, was more tolerable.*

The other difficulty attaches to works of virtue as to interior acts: for instance, that a virtuous deed be done with promptitude and pleasure. It is this difficulty that virtue solves: because to act thus is difficult for a man without virtue: but through virtue it becomes easy for him. In this respect the precepts of the New Law are more burdensome than those of the Old; because the New Law prohibits certain interior movements of the soul, which were not expressly forbidden in the Old Law in all cases, although they were forbidden in some, without, however, any punishment being attached to the prohibition. Now this is very difficult to a man without virtue: thus even the Philosopher states (*Ethic.* v, 9) that it is easy to do what a righteous man does; but that to do it in the same way, viz., with pleasure and promptitude, is difficult to a man who is not righteous. Accordingly we read also (1 John 5:3) that *His commandments are not heavy*: which words Augustine expounds by saying that *they are not heavy to the man that loveth; whereas they are a burden to him that loveth not.*

REPLY OBJ. 1: The passage quoted speaks expressly of the difficulty of the New Law as to the deliberate curbing of interior movements.

REPLY OBJ. 2: The tribulations suffered by those who observe the New Law are not imposed by the Law itself. Moreover they are easily borne, on account of the love in which the same Law consists: since, as Augustine says (*De Verb. Dom.*, Serm. lxx), *love makes light and nothing of things that seem arduous and beyond our power.*

REPLY OBJ. 3: The object of these additions to the precepts of the Old Law was to render it easier to do what it prescribed, as Augustine states. Accordingly this does not prove that the New Law is more burdensome, but rather that it is a lighter burden.

QUESTION 108

OF THOSE THINGS THAT ARE CONTAINED IN THE NEW LAW

Deinde considerandum est de his quae continentur in lege nova. Et circa hoc quaeruntur quatuor.

Primo, utrum lex nova debeat aliqua opera exteriora praecipere vel prohibere.

Secundo, utrum sufficienter se habeat in exterioribus actibus praecipiendis vel prohibendis.

Tertio, utrum convenienter instituat homines quantum ad actus interiores.

Quarto, utrum convenienter superaddat consilia praeceptis.

We must now consider those things that are contained in the New Law: under which head there are four points of inquiry:

(1) Whether the New Law ought to prescribe or to forbid any outward works?

(2) Whether the New Law makes sufficient provision in prescribing and forbidding external acts?

(3) Whether in the matter of internal acts it directs man sufficiently?

(4) Whether it fittingly adds counsels to precepts?

Article 1

Whether the New Law Ought to Prescribe or Prohibit Any External Acts?

AD PRIMUM SIC PROCEDITUR. Videtur quod lex nova nullos exteriores actus debeat praecipere vel prohibere. Lex enim nova est Evangelium regni; secundum illud Matth. XXIV, *praedicabitur hoc Evangelium regni in universo orbe*. Sed regnum Dei non consistit in exterioribus actibus, sed solum in interioribus; secundum illud Luc. XVII, *regnum Dei intra vos est*; et Rom. XIV, *non est regnum Dei esca et potus, sed iustitia et pax et gaudium in spiritu sancto*. Ergo lex nova non debet praecipere vel prohibere aliquos exteriores actus.

PRAETEREA, *lex nova est lex spiritus*, ut dicitur Rom. VIII. Sed *ubi spiritus domini, ibi libertas*, ut dicitur II ad Cor. III. Non est autem libertas ubi homo obligatur ad aliqua exteriora opera facienda vel vitanda. Ergo lex nova non continet aliqua praecepta vel prohibitiones exteriorum actuum.

PRAETEREA, omnes exteriores actus pertinere intelliguntur ad manum, sicut interiores actus pertinent ad animum. Sed haec ponitur differentia inter novam legem et veterem, quod *vetus lex cohibet manum, sed lex nova cohibet animum*. Ergo in lege nova non debent poni prohibitiones et praecepta exteriorum actuum, sed solum interiorum.

SED CONTRA est quod per legem novam efficiuntur homines filii lucis, unde dicitur Ioan. XII, *credite in lucem, ut filii lucis sitis*. Sed filios lucis decet opera lucis facere, et opera tenebrarum abiicere; secundum illud Ephes. V, *eratis aliquando tenebrae, nunc autem lux in domino. Ut filii lucis ambulate*. Ergo lex nova quaedam

OBJECTION 1: It would seem that the New Law should not prescribe or prohibit any external acts. For the New Law is the Gospel of the kingdom, according to Mt. 24:14: *This Gospel of the kingdom shall be preached in the whole world*. But the kingdom of God consists not in exterior, but only in interior acts, according to Lk. 17:21: *The kingdom of God is within you*; and Rm. 14:17: *The kingdom of God is not meat and drink; but justice and peace and joy in the Holy Spirit*. Therefore the New Law should not prescribe or forbid any external acts.

OBJ. 2: Further, the New Law is *the law of the Spirit* (Rom 8:2). But *where the Spirit of the Lord is, there is liberty* (2 Cor 3:17). Now there is no liberty when man is bound to do or avoid certain external acts. Therefore the New Law does not prescribe or forbid any external acts.

OBJ. 3: Further, all external acts are understood as referable to the hand, just as interior acts belong to the mind. But this is assigned as the difference between the New and Old Laws that the *Old Law restrains the hand, whereas the New Law curbs the will*. Therefore the New Law should not contain prohibitions and commands about exterior deeds, but only about interior acts.

ON THE CONTRARY, Through the New Law, men are made *children of light*: wherefore it is written (John 12:36): *Believe in the light that you may be the children of light*. Now it is becoming that children of the light should do deeds of light and cast aside deeds of darkness, according to Eph. 5:8: *You were heretofore darkness, but now light in the Lord*.

exteriora opera debuit prohibere, et quaedam praecipere.

RESPONDEO dicendum quod, sicut dictum est, principalitas legis novae est gratia spiritus sancti, quae manifestatur in fide per dilectionem operante. Hanc autem gratiam consequuntur homines per Dei filium hominem factum, cuius humanitatem primo replevit gratia, et exinde est ad nos derivata. Unde dicitur Ioan. I, *verbum caro factum est*; et postea subditur, *plenum gratiae et veritatis*; et infra, *de plenitudine eius nos omnes accepimus, et gratiam pro gratia.* Unde subditur quod gratia et veritas per Iesum Christum facta est. Et ideo convenit ut per aliqua exteriora sensibilia gratia a verbo incarnato profluens in nos deducatur; et ex hac interiori gratia, per quam caro spiritui subditur, exteriora quaedam opera sensibilia producantur.

Sic igitur exteriora opera dupliciter ad gratiam pertinere possunt. Uno modo, sicut inducentia aliqualiter ad gratiam. Et talia sunt opera sacramentorum quae in lege nova sunt instituta, sicut Baptismus, Eucharistia, et alia huiusmodi.

Alia vero sunt opera exteriora quae ex instinctu gratiae producuntur. Et in his est quaedam differentia attendenda. Quaedam enim habent necessariam convenientiam vel contrarietatem ad interiorem gratiam, quae in fide per dilectionem operante consistit. Et huiusmodi exteriora opera sunt praecepta vel prohibita in lege nova, sicut praecepta est confessio fidei, et prohibita negatio; dicitur enim Matth. X, *qui confitebitur me coram hominibus, confitebor et ego eum coram patre meo. Qui autem negaverit me coram hominibus, negabo et ego eum coram patre meo.* Alia vero sunt opera quae non habent necessariam contrarietatem vel convenientiam ad fidem per dilectionem operantem. Et talia opera non sunt in nova lege praecepta vel prohibita ex ipsa prima legis institutione; sed relicta sunt a legislatore, scilicet Christo, unicuique, secundum quod aliquis curam gerere debet. Et sic unicuique liberum est circa talia determinare quid sibi expediat facere vel vitare; et cuicumque praesidenti, circa talia ordinare suis subditis quid sit in talibus faciendum vel vitandum. Unde etiam quantum ad hoc dicitur lex Evangelii lex libertatis, nam lex vetus multa determinabat, et pauca relinquebat hominum libertati determinanda.

AD PRIMUM ergo dicendum quod regnum Dei in interioribus actibus principaliter consistit, sed ex consequenti etiam ad regnum Dei pertinent omnia illa sine quibus interiores actus esse non possunt. Sicut si regnum Dei est interior iustitia et pax et gaudium spirituale, necesse est quod omnes exteriores actus qui repugnant iustitiae aut paci aut gaudio spirituali, repugnent regno Dei, et ideo sunt in Evangelio regni prohibendi. Illa vero quae indifferenter se habent respectu horum, puta comedere hos vel illos cibos, in his non est regnum

Walk . . . as children of the light. Therefore the New Law had to forbid certain external acts and prescribe others.

I ANSWER THAT, As stated above (Q106, AA1,2), the New Law consists chiefly in the grace of the Holy Spirit, which is shown forth by faith that worketh through love. Now men become receivers of this grace through God's Son made man, Whose humanity grace filled first, and thence flowed forth to us. Hence it is written (John 1:14): *The Word was made flesh*, and afterwards: *full of grace and truth*; and further on: *Of His fullness we all have received, and grace for grace.* Hence it is added that *grace and truth came by Jesus Christ.* Consequently it was becoming that the grace which flows from the incarnate Word should be given to us by means of certain external sensible objects; and that from this inward grace, whereby the flesh is subjected to the Spirit, certain external works should ensue.

Accordingly external acts may have a twofold connection with grace. In the first place, as leading in some way to grace. Such are the sacramental acts which are instituted in the New Law, e.g., Baptism, the Eucharist, and the like.

In the second place there are those external acts which ensue from the promptings of grace: and herein we must observe a difference. For there are some which are necessarily in keeping with, or in opposition to inward grace consisting in faith that worketh through love. Such external works are prescribed or forbidden in the New Law; thus confession of faith is prescribed, and denial of faith is forbidden; for it is written (Matt 10:32,33) *(Every one) that shall confess Me before men, I will also confess him before My Father . . . But he that shall deny Me before men, I will also deny him before My Father.* On the other hand, there are works which are not necessarily opposed to, or in keeping with faith that worketh through love. Such works are not prescribed or forbidden in the New Law, by virtue of its primitive institution; but have been left by the Lawgiver, i.e., Christ, to the discretion of each individual. And so to each one it is free to decide what he should do or avoid; and to each superior, to direct his subjects in such matters as regards what they must do or avoid. Wherefore also in this respect the Gospel is called the *law of liberty*: since the Old Law decided many points and left few to man to decide as he chose.

REPLY OBJ. 1: The kingdom of God consists chiefly in internal acts: but as a consequence all things that are essential to internal acts belong also to the kingdom of God. Thus if the kingdom of God is internal righteousness, peace, and spiritual joy, all external acts that are incompatible with righteousness, peace, and spiritual joy, are in opposition to the kingdom of God; and consequently should be forbidden in the Gospel of the kingdom. On the other hand, those things that are indifferent as regards the aforesaid, for instance, to eat of this or that food, are not part of

Dei, unde apostolus praemittit, *non est regnum Dei esca et potus.*

Ad secundum dicendum quod, secundum philosophum, in I Metaphys., *liber est qui sui causa est.* Ille ergo libere aliquid agit qui ex seipso agit. Quod autem homo agit ex habitu suae naturae convenienti, ex seipso agit, quia habitus inclinat in modum naturae. Si vero habitus esset naturae repugnans, homo non ageret secundum quod est ipse, sed secundum aliquam corruptionem sibi supervenientem. Quia igitur gratia spiritus sancti est sicut interior habitus nobis infusus inclinans nos ad recte operandum, facit nos libere operari ea quae conveniunt gratiae, et vitare ea quae gratiae repugnant.

Sic igitur lex nova dicitur lex libertatis dupliciter. Uno modo, quia non arctat nos ad facienda vel vitanda aliqua, nisi quae de se sunt vel necessaria vel repugnantia saluti, quae cadunt sub praecepto vel prohibitione legis. Secundo, quia huiusmodi etiam praecepta vel prohibitiones facit nos libere implere, inquantum ex interiori instinctu gratiae ea implemus. Et propter haec duo lex nova dicitur *lex perfectae libertatis,* Iac. I.

Ad tertium dicendum quod lex nova, cohibendo animum ab inordinatis motibus, oportet quod etiam cohibeat manum ab inordinatis actibus, qui sunt effectus interiorum motuum.

the kingdom of God; wherefore the Apostle says before the words quoted: *The kingdom of God is not meat and drink.*

Reply Obj. 2: According to the Philosopher (*Metaph.* i, 2), what is *free is cause of itself.* Therefore he acts freely, who acts of his own accord. Now man does of his own accord that which he does from a habit that is suitable to his nature: since a habit inclines one as a second nature. If, however, a habit be in opposition to nature, man would not act according to his nature, but according to some corruption affecting that nature. Since then the grace of the Holy Spirit is like an interior habit bestowed on us and inclining us to act aright, it makes us do freely those things that are becoming to grace, and shun what is opposed to it.

Accordingly the New Law is called the law of liberty in two respects. First, because it does not bind us to do or avoid certain things, except such as are of themselves necessary or opposed to salvation, and come under the prescription or prohibition of the law. Second, because it also makes us comply freely with these precepts and prohibitions, inasmuch as we do so through the promptings of grace. It is for these two reasons that the New Law is called *the law of perfect liberty* (Jas 1:25).

Reply Obj. 3: The New Law, by restraining the mind from inordinate movements, must needs also restrain the hand from inordinate acts, which ensue from inward movements.

Article 2

Whether the New Law Made Sufficient Ordinations About External Acts?

Ad secundum sic proceditur. Videtur quod lex nova insufficienter exteriores actus ordinaverit. Ad legem enim novam praecipue pertinere videtur fides per dilectionem operans; secundum illud ad Gal. V, *in Christo Iesu neque circumcisio aliquid valet neque praeputium, sed fides quae per dilectionem operatur.* Sed lex nova explicavit quaedam credenda quae non erant in veteri lege explicita, sicut de fide Trinitatis. Ergo etiam debuit superaddere aliqua exteriora opera moralia, quae non erant in veteri lege determinata.

Praeterea, in veteri lege non solum instituta sunt sacramenta, sed etiam aliqua sacra, ut supra dictum est. Sed in nova lege, etsi sint instituta aliqua sacramenta, nulla tamen sacra instituta a domino videntur, puta quae pertineant vel ad sanctificationem alicuius templi aut vasorum, vel etiam ad aliquam solemnitatem celebrandam. Ergo lex nova insufficienter exteriora ordinavit.

Praeterea, in veteri lege, sicut erant quaedam observantiae pertinentes ad Dei ministros, ita etiam erant quaedam observantiae pertinentes ad populum; ut supra

Objection 1: It would seem that the New Law made insufficient ordinations about external acts. Because faith that worketh through charity seems chiefly to belong to the New Law, according to Gal. 5:6: *In Christ Jesus neither circumcision availeth anything, nor uncircumcision: but faith that worketh through charity.* But the New Law declared explicitly certain points of faith which were not set forth explicitly in the Old Law; for instance, belief in the Trinity. Therefore it should also have added certain outward moral deeds, which were not fixed in the Old Law.

Obj. 2: Further, in the Old Law not only were sacraments instituted, but also certain sacred things, as stated above (Q101, A4; Q102, A4). But in the New Law, although certain sacraments are instituted by Our Lord; for instance, pertaining either to the sanctification of a temple or of the vessels, or to the celebration of some particular feast. Therefore the New Law made insufficient ordinations about external matters.

Obj. 3: Further, in the Old Law, just as there were certain observances pertaining to God's ministers, so also were there certain observances pertaining to the people: as was

dictum est, cum de caeremonialibus veteris legis ageretur. Sed in nova lege videntur aliquae observantiae esse
datae ministris Dei, ut patet Matth. X, *nolite possidere
aurum neque argentum, neque pecuniam in zonis vestris*,
et cetera quae ibi sequuntur, et quae dicuntur Luc. IX et
X. Ergo etiam debuerunt aliquae observantiae institui in
nova lege ad populum fidelem pertinentes.

PRAETEREA, in veteri lege, praeter moralia et caeremonialia, fuerunt quaedam iudicialia praecepta. Sed
in lege nova non traduntur aliqua iudicialia praecepta.
Ergo lex nova insufficienter exteriora opera ordinavit.

SED CONTRA est quod dominus dicit, Matth. VII,
*omnis qui audit verba mea haec et facit ea, assimilabitur
viro sapienti qui aedificavit domum suam supra petram.*
Sed sapiens aedificator nihil omittit eorum quae sunt necessaria ad aedificium. Ergo in verbis Christi sufficienter
sunt omnia posita quae pertinent ad salutem humanam.

RESPONDEO dicendum quod, sicut dictum est, lex
nova in exterioribus illa solum praecipere debuit vel prohibere, per quae in gratiam introducimur, vel quae pertinent ad rectum gratiae usum ex necessitate. Et quia gratiam ex nobis consequi non possumus, sed per Christum
solum, ideo sacramenta, per quae gratiam consequimur,
ipse dominus instituit per seipsum, scilicet Baptismum,
Eucharistiam, ordinem ministrorum novae legis, instituendo apostolos et septuaginta duos discipulos, et
poenitentiam, et matrimonium indivisibile. Confirmationem etiam promisit per spiritus sancti missionem. Ex
eius etiam institutione apostoli leguntur oleo infirmos
ungendo sanasse, ut habetur Marc. VI. Quae sunt novae
legis sacramenta.

Rectus autem gratiae usus est per opera caritatis.
Quae quidem secundum quod sunt de necessitate virtutis, pertinent ad praecepta moralia, quae etiam in veteri lege tradebantur. Unde quantum ad hoc, lex nova
super veterem addere non debuit circa exteriora agenda.
Determinatio autem praedictorum operum in ordine
ad cultum Dei, pertinet ad praecepta caeremonialia legis; in ordine vero ad proximum, ad iudicialia; ut supra
dictum est. Et ideo, quia istae determinationes non sunt
secundum se de necessitate interioris gratiae, in qua lex
consistit; idcirco non cadunt sub praecepto novae legis,
sed relinquuntur humano arbitrio; quaedam quidem
quantum ad subditos, quae scilicet pertinent singillatim
ad unumquemque; quaedam vero ad praelatos temporales vel spirituales, quae scilicet pertinent ad utilitatem
communem.

Sic igitur lex nova nulla alia exteriora opera determinare debuit praecipiendo vel prohibendo, nisi sacramenta, et moralia praecepta quae de se pertinent ad rationem
virtutis, puta non esse occidendum, non esse furandum,
et alia huiusmodi.

stated above when we were treating of the ceremonial of
the Old Law (Q101, A4; Q102, A6). Now in the New Law
certain observances seem to have been prescribed to the
ministers of God; as may be gathered from Mt. 10:9: *Do not
possess gold, nor silver, nor money in your purses*, nor other
things which are mentioned here and Lk. 9,10. Therefore
certain observances pertaining to the faithful should also
have been instituted in the New Law.

OBJ. 4: Further, in the Old Law, besides moral and ceremonial precepts, there were certain judicial precepts. But
in the New Law there are no judicial precepts. Therefore
the New Law made insufficient ordinations about external
works.

ON THE CONTRARY, Our Lord said (Matt 7:24): *Every
one . . . that heareth these My words, and doth them, shall be
likened to a wise man that built his house upon a rock.* But
a wise builder leaves out nothing that is necessary to the
building. Therefore Christ's words contain all things necessary for man's salvation.

I ANSWER THAT, as stated above (A1), the New Law
had to make such prescriptions or prohibitions alone as are
essential for the reception or right use of grace. And since
we cannot of ourselves obtain grace, but through Christ
alone, hence Christ of Himself instituted the sacraments
whereby we obtain grace: viz., Baptism, Eucharist, Orders
of the ministers of the New Law, by the institution of the
apostles and seventy-two disciples, Penance, and indissol-
uble Matrimony. He promised Confirmation through the
sending of the Holy Spirit: and we read that by His institution the apostles healed the sick by anointing them with oil
(Mark 6:13). These are the sacraments of the New Law.

The right use of grace is by means of works of charity.
These, insofar as they are essential to virtue, pertain to the
moral precepts, which also formed part of the Old Law.
Hence, in this respect, the New Law had nothing to add as
regards external action. The determination of these works
in their relation to the divine worship, belongs to the ceremonial precepts of the Law; and, in relation to our neighbor, to the judicial precepts, as stated above (Q99, A4). And
therefore, since these determinations are not in themselves
necessarily connected with inward grace wherein the Law
consists, they do not come under a precept of the New Law,
but are left to the decision of man; some relating to inferiors—as when a precept is given to an individual; others, relating to superiors, temporal or spiritual, referring, namely,
to the common good.

Accordingly the New Law had no other external works
to determine, by prescribing or forbidding, except the sacraments, and those moral precepts which have a necessary
connection with virtue, for instance, that one must not kill,
or steal, and so forth.

Ad primum ergo dicendum quod ea quae sunt fidei, sunt supra rationem humanam, unde in ea non possumus pervenire nisi per gratiam. Et ideo, abundantiori gratia superveniente, oportuit plura credenda explicari. Sed ad opera virtutum dirigimur per rationem naturalem, quae est regula quaedam operationis humanae, ut supra dictum est. Et ideo in his non oportuit aliqua praecepta dari ultra moralia legis praecepta, quae sunt de dictamine rationis.

Ad secundum dicendum quod in sacramentis novae legis datur gratia, quae non est nisi a Christo, et ideo oportuit quod ab ipso institutionem haberent. Sed in sacris non datur aliqua gratia, puta in consecratione templi vel altaris vel aliorum huiusmodi, aut etiam in ipsa celebritate solemnitatum. Et ideo talia, quia secundum seipsa non pertinent ad necessitatem interioris gratiae, dominus fidelibus instituenda reliquit pro suo arbitrio.

Ad tertium dicendum quod illa praecepta dominus dedit apostolis non tanquam caeremoniales observantias, sed tanquam moralia instituta. Et possunt intelligi dupliciter. Uno modo, secundum Augustinum, in libro de consensu Evangelist., ut non sint praecepta, sed concessiones. Concessit enim eis ut possent pergere ad praedicationis officium sine pera et baculo et aliis huiusmodi, tanquam habentes potestatem necessaria vitae accipiendi ab illis quibus praedicabant, unde subdit, dignus enim est operarius cibo suo. Non autem peccat, sed supererogat, qui sua portat, ex quibus vivat in praedicationis officio, non accipiens sumptum ab his quibus Evangelium praedicat, sicut Paulus fecit.

Alio modo possunt intelligi, secundum aliorum sanctorum expositionem, ut sint quaedam statuta temporalia apostolis data pro illo tempore quo mittebantur ad praedicandum in Iudaea ante Christi passionem. Indigebant enim discipuli, quasi adhuc parvuli sub Christi cura existentes, accipere aliqua specialia instituta a Christo, sicut et quilibet subditi a suis praelatis, et praecipue quia erant paulatim exercitandi ut temporalium sollicitudinem abdicarent, per quod reddebantur idonei ad hoc quod Evangelium per universum orbem praedicarent. Nec est mirum si, adhuc durante statu veteris legis, et nondum perfectam libertatem spiritus consecutis, quosdam determinatos modos vivendi instituit. Quae quidem statuta, imminente passione, removit, tanquam discipulis iam per ea sufficienter exercitatis. Unde Luc. XXII, dixit, *quando misi vos sine sacculo et pera et calceamentis, numquid aliquid defuit vobis? At illi dixerunt, nihil. Dixit ergo eis, sed nunc qui habet sacculum, tollat; similiter et peram.* Iam enim imminebat tempus perfectae libertatis, ut totaliter suo dimitterentur arbitrio in his quae secundum se non pertinent ad necessitatem virtutis.

Reply Obj. 1: Matters of faith are above human reason, and so we cannot attain to them except through grace. Consequently, when grace came to be bestowed more abundantly, the result was an increase in the number of explicit points of faith. On the other hand, it is through human reason that we are directed to works of virtue, for it is the rule of human action, as stated above (Q19, A3; Q63, A2). Wherefore in such matters as these there was no need for any precepts to be given besides the moral precepts of the Law, which proceed from the dictate of reason.

Reply Obj. 2: In the sacraments of the New Law grace is bestowed, which cannot be received except through Christ: consequently they had to be instituted by Him. But in the sacred things no grace is given: for instance, in the consecration of a temple, an altar or the like, or, again, in the celebration of feasts. Wherefore Our Lord left the institution of such things to the discretion of the faithful, since they have not of themselves any necessary connection with inward grace.

Reply Obj. 3: Our Lord gave the apostles those precepts not as ceremonial observances, but as moral statutes: and they can be understood in two ways. First, following Augustine (*De Consensu Evang.* 30), as being not commands but permissions. For He permitted them to set forth to preach without scrip or stick, and so on, since they were empowered to accept their livelihood from those to whom they preached: wherefore He goes on to say: *For the laborer is worthy of his hire.* Nor is it a sin, but a work of supererogation for a preacher to take means of livelihood with him, without accepting supplies from those to whom he preaches; as Paul did (1 Cor 9:4, seqq.).

Second, according to the explanation of other holy men, they may be considered as temporal commands laid upon the apostles for the time during which they were sent to preach in Judea before Christ's Passion. For the disciples, being yet as little children under Christ's care, needed to receive some special commands from Christ, such as all subjects receive from their superiors: and especially so, since they were to be accustomed little by little to renounce the care of temporalities, so as to become fitted for the preaching of the Gospel throughout the whole world. Nor must we wonder if He established certain fixed modes of life, as long as the state of the Old Law endured and the people had not as yet achieved the perfect liberty of the Spirit. These statutes He abolished shortly before His Passion, as though the disciples had by their means become sufficiently practiced. Hence He said (Luke 22:35,36) *When I sent you without purse and scrip and shoes, did you want anything? But they said: Nothing. Then said He unto them: But now, he that hath a purse, let him take it, and likewise a scrip.* Because the time of perfect liberty was already at hand, when they would be left entirely to their own judgment in matters not necessarily connected with virtue.

AD QUARTUM dicendum quod iudicialia etiam, secundum se considerata, non sunt de necessitate virtutis quantum ad talem determinationem sed solum quantum ad communem rationem iustitiae. Et ideo iudicialia praecepta reliquit dominus disponenda his qui curam aliorum erant habituri vel spiritualem vel temporalem. Sed circa iudicialia praecepta veteris legis quaedam explanavit, propter malum intellectum Pharisaeorum, ut infra dicetur.

REPLY OBJ. 4: Judicial precepts also, are not essential to virtue in respect of any particular determination, but only in regard to the common notion of justice. Consequently Our Lord left the judicial precepts to the discretion of those who were to have spiritual or temporal charge of others. But as regards the judicial precepts of the Old Law, some of them He explained, because they were misunderstood by the Pharisees, as we shall state later on (A3, ad 2).

Article 3

Whether the New Law Directed Man Sufficiently As Regards Interior Actions?

AD TERTIUM SIC PROCEDITUR. Videtur quod circa interiores actus lex nova insufficienter hominem ordinaverit. Sunt enim decem praecepta Decalogi ordinantia hominem ad Deum et proximum. Sed dominus solum circa tria illorum aliquid adimplevit, scilicet circa prohibitionem homicidii, et circa prohibitionem adulterii, et circa prohibitionem periurii. Ergo videtur quod insufficienter hominem ordinaverit, adimpletionem aliorum praeceptorum praetermittens.

PRAETEREA, dominus nihil ordinavit in Evangelio de iudicialibus praeceptis nisi circa repudium uxoris, et circa poenam talionis, et circa persecutionem inimicorum. Sed multa sunt alia iudicialia praecepta veteris legis, ut supra dictum est. Ergo quantum ad hoc, insufficienter vitam hominum ordinavit.

PRAETEREA, in veteri lege, praeter praecepta moralia et iudicialia, erant quaedam caeremonialia. Circa quae dominus nihil ordinavit. Ergo videtur insufficienter ordinasse.

PRAETEREA, ad interiorem bonam mentis dispositionem pertinet ut nullum bonum opus homo faciat propter quemcumque temporalem finem. Sed multa sunt alia temporalia bona quam favor humanus, multa etiam alia sunt bona opera quam ieiunium, eleemosyna et oratio. Ergo inconveniens fuit quod dominus docuit solum circa haec tria opera gloriam favoris humani vitari, et nihil aliud terrenorum bonorum.

PRAETEREA, naturaliter homini inditum est ut sollicitetur circa ea quae sunt sibi necessaria ad vivendum, in qua etiam sollicitudine alia animalia cum homine conveniunt, unde dicitur Prov. VI, *vade ad formicam, o piger, et considera vias eius. Parat in aestate cibum sibi, et congregat in messe quod comedat*. Sed omne praeceptum quod datur contra inclinationem naturae, est iniquum, utpote contra legem naturalem existens. Ergo inconvenienter videtur dominus prohibuisse sollicitudinem victus et vestitus.

OBJECTION 1: It would seem that the New Law directed man insufficiently as regards interior actions. For there are ten commandments of the decalogue directing man to God and his neighbor. But Our Lord partly fulfilled only three of them: as regards, namely, the prohibition of murder, of adultery, and of perjury. Therefore it seems that, by omitting to fulfill the other precepts, He directed man insufficiently.

OBJ. 2: Further, as regards the judicial precepts, Our Lord ordained nothing in the Gospel, except in the matter of divorcing of wife, of punishment by retaliation, and of persecuting one's enemies. But there are many other judicial precepts of the Old Law, as stated above (Q104, A4; Q105). Therefore, in this respect, He directed human life insufficiently.

OBJ. 3: Further, in the Old Law, besides moral and judicial, there were ceremonial precepts about which Our Lord made no ordination. Therefore it seems that He ordained insufficiently.

OBJ. 4: Further, in order that the mind be inwardly well disposed, man should do no good deed for any temporal whatever. But there are many other temporal goods besides the favor of man: and there are many other good works besides fasting, alms-deeds, and prayer. Therefore Our Lord unbecomingly taught that only in respect of these three works, and of no other earthly goods ought we to shun the glory of human favor.

OBJ. 5: Further, solicitude for the necessary means of livelihood is by nature instilled into man, and this solicitude even other animals share with man: wherefore it is written (Prov 6:6,8): *Go to the ant, O sluggard, and consider her ways . . . she provideth her meat for herself in the summer, and gathereth her food in the harvest*. But every command issued against the inclination of nature is an unjust command, forasmuch as it is contrary to the law of nature. Therefore it seems that Our Lord unbecomingly forbade solicitude about food and raiment.

Praeterea, nullus actus virtutis est prohibendus. Sed iudicium est actus iustitiae; secundum illud Psalmi XCIII, *quousque iustitia convertatur in iudicium.* Ergo inconvenienter videtur dominus iudicium prohibuisse. Et ita videtur lex nova insufficienter hominem ordinasse circa interiores actus.

Sed contra est quod Augustinus dicit, in libro de Serm. Dom. in monte, *considerandum est quia, cum dixit, qui audit verba mea haec, satis significat sermonem istum domini omnibus praeceptis quibus Christiana vita formatur, esse perfectum.*

Respondeo dicendum quod, sicut ex inducta auctoritate Augustini apparet, sermo quem dominus in monte proposuit, totam informationem Christianae vitae continet. In quo perfecte interiores motus hominis ordinantur. Nam post declaratum beatitudinis finem; et commendata apostolica dignitate, per quos erat doctrina evangelica promulganda; ordinat interiores hominis motus, primo quidem quantum ad seipsum; et deinde quantum ad proximum.

Quantum autem ad seipsum, dupliciter; secundum duos interiores hominis motus circa agenda, qui sunt voluntas de agendis, et intentio de fine. Unde primo ordinat hominis voluntatem secundum diversa legis praecepta, ut scilicet abstineat aliquis non solum ab exterioribus operibus quae sunt secundum se mala, sed etiam ab interioribus, et ab occasionibus malorum. Deinde ordinat intentionem hominis, docens quod in bonis quae agimus, neque quaeramus humanam gloriam, neque mundanas divitias, quod est thesaurizare in terra.

Consequenter autem ordinat interiorem hominis motum quoad proximum, ut scilicet eum non temerarie aut iniuste iudicemus, aut praesumptuose; neque tamen sic simus apud proximum remissi, ut eis sacra committamus, si sint indigni.

Ultimo autem docet modum adimplendi evangelicam doctrinam, scilicet implorando divinum auxilium; et conatum apponendo ad ingrediendum per angustam portam perfectae virtutis; et cautelam adhibendo ne a seductoribus corrumpamur. Et quod observatio mandatorum eius est necessaria ad virtutem, non autem sufficit sola confessio fidei, vel miraculorum operatio, vel solus auditus.

Ad primum ergo dicendum quod dominus circa illa legis praecepta adimpletionem apposuit, in quibus Scribae et Pharisaei non rectum intellectum habebant. Et hoc contingebat praecipue circa tria praecepta Decalogi. Nam circa prohibitionem adulterii et homicidii, aestimabant solum exteriorem actum prohiberi, non autem interiorem appetitum. Quod magis credebant circa homicidium et adulterium quam circa furtum vel falsum testimonium, quia motus irae in homicidium tendens, et

Obj. 6: Further, no act of virtue should be the subject of a prohibition. Now judgment is an act of justice, according to Ps. 18:15: *Until justice be turned into judgment.* Therefore it seems that Our Lord unbecomingly forbade judgment: and consequently that the New Law directed man insufficiently in the matter of interior acts.

On the contrary, Augustine says (*De Serm. Dom. in Monte* i, 1): We should take note that, when He said: '*He that heareth these My words,*' He indicates clearly that this sermon of the Lord is replete with all the precepts whereby a Christian's life is formed.

I answer that, As is evident from Augustine's words just quoted, the sermon, contains the whole process of forming the life of a Christian. Therein man's interior movements are ordered. Because after declaring that his end is Beatitude; and after commending the authority of the apostles, through whom the teaching of the Gospel was to be promulgated, He orders man's interior movements, first in regard to man himself, second in regard to his neighbor.

This he does in regard to man himself, in two ways, corresponding to man's two interior movements in respect of any prospective action, viz., volition of what has to be done, and intention of the end. Wherefore, in the first place, He directs man's will in respect of the various precepts of the Law: by prescribing that man should refrain not merely from those external works that are evil in themselves, but also from internal acts, and from the occasions of evil deeds. In the second place He directs man's intention, by teaching that in our good works, we should seek neither human praise, nor worldly riches, which is to lay up treasures on earth.

Afterwards He directs man's interior movement in respect of his neighbor, by forbidding us, on the one hand, to judge him rashly, unjustly, or presumptuously; and, on the other, to entrust him too readily with sacred things if he be unworthy.

Lastly, He teaches us how to fulfill the teaching of the Gospel; viz., by imploring the help of God; by striving to enter by the narrow door of perfect virtue; and by being wary lest we be led astray by evil influences. Moreover, He declares that we must observe His commandments, and that it is not enough to make profession of faith, or to work miracles, or merely to hear His words.

Reply Obj. 1: Our Lord explained the manner of fulfilling those precepts which the Scribes and Pharisees did not rightly understand: and this affected chiefly those precepts of the decalogue. For they thought that the prohibition of adultery and murder covered the external act only, and not the internal desire. And they held this opinion about murder and adultery rather than about theft and false witness, because the movement of anger tending to murder, and the movement of desire tending to adultery, seem to be

concupiscentiae motus tendens in adulterium, videntur aliqualiter nobis a natura inesse; non autem appetitus furandi, vel falsum testimonium dicendi. Circa periurium vero habebant falsum intellectum, credentes periurium quidem esse peccatum; iuramentum autem per se esse appetendum et frequentandum, quia videtur ad Dei reverentiam pertinere. Et ideo dominus ostendit iuramentum non esse appetendum tanquam bonum; sed melius esse absque iuramento loqui, nisi necessitas cogat.

Ad secundum dicendum quod circa iudicialia praecepta dupliciter Scribae et Pharisaei errabant. Primo quidem, quia quaedam quae in lege Moysi erant tradita tanquam permissiones, aestimabant esse per se iusta, scilicet repudium uxoris, et usuras accipere ab extraneis. Et ideo dominus prohibuit uxoris repudium, Matth. V; et usurarum acceptionem, Luc. VI, dicens, *date mutuum nihil inde sperantes.*

Alio modo errabant credentes quaedam quae lex vetus instituerat facienda propter iustitiam, esse exequenda ex appetitu vindictae; vel ex cupiditate temporalium rerum; vel ex odio inimicorum. Et hoc in tribus praeceptis. Appetitum enim vindictae credebant esse licitum, propter praeceptum datum de poena talionis. Quod quidem fuit datum ut iustitia servaretur, non ut homo vindictam quaereret. Et ideo dominus, ad hoc removendum, docet animum hominis sic debere esse praeparatum ut, si necesse sit, etiam paratus sit plura sustinere. Motum autem cupiditatis aestimabant esse licitum, propter praecepta iudicialia in quibus mandabatur restitutio rei ablatae fieri etiam cum aliqua additione, ut supra dictum est. Et hoc quidem lex mandavit propter iustitiam observandam, non ut daret cupiditati locum. Et ideo dominus docet ut ex cupiditate nostra non repetamus, sed simus parati, si necesse fuerit, etiam ampliora dare. Motum vero odii credebant esse licitum, propter praecepta legis data de hostium interfectione. Quod quidem lex statuit propter iustitiam implendam, ut supra dictum est, non propter odia exsaturanda. Et ideo dominus docet ut ad inimicos dilectionem habeamus, et parati simus, si opus fuerit, etiam benefacere. Haec enim praecepta secundum praeparationem animi sunt accipienda, ut Augustinus exponit.

Ad tertium dicendum quod praecepta moralia omnino in nova lege remanere debebant, quia secundum se pertinent ad rationem virtutis. Praecepta autem iudicialia non remanebant ex necessitate secundum modum quem lex determinavit; sed relinquebatur arbitrio hominum utrum sic vel aliter esset determinandum. Et ideo convenienter dominus circa haec duo genera praeceptorum nos ordinavit. Praeceptorum autem caeremonialium observatio totaliter per rei impletionem

in us from nature somewhat, but not the desire of stealing or bearing false witness. They held a false opinion about perjury, for they thought that perjury indeed was a sin; but that oaths were of themselves to be desired and to be taken frequently, since they seem to proceed from reverence to God. Hence Our Lord shows that an oath is not desirable as a good thing; and that it is better to speak without oaths, unless necessity forces us to have recourse to them.

Reply Obj. 2: The Scribes and Pharisees erred about the judicial precepts in two ways. First, because they considered certain matters contained in the Law of Moses by way of permission, to be right in themselves: namely, divorce of a wife, and the taking of usury from strangers. Wherefore Our Lord forbade a man to divorce his wife (Matt 5:32); and to receive usury (Luke 6:35), when He said: *Lend, hoping for nothing thereby.*

In another way they erred by thinking that certain things which the Old Law commanded to be done for justice's sake, should be done out of desire for revenge, or out of lust for temporal goods, or out of hatred of one's enemies; and this in respect of three precepts. For they thought that desire for revenge was lawful, on account of the precept concerning punishment by retaliation: whereas this precept was given that justice might be safeguarded, not that man might seek revenge. Wherefore, in order to do away with this, Our Lord teaches that man should be prepared in his mind to suffer yet more if necessary. They thought that movements of covetousness were lawful on account of those judicial precepts which prescribed restitution of what had been purloined, together with something added thereto, as stated above (Q105, A2, ad 9); whereas the Law commanded this to be done in order to safeguard justice, not to encourage covetousness. Wherefore Our Lord teaches that we should not demand our goods from motives of cupidity, and that we should be ready to give yet more if necessary. They thought that the movement of hatred was lawful, on account of the commandments of the Law about the slaying of one's enemies: whereas the Law ordered this for the fulfilment of justice, as stated above (Q105, A3, ad 4), not to satisfy hatred. Wherefore Our Lord teaches us that we ought to love our enemies, and to be ready to do good to them if necessary. For these precepts are to be taken as binding *the mind to be prepared to fulfill them*, as Augustine says (*De Serm. Dom. in Monte* i, 19).

Reply Obj. 3: The moral precepts necessarily retained their force under the New Law, because they are of themselves essential to virtue: whereas the judicial precepts did not necessarily continue to bind in exactly the same way as had been fixed by the Law: this was left to man to decide in one way or another. Hence Our Lord directed us becomingly with regard to these two kinds of precepts. On the other hand, the observance of the ceremonial precepts was totally abolished by the advent of the reality; wherefore in

tollebatur. Et ideo circa huiusmodi praecepta, in illa communi doctrina, nihil ordinavit. Ostendit tamen alibi quod totus corporalis cultus qui erat determinatus in lege, erat in spiritualem commutandus; ut patet Ioan. IV, ubi dixit, *venit hora quando neque in monte hoc neque in Ierosolymis adorabitis patrem; sed veri adoratores adorabunt patrem in spiritu et veritate.*

Ad quartum dicendum quod omnes res mundanae ad tria reducuntur, scilicet ad honores, divitias et delicias; secundum illud I Ioan. II, *omne quod est in mundo, concupiscentia carnis est*, quod pertinet ad delicias carnis; et concupiscentia oculorum, quod pertinet ad divitias; et superbia vitae, quod pertinet ad ambitum gloriae et honoris. Superfluas autem carnis delicias lex non repromisit, sed magis prohibuit. Repromisit autem celsitudinem honoris, et abundantiam divitiarum, dicitur enim Deut. XXVIII, *si audieris vocem domini Dei tui, faciet te excelsiorem cunctis gentibus*, quantum ad primum; et post pauca subdit, *abundare te faciet omnibus bonis*, quantum ad secundum. Quae quidem promissa sic prave intelligebant Iudaei, ut propter ea esset Deo serviendum, sicut propter finem. Et ideo dominus hoc removit, docens primo, quod opera virtutis non sunt facienda propter humanam gloriam. Et ponit tria opera, ad quae omnia alia reducuntur, nam omnia quae aliquis facit ad refrenandum seipsum in suis concupiscentiis, reducuntur ad ieiunium; quaecumque vero fiunt propter dilectionem proximi, reducuntur ad eleemosynam; quaecumque vero propter cultum Dei fiunt, reducuntur ad orationem. Ponit autem haec tria specialiter quasi praecipua, et per quae homines maxime solent gloriam venari. Secundo, docuit quod non debemus finem constituere in divitiis, cum dixit, *nolite thesaurizare vobis thesauros in terra.*

Ad quintum dicendum quod dominus sollicitudinem necessariam non prohibuit, sed sollicitudinem inordinatam. Est autem quadruplex inordinatio sollicitudinis vitanda circa temporalia. Primo quidem, ut in eis finem non constituamus, neque Deo serviamus propter necessaria victus et vestitus. Unde dicit, *nolite thesaurizare vobis* et cetera. Secundo, ut non sic sollicitemur de temporalibus, cum desperatione divini auxilii. Unde dominus dicit, *scit pater vester quia his omnibus indigetis.* Tertio, ne sit sollicitudo praesumptuosa, ut scilicet homo confidat se necessaria vitae per suam sollicitudinem posse procurare, absque divino auxilio. Quod dominus removet per hoc quod *homo non potest aliquid adiicere ad staturam suam.* Quarto, per hoc quod homo sollicitudinis tempus praeoccupat, quia scilicet de hoc sollicitus est

regard to these precepts He commanded nothing on this occasion when He was giving the general points of His doctrine. Elsewhere, however, He makes it clear that the entire bodily worship which was fixed by the Law, was to be changed into spiritual worship: as is evident from Jn. 4:21,23, where He says: *The hour cometh when you shall neither on this mountain, nor in Jerusalem adore the Father . . . but . . . the true adorers shall adore the Father in spirit and in truth.*

Reply Obj. 4: All worldly goods may be reduced to three—honors, riches, and pleasures; according to 1 Jn. 2:16: *All that is in the world is the concupiscence of the flesh*, which refers to pleasures of the flesh, *and the concupiscence of the eyes*, which refers to riches, *and the pride of life*, which refers to ambition for renown and honor. Now the Law did not promise an abundance of carnal pleasures; on the contrary, it forbade them. But it did promise exalted honors and abundant riches; for it is written in reference to the former (Deut 28:1): *If thou wilt hear the voice of the Lord thy God . . . He will make thee higher than all the nations*; and in reference to the latter, we read a little further on (Deut 28:11): *He will make thee abound with all goods*. But the Jews so distorted the true meaning of these promises, as to think that we ought to serve God, with these things as the end in view. Wherefore Our Lord set this aside by teaching, first of all, that works of virtue should not be done for human glory. And He mentions three works, to which all others may be reduced: since whatever a man does in order to curb his desires, comes under the head of fasting; and whatever a man does for the love of his neighbor, comes under the head of alms-deeds; and whatever a man does for the worship of God, comes under the head of prayer. And He mentions these three specifically, as they hold the principal place, and are most often used by men in order to gain glory. In the second place He taught us that we must not place our end in riches, when He said: *Lay not up to yourselves treasures on earth* (Matt 6:19).

Reply Obj. 5: Our Lord forbade, not necessary, but inordinate solicitude. Now there is a fourfold solicitude to be avoided in temporal matters. First, we must not place our end in them, nor serve God for the sake of the necessities of food and raiment. Wherefore He says: *Lay not up for yourselves*, etc. Second, we must not be so anxious about temporal things, as to despair of God's help: wherefore Our Lord says (Matt 6:32): *Your Father knoweth that you have need of all these things*. Third, we must not add presumption to our solicitude; in other words, we must not be confident of getting the necessaries of life by our own efforts without God's help: such solicitude Our Lord sets aside by saying that *a man cannot add anything to his stature* (Matt 6:27). We must not anticipate the time for anxiety; namely, by being solicitous now, for the needs, not of the present, but of

nunc, quod non pertinet ad curam praesentis temporis, sed ad curam futuri. Unde dicit, *nolite solliciti esse in crastinum.*

Ad sextum dicendum quod dominus non prohibet iudicium iustitiae, sine quo non possent sancta subtrahi ab indignis. Sed prohibet iudicium inordinatum, ut dictum est.

a future time: wherefore He says (Matt 6:34): *Be not . . . solicitous for tomorrow.*

Reply Obj. 6: Our Lord did not forbid the judgment of justice, without which holy things could not be withdrawn from the unworthy. But he forbade inordinate judgment, as stated above.

Article 4

Whether Certain Definite Counsels Are Fittingly Proposed in the New Law?

Ad quartum sic proceditur. Videtur quod inconvenienter in lege nova consilia quaedam determinata sint proposita. Consilia enim dantur de rebus expedientibus ad finem; ut supra dictum est, cum de consilio ageretur. Sed non eadem omnibus expediunt. Ergo non sunt aliqua consilia determinata omnibus proponenda.

Praeterea, consilia dantur de meliori bono. Sed non sunt determinati gradus melioris boni. Ergo non debent aliqua determinata consilia dari.

Praeterea, consilia pertinent ad perfectionem vitae. Sed obedientia pertinet ad perfectionem vitae. Ergo inconvenienter de ea consilium non datur in Evangelio.

Praeterea, multa ad perfectionem vitae pertinentia inter praecepta ponuntur, sicut hoc quod dicitur, *diligite inimicos vestros*; et praecepta etiam quae dedit dominus apostolis, Matth. X. Ergo inconvenienter traduntur consilia in nova lege, tum quia non omnia ponuntur; tum etiam quia a praeceptis non distinguuntur.

Sed contra, consilia sapientis amici magnam utilitatem afferunt; secundum illud Prov. XXVII, *unguento et variis odoribus delectatur cor, et bonis amici consiliis anima dulcoratur.* Sed Christus maxime est sapiens et amicus. Ergo eius consilia maximam utilitatem continent, et convenientia sunt.

Respondeo dicendum quod haec est differentia inter consilium et praeceptum, quod praeceptum importat necessitatem, consilium autem in optione ponitur eius cui datur. Et ideo convenienter in lege nova, quae est lex libertatis, supra praecepta sunt addita consilia, non autem in veteri lege, quae erat lex servitutis. Oportet igitur quod praecepta novae legis intelligantur esse data de his quae sunt necessaria ad consequendum finem aeternae beatitudinis, in quem lex nova immediate introducit. Consilia vero oportet esse de illis per quae melius et expeditius potest homo consequi finem praedictum.

Est autem homo constitutus inter res mundi huius et spiritualia bona, in quibus beatitudo aeterna consistit,

Objection 1: It would seem that certain definite counsels are not fittingly proposed in the New Law. For counsels are given about that which is expedient for an end, as we stated above, when treating of counsel (Q14, A2). But the same things are not expedient for all. Therefore certain definite counsels should not be proposed to all.

Obj. 2: Further, counsels regard a greater good. But there are no definite degrees to the greater good. Therefore definite counsels should not be given.

Obj. 3: Further, counsels pertain to the life of perfection. But obedience pertains to the life of perfection. Therefore it was unfitting that no counsel of obedience should be contained in the Gospel.

Obj. 4: Further, many matters pertaining to the life of perfection are found among the commandments, as, for instance, *Love your enemies* (Matt 5:44), and those precepts which Our Lord gave His apostles (Matt 10). Therefore the counsels are unfittingly given in the New Law: both because they are not all mentioned; and because they are not distinguished from the commandments.

On the contrary, The counsels of a wise friend are of great use, according to Prov. (27:9): *Ointment and perfumes rejoice the heart: and the good counsels of a friend rejoice the soul.* But Christ is our wisest and greatest friend. Therefore His counsels are supremely useful and becoming.

I answer that, The difference between a counsel and a commandment is that a commandment implies obligation, whereas a counsel is left to the option of the one to whom it is given. Consequently in the New Law, which is the law of liberty, counsels are added to the commandments, and not in the Old Law, which is the law of bondage. We must therefore understand the commandments of the New Law to have been given about matters that are necessary to gain the end of eternal bliss, to which end the New Law brings us forthwith: but that the counsels are about matters that render the gaining of this end more assured and expeditious.

Now man is placed between the things of this world, and spiritual goods wherein eternal happiness consists: so

ita quod quanto plus inhaeret uni eorum, tanto plus recedit ab altero, et e converso. Qui ergo totaliter inhaeret rebus huius mundi, ut in eis finem constituat, habens eas quasi rationes et regulas suorum operum, totaliter excidit a spiritualibus bonis. Et ideo huiusmodi inordinatio tollitur per praecepta. Sed quod homo totaliter ea quae sunt mundi abiiciat, non est necessarium ad perveniendum in finem praedictum, quia potest homo utens rebus huius mundi, dummodo in eis finem non constituat, ad beatitudinem aeternam pervenire. Sed expeditius perveniet totaliter bona huius mundi abdicando. Et ideo de hoc dantur consilia Evangelii.

Bona autem huius mundi, quae pertinent ad usum humanae vitae, in tribus consistunt, scilicet in divitiis exteriorum bonorum, quae pertinent ad concupiscentiam oculorum; in deliciis carnis, quae pertinent ad concupiscentiam carnis; et in honoribus, quae pertinent ad superbiam vitae; sicut patet I Ioan. II. Haec autem tria totaliter derelinquere, secundum quod possibile est, pertinet ad consilia evangelica. In quibus etiam tribus fundatur omnis religio, quae statum perfectionis profitetur, nam divitiae abdicantur per paupertatem; deliciae carnis per perpetuam castitatem; superbia vitae per obedientiae servitutem.

Haec autem simpliciter observata pertinent ad consilia simpliciter proposita. Sed observatio uniuscuiusque eorum in aliquo speciali casu, pertinet ad consilium secundum quid, scilicet in casu illo. Puta cum homo dat aliquam eleemosynam pauperi quam dare non tenetur, consilium sequitur quantum ad factum illud. Similiter etiam quando aliquo tempore determinato a delectationibus carnis abstinet ut orationibus vacet, consilium sequitur pro tempore illo. Similiter etiam quando aliquis non sequitur voluntatem suam in aliquo facto quod licite posset facere, consilium sequitur in casu illo, puta si benefaciat inimicis quando non tenetur, vel si offensam remittat cuius iuste posset exigere vindictam. Et sic etiam omnia consilia particularia ad illa tria generalia et perfecta reducuntur.

Ad primum ergo dicendum quod praedicta consilia, quantum est de se sunt omnibus expedientia, sed ex indispositione aliquorum contingit quod alicui expedientia non sunt, quia eorum affectus ad haec non inclinatur. Et ideo dominus, consilia evangelica proponens, semper facit mentionem de idoneitate hominum ad observantiam consiliorum. Dans enim consilium perpetuae paupertatis, Matth. XIX, praemittit, *si vis perfectus esse*; et postea subdit, *vade et vende omnia quae habes*. Similiter, dans consilium perpetuae castitatis, cum dixit, *sunt eunuchi qui castraverunt seipsos propter regnum caelorum*, statim subdit, *qui potest capere, capiat*. Et similiter apostolus, I ad Cor. VII, praemisso consilio virginitatis,

that the more he cleaves to the one, the more he withdraws from the other, and conversely. Wherefore he that cleaves wholly to the things of this world, so as to make them his end, and to look upon them as the reason and rule of all he does, falls away altogether from spiritual goods. Hence this disorder is removed by the commandments. Nevertheless, for man to gain the end aforesaid, he does not need to renounce the things of the world altogether: since he can, while using the things of this world, attain to eternal happiness, provided he does not place his end in them: but he will attain more speedily thereto by giving up the goods of this world entirely: wherefore the evangelical counsels are given for this purpose.

Now the goods of this world which come into use in human life, consist in three things: viz., in external wealth pertaining to the *concupiscence of the eyes*; carnal pleasures pertaining to the *concupiscence of the flesh*; and honors, which pertain to the *pride of life*, according to 1 Jn. 2:16: and it is in renouncing these altogether, as far as possible, that the evangelical counsels consist. Moreover, every form of the religious life that professes the state of perfection is based on these three: since riches are renounced by poverty; carnal pleasures by perpetual chastity; and the pride of life by the bondage of obedience.

Now if a man observe these absolutely, this is in accordance with the counsels as they stand. But if a man observe any one of them in a particular case, this is taking that counsel in a restricted sense, namely, as applying to that particular case. For instance, when anyone gives an alms to a poor man, not being bound so to do, he follows the counsels in that particular case. In like manner, when a man for some fixed time refrains from carnal pleasures that he may give himself to prayer, he follows the counsel for that particular time. And again, when a man follows not his will as to some deed which he might do lawfully, he follows the counsel in that particular case: for instance, if he do good to his enemies when he is not bound to, or if he forgive an injury of which he might justly seek to be avenged. In this way, too, all particular counsels may be reduced to these three general and perfect counsels.

Reply Obj. 1: The aforesaid counsels, considered in themselves, are expedient to all; but owing to some people being ill-disposed, it happens that some of them are inexpedient, because their disposition is not inclined to such things. Hence Our Lord, in proposing the evangelical counsels, always makes mention of man's fitness for observing the counsels. For in giving the counsel of perpetual poverty (Matt 19:21), He begins with the words: *If thou wilt be perfect*, and then He adds: *Go, sell all thou hast*. In like manner when He gave the counsel of perpetual chastity, saying (Matt 19:12): *There are eunuchs who have made themselves eunuchs for the kingdom of heaven*, He adds straightway: *He that can take, let him take it*. And again, the Apostle

dicit, *porro hoc ad utilitatem vestram dico, non ut laqueum vobis iniiciam.*

AD SECUNDUM dicendum quod meliora bona particulariter in singulis sunt indeterminata. Sed illa quae sunt simpliciter et absolute meliora bona in universali, sunt determinata. Ad quae etiam omnia illa particularia reducuntur, ut dictum est.

AD TERTIUM dicendum quod etiam consilium obedientiae dominus intelligitur dedisse in hoc quod dixit, *et sequatur me;* quem sequimur non solum imitando opera, sed etiam obediendo mandatis ipsius; secundum illud Ioan. X. *Oves meae vocem meam audiunt, et sequuntur me.*

AD QUARTUM dicendum quod ea quae de vera dilectione inimicorum, et similibus, dominus dicit Matth. V et Luc. VI, si referantur ad praeparationem animi, sunt de necessitate salutis, ut scilicet homo sit paratus benefacere inimicis, et alia huiusmodi facere, cum necessitas hoc requirat. Et ideo inter praecepta ponuntur. Sed ut aliquis hoc inimicis exhibeat prompte in actu, ubi specialis necessitas non occurrit, pertinet ad consilia particularia, ut dictum est. Illa autem quae ponuntur Matth. X, et Luc. IX, et X, fuerunt quaedam praecepta disciplinae pro tempore illo, vel concessiones quaedam, ut supra dictum est. Et ideo non inducuntur tanquam consilia.

(1 Cor 7:35), after giving the counsel of virginity, says: *And this I speak for your profit; not to cast a snare upon you.*

REPLY OBJ. 2: The greater goods are not definitely fixed in the individual; but those which are simply and absolutely the greater good in general are fixed: and to these all the above particular goods may be reduced, as stated above.

REPLY OBJ. 3: Even the counsel of obedience is understood to have been given by Our Lord in the words: *And follow Me.* For we follow Him not only by imitating His works, but also by obeying His commandments, according to Jn. 10:27: *My sheep hear My voice . . . and they follow Me.*

REPLY OBJ. 4: Those things which Our Lord prescribed about the true love of our enemies, and other similar sayings (Matt 5; Lk. 6), may be referred to the preparation of the mind, and then they are necessary for salvation; for instance, that man be prepared to do good to his enemies, and other similar actions, when there is need. Hence these things are placed among the precepts. But that anyone should actually and promptly behave thus towards an enemy when there is no special need, is to be referred to the particular counsels, as stated above. As to those matters which are set down in Mt. 10 and Lk. 9 and 10, they were either disciplinary commands for that particular time, or concessions, as stated above (A2, ad 3). Hence they are not set down among the counsels.

QUESTION 109

OF THE NECESSITY OF GRACE

Consequenter considerandum est de exteriori principio humanorum actuum, scilicet de Deo, prout ab ipso per gratiam adiuvamur ad recte agendum. Et primo, considerandum est de gratia Dei; secundo, de causa eius; tertio, de eius effectibus.

Prima autem consideratio erit tripartita, nam primo considerabimus de necessitate gratiae; secundo, de ipsa gratia quantum ad eius essentiam; tertio, de eius divisione.

Circa primum quaeruntur decem.

Primo, utrum absque gratia possit homo aliquod verum cognoscere.

Secundo, utrum absque gratia Dei possit homo aliquod bonum facere vel velle.

Tertio, utrum homo absque gratia possit Deum diligere super omnia.

Quarto, utrum absque gratia possit praecepta legis observare.

Quinto, utrum absque gratia possit mereri vitam aeternam.

Sexto, utrum homo possit se ad gratiam praeparare sine gratia.

Septimo, utrum homo sine gratia possit resurgere a peccato.

Octavo, utrum absque gratia possit homo vitare peccatum.

Nono, utrum homo gratiam consecutus possit, absque alio divino auxilio, bonum facere et vitare peccatum.

Decimo, utrum possit perseverare in bono per seipsum.

We must now consider the exterior principle of human acts, i.e., God, insofar as, through grace, we are helped by Him to do right: and, first, we must consider the grace of God; second, its cause; third, its effects.

The first point of consideration will be threefold: for we shall consider (1) The necessity of grace; (2) grace itself, as to its essence; (3) its division.

Under the first head there are ten points of inquiry:

(1) Whether without grace man can know anything?

(2) Whether without God's grace man can do or wish any good?

(3) Whether without grace man can love God above all things?

(4) Whether without grace man can keep the commandments of the Law?

(5) Whether without grace he can merit eternal life?

(6) Whether without grace man can prepare himself for grace?

(7) Whether without grace he can rise from sin?

(8) Whether without grace man can avoid sin?

(9) Whether man having received grace can do good and avoid sin without any further Divine help?

(10) Whether he can of himself persevere in good?

Article 1

Whether Without Grace Man Can Know Any Truth?

AD PRIMUM SIC PROCEDITUR. Videtur quod homo sine gratia nullum verum cognoscere possit. Quia super illud I Cor. XII, *nemo potest dicere, dominus Iesus, nisi in spiritu sancto*, dicit Glossa Ambrosii, *omne verum, a quocumque dicatur, a spiritu sancto est.* Sed Spiritus Sanctus habitat in nobis per gratiam. Ergo veritatem cognoscere non possumus sine gratia.

PRAETEREA, Augustinus dicit, in I Soliloq., quod *disciplinarum certissima talia sunt qualia illa quae a sole illustrantur ut videri possint; Deus autem ipse est qui*

OBJECTION 1: It would seem that without grace man can know no truth. For, on 1 Cor. 12:3: *No man can say, the Lord Jesus, but by the Holy Spirit*, a gloss says: *Every truth, by whomsoever spoken is from the Holy Spirit.* Now the Holy Spirit dwells in us by grace. Therefore we cannot know truth without grace.

OBJ. 2: Further, Augustine says (*Solil.* i, 6) that *the most certain sciences are like things lit up by the sun so as to be seen. Now God Himself is He Whom sheds the light. And*

illustrat; ratio autem ita est in mentibus ut in oculis est aspectus; mentis autem oculi sunt sensus animae. Sed sensus corporis, quantumcumque sit purus, non potest aliquod visibile videre sine solis illustratione. Ergo humana mens, quantumcumque sit perfecta, non potest ratiocinando veritatem cognoscere absque illustratione divina. Quae ad auxilium gratiae pertinet.

PRAETEREA, humana mens non potest veritatem intelligere nisi cogitando; ut patet per Augustinum XIV de Trin. Sed apostolus dicit, II ad Cor. III, *non sufficientes sumus aliquid cogitare a nobis, quasi ex nobis.* Ergo homo non potest cognoscere veritatem per seipsum sine auxilio gratiae.

SED CONTRA est quod Augustinus dicit, in I Retract., *non approbo quod in oratione dixi, Deus, qui non nisi mundos verum scire voluisti. Responderi enim potest multos etiam non mundos multa scire vera.* Sed per gratiam homo mundus efficitur; secundum illud Psalmi l, *cor mundum crea in me, Deus; et spiritum rectum innova in visceribus meis.* Ergo sine gratia potest homo per seipsum veritatem cognoscere.

RESPONDEO dicendum quod cognoscere veritatem est usus quidam, vel actus, intellectualis luminis, quia secundum apostolum, ad Ephes. V, *omne quod manifestatur, lumen est.* Usus autem quilibet quendam motum importat, large accipiendo motum secundum quod intelligere et velle motus quidam esse dicuntur, ut patet per philosophum in III de anima. Videmus autem in corporalibus quod ad motum non solum requiritur ipsa forma quae est principium motus vel actionis; sed etiam requiritur motio primi moventis. Primum autem movens in ordine corporalium est corpus caeleste. Unde quantumcumque ignis habeat perfectum calorem, non alteraret nisi per motionem caelestis corporis. Manifestum est autem quod, sicut omnes motus corporales reducuntur in motum caelestis corporis sicut in primum movens corporale; ita omnes motus tam corporales quam spirituales reducuntur in primum movens simpliciter, quod est Deus. Et ideo quantumcumque natura aliqua corporalis vel spiritualis ponatur perfecta, non potest in suum actum procedere nisi moveatur a Deo. Quae quidem motio est secundum suae providentiae rationem; non secundum necessitatem naturae, sicut motio corporis caelestis. Non solum autem a Deo est omnis motio sicut a primo movente; sed etiam ab ipso est omnis formalis perfectio sicut a primo actu. Sic igitur actio intellectus, et cuiuscumque entis creati, dependet a Deo quantum ad duo, uno modo, inquantum ab ipso habet formam per quam agit; alio modo, inquantum ab ipso movetur ad agendum.

Unaquaeque autem forma indita rebus creatis a Deo, habet efficaciam respectu alicuius actus determinati, in quem potest secundum suam proprietatem, ultra autem non potest nisi per aliquam formam superadditam, sicut

reason is in the mind as sight is in the eye. And the eyes of the mind are the senses of the soul. Now the bodily senses, however pure, cannot see any visible object, without the sun's light. Therefore the human mind, however perfect, cannot, by reasoning, know any truth without Divine light: and this pertains to the aid of grace.

OBJ. 3: Further, the human mind can only understand truth by thinking, as is clear from Augustine (*De Trin.* xiv, 7). But the Apostle says (2 Cor 3:5): *Not that we are sufficient to think anything of ourselves, as of ourselves; but our sufficiency is from God.* Therefore man cannot, of himself, know truth without the help of grace.

ON THE CONTRARY, Augustine says (*Retract.* i, 4): *I do not approve having said in the prayer, O God, Who dost wish the sinless alone to know the truth; for it may be answered that many who are not sinless know many truths.* Now man is cleansed from sin by grace, according to Ps. 50:12: *Create a clean heart in me, O God, and renew a right spirit within my bowels.* Therefore without grace man of himself can know truth.

I ANSWER THAT, To know truth is a use or act of intellectual light, since, according to the Apostle (Eph 5:13): *All that is made manifest is light.* Now every use implies movement, taking movement broadly, so as to call thinking and willing movements, as is clear from the Philosopher (*De Anima* iii, 4). Now in corporeal things we see that for movement there is required not merely the form which is the principle of the movement or action, but there is also required the motion of the first mover. Now the first mover in the order of corporeal things is the heavenly body. Hence no matter how perfectly fire has heat, it would not bring about alteration, except by the motion of the heavenly body. But it is clear that as all corporeal movements are reduced to the motion of the heavenly body as to the first corporeal mover, so all movements, both corporeal and spiritual, are reduced to the simple First Mover, Who is God. And hence no matter how perfect a corporeal or spiritual nature is supposed to be, it cannot proceed to its act unless it be moved by God; but this motion is according to the plan of His providence, and not by necessity of nature, as the motion of the heavenly body. Now not only is every motion from God as from the First Mover, but all formal perfection is from Him as from the First Act. And thus the act of the intellect or of any created being whatsoever depends upon God in two ways: first, inasmuch as it is from Him that it has the form whereby it acts; second, inasmuch as it is moved by Him to act.

Now every form bestowed on created things by God has power for a determined act, which it can bring about in proportion to its own proper endowment; and beyond which it is powerless, except by a superadded form, as water

aqua non potest calefacere nisi calefacta ab igne. Sic igitur intellectus humanus habet aliquam formam, scilicet ipsum intelligibile lumen, quod est de se sufficiens ad quaedam intelligibilia cognoscenda, ad ea scilicet in quorum notitiam per sensibilia possumus devenire. Altiora vero intelligibilia intellectus humanus cognoscere non potest nisi fortiori lumine perficiatur, sicut lumine fidei vel prophetiae; quod dicitur lumen gratiae, inquantum est naturae superadditum.

Sic igitur dicendum est quod ad cognitionem cuiuscumque veri, homo indiget auxilio divino ut intellectus a Deo moveatur ad suum actum. Non autem indiget ad cognoscendam veritatem in omnibus, nova illustratione superaddita naturali illustrationi; sed in quibusdam, quae excedunt naturalem cognitionem. Et tamen quandoque Deus miraculose per suam gratiam aliquos instruit de his quae per naturalem rationem cognosci possunt, sicut et quandoque miraculose facit quaedam quae natura facere potest.

AD PRIMUM ergo dicendum quod omne verum, a quocumque dicatur, est a spiritu sancto sicut ab infundente naturale lumen, et movente ad intelligendum et loquendum veritatem. Non autem sicut ab inhabitante per gratiam gratum facientem, vel sicut a largiente aliquod habituale donum naturae superadditum, sed hoc solum est in quibusdam veris cognoscendis et loquendis; et maxime in illis quae pertinent ad fidem, de quibus apostolus loquebatur.

AD SECUNDUM dicendum quod sol corporalis illustrat exterius; sed sol intelligibilis, qui est Deus, illustrat interius. Unde ipsum lumen naturale animae inditum est illustratio Dei, qua illustramur ab ipso ad cognoscendum ea quae pertinent ad naturalem cognitionem. Et ad hoc non requiritur alia illustratio, sed solum ad illa quae naturalem cognitionem excedunt.

AD TERTIUM dicendum quod semper indigemus divino auxilio ad cogitandum quodcumque, inquantum ipse movet intellectum ad agendum, actu enim intelligere aliquid est cogitare, ut patet per Augustinum, XIV de Trin.

can only heat when heated by the fire. And thus the human understanding has a form, viz., intelligible light, which of itself is sufficient for knowing certain intelligible things, viz., those we can come to know through the senses. Higher intelligible things of the human intellect cannot know, unless it be perfected by a stronger light, viz., the light of faith or prophecy which is called the *light of grace*, inasmuch as it is added to nature.

Hence we must say that for the knowledge of any truth whatsoever man needs Divine help, that the intellect may be moved by God to its act. But he does not need a new light added to his natural light, in order to know the truth in all things, but only in some that surpass his natural knowledge. And yet at times God miraculously instructs some by His grace in things that can be known by natural reason, even as He sometimes brings about miraculously what nature can do.

REPLY OBJ. 1: Every truth by whomsoever spoken is from the Holy Spirit as bestowing the natural light, and moving us to understand and speak the truth, but not as dwelling in us by sanctifying grace, or as bestowing any habitual gift superadded to nature. For this only takes place with regard to certain truths that are known and spoken, and especially in regard to such as pertain to faith, of which the Apostle speaks.

REPLY OBJ. 2: The material sun sheds its light outside us; but the intelligible Sun, Who is God, shines within us. Hence the natural light bestowed upon the soul is God's enlightenment, whereby we are enlightened to see what pertains to natural knowledge; and for this there is required no further knowledge, but only for such things as surpass natural knowledge.

REPLY OBJ. 3: We always need God's help for every thought, inasmuch as He moves the understanding to act; for actually to understand anything is to think, as is clear from Augustine (*De Trin.* xiv, 7).

Article 2

Whether Man Can Wish or Do Any Good Without Grace?

AD SECUNDUM SIC PROCEDITUR. Videtur quod homo possit velle et facere bonum absque gratia. Illud enim est in hominis potestate cuius ipse est dominus. Sed homo est dominus suorum actuum, et maxime eius quod est velle, ut supra dictum est. Ergo homo potest velle et facere bonum per seipsum absque auxilio gratiae.

OBJECTION 1: It would seem that man can wish and do good without grace. For that is in man's power, whereof he is master. Now man is master of his acts, and especially of his willing, as stated above (Q1, A1; Q13, A6). Hence man, of himself, can wish and do good without the help of grace.

PRAETEREA, unumquodque magis potest in id quod est sibi secundum naturam, quam in id quod est sibi praeter naturam. Sed peccatum est contra naturam, ut Damascenus dicit, in II libro, opus autem virtutis est homini secundum naturam, ut supra dictum est. Cum igitur homo per seipsum possit peccare, videtur quod multo magis per seipsum possit bonum velle et facere.

PRAETEREA, bonum intellectus est verum, ut philosophus dicit, in VI Ethic. Sed intellectus potest cognoscere verum per seipsum, sicut et quaelibet alia res potest suam naturalem operationem per se facere. Ergo multo magis homo potest per seipsum facere et velle bonum.

SED CONTRA est quod apostolus dicit, Rom. IX, non est volentis, scilicet velle, neque currentis, scilicet currere, sed miserentis Dei. Et Augustinus dicit, in libro de Corrept. et gratia, quod *sine gratia nullum prorsus, sive cogitando, sive volendo et amando, sive agendo, faciunt homines bonum.*

RESPONDEO dicendum quod natura hominis dupliciter potest considerari, uno modo, in sui integritate, sicut fuit in primo parente ante peccatum; alio modo, secundum quod est corrupta in nobis post peccatum primi parentis. Secundum autem utrumque statum, natura humana indiget auxilio divino ad faciendum vel volendum quodcumque bonum, sicut primo movente, ut dictum est. Sed in statu naturae integrae, quantum ad sufficientiam operativae virtutis, poterat homo per sua naturalia velle et operari bonum suae naturae proportionatum, quale est bonum virtutis acquisitae, non autem bonum superexcedens, quale est bonum virtutis infusae. Sed in statu naturae corruptae etiam deficit homo ab hoc quod secundum suam naturam potest, ut non possit totum huiusmodi bonum implere per sua naturalia. Quia tamen natura humana per peccatum non est totaliter corrupta, ut scilicet toto bono naturae privetur; potest quidem etiam in statu naturae corruptae, per virtutem suae naturae aliquod bonum particulare agere, sicut aedificare domos, plantare vineas, et alia huiusmodi; non tamen totum bonum sibi connaturale, ita quod in nullo deficiat. Sicut homo infirmus potest per seipsum aliquem motum habere; non tamen perfecte potest moveri motu hominis sani, nisi sanetur auxilio medicinae.

Sic igitur virtute gratuita superaddita virtuti naturae indiget homo in statu naturae integrae quantum ad unum, scilicet ad operandum et volendum bonum supernaturale. Sed in statu naturae corruptae, quantum ad duo, scilicet ut sanetur; et ulterius ut bonum supernaturalis virtutis operetur, quod est meritorium. Ulterius autem in utroque statu indiget homo auxilio divino ut ab ipso moveatur ad bene agendum.

AD PRIMUM ergo dicendum quod homo est dominus suorum actuum, et volendi et non volendi, propter deliberationem rationis, quae potest flecti ad unam partem vel ad aliam. Sed quod deliberet vel non deliberet, si

OBJ. 2: Further, man has more power over what is according to his nature than over what is beyond his nature. Now sin is against his nature, as Damascene says (*De Fide Orth.* ii, 30); whereas deeds of virtue are according to his nature, as stated above (Q71, A1). Therefore since man can sin of himself he can wish and do good.

OBJ. 3: Further, the understanding's good is truth, as the Philosopher says (*Ethic.* vi, 2). Now the intellect can of itself know truth, even as every other thing can work its own operation of itself. Therefore, much more can man, of himself, do and wish good.

ON THE CONTRARY, The Apostle says (Rom 9:16): *It is not of him that willeth*, namely, to will, *nor of him that runneth*, namely, to run, *but of God that showeth mercy.* And Augustine says (*De Corrept. et Gratia* ii) that *without grace men do nothing good when they either think or wish or love or act.*

I ANSWER THAT, Man's nature may be looked at in two ways: first, in its integrity, as it was in our first parent before sin; second, as it is corrupted in us after the sin of our first parent. Now in both states human nature needs the help of God as First Mover, to do or wish any good whatsoever, as stated above (A1). But in the state of integrity, as regards the sufficiency of the operative power, man by his natural endowments could wish and do the good proportionate to his nature, such as the good of acquired virtue; but not surpassing good, as the good of infused virtue. But in the state of corrupt nature, man falls short of what he could do by his nature, so that he is unable to fulfill it by his own natural powers. Yet because human nature is not altogether corrupted by sin, so as to be shorn of every natural good, even in the state of corrupted nature it can, by virtue of its natural endowments, work some particular good, as to build dwellings, plant vineyards, and the like; yet it cannot do all the good natural to it, so as to fall short in nothing; just as a sick man can of himself make some movements, yet he cannot be perfectly moved with the movements of one in health, unless by the help of medicine he be cured.

And thus in the state of perfect nature man needs a gratuitous strength superadded to natural strength for one reason, viz., in order to do and wish supernatural good; but for two reasons, in the state of corrupt nature, viz., in order to be healed, and furthermore in order to carry out works of supernatural virtue, which are meritorious. Beyond this, in both states man needs the Divine help, that he may be moved to act well.

REPLY OBJ. 1: Man is master of his acts and of his willing or not willing, because of his deliberate reason, which can be bent to one side or another. And although he is master of his deliberating or not deliberating, yet this can only

huius etiam sit dominus, oportet quod hoc sit per deliberationem praecedentem. Et cum hoc non procedat in infinitum, oportet quod finaliter deveniatur ad hoc quod liberum arbitrium hominis moveatur ab aliquo exteriori principio quod est supra mentem humanam, scilicet a Deo; ut etiam philosophus probat in cap. de bona fortuna. Unde mens hominis etiam sani non ita habet dominium sui actus quin indigeat moveri a Deo. Et multo magis liberum arbitrium hominis infirmi post peccatum, quod impeditur a bono per corruptionem naturae.

AD SECUNDUM dicendum quod peccare nihil aliud est quam deficere a bono quod convenit alicui secundum suam naturam. Unaquaeque autem res creata, sicut esse non habet nisi ab alio, et in se considerata est nihil, ita indiget conservari in bono suae naturae convenienti ab alio. Potest autem per seipsam deficere a bono, sicut et per seipsam potest deficere in non esse, nisi divinitus conservaretur.

AD TERTIUM dicendum quod etiam verum non potest homo cognoscere sine auxilio divino, sicut supra dictum est. Et tamen magis est natura humana corrupta per peccatum quantum ad appetitum boni, quam quantum ad cognitionem veri.

be by a previous deliberation; and since it cannot go on to infinity, we must come at length to this, that man's free-will is moved by an extrinsic principle, which is above the human mind, to wit by God, as the Philosopher proves in the chapter *On Good Fortune* (*Ethic. Eudem.* vii). Hence the mind of man still unweakened is not so much master of its act that it does not need to be moved by God; and much more the free-will of man weakened by sin, whereby it is hindered from good by the corruption of the nature.

REPLY OBJ. 2: To sin is nothing else than to fail in the good which belongs to any being according to its nature. Now as every created thing has its being from another, and, considered in itself, is nothing, so does it need to be preserved by another in the good which pertains to its nature. For it can of itself fail in good, even as of itself it can fall into non-existence, unless it is upheld by God.

REPLY OBJ. 3: Man cannot even know truth without Divine help, as stated above (A1). And yet human nature is more corrupt by sin in regard to the desire for good, than in regard to the knowledge of truth.

Article 3

Whether by His Own Natural Powers and Without Grace Man Can Love God Above All Things?

AD TERTIUM SIC PROCEDITUR. Videtur quod homo non possit diligere Deum super omnia ex solis naturalibus sine gratia. Diligere enim Deum super omnia est proprius et principalis caritatis actus. Sed caritatem homo non potest habere per seipsum, quia *caritas Dei diffusa est in cordibus nostris per spiritum sanctum, qui datus est nobis*, ut dicitur Rom. V. Ergo homo ex solis naturalibus non potest Deum diligere super omnia.

PRAETEREA, nulla natura potest supra seipsam. Sed diligere aliquid plus quam se, est tendere in aliquid supra seipsum. Ergo nulla natura creata potest Deum diligere supra seipsam sine auxilio gratiae.

PRAETEREA, Deo, cum sit summum bonum, debetur summus amor, qui est ut super omnia diligatur. Sed ad summum amorem Deo impendendum, qui ei a nobis debetur, homo non sufficit sine gratia, alioquin frustra gratia adderetur. Ergo homo non potest sine gratia ex solis naturalibus diligere Deum super omnia.

SED CONTRA, primus homo in solis naturalibus constitutus fuit, ut a quibusdam ponitur. In quo statu manifestum est quod aliqualiter Deum dilexit. Sed non dilexit Deum aequaliter sibi, vel minus se, quia secundum hoc peccasset. Ergo dilexit Deum supra se. Ergo homo ex

OBJECTION 1: It would seem that without grace man cannot love God above all things by his own natural powers. For to love God above all things is the proper and principal act of charity. Now man cannot of himself possess charity, since the *charity of God is poured forth in our hearts by the Holy Spirit Who is given to us*, as is said Rm. 5:5. Therefore man by his natural powers alone cannot love God above all things.

OBJ. 2: Further, no nature can rise above itself. But to love God above all things is to tend above oneself. Therefore without the help of grace no created nature can love God above itself.

OBJ. 3: Further, to God, Who is the Highest Good, is due the best love, which is that He be loved above all things. Now without grace man is not capable of giving God the best love, which is His due; otherwise it would be useless to add grace. Hence man, without grace and with his natural powers alone, cannot love God above all things.

ON THE CONTRARY, As some maintain, man was first made with only natural endowments; and in this state it is manifest that he loved God to some extent. But he did not love God equally with himself, or less than himself, otherwise he would have sinned. Therefore he loved God above

solis naturalibus potest Deum diligere plus quam se, et super omnia.

RESPONDEO dicendum quod, sicut supra dictum est in primo, in quo etiam circa naturalem dilectionem Angelorum diversae opiniones sunt positae; homo in statu naturae integrae poterat operari virtute suae naturae bonum quod est sibi connaturale, absque superadditione gratuiti doni, licet non absque auxilio Dei moventis. Diligere autem Deum super omnia est quiddam connaturale homini; et etiam cuilibet creaturae non solum rationali, sed irrationali et etiam inanimatae, secundum modum amoris qui unicuique creaturae competere potest. Cuius ratio est quia unicuique naturale est quod appetat et amet aliquid, secundum quod aptum natum est esse, *sic enim agit unumquodque, prout aptum natum est*, ut dicitur in II Physic. Manifestum est autem quod bonum partis est propter bonum totius. Unde etiam naturali appetitu vel amore unaquaeque res particularis amat bonum suum proprium propter bonum commune totius universi, quod est Deus. Unde et Dionysius dicit, in libro de Div. Nom., quod *Deus convertit omnia ad amorem sui ipsius*. Unde homo in statu naturae integrae dilectionem sui ipsius referebat ad amorem Dei sicut ad finem, et similiter dilectionem omnium aliarum rerum. Et ita Deum diligebat plus quam seipsum, et super omnia. Sed in statu naturae corruptae homo ab hoc deficit secundum appetitum voluntatis rationalis, quae propter corruptionem naturae sequitur bonum privatum, nisi sanetur per gratiam Dei. Et ideo dicendum est quod homo in statu naturae integrae non indigebat dono gratiae superadditae naturalibus bonis ad diligendum Deum naturaliter super omnia; licet indigeret auxilio Dei ad hoc eum moventis. Sed in statu naturae corruptae indiget homo etiam ad hoc auxilio gratiae naturam sanantis.

AD PRIMUM ergo dicendum quod caritas diligit Deum super omnia eminentius quam natura. Natura enim diligit Deum super omnia, prout est principium et finis naturalis boni, caritas autem secundum quod est obiectum beatitudinis, et secundum quod homo habet quandam societatem spiritualem cum Deo. Addit etiam caritas super dilectionem naturalem Dei promptitudinem quandam et delectationem, sicut et quilibet habitus virtutis addit supra actum bonum qui fit ex sola naturali ratione hominis virtutis habitum non habentis.

AD SECUNDUM dicendum quod, cum dicitur quod nulla natura potest supra seipsam, non est intelligendum quod non possit ferri in aliquod obiectum quod est supra se, manifestum est enim quod intellectus noster naturali cognitione potest aliqua cognoscere quae sunt supra seipsum, ut patet in naturali cognitione Dei. Sed intelligendum est quod natura non potest in actum excedentem proportionem suae virtutis. Talis autem actus non est diligere Deum super omnia, hoc enim est naturale cuilibet naturae creatae, ut dictum est.

himself. Therefore man, by his natural powers alone, can love God more than himself and above all things.

I ANSWER THAT, As was said above (FP, Q60, A5), where the various opinions concerning the natural love of the angels were set forth, man in a state of perfect nature, could by his natural power, do the good natural to him without the addition of any gratuitous gift, though not without the help of God moving him. Now to love God above all things is natural to man and to every nature, not only rational but irrational, and even to inanimate nature according to the manner of love which can belong to each creature. And the reason of this is that it is natural to all to seek and love things according as they are naturally fit (to be sought and loved) since *all things act according as they are naturally fit* as stated in *Phys.* ii, 8. Now it is manifest that the good of the part is for the good of the whole; hence everything, by its natural appetite and love, loves its own proper good on account of the common good of the whole universe, which is God. Hence Dionysius says (*Div. Nom.* iv) that *God leads everything to love of Himself*. Hence in the state of perfect nature man referred the love of himself and of all other things to the love of God as to its end; and thus he loved God more than himself and above all things. But in the state of corrupt nature man falls short of this in the appetite of his rational will, which, unless it is cured by God's grace, follows its private good, on account of the corruption of nature. And hence we must say that in the state of perfect nature man did not need the gift of grace added to his natural endowments, in order to love God above all things naturally, although he needed God's help to move him to it; but in the state of corrupt nature man needs, even for this, the help of grace to heal his nature.

REPLY OBJ. 1: Charity loves God above all things in a higher way than nature does. For nature loves God above all things inasmuch as He is the beginning and the end of natural good; whereas charity loves Him, as He is the object of beatitude, and inasmuch as man has a spiritual fellowship with God. Moreover charity adds to natural love of God a certain quickness and joy, in the same way that every habit of virtue adds to the good act which is done merely by the natural reason of a man who has not the habit of virtue.

REPLY OBJ. 2: When it is said that nature cannot rise above itself, we must not understand this as if it could not be drawn to any object above itself, for it is clear that our intellect by its natural knowledge can know things above itself, as is shown in our natural knowledge of God. But we are to understand that nature cannot rise to an act exceeding the proportion of its strength. Now to love God above all things is not such an act; for it is natural to every creature, as was said above.

AD TERTIUM dicendum quod amor dicitur summus non solum quantum ad gradum dilectionis, sed etiam quantum ad rationem diligendi, et dilectionis modum. Et secundum hoc, supremus gradus dilectionis est quo caritas diligit Deum ut beatificantem, sicut dictum est.

REPLY OBJ. 3: Love is said to be best, both with respect to degree of love, and with regard to the motive of loving, and the mode of love. And thus the highest degree of love is that whereby charity loves God as the giver of beatitude, as was said above.

Article 4

Whether Man Without Grace and by His Own Natural Powers Can Fulfill the Commandments of the Law?

AD QUARTUM SIC PROCEDITUR. Videtur quod homo sine gratia per sua naturalia possit praecepta legis implere. Dicit enim apostolus, ad Rom. II, quod *gentes, quae legem non habent, naturaliter ea quae legis sunt faciunt.* Sed illud quod naturaliter homo facit, potest per seipsum facere absque gratia. Ergo homo potest legis praecepta facere absque gratia.

PRAETEREA, Hieronymus dicit, in expositione Catholicae fidei, *illos esse maledicendos qui Deum praecepisse homini aliquid impossibile dicunt.* Sed impossibile est homini quod per seipsum implere non potest. Ergo homo potest implere omnia praecepta legis per seipsum.

PRAETEREA, inter omnia praecepta legis maximum est illud, *diliges dominum Deum tuum ex toto corde tuo*; ut patet Matth. XXII. Sed hoc mandatum potest homo implere ex solis naturalibus, diligendo Deum super omnia, ut supra dictum est. Ergo omnia mandata legis potest homo implere sine gratia.

SED CONTRA est quod Augustinus dicit, in libro de haeresibus, hoc pertinere ad haeresim Pelagianorum, ut credant *sine gratia posse hominem facere omnia divina mandata.*

RESPONDEO dicendum quod implere mandata legis contingit dupliciter. Uno modo, quantum ad substantiam operum, prout scilicet homo operatur iusta et fortia, et alia virtutis opera. Et hoc modo homo in statu naturae integrae potuit omnia mandata legis implere, alioquin non potuisset in statu illo non peccare, cum nihil aliud sit peccare quam transgredi divina mandata. Sed in statu naturae corruptae non potest homo implere omnia mandata divina sine gratia sanante. Alio modo possunt impleri mandata legis non solum quantum ad substantiam operis, sed etiam quantum ad modum agendi, ut scilicet ex caritate fiant. Et sic neque in statu naturae integrae, neque in statu naturae corruptae, potest homo implere absque gratia legis mandata. Unde Augustinus, in libro de Corrept. et Grat., cum dixisset quod sine gratia nullum prorsus bonum homines faciunt, subdit, *non solum ut, monstrante ipsa quid faciendum sit, sciant; verum etiam ut, praestante ipsa, faciant cum dilectione*

OBJECTION 1: It would seem that man without grace, and by his own natural powers, can fulfill the commandments of the Law. For the Apostle says (Rom 2:14) that *the Gentiles who have not the law, do by nature those things that are of the Law.* Now what a man does naturally he can do of himself without grace. Hence a man can fulfill the commandments of the Law without grace.

OBJ. 2: Further, Jerome says (*Expos. Cathol. Fide*) that *they are anathema who say God has laid impossibilities upon man.* Now what a man cannot fulfill by himself is impossible to him. Therefore a man can fulfill all the commandments of himself.

OBJ. 3: Further, of all the commandments of the Law, the greatest is this, *Thou shalt love the Lord thy God with thy whole heart* (Matt 27:37). Now man with his natural endowments can fulfill this command by loving God above all things, as stated above (A3). Therefore man can fulfill all the commandments of the Law without grace.

ON THE CONTRARY, Augustine says (*De Haeres.* lxxxviii) that it is part of the Pelagian heresy that *they believe that without grace man can fulfill all the Divine commandments.*

I ANSWER THAT, There are two ways of fulfilling the commandments of the Law. The first regards the substance of the works, as when a man does works of justice, fortitude, and of other virtues. And in this way man in the state of perfect nature could fulfill all the commandments of the Law; otherwise he would have been unable to sin in that state, since to sin is nothing else than to transgress the Divine commandments. But in the state of corrupted nature man cannot fulfill all the Divine commandments without healing grace. Second, the commandments of the law can be fulfilled, not merely as regards the substance of the act, but also as regards the mode of acting, i.e., their being done out of charity. And in this way, neither in the state of perfect nature, nor in the state of corrupt nature can man fulfill the commandments of the law without grace. Hence, Augustine (*De Corrupt. et Grat.* ii) having stated that *without grace men can do no good whatever*, adds: *Not only do they know by its light what to do, but by its help they do lovingly*

quod sciunt. Indigent insuper in utroque statu auxilio Dei moventis ad mandata implenda, ut dictum est.

Ad primum ergo dicendum quod, sicut Augustinus dicit, in libro de Spir. et Litt., *non moveat quod naturaliter eos dixit quae legis sunt facere, hoc enim agit spiritus gratiae, ut imaginem Dei, in qua naturaliter facti sumus, instauret in nobis.*

Ad secundum dicendum quod illud quod possumus cum auxilio divino, non est nobis omnino impossibile; secundum illud philosophi, in III Ethic., *quae per amicos possumus, aliqualiter per nos possumus.* Unde et Hieronymus ibidem *confitetur sic nostrum liberum esse arbitrium, ut dicamus nos semper indigere Dei auxilio.*

Ad tertium dicendum quod praeceptum de dilectione Dei non potest homo implere ex puris naturalibus secundum quod ex caritate impletur, ut ex supradictis patet.

what they know. Beyond this, in both states they need the help of God's motion in order to fulfill the commandments, as stated above (AA2,3).

Reply Obj. 1: As Augustine says (*De Spir. et Lit.* xxvii), *do not be disturbed at his saying that they do by nature those things that are of the Law; for the Spirit of grace works this, in order to restore in us the image of God, after which we were naturally made.*

Reply Obj. 2: What we can do with the Divine assistance is not altogether impossible to us; according to the Philosopher (*Ethic.* iii, 3): *What we can do through our friends, we can do, in some sense, by ourselves.* Hence Jerome concedes that *our will is in such a way free that we must confess we still require God's help.*

Reply Obj. 3: Man cannot, with his purely natural endowments, fulfill the precept of the love of God, as stated above (A3).

Article 5

Whether Man Can Merit Everlasting Life Without Grace?

Ad quintum sic proceditur. Videtur quod homo possit mereri vitam aeternam sine gratia. Dicit enim dominus, Matth. XIX, *si vis ad vitam ingredi, serva mandata,* ex quo videtur quod ingredi in vitam aeternam sit constitutum in hominis voluntate. Sed id quod in nostra voluntate constitutum est, per nos ipsos possumus. Ergo videtur quod homo per seipsum possit vitam aeternam mereri.

Praeterea, vita aeterna est praemium vel merces quae hominibus redditur a Deo; secundum illud Matth. V, *merces vestra multa est in caelis.* Sed merces vel praemium redditur a Deo homini secundum opera eius; secundum illud Psalmi LXI, *tu reddes unicuique secundum opera eius.* Cum igitur homo sit dominus suorum operum, videtur quod in eius potestate constitutum sit ad vitam aeternam pervenire.

Praeterea, vita aeterna est ultimus finis humanae vitae. Sed quaelibet res naturalis per sua naturalia potest consequi finem suum. Ergo multo magis homo, qui est altioris naturae, per sua naturalia potest pervenire ad vitam aeternam absque aliqua gratia.

Sed contra est quod apostolus dicit, ad Rom. VI, *gratia Dei vita aeterna.* Quod ideo dicitur, sicut Glossa ibidem dicit, *ut intelligeremus Deum ad aeternam vitam pro sua miseratione nos perducere.*

Respondeo dicendum quod actus perducentes ad finem oportet esse fini proportionatos. Nullus autem actus excedit proportionem principii activi. Et ideo videmus in rebus naturalibus quod nulla res potest perficere

Objection 1: It would seem that man can merit everlasting life without grace. For Our Lord says (Matt 19:17): *If thou wilt enter into life, keep the commandments*; from which it would seem that to enter into everlasting life rests with man's will. But what rests with our will, we can do of ourselves. Hence it seems that man can merit everlasting life of himself.

Obj. 2: Further, eternal life is the wage of reward bestowed by God on men, according to Mt. 5:12: *Your reward is very great in heaven.* But wage or reward is meted by God to everyone according to his works, according to Ps. 61:12: *Thou wilt render to every man according to his works.* Hence, since man is master of his works, it seems that it is within his power to reach everlasting life.

Obj. 3: Further, everlasting life is the last end of human life. Now every natural thing by its natural endowments can attain its end. Much more, therefore, may man attain to life everlasting by his natural endowments, without grace.

On the contrary, The Apostle says (Rom 6:23): *The grace of God is life everlasting.* And as a gloss says, this is said *that we may understand that God, of His own mercy, leads us to everlasting life.*

I answer that, Acts conducing to an end must be proportioned to the end. But no act exceeds the proportion of its active principle; and hence we see in natural things, that nothing can by its operation bring about an effect which

effectum per suam operationem qui excedat virtutem activam, sed solum potest producere per operationem suam effectum suae virtuti proportionatum. Vita autem aeterna est finis excedens proportionem naturae humanae, ut ex supradictis patet. Et ideo homo per sua naturalia non potest producere opera meritoria proportionata vitae aeternae, sed ad hoc exigitur altior virtus, quae est virtus gratiae. Et ideo sine gratia homo non potest mereri vitam aeternam. Potest tamen facere opera perducentia ad aliquod bonum homini connaturale, sicut laborare in agro, bibere, manducare, et habere amicum, et alia huiusmodi; ut Augustinus dicit, in tertia responsione contra Pelagianos.

AD PRIMUM ergo dicendum quod homo sua voluntate facit opera meritoria vitae aeternae, sed, sicut Augustinus in eodem libro dicit, ad hoc exigitur quod voluntas hominis praeparetur a Deo per gratiam.

AD SECUNDUM dicendum quod, sicut Glossa dicit Rom. VI, super illud, *gratia Dei vita aeterna, certum est vitam aeternam bonis operibus reddi, sed ipsa opera quibus redditur, ad Dei gratiam pertinent*, cum etiam supra dictum sit quod ad implendum mandata legis secundum debitum modum, per quem eorum impletio est meritoria, requiritur gratia.

AD TERTIUM dicendum quod obiectio illa procedit de fine homini connaturali. Natura autem humana, ex hoc ipso quod nobilior est, potest ad altiorem finem perduci, saltem auxilio gratiae, ad quem inferiores naturae nullo modo pertingere possunt. Sicut homo est melius dispositus ad sanitatem qui aliquibus auxiliis medicinae potest sanitatem consequi, quam ille qui nullo modo; ut philosophus introducit in II de caelo.

exceeds its active force, but only such as is proportionate to its power. Now everlasting life is an end exceeding the proportion of human nature, as is clear from what we have said above (Q5, A5). Hence man, by his natural endowments, cannot produce meritorious works proportionate to everlasting life; and for this a higher force is needed, viz., the force of grace. And thus without grace man cannot merit everlasting life; yet he can perform works conducing to a good which is natural to man, as *to toil in the fields, to drink, to eat, or to have friends*, and the like, as Augustine says in his third Reply to the Pelagians.

REPLY OBJ. 1: Man, by his will, does works meritorious of everlasting life; but as Augustine says, in the same book, for this it is necessary that the will of man should be prepared with grace by God.

REPLY OBJ. 2: As the gloss upon Rm. 6:23, *The grace of God is life everlasting*, says, *It is certain that everlasting life is meter to good works; but the works to which it is meted, belong to God's grace*. And it has been said (A4), that to fulfill the commandments of the Law, in their due way, whereby their fulfilment may be meritorious, requires grace.

REPLY OBJ. 3: This objection has to do with the natural end of man. Now human nature, since it is nobler, can be raised by the help of grace to a higher end, which lower natures can nowise reach; even as a man who can recover his health by the help of medicines is better disposed to health than one who can nowise recover it, as the Philosopher observes (*De Coelo* ii, 12).

Article 6

Whether a Man, by Himself and Without the External Aid of Grace, Can Prepare Himself for Grace?

AD SEXTUM SIC PROCEDITUR. Videtur quod homo possit seipsum ad gratiam praeparare per seipsum, absque exteriori auxilio gratiae. Nihil enim imponitur homini quod sit ei impossibile, ut supra dictum est. Sed Zach. I dicitur, *convertimini ad me, et ego convertar ad vos*, nihil autem est aliud se ad gratiam praeparare quam ad Deum converti. Ergo videtur quod homo per seipsum possit se ad gratiam praeparare absque auxilio gratiae.

PRAETEREA, homo se ad gratiam praeparat faciendo quod in se est, quia si homo facit quod in se est, Deus ei non denegat gratiam; dicitur enim Matth. VII, quod Deus dat spiritum bonum petentibus se. Sed illud in nobis esse dicitur quod est in nostra potestate. Ergo videtur quod in nostra potestate sit constitutum ut nos ad gratiam praeparemus.

OBJECTION 1: It would seem that man, by himself and without the external help of grace, can prepare himself for grace. For nothing impossible is laid upon man, as stated above (A4, ad 1). But it is written (Zech 1:3): *Turn ye to Me . . . and I will turn to you*. Now to prepare for grace is nothing more than to turn to God. Therefore it seems that man of himself, and without the external help of grace, can prepare himself for grace.

OBJ. 2: Further, man prepares himself for grace by doing what is in him to do, since if man does what is in him to do, God will not deny him grace, for it is written (Matt 7:11) that God gives His good Spirit *to them that ask Him*. But what is in our power is in us to do. Therefore it seems to be in our power to prepare ourselves for grace.

PRAETEREA, si homo indiget gratia ad hoc quod praeparet se ad gratiam, pari ratione indigebit gratia ad hoc quod praeparet se ad illam gratiam, et sic procederetur in infinitum, quod est inconveniens. Ergo videtur standum in primo, ut scilicet homo sine gratia possit se ad gratiam praeparare.

PRAETEREA, Prov. XVI dicitur, hominis est praeparare animum. Sed illud dicitur esse hominis quod per seipsum potest. Ergo videtur quod homo per seipsum se possit ad gratiam praeparare.

SED CONTRA est quod dicitur Ioan. VI, *nemo potest venire ad me, nisi pater, qui misit me, traxerit eum.* Si autem homo seipsum praeparare posset, non oporteret quod ab alio traheretur. Ergo homo non potest se praeparare ad gratiam absque auxilio gratiae.

RESPONDEO dicendum quod duplex est praeparatio voluntatis humanae ad bonum. Una quidem qua praeparatur ad bene operandum et ad Deo fruendum. Et talis praeparatio voluntatis non potest fieri sine habituali gratiae dono, quod sit principium operis meritorii, ut dictum est. Alio modo potest intelligi praeparatio voluntatis humanae ad consequendum ipsum gratiae habitualis donum. Ad hoc autem quod praeparet se ad susceptionem huius doni, non oportet praesupponere aliquod aliud donum habituale in anima, quia sic procederetur in infinitum, sed oportet praesupponi aliquod auxilium gratuitum Dei interius animam moventis, sive inspirantis bonum propositum. His enim duobus modis indigemus auxilio divino, ut supra dictum est. Quod autem ad hoc indigeamus auxilio Dei moventis, manifestum est. Necesse est enim, cum omne agens agat propter finem, quod omnis causa convertat suos effectus ad suum finem. Et ideo, cum secundum ordinem agentium sive moventium sit ordo finium, necesse est quod ad ultimum finem convertatur homo per motionem primi moventis, ad finem autem proximum per motionem alicuius inferiorum moventium, sicut animus militis convertitur ad quaerendum victoriam ex motione ducis exercitus, ad sequendum autem vexillum alicuius aciei ex motione tribuni. Sic igitur, cum Deus sit primum movens simpliciter, ex eius motione est quod omnia in ipsum convertantur secundum communem intentionem boni, per quam unumquodque intendit assimilari Deo secundum suum modum. Unde et Dionysius, in libro de Div. Nom., dicit quod Deus convertit omnia ad seipsum. Sed homines iustos convertit ad seipsum sicut ad specialem finem, quem intendunt, et cui cupiunt adhaerere sicut bono proprio; secundum illud Psalmi LXXII, mihi adhaerere Deo bonum est. Et ideo quod homo convertatur ad Deum, hoc non potest esse

OBJ. 3: Further, if a man needs grace in order to prepare for grace, with equal reason will he need grace to prepare himself for the first grace; and thus to infinity, which is impossible. Hence it seems that we must not go beyond what was said first, viz., that man, of himself and without grace, can prepare himself for grace.

OBJ. 4: Further, it is written (Prov 16:1) that *it is the part of man to prepare the soul.* Now an action is said to be part of a man, when he can do it by himself. Hence it seems that man by himself can prepare himself for grace.

ON THE CONTRARY, It is written (John 6:44): *No man can come to Me except the Father, Who hath sent Me, draw him.* But if man could prepare himself, he would not need to be drawn by another. Hence man cannot prepare himself without the help of grace.

I ANSWER THAT, The preparation of the human will for good is twofold: the first, whereby it is prepared to operate rightly and to enjoy God; and this preparation of the will cannot take place without the habitual gift of grace, which is the principle of meritorious works, as stated above (A5). There is a second way in which the human will may be taken to be prepared for the gift of habitual grace itself. Now in order that man prepare himself to receive this gift, it is not necessary to presuppose any further habitual gift in the soul, otherwise we should go on to infinity. But we must presuppose a gratuitous gift of God, Who moves the soul inwardly or inspires the good wish. For in these two ways do we need the Divine assistance, as stated above (AA2,3). Now that we need the help of God to move us, is manifest. For since every agent acts for an end, every cause must direct is effect to its end, and hence since the order of ends is according to the order of agents or movers, man must be directed to the last end by the motion of the first mover, and to the proximate end by the motion of any of the subordinate movers; as the spirit of the soldier is bent towards seeking the victory by the motion of the leader of the army—and towards following the standard of a regiment by the motion of the standard-bearer. And thus since God is the First Mover, simply, it is by His motion that everything seeks to be likened to God in its own way. Hence Dionysius says (*Div. Nom.* iv) that *God turns all to Himself.* But He directs righteous men to Himself as to a special end, which they seek, and to which they wish to cling, according to Ps. 72:28, *it is good for Me to adhere to my God.* And that they are *turned* to God can only spring from God's having *turned* them. Now to prepare oneself for grace is, as it were, to be turned to God; just as, whoever has his eyes turned away from the light of the sun, prepares himself to receive the sun's light, by turning his eyes towards the sun. Hence it is clear that man cannot prepare himself to receive the

nisi Deo ipsum convertente. Hoc autem est praeparare se ad gratiam, quasi ad Deum converti, sicut ille qui habet oculum aversum a lumine solis, per hoc se praeparat ad recipiendum lumen solis, quod oculos suos convertit versus solem. Unde patet quod homo non potest se praeparare ad lumen gratiae suscipiendum, nisi per auxilium gratuitum Dei interius moventis.

AD PRIMUM ergo dicendum quod conversio hominis ad Deum fit quidem per liberum arbitrium; et secundum hoc homini praecipitur quod se ad Deum convertat. Sed liberum arbitrium ad Deum converti non potest nisi Deo ipsum ad se convertente; secundum illud Ierem. XXXI, *converte me, et convertar, quia tu dominus Deus meus*; et Thren. ult., *converte nos, domine, ad te, et convertemur.*

AD SECUNDUM dicendum quod nihil homo potest facere nisi a Deo moveatur; secundum illud Ioan. XV, *sine me nihil potestis facere.* Et ideo cum dicitur homo facere quod in se est, dicitur hoc esse in potestate hominis secundum quod est motus a Deo.

AD TERTIUM dicendum quod obiectio illa procedit de gratia habituali, ad quam requiritur aliqua praeparatio, quia omnis forma requirit susceptibile dispositum. Sed hoc quod homo moveatur a Deo non praeexigit aliquam aliam motionem, cum Deus sit primum movens. Unde non oportet abire in infinitum.

AD QUARTUM dicendum quod hominis est praeparare animum, quia hoc facit per liberum arbitrium, sed tamen hoc non facit sine auxilio Dei moventis et ad se attrahentis, ut dictum est.

light of grace except by the gratuitous help of God moving him inwardly.

REPLY OBJ. 1: Man's turning to God is by free-will; and thus man is bidden to turn himself to God. But free-will can only be turned to God, when God turns it, according to Jer. 31:18: *Convert me and I shall be converted, for Thou art the Lord, my God*; and Lam. 5:21: *Convert us, O Lord, to Thee, and we shall be converted.*

REPLY OBJ. 2: Man can do nothing unless moved by God, according to Jn. 15:5: *Without Me, you can do nothing.* Hence when a man is said to do what is in him to do, this is said to be in his power according as he is moved by God.

REPLY OBJ. 3: This objection regards habitual grace, for which some preparation is required, since every form requires a disposition in that which is to be its subject. But in order that man should be moved by God, no further motion is presupposed since God is the First Mover. Hence we need not go to infinity.

REPLY OBJ. 4: It is the part of man to prepare his soul, since he does this by his free-will. And yet he does not do this without the help of God moving him, and drawing him to Himself, as was said above.

Article 7

Whether Man Can Rise from Sin Without the Help of Grace?

AD SEPTIMUM SIC PROCEDITUR. Videtur quod homo possit resurgere a peccato sine auxilio gratiae. Illud enim quod praeexigitur ad gratiam, fit sine gratia. Sed resurgere a peccato praeexigitur ad illuminationem gratiae, dicitur enim ad Ephes. V, *exurge a mortuis, et illuminabit te Christus.* Ergo homo potest resurgere a peccato sine gratia.

PRAETEREA, peccatum virtuti opponitur sicut morbus sanitati, ut supra dictum est. Sed homo per virtutem naturae potest resurgere de aegritudine ad sanitatem sine auxilio exterioris medicinae, propter hoc quod intus manet principium vitae, a quo procedit operatio naturalis. Ergo videtur quod, simili ratione, homo possit reparari per seipsum, redeundo de statu peccati ad statum iustitiae, absque auxilio exterioris gratiae.

PRAETEREA, quaelibet res naturalis potest redire ad actum convenientem suae naturae, sicut aqua calefacta

OBJECTION 1: It would seem that man can rise from sin without the help of grace. For what is presupposed to grace, takes place without grace. But to rise to sin is presupposed to the enlightenment of grace; since it is written (Eph 5:14): *Arise from the dead and Christ shall enlighten thee.* Therefore man can rise from sin without grace.

OBJ. 2: Further, sin is opposed to virtue as illness to health, as stated above (Q71, A1, ad 3). Now, man, by force of his nature, can rise from illness to health, without the external help of medicine, since there still remains in him the principle of life, from which the natural operation proceeds. Hence it seems that, with equal reason, man may be restored by himself, and return from the state of sin to the state of justice without the help of external grace.

OBJ. 3: Further, every natural thing can return by itself to the act befitting its nature, as hot water returns by itself

per seipsam redit ad naturalem frigiditatem, et lapis sursum proiectus per seipsum redit ad suum naturalem motum. Sed peccatum est quidam actus contra naturam; ut patet per Damascenus, in II libro. Ergo videtur quod homo possit per seipsum redire de peccato ad statum iustitiae.

SED CONTRA est quod apostolus dicit, ad Gal. II, *si data est lex quae potest iustificare, ergo Christus gratis mortuus est*, idest sine causa. Pari ergo ratione, si homo habet naturam per quam potest iustificari, Christus gratis, idest sine causa, mortuus est. Sed hoc est inconveniens dicere. Ergo non potest homo per seipsum iustificari, idest redire de statu culpae ad statum iustitiae.

RESPONDEO dicendum quod homo nullo modo potest resurgere a peccato per seipsum sine auxilio gratiae. Cum enim peccatum transiens actu remaneat reatu, ut supra dictum est; non est idem resurgere a peccato quod cessare ab actu peccati. Sed resurgere a peccato est reparari hominem ad ea quae peccando amisit. Incurrit autem homo triplex detrimentum peccando, ut ex supradictis patet, scilicet maculam, corruptionem naturalis boni, et reatum poenae. Maculam quidem incurrit, inquantum privatur decore gratiae ex deformitate peccati. Bonum autem naturae corrumpitur, inquantum natura hominis deordinatur voluntate hominis Deo non subiecta, hoc enim ordine sublato, consequens est ut tota natura hominis peccantis inordinata remaneat. Reatus vero poenae est per quem homo peccando mortaliter meretur damnationem aeternam.

Manifestum est autem de singulis horum trium, quod non possunt reparari nisi per Deum. Cum enim decor gratiae proveniat ex illustratione divini luminis, non potest talis decor in anima reparari, nisi Deo denuo illustrante, unde requiritur habituale donum, quod est gratiae lumen. Similiter ordo naturae reparari non potest, ut voluntas hominis Deo subiiciatur, nisi Deo voluntatem hominis ad se trahente, sicut dictum est. Similiter etiam reatus poenae aeternae remitti non potest nisi a Deo, in quem est offensa commissa, et qui est hominum iudex. Et ideo requiritur auxilium gratiae ad hoc quod homo a peccato resurgat, et quantum ad habituale donum, et quantum ad interiorem Dei motionem.

AD PRIMUM ergo dicendum quod illud indicitur homini quod pertinet ad actum liberi arbitrii qui requiritur in hoc quod homo a peccato resurgat. Et ideo cum dicitur, exsurge, et illuminabit te Christus, non est intelligendum quod tota exurrectio a peccato praecedat illuminationem gratiae, sed quia cum homo per liberum arbitrium a Deo motum surgere conatur a peccato, recipit lumen gratiae iustificantis.

AD SECUNDUM dicendum quod naturalis ratio non est sufficiens principium huius sanitatis quae est in homine per gratiam iustificantem; sed huius principium

to its natural coldness, and a stone cast upwards returns by itself to its natural movement. Now a sin is an act against nature, as is clear from Damascene (*De Fide* Orth. ii, 30). Hence it seems that man by himself can return from sin to the state of justice.

ON THE CONTRARY, The Apostle says (Gal 2:21; Cf. Gal. 3:21): *For if there had been a law given which could give life—then Christ died in vain*, i.e., to no purpose. Hence with equal reason, if man has a nature, whereby he can he justified, *Christ died in vain*, i.e., to no purpose. But this cannot fittingly be said. Therefore by himself he cannot be justified, i.e., he cannot return from a state of sin to a state of justice.

I ANSWER THAT, Man by himself can no wise rise from sin without the help of grace. For since sin is transient as to the act and abiding in its guilt, as stated above (Q87, A6), to rise from sin is not the same as to cease the act of sin; but to rise from sin means that man has restored to him what he lost by sinning. Now man incurs a triple loss by sinning, as was clearly shown above (Q85, A1; Q86, A1; Q87, A1), viz., stain, corruption of natural good, and debt of punishment. He incurs a stain, inasmuch as he forfeits the lustre of grace through the deformity of sin. Natural good is corrupted, inasmuch as man's nature is disordered by man's will not being subject to God's; and this order being overthrown, the consequence is that the whole nature of sinful man remains disordered. Lastly, there is the debt of punishment, inasmuch as by sinning man deserves everlasting damnation.

Now it is manifest that none of these three can be restored except by God. For since the lustre of grace springs from the shedding of Divine light, this lustre cannot be brought back, except God sheds His light anew: hence a habitual gift is necessary, and this is the light of grace. Likewise, the order of nature can only be restored, i.e., man's will can only be subject to God when God draws man's will to Himself, as stated above (A6). So, too, the guilt of eternal punishment can be remitted by God alone, against Whom the offense was committed and Who is man's Judge. And thus in order that man rise from sin there is required the help of grace, both as regards a habitual gift, and as regards the internal motion of God.

REPLY OBJ. 1: To man is bidden that which pertains to the act of free-will, as this act is required in order that man should rise from sin. Hence when it is said, *Arise, and Christ shall enlighten thee*, we are not to think that the complete rising from sin precedes the enlightenment of grace; but that when man by his free-will, moved by God, strives to rise from sin, he receives the light of justifying grace.

REPLY OBJ. 2: The natural reason is not the sufficient principle of the health that is in man by justifying grace. This principle is grace which is taken away by sin. Hence

est gratia, quae tollitur per peccatum. Et ideo non potest homo per seipsum reparari, sed indiget ut denuo ei lumen gratiae infundatur, sicut si corpori mortuo resuscitando denuo infunderetur anima.

AD TERTIUM dicendum quod, quando natura est integra, per seipsam potest reparari ad id quod est sibi conveniens et proportionatum, sed ad id quod superexcedit suam proportionem, reparari non potest sine exteriori auxilio. Sic igitur humana natura defluens per actum peccati, quia non manet integra sed corrumpitur, ut supra dictum est, non potest per seipsam reparari neque etiam ad bonum sibi connaturale; et multo minus ad bonum supernaturalis iustitiae.

man cannot be restored by himself; but he requires the light of grace to be poured upon him anew, as if the soul were infused into a dead body for its resurrection.

REPLY OBJ. 3: When nature is perfect, it can be restored by itself to its befitting and proportionate condition; but without exterior help it cannot be restored to what surpasses its measure. And thus human nature undone by reason of the act of sin, remains no longer perfect, but corrupted, as stated above (Q85); nor can it be restored, by itself, to its connatural good, much less to the supernatural good of justice.

Article 8

Whether Man Without Grace Can Avoid Sin?

AD OCTAVUM SIC PROCEDITUR. Videtur quod homo sine gratia possit non peccare. *Nullus enim peccat in eo quod vitare non potest*; ut Augustinus dicit, in libro de Duab. Animab., et de Lib. Arb. Si ergo homo existens in peccato mortali non possit vitare peccatum, videtur quod peccando non peccet. Quod est inconveniens.

PRAETEREA, ad hoc corripitur homo ut non peccet. Si igitur homo in peccato mortali existens non potest non peccare, videtur quod frustra ei correptio adhibeatur. Quod est inconveniens.

PRAETEREA, Eccli. XV dicitur, *ante hominem vita et mors, bonum et malum, quod placuerit ei, dabitur illi*. Sed aliquis peccando non desinit esse homo. Ergo adhuc in eius potestate est eligere bonum vel malum. Et ita potest homo sine gratia vitare peccatum.

SED CONTRA est quod Augustinus dicit, in libro de Perfect. Iustit., *quisquis negat nos orare debere ne intremus in tentationem (negat autem hoc qui contendit ad non peccandum gratiae Dei adiutorium non esse homini necessarium, sed, sola lege accepta, humanam sufficere voluntatem), ab auribus omnium removendum, et ore omnium anathematizandum esse non dubito.*

RESPONDEO dicendum quod de homine dupliciter loqui possumus, uno modo, secundum statum naturae integrae; alio modo, secundum statum naturae corruptae. Secundum statum quidem naturae integrae, etiam sine gratia habituali, poterat homo non peccare nec mortaliter nec venialiter, quia peccare nihil aliud est quam recedere ab eo quod est secundum naturam, quod vitare homo poterat in integritate naturae. Non tamen hoc poterat sine auxilio Dei in bono conservantis, quo subtracto, etiam ipsa natura in nihilum decideret.

In statu autem naturae corruptae, indiget homo gratia habituali sanante naturam, ad hoc quod omnino

OBJECTION 1: It would seem that without grace man can avoid sin. Because *no one sins in what he cannot avoid*, as Augustine says (*De Duab. Anim.* x, xi; *De Libero Arbit.* iii, 18). Hence if a man in mortal sin cannot avoid sin, it would seem that in sinning he does not sin, which is impossible.

OBJ. 2: Further, men are corrected that they may not sin. If therefore a man in mortal sin cannot avoid sin, correction would seem to be given to no purpose; which is absurd.

OBJ. 3: Further, it is written (Sir 15:18): *Before man is life and death, good and evil; that which he shall choose shall be given him*. But by sinning no one ceases to be a man. Hence it is still in his power to choose good or evil; and thus man can avoid sin without grace.

ON THE CONTRARY, Augustine says (*De Perfect. Just.* xxi): *Whoever denies that we ought to say the prayer 'Lead us not into temptation' (and they deny it who maintain that the help of God's grace is not necessary to man for salvation, but that the gift of the law is enough for the human will) ought without doubt to be removed beyond all hearing, and to be anathematized by the tongues of all.*

I ANSWER THAT, We may speak of man in two ways: first, in the state of perfect nature; second, in the state of corrupted nature. Now in the state of perfect nature, man, without habitual grace, could avoid sinning either mortally or venially; since to sin is nothing else than to stray from what is according to our nature—and in the state of perfect nature man could avoid this. Nevertheless he could not have done it without God's help to uphold him in good, since if this had been withdrawn, even his nature would have fallen back into nothingness.

But in the state of corrupt nature man needs grace to heal his nature in order that he may entirely abstain from

a peccato abstineat. Quae quidem sanatio primo fit in praesenti vita secundum mentem, appetitu carnali nondum totaliter reparato, unde apostolus, ad Rom. VII, in persona hominis reparati, dicit, *ego ipse mente servio legi Dei, carne autem legi peccati.* In quo quidem statu potest homo abstinere a peccato mortali quod in ratione consistit, ut supra habitum est. Non autem potest homo abstinere ab omni peccato veniali, propter corruptionem inferioris appetitus sensualitatis, cuius motus singulos quidem ratio reprimere potest (et ex hoc habent rationem peccati et voluntarii), non autem omnes, quia dum uni resistere nititur, fortassis alius insurgit; et etiam quia ratio non semper potest esse pervigil ad huiusmodi motus vitandos; ut supra dictum est.

Similiter etiam antequam hominis ratio, in qua est peccatum mortale, reparetur per gratiam iustificantem, potest singula peccata mortalia vitare, et secundum aliquod tempus, quia non est necesse quod continuo peccet in actu. Sed quod diu maneat absque peccato mortali, esse non potest. Unde et Gregorius dicit, super Ezech., quod *peccatum quod mox per poenitentiam non deletur, suo pondere ad aliud trahit.* Et huius ratio est quia, sicut rationi subdi debet inferior appetitus, ita etiam ratio debet subdi Deo, et in ipso constituere finem suae voluntatis. Per finem autem oportet quod regulentur omnes actus humani, sicut per rationis iudicium regulari debent motus inferioris appetitus. Sicut ergo, inferiori appetitu non totaliter subiecto rationi, non potest esse quin contingant inordinati motus in appetitu sensitivo; ita etiam, ratione hominis non existente subiecta Deo, consequens est ut contingant multae inordinationes in ipsis actibus rationis. Cum enim homo non habet cor suum firmatum in Deo, ut pro nullo bono consequendo vel malo vitando ab eo separari vellet; occurrunt multa propter quae consequenda vel vitanda homo recedit a Deo contemnendo praecepta ipsius, et ita peccat mortaliter, praecipue quia in repentinis homo operatur secundum finem praeconceptum, et secundum habitum praeexistentem, ut philosophus dicit, in III Ethic.; quamvis ex praemeditatione rationis homo possit aliquid agere praeter ordinem finis praeconcepti, et praeter inclinationem habitus. Sed quia homo non potest semper esse in tali praemeditatione, non potest contingere ut diu permaneat quin operetur secundum consequentiam voluntatis deordinatae a Deo, nisi cito per gratiam ad debitum ordinem reparetur.

AD PRIMUM ergo dicendum quod homo potest vitare singulos actus peccati, non tamen omnes, nisi per gratiam, ut dictum est. Et tamen quia ex eius defectu est quod homo se ad gratiam habendam non praeparet, per hoc a peccato non excusatur, quod sine gratia peccatum vitare non potest.

AD SECUNDUM dicendum quod correptio utilis est *ut ex dolore correptionis voluntas regenerationis oriatur. Si tamen qui corripitur filius est promissionis, ut, strepitu*

sin. And in the present life this healing is wrought in the mind—the carnal appetite being not yet restored. Hence the Apostle (Rom 7:25) says in the person of one who is restored: *I myself, with the mind, serve the law of God, but with the flesh, the law of sin.* And in this state man can abstain from all mortal sin, which takes its stand in his reason, as stated above (Q74, A5); but man cannot abstain from all venial sin on account of the corruption of his lower appetite of sensuality. For man can, indeed, repress each of its movements (and hence they are sinful and voluntary), but not all, because whilst he is resisting one, another may arise, and also because the reason is always alert to avoid these movements, as was said above (Q74, A3, ad 2).

So, too, before man's reason, wherein is mortal sin, is restored by justifying grace, he can avoid each mortal sin, and for a time, since it is not necessary that he should be always actually sinning. But it cannot be that he remains for a long time without mortal sin. Hence Gregory says (*Super Ezech. Hom. xi*) that *a sin not at once taken away by repentance, by its weight drags us down to other sins*: and this because, as the lower appetite ought to be subject to the reason, so should the reason be subject to God, and should place in Him the end of its will. Now it is by the end that all human acts ought to be regulated, even as it is by the judgment of the reason that the movements of the lower appetite should be regulated. And thus, even as inordinate movements of the sensitive appetite cannot help occurring since the lower appetite is not subject to reason, so likewise, since man's reason is not entirely subject to God, the consequence is that many disorders occur in the reason. For when man's heart is not so fixed on God as to be unwilling to be parted from Him for the sake of finding any good or avoiding any evil, many things happen for the achieving or avoiding of which a man strays from God and breaks His commandments, and thus sins mortally: especially since, when surprised, a man acts according to his preconceived end and his pre-existing habits, as the Philosopher says (*Ethic.* iii); although with premeditation of his reason a man may do something outside the order of his preconceived end and the inclination of his habit. But because a man cannot always have this premeditation, it cannot help occurring that he acts in accordance with his will turned aside from God, unless, by grace, he is quickly brought back to the due order.

REPLY OBJ. 1: Man can avoid each but every act of sin, except by grace, as stated above. Nevertheless, since it is by his own shortcoming that he does not prepare himself to have grace, the fact that he cannot avoid sin without grace does not excuse him from sin.

REPLY OBJ. 2: Correction is useful *in order that out of the sorrow of correction may spring the wish to be regenerate; if indeed he who is corrected is a son of promise, in such*

correptionis forinsecus insonante ac flagellante, Deus in illo intrinsecus occulta inspiratione operetur et velle; ut Augustinus dicit, in libro de Corrept. et Grat. Ideo ergo necessaria est correptio, quia voluntas hominis requiritur ad hoc quod a peccato abstineat. Sed tamen correptio non est sufficiens sine Dei auxilio, unde dicitur Eccle. VII, *considera opera Dei, quod nemo possit corrigere quem ille despexerit.*

Ad tertium dicendum quod, sicut Augustinus dicit, in Hypognost., verbum illud intelligitur de homine secundum statum naturae integrae, quando nondum erat servus peccati, unde poterat peccare et non peccare. Nunc etiam quodcumque vult homo, datur ei. Sed hoc quod bonum velit, habet ex auxilio gratiae.

sort that whilst the noise of correction is outwardly resounding and punishing, God by hidden inspirations is inwardly causing to will, as Augustine says (*De Corr. et Gratia* vi). Correction is therefore necessary, from the fact that man's will is required in order to abstain from sin; yet it is not sufficient without God's help. Hence it is written (Eccl 7:14): *Consider the works of God that no man can correct whom He hath despised.*

Reply Obj. 3: As Augustine says (*Hypognosticon* iii), this saying is to be understood of man in the state of perfect nature, when as yet he was not a slave of sin. Hence he was able to sin and not to sin. Now, too, whatever a man wills, is given to him; but his willing good, he has by God's assistance.

Article 9

Whether One Who Has Already Obtained Grace, Can, of Himself and Without Further Help of Grace, Do Good and Avoid Sin?

Ad nonum sic proceditur. Videtur quod ille qui iam consecutus est gratiam, per seipsum possit operari bonum et vitare peccatum, absque alio auxilio gratiae. Unumquodque enim aut frustra est, aut imperfectum, si non implet illud ad quod datur. Sed gratia ad hoc datur nobis ut possimus bonum facere et vitare peccatum. Si igitur per gratiam hoc homo non potest, videtur quod vel gratia sit frustra data, vel sit imperfecta.

Praeterea, per gratiam ipse Spiritus Sanctus in nobis habitat; secundum illud I ad Cor. III, *nescitis quia templum Dei estis, et spiritus Dei habitat in vobis?* Sed Spiritus Sanctus, cum sit omnipotens, sufficiens est ut nos inducat ad bene operandum, et ut nos a peccato custodiat. Ergo homo gratiam consecutus potest utrumque praedictorum absque alio auxilio gratiae.

Praeterea, si homo consecutus gratiam adhuc alio auxilio gratiae indiget ad hoc quod recte vivat et a peccato abstineat, pari ratione et si illud aliud auxilium gratiae consecutus fuerit, adhuc alio auxilio indigebit. Procedetur ergo in infinitum, quod est inconveniens. Ergo ille qui est in gratia, non indiget alio auxilio gratiae ad hoc quod bene operetur et a peccato abstineat.

Sed contra est quod Augustinus dicit, in libro de natura et gratia, quod *sicut oculus corporis plenissime sanus, nisi candore lucis adiutus, non potest cernere; sic et homo perfectissime etiam iustificatus, nisi aeterna luce iustitiae divinitus adiuvetur, recte non potest vivere.* Sed iustificatio fit per gratiam; secundum illud Rom. III. *Iustificati gratis per gratiam ipsius.* Ergo etiam homo iam habens gratiam indiget alio auxilio gratiae ad hoc quod recte vivat.

Objection 1: It would seem that whoever has already obtained grace, can by himself and without further help of grace, do good and avoid sin. For a thing is useless or imperfect, if it does not fulfill what it was given for. Now grace is given to us that we may do good and keep from sin. Hence if with grace man cannot do this, it seems that grace is either useless or imperfect.

Obj. 2: Further, by grace the Holy Spirit dwells in us, according to 1 Cor. 3:16: *Know you not that you are the temple of God, and that the Spirit of God dwelleth in you?* Now since the Spirit of God is omnipotent, He is sufficient to ensure our doing good and to keep us from sin. Hence a man who has obtained grace can do the above two things without any further assistance of grace.

Obj. 3: Further, if a man who has obtained grace needs further aid of grace in order to live righteously and to keep free from sin, with equal reason, will he need yet another grace, even though he has obtained this first help of grace. Therefore we must go on to infinity; which is impossible. Hence whoever is in grace needs no further help of grace in order to do righteously and to keep free from sin.

On the contrary, Augustine says (*De Natura et Gratia* xxvi) that *as the eye of the body though most healthy cannot see unless it is helped by the brightness of light, so, neither can a man, even if he is most righteous, live righteously unless he be helped by the eternal light of justice.* But justification is by grace, according to Rm. 3:24: *Being justified freely by His grace.* Hence even a man who already possesses grace needs a further assistance of grace in order to live righteously.

RESPONDEO dicendum quod, sicut supra dictum est, homo ad recte vivendum dupliciter auxilio Dei indiget. Uno quidem modo, quantum ad aliquod habituale donum, per quod natura humana corrupta sanetur; et etiam sanata elevetur ad operandum opera meritoria vitae aeternae, quae excedunt proportionem naturae. Alio modo indiget homo auxilio gratiae ut a Deo moveatur ad agendum.

Quantum igitur ad primum auxilii modum, homo in gratia existens non indiget alio auxilio gratiae quasi aliquo alio habitu infuso. Indiget tamen auxilio gratiae secundum alium modum, ut scilicet a Deo moveatur ad recte agendum. Et hoc propter duo. Primo quidem, ratione generali, propter hoc quod, sicut supra dictum est, nulla res creata potest in quemcumque actum prodire nisi virtute motionis divinae. Secundo, ratione speciali, propter conditionem status humanae naturae. Quae quidem licet per gratiam sanetur quantum ad mentem, remanet tamen in ea corruptio et infectio quantum ad carnem, per quam servit legi peccati, ut dicitur ad Rom. VII. Remanet etiam quaedam ignorantiae obscuritas in intellectu, secundum quam, ut etiam dicitur Rom. VIII, *quid oremus sicut oportet, nescimus.* Propter varios enim rerum eventus, et quia etiam nosipsos non perfecte cognoscimus, non possumus ad plenum scire quid nobis expediat; secundum illud Sap. IX, *cogitationes mortalium timidae, et incertae providentiae nostrae.* Et ideo necesse est nobis ut a Deo dirigamur et protegamur, qui omnia novit et omnia potest. Et propter hoc etiam renatis in filios Dei per gratiam, convenit dicere, *et ne nos inducas in tentationem, et, fiat voluntas tua sicut in caelo et in terra,* et cetera quae in oratione dominica continentur ad hoc pertinentia.

AD PRIMUM ergo dicendum quod donum habitualis gratiae non ad hoc datur nobis ut per ipsum non indigeamus ulterius divino auxilio, indiget enim quaelibet creatura ut a Deo conservetur in bono quod ab ipso accepit. Et ideo si post acceptam gratiam homo adhuc indiget divino auxilio, non potest concludi quod gratia sit in vacuum data, vel quod sit imperfecta. Quia etiam in statu gloriae, quando gratia erit omnino perfecta, homo divino auxilio indigebit. Hic autem aliqualiter gratia imperfecta est, inquantum hominem non totaliter sanat, ut dictum est.

AD SECUNDUM dicendum quod operatio spiritus sancti qua nos movet et protegit, non circumscribitur per effectum habitualis doni quod in nobis causat; sed praeter hunc effectum nos movet et protegit, simul cum patre et filio.

AD TERTIUM dicendum quod ratio illa concludit quod homo non indigeat alia habituali gratia.

I ANSWER THAT, As stated above (A5), in order to live righteously a man needs a twofold help of God—first, a habitual gift whereby corrupted human nature is healed, and after being healed is lifted up so as to work deeds meritoriously of everlasting life, which exceed the capability of nature. Second, man needs the help of grace in order to be moved by God to act.

Now with regard to the first kind of help, man does not need a further help of grace, e.g., a further infused habit. Yet he needs the help of grace in another way, i.e., in order to be moved by God to act righteously, and this for two reasons: first, for the general reason that no created thing can put forth any act, unless by virtue of the Divine motion. Second, for this special reason—the condition of the state of human nature. For although healed by grace as to the mind, yet it remains corrupted and poisoned in the flesh, whereby it serves *the law of sin*, Rm. 7:25. In the intellect, too, there seems the darkness of ignorance, whereby, as is written (Rom 8:26): *We know not what we should pray for as we ought;* since on account of the various turns of circumstances, and because we do not know ourselves perfectly, we cannot fully know what is for our good, according to Wis. 9:14: *For the thoughts of mortal men are fearful and our counsels uncertain.* Hence we must be guided and guarded by God, Who knows and can do all things. For which reason also it is becoming in those who have been born again as sons of God, to say: *Lead us not into temptation,* and *Thy Will be done on earth as it is in heaven,* and whatever else is contained in the Lord's Prayer pertaining to this.

REPLY OBJ. 1: The gift of habitual grace is not therefore given to us that we may no longer need the Divine help; for every creature needs to be preserved in the good received from Him. Hence if after having received grace man still needs the Divine help, it cannot be concluded that grace is given to no purpose, or that it is imperfect, since man will need the Divine help even in the state of glory, when grace shall be fully perfected. But here grace is to some extent imperfect, inasmuch as it does not completely heal man, as stated above.

REPLY OBJ. 2: The operation of the Holy Spirit, which moves and protects, is not circumscribed by the effect of habitual grace which it causes in us; but beyond this effect He, together with the Father and the Son, moves and protects us.

REPLY OBJ. 3: This argument merely proves that man needs no further habitual grace.

Article 10

Whether Man Possessed of Grace Needs the Help of Grace in Order to Persevere?

AD DECIMUM SIC PROCEDITUR. Videtur quod homo in gratia constitutus non indigeat auxilio gratiae ad perseverandum. Perseverantia enim est aliquid minus virtute, sicut et continentia, ut patet per philosophum in VII Ethic. Sed homo non indiget alio auxilio gratiae ad habendum virtutes, ex quo est iustificatus per gratiam. Ergo multo minus indiget auxilio gratiae ad habendum perseverantiam.

PRAETEREA, omnes virtutes simul infunduntur. Sed perseverantia ponitur quaedam virtus. Ergo videtur quod, simul cum gratia infusis aliis virtutibus, perseverantia detur.

PRAETEREA, sicut apostolus dicit, ad Rom. V, plus restitutum est homini per donum Christi, quam amiserit per peccatum Adae. Sed Adam accepit unde posset perseverare. Ergo multo magis nobis restituitur per gratiam Christi ut perseverare possimus. Et ita homo non indiget gratia ad perseverandum.

SED CONTRA est quod Augustinus dicit, in libro de perseverantia, *cur perseverantia poscitur a Deo, si non datur a Deo? An et ista irrisoria petitio est, cum id ab eo petitur quod scitur non ipsum dare, sed, ipso non dante, esse in hominis potestate?* Sed perseverantia petitur etiam ab illis qui sunt per gratiam sanctificati, quod intelligitur cum dicimus, sanctificetur nomen tuum, ut ibidem Augustinus confirmat per verba Cypriani. Ergo homo etiam in gratia constitutus, indiget ut ei perseverantia a Deo detur.

RESPONDEO dicendum quod perseverantia tripliciter dicitur. Quandoque enim significat habitum mentis per quem homo firmiter stat, ne removeatur ab eo quod est secundum virtutem, per tristitias irruentes, ut sic se habeat perseverantia ad tristitias sicut continentia ad concupiscentias et delectationes ut philosophus dicit, in VII Ethic. Alio modo potest dici perseverantia habitus quidam secundum quem habet homo propositum perseverandi in bono usque in finem. Et utroque istorum modorum, perseverantia simul cum gratia infunditur sicut et continentia et ceterae virtutes. Alio modo dicitur perseverantia continuatio quaedam boni usque ad finem vitae. Et ad talem perseverantiam habendam homo in gratia constitutus non quidem indiget aliqua alia habituali gratia, sed divino auxilio ipsum dirigente et protegente contra tentationum impulsus, sicut ex praecedenti quaestione apparet. Et ideo postquam aliquis est iustificatus per gratiam, necesse habet a Deo petere praedictum perseverantiae donum, ut scilicet custodiatur a malo usque ad finem vitae. Multis enim datur gratia, quibus non datur perseverare in gratia.

OBJECTION 1: It would seem that man possessed of grace needs no help to persevere. For perseverance is something less than virtue, even as continence is, as is clear from the Philosopher (*Ethic.* vii, 7,9). Now since man is justified by grace, he needs no further help of grace in order to have the virtues. Much less, therefore, does he need the help of grace to have perseverance.

OBJ. 2: Further, all the virtues are infused at once. But perseverance is put down as a virtue. Hence it seems that, together with grace, perseverance is given to the other infused virtues.

OBJ. 3: Further, as the Apostle says (Rom 5:20) more was restored to man by Christ's gift, than he had lost by Adam's sin. But Adam received what enabled him to persevere; and thus man does not need grace in order to persevere.

ON THE CONTRARY, Augustine says (*De Persev.* ii): *Why is perseverance besought of God, if it is not bestowed by God? For is it not a mocking request to seek what we know He does not give, and what is in our power without His giving it?* Now perseverance is besought by even those who are hallowed by grace; and this is seen, when we say *Hallowed be Thy name,* which Augustine confirms by the words of Cyprian (*De Correp. et Grat.* xii). Hence man, even when possessed of grace, needs perseverance to be given to him by God.

I ANSWER THAT, Perseverance is taken in three ways. First, to signify a habit of the mind whereby a man stands steadfastly, lest he be moved by the assault of sadness from what is virtuous. And thus perseverance is to sadness as continence is to concupiscence and pleasure, as the Philosopher says (*Ethic.* vii, 7). Second, perseverance may be called a habit, whereby a man has the purpose of persevering in good unto the end. And in both these ways perseverance is infused together with grace, even as continence and the other virtues are. Third, perseverance is called the abiding in good to the end of life. And in order to have this perseverance man does not, indeed, need another habitual grace, but he needs the Divine assistance guiding and guarding him against the attacks of the passions, as appears from the preceding article. And hence after anyone has been justified by grace, he still needs to beseech God for the aforesaid gift of perseverance, that he may be kept from evil till the end of his life. For to many grace is given to whom perseverance in grace is not given.

AD PRIMUM ergo dicendum quod obiectio illa procedit de primo modo perseverantiae, sicut et secunda obiectio procedit de secundo.

UNDE PATET solutio ad secundum.

AD TERTIUM dicendum quod, sicut Augustinus dicit, in libro de natura et gratia, *homo in primo statu accepit donum per quod perseverare posset, non autem accepit ut perseveraret. Nunc autem per gratiam Christi multi accipiunt et donum gratiae quo perseverare possunt, et ulterius eis datur quod perseverent.* Et sic donum Christi est maius quam delictum Adae. Et tamen facilius homo per gratiae donum perseverare poterat in statu innocentiae, in quo nulla erat rebellio carnis ad spiritum, quam nunc possumus, quando reparatio gratiae Christi, etsi sit inchoata quantum ad mentem, nondum tamen est consummata quantum ad carnem. Quod erit in patria, ubi homo non solum perseverare poterit, sed etiam peccare non poterit.

REPLY OBJ. 1: This objection regards the first mode of perseverance, as the second objection regards the second.

HENCE the solution of the second objection is clear.

REPLY OBJ. 3: As Augustine says (*De Natura et Gratia* xliii): *in the original state man received a gift whereby he could persevere, but to persevere was not given him. But now, by the grace of Christ, many receive both the gift of grace whereby they may persevere, and the further gift of persevering*, and thus Christ's gift is greater than Adam's fault. Nevertheless it was easier for man to persevere, with the gift of grace in the state of innocence in which the flesh was not rebellious against the spirit, than it is now. For the restoration by Christ's grace, although it is already begun in the mind, is not yet completed in the flesh, as it will be in heaven, where man will not merely be able to persevere but will be unable to sin.

QUESTION 110

OF THE GRACE OF GOD AS REGARDS ITS ESSENCE

Deinde considerandum est de gratia Dei quantum ad eius essentiam. Et circa hoc quaeruntur quatuor.

Primo, utrum gratia ponat aliquid in anima.
Secundo, utrum gratia sit qualitas.
Tertio, utrum gratia differat a virtute infusa.
Quarto, de subiecto gratiae.

We must now consider the grace of God as regards its essence; and under this head there are four points of inquiry:

(1) Whether grace implies something in the soul?
(2) Whether grace is a quality?
(3) Whether grace differs from infused virtue?
(4) Of the subject of grace.

Article 1

Whether Grace Implies Anything in the Soul?

AD PRIMUM SIC PROCEDITUR. Videtur quod gratia non ponat aliquid in anima. Sicut enim homo dicitur habere gratiam Dei, ita etiam gratiam hominis, unde dicitur Gen. XXXIX, quod *dominus dedit Ioseph gratiam in conspectu principis carceris.* Sed per hoc quod homo dicitur habere gratiam hominis, nihil ponitur in eo qui gratiam alterius habet; sed in eo cuius gratiam habet, ponitur acceptatio quaedam. Ergo per hoc quod homo dicitur gratiam Dei habere, nihil ponitur in anima, sed solum significatur acceptatio divina.

PRAETEREA, sicut anima vivificat corpus, ita Deus vivificat animam, unde dicitur Deut. XXX, *ipse est vita tua.* Sed anima vivificat corpus immediate. Ergo etiam nihil cadit medium inter Deum et animam. Non ergo gratia ponit aliquid creatum in anima.

PRAETEREA, ad Rom. I, super illud, *gratia vobis et pax,* dicit Glossa. Gratia, idest remissio peccatorum, sed remissio peccatorum non ponit in anima aliquid, sed solum in Deo, non imputando peccatum; secundum illud Psalmi XXXI, *beatus vir cui non imputavit dominus peccatum.* Ergo nec gratia ponit aliquid in anima.

SED CONTRA, lux ponit aliquid in illuminato. Sed gratia est quaedam lux animae, unde Augustinus dicit, in libro de natura et gratia, *praevaricatorem legis digne lux deserit veritatis, qua desertus utique fit caecus.* Ergo gratia ponit aliquid in anima.

RESPONDEO dicendum quod secundum communem modum loquendi, gratia tripliciter accipi consuevit. Uno modo, pro dilectione alicuius, sicut consuevimus dicere quod iste miles habet gratiam regis, idest, rex habet eum gratum. Secundo sumitur pro aliquo dono gratis dato, sicut consuevimus dicere, hanc gratiam facio

OBJECTION 1: It would seem that grace does not imply anything in the soul. For man is said to have the grace of God even as the grace of man. Hence it is written (Gen 39:21) that the Lord gave to Joseph *grace in the sight of the chief keeper of the prison.* Now when we say that a man has the favor of another, nothing is implied in him who has the favor of the other, but an acceptance is implied in him whose favor he has. Hence when we say that a man has the grace of God, nothing is implied in his soul; but we merely signify the Divine acceptance.

OBJ. 2: Further, as the soul quickens the body so does God quicken the soul; hence it is written (Deut 30:20): *He is thy life.* Now the soul quickens the body immediately. Therefore nothing can come as a medium between God and the soul. Hence grace implies nothing created in the soul.

OBJ. 3: Further, on Rm. 1:7, *Grace to you and peace,* the gloss says: *Grace, i.e., the remission of sins.* Now the remission of sin implies nothing in the soul, but only in God, Who does not impute the sin, according to Ps. 31:2: *Blessed is the man to whom the Lord hath not imputed sin.* Hence neither does grace imply anything in the soul.

ON THE CONTRARY, Light implies something in what is enlightened. But grace is a light of the soul; hence Augustine says (*De Natura et Gratia* xxii): *The light of truth rightly deserts the prevaricator of the law, and those who have been thus deserted become blind.* Therefore grace implies something in the soul.

I ANSWER THAT, According to the common manner of speech, grace is usually taken in three ways. First, for anyone's love, as we are accustomed to say that the soldier is in the good graces of the king, i.e., the king looks on him with favor. Second, it is taken for any gift freely bestowed, as we are accustomed to say: I do you this act of grace. Third, it is

tibi. Tertio modo sumitur pro recompensatione beneficii gratis dati, secundum quod dicimur agere gratias beneficiorum. Quorum trium secundum dependet ex primo, ex amore enim quo aliquis alium gratum habet, procedit quod aliquid ei gratis impendat. Ex secundo autem procedit tertium, quia ex beneficiis gratis exhibitis gratiarum actio consurgit.

Quantum igitur ad duo ultima, manifestum est quod gratia aliquid ponit in eo qui gratiam accipit, primo quidem, ipsum donum gratis datum; secundo, huius doni recognitionem. Sed quantum ad primum, est differentia attendenda circa gratiam Dei et gratiam hominis. Quia enim bonum creaturae provenit ex voluntate divina, ideo ex dilectione Dei qua vult creaturae bonum, profluit aliquod bonum in creatura. Voluntas autem hominis movetur ex bono praeexistente in rebus, et inde est quod dilectio hominis non causat totaliter rei bonitatem, sed praesupponit ipsam vel in parte vel in toto. Patet igitur quod quamlibet Dei dilectionem sequitur aliquod bonum in creatura causatum quandoque, non tamen dilectioni aeternae coaeternum. Et secundum huiusmodi boni differentiam, differens consideratur dilectio Dei ad creaturam. Una quidem communis, secundum quam diligit omnia quae sunt, ut dicitur Sap. XI; secundum quam esse naturale rebus creatis largitur. Alia autem est dilectio specialis, secundum quam trahit creaturam rationalem supra conditionem naturae, ad participationem divini boni. Et secundum hanc dilectionem dicitur aliquem diligere simpliciter, quia secundum hanc dilectionem vult Deus simpliciter creaturae bonum aeternum, quod est ipse.

Sic igitur per hoc quod dicitur homo gratiam Dei habere, significatur quiddam supernaturale in homine a Deo proveniens. Quandoque tamen gratia Dei dicitur ipsa aeterna Dei dilectio, secundum quod dicitur etiam gratia praedestinationis, inquantum Deus gratuito, et non ex meritis, aliquos praedestinavit sive elegit; dicitur enim ad Ephes. I, *praedestinavit nos in adoptionem filiorum, in laudem gloriae gratiae suae.*

AD PRIMUM ergo dicendum quod etiam in hoc quod dicitur aliquis habere gratiam hominis, intelligitur in aliquo esse aliquid quod sit homini gratum, sicut et in hoc quod dicitur aliquis gratiam Dei habere; sed differenter. Nam illud quod est homini gratum in alio homine, praesupponitur eius dilectioni, causatur autem ex dilectione divina quod est in homine Deo gratum, ut dictum est.

AD SECUNDUM dicendum quod Deus est vita animae per modum causae efficientis, sed anima est vita corporis per modum causae formalis inter formam autem et materiam non cadit aliquod medium, quia forma per seipsam informat materiam vel subiectum. Sed agens informat subiectum non per suam substantiam, sed per formam quam in materia causat.

taken for the recompense of a gift given *gratis*, inasmuch as we are said to be *grateful* for benefits. Of these three the second depends on the first, since one bestows something on another *gratis* from the love wherewith he receives him into his good *graces*. And from the second proceeds the third, since from benefits bestowed *gratis* arises *gratitude*.

Now as regards the last two, it is clear that grace implies something in him who receives grace: first, the gift given gratis; second, the acknowledgment of the gift. But as regards the first, a difference must be noted between the grace of God and the grace of man; for since the creature's good springs from the Divine will, some good in the creature flows from God's love, whereby He wishes the good of the creature. On the other hand, the will of man is moved by the good pre-existing in things; and hence man's love does not wholly cause the good of the thing, but pre-supposes it either in part or wholly. Therefore it is clear that every love of God is followed at some time by a good caused in the creature, but not co-eternal with the eternal love. And according to this difference of good the love of God to the creature is looked at differently. For one is common, whereby He loves *all things that are* (Wis 11:25), and thereby gives things their natural being. But the second is a special love, whereby He draws the rational creature above the condition of its nature to a participation of the Divine good; and according to this love He is said to love anyone simply, since it is by this love that God simply wishes the eternal good, which is Himself, for the creature.

Accordingly when a man is said to have the grace of God, there is signified something bestowed on man by God. Nevertheless the grace of God sometimes signifies God's eternal love, as we say the grace of predestination, inasmuch as God gratuitously and not from merits predestines or elects some; for it is written (Eph 1:5): *He hath predestined us into the adoption of children . . . unto the praise of the glory of His grace.*

REPLY OBJ. 1: Even when a man is said to be in another's good graces, it is understood that there is something in him pleasing to the other; even as anyone is said to have God's grace—with this difference, that what is pleasing to a man in another is presupposed to his love, but whatever is pleasing to God in a man is caused by the Divine love, as was said above.

REPLY OBJ. 2: God is the life of the soul after the manner of an efficient cause; but the soul is the life of the body after the manner of a formal cause. Now there is no medium between form and matter, since the form, of itself, *informs* the matter or subject; whereas the agent *informs* the subject, not by its substance, but by the form, which it causes in the matter.

AD TERTIUM dicendum quod Augustinus dicit, in libro Retract., *ubi dixi gratiam esse remissionem peccatorum, pacem vero in reconciliatione Dei, non sic accipiendum est ac si pax ipsa et reconciliatio non pertineant ad gratiam generalem; sed quod specialiter nomine gratiae remissionem significaverit peccatorum.* Non ergo sola remissio peccatorum ad gratiam pertinet, sed etiam multa alia Dei dona. Et etiam remissio peccatorum non fit sine aliquo effectu divinitus in nobis causato, ut infra patebit.

REPLY OBJ. 3: Augustine says (*Retract.* i, 25): *When I said that grace was for the remission of sins, and peace for our reconciliation with God, you must not take it to mean that peace and reconciliation do not pertain to general peace, but that the special name of grace signifies the remission of sins.* Not only grace, therefore, but many other of God's gifts pertain to grace. And hence the remission of sins does not take place without some effect divinely caused in us, as will appear later (Q113, A2).

Article 2

Whether Grace Is a Quality of the Soul?

AD SECUNDUM SIC PROCEDITUR. Videtur quod gratia non sit qualitas animae. Nulla enim qualitas agit in suum subiectum, quia actio qualitatis non est absque actione subiecti, et sic oporteret quod subiectum ageret in seipsum. Sed gratia agit in animam, iustificando ipsam. Ergo gratia non est qualitas.

PRAETEREA, substantia est nobilior qualitate. Sed gratia est nobilior quam natura animae, multa enim possumus per gratiam ad quae natura non sufficit, ut supra dictum est. Ergo gratia non est qualitas.

PRAETEREA, nulla qualitas remanet postquam desinit esse in subiecto. Sed gratia remanet. Non enim corrumpitur, quia sic in nihilum redigeretur, sicut ex nihilo creatur, unde et dicitur nova creatura, ad Gal. ult. Ergo gratia non est qualitas.

SED CONTRA est quod, super illud Psalmi CIII, *ut exhilaret faciem in oleo*, dicit Glossa quod *gratia est nitor animae, sanctum concilians amorem.* Sed nitor animae est quaedam qualitas, sicut et pulchritudo corporis. Ergo gratia est quaedam qualitas.

RESPONDEO dicendum quod, sicut iam dictum est, in eo qui dicitur gratiam Dei habere, significatur esse quidam effectus gratuitae Dei voluntatis. Dictum est autem supra quod dupliciter ex gratuita Dei voluntate homo adiuvatur. Uno modo, inquantum anima hominis movetur a Deo ad aliquid cognoscendum vel volendum vel agendum. Et hoc modo ipse gratuitus effectus in homine non est qualitas, sed motus quidam animae, actus enim moventis in moto est motus, ut dicitur in III Physic. Alio modo adiuvatur homo ex gratuita Dei voluntate, secundum quod aliquod habituale donum a Deo animae infunditur. Et hoc ideo, quia non est conveniens quod Deus minus provideat his quos diligit ad supernaturale bonum habendum, quam creaturis quas diligit ad bonum naturale habendum. Creaturis autem naturalibus sic providet ut non solum moveat eas ad actus naturales, sed etiam largiatur eis formas et virtutes quasdam, quae

OBJECTION 1: It would seem that grace is not a quality of the soul. For no quality acts on its subject, since the action of a quality is not without the action of its subject, and thus the subject would necessarily act upon itself. But grace acts upon the soul, by justifying it. Therefore grace is not a quality.

OBJ. 2: Furthermore, substance is nobler than quality. But grace is nobler than the nature of the soul, since we can do many things by grace, to which nature is not equal, as stated above (Q109, AA1,2,3). Therefore grace is not a quality.

OBJ. 3: Furthermore, no quality remains after it has ceased to be in its subject. But grace remains; since it is not corrupted, for thus it would be reduced to nothing, since it was created from nothing; hence it is called a *new creature* (Gal 6:15).

ON THE CONTRARY, on Ps. 103:15: *That he may make the face cheerful with oil*; the gloss says: *Grace is a certain beauty of soul, which wins the Divine love.* But beauty of soul is a quality, even as beauty of body. Therefore grace is a quality.

I ANSWER THAT, As stated above (A1), there is understood to be an effect of God's gratuitous will in whoever is said to have God's grace. Now it was stated (Q109, A1) that man is aided by God's gratuitous will in two ways: first, inasmuch as man's soul is moved by God to know or will or do something, and in this way the gratuitous effect in man is not a quality, but a movement of the soul; for *motion is the act of the mover in the moved*. Second, man is helped by God's gratuitous will, inasmuch as a habitual gift is infused by God into the soul; and for this reason, that it is not fitting that God should provide less for those He loves, that they may acquire supernatural good, than for creatures, whom He loves that they may acquire natural good. Now He so provides for natural creatures, that not merely does He move them to their natural acts, but He bestows upon them certain forms and powers, which are the principles of acts, in order that they may of themselves be inclined to

sunt principia actuum, ut secundum seipsas inclinentur ad huiusmodi motus. Et sic motus quibus a Deo moventur, fiunt creaturis connaturales et faciles; secundum illud Sap. VIII, et disponit omnia suaviter. Multo igitur magis illis quos movet ad consequendum bonum supernaturale aeternum, infundit aliquas formas seu qualitates supernaturales, secundum quas suaviter et prompte ab ipso moveantur ad bonum aeternum consequendum. Et sic donum gratiae qualitas quaedam est.

AD PRIMUM ergo dicendum quod gratia, secundum quod est qualitas, dicitur agere in animam non per modum causae efficientis, sed per modum causae formalis, sicut albedo facit album, et iustitia iustum.

AD SECUNDUM dicendum quod omnis substantia vel est ipsa natura rei cuius est substantia, vel est pars naturae, secundum quem modum materia vel forma substantia dicitur. Et quia gratia est supra naturam humanam, non potest esse quod sit substantia aut forma substantialis, sed est forma accidentalis ipsius animae. Id enim quod substantialiter est in Deo, accidentaliter fit in anima participante divinam bonitatem, ut de scientia patet. Secundum hoc ergo, quia anima imperfecte participat divinam bonitatem, ipsa participatio divinae bonitatis quae est gratia, imperfectiori modo habet esse in anima quam anima in seipsa subsistat. Est tamen nobilior quam natura animae, inquantum est expressio vel participatio divinae bonitatis, non autem quantum ad modum essendi.

AD TERTIUM dicendum quod, sicut dicit Boetius, accidentis esse est inesse. Unde omne accidens non dicitur ens quasi ipsum esse habeat, sed quia eo aliquid est, unde et magis dicitur esse entis quam ens, ut dicitur in VII Metaphys. Et quia eius est fieri vel corrumpi cuius est esse, ideo, proprie loquendo, nullum accidens neque fit neque corrumpitur, sed dicitur fieri vel corrumpi, secundum quod subiectum incipit vel desinit esse in actu secundum illud accidens. Et secundum hoc etiam gratia dicitur creari, ex eo quod homines secundum ipsam creantur, idest in novo esse constituuntur, ex nihilo, idest non ex meritis; secundum illud ad Ephes. II, *creati in Christo Iesu in operibus bonis.*

these movements, and thus the movements whereby they are moved by God become natural and easy to creatures, according to Wis. 8:1: *she . . . ordereth all things sweetly.* Much more therefore does He infuse into such as He moves towards the acquisition of supernatural good, certain forms or supernatural qualities, whereby they may be moved by Him sweetly and promptly to acquire eternal good; and thus the gift of grace is a quality.

REPLY OBJ. 1: Grace, as a quality, is said to act upon the soul, not after the manner of an efficient cause, but after the manner of a formal cause, as whiteness makes a thing white, and justice, just.

REPLY OBJ. 2: Every substance is either the nature of the thing whereof it is the substance or is a part of the nature, even as matter and form are called substance. And because grace is above human nature, it cannot be a substance or a substantial form, but is an accidental form of the soul. Now what is substantially in God, becomes accidental in the soul participating the Divine goodness, as is clear in the case of knowledge. And thus because the soul participates in the Divine goodness imperfectly, the participation of the Divine goodness, which is grace, has its being in the soul in a less perfect way than the soul subsists in itself. Nevertheless, inasmuch as it is the expression or participation of the Divine goodness, it is nobler than the nature of the soul, though not in its mode of being.

REPLY OBJ. 3: As Boethius says, the *being of an accident is to inhere.* Hence no accident is called being as if it had being, but because by it something is; hence it is said to belong to a being rather to be a being (*Metaph.* vii, text. 2). And because to become and to be corrupted belong to what is, properly speaking, no accident comes into being or is corrupted, but is said to come into being and to be corrupted inasmuch as its subject begins or ceases to be in act with this accident. And thus grace is said to be created inasmuch as men are created with reference to it, i.e., are given a new being out of nothing, i.e., not from merits, according to Eph. 2:10, *created in Jesus Christ in good works.*

Article 3

Whether Grace Is the Same As Virtue?

AD TERTIUM SIC PROCEDITUR. Videtur quod gratia sit idem quod virtus. Dicit enim Augustinus quod *gratia operans est fides quae per dilectionem operatur*; ut habetur in libro de spiritu et littera. Sed fides quae per dilectionem operatur, est virtus. Ergo gratia est virtus.

OBJECTION 1: It would seem that grace is the same as virtue. For Augustine says (*De Spir. et Lit.* xiv) that *operating grace is faith that worketh by charity*. But faith that worketh by charity is a virtue. Therefore grace is a virtue.

PRAETEREA, cuicumque convenit definitio, et definitum. Sed definitiones de virtute datae sive a sanctis sive a philosophis, conveniunt gratiae, ipsa enim bonum facit habentem et opus eius bonum reddit; ipsa etiam est bona qualitas mentis qua recte vivitur, et cetera. Ergo gratia est virtus.

PRAETEREA, gratia est qualitas quaedam. Sed manifestum est quod non est in quarta specie qualitatis, quae est forma et circa aliquid constans figura, quia non pertinet ad corpus. Neque etiam in tertia est, quia non est passio vel passibilis qualitas, quae est in parte animae sensitiva, ut probatur in VII Physic.; ipsa autem gratia principaliter est in mente. Neque iterum est in secunda specie, quae est potentia vel impotentia naturalis, quia gratia est supra naturam; et non se habet ad bonum et malum, sicut potentia naturalis. Ergo relinquitur quod sit in prima specie, quae est habitus vel dispositio. Habitus autem mentis sunt virtutes, quia etiam ipsa scientia quodammodo est virtus, ut supra dictum est. Ergo gratia est idem quod virtus.

SED CONTRA, si gratia est virtus, maxime videtur quod sit aliqua trium theologicarum virtutum. Sed gratia non est fides vel spes, quia haec possunt esse sine gratia gratum faciente. Neque etiam caritas, quia gratia praevenit caritatem, ut Augustinus dicit, in libro de Praedest. sanctorum. Ergo gratia non est virtus.

RESPONDEO dicendum quod quidam posuerunt idem esse gratiam et virtutem secundum essentiam, sed differre solum secundum rationem, ut gratia dicatur secundum quod facit hominem Deo gratum, vel secundum quod gratis datur; virtus autem, secundum quod perficit ad bene operandum. Et hoc videtur sensisse Magister, in II Sent.

Sed si quis recte consideret rationem virtutis, hoc stare non potest. Quia ut philosophus dicit, in VII Physic., *virtus est quaedam dispositio perfecti, dico autem perfectum, quod est dispositum secundum naturam.* Ex quo patet quod virtus uniuscuiusque rei dicitur in ordine ad aliquam naturam praeexistentem, quando scilicet unumquodque sic est dispositum, secundum quod congruit suae naturae. Manifestum est autem quod virtutes acquisitae per actus humanos, de quibus supra dictum est, sunt dispositiones quibus homo convenienter disponitur in ordine ad naturam qua homo est. Virtutes autem infusae disponunt hominem altiori modo, et ad altiorem finem, unde etiam oportet quod in ordine ad aliquam altiorem naturam. Hoc autem est in ordine ad naturam divinam participatam; secundum quod dicitur II Petr. I, *maxima et pretiosa nobis promissa donavit, ut per haec efficiamini divinae consortes naturae.* Et secundum acceptionem huius naturae, dicimur regenerari in filios Dei.

OBJ. 2: Further, what fits the definition, fits the defined. But the definitions of virtue given by saints and philosophers fit grace, since *it makes its subject good, and his work good*, and *it is a good quality of the mind, whereby we live righteously*, etc. Therefore grace is virtue.

OBJ. 3: Further, grace is a quality. Now it is clearly not in the *fourth* species of quality; viz., *form* which is the *abiding figure of things*, since it does not belong to bodies. Nor is it in the *third*, since it is not a *passion nor a passion-like quality*, which is in the sensitive part of the soul, as is proved in Physic. viii; and grace is principally in the mind. Nor is it in the *second* species, which is *natural power* or *impotence*; since grace is above nature and does not regard good and evil, as does natural power. Therefore it must be in the *first* species which is *habit* or *disposition*. Now habits of the mind are virtues; since even knowledge itself is a virtue after a manner, as stated above (Q57, AA1,2). Therefore grace is the same as virtue.

ON THE CONTRARY, If grace is a virtue, it would seem before all to be one of the three theological virtues. But grace is neither faith nor hope, for these can be without sanctifying grace. Nor is it charity, since *grace foreruns charity*, as Augustine says in his book on the Predestination of the Saints (*De Dono Persev.* xvi). Therefore grace is not virtue.

I ANSWER THAT, Some held that grace and virtue were identical in essence, and differed only logically—in the sense that we speak of grace inasmuch as it makes man pleasing to God, or is given gratuitously—and of virtue inasmuch as it empowers us to act rightly. And the Master seems to have thought this (*Sent.* ii, D 27).

But if anyone rightly considers the nature of virtue, this cannot hold, since, as the Philosopher says (*Physic.* vii, text. 17), *virtue is disposition of what is perfect—and I call perfect what is disposed according to its nature.* Now from this it is clear that the virtue of a thing has reference to some pre-existing nature, from the fact that everything is disposed with reference to what befits its nature. But it is manifest that the virtues acquired by human acts of which we spoke above (Q55, seqq.) are dispositions, whereby a man is fittingly disposed with reference to the nature whereby he is a man; whereas infused virtues dispose man in a higher manner and towards a higher end, and consequently in relation to some higher nature, i.e., in relation to a participation of the Divine Nature, according to 2 Pt. 1:4: *He hath given us most great and most precious promises; that by these you may be made partakers of the Divine Nature.* And it is in respect of receiving this nature that we are said to be born again sons of God.

Sicut igitur lumen naturale rationis est aliquid praeter virtutes acquisitas, quae dicuntur in ordine ad ipsum lumen naturale; ita etiam ipsum lumen gratiae, quod est participatio divinae naturae, est aliquid praeter virtutes infusas, quae a lumine illo derivantur, et ad illud lumen ordinantur. Unde et apostolus dicit, ad Ephes. V, *eratis aliquando tenebrae, nunc autem lux in domino, ut filii lucis ambulate.* Sicut enim virtutes acquisitae perficiunt hominem ad ambulandum congruenter lumini naturali rationis; ita virtutes infusae perficiunt hominem ad ambulandum congruenter lumini gratiae.

AD PRIMUM ergo dicendum quod Augustinus nominat fidem per dilectionem operantem gratiam, quia actus fidei per dilectionem operantis est primus actus in quo gratia gratum faciens manifestatur.

AD SECUNDUM dicendum quod bonum positum in definitione virtutis, dicitur secundum convenientiam ad aliquam naturam praeexistentem, vel essentialem vel participatam. Sic autem bonum non attribuitur gratiae, sed sicut radici bonitatis in homine, ut dictum est.

AD TERTIUM dicendum quod gratia reducitur ad primam speciem qualitatis. Nec tamen est idem quod virtus, sed habitudo quaedam quae praesupponitur virtutibus infusis, sicut earum principium et radix.

And thus, even as the natural light of reason is something besides the acquired virtues, which are ordained to this natural light, so also the light of grace which is a participation of the Divine Nature is something besides the infused virtues which are derived from and are ordained to this light, hence the Apostle says (Eph 5:8): *For you were heretofore darkness, but now light in the Lord. Walk then as children of the light.* For as the acquired virtues enable a man to walk, in accordance with the natural light of reason, so do the infused virtues enable a man to walk as befits the light of grace.

REPLY OBJ. 1: Augustine calls *faith that worketh by charity* grace, since the act of faith of him that worketh by charity is the first act by which sanctifying grace is manifested.

REPLY OBJ. 2: Good is placed in the definition of virtue with reference to its fitness with some pre-existing nature essential or participated. Now good is not attributed to grace in this manner, but as to the root of goodness in man, as stated above.

REPLY OBJ. 3: Grace is reduced to the first species of quality; and yet it is not the same as virtue, but is a certain disposition which is presupposed to the infused virtues, as their principle and root.

Article 4

Whether Grace Is in the Essence of the Soul As in a Subject, or in One of the Powers?

AD QUARTUM SIC PROCEDITUR. Videtur quod gratia non sit in essentia animae sicut in subiecto, sed in aliqua potentiarum. Dicit enim Augustinus, in Hypognost., quod gratia comparatur ad voluntatem, sive ad liberum arbitrium, sicut sessor ad equum. Sed voluntas, sive liberum arbitrium, est potentia quaedam, ut in primo dictum est. Ergo gratia est in potentia animae sicut in subiecto.

PRAETEREA, ex gratia incipiunt merita hominis, ut Augustinus dicit. Sed meritum consistit in actu, qui ex aliqua potentia procedit. Ergo videtur quod gratia sit perfectio alicuius potentiae animae.

PRAETEREA, si essentia animae sit proprium subiectum gratiae, oportet quod anima inquantum habet essentiam, sit capax gratiae. Sed hoc est falsum, quia sic sequeretur quod omnis anima esset gratiae capax. Non ergo essentia animae est proprium subiectum gratiae.

PRAETEREA, essentia animae est prior potentiis eius. Prius autem potest intelligi sine posteriori. Ergo sequetur quod gratia possit intelligi in anima, nulla parte vel potentia animae intellecta, scilicet neque voluntate neque intellectu neque aliquo huiusmodi. Quod est inconveniens.

OBJECTION 1: It would seem that grace is not in the essence of the soul, as in a subject, but in one of the powers. For Augustine says (*Hypognosticon* iii) that grace is related to the will or to the free will *as a rider to his horse.* Now the will or the free will is a power, as stated above (FP, Q83, A2). Hence grace is in a power of the soul, as in a subject.

OBJ. 2: Further, *Man's merit springs from grace* as Augustine says (*De Gratia et Lib. Arbit.* vi). Now merit consists in acts, which proceed from a power. Hence it seems that grace is a perfection of a power of the soul.

OBJ. 3: Further, if the essence of the soul is the proper subject of grace, the soul, inasmuch as it has an essence, must be capable of grace. But this is false; since it would follow that every soul would be capable of grace. Therefore the essence of the soul is not the proper subject of grace.

OBJ. 4: Further, the essence of the soul is prior to its powers. Now what is prior may be understood without what is posterior. Hence it follows that grace may be taken to be in the soul, although we suppose no part or power of the soul—viz., neither the will, nor the intellect, nor anything else; which is impossible.

SED CONTRA est quod per gratiam regeneramur in filios Dei. Sed generatio per prius terminatur ad essentiam quam ad potentias. Ergo gratia per prius est in essentia animae quam in potentiis.

RESPONDEO dicendum quod ista quaestio ex praecedenti dependet. Si enim gratia sit idem quod virtus, necesse est quod sit in potentia animae sicut in subiecto, nam potentia animae est proprium subiectum virtutis, ut supra dictum est. Si autem gratia differt a virtute, non potest dici quod potentia animae sit gratiae subiectum, quia omnis perfectio potentiae animae habet rationem virtutis, ut supra dictum est. Unde relinquitur quod gratia, sicut est prius virtute, ita habeat subiectum prius potentiis animae, ita scilicet quod sit in essentia animae. Sicut enim per potentiam intellectivam homo participat cognitionem divinam per virtutem fidei; et secundum potentiam voluntatis amorem divinum, per virtutem caritatis; ita etiam per naturam animae participat, secundum quandam similitudinem, naturam divinam, per quandam regenerationem sive recreationem.

AD PRIMUM ergo dicendum quod, sicut ab essentia animae effluunt eius potentiae, quae sunt operum principia; ita etiam ab ipsa gratia effluunt virtutes in potentias animae, per quas potentiae moventur ad actus. Et secundum hoc gratia comparatur ad voluntatem ut movens ad motum, quae est comparatio sessoris ad equum, non autem sicut accidens ad subiectum.

ET PER HOC etiam patet solutio ad secundum. Est enim gratia principium meritorii operis mediantibus virtutibus, sicut essentia animae est principium operum vitae mediantibus potentiis.

AD TERTIUM dicendum quod anima est subiectum gratiae secundum quod est in specie intellectualis vel rationalis naturae. Non autem constituitur anima in specie per aliquam potentiam, cum potentiae sint proprietates naturales animae speciem consequentes. Et ideo anima secundum suam essentiam differt specie ab aliis animabus, scilicet brutorum animalium et plantarum. Et propter hoc, non sequitur, si essentia animae humanae sit subiectum gratiae, quod quaelibet anima possit esse gratiae subiectum, hoc enim convenit essentiae animae inquantum est talis speciei.

AD QUARTUM dicendum quod, cum potentiae animae sint naturales proprietates speciem consequentes, anima non potest sine his esse. Dato autem quod sine his esset, adhuc tamen anima diceretur secundum speciem suam intellectualis vel rationalis, non quia actu haberet has potentias; sed propter speciem talis essentiae ex qua natae sunt huiusmodi potentiae effluere.

ON THE CONTRARY, By grace we are born again sons of God. But generation terminates at the essence prior to the powers. Therefore grace is in the soul's essence prior to being in the powers.

I ANSWER THAT, This question depends on the preceding. For if grace is the same as virtue, it must necessarily be in the powers of the soul as in a subject; since the soul's powers are the proper subject of virtue, as stated above (Q56, A1). But if grace differs from virtue, it cannot be said that a power of the soul is the subject of grace, since every perfection of the soul's powers has the nature of virtue, as stated above (Q55, A1; Q56, A1). Hence it remains that grace, as it is prior to virtue, has a subject prior to the powers of the soul, so that it is in the essence of the soul. For as man in his intellective powers participates in the Divine knowledge through the virtue of faith, and in his power of will participates in the Divine love through the virtue of charity, so also in the nature of the soul does he participate in the Divine Nature, after the manner of a likeness, through a certain regeneration or re-creation.

REPLY OBJ. 1: As from the essence of the soul flows its powers, which are the principles of deeds, so likewise the virtues, whereby the powers are moved to act, flow into the powers of the soul from grace. And thus grace is compared to the will as the mover to the moved, which is the same comparison as that of a horseman to the horse—but not as an accident to a subject.

AND THEREBY is made clear the Reply to the Second Objection. For grace is the principle of meritorious works through the medium of virtues, as the essence of the soul is the principal of vital deeds through the medium of the powers.

REPLY OBJ. 3: The soul is the subject of grace, as being in the species of intellectual or rational nature. But the soul is not classed in a species by any of its powers, since the powers are natural properties of the soul following upon the species. Hence the soul differs specifically in its essence from other souls, viz., of dumb animals, and of plants. Consequently it does not follow that, if the essence of the human soul is the subject of grace, every soul may be the subject of grace; since it belongs to the essence of the soul, inasmuch as it is of such a species.

REPLY OBJ. 4: Since the powers of the soul are natural properties following upon the species, the soul cannot be without them. Yet, granted that it was without them, the soul would still be called intellectual or rational in its species, not that it would actually have these powers, but on account of the essence of such a species, from which these powers naturally flow.

QUESTION 111

OF THE DIVISION OF GRACE

Deinde considerandum est de divisione gratiae. Et circa hoc quaeruntur quinque.

Primo, utrum convenienter dividatur gratia per gratiam gratis datam et gratiam gratum facientem.

Secundo, de divisione gratiae gratum facientis per operantem et cooperantem.

Tertio, de divisione eiusdem per gratiam praevenientem et subsequentem.

Quarto, de divisione gratiae gratis datae.

Quinto, de comparatione gratiae gratum facientis et gratis datae.

We must now consider the division of grace; under which head there are five points of inquiry:

(1) Whether grace is fittingly divided into gratuitous grace and sanctifying grace?

(2) Of the division into operating and cooperating grace;

(3) Of the division of it into prevenient and subsequent grace;

(4) Of the division of gratuitous grace;

(5) Of the comparison between sanctifying and gratuitous grace.

Article 1

Whether Grace Is Fittingly Divided into Sanctifying Grace and Gratuitous Grace?

AD PRIMUM SIC PROCEDITUR. Videtur quod gratia non convenienter dividatur per gratiam gratum facientem et gratiam gratis datam. Gratia enim est quoddam Dei donum, ut ex supradictis patet. Homo autem ideo non est Deo gratus quia aliquid est ei datum a Deo, sed potius e converso, ideo enim aliquid datur alicui gratis a Deo, quia est homo gratus ei. Ergo nulla est gratia gratum faciens.

PRAETEREA, quaecumque non dantur ex meritis praecedentibus, dantur gratis. Sed etiam ipsum bonum naturae datur homini absque merito praecedenti, quia natura praesupponitur ad meritum. Ergo ipsa natura est etiam gratis data a Deo. Natura autem dividitur contra gratiam. Inconvenienter igitur hoc quod est gratis datum, ponitur ut gratiae differentia, quia invenitur etiam extra gratiae genus.

PRAETEREA, omnis divisio debet esse per opposita. Sed etiam ipsa gratia gratum faciens, per quam iustificamur, gratis nobis a Deo conceditur; secundum illud Rom. III, *iustificati gratis per gratiam ipsius.* Ergo gratia gratum faciens non debet dividi contra gratiam gratis datam.

SED CONTRA est quod apostolus utrumque attribuit gratiae, scilicet et gratum facere, et esse gratis datum. Dicit enim quantum ad primum, ad Ephes. I, *gratificavit nos in dilecto filio suo.* Quantum vero ad secundum, dicitur ad Rom. XI, *si autem gratia, iam non ex operibus, alioquin gratia iam non est gratia.* Potest ergo distingui gratia quae vel habet unum tantum, vel utrumque.

OBJECTION 1: It would seem that grace is not fittingly divided into sanctifying grace and gratuitous grace. For grace is a gift of God, as is clear from what has been already stated (Q110, A1). But man is not therefore pleasing to God because something is given him by God, but rather on the contrary; since something is freely given by God, because man is pleasing to Him. Hence there is no sanctifying grace.

OBJ. 2: Further, whatever is not given on account of preceding merits is given gratis. Now even natural good is given to man without preceding merit, since nature is presupposed to merit. Therefore nature itself is given gratuitously by God. But nature is condivided with grace. Therefore to be gratuitously given is not fittingly set down as a difference of grace, since it is found outside the genus of grace.

OBJ. 3: Further, members of a division are mutually opposed. But even sanctifying grace, whereby we are justified, is given to us gratuitously, according to Rm. 3:24: *Being justified freely by His grace.* Hence sanctifying grace ought not to be divided against gratuitous grace.

ON THE CONTRARY, The Apostle attributes both to grace, viz., to sanctify and to be gratuitously given. For with regard to the first he says (Eph 1:6): *He hath graced us in His beloved son.* And with regard to the second (Rom 2:6): *And if by grace, it is not now by works, otherwise grace is no more grace.* Therefore grace can be distinguished by its having one only or both.

RESPONDEO dicendum quod, sicut apostolus dicit, ad Rom. XIII, *quae a Deo sunt, ordinata sunt.* In hoc autem ordo rerum consistit, quod quaedam per alia in Deum reducuntur; ut Dionysius dicit, in Cael. Hier. Cum igitur gratia ad hoc ordinetur ut homo reducatur in Deum, ordine quodam hoc agitur, ut scilicet quidam per alios in Deum reducantur.

Secundum hoc igitur duplex est gratia. Una quidem per quam ipse homo Deo coniungitur, quae vocatur gratia gratum faciens. Alia vero per quam unus homo cooperatur alteri ad hoc quod ad Deum reducatur. Huiusmodi autem donum vocatur gratia gratis data, quia supra facultatem naturae, et supra meritum personae, homini conceditur, sed quia non datur ad hoc ut homo ipse per eam iustificetur, sed potius ut ad iustificationem alterius cooperetur, ideo non vocatur gratum faciens. Et de hac dicit apostolus, I ad Cor. XII, *unicuique datur manifestatio spiritus ad utilitatem,* scilicet aliorum.

AD PRIMUM ergo dicendum quod gratia non dicitur facere gratum effective, sed formaliter, scilicet quia per hanc homo iustificatur, et dignus efficitur vocari Deo gratus; secundum quod dicitur ad Coloss. I, *dignos nos fecit in partem sortis sanctorum in lumine.*

AD SECUNDUM dicendum quod gratia, secundum quod gratis datur, excludit rationem debiti. Potest autem intelligi duplex debitum. Unum quidem ex merito proveniens, quod refertur ad personam, cuius est agere meritoria opera; secundum illud ad Rom. IV, *ei qui operatur, merces imputatur secundum debitum, non secundum gratiam.* Aliud est debitum ex conditione naturae, puta si dicamus debitum esse homini quod habeat rationem et alia quae ad humanam pertinent naturam. Neutro autem modo dicitur debitum propter hoc quod Deus creaturae obligatur, sed potius inquantum creatura debet subiici Deo ut in ea divina ordinatio impleatur, quae quidem est ut talis natura tales conditiones vel proprietates habeat, et quod talia operans talia consequatur. Dona igitur naturalia carent primo debito, non autem carent secundo debito. Sed dona supernaturalia utroque debito carent, et ideo specialius sibi nomen gratiae vindicant.

AD TERTIUM dicendum quod gratia gratum faciens addit aliquid supra rationem gratiae gratis datae quod etiam ad rationem gratiae pertinet, quia scilicet hominem gratum facit Deo. Et ideo gratia gratis data, quae hoc non facit, retinet sibi nomen commune, sicut in pluribus aliis contingit. Et sic opponuntur duae partes divisionis sicut gratum faciens et non faciens gratum.

I ANSWER THAT, As the Apostle says (Rom 13:1), *those things that are of God are well ordered.* Now the order of things consists in this, that things are led to God by other things, as Dionysius says (*Coel. Hier.* iv). And hence since grace is ordained to lead men to God, this takes place in a certain order, so that some are led to God by others.

And thus there is a twofold grace: one whereby man himself is united to God, and this is called *sanctifying grace*; the other is that whereby one man cooperates with another in leading him to God, and this gift is called *gratuitous grace*, since it is bestowed on a man beyond the capability of nature, and beyond the merit of the person. But whereas it is bestowed on a man, not to justify him, but rather that he may cooperate in the justification of another, it is not called sanctifying grace. And it is of this that the Apostle says (1 Cor 12:7): *And the manifestation of the Spirit is given to every man unto utility,* i.e., of others.

REPLY OBJ. 1: Grace is said to make pleasing, not efficiently but formally, i.e., because thereby a man is justified, and is made worthy to be called pleasing to God, according to Col. 1:21: *He hath made us worthy to be made partakers of the lot of the saints in light.*

REPLY OBJ. 2: Grace, inasmuch as it is gratuitously given, excludes the notion of debt. Now debt may be taken in two ways: first, as arising from merit; and this regards the person whose it is to do meritorious works, according to Rm. 4:4: *Now to him that worketh, the reward is not reckoned according to grace, but according to debt.* The second debt regards the condition of nature. Thus we say it is due to a man to have reason, and whatever else belongs to human nature. Yet in neither way is debt taken to mean that God is under an obligation to His creature, but rather that the creature ought to be subject to God, that the Divine ordination may be fulfilled in it, which is that a certain nature should have certain conditions or properties, and that by doing certain works it should attain to something further. And hence natural endowments are not a debt in the first sense but in the second. Hence they especially merit the name of grace.

REPLY OBJ. 3: Sanctifying grace adds to the notion of gratuitous grace something pertaining to the nature of grace, since it makes man pleasing to God. And hence gratuitous grace which does not do this keeps the common name, as happens in many other cases; and thus the two parts of the division are opposed as sanctifying and nonsanctifying grace.

Article 2

Whether Grace Is Fittingly Divided into Operating and Cooperating Grace?

Ad secundum sic proceditur. Videtur quod gratia inconvenienter dividatur per operantem et cooperantem. Gratia enim accidens quoddam est, ut supra dictum est. Sed accidens non potest agere in subiectum. Ergo nulla gratia debet dici operans.

Praeterea, si gratia aliquid operetur in nobis, maxime operatur iustificationem. Sed hoc non sola gratia operatur in nobis, dicit enim Augustinus, super illud Ioan. XIV, *opera quae ego facio, et ipse faciet, qui creavit te sine te, non iustificabit te sine te.* Ergo nulla gratia debet dici simpliciter operans.

Praeterea, cooperari alicui videtur pertinere ad inferius agens, non autem ad principalius. Sed gratia principalius operatur in nobis quam liberum arbitrium; secundum illud Rom. IX, *non est volentis neque currentis, sed miserentis Dei.* Ergo gratia non debet dici cooperans.

Praeterea, divisio debet dari per opposita. Sed operari et cooperari non sunt opposita, idem enim potest operari et cooperari. Ergo inconvenienter dividitur gratia per operantem et cooperantem.

Sed contra est quod Augustinus dicit, in libro de Grat. et Lib. Arb., *cooperando Deus in nobis perficit quod operando incipit, quia ipse ut velimus operatur incipiens, qui volentibus cooperatur perficiens.* Sed operationes Dei quibus movet nos ad bonum, ad gratiam pertinent. Ergo convenienter gratia dividitur per operantem et cooperantem.

Respondeo dicendum quod, sicut supra dictum est, gratia dupliciter potest intelligi, uno modo, divinum auxilium quo nos movet ad bene volendum et agendum; alio modo, habituale donum nobis divinitus inditum.

Utroque autem modo gratia dicta convenienter dividitur per operantem et cooperantem. Operatio enim alicuius effectus non attribuitur mobili, sed moventi. In illo ergo effectu in quo mens nostra est mota et non movens, solus autem Deus movens, operatio Deo attribuitur, et secundum hoc dicitur gratia operans. In illo autem effectu in quo mens nostra et movet et movetur, operatio non solum attribuitur Deo, sed etiam animae, et secundum hoc dicitur gratia cooperans. Est autem in nobis duplex actus. Primus quidem, interior voluntatis. Et quantum ad istum actum, voluntas se habet ut mota, Deus autem ut movens, et praesertim cum voluntas incipit bonum velle quae prius malum volebat. Et ideo secundum quod Deus movet humanam mentem ad hunc actum, dicitur gratia operans. Alius autem actus est exterior; qui cum a voluntate imperetur, ut supra habitum est, consequens est ut ad hunc actum operatio attribuatur voluntati. Et

Objection 1: It would seem that grace is not fittingly divided into operating and cooperating grace. For grace is an accident, as stated above (Q110, A2). Now no accident can act upon its subject. Therefore no grace can be called operating.

Obj. 2: Further, if grace operates anything in us it assuredly brings about justification. But not only grace works this. For Augustine says, on Jn. 14:12, *the works that I do he also shall do,* says (*Serm. clxix*): *He Who created thee without thyself, will not justify thee without thyself.* Therefore no grace ought to be called simply operating.

Obj. 3: Further, to cooperate seems to pertain to the inferior agent, and not to the principal agent. But grace works in us more than free-will, according to Rm. 9:16: *It is not of him that willeth, nor of him that runneth, but of God that showeth mercy.* Therefore no grace ought to be called cooperating.

Obj. 4: Further, division ought to rest on opposition. But to operate and to cooperate are not opposed; for one and the same thing can both operate and cooperate. Therefore grace is not fittingly divided into operating and cooperating.

On the contrary, Augustine says (*De Gratia et Lib. Arbit.* xvii): *God by cooperating with us, perfects what He began by operating in us, since He who perfects by cooperation with such as are willing, beings by operating that they may will.* But the operations of God whereby He moves us to good pertain to grace. Therefore grace is fittingly divided into operating and cooperating.

I answer that, As stated above (Q110, A2) grace may be taken in two ways; first, as a Divine help, whereby God moves us to will and to act; second, as a habitual gift divinely bestowed on us.

Now in both these ways grace is fittingly divided into operating and cooperating. For the operation of an effect is not attributed to the thing moved but to the mover. Hence in that effect in which our mind is moved and does not move, but in which God is the sole mover, the operation is attributed to God, and it is with reference to this that we speak of *operating grace.* But in that effect in which our mind both moves and is moved, the operation is not only attributed to God, but also to the soul; and it is with reference to this that we speak of *cooperating grace.* Now there is a double act in us. First, there is the interior act of the will, and with regard to this act the will is a thing moved, and God is the mover; and especially when the will, which hitherto willed evil, begins to will good. And hence, inasmuch as God moves the human mind to this act, we speak of operating grace. But there is another, exterior act; and since it is commanded by the will, as was shown above (Q17, A9) the operation of

quia etiam ad hunc actum Deus nos adiuvat, et interius confirmando voluntatem ut ad actum perveniat, et exterius facultatem operandi praebendo; respectu huius actus dicitur gratia cooperans. Unde post praemissa verba subdit Augustinus, *ut autem velimus operatur, cum autem volumus, ut perficiamus nobis cooperatur.* Sic igitur si gratia accipiatur pro gratuita Dei motione qua movet nos ad bonum meritorium, convenienter dividitur gratia per operantem et cooperantem.

Si vero accipiatur gratia pro habituali dono, sic etiam duplex est gratiae effectus, sicut et cuiuslibet alterius formae, quorum primus est esse, secundus est operatio; sicut caloris operatio est facere calidum, et exterior calefactio. Sic igitur habitualis gratia, inquantum animam sanat vel iustificat, sive gratam Deo facit, dicitur gratia operans, inquantum vero est principium operis meritorii, quod etiam ex libero arbitrio procedit, dicitur cooperans.

AD PRIMUM ergo dicendum quod, secundum quod gratia est quaedam qualitas accidentalis, non agit in animam effective; sed formaliter, sicut albedo dicitur facere albam superficiem.

AD SECUNDUM dicendum quod Deus non sine nobis nos iustificat, quia per motum liberi arbitrii, dum iustificamur, Dei iustitiae consentimus. Ille tamen motus non est causa gratiae, sed effectus. Unde tota operatio pertinet ad gratiam.

AD TERTIUM dicendum quod cooperari dicitur aliquis alicui non solum sicut secundarium agens principali agenti, sed sicut adiuvans ad praesuppositum finem. Homo autem per gratiam operantem adiuvatur a Deo ut bonum velit. Et ideo, praesupposito iam fine, consequens est ut gratia nobis cooperetur.

AD QUARTUM dicendum quod gratia operans et cooperans est eadem gratia, sed distinguitur secundum diversos effectus, ut ex dictis patet.

this act is attributed to the will. And because God assists us in this act, both by strengthening our will interiorly so as to attain to the act, and by granting outwardly the capability of operating, it is with respect to this that we speak of cooperating grace. Hence after the aforesaid words Augustine subjoins: *He operates that we may will; and when we will, He cooperates that we may perfect.* And thus if grace is taken for God's gratuitous motion whereby He moves us to meritorious good, it is fittingly divided into operating and cooperating grace.

But if grace is taken for the habitual gift, then again there is a double effect of grace, even as of every other form; the first of which is *being*, and the second, *operation*; thus the work of heat is to make its subject hot, and to give heat outwardly. And thus habitual grace, inasmuch as it heals and justifies the soul, or makes it pleasing to God, is called operating grace; but inasmuch as it is the principle of meritorious works, which spring from the free-will, it is called cooperating grace.

REPLY OBJ. 1: Inasmuch as grace is a certain accidental quality, it does not act upon the soul efficiently, but formally, as whiteness makes a surface white.

REPLY OBJ. 2: God does not justify us without ourselves, because whilst we are being justified we consent to God's justification by a movement of our free-will. Nevertheless this movement is not the cause of grace, but the effect; hence the whole operation pertains to grace.

REPLY OBJ. 3: One thing is said to cooperate with another not merely when it is a secondary agent under a principal agent, but when it helps to the end intended. Now man is helped by God to will the good, through the means of operating grace. And hence, the end being already intended, grace cooperates with us.

REPLY OBJ. 4: Operating and cooperating grace are the same grace; but are distinguished by their different effects, as is plain from what has been said.

Article 3

Whether Grace Is Fittingly Divided into Prevenient and Subsequent Grace?

AD TERTIUM SIC PROCEDITUR. Videtur quod gratia inconvenienter dividatur in praevenientem et subsequentem. Gratia enim est divinae dilectionis effectus. Sed Dei dilectio nunquam est subsequens, sed semper praeveniens; secundum illud I Ioan. IV, *non quasi nos dilexerimus Deum, sed quia ipse prior dilexit nos.* Ergo gratia non debet poni praeveniens et subsequens.

PRAETEREA, gratia gratum faciens est una tantum in homine, cum sit sufficiens, secundum illud II ad Cor. XII, *sufficit tibi gratia mea.* Sed idem non potest esse

OBJECTION 1: It would seem that grace is not fittingly divided into prevenient and subsequent. For grace is an effect of the Divine love. But God's love is never subsequent, but always prevenient, according to 1 Jn. 4:10: *Not as though we had loved God, but because He hath first loved us.* Therefore grace ought not to be divided into prevenient and subsequent.

OBJ. 2: Further, there is but one sanctifying grace in man, since it is sufficient, according to 2 Cor. 12:9: *My grace is sufficient for thee.* But the same thing cannot be before

prius et posterius. Ergo gratia inconvenienter dividitur in praevenientem et subsequentem.

PRAETEREA, gratia cognoscitur per effectus. Sed infiniti sunt effectus gratiae, quorum unus praecedit alium. Ergo si penes hoc gratia deberet dividi in praevenientem et subsequentem, videtur quod infinitae essent species gratiae. Infinita autem relinquuntur a qualibet arte. Non ergo gratia convenienter dividitur in praevenientem et subsequentem.

SED CONTRA est quod gratia Dei ex eius misericordia provenit. Sed utrumque in Psalmo legitur, *misericordia eius praeveniet me*; et iterum, *misericordia eius subsequetur me*. Ergo gratia convenienter dividitur in praevenientem et subsequentem.

RESPONDEO dicendum quod, sicut gratia dividitur in operantem et cooperantem secundum diversos effectus, ita etiam in praevenientem et subsequentem, qualitercumque gratia accipiatur. Sunt autem quinque effectus gratiae in nobis, quorum primus est ut anima sanetur; secundus est ut bonum velit; tertius est ut bonum quod vult, efficaciter operetur; quartus est ut in bono perseveret; quintus est ut ad gloriam perveniat. Et ideo gratia secundum quod causat in nobis primum effectum, vocatur praeveniens respectu secundi effectus; et prout causat in nobis secundum, vocatur subsequens respectu primi effectus. Et sicut unus effectus est posterior uno effectu et prior alio, ita gratia potest dici et praeveniens et subsequens secundum eundem effectum, respectu diversorum. Et hoc est quod Augustinus dicit, in libro de Nat. et Grat., *praevenit ut sanemur, subsequitur ut sanati vegetemur, praevenit ut vocemur, subsequitur ut glorificemur.*

AD PRIMUM ergo dicendum quod dilectio Dei nominat aliquid aeternum, et ideo nunquam potest dici nisi praeveniens. Sed gratia significat effectum temporalem, qui potest praecedere aliquid et ad aliquid subsequi. Et ideo gratia potest dici praeveniens et subsequens.

AD SECUNDUM dicendum quod gratia non diversificatur per hoc quod est praeveniens et subsequens, secundum essentiam, sed solum secundum effectum, sicut et de operante et cooperante dictum est. Quia etiam secundum quod gratia subsequens ad gloriam pertinet, non est alia numero a gratia praeveniente per quam nunc iustificamur. Sicut enim caritas viae non evacuatur, sed perficitur in patria, ita etiam et de lumine gratiae est dicendum, quia neutrum in sui ratione imperfectionem importat.

AD TERTIUM dicendum quod, quamvis effectus gratiae possint esse infiniti numero, sicut sunt infiniti actus humani; tamen omnes reducuntur ad aliqua determinata in specie. Et praeterea omnes conveniunt in hoc quod unus alium praecedit.

and after. Therefore grace is not fittingly divided into prevenient and subsequent.

OBJ. 3: Further, grace is known by its effects. Now there are an infinite number of effects—one preceding another. Hence it with regard to these, grace must be divided into prevenient and subsequent, it would seem that there are infinite species of grace. Now no art takes note of the infinite in number. Hence grace is not fittingly divided into prevenient and subsequent.

ON THE CONTRARY, God's grace is the outcome of His mercy. Now both are said in Ps. 58:11: *His mercy shall prevent me*, and again, Ps. 22:6: *Thy mercy will follow me.* Therefore grace is fittingly divided into prevenient and subsequent.

I ANSWER THAT, As grace is divided into operating and cooperating, with regard to its diverse effects, so also is it divided into prevenient and subsequent, howsoever we consider grace. Now there are five effects of grace in us: of these, the first is, to heal the soul; the second, to desire good; the third, to carry into effect the good proposed; the fourth, to persevere in good; the fifth, to reach glory. And hence grace, inasmuch as it causes the first effect in us, is called prevenient with respect to the second, and inasmuch as it causes the second, it is called subsequent with respect to the first effect. And as one effect is posterior to this effect, and prior to that, so may grace be called prevenient and subsequent on account of the same effect viewed relatively to diverse others. And this is what Augustine says (*De Natura et Gratia* xxxi): *It is prevenient, inasmuch as it heals, and subsequent, inasmuch as, being healed, we are strengthened; it is prevenient, inasmuch as we are called, and subsequent, inasmuch as we are glorified.*

REPLY OBJ. 1: God's love signifies something eternal; and hence can never be called anything but prevenient. But grace signifies a temporal effect, which can precede and follow another; and thus grace may be both prevenient and subsequent.

REPLY OBJ. 2: The division into prevenient and subsequent grace does not divide grace in its essence, but only in its effects, as was already said of operating and cooperating grace. For subsequent grace, inasmuch as it pertains to glory, is not numerically distinct from prevenient grace whereby we are at present justified. For even as the charity of the earth is not voided in heaven, so must the same be said of the light of grace, since the notion of neither implies imperfection.

REPLY OBJ. 3: Although the effects of grace may be infinite in number, even as human acts are infinite, nevertheless all reduced to some of a determinate species, and moreover all coincide in this—that one precedes another.

Article 4

Whether Gratuitous Grace Is Rightly Divided by the Apostle?

AD QUARTUM SIC PROCEDITUR. Videtur quod gratia gratis data inconvenienter ab apostolo distinguatur. Omne enim donum quod nobis a Deo gratis datur, potest dici gratia gratis data. Sed infinita sunt dona quae nobis gratis a Deo conceduntur, tam in bonis animae quam in bonis corporis, quae tamen nos Deo gratos non faciunt. Ergo gratiae gratis datae non possunt comprehendi sub aliqua certa divisione.

PRAETEREA, gratia gratis data distinguitur contra gratiam gratum facientem. Sed fides pertinet ad gratiam gratum facientem, quia per ipsam iustificamur, secundum illud Rom. V, *iustificati ergo ex fide*, et cetera. Ergo inconvenienter fides ponitur inter gratias gratis datas, praesertim cum aliae virtutes ibi non ponantur, ut spes et caritas.

PRAETEREA, operatio sanitatum, et loqui diversa genera linguarum, miracula quaedam sunt. Interpretatio etiam sermonum ad sapientiam vel scientiam pertinet; secundum illud Dan. I, *pueris his dedit Deus scientiam et disciplinam in omni libro et sapientia*. Ergo inconvenienter dividitur gratia sanitatum, et genera linguarum, contra operationem virtutum; et interpretatio sermonum contra sermonem sapientiae et scientiae.

PRAETEREA, sicut sapientia et scientia sunt quaedam dona spiritus sancti, ita etiam intellectus et consilium, pietas, fortitudo et timor, ut supra dictum est. Ergo haec etiam deberent poni inter gratias gratis datas.

SED CONTRA est quod apostolus dicit, I ad Cor. XII, *alii per spiritum datur sermo sapientiae, alii autem sermo scientiae secundum eundem spiritum, alteri fides in eodem spiritu, alii gratia sanitatum, alii operatio virtutum, alii prophetia, alii discretio spirituum, alii genera linguarum, alii interpretatio sermonum*.

RESPONDEO dicendum quod, sicut supra dictum est, gratia gratis data ordinatur ad hoc quod homo alteri cooperetur ut reducatur ad Deum. Homo autem ad hoc operari non potest interius movendo, hoc enim solius Dei est; sed solum exterius docendo vel persuadendo. Et ideo gratia gratis data illa sub se continet quibus homo indiget ad hoc quod alterum instruat in rebus divinis, quae sunt supra rationem. Ad hoc autem tria requiruntur. Primo quidem, quod homo sit sortitus plenitudinem cognitionis divinorum, ut ex hoc possit alios instruere. Secundo, ut possit confirmare vel probare ea quae dicit, alias non esset efficax eius doctrina. Tertio, ut ea quae concipit, possit convenienter auditoribus proferre.

Quantum igitur ad primum, tria sunt necessaria, sicut etiam apparet in magisterio humano. Oportet enim quod ille qui debet alium instruere in aliqua scientia,

OBJECTION 1: It would seem that gratuitous grace is not rightly divided by the Apostle. For every gift vouchsafed to us by God, may be called a gratuitous grace. Now there are an infinite number of gifts freely bestowed on us by God as regards both the good of the soul and the good of the body—and yet they do not make us pleasing to God. Hence gratuitous graces cannot be contained under any certain division.

OBJ. 2: Further, gratuitous grace is distinguished from sanctifying grace. But faith pertains to sanctifying grace, since we are justified by it, according to Rm. 5:1: *Being justified therefore by faith*. Hence it is not right to place faith amongst the gratuitous graces, especially since the other virtues are not so placed, as hope and charity.

OBJ. 3: Further, the operation of healing, and speaking diverse tongues are miracles. Again, the interpretation of speeches pertains either to wisdom or to knowledge, according to Dan. 1:17: *And to these children God gave knowledge and understanding in every book and wisdom*. Hence it is not correct to divide the grace of healing and kinds of tongues against the working of miracles; and the interpretation of speeches against the word of wisdom and knowledge.

OBJ. 4: Further, as wisdom and knowledge are gifts of the Holy Spirit, so also are understanding, counsel, piety, fortitude, and fear, as stated above (Q68, A4). Therefore these also ought to be placed amongst the gratuitous gifts.

ON THE CONTRARY, The Apostle says (1 Cor 12:8,9,10): *To one indeed by the Spirit is given the word of wisdom; and to another the word of knowledge, according to the same Spirit; to another, the working of miracles; to another, prophecy; to another, the discerning of spirits; to another diverse kinds of tongues; to another interpretation of speeches.*

I ANSWER THAT, As was said above (A1), gratuitous grace is ordained to this, viz., that a man may help another to be led to God. Now no man can help in this by moving interiorly (for this belongs to God alone), but only exteriorly by teaching or persuading. Hence gratuitous grace embraces whatever a man needs in order to instruct another in Divine things which are above reason. Now for this three things are required: first, a man must possess the fullness of knowledge of Divine things, so as to be capable of teaching others. Second, he must be able to confirm or prove what he says, otherwise his words would have no weight. Third, he must be capable of fittingly presenting to his hearers what he knows.

Now as regards the first, three things are necessary, as may be seen in human teaching. For whoever would teach another in any science must first be certain of the principles

primo quidem, ut principia illius scientiae sint ei certissima. Et quantum ad hoc ponitur fides, quae est certitudo de rebus invisibilibus, quae supponuntur ut principia in Catholica doctrina. Secundo, oportet quod doctor recte se habeat circa principales conclusiones scientiae. Et sic ponitur sermo sapientiae, quae est cognitio divinorum. Tertio, oportet ut etiam abundet exemplis et cognitione effectuum, per quos interdum oportet manifestare causas. Et quantum ad hoc ponitur sermo scientiae, quae est cognitio rerum humanarum, quia invisibilia Dei per ea quae facta sunt, conspiciuntur.

Confirmatio autem in his quae subduntur rationi, est per argumenta. In his autem quae sunt supra rationem divinitus revelata, confirmatio est per ea quae sunt divinae virtuti propria. Et hoc dupliciter. Uno quidem modo, ut doctor sacrae doctrinae faciat quae solus Deus facere potest, in operibus miraculosis, sive sint ad salutem corporum, et quantum ad hoc ponitur gratia sanitatum; sive ordinentur ad solam divinae potestatis manifestationem, sicut quod sol stet aut tenebrescat, quod mare dividatur; et quantum ad hoc ponitur operatio virtutum. Secundo, ut possit manifestare ea quae solius Dei est scire. Et haec sunt contingentia futura, et quantum ad hoc ponitur prophetia; et etiam occulta cordium, et quantum ad hoc ponitur discretio spirituum.

Facultas autem pronuntiandi potest attendi vel quantum ad idioma in quo aliquis intelligi possit, et secundum hoc ponuntur genera linguarum, vel quantum ad sensum eorum quae sunt proferenda, et quantum ad hoc ponitur interpretatio sermonum.

AD PRIMUM ergo dicendum quod, sicut supra dictum est, non omnia beneficia quae nobis divinitus conceduntur, gratiae gratis datae dicuntur, sed solum illa quae excedunt facultatem naturae, sicut quod piscator abundet sermone sapientiae et scientiae et aliis huiusmodi. Et talia ponuntur hic sub gratia gratis data.

AD SECUNDUM dicendum quod fides non numeratur hic inter gratias gratis datas secundum quod est quaedam virtus iustificans hominem in seipso, sed secundum quod importat quandam supereminentem certitudinem fidei, ex qua homo sit idoneus ad instruendum alios de his quae ad fidem pertinent. Spes autem et caritas pertinent ad vim appetitivam, secundum quod per eam homo in Deum ordinatur.

AD TERTIUM dicendum quod gratia sanitatum distinguitur a generali operatione virtutum, quia habet specialem rationem inducendi ad fidem; ad quam aliquis magis promptus redditur per beneficium corporalis sanitatis quam per fidei virtutem assequitur. Similiter etiam loqui variis linguis, et interpretari sermones, habent speciales quasdam rationes movendi ad fidem, et ideo ponuntur speciales gratiae gratis datae.

AD QUARTUM dicendum quod sapientia et scientia non computantur inter gratias gratis datas secundum

of the science, and with regard to this there is *faith*, which is certitude of invisible things, the principles of Catholic doctrine. Second, it behooves the teacher to know the principal conclusions of the science, and hence we have the word of *wisdom*, which is the knowledge of Divine things. Third, he ought to abound with examples and a knowledge of effects, whereby at times he needs to manifest causes; and thus we have the word of *knowledge*, which is the knowledge of human things, since *the invisible things of Him . . . are clearly seen, being understood by the things that are made* (Rom 1:20).

Now the confirmation of such things as are within reason rests upon arguments; but the confirmation of what is above reason rests on what is proper to the Divine power, and this in two ways: first, when the teacher of sacred doctrine does what God alone can do, in miraculous deeds, whether with respect to bodily health—and thus there is the *grace of healing*, or merely for the purpose of manifesting the Divine power; for instance, that the sun should stand still or darken, or that the sea should be divided—and thus there is the *working of miracles*. Second, when he can manifest what God alone can know, and these are either future contingents—and thus there is *prophecy*, or also the secrets of hearts—and thus there is the *discerning of spirits*.

But the capability of speaking can regard either the idiom in which a person can be understood, and thus there is *kinds of tongues*; or it can regard the sense of what is said, and thus there is the *interpretation of speeches*.

REPLY OBJ. 1: As stated above (A1), not all the benefits divinely conferred upon us are called gratuitous graces, but only those that surpass the power of nature—e.g., that a fisherman should be replete with the word of wisdom and of knowledge and the like; and such as these are here set down as gratuitous graces.

REPLY OBJ. 2: Faith is enumerated here under the gratuitous graces, not as a virtue justifying man in himself, but as implying a super-eminent certitude of faith, whereby a man is fitted for instructing others concerning such things as belong to the faith. With regard to hope and charity, they belong to the appetitive power, according as man is ordained thereby to God.

REPLY OBJ. 3: The grace of healing is distinguished from the general working of miracles because it has a special reason for inducing one to the faith, since a man is all the more ready to believe when he has received the gift of bodily health through the virtue of faith. So, too, to speak with diverse tongues and to interpret speeches have special efficacy in bestowing faith. Hence they are set down as special gratuitous graces.

REPLY OBJ. 4: Wisdom and knowledge are not numbered among the gratuitous graces in the same way as they

quod enumerantur inter dona spiritus sancti, prout scilicet mens hominis est bene mobilis per spiritum sanctum ad ea quae sunt sapientiae vel scientiae, sic enim sunt dona spiritus sancti, ut supra dictum est. Sed computantur inter gratias gratis datas secundum quod important quandam abundantiam scientiae et sapientiae, ut homo possit non solum in seipso recte sapere de divinis, sed etiam alios instruere et contradicentes revincere. Et ideo inter gratias gratis datas signanter ponitur sermo sapientiae, et sermo scientiae, quia ut Augustinus dicit, XIV de Trin., *aliud est scire tantummodo quid homo credere debeat propter adipiscendam vitam beatam; aliud, scire quemadmodum hoc ipsum et piis opituletur, et contra impios defendatur.*

are reckoned among the gifts of the Holy Spirit, i.e., inasmuch as man's mind is rendered easily movable by the Holy Spirit to the things of wisdom and knowledge; for thus they are gifts of the Holy Spirit, as stated above (Q68, AA1,4). But they are numbered amongst the gratuitous graces, inasmuch as they imply such a fullness of knowledge and wisdom that a man may not merely think aright of Divine things, but may instruct others and overpower adversaries. Hence it is significant that it is the *word* of wisdom and the *word* of knowledge that are placed in the gratuitous graces, since, as Augustine says (*De Trin.* xiv, 1), *It is one thing merely to know what a man must believe in order to reach everlasting life, and another thing to know how this may benefit the godly and may be defended against the ungodly.*

Article 5

Whether Gratuitous Grace Is Nobler Than Sanctifying Grace?

AD QUINTUM SIC PROCEDITUR. Videtur quod gratia gratis data sit dignior quam gratia gratum faciens. *Bonum enim gentis est melius quam bonum unius*; ut philosophus dicit, in I Ethic. Sed gratia gratum faciens ordinatur solum ad bonum unius hominis, gratia autem gratis data ordinatur ad bonum commune totius Ecclesiae, ut supra dictum est. Ergo gratia gratis data est dignior quam gratia gratum faciens.

PRAETEREA, maioris virtutis est quod aliquid possit agere in aliud, quam quod solum in seipso perficiatur, sicut maior est claritas corporis quod potest etiam alia corpora illuminare, quam eius quod ita in se lucet quod alia illuminare non potest. Propter quod etiam philosophus dicit, in V Ethic., quod iustitia est praeclarissima virtutum, per quam homo recte se habet etiam ad alios. Sed per gratiam gratum facientem homo perficitur in seipso, per gratiam autem gratis datam homo operatur ad perfectionem aliorum. Ergo gratia gratis data est dignior quam gratia gratum faciens.

PRAETEREA, id quod est proprium meliorum, dignius est quam id quod est commune omnium, sicut ratiocinari, quod est proprium hominis, dignius est quam sentire, quod est commune omnibus animalibus. Sed gratia gratum faciens est communis omnibus membris Ecclesiae, gratia autem gratis data est proprium donum digniorum membrorum Ecclesiae. Ergo gratia gratis data est dignior quam gratia gratum faciens.

SED CONTRA est quod apostolus, I ad Cor. XII, enumeratis gratiis gratis datis, subdit, *adhuc excellentiorem viam vobis demonstro*, et sicut per subsequentia patet, loquitur de caritate, quae pertinet ad gratiam gratum facientem. Ergo gratia gratum faciens excellentior est quam gratia gratis data.

OBJECTION 1: It would seem that gratuitous grace is nobler than sanctifying grace. For *the people's good is better than the individual good*, as the Philosopher says (*Ethic.* i, 2). Now sanctifying grace is ordained to the good of one man alone, whereas gratuitous grace is ordained to the common good of the whole Church, as stated above (AA1,4). Hence gratuitous grace is nobler than sanctifying grace.

OBJ. 2: Further, it is a greater power that is able to act upon another, than that which is confined to itself, even as greater is the brightness of the body that can illuminate other bodies, than of that which can only shine but cannot illuminate; and hence the Philosopher says (*Ethic.* v, 1) *that justice is the most excellent of the virtues*, since by it a man bears himself rightly towards others. But by sanctifying grace a man is perfected only in himself; whereas by gratuitous grace a man works for the perfection of others. Hence gratuitous grace is nobler than sanctifying grace.

OBJ. 3: Further, what is proper to the best is nobler than what is common to all; thus to reason, which is proper to man is nobler than to feel, which is common to all animals. Now sanctifying grace is common to all members of the Church, but gratuitous grace is the proper gift of the more exalted members of the Church. Hence gratuitous grace is nobler than sanctifying grace.

ON THE CONTRARY, The Apostle (1 Cor 12:31), having enumerated the gratuitous graces adds: *And I show unto you yet a more excellent way*; and as the sequel proves he is speaking of charity, which pertains to sanctifying grace. Hence sanctifying grace is more noble than gratuitous grace.

Respondeo dicendum quod unaquaeque virtus tanto excellentior est, quanto ad altius bonum ordinatur. Semper autem finis potior est his quae sunt ad finem. Gratia autem gratum faciens ordinat hominem immediate ad coniunctionem ultimi finis. Gratiae autem gratis datae ordinant hominem ad quaedam praeparatoria finis ultimi, sicut per prophetiam et miracula et alia huiusmodi homines inducuntur ad hoc quod ultimo fini coniungantur. Et ideo gratia gratum faciens est multo excellentior quam gratia gratis data.

Ad primum ergo dicendum quod, sicut philosophus dicit, in XII Metaphys., bonum multitudinis, sicut exercitus, est duplex. Unum quidem quod est in ipsa multitudine, puta ordo exercitus. Aliud autem quod est separatum a multitudine, sicut bonum ducis, et hoc melius est, quia ad hoc etiam illud aliud ordinatur. Gratia autem gratis data ordinatur ad bonum commune Ecclesiae quod est ordo ecclesiasticus, sed gratia gratum faciens ordinatur ad bonum commune separatum, quod est ipse Deus. Et ideo gratia gratum faciens est nobilior.

Ad secundum dicendum quod, si gratia gratis data posset hoc agere in altero quod homo per gratiam gratum facientem consequitur, sequeretur quod gratia gratis data esset nobilior, sicut excellentior est claritas solis illuminantis quam corporis illuminati. Sed per gratiam gratis datam homo non potest causare in alio coniunctionem ad Deum, quam ipse habet per gratiam gratum facientem; sed causat quasdam dispositiones ad hoc. Et ideo non oportet quod gratia gratis data sit excellentior, sicut nec in igne calor manifestativus speciei eius, per quam agit ad inducendum calorem in alia, est nobilior quam forma substantialis ipsius.

Ad tertium dicendum quod sentire ordinatur ad ratiocinari sicut ad finem, et ideo ratiocinari est nobilius. Hic autem est e converso, quia id quod est proprium, ordinatur ad id quod est commune sicut ad finem. Unde non est simile.

I answer that, The higher the good to which a virtue is ordained, the more excellent is the virtue. Now the end is always greater than the means. But sanctifying grace ordains a man immediately to a union with his last end, whereas gratuitous grace ordains a man to what is preparatory to the end; i.e., by prophecy and miracles and so forth, men are induced to unite themselves to their last end. And hence sanctifying grace is nobler than gratuitous grace.

Reply Obj. 1: As the Philosopher says (*Metaph.* xii, text. 52), a multitude, as an army, has a double good; the first is in the multitude itself, viz., the order of the army; the second is separate from the multitude, viz., the good of the leader—and this is better good, since the other is ordained to it. Now gratuitous grace is ordained to the common good of the Church, which is ecclesiastical order, whereas sanctifying grace is ordained to the separate common good, which is God. Hence sanctifying grace is the nobler.

Reply Obj. 2: If gratuitous grace could cause a man to have sanctifying grace, it would follow that the gratuitous grace was the nobler; even as the brightness of the sun that enlightens is more excellent than that of an object that is lit up. But by gratuitous grace a man cannot cause another to have union with God, which he himself has by sanctifying grace; but he causes certain dispositions towards it. Hence gratuitous grace needs not to be the more excellent, even as in fire, the heat, which manifests its species whereby it produces heat in other things, is not more noble than its substantial form.

Reply Obj. 3: Feeling is ordained to reason, as to an end; and thus, to reason is nobler. But here it is the contrary; for what is proper is ordained to what is common as to an end. Hence there is no comparison.

QUESTION 112

OF THE CAUSE OF GRACE

Deinde considerandum est de causa gratiae. Et circa hoc quaeruntur quinque.

Primo, utrum solus Deus sit causa efficiens gratiae.

Secundo, utrum requiratur aliqua dispositio ad gratiam ex parte recipientis ipsam, per actum liberi arbitrii.

Tertio, utrum talis dispositio possit esse necessitas ad gratiam.

Quarto, utrum gratia sit aequalis in omnibus.

Quinto, utrum aliquis possit scire se habere gratiam.

We must now consider the cause of grace; and under this head there are five points of inquiry:

(1) Whether God alone is the efficient cause of grace?

(2) Whether any disposition towards grace is needed on the part of the recipient, by an act of free-will?

(3) Whether such a disposition can make grace follow of necessity?

(4) Whether grace is equal in all?

(5) Whether anyone may know that he has grace?

Article 1

Whether God Alone Is the Cause of Grace?

AD PRIMUM SIC PROCEDITUR. Videtur quod non solus Deus sit causa gratiae. Dicitur enim Ioan. I, *gratia et veritas per Iesum Christum facta est*. Sed in nomine Iesu Christi intelligitur non solum natura divina assumens, sed etiam natura creata assumpta. Ergo aliqua creatura potest esse causa gratiae.

PRAETEREA, ista differentia ponitur inter sacramenta novae legis et veteris, quod sacramenta novae legis causant gratiam, quam sacramenta veteris legis solum significant. Sed sacramenta novae legis sunt quaedam visibilia elementa. Ergo non solus Deus est causa gratiae.

PRAETEREA, secundum Dionysium, in libro Cael. Hier., Angeli purgant et illuminant et perficiunt et Angelos inferiores et etiam homines. Sed rationalis creatura purgatur, illuminatur et perficitur per gratiam. Ergo non solus Deus est causa gratiae.

SED CONTRA est quod in Psalmo LXXXIII dicitur, *gratiam et gloriam dabit dominus*.

RESPONDEO dicendum quod nulla res agere potest ultra suam speciem, quia semper oportet quod causa potior sit effectu. Donum autem gratiae excedit omnem facultatem naturae creatae, cum nihil aliud sit quam quaedam participatio divinae naturae, quae excedit omnem aliam naturam. Et ideo impossibile est quod aliqua creatura gratiam causet. Sic enim necesse est quod solus Deus deificet, communicando consortium divinae naturae per quandam similitudinis participationem, sicut impossibile est quod aliquid igniat nisi solus ignis.

AD PRIMUM ergo dicendum quod humanitas Christi est sicut quoddam organum divinitatis eius; ut

OBJECTION 1: It would seem that God alone is not the cause of grace. For it is written (John 1:17): *Grace and truth came by Jesus Christ*. Now, by the name of Jesus Christ is understood not merely the Divine Nature assuming, but the created nature assumed. Therefore a creature may be the cause of grace.

OBJ. 2: Further, there is this difference between the sacraments of the New Law and those of the Old, that the sacraments of the New Law cause grace, whereas the sacraments of the Old Law merely signify it. Now the sacraments of the New Law are certain visible elements. Therefore God is not the only cause of grace.

OBJ. 3: Further, according to Dionysius (*Coel. Hier.* iii, iv, vii, viii), *Angels cleanse, enlighten, and perfect both lesser angels and men*. Now the rational creature is cleansed, enlightened, and perfected by grace. Therefore God is not the only cause of grace.

ON THE CONTRARY, It is written (Ps 83:12): *The Lord will give grace and glory*.

I ANSWER THAT, Nothing can act beyond its species, since the cause must always be more powerful than its effect. Now the gift of grace surpasses every capability of created nature, since it is nothing short of a partaking of the Divine Nature, which exceeds every other nature. And thus it is impossible that any creature should cause grace. For it is as necessary that God alone should deify, bestowing a partaking of the Divine Nature by a participated likeness, as it is impossible that anything save fire should enkindle.

REPLY OBJ. 1: Christ's humanity is an *organ of His Godhead*, as Damascene says (*De Fide Orth.* iii, 19). Now an

Damascenus dicit, in III libro. Instrumentum autem non agit actionem agentis principalis propria virtute, sed virtute principalis agentis. Et ideo humanitas Christi non causat gratiam propria virtute, sed virtute divinitatis adiunctae, ex qua actiones humanitatis Christi sunt salutares.

AD SECUNDUM dicendum quod, sicut in ipsa persona Christi humanitas causat salutem nostram per gratiam, virtute divina principaliter operante; ita etiam in sacramentis novae legis, quae derivantur a Christo, causatur gratia instrumentaliter quidem per ipsa sacramenta, sed principaliter per virtutem spiritus sancti in sacramentis operantis; secundum illud Ioan. III, *nisi quis renatus fuerit ex aqua et spiritu sancto*, et cetera.

AD TERTIUM dicendum quod Angelus purgat, illuminat et perficit Angelum vel hominem, per modum instructionis cuiusdam, non autem iustificando per gratiam. Unde Dionysius dicit, VII cap. de Div. Nom., quod *huiusmodi purgatio, illuminatio et perfectio nihil est aliud quam divinae scientiae assumptio*.

instrument does not bring forth the action of the principal agent by its own power, but in virtue of the principal agent. Hence Christ's humanity does not cause grace by its own power, but by virtue of the Divine Nature joined to it, whereby the actions of Christ's humanity are saving actions.

REPLY OBJ. 2: As in the person of Christ the humanity causes our salvation by grace, the Divine power being the principal agent, so likewise in the sacraments of the New Law, which are derived from Christ, grace is instrumentally caused by the sacraments, and principally by the power of the Holy Spirit working in the sacraments, according to Jn. 3:5: *Unless a man be born again of water and the Holy Spirit he cannot enter into the kingdom of God.*

REPLY OBJ. 3: Angels cleanse, enlighten, and perfect angels or men, by instruction, and not by justifying them through grace. Hence Dionysius says (*Coel. Hier.* vii) that *this cleansing and enlightenment and perfecting is nothing else than the assumption of Divine knowledge.*

Article 2

Whether Any Preparation and Disposition for Grace Is Required on Man's Part?

AD SECUNDUM SIC PROCEDITUR. Videtur quod non requiratur aliqua praeparatio sive dispositio ad gratiam ex parte hominis. Quia ut apostolus dicit, Rom. IV, *ei qui operatur, merces non imputatur secundum gratiam, sed secundum debitum*. Sed praeparatio hominis per liberum arbitrium non est nisi per aliquam operationem. Ergo tolleretur ratio gratiae.

PRAETEREA, ille qui in peccato progreditur, non se praeparat ad gratiam habendam. Sed aliquibus in peccato progredientibus data est gratia, sicut patet de Paulo, qui gratiam consecutus est *dum esset spirans minarum et caedis in discipulos domini*, ut dicitur Act. IX. Ergo nulla praeparatio ad gratiam requiritur ex parte hominis.

PRAETEREA, agens infinitae virtutis non requirit dispositionem in materia, cum nec ipsam materiam requirat, sicut in creatione apparet; cui collatio gratiae comparatur, quae dicitur nova creatura, ad Gal. ult. Sed solus Deus, qui est infinitae virtutis, gratiam causat, ut dictum est. Ergo nulla praeparatio requiritur ex parte hominis ad gratiam consequendam.

SED CONTRA est quod dicitur Amos IV, *praeparare in occursum Dei tui, Israel*. Et I Reg. VII dicitur, *praeparate corda vestra domino*.

RESPONDEO dicendum quod, sicut supra dictum est, gratia dupliciter dicitur, quandoque quidem ipsum habituale donum Dei; quandoque autem ipsum auxilium Dei moventis animam ad bonum. Primo igitur

OBJECTION 1: It would seem that no preparation or disposition for grace is required on man's part, since, as the Apostle says (Rom 4:4), *To him that worketh, the reward is not reckoned according to grace, but according to debt*. Now a man's preparation by free-will can only be through some operation. Hence it would do away with the notion of grace.

OBJ. 2: Further, whoever is going on sinning, is not preparing himself to have grace. But to some who are going on sinning grace is given, as is clear in the case of Paul, who received grace whilst he was *breathing our threatenings and slaughter against the disciples of the Lord* (Acts 9:1). Hence no preparation for grace is required on man's part.

OBJ. 3: Further, an agent of infinite power needs no disposition in matter, since it does not even require matter, as appears in creation, to which grace is compared, which is called *a new creature* (Gal 6:15). But only God, Who has infinite power, causes grace, as stated above (A1). Hence no preparation is required on man's part to obtain grace.

ON THE CONTRARY, It is written (Amos 4:12): *Be prepared to meet thy God, O Israel*, and (1 Kgs 7:3): *Prepare your hearts unto the Lord.*

I ANSWER THAT, As stated above (Q111, A2), grace is taken in two ways: first, as a habitual gift of God. Second, as a help from God, Who moves the soul to good. Now taking grace in the first sense, a certain preparation of grace is

modo accipiendo gratiam, praeexigitur ad gratiam aliqua gratiae praeparatio, quia nulla forma potest esse nisi in materia disposita. Sed si loquamur de gratia secundum quod significat auxilium Dei moventis ad bonum, sic nulla praeparatio requiritur ex parte hominis quasi praeveniens divinum auxilium, sed potius quaecumque praeparatio in homine esse potest, est ex auxilio Dei moventis animam ad bonum. Et secundum hoc, ipse bonus motus liberi arbitrii quo quis praeparatur ad donum gratiae suscipiendum, est actus liberi arbitrii moti a Deo, et quantum ad hoc, dicitur homo se praeparare, secundum illud Prov. XVI, *hominis est praeparare animum*. Et est principaliter a Deo movente liberum arbitrium, et secundum hoc, dicitur a Deo voluntas hominis praeparari, et a domino gressus hominis dirigi.

AD PRIMUM ergo dicendum quod praeparatio hominis ad gratiam habendam, quaedam est simul cum ipsa infusione gratiae. Et talis operatio est quidem meritoria; sed non gratiae, quae iam habetur, sed gloriae, quae nondum habetur. Est autem alia praeparatio gratiae imperfecta, quae aliquando praecedit donum gratiae gratum facientis, quae tamen est a Deo movente. Sed ista non sufficit ad meritum, nondum homine per gratiam iustificato, quia nullum meritum potest esse nisi ex gratia, ut infra dicetur.

AD SECUNDUM dicendum quod, cum homo ad gratiam se praeparare non possit nisi Deo eum praeveniente et movente ad bonum, non refert utrum subito vel paulatim aliquis ad perfectam praeparationem perveniat, dicitur enim Eccli. XI, quod *facile est in oculis Dei subito honestare pauperem*. Contingit autem quandoque quod Deus movet hominem ad aliquod bonum, non tamen perfectum, et talis praeparatio praecedit gratiam. Sed quandoque statim perfecte movet ipsum ad bonum, et subito homo gratiam accipit; secundum illud Ioan. VI, *omnis qui audivit a patre et didicit, venit ad me*. Et ita contigit Paulo, quia subito, cum esset in progressu peccati, perfecte motum est cor eius a Deo, audiendo et addiscendo et veniendo; et ideo subito est gratiam consecutus.

AD TERTIUM dicendum quod agens infinitae virtutis non exigit materiam, vel dispositionem materiae, quasi praesuppositam ex alterius causae actione. Sed tamen oportet quod, secundum conditionem rei causandae, in ipsa re causet et materiam et dispositionem debitam ad formam. Et similiter ad hoc quod Deus gratiam infundat animae, nulla praeparatio exigitur quam ipse non faciat.

required for it, since a form can only be in disposed matter. But if we speak of grace as it signifies a help from God to move us to good, no preparation is required on man's part, that, as it were, anticipates the Divine help, but rather, every preparation in man must be by the help of God moving the soul to good. And thus even the good movement of the free-will, whereby anyone is prepared for receiving the gift of grace is an act of the free-will moved by God. And thus man is said to prepare himself, according to Prov. 16:1: *It is the part of man to prepare the soul*; yet it is principally from God, Who moves the free-will. Hence it is said that man's will is prepared by God, and that man's steps are guided by God.

REPLY OBJ. 1: A certain preparation of man for grace is simultaneous with the infusion of grace; and this operation is meritorious, not indeed of grace, which is already possessed—but of glory which is not yet possessed. But there is another imperfect preparation, which sometimes precedes the gift of sanctifying grace, and yet it is from God's motion. But it does not suffice for merit, since man is not yet justified by grace, and merit can only arise from grace, as will be seen further on (Q114, A2).

REPLY OBJ. 2: Since a man cannot prepare himself for grace unless God prevent and move him to good, it is of no account whether anyone arrive at perfect preparation instantaneously, or step by step. For it is written (Sir 11:23): *It is easy in the eyes of God on a sudden to make the poor man rich*. Now it sometimes happens that God moves a man to good, but not perfect good, and this preparation precedes grace. But He sometimes moves him suddenly and perfectly to good, and man receives grace suddenly, according to Jn. 6:45: *Every one that hath heard of the Father, and hath learned, cometh to Me*. And thus it happened to Paul, since, suddenly when he was in the midst of sin, his heart was perfectly moved by God to hear, to learn, to come; and hence he received grace suddenly.

REPLY OBJ. 3: An agent of infinite power needs no matter or disposition of matter, brought about by the action of something else; and yet, looking to the condition of the thing caused, it must cause, in the thing caused, both the matter and the due disposition for the form. So likewise, when God infuses grace into a soul, no preparation is required which He Himself does not bring about.

Article 3

Whether Grace Is Necessarily Given to Whoever Prepares Himself for It, or to Whoever Does What He Can?

AD TERTIUM SIC PROCEDITUR. Videtur quod ex necessitate detur gratia se praeparanti ad gratiam, vel facienti quod in se est. Quia super illud Rom. V, *iustificati ex fide pacem habeamus* etc., dicit Glossa, *Deus recipit eum qui ad se confugit, aliter esset in eo iniquitas*. Sed impossibile est in Deo iniquitatem esse. Ergo impossibile est quod Deus non recipiat eum qui ad se confugit. Ex necessitate igitur gratiam assequitur.

PRAETEREA, Anselmus dicit, in libro de casu Diaboli, quod ista est causa quare Deus non concedit Diabolo gratiam, quia ipse non voluit accipere, nec paratus fuit. Sed remota causa, necesse est removeri effectum. Ergo si aliquis velit accipere gratiam, necesse est quod ei detur.

PRAETEREA, bonum est communicativum sui; ut patet per Dionysium, in IV cap. de Div. Nom. Sed bonum gratiae est melius quam bonum naturae. Cum igitur forma naturalis ex necessitate adveniat materiae dispositae, videtur quod multo magis gratia ex necessitate detur praeparanti se ad gratiam.

SED CONTRA est quod homo comparatur ad Deum sicut lutum ad figulum; secundum illud Ierem. XVIII, *sicut lutum in manu figuli, sic vos in manu mea*. Sed lutum non ex necessitate accipit formam a figulo, quantumcumque sit praeparatum. Ergo neque homo recipit ex necessitate gratiam a Deo, quantumcumque se praeparet.

RESPONDEO dicendum quod, sicut supra dictum est, praeparatio ad hominis gratiam est a Deo sicut a movente, a libero autem arbitrio sicut a moto. Potest igitur praeparatio dupliciter considerari. Uno quidem modo, secundum quod est a libero arbitrio. Et secundum hoc, nullam necessitatem habet ad gratiae consecutionem, quia donum gratiae excedit omnem praeparationem virtutis humanae. Alio modo potest considerari secundum quod est a Deo movente. Et tunc habet necessitatem ad id ad quod ordinatur a Deo, non quidem coactionis, sed infallibilitatis, quia intentio Dei deficere non potest; secundum quod et Augustinus dicit, in libro de Praedest. Sanct., *quod per beneficia Dei certissime liberantur quicumque liberantur*. Unde si ex intentione Dei moventis est quod homo cuius cor movet, gratiam consequatur, infallibiliter ipsam consequitur; secundum illud Ioan. VI, *omnis qui audivit a patre et didicit, venit ad me*.

AD PRIMUM ergo dicendum quod Glossa illa loquitur de illo qui confugit ad Deum per actum meritorium liberi arbitrii iam per gratiam informati, quem si non reciperet, esset contra iustitiam quam ipse statuit. Vel si referatur ad motum liberi arbitrii ante gratiam, loquitur

OBJECTION 1: It would seem that grace is necessarily given to whoever prepares himself for grace, or to whoever does what he can, because, on Rom. 5:1, *Being justified . . . by faith, let us have peace*, etc. the gloss says: *God welcomes whoever flies to Him, otherwise there would be injustice with Him.* But it is impossible for injustice to be with God. Therefore it is impossible for God not to welcome whoever flies to Him. Hence he receives grace of necessity.

OBJ. 2: Further, Anselm says (*De Casu Diaboli.* iii) that the reason why God does not bestow grace on the devil, is that he did not wish, nor was he prepared, to receive it. But if the cause be removed, the effect must needs be removed also. Therefore, if anyone is willing to receive grace it is bestowed on them of necessity.

OBJ. 3: Further, good is diffusive of itself, as appears from Dionysius (*Div. Nom.* iv). Now the good of grace is better than the good of nature. Hence, since natural forms necessarily come to disposed matter, much more does it seem that grace is necessarily bestowed on whoever prepares himself for grace.

ON THE CONTRARY, Man is compared to God as clay to the potter, according to Jer. 18:6: *As clay is in the hand of the potter, so are you in My hand.* But however much the clay is prepared, it does not necessarily receive its shape from the potter. Hence, however much a man prepares himself, he does not necessarily receive grace from God.

I ANSWER THAT, As stated above (A2), man's preparation for grace is from God, as Mover, and from the free-will, as moved. Hence the preparation may be looked at in two ways: first, as it is from free-will, and thus there is no necessity that it should obtain grace, since the gift of grace exceeds every preparation of human power. But it may be considered, second, as it is from God the Mover, and thus it has a necessity—not indeed of coercion, but of infallibility—as regards what it is ordained to by God, since God's intention cannot fail, according to the saying of Augustine in his book on the Predestination of the Saints (*De Dono Persev.* xiv) that *by God's good gifts whoever is liberated, is most certainly liberated.* Hence if God intends, while moving, that the one whose heart He moves should attain to grace, he will infallibly attain to it, according to Jn. 6:45: *Every one that hath heard of the Father, and hath learned, cometh to Me.*

REPLY OBJ. 1: This gloss is speaking of such as fly to God by a meritorious act of their free-will, already *informed* with grace; for if they did not receive grace, it would be against the justice which He Himself established. Or if it refers to the movement of free-will before grace, it is

secundum quod ipsum confugium hominis ad Deum est per motionem divinam, quam iustum est non deficere.

AD SECUNDUM dicendum quod defectus gratiae prima causa est ex nobis, sed collationis gratiae prima causa est a Deo; secundum illud Osee XIII, *perditio tua, Israel, tantummodo ex me auxilium tuum.*

AD TERTIUM dicendum quod etiam in rebus naturalibus dispositio materiae non ex necessitate consequitur formam, nisi per virtutem agentis qui dispositionem causat.

speaking in the sense that man's flight to God is by a Divine motion, which ought not, in justice, to fail.

REPLY OBJ. 2: The first cause of the defect of grace is on our part; but the first cause of the bestowal of grace is on God's according to Osee 13:9: *Destruction is thy own, O Israel; thy help is only in Me.*

REPLY OBJ. 3: Even in natural things, the form does not necessarily ensue the disposition of the matter, except by the power of the agent that causes the disposition.

Article 4

Whether Grace Is Greater in One Than in Another?

AD QUARTUM SIC PROCEDITUR. Videtur quod gratia non sit maior in uno quam in alio. Gratia enim causatur in nobis ex dilectione divina, ut dictum est. Sed Sap. VI dicitur, *pusillum et magnum ipse fecit, et aequaliter est illi cura de omnibus.* Ergo omnes aequaliter gratiam ab eo consequuntur.

PRAETEREA, ea quae in summo dicuntur, non recipiunt magis et minus. Sed gratia in summo dicitur, quia coniungit ultimo fini. Ergo non recipit magis et minus. Non ergo est maior in uno quam in alio.

PRAETEREA, gratia est vita animae, ut supra dictum est. Sed vivere non dicitur secundum magis et minus. Ergo etiam neque gratia.

SED CONTRA est quod dicitur ad Ephes. IV, *unicuique data est gratia secundum mensuram donationis Christi.* Quod autem mensurate datur, non omnibus aequaliter datur. Ergo non omnes aequalem gratiam habent.

RESPONDEO dicendum quod, sicut supra dictum est, habitus duplicem magnitudinem habere potest, unam ex parte finis vel obiecti, secundum quod dicitur una virtus alia nobilior inquantum ad maius bonum ordinatur; aliam vero ex parte subiecti, quod magis vel minus participat habitum inhaerentem.

Secundum igitur primam magnitudinem, gratia gratum faciens non potest esse maior et minor, quia gratia secundum sui rationem coniungit hominem summo bono, quod est Deus. Sed ex parte subiecti, gratia potest suscipere magis vel minus, prout scilicet unus perfectius illustratur a lumine gratiae quam alius. Cuius diversitatis ratio quidem est aliqua ex parte praeparantis se ad gratiam, qui enim se magis ad gratiam praeparat, pleniorem gratiam accipit. Sed ex hac parte non potest accipi prima ratio huius diversitatis, quia praeparatio ad gratiam non est hominis nisi inquantum liberum arbitrium eius praeparatur a Deo. Unde prima causa huius diversitatis accipienda est ex parte ipsius Dei, qui diversimode suae gratiae dona dispensat, ad hoc quod ex diversis gradibus

OBJECTION 1: It would seem that grace is not greater in one than in another. For grace is caused in us by the Divine love, as stated above (Q110, A1). Now it is written (Wis 6:8): *He made the little and the great and He hath equally care of all.* Therefore all obtain grace from Him equally.

OBJ. 2: Further, whatever is the greatest possible, cannot be more or less. But grace is the greatest possible, since it joins us with our last end. Therefore there is no greater or less in it. Hence it is not greater in one than in another.

OBJ. 3: Further, grace is the soul's life, as stated above (Q110, A1, ad 2). But there is no greater or less in life. Hence, neither is there in grace.

ON THE CONTRARY, It is written (Eph 4:7): *But to every one of us is given grace according to the measure of the giving of Christ.* Now what is given in measure, is not given to all equally. Hence all have not an equal grace.

I ANSWER THAT, As stated above (Q52, AA1,2; Q56, AA1,2), habits can have a double magnitude: one, as regards the end or object, as when a virtue is said to be more noble through being ordained to a greater good; the other on the part of the subject, which more or less participates in the habit inhering to it.

Now as regards the first magnitude, sanctifying grace cannot be greater or less, since, of its nature, grace joins man to the Highest Good, which is God. But as regards the subject, grace can receive more or less, inasmuch as one may be more perfectly enlightened by grace than another. And a certain reason for this is on the part of him who prepares himself for grace; since he who is better prepared for grace, receives more grace. Yet it is not here that we must seek the first cause of this diversity, since man prepares himself, only inasmuch as his free-will is prepared by God. Hence the first cause of this diversity is to be sought on the part of the God, Who dispenses His gifts of grace variously, in order that the beauty and perfection of the Church may result from these various degree; even as He instituted the

pulchritudo et perfectio Ecclesiae consurgat, sicut etiam diversos gradus rerum instituit ut esset universum perfectum. Unde apostolus, ad Ephes. IV, postquam dixerat, *unicuique data est gratia secundum mensuram donationis Christi*, enumeratis diversis gratiis, subiungit, *ad consummationem sanctorum, in aedificationem corporis Christi*.

AD PRIMUM ergo dicendum quod cura divina dupliciter considerari potest. Uno modo, quantum ad ipsum divinum actum, qui est simplex et uniformis. Et secundum hoc, aequaliter se habet eius cura ad omnes, quia scilicet uno actu et simplici et maiora et minora dispensat. Alio modo potest considerari ex parte eorum quae in creaturis ex divina cura proveniunt. Et secundum hoc invenitur inaequalitas, inquantum scilicet Deus sua cura quibusdam maiora, quibusdam minora providet dona.

AD SECUNDUM dicendum quod ratio illa procedit secundum primum modum magnitudinis gratiae. Non enim potest gratia secundum hoc maior esse, quod ad maius bonum ordinet, sed ex eo quod magis vel minus ordinat ad idem bonum magis vel minus participandum. Potest enim esse diversitas intensionis et remissionis secundum participationem subiecti, et in ipsa gratia et in finali gloria.

AD TERTIUM dicendum quod vita naturalis pertinet ad substantiam hominis, et ideo non recipit magis et minus. Sed vitam gratiae participat homo accidentaliter, et ideo eam potest homo magis vel minus habere.

various conditions of things, that the universe might be perfect. Hence after the Apostle had said (Eph 4:7): *To every one of us is given grace according to the measure of the giving of Christ*, having enumerated the various graces, he adds (Eph 4:12): *For the perfecting of the saints . . . for the edifying of the body of Christ*.

REPLY OBJ. 1: The Divine care may be looked at in two ways: first, as regards the Divine act, which is simple and uniform; and thus His care looks equally to all, since by one simple act He administers great things and little. But, *second*, it may be considered in those things which come to be considered by the Divine care; and thus, inequality is found, inasmuch as God by His care provides greater gifts to some, and lesser gifts for others.

REPLY OBJ. 2: This objection is based on the first kind of magnitude of grace; since grace cannot be greater by ordaining to a greater good, but inasmuch as it more or less ordains to a greater or less participation of the same good. For there may be diversity of intensity and remissness, both in grace and in final glory as regards the subjects' participation.

REPLY OBJ. 3: Natural life pertains to man's substance, and hence cannot be more or less; but man partakes of the life of grace accidentally, and hence man may possess it more or less.

Article 5

Whether Man Can Know That He Has Grace?

AD QUINTUM SIC PROCEDITUR. Videtur quod homo possit scire se habere gratiam. Gratia enim est in anima per sui essentiam. Sed certissima cognitio animae est eorum quae sunt in anima per sui essentiam; ut patet per Augustinum, XII super Gen. ad Litt. Ergo gratia certissime potest cognosci a Deo qui gratiam habet.

PRAETEREA, sicut scientia est donum Dei, ita et gratia. Sed qui a Deo scientiam accipit, scit se scientiam habere; secundum illud Sap. VII, *dominus dedit mihi horum quae sunt veram scientiam*. Ergo pari ratione qui accipit gratiam a Deo, scit se gratiam habere.

PRAETEREA, lumen est magis cognoscibile quam tenebra, quia secundum apostolum, ad Ephes. V, *omne quod manifestatur, lumen est*. Sed peccatum, quod est spiritualis tenebra, per certitudinem potest sciri ab eo qui habet peccatum. Ergo multo magis gratia, quae est spirituale lumen.

OBJECTION 1: It would seem that man can know that he has grace. For grace by its physical reality is in the soul. Now the soul has most certain knowledge of those things that are in it by their physical reality, as appears from Augustine (*Gen ad lit.* xii, 31). Hence grace may be known most certainly by one who has grace.

OBJ. 2: Further, as knowledge is a gift of God, so is grace. But whoever receives knowledge from God, knows that he has knowledge, according to Wis. 7:17: The Lord *hath given me the true knowledge of the things that are*. Hence, with equal reason, whoever receives grace from God, knows that he has grace.

OBJ. 3: Further, light is more knowable than darkness, since, according to the Apostle (Eph 5:13), *all that is made manifest is light*, Now sin, which is spiritual darkness, may be known with certainty by one that is in sin. Much more, therefore, may grace, which is spiritual light, be known.

PRAETEREA, apostolus dicit, I ad Cor. II, *nos autem non spiritum huius mundi accepimus, sed spiritum qui a Deo est, ut sciamus quae a Deo donata sunt nobis.* Sed gratia est praecipuum donum Dei. Ergo homo qui accepit gratiam per spiritum sanctum, per eundem spiritum scit gratiam esse sibi datam.

PRAETEREA, Gen. XXII, ex persona domini dicitur ad Abraham, *nunc cognovi quod timeas dominum, idest, cognoscere te feci.* Loquitur autem ibi de timore casto, qui non est sine gratia. Ergo homo potest cognoscere se habere gratiam.

SED CONTRA est quod dicitur Eccle. IX, *nemo scit utrum sit dignus odio vel amore.* Sed gratia gratum faciens facit hominem dignum Dei amore. Ergo nullus potest scire utrum habeat gratiam gratum facientem.

RESPONDEO dicendum quod tripliciter aliquid cognosci potest. Uno modo, per revelationem. Et hoc modo potest aliquis scire se habere gratiam. Revelat enim Deus hoc aliquando aliquibus ex speciali privilegio, ut securitatis gaudium etiam in hac vita in eis incipiat, et confidentius et fortius magnifica opera prosequantur, et mala praesentis vitae sustineant, sicut Paulo dictum est, II ad Cor. XII, *sufficit tibi gratia mea.*

Alio modo homo cognoscit aliquid per seipsum, et hoc certitudinaliter. Et sic nullus potest scire se habere gratiam. Certitudo enim non potest haberi de aliquo, nisi possit diiudicari per proprium principium, sic enim certitudo habetur de conclusionibus demonstrativis per indemonstrabilia universalia principia; nullus autem posset scire se habere scientiam alicuius conclusionis, si principium ignoraret. Principium autem gratiae, et obiectum eius, est ipse Deus, qui propter sui excellentiam est nobis ignotus; secundum illud Iob XXXVI, *ecce, Deus magnus, vincens scientiam nostram.* Et ideo eius praesentia in nobis vel absentia per certitudinem cognosci non potest; secundum illud Iob IX, *si venerit ad me, non videbo eum, si autem abierit, non intelligam.* Et ideo homo non potest per certitudinem diiudicare utrum ipse habeat gratiam; secundum illud I ad Cor. IV, *sed neque meipsum iudico, qui autem iudicat me, dominus est.*

Tertio modo cognoscitur aliquid coniecturaliter per aliqua signa. Et hoc modo aliquis cognoscere potest se habere gratiam, inquantum scilicet percipit se delectari in Deo, et contemnere res mundanas; et inquantum homo non est conscius sibi alicuius peccati mortalis. Secundum quem modum potest intelligi quod habetur Apoc. II, *vincenti dabo manna absconditum, quod nemo novit nisi qui accipit,* quia scilicet ille qui accipit, per quandam experientiam dulcedinis novit, quam non experitur ille qui non accipit. Ista tamen cognitio imperfecta est. Unde apostolus dicit, I ad Cor. IV, *nihil mihi conscius sum, sed non in hoc iustificatus sum.* Quia ut

OBJ. 4: Further, the Apostle says (1 Cor 2:12): *Now we have received not the Spirit of this world, but the Spirit that is of God; that we may know the things that are given us from God.* Now grace is God's first gift. Hence, the man who receives grace by the Holy Spirit, by the same Holy Spirit knows the grace given to him.

OBJ. 5: Further, it was said by the Lord to Abraham (Gen 22:12): *Now I know that thou fearest God,* i.e., *I have made thee know.* Now He is speaking there of chaste fear, which is not apart from grace. Hence a man may know that he has grace.

ON THE CONTRARY, It is written (Eccl 9:1): *Man knoweth not whether he be worthy of love or hatred.* Now sanctifying grace maketh a man worthy of God's love. Therefore no one can know whether he has sanctifying grace.

I ANSWER THAT, There are three ways of knowing a thing: first, by revelation, and thus anyone may know that he has grace, for God by a special privilege reveals this at times to some, in order that the joy of safety may begin in them even in this life, and that they may carry on toilsome works with greater trust and greater energy, and may bear the evils of this present life, as when it was said to Paul (2 Cor 12:9): *My grace is sufficient for thee.*

Second, a man may, of himself, know something, and with certainty; and in this way no one can know that he has grace. For certitude about a thing can only be had when we may judge of it by its proper principle. Thus it is by undemonstrable universal principles that certitude is obtained concerning demonstrative conclusions. Now no one can know he has the knowledge of a conclusion if he does not know its principle. But the principle of grace and its object is God, Who by reason of His very excellence is unknown to us, according to Job 36:26: *Behold God is great, exceeding our knowledge.* And hence His presence in us and His absence cannot be known with certainty, according to Job 9:11: *If He come to me, I shall not see Him; if He depart I shall not understand.* And hence man cannot judge with certainty that he has grace, according to 1 Cor. 4:3,4: *But neither do I judge my own self . . . but He that judgeth me is the Lord.*

Third, things are known conjecturally by signs; and thus anyone may know he has grace, when he is conscious of delighting in God, and of despising worldly things, and inasmuch as a man is not conscious of any mortal sin. And thus it is written (Rev 2:17): *To him that overcometh I will give the hidden manna . . . which no man knoweth, but he that receiveth it,* because whoever receives it knows, by experiencing a certain sweetness, which he who does not receive it, does not experience. Yet this knowledge is imperfect; hence the Apostle says (1 Cor 4:4): *I am not conscious to myself of anything, yet am I not hereby justified,* since, according to Ps. 18:13: *Who can understand sins? From my*

dicitur in Psalmo XVIII, *delicta quis intelligit? Ab occultis meis munda me, domine.*

AD PRIMUM ergo dicendum quod illa quae sunt per essentiam sui in anima, cognoscuntur experimentali cognitione, inquantum homo experitur per actus principia intrinseca, sicut voluntatem percipimus volendo, et vitam in operibus vitae.

AD SECUNDUM dicendum quod de ratione scientiae est quod homo certitudinem habeat de his quorum habet scientiam, et similiter de ratione fidei est quod homo sit certus de his quorum habet fidem. Et hoc ideo, quia certitudo pertinet ad perfectionem intellectus, in quo praedicta dona existunt. Et ideo quicumque habet scientiam vel fidem, certus est se habere. Non est autem similis ratio de gratia et caritate et aliis huiusmodi, quae perficiunt vim appetitivam.

AD TERTIUM dicendum quod peccatum habet pro principio et pro obiecto bonum commutabile, quod nobis est notum. Obiectum autem vel finis gratiae est nobis ignotum, propter sui luminis immensitatem; secundum illud I ad Tim. ult., *lucem habitat inaccessibilem.*

AD QUARTUM dicendum quod apostolus ibi loquitur de donis gloriae, quae sunt nobis data in spe, quae certissime cognoscimus per fidem; licet non cognoscamus per certitudinem nos habere gratiam, per quam nos possumus ea promereri. Vel potest dici quod loquitur de notitia privilegiata, quae est per revelationem. Unde subdit, *nobis autem revelavit Deus per spiritum sanctum.*

AD QUINTUM dicendum quod illud etiam verbum Abrahae dictum, potest referri ad notitiam experimentalem, quae est per exhibitionem operis. In opere enim illo quod fecerat Abraham, cognoscere potuit experimentaliter se Dei timorem habere. Vel potest etiam ad revelationem referri.

secret ones cleanse me, O Lord, and from those of others spare Thy servant.

REPLY OBJ. 1: Those things which are in the soul by their physical reality, are known through experimental knowledge; insofar as through acts man has experience of their inward principles: thus when we wish, we perceive that we have a will; and when we exercise the functions of life, we observe that there is life in us.

REPLY OBJ. 2: It is an essential condition of knowledge that a man should have certitude of the objects of knowledge; and again, it is an essential condition of faith that a man should be certain of the things of faith, and this, because certitude belongs to the perfection of the intellect, wherein these gifts exist. Hence, whoever has knowledge or faith is certain that he has them. But it is otherwise with grace and charity and such like, which perfect the appetitive faculty.

REPLY OBJ. 3: Sin has for its principal object commutable good, which is known to us. But the object or end of grace is unknown to us on account of the greatness of its light, according to 1 Tim. 6:16: *Who . . . inhabiteth light inaccessible.*

REPLY OBJ. 4: The Apostle is here speaking of the gifts of glory, which have been given to us in hope, and these we know most certainly by faith, although we do not know for certain that we have grace to enable us to merit them. Or it may be said that he is speaking of the privileged knowledge, which comes of revelation. Hence he adds (1 Cor 2:10): *But to us God hath revealed them by His Spirit.*

REPLY OBJ. 5: What was said to Abraham may refer to experimental knowledge which springs from deeds of which we are cognizant. For in the deed that Abraham had just wrought, he could know experimentally that he had the fear of God. Or it may refer to a revelation.

QUESTION 113

OF THE EFFECTS OF GRACE

Deinde considerandum est de effectibus gratiae. Et primo, de iustificatione impii, quae est effectus gratiae operantis; secundo, de merito, quod est effectus gratiae cooperantis. Circa primum quaeruntur decem.

Primo, quid sit iustificatio impii.

Secundo, utrum ad eam requiratur gratiae infusio.

Tertio, utrum ad eam requiratur aliquis motus liberi arbitrii.

Quarto, utrum ad eam requiratur motus fidei.

Quinto, utrum ad eam requiratur motus liberi arbitrii contra peccatum.

Sexto, utrum praemissis sit connumeranda remissio peccatorum.

Septimo, utrum in iustificatione impii sit ordo temporis, aut sit subito.

Octavo, de naturali ordine eorum quae ad iustificationem concurrunt.

Nono, utrum iustificatio impii sit maximum opus Dei.

Decimo, utrum iustificatio impii sit miraculosa.

We have now to consider the effect of grace; (1) the justification of the ungodly, which is the effect of operating grace; and (2) merit, which is the effect of cooperating grace. Under the first head there are ten points of inquiry:

(1) What is the justification of the ungodly?

(2) Whether grace is required for it?

(3) Whether any movement of the free-will is required?

(4) Whether a movement of faith is required?

(5) Whether a movement of the free-will against sin is required?

(6) Whether the remission of sins is to be reckoned with the foregoing?

(7) Whether the justification of the ungodly is a work of time or is sudden?

(8) Of the natural order of the things concurring to justification;

(9) Whether the justification of the ungodly is God's greatest work?

(10) Whether the justification of the ungodly is miraculous?

Article 1

Whether the Justification of the Ungodly Is the Remission of Sins?

AD PRIMUM SIC PROCEDITUR. Videtur quod iustificatio impii non sit remissio peccatorum. Peccatum enim non solum iustitiae opponitur, sed omnibus virtutibus; ut ex supradictis patet. Sed iustificatio significat motum quendam ad iustitiam. Non ergo omnis peccati remissio est iustificatio, cum omnis motus sit de contrario in contrarium.

PRAETEREA, unumquodque debet denominari ab eo quod est potissimum in ipso, ut dicitur in II de anima. Sed remissio peccatorum praecipue fit per fidem, secundum illud Act. XV, *fide purificans corda eorum*; et per caritatem, secundum illud Prov. X, *universa delicta operit caritas*. Magis ergo remissio peccatorum debuit denominari a fide vel a caritate, quam a iustitia.

PRAETEREA, remissio peccatorum idem esse videtur quod vocatio, vocatur enim qui distat; distat autem aliquis a Deo per peccatum. Sed vocatio iustificationem praecedit; secundum illud Rom. VIII, *quos vocavit, hos et iustificavit*. Ergo iustificatio non est remissio peccatorum.

OBJECTION 1: It would seem that the justification of the ungodly is not the remission of sins. For sin is opposed not only to justice, but to all the other virtues, as stated above (Q71, A1). Now justification signifies a certain movement towards justice. Therefore not even remission of sin is justification, since movement is from one contrary to the other.

OBJ. 2: Further, everything ought to be named from what is predominant in it, according to *De Anima* ii, text. 49. Now the remission of sins is brought about chiefly by faith, according to Acts 15:9: *Purifying their hearts by faith*; and by charity, according to Prov. 10:12: *Charity covereth all sins*. Therefore the remission of sins ought to be named after faith or charity rather than justice.

OBJ. 3: Further, the remission of sins seems to be the same as being called, for whoever is called is afar off, and we are afar off from God by sin. But one is called before being justified according to Rm. 8:30: *And whom He called, them He also justified*. Therefore justification is not the remission of sins.

SED CONTRA est quod, Rom. VIII super illud, *quos vocavit, hos et iustificavit*, dicit Glossa, remissione peccatorum. Ergo remissio peccatorum est iustificatio.

RESPONDEO dicendum quod iustificatio passive accepta importat motum ad iustitiam; sicut et calefactio motum ad calorem. Cum autem iustitia de sui ratione importet quandam rectitudinem ordinis, dupliciter accipi potest. Uno modo, secundum quod importat ordinem rectum in ipso actu hominis. Et secundum hoc iustitia ponitur virtus quaedam, sive sit particularis iustitia, quae ordinat actum hominis secundum rectitudinem in comparatione ad alium singularem hominem; sive sit iustitia legalis, quae ordinat secundum rectitudinem actum hominis in comparatione ad bonum commune multitudinis; ut patet in V Ethic.

Alio modo dicitur iustitia prout importat rectitudinem quandam ordinis in ipsa interiori dispositione hominis, prout scilicet supremum hominis subditur Deo, et inferiores vires animae subduntur supremae, scilicet rationi. Et hanc etiam dispositionem vocat philosophus, in V Ethic., iustitiam metaphorice dictam. Haec autem iustitia in homine potest fieri dupliciter. Uno quidem modo, per modum simplicis generationis, quae est ex privatione ad formam. Et hoc modo iustificatio posset competere etiam ei qui non esset in peccato, dum huiusmodi iustitiam a Deo acciperet, sicut Adam dicitur accepisse originalem iustitiam. Alio modo potest fieri huiusmodi iustitia in homine secundum rationem motus qui est de contrario in contrarium. Et secundum hoc, iustificatio importat transmutationem quandam de statu iniustitiae ad statum iustitiae praedictae. Et hoc modo loquimur hic de iustificatione impii; secundum illud apostoli, ad Rom. IV, *ei qui non operatur, credenti autem in eum qui iustificat impium*, et cetera. Et quia motus magis denominatur a termino ad quem quam a termino a quo, ideo huiusmodi transmutatio, qua aliquis transmutatur a statu iniustitiae per remissionem peccati, sortitur nomen a termino ad quem, et vocatur iustificatio impii.

AD PRIMUM ergo dicendum quod omne peccatum, secundum quod importat quandam inordinationem mentis non subditae Deo, iniustitia potest dici praedictae iustitiae contraria; secundum illud I Ioan. III, *omnis qui facit peccatum, et iniquitatem facit, et peccatum est iniquitas*. Et secundum hoc, remotio cuiuslibet peccati dicitur iustificatio.

AD SECUNDUM dicendum quod fides et caritas dicunt ordinem specialem mentis humanae ad Deum secundum intellectum vel affectum. Sed iustitia importat generaliter totam rectitudinem ordinis. Et ideo magis denominatur huiusmodi transmutatio a iustitia quam a caritate vel fide.

ON THE CONTRARY, On Rm. 8:30, *Whom He called, them He also justified*, the gloss says i.e., *by the remission of sins*. Therefore the remission of sins is justification.

I ANSWER THAT, Justification taken passively implies a movement towards justice; as heating implies movement towards heat. But since justice, by its nature, implies a certain rectitude of order, it may be taken in two ways: first, inasmuch as it implies a right order in man's act, and thus justice is placed amongst the virtues—either as particular justice, which directs a man's acts by regulating them in relation to his fellowman—or as legal justice, which directs a man's acts by regulating them in their relation to the common good of society, as appears from *Ethic.* v, 1.

Second, justice is so-called inasmuch as it implies a certain rectitude of order in the interior disposition of a man, insofar as what is highest in man is subject to God, and the inferior powers of the soul are subject to the superior, i.e., to the reason; and this disposition the Philosopher calls *justice metaphorically speaking* (*Ethic.* v, 11). Now this justice may be in man in two ways: first, by simple generation, which is from privation to form; and thus justification may belong even to such as are not in sin, when they receive this justice from God, as Adam is said to have received original justice. Second, this justice may be brought about in man by a movement from one contrary to the other, and thus justification implies a transmutation from the state of injustice to the aforesaid state of justice. And it is thus we are now speaking of the justification of the ungodly, according to the Apostle (Rom 4:5): *But to him that worketh not, yet believeth in Him that justifieth the ungodly*, etc. And because movement is named after its term *whereto* rather than from its term *whence*, the transmutation whereby anyone is changed by the remission of sins from the state of ungodliness to the state of justice, borrows its name from its term *whereto*, and is called *justification of the ungodly*.

REPLY OBJ. 1: Every sin, inasmuch as it implies the disorder of a mind not subject to God, may be called injustice, as being contrary to the aforesaid justice, according to 1 Jn. 3:4: *Whosoever committeth sin, committeth also iniquity; and sin is iniquity*. And thus the removal of any sin is called the justification of the ungodly.

REPLY OBJ. 2: Faith and charity imply a special directing of the human mind to God by the intellect and will; whereas justice implies a general rectitude of order. Hence this transmutation is named after justice rather than after charity or faith.

AD TERTIUM dicendum quod vocatio refertur ad auxilium Dei interius moventis et excitantis mentem ad deserendum peccatum. Quae quidem motio Dei non est ipsa remissio peccati, sed causa eius.

REPLY OBJ. 3: Being called refers to God's help moving and exciting our mind to give up sin, and this motion of God is not the remission of sins, but its cause.

Article 2

Whether the Infusion of Grace Is Required for the Remission of Guilt, i.e., for the Justification of the Ungodly?

AD SECUNDUM SIC PROCEDITUR. Videtur quod ad remissionem culpae, quae est iustificatio impii, non requiratur gratiae infusio. Potest enim aliquis removeri ab uno contrario sine hoc quod perducatur ad alterum, si contraria sint mediata. Sed status culpae et status gratiae sunt contraria mediata, est enim medius status innocentiae, in quo homo nec gratiam habet nec culpam. Ergo potest alicui remitti culpa sine hoc quod perducatur ad gratiam.

PRAETEREA, remissio culpae consistit in reputatione divina; secundum illud Psalmi XXXI, *beatus vir cui non imputavit dominus peccatum*. Sed infusio gratiae ponit etiam aliquid in nobis, ut supra habitum est. Ergo infusio gratiae non requiritur ad remissionem culpae.

PRAETEREA, nullus subiicitur simul duobus contrariis. Sed quaedam peccata sunt contraria, sicut prodigalitas et illiberalitas. Ergo qui subiicitur peccato prodigalitatis, non simul subiicitur peccato illiberalitatis. Potest tamen contingere quod prius ei subiiciebatur. Ergo peccando vitio prodigalitatis, liberatur a peccato illiberalitatis. Et sic remittitur aliquod peccatum sine gratia.

SED CONTRA est quod dicitur Rom. III, *iustificati gratis per gratiam ipsius*.

RESPONDEO dicendum quod homo peccando Deum offendit, sicut ex supradictis patet. Offensa autem non remittitur alicui nisi per hoc quod animus offensi pacatur offendenti. Et ideo secundum hoc peccatum nobis remitti dicitur, quod Deus nobis pacatur. Quae quidem pax consistit in dilectione qua Deus nos diligit. Dilectio autem Dei, quantum est ex parte actus divini, est aeterna et immutabilis, sed quantum ad effectum quem nobis imprimit, quandoque interrumpitur, prout scilicet ab ipso quandoque deficimus et quandoque iterum recuperamus. Effectus autem divinae dilectionis in nobis qui per peccatum tollitur, est gratia, qua homo fit dignus vita aeterna, a qua peccatum mortale excludit. Et ideo non posset intelligi remissio culpae, nisi adesset infusio gratiae.

AD PRIMUM ergo dicendum quod plus requiritur ad hoc quod offendenti remittatur offensa, quam ad hoc quod simpliciter aliquis non offendens non habeatur

OBJECTION 1: It would seem that for the remission of guilt, which is the justification of the ungodly, no infusion of grace is required. For anyone may be moved from one contrary without being led to the other, if the contraries are not immediate. Now the state of guilt and the state of grace are not immediate contraries; for there is the middle state of innocence wherein a man has neither grace nor guilt. Hence a man may be pardoned his guilt without his being brought to a state of grace.

OBJ. 2: Further, the remission of guilt consists in the Divine imputation, according to Ps. 31:2: *Blessed is the man to whom the Lord hath not imputed sin*. Now the infusion of grace puts something into our soul, as stated above (Q110, A1). Hence the infusion of grace is not required for the remission of guilt.

OBJ. 3: Further, no one can be subject to two contraries at once. Now some sins are contraries, as wastefulness and miserliness. Hence whoever is subject to the sin of wastefulness is not simultaneously subject to the sin of miserliness, yet it may happen that he has been subject to it hitherto. Hence by sinning with the vice of wastefulness he is freed from the sin of miserliness. And thus a sin is remitted without grace.

ON THE CONTRARY, It is written (Rom 3:24): *Justified freely by His grace*.

I ANSWER THAT, by sinning a man offends God as stated above (Q71, A5). Now an offense is remitted to anyone, only when the soul of the offender is at peace with the offended. Hence sin is remitted to us, when God is at peace with us, and this peace consists in the love whereby God loves us. Now God's love, considered on the part of the Divine act, is eternal and unchangeable; whereas, as regards the effect it imprints on us, it is sometimes interrupted, inasmuch as we sometimes fall short of it and once more require it. Now the effect of the Divine love in us, which is taken away by sin, is grace, whereby a man is made worthy of eternal life, from which sin shuts him out. Hence we could not conceive the remission of guilt, without the infusion of grace.

REPLY OBJ. 1: More is required for an offender to pardon an offense, than for one who has committed no offense, not to be hated. For it may happen amongst men that

odio. Potest enim apud homines contingere quod unus homo aliquem alium nec diligat nec odiat; sed si eum offendat, quod ei dimittat offensam, hoc non potest contingere absque speciali benevolentia. Benevolentia autem Dei ad hominem reparari dicitur per donum gratiae. Et ideo licet, antequam homo peccet, potuerit esse sine gratia et sine culpa; tamen post peccatum, non potest esse sine culpa nisi gratiam habeat.

AD SECUNDUM dicendum quod, sicut dilectio Dei non solum consistit in actu voluntatis divinae, sed etiam importat quendam gratiae effectum, ut supra dictum est; ita etiam et hoc quod est Deum non imputare peccatum homini, importat quendam effectum in ipso cuius peccatum non imputatur. Quod enim alicui non imputetur peccatum a Deo, ex divina dilectione procedit.

AD TERTIUM dicendum quod, sicut Augustinus dicit, in libro de nuptiis et Concup., *si a peccato desistere, hoc esset non habere peccatum, sufficeret ut hoc moneret Scriptura, fili, peccasti, non adiicias iterum. Non autem sufficit, sed additur, et de pristinis deprecare, ut tibi remittantur.* Transit enim peccatum actu, et remanet reatu, ut supra dictum est. Et ideo cum aliquis a peccato unius vitii transit in peccatum contrarii vitii, desinit quidem habere actum praeteriti, sed non desinit habere reatum, unde simul habet reatum utriusque peccati. Non enim peccata sunt sibi contraria ex parte aversionis a Deo, ex qua parte peccatum reatum habet.

one man neither hates nor loves another. But if the other offends him, then the forgiveness of the offense can only spring from a special goodwill. Now God's goodwill is said to be restored to man by the gift of grace; and hence although a man before sinning may be without grace and without guilt, yet that he is without guilt after sinning can only be because he has grace.

REPLY OBJ. 2: As God's love consists not merely in the act of the Divine will but also implies a certain effect of grace, as stated above (Q110, A1), so likewise, when God does not impute sin to a man, there is implied a certain effect in him to whom the sin is not imputed; for it proceeds from the Divine love, that sin is not imputed to a man by God.

REPLY OBJ. 3: As Augustine says (*De Nup. et Concup.* i, 26), if to leave off sinning was the same as to have no sin, it would be enough if Scripture warned us thus: '*My son, hast thou sinned? do so no more?*' Now this is not enough, but it is added: '*But for thy former sins also pray that they may be forgiven thee.*' For the act of sin passes, but the guilt remains, as stated above (Q87, A6). Hence when anyone passes from the sin of one vice to the sin of a contrary vice, he ceases to have the act of the former sin, but he does not cease to have the guilt, hence he may have the guilt of both sins at once. For sins are not contrary to each other on the part of their turning from God, wherein sin has its guilt.

Article 3

Whether for the Justification of the Ungodly Is Required a Movement of the Free-Will?

AD TERTIUM SIC PROCEDITUR. Videtur quod ad iustificationem impii non requiratur motus liberi arbitrii. Videmus enim quod per sacramentum Baptismi iustificantur pueri absque motu liberi arbitrii, et etiam interdum adulti, dicit enim Augustinus, in IV Confess., quod cum quidam suus amicus laboraret febribus, *iacuit diu sine sensu in sudore letali; et dum desperaretur, baptizatus est nesciens, et recreatus est*; quod fit per gratiam iustificantem. Sed Deus potentiam suam non alligavit sacramentis. Ergo etiam potest iustificare hominem sine sacramentis absque omni motu liberi arbitrii.

PRAETEREA, in dormiendo homo non habet usum rationis, sine quo non potest esse motus liberi arbitrii. Sed Salomon in dormiendo consecutus est a Deo donum sapientiae; ut habetur III Reg. III, et II Paral. I. Ergo etiam, pari ratione, donum gratiae iustificantis quandoque datur homini a Deo absque motu liberi arbitrii.

OBJECTION 1: It would seem that no movement of the free-will is required for the justification of the ungodly. For we see that by the sacrament of Baptism, infants and sometimes adults are justified without a movement of their free-will: hence Augustine says (*Confess.* iv) that when one of his friends was taken with a fever, *he lay for a long time senseless and in a deadly sweat, and when he was despaired of, he was baptized without his knowing, and was regenerated*; which is effected by sanctifying grace. Now God does not confine His power to the sacraments. Hence He can justify a man without the sacraments, and without any movement of the free-will.

OBJ. 2: Further, a man has not the use of reason when asleep, and without it there can be no movement of the free-will. But Solomon received from God the gift of wisdom when asleep, as related in 3 Kgs. 3 and 2 Paral 1. Hence with equal reason the gift of sanctifying grace is sometimes bestowed by God on man without the movement of his free-will.

PRAETEREA, per eandem causam gratia producitur in esse et conservatur, dicit enim Augustinus, VIII super Gen. ad Litt., quod *ita se debet homo ad Deum convertere, ut ab illo semper fiat iustus.* Sed absque motu liberi arbitrii gratia in homine conservatur. Ergo absque motu liberi arbitrii potest a principio infundi.

SED CONTRA est quod dicitur Ioan. VI, *omnis qui audit a patre et didicit, venit ad me.* Sed discere non est sine motu liberi arbitrii, addiscens enim consentit docenti. Ergo nullus venit ad Deum per gratiam iustificantem absque motu liberi arbitrii.

RESPONDEO dicendum quod iustificatio impii fit Deo movente hominem ad iustitiam, ipse enim est qui iustificat impium, ut dicitur Rom. IV. Deus autem movet omnia secundum modum uniuscuiusque, sicut in naturalibus videmus quod aliter moventur ab ipso gravia et aliter levia, propter diversam naturam utriusque. Unde et homines ad iustitiam movet secundum conditionem naturae humanae. Homo autem secundum propriam naturam habet quod sit liberi arbitrii. Et ideo in eo qui habet usum liberi arbitrii, non fit motio a Deo ad iustitiam absque motu liberi arbitrii; sed ita infundit donum gratiae iustificantis, quod etiam simul cum hoc movet liberum arbitrium ad donum gratiae acceptandum, in his qui sunt huius motionis capaces.

AD PRIMUM ergo dicendum quod pueri non sunt capaces motus liberi arbitrii, et ideo moventur a Deo ad iustitiam per solam informationem animae ipsorum. Non autem hoc fit sine sacramento, quia sicut peccatum originale, a quo iustificantur, non propria voluntate ad eos pervenit, sed per carnalem originem; ita etiam per spiritualem regenerationem a Christo in eos gratia derivatur. Et eadem ratio est de furiosis et amentibus qui nunquam usum liberi arbitrii habuerunt. Sed si quis aliquando habuerit usum liberi arbitrii, et postmodum eo careat vel per infirmitatem vel per somnum; non consequitur gratiam iustificantem per Baptismum exterius adhibitum, aut per aliquod aliud sacramentum, nisi prius habuerit sacramentum in proposito; quod sine usu liberi arbitrii non contingit. Et hoc modo ille de quo loquitur Augustinus, recreatus fuit, quia et prius et postea Baptismum acceptavit.

AD SECUNDUM dicendum quod etiam Salomon dormiendo non meruit sapientiam, nec accepit. Sed in somno declaratum est ei quod, propter praecedens desiderium, ei a Deo sapientia infunderetur, unde ex eius persona dicitur, Sap. VII, optavi, et datus est mihi sensus.

Vel potest dici quod ille somnus non fuit naturalis, sed somnus prophetiae; secundum quod dicitur Num. XII, *si quis fuerit inter vos propheta domini, per somnium aut in visione loquar ad eum.* In quo casu aliquis usum liberi arbitrii habet.

OBJ. 3: Further, grace is preserved by the same cause as brings it into being, for Augustine says (*Gen ad lit.* viii, 12) that *so ought man to turn to God as he is ever made just by Him.* Now grace is preserved in man without a movement of his free-will. Hence it can be infused in the beginning without a movement of the free-will.

ON THE CONTRARY, It is written (John 6:45): *Every one that hath heard of the Father, and hath learned, cometh to Me.* Now to learn cannot be without a movement of the free-will, since the learner assents to the teacher. Hence, no one comes to the Father by justifying grace without a movement of the free-will.

I ANSWER THAT, The justification of the ungodly is brought about by God moving man to justice. For He it is *that justifieth the ungodly* according to Rm. 4:5. Now God moves everything in its own manner, just as we see that in natural things, what is heavy and what is light are moved differently, on account of their diverse natures. Hence He moves man to justice according to the condition of his human nature. But it is man's proper nature to have free-will. Hence in him who has the use of reason, God's motion to justice does not take place without a movement of the free-will; but He so infuses the gift of justifying grace that at the same time He moves the free-will to accept the gift of grace, in such as are capable of being moved thus.

REPLY OBJ. 1: Infants are not capable of the movement of their free-will; hence it is by the mere infusion of their souls that God moves them to justice. Now this cannot be brought about without a sacrament; because as original sin, from which they are justified, does not come to them from their own will, but by carnal generation, so also is grace given them by Christ through spiritual regeneration. And the same reason holds good with madmen and idiots that have never had the use of their free-will. But in the case of one who has had the use of his free-will and afterwards has lost it either through sickness or sleep, he does not obtain justifying grace by the exterior rite of Baptism, or of any other sacrament, unless he intended to make use of this sacrament, and this can only be by the use of his free-will. And it was in this way that he of whom Augustine speaks was regenerated, because both previously and afterwards he assented to the Baptism.

REPLY OBJ. 2: Solomon neither merited nor received wisdom whilst asleep; but it was declared to him in his sleep that on account of his previous desire wisdom would be infused into him by God. Hence it is said in his person (Wis 7:7): *I wished, and understanding was given unto me.*

Or it may be said that his sleep was not natural, but was the sleep of prophecy, according to Num. 12:6: *If there be among you a prophet of the Lord, I will appear to him in a vision, or I will speak to him in a dream.* In such cases the use of free-will remains.

Et tamen sciendum est quod non est eadem ratio de dono sapientiae et de dono gratiae iustificantis. Nam donum gratiae iustificantis praecipue ordinat hominem ad bonum, quod est obiectum voluntatis, et ideo ad ipsum movetur homo per motum voluntatis, qui est motus liberi arbitrii. Sed sapientia perficit intellectum, qui praecedit voluntatem, unde absque completo motu liberi arbitrii, potest intellectus dono sapientiae illuminari. Sicut etiam videmus quod in dormiendo aliqua hominibus revelantur, sicut dicitur Iob XXXIII, *quando irruit sopor super homines et dormiunt in lectulo, tunc aperit aures virorum, et erudiens eos instruit disciplina.*

AD TERTIUM dicendum quod in infusione gratiae iustificantis est quaedam transmutatio animae, et ideo requiritur motus proprius animae humanae, ut anima moveatur secundum modum suum. Sed conservatio gratiae est absque transmutatione, unde non requiritur aliquis motus ex parte animae, sed sola continuatio influxus divini.

And yet it must be observed that the comparison between the gift of wisdom and the gift of justifying grace does not hold. For the gift of justifying grace especially ordains a man to good, which is the object of the will; and hence a man is moved to it by a movement of the will which is a movement of free-will. But wisdom perfects the intellect which precedes the will; hence without any complete movement of the free-will, the intellect can be enlightened with the gift of wisdom, even as we see that things are revealed to men in sleep, according to Job 33:15,16: *When deep sleep falleth upon men and they are sleeping in their beds, then He openeth the ears of men, and teaching, instructeth them in what they are to learn.*

REPLY OBJ. 3: In the infusion of justifying grace there is a certain transmutation of the human soul, and hence a proper movement of the human soul is required in order that the soul may be moved in its own manner. But the conservation of grace is without transmutation: no movement on the part of the soul is required but only a continuation of the Divine influx.

Article 4

Whether a Movement of Faith Is Required for the Justification of the Ungodly?

AD QUARTUM SIC PROCEDITUR. Videtur quod ad iustificationem impii non requiratur motus fidei. Sicut enim per fidem iustificatur homo, ita etiam et per quaedam alia. Scilicet per timorem; de quo dicitur Eccli. I, *timor domini expellit peccatum, nam qui sine timore est, non poterit iustificari.* Et iterum per caritatem; secundum illud Luc. VII, *dimissa sunt ei peccata multa, quoniam dilexit multum.* Et iterum per humilitatem; secundum illud Iac. IV, *Deus superbis resistit, humilibus autem dat gratiam.* Et iterum per misericordiam; secundum illud Prov. XV, *per misericordiam et fidem purgantur peccata.* Non ergo magis motus fidei requiritur ad iustificationem quam motus praedictarum virtutum.

PRAETEREA, actus fidei non requiritur ad iustificationem nisi inquantum per fidem homo cognoscit Deum. Sed etiam aliis modis potest homo Deum cognoscere, scilicet per cognitionem naturalem, et per donum sapientiae. Ergo non requiritur actus fidei ad iustificationem impii.

PRAETEREA, diversi sunt articuli fidei. Si igitur actus fidei requiratur ad iustificationem impii, videtur quod oporteret hominem, quando primo iustificatur, de omnibus articulis fidei cogitare. Sed hoc videtur inconveniens, cum talis cogitatio longam temporis moram requirat. Ergo videtur quod actus fidei non requiratur ad iustificationem.

OBJECTION 1: It would seem that no movement of faith is required for the justification of the ungodly. For as a man is justified by faith, so also by other things, viz., by fear, of which it is written (Sir 1:27): *The fear of the Lord driveth out sin, for he that is without fear cannot be justified*; and again by charity, according to Lk. 7:47: *Many sins are forgiven her because she hath loved much*; and again by humility, according to James 4:6: *God resisteth the proud and giveth grace to the humble*; and again by mercy, according to Prov. 15:27: *By mercy and faith sins are purged away*. Hence the movement of faith is no more required for the justification of the ungodly, than the movements of the aforesaid virtues.

OBJ. 2: Further, the act of faith is required for justification only inasmuch as a man knows God by faith. But a man may know God in other ways, viz., by natural knowledge, and by the gift of wisdom. Hence no act of faith is required for the justification of the ungodly.

OBJ. 3: Further, there are several articles of faith. Therefore if the act of faith is required for the justification of the ungodly, it would seem that a man ought to think on every article of faith when he is first justified. But this seems inconvenient, since such thought would require a long delay of time. Hence it seems that an act of faith is not required for the justification of the ungodly.

SED CONTRA est quod dicitur Rom. V, *iustificati igitur ex fide, pacem habeamus ad Deum.*

RESPONDEO dicendum quod, sicut dictum est, motus liberi arbitrii requiritur ad iustificationem impii, secundum quod mens hominis movetur a Deo. Deus autem movet animam hominis convertendo eam ad seipsum; ut dicitur in Psalmo LXXXIV, secundum aliam litteram, *Deus, tu convertens vivificabis nos.* Et ideo ad iustificationem impii requiritur motus mentis quo convertitur in Deum. Prima autem conversio in Deum fit per fidem; secundum illud ad Heb. XI, *accedentem ad Deum oportet credere quia est.* Et ideo motus fidei requiritur ad iustificationem impii.

AD PRIMUM ergo dicendum quod motus fidei non est perfectus nisi sit caritate informatus, unde simul in iustificatione impii cum motu fidei, est etiam motus caritatis. Movetur autem liberum arbitrium in Deum ad hoc quod ei se subiiciat, unde etiam concurrit actus timoris filialis, et actus humilitatis. Contingit enim unum et eundem actum liberi arbitrii diversarum virtutum esse, secundum quod una imperat et alia imperatur, prout scilicet actus est ordinabilis ad diversos fines. Actus autem misericordiae operatur contra peccatum per modum satisfactionis, et sic sequitur iustificationem, vel per modum praeparationis, inquantum misericordes misericordiam consequuntur, et sic etiam potest praecedere iustificationem; vel etiam ad iustificationem concurrere simul cum praedictis virtutibus, secundum quod misericordia includitur in dilectione proximi.

AD SECUNDUM dicendum quod per cognitionem naturalem homo non convertitur in Deum inquantum est obiectum beatitudinis et iustificationis causa, unde talis cognitio non sufficit ad iustificationem. Donum autem sapientiae praesupponit cognitionem fidei, ut ex supradictis patet.

AD TERTIUM dicendum quod, sicut apostolus dicit, ad Rom. IV, *credenti in eum qui iustificat impium, reputabitur fides eius ad iustitiam, secundum propositum gratiae Dei.* Ex quo patet quod in iustificatione impii requiritur actus fidei quantum ad hoc, quod homo credat Deum esse iustificatorem hominum per mysterium Christi.

ON THE CONTRARY, It is written (Rom 5:1): *Being justified therefore by faith, let us have peace with God.*

I ANSWER THAT, As stated above (A3) a movement of free-will is required for the justification of the ungodly, inasmuch as man's mind is moved by God. Now God moves man's soul by turning it to Himself according to Ps. 84:7 (Septuagint): *Thou wilt turn us, O God, and bring us to life.* Hence for the justification of the ungodly a movement of the mind is required, by which it is turned to God. Now the first turning to God is by faith, according to Heb. 11:6: *He that cometh to God must believe that He is.* Hence a movement of faith is required for the justification of the ungodly.

REPLY OBJ. 1: The movement of faith is not perfect unless it is quickened by charity; hence in the justification of the ungodly, a movement of charity is infused together with the movement of faith. Now free-will is moved to God by being subject to Him; hence an act of filial fear and an act of humility also concur. For it may happen that one and the same act of free-will springs from different virtues, when one commands and another is commanded, inasmuch as the act may be ordained to various ends. But the act of mercy counteracts sin either by way of satisfying for it, and thus it follows justification; or by way of preparation, inasmuch as the merciful obtain mercy; and thus it can either precede justification, or concur with the other virtues towards justification, inasmuch as mercy is included in the love of our neighbor.

REPLY OBJ. 2: By natural knowledge a man is not turned to God, according as He is the object of beatitude and the cause of justification. Hence such knowledge does not suffice for justification. But the gift of wisdom presupposes the knowledge of faith, as stated above (Q68, A4, ad 3).

REPLY OBJ. 3: As the Apostle says (Rom 4:5), *to him that . . . believeth in Him that justifieth the ungodly his faith is reputed to justice, according to the purpose of the grace of God.* Hence it is clear that in the justification of the ungodly an act of faith is required in order that a man may believe that God justifies man through the mystery of Christ.

Article 5

Whether for the Justification of the Ungodly There Is Required a Movement of the Free-Will Towards Sin?

AD QUINTUM SIC PROCEDITUR. Videtur quod ad iustificationem impii non requiratur motus liberi arbitrii in peccatum. Sola enim caritas sufficit ad deletionem peccati, secundum illud Prov. X, *universa delicta operit caritas.* Sed caritatis obiectum non est peccatum. Ergo

OBJECTION 1: It would seem that no movement of the free-will towards sin is required for the justification of the ungodly. For charity alone suffices to take away sin, according to Prov. 10:12: *Charity covereth all sins.* Now the object of charity is not sin. Therefore for this justification of

non requiritur ad iustificationem impii motus liberi arbitrii in peccatum.

PRAETEREA, qui in anteriora tendit, ad posteriora respicere non debet; secundum illud apostoli, ad Philipp. III, *quae quidem retro sunt obliviscens, ad ea vero quae sunt priora extendens meipsum, ad destinatum persequor bravium supernae vocationis.* Sed tendenti in iustitiam retrorsum sunt peccata praeterita. Ergo eorum debet oblivisci, nec in ea se debet extendere per motum liberi arbitrii.

PRAETEREA, in iustificatione impii non remittitur unum peccatum sine alio, impium enim est a Deo dimidiam sperare veniam. Si igitur in iustificatione impii oporteat liberum arbitrium moveri contra peccatum, oporteret quod de omnibus peccatis suis cogitaret. Quod videtur inconveniens, tum quia requireretur magnum tempus ad huiusmodi cogitationem; tum etiam quia peccatorum quorum est homo oblitus, veniam habere non posset. Ergo motus liberi arbitrii in peccatum non requiritur ad iustificationem impii.

SED CONTRA est quod dicitur in Psalmo XXXI, *dixi, confitebor adversum me iniustitiam meam domino, et tu remisisti impietatem peccati mei.*

RESPONDEO dicendum quod, sicut supra dictum est, iustificatio impii est quidam motus quo humana mens movetur a Deo a statu peccati in statum iustitiae. Oportet igitur quod humana mens se habeat ad utrumque extremorum secundum motum liberi arbitrii, sicut se habet corpus localiter motum ab aliquo movente ad duos terminos motus. Manifestum est autem in motu locali corporum quod corpus motum recedit a termino a quo, et accedit ad terminum ad quem. Unde oportet quod mens humana, dum iustificatur, per motum liberi arbitrii recedat a peccato, et accedat ad iustitiam.

Recessus autem et accessus in motu liberi arbitrii accipitur secundum detestationem et desiderium, dicit enim Augustinus, super Ioan. exponens illud, *mercenarius autem fugit, affectiones nostrae motus animorum sunt, laetitia animi diffusio, timor animi fuga est; progrederis animo cum appetis, fugis animo cum metuis.* Oportet igitur quod in iustificatione impii sit motus liberi arbitrii duplex, unus quo per desiderium tendat in Dei iustitiam; et alius quo detestetur peccatum.

AD PRIMUM ergo dicendum quod ad eandem virtutem pertinet prosequi unum oppositorum, et refugere aliud. Et ideo sicut ad caritatem pertinet diligere Deum, ita etiam detestari peccata, per quae anima separatur a Deo.

AD SECUNDUM dicendum quod ad posteriora non debet homo regredi per amorem; sed quantum ad hoc debet ea oblivisci, ut ad ea non afficiatur. Debet tamen eorum recordari per considerationem ut ea detestetur, sic enim ab eis recedit.

the ungodly no movement of the free-will towards sin is required.

OBJ. 2: Further, whoever is tending onward, ought not to look back, according to Phil. 3:13, 14: *Forgetting the things that are behind, and stretching forth myself to those that are before, I press towards the mark, to the prize of the supernal vocation.* But whoever is stretching forth to righteousness has his sins behind him. Hence he ought to forget them, and not stretch forth to them by a movement of his free-will.

OBJ. 3: Further, in the justification of the ungodly one sin is not remitted without another, for *it is irreverent to expect half a pardon from God.* Hence, in the justification of the ungodly, if man's free-will must move against sin, he ought to think of all his sins. But this is unseemly, both because a great space of time would be required for such thought, and because a man could not obtain the forgiveness of such sins as he had forgotten. Hence for the justification of the ungodly no movement of the free-will is required.

ON THE CONTRARY, It is written (Ps 31:5): *I will confess against myself my injustice to the Lord; and Thou hast forgiven the wickedness of my sin.*

I ANSWER THAT, As stated above (A1), the justification of the ungodly is a certain movement whereby the human mind is moved by God from the state of sin to the state of justice. Hence it is necessary for the human mind to regard both extremes by an act of free-will, as a body in local movement is related to both terms of the movement. Now it is clear that in local movement the moving body leaves the term whence and nears the term whereto. Hence the human mind whilst it is being justified, must, by a movement of its free-will withdraw from sin and draw near to justice.

Now to withdraw from sin and to draw near to justice, in an act of free-will, means detestation and desire. For Augustine says on the words *the hireling fleeth*, etc. (John 10:12): *Our emotions are the movements of our soul; joy is the soul's outpouring; fear is the soul's flight; your soul goes forward when you seek; your soul flees, when you are afraid.* Hence in the justification of the ungodly there must be two acts of the free-will—one, whereby it tends to God's justice; the other whereby it hates sin.

REPLY OBJ. 1: It belongs to the same virtue to seek one contrary and to avoid the other; and hence, as it belongs to charity to love God, so likewise, to detest sin whereby the soul is separated from God.

REPLY OBJ. 2: A man ought not to return to those things that are behind, by loving them; but, for that matter, he ought to forget them, lest he be drawn to them. Yet he ought to recall them to mind, in order to detest them; for this is to fly from them.

AD TERTIUM dicendum quod in tempore praecedente iustificationem, oportet quod homo singula peccata quae commisit detestetur, quorum memoriam habet. Et ex tali consideratione praecedenti subsequitur in anima quidam motus detestantis universaliter omnia peccata commissa, inter quae etiam includuntur peccata oblivioni tradita, quia homo in statu illo est sic dispositus ut etiam de his quae non meminit, contereretur, si memoriae adessent. Et iste motus concurrit ad iustificationem.

REPLY OBJ. 3: Previous to justification a man must detest each sin he remembers to have committed, and from this remembrance the soul goes on to have a general movement of detestation with regard to all sins committed, in which are included such sins as have been forgotten. For a man is then in such a frame of mind that he would be sorry even for those he does not remember, if they were present to his memory; and this movement cooperates in his justification.

Article 6

Whether the Remission of Sins Ought to Be Reckoned Amongst the Things Required for Justification?

AD SEXTUM SIC PROCEDITUR. Videtur quod remissio peccatorum non debeat numerari inter ea quae requiruntur ad iustificationem impii. Substantia enim rei non connumeratur his quae ad rem requiruntur, sicut homo non debet connumerari animae et corpori. Sed ipsa iustificatio impii est remissio peccatorum, ut dictum est. Ergo remissio peccatorum non debet computari inter ea quae ad iustificationem impii requiruntur.

PRAETEREA, idem est gratiae infusio et culpae remissio, sicut idem est illuminatio et tenebrarum expulsio. Sed idem non debet connumerari sibi ipsi, unum enim multitudini opponitur. Ergo non debet culpae remissio connumerari infusioni gratiae.

PRAETEREA, remissio peccatorum consequitur ad motum liberi arbitrii in Deum et in peccatum, sicut effectus ad causam, per fidem enim et contritionem remittuntur peccata. Sed effectus non debet connumerari suae causae, quia ea quae connumerantur quasi ad invicem condivisa, sunt simul natura. Ergo remissio culpae non debet connumerari aliis quae requiruntur ad iustificationem impii.

SED CONTRA est quod in enumeratione eorum quae requiruntur ad rem, non debet praetermitti finis, qui est potissimum in unoquoque. Sed remissio peccatorum est finis in iustificatione impii, dicitur enim Isaiae XXVII, *iste est omnis fructus, ut auferatur peccatum eius*. Ergo remissio peccatorum debet connumerari inter ea quae requiruntur ad iustificationem impii.

RESPONDEO dicendum quod quatuor enumerantur quae requiruntur ad iustificationem impii, scilicet gratiae infusio; motus liberi arbitrii in Deum per fidem; et motus liberi arbitrii in peccatum; et remissio culpae. Cuius ratio est quia, sicut dictum est, iustificatio est quidam motus quo anima movetur a Deo a statu culpae in statum iustitiae. In quolibet autem motu quo aliquid ab altero movetur, tria requiruntur, primo quidem, motio

OBJECTION 1: It would seem that the remission of sins ought not to be reckoned amongst the things required for justification. For the substance of a thing is not reckoned together with those that are required for a thing; thus a man is not reckoned together with his body and soul. But the justification of the ungodly is itself the remission of sins, as stated above (A1). Therefore the remission of sins ought not to be reckoned among the things required for the justification of the ungodly.

OBJ. 2: Further, infusion of grace and remission of sins are the same; as illumination and expulsion of darkness are the same. But a thing ought not to be reckoned together with itself; for unity is opposed to multitude. Therefore the remission of sins ought not to be reckoned with the infusion of grace.

OBJ. 3: Further, the remission of sin follows as effect from cause, from the free-will's movement towards God and sin; since it is by faith and contrition that sin is forgiven. But an effect ought not to be reckoned with its cause; since things thus enumerated together, and, as it were, condivided, are by nature simultaneous. Hence the remission of sins ought not to be reckoned with the things required for the justification of the ungodly.

ON THE CONTRARY, In reckoning what is required for a thing we ought not to pass over the end, which is the chief part of everything. Now the remission of sins is the end of the justification of the ungodly; for it is written (Isa 27:9): *This is all the fruit, that the sin thereof should be taken away.* Hence the remission of sins ought to be reckoned amongst the things required for justification.

I ANSWER THAT, There are four things which are accounted to be necessary for the justification of the ungodly, viz., the infusion of grace, the movement of the free-will towards God by faith, the movement of the free-will towards sin, and the remission of sins. The reason for this is that, as stated above (A1), the justification of the ungodly is a movement whereby the soul is moved by God from a state of sin to a state of justice. Now in the movement whereby

ipsius moventis; secundo, motus mobilis; et tertio, consummatio motus, sive perventio ad finem. Ex parte igitur motionis divinae, accipitur gratiae infusio; ex parte vero liberi arbitrii moti, accipiuntur duo motus ipsius, secundum recessum a termino a quo, et accessum ad terminum ad quem; consummatio autem, sive perventio ad terminum huius motus, importatur per remissionem culpae, in hoc enim iustificatio consummatur.

AD PRIMUM ergo dicendum quod iustificatio impii dicitur esse ipsa remissio peccatorum, secundum quod omnis motus accipit speciem a termino. Et tamen ad terminum consequendum multa alia requiruntur, ut ex supradictis patet.

AD SECUNDUM dicendum quod gratiae infusio et remissio culpae dupliciter considerari possunt. Uno modo, secundum ipsam substantiam actus. Et sic idem sunt, eodem enim actu Deus et largitur gratiam et remittit culpam. Alio modo possunt considerari ex parte obiectorum. Et sic differunt, secundum differentiam culpae quae tollitur, et gratiae quae infunditur. Sicut etiam in rebus naturalibus generatio et corruptio differunt, quamvis generatio unius sit corruptio alterius.

AD TERTIUM dicendum quod ista non est connumeratio secundum divisionem generis in species, in qua oportet quod connumerata sint simul, sed secundum differentiam eorum quae requiruntur ad completionem alicuius. In qua quidem enumeratione aliquid potest esse prius, et aliquid posterius, quia principiorum et partium rei compositae potest esse aliquid alio prius.

one thing is moved by another, three things are required: first, the motion of the mover; second, the movement of the moved; third, the consummation of the movement, or the attainment of the end. On the part of the Divine motion, there is the infusion of grace; on the part of the free-will which is moved, there are two movements—of departure from the term whence, and of approach to the term whereto; but the consummation of the movement or the attainment of the end of the movement is implied in the remission of sins; for in this is the justification of the ungodly completed.

REPLY OBJ. 1: The justification of the ungodly is called the remission of sins, even as every movement has its species from its term. Nevertheless, many other things are required in order to reach the term, as stated above (A5).

REPLY OBJ. 2: The infusion of grace and the remission of sin may be considered in two ways: first, with respect to the substance of the act, and thus they are the same; for by the same act God bestows grace and remits sin. Second, they may be considered on the part of the objects; and thus they differ by the difference between guilt, which is taken away, and grace, which is infused; just as in natural things generation and corruption differ, although the generation of one thing is the corruption of another.

REPLY OBJ. 3: This enumeration is not the division of a genus into its species, in which the things enumerated must be simultaneous; but it is division of the things required for the completion of anything; and in this enumeration we may have what precedes and what follows, since some of the principles and parts of a composite thing may precede and some follow.

Article 7

Whether the Justification of the Ungodly Takes Place in an Instant or Successively?

AD SEPTIMUM SIC PROCEDITUR. Videtur quod iustificatio impii non fiat in instanti, sed successive. Quia ut dictum est, ad iustificationem impii requiritur motus liberi arbitrii. Actus autem liberi arbitrii est eligere, qui praeexigit deliberationem consilii, ut supra habitum est. Cum igitur deliberatio discursum quendam importet, qui successionem quandam habet, videtur quod iustificatio impii sit successiva.

PRAETEREA, motus liberi arbitrii non est absque actuali consideratione. Sed impossibile est simul multa intelligere in actu, ut in primo dictum est. Cum igitur ad iustificationem impii requiratur motus liberi arbitrii in

OBJECTION 1: It would seem that the justification of the ungodly does not take place in an instant, but successively, since, as already stated (A3), for the justification of the ungodly, there is required a movement of free-will. Now the act of the free-will is choice, which requires the deliberation of counsel, as stated above (Q13, A1). Hence, since deliberation implies a certain reasoning process, and this implies succession, the justification of the ungodly would seem to be successive.

OBJ. 2: Further, the free-will's movement is not without actual consideration. But it is impossible to understand many things actually and at once, as stated above (I, Q85, A4). Hence, since for the justification of the

diversa, scilicet in Deum et in peccatum, videtur quod iustificatio impii non possit esse in instanti.

PRAETEREA, forma quae suscipit magis et minus, successive recipitur in subiecto, sicut patet de albedine et nigredine. Sed gratia suscipit magis et minus, ut supra dictum est. Ergo non recipitur subito in subiecto. Cum igitur ad iustificationem impii requiratur gratiae infusio, videtur quod iustificatio impii non possit esse in instanti.

PRAETEREA, motus liberi arbitrii qui ad iustificationem impii concurrit, est meritorius, et ita oportet quod procedat a gratia, sine qua nullum est meritum, ut infra dicetur. Sed prius est aliquid consequi formam, quam secundum formam operari. Ergo prius infunditur gratia, et postea liberum arbitrium movetur in Deum et in detestationem peccati. Non ergo iustificatio est tota simul.

PRAETEREA, si gratia infundatur animae, oportet dare aliquod instans in quo primo animae insit. Similiter si culpa remittitur, oportet ultimum instans dare in quo homo culpae subiaceat. Sed non potest esse idem instans, quia sic opposita simul inessent eidem. Ergo oportet esse duo instantia sibi succedentia, inter quae, secundum philosophum, in VI Physic., oportet esse tempus medium. Non ergo iustificatio fit tota simul, sed successive.

SED CONTRA est quod iustificatio impii fit per gratiam spiritus sancti iustificantis. Sed Spiritus Sanctus subito advenit mentibus hominum; secundum illud Act. II, *factus est repente de caelo sonus tanquam advenientis spiritus vehementis*; ubi dicit Glossa quod *nescit tarda molimina spiritus sancti gratia*. Ergo iustificatio impii non est successiva, sed instantanea.

RESPONDEO dicendum quod tota iustificatio impii originaliter consistit in gratiae infusione, per eam enim et liberum arbitrium movetur, et culpa remittitur. Gratiae autem infusio fit in instanti absque successione. Cuius ratio est quia quod aliqua forma non subito imprimatur subiecto, contingit ex hoc quod subiectum non est dispositum, et agens indiget tempore ad hoc quod subiectum disponat. Et ideo videmus quod statim cum materia est disposita per alterationem praecedentem, forma substantialis acquiritur materiae, et eadem ratione, quia diaphanum est secundum se dispositum ad lumen recipiendum, subito illuminatur a corpore lucido in actu. Dictum est autem supra quod Deus ad hoc quod gratiam infundat animae, non requirit aliquam dispositionem nisi quam ipse facit. Facit autem huiusmodi dispositionem sufficientem ad susceptionem gratiae, quandoque quidem subito, quandoque autem paulatim et successive, ut supra dictum est. Quod enim agens naturale non subito possit disponere materiam, contingit ex hoc quod

ungodly there is required a movement of the free-will towards several things, viz., towards God and towards sin, it would seem impossible for the justification of the ungodly to be in an instant.

OBJ. 3: Further, a form that may be greater or less, e.g., blackness or whiteness, is received successively by its subject. Now grace may be greater or less, as stated above (Q112, A4). Hence it is not received suddenly by its subject. Therefore, seeing that the infusion of grace is required for the justification of the ungodly, it would seem that the justification of the ungodly cannot be in an instant.

OBJ. 4: Further, the free-will's movement, which co-operates in justification, is meritorious; and hence it must proceed from grace, without which there is no merit, as we shall state further on (Q114, A2). Now a thing receives its form before operating by this form. Hence grace is first infused, and then the free-will is moved towards God and to detest sin. Hence justification is not all at once.

OBJ. 5: Further, if grace is infused into the soul, there must be an instant when it first dwells in the soul; so, too, if sin is forgiven there must be a last instant that man is in sin. But it cannot be the same instant, otherwise opposites would be in the same simultaneously. Hence they must be two successive instants; between which there must be time, as the Philosopher says (*Phys.* vi, 1). Therefore the justification of the ungodly takes place not all at once, but successively.

ON THE CONTRARY, The justification of the ungodly is caused by the justifying grace of the Holy Spirit. Now the Holy Spirit comes to men's minds suddenly, according to Acts 2:2: *And suddenly there came a sound from heaven as of a mighty wind coming*, upon which the gloss says that *the grace of the Holy Spirit knows no tardy efforts*. Hence the justification of the ungodly is not successive, but instantaneous.

I ANSWER THAT, The entire justification of the ungodly consists as to its origin in the infusion of grace. For it is by grace that free-will is moved and sin is remitted. Now the infusion of grace takes place in an instant and without succession. And the reason of this is that if a form be not suddenly impressed upon its subject, it is either because that subject is not disposed, or because the agent needs time to dispose the subject. Hence we see that immediately the matter is disposed by a preceding alteration, the substantial form accrues to the matter; thus because the atmosphere of itself is disposed to receive light, it is suddenly illuminated by a body actually luminous. Now it was stated (Q112, A2) that God, in order to infuse grace into the soul, needs no disposition, save what He Himself has made. And sometimes this sufficient disposition for the reception of grace He makes suddenly, sometimes gradually and successively, as stated above (Q112, A2, ad 2). For the reason why a natural agent cannot suddenly dispose matter is that in the matter there is a resistant which has some disproportion with

est aliqua disproportio eius quod in materia resistit, ad virtutem agentis, et propter hoc videmus quod quanto virtus agentis fuerit fortior, tanto materia citius disponitur. Cum igitur virtus divina sit infinita, potest quamcumque materiam creatam subito disponere ad formam, et multo magis liberum arbitrium hominis, cuius motus potest esse instantaneus secundum naturam. Sic igitur iustificatio impii fit a Deo in instanti.

AD PRIMUM ergo dicendum quod motus liberi arbitrii qui concurrit ad iustificationem impii, est consensus ad detestandum peccatum et ad accedendum ad Deum, qui quidem consensus subito fit. Contingit autem quandoque quod praecedit aliqua deliberatio, quae non est de substantia iustificationis, sed via in iustificationem, sicut motus localis est via ad illuminationem, et alteratio ad generationem.

AD SECUNDUM dicendum quod, sicut in primo dictum est, nihil prohibet duo simul intelligere actu, secundum quod sunt quodammodo unum, sicut simul intelligimus subiectum et praedicatum, inquantum uniuntur in ordine affirmationis unius. Et per eundem modum liberum arbitrium potest in duo simul moveri, secundum quod unum ordinatur in aliud. Motus autem liberi arbitrii in peccatum, ordinatur ad motum liberi arbitrii in Deum, propter hoc enim homo detestatur peccatum, quia est contra Deum, cui vult adhaerere. Et ideo liberum arbitrium in iustificatione impii simul detestatur peccatum et convertit se ad Deum, sicut etiam corpus simul, recedendo ab uno loco, accedit ad alium.

AD TERTIUM dicendum quod non est ratio quare forma subito in materia non recipiatur, quia magis et minus inesse potest, sic enim lumen non subito reciperetur in aere, qui potest magis et minus illuminari. Sed ratio est accipienda ex parte dispositionis materiae vel subiecti, ut dictum est.

AD QUARTUM dicendum quod in eodem instanti in quo forma acquiritur, incipit res operari secundum formam, sicut ignis statim cum est generatus, movetur sursum; et si motus eius esset instantaneus, in eodem instanti compleretur. Motus autem liberi arbitrii, qui est velle, non est successivus, sed instantaneus. Et ideo non oportet quod iustificatio impii sit successiva.

AD QUINTUM dicendum quod successio duorum oppositorum in eodem subiecto aliter est consideranda in his quae subiacent tempori, et aliter in his quae sunt supra tempus. In his enim quae subiacent tempori, non est dare ultimum instans in quo forma prior subiecto inest, est autem dare ultimum tempus, et primum instans in quo forma sequens inest materiae vel subiecto. Cuius ratio est quia in tempore non potest accipi ante unum instans aliud instans praecedens immediate, eo quod instantia non consequenter se habeant in tempore, sicut nec puncta in linea, ut probatur in VI Physic. Sed tempus terminatur ad instans. Et ideo in toto tempore

the power of the agent; and hence we see that the stronger the agent, the more speedily is the matter disposed. Therefore, since the Divine power is infinite, it can suddenly dispose any matter whatsoever to its form; and much more man's free-will, whose movement is by nature instantaneous. Therefore the justification of the ungodly by God takes place in an instant.

REPLY OBJ. 1: The movement of the free-will, which concurs in the justification of the ungodly, is a consent to detest sin, and to draw near to God; and this consent takes place suddenly. Sometimes, indeed, it happens that deliberation precedes, yet this is not of the substance of justification, but a way of justification; as local movement is a way of illumination, and alteration to generation.

REPLY OBJ. 2: As stated above (I, Q85, A5), there is nothing to prevent two things being understood at once, insofar as they are somehow one; thus we understand the subject and predicate together, inasmuch as they are united in the order of one affirmation. And in the same manner can the free-will be moved to two things at once insofar as one is ordained to the other. Now the free-will's movement towards sin is ordained to the free-will's movement towards God, since a man detests sin, as contrary to God, to Whom he wishes to cling. Hence in the justification of the ungodly the free-will simultaneously detests sin and turns to God, even as a body approaches one point and withdraws from another simultaneously.

REPLY OBJ. 3: The reason why a form is not received instantaneously in the matter is not the fact that it can inhere more or less; for thus the light would not be suddenly received in the air, which can be illumined more or less. But the reason is to be sought on the part of the disposition of the matter or subject, as stated above.

REPLY OBJ. 4: The same instant the form is acquired, the thing begins to operate with the form; as fire, the instant it is generated moves upwards, and if its movement was instantaneous, it would be terminated in the same instant. Now to will and not to will—the movements of the free-will—are not successive, but instantaneous. Hence the justification of the ungodly must not be successive.

REPLY OBJ. 5: The succession of opposites in the same subject must be looked at differently in the things that are subject to time and in those that are above time. For in those that are in time, there is no last instant in which the previous form inheres in the subject; but there is the last time, and the first instant that the subsequent form inheres in the matter or subject; and this for the reason, that in time we are not to consider one instant, since neither do instants succeed each other immediately in time, nor points in a line, as is proved in *Physic.* vi, 1. But time is terminated by an instant. Hence in the whole of the previous time wherein anything is moving towards its form, it is under

praecedenti, quo aliquid movetur ad unam formam, subest formae oppositae, et in ultimo instanti illius temporis, quod est primum instans sequentis temporis, habet formam, quae est terminus motus.

Sed in his quae sunt supra tempus, aliter se habet. Si qua enim successio sit ibi affectuum vel intellectualium conceptionum, puta in Angelis, talis successio non mensuratur tempore continuo, sed tempore discreto, sicut et ipsa quae mensurantur non sunt continua, ut in primo habitum est. Unde in talibus est dandum ultimum instans in quo primum fuit, et primum instans in quo est id quod sequitur, nec oportet esse tempus medium, quia non est ibi continuitas temporis, quae hoc requirebat.

Mens autem humana quae iustificatur, secundum se quidem est supra tempus, sed per accidens subditur tempori, inquantum scilicet intelligit cum continuo et tempore secundum phantasmata, in quibus species intelligibiles considerat, ut in primo dictum est. Et ideo iudicandum est, secundum hoc, de eius mutatione secundum conditionem temporalium motuum, ut scilicet dicamus quod non est dare ultimum instans in quo culpa infuit, sed ultimum tempus; est autem dare primum instans in quo gratia inest, in toto autem tempore praecedenti inerat culpa.

the opposite form; but in the last instant of this time, which is the first instant of the subsequent time, it has the form which is the term of the movement.

But in those that are above time, it is otherwise. For if there be any succession of affections or intellectual conceptions in them (as in the angels), such succession is not measured by continuous time, but by discrete time, even as the things measured are not continuous, as stated above (I, Q53, AA2,3). In these, therefore, there is a last instant in which the preceding is, and a first instant in which the subsequent is. Nor must there be time in between, since there is no continuity of time, which this would necessitate.

Now the human mind, which is justified, is, in itself, above time, but is subject to time accidentally, inasmuch as it understands with continuity and time, with respect to the phantasms in which it considers the intelligible species, as stated above (I, Q85, AA1,2). We must, therefore, decide from this about its change as regards the condition of temporal movements, i.e., we must say that there is no last instant that sin inheres, but a last time; whereas there is a first instant that grace inheres; and in all the time previous sin inhered.

Article 8

Whether the Infusion of Grace Is Naturally the First of the Things Required for the Justification of the Ungodly?

AD OCTAVUM SIC PROCEDITUR. Videtur quod gratiae infusio non sit prima ordine naturae inter ea quae requiruntur ad iustificationem impii. Prius enim est recedere a malo quam accedere ad bonum; secundum illud Psalmi XXXVI, *declina a malo, et fac bonum.* Sed remissio culpae pertinet ad recessum a malo, infusio autem gratiae pertinet ad prosecutionem boni. Ergo naturaliter prius est remissio culpae quam infusio gratiae.

PRAETEREA, dispositio praecedit naturaliter formam ad quam disponit. Sed motus liberi arbitrii est quaedam dispositio ad susceptionem gratiae. Ergo naturaliter praecedit infusionem gratiae.

PRAETEREA, peccatum impedit animam ne libere tendat in Deum. Sed prius est removere id quod prohibet motum, quam motus sequatur. Ergo prius est naturaliter remissio culpae et motus liberi arbitrii in peccatum, quam motus liberi arbitrii in Deum, et quam infusio gratiae.

SED CONTRA, causa naturaliter est prior effectu. Sed gratiae infusio causa est omnium aliorum quae requiruntur ad iustificationem impii, ut supra dictum est. Ergo est naturaliter prior.

OBJECTION 1: It would seem that the infusion of grace is not what is naturally required first for the justification of the ungodly. For we withdraw from evil before drawing near to good, according to Ps. 33:15: *Turn away from evil, and do good.* Now the remission of sins regards the turning away from evil, and the infusion of grace regards the turning to good. Hence the remission of sin is naturally before the infusion of grace.

OBJ. 2: Further, the disposition naturally precedes the form to which it disposes. Now the free-will's movement is a disposition for the reception of grace. Therefore it naturally precedes the infusion of grace.

OBJ. 3: Further, sin hinders the soul from tending freely to God. Now a hindrance to movement must be removed before the movement takes place. Hence the remission of sin and the free-will's movement towards sin are naturally before the infusion of grace.

ON THE CONTRARY, The cause is naturally prior to its effect. Now the infusion of grace is the cause of whatever is required for the justification of the ungodly, as stated above (A7). Therefore it is naturally prior to it.

RESPONDEO dicendum quod praedicta quatuor quae requiruntur ad iustificationem impii, tempore quidem sunt simul, quia iustificatio impii non est successiva, ut dictum est, sed ordine naturae unum eorum est prius altero. Et inter ea naturali ordine primum est gratiae infusio; secundum, motus liberi arbitrii in Deum; tertium est motus liberi arbitrii in peccatum; quartum vero est remissio culpae.

Cuius ratio est quia in quolibet motu naturaliter primum est motio ipsius moventis; secundum autem est dispositio materiae, sive motus ipsius mobilis; ultimum vero est finis vel terminus motus, ad quem terminatur motio moventis. Ipsa igitur Dei moventis motio est gratiae infusio, ut dictum est supra; motus autem vel dispositio mobilis est duplex motus liberi arbitrii; terminus autem vel finis motus est remissio culpae, ut ex supradictis patet. Et ideo naturali ordine primum in iustificatione impii est gratiae infusio; secundum est motus liberi arbitrii in Deum; tertium vero est motus liberi arbitrii in peccatum (propter hoc enim ille qui iustificatur, detestatur peccatum, quia est contra Deum, unde motus liberi arbitrii in Deum, praecedit naturaliter motum liberi arbitrii in peccatum, cum sit causa et ratio eius); quartum vero et ultimum est remissio culpae, ad quam tota ista transmutatio ordinatur sicut ad finem, ut dictum est.

AD PRIMUM ergo dicendum quod recessus a termino et accessus ad terminum dupliciter considerari possunt. Uno modo, ex parte mobilis. Et sic naturaliter recessus a termino praecedit accessum ad terminum, prius enim est in subiecto mobili oppositum quod abiicitur, et postmodum est id quod per motum assequitur mobile. Sed ex parte agentis, est e converso. Agens enim per formam quae in eo praeexistit, agit ad removendum contrarium, sicut sol per suam lucem agit ad removendum tenebras. Et ideo ex parte solis, prius est illuminare quam tenebras removere; ex parte autem aeris illuminandi, prius est purgari a tenebris quam consequi lumen, ordine naturae; licet utrumque sit simul tempore. Et quia infusio gratiae et remissio culpae dicuntur ex parte Dei iustificantis, ideo ordine naturae prior est gratiae infusio quam culpae remissio. Sed si sumantur ea quae sunt ex parte hominis iustificati, est e converso, nam prius est naturae ordine liberatio a culpa, quam consecutio gratiae iustificantis. Vel potest dici quod termini iustificationis sunt culpa sicut a quo, et iustitia sicut ad quem, gratia vero est causa remissionis culpae, et adeptionis iustitiae.

AD SECUNDUM dicendum quod dispositio subiecti praecedit susceptionem formae ordine naturae, sequitur tamen actionem agentis, per quam etiam ipsum subiectum disponitur. Et ideo motus liberi arbitrii naturae

I ANSWER THAT, The aforesaid four things required for the justification of the ungodly are simultaneous in time, since the justification of the ungodly is not successive, as stated above (A7); but in the order of nature, one is prior to another; and in their natural order the first is the infusion of grace; the second, the free-will's movement towards God; the third, the free-will's movement towards sin; the fourth, the remission of sin.

The reason for this is that in every movement the motion of the mover is naturally first; the disposition of the matter, or the movement of the moved, is second; the end or term of the movement in which the motion of the mover rests, is last. Now the motion of God the Mover is the infusion of grace, as stated above (A6); the movement or disposition of the moved is the free-will's double movement; and the term or end of the movement is the remission of sin, as stated above (A6). Hence in their natural order the first in the justification of the ungodly is the infusion of grace; the second is the free-will's movement towards God; the third is the free-will's movement towards sin, for he who is being justified detests sin because it is against God, and thus the free-will's movement towards God naturally precedes the free-will's movement towards sin, since it is its cause and reason; the fourth and last is the remission of sin, to which this transmutation is ordained as to an end, as stated above (AA1,6).

REPLY OBJ. 1: The withdrawal from one term and approach to another may be looked at in two ways: first, on the part of the thing moved, and thus the withdrawal from a term naturally precedes the approach to a term, since in the subject of movement the opposite which is put away is prior to the opposite which the subject moved attains to by its movement. But on the part of the agent it is the other way about, since the agent, by the form pre-existing in it, acts for the removal of the opposite form; as the sun by its light acts for the removal of darkness, and hence on the part of the sun, illumination is prior to the removal of darkness; but on the part of the atmosphere to be illuminated, to be freed from darkness is, in the order of nature, prior to being illuminated, although both are simultaneous in time. And since the infusion of grace and the remission of sin regard God Who justifies, hence in the order of nature the infusion of grace is prior to the freeing from sin. But if we look at what is on the part of the man justified, it is the other way about, since in the order of nature the being freed from sin is prior to the obtaining of justifying grace. Or it may be said that the term whence of justification is sin; and the term whereto is justice; and that grace is the cause of the forgiveness of sin and of obtaining of justice.

REPLY OBJ. 2: The disposition of the subject precedes the reception of the form, in the order of nature; yet it follows the action of the agent, whereby the subject is disposed. And hence the free-will's movement precedes the

ordine praecedit consecutionem gratiae, sequitur autem gratiae infusionem.

AD TERTIUM dicendum quod, sicut philosophus dicit, in II Physic., in motibus animi omnino praecedit motus in principium speculationis, vel in finem actionis, sed in exterioribus motibus remotio impedimenti praecedit assecutionem finis. Et quia motus liberi arbitrii est motus animi, prius naturae ordine movetur in Deum sicut in finem, quam ad removendum impedimentum peccati.

reception of grace in the order of nature, and follows the infusion of grace.

REPLY OBJ. 3: As the Philosopher says (*Phys.* ii, 9), in movements of the soul the movement toward the speculative principle or the practical end is the very first, but in exterior movements the removal of the impediment precedes the attainment of the end. And as the free-will's movement is a movement of the soul, in the order of nature it moves towards God as to its end, before removing the impediment of sin.

Article 9

Whether the Justification of the Ungodly Is God's Greatest Work?

AD NONUM SIC PROCEDITUR. Videtur quod iustificatio impii non sit maximum opus Dei. Per iustificationem enim impii consequitur aliquis gratiam viae. Sed per glorificationem consequitur aliquis gratiam patriae, quae maior est. Ergo glorificatio Angelorum vel hominum est maius opus quam iustificatio impii.

PRAETEREA, iustificatio impii ordinatur ad bonum particulare unius hominis. Sed bonum universi est maius quam bonum unius hominis; ut patet in I Ethic. Ergo maius opus est creatio caeli et terrae quam iustificatio impii.

PRAETEREA, maius est ex nihilo aliquid facere, et ubi nihil cooperatur agenti, quam ex aliquo facere aliquid cum aliqua cooperatione patientis. Sed in opere creationis ex nihilo fit aliquid, unde nihil potest cooperari agenti. Sed in iustificatione impii Deus ex aliquo aliquid facit, idest ex impio iustum, et est ibi aliqua cooperatio ex parte hominis, quia est ibi motus liberi arbitrii, ut dictum est. Ergo iustificatio impii non est maximum opus Dei.

SED CONTRA est quod in Psalmo CXLIV, dicitur, *miserationes eius super omnia opera eius.* Et in collecta dicitur, *Deus, qui omnipotentiam tuam parcendo maxime et miserando manifestas.* Et Augustinus dicit exponens illud Ioan. XIV, maiora horum faciet, *quod maius opus est ut ex impio iustus fiat, quam creare caelum et terram.*

RESPONDEO dicendum quod opus aliquod potest dici magnum dupliciter. Uno modo, ex parte modi agendi. Et sic maximum est opus creationis, in quo ex nihilo fit aliquid. Alio modo potest dici opus magnum propter magnitudinem eius quod fit. Et secundum hoc, maius opus est iustificatio impii, quae terminatur ad bonum aeternum divinae participationis, quam creatio caeli et terrae, quae terminatur ad bonum naturae mutabilis. Et ideo Augustinus, cum dixisset quod *maius est quod ex*

OBJECTION 1: It would seem that the justification of the ungodly is not God's greatest work. For it is by the justification of the ungodly that we attain the grace of a wayfarer. Now by glorification we receive heavenly grace, which is greater. Hence the glorification of angels and men is a greater work than the justification of the ungodly.

OBJ. 2: Further, the justification of the ungodly is ordained to the particular good of one man. But the good of the universe is greater than the good of one man, as is plain from *Ethic.* i, 2. Hence the creation of heaven and earth is a greater work than the justification of the ungodly.

OBJ. 3: Further, to make something from nothing, where there is naught to cooperate with the agent, is greater than to make something with the cooperation of the recipient. Now in the work of creation something is made from nothing, and hence nothing can cooperate with the agent; but in the justification of the ungodly God makes something from something, i.e., a just man from a sinner, and there is a cooperation on man's part, since there is a movement of the free-will, as stated above (A3). Hence the justification of the ungodly is not God's greatest work.

ON THE CONTRARY, It is written (Ps 144:9): *His tender mercies are over all His works,* and in a collect we say: *O God, Who dost show forth Thine all-mightiness most by pardoning and having mercy,* and Augustine, expounding the words, *greater than these shall he do* (John 14:12) says that *for a just man to be made from a sinner, is greater than to create heaven and earth.*

I ANSWER THAT, A work may be called great in two ways: first, on the part of the mode of action, and thus the work of creation is the greatest work, wherein something is made from nothing; second, a work may be called great on account of what is made, and thus the justification of the ungodly, which terminates at the eternal good of a share in the Godhead, is greater than the creation of heaven and earth, which terminates at the good of mutable nature. Hence, Augustine, after saying that *for a just man to*

impio fiat iustus, quam creare caelum et terram, subiungit, *caelum enim et terra transibit, praedestinatorum autem salus et iustificatio permanebit.*

Sed sciendum est quod aliquid magnum dicitur dupliciter. Uno modo, secundum quantitatem absolutam. Et hoc modo donum gloriae est maius quam donum gratiae iustificantis impium. Et secundum hoc, glorificatio iustorum est maius opus quam iustificatio impii. Alio modo dicitur aliquid magnum quantitate proportionis, sicut dicitur mons parvus, et milium magnum. Et hoc modo donum gratiae impium iustificantis est maius quam donum gloriae beatificantis iustum, quia plus excedit donum gratiae dignitatem impii, qui erat dignus poena, quam donum gloriae dignitatem iusti, qui ex hoc ipso quod est iustificatus, est dignus gloria. Et ideo Augustinus dicit ibidem, *iudicet qui potest, utrum maius sit iustos Angelos creare quam impios iustificare. Certe, si aequalis est utrumque potentiae, hoc maioris est misericordiae.*

ET PER HOC patet responsio ad primum.

AD SECUNDUM dicendum quod bonum universi est maius quam bonum particulare unius, si accipiatur utrumque in eodem genere. Sed bonum gratiae unius maius est quam bonum naturae totius universi.

AD TERTIUM dicendum quod ratio illa procedit ex parte modi agendi, secundum quem creatio est maximum opus Dei.

be made from a sinner is greater than to create heaven and earth, adds, *for heaven and earth shall pass away, but the justification of the ungodly shall endure.*

Again, we must bear in mind that a thing is called great in two ways: first, in an absolute quantity, and thus the gift of glory is greater than the gift of grace that sanctifies the ungodly; and in this respect the glorification of the just is greater than the justification of the ungodly. Second, a thing may be said to be great in proportionate quantity, and thus the gift of grace that justifies the ungodly is greater than the gift of glory that beatifies the just, for the gift of grace exceeds the worthiness of the ungodly, who are worthy of punishment, more than the gift of glory exceeds the worthiness of the just, who by the fact of their justification are worthy of glory. Hence Augustine says: *Let him that can, judge whether it is greater to create the angels just, than to justify the ungodly. Certainly, if they both betoken equal power, one betokens greater mercy.*

AND THUS the reply to the first is clear.

REPLY OBJ. 2: The good of the universe is greater than the particular good of one, if we consider both in the same genus. But the good of grace in one is greater than the good of nature in the whole universe.

REPLY OBJ. 3: This objection rests on the manner of acting, in which way creation is God's greatest work.

Article 10

Whether the Justification of the Ungodly Is a Miraculous Work?

AD DECIMUM SIC PROCEDITUR. Videtur quod iustificatio impii sit opus miraculosum. Opera enim miraculosa sunt maiora non miraculosis. Sed iustificatio impii est maius opus quam alia opera miraculosa; ut patet per Augustinum in auctoritate inducta. Ergo iustificatio impii est opus miraculosum.

PRAETEREA, motus voluntatis ita est in anima, sicut inclinatio naturalis in rebus naturalibus. Sed quando Deus aliquid operatur in rebus naturalibus contra inclinationem naturae, est opus miraculosum, sicut cum illuminat caecum, vel suscitat mortuum. Voluntas autem impii tendit in malum. Cum igitur Deus, iustificando hominem, moveat eum in bonum, videtur quod iustificatio impii sit miraculosa.

PRAETEREA, sicut sapientia est donum Dei, ita et iustitia. Sed miraculosum est quod aliquis subito sine studio sapientiam assequatur a Deo. Ergo miraculosum est quod aliquis impius iustificetur a Deo.

SED CONTRA, opera miraculosa sunt supra potentiam naturalem. Sed iustificatio impii non est supra

OBJECTION 1: It would seem that the justification of the ungodly is a miraculous work. For miraculous works are greater than non-miraculous. Now the justification of the ungodly is greater than the other miraculous works, as is clear from the quotation from Augustine (A9). Hence the justification of the ungodly is a miraculous work.

OBJ. 2: Further, the movement of the will in the soul is like the natural inclination in natural things. But when God works in natural things against their inclination of their nature, it is a miraculous work, as when He gave sight to the blind or raised the dead. Now the will of the ungodly is bent on evil. Hence, since God in justifying a man moves him to good, it would seem that the justification of the ungodly is miraculous.

OBJ. 3: Further, as wisdom is a gift of God, so also is justice. Now it is miraculous that anyone should suddenly obtain wisdom from God without study. Therefore it is miraculous that the ungodly should be justified by God.

ON THE CONTRARY, Miraculous works are beyond natural power. Now the justification of the ungodly is not

potentiam naturalem, dicit enim Augustinus, in libro de Praedest. Sanct., quod *posse habere fidem, sicut posse habere caritatem, naturae est hominum, habere autem gratiae est fidelium.* Ergo iustificatio impii non est miraculosa.

RESPONDEO dicendum quod in operibus miraculosis tria consueverunt inveniri. Quorum unum est ex parte potentiae agentis, quia sola divina virtute fieri possunt. Et ideo sunt simpliciter mira, quasi habentia causam occultam, ut in primo dictum est. Et secundum hoc, tam iustificatio impii quam creatio mundi, et universaliter omne opus quod a solo Deo fieri potest, miraculosum dici potest.

Secundo, in quibusdam miraculosis operibus invenitur quod forma inducta est supra naturalem potentiam talis materiae, sicut in suscitatione mortui vita est supra naturalem potentiam talis corporis. Et quantum ad hoc, iustificatio impii non est miraculosa, quia naturaliter anima est gratiae capax; *eo enim ipso quod facta est ad imaginem Dei, capax est Dei per gratiam,* ut Augustinus dicit.

Tertio modo, in operibus miraculosis invenitur aliquid praeter solitum et consuetum ordinem causandi effectum, sicut cum aliquis infirmus sanitatem perfectam assequitur subito, praeter solitum cursum sanationis quae fit a natura vel arte. Et quantum ad hoc, iustificatio impii quandoque est miraculosa, et quandoque non. Est enim iste consuetus et communis cursus iustificationis, ut, Deo movente interius animam, homo convertatur ad Deum, primo quidem conversione imperfecta, et postmodum ad perfectam deveniat, quia *caritas inchoata meretur augeri, ut aucta mereatur perfici,* sicut Augustinus dicit. Quandoque vero tam vehementer Deus animam movet ut statim quandam perfectionem iustitiae assequatur, sicut fuit in conversione Pauli, adhibita etiam exterius miraculosa prostratione. Et ideo conversio Pauli, tanquam miraculosa, in Ecclesia commemoratur celebriter.

AD PRIMUM ergo dicendum quod quaedam miraculosa opera, etsi sint minora quam iustificatio impii quantum ad bonum quod fit, sunt tamen praeter consuetum ordinem talium effectuum. Et ideo plus habent de ratione miraculi.

AD SECUNDUM dicendum quod non quandocumque res naturalis movetur contra suam inclinationem, est opus miraculosum, alioquin miraculosum esset quod aqua calefieret, vel quod lapis sursum proiiceretur, sed quando hoc fit praeter ordinem propriae causae, quae nata est hoc facere. Iustificare autem impium nulla alia causa potest nisi Deus, sicut nec aquam calefacere nisi ignis. Et ideo iustificatio impii a Deo, quantum ad hoc, non est miraculosa.

AD TERTIUM dicendum quod sapientiam et scientiam homo natus est acquirere a Deo per proprium

beyond natural power; for Augustine says (*De Praed. Sanct.* v) that *to be capable of having faith and to be capable of having charity belongs to man's nature; but to have faith and charity belongs to the grace of the faithful.* Therefore the justification of the ungodly is not miraculous.

I ANSWER THAT, In miraculous works it is usual to find three things: the first is on the part of the active power, because they can only be performed by Divine power; and they are simply wondrous, since their cause is hidden, as stated above (I, Q105, A7). And thus both the justification of the ungodly and the creation of the world, and, generally speaking, every work that can be done by God alone, is miraculous.

Second, in certain miraculous works it is found that the form introduced is beyond the natural power of such matter, as in the resurrection of the dead, life is above the natural power of such a body. And thus the justification of the ungodly is not miraculous, because the soul is naturally capable of grace; since from its having been made to the likeness of God, it is fit to receive God by grace, as Augustine says, in the above quotation.

Third, in miraculous works something is found besides the usual and customary order of causing an effect, as when a sick man suddenly and beyond the wonted course of healing by nature or art, receives perfect health; and thus the justification of the ungodly is sometimes miraculous and sometimes not. For the common and wonted course of justification is that God moves the soul interiorly and that man is converted to God, first by an imperfect conversion, that it may afterwards become perfect; because *charity begun merits increase, and when increased merits perfection,* as Augustine says (*In Epist. Joan. Tract. v*). Yet God sometimes moves the soul so vehemently that it reaches the perfection of justice at once, as took place in the conversion of Paul, which was accompanied at the same time by a miraculous external prostration. Hence the conversion of Paul is commemorated in the Church as miraculous.

REPLY OBJ. 1: Certain miraculous works, although they are less than the justification of the ungodly, as regards the good caused, are beyond the wonted order of such effects, and thus have more of the nature of a miracle.

REPLY OBJ. 2: It is not a miraculous work, whenever a natural thing is moved contrary to its inclination, otherwise it would be miraculous for water to be heated, or for a stone to be thrown upwards; but only whenever this takes place beyond the order of the proper cause, which naturally does this. Now no other cause save God can justify the ungodly, even as nothing save fire can heat water. Hence the justification of the ungodly by God is not miraculous in this respect.

REPLY OBJ. 3: A man naturally acquires wisdom and knowledge from God by his own talent and study. Hence it

ingenium et studium, et ideo quando praeter hunc modum homo sapiens vel sciens efficitur, est miraculosum. Sed gratiam iustificantem non est homo natus acquirere per suam operationem, sed Deo operante. Unde non est simile.

is miraculous when a man is made wise or learned outside this order. But a man does not naturally acquire justifying grace by his own action, but by God's. Hence there is no parity.

QUESTION 114

OF MERIT

Deinde considerandum est de merito, quod est effectus gratiae cooperantis. Et circa hoc quaeruntur decem.

Primo, utrum homo possit aliquid mereri a Deo.

Secundo, utrum aliquis sine gratia possit mereri vitam aeternam.

Tertio, utrum aliquis per gratiam possit mereri vitam aeternam ex condigno.

Quarto, utrum gratia sit principium merendi mediante caritate principaliter.

Quinto, utrum homo possit sibi mereri primam gratiam.

Sexto, utrum homo possit eam mereri alii.

Septimo, utrum possit sibi aliquis mereri reparationem post lapsum.

Octavo, utrum possit sibi mereri augmentum gratiae vel caritatis.

Nono, utrum possit sibi mereri finalem perseverantiam.

Decimo, utrum bona temporalia cadant sub merito.

We must now consider merit, which is the effect of co-operating grace; and under this head there are ten points of inquiry:

(1) Whether a man can merit anything from God?

(2) Whether without grace anyone can merit eternal life?

(3) Whether anyone with grace may merit eternal life condignly?

(4) Whether it is chiefly through the instrumentality of charity that grace is the principle of merit?

(5) Whether a man may merit the first grace for himself?

(6) Whether he may merit it for someone else?

(7) Whether anyone can merit restoration after sin?

(8) Whether he can merit for himself an increase of grace or charity?

(9) Whether he can merit final perseverance?

(10) Whether temporal goods fall under merit?

Article 1

Whether a Man May Merit Anything from God?

Ad primum sic proceditur. Videtur quod homo non possit aliquid mereri a Deo. Nullus enim videtur mercedem mereri ex hoc quod reddit alteri quod debet. Sed *per omnia bona quae facimus, non possumus sufficienter recompensare Deo quod debemus, quin semper amplius debeamus*; ut etiam philosophus dicit, in VIII Ethic. Unde et Luc. XVII, dicitur, *cum omnia quae praecepta sunt, feceritis, dicite, servi inutiles sumus, quod debuimus facere, fecimus.* Ergo homo non potest aliquid mereri a Deo.

Praeterea, ex eo quod aliquis sibi proficit, nihil videtur mereri apud eum cui nihil proficit. Sed homo bene operando sibi proficit, vel alteri homini, non autem Deo, dicitur enim Iob XXXV, *si iuste egeris, quid donabis ei, aut quid de manu tua accipiet?* Ergo homo non potest aliquid a Deo mereri.

Praeterea, quicumque apud aliquem aliquid meretur, constituit eum sibi debitorem, debitum enim est ut aliquis merendi mercedem rependat. Sed Deus nulli est debitor, unde dicitur Rom. XI, *quis prior dedit ei, et retribuetur ei?* Ergo nullus a Deo potest aliquid mereri.

Objection 1: It would seem that a man can merit nothing from God. For no one, it would seem, merits by giving another his due. But by all the good we do, we cannot make sufficient return to God, since yet more is His due, as also the Philosopher says (*Ethic.* viii, 14). Hence it is written (Luke 17:10): *When you have done all these things that are commanded you, say: We are unprofitable servants; we have done that which we ought to do.* Therefore a man can merit nothing from God.

Obj. 2: Further, it would seem that a man merits nothing from God, by what profits himself only, and profits God nothing. Now by acting well, a man profits himself or another man, but not God, for it is written (Job 35:7): *If thou do justly, what shalt thou give Him, or what shall He receive of thy hand.* Hence a man can merit nothing from God.

Obj. 3: Further, whoever merits anything from another makes him his debtor; for a man's wage is a debt due to him. Now God is no one's debtor; hence it is written (Rom 11:35): *Who hath first given to Him, and recompense shall be made to him?* Hence no one can merit anything from God.

S<small>ED CONTRA</small> est quod dicitur Ierem. XXXI, *est merces operi tuo*. Sed merces dicitur quod pro merito redditur. Ergo videtur quod homo possit a Deo mereri.

R<small>ESPONDEO</small> dicendum quod meritum et merces ad idem referuntur, id enim merces dicitur quod alicui recompensatur pro retributione operis vel laboris, quasi quoddam pretium ipsius. Unde sicut reddere iustum pretium pro re accepta ab aliquo, est actus iustitiae; ita etiam recompensare mercedem operis vel laboris, est actus iustitiae. Iustitia autem aequalitas quaedam est; ut patet per philosophum, in V Ethic. Et ideo simpliciter est iustitia inter eos quorum est simpliciter aequalitas, eorum vero quorum non est simpliciter aequalitas, non est simpliciter iustitia, sed quidam iustitiae modus potest esse, sicut dicitur quoddam ius paternum vel dominativum, ut in eodem libro philosophus dicit. Et propter hoc, in his in quibus est simpliciter iustum, est etiam simpliciter ratio meriti et mercedis. In quibus autem est secundum quid iustum, et non simpliciter, in his etiam non simpliciter est ratio meriti, sed secundum quid, inquantum salvatur ibi iustitiae ratio, sic enim et filius meretur aliquid a patre, et servus a domino.

Manifestum est autem quod inter Deum et hominem est maxima inaequalitas, in infinitum enim distant, et totum quod est hominis bonum, est a Deo. Unde non potest hominis ad Deum esse iustitia secundum absolutam aequalitatem, sed secundum proportionem quandam, inquantum scilicet uterque operatur secundum modum suum. Modus autem et mensura humanae virtutis homini est a Deo. Et ideo meritum hominis apud Deum esse non potest nisi secundum praesuppositionem divinae ordinationis, ita scilicet ut id homo consequatur a Deo per suam operationem quasi mercedem, ad quod Deus ei virtutem operandi deputavit. Sicut etiam res naturales hoc consequuntur per proprios motus et operationes, ad quod a Deo sunt ordinatae. Differenter tamen, quia creatura rationalis seipsam movet ad agendum per liberum arbitrium, unde sua actio habet rationem meriti; quod non est in aliis creaturis.

A<small>D PRIMUM</small> ergo dicendum quod homo inquantum propria voluntate facit illud quod debet, meretur. Alioquin actus iustitiae quo quis reddit debitum, non esset meritorius.

A<small>D SECUNDUM</small> dicendum quod Deus ex bonis nostris non quaerit utilitatem, sed gloriam, idest manifestationem suae bonitatis, quod etiam ex suis operibus quaerit. Ex hoc autem quod eum colimus, nihil ei accrescit, sed nobis. Et ideo meremur aliquid a Deo, non quasi ex nostris operibus aliquid ei accrescat, sed inquantum propter eius gloriam operamur.

A<small>D TERTIUM</small> dicendum quod, quia actio nostra non habet rationem meriti nisi ex praesuppositione divinae ordinationis, non sequitur quod Deus efficiatur

O<small>N THE CONTRARY</small>, It is written (Jer 31:16): *There is a reward for thy work*. Now a reward means something bestowed by reason of merit. Hence it would seem that a man may merit from God.

I <small>ANSWER THAT</small>, Merit and reward refer to the same, for a reward means something given anyone in return for work or toil, as a price for it. Hence, as it is an act of justice to give a just price for anything received from another, so also is it an act of justice to make a return for work or toil. Now justice is a kind of equality, as is clear from the Philosopher (*Ethic.* v, 3), and hence justice is simply between those that are simply equal; but where there is no absolute equality between them, neither is there absolute justice, but there may be a certain manner of justice, as when we speak of a father's or a master's right (*Ethic.* v, 6), as the Philosopher says. And hence where there is justice simply, there is the character of merit and reward simply. But where there is no simple right, but only relative, there is no character of merit simply, but only relatively, insofar as the character of justice is found there, since the child merits something from his father and the slave from his lord.

Now it is clear that between God and man there is the greatest inequality: for they are infinitely apart, and all man's good is from God. Hence there can be no justice of absolute equality between man and God, but only of a certain proportion, inasmuch as both operate after their own manner. Now the manner and measure of human virtue is in man from God. Hence man's merit with God only exists on the presupposition of the Divine ordination, so that man obtains from God, as a reward of his operation, what God gave him the power of operation for, even as natural things by their proper movements and operations obtain that to which they were ordained by God; differently, indeed, since the rational creature moves itself to act by its free-will, hence its action has the character of merit, which is not so in other creatures.

R<small>EPLY OBJ.</small> 1: Man merits, inasmuch as he does what he ought, by his free-will; otherwise the act of justice whereby anyone discharges a debt would not be meritorious.

R<small>EPLY OBJ.</small> 2: God seeks from our goods not profit, but glory, i.e., the manifestation of His goodness; even as He seeks it also in His own works. Now nothing accrues to Him, but only to ourselves, by our worship of Him. Hence we merit from God, not that by our works anything accrues to Him, but inasmuch as we work for His glory.

R<small>EPLY OBJ.</small> 3: Since our action has the character of merit, only on the presupposition of the Divine ordination, it does not follow that God is made our debtor simply, but

simpliciter debitor nobis, sed sibi ipsi, inquantum debitum est ut sua ordinatio impleatur.

His own, inasmuch as it is right that His will should be carried out.

Article 2

Whether Anyone Without Grace Can Merit Eternal Life?

AD SECUNDUM SIC PROCEDITUR. Videtur quod aliquis sine gratia possit mereri vitam aeternam. Illud enim homo a Deo meretur ad quod divinitus ordinatur, sicut dictum est. Sed homo secundum suam naturam ordinatur ad beatitudinem sicut ad finem, unde etiam naturaliter appetit esse beatus. Ergo homo per sua naturalia, absque gratia, mereri potest beatitudinem, quae est vita aeterna.

PRAETEREA, idem opus quanto est minus debitum, tanto est magis meritorium. Sed minus debitum est bonum quod fit ab eo qui minoribus beneficiis est praeventus. Cum igitur ille qui habet solum bona naturalia, minora beneficia sit consecutus a Deo quam ille qui cum naturalibus habet gratuita; videtur quod eius opera sint apud Deum magis meritoria. Et ita, si ille qui habet gratiam, potest mereri aliquo modo vitam aeternam, multo magis ille qui non habet.

PRAETEREA, misericordia et liberalitas Dei in infinitum excedit misericordiam et liberalitatem humanam. Sed unus homo potest apud alium mereri, etiam si nunquam suam gratiam ante habuerit. Ergo videtur quod multo magis homo absque gratia vitam aeternam possit a Deo mereri.

SED CONTRA est quod apostolus dicit, Rom. VI, *gratia Dei vita aeterna*.

RESPONDEO dicendum quod hominis sine gratia duplex status considerari potest sicut supra dictum est, unus quidem naturae integrae, qualis fuit in Adam ante peccatum; alius autem naturae corruptae, sicut est in nobis ante reparationem gratiae. Si ergo loquamur de homine quantum ad primum statum, sic una ratione non potest mereri absque gratia vitam aeternam per pura naturalia. Quia scilicet meritum hominis dependet ex praeordinatione divina. Actus autem cuiuscumque rei non ordinatur divinitus ad aliquid excedens proportionem virtutis quae est principium actus, hoc enim est ex institutione divinae providentiae, ut nihil agat ultra suam virtutem. Vita autem aeterna est quoddam bonum excedens proportionem naturae creatae, quia etiam excedit cognitionem et desiderium eius, secundum illud I ad Cor. II, *nec oculus vidit, nec auris audivit, nec in cor hominis ascendit*. Et inde est quod nulla natura creata est sufficiens principium actus meritorii vitae aeternae, nisi superaddatur aliquod supernaturale donum, quod gratia dicitur. Si vero loquamur de homine sub peccato

OBJECTION 1: It would seem that without grace anyone can merit eternal life. For man merits from God what he is divinely ordained to, as stated above (A1). Now man by his nature is ordained to beatitude as his end; hence, too, he naturally wishes to be blessed. Hence man by his natural endowments and without grace can merit beatitude which is eternal life.

OBJ. 2: Further, the less a work is due, the more meritorious it is. Now, less due is that work which is done by one who has received fewer benefits. Hence, since he who has only natural endowments has received fewer gifts from God, than he who has gratuitous gifts as well as nature, it would seem that his works are more meritorious with God. And thus if he who has grace can merit eternal life to some extent, much more may he who has no grace.

OBJ. 3: Further, God's mercy and liberality infinitely surpass human mercy and liberality. Now a man may merit from another, even though he has not hitherto had his grace. Much more, therefore, would it seem that a man without grace may merit eternal life.

ON THE CONTRARY, The Apostle says (Rom 6:23): *The grace of God, life everlasting*.

I ANSWER THAT, Man without grace may be looked at in two states, as was said above (Q109, A2): the first, a state of perfect nature, in which Adam was before his sin; the second, a state of corrupt nature, in which we are before being restored by grace. Therefore, if we speak of man in the first state, there is only one reason why man cannot merit eternal life without grace, by his purely natural endowments, viz., because man's merit depends on the Divine pre-ordination. Now no act of anything whatsoever is divinely ordained to anything exceeding the proportion of the powers which are the principles of its act; for it is a law of Divine providence that nothing shall act beyond its powers. Now everlasting life is a good exceeding the proportion of created nature; since it exceeds its knowledge and desire, according to 1 Cor. 2:9: *Eye hath not seen, nor ear heard, neither hath it entered into the heart of man*. And hence it is that no created nature is a sufficient principle of an act meritorious of eternal life, unless there is added a supernatural gift, which we call grace. But if we speak of man as existing in sin, a second reason is added to this, viz.,

existente, additur cum hac secunda ratio, propter impedimentum peccati. Cum enim peccatum sit quaedam Dei offensa excludens a vita aeterna, ut patet per supradicta; nullus in statu peccati existens potest vitam aeternam mereri, nisi prius Deo reconcilietur, dimisso peccato, quod fit per gratiam. Peccatori enim non debetur vita, sed mors; secundum illud Rom. VI, *stipendia peccati mors*.

AD PRIMUM ergo dicendum quod Deus ordinavit humanam naturam ad finem vitae aeternae consequendum non propria virtute, sed per auxilium gratiae. Et hoc modo eius actus potest esse meritorius vitae aeternae.

AD SECUNDUM dicendum quod homo sine gratia non potest habere aequale opus operi quod ex gratia procedit, quia quanto est perfectius principium actionis, tanto est perfectior actio. Sequeretur autem ratio, supposita aequalitate operationis utrobique.

AD TERTIUM dicendum quod, quantum ad primam rationem inductam, dissimiliter se habet in Deo et in homine. Nam homo omnem virtutem benefaciendi habet a Deo, non autem ab homine. Et ideo a Deo non potest homo aliquid mereri nisi per donum eius, quod apostolus signanter exprimit, dicens, *quis prior dedit ei, et retribuetur illi?* Sed ab homine potest aliquis mereri antequam ab eo acceperit, per id quod accepit a Deo.

Sed quantum ad secundam rationem, sumptam ex impedimento peccati, simile est de homine et de Deo, quia etiam homo ab alio mereri non potest quem offendit prius, nisi ei satisfaciens reconcilietur.

the impediment of sin. For since sin is an offense against God, excluding us from eternal life, as is clear from what has been said above (Q71, A6; Q113, A2), no one existing in a state of mortal sin can merit eternal life unless first he be reconciled to God, through his sin being forgiven, which is brought about by grace. For the sinner deserves not life, but death, according to Rm. 6:23: *The wages of sin is death.*

REPLY OBJ. 1: God ordained human nature to attain the end of eternal life, not by its own strength, but by the help of grace; and in this way its act can be meritorious of eternal life.

REPLY OBJ. 2: Without grace a man cannot have a work equal to a work proceeding from grace, since the more perfect the principle, the more perfect the action. But the objection would hold good, if we supposed the operations equal in both cases.

REPLY OBJ. 3: With regard to the first reason adduced, the case is different in God and in man. For a man receives all his power of well-doing from God, and not from man. Hence a man can merit nothing from God except by His gift, which the Apostle expresses aptly saying (Rom 11:35): *Who hath first given to Him, and recompense shall be made to him?* But man may merit from man, before he has received anything from him, by what he has received from God.

But as regards the second proof taken from the impediment of sin, the case is similar with man and God, since one man cannot merit from another whom he has offended, unless he makes satisfaction to him and is reconciled.

Article 3

Whether a Man in Grace Can Merit Eternal Life Condignly?

AD TERTIUM SIC PROCEDITUR. Videtur quod homo in gratia constitutus non possit mereri vitam aeternam ex condigno. Dicit enim apostolus, ad Rom. VIII, *non sunt condignae passiones huius temporis ad futuram gloriam quae revelabitur in nobis.* Sed inter alia opera meritoria maxime videntur esse meritoriae sanctorum passiones. Ergo nulla opera hominum sunt meritoria vitae aeternae ex condigno.

PRAETEREA, super illud Rom. VI, *gratia Dei vita aeterna*, dicit Glossa, *posset recte dicere, stipendium iustitiae vita aeterna, sed maluit dicere, gratia Dei vita aeterna, ut intelligeremus Deum ad aeternam vitam pro sua miseratione nos perducere, non meritis nostris.* Sed id quod ex condigno quis meretur, non ex miseratione, sed ex merito accipit. Ergo videtur quod homo non possit per gratiam mereri vitam aeternam ex condigno.

OBJECTION 1: It would seem that a man in grace cannot merit eternal life condignly, for the Apostle says (Rom 8:18): *The sufferings of this time are not worthy to be compared with the glory to come, that shall be revealed in us.* But of all meritorious works, the sufferings of the saints would seem the most meritorious. Therefore no works of men are meritorious of eternal life condignly.

OBJ. 2: Further, on Rm. 6:23, *The grace of God, life everlasting*, a gloss says: *He might have truly said: 'The wages of justice, life everlasting'; but He preferred to say 'The grace of God, life everlasting,' that we may know that God leads us to life everlasting of His own mercy and not by our merits.* Now when anyone merits something condignly he receives it not from mercy, but from merit. Hence it would seem that a man with grace cannot merit life everlasting condignly.

PRAETEREA, illud meritum videtur esse condignum quod aequatur mercedi. Sed nullus actus praesentis vitae potest aequari vitae aeternae, quae cognitionem et desiderium nostrum excedit. Excedit etiam caritatem vel dilectionem viae, sicut et excedit naturam. Ergo homo non potest per gratiam mereri vitam aeternam ex condigno.

SED CONTRA, id quod redditur secundum iustum iudicium, videtur esse merces condigna. Sed vita aeterna redditur a Deo secundum iudicium iustitiae; secundum illud II ad Tim. IV, *in reliquo reposita est mihi corona iustitiae, quam reddet mihi dominus in illa die, iustus iudex.* Ergo homo meretur vitam aeternam ex condigno.

RESPONDEO dicendum quod opus meritorium hominis dupliciter considerari potest, uno modo, secundum quod procedit ex libero arbitrio; alio modo, secundum quod procedit ex gratia spiritus sancti. Si consideretur secundum substantiam operis, et secundum quod procedit ex libero arbitrio, sic non potest ibi esse condignitas, propter maximam inaequalitatem. Sed est ibi congruitas, propter quandam aequalitatem proportionis, videtur enim congruum ut homini operanti secundum suam virtutem, Deus recompenset secundum excellentiam suae virtutis.

Si autem loquamur de opere meritorio secundum quod procedit ex gratia spiritus sancti, sic est meritorium vitae aeternae ex condigno. Sic enim valor meriti attenditur secundum virtutem spiritus sancti moventis nos in vitam aeternam; secundum illud Ioan. IV, *fiet in eo fons aquae salientis in vitam aeternam.* Attenditur etiam pretium operis secundum dignitatem gratiae, per quam homo, consors factus divinae naturae, adoptatur in filium Dei, cui debetur hereditas ex ipso iure adoptionis, secundum illud Rom. VIII, *si filii, et heredes.*

AD PRIMUM ergo dicendum quod apostolus loquitur de passionibus sanctorum secundum eorum substantiam.

AD SECUNDUM dicendum quod verbum Glossae intelligendum est quantum ad primam causam perveniendi ad vitam aeternam, quae est miseratio Dei. Meritum autem nostrum est causa subsequens.

AD TERTIUM dicendum quod gratia spiritus sancti quam in praesenti habemus, etsi non sit aequalis gloriae in actu, est tamen aequalis in virtute, sicut et semen arborum, in quo est virtus ad totam arborem. Et similiter per gratiam inhabitat hominem Spiritus Sanctus, qui est sufficiens causa vitae aeternae, unde et dicitur esse pignus hereditatis nostrae, II ad Cor. I.

OBJ. 3: Further, merit that equals the reward, would seem to be condign. Now no act of the present life can equal everlasting life, which surpasses our knowledge and our desire, and moreover, surpasses the charity or love of the wayfarer, even as it exceeds nature. Therefore with grace a man cannot merit eternal life condignly.

ON THE CONTRARY, What is granted in accordance with a fair judgment, would seem a condign reward. But life everlasting is granted by God, in accordance with the judgment of justice, according to 2 Tim. 4:8: *As to the rest, there is laid up for me a crown of justice, which the Lord, the just judge, will render to me in that day.* Therefore man merits everlasting life condignly.

I ANSWER THAT, Man's meritorious work may be considered in two ways: first, as it proceeds from free-will; second, as it proceeds from the grace of the Holy Spirit. If it is considered as regards the substance of the work, and inasmuch as it springs from the free-will, there can be no condignity because of the very great inequality. But there is congruity, on account of an equality of proportion: for it would seem congruous that, if a man does what he can, God should reward him according to the excellence of his power.

If, however, we speak of a meritorious work, inasmuch as it proceeds from the grace of the Holy Spirit moving us to life everlasting, it is meritorious of life everlasting condignly. For thus the value of its merit depends upon the power of the Holy Spirit moving us to life everlasting according to Jn. 4:14: *Shall become in him a fount of water springing up into life everlasting.* And the worth of the work depends on the dignity of grace, whereby a man, being made a partaker of the Divine Nature, is adopted as a son of God, to whom the inheritance is due by right of adoption, according to Rm. 8:17: *If sons, heirs also.*

REPLY OBJ. 1: The Apostle is speaking of the substance of these sufferings.

REPLY OBJ. 2: This saying is to be understood of the first cause of our reaching everlasting life, viz., God's mercy. But our merit is a subsequent cause.

REPLY OBJ. 3: The grace of the Holy Spirit which we have at present, although unequal to glory in act, is equal to it virtually as the seed of a tree, wherein the whole tree is virtually. So likewise by grace the Holy Spirit dwells in man; and He is a sufficient cause of life everlasting; hence, 2 Cor. 1:22, He is called the *pledge* of our inheritance.

Article 4

Whether Grace Is the Principle of Merit Through Charity Rather Than the Other Virtues?

AD QUARTUM SIC PROCEDITUR. Videtur quod gratia non sit principium meriti principalius per caritatem quam per alias virtutes. Merces enim operi debetur; secundum illud Matth. XX, *voca operarios, et redde illis mercedem suam.* Sed quaelibet virtus est principium alicuius operis, est enim virtus habitus operativus, ut supra habitum est. Ergo quaelibet virtus est aequaliter principium merendi.

PRAETEREA, apostolus dicit, I ad Cor. III, *unusquisque propriam mercedem accipiet secundum proprium laborem.* Sed caritas magis diminuit laborem quam augeat, quia sicut Augustinus dicit, in libro de verbis Dom., *omnia saeva et immania, facilia et prope nulla facit amor.* Ergo caritas non est principalius principium merendi quam alia virtus.

PRAETEREA, illa virtus videtur principalius esse principium merendi, cuius actus sunt maxime meritorii. Sed maxime meritorii videntur esse actus fidei et patientiae, sive fortitudinis, sicut patet in martyribus, qui pro fide patienter et fortiter usque ad mortem certaverunt. Ergo aliae virtutes principalius sunt principium merendi quam caritas.

SED CONTRA est quod dominus, Ioan. XIV, dicit, *si quis diligit me, diligetur a patre meo, et ego diligam eum, et manifestabo ei meipsum.* Sed in manifesta Dei cognitione consistit vita aeterna; secundum illud Ioan. XVII, *haec est vita aeterna, ut cognoscant te solum Deum verum et vivum.* Ergo meritum vitae aeternae maxime residet penes caritatem.

RESPONDEO dicendum quod, sicut ex dictis accipi potest, humanus actus habet rationem merendi ex duobus, primo quidem et principaliter, ex divina ordinatione, secundum quod actus dicitur esse meritorius illius boni ad quod homo divinitus ordinatur; secundo vero, ex parte liberi arbitrii, inquantum scilicet homo habet prae ceteris creaturis ut per se agat, voluntarie agens. Et quantum ad utrumque, principalitas meriti penes caritatem consistit. Primo enim considerandum est quod vita aeterna in Dei fruitione consistit. Motus autem humanae mentis ad fruitionem divini boni, est proprius actus caritatis, per quem omnes actus aliarum virtutum ordinantur in hunc finem, secundum quod aliae virtutes imperantur a caritate. Et ideo meritum vitae aeternae primo pertinet ad caritatem, ad alias autem virtutes secundario, secundum quod eorum actus a caritate imperantur. Similiter etiam manifestum est quod id quod ex amore facimus, maxime voluntarie facimus. Unde etiam secundum quod ad rationem meriti requiritur quod sit voluntarium, principaliter meritum caritati attribuitur.

OBJECTION 1: It would seem that grace is not the principle of merit through charity rather than the other virtues. For wages are due to work, according to Mt. 20:8: *Call the laborers and pay them their hire.* Now every virtue is a principle of some operation, since virtue is an operative habit, as stated above (Q55, A2). Hence every virtue is equally a principle of merit.

OBJ. 2: Further, the Apostle says (1 Cor 3:8): *Every man shall receive his own reward according to his labor.* Now charity lessens rather than increases the labor, because as Augustine says (*De Verbis Dom., Serm. lxx*), *love makes all hard and repulsive tasks easy and next to nothing.* Hence charity is no greater principle of merit than any other virtue.

OBJ. 3: Further, the greatest principle of merit would seem to be the one whose acts are most meritorious. But the acts of faith and patience or fortitude would seem to be the most meritorious, as appears in the martyrs, who strove for the faith patiently and bravely even till death. Hence other virtues are a greater principle of merit than charity.

ON THE CONTRARY, Our Lord said (John 14:21): *He that loveth Me, shall be loved of My Father; and I will love him and will manifest Myself to him.* Now everlasting life consists in the manifest knowledge of God, according to Jn. 17:3: *This is eternal life: that they may know Thee, the only true and living God.* Hence the merit of eternal life rests chiefly with charity.

I ANSWER THAT, As we may gather from what has been stated above (A1), human acts have the nature of merit from two causes: first and chiefly from the Divine ordination, inasmuch as acts are said to merit that good to which man is divinely ordained. Second, on the part of free-will, inasmuch as man, more than other creatures, has the power of voluntary acts by acting by himself. And in both these ways does merit chiefly rest with charity. For we must bear in mind that everlasting life consists in the enjoyment of God. Now the human mind's movement to the fruition of the Divine good is the proper act of charity, whereby all the acts of the other virtues are ordained to this end, since all the other virtues are commanded by charity. Hence the merit of life everlasting pertains first to charity, and second, to the other virtues, inasmuch as their acts are commanded by charity. So, likewise, is it manifest that what we do out of love we do most willingly. Hence, even inasmuch as merit depends on voluntariness, merit is chiefly attributed to charity.

AD PRIMUM ergo dicendum quod caritas, inquantum habet ultimum finem pro obiecto, movet alias virtutes ad operandum. Semper enim habitus ad quem pertinet finis, imperat habitibus ad quos pertinent ea quae sunt ad finem; ut ex supradictis patet.

AD SECUNDUM dicendum quod opus aliquod potest esse laboriosum et difficile dupliciter. Uno modo, ex magnitudine operis. Et sic magnitudo laboris pertinet ad augmentum meriti. Et sic caritas non diminuit laborem, immo facit aggredi opera maxima; magna enim operatur, si est, ut Gregorius dicit in quadam homilia. Alio modo ex defectu ipsius operantis, unicuique enim est laboriosum et difficile quod non prompta voluntate facit. Et talis labor diminuit meritum, et a caritate tollitur.

AD TERTIUM dicendum quod fidei actus non est meritorius nisi fides per dilectionem operetur, ut dicitur ad Gal. V. Similiter etiam actus patientiae et fortitudinis non est meritorius nisi aliquis ex caritate haec operetur; secundum illud I ad Cor. XIII, *si tradidero corpus meum ita ut ardeam, caritatem autem non habuero, nihil mihi prodest.*

REPLY OBJ. 1: Charity, inasmuch as it has the last end for object, moves the other virtues to act. For the habit to which the end pertains always commands the habits to which the means pertain, as was said above (Q9, A1).

REPLY OBJ. 2: A work can be toilsome and difficult in two ways: first, from the greatness of the work, and thus the greatness of the work pertains to the increase of merit; and thus charity does not lessen the toil—rather, it makes us undertake the greatest toils, *for it does great things, if it exists,* as Gregory says (*Hom. in Evang. xxx*). Second, from the defect of the operator; for what is not done with a ready will is hard and difficult to all of us, and this toil lessens merit and is removed by charity.

REPLY OBJ. 3: The act of faith is not meritorious unless *faith . . . worketh by charity* (Gal 5:6). So, too, the acts of patience and fortitude are not meritorious unless a man does them out of charity, according to 1 Cor. 13:3: *If I should deliver my body to be burned, and have not charity, it profiteth me nothing.*

Article 5

Whether a Man May Merit for Himself the First Grace?

AD QUINTUM SIC PROCEDITUR. Videtur quod homo possit sibi mereri primam gratiam. Quia ut Augustinus dicit, *fides meretur iustificationem.* Iustificatur autem homo per primam gratiam. Ergo homo potest sibi mereri primam gratiam.

PRAETEREA, Deus non dat gratiam nisi dignis. Sed non dicitur aliquis dignus aliquo dono, nisi qui ipsum promeruit ex condigno. Ergo aliquis ex condigno potest mereri primam gratiam.

PRAETEREA, apud homines aliquis potest promereri donum iam acceptum, sicut qui accepit equum a domino, meretur ipsum bene utendo eo in servitio domini. Sed Deus est liberalior quam homo. Ergo multo magis primam gratiam iam susceptam potest homo promereri a Deo per subsequentia opera.

SED CONTRA est quod ratio gratiae repugnat mercedi operum; secundum illud Rom. IV, *ei qui operatur, merces non imputatur secundum gratiam, sed secundum debitum.* Sed illud meretur homo quod imputatur quasi merces operis eius. Ergo primam gratiam non potest homo mereri.

RESPONDEO dicendum quod donum gratiae considerari potest dupliciter. Uno modo, secundum rationem gratuiti doni. Et sic manifestum est quod omne meritum repugnat gratiae, quia ut ad Rom. XI apostolus dicit, *si ex operibus, iam non ex gratia.* Alio modo potest

OBJECTION 1: It would seem that a man may merit for himself the first grace, because, as Augustine says (*Ep. clxxxvi*), *faith merits justification.* Now a man is justified by the first grace. Therefore a man may merit the first grace.

OBJ. 2: Further, God gives grace only to the worthy. Now, no one is said to be worthy of some good, unless he has merited it condignly. Therefore we may merit the first grace condignly.

OBJ. 3: Further, with men we may merit a gift already received. Thus if a man receives a horse from his master, he merits it by a good use of it in his master's service. Now God is much more bountiful than man. Much more, therefore, may a man, by subsequent works, merit the first grace already received from God.

ON THE CONTRARY, The nature of grace is repugnant to reward of works, according to Rm. 4:4: *Now to him that worketh, the reward is not reckoned according to grace but according to debt.* Now a man merits what is reckoned to him according to debt, as the reward of his works. Hence a man may not merit the first grace.

I ANSWER THAT, The gift of grace may be considered in two ways: first in the nature of a gratuitous gift, and thus it is manifest that all merit is repugnant to grace, since as the Apostle says (Rom 11:6), *if by grace, it is not now by works.* Second, it may be considered as regards the nature

considerari secundum naturam ipsius rei quae donatur. Et sic etiam non potest cadere sub merito non habentis gratiam, tum quia excedit proportionem naturae; tum etiam quia ante gratiam, in statu peccati, homo habet impedimentum promerendi gratiam, scilicet ipsum peccatum. Postquam autem iam aliquis habet gratiam, non potest gratia iam habita sub merito cadere, quia merces est terminus operis, gratia vero est principium cuiuslibet boni operis in nobis, ut supra dictum est. Si vero aliud donum gratuitum aliquis mereatur virtute gratiae praecedentis, iam non erit prima. Unde manifestum est quod nullus potest sibi mereri primam gratiam.

Ad primum ergo dicendum quod, sicut Augustinus dicit in libro Retract., ipse aliquando in hoc fuit deceptus, quod credidit initium fidei esse ex nobis, sed consummationem nobis dari ex Deo, quod ipse ibidem retractat. Et ad hunc sensum videtur pertinere quod fides iustificationem mereatur. Sed si supponamus, sicut fidei veritas habet, quod initium fidei sit in nobis a Deo; iam etiam ipse actus fidei consequitur primam gratiam, et ita non potest esse meritorius primae gratiae. Per fidem igitur iustificatur homo, non quasi homo credendo mereatur iustificationem, sed quia, dum iustificatur, credit; eo quod motus fidei requiritur ad iustificationem impii, ut supra dictum est.

Ad secundum dicendum quod Deus non dat gratiam nisi dignis. Non tamen ita quod prius digni fuerint, sed quia ipse per gratiam eos facit dignos, *qui solus potest facere mundum de immundo conceptum semine.*

Ad tertium dicendum quod omne bonum opus hominis procedit a prima gratia sicut a principio. Non autem procedit a quocumque humano dono. Et ideo non est similis ratio de dono gratiae et de dono humano.

of the thing given, and thus, also, it cannot come under the merit of him who has not grace, both because it exceeds the proportion of nature, and because previous to grace a man in the state of sin has an obstacle to his meriting grace, viz., sin. But when anyone has grace, the grace already possessed cannot come under merit, since reward is the term of the work, but grace is the principle of all our good works, as stated above (Q109). But of anyone merits a further gratuitous gift by virtue of the preceding grace, it would not be the first grace. Hence it is manifest that no one can merit for himself the first grace.

Reply Obj. 1: As Augustine says (*Retract.* i, 23), he was deceived on this point for a time, believing the beginning of faith to be from us, and its consummation to be granted us by God; and this he here retracts. And seemingly it is in this sense that he speaks of faith as meriting justification. But if we suppose, as indeed it is a truth of faith, that the beginning of faith is in us from God, the first act must flow from grace; and thus it cannot be meritorious of the first grace. Therefore man is justified by faith, not as though man, by believing, were to merit justification, but that, he believes, whilst he is being justified; inasmuch as a movement of faith is required for the justification of the ungodly, as stated above (Q113, A4).

Reply Obj. 2: God gives grace to none but to the worthy, not that they were previously worthy, but that by His grace He makes them worthy, Who alone *can make him clean that is conceived of unclean seed* (Job 14:4).

Reply Obj. 3: Man's every good work proceeds from the first grace as from its principle; but not from any gift of man. Consequently, there is no comparison between gifts of grace and gifts of men.

Article 6

Whether a Man Can Merit the First Grace for Another?

Ad sextum sic proceditur. Videtur quod homo possit alteri mereri primam gratiam. Quia Matth. IX, super illud, *videns Iesus fidem illorum* etc., dicit Glossa, *quantum valet apud Deum fides propria, apud quem sic valuit aliena ut intus et extra sanaret hominem.* Sed interior sanatio hominis est per primam gratiam. Ergo homo potest alteri mereri primam gratiam.

Praeterea, orationes iustorum non sunt vacuae, sed efficaces; secundum illud Iac. ult., *multum valet deprecatio iusti assidua.* Sed ibidem praemittitur, *orate pro invicem ut salvemini.* Cum igitur salus hominis non possit esse nisi per gratiam, videtur quod unus homo possit alteri mereri primam gratiam.

Objection 1: It would seem that a man can merit the first grace for another. Because on Mt. 9:2: *Jesus seeing their faith*, etc. a gloss says: *How much is our personal faith worth with God, Who set such a price on another's faith, as to heal the man both inwardly and outwardly!* Now inward healing is brought about by grace. Hence a man can merit the first grace for another.

Obj. 2: Further, the prayers of the just are not void, but efficacious, according to James 5:16: *The continued prayer of a just man availeth much.* Now he had previously said: *Pray one for another, that you may be saved.* Hence, since man's salvation can only be brought about by grace, it seems that one man may merit for another his first grace.

Praeterea, Luc. XVI dicitur, *facite vobis amicos de mammona iniquitatis, ut cum defeceritis, recipiant vos in aeterna tabernacula.* Sed nullus recipitur in aeterna tabernacula nisi per gratiam, per quam solam aliquis meretur vitam aeternam, ut supra dictum est. Ergo unus homo potest alteri acquirere, merendo, primam gratiam.

Sed contra est quod dicitur Ierem. XV, *si steterint Moyses et Samuel coram me, non est anima mea ad populum istum*, qui tamen fuerunt maximi meriti apud Deum. Videtur ergo quod nullus possit alteri mereri primam gratiam.

Respondeo dicendum quod, sicut ex supradictis patet, opus nostrum habet rationem meriti ex duobus. Primo quidem, ex vi motionis divinae, et sic meretur aliquis ex condigno. Alio modo habet rationem meriti, secundum quod procedit ex libero arbitrio, inquantum voluntarie aliquid facimus. Et ex hac parte est meritum congrui, quia congruum est ut, dum homo bene utitur sua virtute, Deus secundum superexcellentem virtutem excellentius operetur. Ex quo patet quod merito condigni nullus potest mereri alteri primam gratiam nisi solus Christus. Quia unusquisque nostrum movetur a Deo per donum gratiae ut ipse ad vitam aeternam perveniat, et ideo meritum condigni ultra hanc motionem non se extendit. Sed anima Christi mota est a Deo per gratiam non solum ut ipse perveniret ad gloriam vitae aeternae, sed etiam ut alios in eam adduceret, inquantum est caput Ecclesiae et auctor salutis humanae; secundum illud ad Heb. II, *qui multos filios in gloriam adduxerat, auctorem salutis* et cetera.

Sed merito congrui potest aliquis alteri mereri primam gratiam. Quia enim homo in gratia constitutus implet Dei voluntatem, congruum est, secundum amicitiae proportionem, ut Deus impleat hominis voluntatem in salvatione alterius, licet quandoque possit habere impedimentum ex parte illius cuius aliquis sanctus iustificationem desiderat. Et in hoc casu loquitur auctoritas Ieremiae ultimo inducta.

Ad primum ergo dicendum quod fides aliorum valet alii ad salutem merito congrui, non merito condigni.

Ad secundum dicendum quod impetratio orationis innititur misericordiae, meritum autem condigni innititur iustitiae. Et ideo multa orando impetrat homo ex divina misericordia, quae tamen non meretur secundum iustitiam; secundum illud Dan. IX, *neque enim in iustificationibus nostris prosternimus preces ante faciem tuam, sed in miserationibus tuis multis.*

Ad tertium dicendum quod pauperes eleemosynas recipientes dicuntur recipere alios in aeterna tabernacula, vel impetrando eis veniam orando; vel merendo per alia bona ex congruo; vel etiam materialiter loquendo, quia per ipsa opera misericordiae quae quis in pauperes exercet, meretur recipi in aeterna tabernacula.

Obj. 3: Further, it is written (Luke 16:9): *Make unto you friends of the mammon of iniquity, that when you shall fail they may receive you into everlasting dwellings.* Now it is through grace alone that anyone is received into everlasting dwellings, for by it alone does anyone merit everlasting life as stated above (A2; Q109, A5). Hence one man may by merit obtain for another his first grace.

On the contrary, It is written (Jer 15:1): *If Moses and Samuel shall stand before Me, My soul is not towards this people*—yet they had great merit with God. Hence it seems that no one can merit the first grace for another.

I answer that, As shown above (AA1,3,4), our works are meritorious from two causes: first, by virtue of the Divine motion; and thus we merit condignly; second, according as they proceed from free-will insofar as we do them willingly, and thus they have congruous merit, since it is congruous that when a man makes good use of his power God should by His super-excellent power work still higher things. And therefore it is clear that no one can merit condignly for another his first grace, save Christ alone; since each one of us is moved by God to reach life everlasting through the gift of grace; hence condign merit does not reach beyond this motion. But Christ's soul is moved by God through grace, not only so as to reach the glory of life everlasting, but so as to lead others to it, inasmuch as He is the Head of the Church, and the Author of human salvation, according to Heb. 2:10: *Who hath brought many children into glory, the Author of their salvation.*

But one may merit the first grace for another congruously; because a man in grace fulfils God's will, and it is congruous and in harmony with friendship that God should fulfill man's desire for the salvation of another, although sometimes there may be an impediment on the part of him whose salvation the just man desires. And it is in this sense that the passage from Jeremias speaks.

Reply Obj. 1: A man's faith avails for another's salvation by congruous and not by condign merit.

Reply Obj. 2: The impetration of prayer rests on mercy, whereas condign merit rests on justice; hence a man may impetrate many things from the Divine mercy in prayer, which he does not merit in justice, according to Dan. 9:18: *For it is not for our justifications that we present our prayers before Thy face, but for the multitude of Thy tender mercies.*

Reply Obj. 3: The poor who receive alms are said to receive others into everlasting dwellings, either by impetrating their forgiveness in prayer, or by meriting congruously by other good works, or materially speaking, inasmuch as by these good works of mercy, exercised towards the poor, we merit to be received into everlasting dwellings.

Article 7

Whether a Man May Merit Restoration After a Fall?

AD SEPTIMUM SIC PROCEDITUR. Videtur quod aliquis possit mereri sibi ipsi reparationem post lapsum. Illud enim quod iuste a Deo petitur, homo videtur posse mereri. Sed nihil iustius a Deo petitur, ut Augustinus dicit, quam quod reparetur post lapsum; secundum illud Psalmi LXX, *cum defecerit virtus mea, ne derelinquas me, domine.* Ergo homo potest mereri ut reparetur post lapsum.

PRAETEREA, multo magis homini prosunt opera sua quam prosint alii. Sed homo potest aliquo modo alteri mereri reparationem post lapsum, sicut et primam gratiam. Ergo multo magis sibi potest mereri ut reparetur post lapsum.

PRAETEREA, homo qui aliquando fuit in gratia, per bona opera quae fecit, meruit sibi vitam aeternam; ut ex supradictis patet. Sed ad vitam aeternam non potest quis pervenire nisi reparetur per gratiam. Ergo videtur quod sibi meruit reparationem per gratiam.

SED CONTRA est quod dicitur Ezech. XVIII, *si averterit se iustus a iustitia sua, et fecerit iniquitatem; omnes iustitiae eius quas fecerat, non recordabuntur.* Ergo nihil valebunt ei praecedentia merita ad hoc quod resurgat. Non ergo aliquis potest sibi mereri reparationem post lapsum futurum.

RESPONDEO dicendum quod nullus potest sibi mereri reparationem post lapsum futurum, neque merito condigni, neque merito congrui. Merito quidem condigni hoc sibi mereri non potest, quia ratio huius meriti dependet ex motione divinae gratiae, quae quidem motio interrumpitur per sequens peccatum. Unde omnia beneficia quae postmodum aliquis a Deo consequitur, quibus reparatur, non cadunt sub merito; tanquam motione prioris gratiae usque ad hoc non se extendente. Meritum etiam congrui quo quis alteri primam gratiam meretur, impeditur ne consequatur effectum, propter impedimentum peccati in eo cui quis meretur. Multo igitur magis impeditur talis meriti efficacia per impedimentum quod est et in eo qui meretur et in eo cui meretur, hic enim utrumque in unam personam concurrit. Et ideo nullo modo aliquis potest sibi mereri reparationem post lapsum.

AD PRIMUM ergo dicendum quod desiderium quo quis desiderat reparationem post lapsum, iustum dicitur, et similiter oratio, quia tendit ad iustitiam. Non tamen ita quod iustitiae innitatur per modum meriti, sed solum misericordiae.

AD SECUNDUM dicendum quod aliquis potest alteri mereri ex congruo primam gratiam, quia non est ibi impedimentum saltem ex parte merentis. Quod invenitur dum aliquis post meritum gratiae a iustitia recedit.

OBJECTION 1: It would seem that anyone may merit for himself restoration after a fall. For what a man may justly ask of God, he may justly merit. Now nothing may more justly be besought of God than to be restored after a fall, as Augustine says, according to Ps. 70:9: *When my strength shall fail, do not Thou forsake me.* Hence a man may merit to be restored after a fall.

OBJ. 2: Further, a man's works benefit himself more than another. Now a man may, to some extent, merit for another his restoration after a fall, even as his first grace. Much more, therefore, may he merit for himself restoration after a fall.

OBJ. 3: Further, when a man is once in grace he merits life everlasting by the good works he does, as was shown above (A2; Q109, A5). Now no one can attain life everlasting unless he is restored by grace. Hence it would seem that he merits for himself restoration.

ON THE CONTRARY, It is written (Ezek 18:24): *If the just man turn himself away from his justice and do iniquity . . . all his justices which he hath done shall not be remembered.* Therefore his previous merits will nowise help him to rise again. Hence no one can merit for himself restoration after a fall.

I ANSWER THAT, No one can merit for himself restoration after a future fall, either condignly or congruously. He cannot merit for himself condignly, since the reason of this merit depends on the motion of Divine grace, and this motion is interrupted by the subsequent sin; hence all benefits which he afterwards obtains from God, whereby he is restored, do not fall under merit—the motion of the preceding grace not extending to them. Again, congruous merit, whereby one merits the first grace for another, is prevented from having its effect on account of the impediment of sin in the one for whom it is merited. Much more, therefore, is the efficacy of such merit impeded by the obstacle which is in him who merits, and in him for whom it is merited; for both these are in the same person. And therefore a man can nowise merit for himself restoration after a fall.

REPLY OBJ. 1: The desire whereby we seek for restoration after a fall is called just, and likewise the prayer whereby this restoration is besought is called just, because it tends to justice; and not that it depends on justice by way of merit, but only on mercy.

REPLY OBJ. 2: Anyone may congruously merit for another his first grace, because there is no impediment (at least, on the part of him who merits), such as is found when anyone recedes from justice after the merit of grace.

AD TERTIUM dicendum quod quidam dixerunt quod nullus meretur absolute vitam aeternam, nisi per actum finalis gratiae; sed solum sub conditione, si perseverat. Sed hoc irrationabiliter dicitur, quia quandoque actus ultimae gratiae non est magis meritorius, sed minus, quam actus praecedentis, propter aegritudinis oppressionem. Unde dicendum quod quilibet actus caritatis meretur absolute vitam aeternam. Sed per peccatum sequens ponitur impedimentum praecedenti merito, ut non sortiatur effectum, sicut etiam causae naturales deficiunt a suis effectibus propter superveniens impedimentum.

REPLY OBJ. 3: Some have said that no one *absolutely* merits life everlasting except by the act of final grace, but only *conditionally*, i.e., if he perseveres. But it is unreasonable to say this, for sometimes the act of the last grace is not more, but less meritorious than preceding acts, on account of the prostration of illness. Hence it must be said that every act of charity merits eternal life absolutely; but by subsequent sin, there arises an impediment to the preceding merit, so that it does not obtain its effect; just as natural causes fail of their effects on account of a supervening impediment.

Article 8

Whether a Man May Merit the Increase of Grace or Charity?

AD OCTAVUM SIC PROCEDITUR. Videtur quod homo non possit mereri augmentum gratiae vel caritatis. Cum enim aliquis acceperit praemium quod meruit, non debetur ei alia merces, sicut de quibusdam dicitur Matth. VI, *receperunt mercedem suam*. Si igitur aliquis mereretur augmentum caritatis vel gratiae, sequeretur quod, gratia augmentata, non posset ulterius expectare aliud praemium. Quod est inconveniens.

PRAETEREA, nihil agit ultra suam speciem. Sed principium meriti est gratia vel caritas, ut ex supradictis patet. Ergo nullus potest maiorem gratiam vel caritatem mereri quam habeat.

PRAETEREA, id quod cadit sub merito, meretur homo per quemlibet actum a gratia vel caritate procedentem, sicut per quemlibet talem actum meretur homo vitam aeternam. Si igitur augmentum gratiae vel caritatis cadat sub merito, videtur quod per quemlibet actum caritate informatum aliquis meretur augmentum caritatis. Sed id quod homo meretur, infallibiliter a Deo consequitur, nisi impediatur per peccatum sequens, dicitur enim II ad Tim. I, *scio cui credidi, et certus sum quia potens est depositum meum servare*. Sic ergo sequeretur quod per quemlibet actum meritorium gratia vel caritas augeretur. Quod videtur esse inconveniens, cum quandoque actus meritorii non sint multum ferventes, ita quod sufficiant ad caritatis augmentum. Non ergo augmentum caritatis cadit sub merito.

SED CONTRA est quod Augustinus dicit, super Epist. Ioan., quod *caritas meretur augeri, ut aucta mereatur perfici*. Ergo augmentum caritatis vel gratiae cadit sub merito.

RESPONDEO dicendum quod, sicut supra dictum est, illud cadit sub merito condigni, ad quod motio gratiae se extendit. Motio autem alicuius moventis non solum se extendit ad ultimum terminum motus, sed etiam ad totum progressum in motu. Terminus autem motus

OBJECTION 1: It would seem that a man cannot merit an increase of grace or charity. For when anyone receives the reward he merited no other reward is due to him; thus it was said of some (Matt 6:2): *They have received their reward*. Hence, if anyone were to merit the increase of charity or grace, it would follow that, when his grace has been increased, he could not expect any further reward, which is unfitting.

OBJ. 2: Further, nothing acts beyond its species. But the principle of merit is grace or charity, as was shown above (AA2, 4). Therefore no one can merit greater grace or charity than he has.

OBJ. 3: Further, what falls under merit a man merits by every act flowing from grace or charity, as by every such act a man merits life everlasting. If, therefore, the increase of grace or charity falls under merit, it would seem that by every act quickened by charity a man would merit an increase of charity. But what a man merits, he infallibly receives from God, unless hindered by subsequent sin; for it is written (2 Tim 1:12): *I know Whom I have believed, and I am certain that He is able to keep that which I have committed unto Him*. Hence it would follow that grace or charity is increased by every meritorious act; and this would seem impossible since at times meritorious acts are not very fervent, and would not suffice for the increase of charity. Therefore the increase of charity does not come under merit.

ON THE CONTRARY, Augustine says (*super Ep. Joan.*; cf. *Ep. clxxxvi*) that *charity merits increase, and being increased merits to be perfected*. Hence the increase of grace or charity falls under merit.

I ANSWER THAT, As stated above (AA6,7), whatever the motion of grace reaches to, falls under condign merit. Now the motion of a mover extends not merely to the last term of the movement, but to the whole progress of the movement. But the term of the movement of grace is eternal life;

gratiae est vita aeterna, progressus autem in hoc motu est secundum augmentum caritatis vel gratiae, secundum illud Prov. IV, *iustorum semita quasi lux splendens procedit, et crescit usque ad perfectum diem*, qui est dies gloriae. Sic igitur augmentum gratiae cadit sub merito condigni.

AD PRIMUM ergo dicendum quod praemium est terminus meriti. Est autem duplex terminus motus, scilicet ultimus; et medius, qui est et principium et terminus. Et talis terminus est merces augmenti. Merces autem favoris humani est sicut ultimus terminus his qui finem in hoc constituunt, unde tales nullam aliam mercedem recipiunt.

AD SECUNDUM dicendum quod augmentum gratiae non est supra virtutem praeexistentis gratiae, licet sit supra quantitatem ipsius, sicut arbor, etsi sit supra quantitatem seminis, non est tamen supra virtutem ipsius.

AD TERTIUM dicendum quod quolibet actu meritorio meretur homo augmentum gratiae, sicut et gratiae consummationem, quae est vita aeterna. Sed sicut vita aeterna non statim redditur, sed suo tempore; ita nec gratia statim augetur, sed suo tempore; cum scilicet aliquis sufficienter fuerit dispositus ad gratiae augmentum.

and progress in this movement is by the increase of charity or grace according to Prov. 4:18: *But the path of the just as a shining light, goeth forward and increaseth even to perfect day*, which is the day of glory. And thus the increase of grace falls under condign merit.

REPLY OBJ. 1: Reward is the term of merit. But there is a double term of movement, viz., the last, and the intermediate, which is both beginning and term; and this term is the reward of increase. Now the reward of human favor is as the last end to those who place their end in it; hence such as these receive no other reward.

REPLY OBJ. 2: The increase of grace is not above the virtuality of the pre-existing grace, although it is above its quantity, even as a tree is not above the virtuality of the seed, although above its quantity.

REPLY OBJ. 3: By every meritorious act a man merits the increase of grace, equally with the consummation of grace which is eternal life. But just as eternal life is not given at once, but in its own time, so neither is grace increased at once, but in its own time, viz., when a man is sufficiently disposed for the increase of grace.

Article 9

Whether a Man May Merit Perseverance?

AD NONUM SIC PROCEDITUR. Videtur quod aliquis possit perseverantiam mereri. Illud enim quod homo obtinet petendo, potest cadere sub merito habentis gratiam. Sed perseverantiam petendo homines a Deo obtinent, alioquin frustra peteretur a Deo in petitionibus orationis dominicae, ut Augustinus exponit, in libro de dono Persever. Ergo perseverantia potest cadere sub merito habentis gratiam.

PRAETEREA, magis est non posse peccare quam non peccare. Sed non posse peccare cadit sub merito, meretur enim aliquis vitam aeternam, de cuius ratione est impeccabilitas. Ergo multo magis potest aliquis mereri ut non peccet, quod est perseverare.

PRAETEREA, maius est augmentum gratiae quam perseverantia in gratia quam quis habet. Sed homo potest mereri augmentum gratiae, ut supra dictum est. Ergo multo magis potest mereri perseverantiam in gratia quam quis habet.

SED CONTRA est quod omne quod quis meretur, a Deo consequitur, nisi impediatur per peccatum. Sed multi habent opera meritoria, qui non consequuntur perseverantiam. Nec potest dici quod hoc fiat propter impedimentum peccati, quia hoc ipsum quod est peccare, opponitur perseverantiae; ita quod, si aliquis

OBJECTION 1: It would seem that anyone may merit perseverance. For what a man obtains by asking, can come under the merit of anyone that is in grace. Now men obtain perseverance by asking it of God; otherwise it would be useless to ask it of God in the petitions of the Lord's Prayer, as Augustine says (*De Dono Persev.* ii). Therefore perseverance may come under the merit of whoever has grace.

OBJ. 2: Further, it is more not to be able to sin than not to sin. But not to be able to sin comes under merit, for we merit eternal life, of which impeccability is an essential part. Much more, therefore, may we merit not to sin, i.e., to persevere.

OBJ. 3: Further, increase of grace is greater than perseverance in the grace we already possess. But a man may merit an increase of grace, as was stated above (A8). Much more, therefore, may he merit perseverance in the grace he has already.

ON THE CONTRARY, What we merit, we obtain from God, unless it is hindered by sin. Now many have meritorious works, who do not obtain perseverance; nor can it be urged that this takes place because of the impediment of sin, since sin itself is opposed to perseverance; and thus if anyone were to merit perseverance, God would not permit

perseverantiam mereretur, Deus non permitteret aliquem cadere in peccatum. Non igitur perseverantia cadit sub merito.

Respondeo dicendum quod, cum homo naturaliter habeat liberum arbitrium flexibile ad bonum et ad malum, dupliciter potest aliquis perseverantiam in bono obtinere a Deo. Uno quidem modo, per hoc quod liberum arbitrium determinatur ad bonum per gratiam consummatam, quod erit in gloria. Alio modo, ex parte motionis divinae, quae hominem inclinat ad bonum usque in finem. Sicut autem ex dictis patet, illud cadit sub humano merito, quod comparatur ad motum liberi arbitrii directi a Deo movente, sicut terminus, non autem id quod comparatur ad praedictum motum sicut principium. Unde patet quod perseverantia gloriae, quae est terminus praedicti motus, cadit sub merito, perseverantia autem viae non cadit sub merito, quia dependet solum ex motione divina, quae est principium omnis meriti. Sed Deus gratis perseverantiae bonum largitur, cuicumque illud largitur.

Ad primum ergo dicendum quod etiam ea quae non meremur, orando impetramus. Nam et peccatores Deus audit, peccatorum veniam petentes, quam non merentur, ut patet per Augustinum, super illud Ioan. IX, scimus quia peccatores Deus non exaudit; alioquin frustra dixisset publicanus, Deus, propitius esto mihi peccatori, ut dicitur Luc. XVIII. Et similiter perseverantiae donum aliquis petendo a Deo impetrat vel sibi vel alii, quamvis sub merito non cadat.

Ad secundum dicendum quod perseverantia quae erit in gloria, comparatur ad motum liberi arbitrii meritorium sicut terminus, non autem perseverantia viae, ratione praedicta.

Et similiter dicendum est ad tertium, de augmento gratiae, ut per praedicta patet.

him to fall into sin. Hence perseverance does not come under merit.

I answer that, Since man's free-will is naturally flexible towards good and evil, there are two ways of obtaining from God perseverance in good: first, inasmuch as free-will is determined to good by consummate grace, which will be in glory; second, on the part of the Divine motion, which inclines man to good unto the end. Now as explained above (AA6,7,8), that which is related as a term to the free-will's movement directed to God the mover, falls under human merit; and not what is related to the aforesaid movement as principle. Hence it is clear that the perseverance of glory which is the term of the aforesaid movement falls under merit; but perseverance of the wayfarer does not fall under merit, since it depends solely on the Divine motion, which is the principle of all merit. Now God freely bestows the good of perseverance, on whomsoever He bestows it.

Reply Obj. 1: We impetrate in prayer things that we do not merit, since God hears sinners who beseech the pardon of their sins, which they do not merit, as appears from Augustine on Jn. 11:31, *Now we know that God doth not hear sinners*, otherwise it would have been useless for the publican to say: *O God, be merciful to me a sinner*, Lk. 18:13. So too may we impetrate of God in prayer the grace of perseverance either for ourselves or for others, although it does not fall under merit.

Reply Obj. 2: The perseverance which is in heaven is compared as term to the free-will's movement; not so, the perseverance of the wayfarer, for the reason given in the body of the article.

In the same way may we answer the third objection which concerns the increase of grace, as was explained above.

Article 10

Whether Temporal Goods Fall Under Merit?

Ad decimum sic proceditur. Videtur quod temporalia bona cadant sub merito. Illud enim quod promittitur aliquibus ut praemium iustitiae, cadit sub merito. Sed temporalia bona promissa sunt in lege veteri sicut merces iustitiae, ut patet Deut. XXVIII. Ergo videtur quod bona temporalia cadant sub merito.

Praeterea, illud videtur sub merito cadere, quod Deus alicui retribuit pro aliquo servitio quod fecit. Sed Deus aliquando recompensat hominibus pro servitio sibi facto, aliqua bona temporalia. Dicitur enim Exod. I, *et quia timuerunt obstetrices Deum, aedificavit illis*

Objection 1: It would seem that temporal goods fall under merit. For what is promised to some as a reward of justice, falls under merit. Now, temporal goods were promised in the Old Law as the reward of justice, as appears from Dt. 28. Hence it seems that temporal goods fall under merit.

Obj. 2: Further, that would seem to fall under merit, which God bestows on anyone for a service done. But God sometimes bestows temporal goods on men for services done for Him. For it is written (Exod 1:21): *And because the midwives feared God, He built them houses*; on which a gloss

domos; ubi Glossa Gregorii dicit quod *benignitatis earum merces potuit in aeterna vita retribui, sed pro culpa mendacii, terrenam recompensationem accepit.* Et Ezech. XXIX dicitur, *rex Babylonis servire fecit exercitum suum servitute magna adversus Tyrum, et merces non est reddita ei*; et postea subdit, *erit merces exercitui illius, et dedi ei terram Aegypti, pro eo quod laboraverit mihi.* Ergo bona temporalia cadunt sub merito.

PRAETEREA, sicut bonum se habet ad meritum, ita malum se habet ad demeritum. Sed propter demeritum peccati aliqui puniuntur a Deo temporalibus poenis, sicut patet de Sodomitis, Gen. XIX. Ergo et bona temporalia cadunt sub merito.

SED CONTRA est quod illa quae cadunt sub merito, non similiter se habent ad omnes. Sed bona temporalia et mala similiter se habent ad bonos et malos; secundum illud Eccle. IX, *universa aeque eveniunt iusto et impio, bono et malo, mundo et immundo, immolanti victimas et sacrificia contemnenti.* Ergo bona temporalia non cadunt sub merito.

RESPONDEO dicendum quod illud quod sub merito cadit, est praemium vel merces, quod habet rationem alicuius boni. Bonum autem hominis est duplex, unum simpliciter, et aliud secundum quid. Simpliciter quidem bonum hominis est ultimus finis eius, secundum illud Psalmi LXXII, *mihi autem adhaerere Deo bonum est*, et per consequens omnia illa quae ordinantur ut ducentia ad hunc finem. Et talia simpliciter cadunt sub merito. Bonum autem secundum quid et non simpliciter hominis, est quod est bonum ei ut nunc, vel quod ei est secundum aliquid bonum. Et huiusmodi non cadunt sub merito simpliciter, sed secundum quid.

Secundum hoc ergo dicendum est quod, si temporalia bona considerentur prout sunt utilia ad opera virtutum, quibus perducimur in vitam aeternam, secundum hoc directe et simpliciter cadunt sub merito, sicut et augmentum gratiae, et omnia illa quibus homo adiuvatur ad perveniendum in beatitudinem, post primam gratiam. Tantum enim dat Deus viris iustis de bonis temporalibus, et etiam de malis, quantum eis expedit ad perveniendum ad vitam aeternam. Et intantum sunt simpliciter bona huiusmodi temporalia. Unde dicitur in Psalmo, *timentes autem dominum non minuentur omni bono*; et alibi, *non vidi iustum derelictum.*

Si autem considerentur huiusmodi temporalia bona secundum se, sic non sunt simpliciter bona hominis, sed secundum quid. Et ita non simpliciter cadunt sub merito, sed secundum quid, inquantum scilicet homines moventur a Deo ad aliqua temporaliter agenda, in quibus suum propositum consequuntur, Deo favente. Ut sicut vita aeterna est simpliciter praemium operum iustitiae per relationem ad motionem divinam, sicut supra dictum est; ita temporalia bona in se considerata habeant

of Gregory (*Moral.* xviii, 4) says that *life everlasting might have been awarded them as the fruit of their goodwill, but on account of their sin of falsehood they received an earthly reward.* And it is written (Ezek 29:18): *The King of Babylon hath made his army to undergo hard service against Tyre ... and there hath been no reward given him*, and further on: *And it shall be wages for his army ... I have given him the land of Egypt because he hath labored for me.* Therefore temporal goods fall under merit.

OBJ. 3: Further, as good is to merit so is evil to demerit. But on account of the demerit of sin some are punished by God with temporal punishments, as appears from the Sodomites, Gn. 19. Hence temporal goods fall under merit.

ON THE CONTRARY: On the contrary, What falls under merit does not come upon all alike. But temporal goods regard the good and the wicked alike; according to Eccles. 9:2: *All things equally happen to the just and the wicked, to the good and to the evil, to the clean and to the unclean, to him that offereth victims and to him that despiseth sacrifices.* Therefore temporal goods do not fall under merit.

I ANSWER THAT, What falls under merit is the reward or wage, which is a kind of good. Now man's good is twofold: the first, simply; the second, relatively. Now man's good simply is his last end, according to Ps. 72:27: *But it is good for men to adhere to my God*, and consequently what is ordained and leads to this end; and these fall simply under merit. But the relative, not the simple, good of man is what is good to him now, or what is a good to him relatively; and this does not fall under merit simply, but relatively.

Hence we must say that if temporal goods are considered as they are useful for virtuous works, whereby we are led to heaven, they fall directly and simply under merit, even as increase of grace, and everything whereby a man is helped to attain beatitude after the first grace. For God gives men, both just and wicked, enough temporal goods to enable them to attain to everlasting life; and thus these temporal goods are simply good. Hence it is written (Ps 33:10): *For there is no want to them that fear Him*, and again, Ps. 36:25: *I have not seen the just forsaken*, etc.

But if these temporal goods are considered in themselves, they are not man's good simply, but relatively, and thus they do not fall under merit simply, but relatively, inasmuch as men are moved by God to do temporal works, in which with God's help they reach their purpose. And thus as life everlasting is simply the reward of the works of justice in relation to the Divine motion, as stated above (AA3,6), so have temporal goods, considered in themselves, the nature of reward, with respect to the Divine motion,

rationem mercedis, habito respectu ad motionem divinam qua voluntates hominum moventur ad haec prosequenda; licet interdum in his non habeant homines rectam intentionem.

AD PRIMUM ergo dicendum quod, sicut Augustinus dicit, contra Faust., libro IV, *in illis temporalibus promissis figurae fuerunt futurorum spiritualium, quae implentur in nobis. Carnalis enim populus promissis vitae praesentis inhaerebat, et illorum non tantum lingua, sed etiam vita prophetica fuit.*

AD SECUNDUM dicendum quod illae retributiones dicuntur esse divinitus factae secundum comparationem ad divinam motionem, non autem secundum respectum ad malitiam voluntatis. Praecipue quantum ad regem Babylonis, qui non impugnavit Tyrum quasi volens Deo servire, sed potius ut sibi dominium usurparet. Similiter etiam obstetrices, licet habuerunt bonam voluntatem quantum ad liberationem puerorum, non tamen fuit earum recta voluntas quantum ad hoc quod mendacium confinxerunt.

AD TERTIUM dicendum quod temporalia mala infliguntur in poenam impiis, inquantum per ea non adiuvantur ad consecutionem vitae aeternae. Iustis autem, qui per huiusmodi mala iuvantur, non sunt poenae, sed magis medicinae, ut etiam supra dictum est.

AD QUARTUM dicendum quod omnia aeque eveniunt bonis et malis, quantum ad ipsam substantiam bonorum vel malorum temporalium. Sed non quantum ad finem, quia boni per huiusmodi manuducuntur ad beatitudinem, non autem mali.

Et haec de moralibus in communi dicta sufficiant.

whereby men's wills are moved to undertake these works, even though, sometimes, men have not a right intention in them.

REPLY OBJ. 1: As Augustine says (*Contra Faust.* iv, 2), *in these temporal promises were figures of spiritual things to come. For the carnal people were adhering to the promises of the present life; and not merely their speech but even their life was prophetic.*

REPLY OBJ. 2: These rewards are said to have been divinely brought about in relation to the Divine motion, and not in relation to the malice of their wills, especially as regards the King of Babylon, since he did not besiege Tyre as if wishing to serve God, but rather in order to usurp dominion. So, too, although the midwives had a good will with regard to saving the children, yet their will was not right, inasmuch as they framed falsehoods.

REPLY OBJ. 3: Temporal evils are imposed as a punishment on the wicked, inasmuch as they are not thereby helped to reach life everlasting. But to the just who are aided by these evils they are not punishments but medicines as stated above (Q87, A8).

REPLY OBJ. 4: All things happen equally to the good and the wicked, as regards the substance of temporal good or evil; but not as regards the end, since the good and not the wicked are led to beatitude by them.

And now enough has been said regarding morals in general.